Criminological Theory

Second Edition

Dedication

Stephen G. Tibbetts dedicates this book to his daughter, Rian Sage, who has been really cool to hang out with watching SpongeBob over the last few years; Rian has been the best daughter anyone could ask for.

Craig Hemmens dedicates this book, all the books in this series, and everything of value he has ever done to his father, George Hemmens, who showed him the way; James Marquart and Rolando del Carmen, who taught him how; and Mary and Emily, for giving him something he loves even more than his work.

Criminological Theory

A Text/Reader

Second Edition

Stephen G. Tibbetts
California State University, San Bernardino

Craig Hemmens
Washington State University

Los Angeles | London | New Delhi
Singapore | Washington DC

Los Angeles | London | New Delhi
Singapore | Washington DC

FOR INFORMATION:

SAGE Publications, Inc.
2455 Teller Road
Thousand Oaks, California 91320
E-mail: order@sagepub.com

SAGE Publications Ltd.
1 Oliver's Yard
55 City Road
London, EC1Y 1SP
United Kingdom

SAGE Publications India Pvt. Ltd.
B 1/I 1 Mohan Cooperative Industrial Area
Mathura Road, New Delhi 110 044
India

SAGE Publications Asia-Pacific Pte. Ltd.
3 Church Street
#10-04 Samsung Hub
Singapore 048763

Acquisitions Editor: Jerry Westby
Associate Editor: MaryAnn Vail
Editorial Assistant: Laura Kirkhuff
Production Editor: Libby Larson
Copy Editor: Rachel Keith
Typesetter: C&M Digitals (P) Ltd.
Proofreader: Dennis W. Webb
Indexer: David Luljak
Cover Designer: Michael Dubowe
Marketing Manager: Terra Schultz

Printed in the United States of America

Library of Congress Cataloging-in-Publication Data

Tibbetts, Stephen G.

Criminological theory : a text/reader / Stephen G. Tibbetts, California State University, San Bernadino, Craig Hemmens, Washington State University. — Second edition.

pages cm
Includes bibliographical references and index.

ISBN 978-1-4522-5815-7 (pbk. : alk. paper) 1. Criminology. 2. Crime. I. Hemmens, Craig. II. Title.

HV6018.T53 2015
364.01—dc23   2014020164

This book is printed on acid-free paper.

14 15 16 17 18 10 9 8 7 6 5 4 3 2 1

Brief Contents

Foreword   xvii

Preface   xix

Section I. Introduction to the Book: An Overview of Issues in Criminological Theory   1

Section II. Preclassical and Classical Theories of Crime   39

Section III. Modern Applications of the Classical Perspective:
Deterrence, Rational Choice, and Routine Activities or Lifestyle Theories of Crime   73

Section IV. Early Positive School Perspectives of Criminality   133

Section V. Modern Biosocial Perspectives of Criminal Behavior   173

Section VI. Early Social Structure and Strain Theories of Crime   215

Section VII. The Chicago School and Cultural and Subcultural Theories of Crime   261

Section VIII. Social Process and Learning Theories of Crime   297

Section IX. Social Reaction, Critical, and Feminist Models of Crime   357

Section X. Life-Course Perspectives of Criminality   399

Section XI. Integrated Theoretical Models and New Perspectives of Crime   439

Section XII. Applying Criminological Theory to Policy   499

Glossary   529

Index   539

About the Authors   551

Detailed Contents

Foreword   xvii

Preface   xix

SECTION I. INTRODUCTION TO THE BOOK: AN OVERVIEW
OF ISSUES IN CRIMINOLOGICAL THEORY   1

What Is Criminology, and How Does It Differ from Other Examinations of Crime?   2

What Is Theory?   2

What Is Crime?   3

How Are Criminological Theories Classified? The Major Theoretical Paradigms   4

Additional Ways to Classify Criminological Theories   5

Characteristics of Good Theories   6

Criteria for Determining Causality   8

Measures of Crime   10

The Uniform Crime Report   11

The National Crime Victimization Survey   14

Self-Report Studies of Crime   15

What Do the Measures of Crime Show regarding the Distribution of Crime?   16

The Baby-Boom Effect   19

Regional and City Differences in Rates of Crime   20

Rates of Crime according to Time of Day and Time of Year   20

Rates of Crime according to Age and Gender   21

Rates of Crime according to Population Density   22

Rates of Crime according to Race/Ethnicity   23

Policy Implications   24

Section Summary   24

Key Terms   25

Discussion Questions   26

Web Resources   26

How to Read a Research Article   27

READING

    1. The Use and Usefulness of Criminology, 1751–2005: Enlightened Justice and Its Failures   30
       Lawrence W. Sherman
         This reading discusses the evolution of many key policy implications that have been derived from criminological theories over the last few centuries.

SECTION II. PRECLASSICAL AND CLASSICAL THEORIES OF CRIME   39
    Preclassical Perspectives of Crime and Punishment   40
    The Age of Enlightenment   42
    The Classical School of Criminology   44
       Influences on Beccaria and His Writings   44
       Beccaria's Proposed Reforms and Ideas of Justice   44
       Beccaria's Ideas regarding the Death Penalty   47
       Beccaria's Concept of Deterrence and the Three Key Elements of Punishment   49
       Beccaria's Conceptualization of Specific and General Deterrence   51
       A Summary of Beccaria's Ideas and His Influence on Policy   52
       The Impact of Beccaria's Work on Other Theorists   53
    The Neoclassical School of Criminology   54
    Loss of Dominance of Classical and Neoclassical Theory   55
    Policy Implications   56
    Conclusion   57
    Section Summary   58
    Key Terms   58
    Discussion Questions   58
    Web Resources   59

READINGS

    2. On Crimes and Punishments   61
       Cesare Beccaria
         Perhaps the most important work in criminal justice, this selection presents a deterrence theory explaining criminal behavior.
    3. Capital Punishment and Deterrence: Examining the Effect of Executions on Murder in Texas   66
       Jon Sorensen, Robert Wrinkle, Victoria Brewer, and James Marquart
         In this study, the authors examine the extent to which capital punishment has a significant deterrent effect on murder rates in Texas.

SECTION III. MODERN APPLICATIONS OF THE CLASSICAL PERSPECTIVE: DETERRENCE, RATIONAL CHOICE, AND ROUTINE ACTIVITIES OR LIFESTYLE THEORIES OF CRIME   73
    The Rebirth of Deterrence Theory and Contemporary Research   74
    Rational Choice Theory   78
    Routine Activities Theory   80
    Policy Implications   83
    Conclusion   84
    Section Summary   84
    Key Terms   85
    Discussion Questions   85
    Web Resources   86

READINGS

4. The Effects of Focused Deterrence Strategies on Crime: A Systematic
   Review and Meta-analysis of the Empirical Evidence   87
   Anthony A. Braga and David L. Weisburd
      In this reading, Braga and Weisburd present a comprehensive review and meta-analysis of
         various programs that attempted to reduce crime activity in the areas of gang- or group-
         involved violence, repeat offenders, and the drug market.

5. Specifying the Direct and Indirect Effects of Low Self-Control and Situational
   Factors in Offenders' Decision Making: Toward a More Complete Model of Rational Offending   95
   Alex R. Piquero and Stephen G. Tibbetts
      This selection examines the need to merge rational choice/deterrence theories of crime with
         contextual factors and individual propensities for low self-control and provides a test of
         the integration of these theoretical perspectives.

6. Hot Spots of Predatory Crime: Routine Activities and the Criminology of Place   109
   Lawrence W. Sherman, Patrick R. Gartin, and Michael E. Buerger
      This reading provides one of the seminal empirical investigations of hot spots of crime by
         examining police calls for service at specific addresses in a large city utilizing the routine
         activities framework.

7. The Impact of Neighborhoods, Schools, and Malls on the
   Spatial Distribution of Property Damage   118
   Teresa C. LaGrange
      This selection provides an example of the contemporary use of geospatial modeling of
         crimes occurring in certain areas, illustrating the importance of lifestyle and routine
         activities perspectives of criminal behavior.

SECTION IV. EARLY POSITIVE SCHOOL PERSPECTIVES OF CRIMINALITY   133
   Lombroso's Theory of Atavism and Born Criminals   136
      Lombroso's Theory of Crime   136
      Lombroso's List of Stigmata   137
      Lombroso's as the Father of Criminology and the Father of the Positive School   138
      Lombroso's Policy Implications   139
   The IQ Testing Era   140
   Body Type Theory: Sheldon's Model of Somatotyping   144
   Policy Implications   147
   Conclusion   148
   Section Summary   149
   Key Terms   149
   Discussion Questions   150
   Web Resources   150

READINGS

8. The Criminal Man (L'uomo delinquente)   151
   Cesare Lombroso (as translated by Mary Gibson and Nicole H. Rafter)
      This reading provides excerpts of the original work of Lombroso, who is generally
         considered the father of criminology and the father of the Positive School of criminology,
         emphasizing the "born criminal" and stigmata aspects of his theory.

9. The Contribution of Family Adversity and Verbal IQ to Criminal Behavior   161
Chris L. Gibson, Alex R. Piquero, and Stephen G. Tibbetts

> This reading describes an empirical test of the association between low IQ scores and criminal offending, particularly when coupled with family problems in early life, and discusses the issues involved in such research and the implications of these effects.

SECTION V. MODERN BIOSOCIAL PERSPECTIVES OF CRIMINAL BEHAVIOR   173

Nature versus Nurture: Studies Examining the Influence of Genetics and Environment   174
    Family Studies   174
    Twin Studies   174
    Adoption Studies   176
    Twins Separated at Birth   177
Cytogenetic Studies: The XYY Factor   178
Hormones and Neurotransmitters: Chemicals That Determine Criminal Behavior   179
Brain Injuries   182
Central and Autonomic Nervous System Activity   183
Biosocial Approaches to Explaining Criminal Behavior   186
Policy Implications   187
Conclusion   188
Section Summary   188
Key Terms   189
Discussion Questions   189
Web Resources   190

READINGS

10. A Theory Explaining Biological Correlates of Criminality   191
Lee Ellis

> This piece presents a recent theoretical framework that incorporates many of the biological predictors of criminal propensity, as well as the interactions among them, into a single theoretical perspective.

11. Neuroimaging Studies of Aggressive and Violent Behavior: Current Findings and Implications for Criminology and Criminal Justice   198
Jana L. Bufkin and Vickie R. Luttrell

> This selection examines the modern research comparing brain images of chronic offenders with those of normal brain images, with an emphasis on the significant differences across such images and the implications for future research.

12. A Life-Course Analysis of the Criminogenic Effects of Maternal Cigarette Smoking during Pregnancy: A Research Note on the Mediating Impact of Neuropsychological Deficit   206
Jean Marie McGloin, Travis C. Pratt, and Alex R. Piquero

> This reading provides a review of previous studies that have examined the effect of mothers' cigarette smoking on their offspring's future criminality and discusses various issues and implications that can be derived from these findings from a developmental perspective.

SECTION VI. EARLY SOCIAL STRUCTURE AND STRAIN THEORIES OF CRIME   215

Early Theories of Social Structure: Early to Mid 1800s   216
    Auguste Comte   216
    André-Michel Guerry and Adolphe Quetelet   217
    Durkheim and the Concept of Anomie   218

Strain Theories   222
    Merton's Strain Theory   222
    Cultural Context and Assumptions of Strain Theory   222
    Variations of Merton's Strain Theory: Cohen, and Cloward and Ohlin   228
    General Strain Theory   232
    Summary of Strain Theories   235
Policy Implications   236
Conclusion   236
Section Summary   236
Key Terms   237
Discussion Questions   237
Web Resources   237

READINGS

13. Social Structure and Anomie   238
    Robert K. Merton
    This piece is the first proposition of strain theory and one of the most cited and highly respected pieces in criminological and sociological literature; in it, Merton explains adaptations to strain.

14. There's a Darkness on the Edge of Town: Merton's Five Modes of Adaptation
    in the Lyrics of Bruce Springsteen   244
    Craig Hemmens
    This reading applies the lyrics of a modern poet and rock-artist to the various ways that individuals cope with the pressures of economic stress; each person deals with such strains in his or her own way.

15. Building on the Foundation of General Strain Theory: Specifying the Types of
    Strain Most Likely to Lead to Crime and Delinquency   250
    Robert Agnew
    Agnew revises and updates his general strain theory in light of empirical evidence that is both supporting and not supporting of the theory. Acknowledging scientific research and revising one's theory accordingly promotes good theoretical development, and this piece provides a good example of this process.

SECTION VII. THE CHICAGO SCHOOL AND CULTURAL AND
SUBCULTURAL THEORIES OF CRIME   261
The Ecological School and the Chicago School of Criminology   262
    Cultural Context: Chicago in the 1800s and Early 1900s   262
    Ecological Principles in City Growth and Concentric Circles   263
    Shaw and McKay's Theory of Social Disorganization   266
    Reaction and Research on Social Disorganization Theory   268
Cultural and Subcultural Theories of Crime   270
    Early Theoretical Developments and Research in Cultural and Subcultural Theory 271
    Criticisms of Cultural Theories of Crime   271
Policy Implications   272
Conclusion   273
Section Summary   273

Key Terms   274
Discussion Questions   274
Web Resources   274

READINGS

16. Delinquency Rates and Community Characteristics   275
Clifford R. Shaw and Henry D. McKay

This selection proposes a theory regarding high delinquency and crime rates in certain neighborhoods, especially those that have high levels of poverty and mobility and, perhaps most important, a lack of caring about their local community.

17. Replicating Sampson and Groves's Test of Social Disorganization Theory: Revisiting a Criminological Classic   279
Christopher T. Lowenkamp, Francis T. Cullen, and Travis C. Pratt

This selection reviews some modern studies that have examined the various propositions of the Chicago School/social disorganization model of crime; the authors provide their own analysis of this theoretical model.

18. Peaceful Warriors: Codes for Violence among Adult Male Bar Fighters   288
Heith Copes, Andy Hochstetler, and Craig Forsyth

In this piece, the authors examine a type of subcultural normative code applied to the behavior of males who fight in bars.

SECTION VIII. SOCIAL PROCESS AND LEARNING THEORIES OF CRIME   297

Learning Theories   298
  Differential Association Theory   298
  Differential Reinforcement Theory   302
  Neutralization Theory   306
  Summary of Learning Theories   307
Control Theories   307
  Early Control Theories of Human Behavior   309
  Early Control Theories of Crime   311
  Modern Social Control Theories   314
  Integrated Social Control Theories   319
  A General Theory of Crime: Low Self-Control   321
  Summary of Control Theories   322
Policy Implications   322
Conclusion   323
Section Summary   324
Key Terms   324
Discussion Questions   324
Web Resources   **325**

READINGS

19. A Sociological Theory of Criminal Behavior   326
Edwin H. Sutherland

This is the first major social learning theory of crime; it focuses on the association with significant others. Sutherland's theoretical model was the basis of all other learning models that followed.

20. A Social Learning Theory of Crime 329
  Ronald L. Akers
    Using the previous framework by Sutherland, this theoretical model incorporates all of the
      concepts and propositions proposed by Sutherland but also includes many other key
      concepts and propositions that come from more modern psychological theories, such as
      imitation/modeling and positive reinforcement.
21. Do Women and Men Differ in Their Neutralizations of Corporate Crime? 337
  Lynne M. Vieraitis, Nicole Leeper Piquero, Alex R. Piquero,
  Stephen G. Tibbetts, and Michael Blankenship
    This selection examines gender differences in the effects of techniques of neutralization in
      decisions to engage in unethical decision making in a corporate setting among a sample
      of students in a master of business administration (MBA) program.
22. Scared Kids, Unattached Kids, or Peer Pressure: Why Do Students Carry Firearms to School? 346
  David C. May
    This piece examines the view that a lack of social bonds, peer pressure, and other factors
      are involved in youths' bringing firearms to school. An analysis reveals which factors are
      most important in determining this behavior.

SECTION IX. SOCIAL REACTION, CRITICAL, AND FEMINIST MODELS OF CRIME 357
  Labeling and Social Reaction Theory 357
  Marxist Theories of Crime 360
    Evidence regarding Marxist Theories of Crime 361
  Conflict Theories of Crime 361
    Evidence regarding Conflict Theories of Crime 363
  Feminist Theories of Crime 363
    Evidence regarding Feminist Theories of Crime 365
  Policy Implications 366
  Conclusion 367
  Section Summary 367
  Key Terms 367
  Discussion Questions 367
  Web Resources 368

READINGS
  23. Informal Reactions and Delinquency 369
    Lening Zhang
      This selection reviews many studies based on labeling theory and suggests that informal
        factors (e.g., family, peers) have the greatest labeling effects in promoting further
        criminal offending. An analysis appears to support this claim.
  24. Conflict Theory and Deviance in Sport 380
    D. Stanley Eitzen
      This reading applies principles and concepts of conflict theory to deviance in the area of
        sports, with an emphasis on the power of certain groups over others.
  25. Intersections of Race, Class, Gender, and Crime: Future Directions for Feminist Criminology 388
    Amanda Burgess-Proctor
      Following the call given in the previous reading, this selection attempts to address many
        of the issues that were noted, namely, to build theoretical links among gender, race, and
        social class regarding criminal offending and treatment by the criminal justice system.

SECTION X. LIFE-COURSE PERSPECTIVES OF CRIMINALITY 399
    Developmental Theories 399
        Antidevelopmental Theory: Low Self-Control Theory 400
        Sampson and Laub's Developmental Model 402
        Moffitt's Developmental Taxonomy 403
    Policy Implications 405
    Conclusion 406
    Section Summary 406
    Key Terms 406
    Discussion Questions 406
    Web Resources 407

READINGS
    26. Criminal Career Paradigm: Background, Recent Developments, and the Way Forward 408
        Alex R. Piquero, David P. Farrington, and Alfred Blumstein
        This reading provides an excellent review of the concepts of developmental theory and
            examines the empirical research that has been done on offending patterns of individuals
            over time.
    27. The Effects of Prenatal Problems, Family Functioning, and Neighborhood Disadvantage
        in Predicting Life-Course-Persistent Offending 421
        Michael G. Turner, Jennifer L. Hartman, and Donna M. Bishop
        In this selection, the authors test a biosocial interaction in predicting life-course persistent
            offending using the National Longitudinal Survey of Youth.
    28. Highlights from Pathways to Desistance: A Longitudinal Study of
        Serious Adolescent Offenders 434
        Edward P. Mulvey
        In this reading, the author reviews a number of studies that have focused on reducing
            offending among youth offenders, and points out a number of intervention strategies
            that have seemed to show effectiveness in reducing recidivism.

SECTION XI. INTEGRATED THEORETICAL MODELS AND NEW PERSPECTIVES OF CRIME 439
    Integrated Theories 440
        The Need for Integrated Theories in Criminology 440
        Different Forms of Integrated Theories 441
        Levels of Analysis of Integrated Theories 445
        Additional Considerations regarding Types of Integration 446
        Criticisms and Weaknesses of Integrated Theories 448
        Examples of Integrated Criminological Theory 452
    Policy Implications 463
    Conclusion 464
    Section Summary 464
    Key Terms 465
    Discussion Questions 465
    Web Resources 465

READINGS
    29. An Integrated Theoretical Perspective on Delinquent Behavior 466
        Delbert S. Elliott, Suzanne S. Ageton, and Rachelle J. Canter

This selection presents one of the earliest and perhaps most influential integrated theoretical models of criminal behavior. This model has received considerable empirical support and has demonstrated that integrated models could contribute much to our understanding of offending.

30. An Exploratory Test of Braithwaite's Reintegrative Shaming Theory   477
    Carter Hay

    This selection tests one of the prominent integrated theories, which emphasizes the way that offenders are treated, specifically, whether they are permanently stigmatized or allowed to be reintegrated into conventional society once they have completed their punishment for the crime they committed.

31. Toward an Interactional Theory of Delinquency   488
    Terence P. Thornberry

    This piece presents an integrated model that is one of the most complicated, yet most useful, to date because it involves "feedback loops" for a number of influences and factors that tend to affect each other in a reciprocal fashion. It is easy to see how these factors could continuously influence the others in ways that don't fit most temporally ordered causal models of criminal offending.

SECTION XII. APPLYING CRIMINOLOGICAL THEORY TO POLICY   499

Policy Applications Derived from the Classical School: Deterrence Theory   499
    Law Enforcement   500
    Courts, Diversion Programs, and Corrections   501
Policy Applications Derived from Biosocial Theories   502
Policy Applications Derived from Social Structure Theories   503
Policy Applications Derived from Social Process Theories   504
Policy Applications Derived from Social Reaction and Conflict Theories   505
Policy Applications Derived from Integrated and Developmental Theories   506
Conclusion   506
Section Summary   506
Discussion Questions   507
Web Resources   507

READINGS

32. Crime and Public Policy   508
    James Q. Wilson

    This piece examines modern policy implications and the frameworks on which such policies are based, as well as evaluations of their effectiveness.

33. Toward an Integrated Theory of Probation   515
    Craig S. Schwalbe

    In this selection, the author proposes a theoretical framework to guide future probation programs and policies, as well as to guide future research development.

Glossary   529

Index   539

About the Authors   551

Foreword

You hold in your hands a book that we think is a different approach to this subject matter and to student learning. It is billed a "text/reader." What that means is that we have blended the two most commonly used types of books, the textbook and the reader, in a way that will appeal to both students and faculty.

Our experience as teachers and scholars has been that textbooks for the core classes in criminal justice (or any other social science discipline) leave many students and professors cold. The textbooks are huge and crammed with photographs, charts, highlighted material, and all sorts of pedagogical devices intended to increase student interest. Too often, however, these books end up creating a sort of sensory overload for students and suffer from their focus on "bells and whistles," such as fancy graphics, at the expense of coverage of the most significant and current research on the subject matter. And, in the end, isn't that what matters most? We study crime and justice to better understand why crime happens and how society processes it, and it is research—not pretty pictures—that inform this process. Our students deserve more than a nicely packaged recitation of boring facts; they need to understand what the research says, and this research needs to be presented in a fashion that does not scare them off.

Readers, on the other hand, are typically composed of recent and classic research articles on the subject matter. They generally suffer, however, from an absence of meaningful explanatory material. Articles are simply lined up and presented to the students with little or no context or explanation. Students, particularly undergraduate students, are often confused and overwhelmed by the jargon and detailed statistical analyses presented in the articles. It is unrealistic to expect students to fully grasp criminal justice research if this research is not placed in context and presented in a manner suited to their knowledge level.

This text/reader represents our attempt to take the best of both textbook and reader approaches. The book includes a combination of previously published articles on criminological theory and of textual material introducing the articles and providing structure and context. The text/reader is intended to serve either as a supplement to a core undergraduate textbook or as a stand-alone text.

The book is divided into a number of sections. The sections of the book track the typical content and structure of a textbook on the subject. Each section of the book has an introductory chapter that introduces, explains, and provides context for the readings that follow. The readings are a selection of the best recent research from academic journals, as well as some classic readings where appropriate. The articles are edited as necessary to make them accessible to students. This variety of research and perspectives will provide the student with a grasp of the development of research, as well as an understanding of the current status of research in the subject area. The approach gives the student the opportunity to learn the basics (in the introductory portion of each section) and to read some of the most interesting research on the subject.

There is also a preface and an introductory chapter. The preface explains the organization and content of the book, and the introductory chapter provides a framework for the material that follows and introduces relevant themes, issues, and concepts to assist the student in understanding the articles.

Each section concludes with a summary of the material covered, as well as a set of discussion questions. Discussion questions also appear at the end of each reading. These summaries and discussion questions should facilitate student thought and class discussion of the material.

Ancillary materials, such as PowerPoint slides, a testbank, and lecture outlines, are available to help assist the instructor in moving from a standard textbook to this hybrid approach.

We acknowledge that this approach may be viewed by some as more challenging than the traditional textbook. To that we say "Yes! It is!" But we believe that, if we raise the bar, our students will rise to the challenge. Research shows that students and faculty often find textbooks boring to read. It is our belief that many criminal justice instructors welcome the opportunity to teach without having to rely on a "standard" textbook that covers only the most basic information and that lacks both depth of coverage and an attention to current research. This book provides an alternative for instructors who want more than a basic textbook aimed at the lowest common denominator and filled with flashy but often useless features that merely drive up its cost. This book is intended for instructors who want their students to be exposed to more than the ordinary, basic coverage of criminal justice.

We also believe students will find this approach more interesting. They are given the opportunity to read current, cutting-edge research on the subject while also being provided with background and context for this research. In addition to including the most topical and relevant research, we have included a short entry, "How to Read a Research Article." The purpose of this entry, placed toward the beginning of the book, is to provide students with an overview of the components of a research article. It helps walk them through the process of reading a research article, lessening their trepidation and increasing their ability to comprehend the material presented therein. Many students will be unfamiliar with reading and deciphering research articles; we hope this feature will help them do so.

In addition, we provide a student study site on the Internet with supplemental research articles, study questions, practice quizzes, and other pedagogical material to assist the student in learning the material. We chose to put these pedagogical tools on a companion study site rather than in the text to allow instructors to focus on the material, while still offering students the opportunity to learn more.

To date, there have been twelve books published in the text/reader series. Many of them have gone into (or are in the process of going into) multiple editions. The feedback we have received from early adopters has been overwhelmingly positive. Instructors have successfully used these books in community colleges and universities at both the undergraduate and graduate levels. Faculty tell us they find the books more interesting to use and teach from, and that students appreciate the different approach.

We hope that this unconventional approach will be more interesting to students and faculty alike and thus make learning and teaching more fun. Criminal justice is a fascinating subject, and the topic deserves to be presented in an interesting manner. We hope you will agree.

Craig Hemmens, JD, PhD, Series Editor
Department of Criminal Justice and Criminology
Washington State University

Preface

Anumber of excellent criminology theory textbooks and readers are available to students and professors, so why this one? The reason is that stand-alone textbooks and readers (often assigned as an expensive addition to a textbook) have a pedagogical fault that we seek to rectify with the present book. Textbooks provide a broad overview of the topic but lack depth and a focus on current research, whereas readers often feature in-depth articles about a single topic but give little or no text to describe the history of each model or the context in which it was proposed, little text to unify the readings, and little in the way of pedagogy. This book, especially in its second edition, provides more in the way of text and pedagogy and uses recent research-based articles to help students understand criminological theory. This book is unique in that it is a hybrid text/reader, offering the best of both worlds. It includes a collection of articles on criminological theory that have previously appeared in a number of leading criminology journals, along with original text that explains and synthesizes the readings. We have selected some of the best recent research and literature reviews and assembled them into this text/reader for an undergraduate or graduate theory class.

Journal articles and book chapters have been chosen based primarily on how they add to and complement the text and on how interesting we perceive them to be for students. Although seminal theoretical pieces are included among the previously published works, we have emphasized contemporary empirical studies that actually test the theories in each respective section. We believe this focus on recent empirical studies and scholarly works regarding the various major theoretical models in criminology, most from leading criminology journals, is a distinguishing feature of this text/reader as compared to other books on criminological theory. In our opinion, these articles are the best contemporary work on the issues they address. For example, in this second edition, we are including eight new readings that are either far more recent or seen as more relevant for applying the theoretical models and concepts presented in the text.

However, journal articles are written for professional audiences, not for students, and thus often contain quantitative material that students are not expected to understand. They also often contain concepts and hair-splitting arguments that tend to turn students glassy-eyed. Mindful of this, the articles contained in this text/reader have been carefully and meticulously edited to make them as student friendly as possible. We have done this without doing injustice to the core points raised by the authors or detracting from the authors' key findings and conclusions. Those wishing to read these articles (and others) in their entirety can do so by accessing the SAGE website provided for users of this book. Research-based quantitative articles are balanced by review/overview essay-type articles and qualitative articles providing subjective insight into criminal behavior from the points of view of offenders.

This book can serve as a supplemental reader or the primary text for an undergraduate course in criminological theory or as the primary text for a graduate course. In a graduate course, it would serve as both an introduction to the extant literature and a sourcebook for additional reading, as well as a springboard for enhanced class discussion. When used in an undergraduate course, this book can serve to provide greater depth than the standard textbook. It is important to note that the readings and the introductory texts provide a comprehensive survey of the existing scientific literature in virtually all areas of criminological theory, as well as giving a history of how we got to this point regarding each theoretical model and each topic.

Structure of the Book

We use a rather typical outline for criminological theory textbook topics/sections, beginning with an introduction of the definitions of crime and criminology and measuring crime, as well as what such measures of crime reveal regarding the various characteristics that are most associated with higher offending rates. This is a very important aspect of the book, because each theory or model must be judged by how well it explains the distribution of crime rates among these various characteristics.

This text/reader is divided into 12 sections that mirror the sections in a typical criminology textbook, each dealing with a particular subject in criminology. These sections are as follows:

I. Introduction to the Book: An Overview of Issues in Criminological Theory

We first provide an introductory section that deals with what criminological theory is, as well as examining the concepts of crime and the criteria used to determine whether a theory is adequate for explaining behavior. This section introduces the facts and criteria by which all of the theoretical models presented in the following sections will be evaluated. We also include a discussion of the criteria involved in determining whether a given factor or variable actually causes criminal behavior.

II. Preclassical and Classical Theories of Crime

In this section, we examine the types of theories that were dominant before logical theories of crime were presented, namely supernatural or demonic theories of crime. Then we examine how the Age of Enlightenment led to more rational approaches to explaining criminal behavior, such as that of the Classical School and neoclassical theory. We also discuss at length the major model that evolved from the Classical School: deterrence theory. We describe studies that have empirically tested deterrence theory.

III. Modern Applications of the Classical Perspective: Deterrence, Rational Choice, and Routine Activities or Lifestyle Theories of Crime

In this section, we review more contemporary theoretical models and empirical findings regarding explanations of crime that focus on deterrence and other recent perspectives—such as rational choice theory, routine activities theory, and the lifestyle perspective—that are based on the assumption that individuals rationally choose their behavior or targets. Some of these perspectives focus more on the perceived costs or benefits of a given act to the individual who carries it out, whereas other models focus on the types of locations that people choose to commit crime or the daily activities or lifestyles that predispose them to certain criminal behavior.

IV. Early Positive School Perspectives of Criminality

This section will examine the early development of theoretical models proposing that certain individuals or groups are predisposed to criminal offending. The earliest theories in the 19th century proposed that certain physical traits are associated with criminal behavior, whereas perspectives in the early 20th century proposed that such criminality is due to level of intelligence. This section also examines body-type theory, which proposes that the physical body type of an individual has an effect on criminality. We will also examine modern applications of this perspective and review the empirical support such theoretical models have received in modern times.

V. Modern Biosocial Perspectives of Criminal Behavior

In this section, we will review the various forms of modern studies that investigate the link between physiology and criminality, including family studies, twin and adoption studies, cytogenetic studies, and studies on hormones and neurotransmitters. We will examine some of the primary methods used to explore this link as well as discuss the findings of more rational and recent empirical studies, which show a relatively consistent link between physiological factors and criminal behavior.

VI. Early Social Structure and Strain Theories of Crime

This section reviews the development of the social structure perspective, which originated in the 19th century and culminated with Merton's theory of strain in the early 20th century. A variety of perspectives based on Merton's strain theory will be examined, but all of these models have a primary emphasis on how the social structure produces criminal behavior. We examine the many empirical studies that have tested the validity of these early social structure theories, as well as discussing policy implications that these models suggested.

VII. The Chicago School and Cultural and Subcultural Theories of Crime

In this section, we examine the evolution and propositions of the scholars at the University of Chicago, the most advanced form of criminological theorizing of the early 20th century. In addition to discussing the evolution of the Chicago School and its application of ecological theory to criminal behavior, we examine the more modern applications of this theoretical framework for explaining criminal behavior among residents of certain neighborhoods. Finally, we discuss several theoretical models that examine cultural or subcultural groups that differ drastically from conventional norms.

VIII. Social Process and Learning Theories of Crime

This section examines the many perspectives that have proposed that criminal behavior is the result of being taught by significant others to commit crime. When these theories were first presented, they were considered quite novel. We examine the evolution of various theories of social learning, starting with the earliest, which were based on somewhat outdated forms of learning theory, and then progressing to more modern theories that incorporate contemporary learning models. We also examine the most recent versions of this theoretical perspective, which incorporates all forms of social learning in explaining criminal behavior.

IX. Social Reaction, Critical, and Feminist Models of Crime

In this section, we examine a large range of theories, with the common assumption that the reason for criminal behavior is factors outside of the traditional criminal justice system. Many social reaction theories, for example, are based on labeling theory, which proposes that it is not the individual offender who is to blame, but rather the societal reaction to such early antisocial behavior. Furthermore, this section examines the critical perspective, which blames the existing legal and economical structure for the "criminal" label that is used against most offenders. Also, we discuss the major perspectives of criminal offending as they pertain to females as compared to males, as well as the differential treatment of the sexes by the formal criminal justice system. Finally, we look at how explaining low levels of female offending might be important for policies regarding males.

X. Life-Course Perspectives of Criminality

This section examines the various theoretical perspectives that emphasize the predisposition and influences present among individuals who begin committing crime at early versus later ages. We also examine the various stages of life that tend to have a high influence on an individual's state of criminality (e.g., marriage), as well as the empirical studies that have examined these types of transitions in life. Finally, we examine the various types of offenders and the kinds of transitions and trajectories that tend to influence their future behavior, along with various policy implications that can be suggested by such models of criminality.

XI. Integrated Theoretical Models and New Perspectives of Crime

In this section, we present the general theoretical framework for integrated models. Then we introduce criticisms of such integration of traditional theoretical models. In addition, we present several integrated models of criminality, some of which are based on micro-level factors and others that are based on macro-level factors. Finally, we examine the weaknesses and strengths of these various models based on empirical studies that have tested their validity.

XII. Applying Criminological Theory to Policy

This final section will review the most recent empirical evidence regarding how the theoretical models and findings reviewed in this book can be used to inform policies to reduce criminal behavior among offenders. These studies show that many theoretical perspectives suggest some effective policy recommendations, whereas other theoretical frameworks have been shown to be less effective in terms of policy applications.

 ## Ancillaries

To enhance the use of this text/reader and to assist those using this book as a core text, we have developed high-quality ancillaries for instructors and students.

Instructor's Resource CD. A variety of instructor's materials are available. For each chapter, these include summaries, PowerPoint slides, chapter activities, web resources, and a complete set of test questions.

Student Study Site. A comprehensive student study site features chapter outlines students can print for class, flashcards, interactive quizzes, web exercises, links to additional journal articles, links to Frontline videos, links to NPR and PBS radio shows, and more.

 ## Acknowledgments

We would first of all like to thank executive editor Jerry Westby. Jerry's faith in and commitment to the project are greatly appreciated, as are those of his very able production editor Libby Larson. They kept up a most useful three-way dialogue among authors, publisher, and a parade of excellent reviewers, making this text the best that it could possibly be. We would also like to thank Erin Conley, who wrote the guide "How to Read a Research Article." Our copy editor, Rachel Keith, spotted every errant comma, dangling participle, and missing reference in the manuscript, for which we are truly thankful. Thank you one and all.

Stephen Tibbetts also would like to thank the various individuals who helped him complete this book. First, he would like to thank the professors he had as an undergraduate at University of Florida, who first exposed him to criminological theory. These professors include Ronald Akers and Lonn Lanza-Kaduce, with a special thanks to

Donna Bishop, who was the instructor in his first criminological theory course. He would also like to thank the influential professors he had at the University of Maryland, including Denise Gottfredson, Colin Loftin, David McDowell, Lawrence Sherman, and Charles Wellford. He gives a very special acknowledgment to Raymond Paternoster, who was his primary mentor and adviser and exerted an influence words can't describe. Ray and his wife, Ronet Bachman, provided rare support as surrogate parents when Tibbetts was in graduate school. Paternoster also introduced him to the passion for criminological theory that he hopes is reflected in this book.

Tibbetts would like to thank Alex Piquero, also at the University of Maryland, with whom he had the great luck of sharing a graduate student office in the mid-1990s, and who is now a professor at the university. Without the many collaborations and discussions about theory that he had with Alex, this book would be quite different and would likely not exist. Alex and his wife, Nicole Leeper Piquero, have consistently been key influences on Tibbetts's perspective on and understanding of theories of crimes, especially contemporary models (and the works of both of the Piqueros are represented in this book).

In addition, Tibbetts would like to thank several colleagues who have helped him subsequent to his education. First, he would like to thank John Paul Wright at the University of Cincinnati and Chris Gibson at the University of Florida for inspiring him to further explore biosocial and developmental areas of criminality. Also, he would like to thank Mary Schmidt and Joseph Schwartz at California State University, San Bernardino (CSUSB), who provided much help in the compilation of materials for this book. In addition, he would like to especially thank Pamela Schram and Larry Gaines, fellow professors at CSUSB, who have provided the highest possible level of support and guidance during his career. Furthermore, it should be noted that Pamela Schram provided key insights and materials that aided in the writing of several sections of this book.

Tibbetts owes the most gratitude to his wife, Kim, who has patiently put up with him typing away for the past few years while working on this book. Her constant support and companionship are what keeps him going.

Both authors are grateful to the many reviewers who spent considerable time reading early drafts of their work and who provided helpful suggestions for improving both the textual material and the edited readings. Trying to please so many individuals is a challenge, but one that is ultimately satisfying and undoubtedly made the book better than it would otherwise have been. Heartfelt thanks to the following experts: Shannon Barton-Bellessa, Indiana State University; Deborah Baskin, Loyola University-Chicago; Michael L. Benson, University of Cincinnati; Robert Brame, University of South Carolina; Tammy Castle, University of West Florida; James Chriss, Cleveland State University; Toni DuPont-Morales, Pennsylvania State University; Joshua D. Freilich, John Jay College; Randy Gainey, Old Dominion University; Evan Gorelick, Germanna Community College; Robert Hanser, Kaplan University; Jay Healey, Simon Fraser University; Heath Hoffman, College of Charleston; Thomas Holt, University of North Carolina, Charlotte; Rebecca Katz, Morehead State University; Dennis Longmire, Sam Houston State University; Gina Luby, DePaul University; Michael J. Lynch, University of South Florida; Michelle Hughes Miller, Southern Illinois University, Carbondale; J. Mitchell Miller, University of Texas, San Antonio; Travis Pratt, Arizona State University; Lois Presser, University of Tennessee; Robert Sarver, University of Texas, Arlington; Joseph Scimecca, George Mason University; Martin S. Schwartz, Ohio University; Victoria Silverwood, Cardiff University; Ira Sommers, California State University, Los Angeles; Amy Thistlethwaite, Northern Kentucky University; Kimberly Tobin, Westfield State College; Michael Turner, University of North Carolina, Charlotte; Scott Vollum, James Madison University; Courtney Waid, North Dakota State University; Barbara Warner, Georgia State University; Mary G Wilson, Kent State University Trumbull Campus; and Sarah Yercich, Northern Arizona University.

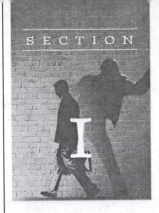

Introduction to the Book

An Overview of Issues in Criminological Theory

Welcome to the world of criminological theory! It is an exciting and complex endeavor that explains why certain individuals and groups commit crimes and why other people do not. This book will explore the conceptual history of this endeavor as well as current theories. Most of us can relate directly to many of these theories; we may know friends or family members who fit dominant models of criminal behavior.

This introduction begins by describing what criminology is; what distinguishes it from other perspectives of crime, such as religion, journalism, and philosophy; and how definitions of crime vary across time and place. Then it examines some of the major issues used to classify different theories of criminology. After exploring the various paradigms and categories of criminological theory, we discuss what characteristics help to make a theory a good one—in criminology or in any scientific field. In addition, we review the specific criteria for proving causality—for showing which predictors or variables actually cause criminal behavior. We also explain why—for logistic and ethical reasons—few theories in criminology will ever meet the strict criteria required to prove that key factors actually cause criminal behavior. Finally, we look at the strengths and weaknesses of the various measures of crime, which are used to test the validity of all criminological theories, and what those measures reveal about how crime is distributed across various individuals and groups. Although the discussion of crime distribution, as shown by various measures of criminality, may seem removed from our primary discussion regarding theories of why certain individuals and groups commit more crime than others, nothing could be further from the truth. Ultimately, all theories of criminal behavior will be judged based on how much each theory can explain the observed rates of crime shown by the measures of criminality among individuals and groups.

What Is Criminology, and How Does It Differ from Other Examinations of Crime?

Criminology is the scientific study of crime, and especially of why people commit crime. Although many textbooks have more complex definitions of crime, the word *scientific* separates our definition from other perspectives and examinations of crime.[1] Philosophical and legal examinations of crime are based on logic and deductive reasoning, for example, by developing propositions for what makes logical sense. Journalists play a vital role in examinations of crime by exploring what is happening in criminal justice and revealing injustices and new forms of crime; however, they tend to examine anecdotes or examples of crime as opposed to objective measures of criminality.

Taken together, philosophical, legal, and journalistic perspectives of crime are not scientific because they do not involve the use of the scientific method. Specifically, they do not develop specific predictions, known scientifically as hypotheses, which are based on prior knowledge and studies, and then go out and test these predictions through observation. Criminology is based on this scientific method, whereas other examinations of crime are not.

Instead, philosophers and journalists tend to examine a specific case, make conclusions based on that one example of a crime incident, and then leave it at that. Experts in these nonscientific disciplines do not typically examine a multitude of stories similar to the one they are considering, nor do they apply the elements of their story to an existing theoretical framework that offers specific predictions or hypotheses. Further, they do not test those predictions by observation. The method of testing predictions through observation and then applying the findings to a larger body of knowledge, as established by theoretical models, is solely the domain of criminologists, and it separates criminology from other fields. The use of the scientific method is a distinguishing criterion for many studies of human behavior, such as psychology, economics, sociology, and anthropology, which is why these disciplines are generally classified as social sciences; criminology is one of them.

To look at another perspective on crime, religious accounts are almost entirely based on dogmatic, authoritarian, or reasoning principles, meaning that they are typically based on what some authority (e.g., the Pope, the Bible, the Torah, or the Koran) has to say about the primary causes of crime and the best ways to deal with such violations. These ideas are not based on observations. A science like criminology is based not on authority or anecdotes but on empirical research, even if that research is conducted by a 15-year-old who performs a methodologically sound study. In other words, the authority of the scientist performing the study does not matter; rather, the observed evidence and the soundness of the methodology—how the study was performed—are of utmost importance. Criminology is based on science, and its work is accomplished through direct observation and testing of hypotheses, even if those findings do not fit neatly into logical principles or the general feelings of the public.

What Is Theory?

Theory can be defined as a set of concepts linked together by a series of statements to explain why an event or phenomenon occurs. A simple way of thinking about theories is that they provide explanations of why the world works the way it does. In other words, a theory is a model of the phenomenon that is being discussed, which in this case is criminal behavior. Sometimes, perhaps quite often, theories are simply wrong, even if the predictions they give are highly accurate.

For example, in the early Middle Ages, most people, including expert scientists, believed the Earth was the center of the universe because everything seemed to rotate and revolve around our home planet. If we wake up day

---

[1]Stephen Brown, Finn Esbensen, and Gilbert Geis, *Criminology*, 8th ed. (Cincinnati: Anderson, 2013).

after day and see the sun (or moon) rise and set in close to the same place, it appears that these celestial bodies are revolving around the Earth, especially considering the fact that we don't feel the world around us moving. Furthermore, calendars predicting the change of seasons, as well as the location and phases of these celestial bodies (such as the moon), were quite accurate. However, although the experts were able to predict the movements of celestial objects quite well and develop extremely accurate calendars, they had absolutely no understanding of what was actually happening. Later, when some individuals tried to convince the majority that they were wrong, specifically that the Earth was not the center of the universe, they were condemned as heretics and persecuted, even though their theoretical models were correct.

The same type of argument could be made about the Earth being flat; at one time, obser-

▲ Image 1.1   Theories of the Earth as the center of the universe were dominant for many centuries, and scientists who proposed that the Earth was not the center of the universe were often persecuted. Over time, the theory was proved false.

Source: © Comstock / Stockbyte / Thinkstock

vations and all existing models seemed to claim it as proven and true. Some disagreed and decided to test their own predictions, which is how America was discovered by European explorers. Still, many who believed the Earth was round were persecuted or cast out of mainstream society in Europe at the time.

Two things should be clear: Theories can be erroneous, and accurate predictions can be made (e.g., early calendars and moon and star charts) using them, even though there is no true understanding of what is actually happening. One way to address both of these issues is to base knowledge and theories on scientific observation and testing. All respected theories of crime in the modern era are based on science; thus, we try to avoid buying into and applying theories that are inaccurate, and we continuously refine and improve our theories (based on findings from scientific testing) to gain a better understanding of what causes people to commit crime. Criminology, as a science, always allows and even welcomes criticism of its existing theoretical models. There is no emphasis on authority but rather on the scientific method and the quality of the observations that take place in testing the predictions. All scientific theories can be improved, and they are improved only through observation and empirical testing.

What Is Crime?

Definitions of crime vary drastically. For example, some take a legalistic approach to defining crime, including only acts that are specifically prohibited in the legal codes of a given jurisdiction. The problem with such a definition is that what is a crime in one jurisdiction is not necessarily a crime in other jurisdictions. To clarify, some acts, such as murder and armed robbery, are against the law in virtually all countries and all regions of the United States, across time and culture. These are known as acts of *mala in se*, literally meaning *evil in itself*.[2] Typically, these crimes involve serious violence and shock the society in which they occur.

Other crimes are known as acts of *mala prohibita*, which has the literal meaning of *evil because prohibited*. This term acknowledges that these crimes are not inherently evil acts; they are bad only because the law says so.[3] A good example is prostitution, which is illegal in most of the United States but is quite legal and even licensed in most

---

[2]Ibid.

[3]Ibid.

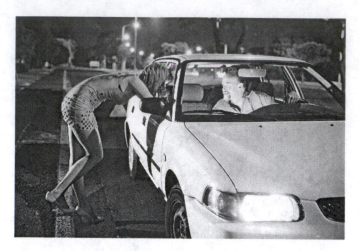

▲ Image 1.2 Prostitution is considered a *mala prohibita* offense because it is not inherently evil, and is even legal in many jurisdictions around the world.

SOURCE: © iStockphoto.com /RapidEye

counties of Nevada. The same can be said about gambling and drug possession or use. These are just examples of acts that are criminal only in certain places or at certain times and thus are not agreed upon by most members of a given community.

This book examines both *mala in se* and *mala prohibita* types of offenses, as well as other acts of deviance, which are not against the law in many places but are statistically atypical and may be considered more immoral than illegal. For example, in Nevada in the 1990s, a young man watched his friend (who was later criminally prosecuted) kill a young girl in the bathroom at a casino, but he told no one. Although most people would claim that this was highly immoral, at that time, the Nevada state laws did not require people who witnessed a killing to report it to authorities. (Note: As a result of this event, Nevada made withholding such information a criminal act.) Therefore, this act was deviant because most people would find it immoral, but it was not criminal because it was not technically against the laws in the jurisdiction at that time.

Other acts of deviance are not necessarily immoral but are certainly statistically unusual and violate social norms, such as purposely "passing gas" at a formal dinner. Such activities are relevant for our discussion, even if they are not defined as criminal by the law, because they show a disposition toward antisocial behavior, which is often found in individuals who are likely to become criminal offenders. Furthermore, some acts are moving from deviant to illegal all the time, such as using cell phones while driving or smoking cigarettes in public; many jurisdictions are moving to have these behaviors made illegal and have been quite successful to date, especially in New York and California.

Most *mala in se* activities (e.g., murder) are highly deviant, too, meaning they are not typically found in society, but many, if not most, *mala prohibita* acts are not deviant because they are committed by most people at some point. Speeding on a highway is a good example of a *mala prohibita* act that is illegal but not deviant. This book will examine theories for all of these types of activities, even those that do not violate the law in a given jurisdiction at the present time.

How Are Criminological Theories Classified? The Major Theoretical Paradigms

Scientific theories of crime can be categorized based on several important concepts, assumptions, and characteristics. To begin, most criminological theories are classified by the paradigm they emphasize. Paradigms are distinctive theoretical models or perspectives; in the case of crime, they vary based largely on opposing assumptions of human behavior. There are four major paradigms.[4]

The first of these, deterrence or rational choice theories, commonly referred to as the Classical School perspective, will be discussed at length later in this book. It assumes that individuals have free will and choose to commit

[4]Thomas J. Bernard, Jeffrey B. Snipes, and Alexander L. Gerould, *Vold's Theoretical Criminology*, 6th ed. (Oxford: Oxford University Press, 2010).

crimes based on rational, hedonistic decisions; they weigh out the potential costs and benefits of offending and then choose what will maximize their pleasure and minimize their pain. The distinguishing characteristic of these theories is that they emphasize the free choice individuals have in committing crime. The other paradigms are based on the influence of factors other than free will or rational decision making—for example, biology, culture, parenting, and economics.

Another category of theories is positivism, which is somewhat the opposite of rational choice theories. These theories argue that individuals do not have free will or rationality in making decisions to commit crime. Rather, the Positive School perspective assumes that individuals are passive subjects of determinism, which means that people do not freely choose their behavior. Instead, their behavior is determined by factors outside of their free will, such as genetics, IQ, education, employment, peer influences, parenting, and economics.[5] Most of the highly respected and scientifically validated criminological theories of the modern era fall into this category.[6]

Another group of criminological theories belongs to the conflict or critical perspective, which emphasizes the use of law as a reaction or tool to enforce restraint on others by those in power or authority; it also involves how society reacts when a person (often a juvenile) is caught doing something wrong. These theories emphasize group behavior over individual behavior: Groups that are in power use the criminal codes as a tool in keeping people who have limited power restrained or confined.

Finally, over the last few decades, a new category has emerged, namely the integrated theoretical models, which attempt to combine the best aspects of explanatory models into a single, better theoretical framework for understanding crime. These models tend to suffer from the logical inconsistencies inherent in integrating theoretical models that have opposing assumptions or propositions. All of these categories will become clearer as we progress through this book.

Additional Ways to Classify Criminological Theories

Although the major paradigms are the primary way criminological theories are classified, there are several other ways that they can be categorized. Specifically, theoretical models can be classified based on whether they focus on individuals or groups as their primary units of examination. For instance, some theories emphasize why certain individuals do or do not commit crime. This level of investigation, in which the focus is on the individual, is often referred to as the micro level of analysis, much as microeconomics is the study of economics on the individual (person) level. When your instructors score each student on an exam, this is a micro-level analysis.

On the other hand, many theories emphasize primarily the group or macro level of analysis, much as macroeconomics is the study of economic principles at the aggregate or group level. In this book, some sections are separated by whether the individual or the group level of analysis is emphasized. For example, social process theories tend to be more micro level oriented, whereas social structure theories are more macro level oriented. Here's a good example: If instructors compare the mean score (or average) of one class to the mean score of another, this is a comparison of group rates, regardless of the performance of any individual in either class. Ultimately, a great theory would explain both the micro and macro levels of analysis, but we will see that very few attempt to explain or account for both levels.

Criminological theories can also be classified by their general perspective on how laws are made. Some theories assume that laws are made to define acts as criminal to the extent that they violate rights of individuals, and thus, virtually everyone agrees that such acts are immoral. This type of perspective is considered a consensual perspective (or nonconflict model). On the other hand, many modern forms of criminological theories fall into an opposite category, commonly known as the conflict theories, which assumes that different groups disagree

---

[5]Ibid.

[6]Lee Ellis and Anthony Walsh, "Criminologists' Opinions about Causes and Theories of Crime and Delinquency," *The Criminologist* 24 (1999):1–4.

about the fairness of laws and that laws are used as a tool by those in power to keep down other, lower-power groups. There are many forms of both consensual and conflict theoretical models, and both will be specifically noted as we progress through the book.

A final, but perhaps most important, way to classify theories is in terms of their assumptions regarding human nature. Some theories assume that people are born good (giving, benevolent, etc.) and are corrupted by social or other developmental influences that lead them to crime. A good example is strain theory, which claims that people are born innocent and with good intentions but that society causes them to commit crime. On the other hand, many of the most popular current theories claim that virtually all individuals are born with a disposition toward being bad (selfish, greedy, etc.) and must be socialized or restrained from following their inherent propensities for engaging in crime.[7] A good example of this is control theory, which assumes that all individuals have a predisposition to be greedy, selfish, violent, and so on (i.e., they are criminally disposed), and therefore that people need to be controlled or prevented from acting on their natural, inherent disposition toward selfish and aggressive behaviors.

A variation of these theories is often referred to as *tabula rasa*, literally translated as *blank slate*. This assumes that people are born with no leaning toward good or bad but are simply influenced by the balance of positive or negative influences that are introduced socially during their development. A good example of this perspective is differential association or reinforcement theory, which assumes that all individuals are born with a blank slate and that they learn whether to be good or bad based on what they experience.

Although the dominant assumption tends to vary across these three models from time to time, the most popular theories today (which are self- and social-control theories) seem to imply the second option, specifically that people are born selfish and greedy and must be socialized and trained to be good and conforming.[8] There are other ways that criminological theories can be classified, but the various characteristics we have discussed in this section summarize the most important factors.

Characteristics of Good Theories

Respected scientific theories in any field, whether it be chemistry, physics, or criminology, tend to have the same characteristics. After all, the same scientific review process (i.e., blind peer review by experts) is used in all sciences to determine which studies and theoretical works are of high quality. The criteria that characterize a good theory in chemistry are the same as those used to judge a criminological theory. Such characteristics include parsimony, scope, logical consistency, testability, empirical validity, and policy implications.[9] Each of these characteristics is examined here. (It should be noted that our discussion and many of the examples provided for the characteristics are taken from Akers and Sellers, 2012).[10]

Parsimony is achieved by explaining a given phenomenon—in our case criminal activity—in the simplest way possible. Other characteristics being equal, the simpler a theory, the better. The problem with criminal behavior is that it is highly complex. However, that has not stopped some criminologists from attempting to explain this convoluted phenomenon in highly simple ways. For example, one of the most recent and most popular theories (as indicated by the amount of related research and by which theories the experts believe are most important) is the theory of low self-control (which we discuss later in this book). This very simple model holds that one personality factor—low self-control—is responsible for all criminal activity. The originators of this theory, Michael Gottfredson and

---

[7]Ibid.

[8]Ibid.

[9]Ronald Akers and Christine Sellers, *Criminological Theories*, 6th ed. (Oxford: Oxford University Press, 2012).

[10]Ibid., 4–19.

Travis Hirschi, assert that every single act of crime and deviance is caused by this same factor: low self-control[11]—everything from speeding, smoking tobacco, not wearing a seat belt while driving, and having numerous sex partners to serious crimes such as murder and armed robbery are caused by low self-control.

Although this theory has been disputed by much of the subsequent research on this model, it remains one of the most popular and accepted models of the modern era.[12] Furthermore, despite the criticisms of this theory, many notable criminologists still believe that this is the best single model of offending that has been presented to date. In addition, there is little doubt that this model has become the most researched theoretical model over the last two decades.[13]

Perhaps the most important reason why so much attention has been given to this theory is its simplicity, putting all of the focus on a single factor. Virtually all other theoretical models have proposed multiple factors that may play major parts in determining why individuals commit crime. After all, how can low self-control explain white-collar crime? Some self-control is required to obtain a white-collar position of employment. It is true that a simple theory is better than a more complex one, as long as other characteristics are equivalent. However, given a complex behavior like criminal behavior, it is unlikely that a simple explanation, such as naming one factor to account for everything, will prove adequate.

Scope, the next characteristic of a theory, indicates how much of a given phenomenon the theory seeks to explain. This is somewhat related to parsimony in the sense that some theories, like the theory of low self-control, seek to explain all crimes and all deviant acts as well. Thus, the theory of low self-control has a very wide scope. Other theories of crime, such as some versions of strain theory, may seek to explain only property crime or drug use. However, the wider the scope of what a theory can explain, the better the theory, assuming other characteristics are equal.

Logical consistency is the extent to which a theory makes sense in terms of its concepts and propositions. It is easier to show what we mean by logical consistency if we give examples of what does not fit this criterion. Some theories simply don't make sense because of the face value of their propositions. For example, Cesare Lombroso, called the father of criminology, claimed that the most serious offenders are "born criminals," biological throwbacks to an earlier stage of evolutionary development who can be identified by their physical features.[14] Lombroso, who is discussed at more length later in this book, claimed that tattoos were one of the physical features that identified these born criminals. This doesn't make sense, however, because tattoos are not biological physical features—no baby has ever been born with a tattoo. This criticism will make even more sense when we discuss the criteria for determining causality later in this section.

Another prominent example of theories that lack logical consistency is the work of early feminist theorists, such as Freda Adler, who argued that, as females gain educational and employment opportunities, their rates of crime will be more likely to converge with those of males.[15] Such hypotheses were logically inconsistent with the data available at the time they were presented and are even more inconsistent with the data available today; the facts show that females who are given the most opportunities commit the fewest crimes, while females who have not been given these benefits commit the most crimes.

These are just two examples of how past theories were logically inconsistent with the data available at the time they were created, not to mention inconsistent with future research findings, which have completely dismissed their hypotheses.

---

[11]Michael Gottfredson and Travis Hirschi, *A General Theory of Crime* (Palo Alto: Stanford University Press, 1990).

[12]Ellis and Walsh, "Criminologists' Opinions," 3–4.

[13]Anthony Walsh and Lee Ellis, "Political Ideology and American Criminologists' Explanations for Criminal Behavior," *The Criminologist* 24 (1999): 1, 14.

[14]Cesare Lombroso, *The Criminal Man* (Milan: Hoepli, 1876).

[15]Freda Adler, *Sisters in Crime* (New York: McGraw-Hill, 1975).

Testability is the extent to which a theory can be put to empirical, scientific testing. Some theories simply cannot be tested. A good example is Freud's theory of the psyche. Freud described three domains of the psyche—the conscious ego, the subconscious id, and the superego—but none of these domains can be observed or tested.[16] Although some theories can be quite influential without being testable (as was Freud's theory), other things being equal, it is a considerable disadvantage for a theoretical model to be untestable and unobservable. Fortunately, most established criminological theories can be examined through empirical testing.

Empirical validity is the extent to which a theoretical model is supported by scientific research. Obviously, this is highly related to the previous characteristic of testability. However, while virtually all accepted modern criminological theories are testable, that does not mean they are equal in terms of empirical validity. Although some integrated models (meaning two or more traditional theories that have been merged together; these will be examined later in this book) have gained a large amount of empirical validity, these models "cheat" because they merge the best of two or more models, even when the assumptions of these models are not compatible. The independent theoretical model that has garnered the most empirical validity is differential reinforcement theory, which has been strongly supported for various crime types (from tobacco usage to violence) among a wide variety of populations (from young children to elderly subjects).[17]

Ultimately, empirical validity is perhaps one of the most important characteristics used in determining how good a theory is at explaining a given phenomenon or behavior. If a theory has good empirical validity, it is an accurate explanation of behavior; if it does not have good empirical validity, it should be revised or dismissed because it is simply not true.

Policy implications refers to the extent to which a theory can create realistic and useful guidance for changing the way society deals with a given phenomenon. In our case, this means providing a useful model for informing authorities of how to deal with crime. An example is the broken windows theory, which says that to reduce serious crimes, authorities should focus on the minor incivilities that occur in a given area. This theory has been used successfully by many police agencies (most notably by New York City police, who reduced their homicide rate by more than 75% in the last decade). Other theories may not be as useful in terms of reducing crime because they are too abstract or propose changes that are far too costly or impossible to implement, such as theories that emphasize changing family structure or the chromosomal makeup of individuals. So, other things being equal, a theory that has readily available policy implications would be more advantageous than theories that do not.

Criteria for Determining Causality

There are several criteria for determining whether a certain variable causes another variable to change—in other words, causality. For this discussion, we will be using standard scientific notation to designate an independent or predictor variable (X) that results in a dependent or explanatory variable (Y). Such criteria are used for all scientific disciplines, whether chemistry, physics, biology, or criminology. In this book, we are discussing crime, so we will concentrate on examples that relate to this goal, but some examples will be given that are not crime related. Unfortunately, we will also see that, given the nature of our field, there are important problems with determining causality, largely because we are dealing with human beings as opposed to a chemical element or biological molecule.

---

[16]See Stephen G. Tibbetts, *Criminological Theory: The Essentials* (Thousand Oaks: Sage, 2012), 8.

[17]See Ronald Akers and Gang Lee, "A Longitudinal Test of Social Learning Theory: Adolescent Smoking," *Journal of Drug Issues* 26 (1996): 317–43; Ronald Akers and Gang Lee, "Age, Social Learning, and Social Bonding in Adolescent Substance Abuse," *Deviant Behavior* 19 (1999): 1–25; Ronald Akers and Anthony J. La Greca, "Alcohol Use among the Elderly: Social Learning, Community Context, and Life Events," in *Society, Culture, and Drinking Patterns Re-examined*, ed. David J. Pittman and Helene Raskin White (New Brunswick: Rutgers Center of Alcohol Studies, 1991), 242–62; Sunghyun Hwang, *Substance Use in a Sample of South Korean Adolescents: A Test of Alternative Theories* (Ann Arbor: University Microfilms, 2000); and Sunghyun Hwang and Ronald Akers, "Adolescent Substance Use in South Korea: A Cross-Cultural Test of Three Theories," in *Social Learning Theory and the Explanation of Crime: A Guide for the New Century*, ed. Ronald Akers and Gary F. Jensen (New Brunswick: Transaction, 2003).

The three criteria that are needed to show causality are (a) temporal ordering, (b) covariation or correlation, and (c) accounting for spuriousness.

Temporal ordering requires that the predictor variable (*X*) precede the explanatory variable (*Y*) if we are to determine that *X* causes *Y*. Although this seems like a no-brainer, it is sometimes violated in criminological theories. For example, you'll remember that Lombroso claimed born criminals could be identified by tattoos, which obviously goes against this principle.

A more recent scientific debate has focused on whether delinquency is an outcome variable (*Y*) due to associations with delinquent peers and associates (*X*), or whether delinquency (*X*) causes associations with delinquent peers and associates (*Y*), which then leads to even more delinquency. This can be seen as the argument of which came first, the chicken or the egg. Studies show that both processes are often taking place, meaning that delinquency and associations with delinquent peers are likely to be both predictor and explanatory variables in most cases, and this forms a reciprocal or feedback loop that encourages both causal paths.[18] Thus, temporal ordering is an important question, and often it is quite complex and must be examined fully before causal order can be understood.

Correlation, or covariation, is the extent to which a change in the predictor (*X*) is associated with a change (either higher or lower) in the explanatory variable (*Y*). In other words, a change in *X* leads to a change in *Y*. For example, a rise in unemployment (*X*) in a given location is likely to lead to a rise in crime rates (*Y*) in the same area; this would be a positive association because both increased. Similarly, an increase in

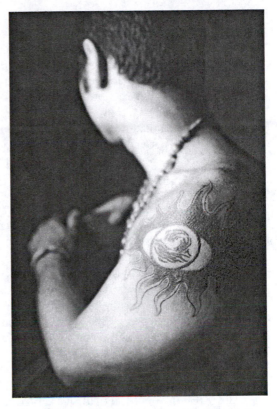

▲ Image 1.3 Early theories identified criminals by whether they had tattoos; at that time, this might have been true. In contemporary times, many individuals have tattoos, so this would not apply.

Source: © Thinkstock / Stockbyte.

employment (*X*) is likely to lead to a decrease in crime rates (*Y*) in that area; this would be a negative, or inverse, association, because one decreased and the other increased. The criterion of covariance is not met when a change in *X* does not produce any change in *Y*. That is, if a statistically significant change in *X* does not lead to a statistically significant change in *Y*, then this criterion is not met.

However, correlation alone does not mean that *X* causes *Y*. For example, if ice cream sales (*X*) tend to be highly associated with crime rates (*Y*), this does not mean that ice cream sales cause higher crime rates. Rather, other factors—in this case, warm weather—lead to increases in both sales of ice cream and the number of people who are outdoors in public areas and interacting, which naturally leads to greater opportunities and tendencies to engage in criminal activity. This brings us to the final criterion for determining causality.

Accounting for spuriousness is a complicated way of saying that, to determine that *X* causes *Y*, other factors (typically called *Z* factors) that could be causing the observed association must be accounted for before we can be sure that it is actually *X* that is causing *Y*. In other words, it is often a third factor (*Z*) that causes two events to occur together in time and place. A good example of a spurious association would be the observation that a greater number

---

[18]Terence Thornberry, "Toward an Interactional Theory of Delinquency," *Criminology* 25 (1987): 863–87.

of firefighters at the scene of a fire is correlated with more damage. If only the first two criteria of causality were followed, this would lead to the conclusion that an increased number of fire officers (X) causes the heavier fire damage (Y). This conclusion meets the temporal ordering and covariance criteria. However, a third Z variable or factor is causing both X and Y to appear together. This Z variable is the size of the fire, which is causing more officers to show up and also causing more damage. Once this Z factor is accounted for, the effect of X on Y becomes nonexistent.

Using the Lombroso example, tattoos may have predicted criminality at the time he wrote (although criminals weren't born with them). However, Lombroso did not account for an important Z factor, namely, associates or friends who also had tattoos. This Z factor caused the simultaneous occurrence of both other factors. To clarify, individuals who had friends or associates with tattoos tended to get tattoos, and (especially at that time in the 1800s) friends or associates who had tattoos also tended to commit more crime. In that era, pirates and incarcerated individuals were most likely to get tattoos. Therefore, had Lombroso controlled for the number of tattooed associates of the criminals he studied, he likely would have found no causal effect on crime from body art.

Ultimately, researchers in criminology are fairly good at determining the first two criteria of causality: temporal ordering and covariance or correlation. Most scientists can perform classical experiments that randomly assign subjects either to receive or not to receive the experimental manipulation to examine the effect on outcomes. However, the dilemma for criminologists is that the factors that appear to be important (according to police officers, parole agents, and corrections officers) are family variables, personality traits, employment variables, intelligence, and other similar characteristics that cannot be experimentally manipulated to control for possible Z factors. After all, how can we randomly assign certain people or groups to bad parents or bad educations, no jobs, low IQs, bad genetics, or delinquent peers? Even if we could manage such manipulations, ethical constraints would prohibit them.

Thus, as criminologists, we may never be able to meet all the criteria of causality, so we are essentially stuck with building a case for the factors we think are causing crime by amassing as much support as we can in terms of temporal ordering and covariance or correlation, and perhaps accounting for other factors in advanced statistical models. Ultimately, social science, especially criminology, is a difficult field in terms of establishing causality, and we shall see that the empirical validity of various criminological theories is hindered by such issues.

 ## Measures of Crime

Crime can be measured in an infinite number of ways. To some extent, readers have measured crime by observing what has been happening in their own neighborhoods or reading or watching the news every day. However, some measures of crime go beyond these anecdotal or personal experiences, and these more exacting measures are what criminologists commonly use to gauge rates of crime across time and place.

Specifically, three major categories of crime measures are used by social scientists to examine crime. The first and most used measure is the Uniform Crime Report (UCR). Police send reports about certain crimes and arrests to the Federal Bureau of Investigation (FBI), which combines the many thousands of reports they receive from across the nation and publishes the UCR annually.

The second measure is the National Crime Victimization Survey (NCVS; prior to the early 1990s, it was known as the National Crime Survey [NCS]). Like the UCR, the report is issued by the U.S. Department of Justice (DOJ), but the data are collected in an entirely different way. Specifically, interviews are conducted with a large, random sample of U.S. households, asking how much crime they have experienced in half-year intervals. The NCVS is collected by the research branch of the DOJ, called the Bureau of Justice Statistics (BJS), in conjunction with the U.S. Bureau of the Census, which was one of the earliest agencies to collect information about citizens and thus is the most experienced at such endeavors.

The third measure, which is perhaps the most important for purposes of this book, is self-report data (SRD), which are primarily collected by independent academic scientists or think tank agencies, such as RAND Corporation. Participating in surveys or interviews, individuals report crimes against themselves or crimes they have committed.

This measure is the most important for the purposes of this book because the UCR and NCVS do not provide in-depth information on the offenders or the victims, such as personality, biology or physiology, family life, and economic information. These factors are of the utmost importance for our purposes because there is a broad consensus that they cause people to commit crime, and yet they are missing from the most commonly used measures of crime. Self-report data are the best, and in most cases the only, measure for figuring out why some people offend and others do not. However, like the other measures, self-reports have numerous weaknesses as well as strengths.

Each of these three measures is briefly examined here. Although the measures are not the primary emphasis of this book, it is important to understand their strengths and weaknesses.

The Uniform Crime Report

The UCR is the oldest and most used measure of crime rates in the United States for purposes of examining trends and distribution of crime. It was first published in the early 1930s, and although changes have been made along the way, it is relatively stable in terms of comparing various years and decades. As mentioned before, the data are collected by many thousands of independent police agencies at federal, state, and local levels. These thousands of agencies send their reports of crimes and arrests to their respective state capitals, which then forward their synthesized reports to FBI headquarters, where all reports are combined to provide an overview of crime in the nation.

FBI definitions of crimes often differ from state categorizations, and how crimes are differentiated will be important in future discussions in this section. The FBI concentrates on eight (four violent and four property) index offenses, or Part I offenses. The four violent crimes are murder and nonnegligent manslaughter, forc-

▲ Image 1.4 The annual UCRs are produced by the FBI. Local, county, and state criminal justice agencies send their annual crime data to the J. Edgar Hoover Building in Washington, DC. UCR data are, by their nature, incomplete, as many crimes are never reported to the police at all. This dark figure of crime might be as high as 90% of all crime incidents.

Source: © Getty Images.

ible (not statutory) rape, robbery, and aggravated assault (which involves intentions of serious injury to the victim). The four property offenses are burglary (which includes a breaking and entering or trespass), motor vehicle theft, larceny (which does not involve a trespass; e.g., shoplifting), and arson (which was added to the crime index count in the late 1970s). All reports to police for these eight offenses are included in the crime index, whether or not they resulted in an arrest. This information is often referred to as crimes known to police (CKP).

The UCR also includes about two dozen other offenses known as nonindex offenses, or Part II offenses, which are reported only if an arrest is made. These offenses range from violent crimes (such as simple assault), to embezzlement and fraud, to offenses that are considered violations of the law only if an individual is under 18 years of age (such as running away from home). The major problem with the estimates of these nonindex offenses is that the likelihood of arresting someone for such crimes is less than 10% of the actual occurrence, so the data regarding nonindex offenses are highly inaccurate. The official count from the FBI is missing at least 90% of the actual offenses that take place in the United States. Therefore, we will primarily concentrate on index offenses for the purposes of our discussion.

Even the count of index offenses has numerous problems. The most important and chronic problem with using the UCR as a measure of crime is that, most of the time, victims fail to report crimes—yes, even aggravated assault, forcible rape, robbery, burglary, and larceny. Recent studies estimate that about 70% to 80% of these serious crimes are not reported to police. Criminologists call this missing amount of crime the dark figure because it never shows up in the police reports that get sent to the FBI.

There are many reasons why victims do not report these serious crimes to the police. One of the most important is that they consider it a personal matter. Many times, the offense is committed by a family member, a close friend, or an acquaintance. For instance, police are rarely informed about aggravated assaults among siblings. Rape victims are often assaulted on a date or by someone they know; they may feel that they contributed to their attack by choosing to go out with the offender, or they may believe that police won't take such a claim seriously. Regardless of the reason, many crime victims prefer to handle it informally and not involve the police.

Another major reason why police are not called is that victims don't feel the crime is important enough to report. For example, a thief may steal a small item that the victim won't miss, so she or he may not see the need to report what the police or FBI would consider a serious crime. This is likely related to another major reason why people do not report crime to the police: They have no confidence that reporting the case to law enforcement will do any good. Many people, often residents of the neighborhoods that are most crime ridden, are likely to feel that the police are not competent or will not seriously investigate their charges.

There are many other reasons why people do not report their victimizations to police. Some may fear retaliation, for example, in cases involving gang activity; many cities, especially those with many gangs, have seen this occur even more in recent years. The victims may also fail to report a crime for fear that their own illegal activities will be exposed; an example is a prostitute who has been brutally beaten by her pimp. In U.S. society, much crime is committed against businesses, but those businesses may be very reluctant to report crimes because they don't want a reputation for being a hot spot for criminal activity. Sometimes when victims do call the police or 911, they leave the scene if the police fail to show up in a reasonable amount of time. This has become a chronic problem despite efforts by police departments to prioritize calls.

Perhaps the most chronic, most important reason for failure to report crimes—but one that is often ignored—can be traced to U.S. school systems. Most studies of crime and victimization in schools show that many and maybe even most juvenile crimes occur in schools, but these offenses almost never get reported to police, even when school resource officers (SROs) are assigned to the school. Schools—and especially private schools—have a vested interest in not reporting crimes that occur on their premises to the police. After all, no school (or school system) wants to become known as crime ridden.

Schools are predisposed to being crime ridden because the most likely offenders and the most likely victims—young people—interact there in close quarters for most of the day. The school is much happier, however, if teachers and administrators deal informally with the parties involved in an on-campus fight; the school doesn't want these activities reported to and by the media. In addition, the student parties involved in the fight don't want to be formally arrested and charged with the offense, so they are also happy with the case being handled informally. Finally, the parents of the students are also generally pleased with the informal process because they don't want their children involved in a formal legal case.

Even universities and colleges follow this model of not reporting crimes when they occur on campus. A good example can be seen on the websites of most major colleges, which are required by federal law to report crimes on campus. Official reports of crimes, ranging from rapes to liquor law violations, are often in the single digits each year for campuses housing many thousands of students. Of course, some crimes may not be reported to the school, and others may be dealt with administratively rather than by calling police. The absence of school data is a big weakness of the UCR.

Besides the dark figure, there are many other criticisms of the UCR as a measure of crime. For example, the way that crimes are counted can be misleading. Specifically, the UCR counts only the most serious crime that is committed in a given incident. For example, if a person or persons rob, rape, and murder a victim, only the murder will show up in the UCR; the robbery and rape will not be recorded. Furthermore, there are inconsistencies in how the UCR counts the incidents; for example, if a person walks into a bar and assaults eight people there, it is counted as eight assaults, but if the same person walks into the bar and robs every person of wallets and purses, it is counted as one robbery. This makes little sense, but it is the official count policy used by the UCR.

Other more important criticisms of the UCR involve political considerations, such as the fact that many police departments (such as in Philadelphia and New York City) have systematically altered the way that crimes are defined, for example, by manipulating the way that classifications and counts of crimes are recorded (e.g., aggravated assault [an index crime] vs. simple assault [a nonindex crime]). Thus, official estimates can make it seem as if major crimes have decreased in the city when in fact they may have actually increased.

It is also important to note the strengths of the UCR. First, it was introduced in 1930, making it the longest-lasting systematic measure of crime in the United States. This is a very important advantage when we want to examine trends in crime over most of the 20th century. We will see later that there have been extremely high crime rates at certain times (such as during the 1930s and the 1970s to 1980) and very low crime rates at other times (such as the early 1940s and recent years [late 1990s to the present]). Other measures, such as the NCVS and national self-report data, did not come into use until much later, so the UCR is important for the fact that it started so early.

Another important strength of this measure is that two of the offenses that the UCR concentrates on are almost always reported and therefore overcome the weakness of the dark figure, or lack of reporting to police. These two offenses are murder or nonnegligent manslaughter and motor vehicle theft. Murder is almost always reported because a dead body is found; very few murders go unreported to authorities. Although a few may elude official recording—for example, if the body is transported elsewhere or carefully hidden—almost all murders are recorded. Similarly, motor vehicle thefts, a property crime, are almost always reported because any insurance claims must provide a police report. Most cars are worth thousands (or at least many hundreds) of dollars, so victims tend to report when their vehicle(s) have been stolen; this provides a rather valid estimate of property crime in specific areas. The rest of the offenses (yes, even the other index crimes) counted by the UCR are far less reliable. If someone is doing a study on homicide or motor vehicle theft, the UCR is likely the best source of data, but for any other crime, researchers should probably look elsewhere.

This is even further advised for studies examining nonindex offenses, which the UCR counts only when someone is arrested for a given offense. The vast majority of nonindex offenses do not result in an arrest. To shed some light on how much actual nonindex crime is not reported to police, it is useful to examine the clearance rate of the index offenses in the UCR, our best indicator of solving crimes. Even for the crimes that the FBI considers most serious, the clearance rate is about 21% of crimes reported to police ("reported to police" meaning that police made a report of the crime). Of course, the more violent offenses have higher clearance rates because (outside of murder) they inherently have a witness, namely the victim, and because police place a higher priority on solving violent crimes. However, for some of the index crimes, especially serious property offenses, the clearance rates are very low. Furthermore, it should be noted that the clearance rate of serious index crimes has not improved at all over the last few decades despite much more advanced resources and technology, such as DNA testing, fingerprints, and faster cars. These data on the clearance rates are only for the most serious, or index, crimes; thus, the reporting of the UCR regarding nonindex crimes is even more inaccurate because there is even less reporting (i.e., the dark figure) and less clearance of these less serious offenses. In other words, the data provided by the UCR regarding nonindex offenses are totally invalid and thus for the most part completely worthless.

Ultimately, the UCR is good for (a) measuring the overall crime rate in the United States over time, (b) examining what crime was like prior to the 1970s, and (c) investigating murder and motor vehicle theft. Outside of these offenses, the UCR has serious problems, and fortunately we have better measures for examining crime rates in the United States.

The National Crime Victimization Survey

Another commonly used measure of crime is the NCVS (the NCS until the early 1990s), which is distinguished from other key measures of crime because it concentrates on the victims of crime, whereas other measures tend to emphasize the offenders. In fact, that is the key reason why this measure was started in 1973 after several years of preparation and pretesting. To clarify, one of the key recommendations of Lyndon Johnson's President's Commission on Law Enforcement and Administration of Justice in the late 1960s was to learn more about the characteristics of victims of crime; at that time, virtually no studies had been done on the subject, whereas much research had been done on criminal offenders. The efforts of this commission set into motion the creation of the NCVS.

Since it began, the NCVS has been designed and collected by two agencies: the U.S. Bureau of the Census and the BJS, which is one of the key research branches of the U.S. DOJ. The NCVS is collected in a completely different way from the other commonly used measures of crimes; the researchers select tens of thousands of U.S. households, and each member of the household who is over 12 years of age is interviewed every six months about crime that occurred in the previous six-month period (each selected household remains in the survey for three years, resulting in seven collection periods, including the initial interview). Although the selection of households is to some extent random, the way the sampling is designed guarantees that a certain proportion of the selected households have certain characteristics. For example, before the households are selected, they are first categorized according to factors such as region of the country, type of area (urban, suburban, rural), income level, and racial or ethnic composition. This type of sampling, called a multistage, stratified cluster sampling design, ensures that enough households are included in the survey to permit conclusions regarding these important characteristics. As you will see later in this section, some of the most victimized groups (by rate) in the United States do not make up a large portion of the population or households. So, if the sampling design were not set up to select a certain number of people from certain groups, it is quite likely the researchers would not obtain enough cases to draw conclusions about them.

The data gathered from this sample are then adjusted, and statistical estimates are made about crime across the United States, with the NCVS estimates showing about three times more crime than the UCR rates. Some may doubt the ability of this selected sample to represent crime in the nation, but most studies find that its estimates are far more accurate than those provided by the UCR (with the exception of homicide and maybe motor vehicle theft). This is largely due to the expertise and professionalism of the agencies that collect and analyze the data, as well as the carefully thought out and well-administered survey design, as indicated by interview completion rates (which are typically more than 90%, higher than those of virtually all other crime and victimization surveys).

One of the biggest strengths of the NCVS is that it directly addresses the worst problem with the previously discussed measure, the UCR. Specifically, the greatest weakness of the UCR is the dark figure, or the crimes that victims fail to report, which happens most of the time (except in cases of homicide or motor vehicle theft). The NCVS interviews victims about crimes that happened to them, even those that were not reported to police. Thus, the NCVS captures far more crime events than the UCR, especially crimes that are highly personal (such as rape). The extent to which the NCVS captures much of this dark figure of crime is its greatest strength.

Despite this important strength, the NCVS, like the other measures of crime, has numerous weaknesses. Probably the biggest problem is that two of the most victimized groups in U.S. society are systematically not included in the NCVS. Specifically, homeless people are completely left out because they do not have a home and the participants are contacted through households, yet they remain one of the most victimized groups per capita in our society. Another highly victimized group in our society that is systematically not included in the NCVS is young children. Studies consistently show that the younger a person is, the more likely she or he is to be victimized. Infants in particular, especially in their first hours or days of life, face great risk of death and other sorts of victimization, typically from parents or caregivers. This is not very surprising, especially in light of the fact that very young children cannot defend themselves or run away. They can't even tell anyone until they are old enough to speak, and then most are too afraid to do so or are not given an opportunity. Although, to some extent, it is understandable to exempt young children from such sensitive questions, the loss of this group is huge in terms of estimating victimization in the United States.

The NCVS also misses the crimes suffered by American businesses, which cumulatively constitute an enormous amount of crime. In the early years of the NCVS, businesses were also sampled, but that practice was discontinued in the late 1970s. Had it continued, it would have provided invaluable information for social scientists and policy makers, not to mention the businesses that are losing billions of dollars each year as a result of crimes committed against them.

Many find it surprising that the NCVS does not collect data on homicide, which most people and agencies consider the most serious and important crime. Researchers studying murder cannot get information from the NCVS but must rely on the UCR, which is most accurate in its reporting for this crime type.

The NCVS also has issues with people accurately reporting the victimization that has occurred to them in the previous six months. However, studies show that their reports are surprisingly accurate most of the time. Often when participants report incidents inaccurately, they make unknowing mistakes rather than intentionally lying. Obviously, victims sometimes forget incidents that occur to them, probably because, most of the time, they know or are related to the person committing the offense against them, so they never think of it as a crime per se but rather as a personal disagreement. When asked if they were victims of theft, they may not think to report the time that a brother or uncle borrowed a tool without asking and never returned it.

Although NCVS researchers go to great lengths to prevent it, a common phenomenon known as telescoping tends to occur, which leads to overreporting of incidents. Telescoping is the human tendency to perceive events as having occurred more recently than they actually did. This is one of the key reasons why NCVS researchers interview household subjects every six months, but telescoping still happens. For instance, a larceny may have occurred eight months ago, but it seems as if it happened just a few months ago to the participant, so it is reported to the researchers as occurring in the last six months when it really didn't. Telescoping thus inflates national crime rate estimates for a given interval.

As mentioned before, an additional weakness is that the NCVS did not start until 1973, so it cannot provide any estimates of victimization prior to that time. A study of national crime rates prior to the 1970s has little choice but to use the UCR. Still, for most crimes, the NCVS has provided a more accurate estimate over the past three decades. Since the NCVS was created, the crime trends it has revealed have tended to be highly consistent with those shown by the UCR. For example, both measures show violent crime rates peaking at the same time (about 1980), and both agree on when the rates increased (the 1970s) and decreased (the late 1990s to the present) most. This is very good, because if they did not agree, that would mean at least one of them was wrong. Before we discuss the national trends in crime rates, however, we will examine the strengths and weaknesses of a third measure of crime.

Self-Report Studies of Crime

The final measure of crime consists of various self-report studies of crime, in which individuals report (either in a written survey or interview) the extent of their own past criminal offending or victimization and other information. There is no one systematic study providing a yearly estimate of crime in the United States; rather, self-report studies tend to be conducted by independent researchers or institutes. Even when they do involve a national sample (such as the National Youth Survey), they almost never use such data to make estimates of the extent of crime or victimization across the nation.

This lack of a long-term, systematic study that can be used to estimate national crime rates may be the greatest weakness of self-report studies; however, this very weakness—not having a universal consistency in collection—is also its greatest strength. To clarify, researchers can develop their questionnaires to best fit the exact purposes of their study. For example, if researchers are doing a study on the relationship between a given personality trait (e.g., narcissism) and criminal offending, they can simply give participants a questionnaire that contains a narcissism scale and items that ask about past criminal behavior. Of course, these scales and items must be checked for their reliability and validity, but this is a relatively easy way to directly measure and test the hypotheses the researcher is most concerned about.

Some question the accuracy of self-report data because they believe participants typically lie, but most studies have concluded that participants generally tell the truth. Specifically, researchers have compared self-reported offenses to lie detector machine results, readministered the same survey to the same individuals to see if they answer the same way each time (called test-retest reliability), and cross-checked self-reported arrests with police arrest data. All of these methods have shown that most people tend to be quite truthful when answering surveys.[19]

The most important aspect of self-report surveys is that they are the only available source of data for determining the social and psychological reasons people commit crime. The UCR and NCVS have virtually no data on the personality, family life, biological development, or other characteristics of criminal offenders, which are generally considered key factors in the development of criminality. Therefore, although we examine the findings of all three measures in the next section, the vast majority of the content we cover in this book will be based on findings from self-report studies.

What Do the Measures of Crime Show regarding the Distribution of Crime?

It is important to examine the most aggregated trends of crime, namely the ups and downs of overall crime rates in the United States across different decades. We will start with crime in the early 1900s, largely because the best data started being collected during this era and also because the 20th century (especially the most recent decades) is most relevant to our understanding of the reasons for our current crime rates. However, most experts believe that the U.S. crime rate, whether in terms of violence or property offending, used to be far higher prior to the 20th century; historians have arrived at this conclusion based on sporadic, poorly recorded documentation from the 18th and 19th centuries. By virtually all accounts, crime per capita (especially homicide) was far higher in the 1700s and 1800s than at any point after 1900, which is likely due to many factors, but perhaps most importantly because formal agencies of justice, such as police and corrections (i.e., prisons, parole, etc.), did not exist in most of the United States until the middle or end of the 1800s. Up to that time, it was up to individual communities or vigilantes to deal with offenders.

Therefore, there was little ability to investigate or apprehend criminals and no means to imprison them. But, as industrialization increased, the need to establish formal police agencies and correctional facilities evolved as a

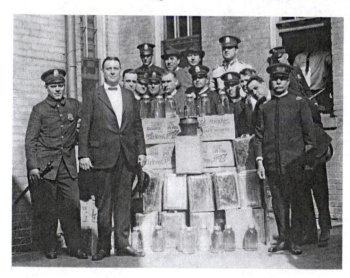

▲ Image 1.5   Group portrait of a police department liquor squad posing with cases of confiscated alcohol and distilling equipment during Prohibition.

SOURCE: © Getty Images / Archive Photos / Archive Photos.

[19]Michael Hindelang, Travis Hirschi, and J. Weis, *Measuring Delinquency* (Beverly Hills: Sage, 1981).

way to deal with people who offended in modern cities. By 1900, most existing states had formed police and prison systems, which is where our discussion will begin.

The level of crime in the United States, particularly homicide, was relatively low at the beginning of the 20th century, perhaps because of the formal justice agencies that had been created during the 19th century. For example, the first metropolitan U.S. police departments were formed in Boston and then New York during the 1830s; in the same decade but a bit earlier, the first state police department, the Texas Rangers, had been established, and the federal marshals service had been founded still earlier. Although prisons started in the late 1790s, they did not begin to resemble their modern form or proliferate rapidly until the mid-1800s. The first juvenile court was formed in the Chicago area in 1899. The development of these formal law enforcement and justice agencies may have contributed to the low levels of crime and homicide in the very early 1900s. (Note: Our discussion of the crime rate in the early 1900s will primarily deal with homicide, because murder records constitute the only valid records of crime from that time; the UCR did not start until the 1930s. Most people consider homicide the most serious crime, and its frequency typically reflects the overall crime rate.)

The effects of the creation of these formal agencies did not persist long into the 20th century. Looking at the level of homicides that occurred in the United States, it is obvious that large increases took place between 1910 and 1920, likely because of extremely high increases in industrialization as the U.S. economy moved from an agricultural to an industrial emphasis. More important, population growth was rapid as a result of urbanization. Whenever high numbers of people move into an area (in this case, cities) and form a far more dense population (think of New York City at that time or Las Vegas in current times), it creates a crime problem. This is likely due to there being more opportunities to commit crimes against others; after all, when people are crammed together, it creates a situation in which there are far more potential offenders in close proximity to far more potential victims. A good modern example of this is high schools, which studies show have higher crime rates than city subways or other crime-ridden areas, largely because they densely pack people together, and in such conditions, opportunities for crime are readily available. Thus, the rapid industrialization and urbanization of the early 1900s is probably the most important reason for the increase in homicide and crime in general in the United States at that time.

The largest increases in U.S. homicide in the early 1900s occurred during the 1920s and early 1930s, with the peak level of homicide coming in the early 1930s. Criminologists and historians have concluded that this huge increase in the homicide rate was primarily due to two factors beyond the industrialization and urbanization that explained the increase prior to the 1920s. First, the U.S. Congress passed a constitutional amendment that banned the distribution and consumption of alcohol beginning in 1920. The period that followed is known as Prohibition. This legal action proved to be a disaster, at least in terms of crime, and Congress later agreed—but not until the 1930s—by passing another amendment to do away with the previous amendment that banned alcohol. For about 14 years, which notably recorded the highest U.S. rates of homicide and crime before 1950, the government attempted to stop people from drinking.

Prior to Prohibition, gangsters had been relatively passive and had not held much power. However, the ban on alcohol gave the black market a lot of potential in terms of monetary profit and reasons for killing off competition. Some of the greatest massacres of rival gangs of organized crime syndicates (e.g., the Italian Mafia) occurred during the Prohibition era. The impact on crime was likely only one of the many problems with Prohibition, but it was a very important and deadly one for our purposes. Once Prohibition ended in the early 1930s, homicide and crime rates decreased significantly, which may have implications for modern drug policies. According to studies, many banned substances today are less violence producing than alcohol, which studies show is the most violence-causing substance. For example, most criminologists believe that the current War on Drugs may actually be causing far more crime than it seeks to prevent (even if it may be lowering the number of drug addicts) due to the black market it creates for drugs that are in demand, much like the case with alcohol during Prohibition.

Another major reason why the homicide rate and overall crime levels increased so much during the early 1930s was the Great Depression, which sent the United States into an unprecedented state of economic upheaval. Most historians and criminologists agree that the stock market crash of the late 1920s was a primary contributor to the large numbers of homicides in the early 1930s. We will return to this subject later when we examine the strain theory of crime, which emphasizes economic structure and poverty as the primary causes of crime.

Although the homicide and crime rate experienced a significant drop after Prohibition was eliminated, another reason for this decrease was likely the social policies of the New Deal, which was implemented by President Franklin D. Roosevelt. Such policies included those that created new jobs for people hit hardest by the Depression through programs such as Job Corps and the Tennessee Valley Authority, both of which still exist today. Although such programs likely aided economic (and thus crime) recovery in the United States, world events of the early 1940s provided the greatest reasons for the huge decreases that were seen at that time.

The entry of the United States into World War II was probably the biggest contributor to decreasing U.S. crime in the early 20th century. As you will notice, homicides decreased dramatically during the four years (1941–1945) that hundreds of thousands of young men (the most likely offenders and victims) were sent overseas to fight on two fronts, Europe and the South Pacific. Any time a society loses a huge portion of the most common offenders, namely young (teenage to twenties) males, it can expect a drop in crime like the one the United States experienced in the 1940s. However, at the end of 1945, most of these men returned and began making babies, which triggered the greatest increase in babies that U.S. society had ever seen. This generation of babies started what historians call the baby boom, which would have the greatest impact on crime levels that has ever been recorded in U.S. history.

Although crime rates increased after soldiers returned home from overseas in the late 1940s, they did not rise to anywhere near the levels present during Prohibition and the Great Depression. Alcohol was legal, and the

Figure 1.1 Homicide rates in the United States in the 20th century and the early years of the 21st century

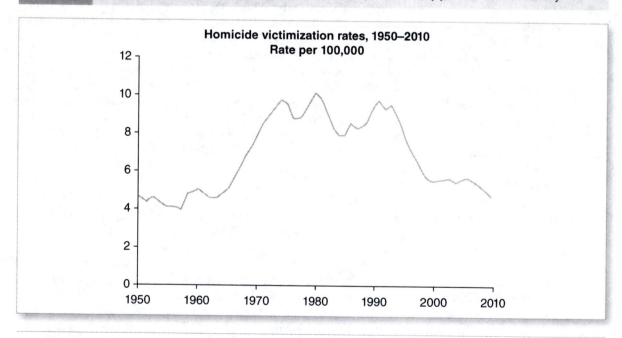

SOURCE: http://www.ericgarland.co/wp-content/uploads/pix/2013/09/US-homocide-victimization-trend-1950-2010.png

NOTE: The 2001 rate includes deaths attributed to the 9/11 terrorist attacks.

economy was doing relatively well after World War II. During the 1950s, the crime level remained relatively low and stable until the early 1960s, when the impact of the baby boom emerged in terms of the crime rate. If a very large share of the population is made up of young people, particularly teenage or early-twenties males, the crime rate will almost inevitably go up. This is exactly what occurred in the United States, starting in the early 1960s, and it led to the largest 10-year increase in crime that the country has ever seen.

The Baby-Boom Effect

The UCR shows that the greatest single-decade increase in the crime rate occurred between 1965 and 1975. In that time, the overall crime rate more than doubled, an unprecedented increase. Notably, this increase occurred during the War on Poverty, which was set into motion by President Lyndon B. Johnson in a program he termed the Great Society; the crime increase thus turned many people and policy makers against having the government address economic issues to better society. However, the demographic factor that these individuals did not take into account was that this was the era in which most people in society belonged to young age groups, which predisposed the nation to the high crime rates experienced at this time. In contrast, the following generation, called Generation X, which includes those individuals born between 1965 and 1978, had a very low birthrate, which may contribute to the low crime rates observed in recent years.

The high numbers of young people in society were not the only societal trend going on during the late 1960s and early 1970s that would lead to higher crime rates. For example, a large number of people were being arrested as a result of their participation in the civil rights movement, the women's rights movement, and anti–Vietnam War activities. Perhaps most important, the 1970s showed the highest levels of drug usage and favorable attitudes toward drugs since accurate national studies had first been conducted. Virtually all measures of drug usage peaked during the 1970s or early 1980s.

So, ultimately, many things came together between the mid-1960s and the late 1970s to usher in the greatest increase in the crime rate that the United States has ever seen, culminating in the peak of crime and homicide in 1980. All of our measures agree that crime, especially homicide, reached its highest level about that year. Although other periods, such as the early 1990s, showed similar increases in crime, largely due to juvenile offending, no other period showed higher rates than the 1980 period, most likely due to the coming of age of many baby boomers and their high drug usage.

Crime levels declined somewhat in the early 1980s and then rose again in the late 1980s and early 1990s, but the crime and homicide rate never exceeded the 1980 peak. Furthermore, after 1994, the crime rate decreased drastically every year for about a decade, to the point that it dropped as low as it had been in the early 1960s. The U.S. crime rate is currently around where it was about 50 years ago.

There are many reasons for this huge decrease over the last two decades. One of the biggest reasons is that the population has a relatively smaller proportion of young people than it did during the 1960s and 1970s, but obviously there is more to the picture. Drug usage, as well as favorable attitudes toward drugs, has dropped a lot in recent years. Furthermore, the incarceration rate of prisoners is about 400% to 500% of what it was in the early 1970s. Although many experts have claimed that locking up criminals does not reduce crime levels in a society, it is hard to deny that imprisoning five times more people will not result in catching many, if not most, of the habitual offenders. It makes sense: By rate, the United States currently locks up more citizens in prison than virtually any other developed country.

Almost all crime tends to be nonrandom. Consistent with this, the crime measures show a number of trends in which crime occurs among certain types of people, in certain places, at certain times, and so on. We turn to an examination of such concentrations of crime, starting with large, macro differences in crime rates across regions of the United States.

Regional and City Differences in Rates of Crime

Crime tends to be higher in certain regions of the country. According to the UCR, the United States is separated into four regions: Northeast, Midwest, South, and West. For the last few decades, crime rates (based on crime per capita) have been significantly higher in two of these regions: the South and the West. These two regions consistently have higher rates than the other regions, with one or the other having the highest rates for violence or property offenses or both each year. Some studies have found that, when poverty levels are accounted for, much of the regional difference is explained away. Although this is a very simple conclusion, the studies seem to be consistent in tying regional differences to variations in social factors, notably socioeconomic levels.

Regardless of the region, there seems to be extreme variation from high to low crime rates across states and cities within each of these large regions. For example, crime measures consistently show that certain U.S. states and jurisdictions have consistently high crime rates. The two standouts are Louisiana and the District of Columbia, with the latter having an extremely high rate, typically more than eight times the national average for homicide. It is quite ironic that arguably the most powerful city in the world has an extremely serious crime problem, certainly one of the worst in our nation.

Another question is why crime rates in states or jurisdictions, or in cities and counties, vary drastically from one region to the next. For instance, Camden, New Jersey, one of the cities in the lower-rate Northeast region according to the UCR, had the highest rate of crime among all U.S. cities in the years 2004 and 2005. Detroit, Michigan, was second worst for both of these years; it used to be number one before Camden outdid it. At the same time, however, New Jersey had some of the safest cities in the nation for these years—two of the 10 safest cities are in New Jersey, which shows how much crime can vary from place to place, even those in relatively close proximity. Notably, in the most recent estimates from the FBI, the cities of St. Louis and New Orleans exhibited the highest rates of serious violent crimes in 2006 and 2007, respectively. An important factor for New Orleans was the devastation of the city's infrastructure after Hurricane Katrina, which essentially wiped out the city's criminal justice system and resources.

Crime has also been found to cluster within a given city, whether the overall city is relatively low crime or high crime. Virtually every area (whether urban, suburban, or rural) has what are known as hot spots, or places that have high levels of crime activity. Such places are often bars or liquor stores or other types of businesses, such as bus stops and depots, convenience stores, shopping malls, motels and hotels, fast-food restaurants, check-cashing businesses, tattoo parlors, or discount stores (such as dollar stores). However, hot spots can also be residential places, such as homes that police are constantly called to for domestic violence or apartment complexes that are crime ridden, something often seen in subsidized housing areas.

Even the nicest of cities and areas have hot spots, and even the worst cities and areas also tend to have most of their police calls coming from specific addresses or businesses. This is one of the best examples of how crime does not tend to be random. Many police agencies have begun using spatial software on computer systems to analyze where the hot spots in a given city are and to predict where certain crimes are likely to occur in the future. This allows more preventive patrols and proactive strategies in such zones. One criminological theory, routine activities theory, is largely based on explaining why hot spots exist.

 ## Rates of Crime according to Time of Day and Time of Year

Another way that crime is known to cluster is by time of day. This varies greatly depending on the type of group being examined. For example, juvenile delinquency and victimization, especially for violence, tends to peak sharply at 3 p.m. on school days (about half of the days of the year for children), which is the time that youths are most likely to lack supervision (i.e., children are let out of school and are often not supervised by adults until they get home). On the other hand, adult crime and victimization, especially for violence, tends to peak much later on, at about 11 p.m. on almost all days, which is a sharp contrast to the juvenile peak in midafternoon. These estimates are primarily based on FBI and UCR data.

To some extent, the peak hour for juveniles is misleading; other non-police-based estimates show that just as much crime is going on during school, but schools tend not to report it. As stated above, this widespread lack of reporting by schools occurs because none of the parties involved wants a formal police report taken. Typically, the youth doesn't want to be arrested, the child's parents don't want their daughter or son to be formally processed by police, and most important, no school wants to become known as a dangerous place. Thus, the police are typically called only in extreme cases, for example, if a student pulls a gun on another student or actually uses a weapon.

This underreporting also occurs in colleges and universities, because such institutions depend largely on tuition for funding, and this goes down if enrollment levels decline. After all, no parents want to send their teenagers to a college that is high in crime. Federal law now requires virtually all colleges to report their crime levels to the public, so there is a lot at stake if police take formal reports on crime events. Thus, most colleges, like K–12 school systems, have an informal process in place so that even violent crimes can often be handled informally.

Crimes tend to peak significantly during the summer. Studies show that criminals tend to be highly opportunistic, meaning that they happen to be going about their normal activities when they see an opportunity to commit a crime, as compared to a more hydraulic model, in which an offender actually goes out looking to commit a crime. Because criminals are like everyone else in most ways, they tend to be out and about more in the summer, so they are more likely to see opportunities at that time. Furthermore, youths are typically out of school during the summer, so they are often bored and not supervised by adults as much as during the traditional school year. Burglary tends to rise 300% during the summer, an increase that may be linked to the fact that people go on vacation and leave their homes vacant for weeks or months at a time. All of these factors come together to produce much higher rates in the summer than in any other season.

A couple of crimes, such as murder and robbery, tend to have a second peak in the winter, which most experts believe is due to high emotions during the holidays, additional social interaction (and often the drinking of alcohol) during the holidays, and an increase in wanting money or goods for gift giving, which would explain robbery increases at that time. These offenses are the exception, however, not the rule. Most offenses, including murder and robbery, tend to have their highest peaks during warmer summer months.

Rates of Crime according to Age and Gender

Age is perhaps the most important way that crime and victimization tend to cluster in certain groups. Almost no individual gets arrested before the age of 10; if one does, it is a huge predictor that the child is likely to become a habitual, chronic offender. However, between the ages of 10 and 17, the offending rate for all serious street crimes (i.e., FBI index crimes) goes up drastically, peaking at an average age of 17. Then the offending rates begin decreasing significantly, such that by the time people reach the age of 20, the likelihood of being arrested has fallen in half as compared to the midteenage years. This offending level continues to decline throughout life for all of the serious index crimes, although other crimes, such as white-collar crimes, tax evasion, and gambling, are likely to be committed more often at later ages,.

The extraordinarily high levels of offending in the teenage years have implications for how we prevent and deal with juvenile delinquency and help explain why we are so bad at preventing habitual offenders from committing so many crimes. We are often good at predicting who the most chronic, serious offenders are by the time they are in their twenties, but that does little good because most offenders have committed most of their crimes before they hit 20 years old.

Another characteristic important in the way crime clusters is gender. In every society, at every time in recorded history, males have committed far more serious street crimes (both violent and property) than females. It appears there is almost no closing of this gap in offending, at least for FBI index crimes. Even in the most recent years, males have been the offenders in 80% to 98% of all serious violent crimes (murder, robbery, aggravated assault, forcible rape) and have made up the vast majority of offenders in property index crimes (burglary, motor vehicle theft, arson, and larceny). The fact that the last offense is committed more frequently by males often surprises people because the most common type of larceny is shoplifting, which people often perceive as being done mostly by women. All studies show that men commit most of the larcenies in the United States. It is important to realize that males in all societies throughout the world commit the vast majority of offenses, and the more violent and serious the crimes are, the more men are represented.

However, there are a few nonindex crimes that females commit as much as, or more than, males. Specifically, in terms of property crimes, embezzlement and fraud are two offenses that females commit at rates comparable to those for men, which likely has to do with enhanced opportunities to commit such crimes. Most of the workforce is now female, which wasn't true in past decades, and many women work in banking and other businesses that tempt employees by having large amounts of money available for embezzling. In terms of public disorder, prostitution arrests tend to be mostly female, which is not too surprising.

The only other offense in which females are well represented is running away from home, which is a status offense (illegal for juveniles only). However, virtually all sources and studies of offending rates (e.g., self-report studies) show that male juveniles run away far more than females, but because of societal norms and values, females get arrested far more than males. Feminist theories of the patriarchal model (in short, men are in charge and dominate or control females) and the chivalry model (females are treated differently because they are seen as more innocent) argue that females are protected as a type of property. This may be important in light of the opposing findings regarding female and male rates of running away versus female and male rates of being arrested for running away. The bottom line is that families are more likely to report missing girls than missing boys, and more likely to press law enforcement agencies to pursue girls who have run away than boys who have done so. We will explore explanations for such differences in later sections, particularly in the section in which we cover conflict and feminist theories of crime.

Rates of Crime according to Population Density

Victimization and offending rates are also clustered according to the density of a given area. All sources of crime data show that rates of offending and victimization are far higher per capita in urban areas than in suburban and rural regions. Furthermore, this trend is linear: The more rural an area, the lower the rates for crime and victimization. To clarify, urban areas have, by far, the highest rates for offending, followed by suburban areas; the least amount of crime and victimization is found in rural (e.g., farming) areas. This trend has been shown for many decades and is undisputed. Keep in mind that such rates are based on population in such areas, so this trend holds true even per capita for citizens in a given region. This is likely due to enhanced opportunities to commit crime in urban and even suburban areas, as well as the fact that rural communities tend to have stronger informal controls, such as family, church, and community ties. Studies consistently show that informal controls are far more effective in preventing and solving crimes than are the formal controls of justice, which include all official aspects of law enforcement and justice, such as police, courts, and corrections (i.e., prisons, probation, parole).

A good example of the effectiveness of informal sanctions can be seen in the early formation of the U.S. colonies, such as the Massachusetts Bay Colony. In the early 1600s, crime per capita was at an all-time low in what would become the United States. It may surprise many that police and prisons did not exist then; rather, the low crime rate was due to high levels of informal controls: When people committed crimes, they were banished from the society or were shunned.

As in Nathaniel Hawthorne's novel *The Scarlet Letter*, even for what would now be considered a relatively minor offense (adultery), people were forced to wear a large letter (such as an *A* for adultery or a *T* for theft), and they were shunned by all others in their social world. Such punishments were (and still are) highly effective deterrents for offenders, but they work only in communities with high levels of informal controls. Studies have shown that, in such societies, crime tends to be extremely low—in fact, so low that such communities may "invent" serious crimes so that they can have an identifiable group on which to blame societal problems. We saw this occur in the Massachusetts Bay Colony with the creation of a new offense, witchcraft, for which hundreds of people were put on trial and many were executed.

Such issues will be raised again later when we discuss the sociological theories of Émile Durkheim. Nevertheless, it is interesting to note that some judges and communities have gone back to public-shaming punishments, such as making people carry signs of their offenses or putting the names of offenders in local newspapers. But the conclusion at this point is that rural communities tend to have far higher informal controls, which keep their crime rates low. On the other hand, urban (especially inner-city) areas tend to have very low levels of informal controls, which lead to few attempts by the community to police itself.

Crime also tends to cluster according to social class, with the lower classes experiencing far more violent offending and victimization. This is now undisputed and consistently shown across all sources of data regarding criminal offending. Interestingly, the characteristics associated with offending tend to be a mirror image of those associated with victimization. To clarify, young, poor urban males tend to have the highest rates of criminal offending—and this group also has the highest rates of victimization as a result of violent offending. This mirror image phenomenon is often referred to as the equivalency hypothesis. However, the equivalency hypothesis does not characterize the relationship between social class and property crimes. Specifically, members of middle- to upper-class households tend to experience more victimization for property crimes than do lower-class households, but the most likely offenders in most property crimes are from the lower class. This makes sense; offenders will tend to steal from the people and places that have the most property or money to steal. This tendency has been found since criminological data were first collected, even back to the early 1800s, and it is often found in present times, although it is not consistently shown each year (e.g., in NCVS data). Nevertheless, the equivalency hypothesis holds true for violent crimes: Lower-class individuals commit more violent crimes, and they are victimized more as a result of such violent crimes.

Rates of Crime according to Race/Ethnicity

Another important way crimes are clustered in U.S. society is by race or ethnicity. In terms of violent crimes, the most victimized group by far in the United States is Native Americans or American Indians. According to NCVS data, Native Americans are victimized at almost twice the rate of any other racial or ethnic group. This is likely due to the extreme levels of poverty, unemployment, and so on, that exist on virtually all American Indian reservations. Although some Indian tribes have recently gained profits from operating gaming casinos on their lands, the vast majority of tribes in most states are not involved in such endeavors, so deprivation and poverty are still the norm.

Although there is little offending data for this group (the UCR does not adequately measure this group in its arrest data), it is generally assumed that Native Americans have the highest rates of offending as well. This is a fairly safe assumption, because research has clearly shown that the vast majority of criminal offending and victimization are intraracial. This means that crime tends to occur within a race or ethnicity (e.g., Whites offending against Whites) as opposed to being interracial, or across races or ethnicities (e.g., Whites offending against Blacks).

Another major group that experiences an extremely high rate of victimization, particularly for homicide, is Blacks. (The term *Black* is used here, as opposed to *African American*, because this is what most measures [e.g., the UCR and NCVS] use and because many African Americans are not Black [e.g., many citizens from Egypt or

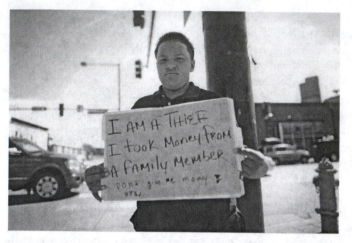

▲ Image 1.6 Offenders being forced to hold signs as part of their punishment is becoming a more popular informal sanction that shames the individual in their community.

Source: © AP Photo/The Denver Post, Joe Amon.

South Africa]). According to UCR data for homicide, which the NCVS does not report, Blacks have by far the highest rates of victimization and offending. Again, this is likely due to the extreme levels of poverty experienced by this group, as well as the high levels of single-headed households among this population (which likely explains much of the poverty).

A good example of the high levels of homicide rates among Blacks, in terms of both offending and victimization, can be seen in certain U.S. cities. Washington, DC, New Orleans, St. Louis, and Detroit have some of the highest murder rates among U.S. cities. They also have some of the highest proportions of Black residents as compared to other U.S. cities. Notably, studies have shown that, when researchers control for poverty rates and single-headed households, the racial and ethnicity effects seem to disappear.

For example, data show that Washington, DC, and the state of Louisiana are the top two jurisdictions for high rates of poverty, with most of the poor being children or teenagers, the latter of whom are most prone to committing crimes, especially violent offenses (such as murder). Thus, the two racial and ethnic groups rated highest for violent crime, both as victims and offenders—Native Americans and Blacks—also tend to have the highest rates in the nation for poverty and broken families. It should be noted that Hispanics, a common ethnic group in the United States, also have relatively high offending and victimization rates as compared to Whites and other minorities, such as Asians, who tend to experience low rates.

Although there are numerous other ways that crime tends to be clustered in our society, we have covered most of the major variables in this section. The rest of this book will examine the various theories of why crime tends to occur in such groups and individuals, and the way that we determine the accuracy of these theories will directly relate to how well they explain the high rates of crime in the groups that we have discussed.

Policy Implications

One of the key elements of a good theory is that it can help inform policy makers in making decisions about how to reduce crime. This theme will be reviewed at the end of each section in this book. After all, a criminological theory is only truly useful in the real world if it helps to reduce criminal offending. Many theories have been used as the basis of such changes in policy, and we will present examples of how the theories of crime discussed in each section have guided policy making. We will also examine empirical evidence for such policies, specifically to determine whether or not such policies have been successful (and many have not).

Section Summary

+ Criminology is the scientific study of crime. It involves the use of the scientific method and testing hypotheses, which distinguishes it from other perspectives of crime (e.g., journalistic, religious, legal) because these fields are not based on science.

- Criminological theory seeks to do more than simply predict criminal behavior; rather, the goal is to more fully understand the reasons why certain individuals offend and others do not.
- Definitions of crime vary drastically across time and place; most criminologists tend to focus on deviant behaviors whether or not they violate criminal codes.
- There are various paradigms, or unique perspectives, pertaining to crime, which have contrasting assumptions and propositions. The Classical School of criminological theory assumes free will and choice among individuals, whereas the Positive School focuses on biological, social, and psychological factors that negate the notion of choice among criminal offenders. Other theoretical paradigms, such as conflict, critical, and integrated models of offending, also exist.
- Criminological theories can be classified by their fundamental assumptions as well as other factors, such as the unit of measure on which they focus—the individual or the group (micro or macro, respectively)—or the assumptions they make regarding basic human nature: good, bad, or blank slate.
- There are more than a handful of characteristics that good criminological theories should have and that bad criminological theories do not have.
- Three criteria are required for determining causality, and thus are essential in determining whether or not an independent (predictive) variable (X) actually affects a dependent (consequent) variable (Y).
- This introduction also discussed the primary measures that are used for estimating the crime committed in the United States; these primary measures are police reports (e.g., the UCR), victimization surveys (e.g., the NCVS), and offenders' self-reports of the crimes they have committed.
- We also discussed in this section what the measures of crime have shown regarding the distribution of criminal offending according to region, race and ethnicity, time of day, time of year, age, gender, socioeconomic status, and period of history. It is important to note that various theories presented in this book will be tested on the extent to which they can explain the clustering of crime among certain individuals and groups.

KEY TERMS

Classical School	index offenses	parsimony
clearance rate	informal controls	policy implications
conflict perspective	interracial	Positive School
consensual perspective	intraracial	scientific method
correlation (or covariation)	legalistic approach	scope
criminology	logical consistency	self-report data (SRD)
dark figure	macro level of analysis	social sciences
deviance	*mala in se*	spuriousness
empirical validity	*mala prohibita*	telescoping
equivalency hypothesis	micro level of analysis	temporal ordering
formal controls	National Crime Victimization Survey (NCVS)	testability
hot spots	nonindex offenses	theory
hypotheses	paradigm	Uniform Crime Report (UCR)

DISCUSSION QUESTIONS

1. How does criminology differ from other perspectives of crime?

2. How does a good theoretical explanation of crime go beyond simply predicting crime?

3. Should criminologists emphasize only crimes made illegal by law, or should they also study acts that are deviant but not illegal? Explain why you feel this way.

4. Even though you haven't been exposed to all the theories in this book, do you favor classical or positive assumptions regarding criminal behavior? Explain why.

5. Which types of theories do you think are most important: those that explain individual behavior (micro) or those that explain criminality among groups (macro)? Explain your decision.

6. Do you tend to favor the idea that human beings are born bad, good, or a blank slate? Discuss your decision and provide an example.

7. Which characteristics of a good theory do you find most important? Which are least important? Make sure to explain why you feel that way.

8. Of the three criteria for determining causality between a predictor variable and a consequent variable, which do you think is easiest to show, and which is hardest to show? Why?

9. Which of the measures of crime do you think is the best estimate of crime in the United States? Why? Also, which measure is the best for determining associations between crime and personality traits? Why?

10. Looking at what the measures of crime show, which finding surprises you the most? Explain why.

11. What types of policies do you feel reduce crime the most? Which do you think have little or no effect in reducing crime?

WEB RESOURCES

Measures of Crime

Overview of Criminological Theory (by Dr. Cecil Greek at Florida State University): http://www.criminology.fsu.edu/crimtheory/

FBI's UCR: http://www.fbi.gov/ucr/ucr.htm

NCVS: http://www.bjs.gov/index.cfm?ty=dcdetail&iid=245

How to Read a Research Article

As you travel through your criminal justice and criminology studies, you will soon learn that some of the best-known and emerging explanations of crime and criminal behavior come from research articles in academic journals. This book is full of research articles, and you may be asking yourself, "How do I read a research article?" It is my hope to answer this question with a quick summary of the key elements of any research article, followed by the questions you should be answering as you read through the assigned sections.

Every research article published in a social science journal will have the following elements: (a) introduction, (b) literature review, (c) methodology, (d) results, and (e) discussion/conclusion.

In the introduction, you will find an overview of the purpose of the research. Within the introduction, you will also find the hypothesis or hypotheses. A hypothesis is most easily defined as an educated statement or guess. In most hypotheses, you will find that the format usually followed is "If *X*, *Y* will occur." For example, a simple hypothesis might be "If the price of gas increases, more people will ride bikes." This is a testable statement that the researcher wants to address in her or his study. Usually authors will state the hypothesis directly, but not always. Therefore, you must be aware of what the author is actually testing in the research project. If you are unable to find the hypothesis, ask yourself what is being tested or manipulated and what are the expected results.

The next section of the research article is the literature review. At times, the literature review will be separated from the text in its own section, and at other times it will be found within the introduction. In any case, the literature review is an examination of what other researchers have already produced in terms of the research question or hypothesis. For example, returning to my hypothesis on the relationship between gas prices and bike riding, we may find that five researchers have previously conducted studies on the increase in gas prices. In the literature review, the author will discuss her or his findings and then discuss what the study will add to the existing research. The literature review may also be used as a platform of support for the hypothesis. For example, one researcher may have already determined that an increase in gas prices causes more people to roller-skate to work. The author can use this study as evidence to support her or his hypothesis that increased gas prices will lead to more bike riding.

The methods used in the research design are found in the next section of the research article. In the methodology section, you will find the following: who/what was studied, how many subjects were studied, the research tool (e.g., interview, survey, observation), how long the subjects were studied, and how the data that were collected were processed. The methods section is usually very concise, with every step of the research project recorded. This is important because a major goal of the researcher is reliability; describing exactly how the research was done allows it to be repeated. Reliability is determined by whether the results are the same.

The results section is an analysis of the researcher's findings. If the researcher conducted a quantitative study, using numbers or statistics to explain the research, you will find statistical tables and analyses that explain whether or not the researcher's hypothesis is supported. If the researcher conducted a qualitative study, nonnumerical research for the purpose of theory construction, the results will usually be displayed as a theoretical analysis or interpretation of the research question.

The research article will conclude with a discussion and summary of the study. In the discussion, you will find that the hypothesis is usually restated, and there may be a small discussion of why this was the hypothesis. You will also find a brief overview of the methodology and results. Finally, the discussion section looks at the implications of the research and what future research is still needed.

Now that you know the key elements of a research article, let us examine a sample article from your text: "The Use and Usefulness of Criminology, 1751–2005: Enlightened Justice and Its Failures" by Lawrence W. Sherman.

1. What is the thesis or main idea from this article?

   ◆ The thesis or main idea is found in the introductory paragraph of this article. Although Sherman does not point out the main idea directly, you may read the introduction and summarize the main idea in your own words. For example: The thesis or main idea is that criminology should move away from strict analysis and toward scientific experimentation to improve the criminal justice system and crime control practices.

2. What is the hypothesis?

   ◆ The hypothesis is found in the introduction of this article. It is first stated in the beginning paragraph: "As experimental criminology provides more comprehensive evidence about responses to crime, the prospects for better basic science—and better policy—will improve accordingly." The hypothesis is also restated in the middle of the second section of the article. Here, Sherman actually distinguishes the hypothesis by stating, "The history of criminology . . . provides an experimental test of this hypothesis about analytic versus experimental social science: *that social science has been most useful, if not most used, when it has been most experimental, with visibly demonstrable benefits (or harm avoidance) from new inventions.*"

3. Is there any prior literature related to the hypothesis?

   ◆ As you may have noticed, this article does not have a separate section for a literature review. However, you will see that Sherman devotes attention to prior literature under the heading "Enlightenment, Criminology, and Justice." Here, he offers literature regarding the analytical and experimental history of criminology. This brief overview helps the reader understand the prior research, which explains why social science became primarily analytic.

4. What methods are used to support the hypothesis?

   ◆ Sherman's methodology is known as a historical analysis. In other words, rather than conducting his own experiment, Sherman is using evidence from history to support his hypothesis regarding analytic and experimental criminology. When conducting a historical analysis, most researchers use archival material from books, newspapers, journals, and so on. Although Sherman does not directly state his source of information, we can see that he is basing his argument on historical essays and books, beginning with Henry Fielding's *An Enquiry into the Causes of the Late Increase of Robbers* (1751) and continuing through the social experiments of the 1980s by the National Institute of Justice. Throughout his methodology, Sherman continues to emphasize his hypothesis about the usefulness of experimental criminology, along with how experiments have also been hidden in the shadows of analytic criminology throughout history.

5. Is this a qualitative study or a quantitative study?

   ◆ To determine whether a study is qualitative or quantitative, you must look at the results. Is Sherman using numbers to support his hypothesis (quantitative), or is he developing a nonnumerical theoretical argument (qualitative)? Because Sherman does not use statistics in this study, we can safely conclude that this is a qualitative study.

6. What are the results, and how does the author present the results?

   ◆ Because this is a qualitative study, as we earlier determined, Sherman offers the results as a discussion of his findings from the historical analysis. The results may be found in the section titled "Criminology: Analytic, Useful, and Used." Here, Sherman explains that "*the vast majority of published criminology remains analytic and nonexperimental.*" He goes on to say that although experimental criminology has been shown to be useful, it has not always been used or used correctly. Because of the misuse of experimental criminology, criminologists have steered toward the safety of analysis rather than experimentation. Therefore, Sherman concludes that "analytic social science still dominates field experiments by 100 to 1 or better in criminology. . . . Future success of the field may depend upon a growing public image based on experimental results."

7. Do you believe that the author/s provided a persuasive argument? Why or why not?

   ◆ This answer is ultimately up to the reader, but looking at this article, I believe that it is safe to assume that readers will agree that Sherman offered a persuasive argument. Let us return to his major premise: The advancement of theory may depend on better experimental evidence, but as history has illustrated, the vast majority of criminology remains analytical. Sherman supports this proposition with a historical analysis of the great thinkers of criminology and the absence of experimental research throughout a major portion of history.

8. Who is the intended audience of this article?

   ◆ A final question that will be useful for the reader deals with the intended audience. As you read the article, ask yourself, to whom is the author wanting to speak? After you read this article, you will see that Sherman is writing for students, professors, criminologists, historians, and criminal justice personnel. The target audience may most easily be identified if you ask yourself, "Who will benefit from reading this article?"

9. What does the article add to your knowledge of the subject?

   ◆ This answer is best left up to the reader because the question is asking how the article improved your knowledge. However, one answer to this question is as follows: This article helps the reader to understand that criminology is not just about theoretical construction. Criminology is both an analytical and experimental social science, and to improve the criminal justice system as well as criminal justice policies, more attention needs to be given to the usefulness of experimental criminology.

10. What are the implications for criminal justice policy that can be derived from this article?

   ◆ Implications for criminal justice policy are most likely to be found in the conclusion or the discussion sections of the article. This article, however, emphasizes the implications throughout. From this article, we are able to derive that crime prevention programs will improve greatly if they are embedded in well-funded, experiment-driven data rather than strictly analytical data. Therefore, it is in the hands of policy makers to fund criminological research and apply the findings in a productive manner to criminal justice policy.

Now that we have gone through the elements of a research article, it is your turn to continue through your text, reading the various articles and answering the same questions. You may find that some articles are easier to follow than others, but do not be dissuaded. Remember that each article will follow the same format: introduction, literature review, methods, results, and discussion. If you have any problems, refer to this introduction for guidance.

READING 1

In this selection, Lawrence Sherman provides an excellent review of the policies that have resulted from the very early stages of classical theories, through the early positivist era, and into modern times. Sherman's primary point is that experimental research is highly important in determining the policies that should be used with offenders and potential offenders. Although many important factors can never be experimentally manipulated—bad parents, poor schooling, negative peer influences—there are, as Sherman asserts, numerous types of variables that can be experimentally manipulated by criminological researchers. The resulting findings can help guide policy makers in pushing forward more efficient and effective policies regarding the prevention of and reaction to various forms of criminal offending. There is no better scholar to present such an argument and support for it; Sherman is perhaps the best-known scholar who has applied the experimental method to criminological research, given his experience with studies regarding domestic violence and other criminal offenses.

Readers are encouraged to consider other variables or aspects of crime that can be examined via experimental forms of research. Furthermore, readers should consider the vast number of variables that are important causes of crime or delinquency but could never be experimentally manipulated for logistic or ethical reasons.

The Use and Usefulness of Criminology, 1751–2005

Enlightened Justice and Its Failures

Lawrence W. Sherman

Criminology was born in a crime wave, raised on a crusade against torture and execution, and then hibernated for two centuries of speculation. Awakened by the rising crime rates of the latter twentieth century, most of its scholars chose to pursue analysis over experiment. The twenty-first century now offers more policy-relevant science than ever, even if basic science still occupies center stage. Its prospects for integrating basic and "clinical" science are growing, with more scholars using multiple tools rather than pursuing single-method work. Criminology contributes only a few drops of science in an ocean of decision making, but the number of drops is growing steadily. As experimental criminology provides more comprehensive evidence about responses to crime, the prospects for better basic science—and better policy—will improve accordingly.

 ## Enlightenment, Criminology, and Justice

The entire history of social science has been shaped by key choices scholars made in that transformative era, choices that are still made today. For criminology more than most disciplines, those Enlightenment choices have had enormous consequences for the use and usefulness of its social science.

Source: Lawrence Sherman, "The Use and Usefulness of Criminology, 1751–2005," *ANNALS of the American Academy of Political and Social Science* 600, no. 1 (2005): 115–35. The selection here is taken from A. Walsh and C. Hemmens, *Introduction to Criminology: A Text/Reader* (Thousand Oaks, CA: Sage, 2008), 24–32. Copyright © 2008 Sage Publications, Inc. Reprinted by permission of Sage Publications, Inc.

The most important of these consequences is that justice still remains largely un-Enlightened by empirical evidence about the effects of its actions on public safety and public trust.

Historians may despair at defining a coherent intellectual or philosophical content in the Age of Enlightenment, but one idea seems paramount: "that we understand nature and man best through the use of our natural faculties" (May 1976, xiv) by systematic empirical methods, rather than through ideology, abstract reasoning, common sense, or claims of divine principles made by competing religious authorities. Kant, in contrast, stressed the receiving end of empirical science in his definition of Enlightenment: the time when human beings regained the courage to "use one's own mind without another's guidance" (Gay 1969, 384).

Rather than becoming *experimental* in method, social science became primarily *analytic*. This distinction between experimental manipulation of some aspect of social behavior versus detached (if systematic) observation of behavioral patterns is crucial to all social science (even though not all questions for social science offer a realistic potential for experiment). The decision to cast social science primarily in the role of critic, rather than of inventor, has had lasting consequences for the enterprise, especially for the credibility of its conclusions. There may be nothing so practical as a good theory, but it is hard to visibly—or convincingly—demonstrate the benefits of social analysis for the reduction of human misery. The absence of "show-and-tell" benefits of analytic social science blurred its boundaries with ideology, philosophy, and even emotion. This problem has plagued analytic social science ever since, with the possible exception of times (like the Progressive Era and the 1960s) when the social order itself was in crisis. As sociologist E. Digby Baltzell (1979) suggested about cities and other social institutions, "as the twig is bent, so grows the tree." Social science may have been forged in the same kind of salon discussions as natural science, but without some kind of empirical reports from factories, clinics, or farm fields. Social science has thus famously "smelled too much of the lamp" of the library (Gay 1969). Even when analytic social science has been most often used, it is rarely praised as useful.

That is not to say that theories (with or without evidence) have lacked influence in criminology, or in any social science. The theory of deterrent effects of sanctions was widely used to reduce the severity of punishment long before the theory could be tested with any evidence. The theories of "anomie" and "differential association" were used to plan the 1960s "War on Poverty" without any clear evidence that opportunity structures could be changed. Psychological theories of personality transformation were used to develop rehabilitation programs in prisons long before any of them were subject to empirical evaluation. Similarly, evidence (without theory) of a high concentration of crime among a small proportion of criminal offenders was used to justify more severe punishment for repeat offenders, also without empirical testing of those policies.

The criminologists' general preference for analysis over experiment has not been universal in social science. Enlightenment political science was, in an important—if revolutionary—sense, experimental, developing and testing new forms of government soon after they were suggested in print. The Federalist Papers, for example, led directly to the "experiment" of the Bill of Rights.

Perhaps the clearest exception to the dominance of analytic social science was within criminology itself in its very first work during the Enlightenment. The fact that criminologists do not remember it this way says more about its subsequent dominance by analytic methods than about the true history of the field. Criminology was born twice in the eighteenth century, first (and forgotten) as an experimental science and then (remembered) as an analytic one. And though experimental criminology in the Enlightenment had an enormous impact on institutions of justice, it was analytic criminology that was preserved by law professors and twentieth-century scholars as the foundation of the field.

The history of criminology thus provides an experimental test of this hypothesis about analytic versus experimental social science: *that social science has been most useful, if not most used, when it has been most experimental, with visibly demonstrable benefits (or harm avoidance) from new inventions.* The evidence for this claim in eighteenth-century criminology is echoed by the facts of criminology in the twentieth century. In both centuries, the fraternal twins of analysis and experiment pursued different pathways through life, while communicating closely with each other. One twin was critical, the other imaginative; one systematically observational, the other actively experimental; one detached with its integrity intact, the other engaged with its integrity under threat. Both twins needed each other to advance their mutual field of inquiry. But it has been experiments in every age that made criminology most useful, as measured by unbiased estimates of the effects of various responses to crime.

The greatest disappointment across these centuries has been the limited usefulness of experimental criminology in achieving "geometric precision" (Beccaria 1764/1964) in the pursuit of "Enlightened Justice," defined as "the administration of sanctions under criminal law guided by (1) inviolate principles protecting human rights of suspects and convicts while seeking (2) consequences reducing human misery, through means known from (3) unbiased empirical evidence of what works best" (Sherman 2005). While some progress has been made, most justice remains unencumbered by empirical evidence on its effects. To understand why this disappointment persists amid great success, we must begin with the Enlightenment itself.

 ## Inventing Criminology: Fielding, Beccaria, and Bentham

The standard account of the origin of criminology locates it as a branch of moral philosophy: part of an aristocratic crusade against torture, the death penalty, and arbitrary punishment, fought with reason, rhetoric, and analysis. This account is true but incomplete. Criminology's forgotten beginnings preceded Cesare Beccaria's famous 1764 essay in the form of Henry Fielding's 1753 experiments with justice in London. Inventing the modern institutions of a salaried police force and prosecutors, of crime reporting, crime records, employee background investigations, liquor licensing, and social welfare policies as crime prevention strategies, Fielding provided the viable preventive alternatives to the cruel excesses of retribution that Beccaria denounced—before Beccaria ever published a word.

The standard account hails a treatise on "the science of justice" (Gay 1969, 440) that was based on Beccaria's occasional visits to courts and prisons, followed by many discussions in a salon. The present alternative account cites a far less famous treatise based on more than a thousand days of Fielding conducting trials and sentencing convicts in the world's (then) largest city, supplemented by his on-site inspections of tenements, gin joints, brothels, and public hangings. The standard account thus chooses a criminology of analytic detachment over a criminology of clinical engagement.

The standard account in twentieth-century criminology textbooks traced the origin of the field to this "classical school" of criminal law and criminology, with Cesare

Beccaria's (1738–1794) treatise *On Crimes and Punishments* (1764) as the first treatise in scientific criminology. (Beccaria is also given credit [incorrectly], even by Enlightenment scholars, for first proposing that utility be measured by "the greatest happiness divided among the greatest number"—which Frances Hutcheson, a mentor to Adam Smith, had published in Glasgow in 1725 before Beccaria was born [Buchan 2003, 68–71]). Beccaria, and later Bentham, contributed the central claims of the deterrence hypothesis on which almost all systems of criminal law now rely: that punishment is more likely to prevent future crime to the extent that it is certain, swift, and proportionate to the offense (Beccaria) or more costly than the benefit derived from the offense (Bentham).

Fielding

This standard account of Beccaria as the *first* criminologist is, on the evidence, simply wrong. Criminology did not begin in a Milanese salon among the group of aristocrats who helped Beccaria formulate and publish his epigrams but more than a decade earlier in a London magistrate's courtroom full of gin-soaked robbery defendants. The first social scientist of crime to publish in the English—and perhaps any—language was Henry Fielding, Esq. (1707–1754). Fielding was appointed by the government as magistrate at the Bow Street Court in London. His years on that bench, supplemented by his visits to the homes of London labor and London poor, provided him with ample qualitative data for his 1751 treatise titled *An Enquiry Into the Causes of the Late Increase of Robbers*.

Fielding's treatise is a remarkable analysis of what would today be called the "environmental criminology" of robbery. Focused on the reasons for a crime wave and the policy alternatives to hanging as the only means of combating crime, Fielding singles out the wave of "that poison called gin" that hit mid-century London like crack hit New York in the 1980s. He theorizes that a drastic price increase (or tax) would make gin too expensive for most people to consume, thereby reducing violent crime. He also proposes more regulation of gambling, based on his interviews with arrested robbers who said they had to rob to pay their gambling debts. Observing the large numbers of poor and homeless people committing crime, he suggests a wider "safety net" of free housing and food. His emphasis is clearly on prevention without punishment as the best policy approach to crime reduction.

Fielding then goes on to document the failures of punishment in three ways. First, the system of compulsory "voluntary policing" by each citizen imposed after the Norman Conquest had become useless: "what is the business of every man is the business of no man." Second, the contemporary system of requiring crime victims to prosecute their own cases (or hire a lawyer at their own expense) was failing to bring many identified offenders to justice. Third, witnesses were intimidated and often unwilling to provide evidence needed for conviction. All this leads him to hint at, but not spell out, a modern system of "socialized" justice in which the state, rather than crime victims, pays for police to investigate and catch criminals, prosecutors to bring evidence to court, and even support for witnesses and crime victims.

His chance to present his new "invention" to the government came two years after he published his treatise on robbery. In August 1753, five different robbery-murders were committed in London in one week. An impatient cabinet secretary summoned Fielding twice from his sickbed and asked him to propose a plan for stopping the murders. In four days, Fielding submitted a "grant proposal" for an experiment in policing that would cost £600 (about £70,000 or $140,000 in current value). The purpose of the money was to retain, on salary, the band of detectives Fielding worked with, and to pay a reward to informants who would provide evidence against the murderers.

Within two weeks, the robberies stopped, and for two months not one murder or robbery was reported in Westminster (Fielding 1755/1964, 191–193). Fielding managed to obtain a "no-cost extension" to the grant, which kept the detectives on salary for several years. After Henry's death, his brother John obtained new funding, so that the small team of "Bow Street Runners" stayed in operation until the foundation of the much larger—and uniformed—Metropolitan Police in 1829.

The birth of the Bow Street Runners was a turning point in the English paradigm of justice. The crime wave accompanying the penny-a-quart gin epidemic of the mid-eighteenth century had demonstrated the failure of relying solely on the *severity* of punishment, so excessive that many juries refused to convict people who were clearly guilty of offenses punishable by death—such as shoplifting. As Bentham would later write, there was good reason to think that the *certainty* of punishment was too low for crime to be deterrable. As Fielding said in his treatise on robbery, "The utmost severity to offenders [will not] be justifiable unless we take every possible method of preventing the offence." Fielding was not the only inventor to propose the idea of a salaried police force to patrol and arrest criminals, but he was the first to conduct an *experiment* testing that invention. While Fielding's police experiment would take decades to be judged successful (seventy-six years for the "Bobbies" to be founded at Scotland Yard in 1829), the role of experimental evidence proved central to changing the paradigm of practice.

Beccaria

In sharp contrast, Beccaria had no clinical practice with offenders, nor was he ever asked to stop a crime wave. Instead, he took aim at a wave of torture and execution that characterized European justice. Arguing the same ideology of prevention as Fielding (whose treatise he did not cite), Beccaria urged abolition of torture, the death penalty, and secret trials. Within two centuries, almost all Europe had adopted his proposals. While many other causes of that result can be cited, there is clear evidence of Beccaria's 1764 treatise creating a "tipping point" of public opinion on justice.

What Beccaria did not do, however, was to supply a shred of scientific evidence in support of his theories of the deterrent effects of non-capital penalties proportionate to the severity of the offense. Nor did he state his theories in a clearly falsifiable way, as Fielding had done. In his method, Beccaria varies little from law professors or judges (then and now) who argue a blend of opinion and factual assumptions they find reasonable, deeming it enlightened truth *ipse dixit* ("because I say so myself"). What he lacked by the light of systematic analysis of data, he made up for by eloquence and "stickiness" of his aphorisms. Criminology by slogan may be more readily communicated than criminology by experiment in terms of fame. But it is worth noting that the founding of the British police appears much more directly linked to Fielding's experiments than the steady abolition of the death penalty was linked to Beccaria's book.

Bentham

Beccaria the moral-empirical theorist stands in sharp contrast to his fellow Utilitarian Jeremy Bentham, who devoted twelve years of his life (and some £10,000) to an invention in prison administration. Working from a book he wrote on a "Panopticon" design for punishment by incarceration (rather than hanging), Bentham successfully lobbied for a

1794 law authorizing such a prison to be built. He was later promised a contract to build and manage such a prison, but landed interests opposed his use of the site he had selected. We can classify Bentham as an experimentalist on the grounds that he invested much of his life in "trying" as well as thinking. Even though he did not build the prison he designed, similar prisons (for better or worse) were built in the United States and elsewhere. Prison design may justifiably be classified as a form of invention and experimental criminology, as distinct from the analytic social science approach Bentham used in his writings—thereby making him as "integrated" as Fielding in terms of theory and practice. The demise of Bentham's plans during the Napoleonic Wars marked the end of an era in criminology, just as the Enlightenment itself went into retreat after the French Revolution and the rise of Napoleon. By 1815, experimentalism in criminology was in hibernation, along with most of criminology itself, not to stir until the 1920s or spring fully to life until the 1960s.

Two Torpid Centuries—With Exceptions

Analytic criminology continued to develop slowly even while experimental criminology slumbered deeply, but neither had any demonstrable utility to the societies that fostered them. One major development was the idea of involuntary causes of crime "determined" by either social (Quetelet 1835/2004) or biological (Lombroso 1876/1918) factors that called into question the legal doctrines of criminal responsibility. The empirical evidence for these claims, however, was weak (and in Lombroso's case, wrong), leaving the theoretical approach to criminology largely unused until President Johnson's War on Poverty in the 1960s.

Cambridge-Somerville

The first fully randomized controlled trial in American criminology appears to have been the Cambridge-Somerville experiment, launched in Massachusetts in the 1930s by Dr. Richard Clark Cabot. This project offered high-risk young males "friendly guidance and social support, healthful activities after school, tutoring when necessary, and medical assistance as needed" (McCord 2001). It also included a

long-term "big brother" mentoring relationship that was abruptly terminated in most cases during World War II. While the long-term effects of the program would not be known until the 1970s, the critical importance of the experimental design was recognized at the outset. It was for that reason that the outcomes test could reach its startling conclusion: "The results showed that as compared with members of the control group, those who had been in the treatment program were more likely to have been convicted for crimes indexed by the Federal Bureau of Investigation as serious street crimes; they had died an average of five years younger; and they were more likely to have received a medical diagnosis as alcoholic, schizophrenic, or manic-depressive" (McCord 2001, 188). In short, the boys offered the program would have been far better off if they had been "deprived" of the program services in the randomly assigned control group.

No study in the history of criminology has ever demonstrated such clear, unintended, criminogenic effects of a program intended to prevent crime. To this day, it is "exhibit A" in discussions with legislators, students, and others skeptical of the value of evaluating government programs of any sort, let alone crime prevention programs. Its early reports in the 1950s also set the stage for a renaissance in experimental criminology, independently of the growth of analytic criminology.

Renaissance: 1950–1982

Amidst growing concern about juvenile delinquency, the Eisenhower administration provided the first federal funding for research on delinquency prevention. Many of the studies funded in that era, with both federal and nonfederal support, adopted experimental designs. What follows is merely a highlighting of the renaissance of experimental criminology in the long twilight of the FDR coalition prior to the advent of the Reagan revolution.

Martinson and Wilson

While experimental evidence was on the rise in policing, it was on the decline in corrections. The comprehensive review of rehabilitation strategies undertaken by Lipton, Martinson, and Wilks (1975) initially focused on the internal validity of the research designs in rehabilitation experiments within prisons. Concluding that these designs were too weak to offer unbiased estimates of treatment effects, the authors essentially said "we don't know" what works to rehabilitate criminals. In a series of less scientific and more popular publications, the summary of the study was transformed into saying that there is no evidence that criminals can be rehabilitated. Even the title "What Works" was widely repeated in 1975 by word of mouth as "nothing works."

The Martinson review soon became the basis for a major change in correctional policies. While the per capita rates of incarceration had been dropping throughout the 1960s and early 1970s, the trend was rapidly reversed after 1975 (Ruth and Reitz 2003). Coinciding with the publication of Wilson's (1975) first edition of *Thinking About Crime*, the Martinson review arguably helped fuel a sea change from treating criminals as victims of society to treating society as the victim of criminals. That, in turn, may have helped to feed a three-decade increase in prisoners (Laub 2004) to more than 2.2 million, the highest incarceration rate in the world.

 ## Warp Speed: 1982–2005

Stewart

In September, 1982, a former Oakland Police captain named James K. Stewart was appointed director of the National Institute of Justice (NIJ). Formerly a White House Fellow who had attended a National Academy of Sciences discussion of the work of NIJ, Stewart had been convinced by James Q. Wilson and others that NIJ needed to invest more of its budget in experimental criminology. He acted immediately by canceling existing plans to award many research grants for analytic criminology, transferring the funds to support experimental work. This work included experiments in policing, probation, drug market disruption, drunk-driving sentences, investigative practices, and shoplifting arrests.

Schools

The 1980s also witnessed the expansion of experimental criminology into the many school-based prevention programs. Extensive experimental and quasi-experimental evidence on their effects—good and bad—has now been published. In one test, for example, a popular peer guidance group that was found effective as an alternative to

incarceration was found to increase crime in a high school setting. Gottfredson (1987) found that high-risk students who were not grouped with other high-risk students in high school group discussions did better than those who were.

Drug Courts

The advent of (diversion from prosecution to medically supervised treatments administered by) "drug courts" during the rapid increase in experimental criminology has led to a large and growing volume of tests of drug court effects on recidivism. Perhaps no other innovation in criminal justice has had so many controlled field tests conducted by so many different independent researchers. The compilations of these findings into meta-analyses will shed increasing light on the questions of when, and how, to divert drug-abusing offenders from prison.

Boot Camps

Much the same can be said about boot camps. The major difference is that boot camp evaluations started off as primarily quasi-experimental in their designs (with matched comparisons or worse), but increasing numbers of fully randomized tests have been conducted in recent years (Mitchell, MacKenzie, and Perez 2005). Many states persist in using boot camps for thousands of offenders, despite fairly consistent evidence that they are no more effective than regular correctional programs.

Child Raising

Criminology has also claimed a major experiment in child raising as one of its own. Beginning at the start of the "warp speed" era, the program of nurse home visits to at-risk first mothers designed by Dr. David Olds and his colleagues (1986) has now been found to have long-term crime prevention effects. Both mothers and children show these effects, which may be linked to lower levels of child abuse or better anger management practices in child raising.

 ## Criminology: Analytic, Useful, and Used

This recitation of a selected list of experiments in criminology must be labeled with a consumer warning: *the*

vast majority of published criminology remains analytic and nonexperimental. While criminology was attracting funding and students during the period of rising crime of the 1960s to 1990s, criminologists put most of their efforts into the basic science of crime patterns and theories of criminality. Studies of the natural life course of crime among cohorts of males became the central focus of the field, as measured by citation patterns (Wolfgang, Figlio, and Thornberry 1978). Despite standing concerns that criminology would be "captured" by governments to become a tool for developing repressive policies, the evidence suggests that the greatest (or largest) generation of criminologists in history captured the field away from policymakers.

The renaissance in experimental criminology therefore addressed very intense debates over many key issues in crime and justice, providing the first unbiased empirical guidance available to inform those debates. That much made criminology increasingly useful, at least potentially. Usefulness alone, of course, does not guarantee that the information will be *used.* Police agencies today do make extensive use of the research on concentrating patrols in crime hot spots, yet they have few repeat offender units, despite two successful tests of the "invention." Correctional agencies make increasing use of the "what works" literature in the United States and United Kingdom, yet prison populations are still fed by people returned to prison on the unevaluated policy of incarcerating "technical" violators of the conditions of their release (who have not committed new crimes). Good evidence alone is not enough to change policy in any context. Yet absent good evidence, there is a far greater danger that bad policies will win out. Analytic criminology—well or badly done—poses fewer risks for society than badly done experimental criminology. It is not clear that another descriptive test of differential association theory will have any effect on policy making, unless it is embedded in a program evaluation. But misleading or biased evidence from poor-quality research designs—or even unreplicated experiments—may well cause the adoption of policies that ultimately prove harmful.

This danger is, in turn, reduced by the lack of influence criminology usually has on policy making or operational decisions. That, in turn, is linked to the absence of clear conclusions about the vast majority of criminal justice policies and decisions. Until experimental criminology can develop a more comprehensive basis of evidence for guiding operations, practitioners are unlikely to develop the habit of checking the literature before making a decision. The possibility of improving the quality of both primary evidence and systematic reviews offers hope for a future in which criminology itself may entail less risk of causing harm.

This is by no means a suggestion that analytic criminology be abandoned; the strength of experimental criminology may depend heavily on the continued advancement of basic (analytic) criminology. Yet the full partnership between the two has yet to be realized. Analytic social science still dominates field experiments by 100 to 1 or better in criminology, just as in any other field of research on human behavior. Future success of the field may depend upon a growing public image based on experimental results, just as advances in treatment attract funding for basic science in medicine.

Conclusion

Theoretical criminology will hold center stage for many years to come. But as Farrington (2000) has argued, the advancement of theory may depend on better experimental evidence. And that, in turn, may depend on a revival in the federal funding that has recently dropped to its lowest level in four decades. Such a revival may well depend on exciting public interest in the practical value of research, as perhaps only experiments can do.

"Show and tell" is hard to do while it is happening. Yet it is not impossible. Whether anyone ever sees a crime prevention program delivered, it is at least possible to embed an experimental design into every long-term analytic study of crime in the life course. As Joan McCord (2003) said in her final words to the American Society of Criminology, the era of purely observational criminology should come to an end. Given what we now know about the basic life-course patterns, McCord suggested, "all longitudinal studies should now have experiments embedded within them."

Doing what McCord proposed would become an experiment *in* social science as well as *of* social science. That experiment is already under way, in a larger sense. Criminology is rapidly becoming more multi-method, as well as multi-level and multi-theoretical. Criminology may soon resemble medicine more than economics, with analysts closely integrated with clinical researchers to develop basic science as well as treatment. The integration of diverse forms and levels of knowledge in "consilience" with each other, rather than a hegemony of any one approach, is within our grasp. It awaits only a generation of broadly educated criminologists prepared to do many things, or at least prepared to work in collaboration with other people who bring diverse talents to science.

✕ References

Baltzell, D. (1979). *Puritan Boston and Quaker Philadelphia: Two Protestant ethics and the spirit of class authority and leadership.* New York: Free Press.

Beccaria, C. (1964). *On crimes and punishments* (J. Grigson, Trans.). Milan, Italy: Oxford University Press. (Original work published 1764)

Buchan, J. (2003). *Crowded with genius: The Scottish Enlightenment: Edinburgh's moment of the mind.* New York: HarperCollins.

Farrington, D. (2000). Explaining and preventing crime: The globalization of knowledge. The American Society of Criminology 1999 Presidential Address. *Criminology, 38,* 1–24.

Fielding, H. (1964). *The journal of a voyage to Lisbon.* London: Dent. (Original work published 1755)

Gay, P. (1969). *The Enlightenment: An interpretation. Vol. 2, The science of freedom.* New York: Knopf.

Gottfredson, G. (1987). Peer group interventions to reduce the risk of delinquent behavior: A selective review and a new evaluation. *Criminology, 25,* 671–714.

Laub, J. (2004). The life course of criminology in the United States: The American Society of Criminology 2003 Presidential Address. *Criminology, 42,* 1–26.

Lipton, D., Martinson, R., & Wilks, J. (1975). *The effectiveness of correctional treatment: A survey of treatment evaluation studies.* New York: Praeger.

Lombroso, C. (1918). *Crime, its causes and remedies.* Boston: Little, Brown. (Original work published 1876)

May, H. (1976). *The Enlightenment in America.* New York: Oxford University Press.

McCord, J. (2001). *Crime prevention: A cautionary tale.* Proceedings of the Third International, Inter-Disciplinary Evidence-Based Policies and Indicator Systems Conference, University of Durham. Retrieved April 22, 2005, from http://cem.dur.ac.uk

McCord, J. (2003). *Discussing age, crime, and human development. The future of life-course criminology.* Denver, CO: American Society of Criminology.

Mitchell, O., MacKenzie, D., & Perez, D. (2005). A randomized evaluation of the Maryland correctional boot camp for adults: Effects on offender anti-social attitudes and cognitions. *Journal of Offender Rehabilitation, 40*(4).

Olds, D., Henderson, C., Chamberlin, R., & Tatelbaum, R. (1986). *Pediatrics, 78,* 65–78.

Quetelet, A. (2004). A treatise on man. As cited in F. Adler, G. O. W. Mueller, and W. S. Laufer, *Criminology and the criminal justice system* (5th ed., p. N-6). New York: McGraw-Hill. (Original work published 1835)

Ruth, H., & Reitz, K. (2003). *The challenge of crime: Rethinking our response.* Cambridge, MA: Harvard University Press.

Sherman, L. (2005). *Enlightened justice: Consequentialism and empiricism from Beccaria to Braithwaite.* Address to the 14th World Congress of Criminology, International Society of Criminology, Philadelphia, August 8.

Wilson, J. (1975). *Thinking about crime.* New York: Basic Books.

Wolfgang, M., Figlio, R., & Thornberry, T. (1978). *Evaluating criminology.* New York: Elsevier.

REVIEW QUESTIONS

1. According to Sherman, what part did Henry Fielding's research play in the early stages of research on crime and the influence it had on stopping robberies in London? Explain in detail. What implications can be drawn about using resources (i.e., money) to stop a given crime in a certain location?

2. According to Sherman, what impact did the "Bow Street Runners" have?

3. What does Sherman have to say about what Beccaria and Bentham contributed to policies regarding crime? Do you agree with Sherman's assessment?

4. What does Sherman have to say about Martinson's review of rehabilitation programs and its impact on policy?

5. What does Sherman have to say about criminological research regarding schools, drug courts, boot camps, and child raising? Which recent programs does he claim had success? Which recent programs or designs does he suggest do not work?

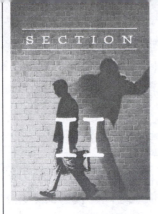

Preclassical and Classical Theories of Crime

This section will examine the earliest logical theories of rule breaking, namely, explanations of criminal conduct that emphasize free will and the ability of individuals to make rational decisions regarding the consequences of their behavior. The natural capabilities of human beings to make decisions based on expected costs and benefits were acknowledged during the Age of Enlightenment in the 17th and 18th centuries. This understanding of human capabilities led to what is considered the first rational theory of criminal activity, deterrence theory. This theory has had a more profound impact on justice systems in the United States than any other perspective to date. Furthermore, virtually all criminal justice systems (e.g., policing, courts, corrections) are based on this theoretical model even today.

Such theories of human rationality were in stark contrast to the theories focusing on religious or supernatural causes of crime, which had prevailed through most of human civilization up to the Age of Enlightenment. In addition, the Classical School theories of crime are distinguished from theories in subsequent sections of this book by their emphasis on the free will and rational decision making of individuals, which modern theories of crime tend to ignore. The theoretical perspectives discussed in this section all focus on the ability of human beings to choose their own behavior and destinies, whereas paradigms that existed before and after this period tend to emphasize the inability of individuals to control their behavior due to external factors. Therefore, the Classical School is perhaps the paradigm best suited for analysis of what types of calculations are going on in someone's head before he or she commits a crime.

The different Classical School theories presented in this section vary in many ways, most notably in what they propose as the primary constructs and processes individuals use to determine whether they are going to commit a crime. For example, some Classical School theories emphasize the potential negative consequences of their actions, whereas others focus on the possible benefits of such activity. Still others concentrate on the opportunities and existing situations that predispose people to engage in criminal activity. Regardless of their differences, all of the theories examined in this section emphasize a common theme: Individuals commit crime because they identify certain situations and acts as beneficial due to the perceived lack of punishment and the perceived likelihood of profits, such as money or peer status. In other words, the potential offender weighs out the possible costs and pleasures of committing a given act and then behaves in a rational way based on this analysis.

The most important distinction of these Classical School theories, as opposed to those discussed in future sections, is that they emphasize individuals making their own decisions regardless of extraneous influences, such as the economy or bonding with society. Although many extraneous factors may influence the ability of an individual to rationally consider offending situations, the Classical School assumes that the individual takes all these influences into account when making the decision about whether or not to engage in criminal behavior. Given the focus placed on individual responsibility, it is not surprising that Classical School theories are used as the basis for U.S. policies on punishment for criminal activity. The Classical School theories are highly compatible and consistent with the conservative, get-tough movement that has existed since the mid-1970s. Thus, the Classical School still retains the highest importance in terms of policy and pragmatic punishment in the United States, as well as throughout all countries in the Western world.

As you will see, the Classical School theoretical paradigm was presented as early as the mid-1700s, and its prominence as a model of offending behavior in criminal justice systems is still dominant. Scientific and academic circles, however, have dismissed many of the claims of this perspective. For reasons we shall explore in this section, the assumptions and primary propositions of Classical School theories have been neglected by most recent theoretical models of criminologists. This dismissal is likely premature, given the impact that this perspective has had on understanding human nature, as well as the profound influence it has had on most criminal justice systems, especially in the United States.

Preclassical Perspectives of Crime and Punishment

Over the long course of human civilization, people have mostly believed that criminal activity is caused by supernatural causes or religious factors. It has been documented that some primitive societies believed that crime increased during major thunderstorms or major droughts. Most primitive cultures believed that, when a person engaged in behavior that violated the tribe's or clan's rules, the devil or evil spirits were making him or her do it.[1] For example, in many societies, if someone committed criminal activity, it was common to perform exorcisms or primitive surgery, such as breaking open the skull of the perpetrator to allow the demons to leave his or her head. Of course, this almost always resulted in the death of the accused person, but it was seen as a liberating experience for the offender.

This was just one form of dealing with criminal behavior, but it epitomizes how primitive cultures understood the causes of crime. As the movie *The Exorcist* revealed, exorcisms were still being performed on offenders by representatives of a number of religions, including Catholicism, in the 21st century to get the devil out of them. In June 2005, a Romanian monk and four nuns acknowledged engaging in an exorcism that led to the death of the victim, who was crucified, a towel stuffed in her mouth, and left without food for many days.[2] When the monk and nuns were asked to explain why they did this, they defiantly said they were trying to take the devils out of the 23-year-old woman. Although they were prosecuted by Romanian authorities, many governments might not have done so because many societies around the world still believe in and condone such practices.

Readers may be surprised to learn that the Roman Catholic Church still authorizes college-level courses on how to perform exorcisms. Specifically, news reports revealed that a Vatican-recognized university was offering a course in exorcism and demonic possession for a second year because of its concern about the "devil's lure."[3] In fact, Pope

[1]Stephen E. Brown, Finn-Aage Esbensen, and Gilbert Geis, *Criminology: Explaining Crime and Its Context*, 8th ed. (Cincinnati: Anderson, 2012).

[2]Associated Press, "Five Charged in Deadly Exorcism," June 24, 2005.

[3]Associated Press, "University Offering Course on Exorcism," July 9, 2005.

Benedict XVI welcomed a large group of Italian exorcists who visited the Vatican in September 2005 and encouraged them to carry on their work for the Catholic Church.[4] Furthermore, in 1999, the Roman Catholic Church issued revised guidelines for conducting exorcisms, which recommend consulting physicians when exorcisms are performed; it also provides an 84-page description of the language (in Latin) to be used in such rituals. It should be noted that the use of such exorcisms is quite rare, especially in more developed nations. However, U.S. Catholic bishops recently (in November 2010) cited the need for more trained exorcists and even held a conference in Baltimore, Maryland, on how to conduct them. This two-day training session instructed clergy on evaluating evil possession, as well as reviewing the rituals that comprise an exorcism. More than 50 bishops and 60 priests attended this training session, despite the tendency for exorcists in U.S. dioceses to keep a very low profile.[5]

▲ Image 2.1   Although more common in ancient times, exorcisms are still approved and carried out by certain groups in attempts to remove evil spirits from individuals.

Source: © iStockphoto.com / KatarzynaBialasiewicz.

One of the most common supernatural beliefs in primitive cultures was that the full moon caused criminal activity. Then, as now, there was much truth to the full-moon theory. In primitive times, people believed that crime was related to the influence of higher powers, including the destructive influence of the moon itself. Modern studies have shown, however, that the increase in crime is primarily due to a Classical School theoretical model: There are simply more opportunities to commit crime when the moon is full because there is more light at night, which results in more people being out on the streets. In any case, nighttime is well established as a high-risk period for adult crimes, such as sexual assault.

Although some primitive theories had some validity in determining when crime would be more common, virtually none of them accurately predicted who would commit the offenses. During the Middle Ages, just about everyone was from the lower classes, and only a minority of that group engaged in offending against the normative society. So, for most of human civilization, there was virtually no rational theoretical understanding of why individuals violate the laws of society; instead, people believed crime was caused by supernatural or religious factors of the devil-made-me-do-it variety.

Consistent with these views, the punishments related to offending during this period were quite harsh by modern standards. Given the assumption that evil spirits drove the motivations for criminal activity, the punishments for criminal acts, especially those deemed particularly offensive to the norms of a given society, were often quite inhumane. Common punishments at that time were beheading, torture, being burned alive at the stake, and being drowned, stoned, or quartered. Good discussions of such harsh examples of punishment, such as quartering, can be found in Brown et al.'s discussion of punishment.[6]

---

[4]Reuters, "Pope Benedict XVI Warmly Greets Exorcist Convention," September 17, 2005.

[5]Associated Press, "Catholic Bishops: More Exorcists Needed," November 13, 2010.

[6]Brown et al., *Criminology*, 170–184.

Although many would find the primitive forms of punishment and execution to be quite barbaric, some modern societies still practice them. For example, Islamic court systems, as well as other religious and ethnic cultures, are often allowed to carry out executions and other forms of corporal punishment. Fifteen individuals were whipped with a cane for gambling in Aceh, Indonesia, a highly conservative Muslim region. The caning was held in public and outside a mosque.[7] In the United States, gambling is a relatively minor crime—when it is not totally legal, as in many places in the United States. It is interesting to note, however, that a relatively recent Gallup poll regarding the use of caning (i.e., public whipping) of convicted individuals was supported by most of the American public.[8]

▲ Image 2.2   Public stoning and caning are still used as punishment by certain societies around the world.

Source: © Design Pics / SuperStock.

Compared to U.S. standards, the more extreme forms of corporal punishment, particularly public executions carried out by many religious courts and countries, are drawn out and very painful. An example is stoning, in which people are buried up to the waist and local citizens throw small stones at them until they die (large stones are not allowed because they would lead to death too quickly). In most of the Western world, such brutal forms of punishment and execution were done away with in the 1700s due to the impact of the Age of Enlightenment.

The Age of Enlightenment

In the midst of the extremely draconian times of the mid-1600s, Thomas Hobbes, in his book *Leviathan* (1651), proposed a rational theory of why people are motivated to form democratic states of governance.[9] Hobbes started with the basic framework that all individuals are in a constant state of warfare with all other individuals. He used the extreme examples of primitive tribes and sects. He argued that the primitive state of man is selfish and greedy, so people live in a constant state of fear of everyone else. However, Hobbes also proclaimed that people are also rational, so they will rationally organize sound forms of governance, which can create rules to avoid this constant state of fear. Interestingly, once a government is created, the state of warfare mutates from one waged among individuals or families to one waged between nations. This can be seen in modern times; after all, it is quite rare that a person or family declares war against another (although gangs may be an exception), but we often hear of governments declaring war.

Hobbes stated that the primitive state of fear—of constant warfare of everyone against everyone else—was the motivation for entering into a contract with others to create a common authority. At the same time, Hobbes specified that it was this exact emotion—fear—that was needed to make citizens conform to the given rules or laws in society. Strangely, it appears that the very emotion that inspires people to enter into an agreement to form a government is the same emotion that inspires these same individuals to follow the rules of the government that is created. It is ironic, but it is quite true.

---

[7]Irwan Firdaus, "Gamblers Whipped in Muslim Indonesia," Associated Press, June 25, 2005.

[8]Philip Shenon, "U.S. Youth in Singapore Loses Appeal on Flogging," *New York Times*, April 1, 1994.

[9]Thomas Hobbes, *Leviathan* (New York: Library of Liberal Arts, 1651/1958).

Given the social conditions during the 1600s, this model appears somewhat accurate; there was little sense of community in terms of working toward progress as a group. It had not been that long since the Middle Ages, when a third of the world's population had died from sickness, and many cultures were severely deprived or in an extreme state of poverty. Prior to the 1600s, the feudal system had been the dominant model of governance in most of the Western world. During this feudal era, a very small group of aristocrats (less than 1% of the population) owned and operated the largely agricultural economy that existed. Virtually no rights were afforded to individuals in the Middle Ages or at the time Hobbes wrote his book. Most people had no individual rights in terms of criminal justice, let alone a say in the existing governments of the time. Hobbes's book clearly took issue with this lack of say in the government, which had profound implications for the justice systems of that time.

Hobbes clearly stated that, until the citizens were entitled to a certain degree of respect from their governing bodies as well as their justice systems, they would never fully buy into the authority of government or the system of justice. Hobbes proposed a number of extraordinary ideas that came to define the Age of Enlightenment. He presented a drastic paradigm shift for social structure, which had extreme implications for justice systems throughout the world.

Hobbes explicitly declared that people are rational beings who choose their destinies by creating societies. Hobbes further proposed that individuals in such societies democratically create rules of conduct that all members of that society must follow. These rules, which all citizens decide upon, become laws, and the result of not following the laws is punishment determined by the democratically instituted government. It is clear from Hobbes's statements that the government, as instructed by the citizens, not only has the authority to punish individuals who violate the rules of the society but, more important, has a duty to punish them. When such an authority fails to fulfill this duty, breakdown in the social order can quickly result.

The arrangement of citizens promising to abide by the rules or laws set forth by a given society in return for protection is commonly referred to as the social contract. Hobbes introduced this idea, but it was also emphasized by all other Enlightenment theorists after him, such as Rousseau, Locke, Voltaire, and Montesquieu. The idea of the social contract is an extraordinarily important part of Enlightenment philosophy. Although Enlightenment philosophers had significant differences in what they believed, the one thing they had in common was the belief in the social contract: the idea that people invest in the laws of their society with the guarantee that they will be protected from others who violate such rules.

Another shared belief among Enlightenment philosophers was that the people should be given a say in the government, especially the justice system. All of them emphasized fairness in determining who was guilty, as well as appropriate punishments or sentences. During the time in which Enlightenment philosophers wrote, individuals who stole a loaf of bread to feed their families were sentenced to death, whereas upper-class individuals who stole large sums of money or committed murder were pardoned. This goes against common sense; moreover, it violates the social contract. If citizens observe people being excused for violating the law, then their belief in the social contract breaks down. This same feeling can be applied to modern times. When the Los Angeles police officers who were filmed beating suspect Rodney King were acquitted of criminal charges in 1992, a massive riot erupted among the citizens of the community. This is a good example of the social contract breaking down when people realize that the government is failing to punish members of the community (in this case, ironically, and significantly, police officers) who have violated its rules.[10]

The concept of the social contract was likely the most important contribution of Enlightenment philosophers, but there were others. Another key concept of Enlightenment philosophers focused on democracy, emphasizing that every person in society should have a say via the government; specifically, they promoted the ideal of *one person, one vote*. Granted, at the time they wrote, this meant one vote for each White, landowning male, and not for women, minorities, or the poor, but it was a step in the right direction. Until then, no individuals outside of the aristocracy had had any say in government or the justice system.

---

[10]Ruben Castaneda, "Rodney King Rewind: L.A. Riots, Crips, Armed Koreans and Two Heroes," *Baltimore Post-Examiner*, May 1, 2012, http://baltimore postexaminer.com/rodney-king-rewind-l-a-riots-crips-armed-koreans-and-two-heroes/2012/05/01

The Enlightenment philosophers also talked about each individual's right to life, liberty, and the pursuit of happiness. This probably sounds familiar because it is contained in the U.S. Declaration of Independence. Until the Enlightenment, individuals were not considered to have these rights; rather, they were seen as instruments for serving totalitarian governments. Although most citizens of the Western world take these rights for granted, they did not exist prior to the Age of Enlightenment.

Perhaps the most relevant concept that Enlightenment philosophers emphasized, as mentioned above, was the idea that human beings are rational and therefore have free will. The philosophers of this age focused on the ability of individuals to consider the consequences of their actions, and they assumed that people freely choose their behavior (or lack thereof), especially in regard to criminal activity. Beccaria, the father of criminal justice, made this assumption in his formulation of what is considered to be the first bona fide theory of why people commit crime, described below.

The Classical School of Criminology

The foundation of the Classical School of criminological theorizing is typically traced to the Enlightenment philosophers, but the specific origin of the Classical School is considered to be the 1764 publication of *On Crimes and Punishments* by Italian scholar Cesare Bonesana, Marchese di Beccaria (1738–1794), commonly known as Cesare Beccaria. Amazingly, he wrote this book at the age of 26 and published it anonymously, but its almost instant popularity persuaded him to come forward as the author. Due to this significant work, most experts consider Beccaria the father of criminal justice and the father of the Classical School of criminology, but perhaps most importantly, the father of deterrence theory. This section provides a comprehensive survey of the ideas and impact of Cesare Beccaria and the Classical School.

Influences on Beccaria and His Writings

The Enlightenment philosophers had a profound impact on the social and political climate of the late 1600s and 1700s. Growing up in this time period, Beccaria was a child of the Enlightenment, and as such, he was highly influenced by the concepts and propositions that these great thinkers proposed. The Enlightenment philosophy is readily evident in Beccaria's essay, and he incorporates much of its assumptions into his work. As a student of law, Beccaria had a good background for determining what was and was not rational in legal policy. But his loyalty to the Enlightenment ideal was ever present throughout his work.

Beccaria emphasizes the concept of the social contract and incorporates the idea that citizens give up certain rights in exchange for the state's or government's protection. He also asserts that acts or punishments by the government that violate the overall sense of unity will not be accepted by the populace, largely due to the need for the social contract to be a fair deal. Beccaria explicitly states that laws are compacts of free individuals in a society. In addition, he specifically notes his appeal to the ideal of the greatest happiness shared by the greatest number, which is otherwise known as utilitarianism. This, too, was a focus of Enlightenment philosophers. Finally, the emphasis on free will and individual choice is key to his propositions and theorizing. Indeed, as we shall see, Enlightenment philosophy is present in virtually all of his propositions; he directly cites Hobbes, Montesquieu, and other Enlightenment thinkers in his work.[11]

Beccaria's Proposed Reforms and Ideas of Justice

When Beccaria wrote, authoritarian governments ruled the justice systems, which were actually quite unjust during that time. For example, it was not uncommon for a person who stole a loaf of bread to feed his or her family to be

---

[11]Hobbes, *Leviathan*; Charles Louis de Secondat, Baron de la Brède et de Montesquieu, *The Spirit of the Laws* (New York: Library of Liberal Arts, 1748/1949).

imprisoned for life or executed. A good example of this is seen in the story of Victor Hugo's *Les Misérables*: The protagonist, Jean Valjean, gets a lengthy prison sentence for stealing food for his starving loved ones. On the other hand, a judge might excuse a person who had committed several murders because the confessed killer was from a prominent family.

Beccaria sought to rid the justice system of such arbitrary acts on the part of individual judges. Specifically, Beccaria claimed in his essay that "only laws can decree punishments for crimes . . . judges in criminal cases cannot have the authority to interpret laws."[12] Rather, he believed that legislatures, elected by the citizens, must define crimes and the specific punishment for each criminal offense. One of his main goals was to prevent a single person from assigning an overly harsh sentence on a defendant and allowing another defendant in a similar case to walk free for the same criminal act, which was quite common at that time. Thus, Beccaria's writings call for a set punishment for a given offense without consideration of the presiding judge's personal attitudes or the defendant's background.

Beccaria believed that "the true measure of crimes is namely the harm done to society."[13] Thus, anyone at all who committed a given act against the society should face the same consequence. He was very clear that the law should impose a specific punishment for a given act, regardless of

▲ Image 2.3   Cesare Beccaria (1738–1794).

Source: © Kean Collection / Archive Photos / Getty Images.

the circumstances. One aspect of this principle was that it ignored the intent the offender had in committing the crime. Obviously, this principle is not followed in most modern justice systems; intent often plays a key role in the charges and sentencing of defendants in many types of crimes. Most notably, the different degrees of homicide in most U.S. jurisdictions include first-degree murder, which requires proof of planning or *malice aforethought*; second-degree murder, which typically involves no evidence of planning but rather a spontaneous act of killing; and various degrees of manslaughter, which generally include some level of provocation on the part of the victim. This is just one example of the importance of intent, legally known as *mens rea* (literally, *guilty mind*), in most modern justice systems. Many types of offending are graded by degree of intent as opposed to being categorized based only on the act itself, known legally as *actus reus* (literally, *guilty act*). Beccaria's propositions focus on only the *actus reus* because he claimed that an act against society was just as harmful, regardless of the intent, or *mens rea*. Despite his recommendations, most societies factor in the intent of the offender in criminal activity. Still, his proposal that *a given act should always receive the same punishment* certainly seemed to represent a significant improvement over the arbitrary punishments handed out by the regimes and justice systems of the 1700s.

Another important reform that Beccaria proposed was to do away with practices that were common in "justice" systems of the time (the word *justice* is in quotation marks because they were largely systems of injustice). Specifically, Beccaria claimed that secret accusations should not be permitted; rather, defendants should be able to confront and cross-examine witnesses. Writing about secret accusations, he said, "Their customary use makes men false and deceptive"; he asked, "Who can defend himself against calumny when it comes armed with tyranny's

[12]Cesare Beccaria, *On Crimes and Punishments*, trans. Henry Paolucci (New York: MacMillan, 1963), 14.

[13]Ibid., 64.

strongest shield, *secrecy*?"[14] Although some modern countries still accept and use secret accusations and disallow the cross-examination of witnesses, Beccaria set the standard in guaranteeing such rights to defendants in the United States and most Western societies.

In addition, Beccaria argued that torture should not be used against defendants:

> A cruelty consecrated by the practice of most nations is torture of the accused . . . either to make him confess the crime or to clear up contradictory statements, or to discover accomplices . . . to discover other crimes of which he might be guilty but of which he is not accused.[15]

Although some countries, such as Israel and Mexico, currently allow the use of torture for eliciting information or confessions, most countries abstain from the practice. There has been wide discussion about a memo, written by former U.S. attorney general Alberto Gonzales when he was President George W. Bush's lead counsel at the White House, claiming that the U.S. military could use torture against terrorist suspects. However, at least in terms of domestic criminal defendants, the United States has traditionally agreed with Beccaria, who believed that any information or oaths obtained under torture are relatively worthless. Beccaria's belief in the worthlessness of torture is further seen in his statement that "it is useless to reveal the author of a crime that lies deeply buried in darkness."[16]

It is likely that Beccaria believed the use of torture was one of the worst aspects of the criminal justice systems of his time and a horrible manifestation of the barbarousness common in the Middle Ages. This is seen in his further elaboration of torture:

> This infamous crucible of truth is a still-standing memorial of the ancient and barbarous legislation of a time when trials by fire and by boiling water, as well as the uncertain outcomes of duels, were called "judgments of God."[17]

Beccaria also expressed his doubt of the relevance of any information received via torture:

> Thus the impression of pain may become so great that, filling the entire sensory capacity of the tortured person, it leaves him free only to choose what for the moment is the shortest way of escape from pain.[18]

As Beccaria saw it, the policy implications from such use of torture are that "of two men, equally innocent or equally guilty, the strong and courageous will be acquitted, the weak and timid condemned."[19]

Beccaria also claimed that defendants should be tried by fellow citizens or peers, not by judges:

> I consider an excellent law that which assigns popular jurors, taken by lot, to assist the chief judge . . . each man ought to be judged by his peers.[20]

It is clear that Beccaria felt that the responsibility of determining the facts of a case should be placed in the hands of more than one person, a belief driven by his Enlightenment beliefs about democratic philosophy, namely,

---

[14]Ibid., 25–26.

[15]Ibid., 30.

[16]Ibid., 30–31.

[17]Ibid., 31.

[18]Ibid., 32.

[19]Ibid., 32.

[20]Ibid., 21.

that citizens of the society should have a voice in judging the facts and deciding the verdicts of criminal cases. This proposition is representative of Beccaria's overall leaning toward fairness and democratic processes, which Enlightenment philosophers shared.

Today, U.S. citizens often take for granted the right to have a trial by a jury of their peers. It may surprise some readers to know that some modern, developed countries have not provided this right. For example, in the 1990s, Russia held jury trials for the first time in 85 years. When Vladimir Lenin was in charge of Russia, he had banished jury trials. Over the course of several decades, the bench trials in Russia produced a 99.6% rate of convictions. This means that virtually every person in Russia who was accused of a crime was found guilty. Given the relatively high percentage of defendants found to be innocent of crimes in the United States, not to mention the numerous people who have been released from death row after DNA analysis showed that they were not guilty, it is rather frightening to think of how many falsely accused individuals have been convicted and unjustly sentenced in Russia over the last century.

Another important aspect of Beccaria's reforms involved making the justice system, particularly its laws and decisions, more public and better understood. This fits the Enlightenment assumption that individuals are rational: If people know the consequences of their actions, they will act accordingly. Beccaria stated that "when the number of those who can understand the sacred code of laws and hold it in their hands increases, the frequency of crimes will be found to decrease."[21] At the time, the laws were often unknown to the populace, in part because of widespread illiteracy but perhaps more as a result of the failure to publicly declare what the laws were. Even when laws were posted, they were often in languages that the citizens did not read or speak (e.g., Latin). Thus, Beccaria stressed the need for society to ensure that its citizens are educated about what the laws are; he believed that this alone would lead to a significant decrease in law violations.

Furthermore, Beccaria believed that the important stages and decision-making processes of any justice system should be made public knowledge rather than being held in secret or carried out behind closed doors. He stated, "Punishment . . . must be essentially public."[22] This has a highly democratic and Enlightenment ring to it, in the sense that citizens of a society are assumed to have the right to know what vital judgments are being made. After all, in a democratic society, citizens give the government the profound responsibility of distributing punishment for crimes against the society. The citizens are entitled to know what decisions their government officials are making, particularly regarding justice. Besides providing knowledge and understanding of what is going on, this sets in place a form of checks and balances on what is happening. Furthermore, the public nature of trials and punishments inherently produces a form of deterrence for those individuals who may be considering criminal activity.

One of Beccaria's most profound and important proposed reforms is one of the least noted. Beccaria said, "The surest but most difficult way to prevent crimes is by perfecting education."[23] We know of no other review of his work that notes this hypothesis, which is quite amazing, because most of the reviews are done for an educational audience. Furthermore, this emphasis on education makes sense, given Beccaria's focus on knowledge of laws and consequences of criminal activity as well as his focus on deterrence.

Beccaria's Ideas regarding the Death Penalty

Another primary area of Beccaria's reforms dealt with the use—and, in his day, the abuse—of the death penalty. First, let it be said that Beccaria was against the use of capital punishment. (Interestingly, he was not against corporal punishment, which he explicitly stated was appropriate for violent offenders.) Perhaps this was due to the times in which he wrote, in which a large number of people were put to death, often by harsh methods. Still, Beccaria had several rational reasons for why he felt the death penalty was not an efficient and effective punishment.

[21]Ibid., 17.

[22]Ibid., 99.

[23]Ibid., 98.

First, Beccaria argued that the use of capital punishment inherently violated the social contract:

Is it conceivable that the least sacrifice of each person's liberty should include sacrifice of the greatest of all goods, life? . . . The punishment of death, therefore, is not a right, for I have demonstrated that it cannot be such; but it is the war of a nation against a citizen whose destruction it judges to be necessary or useful.[24]

The second reason that Beccaria felt that the death penalty was an inappropriate form of punishment was along the same lines: If the government endorsed the death of a citizen, it would provide a negative example to the rest of society. He said, "The death penalty cannot be useful, because of the example of barbarity it gives men."[25] Although some studies show some evidence that use of the death penalty in the United States deters crime,[26] most studies show no effect or even a positive effect on homicides.[27] Researchers have called this increase of homicides after executions the brutalization effect, and a similar phenomenon can be seen at numerous sporting events (boxing matches, hockey games, soccer or football games, etc.) when violence breaks out among spectators. There have even been incidents in recent years at youth sporting events.

To further complicate the possibly contradictory effects of capital punishment, some analyses show that both deterrence and brutalization occur at the same time for different types of murder or crime, depending on the level of planning or spontaneity of a given act. For example, a sophisticated analysis of homicide data from California examined the effects of a high-profile execution in 1992, largely because it was the first one in the state in 25 years.[28] As predicted, the authors found that nonstranger felony murders, which typically involve some planning, significantly decreased after the high-profile execution, whereas the level of argument-based, stranger murders, which are typically more spontaneous, significantly increased during the same period. Thus, both deterrence and brutalization effects were observed at the same time and location following a given execution.

Another primary reason that Beccaria was against the use of capital punishment was that he believed it was an ineffective deterrent. Specifically, he thought that a punishment that was quick, such as the death penalty, could not be as effective a deterrent as a drawn-out penalty. He stated, "It is not the intensity of punishment

---

[24]Ibid., 45.

[25]Ibid., 50.

[26]For a review and analysis, respectively, showing deterrent effects of capital punishment, see Charles F. Manski and John V. Pepper, "Deterrence and the Death Penalty: Partial Identification Analysis Using Repeated Cross Sections," *Journal of Quantitative Criminology* 29 (2013): 123–41; and Steven Stack, "The Effect of Publicized Executions on Homicides in California," *Journal of Crime and Justice* 21 (1998): 1–16. See also Isaac Ehrlich, "Capital Punishment and Deterrence," *Journal of Political Economy* 85 (1977): 741–88; Isaac Ehrlich, "The Deterrent Effect of Capital Punishment: A Question of Life and Death," *American Economic Review* 65 (1975): 397–417; Stephen K. Layson, "Homicide and Deterrence: A Reexamination of United States Time-Series Evidence," *Southern Economic Journal* 52 (1985): 68–89; David P. Phillips, "The Deterrent Effect of Capital Punishment: Evidence on an Old Controversy," *American Journal of Sociology* 86 (1980): 139–48; Steven Stack, "Execution Publicity and Homicide in South Carolina," *Sociological Quarterly* 31 (1990): 599–611; Steven Stack, "The Impact of Publicized Executions on Homicide," *Criminal Justice and Behavior* 22 (1995): 172–86; and Steven Stack, "Publicized Executions and Homicide, 1950–1980," *American Sociological Review* 52 (1987): 532–40.

[27]William C. Bailey, "The Deterrent Effect of the Death Penalty for Murder in California," *Southern California Law Review* 52 (1979): 743–64; William C. Bailey and Ruth D. Peterson, "Murder and Capital Punishment: A Monthly Time Series Analysis of Execution Publicity," *American Sociological Review* 54 (1989): 722–43; William J. Bowers, "The Effect of Execution Is Brutalization, Not Deterrence," *Capital Punishment: Legal and Social Science Approaches*, ed. Kenneth C. Haas and James A. Inciardi (Newbury Park: Sage, 1988), 49–89; John K. Cochran, Mitchell Chamlin, and Mark Seth, "Deterrence or Brutalization? An Impact Assessment of Oklahoma's Return to Capital Punishment," *Criminology* 32 (1994): 107–34; James A. Fox and Michael L. Radelet, "Persistent Flaws in Econometric Studies of the Deterrent Effect of the Death Penalty," *Loyola of Los Angeles Law Review* 23 (1990): 29–44; David Lester, "The Deterrent Effect of Execution on Homicide," *Psychological Reports* 64 (1989): 306–14. For a review, see William C. Bailey and Ruth D. Peterson, "Capital Punishment, Homicide, and Deterrence: An Assessment of the Evidence," in *Studying and Preventing Homicide*, ed. M. Dwayne Smith and Margaret A. Zahn (Thousand Oaks: Sage, 1999), 223–45.

[28]John K. Cochran and Mitchell B. Chamlin, "Deterrence and Brutalization: The Dual Effects of Executions," *Justice Quarterly* (2000): 685–706; Eric G. Lambert, Scott D. Camp, Alan Clarke, and Shanhe Jiang, "The Impact of Information on Death Penalty Support, Revisited," *Crime and Delinquency* 57 (2011): 572–99.

that has the greatest effect on the human spirit, but its duration."[29] It is likely that many readers can relate to this type of argument, not that they necessarily agree with it; the idea of spending the rest of one's life in a cell is a very scary concept to most people. To many people, such a concept is more frightening than death, which supports Beccaria's idea that the duration of the punishment may be more of a deterrent than the short, albeit extremely intense, punishment of execution.

Beccaria's Concept of Deterrence and the Three Key Elements of Punishment

Beccaria is generally considered the father of deterrence theory for good reason. Beccaria was the first known scholar to write a work that summarized such extravagant ideas regarding the direction of human behavior toward choice as opposed to fate or destiny. Prior to his work, the common wisdom on the issue of human destiny was that it was chosen by the gods or God. At that time, governments and societies generally believed that people are born either good or bad. Beccaria, as a child of the Enlightenment, defied this belief in proclaiming that people freely choose their destinies and thus their decisions to commit or not commit criminal behavior.

Beccaria suggested three characteristics of punishment that make a significant difference in whether an individual decides to commit a criminal act: celerity (swiftness), certainty, and severity.

Swiftness

The first of these characteristics was celerity, which we will refer to as swiftness of punishment. Beccaria saw two reasons why swiftness of punishment is important. At the time he wrote, some defendants were spending many years awaiting trial. Often, this was a longer time than they would have been locked up as punishment for their alleged offenses, even if the maximum penalty had been imposed. As Beccaria stated, "The more promptly and the more closely punishment follows upon the commission of a crime, the more just and useful will it be."[30] Thus, the first reason that Beccaria recommended swiftness of punishment was to reform a system that was slow to respond to offenders.

The second reason that Beccaria emphasized swift sentencing was related to the deterrence aspect of punishment. A swift trial and swift punishment were important, Beccaria said, "because of privation of liberty, being itself a punishment, should not precede the sentence."[31] He felt that not only was this "privation of liberty" unjust, in the sense that some of these defendants would not have been incarcerated for such a long period even if they had been convicted and sentenced to the maximum for the charges they were accused of committing, but it was detrimental because the individual would not link the sanction with the violation(s) committed. Specifically, Beccaria believed that people build an association between the pains of punishment and their criminal acts. He asserted

> Promptness of punishments is more useful because when the length of time that passes between the punishment and the misdeed is less, so much the stronger and more lasting in the human mind is the association of these two ideas, crime and punishment; they then come insensibly to be considered, one as the cause, the other as the necessary inevitable effect. It has been demonstrated that the association of ideas is the cement that forms the entire fabric of the human intellect.[32]

An analogy can be made to training animals or children; you have to catch them in the act, or soon after, or the punishment doesn't matter because the offender doesn't know why he or she is being punished. Ultimately,

---

[29]Beccaria, *Crimes and Punishments*, 46–47.

[30]Ibid., 55.

[31]Ibid., 55.

[32]Ibid., 56.

Beccaria argued that, for both reform and deterrence reasons, punishment should occur quickly after the act. Despite the commonsense aspects of making punishments swift, this has not been examined by modern empirical research and therefore is the most neglected of the three elements of punishment Beccaria emphasized.

Certainty

The second characteristic that Beccaria felt was vital to the effectiveness of deterrence was certainty of punishment. Beccaria considered this the most important quality of punishment: "Even the least of evils, when they are certain, always terrify men's minds."[33] He also said, "The certainty of punishment, even if it be moderate, will always make a stronger impression than the fear of another which is more terrible but combined with the hope of impunity."[34] As scientific studies later showed, Beccaria was accurate in his assumption that perceived certainty or risk of punishment was the most important aspect of deterrence.

It is interesting to note that certainty is the least likely characteristic of punishment to be enhanced in modern criminal justice policy. Over the last few decades, the likelihood that criminals will be caught and arrested has not increased. Law enforcement officials have been able to clear only about 21% of known felonies. Such clearance rates are based on the rate at which known suspects are apprehended for crimes reported to police. Law enforcement officials are no better at solving serious crimes known to police than they were in past decades, despite increased knowledge and resources put toward solving such crimes.

Severity

The third characteristic that Beccaria emphasized was severity of punishment. Specifically, Beccaria claimed that, for a punishment to be effective, the possible penalty must outweigh the potential benefits (e.g., financial payoff) of a given crime. However, this criterion came with a caveat. This aspect of punishment was perhaps the most complicated part of Beccaria's philosophy, primarily because he thought that too much severity would lead to more crime, but the punishment must exceed any benefits expected from the crime. Beccaria said

> For a punishment to attain its end, the evil which it inflicts has only to exceed the advantage derivable from the crime; in this excess of evil one should include the . . . loss of the good which the crime might have produced. All beyond this is superfluous and for that reason tyrannical.[35]

Beccaria makes clear in this statement that punishments should equal or outweigh any benefits of a crime to deter individuals from engaging in such acts. However, he also explicitly states that any punishments that largely exceed the reasonable punishment for a given crime are inhumane and may lead to further criminality.

A modern example of how punishments can be taken to an extreme and thereby cause more crime rather than deter it is the current *three-strikes-you're-out* approach to sentencing. Such laws have become common in many states, such as California. In such jurisdictions, individuals who have committed two prior felonies can be sentenced to life imprisonment for committing a crime, even a nonviolent crime, that the state statutes consider a *serious felony*. Such laws have been known to drive some relatively minor property offenders to become violent when they know that they will be incarcerated for life when they are caught. A number of offenders have even wounded or killed people to avoid apprehension, knowing that they would face life imprisonment even for a relatively minor property offense. In a recent study, the authors analyzed the impact of three-strikes laws in 188 large

---

[33]Ibid., 58.

[34]Ibid., 58.

[35]Ibid., 43.

cities in the 25 states that have such laws and concluded that there was no significant reduction in crime rates as a result. Furthermore, the areas with three-strikes laws typically had higher rates of homicide.[36]

Ultimately, Beccaria's philosophy on the three characteristics of good punishment in terms of deterrence—swiftness, certainty, and severity—is still highly respected and followed in most Western criminal justice systems. Despite its contemporary flaws and caveats, perhaps no other traditional framework is so widely adopted. With only one exception—namely, his proposal that a given act should always be punished in exactly the same way (see below)—Beccaria's concepts and propositions are still considered the ideal in virtually all Western criminal justice systems.

Beccaria's Conceptualization of Specific and General Deterrence

Beccaria also defined two identifiable forms of deterrence: specific and general. Although these two forms of deterrence tend to overlap in most sentences given by judges, they can be distinguished in terms of the intended target of the punishment. Sometimes the emphasis is clearly on one or the other, as Beccaria noted in his work.

Although Beccaria did not coin the terms specific deterrence and general deterrence, he clearly makes the case that both are important. Regarding punishment, he said, "The purpose can only be to prevent the criminal from inflicting new injuries on its citizens and to deter others from similar acts."[37] The first portion of this statement—preventing the criminal from reoffending—focuses on the defendant and the defendant alone, regardless of any possible offending by others. Punishments that focus primarily on the individual are considered specific deterrence, also referred to as special or individual deterrence. This concept is appropriately labeled because the emphasis is on the specific individual who offended. On the other hand, the latter portion of Beccaria's quotation emphasizes the deterrence of others, regardless of whether the individual criminal is deterred. Punishments that focus primarily on other potential criminals and not on the actual criminal are referred to as general deterrence.

Readers may wonder how a punishment would not be inherently both a specific and general deterrent. After all, in today's society, virtually all criminal punishments given to individuals (i.e., specific deterrence) are prescribed in court, a public venue, so people are somewhat aware of the sanctions (i.e., general deterrence). However, when Beccaria wrote in the 18th century, many if not most of sentencing was done behind closed doors and was not known to the public and had no way to deter other potential offenders. Therefore, Beccaria saw much utility in letting the public know what punishments were handed out for given crimes. This fulfilled the goal of general deterrence, which was essentially scaring others into not committing such criminal acts, while it also furthered his reforms by letting the public know whether fair and balanced justice was being administered.

Despite the obvious overlap, there are identifiable distinctions between specific and general deterrence seen in modern sentencing strategy. For example, some judges have chosen to hand out punishments to defendants in which they are obligated, as a condition of their probation or parole, to walk along their towns' main streets while wearing signs that say "Convicted Child Molester" or "Convicted Shoplifter." Other cities have implemented policies in which pictures and identifying information of those individuals who are arrested, such as prostitutes or men who solicit them, are put in newspapers or placed on billboards.

These punishment strategies are not likely to be much of a specific deterrent. Having now been labeled, these individuals may actually be psychologically encouraged to engage in doing what the public expects them to do. The specific deterrent effect may not be particularly strong. However, authorities are hoping for a strong general deterrent effect in most of these cases. They expect that many of the people who see these sign-laden individuals on the streets or in public pictures are going to be frightened away from engaging in similar activity.

---

[36]Tomislav V. Kovandzic, John J. Sloan III, and Lynne M. Vieraitis, "'Striking Out' as Crime Reduction Policy: The Impact of 'Three-Strikes' Laws on Crime Rates in the U.S. Cities," *Justice Quarterly* 21 (2004): 207–40. See also Steven N. Durlauf and Daniel S. Nagin, "Imprisonment and Crime: Can Both Be Reduced?," *Criminology and Public Policy* 10 (2011): 13–54.

[37]Ibid., 42.

There are also numerous diversion programs, particularly for juvenile, first-time, and minor offenders, which seek to punish offenders without engaging them in public hearings or trials. The goal of such programs is to hold the individuals accountable and have them fulfill certain obligations without having them dragged through the system, which is often public. Thus, the goal is obviously to instill specific deterrence without using the person as a poster child for the public, which obviously negates any aspects of general deterrence.

Although most judges invoke both specific and general deterrence in many of the criminal sentences that they hand out, there are notable cases in which either specific or general deterrence is emphasized, sometime exclusively. Ultimately, Beccaria seemed to emphasize general deterrence and overall crime prevention, as suggested by his statement that "it is better to prevent crimes than to punish them. This is the ultimate end of every good legislation."[38] This claim implies that it is better to deter potential offenders before they offend rather than imposing sanctions on already convicted criminals. Beccaria's emphasis on prevention (over reaction) and general deterrence is also evident in his claim that education is likely the best way to reduce crime. After all, the more educated an individual is regarding the law and potential punishments, as well as public cases in which offenders have been punished, the less likely he or she will be to engage in such activity. Beccaria's identification of the differential emphases in terms of punishment was a key element in his work that continues to be important in modern times.

A Summary of Beccaria's Ideas and His Influence on Policy

Ultimately, Beccaria summarized his ideas on reforms and deterrence with this statement:

> In order for punishment not to be, in every instance, an act of violence of one or of many against a private citizen, it must be essentially public, prompt, necessary, the least possible in the given circumstances, proportionate to the crimes, dictated by the laws.[39]

In this statement, Beccaria is saying that the processing and punishment administered by justice systems must be known to the public, which delegates to the state the authority to make such decisions. Furthermore, he asserts that the punishment must be appropriately swift, certain (i.e., necessary), and appropriately severe, which fits his concept of deterrence. Finally, he reiterates the need to administer the same punishment every time for a given criminal act, as opposed to having arbitrary punishments imposed by one judge. These are just some of many ideas that Beccaria proposed, but he apparently saw these points as being the most important.

Although we, as U.S. citizens, take for granted the rights proposed by Beccaria, they were quite unique concepts during the 18th century. In fact, the ideas proposed by Beccaria were so unusual and revolutionary then that he published his book anonymously. It is obvious that Beccaria was considerably worried about being accused of blasphemy by the church and of being persecuted by governments for his views.

Regarding the first claim, Beccaria was right; the Roman Catholic Church excommunicated Beccaria when it became known that he wrote the book. In fact, his book remained on the list of condemned works until relatively recently (the 1960s). On the other hand, government officials of the time surprisingly embraced his work. The Italian government and most European and other world officials, particularly dictators, embraced his work as well. Beccaria was invited to visit many other country capitals, even those of the most authoritarian states at that time, to help reform their criminal justice systems. For example, Beccaria was invited to meet with Catherine the Great, the czarina of Russia during the late 1700s, to help revise and improve Russia's justice system. Most historical records

---

[38]Beccaria, *Crimes and Punishments*, 93.

[39]Ibid., 99.

suggest that Beccaria was not a great diplomat or representative of his ideas, largely because he was not physically or socially adequate for such endeavors. However, his ideas were strong and stood on their own merit.

Dictators and authoritarian governments may have liked Beccaria's reform framework so much because it explicitly stated that treason was the most serious crime. He said

> The first class of crime, which are the gravest because most injurious, are those known as crimes of *lese majesty* [high treason]. . . . Every crime . . . injures society, but it is not every crime that aims at its immediate destruction.[40]

According to Enlightenment philosophy, violations of law are criminal acts not only against the direct victims but also against the entire society because they break the social contract. As Beccaria stated, the most heinous criminal acts are those that directly violate the social contract, which would be treason and espionage. In Beccaria's reform proposals, dictators may have seen a chance to pacify revolutionary citizens who might be aiming to overthrow their governments. In many cases, reforms were only a temporary solution. After all, the American Revolution occurred in the 1770s, the French Revolution occurred in the 1780s, and other revolutions occurred soon after this period.

Governments that tried to apply Beccaria's ideas to the letter experienced problems, but generally, most European (and American) societies that incorporated his ideas had fairer and more democratic justice systems than they'd had before Beccaria. This is why, to this day, he is considered the father of criminal justice.

The Impact of Beccaria's Work on Other Theorists

Beccaria's work had an immediate impact on the political and philosophical state of affairs in the late 18th century. He was invited to many other countries to reform their justice systems, and his propositions and theoretical model of deterrence were incorporated into many of the new constitutions of countries, most of them formed after major revolutions. The most notable of these was the Constitution and Bill of Rights of the United States.

It is quite obvious that the many founding documents constructed before and during the American Revolution in the late 1700s were heavily influenced by Beccaria and other Enlightenment philosophers. Specifically, the concept that the U.S. government is "of the people, by the people, and for the people" makes it clear that the Enlightenment idea of democracy and voice in government is of utmost importance. Another clear example is the emphasis on due process and individual rights in the U.S. Bill of Rights. Among the important concepts derived from Beccaria's work are the right to trial by jury, the right to confront and cross-examine witnesses, the right to a speedy trial, and the right to be informed about decisions of the justice system (charges, pleas, trials, verdicts, sentences, etc.).

The impact of Beccaria's ideas on the working ideology of our system of justice cannot be overstated. The public nature of our justice system comes from Beccaria, as does the emphasis on deterrence. The United States, as well as virtually all Western countries, incorporates in its justice system the certainty and severity of punishment to reduce crime. This system of deterrence remains the dominant model in criminal justice: The goal is to deter potential and previous offenders from committing crime by enforcing punishments that will make them reconsider the next time they think about engaging in such activity. This model assumes a rationally thinking human being, as described by Enlightenment philosophy, who can learn from past experiences or from seeing others punished for offenses that he or she is rationally thinking about committing. Thus, Beccaria's work has had a profound impact on the existing philosophy and workings of most justice systems throughout the world.

---

[40]Ibid., 68.

▲ Image 2.4   Jeremy Bentham, often credited as the founder of University College London, insisted that his body be put on display there after his death. You can visit a replica of it today.

Source: © Popperfoto / Popperfoto / Getty Images.

Beyond this, Beccaria also had a large impact on further theorizing about human decision making related to committing criminal behavior. One of the more notable theorists inspired by Beccaria's ideas was Jeremy Bentham (1748–1832) of England, who has become a well-known classical theorist in his own right, perhaps because he helped spread the Enlightenment/Beccarian philosophy to Britain. His influence in the development of classical theorizing is debated, and a number of major texts do not cover his writings at all.[41] Although he did not add a significant amount of theorizing beyond Beccaria's propositions regarding reform and deterrence, Bentham did further refine the ideas presented by previous theorists, and his legacy is well known.

One of the more important contributions of Bentham was the concept of *hedonistic calculus*, which is essentially the weighing of pleasure versus pain. This, of course, is strongly based on the Enlightenment/Beccarian concept of rational choice and utility. After all, if the expected pain outweighs the expected benefit of doing a given act, the rational individual is far less likely to do it. On the other hand, if the expected pleasure outweighs the expected pain, a rational person will engage in the act. Bentham listed a set of criteria that he thought would go into the decision making of a rational individual. An analogy would be an imagined two-sided balance scale on which the pros and cons of crimes are considered, and then the individual makes a rational decision about whether to commit the crime.

Beyond the idea of hedonistic calculus, Bentham's contributions to the overall assumptions of classical theorizing did not significantly revise the theoretical model. Perhaps the most important contribution he made to the Classical School was helping to popularize the framework in Britain. In fact, Bentham became better known for his design of a prison structure, known as the *panopticon*, which was used in several countries and in early Pennsylvania penitentiaries. This model of prisons used a type of wagon wheel design, in which a post at the center allowed 360-degree visual observation of the various "spokes," that is, hallways that contained all of the inmate cells.

The Neoclassical School of Criminology

A number of governments, including the newly formed United States, incorporated Beccaria's concepts and propositions in the development of their justice systems. The government that most strictly applied Beccaria's ideas—France after the revolution of the late 1780s—found that it worked pretty well except for one concept. Beccaria believed that every individual who committed a certain act against the law should be punished the same way. Although equality in punishment sounds like a good philosophy, the French realized very quickly that not everyone should be punished equally for a certain act.

[41]See, for example, Thomas J. Bernard, Jeffrey B. Snipes, and Alexander L. Gerould, *Vold's Theoretical Criminology*, 6th ed. (Oxford: Oxford University Press, 2009).

The French system found that giving a first-time offender the same sentence as a repeat offender did not make much sense, especially when the first-time offender was a juvenile. Furthermore, there were many circumstances in which a defendant appeared to be unmalicious in doing an act, such as when he or she had limited mental capacity or acted out of necessity. Perhaps most important, Beccaria's framework specifically dismissed the intent (i.e., *mens rea*) of criminal offenders while focusing only on the harm done to society by a given act (i.e., *actus reus*). French society, as well as most modern societies such as the United States, deviated from Beccaria's framework in taking the intent of offenders into account, often in a very important way, such as in determining what type of charges should be filed against those accused of homicide. Therefore, a new school of thought regarding the classical or deterrence model developed, which became known as the Neoclassical School of criminology.

The only significant difference between the Neoclassical School and the Classical School of criminology is that the Neoclassical (*neo* means new) School takes into account contextual circumstances of the individual or situation, allowing for increases or decreases in the punishment. For example, would a society want to punish a 12-year-old first-time offender the same way they would punish a 35-year-old who shoplifted the same item a second time? Does a society want to punish a mentally challenged person for stealing a car once as much as they would punish a person without disabilities who has been convicted of stealing more than a dozen cars? The answer is probably not—or at least, that is what most modern criminal justice authorities have decided, including those in the United States.

This was also the conclusion of French society, which quickly realized that, in this respect, Beccaria's system was neither fair nor effective in terms of deterrence. They came to acknowledge that circumstantial factors play an important part in how malicious or guilty a certain defendant is in committing a given crime. The French revised their laws to take into account both mitigating and aggravating circumstances. This neoclassical concept became the standard in all Western justice systems.

The United States also followed this model and considers contextual factors in virtually all of its charges and sentencing decisions. For example, juvenile defendants are actually processed in completely different courts. Furthermore, defendants who are first-time offenders are generally given options for diversion programs or probation as long as their offenses are not serious.

While the Neoclassical School added an important caveat to the previously important Classical School, it assumes virtually all other concepts and propositions of the Classical School: the social contract, due process rights, and the idea that rational beings will be deterred by the certainty, swiftness, and severity of punishment. This neoclassical framework had, and continues to have, an extremely important impact on the world.

Loss of Dominance of Classical and Neoclassical Theory

For about 100 years after Beccaria wrote his book, the Classical and Neoclassical Schools were dominant in criminological theorizing. During this time, most governments, especially those in the Western world, shifted their justice frameworks toward the neoclassical model. This has not changed, even in modern times. For example, when officials attempt to reduce certain illegal behaviors, they increase the punishments or put more effort into catching relevant offenders.

However, the classical and neoclassical frameworks lost dominance among academics and scientists in the 19th century, especially after Darwin's publication in the 1860s of *The Origin of Species*, which introduced the concept of evolution and natural selection. This perspective shed new light on other influences on human behavior beyond free will and rational choice (e.g., genetics, psychological deficits). Despite this shift in emphasis among academic and scientific circles, the actual workings of the justice systems of most Western societies still retain the framework of classical and neoclassical models as their model of justice.

Three-strikes laws are an example; others include police department gang units and injunctions that condemn any observed loitering by or gathering among gang members in a specified region. Furthermore, some jurisdictions, such as California, have created gang enhancements for sentencing; after the jury decides whether the

▲ Image 2.5 Charles Darwin (1809–1882), author of evolutionary theory.

SOURCE: © Photos.com / Photos.com / Thinkstock.

defendant is guilty of a given crime, it then considers whether the person is a gang member. If a jury in California decides that the defendant is a gang member, which is usually determined by evidence provided by local police gang units, it automatically adds more time to any sentence the judge gives. These are just some examples of how Western justice systems still rely primarily on deterrence of criminal activity through increased enforcement and enhanced sentencing. The bottom line is that modern justice systems still base most of their policies on classical or neoclassical theoretical frameworks that fell out of favor among scientists and philosophers in the late 1800s.

Policy Implications

Many policies are based on deterrence theory: the premise that increasing the severity of sanctions will deter crime.[42] This is seen throughout our system of law enforcement, courts, and corrections. This is rather interesting, given the fact that classical deterrence theory has not been the dominant explanatory model among criminologists for decades. In fact, a recent poll of close to 400 criminologists in the nation ranked classical theory 22nd out of 24 theories in terms of being the most valid explanation of serious and persistent offending.[43] Still, given the dominance of classical deterrence theory in most criminal justice policies, it is very important to discuss the most common strategies.

First, the death penalty is used as a general deterrent for committing crime. As the father of deterrence theory predicted, most studies show that capital punishment has a negligible effect on criminality. A recent review of the extant literature concluded that "the death penalty does not deter crime."[44] In fact, some studies show evidence for a brutalization effect, an increase in homicides after a high-profile execution.[45] Although the evidence is somewhat mixed, it is safe to say that the death penalty is not a consistent deterrent.

Another policy flowing from classical and neoclassical models is adding more police officers to deter crime in a given area. A recent review of the existing literature concluded that simply "adding more police officers will not reduce crime."[46] Rather, it is generally up to communities to police themselves via informal factors of control (family, church, community ties, etc.). However, this same review did find that police engagement in problem-solving activities at a specific location can sometimes reduce crime, but at that point the strategy is not based

[42]Stephen G. Tibbetts, *Criminological Theory: The Essentials* (Thousand Oaks: Sage, 2012), 46–48.

[43]Lee Ellis, Jonathan Cooper, and Anthony Walsh, "Criminologists' Opinions about Causes and Theories of Crime and Delinquency: A Follow-up," *The Criminologist* 33 (2008): 23–6.

[44]Samuel Walker, *Sense and Nonsense about Crime and Drugs*, 7th ed. (Stamford, CN: Cengage, 2010).

[45]Bowers, "Effect of Execution."

[46]Walker, *Sense and Nonsense.*

on deterrence.[47] Furthermore, a recent report concluded that proactive arrests for drunk driving have consistently been found to reduce such behavior, as does arresting offenders for domestic violence, but only if these measures are employed consistently.[48]

One example of court and correctional strategies is the "scared straight" approach that became popular several decades ago.[49] These programs essentially sought to scare or deter juvenile offenders into going "straight" by showing them the harshness and realities of prison life. However, nearly all evaluations of these programs showed that they were ineffective, and some evaluations indicated that these programs led to higher rates of recidivism.[50] There seem to be few successful deterrent policies in the court and corrections components of the criminal justice system. A recent review found that one of the only court-mandated policies that seem promising is the provision of protection orders for battered women.[51]

The policies, programs, and strategies based on classical deterrence theory will be examined more thoroughly in the final section of this book. To sum up, however, most of these strategies don't seem to work consistently to deter. This is because such a model assumes that people are rational and think carefully before choosing their behavior, whereas most research findings suggest that people often carry out behaviors that they know are irrational or without engaging in rational decision making,[52] which criminologists often refer to as *bounded rationality*.[53] Therefore, it is not surprising that many attempts by police and other criminal justice authorities to deter potential offenders do not seem to have much effect in preventing crime. This explanation will be more fully discussed in the final section of the book.

 ## Conclusion

This section examined the earliest period of theorizing about criminological theory. The Classical School of criminology evolved out of ideas from the Enlightenment era in the mid to late 18th century. This school of thought emphasized free will and rational choices that individuals make, from the perspective that people make choices regarding criminal behavior based on the potential costs and benefits that could result from such behavior. This section also explored the concepts and propositions of the father of the Classical School, which built the framework on which deterrence theory is based. We also discussed the various reforms that Beccaria proposed, many of which were adopted in the formation of the U.S. Constitution and Bill of Rights. The significance of the Classical School in both theorizing about crime and in actual administration of justice in the United States cannot be overestimated. The Classical and Neoclassical Schools of criminology remain to this day the primary framework within which justice is administered, despite the fact that scientific researchers and academics have, for the most part, moved past this perspective to consider social and economic factors.

---

[47]Ibid.

[48]Lawrence Sherman, Denise Gottfredson, Doris MacKenzie, John Eck, Peter Reuter, and Shawn Bushway, *Preventing Crime: What Works, What Doesn't, What's Promising: A Report to the United States Congress* (Washington, DC: U.S. Department of Justice, 1997).

[49]For a review of these programs and evaluations of them, see Richard Lundman, *Prevention and Control of Juvenile Delinquency*, 3rd ed. (Oxford: Oxford University Press, 2001).

[50]Ibid.

[51]Sherman et al., *Preventing Crime*.

[52]For a review of the extant research on this topic, see Alex Piquero and Stephen Tibbetts, *Rational Choice and Criminal Behavior* (New York: Routledge, 2002).

[53]For a more recent discussion on the complexity of developing policies based on deterrence and rational choice models, see Travis Pratt, "Rational Choice Theory, Crime Control Policy, and Criminological Relevance," *Criminology and Public Policy* 7 (2008): 43–52.

Section Summary

- The dominant theory of criminal behavior for most of the history of human civilization used demonic, supernatural, or other metaphysical explanations of behavior.
- The Age of Enlightenment was important because it brought a new logic and rationality to understanding human behavior, especially regarding the ability of individual human beings to think for themselves. Hobbes and Rousseau were two of the more important Enlightenment philosophers, and both stressed the importance of the social contract.
- Cesare Beccaria, who is generally considered the father of criminal justice, laid out a series of recommendations for reforming the brutal justice systems that existed throughout the world in the 1700s.
- Beccaria is also widely considered the father of the Classical School or deterrence theory; he based virtually all of his theoretical framework on the work of Enlightenment philosophers, especially their emphasis on humans as rational beings who consider perceived risks and benefits before committing criminal behaviors. This is the fundamental assumption of deterrence models of crime reduction.
- Beccaria discussed three key elements that punishments should have to be effective deterrents: certainty, swiftness, and severity.
- Specific deterrence involves sanctioning an individual to deter that particular individual from offending in the future. General deterrence involves sanctioning an individual to deter other potential offenders by making an example out of the individual being punished.
- The Neoclassical School was formed because societies found it nearly impossible to punish offenders equally for a given offense. The significant difference between the Classical and Neoclassical Schools is that the neoclassical model takes aggravating and mitigating circumstances into account when an individual is sentenced.
- Jeremy Bentham helped reinforce and popularize Beccaria's ideas in the English-speaking world, and he further developed the theory by proposing hedonistic calculus, a formula for understanding criminal behavior.
- Despite falling out of favor among most criminologists in the late 1800s, the classical and neoclassical framework remains the dominant model and philosophy of all modern Western justice systems.

KEY TERMS

actus reus	general deterrence	specific deterrence
Age of Enlightenment	*mens rea*	swiftness of punishment
brutalization effect	Neoclassical School	utilitarianism
certainty of punishment	severity of punishment	
deterrence theory	social contract	

DISCUSSION QUESTIONS

1. Do you see any validity to the supernatural or religious explanations of criminal behavior? Provide examples of why you feel the way you do. Is your position supported by scientific research?

2. Which portions of Enlightenment thought do you believe are most valid in modern times? Which portions do you find least valid?

3. Of all of Beccaria's reforms, which do you think made the most significant improvement to modern criminal justice systems and why? Which do you think had the least impact and why?

4. Of the three elements of deterrence that Beccaria described, which do you think has the most important impact on deterring individuals from committing crime? Which of the three do you think has the least impact on deterring potential criminals? Back up your selections with personal experience.

5. Between general and specific deterrence, which do you think is more important for a judge to consider when sentencing a convicted individual? Why do you feel that way?

6. Provide examples of general and specific deterrence in your local community or state. Use the Internet if you can't find examples from your local community. Do you think such deterrence is effective?

7. Given the modern interpretation by the U.S. government of the definition of torture in context with what Beccaria thought about this issue, do you think that the father of criminal justice and deterrence would agree with the interrogation policies of the Bush administration during the Iraq War, which indisputably violated the guidelines set by the Geneva Conventions? Explain your position.

8. Regarding the use of the death penalty, list and explain at least three reasons why the father of criminal justice and deterrence theory felt the way he did. Which of these arguments do you agree with the most? Which argument do you disagree with the most? Ultimately, are you more strongly for or against the death penalty after reading the arguments of Beccaria?

9. Regarding the Neoclassical School, which mitigating factors do you think should reduce the punishment of a criminal defendant the most? Which aggravating circumstances do you think should increase the sentence of a criminal defendant the most? Do you believe that all persons who commit the same act should be punished exactly the same, regardless of age, experience, or gender?

10. What types of policy strategies based on classical and deterrence theory do you support? Which don't you support? Why?

WEB RESOURCES

Age of Enlightenment

http://history-world.org/age_of_enlightenment.htm

Cesare Beccaria

http://www.constitution.org/cb/beccaria_bio.htm

http://www.criminology.fsu.edu/crimtheory/beccaria.htm

Jeremy Bentham

http://www.ucl.ac.uk/Bentham-Project/who

http://www.utilitarianism.com/bentham.htm

Demonic Theories of Crime

http://www.criminology.fsu.edu/crimtheory/week2.htm

http://www.salemweb.com/memorial/

Deterrence

http://www.deathpenaltyinfo.org/article.php?scid=12&did=167

http://www.sentencingproject.org/doc/deterrence%20briefing%20.pdf

Thomas Hobbes

http://oregonstate.edu/instruct/phl302/philosophers/hobbes.html

http://www.philosophypages.com/hy/3x.htm

Neoclassical School

http://www.answers.com/topic/neo-classical-school

Rousseau

http://www.philosophypages.com/ph/rous.htm

http://www.rousseauassociation.org/

READING 2

This entry, passages from Beccaria's *On Crimes and Punishments* (originally published in 1764), is perhaps the most important in the entire book because it provides the framework on which all societies in the Western world have based their criminal justice systems. This is the model presented by the father of criminal justice, Cesare Beccaria, who published his work anonymously at first and then, once it became a widespread success, came forward as the author. The reforms that he presents in the passages excerpted here are examples of his attempts to make justice systems more fair and rational in the time that he wrote, as a son of the Enlightenment Age, which stressed rationality, fairness, and free will among individuals.

Beccaria proposed numerous reforms for justice systems that many of us take for granted, such as trial by peers, the right to confront and cross-examine accusers, the right to public notification of laws, and barring of torture and secret accusations. These reforms made him generally recognized as the father of criminal justice. Furthermore, Beccaria is widely considered the father of the Classical School and the father of deterrence theory because he was the first to be recognized as emphasizing the importance of individuals' free will and rationale in choosing to engage in criminal behavior after considering the perceived costs and benefits. Although it is likely that he was not the first person to come to this realization, he was the first to get credit for explicitly stating this rational, decision-making process in individuals before they commit criminal acts and for identifying the three elements that make a punishment a good deterrent.

On Crimes and Punishments

Cesare Beccaria

 ## I. Origin of Punishments

Laws are the conditions by which independent and isolated men, tired of living in a constant state of war and of enjoying a freedom made useless by the uncertainty of keeping it, unite in society.[1] They sacrifice a portion of this liberty in order to enjoy the remainder in security and tranquility. The sum of all these portions of liberty sacrificed for the good of everyone constitutes the sovereignty of a nation, and the sovereign is its legitimate depository and administrator. The mere formation of this deposit, however, was not sufficient; it had to be defended against the private usurpations of each particular individual, for everyone always seeks to withdraw not only his own share of liberty from the common store, but to expropriate the portions of other men besides. Tangible motives were required sufficient to dissuade the despotic spirit of each man from plunging the laws of society back into the original chaos. These tangible motives are the punishments established for lawbreakers. I say "tangible motives," since experience has shown that the common crowd does not adopt stable principles of conduct, and the universal principle of dissolution which we see in the physical and the moral world cannot be avoided except by motives that have a direct impact on the senses and appear continually to the mind to counterbalance the

Source: Cesare Beccaria, *On Crimes and Punishments*, with notes and introduction by David Young (Indianapolis, IN: Hackett, 1985). The selection here has been abridged from the original.

strong impressions of individual passions opposed to the general good. Neither eloquence nor declamations nor even the sublime truths have sufficed for long to check the emotions aroused by the vivid impressions of immediately present objects.[2]

II. The Right to Punish

Every punishment which does not derive from absolute necessity, says the great Montesquieu, is tyrannical.[3] The proposition may be made general thus: every act of authority between one man and another that does not derive from absolute necessity is tyrannical. Here, then, is the foundation of the sovereign's right to punish crimes: the necessity of defending the depository of the public welfare against the usurpations of private individuals. Further, the more just punishments are, the more sacred and inviolable is personal security, and the greater is the liberty that the sovereign preserves for his subjects. Let us consult the human heart, and there we shall find the fundamental principles of the sovereign's right to punish crimes, for no lasting advantage is to be expected from political morality if it is not founded upon man's immutable sentiments. Any law that deviates from them will always encounter a resistance that will overpower it sooner or later, just as a continually applied force, however slight, eventually overcomes any violent movement communicated to a physical body.

No man freely gave up a part of his own liberty for the sake of the public good; such an illusion exists only in romances. If it were possible, each of us would wish that the agreements binding on others were not binding on himself. Every man thinks of himself as the center of all the world's affairs.

The increase in the numbers of mankind, slight in itself but too much for the means that sterile and uncultivated nature offered to satisfy increasingly interrelated needs, led the first savages to unite. These initial groups necessarily created others to resist the former, and thus the state of war was transposed from individuals to nations.[4]

It was necessity, then, that constrained men to give up part of their personal liberty; hence, it is certain that each man wanted to put only the least possible portion intothe public deposit, only as much as necessary to induce others to defend it.[5] The aggregate of these smallest possible portions of individual liberty constitutes the right to punish; everything beyond that is an abuse and not justice, a fact but scarcely a right. Note that the word "right" is not a contradiction of the word "force"; the former is, rather, a modification of the latter—namely, the modification most useful to the greatest number. By "justice," moreover, I do not mean anything but the bond necessary to hold private interests together. Without it, they would dissolve into the earlier state of incompatibility. All punishments that exceed what is necessary to preserve this bond are unjust by their very nature. One must beware of attaching the idea of something real to this word "justice," as though it were a physical force or a being that actually exists. It is simply a human manner of conceiving things, a manner that has an infinite influence on the happiness of everybody.[6] Most certainly I am not speaking of the other sort of justice that comes from God and that is directly related to the rewards and punishments of the life to come.

XIX. Promptness of Punishment

The more prompt the punishment is and the sooner it follows the crime, the more just and useful it will be. I say more just, because it spares the criminal the useless and cruel torments of uncertainty, which grow with the vigor of one's imagination and the sense of one's own weakness; more just, because being deprived of one's liberty is a punishment, and this cannot precede the sentence except when necessity demands it. Imprisonment, then, simply means taking someone into custody until he is found guilty, and, as such custody is essentially punitive, it should last as short a time as possible and be as lenient as possible. The duration of imprisonment should be determined both by the time necessary for the trial and by the right of those who have been detained the longest to be tried first. The rigor of detention must not exceed what is necessary to forestall escape or the concealment of evidence. The trial itself must be completed in the shortest possible time. Can there be a more cruel contrast than the one between the indolence of a judge and the anguish of someone accused of a crime—between the comforts and pleasures of an unfeeling magistrate on the one hand, and, on the other, the tears and squalid condition of a prisoner? In general, the burden of a punishment and the consequence of a crime should have the greatest impact on others and yet be as mild as possible for the person who suffers it; for one cannot call any society "legitimate" if it does not recognize as an indisputable principle that men have wanted to subject themselves only to the least possible evils.

I have said that promptness of punishment is more useful, for the less time that passes between the misdeed and its chastisement, the stronger and more permanent is the human mind's association of the two ideas of *crime* and *punishment*, so that imperceptibly the one will come to be considered as the cause and the other as the necessary and inevitable result. It is well established that the association of ideas is the cement that shapes the whole structure of the human intellect; without it, pleasure and pain would be isolated feelings with no consequences. The farther removed men are from general ideas and universal principles—in other words, the more uneducated men are—the more they act on the basis of immediate and very familiar associations, neglecting the more remote and complicated ones. The latter are useful only to men strongly impassioned for the object after which they are striving. The light of their attention illuminates this one object only, leaving all others in darkness. Such remote and complicated associations are likewise useful to more lofty minds, for they have acquired the habit of rapidly surveying many objects at once, and they have the ability to contrast many partial sentiments with one another, so that the outcome, which is action, is less dangerous and uncertain.

The temporal proximity of crime and punishment, then, is of the utmost importance if one desires to arouse in crude and uneducated minds the idea of punishment in association with the seductive image of a certain advantageous crime. Long delay only serves to disconnect those two ideas, and whatever impression the chastisement of a crime may make, that impression will be made more as a spectacle than a punishment. Further, the impression will come only after the horror of a given crime, which ought to reinforce the feeling of punishment, has grown weak in the minds of the spectators.

Another principle serves admirably to tighten even further the connection between the misdeed and its punishment, namely, that the latter should conform as closely as possible to the nature of the crime. This analogy marvelously facilitates the contrast that should exist between the motive for a crime and the consequent impact of punishment, so that the latter draws the mind away and leads it to quite a different end than the one toward which the seductive idea of breaking the law seeks to direct it.

XXVII. Mildness of Punishments

But my train of thought has taken me away from my subject, and I hasten to return in order to clarify it. One of the greatest checks on crime is not the cruelty of punishments but their inevitability. Consequently, in order to be effective, virtues, magisterial vigilance and inexorable judicial severity must be accompanied by mild legislation. The certainty of a chastisement, even if it be moderate, will always make a greater impression than the fear of a more terrible punishment that is united with the hope of impunity; for, when they are certain, even the least of evils always terrifies men's minds, while hope, that heavenly gift that often fills us completely, always removes from us the idea of worse punishments, especially if that hope is reinforced by the examples of impunity which weakness and greed frequently accord. The very savagery of a punishment makes the criminal all the bolder in taking risks to avoid it precisely because the evil with which he is threatened is so great, so much so that he commits several crimes in order to escape the punishment for a single one of them. The countries and ages in which punishments have been most atrocious have always been the scene of the bloodiest and most inhuman actions, for the same spirit of ferocity that guided the hand of the legislator governed the hand of the parricide and the assassin. Seated on the throne, this spirit dictated iron laws for savage and slavish souls to obey; in private darkness, it moved men to destroy one tyrant in order to create another.[7]

To the degree that punishments become more cruel, men's souls become hardened, just as fluids always seek the level of surrounding objects, and the constantly active force of the passions leads to this: after a hundred years of cruel punishments, breaking on the wheel[8] occasions no more fright than imprisonment did at first. In order for a penalty to achieve its objective all that is required is that the harm of the punishment should exceed the benefit resulting from the crime. Further, the inevitability of the punishment and the loss of the anticipated advantage of the crime should enter into this calculation of the excess of harm.[9] Everything more than this is thus superfluous and therefore tyrannical. Men regulate their conduct by the repeated experience of evils which they know, not by those of which they are ignorant. Let us imagine two nations, each having a scale of punishments proportional to crimes; in one, the maximum penalty is perpetual slavery, and, in the other, breaking on the wheel. I maintain that the first nation will have as much fear of its greatest punishment as the second.[10] If for some reason the first of these nations were to adopt the more severe penalties of the second, the same reason might lead the latter to increase its punishments, passing gradually from breaking on the wheel to slower and more deliberate torments, and finally to the ultimate refinements of that science that tyrants know all too well.

Cruelty of punishments leads to two other ruinous consequences that are contrary to the very purpose of preventing crimes. The first is that it is far from easy to maintain the essential proportion between crime and punishment, for no matter how much industrious cruelty may have multiplied the forms of chastisement, they still cannot exceed the limit that the human physique and sensory capacity can endure.[11] Once this limit has been reached, it would not be possible to devise greater punishments for more harmful and atrocious crimes, and yet such punishments would be required to deter them. The second consequence is that impunity itself arises from the barbarity of punishments. There are limits to human capacities both for good and for evil, and a spectacle that is too brutal for humanity can only be a passing frenzy, never a permanent system such as the law must be. If the laws are indeed cruel, either they are changed or else fatal impunity results from the laws themselves.

Who would not tremble with horror when he reads in history books of the barbarous and useless torments that were devised and carried out in cold blood by men who were deemed wise? Who would not shudder to the depths of his being at the sight of thousands of poor wretches forced into a desperate return to the original state of nature by a misery that the law—which has always favored the few and trampled on the many—has either willed or permitted? Or at the spectacle of people accused of impossible crimes fabricated by timid ignorance? Or at the sight of persons whose only crime has been their fidelity to their own principles lacerated with deliberate formality and slow torture by men endowed with the same senses and hence with the same passions, providing a diverting show for a fanatical crowd?

 ## XLVII. Conclusion

I conclude with the reflection that the magnitude of punishment ought to be relative to the condition of the nation itself. Stronger and more obvious impressions are required for the hardened spirits of a people who have scarcely emerged from a savage state. A thunderbolt is needed to fell a ferocious lion who is merely angered by a gun shot. But, to the extent that human spirits are made gentle by the social state, sensibility increases; as it increases, the severity of punishment must diminish if one wishes to maintain a constant relationship between object and feeling.[12]

From all that has been seen hitherto, one can deduce a very useful theorem, but one that scarcely conforms to custom, the usual lawgiver of nations. It is this: *In order that any punishment should not be an act of violence committed by one person or many against a private citizen, it is essential that it should be public, prompt, necessary, the minimum possible under the given circumstances, proportionate to the crimes, and established by law.*

Notes

1.   The idea of laws as conditions of the social contract was fundamental to Rousseau. Jean-Jacques Rousseau, *Du contrat social*, in Jean-Jacques Rousseau, *Oeuvres complètes*, ed. Brenard Gagnebin and Marcel Raymond, vol. 3 (Paris, 1964), bk. 2, chap. 6, pp. 378–380.

2. This view of human nature as motivated chiefly by self-interest was common among eighteenth-century utilitarians. Helvétius had declared that all men seek to become despots and that tangible motives are necessary to check this tendency. Helvétius, *D l'esprit*, disc. 3, chap. 17, pp. 284–289. Beccaria frankly admitted that he owed a large part of his ideas to Helvétius. Beccaria to Morellet, 26 Jan. 1766, in *Opere* (Romangnoli ed.), 2:865. Kant and Hegel, of course, vehemently objected to such a theory of punishment, and it must be noted that it was not always typical of Beccaria. Immanuel Kant, *The Metaphysical Elements of Justice. Part I of the Metaphysics of Morals*, ed. and trans. John Ladd (Indianapolis, 1965), p. 100;G. W. Hegel, *Hegel's Philosophy of Right*, ed. and trans. T. M. Knox (London, 1967), p. 246.

3. Montesquieu had held that excessive and unnecessary penalties are suitable only for a despotic government. Montesquieu, *De l'esprit des lois* (Caillois ed.), bk. 6, chap. 9, 2:318–319.

4. This account of the formation of societies closely parallels the one which Montesquieu gave in his *De l'esprit des lois* (Caillois ed.), bk 1, chap. 3, 2:236–238.

5. Beccaria's account of the social contract is quite unlike the total surrender of rights of which Rousseau spoke. Rousseau, *Du contrat social* (Gagnebin and Raymond ed.), bk. 1, chap. 6, 3:360–362. It is, rather, much closer to Locke's idea that the sovereign is purely fiduciary and that the people forming a state make only a minimal surrender of their liberty. John Locke, *The Second Treatise of Government*, ed. Thomas P. Peardon (Indianapolis, 1952), chap. 3, para 21, p. 14; chap 8, paras. 95–101, pp. 54–57.

6. Beccaria's utilitarian view of justice appears very similar to the ideas expounded by Helvétius. Helvétius, *D l'esprit*, disc. 2, chap. 5, pp. 55–57; chap. 8, pp. 69–74; chap. 12, pp. 89–97.

7. On several occasions, Montesquieu remarked that cruel punishments are suitable only in a despotic state, which is based upon fear, and that excessive penalties are most likely to be found in such a regime. Montesquieu, *Lettres persanes* (Callois ed.), vol. 1 (Paris, 1949) letter 80, pp. 252—253, Montesquieu, *De l'esprit des lois* (Callois ed.), bk. 12, chap 4 2:433—435.

8. Breaking on the wheel was a common form of execution in the eighteenth century. An English traveler in France described such an execution: "On the scaffold was erected a large cross exactly in the form of that commonly represented for Saint Andrew's. The executioner and his assistants then placed the prisoner on it, in such a manner that his arms and legs were extended exactly agreeable to the form of the cross, and strongly tied down; under each arm, leg, etc., was cut a notch in the wood, as a mark where the executioner might strike, and break the bone with greater facility. He held in his hand a large iron bar . . . and in the first place broke his arms, then in a moment after both his thighs; it was a melancholy, shocking sight, to see him heave his body up and down in extreme agony, and hideous to behold the terrible distortions of his face; it was a considerable time before he expired. . . ." Sacheverell Stevens, *Miscellaneous Remarks Made on . . . France, Italy, Germany, and Holland* (London, 1756) as cited in Jerry Kaplow, *The Names of Kings: The Parisian Laboring Poor in the Eighteenth Century* (New York, 1972), p. 135.

9. Bentham later elaborated on the calculation of the excess of harm over the profit of the crime, citing Beccaria in the process. Bentham, *Principles* (Burns and Hart ed.), chap. 14,pp. 165–174, esp. sec. 8, n.

10. Montesquieu had made precisely this point as early as 1721. Montesquieu, *Lettres persanes* (Callois ed.), letter 80, 1:252–253.

11. The point Beccaria is making here is based on the psychology of Helvétius, Helvétius, *D l'esprit* (1759 ed.), disc. 1, pp. 1–32; disc. 3, chaps. 1–3, pp. 187–202.

12. Hegel fully agreed with Beccaria on this score, arguing that punishments can and should vary according to the degree of a society's refinement or barbarism. "A penal code, then," concluded Hegel, "is primarily the child of its age and the state of civil society at the time." Hegel, *Philosophy of Right* (Knox ed.), p. 140. For a modern view substantially like Beccaria's, see Jan Gorecki, *Capital Punishment: Criminal Law and Social Evolution* (New York, 1983), esp. pp. 31–80.

REVIEW QUESTIONS

1. What two reasons did Beccaria have for arguing that punishments should be prompt or swift? Which of these relates to deterrence theory (whereas the other is a reform for fairness and due process)?

2. Of the three aspects of deterrence theory—swiftness, severity, and certainty—which did Beccaria say was most important? Provide a quotation that summarizes his feelings regarding this belief.

3. What did Beccaria say about the death penalty? Was he for it or against it? Provide at least three reasons he took this position.

4. Discuss two or more reforms that Beccaria proposed that would make a justice system more fair.

5. Discuss how Beccaria might have felt regarding how Iraqi war suspects have been tortured or held for many years without trial. Would he agree or disagree with their treatment? Why?

READING 3

In this study, Jon Sorensen, Robert Wrinkle, Victoria Brewer, and James Marquart examine the extent to which capital punishment has a significant deterrent effect on murder rates in Texas, which executes far more individuals than any other state in the United States. After reviewing the various designs that have been used to estimate the association between the death penalty/executions and murder rates, the authors offer their own test using data from 1984 to 1997. Without giving away the findings of the study, it is notable that this test is consistent with most other studies on the deterrent effects of capital punishment and thus is a good representation of the empirical research existing to date. Readers should keep in mind that the deterrent effect of capital punishment is just one of the many issues in the debate on whether or not we should use the death penalty, just as the evidence of whether executions deter murderers is just one aspect of deterrence theory.

Capital Punishment and Deterrence

Examining the Effect of Executions on Murder in Texas

Jon Sorensen, Robert Wrinkle, Victoria Brewer, and James Marquart

The dominant approach to determining the relationship between deterrence and the death penalty involves comparing the rate of homicide or some subset of homicide and either the legal status of the death penalty or the performance of actual executions within or across particular jurisdictions. The deterrence hypothesis is supported when lower homicide rates are found within time periods or jurisdictions where the death penalty has been available or in use. If homicide rates are higher in the presence of capital punishment, the alternative, or "brutalization hypothesis," is supported (Bowers and Pierce 1980). The third possible outcome is that the death penalty is found to have no influence on homicide rates.

SOURCE: Adapted from Jon Sorensen, Robert Wrinkle, Victoria Brewer, and James Marquart, "Capital Punishment and Deterrence: Examining the Effect of Executions on Murder in Texas," *Crime and Delinquency* 45, no. 4 (1999): 481–93. Copyright © 1999 Sage Publications, Inc. Reprinted by permission of Sage Publications, Inc.

Empirical studies of deterrence and capital punishment are best classified by their research design. Cross-sectional designs compare homicide rates across jurisdictions. The earliest deterrence studies of this kind simply compared rates of homicide in retentionist states that have statutory provisions for the death penalty to the rates in abolitionist states without such provisions. Findings showed that retentionist states typically experienced higher rates of homicide than did abolitionist jurisdictions (Sutherland 1925). However, examination of geographical, social, and economic dissimilarities between abolitionist and retentionist states suggested that factors other than the death penalty could have influenced homicide rates.

Scholars then began making comparisons that are more specific between neighboring states, which were presumed to be comparable on such factors. These studies failed to support the deterrence hypothesis, finding that retentionist states most often experienced higher rates of homicide than did contiguous abolitionist states (Schuessler 1952; Sellin 1967). A new generation of cross-sectional studies has employed multiple regression analyses to predict the rate of homicide across jurisdictions while controlling for extraneous variables (Forst 1977; Passell 1975) and has consistently found executions to have no effect on murder rates (Cheatwood 1993; Peterson and Bailey 1988).

Longitudinal designs are used to study the influence of the death penalty in a single jurisdiction over time. The earliest of these studies examined homicide rates in jurisdictions before and after a legislative change in the legal status of the death penalty that either abolished or reimplemented capital punishment. The deterrence hypothesis would be supported if states experienced lower rates of homicide during retentionist periods and higher rates of homicide during abolitionist periods. These studies failed to support the deterrence hypothesis (Bedau 1967; Sellin 1967) because they found inconsistent changes in murder rates after legislative enactments.

More recently, the advent of sophisticated statistical techniques has influenced the methodology used in testing the deterrence hypothesis. Time series analysis, introduced by economist Isaac Ehrlich in 1975, has proven to be a superior means of testing the deterrent effect of the death penalty over time. Time series analyses typically concentrate on the effect of actual executions and enable the researcher to simultaneously control for the influence of alternative explanatory variables. In his initial study, Ehrlich claimed that executions carried out during 1933 through 1969 had resulted in a significant reduction in the number of homicides occurring throughout the United States. However, reanalyses of his work failed to find support for the deterrence hypothesis; instead, researchers concluded that the reduction in homicides observed by Ehrlich was an artifact of measurement error that resulted from inappropriate design specifications and faulty statistical analysis (Baldus and Cole 1975; Bowers and Pierce 1975; Klein, Forst, and Filatov 1978). Recent time series analyses have confirmed the findings of Ehrlich's critics; they have failed to find evidence of a deterrent effect (Bailey 1983; Cochran, Chamlin, and Seth 1994; Decker and Kohfeld 1984).

Another recent advance in methodology has been to limit analyses to only those types of murder likely to be deterred by capital punishment. Because only certain instances of murder can result in the death penalty, many researchers have disaggregated the universe of homicides to limit the dependent variable to those that have death as a possible sentence. For example, Bailey and Peterson (1987) found that the likelihood of receiving a death sentence was not related to the killing of police officers in the United States during 1973 through 1984. The findings supported those of earlier studies that have failed to find a relationship between capital punishment and police killing (Cardarelli 1968; Sellin 1980). One limitation of these studies was that the researchers were unable to consider the certainty of punishment because very few executions had been carried out during that period.

In a later study that included a measure of the certainty of punishment, Peterson and Bailey (1991) analyzed the relationship between actual executions and the monthly rates of felony murder throughout the United States from 1976 through 1987. The researchers found no consistent relationship between the number of executions, the level of television publicity of these executions, and the rate of felony murder. A study following Oklahoma's return to capital punishment disaggregated homicides into felony murders and murders involving strangers (Cochran et al. 1994). Using an interrupted time series design, Cochran and colleagues found no change in the rate of felony homicides over the 68 weeks following this highly publicized execution, but observed an increase in the rate of stranger homicides. This brutalization effect was recorded in another study that found an increase in several types of homicide in metropolitan areas after Arizona's first execution in 29 years (Thompson 1997).

After thoroughly reviewing the empirical literature, Peterson and Bailey (1998) concluded that the lack of evidence for any deterrent effect of capital punishment was incontrovertible. According to them, no credible empirical studies had ever been able to demonstrate that the severity, certainty, or celerity of capital punishment reduced the rate of homicide. However, they did envision situations that might present unique opportunities to engage the deterrence hypothesis.

One such opportunity presented itself in Texas in recent years. By far the most active death penalty state, Texas has accounted for more than a third of all executions in the United States since the reimplementation of capital punishment in the years following *Furman* v. *Georgia* (1972). In 1997 alone, Texas executed a record number of 37 capital murderers, accounting for half of the 74 U.S. executions in that year. Texas has provided an ideal natural experiment to engage the deterrence hypothesis.

One study of the effect of capital punishment on homicide rates in Texas from 1933 through 1980 found no support for the deterrence hypothesis (Decker and Kohfeld 1990). Although this study did not include the effects of any post-Furman executions in Texas, an update of their research extended the period studied through 1986. Decker and Kohfeld then found that executions were actually followed by an increase in homicide rates, supporting the brutalization hypothesis. Their studies, however, included a limited number of control variables, an aggregate measure of homicide, and the use of years as the unit of analysis. Their updated study captured few of the executions that were to occur in the post-Furman era. The study reported here advances the work of Decker and Kohfeld by examining the deterrence hypothesis in Texas from 1984 through 1997, capturing the most active period of executions in a jurisdiction during the post-Furman period. It also simultaneously incorporates the methodological strengths of recent studies to provide one of the most compelling tests of the deterrence hypothesis completed thus far.

 ## Data and Methods

To examine the deterrence hypothesis during the modern era, data that spanned the years from 1984 through 1997 were collected from official sources. The year 1984 was chosen as the beginning of the data collection period because of the availability of specific data on homicides and the onset of executions.[1] Because no executions took place until December 1982, the period before the onset of executions was eliminated from our analyses due to a lack of variance in the independent variable. Data collection was further limited as a result of the Houston Police Department's failure to report information on homicides in 1983 for inclusion in the *Supplemental Homicide Reports* (SHR).[2] Estimating the murder rate for 1983 would, to some unknown degree, bias measures of the deterrent effect of the lone execution in December 1982, particularly because no further executions were carried out until March 1984.[3] Because of these potential sources of bias, data collection began with the year 1984.

The number of executions served as the independent variable. The number of executions was tabulated from ledgers provided by the Texas Department of Criminal Justice—Institutional Division. The dependent variables included rates of murder and rates of felony murder. Information on the number of murders was collected from the Texas Department of Public Safety—Uniform Crime Reporting Division. The murder rate was based on the number of murders and nonnegligent manslaughters occurring in Texas during the period studied. Excluded from this category were negligent manslaughters, accidental homicides, justifiable homicides committed by citizens and police officers, and executions performed by the state. Murders involving burglary, robbery, or sexual assault were coded as felony murders.[4]

Information on control variables that have most often been found to be related to homicide rates in previous studies was also collected. Information related to homicide in general, including the percentage of the state population living in metropolitan areas, the percentage of the population aged 18 through 34, and the unemployment rate, were culled from the *Statistical Abstracts of the United States* (see Land, McCall, and Cohen 1990; Peterson and Bailey 1991). The number of physicians per 100,000 residents was also coded from the *Statistical Abstracts of the United States* and is included as a proxy for the availability of emergency services, which could prevent an aggravated assault from turning deadly. Other variables available in the *Statistical Abstracts of the United States* that are typically included in homicide studies are the percentage of Blacks and the percentage of divorced individuals. They were excluded from this study because both were constant over the time period studied. Furthermore, these variables were not significant predictors of homicide rates in a recent deterrence study (Peterson and Bailey 1991).

Additional information was collected from alternate sources. The percentage of murders resulting in convictions was collected from the *Annual Reports of the Texas Judicial Council* as an additional measure of the certainty of punishment. The rate of incarceration per 100,000 in the state was gathered from the Bureau of Justice Statistics. The incarceration rate was included to control for possible incapacitation effects resulting from a vast increase in Texas's prison population during the time period studied. Information on the percentage of Texas residents who are on Aid to Families with Dependent Children (AFDC) was gathered from the Texas Department of Human Resources. The direction of its expected relationship to homicide is not specified herein. Although a direct relationship between welfare and homicide rates is typically expected, a recent study found that AFDC is an indicator of available resources that act to mitigate the harshness of poverty, thereby decreasing homicide rates (DeFronzo 1997).

Control variables were also calculated from the SHR data. The percentage of homicides resulting from gunshots was included as a proxy for the availability of firearms. Temporal variables were included to account for surges and lulls in the homicide rate. A high- and low-season variable specified months that were found to be significantly higher or lower in general homicide rates. High season included the months of July and August, whereas low season included only the month of February. Because the state experienced a record number of executions in 1997, an indicator of that year was also included as a control variable. Lagged execution variables, T_1 to T_3, were also calculated.

Following Chamlin, Grasmick, Bursik, and Cochran (1992), the unit of analysis is the month. Although Chamlin and colleagues did not find significant macro-level deterrent effects when their data were aggregated at longer time intervals, they did find deterrent effects when lagging data in shorter temporal aggregations. A month was the shortest time interval available for which information about the dependent variables was recorded. Accordingly, although we aggregated the number of executions by month, control variables were typically observed on a yearly basis; thus, monthly figures were estimated using linear interpolation. These estimation procedures were appropriate because these variables were treated only as control variables, and not as alternative explanatory variables (Peterson and Bailey 1991).

Analysis and Findings

Figure 1 provides an overview of execution and murder rates during the time period encompassed by the study. This figure illustrates the episodic nature of executions. After the first execution, which was that of Charlie Brooks, was carried out in December 1982 (not included in Figure 1), the next one did not take place until James Autry was executed in March 1984. A small wave of executions, which peaked at 10 in 1986, followed. A slump in executions then occurred, with an average of four per year being carried out during 1988 through 1991. The ascendance of executions in 1992 signaled the beginning of a more substantial wave of executions, with an average of 15.5 executions per year during 1992 through 1995.

A legal challenge to Texas's procedures for speeding up the appellate processing of capital cases resulted in a moratorium on executions. With the exception of the voluntary execution of Joe Gonzalez in September 1996, executions were halted to await a decision of the Texas Court of Criminal Appeals on the legality of the new procedures. Executions resumed in February 1997, after the court's pronouncement that the expedited appellate procedures were constitutional. The next wave of executions in Texas would be of historical significance. In dispatching 37 backlogged cases, Texas reached a new record for the number of executions carried out in the state during a single year.

The rate of murder in the state from 1984 through 1991 showed no discernible trend in relation to the execution rate. Although there was a slight decrease in murder rates in 1987 through 1989 after the execution wave of the mid-1980s that could be attributed to a deterrent effect, the homicide rate only began to increase in 1990 and 1991, which was after a 2-year lull in executions during the late 1980s. Although the increase could be attributed to the earlier lull in executions and hence support the deterrence hypothesis, the considerable lag in its increase would suggest that any deterrent effect, or lack thereof, occurred only after a considerable time and is of limited significance.

The greatest amount of support for the deterrence hypothesis is found when the decrease in murder rates is paired with the increase in executions during the 1990s. During the execution wave of the 1990s, the murder rate declined substantially in the state. In the same year that the state reached a historical high in executions, the murder rate fell below what was experienced in decades. Although this seems to provide a strong support for the deterrence hypothesis, the downward trend in homicide rates does not appear to be disturbed by the moratorium on executions in 1996, as the deterrence hypothesis would predict; instead, the downward trend continued. Although a bivariate regression model (not reported in tabular form) produced a significant equation, with executions explaining 7 percent of the variance in murder rates, the estimates were not reliable due to a high degree of serial correlation. Furthermore, murder rates have been declining throughout the United States during this same period, which suggests that factors unrelated to executions were responsible for this pattern.

 ## Conclusions

This study found that recent evidence from the most active execution state in the nation lent no support to the deterrence hypothesis. The number of executions did not appear to influence either the rate of murder in general or the rate of felony murder in particular. At the same time, no support was found for the brutalization hypothesis. Executions did not reduce murder rates; they also did not have the opposite effect of increasing murder rates. The inability to reject the null hypothesis supports findings from the vast majority of studies on deterrence and capital punishment (Peterson and Bailey 1998). From the data presented, it appears that other factors are responsible for the variations and trends in murder rates.

Once this argument is accepted, several implications can arise. Some may infer, for example, that these results suggest the repeal of the death penalty because it fails to

| Figure 1 | Murders and live executions in Texas |

NOTE: This graph shows the murder rate per population of 100,000 and the number of executions per year.

serve the penological function that is so often offered in its defense. Others would argue that various other goals must also be taken into consideration before making this determination, such as whether the public supports its use, whether it serves the goals of retribution, whether it saves money over life imprisonment, whether it serves to provide justice to the families of victims, and whether it serves the interests of the criminal justice system in general. However, these justifications have also been challenged by research (Acker, Bohm, and Lanier 1998; Bedau 1997). Along with the steady stream of consistent findings on the failure of capital punishment in all of these areas, this study cannot help but support the abolitionist argument.

Notes

1. Detailed information on homicides, a necessity in disaggregating felony murders from more general ones, has been routinely kept by the state since 1976 in the *Supplemental Homicide Reports.*

2. In addition to being the largest jurisdiction in Texas, Houston is the most significant contributor to the number of murders, particularly felony murders, in the state.

3. Information from Houston would be crucial in estimating statewide murder rates, especially felony murder rates, for 1983, the year immediately following the first post-Furman execution,

4. Disaggregating murders into a felony murder category was imperative, because this type of murder was eligible for capital punishment. Felony-related murders have also been the category of capital murders that have most often resulted in death sentences and eventual executions in Texas (Marquart, Ekland-Olson, and Sorensen 1994). Noncapital murders, especially those occurring in the heat of passion, should not be expected to decline in response to executions because they are not punishable by death. Death-eligible homicides, particularly those involving the premeditation of felony-related murders, should reasonably be expected to decrease in response to executions if the deterrence hypothesis is correct.

References

Acker, James R., Robert M. Bohm, and Charles S. Lanier. 1998. *America's Experiment with Capital Punishment: Reflections on the Past, Present, and Future of the Ultimate Sanction.* Durham, NC: Carolina Academic Press.

Bailey, William C. 1983. "Disaggregation in Deterrence and Death Penalty Research: The Case of Murder in Chicago." *Journal of Criminal Law and Criminology* 74:827–59.

Bailey, William C. and Ruth D. Peterson. 1987. "Police Killings and Capital Punishment: The Post-Furman Period." *Criminology* 25:1–25.

Baldus, David C. and James W. L. Cole. 1975. "A Comparison of the Work of Thorsten Sellin and Isaac Ehrlich on the Deterrent Effect of Capital Punishment." *Yale Law Journal* 85:170–86.

Bedau, Hugo A. 1967. *The Death Penalty in America.* Rev. ed. New York: Doubleday.

———. 1997. *The Death Penalty in America: Current Controversies.* New York: Oxford University Press.

Bowers, William J. and Glenn Pierce. 1975. "The Illusion of Deterrence in Isaac Ehrlich's Research on Capital Punishment." *Yale Law Journal* 85:187–208.

———.1980. "Deterrence or Brutalization: What Is the Effect of Executions?" *Crime & Delinquency* 26:453–84.

Cardarelli, Albert P. 1968. "An Analysis of Police Killed in Criminal Action: 1961–1963." *Journal of Criminal Law, Criminology and Police Science* 59:447–53.

Chamlin, Mitchell B., Harold G. Grasmick, Robert J. Bursik, Jr., and John K. Cochran. 1992. "Time Aggregation and Time Lag in Macro-Level Deterrence Research." *Criminology* 30:377–95.

Cheatwood, Derral. 1993. "Capital Punishment and the Deterrence of Violent Crime in Comparable Counties." *Criminal Justice Review* 18:165–79.

Cochran, John K., Mitchell B. Chamlin, and Mark Seth. 1994. "Deterrence or Brutalization? An Assessment of Oklahoma's Return to Capital Punishment." *Criminology* 32:107–34.

Decker, Scott H. and Carol W. Kohfeld. 1984. "A Deterrence Study of the Death Penalty in Illinois, 1933-1980." *Journal of Criminal Justice* 12:367–77.

Decker, Scott H. and Carol W. Kohfeld. 1990. "The Deterrent Effect of Capital Punishment in the Five Most Active Execution States: A Time Series Analysis." *Criminal Justice Review* 15:173–91.

DeFronzo, James. 1997. "Welfare and Homicide." *Journal of Research in Crime & Delinquency* 34:395–406.

Ehrlich, Isaac. 1975. "The Deterrent Effect of Capital Punishment: A Question of Life and Death." *American Economic Review* 65:397–417.

Forst, Brian. 1977. "The Deterrent Effect of Capital Punishment: A Cross-Tabular Analysis of the 1960's." *Minnesota Law Review* 61:743–67.

Furman v. Georgia, 408 U.S. 238 (1972).

Klein, Lawrence R., Brian Forst, and Victor Filatov. 1978. "The Deterrent Effect of Capital Punishment: An Assessment of Estimates." Pp. 331–60 in *Deterrence and Incapacitation: Estimating the Effects of Criminal Sanctions on Crime Rates,* edited by A. Blumstein, J. Cohen, and D. Nagin. Washington, DC: National Academy of Sciences.

Land, Kenneth C., Patricia L. McCall, and Lawrence E. Cohen. 1990. "Structural Covariates of Homicide Rates: Are There Any Invariances Across Time and Social Space?" *American Journal of Sociology* 95:922–63.

Marquart, James W., Sheldon Ekland-Olson, and Jonathan R. Sorensen. 1994. *The Rope, the Chair, and the Needle: Capital Punishment in Texas, 1923–1990.* Austin: University of Texas Press.

Passell, Peter. 1975. "The Deterrent Effect of the Death Penalty: A Statistical Test." *Stanford Law Review* 28:61–80.

Peterson, Ruth D. and William C. Bailey. 1988. "Murder and Capital Punishment in the Evolving Context of the Post-Furman Era." *Social Forces* 66:774–807.

_____. 1991. "Felony Murder and Capital Punishment: An Examination of the Deterrence Question." *Criminology* 29:367–95.

_____. 1998. "Is Capital Punishment an Effective Deterrent for Murder? An Examination of the Social Science Research." Pp. 157–82 in *America's Experiment with Capital Punishment: Reflections on the Past, Present, and Future of the Ultimate Sanction,* edited by J. R. Acker, R. M. Bohm, and C. S. Lanier. Durham, NC: Carolina Academic Press.

Schuessler, Karl F. 1952. "The Deterrent Effect of the Death Penalty." *The Annals of the American Academy of Political and Social Science* 284:54–62.

Sellin, Thorsten. 1967. *Capital Punishment.* New York: Harper & Row.

_____. 1980. *The Penalty of Death.* Beverly Hills, CA: Sage.

Sutherland, Edwin H. 1925. "Murder and the Death Penalty." *Journal of Criminal Law and Criminology* 15:522–29.

Thompson, Ernie. 1997. "Deterrence Versus Brutalization: The Case of Arizona." *Homicide Studies* 1:110–28.

REVIEW QUESTIONS

1. What do the authors conclude toward the end of their discussion of prior studies? Specifically, what did Peterson and Bailey (1998) conclude?

2. What do the authors conclude from their own findings regarding the deterrent effects of capital punishment on murder rates in Texas?

3. What do the authors conclude from their own findings regarding the "brutalization hypothesis"?

❖

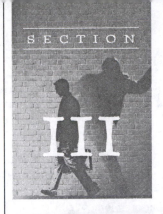

III

Modern Applications of the Classical Perspective

Deterrence, Rational Choice, and Routine Activities or Lifestyle Theories of Crime

This section will discuss the early aggregate studies of deterrence in the late 1960s, then the perceptual studies of the 1970s, and finally the longitudinal and scenario studies of the 1980s and 1990s to the present. Other policy applications, such as increased penalties for drunk driving, white-collar crime, and so on, will also be examined. This section will also discuss the development of rational choice theory in economics and its later application to crime. Finally, it will examine the use of routine activities theory or lifestyle theory as a framework for modern research and applications for reducing criminal activity.

In Section II, we discussed the early development of the Classical and Neoclassical Schools of criminological thought. This theoretical perspective has been the dominant framework used by judges and practitioners in the practice of administering justice and punishment even in current times, but beginning in the late 19th century,

73

criminological researchers dismissed the classical and neoclassical frameworks. Rather, criminological research and theorizing began emphasizing factors other than free will and deterrence. Instead, an emphasis was placed on social, biological, or other factors that go beyond free will and deterrence theory. These theories will be discussed in later sections, but first we will examine the recent rebirth of classical and neoclassical theory and deterrence.

The Rebirth of Deterrence Theory and Contemporary Research

As discussed above, the Classical and Neoclassical School frameworks fell out of favor among scientists and philosophers in the late 19th century, largely due to the introduction of Darwin's ideas about evolution and natural selection. However, virtually all Western criminal systems retained the classical and neoclassical frameworks for their model of justice, particularly the United States. Nevertheless, the ideology of Beccaria's work was largely dismissed by academics and theorists after the presentation of Darwin's theory of evolution in the 1860s. Therefore, the Classical and Neoclassical Schools fell out of favor in terms of criminological theorizing for about 100 years. However, in the 1960s, the Beccarian model of offending experienced a rebirth.

In the late 1960s, several studies using aggregate measures of crime and punishment were published that used a deterrence model for explaining why individuals engage in criminal behavior. These studies revealed a new interest in the deterrent aspects of criminal behavior and further supported the importance of certainty and severity of punishment in deterring individuals from committing crime, particularly homicide. In particular, evidence was presented that showed that increased risk or certainty of punishment was associated with less crime for most serious offenses. Plus, it is a fact that most offenders who are arrested once never get arrested again, which provides some basic support for deterrence.

Many of these studies used statistical formulas to measure the degree of certainty and severity of punishment in given jurisdictions. One measure used the ratio between crimes reported to police and number of arrests in a given jurisdiction. Another measure of certainty of punishment was the ratio of arrests to convictions, or findings of guilt, in criminal cases. Other measures were also employed. Most of the studies showed the same result: The higher the rate of arrest compared to reports of crime, or the higher the conviction rate compared to the arrest rate, the lower the crime rate in the jurisdiction. On the other hand, the scientific evidence for severity, which such studies generally indicated by the lengths of sentences for comparable crimes or similar measures, did not show much impact on crime.

Additional aggregate studies examined the prevalence and influence of capital punishment on the crime rate in given states.[1] The evidence showed that the states with death penalty statutes also had higher murder rates than non-death-penalty states. Furthermore, the studies showed that murderers in death penalty states who were not executed actually served less time than murderers in non-death-penalty states. Thus, the evidence regarding increased sanctions, including capital punishment, was mixed. Still, a review of the early deterrence studies by the National Academy of Sciences concluded that, overall, there was more evidence for a deterrent effect than against it, although the finding was reported in a tone that lacked confidence, perhaps cautious of what future studies would show.[2]

It was not long before critics noted that studies incorporating aggregate (i.e., macro-level) statistics are not adequate indicators or valid measures of the deterrence theoretical framework, largely because the model emphasizes the perceptions of individuals. Using aggregate or group statistics is flawed because different regions may have higher or lower crime rates than others, thereby creating bias in the ratios for certainty or severity of punishment.

---

[1]Daniel Glaser and Max S. Zeigler, "Use of the Death Penalty v. Outrage at Murder," *Crime and Delinquency* 20 (1974): 333–38; Charles Tittle, Franklin E. Zimring, and Gordon J. Hawkins, *Deterrence—The Legal Threat in Crime Control* (Chicago: University of Chicago Press, 1973); Johannes Andenaes, *Punishment and Deterrence* (Ann Arbor: University of Michigan Press, 1974); Jack P. Gibbs, *Crime, Punishment and Deterrence* (New York: Elsevier, 1975).

[2]Alfred Blumstein, Jacqueline Cohen, and Daniel Nagin, eds., *Deterrence and Incapacitation: Estimating the Effects of Criminal Sanctions on Crime Rates* (Washington, DC: National Academy of Sciences, 1978).

Furthermore, the group measures produced by these studies provide virtually no information on the degree to which individuals in those regions perceive sanctions as being certain, severe, or swift. Therefore, the emphasis on the unit of analysis in deterrence research shifted from the aggregate level to a more micro, individual level.

The following phase of deterrence research focused on individual perceptions of certainty and severity of sanctions, primarily drawn at one point in time, known as cross-sectional studies. A number of cross-sectional studies of individual perceptions of deterrence showed that perceptions of the risk or certainty of punishment were strongly associated with intentions to commit future crimes, but individual perceptions of the severity of punishments were mixed. Furthermore, it readily became evident that it was not clear whether perceptions were causing changes in behavior or whether behavior was causing changes in perception. This led to the next wave of research, longitudinal studies of individual perceptions and deterrence, which measured behavior as well as perceptions of risk and severity over time.[3]

One of the primary concepts revealed by longitudinal research was that behavior was influencing perceptions of the risk and severity of punishment more than perceptions were influencing behavior. This was referred to as the experiential effect, which is appropriately named because people's previous experience highly influences their expectations regarding their chances of being caught and suffering the resulting penalties.

A common example is that of people who drive under the influence of alcohol (or other substances). Studies show that if you ask people who have never driven drunk how likely they would be to get caught if they drove home drunk, most predict an unrealistically high chance of getting caught. However, if you ask people who have been arrested for driving drunk, even those who have been arrested several times for this offense, they typically predict that the chance is very low. The reason for this is that these chronic drunk drivers have typically been driving under the influence for many years, mostly without being caught. It is estimated that more than 1 million miles are driven collectively by drunk drivers before one person is arrested.[4] If anything, this is likely a conservative estimate. Thus, people who drive drunk, some of whom do so every day, are not likely to be deterred even when they are arrested more than once because they have done so for years. In fact, perhaps the most notable experts on the deterrence of drunk drivers, H. L. Ross and his colleagues, have concluded that drunk drivers who "perceive a severe punishment if caught, but a near-zero chance of being caught, are being rational in ignoring the threat."[5] Thus, even the most respected scholars in this area admit that sanctions against drunk driving are nowhere near certain enough, even if they are growing in severity.

Another common example is seen with white-collar criminals. Some researchers have theorized that being caught by authorities for violating government rules enforced by the Securities and Exchange Commission (SEC) will make these organizations less likely to commit future offenses.[6] However, business organizations have been in violation of established practices for years by the time they get caught, so it is likely that they will continue to ignore the rules in the future more than organizations that have never violated the rules. Thus, the certainty of punishment for white-collar violations is so low—and many would argue that the severity is also quite low—that it is quite rational for businesses and business professionals to take the risk of engaging in white-collar crime.

---

[3]Raymond Paternoster, Linda E. Saltzman, Gordon P. Waldo, and Theodore G. Chiricos, "Perceived Risk and Social Control: Do Sanctions Really Deter?" *Law and Society Review* 17 (1983): 457–80; Raymond Paternoster, "The Deterrent Effect of the Perceived Certainty and Severity of Punishment: A Review of the Evidence and Issues," *Justice Quarterly* 4 (1987): 173–217; Charles F. Manski and John V. Pepper, "Deterrence and the Death Penalty: Partial Identification Analysis Using Repeated Cross Sections," *Journal of Quantitative Criminology* 29 (2013): 123–44.

[4]Benjamin Hansen, "Punishment and Deterrence: Evidence from Drunk Driving," paper presented at the 7th Annual Conference on Empirical Legal Studies (April 2013); H. Laurence Ross, *Deterring the Drunk Driver: Legal Policy and Social Control* (Lexington: Lexington Books, 1982); H. Laurence Ross, *Confronting Drunk Driving: Social Policy for Saving Lives* (New Haven: Yale University Press, 1992); H. Laurence Ross, "Sobriety Checkpoints, American Style," *Journal of Criminal Justice* 22 (1994): 437–44; H. Laurence Ross, Richard McCleary, and Gary LaFree, "Can Mandatory Jail Laws Deter Drunk Driving? The Arizona Case," *Journal of Criminal Law and Criminology* 81 (1990): 156–70.

[5]H. Laurence Ross, "Sobriety Checkpoints," 164.

[6]See review in Sally Simpson and Christopher S. Koper, "Deterring Corporate Crime," *Criminology* 30 (1992): 347–76.

13

It is interesting to note that white-collar criminals and drunk drivers are two types of offenders who are considered more likely to be deterred because they are mostly of the middle- to upper-level socioeconomic class. The extant research on deterrence has shown that individuals who have something to lose are the most likely to be deterred by sanctions. This makes sense: Those who are unemployed or poor or both do not have much to lose, and for them, as well as for some minorities, incarceration may not present a significant departure from the deprived lives that they lead.

The fact that official sanctions have limitations in deterring individuals from drunk driving and white-collar crime is not a good indication of the effectiveness of deterrence-based policies. Their usefulness becomes even more questionable when other populations are considered, particularly the offenders in most predatory street crimes (robbery, burglary, etc.), in which offenders typically have nothing to lose because they come from poverty-stricken areas and are often unemployed. One recent study showed that being arrested had little effect on perceptions of the certainty of punishment; offending actually corresponded with decreases in such perceptions.[7]

Some people don't see incarceration as that much of a step down in life, given the three meals a day, shelter, and relative stability provided by such punishment. This fact epitomizes one of the most notable paradoxes we have in criminology: The individuals we most want to deter are the least likely to be deterred, primarily because they have nothing to fear. In early Enlightenment thought, Hobbes asserted that, although fear was the tool used to enforce the social contract, people who weren't afraid of punishment could not effectively be deterred. That remains true in modern days.

Along the same lines, studies have consistently shown that for young male offenders—at higher risk, with low emotional or moral inhibitions, low self-control, and high impulsivity—official deterrence is highly ineffective in preventing crimes with immediate payoffs.[8] Thus, many factors go into the extent to which official sanctions can deter. As we have seen, even among those offenders who are in theory the most deterrable, official sanctions have little impact because their experience of not being caught weakens the value of deterrence.

The identification and understanding of the experiential effect had a profound influence on the interpretation of evidence regarding the impact of deterrence. Researchers saw that, to account for such an experiential effect, any estimation of the influence of perceived certainty or severity of punishment must control for previous experiences of engaging in unlawful behavior. The identification of the experiential effect was the primary contribution of the longitudinal studies of deterrence, but such studies faced even further criticism.

Longitudinal studies of deterrence provided a significant improvement over the cross-sectional studies that preceded this advanced methodology. However, such longitudinal studies typically involved designs in which

---

[7]Greg Pogarsky, KiDeuk Kim, and Raymond Paternoster, "Perceptual Change in the National Youth Survey: Lessons for Deterrence Theory and Offender Decision-Making," *Justice Quarterly* 22 (2005): 1–29.

[8]For reviews, see Stephen Brown, Finn Esbensen, and Gilbert Geis, *Criminology*, 8th ed. (Cincinnati: Anderson, 2012); Nancy Finley and Harold Grasmick, "Gender Roles and Social Control," *Sociological Spectrum* 5 (1985): 317–30; Harold Grasmick, Robert Bursik, and Karla Kinsey, "Shame and Embarrassment as Deterrents to Noncompliance with the Law: The Case of an Antilittering Campaign," *Environment and Behavior* 23 (1991): 233–51; Harold Grasmick, Brenda Sims Blackwell, and Robert Bursik, "Changes in the Sex Patterning of Perceived Threats of Sanctions," *Law and Society Review* 27 (1993): 679–705; Pamela Richards and Charles Tittle, "Gender and Perceived Chances of Arrest," *Social Forces* 59 (1981): 1182–99; George Loewenstein, Daniel Nagin, and Raymond Paternoster, "The Effect of Sexual Arousal on Expectations of Sexual Forcefulness," *Journal of Research in Crime and Delinquency* 34 (1997): 209–28; Toni Makkai and John Braithwaite, "The Dialects of Corporate Deterrence," *Journal of Research in Crime and Delinquency* 31 (1994): 347–73; Daniel Nagin and Raymond Paternoster, "Enduring Individual Differences and Rational Choice Theories of Crime," *Law and Society Review* 27 (1993): 467–96; Alex Piquero and Stephen Tibbetts, "Specifying the Direct and Indirect Effects of Low Self-Control and Situational Factors in Offenders' Decision Making: Toward a More Complete Model of Rational Offending," *Justice Quarterly* 13 (1996): 481–510; Raymond Paternoster and Sally Simpson, "Sanction Threats and Appeals to Morality: Testing a Rational Choice Model of Corporate Crime," *Law and Society Review* 30 (1996): 549–83; Daniel Nagin and Greg Pogarsky, "Integrating Celerity, Impulsivity, and Extralegal Sanction Threats into a Model of General Deterrence: Theory and Evidence," *Criminology* 39 (2001): 404–30; and Alex Piquero and Greg Pogarsky, "Beyond Stanford and Warr's Reconceptualization of Deterrence: Personal and Vicarious Experiences, Impulsivity, and Offending Behavior," *Journal of Research in Crime and Delinquency* 39 (2002): 153–86. For a recent review and a different explanation of these conclusions, see Greg Pogarsky, "Identifying 'Deterrable' Offenders: Implications for Research on Deterrence," *Justice Quarterly* 19 (2002): 431–52.

measures of perceptions of certainty and severity of punishment were collected at points in time that were separated by up to a year, including long stretches between when the crime was committed and when the offenders were asked about their perceptions of punishment. Psychological studies have clearly established that perceptions of the likelihood and severity of sanctions vary significantly from day to day, not to mention month to month and year to year.[9] Therefore, in the late 1980s and early 1990s, a new wave of deterrence research evolved, which asked study participants to estimate their likelihood of committing a criminal act in a given situation, as well as their immediate perceptions of the certainty and severity of punishment in the same situation. This wave of research was known as scenario (vignette) research.[10]

Scenario research (i.e., vignette design) was created to deal with the limitations of previous methodological strategies for studying the effects of deterrence on criminal offending, specifically, the criticism that individuals' perceptions of the certainty and severity of punishment change drastically from time to time and across different situations. The scenario method dealt with this criticism directly by providing a specific, realistic (albeit hypothetical) situation in which a person engages in a criminal act. Participants in the study are then asked to estimate the chance that they would engage in such activity in the given circumstances and to respond to questions regarding their perceptions of the risk of getting caught (i.e., certainty of punishment) and the degree of severity of punishment they expect.

Another important and valuable aspect of scenario research was that it promoted contemporaneous (i.e., instantaneous) responses about perceptions of risk and the severity of perceived sanctions. In comparison, previous studies (e.g., aggregate, cross-sectional, longitudinal) had always relied on either group or individual measures of perceptions over long periods of time. While some argue that intentions to commit a crime given a hypothetical situation are not accurate measures of what people would do in reality, studies have shown an extremely high correlation between what people report doing in a given scenario and what they would do in real life.[11] A recent review of criticisms of this research method showed that one weakness was that it did not allow respondents to offer their own perceptions of the risk and costs associated with each offense.[12] Despite such criticisms, the scenario method appears to be the most accurate that we have to date to estimate the effects of individuals' perceptions on the likelihood of their engaging in given criminal activity at a given point in time. This is something that the previous waves of deterrence research—aggregate, cross-sectional, and longitudinal studies—could not estimate.

---

[9]Icek Ajzen and Martin Fishbein, *Understanding Attitudes and Predicting Social Behavior* (Englewood Cliffs: Prentice Hall, 1980); Martin Fishbein and Icek Ajzen, *Belief, Attitude, Intention, and Behavior* (Reading: Addison-Wesley, 1975); Icek Ajzen and Martin Fishbein, "Attitude–Behavior Relations: A Theoretical Analysis and Review of Empirical Research," *Psychological Bulletin* 84 (1977): 888–918. For a recent review, see Pogarsky et al., "Perceptual Change."

[10]Loewenstein et al., "The Effect of Sexual Arousal"; Nagin and Paternoster, "Enduring Individual Differences"; Piquero and Tibbetts, "Specifying the Direct"; Paternoster and Simpson, "Sanction Threats"; Stephen G. Tibbetts, "Traits and States of Self-Conscious Emotions in Criminal Decision Making," in *Affect and Cognition in Criminal Decision Making*, ed. Jean-Louis Van Gelder, Henk Elffers, Danielle Reynald, and Daniel Nagin (London: Routledge, 2014), 221–38; Ronet Bachman, Raymond Paternoster, and Sally Ward, "The Rationality of Sexual Offending: Testing a Deterrence/Rational Choice Conception of Sexual Assault," *Law and Society Review* 26 (1992): 343–72; Harold Grasmick and Robert Bursik, "Conscience, Significant Others, and Rational Choice: Extending the Deterrence Model," *Law and Society Review* 24 (1990): 837–61; Harold Grasmick and Donald E. Green, "Legal Punishment, Social Disapproval, and Internalization as Inhibitors of Illegal Behavior," *Journal of Criminal Law and Criminology* 71 (1980): 325–35; Stephen Klepper and Daniel Nagin, "The Deterrent Effects of Perceived Certainty and Severity of Punishment Revisited, *Criminology* 27 (1989): 721–46; Stephen Tibbetts and Denise Herz, "Gender Differences in Students' Rational Decisions to Cheat," *Deviant Behavior* 18 (1996): 393–414; Stephen Tibbetts and David Myers, "Low Self-Control, Rational Choice, and Student Test Cheating," *American Journal of Criminal Justice* 23 (1999): 179–200; Stephen Tibbetts, "Shame and Rational Choice in Offending Decisions," *Criminal Justice and Behavior 24* (1997): 234–55.

[11]Ajzen and Fishbein, *Understanding Attitudes*; Donald Green, "Measures of Illegal Behavior in Individual Behavior in Individual-Level Deterrence Research," *Journal of Research in Crime and Delinquency* 26 (1989): 253–75; I. Ajzen, "From Intentions to Actions: A Theory of Planned Behavior," in *Action-Control: From Cognition to Behavior*, ed. Julius Kuhl and Jurgen Beckmann (New York: Springer, 1985), 11–39; Icek Ajzen and Martin Fishbein, "The Prediction of Behavioral Intentions in a Choice Situation," *Journal of Experimental Psychology* 5 (1969): 400–16.

[12]Jeffrey A. Bouffard, "Methodological and Theoretical Implications of Using Subject-Generated Consequences in Tests of Rational Choice Theory," *Justice Quarterly* 19 (2002): 747–71.

Ultimately, the studies using the scenario method showed that participants were more affected by perceptions of certainty and less so, albeit sometimes significantly, by perceptions of severity. These findings supported previous methods of estimating the effects of *formal* or *official deterrence*, meaning the deterrent effects of three general groups: law enforcement, courts, and corrections (i.e., prisons and probation or parole). Thus, the overall conclusion regarding the effects of official sanctions on individual decision making remained unaltered. However, one of the more interesting aspects of the scenario research method is that it helped solidify the importance of extralegal variables in deterring criminal behavior, variables that had been neglected by previous methods.

These extralegal or informal deterrence variables, which include any factors beyond the formal sanctions of police, courts, and corrections—such as employment, family, friends, or community—are typically known as informal or unofficial sanctions. The scenario research studies helped show that these informal sanctions provided most of the deterrent effect—if there was any. These findings coincided with the advent of a new model of deterrence, which became commonly known as *rational choice theory*.

Rational Choice Theory

Rational choice theory is a perspective that criminologists adapted from economists, who used it to explain a variety of individual decisions regarding a variety of behaviors. This framework emphasizes all the important factors that go into a person's decision to engage or not engage in a particular act. In terms of criminological research, the rational choice model emphasized both official or formal forms of deterrence, as well as the informal factors that influence individual decisions regarding criminal behavior. This represented a profound advance in the understanding of human behavior. After all, as studies showed, most individuals are more affected by informal factors than they are by official or formal factors.

Although there were several previous attempts to apply the rational choice model to the understanding of criminal activity, the most significant work, which brought rational choice theory into the mainstream of criminological research, was Cornish and Clarke's *The Reasoning Criminal: Rational Choice Perspectives on Offending* in 1986.[13] Furthermore, in 1988, Katz published his work *Seductions of Crime*, which, for the first time, placed an emphasis on the benefits (mostly the inherent physiological pleasure) of committing crime;[14] before Katz's publication, virtually no attention had been paid to the benefits of offending, let alone the fun that people feel when they engage in criminal behavior. A recent study showed that the publication of Cornish and Clarke's book, as well as the timing of other publications such as Katz's, led to an influx of criminological studies in the late 1980s to mid-1990s based on the rational choice model.[15]

These studies on rational choice showed that while official or formal sanctions tend to have some effect on individuals' decisions to commit crime, they almost always are relatively unimportant compared to extralegal or informal factors. The effects of people's perceptions of how much shame or loss of self-esteem they would experience, even if no one else found out that they committed the crime, was one of the most important variables in determining whether or not they would do so.[16] Additional evidence indicated that females were more influenced

[13]Derek Cornish and Ron Clarke, *The Reasoning Criminal: Rational Choice Perspectives on Offending* (New York: Springer-Verlag, 1986).

[14]Jack Katz, *Seductions of Crime* (New York: Basic Books, 1988).

[15]Stephen Tibbetts and Chris Gibson, "Individual Propensities and Rational Decision-Making: Recent Findings and Promising Approaches," in *Rational Choice and Criminal Behavior*, eds. Alex Piquero and Stephen Tibbetts (New York: Routledge, 2002), 3–24. See recent review by Jean-Louis Van Gelder, Henk Elffers, Danielle Reynald, and Daniel Nagin (eds.), *Affect and Cognition in Criminal Decision Making* (2014; London: Routledge).

[16]Grasmick and Bursik, "Conscience"; Pogarsky, "Identifying 'Deterrable' Offenders"; Tibbetts, "Shame and Rational Choice"; Nagin and Paternoster, "Enduring Individual Differences"; Tibbetts and Herz, "Gender Differences"; Tibbetts and Myers, "Low Self-Control"; Harold Grasmick, Brenda Sims Blackwell, and Robert Bursik, "Changes over Time in Gender Differences in Perceived Risk of Sanctions," *Law and Society Review* 27

▲ Image 3.1   There are both formal and informal elements of deterrence that influence decisions of whether or not to commit criminal behavior.

Source: © Brand X Pictures / Stockbyte / Thinkstock; © Stockbyte / Photodisc / Thinkstock; © Digital Vision / Photos.com / Thinkstock; © Jack Hollingsworth / Photodisc / Thinkstock; © Kim Steele / Photodisc / Thinkstock; © Darrin Klimek / Digital Vision / Thinkstock.

by the effects of shame and moral beliefs in this regard than were males.[17] Recent studies have shown that differing levels of certain personality traits, especially self-control and empathy, are likely the reason why males and females differ so much in engaging in criminal activity.[18] Finally, the influence of peers has a profound impact on individual perceptions of the pros and cons of offending, because seeing friends get away with crimes significantly decreases the perceived risk of punishment.[19]

Another area of rational choice research dealt with the influence that an individual's behavior would have on those around her or him. A recent review and test of perceived social disapproval showed that this was one of the most important variables in decisions to commit crime.[20] In addition to self-sanctions, such as feelings of shame and embarrassment, the perception of how loved ones, friends, and employers, would respond is perhaps the most important factor that goes into a person's decision to engage in criminal activity. These are the people we deal with every day, and some of them are the source of our livelihoods, so it should not be too surprising that our perceptions of how they will react strongly affect how we behave.

(1993): 679–705; Harold Grasmick, Robert Bursik, and Bruce Arneklev, "Reduction in Drunk Driving as a Response to Increased Threats of Shame, Embarrassment, and Legal Sanctions," *Criminology* 31 (1993): 41–67; Stephen Tibbetts, "Self-Conscious Emotions and Criminal Offending," *Psychological Reports* 93 (2004): 101–31.

[17]Tibbetts and Herz, "Gender Differences"; Grasmick et al., "Changes in the Sex Patterning"; Finley and Grasmick, "Gender Roles"; Pogarsky et al., "Perceptual Change"; Stephen Tibbetts, "Gender Differences in Students' Rational Decisions to Cheat," *Deviant Behavior* 18 (1997): 393–414.

[18]Nagin and Paternoster, "Enduring Individual Differences"; Grasmick et al., "Changes over Time"; Tibbetts, "Self-Conscious Emotions"; Tibbetts, "Traits and States."

[19]Pogarsky et al., "Perceptual Change."

[20]Pogarsky, "Identifying 'Deterrable' Offenders."

Perhaps the most important finding of rational choice research was that the expected benefits, particularly the pleasure offenders would get from offending, had one of the most significant effects on their decisions to offend. Many other conclusions have been made regarding the influence of extralegal or informal factors on criminal offending, but the ultimate conclusion that can be made is that these informal deterrent variables typically hold more influence on individual decision making regarding deviant activity than the official or formal factors that were emphasized by traditional Classical School models of behavior.

The rational choice model of criminal offending became the modern framework of deterrence. Official authorities acknowledged the influence of extralegal or informal factors, as seen in modern efforts to incorporate the family, employment, and community in rehabilitation efforts. Such efforts are highly consistent with the current understanding of the Classical School and rational choice frameworks, namely, that individuals are more deterred by the perceived impact of their actions on informal aspects of their lives than they are by the formal punishments they might face if they carry out illegal acts.

 ## Routine Activities Theory

▲ Image 3.2   Marcus Felson, 1947– , Rutgers University, author of routine activities theory.

Routine activities theory, or lifestyle theory, is another contemporary form of the Classical School framework in the sense that it assumes an offender who makes rational decisions. The general model of routine activities theory was originally presented by Lawrence Cohen and Marcus Felson in 1979.[21] This theoretical framework emphasized the presence of three factors that come together in time and place to create a high likelihood of crime and victimization. These three factors are: motivated offender(s), suitable target(s), and lack of guardianship. Overall, the theory is appropriately named, in the sense that it assumes that most crime occurs in the daily routine of people who happen to see—and then seize—tempting opportunities to commit crime. Studies tend to support this idea, as opposed to the idea that most offenders leave their home knowing they are going to commit a crime; the latter offenders are called *hydraulic* and are relatively rare compared to the opportunistic type.

Regarding the first factor noted as being important for increasing the likelihood of criminal activity—a motivated offender—the routine activities theory does not provide much insight. Rather, the model simply assumes that some individuals tend to be motivated and leaves it at that. Fortunately, we have many other theories that can fill this notable absence. The strength of routine activities theory lies in its elaboration of the other two aspects of a crime-prone environment: suitable targets and lack of guardianship.

Suitable targets can include a variety of situations. For example, a very suitable target can be a vacant house in the

[21]Lawrence Cohen and Marcus Felson, "Social Change and Crime Rates: A Routine Activities Approach," *American Sociological Review* 44 (1979): 214–41.

suburbs, which the family has left for summer vacation. Data clearly show that burglaries more than double in the summer when many families are on vacation. Other forms of suitable targets range from an unlocked car to a female alone at a shopping mall carrying a lot of cash and credit cards or purchased goods. Other likely targets are bars or other places that serve alcohol. Offenders have traditionally targeted drunk persons because they are less likely to be able to defend themselves, as illustrated by a history of lawbreakers rolling drunks for their wallets that extends back to the early part of the 20th century. This is only a short list of the many types of suitable targets that are available to motivated offenders in everyday life.

The third and final aspect of the routine activities model for increased likelihood of criminal activity is the lack of guardianship. Guardianship is often thought of as a police officer or security guard, which is often the case. There are many other forms of guardianship, however, such as owning a dog to protect a house, which studies demonstrate can be quite effective. Just having a car or house alarm constitutes a form of guardianship. Furthermore, the presence of an adult, neighbor, or teacher can effectively guard an area against crime. In fact, recent studies show that increased lighting in the area can prevent a significant amount of crime, with one study showing a 20% reduction in overall crime in areas randomly chosen to receive improved lighting as compared to control areas that did not.[22] Regardless of the type of guardianship, it is the absence of adequate guardianship that sets the stage for crime; on the other hand, each step taken toward protecting a place or person is likely to deter offenders from choosing the target in relation to others. Locations that have a high convergence of motivated offenders, suitable targets, and lack of guardianship are typically referred to as *hot spots*.

Perhaps the most supportive evidence for routine activities theory and hot spots was the study of 911 calls for service in Minneapolis, Minnesota.[23] This study examined all serious calls (as well as total calls) to police for a one-year period. Half of the top 10 places from which police were called were bars or locations where alcohol was served. As mentioned above, establishments that serve alcohol are often targeted by motivated offenders because of their high proportion of suitable targets. Furthermore, a number of bars tend to have a low level of guardianship in relation to the number of people they serve. Readers of this book may well relate to this situation. Most college towns and cities have certain drinking establishments that are known as being hot spots for crime.

Still, the Minneapolis hot spot study showed other types of establishments that made the top 10 rankings. These included places such as bus depots, convenience stores, run-down motels and hotels, downtown malls, and strip malls. The common theme linking these locations and the bars was the convergence of the three aspects described by routine activities theory as being predictive of criminal activity. Specifically, these places attracted motivated offenders, largely because they have a lot of vulnerable targets and lack sufficient levels of security or guardianship.

The routine activities framework has been applied in many contexts and places, many of them international.[24]

---

[22]David P. Farrington and Brandon C. Welsh, "Improved Street Lighting and Crime Prevention," *Justice Quarterly* 19 (2002): 313–43; Spiros Kitsinelisa and Georges Zissisa, "A Short Review on Lighting and Security," *Journal of Applied Security Research* 7 (2012): 341–353.

[23]Lawrence Sherman, Patrick R. Gartin, and Michael Buerger, "Hot Spots of Predatory Crime: Routine Activities and the Criminology of Place," *Criminology* 27 (1989): 27–56.

[24]Anthony A. Braga, Andrew V. Papachristos, and David M. Hureau, "The Effects of Hot Spots Policing on Crime: An Updated Systematic Review and Meta-Analysis," *Justice Quarterly* 29 (2012): 1–31; Jon Gunnar Bernburg and Thorolfur Thorlindsson, "Routine Activities in Social Context: A Closer Look at the Role of Opportunity in Deviant Behavior," *Justice Quarterly* 18 (2001): 543–67. See also Richard Bennett, "Routine Activity: A Cross-National Assessment of a Criminological Perspective," *Social Forces* 70 (1991): 147–63; James Hawdon, "Deviant Lifestyles: The Social Control of Routine Activities," *Youth and Society* 28 (1996): 162–88; James L. Massey, Marvin Krohn, and Lisa Bonati, "Property Crime and the Routine Activities of Individuals," *Journal of Research in Crime and Delinquency* 26 (1989): 378–400; Terrance Miethe, Mark Stafford, and J. Scott Long, "Social Differences in Criminological Victimization: A Test of Routine Activities/Lifestyles Theories," *American Sociological Review* 52 (1987): 184–94; Elizabeth Mustaine and Richard Tewksbury, "Predicting Risks of Larceny Theft Victimization: A Routine Activity Analysis Using Refined Lifestyle Measures," *Criminology* 36 (1998): 829–57; D. Wayne Osgood, Janet Wilson, Patrick M. O'Malley, Jerald Bachman, and Lloyd Johnston, "Routine Activities and Individual

Figure 3.1   Routine activities theory

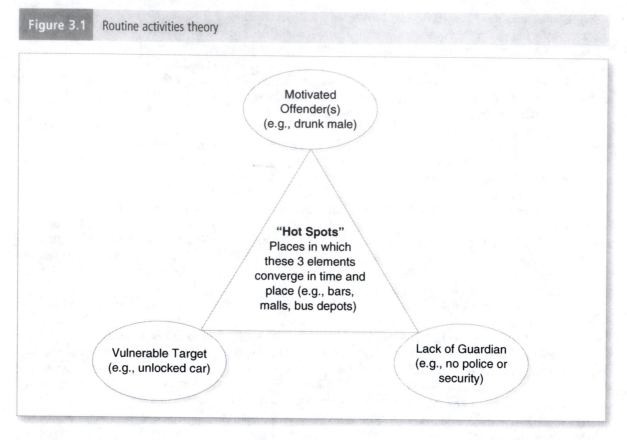

Modern applications of routine activities theory include geographic profiling, which uses satellite positioning systems in perhaps the most attractive and marketable aspect of criminological research in contemporary times. Essentially, such research incorporates computer software for global positioning systems (GPS) to identify the exact location of every crime that takes place in a given jurisdiction. Such information has been used to solve or predict various crimes, to the point where serial killers have been caught by triangulating the sites where the victims were found to show the most likely place where the killer lived.

Some theorists have proposed a theoretical model based on individuals' lifestyles, which has a large overlap with routine activities theory, as shown in studies previously reviewed.[25] It only makes sense that a person who lives a more risky lifestyle, for example, by frequenting bars or living in a high-crime area, will be at more risk because she or he is close to various hot spots as identified by routine activities theory. Although some criminologists label this phenomenon a lifestyle perspective, it is virtually synonymous with the routine activities model because such lifestyles incorporate the same conceptual and causal factors in routine activities.

Deviant Behavior," *American Sociological Review* 61 (1996): 635–55; Dennis Roncek and Pamela Maier, "Bars, Blocks, and Crimes Revisited: Linking the Theory of Routine Activities to the Empiricism of Hot Spots," *Criminology* 29 (1991): 725–53; and Robert Sampson and John Wooldredge, "Linking the Micro- and Macro-Level Dimensions of Lifestyle-Routine Activity and Opportunity Models of Predatory Victimization," *Journal of Quantitative Criminology* 3 (1987): 371–93.

[25]Hawdon, "Deviant Lifestyles"; Sampson and Wooldredge, "Linking the Micro"; Brown et al., *Criminology.*

Policy Implications

There are numerous policy implications that can be derived from the theories and scientific findings in this section. Here we will concentrate on some of the most important policies. First, we look at the policy of broken windows, which has many assumptions similar to those of the routine activities and rational choice theories. The broken windows perspective emphasizes the need for police to crack down on minor offenses to reduce major crimes.[26] Although many cities (e.g., New York and Los Angeles) have claimed reductions in serious crimes by using this theory, crime was reduced by the same amount across most U.S. cities during the same time (the late 1990s to mid 2000s).

Other policies derived from the theories in this section include the *three-strikes-you're-out* policy, which assumes that offenders will make a rational choice not to commit future offenses because they could go to prison for life if they commit three felonies; the negatives certainly outweigh the expected benefits for the third crime. Remember Beccaria's view that for deterrence to be extremely effective, punishment must be swift, certain, and severe. Where does the three-strikes policy fall in this equation? The bottom line is that it is much more severe than it is swift or certain. Given Beccaria's philosophy (see Section II), this policy will probably not work because it is not certain or swift. However, it is severe in the sense that a person can be sentenced to life if she or he commits three felony offenses over time.

A controversial three-strikes law was passed by voter initiative in California, and other states have adopted similar types of laws.[27] It sends third-time felons to prison for the rest of their lives regardless of the nature of that third felony. California first requires convictions for two *strikable* felonies, crimes like murder, rape, aggravated assault, burglary, drug offenses, and so on. Then, any third felony can trigger a life sentence. The stories about people going to prison for the rest of their lives for stealing pieces of pizza or shoplifting DVDs, while rare, are quite true.

The question we are concerned with here is, does the three-strikes policy work? As a specific deterrent, the answer is clearly yes; offenders who are in prison for the rest of their lives cannot commit more crimes on the streets. In that regard, three-strikes works very well. Some people feel, however, that laws like three-strikes need to have a general deterrent effect to be considered successful, meaning that this law should deter everyone from engaging in multiple crimes. So, is three-strikes a general deterrent? Unfortunately, there are no easy answers to this question because laws vary from state to state, the laws are used at different rates across the counties in a given state, and so forth.

There is at least some consensus in the literature, however. One study from California suggests that three-strikes has reduced crime,[28] but the remaining studies show that three-strikes either has had no effect on crime or has actually increased crime.[29] How could three-strikes increase crime? The authors attributed the increase in homicide following the enactment of three-strikes laws to the possibility that third-strikers have an incentive to kill victims and any witnesses in an effort to avoid apprehension. Although this argument is tentative, it may be true.[30]

---

[26]James Q. Wilson and George Kelling, "Broken Windows: The Police and Neighborhood Safety," *Atlantic Monthly* (March 1982): 29–38.

[27]David Shichor and Dale K. Sechrest, eds., *Three Strikes and You're Out: Vengeance as Social Policy* (Thousand Oaks: Sage, 1996).

[28]Joanna M. Shepherd, "Fear of the First Strike: The Full Deterrent Effect of California's Two- and Three-Strikes Legislation," *Journal of Legal Studies* 31 (2002): 159–201.

[29]See Lisa Stolzenberg and Stewart J. D'Alessio, "Three Strikes and You're Out: The Impact of California's New Mandatory Sentencing Law on Serious Crime Rates," *Crime and Delinquency* 43 (1997): 457–69; and Mike Males and Dan Macallair, "Striking Out: The Failure of California's 'Three-Strikes and You're Out Law," *Stanford Law and Policy Review* 11 (1999): 65–72.

[30]Steven N. Durlauf and Daniel S. Nagin, "Imprisonment and Crime: Can Both Be Reduced?," *Criminology and Public Policy* 10 (2011): 13–54; Thomas B. Marvell and Carlisle E. Moody, "The Lethal Effects of Three-Strikes Laws," *Journal of Legal Studies* 30 (2001): 89–106. See also Tomislav Kovandzic, John J. Sloan III, and Lynne M. Vieraitis, "Unintended Consequences of Politically Popular Sentencing Policy: The Homicide-Promoting Effects of 'Three Strikes' in U.S. Cities (1980–1999)," *Criminology and Public Policy* 1 (2002): 399–424. For a review of empirical evaluations of three-strikes laws, see John Worrall, "The Effect of Three-Strikes Legislation on Serious Crime in California," *Journal of Criminal Justice* 32 (2004): 283–96.

This is just one of the many policy implications that can be derived from this section. We expect that readers of this book will come up with many more policy implications, but it is vital to examine the empirical literature to determine these policies' usefulness in reducing criminal activity. Other policy implications of the theories and findings described in this section will be discussed in the final section of this book.

In a strategy that is also strongly based on the rational choice model, a number of judges have started using shaming strategies to deter offenders from recidivating.[31] They have ordered everything from publicly posting pictures of men arrested for soliciting prostitutes to forcing offenders to walk down main streets of towns wearing signs that announce that they've committed crimes. These are just two examples of an increasing trend that emphasizes the informal or community factors required to deter crime. Unfortunately, to date, there have been virtually no empirical evaluations of the effectiveness of such shaming penalties, although studies of expected shame for doing an act consistently show a deterrent effect.[32]

 ## Conclusion

This section reviewed the more recent forms of classical and deterrence theory, such as rational choice theory, which emphasizes the effects of informal sanctions (e.g., family, friends, employment) and the benefits and costs of offending; and a framework called routine activities theory, which explains why victimization tends to occur far more often in certain locations (i.e., hot spots) due to the convergence of three key elements in time and place—motivated offender(s), vulnerable target(s), and lack of guardianship—which create attractive opportunities for crime as individuals go about their everyday activities. The common element across all of these perspectives is the underlying assumption that individuals are rational beings who have free will and thus choose their behavior based on assessment of a given situation, such as by weighing possible risks versus potential payoffs. Although the studies examined in this section lend support to many of the assumptions and propositions of the classical framework, it is also clear that there is a lot more involved in explaining criminal human behavior than the individual decision making that goes on before a person engages in rule violation. After all, human beings, especially chronic offenders, are often not rational and often do things spontaneously without considering the potential risks beforehand. So, despite the use of the classical and neoclassical models in most systems of justice in the modern world, such theoretical models of criminal activity largely fell out of favor among experts in the mid-19th century, when an entirely new paradigm of human behavior became dominant. This new perspective became known as the Positive School, and we will discuss the origin and development of this paradigm in the following section.

Section Summary

- After 100 years of neglect by criminologists, the classical and deterrence models experienced a rebirth in the late 1960s.
- The seminal studies in the late 1960s and early 1970s were largely based on aggregate and group rates of crime, as well as group rates of certainty and severity of punishment, which showed that levels of actual punishment and especially certainty of punishment were associated with lower levels of crime.
- A subsequent wave of deterrence research, cross-sectional surveys, which were collected at one time, supported previous findings that perceptions of certainty of punishment had a strong, inverse association with offending, whereas findings regarding severity were mixed.

---

[31]Alex Piquero and Stephen Tibbetts, eds., *Rational Choice and Criminal Behavior* (New York: Routledge, 2002).

[32]Tibbetts, "Gender Differences."

- Longitudinal studies showed that much of the observed association between perceived levels of punishment and offending could be explained by the experiential effect, which is the phenomenon whereby behavior, rather than deterrence, affects perceptions (i.e., as opposed to perceptions affecting behavior).
- Scenario studies addressed the experiential effect by supplying a specific context, that is, through presenting a detailed vignette and then asking what subjects would do in that specific circumstance and what their perceptions of the event were.
- Rational choice theory emphasizes not only the formal and official aspects of criminal sanctions but also the informal or unofficial aspects, such as family and community.
- Whereas traditional classical deterrence theory ignored the benefits of offending, rational choice theory emphasizes them, such as the thrill offending produces, as well as the social benefits of committing crime.
- Routine activities theory provides a theoretical model that explains why certain places have far more crime than others and why some locations have hundreds of calls to police each year, whereas others have none.
- Lifestyle theories of crime reveal that the way people live may predispose them to both crime and victimization.
- Routine activities theory and the lifestyle perspective are becoming key in one of the most modern approaches to predicting and reducing crime and victimization. Specifically, GPS and other forms of geographical mapping of crime events have contributed to an elevated level of research and attention given to these theoretical models, due to their importance in specifically documenting where crime occurs and, in some cases, predicting where future crimes will occur.
- All of the theoretical models and studies reviewed in this section were based on classical and deterrence models, which assume that individuals consider the potential benefits and costs of punishment and then make their decisions about whether or not to engage in the criminal act.

KEY TERMS

cross-sectional studies

experiential effect

rational choice theory

routine activities
   theory (lifestyle theory)

scenario (vignette) research

DISCUSSION QUESTIONS

1. Do you think it was good that the deterrence model was reborn, or do you think it should have been left for dead? Explain why you feel this way.

2. Considering the aggregate level of research in deterrence studies, do you find such studies valid? Explain why or why not.

3. In comparing longitudinal studies to scenario (vignette) studies, which do you think offers the most valid method for examining individual perceptions regarding the costs and benefits of committing offenses? Explain why you feel this way.

4. Can you relate to the experiential effect? If you can't, do you know someone whose behavior seems to resemble that which results from this phenomenon? Make sure to articulate what the experiential effect is.

5. With rational choice theory in mind, consider whether you would rather be subject to formal sanctions if none of your family, friends, or employers found out that you had engaged in shoplifting, or face the informal sanctions but receive no formal punishment (other than being arrested) for such a crime. Explain your decision.

6. As a teenager, did you or family or friends get a rush out of doing things that were deviant or wrong? If so, did that feeling seem to outweigh any legal or informal consequences that might have deterred you or people you knew?

7. With routine activities theory in mind, consider which places, residences, or areas of your hometown fit the idea that certain places have more crime than others (i.e., are hot spots)? Explain how you, friends, or others (including police) in your community deal with such areas. Does it work?

8. Which of the three elements of routine activities theory do you feel is the most important to address in efforts to reduce crime in the hot spots?

9. What lifestyle characteristics lead to the highest offending or victimizing rates? List at least five factors that lead to such propensities.

10. Find at least one study that uses mapping and geographical (GPS) data, and report the conclusions of that study. Do the findings and conclusions fit the routine activities theoretical framework? Why or why not?

11. What types of policy strategies derived from rational choice and routine activities theories do you think would be most effective? Least effective?

WEB RESOURCES

Modern Testing of Deterrence

http://www.deathpenaltyinfo.org/

Rational Choice Theory

http://www.answers.com/topic/rational-choice-theory-criminology

Routine Activities and Lifestyle Theory

http://www.popcenter.org/learning/pam/help/theory.cfm

READING 4

In this reading, Anthony Braga and David Weisburd present a review and analysis of various programs that emphasized reducing crime activity in the following areas: gang- or group-involved violence, repeat offenders, and the drug market. They carried out a systematic review to examine the evidence found from such strategies of focused deterrence, applying an advanced form of statistical analysis, called a meta-analysis, to combine the findings from numerous studies. Their findings contribute to our knowledge of the effectiveness of focused deterrence strategies for dealing with crime, especially in certain situations.

The Effects of Focused Deterrence Strategies on Crime

A Systematic Review and Meta-analysis of the Empirical Evidence

Anthony A. Braga[1,2] and David L. Weisburd[3,4]

 ## Introduction

Deterrence theory posits that crimes can be prevented when the costs of committing the crime are perceived by the offender to outweigh the benefits (Gibbs 1975; Zimring and Hawkins 1973). Most discussions of the deterrence mechanism distinguish between "general" and "special" deterrence (Cook 1980). General deterrence is the idea that the general population is dissuaded from committing crime when it sees that punishment necessarily follows the commission of a crime. Special deterrence involves punishment administered to criminals with the intent to discourage them from committing crimes in the future. Much of the literature evaluating deterrence focuses on the effect of changing certainty, swiftness, and severity of punishment associated with certain acts on the prevalence of those crimes (see, e.g., Apel and Nagin 2011; Blumstein, Cohen, and Nagin 1978; Cook 1980; Nagin 1998; Paternoster 1987).

In recent years, scholars have begun to argue that police interventions provide an effective approach for gaining both special and general deterrence against crime. A series of experimental and quasi-experimental studies has shown that the police can be effective in preventing crime (Braga 2001, 2005; Skogan and Frydl 2004; Weisburd and Eck 2004) and that such crime prevention benefits are not offset by displacement of crime to areas near to police interventions (Braga 2001; Weisburd et al. 2006). Durlauf and Nagin have drawn from this literature to argue that "(i)ncreasing the visibility of the police by hiring more officers and by allocating existing officers in ways that heighten the perceived risk of apprehension consistently seem to have substantial marginal deterrent effects" (2011:14). Indeed, they conclude that crime prevention

SOURCE: Anthony A. Braga and David L. Weisburd, "The Effects of Focused Deterrence Strategies on Crime: A Systematic Review and Meta-analysis of the Empirical Evidence," *Journal of Research in Crime and Delinquency* 49 (2012): 323–58 (Sage).

[1]Rutgers University, Newark, NJ, USA

[2]Harvard University, Cambridge, MA, USA

[3]Hebrew University Law School, Jerusalem, Israel

[4]George Mason University, Fairfax, VA, USA

in the United States would be improved by "shifting resources from imprisonment to policing" (2011:9–10).

A recent innovation in policing that capitalizes on the growing evidence of the effectiveness of police deterrence strategies is the "focused deterrence" framework, often referred to as "pulling-levers policing" (Kennedy 1997, 2008). Pioneered in Boston as a problem-oriented policing project to halt serious gang violence during the 1990s (Kennedy, Piehl, and Braga 1996), the focused deterrence framework has been applied in many U.S. cities through federally sponsored violence prevention programs such as the Strategic Alternatives to Community Safety Initiative and Project Safe Neighborhoods (Dalton 2002). Focused deterrence strategies honor core deterrence ideas, such as increasing risks faced by offenders, while finding new and creative ways of deploying traditional and nontraditional law enforcement tools to do so, such as directly communicating incentives and disincentives to targeted offenders (Kennedy 1997, 2008). The basic principles of the focused deterrence approach have also been applied to overt drug market problems (Kennedy 2009) and repeat offending by substance-abusing probationers (Hawken and Kleiman 2009) with positive crime control gains reported.

The evaluation of the best-known focused deterrence strategy, Boston's Operation Ceasefire (Braga et al. 2001; Piehl et al. 2003), has been greeted with both a healthy dose of skepticism (Fagan 2002; Rosenfeld, Fornango, and Baumer 2005) and some support (Cook and Ludwig 2006; Morgan and Winship 2007). The National Academy of Sciences' recent report on firearms data and research concluded that the Ceasefire quasi-experimental evaluation was "compelling" in associating the intervention with a 63 percent reduction in youth homicide in Boston (Wellford, Pepper, and Petrie 2005:10); however, the report also stated that the lack of a randomized controlled trial left some doubt over how much of the decline was due to Ceasefire relative to other rival causal factors.

 ## Method

Our examination of the effects of focused deterrence strategies on crime followed the systematic review protocols and conventions of the Campbell Collaboration. It is important to note here that, given limited space, this article focuses on our examination of the crime reduction benefits associated with focused deterrence strategies. We encourage readers interested in a broader range of program operation and evaluation issues to consult our Campbell review (Braga and Weisburd 2011).

Meta-analysis is a method of systematic reviewing and was designed to synthesize empirical relationships across studies, such as the effects of a specific crime prevention intervention on criminal offending behavior (Wilson 2001). Meta-analysis uses specialized statistical methods to analyze the relationships between findings and study features (Lipsey and Wilson 1993; Wilson 2001). The "effect size statistic" is the index used to represent the findings of each study in the overall meta-analysis of study findings and represents the strength and direction (positive or negative) of the relationship observed in a particular study (e.g., the size of the treatment effect found). The "mean effect size" represents the average effect of treatment on the outcome of interest across all eligible studies in a particular area and is estimated by calculating a mean that is weighted by the precision of the effect size for each individual study.

Criteria for Inclusion and Exclusion of Studies in the Review

To be eligible for this review, interventions had to be considered a focused deterrence strategy as described above. Only studies that used comparison group designs involving before and after measures were eligible for the main analyses of this review. The comparison group study had to be either a randomized controlled trial or a quasi-experimental evaluation with comparison groups (Campbell and Stanley 1966; Cook and Campbell 1979). The units of analysis could be areas, such as cities, neighborhoods, or police beats, or individuals. Eligible studies had to measure the effects of the focused deterrence intervention on officially recorded levels of crime at places or crime by individuals. Appropriate crime measures included crime incident reports, citizen emergency calls for service, and arrest data. Particular attention was paid to studies that measured crime displacement effects and diffusion of crime control benefit effects (Clarke and Weisburd 1994; Reppetto 1976). The review considered all forms of displacement and diffusion reported by the studies.

Search Strategies for Identification of Studies

Several strategies were used to perform an exhaustive search for literature fitting the eligibility criteria. First, a keyword search[1] was performed on 15 online abstract databases.[2] Second, we reviewed the bibliographies of past narrative and empirical reviews of literature that examined the effectiveness of focused deterrence programs (Kennedy 2008; Skogan and Frydl 2004; Wellford et al. 2005). Third, we performed forward searches for works that have cited seminal focused deterrence studies (Braga et al. 2001; Kennedy et al. 1996; McGarrell et al. 2006). Fourth, we searched bibliographies of narrative reviews of police crime prevention efforts (Braga 2008a; Sherman 2002; Weisburd and Eck 2004) and past completed Campbell systematic reviews of police crime prevention efforts (Braga 2007; Mazerolle, Soole, and Rombouts 2007; Weisburd et al. 2008). Fifth, we performed hand searches of leading journals in the field.[3] These searches were all completed between May 2010 and September 2010.

After finishing the above searches and reviewing the studies as described later, we e-mailed the list of studies meeting our eligibility criteria in September 2010 to leading criminology and criminal justice scholars knowledgeable in the area of focused deterrence strategies. These 90 scholars were defined as those who authored at least one study that appeared on our inclusion list, anyone involved with the National Academy of Sciences reviews of police research (Skogan and Frydl 2004) and firearms research (Wellford et al. 2005), and other leading scholars identified by the authors (available upon request). This helped us identify unpublished studies that did not appear in conventional databases or other reviews. Finally, we consulted with an information retrieval specialist at the outset of our review and at points along the way in order to ensure that we used appropriate search strategies to identify the studies meeting the criteria of this review.[4]

Statistical Procedures and Conventions

As a preliminary examination of the effects of focused deterrence strategies on crime, we used a vote counting procedure. In this rudimentary approach, each study metaphorically casts a vote for or against the effectiveness of treatment. In our closer examination of program effects, meta-analyses were used to determine the size, direction, and statistical significance of the overall impact of focused deterrence strategies on crime by weighting program effect sizes based on the variance of the effect size and the study sample size (Lipsey and Wilson 2001). We used the standardized mean difference effect size (also known as Cohen's d; see Cohen 1988; Rosenthal 1994) and employed the Effect Size Calculator, developed by David B. Wilson and available on the Campbell Collaboration's Web site, to calculate standardized mean difference effect sizes for reported outcomes in each study. We then used Biostat's Comprehensive Meta Analysis Version 2.2 to conduct the meta-analysis of effect sizes.

One problem in conducting meta-analyses in crime and justice is that investigators often do not prioritize outcomes examined. This is common in studies in the social

---

[1]The following search terms were used: focused deterrence, deterring violent offenders, pulling levers AND police, problem-oriented policing, police AND repeat offenders, police AND gangs, police AND guns, gang violence prevention, strategic gang enforcement, crackdowns AND gangs, enforcement swamping, and drug market intervention.

[2]The following 15 databases were searched: Criminal Justice Periodical Index, Sociological Abstracts, Social Science Abstracts (SocialSciAbs), Social Science Citation Index, Arts and Humanities Search (AHSearch), Criminal Justice Abstracts, National Criminal Justice Reference Service (NCJRS) Abstracts, Educational Resources Information Clearinghouse (ERIC), Legal Resource Index, Dissertation Abstracts, Government Publications Office, Monthly Catalog (GPO Monthly), Google Scholar, Online Computer Library Center (OCLC) SearchFirst, CINCH data search, and C2 SPECTR (The Campbell Collaboration Social, Psychological, Educational and Criminological Trials Register).

[3]These journals were: *Criminology, Criminology & Public Policy, Justice Quarterly, Journal of Research in Crime and Delinquency, Journal of Criminal Justice, Police Quarterly, Policing, Police Practice and Research, British Journal of Criminology, Journal of Quantitative Criminology, Crime & Delinquency, Journal of Criminal Law and Criminology,* and *Policing and Society.* Hand searches covered 1979 to 2010.

[4]Ms. Phyllis Schultze of the Gottfredson Library at the Rutgers University School of Criminal Justice executed the initial abstract search and was consulted throughout on our search strategies.

sciences in which authors view good practice as demanding that all relevant outcomes be reported. However, the lack of prioritization of outcomes in a study raises the question of how to derive an overall effect of treatment. For example, the reporting of one significant result may reflect a type of "creaming" in which the authors focus on one significant finding and ignore the less positive results of other outcomes. But authors commonly view the presentation of multiple findings as a method for identifying the specific contexts in which the treatment is effective. When the number of such comparisons is small and therefore unlikely to affect the error rates for specific comparisons such an approach is often valid.

We analyze the studies using three approaches. The first is conservative in the sense that it combines all reported outcomes reported into an overall average effect size statistic. The second represents the largest effect reported in the studies and gives an upper bound to our findings. It is important to note that in some of the studies with more than one outcome reported, the largest outcome reflected what authors thought would be the most direct program effect. Finally, we present the smallest effect size for each study. This approach is the most conservative and likely underestimates the effect of focused deterrence on crime. We use it here primarily to provide a lower bound to our findings.

 Findings

Search strategies in the systematic review process generate a large number of citations and abstracts for potentially relevant studies that must be closely screened to determine whether the studies meet the eligibility criteria (Farrington and Petrosino 2001). The screening process yields a much smaller pool of eligible studies for inclusion in the review. The four search strategies produced 2,473 distinct abstracts. The contents of these abstracts were reviewed for any suggestion of an evaluation of focused deterrence interventions. About 93 distinct abstracts were selected for closer review and the full-text reports, journal articles, and books for these abstracts were acquired and carefully assessed to determine whether the interventions involved focused

deterrence strategies and whether the studies used randomized controlled trial designs or nonrandomized quasi-experimental designs. Eleven eligible studies were identified and included in this review:

1. Operation Ceasefire in Boston, Massachusetts (Braga et al. 2001)

2. Indianapolis Violence Reduction Partnership in Indianapolis, Indiana (McGarrell et al. 2006)

3. Operation Peacekeeper in Stockton, California (Braga 2008b)

4. Project Safe Neighborhoods in Lowell, Massachusetts (Braga et al. 2008)

5. Cincinnati Initiative to Reduce Violence in Cincinnati, Ohio (Engel, Corsaro, and Skubak Tillyer 2010)

6. Operation Ceasefire in Newark, New Jersey (Boyle et al. 2010)

7. Operation Ceasefire in Los Angeles, California (Tita et al. 2004)

8. Project Safe Neighborhoods in Chicago, Illinois (Papachristos, Meares, and Fagan 2007)

9. Drug Market Intervention in Nashville, Tennessee (Corsaro and McGarrell 2009)

10. Drug Market Intervention in Rockford, Illinois (Corsaro, Brunson, and McGarrell Forthcoming)

11. Hawaii Opportunity with Probation Enforcement in Honolulu, Hawaii (Hawken and Kleiman 2009)

The 11 selected studies examined focused deterrence interventions that were implemented in small, medium, and large U.S. cities. Four of the eligible evaluations (Cincinnati, Honolulu, Nashville, and Newark) were not published at the time the review of abstracts was completed.[5] All 11 evaluations were released after 2000 and 8 were completed after 2007. Six studies evaluated the crime reduction effects of focused deterrence strategies on serious violence generated by street gangs or criminally active

---

[5]During the development of this report, the Newark study was accepted for publication at *Justice Research and Policy* and the Nashville study was accepted for publication at *Evaluation Review*.

street groups (Boston, Cincinnati, Indianapolis, Los Angeles, Lowell, and Stockton). Two studies evaluated strategies focused on reducing crime driven by street-level drug markets (Nashville and Rockford), and three evaluated crime reduction strategies that were focused on individual repeat offenders (Chicago, Honolulu, and Newark).

Ten eligible studies used quasi-experimental designs to analyze the impact of focused deterrence strategies on crime. Seven evaluations used quasi-experimental designs with nonequivalent comparison groups (Boston, Cincinnati, Indianapolis, Lowell, Nashville, Rockford, and Stockton). The comparison units used in these evaluations were selected based on naturally occurring conditions, such as other cities or within-city areas that did not receive treatment, rather than through careful matching or randomization procedures to ensure comparability with treatment units. Two evaluations used quasi-experimental designs with near-equivalent comparison groups created through matching techniques (Chicago and Newark). The Los Angeles evaluation used a quasi-experimental design that included both nonequivalent and near-equivalent comparison groups; for the Los Angeles study, we included only the effects from the more rigorous matched comparison group analysis in our meta-analysis. Only one randomized controlled trial, the evaluation of the HOPE program in Honolulu, was identified. Table 1 provides a brief summary of the treatments, units of analysis, research designs, and results reported by the 11 eligible studies.

Three studies examined possible immediate spatial crime displacement and diffusion of crime control benefits that may have been generated by the focused deterrence interventions (Los Angeles, Nashville, and Newark). The Los Angeles study also examined the criminal behavior of rival gangs socially connected to the targeted gang. Only one study noted potential threats to the integrity of the treatment. Tita et al. (2004) reported that the Los Angeles intervention was not fully implemented as planned. The implementation of the Ceasefire program in the Boyle Heights neighborhood of Los Angeles was negatively affected by the well-known Ramparts LAPD police corruption scandal and a lack of ownership of the intervention by the participating agencies.

The basic findings of our review are very positive. Of the 11 eligible studies, 10 reported strong and statistically significant crime reductions associated with the approach. Nonetheless, we are concerned with the lack of rigorous randomized experimental evaluations of this promising approach. While the biases in quasi-experimental research are not clear (e.g., Campbell and Boruch 1975; Wilkinson and Task Force on Statistical Inference 1999), recent reviews in crime and justice suggest that weaker research designs often lead to more positive outcomes (e.g., see Weisburd, Lum, and Petrosino 2001; Welsh et al. 2011). This does not mean that nonexperimental studies cannot be of high quality, but only that there is evidence that non-experimental designs in crime and justice are likely to overstate outcomes as contrasted with randomized experiments. In his review of situational crime prevention evaluations, Guerette (2009) finds that the conclusions of randomized evaluations were generally consistent with the majority conclusion of the nonrandomized evaluations. While our vote counting review is consistent with Guerette's (2009) conclusion, our calculated effect sizes reveal that less rigorous focused deterrence evaluation designs were associated with stronger reported effects. As such, we think that caution should be used in drawing conclusions regarding population effect sizes for the pulling levers intervention.

At the same time, the effects observed in the studies reviewed were often very large, and such effect sizes are evidenced as well in those studies using strong comparison groups (e.g., Papachristos et al. 2007) and in the sole randomized controlled trial (Hawken and Kleiman 2009). Our review provides strong empirical evidence for the crime prevention effectiveness of focused deterrence strategies. Even if we assume that the effects observed contain some degree of upward bias, it appears that the overall impact of such programs is noteworthy. These findings are certainly encouraging and point to the promises of this approach.

We certainly believe that the positive outcomes of the present studies indicate that additional experimental evaluations, however difficult and costly, are warranted. The potential barriers are real, especially in regard to identifying valid treatment and comparison areas. But existing evidence is strong enough to warrant a large investment in multisite experiments (Weisburd and Taxman 2000). Such experiments could solve the problem of small numbers of places in single jurisdictions and would also allow for examination of variation in effectiveness across contexts.

Despite our concerns over the lack of randomized experiments, we believe that the findings of eligible focused deterrence evaluations fit well within existing research suggesting that deterrence-based strategies, if applied correctly, can reduce crime (Apel and Nagin 2011). The focused deterrence approach seems to have the desirable characteristic of altering offenders' perceptions of sanction risk. Our findings are also supported by the growing body of scientific evidence that suggests police departments, and their partners, can be effective in controlling specific crime problems when they engage a variety of partners, and tailor an array of tactics to address underlying criminogenic conditions and dynamics (Braga 2008a; Weisburd and Eck 2004). Indeed, our study suggests that Durlauf and Nagin (2011) are correct in their conclusion that imprisonment and crime can both be reduced through the noteworthy marginal deterrent effects generated by allocating police officers, and their criminal justice partners, in ways that heighten the perceived risk of apprehension.

While the results of this review are very supportive of deterrence principles, we believe that other complementary crime control mechanisms are at work in the focused deterrence strategies described here that need to be highlighted and better understood (see Weisburd 2011). In Durlauf and Nagin's (2011) article, the focus is on the possibilities for increasing perceived risk and deterrence by increasing police presence. Although this conclusion is warranted by the data and represents an important component of the causal mechanisms that have increased the effectiveness of focused deterrence strategies, we believe it misses an important part of the story. In the focused deterrence approach, the emphasis is not only on increasing the risk of offending but also on decreasing opportunity structures for violence, deflecting offenders away from crime, increasing the collective efficacy of communities, and increasing the legitimacy of police actions. Indeed, we suspect that the large effects we observe come precisely from the multifaceted ways in which this program influences criminals.

In closing, we think it is important to recognize that focused deterrence strategies are a very recent addition to the existing scholarly literature on crime control and prevention strategies. While the evaluation evidence needs to be strengthened and the theoretical underpinnings of the approach needs further refinement, we believe that jurisdictions suffering from gang violence, overt drug markets, and repeat offender problems should add focused deterrence strategies to their existing portfolio of prevention and control interventions. The existing evidence suggests these new approaches to crime prevention and control generate noteworthy crime reductions.

 # References

Apel, R. and D. Nagin. 2011. "General Deterrence: A Review of Recent Evidence." Pp. 411–36 in *Crime and Public Policy*, edited by J. Q. Wilson and J. Petersilia. New York: Oxford University Press.

Blalock, H. 1979. *Social Statistics*. Rev. 2nd ed. New York: McGraw-Hill

Blumstein, A., J. Cohen, and D. Nagin, eds. 1978. *Deterrence and Incapacitation: Estimating the Effects of Criminal Sanctions on Crime Rates*. Washington, DC: National Academy of Sciences.

Boyle, D. J., J. L. Lanterman, J. E. Pascarella, and C.-C. Cheng. 2010. *The Impact of Newark's Operation Ceasefire on Trauma Center Gunshot Wound Admissions*. Newark, NJ: Violence Institute of New Jersey, University of Medicine and Dentistry of New Jersey.

Boyum, D. A., J. P. Caulkins, and M. A. R. Kleiman. 2011. "Drugs, Crime, and Public Policy." Pp. 368–410 in *Crime and Public Policy*, edited by J. Q. Wilson and J. Petersilia. New York: Oxford University Press.

Braga, A. A. 2001. "The Effects of Hot Spots Policing on Crime." *Annals of the American Academy of Political and Social Science* 578:104–25.

Braga, A. A. 2005. "Hot Spots Policing and Crime Prevention: A Systematic Review of Randomized Controlled Trials." *Journal of Experimental Criminology* 1:317–42.

Braga, A. A. 2007. "The Effects of Hot Spots Policing on Crime." *Campbell Systematic Reviews*. DOI:10.4073/csr.2007.1.

Braga, A. A. 2008a. *Problem-Oriented Policing and Crime Prevention*. 2nd ed. Boulder, CO: Lynne Rienner.

Braga, A. A. 2008b. "Pulling Levers Focused Deterrence Strategies and the Prevention of Gun Homicide." *Journal of Criminal Justice* 36:332–43.

Braga, A. A. and D.M. Kennedy. 2012. "Linking Situational Crime Prevention and Focused Deterrence Strategies." Pp. 51–65 in *The Reasoning Criminologist: Essays in Honour of Ronald V. Clarke*, edited by G. Farrell and N. Tilley. London: Taylor and Francis.

Braga, A. A., D. M. Kennedy, E. J. Waring, and A. M. Piehl. 2001. "Problem-Oriented Policing, Deterrence, and Youth Violence: An Evaluation of Boston's Operation Ceasefire." *Journal of Research in Crime and Delinquency* 38:195–225.

Braga, A.A., G. L. Pierce, J. McDevitt, B.J. Bond, and S. Cronin. 2008. "The Strategic Prevention of Gun Violence Among Gang-Involved Offenders." *Justice Quarterly* 25: 132–62.

Braga, A. A. and D. L. Weisburd. 2011. *Systematic Review of the Effects of Focused Deterrence Strategies on Crime*. Report submitted to the Campbell Collaboration Crime and Justice Group (available upon request from author).

Campbell, D. T. and R. F. Boruch. 1975. "Making the Case for Randomized Assignment to Treatment by Considering the Alternatives." Pp. 195–296 in *Evaluation and Experiments: Some Critical Issues in Assessing Social Programs*, edited by C. Bennett and A. Lumsdaine. New York: Academic Press.

Campbell, D. T. and J. Stanley. 1966. *Experimental and Quasi-Experimental Designs for Research.* Chicago, IL: Rand McNally.

Clarke, R. V. and D. L. Weisburd. 1994. "Diffusion of Crime Control Benefits: Observations on the Reverse of Displacement." *Crime Prevention Studies* 2:165–84.

Cohen, J. 1988. *Statistical Power Analysis for the Behavioral Sciences.* 2nd ed. Hillsdale, NJ: Lawrence Erlbaum.

Cook, P. J. 1980. "Research in Criminal Deterrence: Laying the Groundwork for the Second Decade." Pp. 211–68 in *Crime and Justice: An Annual Review of Research.* Vol. 2, edited by Norval Morris and Michael Tonry. Chicago, IL: University of Chicago Press.

Cook, P. J. and J. Ludwig. 2006. "Aiming for Evidence-Based Gun Policy." *Journal of Policy Analysis and Management* 48:691–735.

Cook, T. and D. T. Campbell. 1979. *Quasi-Experimentation: Design and Analysis Issues for Field Settings.* Boston, MA: Houghton Mifflin.

Corsaro, N., R. Brunson, and E. McGarrell. Forthcoming. "Problem-Oriented Policing and Open-Air Drug Markets: Examining the Rockford Pulling Levers Strategy." *Crime & Delinquency.*

Corsaro, N. and E. McGarrell. 2010. *An Evaluation of the Nashville Drug Market Initiative (DMI) Pulling Levers Strategy.* East Lansing, MI: Michigan State University, School of Criminal Justice.

Dalton, E. 2002. "Targeted Crime Reduction Efforts in Ten Communities: Lessons for the Project Safe Neighborhoods Initiative." *U.S. Attorney's Bulletin* 50:16–25.

Durlauf, S. and D. Nagin. 2011. "Imprisonment and Crime: Can Both Be Reduced?" *Criminology & Public Policy* 10:13–54.

Duval, S. and R. Tweedie. 2000. "A Nonparametric 'Trim and Fill' Method of Accounting for Publication Bias in Meta-analysis." *Journal of the American Statistical Association* 95:89–98.

Engel, R.S., N. Corsaro, and M. Skubak Tillyer. 2010. *Evaluation of the Cincinnati Initiative to Reduce Violence (CIRV).* Cincinnati, OH: University of Cincinnati Policing Institute.

Fagan, J. 2002. "Policing Guns and Youth Violence." *The Future of Children* 12: 133–51.

Fagan, J., T. Meares, A. V. Papachristos, and D. Wallace. 2008. "Desistance and Legitimacy: Effect Heterogeneity in a Field Experiment with High-Risk Offenders." Paper presented at the annual meeting of the American Society of Criminology, November, St. Louis, MO.

Farrington, D. and A. Petrosino. 2001. "The Campbell Collaboration Crime and Justice Group." *Annals of the American Academy of Political and Social Science* 578:35-49.

Gibbs, J. P. 1975. *Crime, Punishment, and Deterrence.* New York: Elsevier.

Guerette, R. T. 2009. "The Pull, Push, and Expansion of Situation Crime Prevention Evaluation: An Appraisal of Thirty-Seven Years of Research." Pp 29–58 in *Evaluation Crime Reduction Initiatives, Crime Prevention Studies.* Vol. 24, edited by J. Knutsson and N. Tilley. Monsey, NY: Criminal Justice Press.

Hawken, A. and M. A. R. Kleiman. 2009. *Managing Drug Involved Probationers with Swift and Certain Sanctions: Evaluating Hawaii's HOPE.* Final report submitted to the National Institute of Justice, U.S. Department of Justice.

Horney, J. and I. H. Marshall. 1992. "Risk Perceptions Among Serious Offenders: The Role of Crime and Punishment." *Criminology* 30: 575–94.

Kennedy, D. M. 1997. "Pulling Levers: Chronic Offenders, High-Crime Settings, and a Theory of Prevention." *Valparaiso University Law Review* 31:449–84.

Kennedy, D. M. 2008. *Deterrence and Crime Prevention: Reconsidering the Prospect of Sanction.* London: Routledge.

Kennedy, D. M. 2009. "Drugs, Race, and Common Ground: Reflections on the High Point Intervention." *National Institute of Justice Journal* 262:12–17.

Kennedy, D. M., A. M. Piehl, and A. A. Braga. 1996. "Youth Violence in Boston: Gun Markets, Serious Youth Offenders, and a Use-Reduction Strategy." *Law and Contemporary Problems* 59:147–96.

Kleiman, M. A. R. and K. D. Smith. 1990. "State and Local Drug Enforcement: In Search of a Strategy." Pp. 69–108 in *Drugs and Crime, Crime and Justice: A Review of Research.* Vol. 13, edited by M. Tonry and J. Q. Wilson. Chicago, IL: University of Chicago Press.

Lipsey, M. 2000. "Statistical Conclusion Validity for Intervention Research: A Significant (p<.05) Problem." Pp. 101–20 in *Validity and Social Experimentation: Donald Campbell's Legacy.* Vol. 1, edited by L. Bickman. Thousand Oaks, CA: Sage.

Lipsey, M. 2003. "Those Confounded Moderators in Meta-Analysis: Good, Bad, and Ugly." *Annals of the American Academy of Political and Social Science* 587:69–81.

Lipsey, M. and D. B. Wilson. 2001. *Practical Meta-analysis.* Applied Social Research Methods Series. Vol. 49. Thousand Oaks, CA: Sage.

MacKenzie, D. L. and L. Hickman. 1998. *What Works in Corrections?* Report to the State of Washington Joint Audit and Review Committee. College Park, MD: University of Maryland, Department of Criminology and Criminal Justice.

Mazerolle, L., D. W. Soole, and S. Rombouts. 2007. "Street Level Drug Law Enforcement: A Meta-analytic Review." *Campbell Systematic Reviews.* DOI: 10.4073/csr.2007.2.

McGarrell, E., S. Chermak, J. Wilson, and N. Corsaro. 2006. "Reducing Homicide through a 'Lever-Pulling' Strategy." *Justice Quarterly* 23:214–29.

Morgan, S. L. and C. Winship. 2007. *Counterfactuals and Causal Inference: Methods and Principals for Social Research.* New York: Cambridge University Press.

Nagin, D. 1998. "Criminal Deterrence Research at the Outset of the Twenty-First Century." Pp. 1–42 in *Crime and Justice: A Review of Research.* Vol. 23, edited by M. Tonry. Chicago, IL: University of Chicago Press.

Papachristos, A.V., T. Meares, and J. Fagan. 2007. "Attention Felons: Evaluating Project Safe Neighborhoods in Chicago." *Journal of Empirical Legal Studies* 4:223–72.

Paternoster, R. 1987. "The Deterrent Effect of the Perceived Certainty and Severity of Punishment: A Review of the Evidence and Issues." *Justice Quarterly* 4:173–217.

Paternoster, R., R. Brame, R. Bachman, and L. Sherman. 1997. "Do Fair Procedures Matter? The Effect of Procedural Justice on Spouse Assault." *Law & Society Review* 31:163–204.

Piehl, A. M., S. J. Cooper, A. A. Braga, and D. M. Kennedy. 2003. "Testing for Structural Breaks in the Evaluation of Programs." *Review of Economics and Statistics* 85:550–8.

Reppetto, T. 1976. "Crime Prevention and the Displacement Phenomenon." *Crime & Delinquency* 22:166–77.

Rosenfeld, R., R. Fornango, and E. Baumer. 2005. "Did Ceasefire, Compstat, and Exile Reduce Homicide?" *Criminology & Public Policy* 4:419–50.

Rosenthal, R. 1994. "Parametric Measures of Effect Size." Pp. 231–44 in *The Handbook of Research Synthesis*, edited by H. Cooper and L. Hedges. New York, NY: Russell Sage.

Rothstein, H. R. 2008. "Publication Bias as a Threat to the Validity of Meta-analytic Results." *Journal of Experimental Criminology* 4:61–81.

Sampson, R., S. Raudenbush, and F. Earls. 1997. "Neighborhoods and Violent Crime." *Science* 277:918–24.

Sherman, L. 2002. "Fair and Effective Policing." Pp. 383–412 in *Crime: Public Policies for Crime Control*, edited by J. Q. Wilson and J. Petersilia. Oakland, CA: ICS.

Skogan, W. and K. Frydl, eds. 2004. *Fairness and Effectiveness in Policing: The Evidence*. Committee to Review Research on Police Policy and Practices. Washington, DC: The National Academies Press.

Skubak Tillyer, M. and D. M. Kennedy. 2008. "Locating Focused Deterrence Approaches within a Situational Crime Prevention Framework." *Crime Prevention and Community Safety* 10:75–84.

St. Jean, P. K. B. 2007. *Pockets of Crime: Broken Windows, Collective Efficacy, and the Criminal Point of View*. Chicago, IL: University of Chicago Press.

Tyler, T. R. 1990. *Why People Obey the Law: Procedural Justice, Legitimacy, and Compliance*. New Haven, CT: Yale University Press.

Tyler, T. R. 2004. "Enhancing Police Legitimacy." *Annals of the American Academy of Political and Social Science* 593:84–99.

Tita, G., K. J. Riley, G. Ridgeway, C. Grammich, A. Abrahamse, and P. Greenwood. 2004. *Reducing Gun Violence: Results from an Intervention in East Los Angeles*. Santa Monica, CA: RAND Corporation.

Weisburd, D. L. 1993. "Design Sensitivity in Criminal Justice Experiments." Pp. 337–79 in *Crime and Justice: A Review of Research*.

Vol. 17, edited by Michael Tonry. Chicago, IL: University of Chicago Press.

Weisburd, D. L. 2011. "Shifting Crime and Justice Resources from Prisons to Police: Shifting Police from People to Places." *Criminology & Public Policy* 10:153–64.

Weisburd, D. L. and J. E. Eck. 2004. "What Can Police Do to Reduce Crime, Disorder and Fear?" *Annals of the American Academy of Political and Social Science* 593:42–65.

Weisburd, D. L., C. Lum, and A. Petrosino. 2001. "Does Research Design Affect Study Outcomes in Criminal Justice?" *The Annals of the American Academy of Social and Political Sciences* 578:50–70.

Weisburd, D. L. and F. Taxman. 2000. "Developing a Multi-Center Randomized Trial in Criminology: The Case of HIDTA." *Journal of Quantitative Criminology* 16:315–39.

Weisburd D. L., C. Telep, J. Hinkle, and J. E. Eck. 2008. "The Effects of Problem-Oriented Policing on Crime and Disorder." *Campbell Systematic Reviews*. DOI: 10.4073/csr.2008.14.

Weisburd, D. L., L. Wyckoff, J. Ready, J. Eck, J. Hinkle, and F. Gajewski. 2006. "Does Crime Just Move Around the Corner? A Controlled Study of Spatial Displacement and Diffusion of Crime Control Benefits." *Criminology* 44:549–92.

Wellford, C. F., J. V. Pepper, and C. V. Petrie, eds. 2005. *Firearms and Violence: A Critical Review*. Committee to Improve Research Information and Data on Firearms. Washington, DC: The National Academies Press.

Welsh, B. C. and D. P. Farrington. 2009. *Making Public Places Safer: Surveillance and Crime Prevention*. New York: Oxford University Press.

Welsh, B. C., M. E. Peel, D. P. Farrington, H. Elffers, and A. A. Braga. 2011. "Research Design Influence on Study Outcomes in Crime and Justice: A Partial Replication with Public Area Surveillance." *Journal of Experimental Criminology* 7:183–98.

Wilkinson, L. and Task Force on Statistical Inference. 1999. "Statistical Methods in Psychology Journals: Guidelines and Expectations." *American Psychologist* 54: 594–604.

Wilson, D. B. 2001. "Meta-Analytical Methods for Criminology." *Annals of the American Academy of Political and Social Science* 578:71–89.

Wilson, J. Q. and G. L. Kelling. 1982. "Broken Windows: The Police and Neighborhood Safety." *Atlantic Monthly*, March, 29–38.

Zimring, F. and G. Hawkins. 1973. *Deterrence: The Legal Threat in Crime Control* Chicago, IL: University of Chicago Press.

REVIEW QUESTIONS

1. What do the authors mean by "focused deterrence" strategies?

2. What was the overall finding of this study regarding these strategies for reducing crime?

3. What are some of the concerns or issues with some of the studies used in this meta-analysis?

READING 5

This article uses the scenario design or vignettes to test the compatibility of rational choice theory with what has become the most researched and discussed theory of the last two decades: low self-control theory. Briefly mentioned in the introduction to this section, low self-control theory is a rather simple model that assumes (like other control theories, which we will cover in Section VIII) that all individuals are born with a propensity for crime and that children develop self-control through socialization and discipline. However, some children's parents do not do a good job at monitoring or training their children, so these children never develop self-control and, thus, engage in crime when opportunities present themselves. Alex Piquero and Stephen Tibbetts review other studies that have successfully merged rational choice theory with the low self-control model and then present a test of individuals' perceptions regarding two offenses that most college students are familiar with: drunk driving and shoplifting. As you read this study, try to relate the different theoretical concepts and types of offending to people you know.

Specifying the Direct and Indirect Effects of Low Self-Control and Situational Factors in Offenders' Decision Making

Toward a More Complete Model of Rational Offending

Alex R. Piquero and Stephen G. Tibbetts

It has been argued that criminology is in a state of theoretical paralysis (Wellford 1989:119) and that its theoretical developments have stagnated (Gibbs 1987). Recently, however, theorizing in criminology has undergone two important advances. One of these was proposed by Michael Gottfredson and Travis Hirschi (1990) in *A General Theory of Crime*. Their theory concerns individual differences, or propensities, that predispose an individual toward offending; their central concept is that of low self-control. The other theoretical advancement is the rational choice perspective (Cornish and Clarke 1986, 1987). This framework emphasizes the contextual and situational factors involved in decisions to offend, as well as the "choice-structuring" properties of offenses (Cornish and Clarke 1987:935).

Low self-control is established early and remains relatively stable throughout life. This is a characteristic of individuals who are more likely than others to engage in imprudent behaviors such as smoking, drinking, or gambling and commit criminal offenses such as shoplifting or assault. Gottfredson and Hirschi (1990:89) characterize low self-control as composed of elements such as immediate gratification, risk taking, orientation to the present, acts involving little skill or planning, and self-centeredness.

The rational choice framework focuses on situational inducements and impediments to offending (Cornish and Clarke 1986, 1987; Nagin and Paternoster 1993) such as the perceived costs (e.g., threat of sanctions) and benefits (e.g., pleasure) of crime. The rational choice model is consistent

SOURCE: Alex R. Piquero and Stephen G. Tibbetts, "Specifying the Direct and Indirect Effects of Low Self-Control and Situational Factors in Decision Making: Toward a More Complete Model of Rational Offending," *Justice Quarterly* 13 (3): 481–510. Copyright © 1996 Routledge. Reprinted with permission.

with a deterrence framework, especially in its focus on the perceived costs associated with committing an offense. It also includes the importance of examining an offender's perception of the benefits of offending and of informal and/or internal threats of sanction, which is absent from the traditional deterrence framework (Piliavin et al. 1986). Therefore the rational choice framework provides one way of looking at the influence of situational factors on offending. By the same token, this perspective is not confined to the situational determinants of (perceived) opportunity. Rational choice also examines how motivation is conditioned by situational influences and opportunities to commit crime.

Rational choice emphasizes would-be offenders' subjective perceptions of the expected rewards and costs associated with offending. From this perspective, a crime-specific focus is necessary because the costs and benefits of one crime may be quite different from those of another. This point suggests the importance of examining the choice-structuring properties of particular offenses (Cornish and Clarke 1987:935). Furthermore, the rational choice perspective suggests explanations in terms of those characteristics which promote or hinder gratification of needs, such as low self-control, shame, moral beliefs, threat of formal sanctions, or the pleasure of offending.

Situational factors and individual propensities are related to each other in a way suggested by Harold Grasmick and his colleagues. Grasmick et al. (1993b) noted that situational circumstances and individual characteristics may influence the extent to which low self-control affects criminal behavior. Thus the effect of low self-control depends on the situation; that is, low self-control may condition criminal behavior. Nagin and Paternoster (1993) have examined the compatibility of these perspectives. Using scenario data from a sample of college undergraduates, they found support for the underlying propensity (low self-control) argument advocated by Gottfredson and Hirschi, as well as some support for the effect of situational factors. Attractiveness of the crime target, ease of committing the crime with minimal risk, and perceptions of the costs and benefits of committing the crime were all related significantly to offending decisions. Their analysis, however, consisted solely of examining the direct effects of exogenous variables on the dependent variable (intentions to deviate).

Our analysis builds on Nagin and Paternoster's (1993) paper. We focus on specifying low self-control in an explicit causal model while taking into account the situational factors associated with offending decisions. We believe that low self-control has a direct effect on intentions to deviate, but we also argue that low self-control has indirect effects on these intentions, which operate through a variety of situational factors. These indirect effects are an important step in understanding criminals' decision-making processes.

Whereas Gottfredson and Hirschi distinguish between crime and criminality, Birkbeck and LaFree (1993) argue that theories of crime (situational explanations) should be united with theories of criminality (stable propensities). In this paper, following suggestions emanating from the work of Birkbeck and LaFree (1993) and Nagin and Paternoster (1993), we merge theories of crime (situational factors measured by subjective perceptions) and theories of criminality (low self-control) into a more highly specified causal model of rational offending. We argue that offenders are rational decision makers who are affected by various factors. These factors include not only an individual propensity to offend (i.e., low self-control) but also situational inducements (such as the pleasure of committing the crime) and situational impediments to crime (e.g., sanction threats, shame).

Previous Research

Perceived Sanction Threats and Perceived Pleasure

Deterrence concepts have been modified and expanded (Cornish and Clarke 1986, 1987; Paternoster 1989; Piliavin et al. 1986; Stafford and Warr 1993; Williams and Hawkins 1986), and recent research conducted within the rational choice framework (Bachman, Paternoster, and Ward 1992; Klepper and Nagin 1989b; Nagin and Paternoster 1993), using factorial vignette surveys, has found support for perceptions of certainty and its negative effect on delinquent behavior. Given the consistency with which sanctions may deter certain individuals who commit certain crimes (Bachman et al. 1992; Klepper and Nagin 1989b; Nagin and Paternoster 1993; Smith and Gartin 1989), we contend that these factors are quite important in a general model of rational offending.

The rational choice framework has focused strongly on the pleasure of offending (Bachman et al. 1992; Nagin and Paternoster 1993; Piliavin et al. 1986). Most researchers have found that the perceived benefits of criminal offending are important in a would-be offender's calculations, perhaps even more important than the estimated costs (Nagin and Paternoster 1993:482). The anticipated rewards or gains from offending may be more important than the potential costs to these individuals because the former are more immediate and more characteristic of risk taking and short-term gratification (Gottfredson and Hirschi 1990). Jack Katz (1988) argues that there are "seductions of crime," which result from the thrills and pleasures provided by committing criminal acts. Other research, however, suggests that seductions are influenced by several background factors including age, gender, and the strain associated with inadequate economic opportunities (McCarthy 1995). Almost all previous empirical tests of deterrence models neglected this beneficial dimension of offending; the few studies that have examined this construct find support for perceived pleasure (Nagin and Paternoster 1993; Piliavin et al. 1986).[1]

Shame

Thomas Scheff (1988) labeled shame as an important factor for social control. Scheff's work was followed closely by John Braithwaite's (1989) *Crime, Shame, and Reintegration*, which caused an immediate increase in the attention given to shame in criminology. Early theorizing on shame, however, tended to focus on acts of shaming by others (e.g., disintegrative/reintegrative shaming) rather than on the internal emotion of shame felt by the individual. Therefore those theorists implied that to experience shame, one must be shamed by a social audience. This assumption is not supported by the psychological literature on shame; in fact, the early researchers in this area acknowledged that most experiences of shame are not preceded by an act of shaming (H. Lewis 1971; Piers and Singer 1953). Experiences of shame are the result of a global, internal evaluation of the self in which the actor temporarily loses some of his or her self-esteem (M. Lewis 1992). Although acts of shaming by others may elicit shame in an individual, such an act need not occur to cause the person to feel that emotion (M. Lewis 1992; Piers and Singer 1953). In other words, individuals can be shamed without the presence of an audience (see Grasmick and Bursik 1990).

Despite the lack of criminological theory on the phenomenological nature of shame, researchers recently have attempted to measure the subjective experiences of shame within a rational choice framework. In these studies (Grasmick and Bursik 1990; Grasmick, Bursik, and Kinsey 1991; Grasmick et al. 1993b; Nagin and Paternoster 1993) respondents have been asked to describe the shame they felt, or would feel, if they had committed, or intended to commit, specific criminal offenses such as drunk driving, littering, date rape, tax evasion, or petty theft. Shame was found to have a strong inhibitory effect on the commission of all these offenses. Furthermore, for some of the offenses, shame had the strongest effect of all the variables specified in the model, including formal sanctions (Grasmick and Bursik 1990). Thus, a deterrent effect of shame seems to be strongly evident in the criminological literature.

Low Self-Control

Gottfredson and Hirschi (1990:90) contend that individuals with low self-control will tend to engage in criminal and analogous acts. Their ideas, which have met with some opposition (Akers 1991; Barlow 1991; Polk 1991), have generated a number of empirical studies (Benson and Moore 1992; Brownfield and Sorenson 1993; Gibbs and Giever 1995; Grasmick et al. 1993b; Keane, Maxim, and Teevan 1993; Nagin and Paternoster 1993; Polakowski 1994; Wood, Pfefferbaum, and Arneklev 1993). Although these studies generally support low self-control, some examination of this work is necessary. First, Grasmick et al. (1993b) developed a psychometric scale that measured low self-control, based on the criteria outlined by Gottfredson and Hirschi. The findings of their study, which examined only direct effects, indicated that low self-control was related strongly to offending (force and fraud). Keane et al. (1993) examined the relationship between low self-control and drinking and driving. Employing a behavioral measure of self-control (use of seat belts), they found that for both males and females, low self-control was an important predictor of driving under the influence of alcohol.

Gottfredson and Hirschi (1990:90) also believe that low self-control may manifest itself in various imprudent behaviors such as smoking, drinking, and gambling. Using the same data and measures as found in Grasmick et al. (1993b), Arneklev et al.(1993) tested this proposition. The results were mixed; on one hand, the low self-control index had a direct effect on an individual's participation in various imprudent behaviors. Yet one component of that index (risk taking) was more strongly predictive than the scale as a whole. Furthermore, smoking appeared to be unaffected by low self-control.[2] Similarly, Wood et al. (1993) argued that although low self-control was a significant predictor of imprudent behaviors and some forms of delinquency, their results suggested that the low self-control measure, as well as the different dependent variables, should be disaggregated.

Gibbs and Giever (1995) examined the manifestations of low self-control on a sample of college undergraduates by creating an attitudinal measure of low self-control and examining its impact on two noncriminal behaviors, cutting class and alcohol consumption. They found that low self-control was the strongest predictor of these behaviors. Their study, however, did not include factors other than self-control, such as moral beliefs or perceived threat of sanctions.

Moral Beliefs and Prior Offending

In addition to the variables discussed above, we included two other variables in the model specification: moral beliefs and prior offending. Moral beliefs are necessary in the study of any rational choice framework because such beliefs impede criminal behavior; theorists have stressed the importance of internalized moral constraints (Bachman et al. 1992; Bishop 1984; Grasmick and Bursik 1990; Paternoster et al. 1983; Tittle 1977, 1980). We also included prior offending as a control variable because it could capture the influence of other sources of stable criminality (Nagin and Paternoster 1991, 1993).

Proposed Model

The proposed model assumes that a rational human actor with low self-control encounters situational factors which push him or her toward crime (pleasure of the offense) and/or away from crime (moral beliefs, perceived risk of sanctions, and situational shame). When the push toward crime is greater than the push away from crime, an individual is more likely to choose crime. This idea is summarized by Gottfredson and Hirschi (1990:89) when they observe that a major characteristic of those with low self-control is the tendency to respond to tangible stimuli in the immediate environment and to have a concrete "here and now" orientation (also see Hirschi and Gottfredson 1993).

Although our theoretical model relies heavily on the most recent statement of control theory outlined by Gottfredson and Hirschi, it is not meant to downplay the importance of earlier control theorists, particularly Walter Reckless (1961; also see Toby 1957). In his seminal piece, Reckless noted that inner containment consists mainly of self-control, while outer containment represents the structural buffer in the person's immediate social world which is able to hold him or her within bounds (Reckless 1961:44–45). Expanding upon the idea of outer containment, one could easily infer that sanctions, pleasure, and shame are structural buffers in an individual's immediate social world. Moreover, Block and Flynn (1956:61) state that "there are many variables in the personality of the delinquent and the delinquency-producing situation itself which the investigators may not readily discern and which themselves may constitute the critical factors involved in the delinquent act." Conceivably, then, one could argue that our theoretical model is a refinement, an extension, and an empirical test of Reckless's theory and of Block and Flynn's assertions (also see A. Cohen 1955).

Methods

We collected data through a self-administered questionnaire that presented respondents with a realistic scenario describing in detail the conditions in which an actor commits a crime. The respondents were told only that the actor committed the act, not whether he or she approved of the act. Thus we focus not on the hypothetical actor's perceptions or approval of the act, but rather on the respondent's perceptions and approval. The questions were designed to measure respondents' perceptions of the costs and benefits of committing the offense described in the scenario, to estimate the probability that they would commit that offense, and to estimate the chance that their committing the offense would result in arrest and in exposure without arrest.

The scenario method differs from conventional data collection in perceptual social control/deterrence research in that it uses hypothetical, third-person scenarios of offending to elicit the dependent variable. This strategy has been used successfully in recent research on rational choice (Bachman et al. 1992; Klepper and Nagin 1989a, 1989b; Nagin and Paternoster 1993). The primary weakness of this approach is that an expressed intention to offend is not synonymous with actual offending. Fishbein and Ajzen (1975), however, argue that a person's intention to perform a particular behavior should be highly correlated with the actual performance of that behavior.[3] This proposition is supported empirically by Green (1989), whose two-wave panel design revealed a high correlation ($r = .85$) between intentions and actual performance of deviant behavior. In addition, Kim and Hunter's (1993) recent meta-analysis produced a strong relationship between attitude, intention, and behavior. In all, the scenario method is the best approach available because of its advantages, its realistic nature, and the specificity of the scenarios.[4]

The realistic and specific nature of the scenarios allows us to examine the effect of situational factors on both the intentions to offend and the anticipated risks and rewards of these behaviors. Without these contextual specifications, the respondents would impute their own details; such a situation would "undoubtedly vary across respondents and affect their responses" (Nagin and Paternoster 1993:474). Also, individuals may vary in their definition of illegal behavior. If these differences in definition vary systematically with responses measuring variables of interest, analysis of the effects of such variables on actual behavior may be misrepresented (Nagin and Paternoster 1993).

Another, perhaps more important advantage of the scenario method is its capacity to capture the "instantaneous" relationship between independent variables and the respondent's intentions to offend (Grasmick and Bursik 1990). Previous cross-sectional and panel studies on deterrence used measures of past behavior or behavior within waves to measure the dependent variable (e.g., Bishop 1984). Because perceptions of risk are unstable over time, however, this lagged type of measurement is not appropriate. These designs would tend to find lagged effects for independent variables that remained stable over time, such as moral beliefs, but no lagged effects for independent variables that are not stable, such as perceived of threats sanction (Grasmick and Bursik 1990). Therefore, because the scenario method permits the examination of "instantaneous" relationships, it is preferable to traditional designs.[5]

Sample and Scenario Design

Respondents were undergraduates at a major East Coast university, enrolled in several large introductory criminal justice courses in the fall 1993 semester. A total of 349 males and 293 females (642 in all) completed the questionnaire. Although participation was voluntary, only 4 percent of potential respondents refused to participate; given this small amount, analysis and conclusions appear not to be threatened by response bias. The respondents ranged in age from 17 to 35; the median age was 19. Because we selected introductory classes that fulfill general core requirements for the university curriculum, a substantial majority of students (69 percent) were not criminal justice majors and were currently in their freshman and sophomore years. In addition, questionnaires were administered during the second week of the semester. Therefore it is very unlikely that responses were biased by students' knowledge of deterrence or correctional concerns.[6] Listwise deletion of missing cases resulted in a sample of 604.

The Scenarios

Under an adaptation of the factorial survey methodology developed by Rossi and Anderson (1982), each student was given two scenarios—drunk driving and shoplifting—to which to respond. All of the scenarios were framed in settings familiar to these college student respondents. Selected scenario conditions were varied experimentally across persons. Respondents were asked to estimate the probability that they would commit the act specified in the scenario, to predict the chance that their commission of the offense would result in arrest, and to answer questions designed to measure their perceptions of the costs and benefits of committing the offense described in the scenario. In the present analysis, then, all respondents receive the opportunity to commit the same crimes in the same setting.[7]

 ## Measurement of Variables

Intentions to Deviate

Separate models are estimated for each type of offense. The dependent variable is the respondent's estimate of the chance that he or she will do what the character did in the scenario. We measured intentions to offend on a scale from 0 (no chance at all) to 10 (100 percent chance). Responses were solicited for both the drunk driving (INTENTDD) and the shoplifting (INTENTSH) scenarios.

Shame

Shame is measured by two items following each scenario, which ask the respondent (1) "what is the chance" and (2) "how much of a problem" would loss of self-esteem be if he or she were to do what the actor in the scenario did, even if no one else found out. Responses to both of these items were measured on an 11-point scale (0 = no chance/ no problem to 10 = 100 percent chance/very big problem). We computed shame (SHAME) by multiplying the responses of the two items; higher scores reflect a higher likelihood that the individual would feel shame if he or she were to commit the specified act.

Low Self-Control

We operationalized low self-control with a psychometric scale borrowed from Grasmick et al. (1993b), which includes 24 items intended to measure the six elements of low self-control.[8] We coded these items on a five-point Likert-type scale (1 = never to 5 = very often) and created a composite measure of self-control (SELFCONT) by summing the responses across 24 items. High scores on the scale indicate low self-control. This instrument was used in two previous studies (Grasmick et al. 1993b; Nagin and Paternoster 1993), both of which provided strong reliability and validity support for the scale. The high estimated reliability coefficient (α = .84) gave us confidence in the internal consistency of the scale. Furthermore, the factor loadings provided by a principal-components factor analysis were comparable to those reported by Grasmick et al. (1993b).

Perceived External Sanctions

Respondents were asked to estimate the chance of arrest (*Pf:* risk of formal discovery) and the chance that others would find out if they were not arrested (*Pi:* risk of informal discovery). To measure the perceptions of the implications of discovery, we asked respondents to estimate the probability that discovery by arrest or informal exposure would result in dismissal from the university (*Pdf, Pdi*), loss of respect by close friends (*Pff, Pfi*), loss of respect by parents

and relatives (*Ppf, Ppi*), and diminished job prospects (*Pjf, Pji*). Each of these perceptual measures is intended to measure the risks of informal sanctions that may threaten an individual's "stake in conformity," or bonding to the moral order. To measure the perceived risk of formal sanctions, we asked respondents to estimate the risk of jail (*Pjaf*). The drunk-driving scenario was followed by an additional item measuring the perceived chance of losing one's driver's license (*Plf*) if an arrest was made. All responses were measured on an 11-point scale (0 = no chance at all to 10 = 100 percent chance).

These measures of risk probably would have little effect on intentions unless associated with perceptions of some cost (Grasmick and Bursik 1990). Thus we asked respondents to estimate the perceived severity of each sanction. Specifically, we asked each subject to estimate "how much of a problem" each sanction would pose for them. All responses were measured on an 11-point scale (0 = no problem at all to 10 = a very big problem). To create the composite scale of perceived external sanctions, we multiplied each risk-perception response by the corresponding severity-perception response. Then we summed these separately for drunk driving and for shoplifting (PEREXSAN); higher scores on the scale correspond to a high degree of perceived risk and cost of performing the act in question for that individual. We used the following formula:

$$PEREXSAN = Pi \, [(Pdi) \, (Sd) + (Pfi) \, (Sf) + (Ppi) \, (Sp) + (Pji) \, (Sj)] + Pf \, [(Pdf) \, (Sd) + (Pff) \, (Sf) + (Ppf) \, (Sp) + (Pjf) \, (Sj) + (Plf) \, (Sl) + (Pjaf) \, (Sja)]$$

where *Sd* equals the perceived severity of sanction *d* (dismissal from university) and all other variables are as defined previously.

Moral Beliefs

To measure the perceived immorality of the behavior, we asked respondents to estimate how morally wrong they thought the incident would be if they were to commit drunk driving and shoplifting (MORALS). Response options varied on an 11-point scale (0 = not morally wrong at all to 10 = very morally wrong). Although some may contend that our respondents may not regard the behaviors under study as criminal or morally wrong, the mean moral value was 7.80 against drunk driving and 7.57 against shoplifting. These findings indicate that most of our respondents perceive even these behaviors as morally wrong.

Perceived Pleasure

To measure perceived pleasure, a single item asked respondents to estimate "how much fun or kick" it would be to commit drunk driving and shoplifting under the conditions specified in the scenarios (PLEASURE). Responses varied on an 11-point scale (0 = no fun or kick at all to 10 = a great deal of fun or kick).

Prior Offending

In addition to the variables discussed above, we included prior offending as a control in the model. We did so to capture the influence of sources of stable criminality extraneous to that of persistent individual differences due to personality traits included in the model (such as low self-control). To measure prior offending (PRIOROFF), we included two items (one for each scenario offense) that asked the respondents how many times in the past year they had driven while drunk and how many times they had shoplifted.[9]

Hypotheses

In this paper we postulate and examine three hypotheses:

H_1: Low self-control has both direct and indirect effects via situational factors on intentions to deviate;

H_2: Situational characteristics have both direct and indirect effects on intentions to deviate and on other situational variables;

H_3: The model uniting the effects of low self-control and situational characteristics of crime will provide a good fit to the data.[10]

Analysis of Shoplifting

According to Hypothesis 1, low self-control will have a direct effect on intentions to deviate and indirect effects on intentions to deviate through situational factors. Significant maximum-likelihood estimates for shoplifting may be found in Table 1 and Figure 1. Of the four paths estimated for low self-control, three are significant. Low self-control has a direct positive effect ($b = .153$, $t = 4.438$) on intentions to shoplift and a direct positive effect ($b = .178$, $t = 4.502$) on perceived pleasure, an indication that the higher one scores on the low self-control scale, the more likely one is to intend to shoplift and to perceive pleasure from shoplifting. Low self-control has a direct negative effect ($b = -.102$, $t = -2.889$) on shame, indicating that the higher one scores on the low self-control scale, the less likely one is to experience shame due to shoplifting. The only insignificant effect is the effect of low self-control on perceived risk of sanctions.

Therefore, low self-control not only has a direct effect on intentions to shoplift; it also indirectly affects intentions to shoplift through situational variables (pleasure and shame). These results are consistent with Gottfredson and

| Table 1 | Significant Full-Information Maximum-Likelihood Estimates for Intentions to Shoplift (N = 604) |

Dependent Variables	Independent Variables					
	Shame	Perceived Sanctions	Perceived Pleasure	Moral Beliefs	Prior Offending	Low Self-Control
Intentions to Shoplift	−.214	a	.220	−.186	.176	.153
Shame	—b	—	−.173	.483	—a	−.102
Perceived Sanctions	.434	—	—b	.117	—a	—a
Perceived Pleasure	—b	.153	—b	-.267	.169	.178

NOTE: LISREL shows the effects of columns on rows.

a. Path estimated but not significant.

b. Path not established.

Figure 1

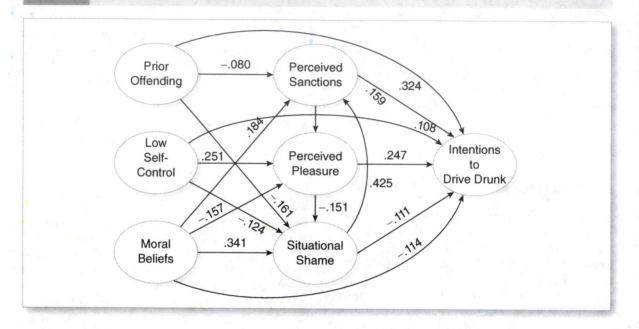

Hirschi's (1990:95) idea that individuals with low self-control will be less likely to consider the consequences of offending.

Hypothesis 2 indicates that situational characteristics should have direct effects on intentions to shoplift and indirect effects on intentions to shoplift which operate through other situational factors. With the exception of perceived sanctions, both shame ($b = -.214$, $t = -5.372$) and perceived pleasure ($b = .220$, $t = 6.270$) have the expected effects on intentions to shoplift. The null results for perceived sanctions are not surprising: Shoplifting is a very common crime and one that can be committed with relative impunity; thus an individual's perception of being caught would likely not be salient.

As for the other effects, shame ($b = .434$, $t = 9.745$) has a positive effect on perceived sanctions, indicating that the more likely one is to perceive shame, the more likely one is to perceive the threat of sanctions as salient. Even though perceived sanctions do not affect intentions to shoplift, they affect perceived pleasure in a rather interesting manner: Perceived sanctions have a positive effect ($b = .153$, $t = 3.398$) on perceived pleasure, in keeping with Katz's (1988) notion of "sneaky thrills." It appears that among our respondents, the more one perceives the risk of sanctions

as high, the more pleasure one perceives from shoplifting. Finally, perceived pleasure has a negative effect on shame ($b = -.173$, $t = -4.468$): The more one perceives pleasure from shoplifting, the less likely one is to feel shame.

Other effects include those of the other two exogenous variables, prior offending and moral beliefs. Prior offending has positive effects on intentions to shoplift ($b = .176$, $t = 5.322$) and on perceived pleasure ($b = .169$, $t = 4.421$), indicating that the more times respondents have shoplifted in the past, the more likely they are to intend to shoplift and to perceive pleasure from shoplifting. Prior behavior does not exert an effect on perceived sanctions. Moral beliefs are the only exogenous variable to be significant and consistent with all effects as predicted. Moral beliefs have the predicted negative effects on intentions to shoplift ($b = -.186$, $t = -4.669$) and on perceived pleasure ($b = -.267$, $t = -6.287$), indicating that the stronger one's moral beliefs against shoplifting, the less likely one is to intend to shoplift or to perceive pleasure from shoplifting. Likewise, moral beliefs have the predicted positive effects on shame ($b = .483$, $t = 13.599$) and on perceived sanctions ($b = .117$, $t = 2.691$), indicating that the stronger one's moral beliefs, the more likely one is to perceive shame and sanctions as important.

To test the third hypothesis, we constructed a model that united the effects of low self-control and of situational characteristics. To determine whether the proposed model fit the data adequately, we examined the chi-square statistic of the model. Because chi-square is sensitive to sample size and to departures from normality in the data, there are alternative methods for assessing the goodness of fit of a model; one such method is the ratio of chi-square to degrees of freedom. Smith and Patterson (1985) suggest that values of 5 or less indicate an adequate fit. For this model the value is 1.01 (4.05/4), indicating an adequate fit to the data.

Analysis of Drunk Driving

The significant maximum-likelihood estimates for drunk driving are shown in Table 2 and Figure 2. For low self-control, three of the four effects are significant. Low self-control has direct positive effects on intentions to drive drunk ($b = .108$, $t = 3.167$) and on perceived pleasure ($b = .251$, $t = 6.308$), indicating that the higher one scores on the low self-control scale, the more likely one is to intend to drive drunk and to perceive pleasure from drunk driving. Low self-control exerts a negative effect on shame ($b = -.124$, $t = -3.257$), indicating that persons with low self-control are less likely to feel shame. As in the analysis of shoplifting, the effect of low self-control on perceived sanctions is insignificant.

All three situational factors have the expected effects on intentions to drive drunk. Shame ($b = -.111$, $t = -2.796$) and perceived sanctions ($b = -.159$, $t = -.4.219$) exert the expected negative effects on intentions to drink and drive, indicating that the more one perceives sanction threats and shame as important, the less likely one is to intend to drive drunk.[11] Perceived pleasure has the expected positive effect ($b = .247$, $t = 7.313$) on intentions to drive drunk, indicating that the more pleasure one perceives from drunk driving, the more likely one is to intend to drive drunk. Other effects for perceived pleasure include a negative effect on shame ($b = -.151$, $t = -4.057$), indicating that the more pleasure one obtains from drinking and driving, the less likely one is to lose self-esteem. Shame has a positive effect ($b = .425$, $t = 11.123$) on perceived sanctions, indicating that the more one perceives shame as salient, the more likely one is to perceive sanction threats as also important.

Figure 2

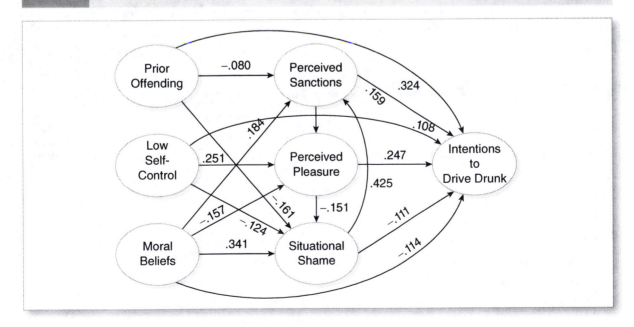

Effects of the other two exogenous variables (prior offending and moral beliefs) are largely as expected. Prior offending has a negative effect on shame ($b = -.161$, $t = -4.498$) and on perceived sanctions ($b = -.080$, $t = -2.295$), indicating that the more one has driven drunk in the past, the less likely one is to feel shame and to perceive sanctions as important. In addition, prior offending has a positive effect on intentions to drive drunk ($b = .324$, $t = 9.946$), which indicates that the more one has driven drunk in the past, the more likely one is to intend to drive drunk. Prior offending has no effect on the perceived pleasure of drunk driving.

All four moral belief effects are significant. Moral beliefs have negative effects on intentions to drink and drive ($b = -.114$, $t = -3.177$) and on perceived pleasure ($b = -.157$, $t = -3.959$), indicating that the stronger one's moral beliefs are against drunk driving, the less likely one is to intend to drive drunk and the less likely one is to derive pleasure from drinking and driving. Moral beliefs also have positive effects on shame ($b = .341$, $t = 9.269$) and on perceived sanctions ($b = .184$, $t = 4.925$), indicating that the stronger one's moral beliefs are, the more likely one is to experience shame and to perceive sanctions as important.

Results concerning Hypothesis 3 in regard to drinking and driving are similar to those for shoplifting. To determine whether the model constructed for drunk driving fit the data adequately, we performed the same two tests as we conducted for shoplifting. The first test examined the ratio of chi-square to degrees of freedom. Values of less than 5 indicate an adequate fit to the data: our value was .33 (1.00/3).

 Conclusion

Building on the early work of Nagin and Paternoster (1993), we set out here to combine two different paths in theoretical criminology into a more complete model of offending. One path attributes crime to individual differences that are established early in life, specifically in low self-control. According to the second path, crime is the result of situational factors associated with criminal offending, such as the perceived costs and benefits of crime. As observed by Nagin and Paternoster (1993:489), these two paths have been explored separately rather than in conjunction. On the basis of our analysis, we find support for a model that integrates these two paths. The model holds after controlling for several important factors and performs well in two different tests designed to measure the fit of the model to the data.

Aside from delineating and testing a more complete model of rational offending, this paper represents the first attempt to examine the indirect effects of low self-control. This attempt is especially important because previous research in low self-control examined only the direct effects of low self-control and rational choice characteristics (Grasmick et al. 1993b; Nagin and Paternoster 1993).

| Table 2 | Significant Full-Information Maximum-Likelihood Estimate for Intention to Drive Drunk (N = 604) |

| | Independent Variables | | | | | |
Dependent Variables	Shame	Perceived Sanctions	Perceived Pleasure	Moral Beliefs	Prior Offending	Low Self-Control
Intentions to Drive Drunk	−.111	−.159	.247	−.114	.324	.108
Shame	—[b]	—[b]	−.151	.341	−.161	−.124
Perceived Sanctions	.425	—[b]	—[b]	.184	−.080	—[a]
Perceived Pleasure	—[b]	—[a]	—[b]	−.157	—[a]	.251

NOTE: LISREL shows the effects of columns on rows.

a. Path estimated but not significant.

b. Path not established.

Of all our findings, ==the indirect effects of low self-control were the most interesting==. In fact, these effects were more complex than we had imagined originally. ==We found that low self-control had similar effects on shame and perceived pleasure across offenses, but exerted no effect on perceived sanctions in either scenario==. Modeling indirect effects of low self-control is a difficult task, which we undertook with almost no previous theoretical guidance. Such effects probably depend on the offense, but currently we have too little information about the indirect effects of low self-control on offending. Additional theoretical work and further modeling of the total effects are priorities in self-control research.

The model we have presented here may be extended in the following ways. First, we would like to see future studies examine a wide array of criminal and deviant behaviors, such as drug use, sexual assault, burglary, and robbery. Insofar as Gottfredson and Hirschi are correct, low self-control should be related to all types of criminal and deviant behaviors. Second, many variables could be interchanged with and/or added to our list of situational variables. We contend that because different offenses require different situational characteristics and circumstances, these mediating factors may change in type—but they will be situational factors nonetheless. ==For example, an examination of marijuana use may require inclusion of a situational variable such as the ease of obtaining marijuana, whereas an examination of breaking and entering would require situational characteristics such as the lack of capable guardians, lack of a security system, and the time of day or night.== Still other examples of situational variables would include peer delinquency and peer associations. Because delinquency is overwhelmingly a group phenomenon (Reiss 1986), inclusion of such a measure has the potential to enhance the predictability of our model. This discussion should make apparent that although situational characteristics may vary in type depending on the crime, the framework of the model will remain the same: Time-stable variables such as low self-control will always precede and influence the situational variables.

 Notes

1. Some may argue that the pleasure associated with offending is only part of the story, and that often the more important situational factors are the amount of time and energy saved (as in drunk driving) and the value of goods stolen (as in shoplifting).

Because of the lack of significant findings from Nagin and Paternoster's (1993) vignettes of these conditions, we did not vary these situational characteristics.

2. This result may be due to the average age of the sample (46.5 years). It could be that these individuals began to smoke before the effects of smoking were known to be undesirable (Arneklev et al. 1993).

3. Fishbein and Ajzen (1975) identify three criteria for maximizing the correspondence between intentions and actual behavior. The first of these criteria is the degree to which the intentions are measured with the same specificity as the behavior that is being predicted. The scenarios presented here include highly specific circumstances, (see). The second criterion is the stability of the expressed intention. In view of the realistic and specific conditions of the scenarios, there is no compelling reason to question the stability of these intentions. The final criterion is the degree to which the respondent can willfully carry out the intention.

4. Our scenarios were designed after those used by Nagin and Paternoster (1993) in regard to detail and contextual specificity. We achieved specificity by presenting details of the circumstance of the offense, such as naming the bar where the actor is drinking or the type of item the actor is shoplifting. The scenario approach has been used as well in research on death penalty juries (Bohm 1991).

5. We systematically varied the location of the intention questions for both the drunk driving and the shoplifting scenarios. In approximately half of these scenarios, the dependent variable item was placed directly after the scenario; other perceptual items (e.g., moral beliefs, perceived certainty) followed (this position was coded 0). In the other half, the dependent variable was located at the end of the battery of perceptual items (this position was coded 1). We adopted this procedure to examine for possible differences due to responses on the dependent variable item affecting the responses on the subsequent perceptual items. For instance, if the dependent variable item is placed directly after the scenario, the respondents may base their perceptions on their previous response to the dependent variable item. In contrast if the dependent variable item is placed after the perceptual items, respondents may respond differently on the dependent variable item if they have thought carefully about their perceptions regarding the offense. Bivariate correlations showed that the location of the dependent variable item did not have a significant effect on respondents' intentions to commit drunk driving or to shoplift ($r = .06$ and $-.05$, respectively). Therefore, we did not include this variable in the multivariate analyses.

6. The use of convenience samples in deterrence research is questionable and has drawn some criticism (Jensen, Erickson, and Gibbs 1978; Williams and Hawkins 1986). The major objection is that of representativeness. Large public universities, however, contain a moderate number of marginal offenders (Matza 1964), particularly for the kinds of offenses that are the focus of this study. In our data, 44 percent of respondents admit to having committed drunk driving in the past year (17 percent committed shoplifting in the past year). Furthermore, a Bureau of Justice Statistics Report (R. Cohen 1992) reveals that the rate of arrest for driving while under the influence of alcohol (DUI) is highest for persons between ages 21 and 24. Those in the 18–20 age range have the second-highest arrest rate for DUI. Also, a survey of 1,287 university students conducted in 1991 revealed that almost one-half were regular users of alcohol; 45 percent of these reported consuming four or more drinks at a time, and more than half reported driving within an hour after consuming their last drink (Kuhn 1992). When subjects in our sample were asked the likelihood of drinking and driving under the conditions of the scenario presented to them, only 33 percent reported "no chance." Shoplifting also has been shown to be quite common among young adults (Empey and Stafford 1991); self-reports show that shoplifting is about as common as drinking (Elliott, et al. 1983; Hindelang, Hirschi, and Weis 1981). When subjects in our sample were asked the likelihood of committing shoplifting under the conditions of the scenario presented to them, only 37 percent reported "no chance." In addition, arrests for theft reported by the university police department totaled 1,267 for 1992; an overwhelming number of these crimes were committed by students. Given this information, one can conclude that college student populations contain frequent offenders in situations involving drunk driving and shoplifting; thus college samples are appealing for studies such as this.

7. We varied the level of risk of exposure (informal and formal) in both the shoplifting and the drunk driving scenarios. Preliminary analysis revealed no effect for these scenario-varied conditions; as a result, they were not estimated in the LISREL equations. Furthermore, we used gender as a control variable in preliminary analyses. After controlling for low self-control, the effect of gender was not significant in predicting intentions to either shoplift or drive drunk. In addition, gender had no significant effect on the other exogenous variables. Thus we did not examine gender in the LISREL models. These results confirm Gottfredson and Hirschi's (1990:144–49) predictions concerning gender, low self-control, and crime and they are consistent with previous research regarding similarity between males and females

in offending behavior regarding shoplifting and drunk driving (Grasmick, Bursik, and Arneklev 1993a; Hindelang et al. 1981; Keane et al. 1993; Nagin and Paternoster 1993; Yu, Essex, and Williford 1992).

8. Persons interested in obtaining a copy of the low self-control scale can write to us or consult Grasmick et al. (1993b) or Nagin and Paternoster (1993).

9. In the models that follow, when we investigate intentions to drive drunk, we use a past behavior measure: the number of times in the past year the respondent has driven drunk. Similarly, when we examine intentions to shoplift, we use a past behavior measure of respondent's previous shoplifting. An anonymous reviewer observed correctly that a situational variable from the perspective of rational choice theory may be a dispositional variable from the perspective of self-control theory, such that one can use the drunk driving (past behavior) variables to predict shoplifting and can use the shoplifting (past behavior) variables to predict drunk driving. Insofar as dispositions rather than situations are at work, the results should be largely the same in either case. For the sake of brevity and because it is not the focus of the present analysis, we did not examine this issue here. We plan on assessing this issue, however, in future work with these data.

10. To examine the validity of this hypothesis, the LISREL computer program provides a chi-square statistic that estimates the goodness of fit of the model.

11. This is the only effect for perceived sanctions and differs from the results for shoplifting. The sanction effects for drunk driving appear to be direct—not indirect, as they were for shoplifting—perhaps because of recent moral campaigns targeting drunk driving and because of the harshness of penalties that are reported by the media. This result is consistent with recent research concerning perceived sanctions on drunk driving (Grasmick et al. 1993a; Nagin and Paternoster 1993).

 ## References

Akers, R. 1991. "Self-Control as a General Theory of Crime." *Journal of Quantitative Criminology* 7:201–11.

Arneklev, B., H. Grasmick, C. Tittle, and R. Bursik, Jr. 1993. "Low Self-Control and Imprudent Behavior." *Journal of Quantitative Criminology* 9:225–47.

Bachman, R., R. Paternoster, and S. Ward. 1992. "The Rationality of Sexual Offending: Testing a Deterrence/Rational Choice Conception of Sexual Assault." *Law and Society Review* 26:343–72.

Barlow, H. 1991. "Explaining Crimes and Analogous Acts, or The Unrestrained Will Grab at Pleasure Whenever They Can." *Journal of Criminal Law and Criminology* 82:229–42.

Benson, M. and E. Moore. 1992. "Are White Collar and Common Offenders the Same?" *Journal of Research in Crime and Delinquency* 29:251–72.

Birkbeck, C. and G. LaFree. 1993. "The Situational Analysis of Crime and Deviance." *Annual Review of Sociology* 19:113–37.

Bishop, D. 1984. "Legal and Extralegal Barriers to Delinquency." *Criminology* 22:403–19.

Block, H. and F. Flynn. 1956. *Delinquency: The Juvenile Offender in America Today.* New York: Random House.

Bohm, R. 1991. *Death Penalty in America: Current Research.* Cincinnati: Anderson.

Braithwaite, J. 1989. *Crime, Shame, and Reintegration.* New York: Cambridge University Press.

Brownfield, D. and A. Sorenson. 1993. "Self-Control and Juvenile Delinquency: Theoretical Issues and an Empirical Assessment of Selected Elements of a General Theory of Crime." *Deviant Behavior* 14:243–64.

Cohen, A. 1955. *Delinquent Boys.* New York: Free Press.

Cohen, R. 1992. *Drunk Driving.* Washington, DC: U.S. Department of Justice.

Cornish, D. and R. Clarke. 1986. *The Reasoning Criminal: Rational Choice Perspectives in Offending.* New York: Springer-Verlag.

———. 1987. "Understanding Crime Displacement: An Application of Rational Choice Theory." *Criminology* 25:933–47.

Elliot, D., S. Ageton, D. Huizinga, W. Knowles, and R. Canter. 1983. *The Prevalence and Incidence of Delinquent Behavior: 1976-1980.* Boulder: University of Colorado.

Empey, L. and M. Stafford. 1991. *American Delinquency: Its Meanings and Construction.* 3rd ed. Belmont, CA: Wadsworth.

Fishbein, M. and I. Ajzen. 1975. *Belief, Attitudes, Intention, and Behavior.* Reading, MA: Addison-Wesley.

Gibbs, J. 1987. "The State of Criminological Theory." *Criminology* 25:821–24.

Gibbs, J. and D. Giever. 1995. "Self-Control and Its Manifestations among University Students: An Empirical Test of Gottfredson and Hirschi's General Theory." *Justice Quarterly* 12:231–55.

Gottfredson, M. and T. Hirschi. 1990. *A General Theory of Crime.* Stanford: Stanford University Press.

Grasmick, H. and R. Bursik, Jr. 1990. "Conscience, Significant Others, and Rational Choice: Extending the Deterrence Model." *Law and Society Review* 24:837–61.

Grasmick, H., R. Bursik, Jr., and B. Arneklev. 1993a. "Reduction in Drunk Driving as a Response to Increased Threats of Shame, Embarrassment, and Legal Sanctions." *Criminology* 31:41–67.

Grasmick, H., R. Bursik, Jr., and K. Kinsey. 1991. "Shame and Embarrassment as Deterrents to Noncompliance with the Law." *Environment and Behavior* 23:233–51.

Grasmick, H., C. Tittle, R. Bursik, Jr., and B. Arneklev. 1993. "Testing the Core Implications of Gottfredson and Hirschi's General Theory of Crime." *Journal of Research in Crime and Delinquency* 30:5–29.

Green, D. 1988. "Measures of Illegal Behavior in Individual-Level Deterrence Research." *Journal of Research in Crime and Delinquency* 26:253–75.

Hindelang, M., T. Hirschi, and J. Weis. 1981. *Measuring Delinquency.* Beverly Hills: Sage.

Hirschi, T. and M. Gottfredson. 1993. "Commentary: Testing the General Theory of Crime." *Journal of Research in Crime and Delinquency* 30:47–54.

Jensen, G., M. Erickson, and J. Gibbs. 1978. "Perceived Risk of Punishment and Self-Reported Delinquency." *Social Forces* 57:57–78.

Katz, J. 1988. *Seductions of Crime.* New York: Basic Books.

Keane, C, P. Maxim, and J. Teevan. 1993. "Drinking and Driving, Self-Control and Gender: Testing a General Theory of Crime." *Journal of Research in Crime and Delinquency* 30:30–46.

Kim, M. and J. Hunter. 1993. "Relationships among Attitudes, Behavioral Intentions, and Behavior: A Meta-Analysis of Past Research. Part 2." *Communications Research* 20:331–64.

Klepper, S. and D. Nagin. 1989a. "Tax Compliance and Perceptions of the Risks of Detection and Criminal Prosecution." *Law and Society Review* 23:209–40.

———. 1989b. "The Deterrent Effect of Perceived Certainty and Severity of Punishment Revisited." *Criminology* 27:721–46.

Kuhn, R. 1992. "1991 Student Drug Survey." College Park: University of Maryland, President's Committee on Alcohol and Drug Policy.

Lewis, H. 1971. *Shame and Guilt in Neurosis.* New York: International Universities Press.

Lewis, M. 1992. *Shame: The Exposed Self.* New York: Macmillan.

Matza, D. 1964. *Delinquency and Drift.* New York: Wiley.

McCarthy, B. 1995. "Not Just 'For the Thrill of It': An Instrumentalist Elaboration of Katz's Explanation of Sneaky Thrill Property Crimes." *Criminology* 33:519–38.

Nagin, D. and R. Paternoster. 1991. "On the Relationship of Past and Future Participation in Delinquency." *Criminology* 29:163–89.

———. 1993. "Enduring Individual Differences and Rational Choice Theories of Crime." *Law and Society Review* 27:467–96.

Paternoster, R. 1989. "Absolute and Restrictive Deterrence in a Panel of Youth: Explaining the Onset, Persistence/Desistence and Frequency of Delinquent Offending." *Social Problems* 36:289–309.

Paternoster, R., L. Saltzman, T. Chiricos, and G. Waldo. 1983. "Estimating Perceptual Stability and Deterrent Effects: The Role of Perceived Legal Punishment in the Inhibition of Criminal Involvement." *Journal of Criminal Law and Criminology* 74:270–97.

Piers, G. and M. Singer. 1953. *Shame and Guilt.* New York: Norton.

Piliavin, I., R. Gartner, C. Thornton, and R. Matsueda. 1986. "Crime Deterrence and Rational Choice." *American Sociological Review* 51:101–19.

Polakowski, M. 1994. "Linking Self-Control and Social Control with Deviance: Illuminating the Structure Underlying a General Theory of Crime and Its Relation to Deviant Activity." *Journal of Quantitative Criminology* 10:41–78.

Polk, K. 1991. "Review of a General Theory of Crime." *Crime and Delinquency* 37:575–81.

Reckless, W. 1961. "A New Theory of Delinquency and Crime." *Federal Probation* 25:42–46.

Reiss, A. 1986. "Co-Offender Influences on Criminal Careers." Pp. 121–60 in *Criminal Careers and "Career Criminals,"* edited by A. Blumstein, J. Cohen, J. Roth, and C. Visher. Washington, DC: National Academy Press.

Rossi, P. and A. Anderson. 1982. "The Factorial Survey Approach: An Introduction." Pp. 15–67 in *Measuring Social Judgments,* edited by P. Rossi and S. Nock. Beverly Hill, CA: Sage.

Scheff, T. 1988. "Shame and Conformity: The Deference-Emotion System." *American Sociological Review* 53:395–406.

Smith, D. and P. Gartin. 1989. "Specifying Specific Deterrence: The Influence *of* Arrest on Future Criminal Activity." *American Sociological Review* 54:94–105.

Smith, D. and B. Patterson. 1985. "Latent-Variable Models in Criminological Research: Applications and a Generalization of Joreskog's LISREL Model." *Journal of Quantitative Criminology* 1:127–58.

Stafford, M. and M. Warr. 1993. "A Reconceptualization of General and Specific Deterrence." *Journal of Research in Crime and Delinquency* 30:123–35.

Tittle, C. 1977. "Sanction Fear and the Maintenance of the Social Order." *Social Forces* 55:579–96.

———. 1980. *Sanctions and Social Deviance.* New York: Praeger.

Toby, J. 1957. "Social Disorganization and Stake in Conformity: Complimentary Factors in the Predatory Behavior of Hoodlums." *Journal of Criminal Law, Criminology and Police Science* 48:12–17.

Wellford, C. 1989. "Towards an Integrated Theory of Criminal Behavior." Pp. 119–28 in *Theoretical Integration in the Study of Deviance and Crime: Problems and Prospects,* edited by S. Messner, M. Krohn, and A. Liska. Albany: SUNY Press.

Williams, K. and R. Hawkins. 1986. "Perceptual Research on General Deterrence: A Critical Review." *Law and Society Review* 20:545–72.

Wood, P., B. Pfefferbaum, and B. Arneklev. 1993. "Risk-Taking and Self-Control: Social Psychological Correlates of Delinquency." *Journal of Crime and Justice* 16:111–30.

Yu, J., D. Essex, and W. Williford. 1992. "DWI/DWAI Offenders and Recidivism by Gender in the Eighties: A Changing Trend?" *International Journal of the Addictions* 27:637–47.

REVIEW QUESTIONS

1. What are some of the elements of the low self-control personality?

2. What do Piquero and Tibbetts say are some of the key concepts of the rational choice framework that go beyond traditional deterrence concepts? Which of these concepts were most supported by their own findings?

3. What finding do Piquero and Tibbetts claim is the "most interesting"?

READING 6

This empirical study on "hot spots" by Lawrence Sherman, Patrick Gartin, and Michael Buerger is generally considered one of the contemporary classics in the literature, perhaps due to its being one of the first tests of routine activities theory to use spatial data, as measured by crime distribution by location of the crime, as opposed to individual or family victimization data.[1] Using data for a single year from Minneapolis, Minnesota, this study found that some locations—both businesses and residences—are responsible for many hundreds of calls for police each year. On the other hand, the vast majority of locations place no calls to police at all. Routine activities theory helps provide a framework for explaining this nonrandom distribution of criminal activity. While reading this selection, consider the place where you grew up or live in now and see if the findings of this study fit with the "hot spots" there.

---

[1]Cohen and Felson, "Social Change."

Hot Spots of Predatory Crime

Routine Activities and the Criminology of Place

Lawrence W. Sherman, Patrick R. Gartin, and Michael E. Buerger

Is crime distributed randomly in space? There is much evidence that it is not. Yet there are many who suggest that it is. In a leading treatise on police innovations, for example, Skolnick and Bayley (1986: 1) observe that "we feel trapped in an environment that is like a madhouse of unpredictable violence and Quixotic threat." People victimized by crime near their homes often feel that there are no safe places and that danger lurks everywhere (Silberman, 1978: 15–16). Even many police we know, who acknowledge that some areas are more dangerous than others, often assume a random distribution of crime within areas. For them, the practical question is not whether crime is concentrated in space, but how much.

Such analysis of variation across space is one of the basic tools of science. Many clues to the environmental causes of cancer, for example, have been revealed by the discovery of carcinogenic "hot spots": locations with extremely high rates of cancer mortality (Mason et al., 1985). Similarly, many factors associated with automobile fatalities (such as low population density and distance from emergency medicine) have been highlighted by the discovery of rural western counties with death rates 350 times higher than those in such eastern states as New Jersey (Baker, Whitfield, and O'Neill 1987). The methodological history of such analyses can be traced to the moral statistics tradition (Guerry, 1831; Quetelet, 1842) and the sociology of crime and deviance, which pioneered the analysis of variation in behavior across space. Durkheim's *Suicide* (1897/1951) and Shaw et al.'s *Delinquency Areas* (1929) are two classic examples. More recently, sociologists have tested income inequality and other structural theories of crime with variation in crime rates across collectivities, at the levels of nation-states (e.g., Krahn, Hartnagel, and Gartrell, 1986; Messner, 1980), regions (e.g., Gastil, 1971; Loftin and Hill, 1974; Messner, 1983), and cities or metropolitan areas (e.g., Blau and Blau, 1982; Messner, 1982; Sampson, 1986).

Collectivities, Communities, and Places

A common problem of spatial analysis is pinpointing the locations of events. The ecological tradition in criminology has been confined to relatively large aggregations of people and space, which may mask important variation and causal properties within those aggregations. This may be especially important for within-city spatial variation.

Unlike the boundaries of nation-states and cities, the boundaries of within-city crime reporting districts do not correspond to theoretically or empirically defined collectivities, such as local communities or ethnic areas (Reiss, 1986: 26). Nor, as Reiss (1986) also points out, do official statistics on communities include many of the variables on collectivity characteristics needed to test theories of crime. The inability of community data to measure those characteristics creates major problems for community crime research (just as it does for this analysis) and leaves it vulnerable to what one sympathetic observer describes as a claim that there is little more here than "a theoretical exercise in the mapping of criminal phenomena" (Bursik, 1986: 36).

Even if collectivity characteristics can be measured at the level of community areas, those characteristics may have very different meanings and causal properties at the level of places. An independent variable like per capita alcohol consumption per hour, for example, means something very different at the street-corner level than it does at a 2-mile-square neighborhood level. It is clearly subject to a much wider range at the place level than it is at greater

SOURCE: Adapted from Lawrence Sherman, Patrick Gartin, and Michael Buerger, "Hot Spots of Predatory Crime: Routine Activities and the Criminology of Place," *Criminology* 27 (1989): 27–56. Reprinted by permission of the American Society of Criminology.

aggregations, with all of the effects of higher levels of consumption being concentrated on behavior in that microsocial space. Focusing on variation across smaller spaces opens up a new level of analysis that can absorb many variables that have previously been shunned as too obvious or not sufficiently sociological: the visibility of cash registers from the street, the availability of public restrooms, the readiness of landlords to evict problem tenants.

The increased range of such independent variables at a micro-place level also means that variation in crime within communities is probably greater than variations across communities (Robinson, 1950). The very meaning of the concept of a bad neighborhood is an open empirical question: whether the risk of crime is randomly or evenly distributed throughout the neighborhood, or so concentrated in some parts of the neighborhood that other parts are relatively safe.

Some recent policy research hints at the latter answer. Taylor and Gottfredson (1986: 410) conclude that there is evidence linking spatial variation in crime to the physical and social environment at the subneighborhood level of street blocks and multiple dwellings (e.g., Jacobs, 1961; Newman, 1972; Newman and Franck, 1980, 1982; but see Merry, 1981a, 1981b). Some 40 years ago, Henry McKay himself made the unpublished discovery that even within high-crime Chicago neighborhoods, entire blocks were free of offenders (Albert J. Reiss, Jr., personal communication).

Other findings suggest microlevel variation within blocks for the predatory stranger crimes of burglary, robbery, and auto theft. Salt Lake City houses with well-tended hedges were found to be less likely than other houses in the same neighborhood to be burglarized (Brown, 1983). Tallahassee apartments near the complex entrance and not facing another building were more likely to be burglarized than apartments inside the development facing other buildings (Molumby, 1976). And apartments in buildings with doormen were also less likely to be burglarized than other apartments (Reppetto, 1974; Waller and Okihiro, 1978).

Microspatial variations in robbery rates also suggest nonrandom distributions. Convenience stores near vacant land or away from other places of commerce were more likely to be robbed than those in dense commercial areas (Duffala, 1976). Over a 5-year period in Gainesville, Florida, 96% of all 47 convenience stores were robbed, compared with 36% of the 67 fast-food establishments, 21% of

the 71 gas stations, and 16% of the 44 liquor stores (Clifton, 1987). Conversely, over a 10-year period in Texas, gas station workers were murdered at a rate of 14.2 per 100,000 workers per year, compared with a rate of 11.9 for convenience-type store workers and 5.1 per 100,000 per year for all retail workers (Davis, 1987). Tallahassee convenience stores with the cashier visibly stationed in the middle of the store were three times more likely to have a low robbery rate as stores with the cashier set less visibly off to the side (Jeffery, Hunter, and Griswold, 1987). Convenience stores with two clerks on duty may be less likely to be robbed than stores with only one (Clifton, 1987; Jeffery et al., 1987; but see Chambers, 1988).

Similar microspatial findings are reported in England. English parking lots with attendants had lower rates of auto theft than unattended parking lots (Clarke, 1983: 239). Pedestrian tunnels in downtown Birmingham, England, accounted for a negligible portion of all public space, but they produced 13% of a sample of 552 criminal attacks on persons (Poyner, 1983: 85).

Traditional collectivity theories may be appropriate for explaining community-level variation, but they seem inappropriate for small, publicly visible places with highly transient populations. Nor is it necessary to give up the explanatory task to the competing perspectives of rational choice (Cornish and Clarke, 1986) and environmental design (Jeffery, 1971; Newman, 1972). A leading recent sociological theory can address these findings, but only with a clearer definition of its unit of analysis. The routine activities approach of Cohen and Felson (1979) can be used to develop a criminology of *places*, rather than its previous restrictions to a criminology of *collectivities* or of the life-styles of victimized *individuals* (Hindelang, Gottfredson, and Garofalo, 1978; Messner and Tardiff, 1985; Miethe et al., 1987) and *households* (Massey, Krohn, and Bonati, 1987).

▧ Routine Activities and Place

In their original statement of the routine activities approach, Cohen and Felson (1979: 589) attempt to account for "direct contact predatory violations," or illegal acts in which "someone definitely and intentionally takes or damages the person or property of another" (Glaser, 1971: 4). They propose that the rate at which such events occur in collectivities is affected by "the convergence in space and time of the three minimal elements of direct-contact predatory violations: (1) motivated offenders, (2) suitable targets, and (3) the absence of capable guardians against a violation" (Cohen and Felson, 1979: 589).

 ## Data Collection

Unfortunately, few if any police departments can provide researchers, or even police chiefs, with a year-long call data base ready to analyze. Computer-aided dispatch systems are designed for operational purposes, so they do not have large storage capacities. The Minneapolis system, for example, can store only about 7,000 call records on line, so the calls must be removed from the mainframe computer about once a week and stored on tape. To construct a single data file for police calls covering 1 year or longer, researchers must generally provide their own computer into which the police backup tapes are read.

Using that procedure in Minneapolis, selected data elements from each complete call record were read from all the available tapes covering the period from December 15, 1985, to December 15, 1986. Missing data were discovered for 28 days, distributed throughout the year in four blocks of about 7 days each. A total of 323,979 call records were copied into a microcomputer, after fire, ambulance, and administrative record calls from police (e.g., out to lunch) were deleted. The findings presented below are derived from those data as well as from a less precise estimate of the number of street addresses and intersections in the city.

Hot Spots of Crime

The analysis reveals substantial concentrations of all police calls, and especially calls for predatory crime, in relatively few "hot spots." Just over half (50.4%) of all calls to the police for which cars were dispatched went to a mere 3.3% of all addresses and intersections A majority (60%) of all addresses generated at least one call over the course of the year, but about half of those addresses produced one call and no more. The top 5% of all locations generated an average of 24 calls each, or 1 every 2 weeks.

The number of calls per location ranged as high as 810 at a large discount store near a poor neighborhood, followed by 686 calls at a large department store, 607 calls at a corner with a 24-hours-a-day convenience store and a

bar, and 479 calls at a public housing apartment building (data not displayed). To test the premise that these concentrations are not merely random clusters, we calculated a simple Poisson model of the expected frequency of locations with each level of call volume. The simple Poisson model assumes that (1) the probability of a dispatched call to police is the same for all places and (2) the probability of a call does not depend on the number of previous calls (Nelson, 1980). For a sample of 115,000 places, the frequencies of repeat calls expected by chance are significantly lower than the observed frequencies, with a maximum of 13 calls expected (and 810 observed) at any one location.

Our findings must be interpreted with great caution, largely because of the enormous heterogeneity across places of both the size of the population and the periods of time at risk. The wide range of risk levels is suggested by capsule qualitative descriptions of the places with highest raw frequencies of predatory crime calls, presented in Table 1.

The nonrandom distribution of crime by place may simply be due to the nonrandom distribution of people. Geographers have long recognized the day-to-day clustering of people residing over a wide area into small "nodes" of activity (Brantingham and Brantingham, 1984: 235). If crime is concentrated in direct proportion to the concentration of people, then there may be nothing particularly criminogenic about those places. It may make sense for police to concentrate their efforts at those nodes, as an experiment in Minneapolis is now attempting to do (Sherman and Weisburd, 1988), but there is no increased per capita risk of crime for people to worry about or for theory to explain.

Two cases in point illustrate the population issue. A Dallas hotel we analyzed looked much like the worst hot spots in Minneapolis. It had a high place rate of predatory crime, with 1,245 crime reports over a 2-year period, 41 of them for violent crimes against persons. Yet the hotel covered 48 acres and had an estimated mean daily population of 3,000 guests, employees, and visitors. The per capita robbery rate was 76% lower than the per capita robbery rate for the entire city (Sherman, Buerger, and Gartin).[1] In contrast, the bar on the Minneapolis hot-spot list (Table 1) with the highest raw frequency of predatory crime also had very high per capita rates of crime. With 25 robberies in 1 year, and an estimated mean daily population of no more

Table 1	Hot Spots in Minneapolis, December 15, 1985–December 15, 1986, with 10 or More Predatory Crimes (adjusted data before aggregation of multiple address listings)	
Rank/Description	**Robberies, Rapes, Auto Thefts**	**All Types**
1. Intersection: bars, liquor store, park	33	461
2. Bus Depot	28	343
3. Intersection: homeless shelters, bars	27	549
4. Downtown Mall	27	445
5. Intersection: adult bookstore, bars	27	431
6. Bar	25	510
7. Intersection: theater, mall, record store	25	458
8. Hotel	23	240
9. Convenience Store	22	607
10. Bar	21	219
11. Intersection: drugstore, adult theater	18	513
12. Intersection: restaurant, bar	15	445
13. Apartment Building	15	177
14. Department Store	15	449
15. Intersection: Burger King, office bldg.	15	365
16. Shopping Mall	15	305
17. Hotel	14	121
18. Bar	14	244
19. Towing Company	14	113
20. Movie Theater	14	251
21. Department Store	14	810
22. High-rise Apartment Building	14	479
23. Intersection: drugstore, adult bookstore	13	290
24. Convenience Store	13	113
25. Intersection: high concentration of bars	13	206
26. Parking Lot	13	31
27. Loring Park	13	212
28. Restaurant	13	25
29. Apartment Building	12	142
30. Restaurant	12	198
31. Homeless Shelter	12	379
32. Detached House	11	190
33. High-rise Apartment Building	11	125

Rank/Description	Robberies, Rapes, Auto Thefts	All Types
34. Apartment Building	10	233
35. Intersection: high residential area	10	156
36. High-rise Apartment Building	10	92
37. Restaurant	10	122
38. Intersection: apartments, gas stations	10	197
39. Intersection: supermarket, liquor store	10	94
40. Lake Harriet	10	171
41. Bar	10	107
42. Apartment Building	10	142
Totals	661	11,760

than 300, Moby Dick's Bar had a robbery call rate of 83 per 1,000 persons—seven times higher than the call rate of 12 per 1,000 for the city's entire 1986 estimated population of 362,000. With 81 assaults, the per capita assault rate at the bar was 270 per 1,000 or more than 1 assault for every 4 persons in the bar over the year. Such an environment can reasonably be labeled as a dangerous place, in which individuals face substantially higher personal risks of criminal victimization than in the "average" place.

The estimates of per capita crime risk by place are further complicated by the varying time at risk. One reason the convenience stores in Gainesville had six times greater prevalence than the liquor stores of at least one armed robbery per location (Clifton 1987) may be that the liquor stores were open for less than half the hours per week of a 24-hour, 7-day convenience store. Just as plane and automobile crash fatalities are computed per passenger mile traveled, the conceptually appropriate indicator for place crimes against persons may be crimes per person-minute spent on the premises. Property crimes would require different adjustments for time at risk. Commercial burglary, for example, should be standardized by the number of hours per week an establishment is closed, and auto theft rates might be standardized by the number of hours each car is present at a place. The violent Minneapolis bar would be even more violent if the annualized violence rates were adjusted for the limited hours per day it was occupied.

Are Places Criminogenic?

The basic theoretical problem for the criminology of place, however, is not just to account for variation in raw frequencies of place crime, or per unit/period crime target risks. The more fundamental issue is whether the routine activities of places, given their physical environment, are actually criminogenic. Do places vary in their capacity to help *cause* crime, or merely in their frequency of *hosting* crime that was going to occur some place inevitably, regardless of the specific place? Are the routine activities of hot spots criminogenic *generators* of crime, or merely more attractive *receptors* of crime? If a crime hot spot is somehow incapacitated from producing its routine activities, would there be a corresponding net decline in total criminal events, or merely a hydraulic displacement of the same events to the next most appropriate locations?

Displacement

A routine activities criminology of place hypothesizes that crime cannot be displaced merely by displacing motivated offenders; the offenders must also be displaced *to* other places with suitable targets and weak guardianship. The findings presented above support that view. If the distribution of crime hot spots was determined solely by the concentration of offenders, then how can we explain the complete 1-year absence of predatory crimes from 73% of the places in high-crime areas in Minneapolis (compared with the expected absence from only 57%)?

Cohen and Felson (1979) support the criminogenic role of place by demonstrating temporal correlations between time spent away from home and collectivity crime rates. Other evidence suggests that variations in area-level guardianship are associated with little displacement of offending from better to more poorly guarded areas (Hakim and Rengert 1981). The entire problem of planned reductions in criminal opportunity unintentionally producing *displacement* of crime may have been exaggerated by policymakers pessimistically resigned to the perseverance of evildoers (Clarke and Mayhew 1988; Cornish and Clarke 1987). But as an empirical question, the generator-versus-receptor problem is far from being resolved.

It seems likely, for example, that the criminogenic influence of place varies by type of offense. Crimes arising out of intimate or market relationships may be much less dependent on place than predatory stranger crimes. The concentration of domestic disturbance calls may simply indicate that certain buildings are receptors for the kinds of people most likely to experience, or at least call police about, domestic problems; such calls might occur at the same rate no matter where they lived. Some market-driven offenses, like the street sale of prostitution and illegal narcotics, may occur independently of the routine activities of places. As the recent failed crackdown on drugs in the District of Columbia suggests (Reuter et al., 1987), market crimes may create their own routine activities in otherwise relatively unorganized public places.

Yet all the literature on robbery discussed above suggests that cash business places open at night generate opportunities for robbery, the absence of which could well mean fewer robberies. The concentration of exposers in Minneapolis parks (7 of the 25 top-ranked places for sex crimes) suggest that there might be fewer exposures if there were fewer places providing both a desirable audience and abundant opportunities for concealment. Predatory stranger offenses, in particular, seem dependent on places where offenders converge with vulnerable victims and low surveillance.

Yet even predatory stranger offenses vary substantially by type of offense, as Table 1 shows, with respect to the magnitude of concentration they display relative to the number of possible locations. One can avoid robbery twice as effectively by staying away from certain places than one

can avoid sex crimes or auto theft. If routine activities of places are criminogenic, they appear to be more powerfully so for some kinds of offenses than others.

Changing Places, Not People

Ironically, Cohen and Felson (1979) concluded their original analysis with an emphasis on individual life-styles as the primary aspect of routine activities affecting crime, implying the inevitability of higher crime with a more mobile life-style (cf. Hindelang et al. 1978). Focusing on the routine activities of places rather than of individual life-styles produces a different conclusion, as Felson (1987) has recently implied. On a place-specific basis, targets may be made less suitable, guardianship may be increased, and the supply of potential offenders may be reduced. Successful efforts to do so might produce net reductions in crime, holding constant the absolute size of the populations of offenders and targets. The routine activities of the person who goes to bars or convenience stores late at night does not have to change for such places to be made less criminogenic.

Many recent examples of such attempts can be found. Local ordinances passed in the late 1980s in Ohio, Florida, and New Jersey require convenience stores to have two or more clerks on duty, for the explicit purpose of reducing armed robbery through better guardianship (Clifton 1987). A 1987 editorial in the *American Journal of Public Health* recommends that the U.S. Occupational Safety and Health Administration regulate workplace environments to reduce target suitability for robbery-homicide by requiring bullet-proof barriers to protect taxi drivers and store clerks and better placement of cash registers to increase surveillability from the street (Dietz and Baker, 1987). The mother of a boy murdered in a 1985 Orlando, Florida, convenience store robbery attempted to create a Mother against Drunk Driving (MADD)-type organization called Victims of Interstate Convenience Enterprises (VOICE) to fight for better convenience store security (Lawrence 1986). New York police developed an Operation Padlock program to close up businesses with repeated crime problems. As part of the developing problem-oriented approach to reinventing police strategies (Eck and Spelman 1987; Goldstein 1979), police in Minneapolis have sought to reduce convergence of offenders and targets under weak guardianship by revoking the liquor licenses of two violent bars, based in part on the data analysis presented above (Sherman et al., 1988). Citizens in Detroit have gone as far as buying up and renovating vacant houses to prevent them from becoming crack houses (Wilkerson, 1988b), and citizens in both Detroit and Miami have burned down crack houses, with an acquittal on arson charges by one Detroit jury (Wilkerson, 1988a).

Whether such measures can produce net reductions in crime (without displacement) may be impossible to determine, given the difficulty of holding constant the collectivity supply of motivated offenders—or even of defining adequately who they are (Massey et al., 1987). But controlled experimentation may be the best means for determining the extent to which routine activities of places can be made less criminogenic. Random assignment of a large sample of clusters of hot spot addresses to different levels of guardianship by police patrol, for example, could determine (1) whether guardianship affects place crime and (2) whether crimes reduced in one place are matched by crimes increased in nearby places (Sherman and Weisburd, 1988). The convenience store industry could experiment with numbers of clerks and other guardianship measures and examine potential displacement of armed robbery to other nighttime commercial establishments in nearby jurisdictions.

At the same time, the criminology of place can be enhanced by longitudinal analysis of the characteristics associated with onset, frequency rates, seriousness, and desistance of crime in places (Blumstein, Cohen, Roth, and Visher, 1986; Wolfgang, Figlio, and Sellin 1972). For example, from 1945 (the birth year of the first Philadelphia cohort) to 1988, one liquor store in Northeast Washington under the same family management experienced 16 robberies and burglaries and 4 robbery-homicides (Mintz, 1988). How does that compare with other liquor stores? How will it compare with future rates under new management? How do liquor stores compare with other types of retail outlets, or other types of places? Such research on the "criminal careers" of places could help to specify the fertile, but still too general, routine activities concepts of target suitability, motivated offenders, and guardianship.

Like the criminology of individuals, a criminology of place could fall prey to the facile notion that getting rid of the "bad apples" will solve the problem. Neither capital punishment of places (as in arson of crack houses) nor incapacitation of the routine activities of criminal hot spots

(as in revocation of liquor licenses) seems likely to eliminate crime. But since the routine activities of places may be regulated far more easily than the routine activities of persons, a criminology of place would seem to offer substantial promise for public policy as well as theory.

 ## Note

1. One possible cause for the actual "coolness" of this apparently hot spot was the much higher level of guardianship at the hotel. The ratio of patrol officers (including the hotel's security officers) to population was three times higher at the hotel than in the city as a whole, and the density of patrol presence per acre was 63 times higher at the hotel than city wide. As Felson (1987: 927) points out, growing inequality of security is characteristic of the modern metropolis. This inequality has arguably made many people into virtual prisoners of their private spaces, or "modern cliff dwellers" (Reiss. 1987: 42).

 ## References

Baker, Susan P., R. A. Whitfield, and Brian O'Neill. 1987. "Geographic Variations in Mortality from Motor Vehicle Crashes". *New England Journal of Medicine* 316:1, 384–87.

Blau, Judith R., and Peter M. Blau. 1982. "The Cost of Inequality: Metropolitan Structure and Violent Crime". *American Sociological Review* 47:114–129.

Blumstein, Alfred, Jacqueline Cohen, Jeffrey A. Roth, and Christy Visher, eds. 1986. *Criminal Careers and "Career Criminals."* Vol. 1. Washington, DC: National Academy Press.

Brantingham, Paul J., and Patricia L. Brantingham. 1984. *Patterns in Crime.* New York: Macmillan.

Brown, Barbara, 1983. Ph.D. dissertation, Department of Psychology, University of Utah. Cited in *The New York Times,* November 17, C11.

Bursik, Robert J., Jr. 1986. "Ecological Stability and the Dynamics of Delinquency". In *Communities and Crime,* edited by Albert J. Reiss, Jr. and Michael Tonry. Chicago: University of Chicago Press.

Chambers, Ray W. 1988. "Gainesville Convenience Store Security Measures Ordinance: A Review and Analysis". Unpublished manuscript.

Clarke, Ronald V. 1983. "Situational Crime Prevention: Its Theoretical Basis and Practical Scope". In *Crime and Justice: An Annual Review of research.* Vol. 4, edited by Michael Tonry and Norval Morris. Chicago: University of Chicago Press.

Clarke, Ronald V., and Pal Mayhew. 1988. "The British Gas Suicide Rate Story and Its Criminological Implications". In *Crime and Justice: An Annual Review of Research.* Vol. 10, edited by Michael Tonry and Norval Morris. Chicago: University of Chicago Press.

Clifton, Wayland, Jr. 1987. "Convenience Store Robberies in Gainesville, Florida: An Intervention Strategy by the Gainesville Police Department". Paper presented at meeting of the American Society of Criminology, Montreal, November.

Cohen, Lawrence E. and Marcus Felson. 1979. "Social Change and Crime Rate Trends: A Routine Activity Approach". *American Sociological Review* 44:588–608.

Cornish, Derek B. and Ronald V. Clarke. 1986. *The Reasoning Criminal: Rational Choice Perspectives on Offending*. New York: Springer-Verlag.

———. 1987. "Understanding Crime Displacement: An Application of Rational Choice Theory". *Criminology* 25:933–48.

Davis, Harold. 1987. "Workplace Homicides of Texas Males". *American Journal of Public Health* 77:1, 290–93.

Dietz, Park Elliott, and Susan P. Baker. 1987. "Murder at Work". *American Journal of Public Health* 77:273–74.

Duffala, Dennis C. 1976. "Convenience Stores, Armed Robbery, and Physical Environmental Features". *American Behavioral Scientist* 20:227–46.

Durkheim, Emile. [1897] 1951. *Suicide: A Study in sociology*. New York: Free Press.

Eck, John, and William Spelman. 1987. *Problem-solving*. Washington, DC: Police Executive Research Forum.

Felson, Marcus. 1987. Routine activities and crime prevention in the developing metropolis. *Criminology* 25:911–32.

Gastil, Raymond D. 1971. "Homicide and a Regional Culture of Violence". *American Sociological Review* 36:412–17.

Glaser, Daniel. 1971. *Social deviance*. Chicago: Markham.

Goldstein, Herman. 1979. "Improving Policing: A Problem-oriented Approach". *Crime and Delinquency* 25:236–38.

Guerry, A. M. 1831. *Essai sur la statistique morale de la France*. Paris: Chez Corchard.

Hakim, Simon, and George F. Rengert, eds. 1981. *Crime Spillover*. Beverly Hills, CA: Sage.

Hindelang, Michael. 1976. *Criminal Victimization in Eight American Cities*. Cambridge, MA: Ballinger.

Hindelang, Michael, Michael Gottfredson, and James Garofalo. 1978. *Victims of Personal Crime*. Cambridge, MA: Ballinger.

Jacobs, Jane. 1961 *The Death and Life of Great American Cities*. New York: Vintage.

Jeffery, C. Ray. 1971. *Crime Prevention through Environmental Design*. Beverly Hills, CA: Sage.

Jeffery, C. Ray, Ronald Hunter, and Jeffery Griswold. 1987. "Crime Analysis, Computers, and Convenience Store Robberies". Appendix D to Wayland Clifton, Jr., "Convenience Store Robberies in Gainesville, Florida: An Intervention Strategy by the Gainesville Police Department". Paper presented at meeting of the American Society of Criminology, Montreal, November.

Krahn, Harvey, Timothy F. Hartnagel, and John W. Gartrell. 1986. "Income Inequality and Homicide Rates: Cross-national Data and Criminological Theories". *Criminology* 24:269–95.

Lawrence, Donna. 1986. "Mad Mother Fights for Tighter C-Store Security". *C-Store Digest*, October 20, 1

Loftin, Colin, and Robert Hill. 1974. "Regional Subculture and Homicide: An Examination of the Gastil-Hackney Hypothesis". *American Sociological Review* 39:714–24.

Mason, T. J., F. W. McKay, R. Hoover, W. J. Blot, and J. F. Fraumeni, Jr. 1985. *Atlas of Cancer Mortality for U.S. Counties: 1950-69*, DHEW Publication (NIH) 75-780. Bethesda, MD: National Cancer Institute.

Massey, James L., Marvin D. Krohn, and Lisa Bonati. 1987. "The Routine Activities of Individuals and Property Crime". Paper presented at meeting of the American Society of Criminology, Montreal.

Merry, Sally E. 1981a. "Defensible Space Undefended: Social Factors in Crime Prevention through Environmental Design". *Urban Affairs Quarterly* 16:397–422.

———. 1981b. *Urban Danger: Life in a Neighborhood of Strangers*. Philadelphia: Temple University Press.

Messner, Steven. 1980. "Income Inequality and Murder Rates: Some Cross-national Findings". *Comparative Social Research* 3: 185–98.

———. 1982. Poverty, Inequality and the Urban Homicide Rate. *Criminology* 20:103–14.

———. 1983. "Regional Differences in the Economic Correlates of the Urban Homicide Rate: Some Evidence on the Importance of Cultural Context". *Criminology* 21:477–88.

Messner, Steven, and Kenneth Tardiff. 1985. "The Social Ecology of Urban Homicide: An Application of the 'Routine Activities' Approach". *Criminology* 23:241–67.

Miethe, Terance D.. Mark C. Stafford, and J. Scott Long. 1987. "Social Differentiation in Criminal Victimization: A Test of Routine Activities Lifestyle Theories". *American Sociological Review* 52: 1984–94.

Mintz, John. 1988. "NE Store Owners Retiring with Stock of Memories". *The Washington Post*, October 17, CI.

Molumby, Thomas. 1976. "Patterns of Crime in a University Housing project". *American Behavioral Scientist* 20:247–59.

Nelson, James F. 1980. "Multiple Victimization in American Cities: A Statistical Analysis of Rare Events". *American Journal of Sociology* 85: 870–91.

Newman, Oscar. 1972. *Defensible Space: Crime Prevention through Urban Design*. New York: Macmillan.

Newman, Oscar, and K. A. Franck. 1980. *Factors Affecting Crime and Instability in Urban Housing Developments*. Washington, DC: Government Printing Office.

———. 1982. "The Effects of Building Size on Personal Crime and Fear of Crime". *Population and Environment* 5: 203–20.

Poyner, Barry. 1983. *Design Against Crime: Beyond Defensible Space*. London: Butterworth.

Quetelet, L. Adolphe J. 1842. *A Treatise on Man and the Development of His Faculties*. Edinburgh: Chambers.

Reiss, Albert J., Jr. 1986. "Why Are Communities Important in Understanding Crime?" In *Communities and Crime*, ed. Albert J. Reiss, Jr., and Michael Tonry. Chicago: University of Chicago Press.

———. 1987. "The Legitimacy of Intrusion into Private Space". In *Sage Criminal Justice Systems Annual Series.*, Vol. 23, *Private Policing*. Newbury Park, CA: Sage.

Reppetto, Thomas A. 1974. *Residential Crime.* Cambridge, MA: Ballinger.

Reuter, Peter, John Haaga, Patrick Murphy, and Amy Praskac. 1987. "Drug Use and Policy in the Washington Metropolitan Area: An Assessment. Draft". Washington, DC: Rand.

Robinson, William S. 1950. "Ecological Correlations and the Behavior of Individuals". *American Sociological Review* 15:351–57.

Sampson, Robert. 1986. "Crime in Cities: Formal and Informal Social Control". In *Communities and Crime,* ed. Albert J. Reiss, Jr., and Michael Tonry. Chicago: University of Chicago Press.

Shaw, Clifford R., Henry D. McKay, Frederick Zorbaugh, and Leonard S. Cottrell. 1929. *Delinquency Areas.* Chicago: University of Chicago Press.

Sherman, Lawrence W. 1988. "Violent Stranger Crime at a Large Hotel: A Case Study in Risk Assessment Methods. Unpublished manuscript, Crime Control Institute, Washington, DC.

Sherman, Lawrence W., and David Weisburd. 1988. "Policing the Hot Spots of Crime: A Redesign of the Kansas City Preventive Patrol Experiment. Unpublished manuscript, Crime Control Institute, Washington, DC.

Sherman, Lawrence, Michael E. Buerger, and Patrick R. Gartin. 1988. "Beyond dial-a-cop: Repeat call addresses policing". Unpublished manuscript, Crime Control Institute, Washington, DC.

Silberman, Charles. 1978. *Criminal Violence, Criminal Justice.* New York: Simon & Schuster.

Skolnick, Jerome, and David Bayley. 1986. *The New Blue Line.* New York: Free Press.

Taylor, Ralph B., and Steven Gottfredson. 1986. "Environmental Design, Crime, and Prevention: An Examination of Community Dynamics". In *Communities and Crime,* ed. Albert J. Reiss, Jr., and Michael Tonry. Chicago: University of Chicago Press.

Waller, Irvin, and Norman Okihiro. 1978. *Burglary: The Victim and the Public.* Toronto: University of Toronto Press.

Wilkerson, Isabel. 1988a. "Crack House Fire: Justice or Vigilantism?" *The New York Times,* October 22.

———. 1988b. "Detroit Citizens Join with Church to Rid Community of Drugs. *The New York Times,* June 29.

Wolfgang, Marvin E., Robert Figlio, and Thorsten Sellin. 1972. *Delinquency in a Birth Cohort.* Chicago: University of Chicago Press.

REVIEW QUESTIONS

1. What measure did Sherman et al. use to measure how crime was distributed? What are the strengths and weaknesses of this measure?

2. Regarding the more serious crimes that Sherman et al. measure, what types of establishments appear the most in the Top 10? Why do such locations appear to epitomize the various elements of routine activities theory?

3. Why would fast-food restaurants or towing companies appear as "hot spots" for crime? What types of characteristics do these locations have that would predispose them to crime/victimization?

READING 7

Like the authors of the previous reading, Teresa LaGrange uses a routine activities theoretical framework for her study of crime in Edmonton, Alberta, and goes a bit further by examining the influence of environmental predictors on why crime tends to be higher in certain areas. Furthermore, she uses more advanced mapping software for her analysis, a relatively new program called MapInfo, which is based on coordinates and geocoding of crime activity. In addition, she reviews the influence of the theory of "broken windows" that was originally presented by Wilson and Kelling.[1] That theory argues that in certain areas, a broken window or other physical eyesore will be fixed very quickly, whereas in other areas, one broken window quickly leads to other broken windows and additional dilapidation because the residents and business owners do not care much about the area or do not have the financial

---

[1]Wilson and Kelling, "Broken Windows."

means to pay for such improvements. Subsequently, this leads to higher crime rates in the area because motivated offenders feel they have less chance of getting caught in run-down areas where residents do not have the inclination or resources to secure the area. This often becomes a serious feedback loop, and physical and crime conditions continue to decline in a rapid cycle. While reading the following selection, consider the importance that environmental planning and the layout of cities have on opportunities for offenders to commit crime.

The Impact of Neighborhoods, Schools, and Malls on the Spatial Distribution of Property Damage

Teresa C. LaGrange

Analysis of the geographic distribution of crime has had a long history in criminology, dating from the work of sociologists at the Chicago School. Most of this research has focused on index crimes such as homicide, robbery, rape, or burglary, and it has linked rates of offending to the social and residential characteristics of the neighborhoods where these crimes occur. Minor crimes, however, such as property damage and vandalism, occur far more frequently in any city than the more widely studied index offenses. Recent research has suggested that these crimes may be significant factors in the occurrence of urban crime in a more general sense, through processes described as the "broken windows" effect or "spiral of decay" (Felson 1998: 131; Skogan 1990:40; see also Kelling and Coles 1996). According to these perspectives, the accumulation of minor property damage sends a subtle signal to potential offenders that guardianship is low and that crimes may be carried out undetected. Thus, crimes of all types are more likely to be committed in run-down areas of a city. An understanding of the geographic distribution of minor offenses like property damage and vandalism, therefore, has the potential to shed light on the spatial patterns of a much broader range of criminal activity.

Although the causal variables that are usually examined in relation to spatial variations in crime rates have been those associated with structural theories of offending (Bursik 1988; Park and Burgess 1933; Shaw and McKay 1942; Snodgrass 1976), the broken windows phenomenon emphasizes that the immediate situational context may also be an important factor in the occurrence of crime. A would-be offender needs a suitable victim or target, and must encounter it in circumstances that permit a crime to be carried out without interruption. Recognition of these fundamental observations has led to the recent development of perspectives such as routine activities theory, which looks beyond the attributes of residents of high-crime areas to consider those social and environmental factors that make such areas conducive to crime (Cohen and Felson 1979; Felson 1986, 1987, 1994, 1998; Felson and Cohen 1980). As formulated and developed by Felson and Cohen, routine activities theory portrays crime as the convergence of the following three elements: motivated offenders, potential victims or targets, and unguarded access (Felson 1998:53). Thus, features of the urban environment that contribute to the convergence of these factors by increasing the concentration of offenders and victims, or reducing guardianship, will result in increased crime rates. Such factors may include characteristics of neighborhoods, such as the age composition of residents or the proportion of rental housing. They may include physical structures in the environment such as bars (Block and Block 1995; Roncek and Maier 1991), schools (Roncek and Faggiani 1985; Roncek and LoBosco 1983),

Source. Teresa C. LaGrange, "The Impact of Neighborhoods, Schools, and Malls on the Spatial Distribution of Property Damage," *Journal of Research in Crime and Delinquency* 36, no. 4 (1999): 393–422. Copyright © 1999 Sage Publications, Inc. Reprinted by permission of Sage Publications, Inc.

or shopping malls (Engstad 1980) that serve as crime attractors or generators (Brantingham and Brantingham 1991, 1994, 1995; Jarvis 1972).

The primary objective of the current study is to apply these concepts, derived from routine activities theory and previous research on the spatial distribution of crime, to the occurrence of minor property damage throughout one city during a single year. The occurrence of damage incidents as recorded by three different city departments or agencies is considered in relationship to neighborhood characteristics, residential composition, and environmental structures (schools and malls) that contribute to the convergence of likely offenders and reduced guardianship. The research has a number of implications. The link between cumulative property damage and more serious crimes means that the analysis of these crimes can make an important contribution to the understanding of urban crime patterns. Furthermore, because property damage and vandalism tend to be directed primarily toward public or impersonal spaces and facilities, an understanding of their etiology may provide a useful model for research into other forms of anonymous environmental damage (Skogan 1990:37). Finally, this research extends the principles of routine activities theory to previously understudied types of criminal activity, and thus sheds further light on the way in which guardianship and opportunity intersect to permit crimes to occur.

 ## Theory and Previous Research

It is well known that crimes tend to cluster in certain areas of a city, so that some areas have higher crime rates than others (Brantingham and Brantingham 1984, 1993; Dunn 1984; Figlio, Hakim, and Rengert 1986; Georges-Abeyie and Harries 1980): This is one of the least disputed facts about crime, and it has been repeatedly supported by numerous studies spanning several decades, different cities, and diverse offenses. Previous research has examined, for example, the locations of homicides in Cleveland (Bensing and Schroeder 1960), Chicago (Block 1976), and Houston (Bullock 1955); robberies in Seattle (Schmid 1960); and burglaries in Washington, D.C. (Scarr 1973). Furthermore, it was the early observation of spatial variations that initially contributed to the development of the

classical perspectives on crime. Early theorists equated areas of the city with neighborhoods having enduring and distinctive features; this conceptualization led to the development of theories that attempted to explain the criminogenic nature of these areas (Kornhauser 1978). Factors associated with higher crime rates included the proportion of unemployed persons, the amount of rental housing, the overall residential density, and the length of time residents remained in the area. Various mechanisms have been identified that link these area characteristics to the criminal inclinations of residents—blocked opportunities and the absence of legitimate pursuits, the attraction of illegitimate opportunities, or a general lack of neighborhood social control (Allan and Steffensmeier 1989; Bursik 1988; Park and Burgess 1933; Sampson and Grove 1989; Shaw and McKay 1942; Snodgrass, 1976).

Contemporary research on when and where crimes occur, however, has been strongly influenced by the recognition that human activities, including crimes, take place within a specific social and physical environment (Hawley 1950, 1971). Thus, contemporary studies have taken into consideration the situational context that surrounds the occurrence of criminal events (Sacco and Kennedy 1994), rather than focusing exclusively on offender motivation. Even highly motivated offenders require certain conditions to complete their crimes—conditions that include such factors as the vulnerability of victims or targets and the presence or absence of witnesses (Sherman, Gartin, and Buerger 1989). Analyses of situational factors that include the routine activities of both likely offenders and potential victims have demonstrated that these requisite elements of crime converge nonrandomly; that is, some areas provide all the components for crime to occur more frequently and more regularly than others. The circumstances, under which crimes occur, from this perspective, are functions of social and structural phenomena that allow people to translate their criminal inclinations into action (Felson 1986, 1994, 1998).

Therefore, the social characteristics of residents of specific areas may not be a direct cause of the crimes rates in those areas (Allan and Steffensmeier 1989). Some, if not all, of the crimes may be committed by outsiders who gravitate to these areas rather than by residents themselves (Costanzo, Halperin, and Gale 1986:74). Crime rates might be high, not because of the criminal inclinations of residents, but because of the criminal opportunities that such areas provide (Dunn 1984; Felson and Cohen 1980). The nature and extent of guardianship in an area is directly related to whether people are at home or away from home and whether there are many people about during different times of day. It is affected by whether residents know their neighbors, and are capable of both recognizing and responding to events that appear out of the ordinary. Social characteristics such as the number of homemakers, single adults, or retired persons living in the area contribute to different patterns of local activity, dictating whether the majority of residents are at home during the day, during the evenings, or only rarely; and whether residents come and go regularly or at all hours.

Residents in their teens or early adulthood are likely to be absent from their homes more frequently, as are those who are single (Felson and Cohen 1980; Hindelang, Gottfredson, and Garofalo 1978). In areas where a large proportion of residents fall into these categories, guardianship may be substantially reduced. Similarly, areas with a high proportion of rental units have a less permanent resident population than well-established owner-occupied housing tracts (Bursik 1988). In areas with a high population turnover, it is less likely that residents will know their neighbors and know who does or does not have a legitimate reason for being in the area. Residents may therefore be unable to exercise informal surveillance by direct observation and by questioning of strangers or suspicious activities (Sampson and Grove 1989). Consistent with a routine activities perspective that emphasizes opportunity; higher crime rates in such areas may be directly related to the inability of residents to exercise suitable guardianship.

The population density of an area, by contrast, may have the opposite effect. Although high density might be hypothesized to increase the convergence of potential offenders and suitable targets, and has been linked by some research to higher crime rates (Hartnagel and Lee 1990), the sheer number of people in an area may make it more difficult for potential offenders to commit a crime without being observed. In general, density may lead to lower rates for crimes that involve secrecy (burglary, for example) and higher rates for crimes that arise from proximity (larceny and muggings) (Decker, Shichor, and O'Brien 1982:52–53; Felson 1998:29; see also Roncek and Faggiani 1985; Roncek and LoBosco 1983; Shlomo 1968).

Physical Structures in the Environment

In addition to the social environment provided by residents and neighborhoods, the urban landscape is shaped by physical structures that influence human activities. Two types of public structures, shopping malls and high schools, have been identified by previous studies as being significantly related to higher crime rates in adjacent areas (Engstad 1980; Roncek and Faggiani 1985; Roncek and LoBosco 1983). Both serve to attract a large number of nonresidents into an area who come and go with little formal supervision—a situation that not only brings potential offenders into the area, but also reduces guardianship.

Shopping malls. Shopping malls exist for the express purpose of attracting potential customers to the shops and services that they shelter. The large number of people who come and go in the streets around a mall works to reduce effective guardianship, because distinguishing between legitimate patrons and persons who are simply loitering may be difficult. It might be predicted that this combination of factors would result in higher crime rates in the areas immediately adjacent to malls. Consistent with this prediction, Engstad (1980) found significantly higher frequencies of auto crimes, thefts, and miscellaneous offenses in three urban census tracts, each of which contained a major shopping center,[1] when compared to surrounding areas with similar social and demographic characteristics. Areas with shopping centers had from 2.1 to 6.5 times as many offenses as the averages recorded for adjacent areas, and 1.5 to 3.7 times as many offenses as the maximum recorded for adjacent areas (Engstad 1980:210–11).

High schools. High schools also contribute to increased traffic and activity in the immediate, surrounding vicinity. Furthermore, this population consists of persons in their teens, who are implicated in higher rates of offending than other demographic groups. Thus, research into the impact of high schools has consistently demonstrated that their presence is associated with higher crime rates in surrounding neighborhoods. In the first of two studies conducted in medium-sized American cities, Roncek and LoBosco (1983) examined crimes occurring in a relatively new, affluent city that ranked lower in crime rates than other cities of comparable size. The authors report higher rates of several types of index crimes[2] in one-block areas immediately adjacent to public high schools,[3] controlling for social, housing, and demographic composition of the areas. Although the size of a school's enrollment was evaluated as a possible predictor, it was found to be nonsignificant.

Routine Activities and Minor Crimes

Although the impact of routine activities of residents and environmental structures such as schools and malls has been investigated for serious crimes such as robbery, burglary, or rape, these factors have not been considered in relation to minor offenses like property damage. One of the primary justifications for the emphasis on serious crimes, without question, is the potential such offenses have for grave social harm. Such crimes typically and understandably arouse the greatest fear and concern among the public, and they receive the greatest attention and resources from criminal justice agencies. Minor crimes do not appear to pose the same sort of immediate social threat, and hence are usually considered to be of secondary concern. Yet, the rate of occurrence for minor crimes far surpasses, in any city, the rates for more serious offenses. Such crimes as vandalism are a constantly occurring and ever present problem in most contemporary North American cities, and their cumulative impact can prove very costly (Bell, Bell, and Godefroy 1988; Skogan 1990). More significant, the accumulation of such incidents has been implicated in the spiral of decay (Felson 1998:131) that leads to the devaluation of urban neighborhoods. The impact is more than economic; the occurrence of minor crimes in an area, especially those that involve visible property damage, may elicit other criminal activity (Chalfant 1992; Challinger 1987; Kelling and Coles 1996).

The assertion that behavior can be formed by the circumstances surrounding it has been criticized as mechanistic at best and environmental determinism at worst (Clarke 1978). It is based, however, on the fundamental tenets of learning theory (Marongiu and Newman 1997; Wortley 1997:66). Specific situational factors can act as eliciting stimuli or behavioral cues to engage in or restrain certain behaviors. For example, in an influential and widely cited study, Zimbardo (1970) demonstrated that "releaser cues," in the form of existing damage, led to the rapid destruction of seemingly abandoned vehicles on the street.

The view that criminal events are contingent on the situation in which they occur is consistent with rational theories that attribute actions, including criminal ones, to a balancing of costs and benefits (Clarke and Felson 1993; Cornish and Clarke 1986). Benefits may be perceived as more likely if there is seemingly a low risk of apprehension. Thus, the perception of opportunity may in fact contribute to the occurrence of crime. Risks, on the other hand, particularly the perceived risks of being caught, may work to suppress such behavior. Areas where minor offenses such as property damage or vandalism occur and accumulate may convey a subtle signal to potential offenders that guardianship and social control are low. This perception may be taken, consciously or unconsciously, as an indication that the risks of detection and apprehension for criminal activity are negligible. That perception, in turn, may lead to an escalation in the rate of other, potentially more serious crimes (Felson 1998:131; Wortley 1997:67).

Social characteristics of areas that contribute to these elements may therefore be associated with higher rates of property damage. Areas that contain many unemployed persons, more young males, more rental than owned housing, and a larger number of transient residents will have greater movement and activity in and around the neighborhood, both during the course of the daily routine and over longer periods of time. These factors, in turn, make it more difficult to distinguish between strangers and residents and to determine the nature of their activities, thereby weakening guardianship. On the other hand, areas of high density and areas where more residents are homemakers or retired, and therefore home for more hours during the day, may not afford anonymous access to unguarded targets. Because potential offenders may feel constrained by the possibility of observation, less damage may occur in such areas.

Beyond the social characteristics of neighborhoods, physical features of the environment, such as malls and schools, that contribute to the convergence of offenders in an area might be expected to result in increased rates of minor crimes, just as with more serious crimes. Malls serve to draw large numbers of people into an area, some of whom may be potential offenders. Malls also impede effective guardianship because of the difficulty in distinguishing between legitimate and illegitimate visitors to the area. The presence of secondary schools within an area can also be expected to result in more crimes of this type because, like malls, such facilities increase local human traffic and thus interfere with guardianship. Furthermore, both malls and schools serve to draw together young people in their teens—the specific age groups most likely to be involved in minor property crime (Beaulieu 1982; Erickson and Jensen 1977; Gladstone 1978; Gold 1970).

The Current Research

In keeping with the foregoing discussion, this study examines the geographic distribution of minor property crime recorded as mischief and vandalism in a medium-sized Canadian city during a 1-year period.[4] Previous studies of the spatial distribution of crime have, for the most part, relied on official crime data as the most widely available and consistent information on crimes throughout all parts of a given geographic area. These statistics usually reflect police activity in response to crime. It is axiomatic that such records undercount crime for a variety of reasons, including the fact that many crimes go unreported and therefore fail to show up in official records, However, underreporting is especially likely to be a problem for official counts of very minor crimes such as property damage and vandalism, because victims may view such incidents as too minor to report. To address the potential methodological issues that arise from reliance on official reports for minor crimes, this study uses three types of data obtained from three departments in the city that served as the study site: the city's Department of Parks and Recreation, its transit department, and its police service.[5] Using census enumeration areas as a unit of aggregation,[6] the geographic patterns of these three types of damage are evaluated using ordinary least square (OLS) regression in relationship to two categories of predictors; the social characteristics of residents of each area, taken from municipal census data, and the presence or absence of two types of environmental structures, shopping malls and secondary schools.

Method

Data for this research was collected in Edmonton, Alberta, a western Canadian city with a population of approximately 600,000. The three agencies cooperating in this research— the police service, the city transit department, and the Department of Parks and Recreation—provided records of

the damage done to the facilities under their supervision during the calendar year of 1992. Each of these data sources was unique due to the nature of the targets, the types of incidents that could occur, and the way in which incidents were recorded; thus, merging them into a single composite index was deemed to be unsuitable. Each measure was therefore retained as a separate indicator of damage.

Mischief. Records were obtained from the Edmonton Police Service on all mischief incidents reported during 1992. Under Canadian law, the offence category of mischief refers to willful, malicious damage or public behavior. Most such incidents are property-related vandalism. Because many of them are relatively minor, however, police data are potentially biased, both by underreporting and by differential response. Research indicates that in Canada, as elsewhere, the extent to which citizens report crime varies. For very minor offenses, and particularly where there is little likelihood of identifying and arresting an offender, reporting is low (Griffiths and Verdun-Jones 1989; Silverman, Teevan, and Sacco 1996). Canadian victimization surveys reveal that most respondents do not report minor property crimes, even when the property is their own. Typically, less than half of such incidents are reported. Most respondents blame their failure to report on the trivial nature of incidents (60 percent) or on the lack of benefit expected from formal police action (47 percent) (Gartner and Doob 1996). Hence, the majority of incidents involving minor property damage does not show up in official police records. In addition, police responses to citizen complaints may vary according to the seriousness of the crime, considerations of the immediate workload, and time pressures. An officer's perception of the neighborhood where the report comes from may also influence the response (Hagan, Gillis, and Chan 1978). These factors can be expected to substantially restrict the number of incidents of minor property damage that show up in official police records, a reduction that may vary considerably for different neighborhoods.

For this study, additional data were obtained from two other contributing agencies. These data consisted of maintenance records to damaged structures, avoiding the difficulties associated with behavior and selective recording of damage. Where damage was observed, maintenance personnel for each department filed a report indicating their assessment of the cause, whether it was an accident, normal wear and tear, theft, or deliberate damage. In contrast to police data, which provided information on single incidents, both of these agencies kept periodic maintenance records that include an unknown amount of cumulative damage.

Transit vandalism. Records obtained from the transit department reported damage to bus stops and shelters throughout the city.[7] These records were compiled on the basis of reports from staff maintenance personnel who made regular visits to each shelter. Given the nature of these structures, assessments on the type of damage were deemed to be fairly accurate—their construction is designed to resist most inadvertent damage and discourage theft. The majority of incidents involved damage to the glass or plexiglass panels from which shelters are constructed; graffiti was excluded from the reports. However, maintenance personnel only visited the shelters on their route on a monthly basis. Any damage that was recorded at that time therefore incorporated an unknown number of actual incidents (D. Kowalchuk, personal communication, June 30, 1993).

Park vandalism. Reports on damage to facilities maintained by the Department of Parks and Recreation reflected periodic visits by maintenance personnel. Unlike the transit department records, however, which listed only a relatively restricted type of damage to specific types of structures, records from the Department of Parks and Recreation included a wide variety of different incidents, reflecting the greater variation in the types of structures and grounds for which the department had responsibility. In addition to all parks within the municipal limits, the Department of Parks and Recreation maintained recreational facilities, cemeteries, the grounds of public buildings, and tracts of public landscaping. Hence, there were potentially many different types of damage done to lawns, flowerbeds, buildings, pools, and other structures. This greater variety, however, renders the issue of determining the exact nature of damage and judging whether it was deliberate more problematic. Although maintenance personnel attempted to discriminate deliberate damage from accidental, the extent to which these judgments were correct is unknown. In addition, there is no way to ascertain whether similar criteria were used in evaluating incidents in different locations. Decisions were made by individual workers who filed reports on damages and classified them

according to the type of incident (W. Gorman, personal communication, June 2, 1993).

Census Enumeration Areas

Data on population and housing characteristics in the city were obtained from the 1992 City of Edmonton Municipal Census, which reported aggregate information for each census enumeration area. Enumeration areas are subdivisions of the permanent statistical units established by Statistics Canada for the national census (Lalu 1989:1). The smaller enumeration areas do not provide as much demographic detail as the larger census tracts. Their smaller size, however, allows for greater variation in population characteristics.

The routine activities perspective that forms the theoretical basis for this research does not equate the concept of neighborhood with that of community or that of the distinctive sociocultural attributes inherent in this term as developed in the earlier ecological tradition. Nevertheless, some minimal assumption about neighborhood is implicit in the expectation that people can potentially come to know their neighbors, that they may become familiar with their neighbors' children and habitual routines, and that these developments are important in informal guardianship. Although the placement of boundaries along naturally occurring lines of demarcation like main roadways, parks, ravines, and commercial strips may appear to be arbitrary, such divisions also tend to create effective barriers that limit guardianship. Residents preoccupied with daily activities are less likely to take note of events that occur across the park, or across the railroad tracks, than those next door or on their own block. It is in this limited sense that the use of census enumeration boundaries provides a basis for comparing areas.

Area characteristics. Area characteristics that are used as predictors of vandalism and mischief for this research included a measure of residents who had lived 1 year or less at their current address (new residents), calculated as a percentage of the total population in each area. Additional population measures included the percentage of the total population identified as homemakers, as retired, and as unemployed at the time of the enumeration. The two following specific segments of the population were included: males between the ages of 10 and 19 and males between the ages of 20 and 24. Both were calculated as a percentage of the total number of males in the area.[8] Housing character-istics were calculated as a percentage of the total number of housing units in the area. These included the percentage of renters, rooming houses, and vacant housing units. A final measure, child density, was calculated as the average num-ber of children per household with ages from 5 to 19.[9]

Environmental structures. Malls included in this study were the 17 largest malls in the city. Commercial strips and smaller neighborhood malls were excluded.[10] Secondary schools included the four following types of schools: the junior and senior high schools of the public school district, and the junior and senior high schools of the Catholic school district. Several schools in the Catholic school dis-trict served students at more than one level, including three junior-senior high schools; these schools were coded as high schools in the analysis. Each of these facilities was coded 0 (absence) or 1 (presence). Previous research on the impact of schools (Roncek and Faggiani 1985; Roncek and LoBosco 1983) had identified a single-block radius as the extent of significant differences. Therefore, schools were introduced as variables only within the enumeration area in which they were located. The impact of malls, however, was expected to be wider, due in part to their greater use of land within a given area and in part to the greater amount of human traffic that they generate. Therefore, malls were introduced both for their presence within an area and for their presence in an adjacent area.[11]

Mapping of Crime Incidents

To obtain area measures of crime rates that might be eval-uated in relation to area-level predictors, crime data were spatially located within the city using a computerized mapping program (MapInfo) that assigns x and y coordi-nates to a reference map.[12] For this study, two base maps were used: a computerized street map containing streets and block numbers for all city addresses, and a map of the boundaries of the census enumeration areas. Mischief inci-dents as reported by the police department were recorded as specific points, in most cases, a street address, and they were geocoded as such. Of the original 13,537 incidents reported to the police, 97 percent (13,131) were success-fully geocoded.[13] Locations for the remaining 259 cases (1.9 percent) could not be identified. Transit vandalism incidents were recorded as occurring at intersections, with

route direction information provided; route direction was used to determine assignment to one of the corners of the intersection. Of the 1,337 incidents, 1,325 were success-fully geocoded. Park vandalism incidents were recorded according to the park or facility where they occurred rather than a street address. Each record also indicated a struc-ture or type of structure, such as a pool house or field house; this portion of the record was used to refine the point of location further. Out of the 402 incidents recorded during 1992, all but 9 were successfully geocoded.[14]

All incidents from each source were separately aggre-gated according to the census enumeration area boundar-ies, resulting in a total figure for each type of damage within each area. These figures represented the actual count of incidents recorded in each enumeration area. In resident populations, areas ranged from 0 (for six areas of the city) to 3,201 (for the most densely populated). They ranged in size from .027 square kilometers to over 55 square kilometers. These two factors are inversely related; that is, the largest areas were low in population, whereas the smaller areas were high.

Area amounts of crime are generally calculated as a population-based rate, obtained by dividing the total num-ber of crimes by the total population and then multiplying by a constant (1,000 or 100,000). Crime rates provide a useful way of comparing units such as cities, states, and even countries, because it is plausible to assume that a larger population would contain a larger number of offend-ers, even if the proportion of such offenders within the population remained constant. For this analysis, however, population-based rates present a number of shortcomings. Although it is logical to calculate a population-based rate of crime for larger geographical units such as a city in com-parison to other cities, because most of the crime in a city can logically be attributed to residents, it is less reasonable to make the same assumption about smaller geographic units such as enumeration areas. Although it may be true that offenders are likely to select targets close to their own residences, the question remains of how close (Costanzo, Halperin, and Gale 1986). Five blocks might be considered close; yet, this is a sufficient distance to place a criminal event two enumeration areas away from the offender's home territory. Following a similar argument, Harries asserts that "most if not all the incidents may be attribut-able to outsiders . . . theoretically, zero events might be 'blamed' on residents, again making nonsense of the rate concept" (Harries 1993:4). This observation is underscored by the fact that crimes can and do occur in areas where there is a very small (or sometimes zero) population. The use of a population-based rate would inflate the amount of crime for these areas.[15]

Difficulties also arise in relation to the physical size of an area. The incidents examined in this research involve crimes, not against individual victims, but against the physical environment. Furthermore, although these crimes are often directed at structures in populated areas such as residences and stores, damage can also occur in parks, ravines, and in industrial or commercial areas. It could therefore be argued that a geographic rate (crimes per square kilometers) would provide a better measure, because larger areas would provide more opportunities for crime. However, the opportunities inherent in available targets, by themselves, are not sufficient to predict crime; it is the convergence of potential offenders with these targets in the absence of suitable guardianship that provides the conditions under which crime is likely to occur. These factors, in turn, are linked to the movements of human activity. Although the empty land around a city's perimeter may theoretically be damaged, areas that are populated, either residentially or because they are activity centers, are likely to experience a greater convergence of all of the components contributing to crime.

These arguments suggest that both the physical size of an area and the number of persons who live there are important considerations; one alone cannot provide an adequate basis for constructing a rate to control for their effects. For this reason, the actual counts of the three types of incidents that occur within each area are retained as measures. To control for the effects of area size and population, these measures are introduced as independent variables in the multiple regression analysis (Agresti and Finlay 1997; Bollen and Ward 1980).[16]

 ## Results

Edmonton, Alberta, had almost three-quarter million residents within its metropolitan limits during 1992, the year for which census data used in this study were gathered. The total area occupied by the city was 690.74 square kilometers.[17] Schools included 13 senior high schools and 26 junior high schools in the public school district, and 9 senior high schools and 11 junior high schools in the Catholic school district. There were, in addition, 17 shopping malls. The municipal enumeration had identified 662 areas. Listwise elimination of missing cases and the removal of one extreme outlier from the analysis[18] resulted in 654 areas that were used in the subsequent analysis. The mapping and aggregating of incidents of mischief and vandalism resulted in positively skewed distributions. Extreme scores at the upper end of the distribution for mischief and transit vandalism were recoded at the 90th percentile (Nagin and Smith 1990).[19] Incidents of recoded mischief ranged from 0 to 37, with a mean of 17.72; recoded transit vandalism ranged from 0 to 5, with a mean of 1.63; and park vandalism ranged from 1 to 29, with a mean of .59.

Ordinary least squares (OLS) regression was used to examine relationships between predictors and dependent variables. Of the residential characteristics, the percentage of unemployed and the percentage of residents who were males aged 20 to 24 were found to be statistically significant predictors of increased mischief. Only the percentage unemployed, however, was identified as a statistically significant predictor for all three crime measures. For transit vandalism, it predicted a small increase, and for park vandalism, a somewhat greater increase. Other measures of residential characteristics, however, had little consistent impact. Those few that were statistically significant for one type of measure proved to be nonsignificant for the other two types. The percentage of new residents was significantly related to mischief, but it predicts lower levels instead of the expected higher levels. For transit and park vandalism, the percentage of new residents was nonsignificant. The percentage of area residences that were rooming houses and the percentage that were vacant were also significant predictors of increased mischief, but not of transit or park damage. The percentage of renters was related to a small but statistically significant increase in both mischief and transit vandalism but it was nonsignificant for park vandalism.

In contrast, the presence or absence of public high schools and shopping malls within an area were consistent and robust predictors for increased damage of all types. Because all these facilities had been coded as dummy variables, the reported coefficients represent the difference between two conditional means—one for those areas with such a structure, and one for those without (Table 1). The presence of a high school predicted a substantial and

| Table 1 | Comparison of Means for Areas with and without Schools and Malls: Independent Sample t Test (N = 654) |

Structure	n	Resident Characteristics (in percentage)					Damage Incidents		
		New Residents	Unemployed	Males Age 10 to 19	Males Age 20 to 24	Renters	Mischief	Transit	Park
Catholic school									
High School									
Present	9	18.07	4.68	11.52	6.94	39.40	23.22	1.00	3.44
Absent	645	20.45	5.57	11.86	9.41*	44.39	17.67	1.64	.56
Junior High									
Present	11	17.20	6.91	11.73	7.93	37.01	21.73	2.72	1.09
Absent	643	20.48	5.54	11.86	9.40*	44.45	17.67	1.61*	.59
Public School									
High School									
Present	12	20.32	4.78	9.97	6.67	54.78	29.16	2.80	6.75
Absent	642	20.42	5.57	11.98	9.39	44.13	17.52**	1.16*	.48
Junior High									
Present	26	14.39	4.08	11.97	7.83	37.49	19.88	2.80	.84
Absent	628	20.67**	5.62**	11.85	9.44**	44.61	17.65	1.59**	.59
Mall									
In Area									
Present	17	24.44	6.55	10.18	9.84	59.89	31.11	3.59	4.41
Absent	637	20.31	5.53	11.90	9.37	43.91	17.38**	1.59**	.50**
Adjacent									
Present	102	21.37	6.32	11.92	9.69	50.01	21.76	2.00	.59
Absent	552	20.24	5.42	11.84	9.32	43.28*	17.00**	1.57*	.60

* $p < .05$. **$p < .01$. Two-tailed tests.

statistically significant increase in mischief incidents, transit incidents, and park vandalism. Effects for a mall in a given area were of greater magnitude, with for mischief, for transit, and for park vandalism. Contrary to expectations, having a mall in an adjacent area did not predict a significant increase in transit or park vandalism, although the reported effect was both robust and statistically significant

for mischief. Consistent with previous literature, the significant relationship identified for high schools applied only to those of the public school system. Catholic schools were associated with a significant increase in park vandalism, but they had little consistent relationship to other types of damage. In contrast to the prominent effect identified for high schools, the presence of a junior high school had a negligible impact. Although these schools were statistically significant for predicting transit vandalism, they did not predict a corresponding increase in mischief or park vandalism.

These differences in incidences reported for high schools and malls cannot be attributed to differences in area characteristics, as measured by the variables included in this study, which summarizes comparisons between areas with and without schools and malls, and is based on independent samples t tests, areas containing high schools did not differ significantly from those without in terms of population characteristics. The same conclusion is apparent for areas containing malls, when they are compared to other areas.[20] These types of structural facilities are dispersed throughout the city in neighborhoods of all kinds. The fact that property crime is consistently higher in surrounding areas appears to be related more to their presence than to any distinctive differences in the residential environment.

 ## Discussion

Damage or vandalism was defined, measured, and counted in widely divergent ways by the agencies that provided data for this research. These three measures of damage, however, yielded very similar results when their spatial patterns throughout the city were examined. In spite of the expectation that residential and neighborhood characteristics would influence the amount of property crime that occurred in an area, these variables had little consistent impact for all types of damage. The unemployment rate, however, was a significant predictor of increased levels of mischief and transit and park vandalism. Other characteristics that were expected to increase the likelihood of property damage were either nonsignificant (the percentage of teen males living in an area) or were predictors of one type of damage but not another (the percentage of local housing that was renter occupied). Those areas with high schools and malls, however, were found to have consistently higher rates of all three types of damage, controlling for differences in social, residential, and demographic characteristics. These results are consistent with a routine activities interpretation of the circumstances in which damage occurs. Routine activities theory argues that crimes will be committed when potential offenders are confronted with the opportunities afforded by available targets in situations of reduced guardianship. This research extends the geographic analysis of crime patterns, which has previously focused on serious index crimes, to study the occurrence of minor property crimes in a Canadian city during a 1-year period. As with the index crimes examined in previous research, the results of this study reveal a marked concentration of criminal incidents in certain areas—specifically, those containing high schools or malls, and those with higher unemployment. Reasons for the concentration of mischief and vandalism in these areas have been framed in terms of routine activities theory's model of crime as arising from the convergence of offenders and targets in the absence of effective guardianship. The results support the conclusion that situational opportunities presented by urban ecological features can account for variations in crime patterns. Some urban areas, due to their residential composition, may be particularly attractive to vandals and to those inclined to minor property crime because they afford inherently low guardianship. Further weakening of guardianship is brought about by the presence of facilities like schools and malls that bring a large number of nonresidents into the vicinity on a daily basis. Furthermore, these facilities attract the segments of population most likely to engage in minor damage and vandalism—people in their teens. Although replication is necessary to confirm these findings, the results of this analysis have implications for crime control. If minor property damage and vandalism are seen as the product of routine activities that arise primarily from the convergence of offenders and reduced guardianship, then prevention may most effectively be focused on disrupting the way in which these factors intersect—through an increase in both active and passive guardianship. Furthermore, the relevance of these findings goes beyond the damage itself. Crimes such as vandalism and mischief are often trivial as single events, but they are collectively significant in their impact on the perception of guardianship, and hence on potential offenders' weighing of the risks and benefits associated with more serious and socially harmful criminal behavior. The accumulation of property crime in an area may provide a signal to the criminally inclined that there is little likelihood of apprehension; therefore, such areas become likely sites for more serious criminal activities. In light of recent research into what has been described as the broken windows effect, an understanding of the circumstances surrounding minor property damage sheds further light on urban crime patterns more generally.

Notes

1. The cited research uses the term *shopping center* to describe the retail facilities studied, in contrast to the current usage of the term *mall*. Although there is a semantic distinction between the two terms based on whether facilities have a common nonretail area (the mall itself), the city in which the current research was conducted does not make such a distinction. The two terms are therefore used interchangeably in this study.

2. The offence categories examined were murder, rape, assault, robbery, burglary, grand theft, and auto theft (Roncek and LoBosco 1983).

3. A similar effect was not observed for private high schools. The authors speculated that "the grounds of public high schools are public property and legitimately available for use by anyone while the grounds of private schools are not" (Roncek and LoBosco 1983).

4. *Vandalism* is defined variously as "intentional acts aimed at damaging or destroying" (Moser 1992); "intentional hostile behavior aimed at damaging environmental objects"; "willful or malicious destruction, injury, disfigurement, or deface-ment" (Federal Bureau of Investigation 1994; see also Cohen 1973; Levy-Leboyer 1984). Although the term vandalism is commonly used in Canada, it is not contained in the Canadian Criminal Code. Instead, instances of vandalism are recorded and prosecuted under the statutes for mischief.

5. Incidents involving property damage and vandalism are recorded under the Canadian Criminal Code as mischief more than or less than $1,000 (Rodrigues 1990:210–211, section 430). Although offences recorded under this section usually refer to property damage, some incidents may refer to other behavior. Section 430.1 of the Canadian Criminal Code states that "Everyone commits mischief who willfully (a) destroys or damages property; (b) renders property dangerous, useless, inoperative or ineffective; (c) obstructs, interrupts or interferes with the lawful use, enjoyment or operation of property" (Rodrigues 1990:210–211). Section 430.1.1 adds that anyone who "destroys or alters data," "renders data meaningless, useless, or ineffective," or otherwise interferes with data is also guilty of mischief (Rodrigues

1990:210–211). Actions falling within the latter subsection would not be considered property damage. It is, however, impossible to determine from the data source whether police records on mischief include offenses of this nature, and, if so, how many.

6. Enumeration areas are subdivisions of the permanent census tracts established by Statistics Canada, and they represent the smallest unit of census aggregation. There are typically several enumeration areas within a tract. Their boundaries are intended to define an area as homogenous as possible in terms of socioeconomic characteristics and to follow, where feasible, well-established natural boundaries (Lalu 1989:1).

7. Although the transit department maintained additional records on damage to buses and Light Rail Transit trains, they were excluded from this study, because they could not be spatially located.

8. Age groupings were chosen to allow a measure of residents in their teens or early adulthood. Actual cutoffs between age groups, however, reflect the limitations of the municipal census data, which recorded age by gender in categories rather than in any substantive or legal distinctions (in Canada, the cutoff between juvenile and adult status is 18 years).

9. Child density was included instead of broader measures of residential or neighborhood density; this was based on previous research that has identified this measure as predictive of increased levels of minor property damage (see Wilson 1978).

10. Commercial strips and smaller neighborhood malls were excluded because an exhaustive, valid measure of their presence or absence in a given area could not be developed for the city in which data were gathered. Many areas contained small, neighborhood strip malls that were identifiable as separate corporate entities. Others had commercial strips of very similar composition (typically centering on fast food outlets or convenience stores) that reflected the clustering of separate facilities within a municipal commercial zone. These latter areas were not identified as malls, although they effectively functioned as such.

11. An adjacent area was operationally defined as one sharing one or more common boundaries with an area containing a mall.

12. More detailed information on the technique of geocoding used for this study is available from the author.

13. This number includes three types of records: (1) those which had been recorded as a specific street address; (2) those recorded as occurring at a particular named building or facility, which in turn had a street address; and (3) those recorded as occurring at an intersection. For the latter group of incidents, a

specific street address could not be identified, nor could it be determined on which of four potential corners an incident had occurred. All incidents of this nature were therefore geocoded to the northwest corner of the intersection.

14. Missing data for the three types of property damage incidents included cases in which an address or specific location could not be identified, cases in which the indicated address or location did not exist (recording agency errors), and cases in which the indicated address or location corresponded to two or more potential locations.

15. The use of a population figure as the denominator in calculating a rate for the dependent variable may lead to spurious positive results if the same population figure is used to compute independent variables. Such a situation might arise in this analysis because predictors include the percentage of area residents falling into certain demographic categories (Bollen and Ward 1980: 61).

16. A further source of potential bias arises from the nature of the data and the possibility of spatial autocorrelation. Multivariate analyses such as the ordinary least squares (OLS) regression models employed in this study are based on the expectation that error terms are independent and do not vary systematically—a requirement that is rarely met with spatial data (Upton and Fingleton 1985:371). Instead, such data are likely to exhibit organized patterns or systematic spatial variation in values across a map (Cliff and Ord 1981:6; Upton and Fingleton 1985:151). High unemployment rates in one area, for example, do not abruptly drop at the border of that area; they tend to continue into neighboring areas. Such facilities as shopping malls, by contrast, will almost universally be absent from any area next to one in which they are present. However, the impact of such potential sources of bias is reduced as n increases (Upton and Fingleton 1985:365), and this study employs a fairly large n of over 650. Although spatial statistics have been developed to correct for such problems (see Anselin 1990a, 1990b; Anselin et al. 1996; Blommestein and Koper 1997), they involve more complex models than OLS regression and thus are appropriate if it appears that autocorrelation contributes to a significant distortion of coefficients. For this analysis, a post-hoc analysis of the differences between theoretically derived (expected) values and the corresponding observed values suggested little consistent spatial patterning that would seriously bias results, and hence regression models were retained (Cliff and Ord 1981:76).

17. The dimensions are those calculated by summing the area per square kilometer for all enumeration areas defined by the City of Edmonton Municipal Census (1992) using mapping software. The size varies somewhat from that reported by other sources.

18. A single enumeration area was excluded from the analysis as an outlier. There were no statistically significant differences in population characteristics when this area was compared to others in the city. All measures were within one standard deviation of the mean for the city as a whole. It differed, however, in that it contains an architectural phenomenon touted as "the world's largest shopping mall." Although the relative size of malls was not included as a variable in this study, the enormity of this structure places it in a category by itself, so that it could not be treated as equivalent to other malls. It should be noted, however, that mischief and vandalism rates recorded for this area were extremely high, consistent with the assumption that such a facility would predict increased amounts of crime.

19. Recoding of park vandalism would have restricted this measure to three categories, which was deemed to provide inadequate variation. This measure was thus retained as recorded in the data.

20. The only exception is size; areas containing malls and schools are significantly smaller than those without. This finding is consistent with the observation, made previously, that there was an inverse relationship between area size and population. Larger areas were the more sparsely populated outlying districts, reflecting their smaller number of residents; they were less likely to contain schools and malls. Densely populated areas closer to the midzones of the city, by contrast, were smaller, but they were more likely to contain such facilities.

 # References

Agresti, A., and B. Finlay. 1997. *Statistical Methods for the Social Sciences*, 3rd ed. Saddle River, NJ: Prentice Hall.

Allan, E. A., and D. J. Steffensmeier. 1989. "Youth, Underemployment, and Property Crime: Differential Effects of Job Availability and Job Quality on Juvenile and Young Adult Arrest Rates." *American Sociological Review* 54:107–23.

Anselin, Luc. 1990a. "Some Robust Approaches to Testing and Estimation in Spatial Econometrics." *Regional Science and Urban Economics* 29:141–63.

———. 1990b. "Spatial Dependence and Spatial Structural Instability in Applied Regression Analysis." *Journal of Regional Science* 30:185–207.

Anselin, Luc, Anil K. Bera, Raymond Florax, and Mann J. Yoon. 1996. "Simple Diagnostic Tests for Spatial Dependence." *Regional Science and Urban Economics* 26:77–104.

Beaulieu, L. 1982. *Vandalism; Responses and Responsibilities.* Report of the Task Force on Vandalism. Ontario, Canada: Queen's Printer.

Bell, M. M., M. M. Bell, and K. Godefroy. 1988. "The Impact of Graffiti on Neighborhoods and One Community's Response." Presented at the International Symposium on Vandalism: Research, Prevention, and Social Policy, April 20–23, Seattle, WA.

Bensing, R.C., and O. Schroeder, Jr. 1960. *Homicide in an Urban Community.* Springfield, IL: Charles C Thomas.

Block, R. 1976. "Homicide in Chicago: A Nine-Year Study (1965–1973)." *Journal of Criminal Law and Criminology* 66:510.

Block, R. L., and C. R. Block. 1995. "Space, Place, and Crime: Hot Spot Areas and Hot Places of Liquor-related Crime." Pp. 145–83 in *Crime Prevention Studies,* Vol. 4, *Crime and Place,* edited by J. E. Eck and D. Weisburd. Monsey, NY: Criminal Justice Press.

Blommestein, Hans J., and Nick A. M. Koper. 1997. "The Influence of Sample Size on the Degree of Redundancy in Spatial Lag Operators." *Journal of Econometrics* 82:317–33.

Bollen, K. A., and S. Ward. 1980, "Ratio Variables in Aggregate Data Analysis." Pp. 60–79 in *Aggregate Data: Analysis and Interpretation,* edited by E. F. Borgatta and D. J. Jackson. Beverly Hills, CA: Sage.

Brantingham, P. J., and P. L. Brantingham, 1991. *Environmental Criminology.* Prospect Heights, IL: Waveland.

———. 1994. "Mobility, Notoriety, and Crime: A Study in Crime Patterns of Urban Nodal Points." *Journal of Environmental Systems* 11:89–99.

Brantingham, P. L., and P. J. Brantingham. 1984. *Patterns in Crime.* New York: Macmillan.

———. 1993. "Environment, Routine and Situation: Toward a Pattern Theory of Crime." Pp. 259–94 in *Routine Activity and Rational Choice: Advances in Criminological Theory,* edited by R. V. Clarke and M. Felson. New Brunswick, NJ: Transaction Books.

———. 1995. "Criminality of Place: Crime Generators and Crime Attractors." *European Journal of Criminal Policy and Research* 3:5–26.

Bullock, H. A. 1955. "Urban Homicide in Theory and Fact." *Journal of Criminal Law, Criminology, and Police Science* 45:565–75.

Bursik, R. J., Jr. 1988. "Social Disorganization and Theories of Crime and Delinquency: Problems and Prospects." *Criminology* 26:519–51.

Chalfant, H. 1992. "No One Is in Control." Pp. 4–11 in *Vandalism: Research, Prevention and Social Policy,* edited by H. H. Chistensen, D. R. Johnson, and M. H. Brookes. Portland, OR: Department of Agriculture Forest Service.

Challinger, D. 1987. *Preventing Property Crime: Proceedings of a Seminar.* Canberra: Australian Institute of Criminology.

City of Edmonton Municipal Census. 1992. Census Summary Data File. Edmonton, Canada: City of Edmonton Computing Resources.

Clarke, R.V.G. 1978. *Tackling Vandalism.* Home Office Research Study No. 47. London, UK: HMSO.

Clarke, R.V.G., and M. Felson. 1993. *Routine Activity and Rational Choice.* New Brunswick, NJ: Transaction Press.

Cliff, Andrew D., and J. K. Ord. 1981. *Spatial Process: Models and Applications.* London, UK: Pion.

Cohen, L. E., and M. Felson. 1979. "Social Change and Crime Rate Trends: A Routine Activity Approach." *American Sociological Review* 44:588–608.

Cohen, S. 1973. "Property Destruction: Motives and Meanings." Pp. 23–54 in *Vandalism,* edited by Colin Ward. New York: Van Nostrand Reinhold.

Cornish, D. B., and R. V. Clarke. 1986. *The Reasoning Criminal: Rational Choice Perspectives on Offending.* New York: Springer-Verlag.

Costanzo, C. M., W. C. Halperin, and N. Gale. 1986. "Criminal Mobility and the Directional Component in Journeys to Crime." Pp. 73-95 in *Metropolitan Crime Patterns,* edited by R. M. Figlio, S. Hakim, and G. F. Rengert. Monsey, NY: Willow Tree Press.

Crowe, T. D. 1991. *Crime Prevention Through Environmental Design: Applications of Architectural Design and Space Management Concepts.* Boston, MA: Butterworth-Heinemann.

Crowe, T. D., and D. Zahm. 1994. "Crime Prevention Through Environmental Design." *Land Management* 7:220-27.

Decker, David L., David Shichor, and Robert M. O'Brien. 1982. *Urban Structure and Victimization.* Lexington, MA: Lexington Books/D. C. Heath and Company.

Dunn, C. S. 1984. "Crime Area Research." Pp. 5–25 in *Patterns in Crime,* edited by P. L. Brantingham and P. J. Brantingham. New York: Macmillan.

Engstad, P. A. 1980. "Environmental Opportunities and the Ecology of Crime." Pp. 206–22 in *Crime in Canadian Society,* 2nd ed., edited by R. A. Silverman and J. J. Teevan, Jr. Toronto, Canada: Butterworths.

Erickson, M. L., and G. F. Jensen. 1977. "Delinquency Is Still Group Behavior!: Toward Revitalizing the Group Premise in the Sociology of Deviance." *Journal of Criminal Law and Criminology.* 68:262–73.

Federal Bureau of Investigation. 1994. *Uniform Crime Reports.* Washington, DC: Government Printing Office.

Felson, M. 1986. "Routine Activities, Social Controls, Rational Decisions and Criminal Outcomes." Pp. 119–28 in *The Reasoning Criminal,* edited by D. Cornish and R. V. Clarke. New York: Springer-Verlag.

———. 1987. "Routine Activities and Crime Prevention in the Developing Metropolis." *Criminology* 25:11–31.

———. 1994. *Crime and Everyday Life.* Thousand Oaks, CA: Pine Forge Press.

———. 1998. *Crime & Everyday Life.* 2nd ed. Thousand Oaks, CA: Pine Forge Press.

Felson, M., and L. E. Cohen. 1980. "Human Ecology and Crime: A Routine Activity Approach." *Human Ecology* 8:389–406.

Figlio, R. M., S. Hakim, and G. F. Rengert. 1986. *Metropolitan Crime Patterns.* Monsey, NY: Willow Tree Press.

Gartner, R., and A. N. Doob. 1996. "Trends in Criminal Victimization: 1988–1993." Pp. 90–104 in *Crime in Canadian Society* (5th ed.), edited by R. A. Silverman, J. J. Teevan Jr., and V. F. Sacco. Toronto, Canada: Butterworths.

Geason, S., and P. R. Wilson. 1990. *Preventing Graffiti and Vandalism.* Canberra: Australian Institute of Criminology.

Georges-Abeyie, D. E., and K. D. Harries. 1980. *Crime: A Spatial Perspective.* New York: Columbia University Press.

Gladstone, F. J. 1978. "Vandalism Amongst Adolescent Schoolboys." Pp. 19–39 in *Tackling Vandalism,* Home Office Research Study No. 47, edited by R. V. G. Clarke. London, UK: HMSO.

Gold, M. 1970. *Delinquent Behavior in an American City.* Belmont, CA: Brooks-Cole.

Gottfredson, M. R., and T. Hirschi. 1990. *A General Theory of Crime.* Stanford, CA: Stanford University Press.

Griffiths, C. T., and S. N. Verdun-Jones. 1989. *Canadian Criminal Justice.* Toronto, Canada: Butterworths.

Hagan, John, A. R. Gillis, and J. Chan. 1978. "Explaining Official Delinquency: A Spatial Study of Class Conflict and Control." *Sociological Quarterly* 19:386–98.

Harries, K. 1993. "The Ecology of Homicide and Assault: Baltimore City and County, 1989-1991." Presented at the American Society of Criminology Annual Meetings, November 4, Phoenix, AZ.

Hartnagel, T. F., and G., Won Lee. 1990. "Urban Crime in Canada." *Canadian Journal of Criminology* (October):591–606.

Hawley, A. H. 1950. *Human Ecology: A Theory of Community Structure.* New York: Ronald Press.

———. 1971. *Urban Society: An Ecological Approach.* New York: Ronald Press.

Hindelang, M. J., M. R. Gottfredson, and J. Garofalo. 1978. *Victims of Personal Crime: An Empirical Foundation for a Theory of Personal Victimization.* Cambridge, MA: Ballinger.

Hirschi, T. 1969. *Causes of Delinquency.* Berkeley: University of California Press.

Hough, M., and P. Mayhew. 1980. *Crime and Public Housing: Proceedings of a Workshop.* London, UK: Home Office.

Jarvis, G. K. 1972. "The Ecological Analysis of Juvenile Delinquency in a Canadian City." Pp. 195–211 in *Deviant Behavior and Society Reaction,* edited by C. L. Boydell, C. F. Grindstaff, and P. C. Whitehead. Toronto, Canada: Holt, Rinehart & Winston.

Kelling, G. L., and C. Coles. 1996. *Fixing Broken Windows: Restoring Order and Reducing Crime in Our Communities.* New York: Free Press.

Kornhauser, R. R. 1978. *Social Sources of Delinquency.* Chicago, IL: University of Chicago Press.

Lalu, N. M. 1989. *Changing Profiles of Edmonton Census Tracts.* Edmonton, Canada: University of Alberta Population Research Laboratory.

Levy-Leboyer, C. 1984. *Vandalism: Behavior and Motivations.* New York: North-Holland.

Marongiu, P., and G. Newman. 1997. "Situational Crime Prevention and the Utilitarian Tradition." Pp. 115–35 in *Rational Choice and Situational Crime Prevention: Theoretical Foundations,* edited by G. Newman, R. V. Clarke, and S. G. Shoham. Dartmouth, VT: Ashgate Publications.

Moser, G. 1992. "What Is Vandalism? Towards a Psycho-social Definition and its Implications." Pp. 49–70 in *Vandalism: Research, Prevention, and Social Policy,* edited by H. H. Chistensen, D. R. Johnson, and M. H. Brookes. Portland, OR: Department of Agriculture Forest Service,

Nagin, D. S., and D. A. Smith. 1990. "Participation in and Frequency of Delinquent Behavior: A Test for Structural Differences." *Quantitative Criminology* 6:335–65.

Newman, O. 1972. *Defensible Space: Crime Prevention Through Urban Design.* New York: Macmillan.

Park, R. E., and E. W. Burgess. 1933. *Introduction to the Science of Sociology.* 2nd ed. Chicago, IL: University of Chicago Press.

Robinson, W. S. 1950. "Ecological Correlation and the Behavior of Individuals." *American Sociological Review* 15:351–57.

Rodrigues, Gary P., ed. 1990. *Canadian Criminal Code: Pocket Criminal Code.* Toronto, Canada: Carswell.

Roncek, D. W., and D. Faggiani. 1985. "High Schools and Crime: a Replication." *The Sociological Quarterly* 26:491–505.

Roncek, D. W., and A. LoBosco. 1983. "The Effect of High Schools on Crime in Their Neighborhoods." *Social Science Quarterly* 64:598–613.

Roncek, D. W., and P. Maier. 1991. "Bars, Blocks, and Crimes Revisited: Linking the Theory of Routine Activities to the Empiricism of Hot Spots." *Criminology* 29:725–53.

Roos, H. 1992. "Vandalism as a Symbolic Act in 'Free-zones.'" Pp. 71–87 in *Vandalism: Research, Prevention, and Social Policy,* edited by H. H. Christensen, D. R. Johnson, and M. H. Brookes. Portland, OR: Department of Agriculture Forest Service.

Sacco, V. F., and L. W. Kennedy. 1994. *The Criminal Event.* Scarborough, Canada: Nelson.

Sampson, R. J., and W. B. Grove. 1989. "Community Structure and Crime: Testing Social Disorganization Theory." *American Journal of Sociology* 94:774–802.

Scarr, H. A. 1973. *Patterns of Burglary.* Washington, DC: Law Enforcement Assistance Administration, National Institute of Law Enforcement and Criminal Justice.

Schmid, C. F. 1960. "Urban Crime Areas, Part I & Part II." *American Sociological Review* 25:527–43, 655–78.

Shaw, C. R., and H. D. McKay, 1942. *Juvenile Delinquency and Urban Areas.* Chicago, IL: University of Chicago Press.

Sherman, L. W., P. R. Gartin, and M. E. Buerger. 1989. "Hot Spots of Predatory Crime: Routine Activities and the Criminology of Place." *Criminology* 17:17–49.

Shlomo, Angel. 1968. "Discouraging Crime Through City Planning." Working Paper No. 75, Space Sciences Laboratory and the Institute of Urban and Regional Development, University of California, Berkeley, CA.

Silverman, R. A., J. J. Teevan, Jr., and V. F. Sacco. 1996. *Crime in Canadian Society.* 5th ed. Toronto, Canada: Harcourt Brace.

Skogan, W. G. 1990. *Disorder and Decline: Crime and the Spiral of Decay in American Neighborhoods.* New York: Free Press.

Snodgrass, J. 1976. "C. R. Shaw and H. D. Mckay: Chicago Criminologists." *The British Journal of Criminology* 16:1–19.

Upton, Graham J. G., and Bernard Fingleton. 1985. *Spatial Data Analysis by Example.* New York: Wiley.

Wilson, S. 1978. "Vandalism and 'Defensible Space' on London Housing Estates." Pp. 41–65 in *Tackling Vandalism.* Home Office Research Study No. 47, edited by R. V. G. Clarke. London, UK: HMSO.

Wortley, R. 1997. "Reconsidering the Role of Opportunity in Situational Crime Prevention." Pp. 65–81 in *Rational Choice and Situational Crime Prevention: Theoretical Foundations,* edited by G. Newman, R. V. Clarke, and S. G. Shoham. Dartmouth, VT: Ashgate Publications.

Zimbardo, Philip. 1970. "The Human Choice: Individuation, Reason, and Order Versus Deindividuation, Impulse, and Chaos." Pp. 237–307 in *Nebraska Symposium on Motivation,* edited by W. Arnold and D. Levine. Lincoln: University of Nebraska Press.

REVIEW QUESTIONS

1. Of the three environmental factors that LaGrange examines, which appears to be the one that most affects high crime levels?

2. To what extent do the findings by LaGrange apply to the broken windows theory?

3. Have you observed such influences of environmental predictors in the place where you live or grew up? Provide details regarding how the proximity of such establishments or demographic characteristics has influenced the crime levels near your residences.

❖

Early Positive School Perspectives of Criminality

In this section, we will discuss the dramatic differences in assumptions between the Classical and Positive Schools of criminological thought. We will also touch on the pre-Darwinian perspectives of human behavior (e.g., phrenology), as well as the influence that Darwin had on the perspectives of all social sciences, particularly criminology. Finally, we will discuss the theories and methods used by early positivists, particularly Cesare Lombroso, IQ theorists, and body type researchers, with an emphasis on the criticisms of these perspectives, methodologies, and resulting policies.

After many decades of dominance by the Classical School (see Sections II and III), academics and scientists were becoming aware that the deterrence framework did not explain the distribution of crime. Their restlessness led to new explanatory models of crime and behavior. Most of these perspectives focused on the fact that certain individuals or groups tend to offend more than others and the idea that such "inferior" individuals should be controlled or even eliminated. This ideological framework fit a more general stance toward eugenics, the study of and policies related to the improvement of the human race via control over reproduction, which as we will see was explicitly mandated for certain groups. Thus, the conclusion was that there must be notable variations across individuals and groups that can help determine who is most at risk of offending.

So, in the early to mid-1800s, several perspectives were offered regarding how to determine which individuals or groups were most likely to commit crime. Many of these theoretical frameworks were made to distinguish the more "superior" individuals or groups from the "inferior" individuals or groups. Such intentions were likely related to the increased use of slavery in the world during the 1800s, as well as imperialism's fight to quell rebellions at that time. For example, slavery was at its peak in the United States during this period, and many European countries controlled many dozens of colonies, which they were trying to retain for profit and domain.

Perhaps the first example of this belief was represented by craniometry. Craniometry was the belief that the size of the brain or skull represents the superiority or inferiority of certain individuals or ethnic or racial groups.[1] The size of the brain and the skull were considered because, at that time, it was believed that a person's skull perfectly conformed to brain structure; thus, the size of the skull was believed to reflect the size of the brain. Modern science has challenged this assumption, but there actually is a significant correlation between the size of the skull and the size of the brain. Still, even according to the assumptions of the craniometrists, it is unlikely that much can be gathered about an individual's intelligence from the overall size of the brain, and certainly the skull, from simple measurements of mass.

The scientists who studied this model, if they were dealing with living subjects, would measure the various sizes or circumferences of the skulls. If they were dealing with recently dead subjects, then they would actually measure the brain weight or volume of the participants. When dealing with subjects who had died long before, craniometrists would measure the volume of skulls by pouring seeds inside and then pouring those that fit into graduated cylinders. Later, when these scientists realized that seeds were not a valid measure of volume, they moved toward using buckshot or ball bearings.

Most studies by the craniometrists tended to show that subjects of White or Western European descent were superior to those of other ethnic groups in terms of brain volume or skull size. Furthermore, the front portion of the brain (i.e., the genu) was thought to be larger in superior individuals or groups, and the hind portion of the brain or skull (i.e., the splenium) was predicted to be larger in inferior individuals or groups. Notably, these researchers typically knew which brains or skulls belonged to which ethnic or racial group before measurements were taken, making for an unethical and improper methodology. Such biased measurements continued throughout the 19th century and into the early 1900s.[2] These examinations were largely done with the intention of furthering the assumptions of eugenics, which aimed to prove under the banner of science that certain individuals and ethnic or racial groups are inferior to others. The fact that this was their intent is underscored by subsequent tests using the same subjects but performed without knowledge of which skulls or brains were from certain ethnic or racial groups; these later studies showed only a small correlation between size of the skull or brain and certain behaviors or personalities.[3]

Furthermore, once some of the early practitioners of craniometry died, their brains were found to have volumes that were less than average or average. The brain of K. F. Gauss, for example, was relatively small but more convoluted, with more gyri and fissures. Craniometrists then switched their postulates to say that more convoluted or complex brain structures, with more fissures and gyri, indicated superior brains.[4] However, this argument was even more tentative and vaguer than the former hypotheses of craniometrists and thus did not last long. The same was true of craniometry in general, thanks to its noticeable lack of validity. However, it is important to note that modern studies show that people who have significantly larger brains tend to score higher on intelligence tests.[5]

Despite the failure of craniometry to explain the difference between criminals and noncriminals, scientists were not ready to give up the assumption that criminal behavior could be explained by visual differences in the skull (or brain), and they certainly weren't ready to give up the assumption that certain ethnic or racial groups were superior or inferior to others. Therefore, the experts of the time created phrenology. Phrenology was the science of determining

---

[1]For a review, see Nicole Rafter, "The Murderous Dutch Fiddler," *Theoretical Criminology* 9, no. 1 (2005): 65–96.

[2]For example, compare Robert Bean, "Some Racial Peculiarities of the Negro Brain," *American Journal of Anatomy* 5 (1906): 353–432, which showed a distinct difference in the brains across race when brains were identified by race before comparison, to Franklin P. Mall, "On Several Anatomical Characters of the Human Brain, Said to Vary According to Race and Sex, with Especial Reference to the Weight of the Frontal Lobe," *American Journal of Anatomy* 9 (1909): 1–32, which showed virtually no differences among the same brains when comparisons were made without knowledge of the races of the brains prior to comparison. See discussion in Stephen Jay Gould, *The Mismeasure of Man*, 2nd ed. (New York: Norton, 1996).

[3]See Mall, "On Several Anatomical Characters"; much of the discussion in this section is taken from Gould, *Mismeasure of Man*.

[4]Edward A. Spitska, "A Study of the Brains of Six Eminent Scientists and Scholars Belonging to the Anthropological Society, Together with a Description of the Skull of Professor E. D. Cope," *Transactions of the American Philosophical Society* 21 (1907): 175–308.

[5]Stanley Coren, *The Left-Hander Syndrome* (New York: Vintage, 1993); James Kalat, *Biological Psychology*, 8th ed. (New York: Wadsworth, 2004).

human dispositions based on distinctions (e.g., bumps) in the skull, which were believed to conform to the shape of the brain.[6] Readers should keep in mind that much of the theorizing by the phrenologists still aimed to support the assumptions of eugenics and show that certain individuals and groups of people are inferior or superior to others.

It is important to keep in mind that, like the craniometrists, phrenologists assumed that the shape of the skull conformed to the shape of the brain. Thus, a bump or other abnormality on the skull directly related to an abnormality in the brain at that spot. Such assumptions have been refuted by modern scientific evidence, so it is not surprising that phrenology fell out of favor in criminological thought rather quickly.

Like its predecessor, however, phrenology got some things right. Certain parts of the brain are indeed responsible for specific tasks. For example, in the original phrenological map, destructiveness was indicated by abnormalities above the left ear. Modern scientific studies show that the most vital part of the brain in terms of criminality associated with trauma is the left temporal lobe, the area above the left ear.[7] Also, most readers know that specific portions of the brain govern the operation of different physical activities; one area governs the action of our hands, whereas other areas govern our arms, legs, and so on. So, the phrenologists had a few things right, but they were completely wrong about the extent to which bumps on the skull could indicate who would be most disposed to criminal behavior.

Once phrenology fell out of favor among scientists, researchers and society in general did not want to depart from the assumption that certain individuals or ethnic groups are inferior to others. Therefore, another discipline, known as physiognomy, became popular in the mid-1800s. Physiognomy is the study of facial and other bodily aspects to indicate developmental problems, such as criminality. Not surprisingly, the early physiognomy studies focused on contrasting various racial or ethnic groups to prove that some were superior or inferior to others.[8]

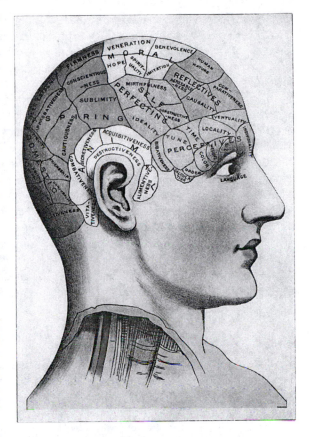

▲ Image 4.1 This diagram shows the sections of the brain as detailed by 19th-century phrenologists, who believed that each section was responsible for a particular human personality trait. If a section was enlarged or shrunken, the personality was assumed to be likewise abnormal. Doctors, particularly those doing entry examinations at American prisons, would examine each new inmate's head for bumps or cavities to develop a criminal profile. For example, if the section of the brain responsible for acquisitiveness was enlarged, the offender was probably a thief. Lombroso and his school combined phrenology with other models that included external physical traits to single out criminals from the general population.

Source: © Photos.com / Photos.com / Thinkstock.

[6]Orson S. Fowler, *Fowler's Practical Phrenology: Giving a Concise Elementary View of Phrenology* (New York: O. S. Fowler, 1842).

[7]For reviews, see Adrian Raine, *The Anatomy of Violence: The Biological Roots of Crime* (New York: Pantheon, 2013), and Adrian Raine, *The Psychopathology of Crime* (San Diego: Academic Press, 1993).

[8]Josiah C. Nott and George R. Gliddon, *Types of Mankind* (Philadelphia: Lippincott/Grambo, 1854); Josiah C. Nott and George R. Gliddon, *Indigenous Races on Earth* (Philadelphia: Lippincott, 1868).

Given modern understandings of science, it is not surprising that physiognomy did not last long as a respected scientific perspective of criminality. At any time other than the late 1800s, their ideas would not have been accepted for long, if at all. However, the theory emerged at an auspicious time. Specifically, Darwin published his work *The Origin of Species* in the late 1800s and made a huge impact on societal views regarding the rank order of groups in societies.

Darwin's model outlined a vague framework suggesting that humans had evolved from more primitive beings and that the human species (like all others) had evolved from a number of adaptations preferred by natural selection. In other words, some species are selected by their ability to adapt to the environment, whereas others do not adapt as well and die off or at least become inferior in terms of dominance. This assumption of Darwin's work, which was quickly and widely accepted by both society and scientists throughout the world, falsely led to an inclination to believe that certain ethnic or racial groups are inferior or superior to other groups. Despite a backlash by many religious authorities, who were likely threatened by the popularity of a theory that promoted natural design as opposed to a higher being or creator, Darwin had created a scientific snowball that spread like wildfire across virtually all scientific disciplines, particularly criminology.

Darwin was not a criminologist, so he is not considered a father or theorist in the field. However, he did set the stage for what followed in criminological thought. Specifically, Darwin's theory laid the groundwork for what would become the first major scientific theory of crime, namely, Cesare Lombroso's theory of born criminals, which also tied together the assumptions and propositions of craniometry, phrenology, and physiognomy.

Lombroso's Theory of Atavism and Born Criminals

Basing his work on Darwin's theory of natural selection, Cesare Lombroso (1835–1909) created what is widely considered the first attempt toward scientific theory in criminological thought. Most previous theorists were not scientists; Beccaria, for example, was trained in law and never tested his propositions. Unlike the craniometrists and phrenologists, Beccaria's goal was not to explain levels of criminality. However, Lombroso was trained in medical science, and he aimed to document his observations and use scientific methodology. Furthermore, timing was on his side in the sense that Darwin's theory was published 15 years prior to Lombroso's major work, and in that time, the idea of evolution had become immensely popular with both scientists and the public.

Lombroso's Theory of Crime

The first edition of Lombroso's *The Criminal Man* was published in 1876 and created an immediate response in most Western societies, influencing both their ideas and policies related to crime and justice.[9] In this work, Lombroso outlined a theory of crime that largely brought together the pre-Darwinian theories of craniometry, phrenology, and physiognomy. Furthermore, Lombroso thought that certain groups and individuals were atavistic, and that they likely were born to commit crime. Atavism refers to the idea that a person or feature of an individual is a throwback to an earlier stage of evolutionary development. In other words, Lombroso thought serious criminals were lower forms of humanity in terms of evolutionary progression. For example, Lombroso would probably have suggested that chronic offenders are more like earlier stages of humankind—that is, like *missing links*—than they are like modern humans.

Lombroso noted other types of offenders, such as the mentally ill and *criminaloids*, who committed minor offenses due to external or environmental circumstances, but he argued that the *born criminals* should be the target in addressing crime, insisting that they were the most serious and violent criminals in any society. These are what

---

[9]Cesare Lombroso, *The Criminal Man* (L'uomo Delinquente), 1st ed. (Milan: Hoepli, 1876), 2nd ed. (Turin: Bocca, 1878).

most criminologists now refer to as *chronic offenders*. Furthermore, Lombroso claimed that born criminals cannot be stopped from their natural tendencies to be antisocial.

On the other hand, Lombroso claimed that, although it was their nature to commit crime, born criminals could be stopped, or at least partially deterred by society. According to Lombroso, societies could identify born criminals, even early in life, through their stigmata. Stigmata were physical manifestations of the atavism of an individual, that is, features indicating a prior evolutionary stage of development.

Lombroso's List of Stigmata

According to Lombroso, more than five stigmata indicate that an individual is atavistic and inevitably will be a born criminal. Understandably, readers may be wondering what these stigmata are, given their importance. This is a great question, but the answer varies. In the beginning, this list was largely based on Lombroso's work as a physician; it included features such as large eyes and large ears. Lombroso changed this list as he went along, however, even in the last edition of his book published well into the 1900s, which might be considered poor science.

▲ Image 4.2 Cesare Lombroso (1837–1909).

Source: © Boyer / Roger Viollet / Getty Images.

For the most part, stigmata consisted of facial and bodily features that deviated from the norm—in other words, abnormally small or large noses, abnormally small or large ears, abnormally small or large eyes, abnormally small or large jaws—almost anything that went outside the bell curve of normal human physical development. Lombroso also threw in some extraphysiological features, such as tattoos and a family history of epilepsy and other disorders.[10] Although tattoos may be somewhat correlated to crime and delinquency, is it likely that they cause antisocial behavior? Given Lombroso's model that people are born criminal, it is quite unlikely that such factors are causally linked to criminality. How many babies are born with tattoos? Ignoring the illogical nature of many of the stigmata, Lombroso professed that people who had more than five of these physical features were born criminals and that something should be done to prevent their inevitable future offending career.

As a physician working for the Italian army, Lombroso examined the bodies of war criminals who had been captured and brought in for analysis. According to Lombroso, he first came to the realization of the nature of criminals when a particular individual was brought in for him to examine:

> This was not merely an idea, but a flash of inspiration. At the sight of that skull, I seemed to see all of a sudden, lighted up as a vast plain under a flaming sky, the problem of the nature of the criminal—an atavistic being who reproduces in his person the ferocious instincts of primitive humanity and the inferior animals.[11]

---

[10]Gould, *Mismeasure of Man*, 153.

[11]Lombroso, *Criminal Man*, as cited and discussed by Ian Taylor, Paul Walton, and Jock Young, *The New Criminology: For a Social Theory of Deviance* (London: Routledge, 1973), 41.

This was Lombroso's first exposure to such a criminal, and this account of it was his first acknowledgment of the theory that he created. He expanded on this theory by specifying some of the physical features he observed in this individual:

Thus were explained anatomically the enormous jaws, high cheek bones . . . solitary lines in the palms, extreme size of the orbits, handle-shaped ears found in criminals, savages and apes, insensibility to pain, extremely acute sight, tattooing, excessive idleness, love of orgies, and the irresponsible craving of evil for its own sake, the desire not only to extinguish life in the victim, but to mutilate the corpse, tear its flesh and drink its blood. [12]

Although most people may now laugh at his words, at the time he wrote this description, it would have rung true to most readers, which is likely why his book was the dominant text for many decades in the criminological field. In this description, Lombroso incorporates many of the core principles of his theory, including the idea that criminals are atavistic or biological throwbacks from evolution as well as the premise that they can be identified by "stigmata."

A good example of the popular acceptance of Lombroso's "scientific" stigmata was Bram Stoker's use of them in the 1896 novel *Dracula*, which featured a character based on Lombrosian traits of a villain, such as a high-bridged, thin nose; arched nostrils; massive eyebrows; and pointed ears. This novel was published in the late 1800s, when Lombroso's theory was highly dominant in society and in science. Lombroso's ideas became quite popular among academics, scientists, philosophers, fiction writers, and those responsible for criminal justice policy.

Beyond identifying born criminals by their stigmata, Lombroso said he could associate the stigmata with certain types of criminals—anarchists, burglars, murderers, shoplifters, and so on. Of course, his work is quite invalid by modern research standards.

Lombroso as the Father of Criminology and the Father of the Positive School

Lombroso's theory came a decade and a half after Darwin's work had been published and had spread rapidly throughout the Western world. Also, Lombroso's model supported what were then the Western world's views on slavery, deportation, and so on. Due to this timing and the fact that Lombroso became known as the first individual who actually tested his hypotheses through observation, Lombroso is widely considered the father of criminology. This title does not indicate respect for his theory, which has been largely rejected, or for his methods, which are considered highly invalid by modern standards. It is deserved, however, in the sense that he was the first person to gain recognition by testing his theoretical propositions. Furthermore, his theory coincided with political movements that became popular at that time: the Fascism and Nazism of the early 1900s.

Beyond being considered the father of criminology, Lombroso is also considered the father of the Positive School of criminology because he was the first to gain prominence in identifying factors beyond free will and free choice, which the Classical School said were the sole cause of crime. Although previous theorists had presented perspectives that went beyond free will, such as craniometrists and phrenologists, Lombroso was the first to gain widespread attention. Lombroso's perspective gained almost immediate support in all developed countries of that time, which is the most likely reason why Lombroso is considered the father of the Positive School of criminology.

It is important to understand the assumptions of *positivism*, which most experts consider somewhat synonymous with the term determinism. Determinism is the assumption that most human behavior is determined by factors beyond free will and free choice. In other words, determinism (i.e., the Positive School) assumes that human beings do not decide how they will act by logically thinking through the costs and benefits of a given situation.

[12]Taylor et al., *New Criminology*, 41–42.

Rather, the Positive School attributes all kinds of behavior, especially crime, on biological, psychological, and sociological variables.

Many readers probably feel they chose their career paths and made most other key decisions in their lives. However, scientific evidence shows otherwise. For example, studies clearly show that far more than 90% of the world's population has adopted the religious affiliation (e.g., Baptist, Buddhist, Catholic, Judaist) of their parents or caretakers. Therefore, what most people consider to be an extremely important decision—the choice of beliefs regarding a higher being or force—is almost completely determined by the environment in which they were brought up. Almost no one sits down and studies various religions before deciding which one suits him or her the best. Rather, in almost all cases, religion is determined by culture, and this finding goes against the Classical School's assumption that free will rules. The same type of argument can be made about the clothes we wear, the food we prefer, and the activities that give us pleasure.

Another way to distinguish positivism and determinism from the Classical School lies in the way scientists view human behavior, which can be seen best in an analogy with chemistry. Specifically, a chemist assumes that, if a certain element is subjected to certain temperatures, pressures, or mixtures with other elements, a predicted response will result. In a highly comparable way, a positivist assumes that, when human beings are subjected to poverty, delinquent peers, low intelligence, or other factors, they will react and behave in predictable ways. Therefore, there is virtually no difference in how a chemist feels about particles and elements and how a positivistic scientist feels about how humans react when exposed to biological and social factors.

In Lombroso's case, the deterministic factor was the biological makeup of the individual. However, we shall see in the next several sections that positivistic theories focus on a large range of variables, from biology to psychology to social aspects. For example, many readers may believe that bad parenting, poverty, and associating with delinquent peers are some of the most important factors in predicting criminality. If you believe that such variables have a significant influence on decisions to commit crime, then you are likely a positive theorist; you believe that crime is caused by factors above and beyond free choice or free will.

Lombroso's Policy Implications

Beyond the theoretical aspects of Lombroso's theory of criminality, it is important to realize that his perspective had profound consequences for policy. Lombroso was called to testify in numerous criminal processes and trials to determine the guilt or innocence of suspects. Under the banner of science (comparable to what we consider DNA or fingerprint analysis in modern times), Lombroso was asked to specify whether or not a suspect had committed a crime.[13] Lombroso based such judgments on the visual stigmata that he could see among suspects.[14] Lombroso documented many of his experiences as an expert witness at criminal trials. Here is one example: "[One suspect] was, in fact, the most perfect type of the born criminal: enormous jaws, frontal sinuses, and zygomata, thin upper lip, huge incisors, unusually large head. . . . [H]e was convicted."[15]

When Lombroso was not available for such "scientific" determinations of the guilty persons, his colleagues or students (often referred to as lieutenants) were often sent. Some of these students, such as Enrico Ferri and Raphael Garrofalo, became quite active in the Fascist regime of Italy in the early 1900s. This model of government, like that of the Nazi Party of Germany, sought to remove the "inferior" groups from society.

Another policy implication in some parts of the world was the identification of young children on the basis of observed stigmata, which often become noticeable in the first 5 to 10 years of life. This led to tracking or isolating of certain children, largely based on physiological features. Although many readers may consider such policies

---

[13]See Gould, *Mismeasure of Man.*

[14]For a review of such identifications, see Gould, *Mismeasure of Man.*

[15]Cesare Lombroso, *Crime: Its Causes and Remedies* (Boston: Little, Brown, 1911), 436.

ridiculous, modern medicine has supported the identification, documentation, and importance of what are termed minor physical anomalies (MPAs), which it holds may indicate high risk of developmental problems. Some of these MPAs include:

- Head circumference out of the normal range
- Fine, "electric" hair
- More than one hair whorl
- Epicanthus, which is observed as a fold of skin extending from the lower eyelids to the nose and appears as droopy eyelids
- Hypertelorism (orbital), which represents an increased interorbital distance
- Malformed ears
- Low-set ears
- Excessively large gap between the first and second toes
- Webbing between toes or fingers
- No earlobes
- Curved fifth finger
- Third toe longer than the second toe
- Asymmetrical ears
- Furrowed tongue
- Simian crease[16]

Given that such visible physical aspects are still correlated with developmental problems, including criminality, it is obvious that Lombroso's model of stigmata for predicting antisocial problems has implications to the present day. Such implications are more accepted by modern medical science than they are in the criminological literature. Furthermore, some modern scientific studies have shown that being unattractive predicts criminal offending, which somewhat supports Lombroso's theory of crime.[17]

About three decades after Lombroso's original work was published, and after a long period of dominance, criminologists began to question his theory of atavism and stigmata. Furthermore, it became clear that more was involved in criminality than just the way people looked, such as psychological aspects of individuals. However, scientists and societies were not ready to depart from theories like Lombroso's, which assumed that certain people or groups of people were inferior to others, so they simply chose another factor to emphasize: intelligence or IQ.

The IQ Testing Era

Despite the evidence that was presented against Lombroso, his theorizing remained dominant until the early 1900s, when criminologists realized that stigmata and the idea of born criminals were not valid. However, even at that time, theorists and researchers were not ready to give up on the eugenics assumption that certain ethnic or racial groups were superior or inferior to others. Thus, a new theory emerged based on a more quantified measure that was originated, with benevolent intentions, by Alfred Binet in France. This new measure was IQ, short for *intelligence quotient*. At that time, IQ was calculated as chronological age divided by mental age, which was then multiplied by 100, with the average score being 100. This scale has changed enormously over time, but the basic premise was that the test could be used to determine whether someone was above or below average intelligence (100).

---

[16]Taken from Mary Waldrop and Charles Halverson, "Minor Physical Anomalies and Hyperactive Behavior in Young Children," in *Exceptional Infant: Studies in Abnormalities*, ed. Jerome Hellmuth (New York: Brunner/Mazel, 1971), 343–81, as cited and reviewed by Diana Fishbein, *Biobehavioral Perspectives on Criminology* (Belmont: Wadsworth, 2001).

[17]Robert Agnew, "Appearance and Delinquency," *Criminology* 22 (1984): 421–40.

As mentioned above, Binet had good intentions: He created IQ scores to identify youths who were not performing up to par on academic skills. Binet was explicit in stating that IQ could be changed; the reason he proposed a score to identify slow learners was so that they could be trained to increase their IQs.[18] However, when Binet's work was brought over to the United States, his basic assumptions and propositions were twisted. One of the most prominent individuals who used Binet's IQ test in the United States for purposes of deporting, incapacitating, sterilizing, and otherwise ridding society of low-IQ individuals was H. H. Goddard.

Goddard is generally considered the leading authority on the use and interpretation of IQ testing in the United States.[19] He adapted Binet's model to examine immigrants who were coming into the United States from foreign lands. It is important to note that Goddard proposed quite different assumptions regarding intelligence or IQ than did Binet. Goddard asserted that IQ was static or innate, meaning that such levels could not be changed, even with training. His assumption was that intelligence was inherited from parents and passed from generation to generation.

Goddard labeled low IQ feeblemindedness, which in the 1900s actually became a technical, scientific term characterizing those who had significantly below-average levels of intelligence. Of course, being a scientist, Goddard specified certain levels of feeblemindedness, which were ranked based on the

▲ Image 4.3　H. H. Goddard (1866–1957)

Source: http://upload.wikimedia.org/wikipedia/commons/4/45/Henry_H._Goddard.jpg

degree to which scores were below average. Ranking from the highest to the lowest intelligence, the first group were the *morons*, the second-lowest group were the *imbeciles*, and the lowest-intelligence group were the *idiots*.

According to Goddard, from a eugenics point of view, the biggest threat to the progress of humanity was not the idiots but the morons. In Goddard's words, "The idiot is not our greatest problem. . . . He does not continue the race with a line of children like himself. . . . It is the moron type that makes for us our great problem."[20] That is, the moron is the one group out of the three categories of feebleminded that is smart enough to slip through the cracks and reproduce.

Goddard received many grants to fund his research to identify the feebleminded. Goddard took his research team to the major immigration center at Ellis Island in the early 1900s to identify the feebleminded as they attempted to enter the United States. Many members of his team were women, who he felt were better at distinguishing the feebleminded by sight:

> The people who are best at this work, and who I believe should do this work, are women. Women seem to have closer observation than men. It was quite impossible for others to see how . . . women could pick out the feeble-minded without the aid of the Binet test at all.[21]

---

[18]Gould, *Mismeasure of Man.*

[19]Again, most of this discussion is taken from Gould, *Mismeasure of Man,* because his review is perhaps the best known in the current literature.

[20]Henry H. Goddard, *The Kallikak Family, a Study of the Heredity of Feeble-Mindedness* (New York: MacMillan, 1912).

[21]Henry H. Goddard, "The Binet Tests in Relation to Immigration," *Journal of Psycho-Asthenics* 18 (1913): 105–7; quote taken from page 106, as cited in Gould, *Mismeasure of Man.*

▲ Image 4.4   Ellis Island.

Source: © Thinkstock / Stockbyte.

Goddard was proud of the increase in the deportation of potential immigrants to the United States, enthusiastically reporting that deportations for the reason of mental deficiency increased by 350% in 1913 and 570% in 1914 over the averages of the preceding five years.[22] However, over time, Goddard realized that his policy recommendations of deportation, incarceration, and sterilization were not based on accurate science.

After consistently validating his IQ test on immigrants and mental patients, Goddard finally tested his intelligence scale on a relatively representative cross-section of American citizens, namely draftees for military service during World War I. The results showed that many of these recruits would score as feebleminded (i.e., as having a mental age of less than 12) on the IQ test. Therefore, Goddard lowered the criterion for determining feeblemindedness from the mental age of 12 to that of age 8. Although this appears to be a clear admission that his scientific method was inaccurate, Goddard continued to promote his model of the feebleminded for many years, and societies used his ideas.

However, toward the end of his career, Goddard admitted that intelligence could be improved, despite his earlier assumptions that it was innate and static.[23] In fact, Goddard actually claimed that he had "gone over to the enemy."[24] However, despite Goddard's admission that his assumptions and testing were not determinant of individuals'

[22]Gould, *Mismeasure of Man*, 198.

[23]Henry H. Goddard, "Feeblemindedness: A Question of Definition," *Journal of Psycho-Asthenics* 33 (1928): 219–27, as discussed in Gould, *Mismeasure of Man*.

[24]Ibid., 224.

intelligence levels, the snowball had been rolling for too long and had gathered too much strength to fight even the most notable theorists' admonishments.

Sterilization of individuals, mostly females, continued in the United States based on scores of intelligence tests. Often the justification was not a person's own intelligence scores but those of his or her mother or father. Goddard had proclaimed that the *germ-plasm* determining feeblemindedness was passed on from one generation to the next, so it inevitably resulted in offspring being feebleminded as well. Thus, the U.S. government typically sterilized individuals, typically women, based on the IQ scores of their parents.

The case of *Buck v. Bell*, brought to the U.S. Supreme Court in 1927, dealt with the issue of sterilizing individuals who had scored, or whose parents had scored, as mentally deficient on intelligence scales. The majority opinion, written by one of the court's most respected jurists, Oliver Wendell Holmes, Jr., stated:

> We have seen more than once that the public welfare may call upon the best citizens for their lives. It would be strange if it could not call upon those who already sap the strength of the state for these lesser sacrifices. . . . Three generations of imbeciles are enough.[25]

Thus, the highest court in the United States upheld the use of sterilization for the purposes of limiting reproduction among individuals who were deemed feebleminded according to an IQ score. Such sterilizations continued until the 1970s, when the practice was finally halted. Governors of many states, such as North Carolina, Virginia, and California, have given public apologies for what was done. For example, in 2002, the governor of California, Gray Davis, apologized for the state law passed almost a century earlier that had resulted in the sterilization of about 19,000 women in California.

Although this aspect of U.S. history is often hidden from the public, it did occur, and it is important to acknowledge this blot on our nation's history, especially at a time when we were fighting abuses of civil rights by the Nazis and other regimes. Ultimately, the sterilizations, deportations, and incarcerations based on IQ testing are an embarrassing episode in the history of the United States.

For decades, the issue of IQ was not researched or discussed much in the literature. However, in the 1970s, a very important study was published in which Travis Hirschi and Michael Hindelang examined the effect of intelligence on youths' behaviors.[26] Hirschi and Hindelang found that, among youths of the same race and social class, intelligence had a significant effect on delinquency and criminality among individuals. This study, as well as others, showed that the IQ of delinquents or criminals is about 10 points lower than that of noncriminals.[27]

This study led to a rebirth in research regarding intelligence testing within the criminological perspective. A number of recent studies have shown that certain types of intelligence are more important than others. For example, several studies have shown that having low verbal intelligence has the most significant impact on predicting delinquent and criminal behavior.[28]

---

[25]As quoted in Gould, *Mismeasure of Man*, 365.

[26]Travis Hirschi and Michael Hindelang, "Intelligence and Delinquency: A Revisionist Review," *American Sociological Review* 42 (1977): 571–87.

[27]For a review, see Raymond Paternoster and Ronet Bachman, *Explaining Criminals and Crime* (Los Angeles: Roxbury, 2001); Also see Raine, *Psychopathology*.

[28]See Joshua Isen, "A Meta-analytic Assessment of Wechsler's P > V Sign in Antisocial Populations," *Clinical Psychology Review* 30 (2010): 423–35; and Chris L. Gibson, Alex R Piquero, and Stephen G. Tibbetts, "The Contribution of Family Adversity and Verbal IQ to Criminal Behavior," *International Journal of Offender Therapy and Comparative Criminology* 45 (2001): 574–92. See also Hirschi and Hindelang, "Intelligence and Delinquency"; Terrie Moffitt, "The Neuropsychology of Delinquency: A Critical Review of Theory and Research," in *Crime and Justice: An Annual Review of Research*, Vol. 12, ed. Michael Tonry and Norval Morris (Chicago: University of Chicago Press, 1990), 99–169; Terrie Moffitt and Bill Henry, "Neuropsychological Studies of Juvenile Delinquency and Juvenile Violence," in *The Neuropsychology of Aggression*, ed. Joel S. Milner (Boston: Kluwer, 1991), 67–91; and the conclusion by Paternoster and Bachman in *Explaining Criminals*, 51.

This tendency makes sense, because verbal skills are important for virtually all aspects of life, from everyday interactions with significant others to filling out forms at work to dealing with people via employment. In contrast, most people do not require advanced math or quantitative skills at their jobs or in day-to-day experiences, let alone spatial and other forms of intelligence that are more abstract. Thus, the fact that low verbal IQ is the type of intelligence that represents the most direct prediction for criminality is most likely due to the general need for verbal skills in routine daily activities. After all, people who lack communication skills will likely find it hard to obtain or retain employment or deal with family and social problems.

This rebirth in studies regarding the link between intelligence and criminality seemed to reach a peak with the publication of Richard Herrnstein and Charles Murray's *The Bell Curve* in 1994.[29] Although this publication changed the terms *moron*, *imbecile*, and *idiot* to relatively benign terms (e.g., *cognitively disadvantaged*), their argument was consistent with that of the feeblemindedness researchers of the early 20th century. Herrnstein and Murray argued that people with low IQ scores are somewhat destined to be unsuccessful in school, become unemployed, produce illegitimate children, and commit crime. They also suggest that IQ or intelligence is primarily innate, or genetically determined, and that there is little chance of improving it. These authors also noted that African Americans tended to score lowest, whereas Asians and Jewish people tended to score highest, and they offered results from social indicators supporting their argument that the intelligence levels of the latter resulted in relative success in life in terms of group-level statistics.

This book produced a public outcry, resulting in symposiums at major universities and other venues in which the authors' postulates were largely condemned. As noted by other reviews of the impact of this work, some professors at public institutions were sued in court because they used this book in their classes.[30] The book received blistering reviews from fellow scientists.[31] However, none of these scientific critics has fully addressed the undisputed fact that African Americans consistently score low on intelligence tests and that Asians and Jews score higher on these examinations. Furthermore, none has adequately addressed the issue that, even within these populations, low IQ scores (especially on verbal tests) predict criminality. For example, in samples of African Americans, the group that scores lowest on verbal intelligence consistently commits more crime and is more likely to become delinquent or criminal. So, despite the harsh criticism of *The Bell Curve*, it is apparent that there is some validity to the authors' arguments.

With the popularity of intelligence testing and IQ scores in the early 20th century, it is not surprising that this was also the period when other psychological models of deviance and criminality became popular. However, one of the most popular involved body type theories.

Body Type Theory: Sheldon's Model of Somatotyping

Although there were numerous theories based on body types in the late 1800s and early 1900s, such as Lombroso's and those of others who called themselves criminal anthropologists, none of these perspectives had a more enduring impact than that of William Sheldon. In the mid-1940s, a new theoretical perspective was proposed that merged the concepts of biology and psychology. Sheldon claimed that, in the embryonic and fetal stages of development,

---

[29]Richard J. Herrnstein and Charles Murray, *The Bell Curve: Intelligence and Class Structure in the United States* (New York: Free Press, 1994).

[30]See Stephen E. Brown, Finn-Aage Esbensen, and Gilbert Geis, *Criminology: Explaining Crime and Its Context*, 8th ed. (Cincinnati: Anderson, 2012), 260 (see chap. 2).

[31]J. Blaine Hudson, "Scientific Racism: The Politics of Tests, Race, and Genes," *Black Scholar* 25 (1995): 1–10; David Perkins, *Outsmarting IQ: The Emerging Science of Learnable Intelligence* (New York: Free Press, 1995); Francis Cullen, Paul Gendreau, G. Roger Jarjoura, and John P. Wright, "Crime and the Bell Curve: Lessons from Intelligent Criminology," *Crime and Delinquency* 43 (1997): 387–411; Robert Hauser, "Review of the Bell Curve," *Contemporary Sociology* 24 (1995): 149–53; Howard Taylor, "Book Review, The Bell Curve," *Contemporary Sociology* 24 (1995): 153–58; Gould, *Mismeasure of Man*, 367–90.

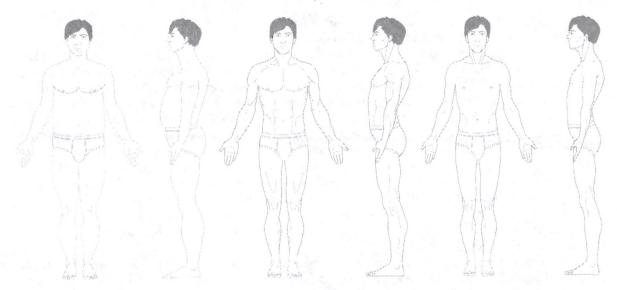

▲ Image 4.4a   Endomorph. Physical traits: soft body, underdeveloped muscles, round shape, overdeveloped digestive system. Associated personality traits: love of food, tolerance, evenness of emotions, love of comfort, sociability, good humor, relaxed mood, need for affection.

Source: © Copyright 2012 Encyclopaedia Britannica.

▲ Image 4.4b   Mesomorph. Physical traits: hard, muscular body; overly mature appearance; rectangular shape; thick skin; upright posture. Associated personality traits: love of adventure, desire for power and dominance, courage, indifference to what others think or want, assertive mien, boldness, zest for physical activity, competitive nature, love of risk and chance.

▲ Image 4.4c   Ectomorph. Physical traits: thin, flat chest; delicate build; young appearance; light muscling; stooped shoulders; large brain. Associated personality traits: self-consciousness, preference for privacy, introversion, inhibition, social anxiety, artistic inclination, mental intensity, emotional restraint.

individuals tend to have an emphasis on certain tissue layers.[32] According to Sheldon, these varying degrees of emphasis are largely due to heredity and lead to the development of certain body types and temperaments or personalities. This became the best-known body type theory, also known as somatotyping.

According to Sheldon, all embryos must develop three distinct tissue layers, and this much is still acknowledged by perinatal medical researchers. The first layer of tissue is the endoderm, which is the inner layer of tissues and includes the internal organs, such as the stomach, large intestine, and small intestine. The middle layer of tissue, called the mesoderm, includes the muscles, bones, ligaments, and tendons. The ectoderm is the outer layer of tissue, which includes the skin, capillaries, and much of the nervous system's sensors.

Sheldon used these medical facts regarding various tissue layers to propose that certain individuals tend to emphasize certain tissue layers relative to others, typically due to inherited dispositions. In turn, Sheldon believed that such emphases lead to certain body types in an individual, such that people who have a focus on their endoderms in embryonic development will inevitably become endomorphic, or obese (see Image 4.4a). According to this theory, individuals who have an emphasis on the middle layer of tissue will typically become mesomorphic, or of an athletic or muscular build (see Image 4.4b), while individuals who have an emphasis on the outer layer will end up with an ectomorphic build, or thin (see Image 4.4c).

Sheldon and his research team graded each subject on three dimensions corresponding to these body types. Each body type was measured on a scale of 1 to 7, with 7 being the highest score. Obviously, no one could score a 0

[32]William Sheldon, E. M. Hartl, and E. McDermott, *Varieties of Delinquent Youth* (New York: Harper, 1949).

for any body type because all tissue layers are needed for survival; we all need our internal organs, bone and muscular structure, and outer systems (skin, capillaries, etc.).

Each somatotype always had the following order: endomorphy, mesomorphy, ectomorphy. Thus, the scores on a typical somatotype might be 3-6-2, which would indicate that this person scored a 3 (a little lower than average) on endomorphy, a 6 (high) on mesomorphy, and a 2 (relatively low) on ectomorphy. According to Sheldon's theory, this hypothetical subject would be a likely candidate for criminality because of the relatively high score on mesomorphy. In fact, the results from his data, as well as all studies that have examined the association of body types with delinquency or criminality, would support this prediction.

Perhaps most important, Sheldon proposed that these body types matched personality traits or temperaments. Individuals who were endomorphic (obese), Sheldon claimed, tended to be more jolly or lazy. The technical term for this temperament is viscerotonic. In contrast, people who were mesomorphic (muscular) typically had risk-taking and aggressive temperaments, called somotonic. Last, individuals who were ectomorphic (thin) tended to have introverted or shy personalities, which is referred to as cerebrotonic. According to Sheldon, members of the middle group, the mesomorphs, obviously had the highest propensity toward criminality because they were disposed toward a risk-taking and aggressive personality.

Interestingly, many politicians were subjects in Sheldon's research. Most entering freshmen at Ivy League schools, especially Harvard, were asked to pose for photos for Sheldon's studies. The Smithsonian Institution still retains a collection of nude photos of George W. Bush, Hillary Rodham Clinton, and many other notable figures.[33]

Sheldon used poor methodology to test his theory. He based his measures of subjects' body types on what he subjectively judged from viewing three perspectives of each subject and often from only three pictures taken of each subject in the three poses. He also had his trained staff view many of the photos and make their determinations of how these individuals scored on each category of body type. The reliability among these scorings has been shown to be weak, meaning that the trained staff did not tend to agree with Sheldon or among themselves on the somatotypes for each participant.

This is not surprising, given the high level of variation in body types and the fact that Sheldon and his colleagues did not employ the technology that is used today, such as caliper tests and submersion in water tanks, which provide the information for which he was searching. People may alter their weights, going from an ectomorphic or mesomorphic build to a more endomorphic form, or vice versa. Presented with the argument that individuals often alter their body types via diet or exercise, Sheldon responded that he could tell what the "natural" body type of each individual was from the three pictures that were taken. Obviously, this position is not a strong one, as demonstrated by the poor inter-rater reliability shown by his staff. Therefore, Sheldon's methodology is questionable, which casts doubt on the entire theoretical framework.

Despite the problems in his methodology, Sheldon clearly showed that mesomorphs, or individuals who had muscular builds and tended to take more risks, were more delinquent and criminal than individuals who had other body types or temperaments.[34] Furthermore, other researchers, even those who despised Sheldon's theory, found the same associations between mesomorphy and criminality, as well as related temperaments (i.e., somotonic) and criminality.[35] Subsequent studies showed that mesomorphic boys were far more likely to have personality traits that predicted criminality, such as aggression, short temper, self-centeredness, and impulsivity.

Recent theorists have also noted the link between an athletic, muscular build and the highly extroverted, aggressive personality that is often associated with this body type.[36] In fact, some recent theorists have gone so far as to claim that chronic offenders, both male and female, can be identified early in life by their relatively V-shaped

---

[33]See discussion in Brown et al., *Criminology*, 246.

[34]Sheldon et al., *Varieties*.

[35]Sheldon Glueck and Eleanor Glueck, *Physique and Delinquency* (New York: Harper & Row, 1956). See also Emil Hartl, *Physique and Delinquent Behavior* (New York: Academic Press, 1982); and Juan Cortes, *Delinquency and Crime* (New York: Seminar Press, 1972). For the most recent applications, see Hans J. Eysenck and G. H. Gudjonsson, *The Causes and Cures of Criminality* (New York: Plenum, 1989).

[36]James Q. Wilson and Richard Herrnstein, *Crime and Human Nature* (New York: Simon & Schuster, 1985).

pelvic structure as opposed to a U-shaped pelvic structure.[37] The V-shaped pelvis is said to indicate relatively high levels of androgens (male hormones, like testosterone) in the system, which predisposes individuals toward crime. On the other hand, a more U-shaped pelvis indicates relatively low levels of such androgens and therefore lower propensity toward aggression and criminality. Using this logic, it may be true that more hair on an individual's arms (whether that person be male or female) is predictive of a high likelihood for committing crime. However, no research exists regarding this factor.

Regarding the use of body types and characteristics in explaining crime, many of the hard-line sociologists who have attempted to examine or replicate Sheldon's results have never been able to refute the association between mesomorphs and delinquency or criminality, nor the association between mesomorphy and the somotonic characteristics of risk-taking and aggression.[38] Thus, the association between being muscular or athletically built and engaging in criminal activities is now undisputed and assumed to be true.

Still, sociologists have taken issue with the reasons for this association. Whereas Sheldon claimed it was due to inherited traits for a certain body type, sociologists argue that this association is due to societal expectations: Muscular male youths would be encouraged to engage in risk-taking and aggressive behavior. For example, a young male with an athletic build would be encouraged to join sports teams and engage in high-risk behaviors by peers. Who would gangs most desire as members? More muscular, athletic individuals would be better at fighting and performing acts that require a certain degree of physical strength and stamina.

Ultimately, it is now established that mesomorphs are more likely to commit crime.[39] Furthermore, the personality traits linked to having an athletic or muscular build are dispositions toward risk-taking and aggressiveness, and few scientists dispute this correlation. No matter which theoretical model is adopted, whether the biopsychologists' or the sociologists', the fact is that mesomorphs are indeed more likely to be risk-taking and aggressive and, thus, to commit more crime than individuals of other body types.

However, whether the cause is biological or sociological is a debate that shows the importance of theory in criminological research. After all, the link between mesomorphy and criminality is now undisputed; the explanation of why this link exists has become a theoretical debate. Readers may make their own determination—if not now, then later.

Our position is that both biology and social environment are likely to interact with one another in explaining this link. Thus, it is most likely that both nature and nurture are at play in this association between mesomorphy and crime, and both Sheldon and his critics may be correct. A middle ground can often be found in theorizing on criminality. It is important to keep in mind that theories in criminology, as a science, are always considered subject to falsification and criticism and can always be improved. Therefore, our stance on the validity and influence of this theory, as well as others, should not be surprising.

Policy Implications

Many policy implications can be derived from the theories presented in this section. First, one could propose more thorough medical screening at birth and in early childhood, especially regarding minor physical anomalies (MPAs). The studies reviewed in this section obviously implicate numerous MPAs in developmental problems (most of them arising in the womb). These MPAs are a red flag signaling problems, especially in cognitive abilities, which are likely to have a significant impact on propensity for criminal behavior.[40]

Other policy implications derived from the theories and findings of this section involve having same-sex classes for children in school because they focus on deficiencies that have been shown for both young boys and

---

[37]Eysenck and Gudjonsson, *Causes and Cures*; Raine, *Psychopathology*.

[38]Cortes, *Delinquency and Crime*; Glueck and Glueck, *Physique and Delinquency*. For a review, see Eysenck and Gudjonsson, *Causes and Cures*.

[39]For a review, see Lee Ellis and Anthony Walsh, *Criminology: A Global Perspective* (Minot: Pyramid Press, 2000), supplemental tables and references.

[40]Fishbein, *Biobehavioral Perspectives*.

girls. Numerous school districts now have policies that specify same-sex math courses for female children. This same strategy might be considered for male children in English or literature courses, because males have a biological disposition for a lower aptitude than females in this area of study. Furthermore, far more screening should be done to determine IQ and aptitude levels of young children in order to identify which children require extra attention, because studies show that such early intervention can make a big difference in improving their IQ and aptitude.

A recent report that reviewed the extant literature regarding what types of programs work best for reducing crime noted the importance of diagnosing early head trauma and further concluded that one of the most consistently supported programs for such at-risk children are those that involve weekly infant home visitation.[41] Another obvious policy implication derived from biosocial theory is mandatory health insurance for pregnant mothers and children, which is quite likely the most efficient way to reduce crime in the long term.[42] Finally, all youths should be screened for abnormal levels of hormones, neurotransmitters, and toxins (especially lead).[43] These and other policy strategies will be discussed in the last section of the book.

 ## Conclusion

In this section, we discussed the development of the early Positive School of criminology. The Positive School can be seen as the opposite of the Classical School perspective, which we covered in Sections II and III, because positivism assumes that individuals have virtually no free will; rather, criminal behavior is considered to be the result of determinism, which means that factors other than rational decision making, such as poverty, intelligence, bad parenting, and unemployment, influence us and determine our behavior.

The earliest positivist theories, such as craniometry and phrenology, were developed in the early 1800s but did not become popular outside of scientific circles, likely because they were presented prior to Charles Darwin's theory of evolution. In the 1860s, Darwin's theory became widely accepted, which set the stage for the father of criminology, Cesare Lombroso, to propose his theory of born criminals. Lombroso's theory was based on Darwin's theory of evolution and argued that the worst criminals are born that way, being biological throwbacks to an earlier stage of evolution. Unfortunately, Lombroso's theory led to numerous policies that fit the philosophy and politics of Fascism, which found useful a theory proposing that certain people were inferior to others. However, Lombroso and many of his contemporaries became aware that the field should shift to a more multifactorial approach, such as one emphasizing how environment and social factors interact with physiological influences.

We also discussed theories regarding low IQ scores, traditionally known as feeblemindedness. Although most recent studies show that there is a correlation between crime and low IQ, this association is not quite as strong as thought in the early 1900s. Modern studies show consistent evidence that low verbal IQ is related with criminality,[44] especially when coupled with sociological factors, such as weak family structure. This is the state of the criminological field today, and it will be discussed in the next section.

Finally, we explored the theories and evidence regarding body types in predisposing an individual toward criminality. Studies have shown that the more athletic or mesomorphic an individual is, the higher the probability that this individual will be involved in criminality. This relationship is likely based on hormonal levels, and this type of association will be explored in the next section.

---

[41]Lawrence Sherman, Denise Gottfredson, Doris MacKenzie, John Eck, Peter Reuter, and Shawn Bushway, *Preventing Crime: What Works, What Doesn't, What's Promising: A Report to the United States Congress* (Washington, DC: U.S. Department of Justice, 1997) (see chap. 2).

[42]John Wright, Stephen Tibbetts, and Leah Daigle, *Criminals in the Making: Criminality across the Life Course*, 2nd ed. (Thousand Oaks: Sage, 2015).

[43]Ibid., 258–63.

[44]Gibson et al., "Contribution of Family Adversity."

Ultimately, we have examined a variety of physiological and psychological factors that predict criminal offending, according to empirical research. Still, the existence of such influence is largely conditional, that is, based on environmental and social factors.

Section Summary

- The Positive School of criminology assumes the opposite of the Classical School. Whereas the Classical School assumes that individuals commit crime because they freely choose to act after rationally considering the expected costs and benefits of the behavior, the Positive School assumes that individuals have virtually no free will or choice in the matter; rather, their behavior is determined by factors outside of free will, such as poverty, low intelligence, bad child rearing, and unemployment.
- The earliest positive theories, such as craniometry and phrenology, emphasized measuring the size and shape of the skull and brain. These perspectives did not become very popular because they preceded Charles Darwin's theory of evolution.
- Cesare Lombroso, the father of criminology, presented a theoretical model that assumed that the worst criminals are born that way. Highly influenced by Darwin, Lombroso claimed that born criminals are evolutionary throwbacks who are not as highly developed as most people.
- Lombroso claimed that these born criminals could be identified by physical features called stigmata. This led to numerous policy implications that fit with the societal beliefs at that time, such as Fascism.
- In the early 1900s, the IQ test was invented in France and was quickly used by American researchers in their quest to identify the feebleminded. This led to massive numbers of deportations, sterilizations, and institutionalizations across the United States and elsewhere.
- Modern studies support a link between low verbal IQ and criminality, even within a given race, social class, or gender.
- Merging elements of the early physiological and psychological perspectives are body type theories. The best known of these is somatotyping, which was proposed by William Sheldon. Sheldon found that an athletic or muscular build (i.e., mesomorphy) is linked to an aggressive, risk-taking personality, which in turn is associated with higher levels of crime.
- Despite the methodological problems with Sheldon's body type theory, many propositions and associations of the perspective hold true in modern studies.
- The early Positive School theories set the stage for most of the other theories we will be covering in this book because they emphasize use of the scientific method for studying and explaining criminal activity.

KEY TERMS

atavism	endomorphic	physiognomy
cerebrotonic	eugenics	somatotyping
craniometry	feeblemindedness	somotonic
determinism	mesoderm	stigmata
ectoderm	mesomorphic	viscerotonic
ectomorphic	minor physical anomalies (MPAs)	
endoderm	phrenology	

DISCUSSION QUESTIONS

1. What characteristics distinguish the Positive School from the Classical School regarding criminal thought? Which of these schools do you lean toward in your own perspective of crime and why?

2. Name and describe the various early schools of positivistic theories that existed in the early to mid-1800s (pre-Darwin), as well as the influence that they had on later schools of thought regarding criminality. Do you see any validity in these approaches (as modern medical science does)? Why or why not?

3. What were the significant reasons that these early schools of positivistic theories did not gain much momentum in societal popularity? Does this lack of popularity relate to the neglect of biological perspectives of crime in modern times?

4. What portion of Lombroso's theory of criminality do you find least valid? Which do you find most valid?

5. Most readers have taken the equivalent of an IQ test (e.g., SAT or ACT tests). Do you believe that this score is a fair representation of your knowledge as compared to that of others? Why or why not? Do your feelings reflect the criticisms of experts regarding the use of IQ (e.g., as in feeblemindedness theory) in identifying potential offenders?

6. In light of scientific findings that show that verbal IQ is a consistent predictor of criminality among virtually all populations and samples, can you provide evidence from your personal experience for why this occurs?

7. What portion of Sheldon's body type theory do you find most valid? What do you find least valid?

8. If you had to give yourself a somatotype (e.g., 3-6-2), what would it be? Explain why your score would be the one you provide, and note whether this would make you likely to be a criminal in Sheldon's model.

9. Provide somatotypes of five of your family members or best friends. Do the somatotypes have any correlation with criminality according to Sheldon's predictions? Either way, describe your findings.

10. Ultimately, do you believe that some of the positive theoretical perspectives presented in this section are valid, or do you think they should be entirely dismissed in terms of understanding or predicting crime? Either way, state your case.

11. What types of policies would you implement if you were in charge, given the theories and findings in this section?

WEB RESOURCES

Body Type Theories/Somatotyping

http://www.innerexplorations.com/psytext/shel.htm

http://www.teachpe.com/multi/somatotyping_eating_disorders_performance.htm

IQ Testing/Feeblemindedness

http://www.eugenicsarchive.org/html/eugenics/static/themes/12.html

Cesare Lombroso

http://www.thenautilus.it/Mu_Lombroso.html

Phrenology/Craniometry

http://www.phrenology.org/index.html

http://skepdic.com/cranial.html

READING 8

Cesare Lombroso is generally considered the father of criminology as well as the father of the Positive School, primarily because he was the first to get credit for testing his theoretical propositions through observation. He emphasized using the scientific method in examining criminal behavior. This selection includes some of the key portions of his evolution-influenced theory of criminals, particularly those he referred to as "born criminals." He also reviews many examples of stigmata, or physical manifestations he believed were signs of evolutionary inferiority. As you read this selection, keep in mind that although most of these ideas have been discredited, at the time they became very popular among both social scientists and society at large. Furthermore, Lombroso's theory was the dominant theory of criminality for several decades, longer than virtually any other theoretical model in over a century.

The Criminal Man (L'uomo delinquente)

Cesare Lombroso (as translated by Mary Gibson and Nicole H. Rafter)

 ## 2. Anthropometry and Physiognomy of 832 Criminals

To many, my attempt to conclude anything at all about the cranial dimensions of the criminal man from a few measurements of cadavers will seem futile and rash. Fortunately, however, I have been able to compare these measurements with those taken from 832 live specimens of criminals, thanks to the help of colleagues who are prison directors and prison physicians.

In terms of height, criminals reproduce their regional types. In Italy, they are very tall in the Veneto (1.69 meters), fairly tall in Umbria and Lombardy (1.66 m), less tall in Emilia, Calabria, and Piedmont (1.63 m), slightly shorter in Naples, Sicily, and the Marehes, and shortest of all in Sardinia (1.59 m).[1] Compared with healthy men in the army, criminals appear to be taller than the average Italian, especially in the Veneto, Umbria, Lombardy, Sicily, and

Calabria. In the Marehes, Naples, and Piedmont, criminals are the same height as healthy men.

These findings, however, are skewed by the preponderance of robbers and murderers in my sample, and thus they conflict with the conclusions of Thomson and Wilson.[2] Robbers and murderers are taller than rapists, forgers, and especially thieves.[a] As for weight, we can compare the findings on 1,331 soldiers, studied by me and Dr. Franchini, with the average for criminals from each region. In the Veneto, healthy men weighed an average of 68 kilograms, while criminals weighed 62.5kg.[3] But in most other regions, most notably Naples, Sicily, and Piedmont, criminals' average weight exceeded that of healthy men.

There are many erroneous ideas in circulation about the physiognomy, or facial expressions, of criminals. Novelists turn them into frightening-looking men with beards that go right up to their eyes, penetrating ferocious gazes, and hawklike noses. More serious observers, such as Casper, err on the other extreme, finding no differences between criminals and normal men.[4] Both are wrong. It is certainly true that there

[a]Thomson found an average weight of 151 pounds among 423 Scottish criminals, 106 pounds among 147 Irish criminals, and 149 pounds among 55 English criminals. The average height was 5 feet 6.9 inches for the Scottish criminals, 5 feet 6.2 inches for the English, and 5 feet 6.6 inches for the Irish.

are criminals with notably large cranial capacity and beautifully formed skulls, just as there are those with perfectly regular physiognomy, particularly among adroit swindlers and gang leaders. Lavater and Polli wrote about a murderer whose face resembled one of the angels painted by Guido (*Saggio di Fisiognomia*, 1837).[5] But criminals whose handsome features make a strong impression can be misleading precisely because they contradict our expectations. They are usually individuals of uncommon intelligence, a trait associated with gracefulness of form.

When, on the other hand, one ignores those rare individuals who form the oligarchy of the criminal world to study the entire spectrum of these wretches, as I have done in various prisons, one has to conclude that while offenders may not look fierce, there is nearly always something strange about their appearance. It can even be said that each type of crime is committed by men with particular physiognomic characteristics, such as lack of a beard or an abundance of hair; this may explain why the overall appearance is neither delicate nor pleasant.

In general, thieves are notable for their expressive faces and manual dexterity, small wandering eyes that are often oblique in form, thick and close eyebrows, distorted or squashed noses, thin beards and hair, and sloping foreheads. Like rapists, they often have jug ears. Rapists, however, nearly always have sparkling eyes, delicate features, and swollen lips and eyelids. Most of them are frail; some are hunchbacked. Pederasts are often distinguished by a feminine elegance of the hair and feminine clothing, which they insist on wearing even under their prison uniforms.

Habitual murderers have a cold, glassy stare and eyes that are sometimes bloodshot and filmy; the nose is often hawklike and always large; the jaw is strong, the cheekbones broad; and their hair is dark, abundant, and crisply textured. Their beards are scanty, their canine teeth very developed, and their lips thin. Often their faces contract, exposing the teeth. Among nearly all arsonists, I have observed a softness of skin, an almost childlike appearance, and an abundance of thick straight hair that is almost feminine. One extremely curious example from Pesaro, known as "the woman," was truly feminine in appearance and behavior.

Nearly all criminals have jug ears, thick hair, thin beards, pronounced sinuses, protruding chins, and broad cheekbones. Dumollard, a rapist and murderer, had a deformed upper lip and very thick black hair.[6] The rapist Mingrat had a low forehead, jug ears, and an enormous square jaw. Archaeologists have established that the cruelest of the Caesars—Commodius, Nero, and Tiberius—had jug ears and swollen temples.

But anthropology needs numbers, not isolated, generic descriptions, especially for use in forensic medicine. Thus I will provide statistics on 390 criminals from the regions of Emilia, the Marehes, and southern Italy. Table 1 compares the hair color of these 390 criminals with that of 868 Italian soldiers from the same regions and 90 insane from Pavia. These figures show that hair color of criminals replicates typical regional characteristics, but only up to a certain point.

Table 1	Hair Color of Soldiers and Criminals							
	Brown (percent)		Black (percent)		Blond (percent)		Red (percent)	
Region	Soldiers	Criminals	Soldiers	Criminals	Soldiers	Criminals	Soldiers	Criminals
Sicily	51	41	25	54	17	0	0	3
Calabria	39	50	20	33	15	0	0	0
Naples	50	50	28	40	22	5	0.3	0
Central Italy	56	66	20	33	21	5	1	5
Piedmont	47	35	13	35	34	29	0	0
Lombardy	38	33	16	33	32	33	0	0
Insane from Pavia	83	–	12	–	4	–	0	–

NOTE: The last category, the insane from Pavia, is not consistent with Lombroso's regional categories but seems to be an attempt to compare the insane with soldiers (normal men) and criminals.

Jug ears are found on 28 percent of criminals, but the proportion varies by region: 47 percent of Sicilian criminals have jug ears, as do 33 percent from Piedmont, 11 percent from Naples, 33 percent from the Romagna, 9 percent from Sardinia, and 36 percent from Lombardy. Nine percent of all criminals have very long ears, although that proportion rises to 10 percent in Lombardy and the Romagna and 18 percent in Sicily and Piedmont.

It is difficult to determine the muscular force of criminals even with the best dynamometers because the subjects are completely out of condition after long periods of detention and inertia.[7] The problem is often compounded by the malignant spirit that characterizes prisoners' whole existence. They pretend to be weaker than they really are and do not put much effort into pushing the dynamometer. In this regard, it is noteworthy that, as I was able to verify in the penitentiary of Ancona, prisoners are more energetic when they work continuously than in institutions that permit them to be idle. Rapists, brigands, and arsonists are the strongest and thieves and forgers the weakest, based on measurements of traction. Murderers and pickpockets differ in strength only by a slight fraction.

Criminal Women

At this point little can be said about female criminals because I have been allowed to examine only twenty-one of them and did so with much less ease than in the case of men. But this does not pose a complete obstacle because, first, I do not have enough information on normal women to make a comparison with criminal women; and, second, Parent-Duchatelet offers us numerous and reliable statistics on prostitutes, a class of women almost identical to criminal women in moral terms.[8] In addition, the esteemed Dr. Soresina has provided me with measurements on fifty-four prostitutes who were patients in the Milan lock hospital for venereal disease.[9]

The average cranial capacity of the twenty-one female criminals in my sample was 1,442 cc, slightly less than that of twenty insane women without dementia (1,468 cc), and above that of nineteen idiots with dementia (1,393 cc).

Table 2 presents these differences more clearly. Female criminals, and especially prostitutes, have oversized heads, but these are found only in a fraction of insane women. The rate of microcephaly, or a cranial circumference of forty-eight centimeters, among prostitutes is four times greater among the insane, who in turn have a rate double that of criminal women.

The only conclusion about the physiognomy of criminal women that I can draw from my sample is that female criminals tend to be masculine. (Among prostitutes even the voice often seems virile.) The only exception was a poisoner. Two out of twenty-one criminal women closely resembled the insane with their protruding and

Table 2   Cranial Circumference of Insane Women, Prostitutes, and Criminal Women

Cranial Circumference (cm.)	Insane Women (86)		Prostitutes (54)		Criminal Women (21)	
	total	percent	total	percent	Total	percent
48	2	0.01	8	4.3	–	
49	16	1.04	9	4.8	1	0.2
50	23	1.09	8	4.8	2	0.2
51	20	1.07	15	8.1	4	0.8
52	20	1.07		–	7	1.4
53	3	0.02	3	1.6	6	1.2
54	1	0.05	1	0.5	1	0.2
55			2	1.0	–	
56			2	1.0	–	

NOTE: The number of insane women in the second column adds to 85 rather than 86; the total number of prostitutes adds to 48 rather than 54. The percentage columns have no relationship to the other data in the table, illustrating Lombroso's statistical ineptitude or general carelessness with detail.

asymmetrical ears. Where criminal women differ most markedly from the insane is in the rich luxuriance of their hair. Not a single woman in my sample was bald, and only one showed precociously graying hair. Thomson, too, has noted rich manes of hair among female criminals.

Summing up in a few words that which scientific exigencies oblige me to express with arid numbers,[10] I conclude:

— The criminal is taller than the normal individual and even more so than the insane, with a broader chest, darker hair and (with the exception of Venetians) greater weight.

— In head volume, the criminal presents a series of submicrocephalic craniums, double the number for normal men, but fewer than in the case of the insane.

— Criminals, especially forgers, also exceed the insane in large-volume heads. But the average head size of criminals never reaches the size of healthy men.

— The cephalic index, or shape of the criminal skull, varies with ethnicity but tends to be brachycephalic, or short-headed, particularly among robbers.[11] Criminal skulls present frequent asymmetry, although less often than among the insane.

— Compared to the insane, criminals have more traumatic lesions of the head and oblique eyes. But they less frequently display degeneration of the temple arteries, abnormalities of the ear, thin beards, tics, virility of appearance (if they are female), dilated pupils, and, still less often, graying hair and baldness.

— Criminals and the insane show equal rates of prognathism, unequally sized pupils, distorted noses, and receding foreheads.

— Measured on the dynamometer, criminals reveal greater weakness than normal men, though they are not as weak as the insane.

— More often than in the healthy population, criminals have brown or dark eyes and thick black hair. Such hair is most frequently found among robbers.

— Hunchbacks are extremely rare among murderers but are more common among rapists, forgers, and arsonists.

— Arsonists, and even more so thieves, tend to have gray irises; members of both groups are always shorter, lighter, weaker, and smaller in cranial capacity than pickpockets, who are in turn shorter, lighter, and weaker than murderers.

Among criminal women, one thing that can be said with certainty is that, like their male counterparts, they are taller than the insane. Yet they are shorter, and, perhaps with the exception of prostitutes, lighter than healthy women. All three female groups are identical in their average cranial circumference. Prostitutes show both a greater than average number of large heads and more microcephaly. In prostitutes, extremely small heads are four times more common than among the mad, and the rates among the mad are twice as high as those of the criminal. Prostitutes have dark, thick hair, and in Lombardy, but not in France, they frequently have dark irises. Female criminals are weaker than the insane and more often masculine looking.

Prognathism, thick and crisp hair, thin beards, dark skin, pointed skulls, oblique eyes, small craniums, overdeveloped jaws, receding foreheads, large ears, similarity between the sexes, muscular weakness—all these characteristics confirm the findings from autopsies to demonstrate that European criminals bear a strong racial resemblance to Australian aborigines and Mongols.

3. Tattoos

One of the most singular characteristics of primitive men and those who still live in a state of nature is the frequency with which they undergo tattooing. This operation, which has both its surgical and aesthetic aspects, derives its name from an Oceanic language. In Italy, the practice is known as *marea* [mark], *nzito, segno* [sign], and *devozione* [devotion]. It occurs only among the lower classes—peasants, sailors, workers, shepherds, soldiers, and even more frequently among criminals. Because of its common occurrence among criminals, tattooing has assumed a new and special anatomico-legal significance that calls for close and careful study. But first we must examine its frequency among normal individuals for the sake of comparison.

To do this, I will use data on 7,114 individuals: 4,380 were soldiers and 2,734 criminals, prostitutes, and criminal soldiers. For this information, I have to thank that valiant student of forensic medicine, Tarehini Bonfanti, as well as the illustrious Dr. Baroffio, Cavaliere Alborghetti of Bergamo, Professor Gamba of Turin, Dr. Soresina of Milan, and Professor De Amicis of Naples. Table 3 summarizes the results of the survey.

In Italy, as among savages, tattooing is infrequent among women. Among noncriminal men, the use of tattoos is decreasing, with rates ten times lower in 1873 than in 1863. On the other hand, the custom persists and indeed reaches enormous proportions among the criminal population, both military and nonmilitary, where among 1,432 individuals examined, 115 or 7.9 percent sported tattoos. The most common place for tattoos is the smooth part of the forearm, followed by the shoulder, the chest (sailors), and the fingers (miners), on which they take the form of a ring. Only men who had been to Oceania or were in prison had tattoos on their backs or pubic regions.

The symbols and meanings of tattoos are generally divisible into the categories of love, religion, war, and profession. Tattoos are external signs of beliefs and passions predominant among working-class men. After a careful study of the designs chosen by 102 criminals, I found that several not only appear frequently but also carry a particular significance. In 2 out of the 102 cases, tattoos marvelously reveal a nature that is violent, vindictive, or divided by conflicting intentions. For example, an old Piedmontese sailor, who had been a swindler and committed murder as part of a vendetta, had inscribed on his chest between two fists the sad phrase "I swear to revenge myself." A Venetian thief who was a recidivist bore the following lugubrious words on his chest: "I will come to a miserable end." It is said that criminals know their own fate and engrave it on their skin.

Other tattoos are obscene, either from their design or the region of the body where they appear. Only a few soldiers, mostly deserters released from prison, had obscene tattoos in the genital region. More significant results are obtained from my direct study of 102 tattooed criminals, of whom four had obscene tattoos.[b] One had a figure of a nude woman traced over the length of his penis. A second had the face of a woman drawn on the glans, in such a way that the woman's mouth was the penis's orifice; higher up on the

Table 3	Tattoos in Soldiers, Criminals, and Prostitutes		
Year	Group (total number)	Medical Examiner	Percentage With Tattoos
1863	Soldiers (1,147)	Dr. Lombroso	11.6
1873	Soldiers (2,739)	Dr. Baroffio	1.4
	Criminal soldiers (150)	Dr. Baroffio	8.6
1872	Criminals (500)	Dr. Lombroso	6.0
1873	Criminals (134)	Dr. Alborghetti	15.0
	Criminals (650)	Dr. Tarehini	7.0
	Criminal women (300)	Dr. Gamba	1.6
1866–1873	Prostitutes (1,000)	Dr. Soresina	–
1871	Prostitutes (small number)	–	a few
1874	Prostitutes (small number)	De Amicis	a few

NOTE: In this eclectic table, Lombroso has combined studies covering different parts of Italy and different years.

penis was the Savoyard flag. A third had the initials of his lover on his penis; a fourth had a bouquet of flowers. All of this reveals not only a shamelessness but also insensitivity, given that the sexual organs are extremely sensitive to pain. Even savages avoid tattooing these areas.

The study of tattoos sometimes helps us track individuals to criminal organizations. Many members of the Camorra, a Neapolitan criminal organization, have tarantula drawn on their arms; and three young arsonists from Milan sported tattoos with the same initials. Even tattoos that do not seem to have anything criminal about them and resemble those of farmers, shepherds, and sailors from the same region can be useful to the legal system and forensic medicine: they may reveal an individual's identity, his origins, and the important events of his life. Criminals, too, are aware of the advantages to the legal system offered by these involuntary revelations; thus the cleverest of them avoid tattoos or try to remove those they already have.

[b]Tardieu has written about a coach driver and an iron smith who had boots tattooed on their penises.

It would be interesting for anthropologists to ponder why such an apparently disadvantageous custom is maintained, given the discomfort and damage it causes. Here are some hypotheses:

— Religion, which tends to preserve ancient habits and customs, certainly perpetuates the practice of tattooing. Those who are devoted to particular saints believe that having their name inscribed on their flesh signifies their devotion and affection.

— A second reason is imitation.[12] Proof of this curious influence is the fact that members of an entire regiment will often sport the same design, such as a heart.

— Laziness also plays a part. For this reason tattoos are often found on deserters, prisoners, and sailors. In one prison, I found that twenty-five out of forty-one inmates had obtained their tattoos while in custody. Idleness is more painful than pain itself.

— Equally if not more influential is vanity. Even those who are not psychiatrists are aware of the way this powerful sentiment, found at all social levels and possibly even among animals, can prompt the most bizarre and damaging behavior. This is why savages who walk around naked have designs on their chests, while those who wear clothes choose to have tattoos in places that are visible or easily revealed, such as the forearm, and more often on the right forearm than on the left.

— Also influential is the sense of camaraderie, and perhaps even, as the initials of those Milanese arsonists suggest, a sense of "sect." I would not be surprised if some *camorristi* adopted, in addition to tattoos of frogs or tarantulas, other primitive ornamentations to distinguish their sect, such as wearing rings, pins, little chains, or sporting a certain style of whiskers. African tribes distinguish themselves by scarring their faces.

— Up to a certain point, noble human passions are also involved. The rites of the paternal village, the image of the patron saint, scenes of infancy, and depictions of distant friends—naturally one does not want to forget these things. Tattoos bring

memories to life in the poor soldier's mind; the "prick of remembrance" overcomes distance, deprivations, and dangers.

— The passion of love, or rather, eroticism, is also important, as indicated by the obscene figures (4 out of 102 cases) or the initials of lovers (10 out of 102 cases) found on our criminals, and similar images on lesbians and prostitutes. Tribal women tattoo themselves to show they are unmarried. In men, too, tattoos often indicate virility. As Darwin puts it somewhat exaggeratedly, tattoos are both a sign and a means of sexual selection.[13]

Among Europeans, the most important reason for tattooing is atavism and that other form of atavism called traditionalism both of which characterize primitive men and men living in a state of nature. There is not a single primitive tribe that does not use tattooing. It is only natural that a custom widespread among savages and prehistoric peoples would reappear among certain lower-class groups. One such group is sailors, who display the same temperament as savages with their violent passions, blunted sensitivity, puerile vanity, and extreme laziness. Sailors even adopt the habits, superstitions, and songs of primitive peoples. In their nudity, prostitutes, too, recall savage customs.

The foregoing should suffice to demonstrate to judges and practitioners of forensic medicine that tattoos can signify a previous incarceration. Criminals' predilection for this custom is sufficient to distinguish them from the insane. Both groups experience forced internment, strong emotion, and long periods of boredom. Although madmen resort to such strange pastimes as rolling stones, snipping their clothes and even their flesh, scribbling on walls, and filling entire reams of paper, they very rarely make designs on their skin. This is yet another proof of the influence of atavism on tattooing because madness is almost never a congenital illness and rarely atavistic.

Forensic medicine should recognize that in the case of the criminal man, who is in constant struggle against society, tattoos—like scars—are professional characteristics.

4. Emotions of Criminals

The unusual predilection of criminals for something as painful as tattooing suggests that they have less sensitivity to pain than ordinary men, a phenomenon that can also be observed in the insane, especially those with dementia. Except in cases of idiocy, what appears as insensitivity to pain is actually the dominance of certain passions. Thus lesbian prostitutes, to reach their lovers in hospital, use red-hot irons to give themselves blisters that resemble pustular eruptions. I once saw two murderers who had for a long time hated one another throw themselves at each other during exercise hour, remaining embroiled for some minutes, one biting the other's lip, the other tearing out the hair of his adversary. When they were finally separated, they were more concerned about their unfinished brawl than their wounds, which became seriously infected.

More generally, criminals exhibit a certain moral insensitivity. It is not so much that they lack all feelings, as bad novelists have led us to believe. But certainly the emotions that are most intense in ordinary men's hearts seem in the criminal man to be almost silent, especially after puberty. The first feeling to disappear is sympathy for the misfortunes of others, an emotion that is, according to some psychologists, profoundly rooted in human nature. The murderer Lacenaire confessed that he had never felt the slightest sense of regret seeing any cadaver except that of his cat: "The sight of agony has no effect on me whatsoever. I would kill a man as easily I would drink a glass of water."[14] Complete indifference to their victims and to the bloody traces of their crimes is a constant characteristic of all true criminals, one that distinguishes them from normal men.

An executioner, Pantoni, told me that nearly all robbers and murderers go to their death laughing. A thief from Voghera, shortly before his execution, ordered a boiled chicken and ate it with gusto. Another inmate wanted to choose his favorite among the three executioners and called him his "professor." While being taken to the gallows, the assassin Valle from Alessandria, who had killed two or three of his companions out of pure caprice, loudly sang the well-known song "It's Not True That Death Is the Worst of All Evils."

The criminal's insensitivity is further proved by the frequency with which an assassin's accomplices will return to murdering people just after he is put to death. Also instructive are the joking words that in criminal jargon are used to name the executioner and his instruments, as well as the tales that are told in prison, where hanging is the favorite theme.[c] This provides one of the strongest arguments for the abolition of the death penalty, which clearly dissuades only a very small number of these wretches from committing crimes. Instead, it may encourage crime thanks to that law of imitation that so dominates among the vulgar classes and to the horrendous prestige that accrues to the person of the condemned. His criminal companions are made envious by the lugubrious and solemn ritual of execution before a crowd of spectators.[15]

Insensitivity to their own and other's pain explains why some criminals can commit acts that seem to be extraordinarily courageous. Thus Holland, Doincau, Mottino, Fieschi, and Saint-Clair had previously won medals for valor on the battlefield. Coppa threw himself into the midst of a battalion firing his gun and came out unharmed. These apparent acts of courage are really only the effect of criminals' insensitivity and infantile impetuousness, which prevent them from recognizing even certain danger. It makes them blind when they have a goal or a passion to satisfy.

Insensitivity combined with precipitous passions explains the lack of logic in crimes and the disjuncture between the gravity of a deed and the motive. For example, a prisoner killed a fellow inmate because he snored too loudly and would not or could not stop (Lauvergne, p. 108). Another, from Alessandria, killed his fellow inmate because he would not polish his shoes. Such moral insensitivity among criminals explains a paradox: the frequent cruelty of criminals who at other times seem capable of kindness.

Criminals' feelings are not always completely gone; some may survive while others disappear. Troppman, a killer of women and children, cried on hearing the name of his mother. D'Avanzo, who roasted and ate a man's calf muscles, later, wrote poetry. Immediately after committing murder, Feron ran to his girlfriend's children and gave them sweets. Holland confessed to a murder committed because he wanted to obtain money for his family, saying, "I did it for my poor child."

Parent-Duchatelet shows that while many prostitutes lose all ties to their own family, others use their ill-gotten gains to provide for their children, their parents, and even friends. They are excessively passionate about their lovers,

---

[c]Fregier. *Des classes dangéreuses*, 1841, p. 111. In German slang, to be hanged is *Heimgangen*, going back home. In Italian there are various terms for being hanged, including "to grimace" or "to squint."

so much so that even violence does not detach them. One unfortunate prostitute, after breaking her leg trying to escape her pimp's beatings, returned to him. Assaulted once again, she suffered a broken arm but lost nothing of her intense affection.

In most criminals, the nobler sentiments tend to be abnormal, excessive, and unstable. Mabille, to entertain a friend he had made one night in a restaurant, committed a murder. A certain Maggin said to me, "The cause of my crimes is that I fall into friendships too easily; I cannot see a companion offended without putting a hand on my dagger to revenge him."

A few tenacious passions dominate criminals in place of their absent or unstable social and family feelings. First among these is pride, or rather, an excessive sense of self-worth, which seems to grow in inverse proportion to merit. It is almost as if the psyche is dominated by the same law that governs reflex reactions, which grow stronger as the nervous system weakens. But in the case of criminals, this disequilibrium reaches gigantic proportions. The vanity of criminals exceeds that of artists, the literati, and flirtatious women. A death sentence did not worry Lacenaire nearly as much as criticism of his dreadful poetry and fear of public ridicule. As he put it, "I do not mind being hated, but do mind being mocked" for verses like the following:

The storm leaves a track

While the humble flower passes without a trace.

The most common motive for modern crimes is vanity, the need to shine in society, which is sadly known as "cutting a fine figure." At the Pallanza prison, a criminal told me, "I killed my sister-in-law because our family was too big, and it was thus difficult to make a show in the world." Denaud killed his wife, and his lover killed her husband, so that they could marry and save their reputation. When an infamous thief adopted a certain type of waistcoat and tie, his fellows imitated him, dressing themselves in the same style. Thus Inspector Vidocq found, among twenty-two thieves caught in one single day, twenty who wore the same color waistcoat.[16] They were vain about their strength, their looks, their courage, their ill-gotten and short-lived gains, and, most distressing of all, their ability to commit crimes.

Criminals resemble prostitutes, who always believe they belong to the highest grade of their profession. To prostitutes, the phrase "you are a one-lira woman" is a deep offense. Male inmates who have stolen thousands of lire laugh at petty thieves; and murderers consider themselves superior to thieves and swindlers.

The excessive vanity of criminals explains why they discuss their crimes before and after committing them, showing incredible lack of foresight and providing the justice system with the best possible weapon for finding and sentencing them. Shortly before killing his father, the patricide Marcellino said, "When my father returns from the fields, he will remain here forever." Berard, before going to commit the last of his crimes—the murder of three rich women—was heard to say: "I want to be connected to something big; oh, how I will be talked about!" But the clearest and most curious example of criminals' incredible vanity is a photograph discovered by the police in Ravenna showing three villains who, after having killed a companion, had themselves portrayed in the positions they had as aimed while striking their blows. They felt the need to immortalize this strange moment at the risk of being reported and apprehended, which in fact happened.

A natural consequence of criminals' limitless vanity and inordinate sense of self is an inclination toward revenge for even the pettiest motives, as in the example of the inmate who killed someone for refusing to polish his shoes. Prostitutes exhibit the same tendency. "They frequently become enraged for the smallest reason, for a comment about being ugly, for example. In this regard they are more childish than their own children. Prostitutes would consider themselves dishonored if they did not react" (Parent-Duchatelet, p. 152). Such violent passions also lie behind the ferocity of ancient and savage peoples, although today they are so rare as to appear monstrous.

Once criminals have experienced the terrible pleasure of blood, violence becomes an uncontrollable addiction. Strangely, criminals are not ashamed of their bloodlust, but treat it with a sort of pride. Thus while he lay dying, Spadolino lamented having killed ninety-nine men instead of reaching a hundred.

Everyone agrees that the few violent women far exceed men in their ferocity and cruelty. The brigand women of southern Italy and the female revolutionaries of Paris invented unspeakable tortures. It was women who sold the flesh of policemen; who forced a man to eat his own roasted penis; and who threaded human bodies on a pike. Thus Shakespeare depicts Lady Macbeth as more cruel and cold than her male accomplice.

After the delights of taking revenge and satisfying his vanity, the criminal finds no greater pleasures than those offered by drinking and gambling. However, the passion for alcohol is very complex, being both a cause and an effect of crime. Indeed, alcohol is a triple cause of crime. First, the children of alcoholics often become criminals, and second, inebriation gives cowards the courage to undertake their dreadful deeds, as well as providing them with a future justification for their crimes. Furthermore, precocious drinking seduces the young into crime.[17] Third, the tavern is a common gathering place for accomplices, where they hatch their plots and upend the proceeds. For many it is their only home. The innkeeper is their banker, with whom criminals deposit their ill-gotten gains.

Few criminals fail to feel a lively passion for gambling, which explains a continual contradiction in the life of the malefactor: he greatly desires the belongings of others but at the same time squanders the money he has stolen, possibly because it was so easily acquired. Love of gambling also explains why most criminals end up poor despite possessing at times enormous sums.

Rarely does a male criminal feel true love for women. His is a carnal love, which almost always takes place in brothels (especially in London, where two-thirds of these are dens of criminals) and which develops at a very young age.[d] Prostitutes experience lesbian love, which distinguishes them from normal women, and they are passionate about flowers, dancing, and dining.

But the pleasures of gambling, eating, sex, and even revenge are nothing but intermediate steps to criminals' predominate passion, that of the orgy. Even though criminals shy away from regular society, they crave a kind of social life all their own, veritable orgies in which they enjoy the jubilant, tumultuous, riotous, and sensuous companionship of other offenders and even police spies.

I will not discuss criminals' many other passions, which vary according to their habits and intelligence. These range from the most terrible, such as pederasty, to the most noble, such as music; collecting books, paintings, and medals; and the enjoyment of flowers—a particular enthusiasm of the prostitute. One can find unusual emotions among criminals as among healthy people; what distinguishes criminal passions is instability, impetuousness, and often violence. In the quest to satisfy themselves, they give no thought to the consequences.

In many of these characteristics, criminals resemble the insane, who also exhibit not only violent and unstable passions but also insensitivity to pain, an exaggerated egotism, and (less frequently) a craving for alcohol. But the insane rarely show a predilection for gambling and orgies, and more than criminals, they will suddenly start to hate those who have hitherto been dearest to them. While the criminal cannot live without his companions and seeks them out even at his peril, the mad prefer to be alone, fleeing from every association with others. Plotting is as rare in the mental hospital as it is common in the prison.

In their emotional intensity, criminals closely resemble not the insane but savages. All travelers know that among the Negroes and savages of America, sensitivity to pain is so limited that the former laugh as they mutilate their hands to escape work, while the latter sing their tribe's praises while being burned alive. During puberty initiations, the young savages of America submit without complaint to cruel tortures that would kill a European. For example, they hang themselves upside down on butchers' hooks over dense columns of smoke. Such insensitivity encourages painful tattooing—something few Europeans can bear—and customs like cutting the lips and the fingers or pulling out teeth during funeral ceremonies.

Even moral sensitivity is weak or nonexistent among savages. The Caesars of the yellow races, called Tamerlanes, made their monuments out of pyramids of dried human heads. The emperor Nero was infamous for his barbarity, but even it paled in comparison to the cruel rites of the Chinese. Savages and criminals are further alike in the impetuosity and instability of their passions. Savages, as Lubbock tells us, have quick and violent emotions; while their strength and passions are those of adults, in character they are children. Similarly, Schaffhausen reports that "in many respects savages are like children: they feel strongly and think little; they love games, dancing and ornaments; and they are sometimes curious and timid. They are unaware of danger, but deep down they are cowards, vengeful

---

[d] Of 3,287 homicides and assaults in Italy, 299 were caused by sexual jealousy and 47 for prostitution and loose behavior. Of 41,454 crimes, 1,499 involved illicit loves. In England, of 10,000 persons sentenced, 3,608 were prostitutes; in Italy, of 383 women sentenced, 12 were prostitutes. Of 208 crimes committed for reasons of love according to Descruret, 91 were for adultery, 96 for concubinage, and 13 for jealousy. Of 10,000 crimes of violence in France and England, 1,477 were for reasons of love (Guerry). Of 10,899 suicides in France, 981 were for love.

and cruel in their vendettas."[e] A Cacique, returning from a failed hunting expedition, was greeted by his young son, who ran between his legs; to vent his rage, the father picked him up by the leg and dashed him against some rocks.

 Notes

1. These heights in meters are equivalent to 5 feet 4.4 inches; 5 feet 3.6 inches; 5 feet 2.8 inches; 5 feet 2.5 inches; and 5 feet 1.8 inches, respectively.

2. James Bruce Thomson (1810–73), chief physician at Scotland's Perth Prison, published influential articles based on degenerationist theory and arguing that many criminals are born criminals; these included "The Psychology of Criminals" in the 1870 issue of the *Journal of Mental Science*. Lombroso was fascinated by Thomson's work and cited it as evidence for his own theory. The Wilson to whom Lombroso refers was probably the British craniometrist George Wilson. The work of both men is discussed in Davie 2004, 2005.

3. These weights in kilograms are equivalent to 150 pounds and 138 pounds, respectively.

4. Johann Ludwig Casper (1787–1853) was a prominent professor of forensic pathology in Berlin.

5. Johann Kasper Lavater (1741–1801) attempted to turn physiognomy, or the reading of character from facial expressions, into a science. In the early nineteenth century, physiognomy flowed into phrenology, and later in the century, phrenology flowed into criminal anthropology. The Guido to whom Lombroso here refers was probably the Italian baroque painter Guido Reni (1575–1642).

6. The French criminal Martin Dumollard, famous for drinking his victims' blood, was executed in 1862.

7. The dynamometer, or strength-testing machine, used by Lombroso was oval in shape with a dial to record results. Subjects had to compress the oval to test "compressive strength" and pull at the oval to test "tractive strength."

8. Alexandre J. B. Parent-Duchatelet (1805–59) was the first European to conduct a large-scale study of prostitution, *De la prostitution dans la ville de Paris* (*Prostitution in the City of Paris*, 1836). Lombroso relied on Parent-Duchatelet's work for most of his early data on female crime. In this first edition of *Criminal Man*, Lombroso begins to establish his theory that prostitution— that is sexual deviancy—constitutes the typical and most widespread form of female crime.

9. Lock hospitals (or *sifilicomi* in Italian) were nineteenth-century institutions for the internment of prostitutes with venereal disease. Although hospitals in name, they resembled prisons to which prostitutes were admitted forcibly by police. Lock hospitals provided criminologists like Lombroso with a captive female population for physical and psychological examinations.

10. In this summary of his conclusions on the anthropometry and physiognomy of criminals, Lombroso is referring (with only a few exceptions) to men. Some of his conclusions are based on material that we cut from this chapter.

11. The cephalic index was an important tool for nineteenth-century criminal anthropologists in their attempts to categorize races and identify born criminals. They obtained the cephalic index by multiplying the width of the skull by one hundred and dividing the result by the length of the skull. The resulting numbers enabled them to classify skulls into various categories including brachycephalic (or short-headed) and dolichocephalic (or long-headed). Born criminals fell into both categories; Lombroso considered their cephalic indices to be abnormal when the numbers deviated from the norm for their geographical region.

12. Imitation became an important criminological concept in the late nineteenth century, especially in explanations of crowd behavior. The French jurist Gabriel Tarde (1843–1904) is best known for applying the concept of imitation to the etiology of crime in his 1890 book *La philosophie pénale* (*Penal Philosophy*). In this first edition of *Criminal Man*, Lombroso anticipates Tarde as well as later criminological debates over imitation. See Barrows 1981.

13. Charles Darwin (1809–82), the British naturalist, elaborated the theory of evolution in his famous work, *The Origin of Species* (1859). For Lombroso, Darwin's theory confirmed his intuition that criminals were atavistic or throwbacks on the evolutionary scale. In the third edition of *Criminal Man*, Lombroso aspires to do for criminals what Darwin had done for plant and animal species.

14. The French thief and poet Pierre-François Lancenair (1800–36) both shocked and fascinated public opinion with his murder of the widow Chardon and her son in 1835. The following year, he was executed by guillotine for his crime.

15. Lombroso was ambivalent about the death penalty, but in general he went from opposition to grudging acceptance of it as a means of social defense against recidivist born criminals and particularly violent members of organized crime like *mafiosi* and brigands. Yet he muffled his support of capital punishment in deference to the opposition of the majority of his positivist colleagues and the public in general. In 1889, Italy abolished the death penalty in its new criminal code.

---

[e]*Uber den Zustand der Wilden*, 1868.

16. The notorious French criminal Eugène François Vidocq (1775–1857) turned informer and finally became head of the French urban police force in 1811. He is the model for both Jean Valjean and Inspector Javert in Victor Hugo's novel *Les misérables* (1862).

17. Lombroso often employs the word *precocity* to mean the premature development of physical or psychological characteristics or early indulgence in adult behaviors. In all cases, precocity signals abnormality for Lombroso.

REVIEW QUESTIONS

1. What are some of the characteristics of the face of habitual murderers, according to Lombroso? What about thieves? Rapists?

2. What does Lombroso claim are key characteristics of female criminals? Do these differ from male criminals?

3. Review some of the tattoos that Lombroso observed on criminals. How do these tattoos relate to the emotions of criminals?

READING 9

In this selection, Chris Gibson, Alex Piquero, and Stephen Tibbetts review the existing research on the link between low verbal IQ and criminality and provide an empirical study to further advance the state of knowledge on this link. They present a test of the interaction between verbal IQ with an environmental factor: family adversity. Thus, this theoretical model assumes a "nature via nurture" perspective (as opposed to "nature versus nurture"), which we will review in more detail in Section IV. While reading this selection, you should keep in mind the contrast between how IQ is viewed and being studied now, as opposed to how it was studied in the early 1900s.

The Contribution of Family Adversity and Verbal IQ to Criminal Behavior

Chris L. Gibson, Alex R. Piquero, and Stephen G. Tibbetts

 ## Correlates of Early Onset and Persistent Offending

Research has shown that adult persistent offending is rooted in early childhood behavioral problems. In concordance with the strong and positive association observed among past and future offending (Gottfredson & Hirschi, 1990; Nagin & Paternoster, 1991; Robins, 1966, 1978; Wilson & Herrnstein, 1985), the age at which a first offense occurs (i.e., onset) has similarly been found to be strongly correlated with future offending, especially serious, habitual, and violent offending (Blumstein, Cohen, Roth, &

SOURCE: Chris L. Gibson, Alex R. Piquero, and Stephen G. Tibbetts, "The Contribution of Family Adversity and Verbal IQ to Criminal Behavior," *International Journal of Offender Therapy and Comparative Criminology* 45, no. 5 (2001): 574–92. © 2001 Sage Publications, Inc. Used by permission of Sage Publications, Inc.

Visher, 1986; Dunford & Elliott, 1984; Farrington, 1986, 1998; Farrington et al., 1990; LeBlanc & Frechette, 1989; Loeber & LeBlanc, 1990; Patterson, Crosby, & Vuchinich, 1992; Reiss & Roth, 1993; Sampson & Laub, 1993; Tolan, 1987; Wolfgang, 1983). In addition, relationships have been observed between early onset, conduct disorder, and oppositional defiant disorder (Wasserman & Miller, 1998).

Although early onset is important to the understanding of homotypic and heterotypic continuity, the risk and protective factors that increase and/or decrease the odds of an early onset is an entirely different question. Acquiring knowledge of the risk and protective factors that increase and/or decrease the probability of an early onset would allow policy makers and researchers to more accurately identify individuals at risk for early onset and persistent offending styles, thus allowing for early implementation of prevention strategies (Farrington, 1998, 2000; Moffitt, 1993). Although few question this agenda and its profound policy implications, reviews of the literature pertaining to early onset suggest that there is limited evidence of risk factors associated with early onset (Farrington, 1998; Farrington et al., 1990).

Research has assessed the influence of several independent risk factors on the development of early offending behavior. Factors such as neuropsychological and psychosocial deficiencies (Gorenstein, 1990; Moffitt, 1990), poor psychomotor skills (Farrington & Hawkins, 1991), as well as family adversity and economic/social deprivation have been identified as predictors of an early onset (Farrington & Hawkins, 1991; Moffitt, 1990). A small number of studies have assessed biosocial interactions between some of the previously mentioned risk factors. Such studies have assessed psychological and environmental factors coupled with various biological and/or physiological traits (e.g., low birth weight, heart rate, and pre/perinatal complications) in predicting early onset of offending behavior (Moffitt, 1990; Raine, Brennan, & Mednick, 1994; Tibbetts & Piquero, 1999) as well as violent offending patterns (Brennan, Mednick, & Raine, 1997; Kandel & Mednick, 1991; Piquero & Tibbetts, 1999; Reiss & Roth, 1993). Although studies that have investigated interactions between individual differences (neuropsychological and personality traits) and environmental factors on offending outcomes are limited, Moffitt (1993) stated, "It is now widely acknowledged that personality and behavior are shaped in large

measure by the interaction between the person and the environment" (p. 682).

Moffitt's Interaction Hypothesis

Moffitt (1993), among others (Wolfgang, Thornberry, & Figlio, 1987), suggested that a relatively small group of offenders (6% to 10%) exhibit criminal behavior early in life and are likely to be chronic in their offending patterns. Specifically, Moffitt claimed that the small groups of individuals who incur an early onset are likely to possess two specific risk factors early in life, neuropsychological problems in early childhood and disadvantaged environments and/or family adversity. Moffitt stated that these risk factors interact to predict early onset of offending behavior, leading to a life-course persistent style of offending.

Moffitt, Lynam, and Silva (1994) claimed that problem behavior begins early in childhood because neuropsychological deficiencies disrupt normal development, and it is these deficits that increase vulnerability to the criminogenic aspects of disadvantaged rearing environments. In agreement with studies on low verbal and communication skills (Tarter, Hegedus, Alterman, & Katz-Garris, 1983; Tarter, Hegedus, Winsten, & Alterman, 1984), Moffitt (1993) noted that children with varying degrees of neuropsychological deficiencies evoke a challenge to the most well-prepared parents. Specifically, these deficiencies may elicit increasingly more physical punishment from caregivers, especially if the family is living in a disadvantaged or distressed environment (Moffitt, 1997).

Preliminary findings from Moffitt's (1990) ongoing New Zealand study showed that young boys who scored low on neuropsychological tests and lived in adverse home environments had a mean aggression score more than four times greater than that of boys with either neuropsychological deficiencies or adverse home environments alone (also see Moffitt et al., 1994). More recently, Moffitt (1997) used data from the Pittsburgh Youth Study to assess the relationship between neuropsychological test scores and delinquency among two groups of African American youth living in "good" and "disadvantaged" urban neighborhoods. The interactive effect of neuropsychological test scores and environmental factors on boys' delinquent behaviors were assessed by categorizing the boys on their mean score, either below or above, on a measure of cognitive impulsivity. The boys were also categorized into good and disadvantaged neighborhoods based on census tract data. Results show that there was a marginally significant interaction effect on delinquency. Moffitt (1997) stated that the results indicate that neuropsychological deficit and delinquency coexist among individuals in disadvantaged inner-city environments. Furthermore, regardless of the type of neighborhood, boys with neuropsychological problems were more likely to be more delinquent.

Moffitt theorized that a variety of factors disrupt the central nervous system of the fetus/infant such as prenatal and perinatal complications. Importantly, these deficits manifest themselves in various ways such as temperament difficulties, lower executive functioning, and poor verbal test scores. Such cognitive deficiencies and temperamental deficits among children are found more pervasively in unsupportive or adverse environments (Moffitt, 1993). In agreement with empirical research (Alexander & Comely, 1987; Caldwell, 1981; Greenberg, 1983), Moffitt (1997) suggested that neuropsychologically vulnerable children are found at higher rates in inner cities because prenatal care is scarce, premature births are more common, infant malnutrition is problematic, and the possibility for exposure to toxic and infectious agents is greater.

Moffitt (1993) suggested that the neuroenvironmental interactions should not be capable of distinguishing offenders from nonoffenders, but should distinguish between types of offenders (i.e., early onset and late onset). In particular, the interaction between neuropsychological deficiencies and disadvantaged environments should predict early onset.

Verbal IQ and Criminal Behavior

Moffitt's (1993) theoretical framework suggests that verbal functioning is one of the two sorts of neuropsychological deficits that are most empirically associated with an early onset, which has been argued to be one manifestation of life-course persistent offending (see Gibson, Piquero, & Tibbetts, 2000). Moffitt (1993) suggested that "the verbal deficits of antisocial children are pervasive, affecting receptive listening and reading, problem solving, expressive speech and writing, and memory" (p. 680). Research has shown that cognitive deficits and criminal behavior share variation that is independent of the effects of social class, race, test motivation, and academic achievement (Lynam, Moffitt, & Stouthamer-Loeber, 1993; Moffitt, 1990).

Moreover, existing empirical evidence supports the conclusion that the association between verbal deficiencies and offending behavior is one of the largest and most robust effects in the investigation of criminal behavior (see Hirschi & Hindelang, 1977; Moffitt, 1990; Moffitt & Henry, 1991; Moffitt & Silva, 1988). The consistency of these findings gives support to the notion that delinquents have a language manipulation deficit and that individuals with such neuropsychological deficiencies tend to be involved in offending at an early age. However, there is limited empirical evidence showing that childhood verbal IQ test scores interact with one's social environment to minimize and/or maximize their likelihood of early offending behavior (Moffitt, 1993, 1997).

Family Adversity and Criminal Behavior

Moffitt (1993) emphasized that children with cognitive and temporal deficiencies are often born into nonsupportive families that are oftentimes saturated with family adversity. For Moffitt (1993), vulnerable children "are disproportionately found in environments that will not be ameliorative because many sources of neural development co-occur with family disadvantage" (p. 681).

Although Moffitt (1993) used the term *criminogenic environment* throughout her theoretical argument, she implied that this is synonymous with family adversity. In defining family adversity, several empirical investigations have employed socioeconomic status (SES), single parenting, age of mother at birth, and multiple family transitions as risk factors that independently and collectively measure family adversity (Loeber & Farrington, 1998; Moffitt, 1990; Nagin, Pogarsky, & Farrington, 1997; Tibbetts & Piquero, 1999).

The aforementioned family adversity risk factors have all been shown to be independently related to several subsequent types of criminal offending. For example, empirical evidence has shown that maternal age at birth is a risk factor for offending behavior for mother's offspring (Nagin et al., 1997). To account for this linkage, scholars argue that young mothers are less likely to have well-developed parenting/role model skills, which oftentimes leads to neglect and poor supervision of offspring, particularly when other family adversity risk factors such as low SES and parental separation are involved (Nagin et al., 1997). Other empirical investigations have documented the adversities of being a young mother. Young mothers are more likely to engage in problem behavior (Elster, Ketterlinus, & Lamb, 1990), head a single-parent household, live in poverty (Grogger & Bronars, 1993), and fail to finish high school (Ahn, 1994), all of which have been used as indicators of family adversity and subsequently have been found to be related to offspring criminal behavior.

Many studies show that children from single-parent families are exposed to an increased risk for behavioral problems. Such studies have shown that broken homes and early separation of parents predict criminal offending (Farrington, 1992, 1993; McCord, 1982). In the New-Castle Thousand Family study, Kolvin and colleagues (Kolvin, Miller, Scott, Gatzanis, & Fleeting, 1990) found a significant association between parental divorce or separation before age 5 and later convictions up to age 33. The importance of the effects of single-parent homes is also shown in the English national longitudinal survey of more than 5,000 children born in 1946 (Wadsworth, 1979). Specifically, boys from broken homes due to divorce or separation were significantly more likely of being convicted or officially cautioned up to age 21. Furthermore, children from single-parent families have been found to have a variety of adverse problems such as conduct disorder and substance abuse (Blum, Boyle, & Offord, 1988; Boyle & Offord, 1986).

Current Effort

In this article, we build on prior research in two ways. First, we examine two different outcome variables that are hypothesized to be related to various risk factors as implicated by Moffitt's theory and other empirical research (Farrington & Loeber, 1999). Second, we more directly measure the role of neuropsychological risk by explicating measures of verbal IQ and expand prior measurement of family adversity by integrating several other risk factors that have been related to offending. Toward this end, we examine two hypotheses from Moffitt's developmental taxonomy that center around the role of neuropsychological risk and family adversity. The following two outcome variables are employed: (a) whether the subject is an offender (no/yes) and (b) given that the subject is an offender, whether he or she exhibited an early onset of offending.

Moffitt hypothesized that the Neuropsychological Risk × Family Adversity interaction would not be predictive of who does/does not offend. For example, several research

efforts have shown that there are important differences (in degree and kind) within the offending population such that offenders are not a homogenous population (D'Unger, Land, McCall, & Nagin, 1998; Nagin, Farrington, & Moffitt, 1995; Nagin & Land, 1993; Piquero et al., 2001). Furthermore, the Neuropsychological Risk × Family Adversity interaction is not meant to distinguish between offenders and nonoffenders; instead, it best predicts a "special sort of delinquency" that is related to styles of life-course persistent offending (Moffitt, 1997). For Moffitt's theory, the Neuropsychological Risk × Family Adversity interaction should be predictive of an early but not late onset of offending because adolescence-limited offenders do not suffer from any individual-level deficits in neuropsychological risk or self-control (whereas the life-course persistent offenders do) (Moffitt, 1993; Moffitt et al., 1994; Moffitt, Caspi, Dickson, Silva, & Stanton, 1996).

Two hypotheses are investigated herein. First, the Neuropsychological Risk × Family Adversity interaction will not be a significant predictor of whether or not individuals offend. Second, the Neuropsychological Risk × Family Adversity interaction will be able to distinguish among the offending population. In particular, the interaction will be a significant predictor of early but not late onset of offending. Because family adversity has independently been found to be related to whether individuals offend or refrain from offending, we expect it to be related to whether subjects offend or do not, but we do not expect it to be a significant discriminator between those who exhibit an early as opposed to late onset of offending. In sum, the key focus of the current analysis lies in understanding the ways in which neuropsychological risk interacts with social and environmental conditions to increase the probability that certain forms of offending will occur (Moffitt, 1997).

Data

Data used to examine these hypotheses are drawn from the Philadelphia portion of the National Collaborative Perinatal Project (NCPP) (Denno, 1990). Designed as a health and development study, the NCPP followed prospectively the course of more than 56,000 pregnancies enrolled between 1959 and 1966 at several university-affiliated medical schools in the United States (Niswander & Gordon, 1972). Pregnancies for the Philadelphia site came from Pennsylvania Hospital.

A wide variety of variables were collected, including events of gestation, labor, and delivery as well as children's mental, motor, sensory, and physical development to 7 years of age. Major findings from the NCPP have been detailed elsewhere (Broman, Nichols, & Kennedy, 1975; Nichols & Chen, 1981), and specific criminological investigations have also been undertaken, primarily with the Philadelphia (Denno, 1990; Piquero, 2000a, 2000b, 2000c; Piquero & Tibbetts, 1999; Tibbetts & Piquero, 1999) and Providence (Lipsett, Buka, & Lipsitt, 1990; Piquero & Buka, 2001) cohorts.

Archived data from the Philadelphia cohort of the NCPP consisted of 987 subjects. All members of this subsample were African American, and the majority was of middle to lower class in socioeconomic status. Detailed criminal history information for this cohort was collected from the Philadelphia Police Department apart from the larger NCPP project by researchers at the University of Pennsylvania in the early 1980s when the cohort was 18 years of age. Several criteria were established for inclusion in the Philadelphia subsample. All subjects were born and raised until young adulthood in Philadelphia, received very similar medical treatment early in life, attended Philadelphia public schools, and shared a predominantly lower to lower-middle socioeconomic status (Denno, 1990).

The Philadelphia NCPP data provide a unique opportunity to study the risk factors associated with the development of criminal offending. In fact, Moffitt (1997) regarded these data as among the best for the study of neuropsychological and cognitive risk factors and their relation to criminal offending.

 ## Variables

Dependent Variables

As stated earlier, we examine the following two distinct outcome variables: (a) whether the participant was/was not an offender by age 18 and (b) if the participant was an offender, the age at first police contact (i.e., early onset). The former variable was measured by the presence of a police contact with the Philadelphia Police Department by age 18. Of the 987 subjects, 220 incurred at least one police contact by age 18. This variable is coded as 0 (nonoffender) and 1 (offender). The latter variable was measured as the age at the first police contact among those individuals incurring at least one police contact by age 18. Following previous research (Patterson et al., 1992; Simons, Wu, Conger, & Lorenz, 1994; Tibbetts & Piquero, 1999), an early onset of offending is measured as onset prior to age 14 (coded 1, $n = 151$), whereas a late onset of offending is measured as onset at or after age 14 (coded 0, $n = 69$). In the Philadelphia data, age 14 marks the peak onset age and occupies the highest hazard, thus providing empirical support for selecting this cutoff.

Independent Variables

Verbal IQ. Verbal IQ is measured by the verbal IQ score on the Wechsler Intelligence Scale for Children (WISC). According to Friedes (1972), the WISC is "the best available test purported to measure intelligence in children," and researchers have established a strong link between verbal IQ and delinquency (Hirschi & Hindelang, 1977; Moffitt, 1997; Wilson & Herrnstein, 1985). Moreover, Caspi and his colleagues (Caspi, Harkness, Moffitt, & Silva, 1996) argued that the WISC is the "most psychometrically trustworthy measure of intellectual performance." The verbal IQ score is a summary measure of verbal ability based on a composite of the following four subtests: (a) information, (b) comprehension, (c) digit span, and (d) vocabulary.

Family adversity. Using the data available in the Philadelphia portion of the NCPP, we measured family adversity in a similar manner to the Dunedin Multidisciplinary Health and Development Study (Pryor & Woodward, 1996; also see Rutter, 1978). All of the variables that comprise the family adversity scale have independently been related to criminal offending (see Loeber & Farrington, 1998; Nagin et al., 1997; Tibbetts & Piquero, 1999). The family adversity scale is composed of the summation of the following four dichotomous items: (a) low socioeconomic status (coded 1 for lowest 25th percentile, coded 0 otherwise), (b) single mother at child birth and at age 7 (coded 1 if single at both ages, 0 otherwise), (c) age of mother at birth of child (younger than 21 coded 1, older than 21 coded 0), and (d) the number of family transitions through age 7 (coded 0 for zero transitions, 1 for one or more transitions). Higher scores indicate more family adversity.

Birth weight. Birth weight was measured immediately on delivery by hospital staff members and ranged from 3 to 12 pounds. Following the literature on low birth weight (Paneth, 1995; World Health Organization, 1950), this variable was recoded to less than 6 pounds (1) and equal to/greater than 6 pounds (0). Research has shown birth weight to be an important correlate of a variety of negative sequelae, including criminal behavior (Tibbetts & Piquero, 1999).

Gender. This variable was coded as male (1) and female (2).

Interaction. Following Jaccard, Turrisi, and Wan (1990), we created an interaction between family adversity and verbal IQ that was based on the multiplicative of the mean-centered scores of these two items. Mean centering is undertaken to avoid problems associated with multicollinearity among the two variables comprising the interaction as well as the interaction itself (descriptive statistics for all variables may be found in Table 1).

Table 1	Descriptive Statistics			
Variable	Mean	Standard Deviation	Minimum	Maximum
Gender	1.50	0.50	1	2
Low birth weight	0.34	0.47	0	1
Verbal IQ	91.92	11.38	57	133
Family adversity	1.17	1.01	0	4
Offender	0.22	0.42	0	1
Early onset	0.36	0.48	0	1

Note: Based on $n = 220$.

Hypotheses

Two key hypotheses are investigated in this article. The first is that the Verbal IQ × Family Adversity interaction will not predict whether an individual is/is not an offender by age 18. We employ logistic regression for this analysis where the outcome variable is nonoffender (0) and offender (1). The second is that the Verbal IQ × Family Adversity interaction will be predictive of the age at first police contact. Specifically, the interaction should be predictive of an early but not late onset of offending. We employ logistic regression for this analysis where the outcome variable is late (0) and early onset (1).

Results

Prior to examining the logistic regression results, we first present some preliminary bivariate analyses to establish the baseline association among the key variables in our analysis. Three ANOVAs were conducted where the family adversity scale was examined with the following three outcome variables: (a) verbal IQ, (b) whether the subject was an offender, and (c) among offenders, whether the subject exhibited an early onset.

Results (not shown) suggest that those individuals scoring highest on the family adversity scale (i.e., more risk factors) scored the lowest on verbal IQ, whereas those individuals scoring lowest on the family adversity scale (i.e., zero risk factors) scored the highest on verbal IQ. In terms of predicting offending, results once again showed the expected effect; that is, those individuals scoring highest on the family adversity scale were the most likely to become offenders, whereas those individuals scoring lowest on the family adversity scale were the least likely to become offenders. The family adversity scale was not related to early onset.

Predicting Offending

The estimates for predicting offending are presented. As can be observed, two variables are statistically significant, gender and family adversity. Specifically, compared to males, females are significantly less likely to become offenders. In terms of family adversity, these results suggest a positive relationship; that is, the higher the score on family adversity, the higher the probability of the subject becoming an offender. Birth weight was not a significant predictor of offending. Most importantly, and in accord with Moffitt's hypothesis, neither the additive effect of verbal IQ nor the interaction between verbal IQ and family adversity were significant predictors of whether a subject was an offender. These results are consistent with Moffitt's hypothesis because the outcome variable speaks only to the prevalence of offending and not to the different types of offenders categorized by their age of onset.

Predicting Early Onset

Since Moffitt anticipated that the Verbal IQ × Family Adversity interaction will be important in differentiating distinct offenders within the age-crime curve, we examine whether such an interaction is present for the prediction of the age at first police contact. Recall that Moffitt's theory hypothesizes that life-course persisters are more likely than adolescent-limited offenders to exhibit an early age of onset (Moffitt et al., 1994, 1996).

Two of the five coefficients in this model are predictive of early onset. Specifically, individuals incurring a low birth weight are significantly more likely to incur an early age of onset. As expected by Moffitt, the interaction between verbal IQ and family adversity is a significant predictor of early onset. The sign of this interaction requires some discussion.

The interaction sign is negative, implying that higher verbal IQ scores serve to inhibit the deleterious consequences of family adversity; thus, individuals who are at most risk for an early onset of offending are those individuals who have the lowest verbal IQ scores and who have the highest family adversity scores.

Thus, when verbal IQ is at its lowest level (57), the effect of family adversity on early onset is −2.213. When verbal IQ is at its highest level (133), the effect of family adversity is at its lowest level (−5.177). This result suggests that subjects who are proficient in verbal abilities are able to ward off the detrimental consequences of family adversity. These results are consistent with those obtained by other research in that exceptionally strong verbal skills can be an asset for resisting the effects of adverse familial environments (Kandel et al., 1988; White, Moffitt, & Silva, 1989). Furthermore, this finding is in concordance with Rutter's (1985) definition of a protective factor in that individuals who have high verbal IQ scores are able to minimize the detrimental effects of family adversity on early onset.

 ## Discussion

This study provides one of the few attempts to assess the prospective link between the interactive effect of two known risk factors, verbal IQ deficiencies and family adversity, on two different forms of criminal offending among a longitudinal sample of urban, inner-city, African American youth. Given the understudied nature of such interactions (Brennan et al., 1997; Raine, 1993; Tibbetts & Piquero, 1999), this assessment should be seen as an important contributor to the risk factor prevention paradigm. At the same time, our findings should be regarded as an empirical contribution to Moffitt's theoretical model as it pertains to the risk factors for differential types of criminal behavior. Not only do our results lend support to Moffitt's interactional hypothesis concerning the correlates of early onset of offending, but our results show that the negative effect of biosocial interactions on early offending are underway or rooted in early childhood.

Our results reveal that the two risk factors under investigation had differential effects on two types of offending behavior (offending prevalence and early onset of offending). First, regarding the model predicting the prevalence of offending, our results are consistent with Moffitt's theory. The interaction of Verbal IQ × Family Adversity did not distinguish between whether or not a youth had committed an offense before age 18, thus lending further support to Moffitt's claim that the interaction cannot distinguish between offenders and nonoffenders. Second, as predicted by Moffitt, our findings show that low verbal IQ scores at age 7 interact with family adversity to predict early onset of offending. Specifically, the odds of incurring an early onset were increased when there was a co-occurrence of both low verbal IQ scores and high family adversity. Further analysis of the interaction term revealed that high verbal IQ scores act as a protective factor because high verbal IQ scores were shown to minimize the deleterious effect that family adversity had on early onset. Neither verbal IQ nor family adversity exerted an independent effect on early onset of offending. In sum, our findings suggest that there may be different risk factors across different types of offending measures.

Although we feel that our findings have made an important contribution, the data used for this investigation suffer from some limitations. First, this study used only WISC verbal IQ scores as an indicator of neuropsychological risk. Although Moffitt (1993) clearly stated that verbal deficiencies are the best risk indicators of neuropsychological problems, future studies should attempt to examine other proxies (e.g., minor physical anomalies, maternal drug use during pregnancy, birth/delivery complications, etc.) or more direct measures (e.g., positron emission tomography scans and magnetic resonance imaging) of neuropsychological risk (Raine, 1993) in concert with criminogenic or disadvantaged environments in predicting early onset. Second, our analysis focused only on one manifestation of life-course persistent offending. Other dimensions such as chronicity, seriousness, and violence were not examined. Future efforts may wish to examine the extent to which the interactions studied herein apply to related life-course persistent offending dimensions. Third, Moffitt's (1993) strategy for research, along with others (Farrington, 1998), suggests that "reports of antisocial behavior should be gathered from multiple sources to tap pervasiveness across circumstances" (p. 694). Due to the original data collection protocol, we were only able to employ official data records. Although many researchers have used official measures for identifying early onset (Moffitt et al., 1994; Simons et al., 1994), such indices would probably best be used in conjunction with multiple measures such as self-reports, teacher reports, and parental reports of early adverse behavioral problems. Different operationalizations of early onset may possibly increase the validity and confidence of the results in this study. Fourth, due to the fact that the sample consisted of only inner-city, African American youth, and the generalizability of our findings may be limited. Therefore, the significant effect of the interaction of risk factors in our study may be diminished (or enhanced) in other populations (e.g., rural Caucasian youth). Finally, future efforts may wish to explore how Moffitt's interaction hypothesis relates to sociopathy. This would be a fruitful research agenda because estimates suggest that sociopaths comprise a small portion of the male population (between 3% and 4%) yet account for 33% to 80% of the chronic offender population (Cohen & Vila, 1996). Information is needed on the extent to which this group of offenders resembles the most extreme end of the life-course persistent continuum.

Given that the present study's results suggest that predictors of life-course persistent types of offending patterns may be underway in early childhood, it would be fruitful to initiate prevention and intervention strategies early in the life course. Programs should place an emphasis on the development of social skills and cognitive tasks when training children to generate multiple alternative solutions to problems, whereas preschool enrichment programs may wish to target the social/cognitive and behavioral correlates of early antisocial behaviors. Continued research into the etiology of life-course persistent styles of offending is likely to provide much more needed information on prevention tactics across various settings and sample compositions.

References

Ahn, N. (1994). Teenage childbearing and high school completion: Accounting for individual heterogeneity. *Family Planning Perspectives, 26,* 17–21.

Alexander, G. R., & Comely, D. A. (1987). Racial disparities in pregnancy outcome role of prenatal care utilization and maternal risk status. *American Journal of Preventive Medicine, 3,* 254–261.

Blum, H. M., Boyle, M. H., & Offord, D. R. (1988). Single-parent families: Child psychiatric disorder and school performance. *Journal of the American Academy of Child and Adolescent Psychiatry, 27,* 214–219.

Blumstein, A., Cohen, J., Roth, J., & Visher, C. (1986). *Criminal careers and "career criminals."* Washington, DC: National Academy Press.

Boyle, M. H., & Offord, D. R. (1986). Smoking, drinking and use of illicit drugs among adolescents in Ontario: Prevalence, patterns of use and socio-demographic correlates. *Canadian Medical Association Journal, 135,* 1113–1121.

Brennan, P., Mednick, S., & Raine, A. (1997). Biosocial interactions and violence: A focus on perinatal factors. In A. Raine, P. Brennan, D. Farrington, & S. Mednick (Eds.), *Biosocial basis of violence* (pp. 163–174). New York: Plenum.

Broman, S. H., Nichols, P. L., & Kennedy, W. A. (1975). *Preschool IQ: Prenatal and early developmental correlates.* New York: John Wiley.

Caldwell, J. (1981). Maternal education as a factor in child mortality. *World Health Organization,* 75–79.

Caspi, A., Harkness, A. R., Moffitt, T. E., & Silva, P. A. (1996). Intellectual performance: Continuity and change. In P. A. Silva & W. R. Stanton (Eds.), *From child to adult: The Dunedin multidisciplinary health and development study* (pp. 59–74). Oxford, UK: Oxford University Press.

Cohen, L., & Vila, B. (1996). Self-control and social control: An exposition of the Gottfredson-Hirschi/Sampson-Laub debate. *Studies on Crime and Crime Prevention, 5,* 125–150.

Denno, D. (1990). *Biology and violence: From birth to adulthood.* Cambridge, UK: Cambridge University Press.

Dunford, F., & Elliott, D. (1984). Identifying career offenders with self-reported data. *Journal of Research in Crime and Delinquency, 21,* 57–86.

D'Unger, A. V., Land, K. C, McCall, P. L., & Nagin, D. S. (1998). How many latent classes of delinquent/criminal careers? Results from mixed poisson regression analyses. *American Journal of Sociology, 103,* 1593–1630.

Elster, A. B., Ketterlinus, R., & Lamb, M. E. (1990). Association between parenthood and problem behavior in a national sample of adolescents. *Pediatrics, 85,* 1044–1055.

Farrington, D. (1986). Age and crime. In M. Tonry & N. Morris (Eds.), *Crime and justice: An annual review of research* (Vol. 7, pp. 189–250). Chicago: University of Chicago Press.

Farrington, D. (1992). Explaining the beginning, progress, and ending of antisocial behavior from birth to adulthood. In J. McCord (Ed.), *Facts, frameworks, and forecasts: Advances in criminological theory* (Vol. 3, pp. 253–286). New Brunswick, NJ: Transaction Books.

Farrington, D. (1993). Childhood origins of teenage antisocial behaviour and adult social dysfunction. *Journal of the Royal Society of Medicine, 86,* 13–70.

Farrington, D. (1998). Predictors, causes, and correlates of male youth violence. In M. Tonry & N. Morris (Eds.), *Crime and justice: A review of research* (Vol. 7, pp. 421–475). Chicago: University of Chicago Press.

Farrington, D. (2000). Explaining and preventing crime: The globalization of knowledge—The American Society of Criminology 1999 presidential address. *Criminology, 38,* 1–24.

Farrington, D., & Hawkins, J. (1991). Predicting participation, early onset, and later persistence in officially recorded offending. *Criminal Behaviour Mental Health, 1,* 1–33.

Farrington, D., & Loeber, R. (1999). Transatlantic replicability of risk factors in the development of delinquency. In P. Cohen, C. Slomkowski, & L. N. Robins (Eds.), *Historical and geographical influences on psychopathology* (pp. 299–329). Hillsdale, NJ: Lawrence Erlbaum.

Farrington, D., Loeber, R., Elliott, D., Hawkins, J., Kandel, D., Klein, M., McCord, L, Rowe, D., & Tremblay, R. (1990). Advancing knowledge about the onset of delinquency and crime. In B. Lahey & A. Kazdin (Eds.), *Advances in clinical and child psychology* (Vol. 13, pp. 283–342). New York: Plenum.

Friedes, D. (1972). Review of the Wechsler Intelligence Scale for Children. In O. K. Buros (Ed.), *The seventh mental measurements yearbook* (pp. 430–432). Highland Park, NJ: Gryphon.

Gibson, C. L., Piquero, A. R., & Tibbetts, S. G. (2000). Assessing the relationship between maternal cigarette smoking during pregnancy and age at first police contact. *Justice Quarterly, 17,* 519–542.

Gorenstein, E. (1990). Neuropsychology of juvenile delinquency. *Forensic Reports, 3,* 15–48.

Gottfredson, M., & Hirschi, T. (1990). *The general theory of crime.* Stanford, CA: Stanford University Press.

Greenberg, R. S. (1983). The impact of prenatal care in different social groups. *American Journal of Obstetrics and Gynecology, 145,* 797–801.

Grogger, J., & Bronars, S. (1993). The socioeconomic consequences of teenage childbearing: Findings from a natural experiment. *Family Planning Perspectives, 25,* 156–161

Hawkins, D. J., & Catalano, R. F. (1992). *Communities that care.* San Francisco: Jossey-Bass.

Hirschi, T., & Hindelang, M. J. (1977). Intelligence and delinquency: A revisionist review. *American Sociological Review, 42,* 571–587.

Jaccard, J., Turrisi, R., & Wan, C. K. (1990). *Interaction effects in multiple regression.* Newbury Park, CA: Sage.

Junger-Tas, J. (1997). *Jeugd en gezin* [Youth and family]. The Hague, the Netherlands: Ministry of Justice.

Kandel, E., & Mednick, S. (1991). Perinatal complications predict violent offending. *Criminology, 29,* 519–530.

Kandel, E., Mednick, S. A., Kirkegaard-Sorenson, L., Hutchings, B., Knop, J., Rosenberg, J. R., & Schulsinger, F. (1988). IQ as a protective factor for subjects at high risk for antisocial behavior. *Journal of Consulting and Clinical Psychology, 56,* 224–226.

Kazdin, A. E., Kraemer, H. C, Kessler, R. S., Kupfer, D. J., & Offord, D. R. (1997). Contributions of risk-factor research to developmental psychopathology. *Clinical Psychology Review, 17,* 375–406.

Kolvin, I., Miller, F. J. W., Scott, D. M., Gatzanis, S. R. M., & Fleeting, M. (1990). *Continuities of deprivation?* Aldershot, UK: Avebury.

LeBlanc, M., & Frechette, M. (1989). *Male criminal activity from childhood through youth.* New York/Berlin: Springer-Verlag.

Lipsett, P. D., Buka, S. L., & Lipsitt, L. P. (1990). Early intelligence scores and subsequent delinquency: A prospective study. *American Journal of Family Therapy, 18,* 197–208.

Loeber, R., & Farrington, D. (1998). *Serious and violent juvenile offenders: Risk factors and successful interventions.* Thousand Oaks, CA: Sage.

Loeber, R., & LeBlanc, M. (1990). Toward a developmental criminology. In M. Tonry & N. Morris (Eds.), *Crime and justice; An annual review of research* (Vol. 12, pp. 375–473). Chicago: University of Chicago Press.

Lynam, D., Moffitt, T. E., & Stouthamer-Loeber, M. (1993). Explaining the relationship between IQ and delinquency: Class, race, test motivation, school failure and self-control. *Journal of Abnormal Psychology, 102,* 187–196.

McCord, J. (1982). A longitudinal view of the relationship between paternal absence and crime. In J. Gunn & D. P. Farrington (Eds.), *Abnormal offenders, delinquency, and the criminal justice system* (pp. 113–128). Chichester, UK: Wiley.

Moffitt, T. E. (1990). The neuropsychology of delinquency: A critical review of theory and research. In M. Tonry & N. Morris (Eds.), *Crime and justice: An annual review of research* (Vol. 12, pp. 99–169). Chicago: University of Chicago Press.

Moffitt, T. E. (1993). Adolescence-limited and life-course persistent antisocial behavior: A developmental taxonomy. *Psychological Review, 100,* 674–701.

Moffitt, T. E. (1994). Natural histories of delinquency. In E. Weitekamp & H. Kerner (Eds.), *Cross-national longitudinal research on human development and criminal behavior* (pp. 3–61). Boston: Kluwer.

Moffitt, T. E. (1997). Neuropsychology, antisocial behavior, and neighborhood context. In J. McCord (Ed.), *Violence and childhood in the inner city* (pp. 116-170). Cambridge, UK: Cambridge University Press.

Moffitt, T. E., Caspi, A., Dickson, N., Silva, P., & Stanton, W. (1996). Childhood-onset versus adolescent-onset antisocial conduct problems in males: Natural history from ages 3 to 18 years. *Development and Psychopathology, 8,* 399–424.

Moffitt, T. E., & Henry, B. (1991). Neuropsychological studies of juvenile delinquency and juvenile violence. In J. S. Milner (Ed.), *The neuropsychology of aggression* (pp. 67–91). Boston: Kluwer.

Moffitt, T. E., Lynam, D., & Silva, P. A. (1994). Neuropsychological tests predicting persistent male delinquency. *Criminology, 32,* 277–300.

Moffitt, T. E., & Silva, P. A. (1988). Neuropsychological deficit and self-reported delinquency in an unselected birth cohort. *Journal of the American Academy of Child and Adolescent Psychiatry, 27,* 233–240.

Nagin, D. S., Farrington, D. P., & Moffitt, T. E. (1995). Life-course trajectories of different types of offenders. *Criminology, 33,* 111–139.

Nagin, D. S., & Land, K. C. (1993). Age, criminal careers, and population heterogeneity: Specification and estimation of a nonparametric, mixed Poisson model. *Criminology, 31,* 327–362.

Nagin, D. S., & Paternoster, R. (1991). On the relationship of past and future offending. *Criminology, 29,* 163–189.

Nagin, D. S., Pogarsky, G., & Farrington, D. (1997). Adolescent mothers and the criminal behaviors of their children. *Law and Society Review, 31,* 137–162.

Nichols, P. L., & Chen, T. C. (1981). *Minimal brain dysfunction: A prospective study.* Hillsdale, NJ: Lawrence Erlbaum.

Niswander, K., & Gordon, M. (1972). *The women and their pregnancies.* Washington, DC: Department of Health, Education, and Welfare.

Nutall, C. P., Goldblatt, P., & Lewis, C. (1998). *Reducing offending: An assessment of research evidence on ways of dealing with offending behaviour.* London: HMSO.

Paneth, N. S. (1995). The problem of low birth weight. *The Future of Children: Low Birth Weight* (Center for the Future of Children), 5, 613–618.

Patterson, G., Crosby, L., & Vuchinich, S. (1992). Predicting risk for early police arrest. *Journal of Quantitative Criminology, 8,* 335–355.

Piquero, A. (2000a). Are chronic offenders the most serious offenders? Exploring the relationship with special attention on offense skewness and gender differences. *Journal of Criminal Justice, 28,* 103–116.

Piquero, A. (2000b). Frequency, specialization and violence in offending careers. *Journal of Research in Crime and Delinquency, 37,* 392–418.

Piquero, A. (2000c). Testing Moffitt's neuropsychological variation hypothesis for the prediction of life-course persistent offending. *Psychology, Crime, and Law, 7,* 193–216.

Piquero, A., Blumstein, A., Brame, R., Haapanen, R., Mulvey, E. P., & Nagin, D. S. (2001). Assessing the impact of exposure time and incapacitation on longitudinal trajectories of criminal offending. *Journal of Adolescent Research, 16,* 54–74.

Piquero, A., & Buka, S. (2001). Investigating race and gender differences in specialization in violence. In B. Cohen, R. A. Silverman, & T. P. Thornberry (Eds.), *Criminology at the millennium.* Boston: Kluwer.

Piquero, A., & Tibbetts, S. (1999). The impact of pre/perinatal disturbances and disadvantaged familial environments in predicting criminal offending. *Studies on Crime and Crime Prevention, 8,* 52–70.

Pryor, J., & Woodward, L. (1996). Families and parenting. In P. A. Silva & W. R. Stanton (Eds.), *From child to adult: The Dunedin multidisciplinary health and development study* (pp. 247–258). Oxford, UK: Oxford University Press.

Raine, A. (1993). *The psychopathology of crime: Criminal behavior as a clinical disorder.* San Diego: Academic Press.

Raine, A., Brennan, P., & Mednick, S. (1994). Birth complications combined with early maternal rejection at age 1 year predispose to violent crime at age 18 years. *Archives of General Psychiatry, 51,* 984–988.

Reiss, A., & Roth, J. (1993). *Understanding and preventing violence.* Washington, DC: National Academy Press.

Robins, L. (1966). *Deviant children grown up.* Baltimore: Williams and Wilkins.

Robins, L. (1978). Sturdy childhood predictors of adult antisocial behavior: Replications from longitudinal studies. *Psychological Medicine, 8,* 611–622.

Rutter, M. (1978). Family, area, and school influences in the genesis of conduct disorders. In L. A. Hersov, M. Berger, & D. Shaffer (Eds.), *Aggression and antisocial behavior in childhood and adolescence* (pp. 95–113). Elmsford, NY: Pergamon.

Rutter, M. (1985). Resilience in the face of adversity: Protective factors and resistance to psychiatric disorders. *British Journal of Psychiatry, 147,* 598–611.

Sampson, R. J., & Laub, J. H. (1993). *Crime in the making: Pathways and turning points through life.* Cambridge, MA: Harvard University Press.

Simons, R., Wu, C, Conger, R., & Lorenz, F. (1994). Two routes to delinquency: Differences between early and late starters in the impact of parenting and deviant peers. *Criminology, 32,* 247–276.

Tarter, R. E., Hegedus, A., Alterman, A. L., & Katz-Garris, L. (1983). Cognitive capabilities of juvenile violent, nonviolent and sexual offenders. *Journal of Nervous and Mental Disease, 171,* 564–567.

Tarter, R. E., Hegedus, A. M., Winsten, N. E., & Alterman, A.I. (1984). Neuropsychological, personality and familial characteristics of physically abused delinquents. *Journal of the American Academy of Child Psychiatry, 23,* 668–674.

Tibbetts, S., & Piquero, A. (1999). The influence of gender, low birth weight, and disadvantaged environment in predicting early onset of offending: A test of Moffitt's interaction hypothesis. *Criminology, 37,* 843–877.

Tolan, P. (1987). Implications of age of onset for delinquency risk. *Journal of Abnormal Child Psychology, 15,* 47–65.

Wadsworth, M. (1979). *Roots of delinquency.* London: Martin Robertson.

Wasserman, G., & Miller, L. (1998). The prevention of serious and violent juvenile offending. In R. Loeber & D. P. Farrington (Eds.), *Serious and violent juvenile offenders* (pp. 197–247). Thousand Oaks, CA: Sage.

White, J., Moffitt, T. E., & Silva, P. A. (1989). A prospective replication of the protective effects of IQ in subjects at high risk for juvenile delinquency. *Journal of Clinical and Consulting Psychology, 57,* 719–724.

Wilson, J. Q., & Herrnstein, R. (1985). *Crime and human nature.* New York: Simon & Schuster.

Wolfgang, M. (1983). Delinquency in two birth cohorts. In K. Van Dusen & S. Mednick (Eds.), *Prospective studies of crime and delinquency* (pp. 7–17). Boston: Kluwer.

Wolfgang, M., Thornberry, T., & Figlio, R. (1987). *From boy to man, from delinquency to crime.* Chicago: University of Chicago Press.

World Health Organization. (1950). *Public health aspects of low birth weight* (WHO Technical Report Series, No. 27). Geneva, Switzerland: Author.

REVIEW QUESTIONS

1. How exactly did Gibson et al. measure family adversity? What type of IQ test did they use? Do these measures reflect the theoretical concepts they are meant to measure?

2. What type of sample did Gibson et al. utilize for this study? What are the strengths and weaknesses in using that type of sample, in terms of supporting the theoretical propositions/hypotheses of this study?

3. What did Gibson et al. conclude based on their findings? Did any of the findings or conclusions surprise you? Do any go against the theoretical assumptions you have regarding criminal behavior?

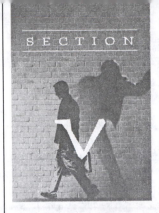

SECTION

Modern Biosocial Perspectives of Criminal Behavior

This section will discuss the more modern biological studies of the 20th century. We will begin with studies from the early 1900s, particularly those that sought to emphasize the influence of biological factors on criminality. Virtually all of these studies have shown a significant biological effect in the development of criminal propensities. Then we will examine the influence of a variety of physiological factors, including chromosomal mutations, hormones, neurotransmitters, brain trauma, and other dispositional aspects of individuals' nervous systems. A special emphasis will be placed on showing the consistent evidence that has been found for the interaction between physiological and environmental factors (i.e., biosocial factors).

This section will examine a variety of perspectives that deal with interactions between physiological and environmental factors, which is currently the dominant model explaining criminal behavior. First, we will discuss the early studies that attempted to emphasize the biological aspects of offending: family, twin, and adoption studies. All of these studies show that biological influences are more important than social and environmental factors, and most also conclude that when both negative biological and disadvantaged environmental variables are combined, these individuals are by far the most likely to offend in the future, which fully supports the interaction between nature and nurture factors.

Later in this section, we will examine other physiological factors, such as hormones and neurotransmitters. We will see that chronic, violent offenders tend to have significantly different levels of hormones and other chemicals in their bodies than do other individuals. Furthermore, we will examine brain trauma and activity among violent offenders, and we will see that habitual violent criminals tend to have slower brain wave patterns and lower anxiety levels than other persons. Ultimately, we will see that numerous physiological distinctions can be made between chronic violent offenders and others but that these differences are most evident when physical factors are combined with being raised in poor, disadvantaged environments.

Nature versus Nurture: Studies Examining the Influence of Genetics and Environment

At the same time that Freud was developing his perspective of psychological deviance, other researchers were busy testing the influence of heredity versus environment to see which of these two components had the strongest effect on predicting criminality. This type of testing produced four waves of research: family studies, twin studies, adoption studies, and in recent years, studies of identical twins separated at birth. Each of these waves of research contributed to our understanding of how much criminality is inherited from our parents (or other ancestors) versus how much is due to cultural norms, such as family or community. Ultimately, all of the studies have shown that the interaction between these two aspects—genetics and environment—is what causes crime among individuals and groups in society.

Family Studies

The most notable family studies were done in the early 1900s by Dugdale, in his study of the Jukes family, and the previously discussed researcher Goddard, who studied the Kallikak family.[1] These studies were supposed to test the proposition that criminality is more likely to be found in certain families, which would indicate that crime is inherited. Due to the similarity of the results, we will focus here on Goddard's work on the Kallikak family.

This study showed that a much higher proportion of children from the Kallikak family became criminal. Furthermore, Goddard thought that many of the individuals (often children) from the Kallikak family actually looked like criminals, which fit Lombroso's theory of stigmata. In fact, Goddard had photographs made of many members of this family to back up these claims. However, follow-up investigations of Goddard's research have shown that many of these photographs were actually altered to make the subjects appear more sinister or evil (fitting Lombroso's stigmata) by altering their facial features, most notably their eyes.[2]

Despite the despicable methodological problems with Goddard's data and subsequent findings, two important conclusions can be made from the family studies that were done in the early 1900s. The first is that criminality is indeed more common in some families; in fact, no study has ever shown otherwise. However, this tendency cannot be shown to be a product of heredity or genetics. After all, individuals from the same family are also products of a similar environment—often a bad one—so this conclusion from the family studies does little to advance knowledge regarding the relative influence of nature versus nurture in terms of predicting criminality.

The second conclusion of family studies was more insightful and interesting. Specifically, they showed that criminality by the mother (or head female caretaker) had a much stronger influence on the future criminality of the children than did the father's criminality. This is likely due to two factors. The first is that the father is often absent most of the time while the children are being raised. Perhaps more important is that it takes much more for a woman to transgress social norms and become a convicted offender, which indicates that the mother is highly antisocial; this gives some (albeit limited) credence to the argument that criminality is somewhat inherited. Despite this conclusion, it should be apparent from the weaknesses in the methodology of family studies that this finding did not hold much weight in the nature-versus-nurture debate. Thus, a new wave of research soon emerged that did a better job of measuring the influence of genetics versus environment, which was twin studies.

Twin Studies

After family studies, the next wave of tests done to determine the relative influence on criminality between nature and nurture involved twin studies, the examination of identical twin pairs versus fraternal twin pairs. Identical twins

---

[1]Stephen Jay Gould, *The Mismeasure of Man*, 2nd ed. (New York: Norton, 1996) (see chap. 4, n. 2).

[2]For an excellent discussion of the alteration of Goddard's photographs, see ibid., 198–204.

are also known as monozygotic twins because they come from a single (hence *mono*) egg (*zygote*); they are typically referred to in scientific literature as MZ (monozygotic) twins. Such twins share 100% of their genotype, meaning they are identical in terms of genetic makeup. Keep in mind that everyone shares approximately 99% of the human genetic makeup, leaving about 1% that can vary over the entire species. On the other hand, fraternal twins are typically referred to as dizygotic twins because they come from two (hence *di*) separate eggs; they are known in the scientific literature as DZ (dizygotic) twins. Such DZ twins share 50% of genes that can vary, which is the same amount that any siblings from the same two parents share. DZ twins can be of different genders and may look and behave quite differently, as many readers have probably observed.

▲ Image 5.1   **Identical twins.**

Source: © Thinkstock / Stockbyte.

The goal of the twin studies was to examine the concordance rates between MZ twin pairs and DZ twin pairs regarding delinquency. Concordance is a count based on whether two people (or a twin pair) share a certain trait (or lack of the trait); for our purposes, the trait is criminal offending. Regarding a count of concordance, if one twin is an offender, then we look to see if the other is also an offender. If that person is, then we say there is concordance given the fact that the first twin was a criminal offender. Also, if neither of the two twins is an offender, that also is concordant, because they both lack the trait. However, if one twin is a criminal offender and the other twin of the pair is not an offender, then this would be discordant, in the sense that one has a trait that the other does not.

Thus, the twin studies focused on comparing the concordance rates of MZ twin pairs versus those of DZ twin pairs, with the assumption that any significant difference in concordance could be attributed to the similarity of the genetic makeup of the MZ twins (which is 100%) versus the DZ twins (which is significantly less, that is, 50%). If genetics plays a major role in determining the criminality of individuals, then it would be expected that MZ twins would have a significantly higher concordance rate for being criminal offenders than would DZ twins. In these studies, it was assumed that each twin in each MZ or DZ twin pair had been raised in more or less the same environment as the other twin, since each pair had been brought up in the same family at the same time.

A number of studies were performed in the early and mid-1900s that examined the concordance rates between MZ and DZ twin pairs. These studies clearly showed that identical twins had far higher concordance rates than did fraternal twins, with most studies showing twice as much concordance or more for MZ twins, even for serious criminality.[3]

However, the studies regarding the comparisons between the twins were strongly criticized for reasons that many readers readily see. Specifically, identical twins, who look almost exactly alike, are typically dressed the same by their parents and treated the same by the public. In addition, they are generally expected to behave the same way. However, this is not true for fraternal twins, who often look very different and quite often are of different genders.

---

[3]See reviews in Adrian Raine, *The Anatomy of Violence* (New York: Pantheon, 2013); Adrian Raine, *The Psychopathology of Crime* (San Diego: Academic Press, 1993); and John P. Wright, Stephen G. Tibbetts, and Leah Daigle, *Criminals in the Making: Criminality across the Life Course*, 2nd ed. (Thousand Oaks, CA: Sage, 2015) (see chap. 4). See also Juan B. Cortes, *Delinquency and Crime* (New York: Seminar Press, 1972); and Karl O. Christiansen, "Seriousness of Criminality and Concordance among Danish Twins," in *Crime, Criminology, and Public Policy*, ed. Roger Hood (New York: Free Press, 1974).

Thus, the foundation for criticism of the twin studies was the very valid argument that the higher rate of concordance among MZ twins could have been due to the extremely similar way they were treated or expected to behave by society. Another criticism of the early twin studies had to do with the questionable accuracy of determinations of whether twins were fraternal or identical, which was often done by sight in the early tests.[4] Although these criticisms were seemingly valid, the most recent meta-analysis, which examined virtually all of the twin studies done up to the 1990s, concluded that the twin studies showed evidence of a significant hereditary basis for criminality.[5] Still, the criticisms of such studies were quite valid; therefore, in the early to mid 1900s, researchers involved in the nature-versus-nurture debate attempted to address these valid criticisms by moving on to another methodological approach to examining this debate: adoption studies.

Adoption Studies

Due to the valid criticisms leveled at twin studies in determining the relative influence of nature (biological) or nurture (environmental), researchers in this area moved on to adoption studies, which examined the predictive influence of the biological parents versus that of the adoptive parents who raised the children from infancy to adulthood. It is important to realize that, in such studies, the adoptees were typically given up for adoption prior to six months of age, meaning that the biological parents had relatively no interaction with their natural children; rather, they were almost completely raised from infancy by the adoptive parents.

Perhaps the most notable of the adoption studies was done by Sarnoff Mednick and his colleagues, in which they examined male children born in Copenhagen between 1927 and 1941 who had been adopted early in life.[6] In this study and virtually all others that have examined adoptees in this light, by far the highest predictability for future criminality was found for adopted youths who had *both* a biological parent and an adoptive parent who were convicted criminals. However, the Mednick study also showed that the criminality of biological parent(s) had a far greater predictive effect on future criminality of offspring than did the criminality of adoptive parents. Still, the adopted children who were least likely to become criminal had no parent with a criminal background. In light of this last conclusion, these findings support the major contentions of this book's authors in the sense that they fully back up the nature-*via*-nurture argument as opposed to the nature-*versus*-nurture argument. They support the idea that both biological *and* environmental factors contribute to the future criminality of youths.

Unfortunately, the researchers who performed these studies focused on the other two groups of youths, those who had either only criminal biological parents or only criminal adoptive parents. Thus, these adoption studies found that the adoptees who had only biological parents who were criminal had a much higher likelihood of becoming criminal compared to the youths who had only adoptive parents who were criminal. Obviously, this finding supports the idea that genetic influence predisposes people toward criminality. However, this methodology was subject to criticism.

Perhaps the most notable criticism of adoption studies was that adoption agencies typically incorporated a policy of selective placement in which adoptees were placed with adoptive families similar in terms of demographics and background to their biological parents. Such selective placement could bias the results of adoption studies. However, recent analyses have examined the impact of such bias, concluding that, even after accounting for the

---

[4]Raine, *Psychopathology of Crime.*

[5]Glenn Walters, "A Meta-analysis of the Gene–Crime Relationship," *Criminology* 30 (1992): 595–613.

[6]Barry Hutchings and Sarnoff A. Mednick, "Criminality in Adoptees and Their Adoptive and Biological Parents: A Pilot Study," in *Biosocial Bases of Criminal Behavior*, ed. Sarnoff Mednick and Karl O. Christiansen (New York: Gardner Press, 1977), 127–41. See recent review and study by Randi Hjalmarsson and Matthew J. Lindquist. "The Origins of Intergenerational Associations in Crime: Lessons from Swedish Adoption Data," *Labour Economics* 20 (2013): 68–81.

influence of selective placement, the ultimate findings of the adoption studies are still somewhat valid.[7] Children's biological parents likely have more influence on their future criminality than the adoptive parents who raise them from infancy to adulthood. Still, the criticism of selective placement was strong enough to encourage a fourth wave of research in the nature-versus-nurture debate, which became studies on identical twins separated at birth.

Twins Separated at Birth

Until recently, studies of identical twins separated at birth were virtually impossible because it was so difficult to get a high number of identical twins who had indeed been separated early. But, since the early 1990s, twins-separated-at-birth studies have been possible. Readers should keep in mind that, in many of the identical twin pairs studied for these investigations, the individuals did not even know they had a twin. Furthermore, the environments in which they were raised were often extremely different; one twin might be raised by a very poor family in an urban environment while the other twin was raised by a middle- to upper-class family in a rural environment.

These studies, the most notable having been done at the University of Minnesota, found that the twin pairs often showed extremely similar tendencies for criminality, sometimes more similar than those seen in concordance rates for identical twins raised together.[8] This finding obviously supports the profound influence of genetics and heredity, which is not surprising to most well-read scientists, who now acknowledge the extreme importance of inheritance of physiological and psychological aspects to human behavior. Perhaps more surprising was why separated identical twins, who had never known that they had a twin and were often raised in extremely different circumstances, had just as high or even higher concordance rates than identical twins who were raised together.

The leading theory for this phenomenon is that identical twins who are raised together actually go out of their way to deviate from their natural tendencies to form an identity separate from their identical twin with whom they have spent their entire lives. As for criticisms of this methodology, none have been presented in the scientific literature. Thus, it is somewhat undisputed at this point that the identical-twins-separated-at-birth studies have shown that genetics has a significant impact on human behavior, especially regarding criminal activity.

Ultimately, taking all of the nature-versus-nurture methodological approaches and subsequent findings together, the best conclusion that can be made is that genetics and heredity both have significant impacts on criminality. Environment simply cannot account for all of the consistent results seen in the comparisons between identical twins and fraternal twins, those of identical twins separated at birth, and those of adoptees with criminal biological parents versus those who did not have such parents. Despite the taboo nature of and controversial response to the findings of such studies, it is quite clear that when nature and nurture are compared, biological rather than environmental factors tend to have the most influence on the criminality of individuals. Still, the authors of this book hope that readers will emphasize the importance of the interaction between nature and nurture (better stated as nature *via* nurture). Ultimately, we hope that we have shown quite convincingly through scientific study that it is the interplay between biology and the environment that is most important in determining human behavior.

Perhaps in response to this nature-versus-nurture debate, a new theoretical perspective was offered in the mid-1900s that merged biological and psychological factors in explaining criminality. Although it leaned more toward the nature side of the debate, critics would use this same perspective to promote the nurture side, so this framework was useful in promoting the interaction between biology and sociological factors.

[7]See James Q. Wilson and Richard J. Herrnstein, *Crime and Human Nature* (New York: Simon & Schuster, 1985); and Walters, "Gene–Crime Relationship."

[8]Thomas J. Bouchard, David T. Lykken, Matthew McGue, Nancy L. Segal, and Auke Tellegen, "Sources of Human Psychological Differences: The Minnesota Study of Twins Reared Apart," *Science* 250 (1990): 223–28. Also see review in Wright et al., *Criminals in the Making* (chap. 4).

Cytogenetic Studies: The XYY Factor

Beyond the body type theories, another model was proposed in the early 1900s regarding biological conditions that predispose individuals toward crime: cytogenetic studies. Cytogenetic studies of crime focus on the genetic makeup of individuals, with a specific focus on abnormalities in chromosomal makeup, and specifically chromosomal abnormalities that occur randomly in the population. Many of the chromosomal mutations that have been studied (such as XYY) typically result not from heredity but from random mutations in chromosomal formation.

The normal chromosomal makeup for women is XX, which represents an X from the mother and an X from the father. The normal chromosomal makeup for men is XY, which represents an X from the mother and a Y from the father. However, as in many species of animals, there are often genetic mutations, which we see in human beings. Consistent with evolutionary theory, virtually all possible variations of chromosomes that are possible have been found in the human population, such as XXY, XYY, and many others. We will focus our discussion on the chromosomal mutations that have been most strongly linked to criminality.

One of the first chromosomal mutations recognized as a predictor of criminal activity was XYY. In 1965, the first major study showed that this mutation was far more common in a Scottish male population of mental patients than in the general population.[9] Specifically, in the general population, XYY occurs in about 1 of every 1,000 males. The first major study that examined the influence of XYY sampled about 200 men in the mental hospital; one occurrence would have been predicted, assuming what was known about the general population. The study, however, found 13 individuals who were XYY, which suggested that individuals who have mental disorders are more likely to have XYY than those who do not. Males who have XYY have at least 13 times the likelihood (or a 1,300% chance) of having behavioral disorders compared with those who do not have this chromosomal abnormality. Subsequent studies have not been able to dismiss the effect of XYY on criminality, but they have concluded that this mutation is more often linked with property crime than with violent crime.[10]

Would knowing this relationship help in policies regarding crime? Probably not, considering the fact that 90% of the male mental patients were not XYY. Still, this study showed the importance of looking at chromosomal mutations as a predictor of criminal behavior.

Such mutations include numerous chromosomal abnormalities, such as XYY, which is a male who is given an extra Y chromosome, making him more "malelike." These individuals are often very tall but slow in terms of social and intelligence skills. Another type of mutation is XXY, which is otherwise known as Klinefelter's syndrome; it results in more feminine males (homosexuality has been linked to this mutation). Many other types of mutations have been observed, but it is the XYY mutation that has been the primary focus of studies, largely due to the higher levels of testosterone produced by this chromosomal mutation (see Figure 5.1).

One study examined the relative criminality and deviance of a group of individuals in each of these groups of chromosomal mutations (see Figure 5.1).[11] This study found that the higher the level of male hormones produced by the chromosomal mutation, the greater the likelihood that people with the mutation would commit criminal and deviant acts. On the other hand, the higher the level of feminine hormones produced by the chromosomal mutation,

---

[9]Patricia A. Jacobs, Muriel Brunton, Marie M. Melville, R. P. Brittian, and W. F. McClemmot, "Aggressive Behavior, Mental Sub-normality, and the XYY Male," *Nature* 208 (1965): 1351–52.

[10]See review in Raymond Paternoster and Ronet Bachman, *Explaining Criminals and Crime* (Los Angeles: Roxbury, 2001), 53.

[11]Anthony Walsh, "Genetic and Cytogenetic Intersex Anomalies: Can They Help Us to Understand Gender Differences in Deviant Behavior?" *International Journal of Offender Therapy and Comparative Criminology* 39 (1995): 151–66. See also Kristine Stochholm, Anders Bojesen, Anne Skakkebæk Jensen, Svend Juul, and Claus Højbjerg Gravholt, "Criminality in Men with Klinefelter's Syndrome and XYY Syndrome: A Cohort Study." *British Medical Journal Open 2* (2012).

| Figure 5.1 | Hypothetical scattergram relating masculinity/androgen level (designated by karyotype) to deviance |

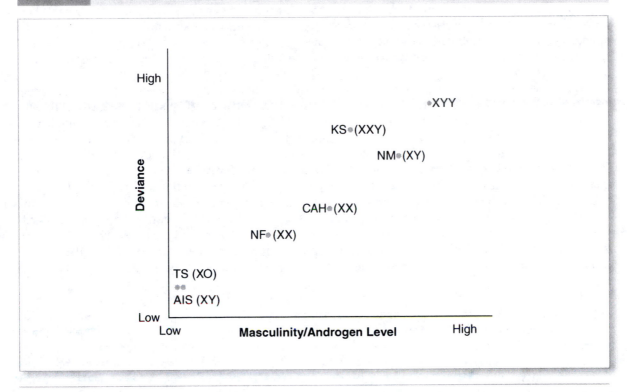

Source: Walsh 1995, 151–66.

Note: TS = Turner's syndrome; AIS = androgen insensitivity syndrome; NF = normal female; KS = Klinefelter's syndrome; CAH = congenital adrenal hyperplasia; NM = normal male; XYY = Jacob's (supermale) syndrome.

the lower the likelihood that the individuals would commit criminal activity. Ultimately, all of these variations in chromosomes show that there is a continuum of femaleness and maleness, and that the more malelike the individual is in terms of chromosomes, the more likely he is to commit criminal behavior.

Ultimately, the cytogenetic studies showed that somewhat random abnormalities in an individual's genetic makeup can have a profound influence on her or his level of criminality. Whether or not this can or should be used in policy related to crime is another matter, but the point is that genetics does indeed contribute to a disposition to commit criminal acts. The extent to which male hormones or androgens are increased by the mutation is an important predictor of criminal traits.

 ## Hormones and Neurotransmitters: Chemicals That Determine Criminal Behavior

Various chemicals in the brain and the rest of the body determine how we think, perceive, and react to various stimuli. Hormones, such as testosterone and estrogen, carry chemical signals to the body as they are released from certain glands and structures. Some studies have shown that a relatively excessive amount of testosterone in the body is consistently linked to criminal or aggressive behavior, with most studies showing a moderate relationship.[12] This relationship is seen even in the early years of life.[13] On the other side of the coin, studies have also shown that hormonal changes in females can cause criminal behavior. Specifically, studies have shown that a high proportion of the women in prison for violent crimes committed their crimes during their premenstrual cycle, at which time women experience a high level of hormones that make them more "malelike" due to relatively low levels of estrogen compared to progesterone.[14]

Anyone who doubts the impact of hormones on behavior should examine the scientific literature regarding performance on intelligence tests at different times of day. Virtually everyone performs better on spatial and mathematical tests early in the day, when people have relatively higher levels of testosterone and other male hormones in their bodies; on the other hand, virtually everyone performs better on verbal tasks in the afternoon or evening, when people have relatively higher levels of estrogen or other female hormones in their systems.[15] Furthermore, studies have shown that individuals who are given shots of androgens (male hormones) before math tests tend to do significantly better on spatial and mathematics tests than they would do otherwise. Scientific studies show that the same is true for people who are given shots of female hormones prior to verbal or reading tests.

It is important to realize that this process of differential levels of hormones begins at a very early age, specifically at about the fifth week after conception. At that time, the Y chromosome of the male tells the developing fetus that it is a male and stimulates production of higher levels of testosterone. So, even during the first few months of gestation, the genes on the Y chromosome significantly alter the course of genital and thus hormonal development.[16]

This level of testosterone alters the genitals of the fetus during gestation, as well as prompting later changes in the genital area, and produces profound increases in testosterone in the teenage and early adult years. This produces not only physical differences but also huge personality and behavioral alterations.[17] High levels of testosterone and other androgens tend to "masculinize" the brain toward risk-taking behavior, whereas the lower levels typically found in females tend to result in the default feminine model.[18] High levels of testosterone have numerous consequences, such as lowered sensitivity to pain, enhanced seeking of sensory stimulation, and a right-hemisphere shift in brain dominance, which has been linked to higher levels of spatial aptitude but lower levels of verbal reasoning and empathy. These consequences have profound implications for criminal activity and are more likely to occur in males than females.[19]

---

[12]Alan Booth and D. Wayne Osgood, "The Influence of Testosterone on Deviance in Adulthood: Assessing and Explaining the Relationship," *Criminology* 31 (1993): 93–117; Richard Ronay and William von Hippel, "Power, Testosterone, and Risk-Taking," *Journal of Behavioral Decision Making* 23 (2010): 473–82; Hosanna Soler, P. Vinayak, and David Quadagno, "Biosocial Aspects of Domestic Violence," *Psychoneuroendocrinology* 25 (2000): 721–73. For a review, see Lee Ellis and Anthony Walsh, *Criminology: A Global Perspective* (Boston: Allyn & Bacon, 2000). See also Raine, *Anatomy of Violence.*

[13]Jose R. Sanchez-Martin, Eduardo Fano, L. Ahedo, Jaione Cardas, Paul F. Brain, and Arantza Azpiroz, "Relating Testosterone Levels and Free Play Social Behavior in Male and Female Preschool Children," *Psychoneuroendocrinology* 25 (2000): 773–83.

[14]Diane Halpern, *Sex Differences in Cognitive Abilities* (Mahwah: Lawrence Erlbaum, 2000).

[15]Ibid.

[16]Lee Ellis, "A Theory Explaining Biological Correlates of Criminality," *European Journal of Criminality* 2 (2005): 287–315.

[17]See ibid.

[18]Chandler Burr, "Homosexuality and Biology," *Atlantic Monthly* 271 (1993): 47–65; Lee Ellis and M. Ashley Ames, "Neurohormonal Functioning and Sexual Orientation: A Theory of Homosexuality-Heterosexuality," *Psychological Bulletin* 101 (1987): 233–58; Ellis, "A Theory."

[19]Martin Reite, C. Munro Cullum, Jeanelle Stocker, Peter Teale, and Elizabeth Kozora, "Neuropsychological Test Performance and MEG-based Brain Lateralization: Sex Differences," *Brain Research Bulletin* 32 (1993): 325–28; Jorge Moll, Ricardo de Oliveira-Souza, Paul J. Eslinger, Ivanei E. Bramanti, Janaina Mourao-Miranda, Pedro Angelo Andreiuolo, and Luiz Pessoa, "The Neural Correlates of Moral Sensitivity: A Functional Magnetic Resonance Imaging Investigation of Basic and Moral Emotions," *Journal of Neuroscience* 22 (2002): 2730–36; Kimberly Badger, Rebecca Simpson Craft, and Larry

Ultimately, hormones have a profound effect on how individuals think and perceive their environments. All criminal behavior comes down to cognitive decisions in our 3-pound brains. So, it should not be surprising that hormones play a highly active role in this decision-making process. Nevertheless, hormones are probably secondary compared to levels of neurotransmitters, which are chemicals in the brain and body that help transmit electric signals from one neuron to another.

Neurotransmitters can be distinguished from hormones in the sense that hormones carry a signal that is not electric, whereas the signals that neurotransmitters carry are indeed electric. Neurotransmitters are chemicals that are released when a neuron, the basic unit of the nervous system, wants to send an electric message to a neighboring neuron(s). Sending such a message requires the creation of neural pathways, which means that neurotransmitters must be activated in processing the signal. At any given moment, healthy levels of various neurotransmitters are needed to pass messages from one neuron to the next across gaps between them, called synapses.

Although there are many types of neurotransmitters, the most studied in relation to criminal activity are dopamine and serotonin. Dopamine is most commonly linked to feeling good. For example, dopamine is the chemical that tells us when we are experiencing good sensations, such as good food, sex, and so on. Most illicit drugs elicit a pleasurable sensation by enhancing the levels of dopamine in our systems. Cocaine and methamphetamine, for example, tell the body to produce more dopamine and inhibit the enzymes that typically mop up the dopamine in our systems after it is used.

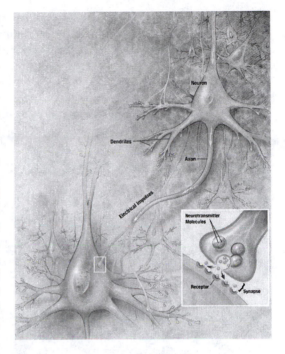

▲ Image 5.2   Neurons are the basic cell in our nervous system, and they communicate via chemicals called neurotransmitters that aid in sending electric messages across gaps between neurons called synapses.

Source: http://en.wikipedia.org/wiki/File:Chemical_synapse_schema.jpg.

Although a number of studies show that low levels of dopamine are linked to high rates of criminality, other studies show no association with—or even a positive link to—criminal behavior.[20] However, the relationship between dopamine and criminal behavior is probably curvilinear, such that both extremely high and extremely low levels of dopamine are associated with deviance. Unfortunately, no conclusion can be made at this point due to the lack of scientific evidence regarding this chemical.

On the other hand, a clear conclusion can be made about the other major neurotransmitter that has been implicated in criminal offending: serotonin. Studies have consistently shown that low levels of serotonin are linked with criminal offending.[21] Serotonin is important in virtually all information processing, whether it be learning or

Jensen, "Age and Gender Differences in Value Orientation among American Adolescents," *Adolescence* 33 (1998): 591–96.

[20]For reviews, see Kevin Beaver, *Biosocial Criminology: A Primer* (Dubuque, IA: Kendall/Hunt, 2008); Raine, *Anatomy of Violence*; and Diana H. Fishbein, *Biobehavioral Perspectives in Criminology* (Belmont: Wadsworth/Thomson Learning, 2001).

[21]For a review, see Ellis, "A Theory." See also Rachel Blumensohn, Gideon Ratzoni, Abraham Weizman, Malka Israeli, Nachman Greuner, Alan Apter, Sam Tyano, and Anat Biegon, "Reduction in Serotonin 5HT Receptor Binding on Platelets of Delinquent Adolescents," *Psychopharmacology* 118 (1995): 354–56; Emil F. Coccaro, Richard J. Kavoussi, Thomas B. Cooper, and Richard L. Hauger, "Central Serotonin Activity and Aggression," *American Journal of Psychiatry* 154 (1997): 1430–35; Mairead Dolan, Bill J. F. Deakin, N. Roberts, and Ian Anderson, "Serotonergic and Cognitive Impairment in Impulsive Aggressive Personality Disordered Offenders: Are There Implications for Treatment?" *Psychological Medicine* 32 (2002): 105–17; and Richard J. Davidson,

emotional; thus, it is vital in most aspects of interacting with the environment. Those who have low levels of serotonin are likely to have problems in everyday communication and life in general. Therefore, it is not surprising that low levels of serotonin are strongly linked to criminal activity.

Brain Injuries

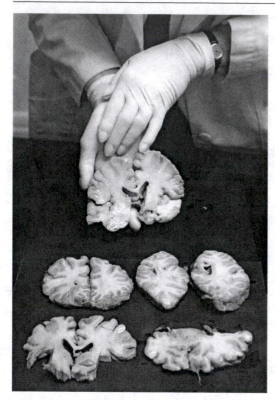

▲ Image 5.3   Harkening back to the 19th century, when postmortem examinations of the brains of criminals were a frequent phenomenon, researchers dissected the brain of serial killer John Wayne Gacy after his execution. The attempt to locate an organic explanation for his monstrous behavior was unsuccessful.

Source: © AP Photo/M. Spencer Green.

Another area of physiological problems associated with criminal activity is that of trauma to the brain. As mentioned before, the brain weighs only 3 pounds, but it is responsible for every criminal act that an individual commits, so any problems related to this structure have profound implications regarding behavior, especially deviance and criminal activity.

Studies have consistently shown that damage to any part of the brain increases the risk of crime by that individual in the future. However, trauma to certain portions of the brain tends to have more serious consequences than injury to other areas. Specifically, damage to the frontal or temporal lobes (particularly those on the left side) appears to have the most consistent associations with criminal offending.[22] These findings make sense primarily because the frontal lobes (which include the prefrontal cortex) are the areas of the brain where the realm of higher-level problem solving and "executive" functioning takes place.[23] Thus, the frontal lobes, especially on the left side, process what we are thinking and inhibit us from doing what we are emotionally charged to do. Thus, any moral reasoning relies on this executive area of the brain because it is the region that considers long-term consequences.[24] If people suffer damage to their frontal lobes, they will be far more inclined to act on their emotional urges because they are not receiving any logical inhibitions from this specialized region.

In a similar vein, the temporal lobe region is highly related to memory and emotion. To clarify, the temporal lobes cover and communicate almost directly with certain structures of our brain's limbic systems. Certain limbic structures govern our memories (the hippocampus) and emotions (the amygdala). Any damage to the temporal lobe, which is

Katherine M. Putnam, and Christine L. Larson, "Dysfunction in the Neural Circuitry of Emotion Regulation: A Possible Prelude to Violence," *Science* 289 (2000): 591–94.

[22]For reviews, see Raine, *Anatomy of Violence*, 80–89; and Raine, *Psychopathology of Crime*, 129–54. See also Joseph M. Tonkonogy, "Violence and Temporal Lobe Lesion: Head CT and MRI Data," *Journal of Neuropsychiatry* 3 (1991): 189–96; and Percy Wright, Jose Nobrega, Ron Langevin, and George Wortzman, "Brain Density and Symmetry in Pedophilic and Sexually Aggressive Offenders," *Annals of Sex Research* 3 (1990): 319–28.

[23]Ellis, "A Theory," 294. See also Diana Fishbein, "Neuropsychological and Emotional Regulatory Processes in Antisocial Behavior," in *Biosocial Criminology: Challenging Environmentalism's Supremacy*, ed. Anthony Walsh and Lee Ellis (New York: Nova Science, 2003), 185–208.

[24]Bobbi Jo Anderson, Malcolm D. Holmes, and Erik Ostresch, "Male and Female Delinquents' Attachments and Effects of Attachments on Severity of Self-Reported Delinquency," *Criminal Justice and Behavior* 26 (1999): 435–52.

generally located above the ear, is likely to damage these structures or the effective communication of these structures to other portions of the brain. Therefore, it is understandable why trauma to the temporal region of the brain is linked to future criminality.

Central and Autonomic Nervous System Activity

The brain is a key player in two different types of neurological systems that have been linked to criminal activity. The first is the central nervous system (CNS), which involves our brains and spinal columns and governs our voluntary motor activities. For example, the fact that you are reading this sentence means that you are in control of this brain-processing activity. Empirical studies of the influence of CNS functioning on criminality have traditionally focused on brain wave patterns, with most using electroencephalograms (EEGs). Although EEGs do not do a good job of describing which areas of the brain are active or inactive, they do reveal how much the brain as an entire organ is performing at certain times.

Studies have compared brain wave patterns of known chronic offenders (e.g., psychopaths, repeat violent offenders) to those of "normal" people (i.e., those who have never been charged with a crime).[25] These studies consistently show that the brain wave patterns of chronic offenders are abnormal compared to those of the normal population, with most studies showing slower brain wave patterns in psychopaths.[26] Four types of brain wave patterns are found, from slowest to fastest: delta, theta, alpha, and beta.[27] Delta waves are often seen when people sleep, whereas theta waves are typically observed in lower levels of wakefulness, such as drowsiness. Alpha waves (which tend to be divided into slow and fast wave patterns, as are beta waves) are usually related to a more relaxed wakefulness, and beta waves are observed with high levels of wakefulness, such as in times of extreme alertness and particularly in times of excited activity.

The studies that have compared brain wave patterns among chronic offenders and normals have shown significant differences. Psychopaths tend to have more activity in the theta (and sometimes slow alpha) patterns, whereas normals tend to show more activity in the fast alpha or beta waves. These consistent findings reveal that the cortical arousal of chronic offenders tends to be significantly slower than that of people who do not typically commit crimes. Thus, it is likely that chronic offenders typically do not have the mental functioning that would dispose them toward accurate assessments regarding the consequences of committing criminal behavior.

The second area of the nervous system that has been most linked to criminal behavior is the autonomic nervous system (ANS), which is primarily responsible for involuntary motor activities, such as heart rate, dilation of pupils, and electric conductivity in the skin. This is the type of physiological activity that is measured by polygraph measures, or lie detector tests. Such measures capitalize on the inability of individuals to control physiological responses to anxiety, which occurs in most normal persons when they lie, especially regarding illegal behavior. However, such measures are not infallible because the individuals who are most at risk of being serious, violent offenders are the most likely to pass such tests even when they are lying.

---

[25]Adrian Raine and Peter H. Venables, "Enhanced P3 Evoked Potentials and Longer P3 Recovery Times in Psychopaths," *Psychophysiology* 25 (1988): 30–38; Lance O. Bauer and Victor M. Hesselbrock, "Frontal P300 Decrements, Childhood Conduct Disorder, Family History, and the Prediction of Relapse among Abstinent Cocaine Abusers," *Drug and Alcohol Dependence* 44 (1997): 1–10. For a review, see Ellis, "A Theory."

[26]For a review, see Raine, *Psychopathology of Crime*, 174–78. See also Robert D. Hare, *Psychopathy: Theory and Practice* (New York: Wiley, 1970); Jan Volavka, "Electroencephalogram among Criminals," in *The Causes of Crime: New Biological Approaches*, ed. Sarnoff A. Mednick, Terrie E. Moffitt, and Susan Stack (Cambridge: Cambridge University Press, 1987), 137–45; Peter H. Venables, "Psychophysiology and Crime: Theory and Data," in *Biological Contributions to Crime Causation*, ed. Terrie E. Moffitt and Sarnoff A. Mednick (Dordrecht: Martinus Nijhoff, 1988); and Peter H. Venables and Adrian Raine, "Biological Theory," in *Applying Psychology to Imprisonment: Theory and Practice*, ed. Barry McGurk, David Thornton, and Mark Williams (London: Her Majesty's Stationery Office, 1987), 3–28.

[27]For further discussion and explanation, see Raine, *Psychopathology of Crime*, 174–77.

Figure 5.2 CNS and ANS

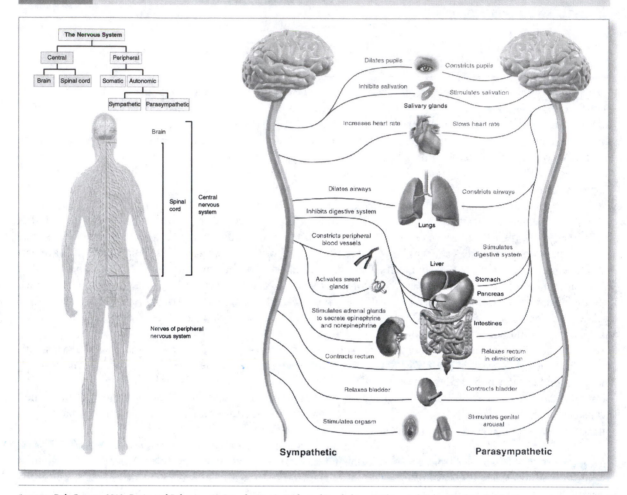

SOURCE: Bob Garrett, 2010. *Brain and Behavior: An Introduction to Biological Psychology, 3e.*Thousand Oaks, CA: Sage Publications.

Consistent with the findings regarding CNS arousal levels, studies have consistently shown that individuals who have significantly low levels of ANS functioning are far more likely to commit criminal acts.[28] For example, studies consistently show that chronic violent offenders tend to have much slower resting heartbeats than normal people, with a number of studies estimating this difference to be as much as 10 beats per minute slower for the offenders.[29]

[28]For a review, see Raine, *Psychopathology of Crime*, 159–73. See also the following reviews and studies: Peter H. Venables, "Childhood Markers for Adult Disorders," *Journal of Child Psychology and Psychiatry and Allied Disciplines* 30 (1989): 347–64; Adrian Raine and Peter H. Venables, "Skin Conductance Responsivity in Psychopaths to Orienting, Defensive, and Consonant-Vowel Stimuli," *Journal of Psychophysiology* 2 (1988): 221–25; and Traci Bice, "Cognitive and Psychophysiological Differences in Proactive and Reactive Aggressive Boys," doctoral dissertation, Department of Psychology, University of Southern California (Ann Arbor: UMI, 1993).

[29]See Enrico Mezzacappa, Richard E. Tremblay, Daniel Kindlon, J. Philip Saul, Louise Arseneault, Jean Seguin, Robert O. Pihl, and Felton Earls, "Anxiety, Antisocial Behavior, and Heart Rate Regulation in Adolescent Males," *Journal of Psychiatry* 38 (1997): 457–69; Graham A. Rogeness, Claudio Cepeda, Carlos A. Macedo, Charles Fischer, and William R. Harris, "Differences in Heart Rate and Blood Pressure in Children with Conduct Disorder, Major

This is a highly significant gap that cannot be explained away by alternative theories—for example, the explanation that offenders are just less excited in laboratory tests.

Furthermore, people who have such low levels of ANS arousal tend to experience what is known in the psychological literature as *stimulus hunger*. Stimulus hunger means that individuals with such a low level of ANS arousal may constantly seek out experiences and stimuli that are risky and thus often illegal. Readers may recall children they have known who can never seem to get enough attention, with some even seeming to enjoy being spanked or other forms of harsh punishment. In addition, people with a low level of ANS arousal may feel no anxiety about punishment, corporal punishment, and thus they may not adequately learn right from wrong through normal forms of discipline. This is perhaps one of the reasons why children who are diagnosed with attention deficit hyperactivity Disorder (ADHD) have a higher likelihood of becoming criminals than their peers.

Because people who are accurately diagnosed with ADHD have a neurological abnormality—a significantly low functioning ANS level of arousal—doctors prescribe stimulants (e.g., Ritalin) for such youths. It may seem counterintuitive to prescribe a hyperactive person a stimulant; however, the medication boosts the individual's ANS functioning to a normal level of arousal. This makes such individuals experience a healthy level of anxiety, which they would not normally experience from wrongdoing. Assuming that the medication is properly prescribed and at the correct dosage, children who are treated tend to become more attuned to the discipline that they face if they engage in rule violation.

Children who do not fear punishment at all—in fact, some of them do not feel anxiety even when being physically punished (e.g., spanking)—are likely to have lower-than-average levels of ANS functioning. Such individuals are likely to become chronic offenders if this disorder is not addressed, because they will not respond to discipline or consider the long-term consequences of their risky behavior. If people don't fear punishment or negative consequences from their behavior, they may be more likely to engage in selfish, greedy behavior. Thus, it is important to address this issue when it becomes evident. On the other hand, children will be children, and ADHD and other disorders have been overly diagnosed in recent years. A well-trained physician should investigate thoroughly to decide whether an individual has such a low level of ANS functioning that medication or therapy is required to curb deviant behavior.

Individuals who have significantly lower ANS arousal are likely to pass lie detector tests because they feel virtually no or little anxiety when they lie; many of them lie all the time. Thus, it is ironic, but the very people whom lie-detecting measures are meant to capture are the most likely to pass such tests, which is probably why they are typically not allowed to be used in court. Only through medication or cognitive behavioral therapy can such individuals learn to consider the long-term consequences of the decisions they make regarding their behavior.

Individuals with low levels of ANS functioning are not always destined to become chronic offenders. Some evidence has shown that people with low ANS arousal often become successful corporate executives, decorated military soldiers, world-champion athletes, and high-level politicians. Most of these occupations require people who constantly seek out exciting, risky behaviors, and others require constant and convincing forms of lying to others. So, there are many legal outlets and productive ways for people with low levels of ANS functioning to use their natural tendencies. These individuals could perhaps be steered toward such occupations and opportunities when they present themselves. This is clearly a better option than committing antisocial acts against others in society.

Ultimately, low levels of cortical arousal in both the CNS and ANS are clearly linked to a predisposition toward criminal activity. However, modern medical research and societal opportunities exist to help such individuals divert their tendencies toward more prosocial outlets.

Depression, and Separation Anxiety," *Psychiatry Research* 33 (1990): 199–206; and Daniel J. Kindlon, Richard E. Tremblay, Enrico Mezzacappa, Felton Earls, Denis Laurent, and Benoist Schaal, "Longitudinal Patterns of Heart Rate and Fighting Behavior in 9- through 12-Year-Old Boys," *Journal of the American Academy of Child and Adolescent Psychiatry* 34 (1995): 371–77.

Biosocial Approaches to Explaining Criminal Behavior

Perhaps the most important and most recent perspective of how criminality is formed is that of biosocial approaches to explaining crime. Specifically, if there is any conclusion that can be made regarding the previous theories and research in this section, it is that both genetics and environment influence behavior, particularly the interaction between the two. Even the most fundamental aspects of life can be explained by these two groups of factors.

For example, if we look at the height of individuals, we can predict with a great amount of accuracy how tall a person will be by looking at the individual's parents and other ancestors because much of height is determined by a person's genotype. However, even for something as physiological as height, the environment plays a large role. As many readers will observe, individuals who are raised in poor, underdeveloped areas (e.g., Mexico, Asia) are shorter than children raised in the United States. However, individuals who descend from parents and relatives in these underdeveloped areas but are raised in the United States tend to be just as tall (if not taller) than children born here. This is largely due to diet, which obviously is an environmental factor.

In other words, our genotype provides a certain range or window that determines the height of an individual based on ancestral factors. But, the extent to which individuals grow to the maximum or minimum, or somewhere in between, is largely dependent on what occurs in the environment as they develop. This is why biologists make a distinction between genotype, which is directly due to genetics, and phenotype, which is a manifestation of genetics interacting with the environment. The same type of biosocial effect is seen for criminal behavior.

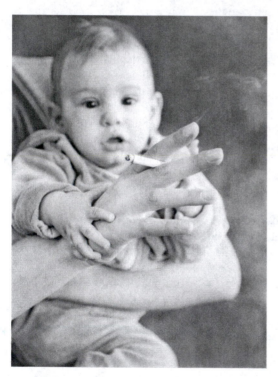

▲ Image 5.4   Young children are particularly vulnerable when exposed to dangerous toxins.

Source: © Photospower / iStock.

Furthermore, over the last decades, a number of empirical investigations have examined the extent to which physiological variables interact with environmental variables, and the findings of these studies have shown consistent predictions regarding criminality. Such studies have been more accurate than those that rely on either physiological and genetic variables or environmental factors separately. For example, findings from a cohort study in Philadelphia showed that individuals who had low birth weights were more likely to commit crime, but that was true primarily if they were raised in a lower-income family or a family with a weak social structure.[30] Those who were raised in a relatively high income household or a strong family structure were unlikely to become criminals. It was the coupling of both a physiological deficiency (i.e., low birth weight) and an environmental deficit (i.e., weak family structure or income) that had a profound effect on propensity for criminal behavior.

In addition, recent studies have shown that when incarcerated juveniles were assigned to diets with limited levels of simple carbohydrates (e.g., sugars), their reported levels of violations during incarceration declined by almost half

---

[30]Stephen Tibbetts and Alex Piquero, "The Influence of Gender, Low Birth Weight, and Disadvantaged Environment in Predicting Early Onset of Offending: A Test of Moffitt's Interactional Hypothesis," *Criminology* 37 (1999): 843–78.

(45%).[31] Furthermore, other studies have reported that various food additives and dyes, such as those commonly found in processed foods, can also have a significant influence on criminal behavior. Thus, the old saying "you are what you eat" appears to have some scientific weight behind it, at least regarding criminal behavior. Additional studies have found that high levels of certain toxins, particularly lead and manganese, can have profound effects on behavior, including criminality. Recent studies have found a consistent, strong effect of high lead levels in predicting criminal behavior. Unfortunately, medical studies have also found many subtle sources of high lead levels, such as the fake jewelry that many children wear as toys. Also unfortunate is that the individuals who are most vulnerable to high levels of lead (like virtually every other toxin) are children, and yet they are the most likely to be exposed. Even more unfortunate is that the populations most susceptible to biosocial interactions (e.g., poor, urban) are most likely to experience high levels of lead, largely due to old paint, which often contains lead, and other household products that contain dangerous toxins.[32]

Consistently, other studies have shown that prenatal and perinatal problems alone do not predict violence very well. However, when such perinatal problems are considered along with environmental deficits, such as weak family structure, this biosocial relationship often predicts violent rather than property crime.[33] Other studies have shown the effects on criminality of a biosocial interaction between the impact of physiological factors within the first minute of life, called Apgar scores, and environmental factors, including exposure to nicotine.[34] Additional studies have also found that the interaction between maternal cigarette smoking and the father's absence from the household is associated with criminal behavior, especially early in life, which is one of the biggest predictors of chronic offending in the future.[35] One of the most revealing studies showed that, although only 4% of a sample of 4,269 individuals had both birth complications and maternal rejection, this relatively small group of people accounted for more than 18% of the total violent crimes committed by the whole sample.[36] So, studies have clearly shown that the interaction between biological factors and environmental deficiencies has the most consistent effect on future criminality.

Policy Implications

The theories in this section have plenty of policy implications; a few of the primary interventions are discussed here. First, there should be universal, funded preschool for all children. This early life stage is important not only for developing academic skills, but also for fostering healthy social and disciplinary skills, which children who do not attend preschool often fail to develop.[37] In addition, there should be funded mental health and drug counseling for all young children and adolescents who exhibit symptoms of mental disorders or drug problems.[38] There should also be universal funding for health care for all expectant mothers, especially those who have risk factors (poverty,

---

[31]Stephen J. Shoenthaler, *Improve Your Child's IQ and Behavior* (London: BBC Books, 1991).

[32]Wright et al., *Criminals in the Making*.

[33]Alex Piquero and Stephen Tibbetts, "The Impact of Pre/Perinatal Disturbances and Disadvantaged Familial Environment in Predicting Criminal Offending," *Studies on Crime and Crime Prevention* 8 (1999): 52–71.

[34]E.g., Chris Gibson and Stephen Tibbetts, "Interaction between Maternal Cigarette Smoking and Apgar Scores in Predicting Offending," *Psychological Reports* 83 (1998): 579–86. For a review, see Stephen G. Tibbetts, "Birth Complications and the Development of Criminality: A Biosocial Perspective," in Kevin Beaver and Anthony Walsh, *The Ashgate Research Companion to Biosocial Theories of Crime* (Burlington, VT: Ashgate, 2012), 273–90.

[35]Chris Gibson and Stephen Tibbetts, "A Biosocial Interaction in Predicting Early Onset of Offending," *Psychological Reports* 86 (2000): 509–18.

[36]Adrian Raine, Pauline A. Brennan, and Sarnoff A. Mednick, "Birth Complications Combined with Early Maternal Rejection at Age 1 Year Predispose to Violent Crime at Age 18 Years," *Archives of General Psychiatry* 51 (1994): 984–88.

[37]Wright et al., *Criminals in the Making*.

[38]Ibid.

inner-city residence, etc.). Also, and perhaps most important, there should be far more thorough examinations of children's physiological makeup in terms of hormones, neurotransmitters, brain formation and functioning, and genetic design so that earlier interventions can take place. It has been shown empirically that the earlier that interventions take place, the better the outcomes.[39] These and other policy implications based on modern biosocial theories will be discussed in the final section of the book.

 ## Conclusion

This section has examined a large range of explanations of criminal behavior that place most of the blame on biological and psychological factors, which are typically intertwined. These types of explanations were primarily popular in the early years of the development of criminology as a science, but they have also been shown in recent years to be quite valid as significant factors in individual decisions to commit crime. This section examined the influence of genetics and environment in family studies, twin studies, adoption studies, and studies of identical twins separated at birth. These studies have ultimately shown the consistent influence of inheritance and genetics in predisposing individuals toward criminal activity. This is supported by the influence of hormones (e.g., testosterone) in human behavior, as well as the influence of variations in chromosomal mutations (e.g., XYY). Recent research has supported both of these theories in showing that people with high levels of male androgens are far more likely to commit crimes than those who do not have high levels of these hormones.

The link between brain trauma and crime was also discussed, with an emphasis on the consistent association between damage to the left or frontal parts of the brain. We also examined theories regarding variations in levels of CNS and ANS functioning; all empirical studies have shown that low levels of functioning of these systems have links to criminality. Finally, we explored the extent to which the interaction between physiological factors and environmental variables contributes to the most consistent prediction of criminal offending. Ultimately, it is interesting that the very theories that were key in the early years of the development of criminology as a science are now showing strong support in studies for being primary influences on criminal behavior.

 ## Section Summary

- Early studies that examined the influence of biology focused on case studies of certain families. These studies showed that criminality was indeed clustered among certain families, but such studies did not separate biology from environment.
- The next stage of studies examined the concordance rates of identical twins versus nonidentical twins. These studies led to the conclusion that genetic makeup was very important, but critics called these conclusions into question.
- The following stage of research examined adoptees to determine which parents (biological or adoptive) had more influence in their future criminal behavior. These studies revealed that biological parents (whom the adoptees never knew) had far more influence than the adoptive parents who raised them. However, there were criticisms of these studies, so the findings were questioned.
- The final stage of the biology-versus-environment debate was that of identical twins separated at birth as compared to identical twins raised together. These studies showed that the twins who were separated at birth were just as similar, if not more so, than the twins who were reared together. To date, there are no criticisms of this method of study. Thus, it appears that all four waves of study are consistent in showing that biological influences are vitally important in explaining the criminality of individuals.

---

[39]Samuel S. Wu, Chang-Xing Ma, Randy L. Carter, Mario Ariet, Edward A. Feaver, Michael B. Resnick, and Jeffrey Roth. "Risk Factors for Infant Maltreatment: A Population-Based Study," *Child Abuse and Neglect* 28 (2004): 1253–64.

◆ This section also examined chromosomal mutations, such as the XYY mutation, which has consistently shown associations with criminality. Much, if not most, of this link is believed to be due to the increased male androgens (e.g., testosterone) produced by individuals who have the XYY chromosomal mutation.

◆ Studies have consistently shown that individuals with higher levels of testosterone and other androgens are more disposed toward criminality; for example, normal males are far more likely than normal females to engage in violent crimes.

◆ This section reviewed findings from studies that show that people with abnormal levels of certain neurotransmitters, such as serotonin, are far more likely to engage in crime than those who have normal levels of these chemicals in their brains or bodies.

◆ Studies show that criminality is more likely among individuals who have experienced brain trauma or have lower levels of brain functioning, especially in certain regions of the brain, such as the frontal and temporal lobes, which are the regions that largely govern higher-level, problem-solving functions.

◆ This section also reviewed the dispositions of individuals regarding two aspects of the nervous system, specifically the CNS and ANS. Those who have significantly slower brain waves and lower anxiety levels are far more likely to commit crimes.

KEY TERMS

adoption studies	dopamine	selective placement
autonomic nervous system (ANS)	family studies	serotonin
central nervous system (CNS)	frontal lobes	temporal lobes
concordance rates	monozygotic twins	twins-separated-at-birth studies
cytogenetic studies	neurotransmitters	twin studies
dizygotic twins	phenotype	

DISCUSSION QUESTIONS

1. Is there any validity to family studies in determining the role of genetics in criminal behavior? Explain why or why not.

2. Explain the rationale of studies that compare the concordance rates of identical twins and fraternal twins who are raised together. What do most of these studies show regarding the influence of genetics on criminal behavior? What are the criticisms of these studies?

3. Explain the rationale of studies that examine the biological and adoptive parents of adopted children. What do most of these studies show regarding the influence of genetics on criminal behavior? What are the criticisms of these studies?

4. What are the general findings in identical twins who are separated at birth? What implications do these findings have for the importance of genetics or heritability regarding criminal behavior? Can you find a criticism for such findings?

5. Explain what cytogenetic disorders are and describe the related disorder that is most linked to criminal behavior. What characteristics of this type of disorder seem to drive the higher propensity for criminal behavior?

6. What types of hormones have been shown by scientific studies to be linked to criminal activity? Give specific examples that show this link to be true.

7. Explain what neurotransmitters are, and describe which neurotransmitters are key in predicting criminal offending. Provide support from previous scientific studies.

8. Which areas of the brain, given trauma, have shown the greatest vulnerability regarding criminal offending? Does the lack of healthy functioning in these areas make sense? Why?

9. How do brain wave patterns differ between chronic, violent criminals and "normal" people? Does this make sense in biosocial models of criminality?

10. How does the ANS differ between chronic, violent criminals and "normal" people? Does this make sense in biosocial models of criminality?

11. What types of policy implications would you support based on the information provided by empirical studies reviewed in this section?

WEB RESOURCES

ANS/CNS

http://www.crimetimes.org/

http://www.mentalhelp.net/poc/view_doc.php?type=doc&id=263

Brain Trauma and Crime

http://www.crimetimes.org/

Cytogenetic Studies

http://en.wikipedia.org/wiki/cytogenetics

Family/Twin/Adoption Studies

http://www.bookrags.com/research/twin-studies-wog/

http://www.criminology.fsu.edu/crimtheory/dugdale.htm

Hormones and Neurotransmitters

http://serendip.brynmawr.edu/biology/b103/f02/web1/kamlin.html

http://www.gender.org.uk/about/06encrn/63faggrs.htm

In Lee Ellis's piece, we see an attempt at integrating many of the factors that we have explored in this section, as well as in Section III, into an explanatory model of offending. In this selection, we will see elements of evolution, early developmental problems, neurology, androgens, nervous systems, IQ/intelligence, emotions, and other factors as leading to various deviant or offending behaviors. This is the most current synthesis and use of the existing biosocial literature in developing a theoretical model of criminality. Although this model has not been tested or incorporated into modern criminological theoretical development, it is a theory that shows promise due to its incorporation of many of the biosocial aspects that have been supported by empirical studies. While reading this piece, consider how many of these factors fit together in a larger framework that helps explain human behavior, specifically criminal activity.

A Theory Explaining Biological Correlates of Criminality

Lee Ellis

Despite growing evidence that biology plays an important role in human behavior, most theories of criminal behavior continue to focus on learning and social environmental variables. This article proposes a biosocial theory of criminality that leads one to expect variables such as age, gender and social status will be associated with offending in very specific ways. According to the theory, androgens (male sex hormones) have the ability to affect the brain in ways that increase the probability of what is termed competitive/victimizing behavior (CVB). This behavior is hypothesized to exist along a continuum, with "crude" (criminal) forms at one end and "sophisticated" (commercial) forms at the other. Theoretically, individuals whose brains receive a great deal of androgen exposure will be prone toward CVB. However, if they have normal or high capabilities to learn and plan, they will transition rapidly from criminal to non-criminal forms of the behavior following the onset of puberty. Individuals with high androgen exposure and poor learning and planning capabilities, on the other hand, often continue to exhibit criminality for decades following the onset of puberty.

The Evolutionary Neuroandrogenic Theory of Criminal Behavior

The theory to be presented is called the evolutionary neuroandrogenic theory (ENA). The main types of offenses it attempts to explain are those that harm others, either by injuring them physically or by depriving them of their property. Two main propositions lie at the heart of ENA theory. The first addresses evolutionary issues by asserting that the commission of victimful crimes evolved as an aspect of human reproduction, especially among males. The second is concerned with identifying the neurochemistry responsible for increasing the probability of criminality among males relative to females. The theory maintains that sex hormones alter male brain functioning in ways that promote CVB, which is hypothesized to include the commission of violent and property crimes.

The concept of CVB is illustrated in Table 1. At one end of the continuum are acts that intentionally and directly either injure others or dispossess them of their property.

SOURCE: Lee Ellis, "A Theory Explaining Biological Correlates of Criminality." *European Journal of Criminology* 2, no. 3 (2005): 287–315. Copyright © 2005 Sage Publications Ltd. Reprinted by permission of Sage Publications Ltd. and the author.

In all societies with written laws, these obviously harmful acts are criminalized. At the other end of the CVB continuum are acts that make no profits on the sale of goods or services, although those who administer and maintain the organizations under which they operate usually receive much higher wages than do those who provide most of the day-to-day labor. In a purely socialist economy, the latter type of minimally competitive activities is all that is allowed; all other forms are criminalized. A capitalist economy, on the other hand, will permit profit-making commerce and often even tolerate commerce that involves significant degrees of deception. With the concept of CVB in mind, the two propositions upon which the theory rests can now be described.

 ## The Evolutionary Proposition

Throughout the world, males engage in victimful crimes (especially those involving violence) to a greater extent than do females. To explain why, ENA theory maintains that female mating preferences play a pivotal role. The nature of this mating preference is that females consider social status criteria much more than males do in making mate choices, a pattern that has been documented throughout the world (Ellis, 2001). From an evolutionary standpoint, this female preference has served to increase the chances of females mating with males who are reliable provisioners of resources, allowing females to focus more of their time and energy on bearing offspring. Another consequence has been that female choice has made it possible for males who are status strivers to pass on their genes at higher rates than males who are not. Such female preferences are found in other mammals, as evidenced by their mating more with dominant males than with subordinate males.

According to ENA theory, female preferences for status-striving males have caused most males to devote considerable time and energy to competing for resources, an endeavor that often victimizes others. In other words, natural selection pressure on females to prefer status-striving mates has resulted in males with an inclination toward CVB. ENA theory maintains that the brains of males have been selected for exhibiting competitive/victimizing behavior to a greater extent than the brains of females, and that one of the manifestations of this evolved sex difference is that males are more prone than females toward victimful criminality.

Theoretically, the same natural selection pressure that has resulted in the evolution of CVB has also favored males who flaunt and even exaggerate their resource-procuring capabilities. More unpleasant consequences of the female bias for resource provisioning mates are male tendencies to seek opportunities to circumvent female caution in mating by using deceptive and even forceful copulation tactics. This implies that rape will always be more prevalent among males than among females. ENA theory also leads one to expect complex social systems to develop in order to prevent crime victimization. In evolutionary terms, these systems are known as *counter-strategies*. An example of a counter-strategy to crude forms of CVB is the evolution of the criminal justice system.

As with any theory founded on neoDarwinian thinking, ENA theory assumes that genes are responsible for substantial proportions of the variation in the traits being investigated. In the present context, the average male is assumed to have a greater genetic propensity toward CVB than is true for the average female. However, this assumption must be compromised with the fact that males and females share nearly all of their genes. Consequently, the only possible way for the theory to be correct is for some of the genes that promote criminality (along with other forms

Table 1	Continuum of Victimizing Behavior (Reflecting Competitive/Victimizing Tendencies)			
The Continuum	very crude _____ intermediate _____ very sophisticated			
Probability of Being Criminalized	virtually certain _____ intermediate _____ exceedingly unlikely			
Examples	Violent and property offenses ("street crime")	Embezzlement, fraud ("white collar crime")	Deceptive business practices, price gouging	Profit-making commerce	Nonprofit-making commerce

of CVB) to be located on the one chromosome that males and females do not share—the Y-chromosome.

The Neuroandrogenic Proposition

The second proposition of ENA theory asserts that three different aspects of brain functioning affect an individual's chances of criminal offending by promoting CVB. Two additional neurological factors help to inhibit offending by speeding up the acquisition of sophisticated forms of CVB. Testosterone's ability to affect brain functioning in ways that promote CVB is not simple, but most of the complexities will not be considered here. The main point to keep in mind is that testosterone production occurs in two distinct phases: the organizational (or perinatal) phase and the activational (or postpubertal) phase. Most of the permanent effects of testosterone occur perinatally. If levels of testosterone are high, the brain will be masculinized; if they are low, the brain will remain in its default feminine mode.

ENA theory asserts that androgens increase the probability of CVB by decreasing an individual's sensitivity to adverse environmental consequences resulting from exhibiting CVB. This lowered sensitivity is accomplished by inclining the brain to be *suboptimally aroused*. Suboptimal arousal manifests itself in terms of individuals seeking elevated levels of sensory stimulation and having diminished sensitivity to pain.

The second way androgens promote CVB according to ENA theory is by inclining the limbic system to seizure more readily, especially under stressful conditions. At the extreme, these seizures include such clinical conditions as epilepsy and Tourette's syndrome. Less extreme manifestations of limbic seizuring are known as *episodic dyscontrol* and *limbic psychotic trigger*. These latter patterns include sudden bursts of rage and other negative emotions, which often trigger forceful actions against a perceived provocateur.

Third, ENA theory asserts that androgen exposure causes neocortical functioning to be less concentrated in the left (language-dominated) hemisphere and to shift more toward a right hemispheric focus. As a result of this so-called *rightward shift in neocortical functioning*, males rely less on language-based reasoning, emphasizing instead

reasoning which involves spatial and temporal calculations of risk and reward probabilities. Coinciding with this evidence are intriguing new research findings based on functional magnetic resonance imaging (fMRI) which suggest that empathy-based moral reasoning occurs primarily in the left hemisphere. Predictably, empathy-based moral reasoning seems to be less pronounced in males than in females. Such evidence suggests that empathy-based moral reasoning is more likely to prevent victimful criminality than so-called justice-based moral reasoning.

Theoretically, the three androgen-enhanced brain processes just described have evolved in males more than in females because these processes contribute to CVB. Furthermore, competitive/victimizing behavior has evolved in males more than in females because it facilitates male reproductive success more than it facilitates female reproductive success.

Inhibiting Criminal Forms of Competitive/Victimizing Behavior

Regarding the inhibiting aspects of brain functioning, two factors are theoretically involved. One has to do with learning ability and the other entails foresight and planning ability. According to ENA theory, the ability to learn will correlate with the rapidity of male transitioning from crude to sophisticated forms of CVB. This means that intelligence and other measures of learning ability should be inversely associated with persistent involvement in criminal behavior. Likewise, neurological underpinnings of intelligence such as brain size and neural efficiency should also correlate negatively with persistent offending. These predictions apply only to persistent victimful offending, with a much weaker link to occasional delinquency and possibly none with victimless criminality.

The frontal lobes, especially their prefrontal regions, play a vital role in coordinating complex sequences of actions intended to accomplish long-term goals. These prefrontal regions tend to keenly monitor the brain's limbic region, where most emotions reside. Then the prefrontal regions devise plans for either maximizing pleasant emotions or minimizing unpleasant ones. In other words, for the brain to integrate experiences into well-coordinated and feedback-contingent strategies for reaching long-term goals, the frontal lobes perform what has come to be called *executive cognitive functioning*. Moral reasoning often draws heavily on executive cognitive functioning since it often requires anticipating the long-term consequences of one's actions.

Factors that can impact executive cognitive functioning include genetics, prenatal complications, and various types of physical and chemical trauma throughout life. According to ENA theory, inefficient executive cognitive functioning contributes to criminal behavior. Similar conclusions have been put forth in recent years by several other researchers.

To summarize, ENA theory asserts that three aspects of brain functioning promote competitive/victimizing behavior, the crudest forms of which are victimful crimes. At least partially counterbalancing these androgen-promoted tendencies are high intelligence and efficient executive cognitive functioning. These latter two factors affect the speed with which individuals quickly learn to express their competitive/victimizing tendencies in sophisticated rather than crude ways. Sophisticated expressions are less likely to elicit retaliation by victims, their relatives, and the criminal justice system than are crude ones. Males with low intelligence and/or with the least efficient executive cognitive functioning will therefore exhibit the highest rates of victimful criminal behavior.

 ## Correlates of Criminal Behavior

Twelve biological correlates of crime with special relevance to ENA theory (testosterone, mesomorphy, maternal smoking during pregnancy, hypoglycemia, epilepsy, heart rate, skin conductivity, cortisol, serotonin, monoamine oxidase, slow brainwave patterns, and P300 amplitude) are discussed below.

Testosterone. ENA theory predicts that correlations will be found between testosterone and CVB. However, the nature of these correlations will not involve a simple one-to-one correspondence between an individual's crime probability and the amount of testosterone in his/her brain at any given point in time. Earlier, a distinction was made between the organizational and activational effects of testosterone on brain functioning, and that the most permanent and irreversible effects of testosterone occur perinatally. For this reason alone, testosterone levels circulating in the blood stream or in saliva following puberty may have little direct correlation with neurological levels, especially within each

sex. Therefore, one should not expect to find a strong correlation between blood or saliva levels of testosterone among, say, 20-year-old males and the number of offenses they have committed even though testosterone levels in the brain at various stages in development are quite influential on offending probabilities.

Numerous studies have investigated the possible relationship between blood levels or saliva levels of testosterone and involvement in criminal behavior, and most have found modest positive correlations (Maras et al. 2003). Additional evidence of a connection between testosterone and aggressive forms of criminality involves a recent study of domestic violence, where offending males had higher levels of saliva testosterone than did males with no history of such violence (Soler, Vinayak, & Quadagno, 2000).

Overall, it is safe to generalize that circulating testosterone levels exhibit a modest positive association with male offending probabilities, particularly in the case of adult violent offenses. According to ENA theory, males are more violent than females, not because of cultural expectations or sex role training, but mainly because of their brains being exposed to much higher levels of testosterone than the brains of females.

Mesomorphy. Body types exist in three extreme forms. These are sometimes represented with a bulging triangle. Most people are located in the center of the triangle, exhibiting what is termed a basically balanced body type. At one corner of the triangle are persons who are extremely muscular, especially in the upper body, called mesomorphs. Ectomorphs occupy a second corner. Individuals with this body type are unusually slender and non-muscular. In the third corner, one finds endomorphs, individuals who are overweight and have little muscularity.

Studies have consistently revealed that offending probabilities are higher among individuals who exhibit a mesomorphic body type than either of the two other extreme body types (e.g., Blackson & Tarter 1994). ENA theory explains this relationship by noting that testosterone affects more than the brain; it also enhances muscle tissue, especially in the upper part of the body.

Maternal Smoking During Pregnancy. There is considerable evidence that maternal smoking may lead to an elevated probability of offspring becoming delinquent (e.g., Räsänes et al. 1999). ENA theory assumes that fetal exposure to carbon monoxide and other neurotoxins found in cigarette smoke disrupt brain development in ways that adversely affects IQ or executive cognitive functioning, thereby making it more difficult for offspring to maintain their behavior within prescribed legal boundaries. However, it is possible that genes contributing to nicotine addiction may also contribute to criminal behavior. In fact, a recent study reported that the link between childhood conduct disorders (a frequent precursor to later criminality) and maternal smoking was mainly the result of mutual genetic influences (Maughan, Taylor, Caspi, & Moffitt, 2004).

Hypoglycemia. Glucose, a type of natural sugar, is the main fuel used by the brain. The production of glucose is largely regulated by the pancreas in response to chemical messages from a portion of the brain called the hypothalamus. When the hypothalamus senses that glucose levels are becoming too high or too low, it sends chemical instructions to the pancreas to either curtail or increase production of glucose by regulating the amount of insulin released into the blood system. In most people, this feedback regulatory process helps to maintain brain glucose at remarkably stable levels. For a variety of reasons, some people have difficulty stabilizing brain glucose levels. These people are said to be hypoglycemic. Dramatic fluctuations in brain glucose can cause temporary disturbances in thoughts and moods, with the most common symptoms being confusion, difficulty concentrating, and irritability.

Studies have indicated that hypoglycemia is associated with an elevated probability of crime, especially of a violent nature (e.g., Virkkunen, 1986). To explain such a connection, ENA theory draws attention to the importance of maintaining communication between the various parts of the brain in order to control emotionality. In particular, if the frontal lobes receive distorted signals from the limbic system, bizarre types of behavioral responses sometimes result, including responses that are violent and antisocial.

Epilepsy. Epilepsy is a neurological disorder typified by seizures. These seizures are tantamount to "electrical storms" in the brain. While people vary in genetic susceptibilities, seizures are usually induced by environmental factors such as physical injuries to the brain, viral infections, birth trauma, and exposure to various chemicals.

The main behavioral symptoms of epilepsy are known as *convulsions* (or *fits*), although not all epileptics have full-blown convulsive episodes. Mild epileptic episodes may manifest themselves as little more than a momentary pause

in an on-going activity accompanied by a glazed stare. Seizures that have little to no noticeable debilitating effects on coordinated movement are called *subconvulsive* (or *subclinical*) *seizures*. Studies of human populations have shown that epilepsy affects only about one in every 150 to 200 persons. In prison populations, however, the prevalence of epilepsy is around one in 50, at least three times higher than in the general population (e.g., Mendez, Doss, & Taylor, 1993).

ENA theory can explain the links between epilepsy and offending by noting that very basic and primitive emotional responses sometimes emanate from the limbic region of the brain. While seizures in motor control centers are most likely to receive a diagnosis of epilepsy, seizures in the limbic region could provoke very basic survival instincts.

Resting Heart and Pulse Rates. Heart and pulse rates rise in response to strenuous exercise along with stressful and frightening experiences. Studies have shown that on average, the resting heart rate and pulse rate of convicted offenders are lower than those of persons in general (e.g., Mezzacappa et al. 1997:463). ENA theory would account for these relationships by stipulating that both low heart and low pulse rates are physiological indicators of suboptimal arousal. Such arousal levels should incline individuals to seek more intense stimulation and to tolerate unpleasant environmental feedback to a greater extent than individuals with normal or superoptimal arousal under most circumstances.

Skin Conductivity (Galvanic Skin Response). Sweat contains high concentrations of sodium, which is a good electrical conductor. A device called a Galvanic Skin Response (GSR) meter was developed nearly a century ago to monitor palm sweat. The GSR works by measuring electrical impulses passing through our bodies from one electrode to another. Thus, by putting one's fingers on two unconnected electrodes of a GSR device, one completes an electrical circuit through which imperceptible amounts of electricity flows. Temperature obviously affects how much people sweat, but so too do emotions. The more intense one's emotions become (especially those of fear and anger), the more one will sweat, and thus the stronger will be the readings on the GSR meter.

Numerous studies have examined the possibility that persons with the greatest propensities toward criminal behavior have distinctive skin conductivity patterns. These studies suggest that offenders exhibit lower skin conductivity under standard testing conditions than do people in general (e.g., Buikhuisen, Eurelings-Bontekoe, & Host, 1989; Raine,

Venables, & Williams, 1996). As in the case of heart and pulse rates, ENA theory can account for such findings by hypothesizing that low GSR readings, especially under stressful testing conditions, are another indication of suboptimal arousal.

Cortisol. So-called stress hormones are secreted mainly by the adrenal glands during times of anxiety, stress, and fear. The stress hormone that has been investigated most in connection with criminality is cortisol. Most of these studies have suggested that offenders have below normal levels (e.g., Lindman, Aromaki, & Eriksson, 1997). As with heart rates and skin conductivity, one could anticipate a low cortisol–high criminality relationship by assuming that low cortisol production even in the face of stress is another indicator of suboptimal arousal. This would suggest that offenders are less intimidated by threatening aspects of their environments than are persons in general.

Serotonin. Serotonin is an important neurotransmitter. When serotonin is relatively active in the synaptic regions connecting adjacent nerve cells, people typically report feeling a sense of contentment and calm. Several drugs that have been designed to treat depression and anxiety disorders operate by either prolonging the presence of serotonin in the synaptic gaps between neurons or by facilitating the ability of receptor sites on the dendrites to bond to the serotonin that is available. Low serotonin activity has been linked to crime by numerous studies, especially impulsive crimes (e.g., Virkkunen, Eggert, Rawlings, & Linnoila, 1996; Matykiewicz, La Grange, Vance, Wang, & Reyes, 1997). Explaining the link between serotonin and criminality from the perspective of ENA theory draws attention to serotonin pathways connecting the brain's prefrontal areas with the emotion-control centers in the limbic system. Serotonin may facilitate the sort of executive cognitive functioning required to restrain impulsive behavior, especially regarding rage and persistent frustration.

Monoamine Oxidase. Monoamine oxidase (MAO) is an enzyme found throughout the body. Within the brain, MAO helps to break down and clear away neurotransmitter molecules (including serotonin), portions of which often linger in the synaptic gap after activating adjacent nerve cells. Studies indicate that MAO activity is unusually low among offenders (e.g., Alm et al. 1996; Klinteberg, 1996). ENA draws attention to the fact that low MAO activity seems to be related to high levels of testosterone. Furthermore, low MAO brain activity may interfere with the brain's ability to manufacture or utilize serotonin.

Brain Waves and Low P300 Amplitude. Brain waves are measured using electrodes placed on the scalp. These electrodes can detect electrical activity occurring close to the surface of the brain fairly clearly. Despite their complexity, brain waves can be roughly classified in terms of ranging from being rapid and regular (alpha brain waves) to being slow and irregular (delta brain waves). Most studies based on electroencephalographic (EEG) readings have found that offenders have slower brain waves than do persons in general (e.g., Petersen, Matousek, Mednick, Volovka, & Pollock, 1982).

Unlike traditional brain wave measurement, modern computerized brain wave detection is able to average responses to dozens of identical stimuli presented to subjects at random intervals. This reveals a distinctive brain wave pattern or "signature" for each individual. Nearly everyone exhibits a noticeable spike in electrical voltage, interrupted by a "dip" approximately one-third of a second following presentation of test stimuli. This is called the P300 amplitude of an event-related evoked potential. From a cognitive standpoint, the P300 amplitude is thought to reflect neurological events central to attention and memory.

While research has been equivocal thus far in the case of criminality, several studies have found a greater dip in P300 responses by individuals diagnosed with antisocial personality disorder than is true for general populations (see Costa et al. 2000). ENA theory can account for slower EEG patterns among offenders and a P300 decrement among persons with antisocial behavior by again focusing on suboptimal arousal. From a neurological standpoint, both slow brain waves and a tendency toward a greater than normal P300 decrement can be considered symptomatic of suboptimal arousal. If ENA theory is correct, both of these conditions will be found associated with elevated brain exposure to testosterone.

Summary and Conclusions

Unlike social environmental theories, the evolutionary neuroandrogenic (ENA) theory can account for statistical associations between biological variables and criminal behavior. Furthermore, ENA theory predicts the universal concentration of offending among males between the ages of 13 and 30, patterns that strictly environmental theories have always had difficulty explaining. As its name implies, ENA theory rests on two over-arching assumptions. The first assumption is an extension of Darwin's theory of evolution by natural selection. It maintains that males on average exhibit CVB more than females because females who prefer to mate with such males increase their chances of having mates who are competent provisioners of resources. These female biases have evolved because females who have had the assistance of competent provisioners have left more offspring in subsequent generations than other females. No comparable reproductive advantage comes to males who select mates based on resource procurement capabilities.

Some forms of CVB are crude in the sense of requiring little learning, nearly all of which are either assaultive or confiscatory in nature. Other forms are sophisticated in the sense that they require complex learning and involve much more subtle types of "victimization." A major expression of sophisticated competitive/victimizing behavior involves profitable business ventures and/or the management of large organizations. In most societies, these expressions are tolerated and even encouraged. However, the vast majority of people in all societies condemn the crudest expressions of CVB, and, in all literate societies, the criminal justice system has evolved to punish such behavior.

The theory's second assumption is that genes on the Y-chromosome have evolved which cause male brains to exhibit higher rates of competitive/victimizing behavior than female brains. These genes operate in part by causing would-be ovaries to develop instead into testes early in fetal development. Once differentiated, the testes produce testosterone and other sex hormones, which have three hypothesized effects upon brain functioning, all of which promote CVB. The three effects are termed *suboptimal arousal, seizuring proneness,* and *a rightward shift in neocortical functioning.* Furthermore, two neurological processes are hypothesized to help individuals shift from crude to sophisticated forms of competitive/victimizing behavior. These are learning ability (or intelligence) and executive cognitive functioning (or planning ability). The better one's learning ability or executive functioning, the quicker he/she will transition from crude to sophisticated forms of the behavior.

References

Alm, P. O., af Klinteberg, B., Humble, K., Leppert, J., Sorensen, S., Thorell, L. H., et al. (1996). Psychopathy, platelet MAO activity and criminality among former juvenile delinquents. *Acta Psychiatrica Scandinavica, 94,* 105–111.

Blackson, T. C., & Tarter, R. E. (1994). Individual, family, and peer affiliation factors predisposing to early-age onset of alcohol and drug use. *Alcoholism: Clinical and Experimental Research, 18,* 813–821.

Buikhuisen, W., Eurelings-Bontekoe, E. H. M., & Host, K. B. (1989). Crime and recovery time: Mednick revisited. *International Journal of Law and Psychiatry, 12,* 29–40.

Costa, L., Bauer, L., Kuperman, S., Porjesz, B., O'Connor, S., & Hesselbrock, V. M. (2000). Frontal P300 decrements, alcohol dependence, and antisocial personality disorder. *Biological Psychiatry, 47,* 1064–1071.

Ellis, L. (2001). The biosocial female choice theory of social stratification. *Social Biology, 48,* 297–319.

Klinteberg, A. (1996). Biology, norms, and personality: A developmental perspective: Psychobiology of sensation seeking. *Neuropsychobiology, 34*(3), 146–154.

Lindman, R. E., Aromaki, A. S., & Eriksson, C. J. P. (1997). Sober-state cortisol as a predictor of drunken violence. *Alcohol and Alcoholism, 32,* 621–626.

Maras, A., Laucht, M., Gerdes, D., Wilhelm, C., Lewicka, S., Haack, D., et al. (2003). Association of testosterone and dihydrotestosterone with externalizing behavior in adolescent boys and girls. *Psychoneuroendocrinology, 28,* 932–940.

Matykiewicz, L., La Grange, L., Vance, P., Wang, M., & Reyes, E. (1997). Adjudicated adolescent males: Measures of urinary 5-hydroxyindoleacetic acid and reactive hypoglycemia. *Personality and Individual Differences, 22,* 327–332.

Maughan, B., Taylor, A., Caspi, A., & Moffitt, T. E. (2004). Prenatal smoking and early childhood conduct problems: Testing genetic and environmental explanations of the association. *Archives of General Psychiatry, 61,* 836.

Mendez, M. F., Doss, R. C., & Taylor, J. (1993). Interictal violence in epilepsy: Relationship to behavior and seizure variables. *The Journal of Nervous and Mental Disease, 181,* 566–569.

Mezzacappa, E., Tremblay, R. E., Kindlon, D., Saul, J. P., Arseneault, L., Seguin, J., et al. (1997). Anxiety, antisocial behavior, and heart rate regulation in adolescent males. *Journal of Psychiatry, 38,* 457–469.

Petersen, K. G. I., Matousek, M., Mednick, S. A., Volovka, J., & Pollock, V. (1982). EEG antecedents of thievery. *Acta Psychiatrica Scandinavica, 65,* 331–338.

Raine, A., Venables, P. H., & Williams, M. (1996). Better autonomic conditioning and faster electrodermal half-recovery time at age 15 years as possible protective factors against crime at age 29 years. *Developmental Psychology, 32,* 624–630.

Rasanes, P., Hakko, H., Isohanni, M., Hodgins, S., Jarvelin, M.-R., & Tiihonen, J. (1999). Maternal smoking during pregnancy and risk of criminal behavior among adult male offspring in the Northern Finland 1966 birth cohort. *American Journal of Psychiatry, 156,* 857–862.

Soler, H., Vinayak, P., & Quadagno, D. (2000). Biosocial aspects of domestic violence. *Psychoneuroendocrinology, 25,* 721–739.

Virkkunen, M. (1986). Reactive hypoglycemic tendency among habitually violent offenders. *Nutrition Reviews, 44*(Supplement), 94–103.

Virkkunen, M., Eggert, M., Rawlings, R., & Linnoila, M. (1996). A prospective follow-up study of alcoholic violent offenders and fire setters. *Archives of General Psychiatry, 53,* 523–529.

REVIEW QUESTIONS

1. What does Ellis call the theoretical model he presents in this piece? Explain why this name is appropriate, given the primary propositions of the theory?

2. Of the 12 biological correlates of crime that Ellis reviews, which three do you feel are the most important or valid? Which three do you feel are least important/valid?

3. What three effects on brain functioning are predicted by Ellis's theory? Do you agree with all three? Which do you think is most important or valid in predicting most criminal behavior?

❖

READING 11

Jana Bufkin and Vickie Luttrell are two of the leading researchers in the area of brain function in criminal behavior. In this selection, they reveal their findings regarding the significant differences they have observed in their neuro-imaging studies of violent criminals. It will be clear that there are notable differences in the 3-pound organ that is the brain that distinguish most violent offenders from normal people (and even nonviolent offenders). While reading this selection, keep in mind that many things can go wrong in the functioning of the brain and that criminologists must be aware of these problems if they wish to understand why some individuals engage in criminal behavior.

Neuroimaging Studies of Aggressive and Violent Behavior

Current Findings and Implications for Criminology and Criminal Justice

Jana L. Bufkin and Vickie R. Luttrell

Aggressive and/or violent behaviors persist as significant social problems. In response, a substantial amount of research has been conducted to determine the roots of such behavior. Case studies of patients with neurological disorders or those who have suffered traumatic brain injury provide provocative insights into which brain regions, when damaged, might predispose to irresponsible, violent behavior. Psychophysiological and neuropsychological assessments have also demonstrated that violent offenders have lower brain functioning than controls, including lower verbal ability and diminished executive functioning. However, until recently it has been impossible to determine which brain areas in particular may be dysfunctional in violent individuals. With the availability of new functional and structural neuroimaging techniques, such as single-photon emission computed tomography (SPECT),

SOURCE: Jana L. Bufkin and Vickie R. Luttrell, "Neuroimaging Studies of Aggressive and Violent Behavior," *Trauma, Violence, and Abuse* 6, no. 2 (2005): 176–91. Copyright © 2005 Sage Publications, Inc. Used by permission of Sage Publications, Inc.

positron emission tomography (PET), magnetic resonance imaging (MRI), and functional MRI (fMRI), it is now possible to examine regional brain dysfunction with a higher sensitivity and accuracy than was possible with previous techniques. This newfound ability to view the brain "in action" has broadened our understanding of the neural circuitry that underlies emotional regulation and affiliated behaviors. In particular, evidence suggests that individuals who are vulnerable to faulty regulation of negative emotion may be at increased risk for aggressive and/or violent behavior.

In this review, we evaluate the proposed link between faulty emotion regulation and aggressive or violent behavior. We define *aggression* as any threatening or physically assaultive behavior directed at persons or the environment. *Violence* refers to behaviors that inflict physical harm in violation of social norms. Specifically, we (a) discuss briefly the neurobiology of emotion regulation and how disruptions in the neural circuitry underlying emotion regulation might predispose to impulsive aggression and violence; (b) summarize the results of modern neuroimaging studies that have directly assessed brain functioning and/or structure in aggressive, violent, and/or antisocial samples and evaluate the consistency of these findings in the context of negative emotion regulation; and (c) discuss theoretical and practical implications for criminology and criminal justice.

Emotion Regulation and Theoretical Links to Impulsive Aggression and Violence

Emotion is regulated by a complex neural circuit that involves several cortical areas, including the prefrontal cortex, the anterior cingulate cortex (ACC), the posterior right hemisphere, and the insular cortex, as well as several subcortical structures, such as the amygdala, hippocampus, and thalamus. These cortical and subcortical areas are intricately and extensively interconnected. In this article, we focus on three key elements of this neural circuitry: the prefrontal cortex, the ACC, and the amygdala.

The prefrontal cortex is a histologically heterogeneous region of the brain and has several (somewhat) functionally distinct sectors, including the ventromedial cortex and the orbitofrontal cortex (OFC). Damage to the

ventromedial cortex and its behavioral affiliations have been assessed in case studies of individuals who experienced traumatic brain injury, either during childhood or adulthood, and in large, systematic studies on cohorts of war veterans with head injury.

Studies have found that patients with early-onset ventromedial lesions experience an insensitivity to future consequences, an inability to modify so-called risky behaviors even when more advantageous options are presented, and defective autonomic responses to punishment contingencies. Studies have also demonstrated that patients with adult-onset ventromedial damage show defects in real-life decision making, are oblivious to the future consequences of their actions, seem to be guided by immediate prospects only, and fail to respond autonomically to anticipated negative future outcomes.

The OFC, also a part of the prefrontal circuit, receives highly processed sensory information concerning a person's environmental experiences. The OFC is hypothesized to play a role in mediating behavior based on social context and appears to play a role in the perception of social signals, in particular, facial expressions of anger. Blair, Morris, Frith, Perrett, and Dolan,(1999), using PET scans, assessed 13 male volunteers as they viewed static images of human faces expressing varying degrees of anger. They found that increasing the intensity of angry facial expressions was associated with enhanced activity in participants' OFC and the ACC. Dougherty et al. (1999) used functional neuroimaging and symptom provocation techniques to study the neurobiology of induced anger states and found that imaginal anger was associated with enhanced activation of the left OFC, right ACC (affective division), and bilateral anterior temporal regions. Also, using imaginal scenarios, Pietrini, Guazzelli, Basso, Jaffe, & Grafman, (2000) found that functional deactivation of OFC areas was strongest when participants were instructed to express unrestrained aggression toward assailants rather than when they tried to inhibit this imaginal aggression. Taken together, these lines of evidence support the suggestion that heightened activity in the left OFC may prevent a behavioral response to induced anger.

Based on these findings, and consistent with fearlessness theories of human aggression, a logical prediction is that OFC and ACC activity in response to provocation may be attenuated in certain individuals, predisposing them to aggression and violence. Consistent with this prediction, patients with OFC damage tend to exhibit poor impulse control, aggressive outbursts, verbal lewdness, and a lack of interpersonal sensitivity, which may increase the probability of sporadic so-called crimes of passion and encounters with the legal system. In contrast, evidence suggests that the ACC plays a role in processing the affective aspects of painful stimuli, such as the perceived unpleasantness that accompanies actual or potential tissue damage.

In addition to the prefrontal cortex and the ACC, another hypothesized neural component of emotion regulation is the amygdala, a subcortical structure, which is located on the medial margin of the temporal lobes. Similar to the OFC, the amygdala appears to play a role in extracting emotional content from environmental stimuli and may also play a role in individuals' ability to regulate negative emotion. However, neuroimaging studies have found that the amygdala is activated in response to cues that connote threat, such as facial expressions of fear (instead of anger), and that increasing the intensity of fearful facial expressions is associated with an increased activation of the left amygdala.

Davidson, Putnam, et al. (2000) suggested that individuals can typically regulate their negative affect and can also profit from restraint-producing cues in their environment, such as others' facial expressions of fear or anger. Information about behaviors that connote threat (e.g., hostile stares, threatening words, or lunging postures) is conveyed to the amygdala, which then projects to other limbic structures, and it is there that information about social context derived from OFC projections is integrated with one's current perceptions. The OFC, through its connections with other prefrontal sectors and with the amygdala, plays an important role in inhibiting impulsive outbursts because prefrontal activations that occur during anger arousal constrain the impulsive expression of emotional behavior.

Davidson, Putnam, and Larson, (2000) also proposed that dysfunctions in one or more of these regions and/or in the interconnections among them may be associated with faulty regulation of negative emotion and an increased propensity for impulsive aggression and violence. First, people with prefrontal and/or amygdalar dysfunction might misinterpret environmental cues, such as the facial expressions of others, and react impulsively, as a preemptive strike, to a misperceived threat. The perception of whether a stimulus is threatening is decisive in the cognitive processing leading to the aggressive behavior. Evidence suggests that individuals vary considerably in their ability to suppress negative

emotion. Therefore, individuals with decreased prefrontal activity may have greater difficulty suppressing negative emotions than those individuals who have greater prefrontal activation. Finally, although prefrontal activity helps one to suppress negative emotion, this negative emotion is generated by subcortical structures, including the amygdala. Therefore, an individual may be more prone to violence in general, and impulsive violence, in particular, if prefrontal functioning is diminished in relation to subcortical activity.

Research on individuals who have suffered traumatic head injury is of key importance in understanding the neural substrates of aggressive and/or violent behavior; however, Brower and Price (2001) noted many limitations of head injury studies, such as inadequate controls for known risk factors, including prior history of aggressive or violent behavior, socioeconomic status, stability of employment, and substance abuse. Research of behavior following head injury is also one step removed from the question of whether aggressive and/or violent individuals (who may have no history of head trauma) have neurological dysfunction localized to specific areas in the brain.

Studies of aggressive, violent, and/or antisocial offenders using functional (SPECT and PET) and structural (MRI) neuroimaging are beginning to reveal abnormalities in these groups (Raine, Lencz, Bihrle, LaCasse, & Colletti, 2000). Specifically, 17 neuroimaging studies have been conducted on samples derived from forensic settings, prisons, psychiatric hospitals, and on violent offenders who are noninstitutionalized. Our review of these works reveals four consistent patterns:

(a) prefrontal dysfunction is associated with aggressive and/or violent behavioral histories;

(b) temporal lobe dysfunction, particularly left-sided medial-temporal (subcortical) activity, is associated with aggression and/or violence;

(c) the relative balance of activity between the prefrontal cortex and the subcortical structures is associated with impulsive aggression and/or violence; and

(d) the neural circuitry underlying the regulation of emotion and its affiliated behaviors is complex. Each of these patterns is described in theoretical context below.

Prefrontal Dysfunction Is Associated With Aggressive and/or Violent Behavioral Histories

Of the 17 studies reviewed, 14 specifically examined possible links between frontal lobe pathology and aggressive and/or violent behavior. In the 10 SPECT and PET studies, 100% reported deficits in either prefrontal (8 of 10 studies) or frontal (2 of 10 studies) functioning in aggressive, violent, and/or antisocial groups compared to nonaggressive patients or healthy controls. Analyses of specific regions in the medial prefrontal cortex revealed that individuals who were aggressive and/or violent had significantly lower prefrontal activity in the OFC (4 of 10 studies), anterior medial cortex (5 of 10 studies), medial frontal cortex (2 of 10 studies), and/ or superior frontal cortex (1 of 10 studies). In the four MRI studies, 50% (2 of 4 studies) reported decreased gray matter volume in prefrontal or frontal regions, and 25% (1 of 4 studies) reported nonspecific white matter abnormalities, not localized to the frontal cortex.

The consistency with which prefrontal disruption occurs across studies, each of which investigated participants with different types of violent behaviors, suggests that prefrontal dysfunction may underlie a predisposition to violence. Evidence is strongest for an association between prefrontal dysfunction and an impulsive subtype of aggressive behavior. Empirical findings concerning the regulation of negative emotion suggest that prefrontal sectors, such as the OFC, appear to play a role in the interpretation of environmental stimuli and the potential for danger. Consequently, disruptions in prefrontal functioning may lead individuals who are impulsive and aggressive to misinterpret situations as threatening and potentially dangerous, which in turn increases the probability of violent behavior against a perceived threat.

Nevertheless, four caveats are noteworthy. First, although prefrontal disruption was consistently related to aggressive and/or violent behavior, this association may reflect a predisposition only, requiring other environmental, psychological, and social factors to enhance or diminish this biological risk. Second, prefrontal dysfunction has also been documented in a wide variety of psychiatric and neurological disorders not associated with violence, and it

may be argued that frontal hypometabolism is a general, nonspecific finding associated with a broad range of conditions. However, Drevets and Raichle (1995) reported that although frontal deficits have been observed in conditions such as major depression, schizophrenia, and obsessive-compulsive disorder, the neurological profile for individuals who are aggressive and/or violent is different from these other groups. For example, while murderers exhibit widespread bilateral prefrontal dysfunction, individuals with depression tend to have disruptions localized in the left hemisphere only and to the left dorsolateral prefrontal cortex, in particular. (See Raine, Buchsbaum, & LaCasse, 1997, for a discussion of alterations in brain functioning across a variety of psychiatric conditions.)

Of the 10 SPECT and PET studies reviewed, 70% reported temporal lobe dysfunction in aggressive and/or violent groups, with reductions in left temporal lobe activity in 6 of 7 studies. Examination of the medial-temporal lobe, which includes subcortical structures such as the amygdala, hippocampus, and basal ganglia, revealed that subcortical disruptions also characterized individuals who were aggressive and/or violent (4 of 7 studies). In the six MRI studies that examined the possibility of temporal lobe abnormalities, 100% (6 of 6 studies) reported temporal irregularities, including asymmetrical gyral patterns in the temporal-parietal region, decreases in anterior-inferior temporal lobe volume (including the amygdala-hippocampal region or adjacent areas), increases in left temporal lobe volume, or pathologies specific to the amygdala.

It is important to note that excessive right subcortical activity or abnormal temporal lobe structure was most common in patients with a history of intense violent behavior, such as that seen in those with intermittent explosive disorder rather than in patients who had aggressive personality types or who had high scores on an aggression scale. In humans, right-hemisphere activation has been suggested to play a role in the generation of negative affect. Therefore, increased subcortical activity in the right hemisphere could lead an individual to experience negative affect that promotes aggressive feelings and acts as a general predisposition to aggression and violence. These findings are generally consistent with current conceptions of emotion regulation and its purported relationship to impulsive violence, in particular.

The Relative Balance of Activity Between the Prefrontal Cortex and the Subcortical Structures Is Associated With Impulsive Aggression and/or Violence

Previous research has suggested that individuals may be predisposed to impulsive violence if prefrontal functioning is diminished relative to subcortical activity. Raine, Meloy, et al. (1998) found that reduced prefrontal functioning relative to subcortical functioning was characteristic of those who commit impulsive acts of aggression and/or violence. By contrast, aggression and/or violence of a predatory nature was not related to reduced prefrontal and/ or subcortical ratios. They also suggest that although most biological studies of aggression and/or violence have not distinguished between impulsive and premeditated aggression, this distinction is likely relevant to understanding the neuroanatomical and functional underpinnings of these behaviors.

An additional line of evidence that lends support to the impulsive and/or predatory distinction comes from investigations regarding the mechanism underlying the suppression of negative emotion. The neurochemical link mediating prefrontal and/or subcortical interactions is purportedly an inhibitory serotonergic connection from the prefrontal cortex to the amygdala. The prefrontal cortex is a region with a high density of serotonin receptors, which sends efferents to the brainstem where most of the brain's serotonin-producing neurons originate. The prefrontal cortex, amygdala, and hippocampus also receive serotonergic innervation. Therefore, it is logical that dysfunction in the prefrontal and/or subcortical regions disrupts serotonergic activity in the brain. Consistent with this hypothesis, the serotonergic system has been shown to be dysfunctional in victims of violent suicide attempts, impulsive violent offenders, impulsive arsonists, violent offender and arson recidivists, children and adolescents with disruptive behavior disorders, and "acting out" hostility in normal volunteers. In all those studies, low serotonin levels were strongly related to the maladaptive behaviors noted.

 ## Implications for Criminology and Criminal Justice

Historically, paradigms guiding criminological programs of study have tended to bypass complex webs of interconnections that produce and reproduce criminality, favoring instead an emphasis on one dimension or level of analysis. The trend has been to maintain a specialized focus, often within the confines of a sociological or a legalistic model. Attempts to expand the image of crime through theory integration, which have surfaced quite frequently since the mid-1970s, shift attention to different realities of crime. The general emphasis, however, has been on the integration of ideas within and/or across the two dominant paradigms rather than on a broader, interdisciplinary strategy.

Resistance to interdisciplinarity or disciplinary cross-fertilization has not been inconsequential. Failure to incorporate interdisciplinary insights has stifled exploration of the intersections among structure, culture, and the body, leaving a knowledge void where provocative social facts "merely hang in space as interesting curiosities" (Pallone & Hennessy, 2000, chap. 22, p. 11), and critical questions go unanswered. More specifically, lack of an imagination of how nurture and nature interact to affect behavior, or what may be understood as biography in historical context, has resulted in an incapacity to either deal with variability or deal with it well. Some male individuals socialized in a patriarchal society rape and some adolescents from poor, urban, single-families chronically offend; however, most do not. In other words, there is individual variation within social contexts, and those differences may be better understood if criminologists begin to consider all pertinent angles or dimensions.

Although the studies in our review may appear to be firmly planted in the tradition of specialization and unidimensional thinking, they should be interpreted within the framework of Barak's (1998) interdisciplinary criminology, where knowledges relevant to a behavioral outcome are treated as complements in an image expansion project. Understanding that each perspective offers a reality of behavior from a different, though interrelated angle, the objective is to develop a logical network of theories that will capture the most dimensions and provide the most accurate information about phenomena of interest. In this vein, our appraisal of knowledge from the field of neuroscience intends to elucidate the image of aggression and/or violence without supplanting other perspectives and paradigms. Our desire is not to reduce aggression and/or violence to brain functioning but to inform of advances in neurological analyses of emotion regulation and their importance to studies of that behavior.

It should be noted that the more comprehensive, inter-disciplinary paradigm has been embraced by some crimi-nologists linked to the biological sciences. In the 17 studies reviewed, researchers attempted to examine (or at least statistically controlled for) a variety of biological, psycholog-ical, and social correlates of aggressive and/or violent behav-ior and, in some cases, analyzed biopsychosocial interac-tions affecting behavior. Across studies, biological variables included history of head injury, substance use/abuse/depen-dence, diseases of the nervous system, left-handedness, body weight, height, head circumference, and sex. Psycho-logical variables included the presence of psychological dis-orders (such as schizophrenia), indices of intellectual func-tioning (such as IQ scores), and performance-related moti-vational differences. Social variables included indices of psychosocial deprivation (such as physical and/or sexual abuse, extreme poverty, neglect, foster home placement, being raised in an institution, parental criminality, parental physical fights, severe family conflict, early parental divorce), family size, and ethnicity.

The benefits of integrating ideas or investigating an image from several angles in a research design is demon-strated in the neuroimaging studies provided. Raine, Lencz, et al. (2000), for example, found that prefrontal and autonomic deficits contributed substantially to the prediction of group membership (antisocial personality disorder vs. control group) over and above 10 demo-graphic and psychosocial measures. The 10 demographic and psychosocial variables accounted for 41.3% of the variance. After the addition of three biological variables into the regression equation (prefrontal gray matter, heart rate, and skin conductance), amount of variance explained increased significantly to 76.7%, and the prediction of group membership increased from 73% to 88.5% classi-fied correctly. These findings suggest that a more contex-tualized theoretical grasp of aggression and/or violence is possible when this behavior is conceptualized as multi-di-mensional. When nature–nurture dichotomies are coun-tered by interdisciplinary image expansion, clues about individual variability emerge, and criminologists come closer to understanding the complexity of aggression and/ or violence.

The compelling evidence about this behavior revealed in the reviewed neuroimaging studies is valuable, then, not because it allows for completely reliable predictions of behavioral outcomes, but because it makes the image of aggression and/or violence a little less murky. Moreover,

when merged with existing knowledges, particularly ideas about social structures and social psychology (sociological model) and rational choice (legalistic model), such find-ings may spawn new visions of justice centered on preven-tion and treatment. Within an interdisciplinary frame-work that values neuroscience, virtually every essential sociological factor elaborated by criminologists, structural and processual, acquires a greater potential to explain aggression and/or violence and influence policy making. According to the works in our review, as well as other research in this area, all forms of child abuse and neglect, direct exposure to violence (including media violence), an unstable family life, poor parenting, lack of prenatal and perinatal services, individual drug use, maternal drug use during pregnancy, poor educational and employment structures, poverty, and even exposure to racism play a vital role in the production of aggression and/or violence. Thus, the inclusion of insights from neuroscience further legitimizes prevention strategies touted by advocates of the sociological paradigm, from social disorganization theory to self-control theory.

When aggression and/or violence is not prevented, the criminal justice system is granted responsibility for social control. . . . Drawing from empirical findings across disci-plines and levels of analysis, a vision of therapeutic justice encourages the development of holistic treatment regi-mens that hold offenders to "scientifically rational and legally appropriate degree[s] of accountability" (Nygaard, 2000, chap. 23, p. 12). The potential for this approach to replace the utilitarian model lies in its continued ability to unveil the often-perplexing ways in which choice is struc-tured. This facilitates an awareness that the legally appro-priate and the scientifically rational are in unity. Human creativity is not ignored in this paradigm; however, the clearer image it provides points to an amalgam of limita-tions. When an individual is brought into the criminal justice system, an inter-disciplinarian seeks to examine those restrictions on behavior and to tailor treatments accordingly.

With varying levels of success, criminologists have sought to qualify choice and diminish the impact of legal-istic factors on conceptions of justice since the advent of positivism in the 19th century. Assessments of measures associated with social psychology, psychology, and psychi-atry, along with input implicating structural concerns, such as unemployment, have been utilized, and a plethora of interventions have evolved. Thus, cracks in the utilitarian mold of justice have accrued, laying the foundation for interdisciplinarity in thought and in treatment. Applied to aggression and/or violence, this translates into the implementation of treatment plans with multidimensional components, to include neurological techniques that address how brain dysfunction affects choice. Although not the sole neurological strategy, the intervention most consistently promoted is drug therapy. Several types of drugs, such as anti-convulsants, psychostimulants, and serotonergic agents, have been successful in reducing aggressive behavior. Inter-disciplinary thinkers should not be hesitant to consider using these pharmacological remedies when bio-psychosocial indicators overwhelmingly suggest that an individual is at risk to violently recidivate, for it is a step in the direction of therapeutic justice.

Other than paradigmatic preferences disallowing an interdisciplinary consideration of aggressive and/or violent crimes and lack of funding, the largest obstacle in attaining therapeutic justice is the inability to predict future behavior. When informed by neuroscience, classification and prediction instruments are fine-tuned. To illustrate, Robinson and Kelley (2000) discovered that, among probationers, indicators of brain dysfunction correlated with repeat violent offending, as opposed to repeat nonviolent offending and first-time offending. Birth complications, family abuse, head injury, parental drug use, abnormal interpersonal characteristics, and offender substance abuse were found to be risk factors for recidivism within this group. Given that it is estimated that less comprehensive prediction models reap false positives in approximately two thirds of all cases, added precision is welcome.

Still, prediction is not foolproof. Shortcomings in this area lead some to conclude that drug therapy and other invasive strategies are unwarranted. Before throwing in the towel, it should be acknowledged that pharmacological remedies already abound in the criminal justice system, along with many other intrusions. Knowledge from neuroscience merely allows for the targeted distribution of services to appropriate populations, a fruitful strategy given the scarcity of resources at the system's disposal. Prevention strategies directed at alleviating environmental conditions that increase the probability for aggression and/or violence are optimal; however, criminologists should not dismiss neuroscientific individual-level interventions in cases where patterns of aggressive and/or violent criminality are detected.

Converging lines of evidence suggest that those patterns are produced by a unique combination of external and internal risk factors, each of which is integral to the construction of treatment regimens intended to effect therapeutic justice.

Blind spots in the image of aggression and/or violence should not deter interventions where they hold promise for enhancing quality of life. It is unfair and unjust to those processed in the criminal justice system and to society at large for criminologists to ignore this evidence and the control strategies proposed.

 ## Conclusion

Functional and morphometric neuroimaging has enhanced our understanding of the distributed neural networks that subserve complex emotional behaviors. Research emanating from affective, behavioral, and clinical neuroscience paradigms is converging on the conclusion that there is a significant neurological basis of aggressive and/or violent behavior over and above contributions from the psychosocial environment. In particular, and consistent with modern theories of emotion regulation, reduced prefrontal and/or subcortical ratios may predispose to impulsive aggression and/or violence. Further progress in the study of these behaviors will require a forensically informed, interdisciplinary approach that integrates neuropsychological and psychophysiological methods for the study of the brain, emotional processing, and behavior.

As this line of interdisciplinary research unfolds, it is vital that criminology and criminal justice begin to incorporate what is known about human behavior into their explanatory models, as well as classrooms. Evidence suggests that brain structure and brain functioning do affect behavior, particularly aggressive and/or violent behavior. It is also the case that neuroscience offers means for curbing aggression and/or violence. Traditional criminology and criminal justice paradigms tend to sidestep these issues because of aversions to less dominant knowledges, especially biological programs of study. Biological insights are often dubbed Lombrosian, suggesting that some behavioral scientists retain notions of a born criminal easily identifiable using some magic test. Continued aversion to anything biological on these grounds is anachronistic and will hamper the development of theory and policy.

The problem is that neurobiological discovery has carried on with little to no input from criminology and criminal justice, and there is every reason to believe that the research will progress. There is also reason to believe that the functioning of the criminal justice system will be affected by the findings produced. The general public is already being widely exposed to such advances through numerous television news clips and articles appearing in newspapers and weekly periodicals. If criminology and criminal justice want to be relevant in more than a historical sense when it comes to theorizing about aggressive and/or violent behavior and formulating policies accordingly, it is imperative that the field embrace the interdisciplinary model.

Implications for Practice, Policy, and Research

Practice

Bridging the gap between nature and nurture, a biopsychosocial model for understanding aggression enhances the explanatory capacity of sociologically based criminological theories by accounting for individual variability within social contexts.

Insights derived from a biopsychosocial model offer the most promise in the realm of crime prevention, which entails devising holistic treatment strategies for those exposed to numerous risk factors.

Policy

The accuracy of risk classification devices, used extensively throughout the criminal justice process, may be enhanced by incorporating what is known about negative emotion regulation.

Research

Research reveals that other cortical and subcortical structures likely play a role in emotion regulation through their inextricable link to the prefrontal and medial-temporal regions. The complexity of this neural circuitry must be explored with greater precision.

References

Barak, G. (1998). *Integrating criminologies*. Needham Heights, MA: Allyn & Bacon.

Blair, R. J. R., Morris, J. S., Frith, C. D., Perrett, D. I., & Dolan, R. J. (1999). Dissociable neural responses to facial expressions of sadness and anger. *Brain, 122*, 883–893.

Brower, M. C., & Price, B. H. (2001). Neuropsychiatry of frontal lobe dysfunction in violent and criminal behavior: A critical review. *Journal of Neurology, Neurosurgery, and Psychiatry, 71*, 720–726.

Davidson, R. J., Putnam, K. M., & Larson, C. L. (2000). Dysfunction in the neural circuitry of emotion regulation: A possible prelude to violence. *Science, 289*(5479), 591–594.

Dougherty, D. D., Shin, L. M., Alpert, N. M., Pitman, R. K., Orr, S. P., Lasko, M., et al. (1999). Anger in healthy men: A PET study using script-driven imagery. *Biological Psychiatry, 46*, 466–472.

Drevets, W. C., & Raichle, M. E. (1995). Positron emission tomographic imaging studies of human emotional disorders. In M. S. Gazzaniga (Ed.), *The cognitive neurosciences* (pp. 1153–1164). Cambridge, MA: MIT Press.

Nygaard, R. L. (2000). The dawn of therapeutic justice. In D. H. Fishbein (Ed.), *The science, treatment, and prevention of antisocial behaviors: Application to the criminal justice system* (chap. 23, pp. 1–18). Kingston, NJ: Civic Research Institute.

Pallone, N. J., & Hennessy, J. J. (2000). Indifferent communication between social science and neuroscience: The case of "biological brain-proneness' for criminal aggression. In D. H. Fishbein (Ed.), *The science, treatment, and prevention of antisocial behaviors: Application to the criminal justice system* (chap. 22, pp. 1–13). Kingston, NJ: Civic Research Institute.

Pietrini, P., Guazzelli, M., Basso, G., Jaffe, K., & Grafman, J. (2000). Neural correlates of imaginal aggressive behavior assessed by positron emission tomography in healthy subjects. *American Journal of Psychiatry, 157*(11), 1772–1781.

Raine, A., Buchsbaum, M., & LaCasse, L. (1997). Brain abnormalities in murderers indicated by positron emission tomography. *Biological Psychiatry, 42*, 495–508.

Raine, A., Lencz, T., Bihrle, S., LaCasse, L., & Colletti, P. (2000). Reduced prefrontal gray matter volume and reduced autonomic activity in antisocial personality disorder. *Archives of General Psychiatry, 57*, 119–127.

Raine, A., Meloy, J. R., Bihrle, S., Stoddard, J., LaCasse, L., & Buchsbaum, M. S. (1998). Reduced prefrontal and increased subcortical brain functioning assessed using positron emission tomography in predatory and affective murderers. *Behavioral Sciences and the Law, 16*, 319–332.

Robinson, M., & Kelley, T. (2000). The identification of neurological correlates of brain dysfunction in offenders by probation officers. In D. H. Fishbein (Ed.), *The science, treatment, and prevention of antisocial behaviors: Application to the criminal justice system* (chap. 12, pp. 12–1–12–20). Kingston, NJ: Civic Research Institute.

1. According to Bufkin and Luttrell, what are four consistent patterns revealed from their review of 17 neuroimaging studies? Which of these do you feel is most valid? Least valid?

2. What types of implications for criminological theory do Bufkin and Luttrell discuss?

3. What types of implications for criminal justice do they discuss?

❖

READING 12

In this selection, Jean Marie McGloin, Travis Pratt, and Alex Piquero present a study that examines the nature of the effects of maternal cigarette smoking during pregnancy. They point out the problems of previous studies, namely, concentrating on measures that are not directly based on neuropsychological problems, but rather on IQ tests. Furthermore, they base their study on a highly respected and influential model of criminal development presented by Terrie Moffitt, which claimed that the most serious, chronic offenders are those that experience both a disadvantaged environment (bad neighborhood, bad parenting, etc.) and early neuropsychological problems (due to maternal cigarette smoking or intake of other toxins, pregnancy/delivery complications, etc.). Although other studies have supported Moffitt's developmental model (which will be discussed at length in Section X), this may be the only study that has directly tested and supported her model. While reading this selection, consider that what happens in the womb may have an effect on what happens much later in life.

A Life-Course Analysis of the Criminogenic Effects of Maternal Cigarette Smoking during Pregnancy

A Research Note on the Mediating Impact of Neuropsychological Deficit

Jean Marie McGloin, Travis C. Pratt, and Alex R. Piquero

Research from a variety of disciplines indicates that maternal cigarette smoking (MCS) during pregnancy is associated with an array of problematic behavioral outcomes in offspring (Cornelius and Day 2000; Wakschlag et al. 2002). Of particular interest to criminologists, this may include such traditional criminological outcomes as violent, persistent, and early-onset offending (Brennan, Grekin, and Mednick 1999; Gibson, Piquero, and Tibbetts 2000; Rasanen et al. 1999). Furthermore, Cotton's (1994) assertion that 20 to 25 percent of pregnant women who smoke continue to do so throughout their pregnancies suggests that this risk factor is worthy of criminologists' attention.

Nevertheless, the question of how MCS risk manifests into criminal behavior still remains. On one hand, some studies have used Moffitt's (1993) developmental taxonomy as a framework for empirical investigation (see Gibson et al. 2000; Gibson and Tibbetts 2000; Piquero et al. 2002). Indeed, MCS fits nicely within the battery of the various congenital risks that serve as the hypothesized roots of life-course-persistent (LCP) offending. Even so, previous investigations that have drawn on Moffitt's framework have not truly tested the developmental pathway specified by her theory. Instead, research has largely focused on the direct relationship between MCS and various measures of LCP offending, which treat MCS as a proxy for neuropsychological deficit (Gibson et al. 2000; Gibson and Tibbetts 2000; Piquero et al. 2002).

The problem with this approach is that Moffitt (1993) did not suggest that MCS is a measure of neuropsychological deficit but rather that MCS is a precursor to such deficits. She specified a mediating relationship in which congenital risks, such as MCS, increase the likelihood of neuropsychological deficits occurring in children, which in turn increase the probability that such youths will eventually engage in LCP offending. Thus, empirical research has yet to be conducted that addresses whether the relationship between MCS and LCP offending is mediated by more direct measures of neuropsychological deficit.

In this research, we addressed this void by determining whether neuropsychological deficit does in fact mediate the connection between MCS and LCP offending. We assessed this relationship while using a number of controls for other early biological risk factors (e.g., low birth weight [LBW]) as well as indicators of social disadvantage at multiple points in time. Our broader purpose, therefore, was to determine whether criminologists should continue to think about MCS in the context of theories that specify neuropsychological deficits—as opposed to, say, parenting effects (i.e., is it simply that mothers who smoke while pregnant also turn out to be inept at shaping prosocial behavior in their kids?)—as a key predictor of criminal behavior.

Despite this goal, we recognize that MCS is, by any reasonable estimation, a distal criminogenic risk factor. To be sure, other variables, such as self-control (Pratt and Cullen 2000), deviant peer influences, and antisocial attitudes (Andrews and Bonta 2001), have all been found to consistently predict antisocial behavior more consistently and robustly than MCS (Wakschlag et al. 2002). Nevertheless, the MCS-crime link provides criminologists with a unique opportunity to examine the relative validity of some

of the claims made by the dominant theoretical traditions in the field. Indeed, a complete explanation of the causal processes underlying the link between MCS and crime or deviance may end up telling us a lot about the compatibility, or lack thereof, of theories that specify biological versus social-psychological causes of crime. Again, we took an initial first step in this process by testing the degree to which the link between MCS and LCP offending is mediated by measures of neuropsychological deficit.

Theoretical Context

Moffitt (1993) argued that two offending trajectories with distinct etiologies are obscured within the aggregate age-crime curve. Individuals on the LCP pathway begin offending at an early age and continue throughout the life course, engaging in an array of deviance, including criminal behavior. Individuals on the adolescence-limited trajectory instead start offending at a relatively older age, have a transitory offending time frame typically defined by minor rebellious offending, and desist on the transition to adulthood (Moffitt 1993; Piquero 2000; Piquero et al. 1999). LCP offending occurs in a small proportion of the population and develops out of an evocative interaction between neuropsychological deficits and a disadvantaged environment. Adolescence-limited offending, in contrast, is found in the majority of the population and develops out of social mimicry during the maturational gap of adolescence. Accordingly, when criminologists concentrate on MCS as a risk factor, they typically do so with a focus on the LCP etiological pathway.

According to Moffitt (1993), developmental disturbances of the fetal brain, which can be caused by various pre- and perinatal risk factors, such as exposure to toxins, poor maternal nutrition, and MCS, produce deficits in the central nervous system. Lynam, Moffitt, and Stouthamer-Loeber (1993) stated that "deficits in the neuropsychological abilities referred to as 'executive functions' interfere with a person's ability to monitor and control his or her own behavior" (p. 188). In short, the hypothesis is that congenital, and therefore biological, risks produce neuropsychological deficits, which can manifest behaviorally in a bad temperament and, later, criminal behavior.

Indeed, neuropsychological deficit, which has also been measured through proxies such as low cognitive ability

(Denno 1990; Moffitt 1990), has emerged as an important discriminating factor between offenders and nonoffenders (see Hirschi and Hindelang 1977; Wolfgang, Figlio, and Sellin 1972) as well as a predictor of more severe markers of offending within criminal populations (McGloin and Pratt 2003; Piquero and White 2003). Moreover, despite criticism about the validity of articulating only two trajectories (Nagin, Farrington, and Moffitt 1995; White, Bates, and Buyske 2001), the main hypothesis that offenders, especially serious offenders, suffer from neuropsychological and/or biological deficits is well supported empirically (Moffitt. Lynam, and Silva 1994; Piquero 2001; Piquero and White 2003).

Even so, in studying the link between MCS and crime or deviance, existing criminological research has used MCS as a proxy of neuropsychological deficit rather than as a precursor to it. For example, Gibson et al. (2000) found a significant relationship between MCS and age at first police contact net of statistical controls,[1] a finding that was echoed by Gibson and Tibbetts[2] (2000) and by Piquero et al. (2002). Although these studies offered some support for the association between MCS and LCP offending, none of them specified the purported mediating mechanism between MCS and neuropsychological deficit.

A substantial gap in the research therefore continues to exist. To be sure, the precise mechanism whereby MCS operates as a criminogenic risk factor is still unknown. Moffitt (1993) argued that neuropsychological deficit is a result of some injury to, or disturbance of, the proper fetal developmental process. She did not suggest that such risks, in this case MCS during pregnancy, should themselves be treated as a proxy for minimal brain dysfunction but rather that they are assumed to represent, among others, the primary causes of neuropsychological deficits. Accordingly, this research explicitly examined the mechanism whereby MCS produces a criminogenic risk (i.e., through its effect on neuropsychological deficits) for LCP offending.

Methods

Data

Data for this project came from both the original Philadelphia portion of the National Collaborative Perinatal Project (NCPP) and a recent criminal history search conducted on the original

cohort of 987 youths born to African American mothers who participated in the NCPP (see Piquero et al. 2002). Moffitt (1997) considered the NCPP data to be particularly well suited to analyses addressing issues associated with neuropsychological deficits, thereby making the use of the NCPP particularly relevant for the questions under investigation in this study. Given the focus on LCP offending, analyses were conducted on the offender subsample ($n = 220$) of the original 987 subjects.[3]

In the early 1980s, information was collected related to school functioning and criminal histories, including all police contacts through age 17 (see Denno 1990).[4] Adult criminal history data, in the form of convictions, are available through age 36 for those sample members born into the 1962 cohort and through age 39 for those born into the 1959 cohort.[5] Some might suggest that conviction data from the adult follow-up are not as reliable as self-report, police contact, or arrest data. All sources of criminal justice data, however, are subject to limitations (see Hindelang et al. 1981; Lauritsen 1998; Wolfgang et al. 1972), and extant theory does not anticipate that certain relationships would be found only when analyzing certain types of outcome data.[6] Moreover, many empirical investigations have used various sources of criminal history data, including self-report and conviction data (Farrington et al. 1996; Ge, Donnellan, and Wenk 2001; Moffitt et al. 1994). To this end, Farrington (1989) showed that self-reports and official conviction data produce "comparable and complementary results on such important topics as prevalence, continuity, versatility, and specialization in different types of offenses" (p. 418).[7]

Dependent Variable

LCP offending. Individuals who exhibited an early onset (prior to age 14) and accumulated at least two adult convictions during the follow-up period (after age 18) were coded 1, and all other sample members were coded 0 (the same approach with these data was taken by Gibson et al. 2000, Gibson and Tibbetts 2000, McGloin and Pratt 2003, Piquero 2001, and Tibbetts and Piquero 1999; see also Piquero and White 2003).

Independent Variables

Neuropsychological deficit. To measure neuropsychological deficit, we used the total battery score of the California Achievement Test (CAT), a measure that has also been used in past criminological research (see Ge et al. 2001; McGloin and Pratt 2003; Piquero and White 2003). The CAT yields total scores in the academic domain of reading, arithmetic, and language (Tiegs and Clark 1970: 14). The total battery score for Grades 7 and 8 (ages 12 to 14), which we used in this study, reflects a student's standing in terms of total achievement level. The CAT is, in general, highly praised in terms of its validity, comprehensive test and interpretive materials, reliability, and standardization procedure (Denno 1990:173).[8]

We used the CAT because we recognized the potential conceptual, empirical, and ideological concerns with using IQ to assess neuropsychological functioning within a sample of economically disadvantaged African American youth. Moreover, Moffitt (1990) argued that the array of cognitive tests is so highly interrelated that interchanging them is acceptable. One could also argue that research on LCP offending should consider measures other than IQ to establish convergent validity (McGloin and Pratt 2003). This is especially true with this data set, which has been subject to much empirical investigation under Moffitt's (1993) framework and has largely relied on IQ as the measure of neuropsychological deficit. Nevertheless, for those who prefer IQ as a measure, we also estimated the models with the verbal subscale of the Wechsler Intelligence Scale for Children (WISC), which was assessed at ages 7 to 8.[9]

Sex. Sex was coded 1 for male and 2 for female. Of these 220 offenders, approximately 70 percent were male.

Low birth weight. LBW was associated with MCS and has been shown to have a relationship with criminal outcomes (see Gibson et al. 2000; McGloin and Pratt 2003; Tibbetts and Piquero 1999). Following designation made by the World Health Organization and used in past research, LBW is a dichotomous variable indicating its presence (1) or absence (0). The cutoff for LBW is five pounds, eight ounces.[10] Of the 220 offenders, 19 percent were LBW.

Risk at birth. Our risk-at-birth composite was a summed index of three dichotomous items measured at birth from the mother: birth complications, marital status, and age at childbirth. Following Farrington and Loeber (2000), these variables were dichotomized to reflect the risk-factor paradigm. Consistent with Nagin, Farrington, and Pogarsky (1997), mother's age at childbirth was coded 0 (18 and older)

or 1 (under 18), and mother's marital status at childbirth was coded 0 (married) or 1 (single). Finally, birth complications were coded 0 (for no birth complications during pregnancy) or 1 (for one or more birth complications during pregnancy). All of these items have been considered indicators of maternal disadvantage and have been related to important offspring problems, including crime (see Farrington and Loeber 2000; Raine 1993).

Risk at age 7. Socioeconomic status was originally measured in a standardized method by all sites of the NCPP with a single-item score, ranging from 0 to 100, that was a composite measure of three indicators collected at age 7 for each child: education of the head of the household, income of the head of the household, and occupation of the head of the household (Myrianthopoulos and French 1968). Those individuals scoring in the lowest 25th percentile (very low socioeconomic status) were coded 1, and all others were coded 0.

Maternal cigarette smoking. MCS was assessed during pregnancy. Mothers were asked to self-report the average number of cigarettes they smoked each day. Although this variable was originally coded continuously, we followed the coding procedure outlined by Brennan et al. (1999) and replicated by others: 0, 1 to 2, 3 to 10, 11 to 20, and 20 or more. This measure, then, assessed a potential dose-response relationship.[11]

Analytic Strategy

The analysis focused on determining whether neuropsychological deficit mediates the relationship between MCS and LCP offending. Given the dichotomous dependent variable of LCP offending, the main analyses estimated the multivariate models via logistic regression techniques. To establish a mediating relationship, three criteria must be satisfied. First, MCS must predict the mediating mechanism of interest, neuropsychological deficit. Second, it must be established that MCS in fact predicts LCP offending. Finally, the inclusion of the potential mediator, neuropsychological deficit, should eliminate much (if not all) of the significance of MCS in the multivariate model.

With this in mind, the first step in the analysis determined whether MCS predicted neuropsychological deficit, net of statistical controls. This analysis relied on ordinary least squares regression techniques, given the continuous measure of neuropsychological deficit. Next, three models were estimated for the prediction of LCP offending. Model 1 included the MCS measure along with the control variables to gauge the relationship between MCS and LCP offending. Model 2 included the measure of neuropsychological deficit to determine if it stripped MCS of its significance and acted as a mediator. Finally, model 3 included the composite of risk at age 7, which was added separately from the other controls given its temporal distinction.

Results

Table 1 presents the results from the ordinary least squares regression model predicting neuropsychological deficit. The findings suggest that the offspring of mothers who smoked (many) cigarettes during pregnancy were more likely to experience lower scores on the CAT.[12]

For the next step in the analysis, three logistic regression models predicting LCP offending. Model 1 revealed that MCS did predict LCP offending were estimated (not shown), net of statistical controls.[13] In particular, it was the most severe category of smoking that held significance: The offspring of mothers who smoked 20 or more cigarettes per day, compared with mothers who did not smoke, were significantly more likely to manifest LCP offending. This suggests that the damage of MCS exists on a spectrum. Others have also confirmed the importance of allowing for a potential dose-response relationship,

finding a growing risk for a certain type of offending as the number of cigarettes a mother smoked during pregnancy increased (Brennan et al. 1999; Gibson et al. 2000; Piquero et al. 2002).

Model 2 included the CAT variable to determine whether introducing an indicator of neuropsychological deficit mediated the effect of the MCS measure. Although the CAT emerged as a significant predictor of LCP offending, it did not affect the significance level of MCS. Thus, neuropsychological deficit did not appear to mediate the relationship between MCS and LCP offending. The same conclusion was reached even with the inclusion of risk at age 7 in model 3, which showed that adding this additional risk factor to the model did not eliminate the significance of the MCS variable.

Discussion

The primary focus of this research was to determine the mechanism whereby MCS manifests itself as a criminogenic risk factor. Despite the fact that previous research has used Moffitt's (1993) theoretical framework, no study has specified this mediating mechanism articulated by Moffitt. The results presented here show that although MCS is a significant precursor to neuropsychological deficit and that neuropsychological deficit significantly predicts LCP offending, this is not the mediating mechanism at work in the relationship between MCS and LCP offending. Indeed, a significant relationship remains between MCS and LCP offending that operates independent of neuropsychological dysfunction.

Table 1	Slopes and Standard Errors for the Ordinary Least Squares Regression Model Predicting Neuropsychological Deficit ($n = 220$)	
Variable	**B**	**SE**
Sex	1.022	2.972
Low birth weight	−2.599	3.642
Risk at birth	2.736	1.660
Maternal cigarette smoking	−2.661**	1.161
Constant	20.399	
F	2.406	
*R*²	.044	

**$p < .05$.

This finding, although somewhat inconsistent with Moffitt's (1993) theoretical predictions, is not necessarily inconsistent with earlier empirical work. Previous research in this area that has used IQ as a control variable has shown that MCS retained its ability to predict criminal outcomes (Gibson et al. 2000; Piquero et al. 2002). Thus, these models provided a hint that Moffitt's theoretical framework was not explaining the nature of the relationship between MCS and LCP offending. The findings offered here, though in a decidedly more explicit fashion, suggest that the risk of MCS does not operate (solely) through the indirect pathway of neuropsychological deficit. At a minimum, these results call into question using an MCS measure as a proxy for neuropsychological deficit.

The question now, therefore, concerns what is in fact the mediating mechanism between MCS and LCP offending. Accordingly, there are two primary potential mediators that should be addressed in future research. First, parenting may play an important role in explaining the empirical relationship between MCS and offending. A mother who smokes cigarettes during pregnancy, particularly a "high-rate" smoker, may illustrate a "foreshadowing" propensity to put her immediate, hedonistic tendencies and desires before long-term considerations for her child's health. Perhaps it is not the toxins inherent to cigarettes that are so damaging to a child (although such toxins certainly provide no known benefit). Rather, it may be that smoking is predictive of poor parenting practices. To be sure, a variety of criminological perspectives highlight the importance of parenting. For example, social learning theorists argue that parents who serve as models of deviance and/or create reinforcement contingencies supportive of such behavior can essentially mold a delinquent child (Akers 1998). Others note that the probability of delinquency increases when parents fail to consistently provide their children with affirming social support (Cullen 1994; Wright and Cullen 2001). Control perspectives, from Hirschi's (1969) original social-bond perspective to Gottfredson and Hirschi's (1990) self-control theory, also rely heavily on the notion of parental efficacy. Although some researchers have highlighted this potential pathway (Gibson et al. 2000), it still remains a hypothesized rather than an empirically confirmed developmental process.

Second, MCS is a known risk for temperamental and conduct problems in childhood. For example, Sadowski and Parish (2005) noted that MCS consistently predicts attention-deficit hyperactivity disorder (ADHD), even when controlling for other important factors, such as maternal socioeconomic status. When combined with the finding that ADHD predicts delinquency (Pratt et al. 2002), mainly through its influence on self-control (Unnever, Cullen, and Pratt 2003), it becomes clear that this is another potential mediating pathway. It is worth noting that these two mediating mechanisms may also act in concert. Given that low self-control is endogenous to ADHD, and that Gottfredson and Hirschi (1990) allowed for variation in temperament, which makes some youth more vulnerable to ineffective parenting practices, a child born to a mother who engages in MCS may have conduct problems and be subject to poor parenting practices. Thus, future research should also investigate a potential interaction between these two pathways.

It is also worth noting a potential genetic explanation, in which the connection between MCS and ADHD in offspring may reflect inherited biological predispositions. For example, recent research suggests that ADHD is highly heritable, with some estimates claiming that up to 80 percent of the variation in the disorder is genetic or biological (see the discussion by Pratt et al. 2002). Thus, the link between MCS and ADHD may potentially reflect mothers who have ADHD and engage in excessive smoking as self-medication. Given the recent focus on genetics with regard to self-control (Wright and Beaver 2005), it would also be wise to consider the role of heredity as another pathway through which the criminogenic effects of MCS may operate.

In the end, though the scope of the present study was modest, our results highlight some important issues. In particular, it should be recognized that the purported link between MCS and LCP offending has been embedded within the larger assumption that damage to a developing fetus is what starts this developmental pathway. The findings presented here, however, question this assumption and instead indicate that our attention should shift elsewhere, perhaps to parenting and/or self-control. Indeed, it seems that the criminogenic risk of MCS, which was supposedly "owned" by one theory, may belong under the heading of another.

 ## Notes

1. This association disappeared in the female subsample with controls, but Gibson et al. argued that this may have been due to the small sample size, because the odds ratio for the women was actually larger than that for the men.

2. Gibson and Tibbetts (2000) did not simply specify a direct relationship. They also included an interaction term with MCS and the absence of a father or husband in the household to specify the neuropsychological deficit and disadvantage environment interaction of which Moffitt wrote.

3. This subsample was defined as those individuals who had at least one official police contact by the age of 18 years.

4. *Police contact* refers to whether a juvenile had contact with police that resulted in either an official arrest or a remedial disposition. This measure of juvenile offending has also been used in the Philadelphia (see Wolfgang et al. 1972; Tracy, Wolfgang, and Figlio 1990) and Racine (see Shannon 1991) cohort studies. More generally, police contacts are positively and moderately correlated with both self-reported offending estimates and other official records of offending such as arrests and convictions (Hindelang, Hirschi, and Weis 1981). Furthermore, Smith and Gartin (1989) noted that "among the domain of official measures, police contacts provide a closer approximation of the true level of offending than arrests or convictions" (p. 102).

5. The criminal history data included offenses committed and officially processed in Philadelphia only. As was the case in another Philadelphia birth cohort study, Tracy and Kempf-Leonard (1996) knew that the sample members were residents of Philadelphia through age 17 but had to assume that the same was true for the adult period as well. In addition, data for women may have been compromised by the fact that women may have married and changed their surnames. Although the original names and social security numbers of the sample subjects were known in the present study, several women changed both. Thus, the analysis may have underestimated the criminal offending of female sample members.

6. Recall that Moffitt et al. (1994) found neuropsychological scores to be related to police, self-report, and court records in very similar ways.

7. As a practical matter, the city of Philadelphia, following the Pennsylvania Crime Code, expunges all arrests from the criminal history database for all of its citizens if the arrests do not lead to convictions within three years; therefore, the use of arrest data would also be limited in the sense that a true arrest for an offense may have in fact occurred but was deleted from the criminal history database because of the three-year rule.

8. Our use of the CAT as a proxy for neuropsychological deficit, although not necessarily ideal (relative to a more direct measure), is consistent with Moffitt's (1990) view that measures such as the CAT serve as adequate proxies for neuropsychological deficit. Our interest in this research, therefore, was to be as

consistent as possible to Moffitt's work, because we were assessing the relative merits of her explanation of the relationship between MCS and crime or delinquency.

9. It is true that measures of executive functioning would also capture neuropsychological deficit. Even so, Moffitt (1990) argued strongly that verbal IQ is a valid measure of neuropsychological deficit.

10. Because LBW is endogenous to MCS, some may view its inclusion in the models as unnecessary. The two variables did not, however, evidence multicollinearity, and failing to include LBW could have overestimated the impact of MCS. Thus, we erred on the conservative side and retained this measure. Additional analyses illustrated that removing LBW did not substantively alter the findings.

11. There were no indications of multicollinearity among the independent variables.

12. When we reestimated this model with the entire sample (*N* = 987), MCS still predicted neuropsychological deficit. It also was a significant predictor when using the WISC measure rather than the CAT.

13. Given the limited regressor space provided by the relatively small sample size (*n* = 220) with fully specified models, we should note that the significance levels for the MCS variable (the category of 20 or more cigarettes per day) were consistently at *p* = .064, below the .10 cutoff but above the "industry standard" of .05. Because *p*-level cutoff points are both theoretically arbitrary and highly dependent on sample size (Tabachnick and Fidell 2001), we maintain that the significance levels reported here indicate a substantively meaningful relationship in the multivariate models.

 # References

Akers, Ronald L. 1998. *Social Learning and Social Structure: A General Theory of Crime and Deviance.* Boston: Northeastern University Press.

Andrews, D. A., and James Bonta. 2001. *The Psychology of Criminal Conduct.* 3rd ed. Cincinnati, OH: Anderson.

Brennan, Patricia A., Emily R. Grekin, and Sarnoff Mednick. 1999. "Maternal Cigarette Smoking During Pregnancy and Adult Male Criminal Outcomes." *Archives of General Psychiatry* 56:215–19.

Cornelius, Marie D. and Nancy Day. 2000. "The Effects of Tobacco Use During and After Pregnancy on Exposed Children." *Alcohol Research and Health* 24:242–49.

Cotton, P. 1994. "Smoking Cigarettes May Do Developing Fetus More Harm Than Ingesting Cocaine, Some Experts Say." *JAMA* 271:576–77.

Cullen, Francis T. 1994, "Social Support as an Organizing Concept for Criminology: Presidential Address to the Academy of Criminal Justice Sciences." *Justice Quarterly* 11:527–59.

Denno, Deborah J. 1990. *Biology and Violence.* Cambridge, UK: Cambridge University Press.

Farrington, David P. 1989. "Self-Reported and Official Offending from Adolescence to Adulthood." Pp. 399–423 in *Cross-National Research in Self-Reported Crime and Delinquency,* edited by M. W. Klein. Boston: Kluwer Academic.

Farrington, David P., and Rolf Loeber. 2000. "Some Benefits of Dichotomization in Psychiatric and Criminological Research." *Criminal Behaviour and Mental Health* 10:100–22.

Farrington, David P., Rolf Loeber, Magda Stouthamer-Loeber, W. B. Van Kammen, and L. Schmidt. 1996. "Self-Report Delinquency and a Combined Seriousness Scale Based on Boys, Mothers, and Teachers: Concurrent and Predictive Validity." *Criminology* 34:493–517.

Ge, Xiaojia, M. Brent Donnellan, and Ernst Wenk. 2001. "The Development of Persistent Criminal Offending in Males." *Criminal Justice and Behavior* 28:731–55.

Gibson, Chris L., Alex R. Piquero, and Stephen G. Tibbetts. 2000. "Assessing the Relationship between Maternal Cigarette Smoking During Pregnancy and Age at First Police Contact." *Justice Quarterly* 17:519–41.

Gibson, Chris L., and Stephen G. Tibbetts. 2000. "A Biosocial Interaction in Predicting Early Onset of Offending." *Psychological Reports* 86:509–18.

Gottfredson, Michael R., and Travis Hirschi. 1990. *A General Theory of Crime.* Stanford, CA: Stanford University Press.

Hindelang, Michael J., Travis Hirschi, and Joseph Weis. 1981. *Measuring Delinquency.* Beverly Hills, CA: Sage.

Hirschi, Travis. 1969. *Causes of Delinquency.* Berkeley: University of California Press.

Hirschi, Travis, and Michael J. Hindelang. 1977. "Intelligence and Delinquency: A Revisionist Review." *American Sociological Review* 42:571–87.

Lauritsen, Janet L. 1998. "The Age-Crime Debate: Assessing the Limits of Longitudinal Self-Report Data." *Social Forces* 77:127–55.

Lynam, Donald R., Terrie E. Moffitt, and Magda Stouthamer-Loeber. 1993. "Explaining the Relationship Between IQ and Delinquency: Class, Race, Test Motivation, School Failure or Self-Control?" *Journal of Abnormal Psychology* 102:187–96.

McGloin, Jean M., and Travis C. Pratt. 2003. "Cognitive Ability and Delinquent Behavior among Inner-City Youth: A Life-Course Analysis of Main, Mediating, and Interaction Effects." *International Journal of Offender Therapy and Comparative Criminology* 47:253–71.

Moffitt, Terrie E. 1990. "The Neuropsychology of Juvenile Delinquency: A Critical Review." Pp. 99–170 in *Crime and Justice: A Review of the Research, Vol. 12,* edited by M. Tonry and N. Morris. Chicago: University of Chicago Press.

———. 1993. "Adolescence-Limited and Life-Course-Persistent Antisocial Behavior: A Developmental Taxonomy." *Psychological Review* 100:674–701.

———. 1997. "Neuropsychology, Antisocial Behavior, and Neighborhood Context." Pp. 116–70 in *Violence,* edited by J. McCord. New York: Cambridge University Press.

Moffitt, Terrie E., Donald Lynam, and Phil A. Silva. 1994. "Neuropsychological Tests Predicting Persistent Male Delinquency." *Criminology* 32:277–300.

Myrianthopoulos, Ntinos C., and K. S. French, 1968. "An Application of the U.S. Bureau of the Census Socioeconomic Index to a Large, Diversified Patient Population." *Social Science Medicine* 2:283–99.

Nagin, Daniel S., David P. Farrington, and Terrie E. Moffitt. 1995. "Life-Course Trajectories of Different Types of Offenders." *Criminology* 33:111–39.

Nagin, Daniel, Daniel P. Farrington, and Greg Pogarsky. 1997. "Adolescent Mothers and the Criminal Behavior of Their Children." *Law and Society Review* 31:137–62.

Piquero, Alex R. 2000. "Frequency, Specialization, and Violence in Offending Careers." *Journal of Research in Crime and Delinquency* 37:392–418.

———. 2001, "Testing Moffitt's Neuropsychological Variation Hypothesis for the Prediction of Life-Course Persistent Offending." *Psychology, Crime and Law* 7:193–215.

Piquero, Alex R., Chris L. Gibson, Stephen G. Tibbetts, Michael G. Turner, and Solomon H. Katz. 2002. "Maternal Cigarette Smoking During Pregnancy and Life Course Persistent Offending." *International Journal of Offender Therapy and Comparative Criminology* 46:231–48.

Piquero, Alex R., Raymond Paternoster, Paul Mazerolle, Robert Brame, and Charles W. Dean. 1999. "Onset Age and Offense Specialization." *Journal of Research in Crime and Delinquency* 36:275–99.

Piquero, Alex R., and Norman A White. 2003. "On the Relationship between Cognitive Abilities and Life Course-Persistent Offending among a Sample of African Americans: A Longitudinal Test of Moffitt's Hypothesis." *Journal of Criminal Justice* 31:399–409.

Pratt, Travis C., and Francis T. Cullen. 2000. "The Empirical Status of Gottfredson and Hirschi's General Theory of Crime: A Meta-Analysis." *Criminology* 38:931–64.

Pratt, Travis C., Francis T. Cullen, Kristie R. Blevins, Leah Daigle, and James D. Unnever. 2002. "The Relationship of Attention Deficit Hyperactivity Disorder to Crime and Delinquency: A Meta-Analysis." *International Journal of Police Science and Management* 4:344–60.

Raine, Adrian. 1993. *The Psychopathology of Crime.* San Diego, CA: Academic Press.

Rasanen, Pirkko, Helina Hakko, Matti Isohanni, Sheilagh Hodgins, Marjo-Ritta Jarvelin, and Jari Tihonen. 1999. "Maternal Smoking during Pregnancy and Risk of Criminal Behavior among Adult Male Offspring in a Northern Finland 1966 Cohort." *American Journal of Psychiatry* 156:857–62.

Sadowski, Kelly, and Thomas G. Parish. 2005. "Maternal Smoking Contributes to the Development of Childhood ADHD." *Internet Journal of Allied Health Sciences and Practice* 3(1). Available at http://ijahsp.nova.edu/articles/vo13num1/sadowski .htm

Shannon, Lyle W. 1991. *Changing Patterns of Delinquency and Crime: A Longitudinal Study in Racine.* Boulder, CO: Westview.

Smith, Douglas A., and Patrick R. Gartin. 1989. "Specifying Specific Deterrence: The Influence of Arrest on Future Criminal Activity." *American Sociological Review* 54:94–105.

Tabachnick, Barbara G., and Linda S. Fidell. 2001. *Using Multivariate Statistics.* 4th ed. Boston: Allyn &. Bacon.

Tibbetts, Stephen G., and Alex R. Piquero, 1999. "The Influence of Gender, Low Birth Weight, and Disadvantaged Environment in Predicting Early Onset of Offending: A Test of Moffitt's Interactional Hypothesis." *Criminology* 37:843–77.

Tiegs, Ernest W., and Willis W. Clark. 1970. *Examiner's Manual and Test Coordinator's Handbook: California Achievement Texts.* New York: McGraw-Hill.

Tracy, Paul E., and Kimberley Kempf-Leonard. 1996. *Continuity and Discontinuity in Criminal Careers.* New York: Plenum.

Tracy, Paul E., Marvin E. Wolfgang, and Robert M. Figlio. 1990. *Delinquency Careen in Two Birth Cohorts.* New York: Plenum.

Unnever, James D., Francis T. Cullen, and Travis C. Pratt. 2003. "Parental Management, ADHD, and Delinquent Involvement: Reassessing Gottfredson and Hirschi's General Theory." *Justice Quarterly* 20:471–500.

Wakschlag, Lauren S., Kate E. Pickett, Edwin Cook, Neal L. Benowitz, and Bennett Leventhal. 2002. "Maternal Smoking during Pregnancy and Severe Antisocial Behavior on Offspring: A Review." *American Journal of Public Health* 92:966–74.

White, Helene R., Marsha E. Bates, and Steven Buyske. 2001. "Adolescence-Limited versus Persistent Delinquency: Extending Moffitt's Hypothesis into Adulthood." *Journal of Abnormal Psychology* 110:600–09.

Wolfgang, Marvin E., Robert Figlio, and Thorstin Sellin. 1972. *Delinquency in a Birth Cohort.* Chicago: University of Chicago Press.

Wright. John P., and Kevin M. Beaver. 2005. "Do Parents Really Matter in Creating Self-Control in Their Children? A Genetically Informed Test of Gottfredson and Hirschi's Theory of Low Self-Control." *Criminology* 43:1169–1202.

Wright. John Paul, and Francis T. Cullen. 2001. "Parental Efficacy and Delinquent Behavior: Do Control and Support Matter?" *Criminology* 39:677–705.

REVIEW QUESTIONS

1. In terms of Moffitt's theoretical framework, name and briefly describe the two distinct offending trajectories, as well as what causes each of them.

2. How did McGloin, Piquero, and Pratt measure neuropsychological deficit? Do you agree that this measure is a valid measure of this concept? Why or why not?

3. One of the major findings of this study is inconsistent with Moffitt's theoretical predictions. What finding is this? What potential explanations do the authors present for this finding?

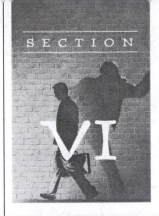

Early Social Structure and Strain Theories of Crime

This section will review the development of anomie or strain theory, starting with early social structure theorists, such as Durkheim, then Merton, and on to the most modern versions (e.g., general strain theory). We will also examine the empirical research findings on this perspective, which remains one of the dominant theoretical explanations of criminal behavior today. We will finish by discussing the policy implications of this research.

We'll begin with a review of explanations of criminal conduct that emphasize the differences among varying groups in societies, particularly in the United States. Such differences are easy to see in everyday life, and many theoretical models place the blame for crime on observed inequalities and cultural differences between groups. In contrast to the theories presented in previous sections, social structure theories disregard any biological or psychological variations across individuals. Instead, social structure theories assume that crime is caused by the way societies are structurally organized.

These social structure theories vary in many ways, most notably in what they propose as the primary constructs and processes responsible for causing criminal activity. For example, some structural models emphasize variations in economic or academic success, whereas others focus on differences in cultural norms and values. Still others concentrate on the actual breakdown of the social structure in certain neighborhoods and the resulting social disorganization that occurs from this process, a topic we will reserve for Section VII. Regardless of their differences, all of the theories examined in this section emphasize a common theme: Certain groups of individuals are more likely to break the law because of disadvantages or cultural differences resulting from the way a society is structured.

The most important distinction between these theories and those discussed in previous sections is that they emphasize group differences instead of individual differences. Structural models tend to focus on the macro level of analysis as opposed to the micro level. Therefore, it is not surprising that social structure theories are commonly used to explain the propensity of certain racial or ethnic groups for committing crime, as well as the overrepresentation of the lower class in criminal activity.

As you will see, these theoretical frameworks were presented as early as the 1800s and reached prominence in the early to mid 1900s, when the political, cultural, and economic climate of society was most conducive to such explanations. Although social structural models of crime have diminished in popularity in recent decades,[1] there is much validity to their propositions in numerous applications to contemporary society.

Early Theories of Social Structure: Early to Mid 1800s

Most criminological and sociological historians trace the origin of social structure theories to the research done in the early to mid-1800s by a number of European researchers, the most important including Auguste Comte, André-Michel Guerry, and Adolphe Quetelet.[2] It is important to understand why structural theories developed in 19th-century Europe. The Industrial Revolution, defined by most historians as beginning in the mid-1700s and ending in the mid-1800s, was in full swing at the turn of the century, so societies were quickly transitioning from primarily agriculturally based economies to industrial based economies. This transition inevitably brought people from rural farmlands to dense urban cities, resulting in an enormous increase in social problems. These social problems ranged from failure to properly dispose of waste and garbage, to constantly losing children and not being able to find them, to much higher rates of crime (which urban areas continue to show today, as compared to suburban and rural areas).

The problems associated with such fast urbanization, as well as the shift in economics, led to drastic changes in the basic social structures in Europe as well as the United States. At the same time, other types of revolutions were also having an effect. Both the American (1776) and French (1789) Revolutions occurred in the last quarter of the 18th century. These two revolutions, inspired by the Enlightenment movement (see Section II), shared an ideology that rejected tyranny and insisted that people should have a voice in how they were governed. Along with the Industrial Revolution, these political revolutions affected intellectual theorizing on social structures, as well as on crime, throughout the 1800s.

Auguste Comte

One of the first important theorists in the area of social structure theory was Auguste Comte (1798–1857), who is widely credited with coining the term *sociology*.[3] Comte distinguished the concepts of social statics and social dynamics. Social statics are aspects of society that relate to stability and social order; they allow societies to continue and endure. Social dynamics are aspects of social life that alter how societies are structured and pattern the development of societal institutions. Although such conceptualization seems elementary by today's standards, it had a significant influence on sociological thinking at the time. Furthermore, the distinction between static and dynamic societal factors was incorporated into several criminological theories in decades to come.

Between 1851 and 1854, Comte published a four-volume work titled *A System of Positive Polity* that encouraged the use of scientific methods to observe and measure societal factors.[4] Although we tend to take this for granted in modern times, the idea of applying such methods to help explain social processes was rather profound at the time;

---

[1] Anthony Walsh and Lee Ellis, "Political Ideology and American Criminologists' Explanations for Criminal Behavior," *The Criminologist* 24 (6) (1999): 1, 4; Lee Ellis and Anthony Walsh, "Criminologists' Opinions about Causes and Theories of Crime and Delinquency," *The Criminologist* 24 (4) (1999): 1–4.

[2] Much of the discussion of the development of structural theories of the 19th century is drawn from James W. Vander Zanden, *Sociology: The Core*, 2nd ed. (New York: McGraw-Hill, 1990), 8–14.

[3] Vander Zanden, *Sociology: The Core*, 8–9.

[4] Auguste Comte, *A System of Positive Polity*, trans. John Henry Bridges (New York: Franklin, 1875).

probably for this reason, Comte is generally considered the founder or father of sociology. Comte's work set the stage for the positivistic perspective, which emphasized social determinism and rejected the notion of free will and individual choice that had been common up until that time.

André-Michel Guerry and Adolphe Quetelet

After the first modern national crime statistics were published in France in the early 1800s, a French lawyer named André-Michel Guerry (1802–1866) published a report that examined these statistics and concluded that property crimes were higher in wealthy areas, but violent crime was much higher in poor areas.[5] Some experts have claimed that this report likely represents the first study of scientific criminology[6]; it was later expanded and published as a book, titled *Essay on the Moral Statistics of France*, in 1833. Ultimately, Guerry concluded that the explanation was opportunity: The wealthy had more to steal, and that is the primary cause of property crime. Interestingly, this conclusion is supported by recent U.S. Department of Justice statistics, which show that, compared to lower-class households, property crime is just as common—and maybe more so—in middle- to upper-class households, but violent crime is not.[7] As Guerry stated centuries ago, there is more to steal in wealthier areas, and poor individuals take the opportunity to steal goods and currency from these households and establishments.

Adolphe Quetelet (1796–1874) was a Belgian researcher who, like Guerry, examined French statistics in the mid-1800s. Besides showing relative stability in the trends of crime rates in France, such as in age distribution and female-to-male ratios of offending, Quetelet also showed that certain types of individuals were more likely to commit crime.[8] Specifically, young, male, poor, uneducated, and unemployed individuals were more likely to commit crime than their counterparts,[9] a finding also supported by modern research. Like Guerry, Quetelet concluded that opportunities, in addition to demographic characteristics, had a lot to do with where crime was concentrated.

▲ Image 6.1   Adolphe Quetelet (1796-1874)

Source: http://commons.wikimedia.org/wiki/File:Adolphe_Quételet_by_ Joseph-Arnold_Demannez.jpg

---

[5]For more thorough discussions of Guerry and Quetelet, see the sources from which I have drawn the information presented here: Piers Beirne, *Inventing Criminology* (Albany: SUNY Press, 1993); Thomas J. Bernard, Jeffrey B. Snipes, and Alexander L. Gerould, *Vold's Theoretical Criminology*, 6th ed. (Oxford: Oxford University Press, 2010) (see chap. 2).

[6]Terrence Morris, *The Criminal Area* (New York: Routledge, 1957), 42–53, as cited in Bernard et al., *Vold's Theoretical Criminology*, 22.

[7]U.S. Department of Justice, Bureau of Justice Statistics, *Sourcebook of Criminal Justice Statistics, 2000, NCJ-190251* (Washington, DC: USGPO, 2001), Table 3.26, 202; U.S. Department of Justice, Bureau of Justice Statistics, *Sourcebook of Criminal Justice Statistics, 2000, NCJ-190251* (Washington, DC: USGPO, 2001), Table 3.13, 194.

[8]Beirne, *Inventing Criminology*, 78–81.

[9]Bernard et al., *Vold's Theoretical Criminology*, 23–26.

However, Quetelet added a special component: Greater inequality or gaps between wealth and poverty in the same place tend to excite temptations and passions. This is a concept referred to as relative deprivation, a condition quite distinct from simple poverty.

For example, a number of deprived areas in the United States do not have high rates of crime, likely because virtually everyone is poor, so people are generally content with their lives relative to their neighbors. However, in areas of the country where very poor people live in close proximity to very wealthy people, animosity and feelings of being deprived develop. Studies have supported this hypothesis.[10] It may well explain why Washington, DC, perhaps the most powerful city in the world and one with many neighborhoods that are severely run-down and poor, has a higher crime rate than any other jurisdiction in the country.[11] Modern studies have also shown a clear linear association between higher crime rates and relative deprivation. For example, David Sang-Yoon Lee found that crime rates were far higher in cities that had wider gaps in income: The larger the gap between the 10th and 90th percentiles, the greater the crime levels.[12]

In addition to the concept of relative deprivation, Quetelet also showed that areas with the most rapidly changing economic conditions have high crime rates. He is perhaps best known for commenting that "the crimes . . . committed seem to be a necessary result of our social organization. . . . Society prepares the crime, and the guilty are only the instruments by which it is executed."[13] This statement makes it clear that crime is a result of societal structure and not the result of individual propensities or personal decision making. Thus, it is not surprising that Quetelet's position was controversial at the time in which he wrote, and he was rigorously attacked by critics for removing all decision-making capabilities from his model of behavior. In response, Quetelet argued that his model could help lower crime rates by leading to social reforms that address the inequalities due to the social structure.[14]

One of the essential points of Guerry's and Quetelet's work is the positivistic nature of their conclusions: that the distribution of crime is not random but rather the result of certain types of people committing certain types of crimes in particular places, largely due to the way society is structured and the way it distributes resources. This perspective of criminality strongly supports the tendency of crime to be clustered in certain neighborhoods as well as among certain people. Such findings support a structural, positivistic perspective of criminality, in which criminality is seen as being deterministic and, thus, caused by factors outside of an individual's control. In some ways, early structural theories were a response to the failure of the classical approach to crime control. As the 19th century drew to a close, classical and deterrence-based perspectives of crime fell out of favor, while social structure theories and other positivist theories of crime, such as the structural models of Guerry and Quetelet, attracted far more attention.

Durkheim and the Concept of Anomie

Although influenced by earlier theorists (e.g., Comte, Guerry, and Quetelet), Émile Durkheim (1858–1916) was perhaps the most influential theorist in the area of modern structural perspectives on criminality.[15] Like most other

---

[10]Velmer Burton and Frank Cullen, "The Empirical Status of Strain Theory," *Journal of Crime and Justice* 15 (1992): 1–30; Nikos Passas, "Continuities in the Anomie Tradition," in *Advances in Criminological Theory, Vol. 6: The Legacy of Anomie Theory*, ed. Freda Adler and William S. Laufer (New Brunswick: Transaction, 1995); Nikos Passas, "Anomie, Reference Groups, and Relative Deprivation," in *The Future of Anomie Theory*, ed. Nikos Passas and Robert Agnew (Boston: Northeastern University Press, 1997).

[11]U.S. Department of Justice, Bureau of Justice Statistics, *Sourcebook of Criminal Justice Statistics, 2000, NCJ-190251* (Washington, DC: USGPO, 2001), Table 3.124, 290.

[12]David Sang-Yoon Lee, "An Empirical Investigation of the Economic Incentives for Criminal Behavior," bachelor's thesis in economics (Boston: Harvard University, 1993), as cited in Richard B. Freeman, "The Labor Market," in *Crime*, ed. James Q. Wilson and Joan Petersilia (San Francisco: ICS Press, 1995), 171–92.

[13]Beirne, *Inventing Criminology*, 88, as cited in Bernard et al., *Vold's Theoretical Criminology*, 25.

[14]Bernard et al., *Vold's Theoretical Criminology*, 25–26.

[15]Much of this discussion of Durkheim is taken from Bernard et al., *Vold's Theoretical Criminology*, 100–16, as well as Vander Zanden, *Sociology: The Core*, 11–13.

social theorists of the 19th century, he was strongly affected by the American and French Revolutions and the Industrial Revolution. In his doctoral dissertation (1893) at the University of Paris, the first sociological dissertation at that institution, Durkheim developed a general model of societal development largely based on economic and labor distribution, in which societies are seen as evolving from a simplistic, mechanical society toward a multilayered, organic society (see Figure 6.1).

As outlined in this dissertation, titled *The Division of Labor in Society*, in primitive mechanical societies, all members essentially perform the same functions, such as hunting (typically done by males) and gathering (typically done by females). Although there are a few anomalies (e.g., medicine men), virtually everyone experiences essentially the same daily routine. Such similarities in work, as well as constant interaction with like members of the society, leads to a strong uniformity in values, which Durkheim called the collective conscience. The collective conscience is the degree to which individuals of a society think alike, or as Durkheim put it, the totality of social likenesses. The similar norms and values among people in these primitive, mechanical societies create *mechanical solidarity*, a very simple-social structure with a very strong collective conscience. In mechanical societies, law functions to enforce the conformity of the group.

However, as societies progress toward more modern, organic societies in the industrial age, the distribution of labor becomes more highly specified. An *organic solidarity* arises in which people tend to depend on other groups because of the highly specified division of labor, and laws have the primary function of regulating interactions and maintaining solidarity among the groups.

For example, modern researchers at universities in the United States tend to be trained in extremely narrow topics—one might be an expert on something as specific as the antennae of certain species of ants. On the other hand, some individuals are still gathering trash from the cans on the same streets every single day. The antennae experts probably have little in common with the garbage collectors and not much interaction with them other than when they pay them. According to Durkheim, moving from the universally shared roles of mechanical societies to the extremely specific roles of organic societal organization results in huge cultural differences and giant contrasts in normative values and attitudes across groups. Thus, the collective conscience in such societies is weak, largely because there is little agreement on moral beliefs or opinions. The preexisting solidarity among members breaks down and the bonds are weakened, which creates a climate for antisocial behavior.

Durkheim was clear in stating that crime is not only normal but necessary in all societies. As a result, his theory is often considered a good representation of structural functionalism. He claimed that all social behaviors, especially crime, provide essential functions in a society. Durkheim thought crime serves several functions. First, it defines the moral boundaries of societies. Few people know or realize what is against societal laws until they see someone punished for a violation. This reinforces their understanding of both what the rules are and what it means to break them. Furthermore, the identification of rule breakers creates a bond among the other

| **Figure 6.1** | Durkheim's Continuum of Development from mechanical to organic societies |

Mechanical Societies	Organic Societies
Industrialization	
Primitive	Modern
Rural	Urban
Agricultural-based economy	Industrial-based economy
Simple division of labor (few divisions)	Complex division of labor (many specialized divisions)
Law used to enforce conformity	Law used to regulate interactions among divisions
Typically stronger collective conscience	Typically weaker collective conscience

▲ Image 6.2   Emile Durkheim (1858-1916)

members of the society, perhaps through a common sense of self-righteousness or superiority.

In later works, Durkheim said the resultant bonding is what makes crime so necessary in a society. Given a community that has no law violators, he thought, society will change the legal definitions of what constitutes a crime to define some of its members as criminals. Examples of this are prevalent, but perhaps the most convincing is that of the Salem witch trials, in which hundreds of individuals were accused and tried for an almost laughable offense, and more than a dozen were executed. Durkheim would say this was inevitable because crime was so low in the Massachusetts Bay Colony, as historical records confirm, that society had to come up with a fabricated criterion for defining certain members of the population as offenders.

Other examples are common in everyday life. The fastest way to have a group of strangers bond is to give them a common enemy, which often means forming into cliques and ganging up on others in the group. In a group of three or more college roommates, for example, two or more of the individuals will quickly join together and complain about the others. This is an inevitable phenomenon of human interaction and group dynamics that has always existed throughout the world across time and place. As Durkheim said, even in "a society of saints . . . crimes . . . will there be unknown; but faults which appear venial to the layman will create there the same scandal that the ordinary offense does in ordinary consciousnesses. . . . This society . . . will define these acts as criminal and will treat them as such."[16]

Law enforcement should always be cautious in cracking down on gangs, especially during relatively inactive periods, because it may make the gang stronger. Like all societal groups, when a common enemy appears, gang members—even those who do not typically get along—will come together and "circle the wagons" to protect themselves via strength in numbers. This very powerful bonding effect is one that many sociologists, and especially gang researchers, have consistently observed.[17]

Traditional, mostly mechanical societies could count on relative consensus about moral values and norms, and this sometimes led to too much control and a stagnation of creative thought. Durkheim thought that progress in society typically depends on deviating from established moral boundaries, especially if the society is in the mechanical stage. Some of the many examples include virtually all religious icons. Jesus, Buddha, and Mohammed were persecuted as criminals for deviating from societal norms in the times they preached. Political heroes have also been prosecuted and incarcerated as criminals, such as Gandhi in India, Mandela in South Africa, and Dr. King in the United States. In one of the most compelling cases, scientist and astronomer Galileo proposed a theory that Earth was not the center of the universe. Even though he was right, he was persecuted for his belief in a society that strictly adhered to its beliefs. Durkheim was clearly accurate in saying that the normative structure in some societies is so strong that it hinders progress and that crime is the price societies pay for progress.

[16]Émile Durkheim, *The Rules of the Sociological Method*, trans. Sarah A. Solovay and John H. Mueller, ed. George E. G. Catlin (New York: Free Press, 1965), as cited in Bernard et al., *Vold's Theoretical Criminology*.

[17]See discussion in Malcolm Klein, "Street Gang Cycles," in *Crime*, ed. James Q. Wilson and Joan Petersilia (San Francisco: ICS Press, 2002), 217–36.

In contrast to mechanical societies, modern societies do not have such extreme restraint against deviations from established norms. Rather, almost the opposite is true; there are too many differences across groups because the division of labor is highly specialized. Thus, the varying roles in society, such as farmers versus scientific researchers, lead to extreme differences in the cultural values and norms of each group. There is a breakdown in the collective conscience because there is really no longer a collective nature in society. Therefore, law focuses not on defining the norms of society but on governing the interactions that take place among the different classes. According to Durkheim, law provides a service in regulating such interactions as societies progress toward more organic (more industrial) forms.

Durkheim emphasized that human beings, unlike other animal species who live according to their spontaneous needs, have no internal mechanism to signal when their needs and desires are satiated. Therefore, the selfish desires of humankind are limitless; the more an individual has, the more he or she wants. People are greedy by nature, and without something to tell them what they need and deserve, they will never feel content.[18] According to Durkheim, society provides the mechanism for limiting this insatiable appetite, having the sole power to create laws that set tangible limits.

Durkheim also noted that in times of rapid change, society fails in this role of regulating desires and expectations. Rapid change can be due to numerous factors, such as war or social movements (like the changes seen in the United States in the 1960s). The transitions Durkheim likely had in mind when he wrote were the American and French Revolutions and the Industrial Revolution. When society's ability to serve as a regulatory mechanism breaks down, the selfish, greedy tendencies of individuals are uncontrolled, causing a state Durkheim called *anomie*, or *normlessness*. Societies in such anomic states experience increases in many social problems, particularly criminal activity.

Durkheim was clear that, whether the rapid change was for good or bad, it would have negative effects on society. For example, whether the U.S. economy was improving, as it did during the late 1960s, or quickly tanking, as it did during the Depression of the 1930s, criminal activity would increase due to the lack of stability in regulating human expectations and desires. Interestingly, these two periods experienced the greatest crime waves of the 20th century, particularly for murder.[19] Another fact that supports Durkheim's predictions is that middle- and upper-class individuals have higher suicide rates than those from lower classes. This is consistent with the idea that it is better to have stability, even if it means always being poor, than it is to have instability at higher levels of income. In his best-known work, *Suicide,* Durkheim took an act that would seem to be the ultimate form of free choice or free will and showed that the decision to take one's own life was largely determined by external social factors. He argued that suicide is a *social fact*, a product of meanings and structural aspects that result from interactions among people.

Durkheim showed that the rate of suicide was significantly lower among individuals who were married, younger, and practiced religions that were more interactive and communal (e.g., Jewish). All of these characteristics boil down to one aspect: The more the social interaction and bonding with the community, the less the suicide. Thus, Durkheim concluded that variations in suicide rates are due to differences in social solidarity or bonding to society. Examples of this are still seen today, as in recent reports of high rates of suicide among people who live in remote areas, like Alaska (which has the highest rate of juvenile suicide), Wyoming, Montana, and the northern portions of Nevada. Another way of looking at the implications of Durkheim's conclusions is that social relationships are what make people happy and fulfilled. If they are isolated or have weak bonds to society, they will likely be depressed and discontented with their lives.

Another reason that Durkheim's examination of suicide was important was that he showed that suicide rates increased in times of rapid economic growth or rapid decline. Although researchers later argued that crime rates did

---

[18]For more details on these issues, see Émile Durkheim's works: *The Division of Labor in Society* (New York: Free Press, 1893/1965) and *Suicide* (New York: Free Press, 1897/1951).

[19]U.S. Department of Justice, Bureau of Justice Statistics, *Violent Crime in the United States* (Washington, DC: Bureau of Justice Statistics, 1996), as illustrated in Joseph P. Senna and Larry G. Siegel, *Introduction to Criminal Justice*, 8th ed. (Belmont: West/Wadsworth, 1999).

not always follow this pattern,[20] Durkheim used quantified measures to test his propositions as the positivistic approach recommended. At the least, Durkheim created a prototype of how theory and empirical research could be combined in testing differences across social groups. This theoretical framework was drawn on heavily for one of the most influential and accepted criminological theories of the 20th century: strain theory.

 ## Strain Theories

All forms of strain theory share an emphasis on frustration as a factor in crime causation, hence the name *strain* theories. Although the theories differ regarding what exactly is causing the frustration—and the way individuals cope (or don't cope) with stress and anger—they all hold that strain is the primary causal factor in the development of criminality. Strain theories all trace their origin to Robert K. Merton's seminal theoretical framework.

Merton's Strain Theory

Working in the 1930s, Merton drew heavily on Durkheim's idea of anomie in developing his own theory of structural strain.[21] Although Merton altered the definition of anomie, Durkheim's theoretical framework was a vital influence in the evolution of strain theory. Combining Durkheimian concepts and propositions with an emphasis on American culture, Merton's structural model became one of the most popular perspectives in criminological thought in the early 1900s and remains one of the most cited theories of crime in criminological literature.

Cultural Context and Assumptions of Strain Theory

Some have claimed that Merton's seminal piece in 1938 was the most influential theoretical formulation in criminological literature, and it is one of the most frequently cited papers in sociology.[22] Although its popularity is partially due to its strong foundation in previous structural theories, Merton's strain theory also benefited from the timing of its publication. Virtually every theory discussed in this book became popular because it was well suited to the political and social climate of the times, fitting perspectives of how the world worked. Perhaps no other theory better represents this phenomenon than strain theory.

Most historians would agree that, in the United States, the most significant social issue of the 1930s was the economy. The influence of the Great Depression, largely a result of a stock market crash in 1929, affected virtually every aspect of life in the United States. Unemployment and extreme poverty soared, along with suicide rates and crime rates, particularly murder rates.[23] American society was fertile ground for a theory of crime that placed virtually all of the blame on the U.S. economic structure.

---

[20]William J. Chambliss, "Functional and Conflict Theories of Crime," in *Whose Law? What Order?*, ed. William J. Chambliss and Milton Mankoff (New York: Wiley, 1976), 11–16.

[21]For reviews of Merton's theory, see both the original and more recent works by Merton himself: Robert K. Merton, "Social Structure and Anomie," *American Sociological Review* 3 (1938): 672–82; Robert K. Merton, *Social Theory and Social Structure* (New York: Free Press, 1968); and Robert K. Merton, "Opportunity Structure: The Emergence, Diffusion, and Differentiation as Sociological Concept, 1930s–1950s," in *Advances in Criminological Theory: The Legacy of Anomie Theory*, Vol. 6, ed. Freda Adler and William Laufer (New Brunswick: Transaction Press, 1995). For reviews by others, see Ronald L. Akers and Christine S. Sellers, *Criminological Theories: Introduction, Evaluation, and Application*, 6th ed. (Oxford: Oxford University Press, 2012), 164–68; Stephen E. Brown, Finn-Aage Esbensen, and Gilbert Geis, *Criminology: Explaining Crime and Its Context*, 8th ed. (Cincinnati: Anderson, 2013), 297–307; Marshall B. Clinard, "The Theoretical Implications of Anomie and Deviant Behavior," in *Anomie and Deviant Behavior*, ed. Marshall B. Clinard (New York: Free Press, 1964), 1–56; and Thomas J. Bernard, "Testing Structural Strain Theories," *Journal of Research in Crime and Delinquency* 24 (1987): 262–80.

[22]Clinard, "Theoretical Implications." See also the discussion in Brown et al., *Criminology*, 297.

[23]Larry J. Siegel, *Introduction to Criminal Justice*, 12th ed. (Belmont: Wadsworth, 2010), 44.

On the other side of the coin, Merton was highly influenced by what he saw happening to the country during the Depression and how much the economic institution impacted almost all other social factors, particularly crime. He watched how the breakdown of the economic structure drove people to kill themselves or others, not to mention the rise in property crimes such as theft. Many once-successful individuals were now poor, and some felt driven to crime for survival. Notably, Durkheim's hypotheses regarding crime and suicide were supported during this time of rapid change, and Merton apparently realized that the framework simply had to be brought up-to-date and supplemented.

One of the key assumptions that distinguishes strain theory from Durkheim's perspective is that Merton altered his version of what anomie means. Merton focused on the nearly universal socialization of the American Dream in U.S. society—the idea that, as long as people work very hard and pay their dues, they will achieve their goals in the end. According to Merton, the socialized image of the goal is material wealth, whereas the socialized concept of the means of achieving the goal is hard work (e.g., education, labor). The conventional model of the American Dream was consistent with the Protestant work ethic, which called for working hard for a long time, knowing that you will be paid off in the distant future.

Furthermore, Merton thought that nearly everyone was socialized to believe in the American Dream, no matter what economic class he or she was raised in as a child. There is some empirical support for this belief, and it makes sense. Virtually all parents, even if they are poor, want to give their children hope for the future if they are willing to work hard in school and at a job. Parents and society usually use celebrities as examples of this process—individuals who started off poor and rose to become wealthy. Modern examples include former secretary of state Colin Powell, owner of the NBA Dallas Mavericks Mark Cuban, Oscar-winning actress Hilary Swank, and Hollywood director and screenwriter Quentin Tarantino, not to mention Arnold Schwarzenegger and his amazing rise from teenage immigrant to Mr. Olympia and California governor.

These stories epitomize the American Dream, but parents and society do not also teach the reality of the situation. As Merton points out, a small percentage of people rise from the lower class to become materially successful, but the vast majority of poor children don't have much chance of ever obtaining such wealth. This near-universal socialization of the American Dream—which turns out not to be true for most people—causes most of the strain and frustration in American society, Merton said. Furthermore, he thought that most of the strain and frustration was due not to the failure to achieve conventional goals (i.e., wealth) but rather to the differential emphasis placed on material goals and the de-emphasizing of the importance of conventional means.

Merton's Concept of Anomie and Strain

Merton claimed that, in an ideal society, there would be an equal emphasis on conventional goals and means. However, in many societies, one is emphasized more than the other. Merton thought the United States epitomized the type of society that emphasized the goals far more than the means. The disequilibrium in emphasis between the goals and means of societies is what Merton called anomie. So, like Durkheim, Merton's anomie was a negative state for society; however, the two men had very different ideas of how this state of society was caused. Whereas Durkheim believed that anomie was primarily caused by a society's transitioning too fast to maintain its regulatory control over its members, for Merton, anomie represented too much focus on the goals of wealth in the United States at the expense of conventional means.

Hypothetical situations can be used to illustrate Merton's view: Which of the following two men would be more respected by youths (or even adults) in our society: (1) John, who has his PhD in physics and lives in a one-bedroom apartment because his job as a postdoctoral student pays $25,000 a year; or (2) Joe, who is a relatively successful drug dealer and owns a four-bedroom home, drives a Hummer, dropped out of school in the 10th grade, and makes about $90,000 a year? In years of asking such a question to our classes, we have found that the answer is usually Joe, the drug dealer. After all, he appears to have obtained the American Dream, and little emphasis is placed on how he achieved it.

▲ Image 6.3   Robert K. Merton (1910–2003)

Source: © Michael Schvel, 1995.

Still another way of supporting Merton's idea that America is too focused on the goal of material success is to ask you, the reader, to think about why you are taking the time to read this book or to attend college. Specifically, the question for you is this: If you knew that studying this book—or earning a college degree—would not lead to a better employment position, would you read it anyway just to increase your own knowledge? In over a decade of putting this question to about 10,000 students in various university courses, one of the authors of this book has found that only about 5% (usually fewer) of respondents say yes. Interestingly, when asked why they put all of this work into attending classes, many of them say it's for the partying or social life. Ultimately, it seems that most college students would not be engaging in the hard work it takes to educate themselves if it weren't for some payoff at the end of the task. In some ways, this supports Merton's claim that there is an emphasis on the goals and little or no intrinsic value placed on the work itself (i.e., means). This phenomenon is not meant to be a disheartening or a negative statement; it is meant only to exhibit the reality of American culture. It is quite common in our society to emphasize the goal of financial success as opposed to hard work or education.

Merton thought that individuals, particularly those in the lower class, eventually realize that the ideal of the American Dream is a lie or at least a false illusion for the vast majority. This revelation will likely take place when people are in their late teens to mid-20s, and according to Merton, this is when the frustration or strain is evident. That is consistent with the age-crime peak of offending at the approximate age of 17. Learning that hard work won't necessarily provide rewards, some individuals begin to innovate ways that they can achieve material success without the conventional means of getting it. Obviously, this is often through criminal activity. However, not all individuals deal with strain in this way; most people who are poor do not resort to crime. To Merton's credit, he explained that individuals deal with the limited economic structure of society in different ways. He referred to these variations as adaptations to strain.

Adaptations to Strain

According to Merton, there are five adaptations to strain. The first of these is conformity, in which people buy into the conventional goals of society and the conventional means of working hard in school or at their labor.[24] Like conformists, most readers of this book would probably like to achieve material success and are willing to use conventional means of achieving success through educational efforts and doing a good job at work. Another adaptation to strain is ritualism. Ritualists do not pursue the goal of material success, probably because they know they don't have a realistic chance of obtaining it. However, they do buy into the conventional means in the sense that they like to do their jobs or are happy

[24]Merton, *Social Theory*.

with just making ends meet through their current positions. For example, studies have shown that some of the most contented and happy people in society are those who don't hope to become rich, are quite content with their blue-collar jobs, and often have a strong sense of pride in their work, even if it is sometimes quite menial. To these people, work is a type of ritual, performed without a goal in mind; rather, it is a form of intrinsic goal in and of itself. Ultimately, conformists and ritualists tend to be at low risk for offending, which is in contrast to the other adaptations to strain.

The other three adaptations to strain are far more likely to be associated with criminal offending: innovation, retreatism, and rebellion. Perhaps most likely to become predatory street criminals are the innovators, who Merton claimed greatly desire the conventional goals of material success but are not willing to engage in conventional means. Obviously, drug dealers and professional auto thieves, as well as many other variations of chronic property criminals (bank robbers, etc.), would fit this category. They are innovating ways to achieve the goals without the hard work that is usually required. However, innovators are not always criminals. In fact, many of them are the most respected individuals in our society. For example, some entrepreneurs have used the capitalistic system of our society to produce useful products and services (e.g., the men who designed Google for the Internet) and have made a fortune at a very young age without advanced college education or years of work at a company. Other examples are successful athletes who sign multimillion-dollar contracts at age 18. So, it should be clear that not all innovators are criminals.

The fourth adaptation to strain is retreatism. Retreatists do not seek to achieve the goals of society, and they also do not buy into the idea of conventional hard work. There are many varieties of this adaptation: for example, people who become homeless by choice or who isolate themselves in desolate places without human contact. A good example of a retreatist is Ted Kaczynski, the Unabomber, who left a good position as a professor at the University of California at Berkeley to live in an isolated cabin in Montana that had no running water or electricity; he did not interact with humans for many months at a time. Other types of retreatists, perhaps the most likely to be criminal, are those who are heavy drug users who actively disengage from social life and try to escape via mind-altering drugs. All of these forms of retreatists seek to drop out of society altogether, thus not buying into its means or goals.

Finally, the last adaptation to strain, according to Merton, is rebellion, which is the most complex of the five adaptations. Interestingly, rebels buy into the idea of societal goals and means, but they do not buy into those currently in place. Most true rebels are criminals by definition, largely because they are trying to overthrow the current societal structure. For example, the founders of the United States were all rebels because they actively fought the governing state—English rule—and clearly committed treason in the process. Had they lost or been caught during the American Revolution, they would have been executed as the criminals they were by law. However, because they won the war, they became heroes and presidents. Another example is Karl Marx. He bought into the idea of goals and means of society, just not those of capitalistic societies. Rather, he proposed socialism or communism as a means to the goal of utopia. So, there are many contexts in which rebels can be criminals, but sometimes they end up being heroes.

Merton also noted that one individual can represent more than one adaptation. Perhaps the best example is that of the Unabomber, who obviously started out as a conformist in that he was a respected professor at the University of California, Berkeley, who was well on his way to tenure and promotion. He then seemed to shift to retreatism in that he isolated himself from society. Later, he became a rebel who bombed innocent people in his quest to implement his own goals and means as described in his manifesto, which he coerced several national newspapers to publish. This subsequently resulted in his apprehension when his brother read it and informed authorities that he thought his brother was the author.

Finally, some have applied a sports analogy to these adaptations.[25] Assuming a basketball game is taking place, conformists will play to win, and they will always play by the rules and won't cheat. Ritualists will play the game just because they like to play; they don't care about winning. Innovators will play to win, and they will

---

[25]Bernard et al., *Vold's Theoretical Criminology*, 140.

break any rules they can to triumph in the game. Retreatists don't like to play and obviously don't care about winning. Finally, rebels won't like the rules on the court, so they will try to steal the ball and go play by their own rules on another court. Although this is a somewhat simplistic analogy, it is likely to help readers remember the adaptations and perhaps enable them to apply these ways of dealing with strain to everyday situations, such as criminal activity.

Evidence and Criticisms of Merton's Strain Theory

Merton's framework, which emphasized the importance of economic structure, had a high degree of face validity during the Great Depression; however, many later scientific studies showed mixed support for strain theory. Although research that examined the effects of poverty on violence and official rates of various crimes has found relatively consistent support for Merton's views (albeit with weaker effects than strain theory implies), a series of studies of self-reported delinquent behavior found little or no relationship between social class and criminality.[26] Furthermore, the idea that unemployment drives people to commit crime has received little support.[27]

On the other hand, some experts have argued that Merton's strain theory is primarily a structural model of crime that is more a theory of societal groups, not individual motivations.[28] Therefore, some modern studies have used aggregated group rates (i.e., macro-level measures) to test the effects of deprivation, as opposed to using individual (micro-level) rates of inequality and crime. Most of these studies provide some support for the hypothesis that social groups and regions with higher rates of deprivation and inequality have higher rates of criminal activity.[29] In sum, there appears to be some support for Merton's strain theory at the macro level of analysis when official measures are being used to indicate criminality.

However, many critics have claimed that these studies do not directly measure perceptions or feelings of strain, so they are only indirect examinations of Merton's theory. In light of these criticisms, some researchers focused on the disparity between what individuals aspire to in various aspects of life (e.g., school, occupation, social life) and what they realistically expect to achieve.[30] The rationale behind these studies was that, if an individual has high

---

[26]For examples and reviews of this research, see F. Ivan Nye, *Family Relationships and Delinquent Behavior* (New York: Wiley, 1958); Ronald L. Akers, "Socio-economic Status and Delinquent Behavior: A Retest," *Journal of Research in Crime and Delinquency* 1 (1964): 38–46; Charles R. Tittle and Wayne J. Villemez, "Social Class and Criminality," *Social Forces* 56 (1977): 474–503; Charles R. Tittle, Wayne J. Villemez, and Douglas A. Smith, "The Myth of Social Class and Criminality: An Empirical Assessment of the Empirical Evidence," *American Sociological Review* 43 (1978): 643–56; Michael J. Hindelang, Travis Hirschi, and Joseph C. Weis, "Correlates of Delinquency: The Illusion of Discrepancy between Self-Report and Official Measures," *American Sociological Review* 44 (1979): 995–1014; Michael J. Hindelang, *Measuring Delinquency* (Beverly Hills: Sage, 1980); Terence P. Thornberry and Margaret Farnworth, "Social Correlates of Criminal Involvement," *American Sociological Review* 47 (1982): 505–17; and Gregory R. Dunaway, Francis T. Cullen, Velmer S. Burton, and T. David Evans, "The Myth of Social Class and Crime Revisited: An Examination of Class and Adult Criminality," *Criminology* 38 (2000): 589–632. For one of the most thorough reviews, see Charles R. Tittle and Robert F. Meier, "Specifying the SES/Delinquency Relationship," *Criminology* 28 (1990): 271–99.

[27]Gary Kleck and Ted Chiricos, "Unemployment and Property Crime: A Target-Specific Assessment of Opportunity and Motivation as Mediating Factors," *Criminology* 40 (2000): 649–680.

[28]Bernard, "Testing Structural Strain Theories"; Steven F. Messner, "Merton's 'Social Structure and Anomie': The Road Not Taken," *Deviant Behavior* 9 (1988): 33–53. See also discussion in Burton and Cullen, "Empirical Status."

[29]For a review of these studies, see Kenneth C. Land, Patricia L. McCall, and Lawrence E. Cohen, "Structural Covariates of Homicide Rates: Are There Any Invariances across Time and Social Space?" *American Journal of Sociology* 95 (1990): 922–63.

[30]For examples and reviews of these types of studies, see Travis Hirschi, *Causes of Delinquency* (Berkeley: University of California Press, 1969), 4–10; Allen E. Liska, "Aspirations, Expectations, and Delinquency: Stress and Additive Models," *Sociological Quarterly* 12 (1971): 99–107; Margaret Farnworth and Michael J. Leiber, "Strain Theory Revisited: Economic Goals, Educational Means, and Delinquency," *American Sociological Review* 54 (1989): 263–74; Burton and Cullen, "Empirical Status"; Velmer S. Burton, Francis T. Cullen, T. David Evans, and R. Gregory Dunaway, "Reconsidering Strain Theory: Operationalization, Rival Theories, and Adult Criminality," *Journal of Quantitative Criminology* 10 (1994): 213–39; and Robert F. Agnew, Francis T. Cullen, Velmer S. Burton, T. David Evans, and R. Gregory Dunaway, "A New Test of Classic Strain Theory," *Justice Quarterly* 13 (1996): 681–704. See also discussion of this issue in Akers and Sellers, *Criminological Theories*, 173–75.

aspirations (i.e., goals) but a low expectation of actually achieving the goals due to structural barriers, then that individual is more likely to experience feelings of frustration and strain. Furthermore, it was predicted that the larger the gap between aspirations and expectations, the stronger the sense of strain. Of the studies that examined discrepancies between aspirations and expectations, most did not find evidence to link a large gap between these two levels with criminal activity. In fact, several studies found that, for most antisocial respondents, there was virtually no gap between aspirations and expectations. Rather, most of the subjects who reported the highest levels of criminal activity (typically young males) tended to report low levels of both aspirations and expectations.

Surprisingly, when aspirations were high, it seemed to inhibit offending, even when expectations to achieve those goals were low. One interpretation of these findings is that individuals who have high goals will not jeopardize their chances even if they are slim. On the other hand, individuals who don't have high goals are likely to be indifferent to their future and, in a sense, have nothing to lose. So, without a stake in conventional society, this predisposes them to crime. While this conclusion supports social control theories, it does not provide support for strain theory.

Some critics have argued that most studies on the discrepancies between aspirations and expectations have not been done correctly. For example, Farnworth and Leiber claimed that it was a mistake to examine differences between educational goals and expectations or differences between occupational goals and expectations, which is what most of these studies did.[31] Rather, they proposed testing the gap between economic aspirations (i.e., goals) and educational expectations (i.e., means of achieving the goals). This makes sense, and Farnworth and Leiber found support for a gap between these two factors and criminality. However, they also found that people who reported low economic aspirations were more likely to be delinquent, which supports the previous studies that they criticized. Another criticism of this type of strain theory study is that simply reporting a gap between expectations and aspirations may not mean that the individuals actually feel strain; rather, researchers have simply, and perhaps wrongfully, assumed that a gap between the two measures indicates feelings of frustration.[32]

Other criticisms of Merton's strain theory include historical evidence and the theory's failure to explain the age-crime curve. Regarding the historical evidence, it is hard to understand why some of the largest increases in crime took place during a period of relative economic prosperity, namely the late 1960s. Between 1965 and 1973, which were generally good economic years in the United States, crime increased more than it had ever done since recording crime rates began. Therefore, if strain theory is presented as the primary explanation for criminal activity, it would probably have a hard time explaining this historical era. On the other hand, the growth in the economy in the 1960s and early 1970s may have caused more disparity between the rich and the poor, thereby producing more relative deprivation.

The other major criticism of strain theory is that it does not explain one of the most established facts in the field: the age-crime curve. In virtually every society in the world, across time and place, predatory street crimes (robbery, rape, murder, burglary, larceny, etc.) tend to peak sharply in the teenage years to early 20s and then drop off very quickly, certainly before age 30. However, most studies show that feelings of stress and frustration tend not to follow this pattern. For example, suicide rates tend to be just as high or higher as one gets older, with middle-aged and elderly people having much higher rates of suicide than those in their teens or early 20s.

On the other hand, it can be argued that crime rates go down even though strain can continue or even increase with age because individuals develop coping mechanisms for dealing with the frustrations they feel. But, even if this is true regarding criminal behavior, apparently this doesn't seem to prevent suicidal tendencies. General strain theory emphasized this concept. However, before we cover general strain theory, we will discuss two other variations of Merton's theory that were both developed between 1955 and 1960 to explain gang formation and behavior using a structural strain framework.

---

[31]Farnworth and Leiber, "Strain Theory."

[32]Agnew et al., "A New Test."

Variations of Merton's Strain Theory: Cohen, and Cloward and Ohlin

Cohen's Theory of Lower-Class Status Frustration and Gang Formation

In 1955, Albert Cohen presented a theory of gang formation that used Merton's strain theory as a basis for why individuals resort to such group behavior.[33] In Cohen's model, young, lower-class males are at a disadvantage in school because they lack the normal interaction, socialization, and discipline instituted by educated parents of the middle class. This is in line with Merton's original framework identifying a disadvantage for underclass youth. According to Cohen, such youths are likely to experience failure in school because they are unprepared to conform with middle-class values and fail to meet the middle-class measuring rod, which emphasizes motivation, accountability, responsibility, deferred gratification, long-term planning, respect for authority and property, controlling emotions, and so on.

Like Merton, Cohen emphasized the youths' internalization of the American Dream and the idea that they had a fair chance of success, which would mean that failure to be successful according to this middle-class standard would be very frustrating for them. The strain felt as a result of failure in school performance and lack of respect among peers is often referred to as *status frustration*. It leads youth to develop a system of values opposed to middle-class standards and values. Some have claimed that this represents a Freudian defense mechanism known as reaction formation, which involves adopting attitudes or committing behaviors that are opposite of what is expected as a form of defiance so as to feel less guilty for not living up to unachievable standards. Specifically, instead of abiding by middle-class norms of obedience to authority, school achievement, and respect for authority, these youths change their normative beliefs to value the opposite characteristics: malicious, negativistic, and nonutilitarian delinquent activity.

Delinquent youths will begin to value destruction of property and skipping school, not because these behaviors lead to a payoff or success in the conventional world, but simply because they defy the conventional order. In other words, they turn middle-class values upside down and consider activity that violates the conventional norms and laws good, thereby psychologically and physically rejecting the cultural system that has been imposed on them without preparation and fair distribution of resources. Furthermore, Cohen claimed that while these behaviors do not appear to have much utility or value, they are quite valuable and important from the perspective of the strained youths. Specifically, they do these acts to gain respect from their peers.

Cohen stated that he believed that this tendency to reject middle-class values is the primary cause of gangs, a classic example of "birds of a feather flock together." Not all lower-class males resort to crime and join a gang in response to this structural disadvantage. Other variations, beyond that of the delinquent boy described above, include the college boy and the corner boy. The college boy responds to his disadvantaged situation by dedicating himself to overcoming the odds and competing in middle-class schools despite his unlikely chances for success. The corner boy responds to the situation by accepting his place as a lower-class individual who will somewhat passively make the best of life at the bottom of the social order.

When compared to Merton's original adaptations, Cohen's delinquent boy is probably best seen as similar to a rebel because he rejects the means and goals of conventional society (i.e., middle-class values and success in school), substituting new means and goals (negativistic behaviors and peer respect in the gang). Some would argue that delinquent boys should be seen as innovators because their goals are ultimately the same: peer respect. However, the actual peers involved completely change, so we argue that, through the reaction formation process, the delinquent boy actually creates his own goals and means that go against the conventional, middle-class goals and means. Regarding the college boy, the adaptation that seems to fit the best is that of conformity, because the college boy continues to believe in the conventional goals (i.e., financial success and achievement) and means (hard work via education or labor) of middle-class society. Finally, the corner boy probably best fits the adaptation of ritualism

---

[33]Albert Cohen, *Delinquent Boys: The Culture of the Gang* (New York: Free Press, 1955).

because he knows that he likely will never achieve the goals of society but resigns himself to not obtaining financial success; at the same time, he does not resort to predatory street crime, but rather holds a stable, blue-collar job or makes ends meet in other typical, legal ways. Some corner boys end up simply collecting welfare and give up working altogether; they may actually become more like the adaptation of retreatism because they have virtually given up on the conventional means of society (hard work) as well as the goals.

At the time that Cohen developed his theory, official statistics showed that virtually all gang violence, and most violence for that matter, was concentrated among lower-class male youth. However, with the development of self-report studies in the 1960s, Cohen's theory was shown to be somewhat overstated: Middle-class youth were well represented among those who committed delinquent acts.[34] Other studies have also been critical of Cohen's theory, particularly the portions that deal with his proposition that crime rates will increase after youths drop out of school and join gangs. Although the findings are mixed, many studies have found that delinquency is often higher before youths drop out of school and may actually decline once they drop out and become employed.[35] Some critics have pointed out that such findings discredit Cohen's theory, but this is not necessarily true. After all, delinquency may peak right before the youths drop out because they feel the most frustrated and strained then, whereas delinquency may decrease after they drop out because some are raising their self-esteem by earning wages and taking pride in having jobs.

Still, studies have clearly shown that lower-class youths are far more likely to have problems in school and that school failure is consistently linked to criminality.[36] Furthermore, there is little dispute that much of delinquency represents malicious, negativistic, and nonutilitarian activity. For example, what do individuals have to gain from destroying mailboxes or spraying graffiti on walls? These acts will never earn much money or any payoff other than peer respect. So, ultimately, it appears that there is some face validity to what Cohen proposed in the sense that some youths engage in behavior that has no value other than earning peer respect, even though that behavior is negativistic and nonutilitarian according to the values of conventional society. Regardless of some criticisms of Cohen's model, he provided an important structural strain theory of the development of gangs and lower-class delinquency.

Cloward and Ohlin's Theory of Differential Opportunity

Five years after Cohen published his theory, Cloward and Ohlin presented yet another structural strain theory of gang formation and behavior.[37] Like Merton and Cohen, Cloward and Ohlin assumed in their model that all youths, including those in the lower class, are socialized to believe in the American Dream, and that when individuals realize that they are blocked from conventional opportunities, they become frustrated and strained. What distinguishes Cloward and Ohlin's theory from that of the previous strain theories is that they identified three different types of gangs based on the characteristics of each neighborhood's social structure. They believed the nature of gangs varied according to the availability of illegal opportunities in the social structure. So, whereas previous strain theories focused only on

[34]Tittle et al., "Myth of Social Class"; Hindelang et al., "Correlates of Delinquency."

[35]See Bernard, "Testing Structural Strain Theories"; Merton, "Opportunity Structure"; Delbert Elliott and Harwin Voss, *Delinquency and Dropout* (Lexington: D. C. Heath, 1974); Terence P. Thornberry, Melanie Moore, and R. L. Christenson, "The Effect of Dropping Out of High School on Subsequent Criminal Behavior," *Criminology* 23 (1985): 3–18; G. Roger Jarjoura, "Does Dropping Out of School Enhance Delinquent Involvement? Results from a Large-Scale National Probability Sample," *Criminology* 31 (1993): 149–72; and G. Roger Jarjoura, "The Conditional Effect of Social Class on the Dropout Delinquency Relationship," *Journal of Research in Crime and Delinquency* 33 (1996): 232–55. See discussion in Donald J. Shoemaker, *Theories of Delinquency*, 6th ed. (New York: Oxford University Press, 2009).

[36]Alexander Liazos, "School, Alienation, and Delinquency," *Crime and Delinquency* 24 (1978): 355–70; Joseph W. Rogers and G. Larry Mays, *Juvenile Delinquency and Juvenile Justice* (New York: Wiley, 1987); Clarence E. Tygart, "Strain Theory and Public School Vandalism: Academic Tracking, School Social Status, and Students' Academic Achievement," *Youth and Society* 20 (1988): 106–18; Hirschi, *Causes of Delinquency*.

[37]Richard A. Cloward and Lloyd E. Ohlin, *Delinquency and Opportunity: A Theory of Delinquent Gangs* (New York: The Free Press, 1960). For a discussion and theoretical critique of the model, see Bernard, "Testing Structural Strain Theories," and Merton, "Opportunity Structure," respectively.

lack of legal opportunities, Cloward and Ohlin's model emphasized both legal and illegal opportunities; the availability or lack of these opportunities largely determined what type of gang would form in that neighborhood, hence the name *differential opportunity theory*. Furthermore, the authors acknowledged Edwin Sutherland's influence on their theory (see Section VIII), and it is evident in their focus on the associations made in the neighborhood.

According to differential opportunity theory, the three types of gangs that form are criminal gangs, conflict gangs, and retreatist gangs. Criminal gangs form in lower-class neighborhoods that have an organized structure of adult criminal behavior. Such neighborhoods are so organized and stable that criminal networks are often known and accepted by the conventional individuals in the area. In these neighborhoods, the adult gangsters mentor the youth and take them under their wings. This can pay off for the adult criminals, too, because youths can often be used to do the dirty work for the criminal enterprises in the neighborhood without risk of serious punishment if they are caught. The successful adult offenders supply the youths with the motives and techniques for committing crime. So, while members of criminal gangs are blocked from legal opportunities, they are offered ample opportunities in the illegal realm.

Criminal gangs tend to reflect the strong organization and stability of such neighborhoods. Therefore, criminal gangs primarily commit property or economic crimes with the goal of making a profit through illegal behavior. These crimes can range from running numbers as local bookies to fencing stolen goods to running businesses that are fronts for vice crimes (e.g., prostitution, drug trading). All of these businesses involve making a profit illegally, and there is often a system or structure in which the criminal activity takes place. Furthermore, these criminal gangs most closely follow Merton's adaptation of innovation because the members still want to achieve the goals of conventional society (financial success). Because of their strong organizational structure, these gangs favor members who have self-control and are good at planning over individuals who are highly impulsive or uncontrolled.

Examples of criminal gangs are seen in movies depicting highly organized neighborhoods that often consist primarily of one ethnicity, including *The Godfather*, *The Godfather II*, *A Bronx Tale*, *State of Grace*, *Sleepers*, *New Jack City*, *Clockers*, *GoodFellas*, *Better Luck Tomorrow*, and many others that were partially based on real events. All of these depictions involve a highly structured hierarchy of a criminal enterprise, which is largely a manifestation of the organization of the neighborhood. Hollywood motion pictures also produce stories about older criminals taking younger males from the neighborhood under their wings and training them in the ways of criminal networks. Furthermore, virtually all ethnic groups offer examples of this type of gang or neighborhood; the list of movies above includes Italian American, Irish American, African American, and Asian American examples. Thus, criminal gangs can be found across the racial and ethnic spectrum, largely because all groups have certain neighborhoods that exhibit strong organization and stability.

▲ Image 6.4 Organized crime syndicates are typically found in neighborhoods with more structured criminal organizations.

Source: © Digital Vision / Photodisc / Thinkstock.

Conflict gangs were another type of gang that Cloward and Ohlin identified. Conflict gangs tend to develop in neighborhoods that have weak stability and little or no organization. In fact, the neighborhood often seems to be in a state of flux, with people constantly moving in and out. Because the youths in the neighborhood do not have a solid crime network or adult criminal mentors, they tend to form as relatively disorganized gangs, and they typically lack the skills and knowledge to make a profit through criminal activity. Therefore, the primary illegal activity of conflict gangs is violence, which they use to gain prominence and respect among themselves and the neighborhood. Due to the disorganized nature of the neighborhoods as well as the gangs themselves, conflict gangs never quite achieve the respect and stability that criminal gangs typically achieve. The members of conflict gangs tend to be more impulsive and lack self-control compared to members of criminal gangs, largely because there are no adult criminal mentors to control them.

According to Cloward and Ohlin, conflict gangs are blocked from both legitimate and illegitimate opportunities. In applying Merton's adaptations, conflict gangs would probably fit the category of rebellion, largely because none of the other categories fit well, but it can also be argued that conflict gangs have rejected the goals and means of conventional society and implemented their own values, which emphasize violence. Examples of motion pictures that depict this type of breakdown in community structure and a mostly violent gang culture are *Menace II Society*, *Boyz n the Hood*, *A Clockwork Orange*, *Colors*, and *The Outsiders*, which all emphasize the chaos and violence that results when neighborhood and family organization is weak.

Finally, if individuals are double failures in both legitimate and illegitimate worlds, meaning that they can't achieve success in school or status in their local gangs, they join together to form retreatist gangs. Because members of retreatist gangs are no good at making a profit from crime or using violence to achieve status, the primary form of offending is usually drug usage. Like individuals who choose Merton's retreatist adaptation to strain, the members of retreatist gangs often want simply to escape from reality. Therefore, the primary activity of the gang when they get together is usually just to get high, which is well represented by Hollywood in such movies as *Trainspotting*, *Drug-Store Cowboy*, and *The Panic in Needle Park*. In all of these movies, the only true goal of the gangs is getting stoned to escape from the worlds where they have failed.

There are a number of empirical studies and critiques of Cloward and Ohlin's theory, with the criticisms being similar to those of Merton's strain theory. Specifically, the critics argue that there is little evidence that gaps between what lower-class youths aspire to and what they expect to achieve produce frustration and strain, nor do such gaps appear predictive of gang membership or criminality.[38] Another criticism of Cloward and Ohlin's theory is the inability to find empirical evidence that supports their model of the formation of three types of gangs and their specializations in offending. While some research supports the existence of gangs that appear to specialize in certain forms of offending, many studies find that the observed specializations of gangs do not exactly follow the categories that Cloward and Ohlin proposed.[39] Additional studies have shown that many gangs tend not to specialize but rather to engage in a wider variety of offending behaviors.

Despite the criticisms of Cloward and Ohlin's model of gang formation, their theoretical framework inspired policy, largely due to the influence that their work had on Attorney General Robert Kennedy, who had read their book. In fact, Kennedy asked Lloyd Ohlin to assist in developing federal policies regarding delinquency,[40] which resulted in the Juvenile Delinquency Prevention and Control Act of 1961. Cloward and Ohlin's theory was a major influence on the Mobilization for Youth project in New York City, which, along with the federal legislation, stressed creating education and work opportunities for youths. Although evaluations of this program showed little effect on

---

[38]James F. Short, "Gang Delinquency and Anomie," in *Anomie and Deviant Behavior*, ed. Marshall B. Clinard (New York: Free Press, 1964), 98–127; James F. Short, Ramon Rivera, and Ray A. Tennyson, "Perceived Opportunities, Gang Membership, and Delinquency," *American Sociological Review* 30 (1965): 56–67; James F. Short and Fred L. Strodtbeck, *Group Processes and Gang Delinquency* (Chicago: University of Chicago Press, 1965); Liska, "Aspirations"; and Hirschi, *Causes of Delinquency*. See discussion in Shoemaker, *Theories of Delinquency*, 121–30.

[39]Irving Spergel, *Racketville, Slumtown, and Haulburg: An Exploratory Study of Delinquent Subcultures* (Chicago: University of Chicago Press, 1964); Short and Strodtbeck, *Group Processes*; Paul E. Tracy, Marvin E. Wolfgang, and Robert M. Figlio, *Delinquency Careers in Two Birth Cohorts* (New York: Plenum, 1990).

[40]Lamar T. Empey, *American Delinquency*, 4th ed. (Belmont, CA: Wadsworth, 1999).

reducing delinquency, it was impressive that such theorizing about lower-class male youths could have such a large impact on policy interventions.

Ultimately, the variations presented by Cohen, as well as Cloward and Ohlin, provided additional revisions that seemed at the time to advance the validity of strain theory. However, most of these revisions were based on official statistics that showed that lower-class male youth committed most crime, which were later shown by self-reports to be exaggerated.[41] Once scholars realized that most of the earlier models were not empirically valid for most criminal activity, strain theory became unpopular for several decades. But during the 1980s, another version was devised by Robert Agnew, who rejuvenated interest in strain theory by devising a way to make it more general and applicable to a larger variety of crimes and forms of deviance.

General Strain Theory

In the 1980s, Robert Agnew proposed general strain theory, which covers a much larger range of behavior by not concentrating on simply the lower class but providing a model more applicable to the frustrations that all individuals feel in everyday life.[42] Unlike other strain theories, general strain theory does not rely on assumptions about the frustration arising when people realize that the American Dream is a false promise to those of the lower classes. Rather, this theoretical framework assumes that people of all social classes and economic positions deal with frustrations in routine daily life.

▲ Image 6.5 Individuals experience stressors every day, and general strain theory emphasizes the importance of stress and anger in increasing the likelihood of engaging in criminal behavior.

Source: © Jupiterimages / Stockbyte / Thinkstock.

Previous strain theories, such as the models proposed by Merton, Cohen, and Cloward and Ohlin, focused on individuals' failure to achieve positively valued goals that they had been socialized to work to obtain. General strain theory also focuses on this source of strain; however, it identifies two additional categories of strain: *presentation of noxious stimuli* and *removal of positively valued stimuli*. In addition to the failure to achieve one's goals, Agnew claimed that the presentation of noxious stimuli (i.e., bad things) in one's life could cause major stress and frustration. Examples of noxious stimuli would include things like an abusive parent, a critical teacher, or an overly demanding boss. These are just some of the many negative factors that can exist in one's life—the number of examples is endless.

The other strain category Agnew identified was the removal of positive stimuli, which is likely the largest cause of frustration. Examples

---

[41]Tittle et al., "Myth of Social Class"; Hindelang et al., "Correlates of Delinquency."

[42]For Agnew's works regarding this theory, see Robert Agnew, "A Revised Strain Theory of Delinquency," *Social Forces* 64 (1985): 151–67; Robert Agnew, "Foundation for a General Strain Theory of Crime and Delinquency," *Criminology* 30 (1992): 47–88; Robert Agnew and Helene Raskin White, "An Empirical Test of General Strain Theory," *Criminology* 30 (1992): 475–500; Robert Agnew, "Controlling Delinquency: Recommendations from General Strain Theory," in *Crime and Public Policy: Putting Theory to Work*, ed. Hugh Barlow (Boulder: Westview Press, 1995), 43–70; Agnew et al., "A New Test," 681–704; Robert Agnew, "Building on the Foundation of General Strain Theory: Specifying the Types of Strain Most Likely to Lead to Crime and Delinquency," *Journal of Research in Crime and Delinquency* 38 (2001): 319–61.

of removal of positively valued stimuli include the loss of a good job, loss of the use of a car for a period of time, or the loss of a loved one. Such losses, like the other two sources of strain, may have varying degrees of influence depending on the individual. One person may not feel much frustration in losing a job or divorcing a spouse, whereas another person may experience severe anxiety or depression from such events.

Ultimately, general strain theory proposes that these three categories of strain (failure to achieve goals, noxious stimuli, and removal of positive stimuli) will lead to stress and that this results in a propensity to feel anger. Anger can be seen as a primary mediating factor in the causal model of the general strain framework. It is predicted that, to the extent that the three sources of strain cause feelings of anger in an individual, he or she will be predisposed to commit crime and deviance. However, Agnew was clear in stating that, if an individual can somehow cope with this anger in a positive way, then such feelings do not necessarily have to result in criminal activity. These coping mechanisms vary widely across individuals, with different strategies working for some people better than others. For example, some people relieve stress by working out or running, whereas others watch television or a movie. One type of activity that has shown relatively consistent success in relieving stress is laughter, which psychologists are now prescribing as a release of tension. Another is yoga, which includes simple breathing techniques such as taking several deep breaths, which has been shown to physiologically enhance release of stress.

Although Agnew did not originally provide details on how coping mechanisms work or explore the extant psychological research on these strategies, Agnew specifically pointed to such mechanisms for dealing with anger in prosocial ways. The primary prediction regarding coping mechanisms is that individuals who find ways to deal with their stress and anger positively will no longer be predisposed to commit crime, whereas individuals who do not find healthy, positive outlets for their anger and frustrations will be far more likely to commit crime. Obviously, the goal is to reduce the use of antisocial and negative coping mechanisms, such as drug usage or aggression, which either are criminal in themselves or increase the likelihood of offending.

Recent research and theoretical development has more fully examined various coping mechanisms and their effectiveness in reducing anger and, thus, preventing criminal activity. Obviously, in focusing on individuals' perceptions of stress and anger, as well as on their personal ability to cope with such feelings, general strain theory places more emphasis on the micro level of analysis. Still, due to its origins in structural strain theory, it is included in this section and is typically classified as belonging to the category of strain theories, which include the earlier theories that are more oriented to the macro level. In addition, recent studies and revisions of the theory have attempted to examine the validity of general strain theory propositions at the macro, structural level.[43]

Since it was first proposed in the mid-1980s, there has been a vast amount of research examining various aspects of the general strain theory.[44] For the most part, studies have generally supported the model. Most studies

[43]Timothy Brezina, Alex Piquero, and Paul Mazerolle, "Student Anger and Aggressive Behavior in School: An Initial Test of Agnew's Macro-Level Strain Theory," *Journal of Research in Crime and Delinquency* 38 (2001): 362–86.

[44]Agnew and White, "An Empirical Test"; Agnew et al., "A New Test"; Justin W. Patchin and Sameer Hinduja, "Traditional and Nontraditional Bullying among Youth: A Test of General Strain Theory," *Youth and Society* 43 (2011): 727–51; Raymond Paternoster and Paul Mazerolle, "General Strain Theory and Delinquency: A Replication and Extension," *Journal of Research in Crime and Delinquency* 31 (1994): 235–63; Timothy Brezina, "Adapting to Strain: An Examination of Delinquent Coping Responses," *Criminology* 34 (1996): 39–60; John P. Hoffman and Alan S. Miller, "A Latent Variable Analysis of General Strain Theory," *Journal of Quantitative Criminology* 14 (1998): 83–110; John P. Hoffman and Felicia Gray Cerbone, "Stressful Life Events and Delinquency Escalation in Early Adolescence," *Criminology* 37 (1999): 343–74; Paul Mazerolle and Alex Piquero, "Linking Exposure to Strain with Anger: An Investigation of Deviant Adaptations," *Journal of Criminal Justice* 26 (1998): 195–211; Paul Mazerolle, "Gender, General Strain, and Delinquency: An Empirical Examination," *Justice Quarterly* 15 (1998): 65–91; John P. Hoffman and S. Susan Su, "Stressful Life Events and Adolescent Substance Use and Depression: Conditional and Gender Differentiated Effects," *Substance Use and Misuse* 33 (1998): 2219–62; Lisa M. Broidy, "A Test of General Strain Theory," *Criminology* 39 (2001): 9–36; Nicole Leeper Piquero and Miriam Sealock, "Generalizing General Strain Theory: An Examination of an Offending Population," *Justice Quarterly* 17 (2000): 449–84; Paul Mazerolle and Jeff Maahs, "General Strain and Delinquency: An Alternative Examination of Conditioning Influences," *Justice Quarterly* 17 (2000): 753–78; Paul Mazerolle, Velmer Burton, Francis Cullen, T. David Evans, and Gary Payne, "Strain, Anger, and Delinquent Adaptations: Specifying General Strain Theory," *Journal of Criminal Justice* 28 (2000): 89–101; Stephen W. Baron and Timothy F. Hartnagel, "Street Youth and Labor Market Strain," *Journal of Criminal Justice* 30 (2002): 519–33; Carter Hay,

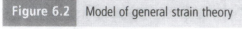

Figure 6.2 Model of general strain theory

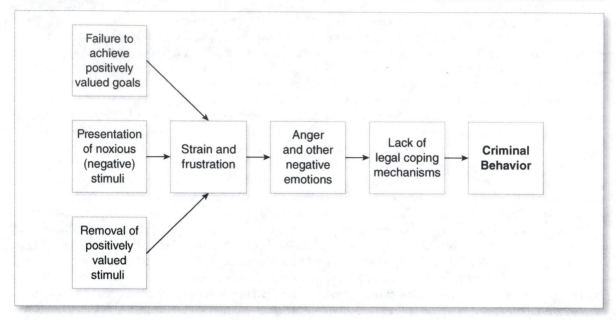

find a link between the three categories of strain and higher rates of criminality, as well as a link between the sources of strain and feelings of anger or other negative emotions (e.g., anxiety, depression).[45] However, the theory and especially the way it has been tested have also been criticized.

It is important for strain research to measure subjects' perceptions and feelings of frustration, not simply the occurrence of certain events themselves. Unfortunately, some studies have only looked at the latter, and the validity of such findings is questionable.[46] Other studies, however, have directly measured subjective perceptions of frustration, as well as personal feelings of anger.[47]

Such studies have found mixed support for the hypothesis that certain events lead to anger[48] but less support for the prediction that anger leads to criminality, and this link is particularly weak for nonviolent offending.[49]

"Family Strain, Gender, and Delinquency," *Sociological Perspectives* 46 (2003): 107–35; Sung Joon Jang and Byron R. Johnson, "Strain, Negative Emotions, and Deviant Coping among African Americans: A Test of General Strain Theory," *Journal of Quantitative Criminology* 19 (2003): 79–105; Paul Mazerolle, Alex Piquero, and George E. Capowich, "Examining the Links between Strain, Situational and Dispositional Anger, and Crime: Further Specifying and Testing General Strain Theory," *Youth and Society* 35 (2003): 131–57; Stephen W. Baron, "General Strain, Street Youth and Crime: A Test of Agnew's Revised Theory," *Criminology* 42 (2004): 457–84.

[45]A recent review of this research can be found in Baron, "General Strain," 457–67.

[46]For examples, see Jean-Louis Van Gelder, Danielle Reynald and Henk Elffers, "Anticipated Emotions and Immediate Affect in Criminal Decision Making: From Shame to Anger," in *Affect and Cognition in Criminal Decision Making*, ed. Jean-Louis Van Gelder, Henk Elffers, Danielle Reynald, and Daniel Nagin (London: Routledge, 2014), 161–78; Paternoster and Mazerolle, "General Strain Theory"; Hoffman and Cerbone, "Stressful Life Events and Delinquency"; and Hoffman and Su, "Stressful Life Events and Adolescent."

[47]Broidy, "A Test"; Baron, "General Strain."

[48]See Brezina, "Adapting to Strain"; Broidy, "A Test"; Mazerolle and Piquero, "Linking Exposure."

[49]Mazerolle and Piquero, "Linking Exposure"; Piquero and Sealock, "Generalizing General Strain Theory"; Mazerolle et al., "Strain, Anger."

On the other hand, the most recent studies have found support for the links between strain and anger, as well as anger and criminal behavior, particularly when coping variables are considered.[50] Still, many of the studies that examine the effects of anger use time-stable, trait measures as opposed to incident-specific, state measures that would be more consistent with the situation-specific emphasis of general strain theory.[51] This is similar to the methodological criticism that has been leveled against studies of self-conscious emotions, particularly shame and guilt; when it comes to measuring emotions such as anger and shame, criminologists should choose their measures carefully and make sure the instruments are consistent with the theory they are testing. Thus, future research on general strain theory should employ more effective, subjective measures of straining events and situational states of anger.

Regardless of the criticisms of general strain theory, it is hard to deny its face validity. After all, virtually everyone can relate to reacting differently to similar situations based on what kind of day they are having. For example, we all have days in which everything seems to be going great—it's a Friday, you receive accolades at work, and you are looking forward to a nice weekend with your friends or family. If someone says something derogatory to you or cuts you off in traffic, you will probably be inclined to let it go because you're in such a good mood. On the other hand, we also all have days in which everything seems to be going horribly—it's Monday, you get blamed for mishaps at work, and you have a fight with your spouse or significant other. At this time, if someone yells at you or cuts you off in traffic, you may be more inclined to respond aggressively in some way. Or perhaps you will overreact and snap at a loved one or friend when he or she really didn't do much to deserve it; this is often a form of displacement in which a cumulative buildup of stressors results in taking frustration out on another individual(s). In many ways, this type of behavior, which is prevalent and easy to see in everyday life, supports general strain theory.

Summary of Strain Theories

The common assumption found across all variations of strain theory is that crime is far more common among individuals who are under a great degree of stress and frustration, especially those who can't cope with stress in a positive way. The origin of most variations of strain theory can be traced to Durkheim's and Merton's concepts of anomie, which essentially means a state of chaos, or normlessness, in society due to a breakdown in the ability of societal institutions to regulate human desires, thereby resulting in feelings of strain.

Although different types of strain theories were proposed and gained popularity at various periods throughout the 20th century, they all became accepted during eras that were politically and culturally conducive to such perspectives, especially in terms of the differences across the strain models. For example, Merton's formulation of strain in the 1930s emphasized the importance of the economic institution, which was developed and became very popular during the Great Depression. Then, in the late 1950s, two strain theories that focused on gang formation were developed, by Cohen and by Cloward and Ohlin; they became popular among politicians and society due to a focus on official statistics suggesting that most crime at that time was being committed by lower-class, inner-city male youths, many of whom were gang members. Finally, Agnew developed his general strain model in the mid to late 1980s, during a time in which a number of general theories of crime were being developed (e.g., Gottfredson and Hirschi's low self-control theory and Sampson and Laub's developmental theory), so such models were popular at that time, particularly those that emphasized personality traits (such as anger) and experiences of individuals. So, all of the variations of strain, like all of the theories discussed in this book, were manifestations of the period in which they were developed and became widely accepted by academics, politicians, and society.

---

[50]Baron, "General Strain"; Mazerolle et al., "Examining the Links."

[51]For examples, see Mazerolle et al., "Strain, Anger"; and Baron, "General Strain." See discussions in Mazerolle et al., "Examining the Links"; and Akers and Sellers, *Criminological Theories*, 180–82.

Policy Implications

Although this section dealt with a wide range of theories regarding social structure, the most applicable policy implications are those suggested by the most recent theoretical models of this genre. Thus, we will focus on the key policy factors in the most modern versions of this perspective. The factors that are most vital for policy implications regarding social structure theories are those regarding educational and vocational opportunities and programs that help people develop healthy coping mechanisms to deal with stress.

Empirical studies have shown that intervention programs are needed for high-risk youths that focus on educational or vocational training and opportunities, because developing motivation for such endeavors can have a significant impact on reducing their offending rates.[52] Providing an individual with a job, or the preparation for one, is key to building a more stable life, even if it is not a high-paying position. As a result, the individual is less likely to feel stressed or strained. In modern times, a person is lucky to have a stable job, and this must be communicated to our youths, and hopefully, they will find some intrinsic value in the work they do.

Another key area of recommendations from this perspective involves developing healthy coping mechanisms. Everyone deals with stress virtually every day. The key is not avoiding stress or strain, because that is inevitable. Rather, the key is to develop healthy, legal ways to cope with such strain. Many programs have been created to train individuals on how to handle stress without resorting to antisocial behavior. There has been some success gained from anger management programs, particularly the ones that take a cognitive behavioral approach and often involve role-playing to teach individuals to think before they act.[53]

Conclusion

This section examined the theories that emphasize inequitable social structure as the primary cause of crime. We examined early perspectives, which established that societies vary in the extent to which they are stratified, and looked at the consequences of the inequalities in and complexities of such structures. Our examination of strain theories explored theoretical models proposing that individuals and groups who are not offered equal opportunities for achieving success can develop stress and frustration and, in turn, dispositions for committing criminal behavior. Finally, we examined the policy recommendations suggested by this theoretical model, which include the need to provide individuals with educational and job opportunities and help them develop healthy coping mechanisms.

Section Summary

- First, we discussed the primary distinction between social structure theories and other types of explanations (e.g., biological or social process theories).
- We examined the importance of the early sociological positivists, particularly Guerry, Quetelet, and Durkheim, and their contributions to the study of deviance and crime.
- We explored reasons why strain theory was developed and became popular in its time and discussed the primary assumptions and propositions of Merton's strain theory.
- We identified, defined, and examined examples of all five adaptations to strain.
- We discussed the variations of strain theory presented by Cohen, Cloward and Ohlin, and Agnew, as well as the empirical support that has been found regarding each.

---

[52]Wright et al., *Criminals in the Making.*

[53]Patricia Van Voorhis and Emily Salisbury, *Correctional Counseling and Rehabilitation*, 8th ed. (Cincinnati: Anderson, 2013).

KEY TERMS

adaptations to strain	delinquent boy	retreatism
anomie	general strain theory	retreatist gangs
collective conscience	innovation	ritualism
college boy	mechanical societies	social dynamics
conflict gangs	organic societies	social statics
conformity	reaction formation	strain theory
corner boy	rebellion	
criminal gangs	relative deprivation	

DISCUSSION QUESTIONS

1. How does sociological positivism differ from biological or psychological positivism?

2. Which of the early sociological positivism theorists do you think contributed most to the evolution of social structure theories of crime? Why? Do you think their ideas still hold up today?

3. Can you think of modern examples of Durkheim's image of mechanical societies? Do you think such societies have more or less crime than modern organic societies?

4. What type of adaptation to strain do you think fits you the best? The least? What adaptation do you think best fits your professor? Your postal delivery worker? Your garbage collector?

5. Do you know school friends who fit Cohen's model of status frustration? What did they do in response to the feelings of strain?

6. How would you describe the neighborhood where you or others you know grew up in terms of Cloward and Ohlin's model of organization or disorganization? Can you relate to the types of gangs they discussed?

WEB RESOURCES

Émile Durkheim

http://www.emile-durkheim.com

Strain Theory

http://www.criminology.fsu.edu/crimtheory/agnew.htm

http://www.oxfordbibliographies.com/view/document/obo-9780195396607/obo-9780195396607-0005.xml

http://www.umsl.edu/~keelr/200/strain.html

READING 13

In this selection, Robert Merton, who is one of the most cited and respected sociologists of the 20th century, explains his theory for why individuals commit crime. Specifically, he asserts that the primary cause of crime is the economy. It plays a large part in determining criminal offending, as well as the many adaptations to strain that Merton proposes. Although strain theory, particularly Merton's framework, emphasizes the macro or group level of analysis, the theory also describes five stereotypical ways that individuals deal with such frustrations or strain.

Social Structure and Anomie

Robert K. Merton

There persists a notable tendency in sociological theory to attribute the malfunctioning of social structure primarily to those of man's imperious biological drives which are not adequately restrained by social control. In this view, the social order is solely a device for "impulse management" and the "social processing" of tensions. These impulses which break through social control, be it noted, are held to be biologically derived. Nonconformity is assumed to be rooted in original nature. Conformity is by implication the result of a utilitarian calculus or unreasoned conditioning. This point of view, whatever its other deficiencies, clearly begs one question. It provides no basis for determining the nonbiological conditions which induce deviations from prescribed patterns of conduct. In this paper, it will be suggested that certain phases of social structure generate the circumstances in which infringement of social codes constitutes a "normal" response.

The conceptual scheme to be outlined is designed to provide a coherent, systematic approach to the study of socio-cultural sources of deviate behavior. Our primary aim lies in discovering how some social structures *exert a definite pressure* upon certain persons in the society to engage in nonconformist rather than conformist conduct. The many ramifications of the scheme cannot all be discussed; the problems mentioned outnumber those explicitly treated.

Among the elements of social and cultural structure, two are important for our purposes. These are analytically separable although they merge imperceptibly in concrete situations. The first consists of culturally defined goals, purposes, and interests. It comprises a frame of aspirational reference. These goals are more or less integrated and involve varying degrees of prestige and sentiment. They constitute a basic, but not the exclusive, component of what Linton aptly has called "designs for group living." Some of these cultural aspirations are related to the original drives of man, but they are not determined by them. The second phase of the social structure defines, regulates, and controls the acceptable modes of achieving these goals. Every social group invariably couples its scale of desired ends with moral or institutional regulation of permissible and required procedures for attaining these ends. These regulatory norms and moral imperatives do not necessarily coincide with technical or efficiency norms. Many procedures which from the standpoint of particular *individuals* would be most efficient in securing desired values, e.g., illicit oil-stock schemes, theft, fraud, are ruled out of the institutional area of permitted conduct. The choice of expedients is limited by the institutional norms.

To say that these two elements, culture goals and institutional norms, operate jointly is not to say that the ranges

SOURCE: Robert Merton, "Social Structure and Anomie," *American Sociological Review* 3, no. 3 (2002): 672–82. Selection taken from S. Cote, ed., *Criminological Theories: Bridging the Past to the Future* (Thousand Oaks, CA: Sage Publications, 2002), 95–103. (Original publication 1938)

of alternative behaviors and aims bear some constant relation to one another. The emphasis upon certain goals may vary independently of the degree of emphasis upon institutional means. There may develop a disproportionate, at times, a virtually exclusive, stress upon the value of specific goals, involving relatively slight concern with the institutionally appropriate modes of attaining these goals. The limiting case in this direction is reached when the range of alternative procedures is limited only by technical rather than institutional considerations. Any and all devices which promise attainment of the all important goal would be permitted in this hypothetical polar case. This constitutes one type of cultural malintegration. A second polar type is found in groups where activities originally conceived as instrumental are transmuted into ends in themselves. The original purposes are forgotten and ritualistic adherence to institutionally prescribed conduct becomes virtually obsessive. Stability is largely ensured while change is flouted. The range of alternative behaviors is severely limited. There develops a tradition-bound, sacred society characterized by neophobia. The occupational psychosis of the bureaucrat may be cited as a case in point. Finally, there are the intermediate types of groups where a balance between culture goals and institutional means is maintained. These are the significantly integrated and relatively stable, though changing groups.

An effective equilibrium between the two phases of the social structure is maintained as long as satisfactions accrue to individuals who conform to both constraints, viz., satisfactions from the achievement of the goals and satisfactions emerging directly from the institutionally canalized modes of striving to attain these ends. Success, in such equilibrated cases, is twofold. Success is reckoned in terms of the product and in terms of the process, in terms of the outcome and in terms of activities. Continuing satisfactions must derive from sheer participation in a competitive order as well as from eclipsing one's competitors if the order itself is to be sustained. The occasional sacrifices involved in institutionalized conduct must be compensated by socialized rewards. The distribution of statuses and roles through competition must be so organized that positive incentives for conformity to roles and adherence to status obligations are provided for every position within the distributive order. Aberrant conduct, therefore, may be viewed as a symptom of dissociation between culturally defined aspirations and socially structured means.

Of the types of groups which result from the independent variation of the two phases of the social structure, we shall be primarily concerned with the first, namely, that involving a disproportionate accent on goals. This statement must be recast in a proper perspective. In no group is there an absence of regulatory codes governing conduct, yet groups do vary in the degree to which these folkways, mores, and institutional controls are effectively integrated with the more diffuse goals which are part of the culture matrix. Emotional convictions may cluster about the complex of socially acclaimed ends, meanwhile shifting their support from the culturally defined implementation of these ends. As we shall see, certain aspects of the social structure may generate countermores and antisocial behavior precisely because of differential emphases on goals and regulations. In the extreme case, the latter may be so vitiated by the goal-emphasis that the range of behavior is limited only by considerations of technical expediency. The sole significant question then becomes, which available means is most efficient in netting the socially approved value? The technically most feasible procedure, whether legitimate or not, is preferred to the institutionally prescribed conduct. As this process continues, the integration of the society becomes tenuous and anomie ensues.

Thus, in competitive athletics, when the aim of victory is shorn of its institutional trappings and success in contests becomes construed as "winning the game" rather than "winning through circumscribed modes of activity," a premium is implicitly set upon the use of illegitimate but technically efficient means. The star of the opposing football team is surreptitiously slugged; the wrestler furtively incapacitates his opponent through ingenious but illicit techniques; university alumni covertly subsidize "students" whose talents are largely confined to the athletic field. The emphasis on the goal has so attenuated the satisfactions deriving from sheer participation in the competitive activity that these satisfactions are virtually confined to a successful outcome. Through the same process, tension generated by the desire to win in a poker game is relieved by successfully dealing oneself four aces, or, when the cult of success has become completely dominant, by sagaciously shuffling the cards in a game of solitaire. The faint twinge of uneasiness in the last instance and the surreptitious nature of public delicts indicate clearly that the institutional rules of the game *are known* to those who evade them, but that the emotional supports of these rules are largely vitiated by cultural exaggeration of the success-goal. They are microcosmic images of the social macrocosm.

Of course, this process is not restricted to the realm of sport. The process whereby exaltation of the end generates a *literal demoralization*, i.e., a deinstitutionalization, of the means is one which characterizes many groups in which the two phases of the social structure are not highly integrated. The extreme emphasis upon the accumulation of wealth as a symbol of success in our own society militates against the completely effective control of institutionally regulated modes of acquiring a fortune. Fraud, corruption, vice, crime, in short, the entire catalogue of proscribed behavior, becomes increasingly common when the emphasis on the *culturally induced* success-goal becomes divorced from a coordinated institutional emphasis. This observation is of crucial theoretical importance in examining the doctrine that antisocial behavior most frequently derives from biological drives breaking through the restraints imposed by society. The difference is one between a strictly utilitarian interpretation which conceives man's ends as random and an analysis which finds these ends deriving from the basic values of the culture.

Our analysis can scarcely stop at this juncture. We must turn to other aspects of the social structure if we are to deal with the social genesis of the varying rates and types of deviate behavior characteristic of different societies. Thus far, we have sketched three ideal types of social orders constituted by distinctive patterns of relations between culture ends and means. Turning from these types of *culture patterning,* we find five logically possible, alternative modes of adjustment or adaptation by *individuals* within the culture-bearing society or group. These are schematically presented in Figure 1, where (+) signifies

Figure 1

	Culture Goals	Institutionalized Means
I. Conformity	+	+
II. Innovation	+	−
III. Ritualism	−	+
IV. Retreatism	−	−
V. Rebellion	±	±

"acceptance," (−) signifies "elimination" and (±) signifies "rejection and substitution of new goals and standards."

Our discussion of the relation between these alternative responses and other phases of the social structure must be prefaced by the observation that persons may shift from one alternative to another as they engage in different social activities. These categories refer to role adjustments in specific situations, not to personality *in toto.* To treat the development of this process in various spheres of conduct would introduce a complexity unmanageable within the confines of this paper. For this reason, we shall be concerned primarily with economic activity in the broad sense, "the production, exchange, distribution and consumption of goods and services" in our competitive society, wherein wealth has taken on a highly symbolic cast. Our task is to search out some of the factors which exert pressure upon individuals to engage in certain of these logically possible alternative responses. This choice, as we shall see, is far from random.

In every society, Adaptation I (conformity to both culture goals and means) is the most common and widely diffused. Were this not so, the stability and continuity of the society could not be maintained. The mesh of expectancies which constitutes every social order is sustained by the modal behavior of its members falling within the first category. Conventional role behavior oriented toward the basic values of the group is the rule rather than the exception. It is this fact alone which permits us to speak of a human aggregate as comprising a group or society.

Conversely, Adaptation IV (rejection of goals and means) is the least common. Persons who "adjust" (or maladjust) in this fashion are, strictly speaking, *in* the society but not *of* it. Sociologically, these constitute the true "aliens." Not sharing the common frame of orientation, they can be included within the societal population merely in a fictional sense. In this category are some of the activities of psychotics, psychoneurotics, chronic autists, pariahs, outcasts, vagrants, vagabonds, tramps, chronic drunkards and drug addicts. These have relinquished, in certain spheres of activity, the culturally defined goals, involving complete aim-inhibition in the polar case, and their adjustments are not in accord with institutional norms. This is not to say that in some cases the source of their behavioral adjustments is not in part the very social structure which they have in effect repudiated nor that their very existence within a social area does not constitute a problem for the socialized population.

This mode of "adjustment" occurs, as far as structural sources are concerned, when both the culture goals and institutionalized procedures have been assimilated thoroughly by the individual and imbued with affect and high positive value, but where those institutionalized procedures which promise a measure of successful attainment of the goals are not available to the individual. In such instances, there results a twofold mental conflict insofar as the moral obligation for adopting institutional means conflicts with the pressure to resort to illegitimate means (which may attain the goal) and inasmuch as the individual is shut off from means which are both legitimate *and* effective. The competitive order is maintained, but the frustrated and handicapped individual who cannot cope with this order drops out.

Defeatism, quietism, and resignation are manifested in escape mechanisms which ultimately lead the individual to "escape" from the requirements of the society. It is an expedient which arises from continued failure to attain the goal by legitimate measures and from an inability to adopt the illegitimate route because of internalized prohibitions and institutionalized compulsives, *during which process the supreme value of the success-goal has as yet not been renounced.* The conflict is resolved by eliminating *both* precipitating elements, the goals and means. The escape is complete, the conflict is eliminated and the individual is asocialized.

Be it noted that where frustration derives from the inaccessibility of effective institutional means for attaining economic or any other type of highly valued "success," that Adaptations II, III, and V (innovation, ritualism and rebellion) are also possible. The result will be determined by the particular personality, and thus, the *particular* cultural background, involved. Inadequate socialization will result in the innovation response whereby the conflict and frustration are eliminated by relinquishing the institutional means and retaining the success-aspiration; an extreme assimilation of institutional demands will lead to ritualism wherein the goal is dropped as beyond one's reach but conformity to the mores persists; and rebellion occurs when emancipation from the reigning standards, due to frustration or to marginalist perspectives, leads to the attempt to introduce a "new social order."

Our major concern is with the illegitimacy adjustment. This involves the use of conventionally proscribed but frequently effective means of attaining at least the simulacrum of culturally defined success—wealth, power, and the like. As we have seen, this adjustment occurs when the individual has assimilated the cultural emphasis on success without equally internalizing the morally prescribed norms governing means for its attainment. The question arises, Which phases of our social structure predispose toward this mode of adjustment? We may examine a concrete instance, effectively analyzed by Lohman, which provides a clue to the answer. Lohman has shown that specialized areas of vice in the near north side of Chicago constitute a "normal" response to a situation where the cultural emphasis upon pecuniary success has been absorbed, but where there is little access to conventional and legitimate means for attaining such success. The conventional occupational opportunities of persons in this area are almost completely limited to manual labor. Given our cultural stigmatization of manual labor, and its correlate, the prestige of white collar work, it is clear that the result is a strain toward innovational practices. The limitation of opportunity to unskilled labor and the resultant low income cannot compete *in terms of conventional standards of achievement* with the high income from organized vice.

For our purposes, this situation involves two important features. First, such antisocial behavior is in a sense "called forth" by certain conventional values of the culture *and* by the class structure involving differential access to the approved opportunities for legitimate, prestige-bearing pursuit of the culture goals. The lack of high integration between the means-and-end elements of the cultural pattern and the particular class structure combine to favor a heightened frequency of antisocial conduct in such groups. The second consideration is of equal significance. Recourse to the first of the alternative responses, legitimate effort, is limited by the fact that actual advance toward desired success-symbols through conventional channels is, despite our persisting open-class ideology, relatively rare and difficult for those handicapped by little formal education and few economic resources. The dominant pressure of group standards of success is, therefore, on the gradual attenuation of legitimate, but by and large ineffective, strivings and the increasing use of illegitimate, but more or less effective, expedients of vice and crime. The cultural demands made on persons in this situation are incompatible. On the one hand, they are asked to orient their conduct toward the prospect of accumulating wealth and on the other, they are largely denied effective opportunities to do so institutionally.

The consequences of such structural inconsistency are psycho-pathological personality, and/or antisocial conduct, and/or revolutionary activities. The equilibrium between culturally designated means and ends becomes highly unstable with the progressive emphasis on attaining the prestige-laden ends by any means whatsoever. Within this context, Capone represents the triumph of amoral intelligence over morally prescribed "failure," when the channels of vertical mobility are closed or narrowed *in a society which places a high premium on economic affluence and social ascent for all its members.*

This last qualification is of primary importance. It suggests that other phases of the social structure besides the extreme emphasis on pecuniary success must be considered if we are to understand the social sources of antisocial behavior. A high frequency of deviate behavior is not generated simply by "lack of opportunity" or by this exaggerated pecuniary emphasis. A comparatively rigidified class structure, a feudalistic or caste order, may limit such opportunities far beyond the point which obtains in our society today. It is only when a system of cultural values extols, virtually above all else, certain common symbols of success for the population at large while its social structure rigorously restricts or completely eliminates access to approved modes of acquiring these symbols for a considerable part of the same population, that antisocial behavior ensues on a considerable scale. In other words, our egalitarian ideology denies by implication the existence of noncompeting groups and individuals in the pursuit of pecuniary success. The same body of success-symbols is held to be desirable for all. These goals are held to transcend class lines, not to be bounded by them, yet the actual social organization is such that there exist class differentials in the accessibility of these common success-symbols. Frustration and thwarted aspiration lead to the search for avenues of escape from a culturally induced intolerable situation; or unrelieved ambition may eventuate in illicit attempts to acquire the dominant values. The American stress on pecuniary success and ambitiousness for all thus invites exaggerated anxieties, hostilities, neuroses and antisocial behavior.

This theoretical analysis may go far toward explaining the varying correlations between crime and poverty. Poverty is not an isolated variable. It is one in a complex of interdependent social and cultural variables. When viewed in such a context, it represents quite different states of affairs. Poverty as such, and consequent limitation of opportunity, are not sufficient to induce a conspicuously high rate of criminal behavior. Even the often mentioned "poverty in the midst of plenty" will not necessarily lead to this result. Only insofar as poverty and associated disadvantages in competition for the culture values approved for *all* members of the society is linked with the assimilation of a cultural emphasis on monetary accumulation as a symbol of success is antisocial conduct a "normal" outcome. Thus, poverty is less highly correlated with crime in southeastern Europe than in the United States. The possibilities of vertical mobility in these European areas would seem to be fewer than in this country, so that neither poverty *per se* nor its association with limited opportunity is sufficient to account for the varying correlations. It is only when the full configuration is considered, poverty, limited opportunity and a commonly shared system of success symbols, that we can explain the higher association between poverty and crime in our society than in others where rigidified class structure is coupled with *differential class symbols of achievement.*

In societies such as our own, then, the pressure of prestige-bearing success tends to eliminate the effective social constraint over means employed to this end. "The-end-justifies-the-means" doctrine becomes a guiding tenet for action when the cultural structure unduly exalts the end and the social organization unduly limits possible recourse to approved means. Otherwise put, this notion and associated behavior reflect a lack of cultural coordination. In international relations, the effects of this lack of integration are notoriously apparent. An emphasis upon national power is not readily coordinated with an inept organization of legitimate, i.e., internationally defined and accepted, means for attaining this goal. The result is a tendency toward the abrogation of international law, treaties become scraps of paper, "undeclared warfare" serves as a technical evasion, the bombing of civilian populations is rationalized, just as the same societal situation induces the same sway of illegitimacy among individuals.

The social order we have described necessarily produces this "strain toward dissolution." The pressure of such an order is upon outdoing one's competitors. The choice of means within the ambit of institutional control will persist as long as the sentiments supporting a competitive system, i.e., deriving from the possibility of outranking competitors and hence enjoying the favorable response of others, are distributed throughout the entire system of activities and are not confined merely to the final result. A stable social structure demands a balanced distribution of affect among its various segments. When there occurs a shift of emphasis from the satisfactions deriving from competition itself to almost exclusive concern with successful competition, the resultant stress leads to the breakdown of the regulatory structure. With the resulting attenuation of the institutional imperatives, there occurs an approximation of the situation erroneously held by utilitarians to be typical of society generally wherein calculations of advantage and fear of punishment are the sole regulating agencies. In such situations, as Hobbes observed, force and fraud come to constitute the sole virtues in view of their relative efficiency in attaining goals, which were for him, of course, not culturally derived.

It should be apparent that the foregoing discussion is not pitched on a moralistic plane. Whatever the sentiments of the writer or reader concerning the ethical desirability of coordinating the means-and-goals phases of the social structure, one must agree that lack of such coordination leads to anomie. Insofar as one of the most general functions of social organization is to provide a basis for calculability and regularity of behavior, it is increasingly limited in effectiveness as these elements of the structure become dissociated. At the extreme, predictability virtually disappears and what may be properly termed cultural chaos or anomie intervenes.

This statement, being brief, is also incomplete. It has not included an exhaustive treatment of the various structural elements which predispose toward one rather than another of the alternative responses open to individuals; it has neglected, but not denied the relevance of, the factors determining the specific incidence of these responses; it has not enumerated the various concrete responses which are constituted by combinations of specific values of the analytical variables; it has omitted, or included only by implication, any consideration of the social functions performed by illicit responses; it has not tested the full explanatory power of the analytical scheme by examining a large number of group variations in the frequency of deviate and conformist behavior; it has not adequately dealt with rebellious conduct which seeks to refashion the social framework radically; it has not examined the relevance of cultural conflict for an analysis of culture-goal and institutional-means malintegration. It is suggested that these and related problems may be profitably analyzed by this scheme.

REVIEW QUESTIONS

1. Why do you think Merton's theory became so popular when it did? Why?

2. Which adaptation to strain do you most identify with?

3. Which types of criminal behavior does Merton's theory have more difficulty explaining? Which types of offending does it explain best?

READING 14

In this selection, Craig Hemmens uses the lyrics of Bruce Springsteen as an analogy for Merton's causes and adaptations to strain and frustration regarding the economical structure to explain and understand the stereotypical experiences of certain individuals. The hypothetical (and/or observed) nature of the strain or frustration that people experience when they are subject to such problems provides a direct analogy to the lyrics of this poet/songwriter, and this provides a good illustration of "real life" intersecting with traditional criminological theory. This entry is an example of how criminological theory can be applied to actual human behaviors and feelings outside of academic theorizing.

There's a Darkness on the Edge of Town

Merton's Five Modes of Adaptation in the Lyrics of Bruce Springsteen

Craig Hemmens

Poor man wanna be rich, rich man wanna be king

And a king ain't satisfied till he rules everything

—Bruce Springsteen (Badlands, 1978)

 ## Introduction

Criminologists have long struggled to explain crime and deviance. A number of sociological theories of crime causation have been posited, including differential association, social control, and labeling. One which has received enormous attention is Robert Merton's "strain" theory. Merton expanded upon Durkheim's concept of "anomie" (Durkheim 1951) and applied it to the modern, capitalist society, as exemplified by America in the mid-twentieth century. Merton's article "Social Structure and Anomie" (1938) is considered one of the most influential works in criminology (Williams & McShane 1994). According to Merton, anomie, or "strain," results when legitimate opportunities to attain success goals are blocked by structural obstacles.

It is often said that art imitates life. Nathaniel Hawthorne's (1962) novels vividly portray the repressed sexuality of the Puritan period, William Faulkner's (1929) work depicts the racial conflict in the South during the early twentieth century, and Arthur Miller's (1949) writing presents the cultural malaise of America in the 1950s. Music is also an art form which often represents life. Rock music is a relatively new musical form, adapted from a number of sources including the blues and gospel music (Barlow 1989; Palmer 1981). While its popularity has eclipsed that of any other popular music form, often it has been criticized by musical scholars for its meaningless lyrics (Bayles 1994; Pollock 1983, 1993). The music of Bruce Springsteen is an exception to the notion that rock music neglects the

realities of everyday life. Much of his work deals with the lack of equity and fairness in American society and the consequent strain experienced by many individuals.

Academic writing is not infrequently criticized as being intended solely for an academic audience. While strain theory is intuitively appealing, the bulk of discussion of the theory has been limited to the pages of academic journals. Bruce Springsteen is a musician, not a criminologist. The significance of his work lies in his ability to articulate, on a popular level, many of the concepts expressed by academicians such as Robert Merton. This article provides a content analysis of the lyrics of one Springsteen album, *Darkness on the Edge of Town* (1978), and discusses how his world view reflects, in popular form, the tenets of Merton's "strain" theory.

 ## Strain Theory

In his articulation of strain theory, Merton focused on the disjuncture between goals and means. Building upon Durkheim's (1951) study of suicide and anomie, Merton saw American society as promulgating the common goal of material success, while failing to provide equal opportunities for all in society to achieve this goal. The lower socio-economic classes had fewer opportunities to get an education and a good job, which Merton saw as the keys to achieving material success. Consequently, the lower classes were more likely to be frustrated in their efforts to achieve the sort of wealth and success that American culture taught

SOURCE: Craig Hemmens, "There's a Darkness on the Edge of Town: Merton's Five Modes of Adaptation in the Lyrics of Bruce Springsteen," *International Journal of Comparative and Applied Criminal Justice* 23, no. 1 (1999): 127–36. Reprinted with permission.

them to want. The result, according to Merton, was anomie, or "strain" (Hirschi 1969). This strain could cause the individual to react to it in one of five ways, what Merton referred to as "modes of adaptation" (Merton 1938).

Merton suggested that there were five possible responses, or "modes of adaptation" to the frustration created by blocked opportunities: conformity, innovation, retreatism, rebellion, and ritualism. Conformists maintain support for both the goals and means of society. This is the largest of the five groups and includes most of mainstream society. Innovators accept the goals but not the means of achieving those goals; instead they find alternative means of achieving them, some of which may be illegal. Retreatists abandon both the goals and means of society and create their own, which may include unlawful activity. Drug addicts are an example. Rebels substitute new goals and means for the original ones endorsed by the wider society. An example is a revolutionary such as Lenin. Ritualists reject society's goals but continue to support the means. An example is treating a job as a form of security rather than a means of achieving success.

Strain theory suggests that the structure of society affects the action of individuals. It is what sociologists refer to as a macro or structural level theory, as it seeks to explain behavior in the aggregate (Farnworth & Leiber 1989). Its proponents do not attempt to make direct predictions about individual behavior (Vold & Bernard 1986). It is also limited in scope. Merton's anomie theory is intended to explain differences in crime by class (Burton 1991). While the theory suggests that massive changes in American social structure might be necessary to remove the barriers to success which lead to strain and deviance, strain theory is essentially conservative. The theory does not reject capitalism per se; it merely challenges the structure of American capitalism. It does not require an overthrow of the government but instead a reworking of the institution (Burton & Cullen 1992).

By the 1970s a sizable portion of the criminological community had turned away from strain theory. The theory was criticized for inadequate operationalization of its concepts and a lack of empirical support (Hirschi 1969; Kornhauser 1978). It has been forcefully argued, however, that such criticisms were based on an imprecise formulation of the theory, one which truncated strain theory and made it susceptible to misinterpretation and inaccurate empirical testing (Burton & Cullen 1992). Despite its apparent limitations, strain theory remains a popular explanation for deviant behavior. Indeed, strain theory has recently received renewed attention from criminologists (Agnew 1985, 1989, 1992).

While strain theory has impacted policy making and continues to provide fertile ground for academic research, its appeal stretches beyond the walls of academia and the halls of government. Part of its success can be attributed to its intuitive appeal. Strain theory, for many, simply makes sense as an explanation for deviant behavior in a capitalistic, materialistic society in which one's reach is always likely to be exceeded by one's goals. Images of strain theory abound in popular culture, from art to literature to film. Perhaps the most forceful exponent of strain theory in popular media is Bruce Springsteen.

 ## The Lyrics of Bruce Springsteen

Bruce Springsteen released his first record, *Greetings From Asbury Park*, in 1973. He was signed to Columbia Records by John Hammond, who also discovered Bob Dylan. Hammond saw Springsteen as a singer-songwriter in the same vein as Dylan, but Springsteen preferred to work within the context of a full rock and roll band (Marsh 1979). His first album and his second, *The Wild, the Innocent,* and *The E Street Shuffle,* also released in 1973, garnered critical acclaim but few sales. Both albums contained songs which celebrated the freedom and exuberance of youth, but also hinted at the difficulty of growing up poor in the modern world. The writing was unpolished, but the lyrics contained a number of powerful images.

In 1975 Springsteen gained a national audience with the release of *Born to Run*. The title song became a staple of rock radio. The album displayed a newfound maturity and songwriting polish. The tone of the album was also darker than the previous albums. While the song "Born to Run" celebrated the possibilities of the open road, it also contained an acknowledgment that the characters in the song had no choice but to flee their humble upbringing:

Baby this town rips the bones from your back

It's a death trap, It's a suicide rap

We gotta get out while we're young

'Cause tramps like us, baby we were born to run

—*Born to Run*

The theme of the album was escape, trying to get out and get what you want and deserve. Escape was possible, but only via a limited number of avenues, some legitimate, others not:

Kids flash guitars just like switchblades

Hustling for the record machine

The hungry and the hunted

Explode into rock'n roll bands

—*Jungleland*

And all we gotta do is hold up our end

Here stuff this in your pocket

It'll look like you're carrying a friend

And remember, just don't smile

Change your shirt, 'cause tonight we got style

—*Meeting Across the River*

Springsteen's songwriting had decidedly taken a turn. The emphasis was on individuals who felt trapped, either in dead-end jobs, failed relationships, or dying industrial towns. The album sold well, and after Springsteen appeared simultaneously on the covers of *Time* and *Newsweek,* he seemed destined to be rock's next superstar (Marsh 1979).

Springsteen's next album, *Darkness on the Edge of Town* (1978), was not released for three years, an unusually long time between albums. The delay was attributable in part to a lawsuit between Springsteen and his producer, which was eventually settled (Marsh 1987). The lawsuit was only part of the reason for the delay, however, as Springsteen spent an enormous amount of time in the studio recording the new album. The cover of the album is a clear indication that the album is different from what had come before. Where Springsteen had posed laughing with his saxophone player on the cover of *Born to Run,* he stands alone on the cover of *Darkness on the Edge of Town,* staring blankly into the camera. Instead of posing in front of a plain white backdrop, as on the previous album, Springsteen is photographed standing in a room, leaning up against a wall covered in fading wallpaper. 1978 was the height of the disco music craze, with its emphasis on outlandish clothes,

a style which many rock acts embraced. Springsteen, by contrast, is dressed in a plain white T-shirt and a black leather jacket. He looks more like a day laborer than a rock star.

Darkness on the Edge of Town continues the exploration of the themes first examined on *Born to Run,* but the tone is different. Where *Born to Run* was dominated by saxophone and piano, *Darkness on the Edge of Town* is driven by guitars. The change in the instrumentation gives the new music a sense of urgency and power. Where *Born to Run* had a tone of frustration and sadness, *Darkness on he Edge of Town* has an angry tone. Lyrically, Springsteen continues to explore the ways that individuals dealt with the inequities of modem society. According to the title song:

Some folks are born into a good life,

Other folks get it anyway, anyhow.

—*Darkness on the Edge of Town*

The entire album is populated with the same characters found in *Born to Run.* But where the individuals in *Born to Run* believed that escape was possible, the protagonists in *Darkness on the Edge of Town* have no illusions:

Through the mansions of fear, through the mansions of pain,

I see my daddy walking through them factory gates in the rain,

Factory takes his hearing, factory gives him life,

The working, the working, just the working life

—*Factory*

Many of the characters on the album are trapped in dead-end jobs, unable to leave but unwilling to quit dreaming of a better life. The hero of "Racing in the Street" has a wife and a job, but neither holds his interest. The only meaning in his life is provided by his car, "a sixty-nine Chevy with a 396." He spends his night racing cars as a means of escaping the drudgery of everyday life:

Some guys they just give up living

And start dying little by little, piece by piece,

Some guys come home from work and wash up,

And go racin' in the street

—*Racing in the Street*

The division between the "haves" and the "have-nots" is clear to the protagonists in these songs, and this class division is viewed as illegitimate:

Poor man wanna be rich,

Rich man wanna be king,

And a king ain't satisfied till he rules everything

—*Badlands*

While some of the protagonists appear to accept responsibility for their failed lives, others look elsewhere, placing the blame on their upbringing:

You're born into this life paying

for the sins of somebody else's past,

Daddy worked his whole life, for nothin' but the pain,

Now he walks these empty rooms, looking for something to blame

—*Adam Raised a Cain*

Some of the protagonists find what they are looking for, an outlet for their rage and frustration:

End of the day, factory whistle cries,

Men walk through these gates with death in their eyes,

And you just better believe, boy,

Somebody's gonna get hurt tonight

—*Factory*

Darkness on the Edge of Town is an angry album. The lyrics are full of rage, and the instrumentation conveys this anger. The protagonists of the album are not criminals, however. Most of them hold jobs and have families. But

they are angry, and the anger is caused by their frustration with being unable to attain what they believe they have been taught to strive for:

Everybody's got a hunger, a hunger they can't resist,

There's so much that you want, you deserve much more than this,

But if dreams came true, oh wouldn't that be nice,

But this ain't no dream we're livin' through tonight

—*Prove It All Night*

Some of Springsteen's characters turn to deviance as a response to stressful life events which anger them. The anger of the speaker in "The Promised Land" is palpable and clearly directed outward:

Sometimes I feel so weak I just want to explode

Explode and tear this whole town apart

Take a knife and cut this pain from my heart

Find somebody itching for something to start

—*The Promised Land*

Most of Springsteen's characters do not become deviant as a consequence of their feelings of strain, however. This is in accord with Merton's writings, which stress that deviance is only one possible response to strain. The angry characters are most likely to become deviant. But others who experience strain, particularly the strain associated with the disjuncture between goals and means, either conform, ritualize, retreat, or rebel.

 ## Discussion

The notion that feelings of societal inequity can create deviance-producing strain is clearly reflected in Springsteen's music, as is the recognition that strain does not necessarily lead to deviance. Many of Springsteen's characters are drawn from the lower classes, from segments of society that

seem to have been abandoned by larger society, or who are trapped living lives of "quiet desperation," to paraphrase Thoreau (1854). These characters are faced with stressful life events ranging from the loss of a job to the loss of a loved one. Some respond with anger, others resign themselves to their lot in life, and others attempt to find a new way. It is those who respond to strain with anger who are most likely to deviate. Springsteen has acknowledged the impact his upbringing in a lower class family in a dying post-industrial town had on him and his songwriting:

> My memory is of my father trying in find work, what that does to you, and how that affects your image of your manhood, as a provider. The loss of that role is devastating. I write coming from that Spot—the spot of disaffection, of loners, outsiders. But not outlaws. It's about people trying to find their way in, but somebody won't let them in. Or they can't find their way in. And what are the actions that leads to? (Corn 1996)

Springsteen's lyrics are filled with images of social injustice and its impact on average working class Americans. And he has made it clear in interviews that social inequality is a major concern of his. Discussing the problems of contemporary society, he said:

> It would take a tremendous concentration of national will, on the order of a domestic Marshall Plan, to do the things that need to be done to achieve a real kind of social justice and equality. (Corn 1996)

Strain theory, for all the blame it places on American society as a cause of deviant behavior, is in many respects a conservative theory. Strain theory does not assert that it is capitalism which is the root cause of crime, as Marxist criminology does (Taylor and Young 1973). Strain theory does not imply that American society is irreparable. According to strain theory, it is the emphasis on material success to the exclusion of all other goals that inevitably leads to a disjunction between goals and means. Recent efforts have been made to demonstrate how strain can be reduced by creating other equally valued societal goals.

This is all in accord with the values Springsteen promotes in his work. Springsteen's lyrics stress the value of community, shared responsibility, and interconnectedness. He has gone to some length to promote these values, even using the concert stage as a vehicle. During the tour in support of his biggest selling album, *Born in the USA* (1984), he spoke during each show about the importance of community and then made a large public donation to a local food bank and encouraged concert attendees to become involved in similar local charities.

Conclusion

Popular music has been the subject of academic ridicule and public disdain since long before Elvis ever stepped into his blue suede shoes. Blues was dismissed as the illiterate ramblings of poor Southern blacks (Gillette 1983; Guralnick 1986). Country and bluegrass music were disparagingly termed "hillbilly music" (Goldrosen & Beecher 1986). In recent years, however, as the first generation raised almost exclusively on popular music has come of age and moved into academia, the reevaluation process has begun. It is now chic to praise the verbal wordplay of country songwriters (Tichi 1994) and the intricacies of blues phraseology (Guralnick 1986, 1994). Rock music has been accorded some credit, but even when it is applauded as technically skillful, its substance is still often dismissed as teenage pabulum.

This paper argues that rock music is sometimes much more than that. Like any art form, rock music is both a creation and a reflection of the culture from which it comes. Its potential impact is undeniably substantial—it reaches a far larger audience than do the works of authors or artists, and it certainly reaches a far greater audience than do the works of academicians. While Robert Merton's strain theory may provide an excellent explanation of how Americans respond to the strain of everyday life, many more Americans listen to the songs of Bruce Springsteen. Thus it is of some interest and import that his songwriting embodies the tenets of strain theory. This is not to suggest that what Bruce Springsteen has to say by itself has resulted in any change in society. It merely indicates that there is some sociological value to his work, and that strain theory, by whatever name it goes or manner in which it is presented, has enormous intuitive appeal, appeal which cuts across layers of discourse.

Finally, it is perhaps strain theory itself which explains why Springsteen's sociological observations would find outlet in popular song rather than academia, for as the

Rolling Stones song "Street Fighting Man" (covered by Springsteen during the *Born in the USA* tour) says: "What can a poor boy do—'cept sing in a rock and roll band?"

References

Agnew, R. 1985. "A Revised Strain Theory of Delinquency." *Social Forces* 64: 151–67.

——. 1989. "A Longitudinal Test of the Revised Strain Theory." *Journal of Quantitative Criminology* 5: 373–387.

——. 1992. "Foundation for A General Strain Theory of Crime and Delinquency." *Criminology* 30: 47–86.

Barlow, W. 1989. *Looking up at Down: The Emergence of Blues Culture.* Philadelphia: Temple University Press.

Bayles, M. 1994. *Hole in Our Soul: The Loss of Beauty and Meaning in American Popular Music.* New York: The Free Press.

Burton, V. S., Jr. 1991. "Explaining Adult Criminality: Testing Strain, Differential Association, and Control Theories." Unpublished dissertation, University of Cincinnati. Ann Arbor, Michigan: University Microfilms.

Burton, V. S., Jr., and F. T. Cullen. 1992. "The Empirical Status of Strain Theory." *Journal of Crime and Justice* 15: 1–30.

Corn, D. 1996. "Springsteen Tells the Story of the Secret America." *Mother Jones.*

Durkheim, E. 1951. *Suicide: A Sociological Study.* New York: The Free Press.

Farnworth, M., and M. J. Leiber. 1989. "Strain Theory Revisited: Economic Goals, Educational Means, and Delinquency." *American Sociological Review* 54: 259–79.

Faulkner, W. 1929. *The Sound and the Fury.* New York: Random House.

Gillette, C. 1983. *The Sound of the City: The Rise of Rock and Roll.* New York: Pantheon.

Goldrosen, J., and J. Beecher. 1986. *Remembering Buddy: The Definitive Biography of Buddy Holly.* New York: Penguin Books.

Guralnick, P. 1986. *Sweet Soul Music: Rhythm and Blues and the Southern Drama of Freedom.* New York: Harper and Row.

——. 1994. *Last Train to Memphis: The Rise of Elvis Presley.* Boston: Little, Brown.

Hawthorne, N. 1962. *The Scarlet Letter.* New York: Knopf.

Hirschi, T. 1969. *Causes of Delinquency.* Berkeley: University of California Press.

Kornhauser, R. R. 1978. *Social Sources of Delinquency.* Chicago: University of Chicago Press.

Marsh, D. 1979. *Born to Run: The Bruce Springsteen Story.* New York: Doubleday.

——1987. *Glory Days.* New York: Pantheon.

Merton, R. K. 1938. "Social Structure and Anomie." *American Sociological Review* 3: 672–82.

Miller, Arthur. 1949. *Death of a Salesman.* New York: Knopf.

Palmer, R. 1981. *Deep Blues.* New York; Viking.

Pollock, B. 1983. *When the Music Mattered: Rock in the 1960's.* New York: Holt, Rinehart & Winston.

——. 1993. *Hipper Than Our Kids: A Rock and Roll Journal of the Baby Boom Generation.* New York: Macmillan.

Taylor, I, P. Walton, and J. Young. 1973. *The New Criminology.* New York: Harper and Row.

Thoreau, H. D. 1854. *Walden, or Life in the Woods.* Boston: Harvard University Press.

Tichi, C. 1994. *High Lonesome: The American Culture of Country Music,* Chapel Hill: University of North Carolina Press.

Vold, G. B., and T. J. Bernard. 1986. *Theoretical Criminology.* New York: Oxford University Press.

Williams, F. P., and M. D. McShane. 1994. *Criminological Theory.* Englewood Cliffs, NJ: Prentice Hall.

Albums Cited

Springsteen, Bruce. (1973). *Greetings from Asbury Park.* New York: Columbia Records.

Springsteen, Bruce. (1973). *The wild, the innocent, and the E Street shuffle.* New York: Columbia Records.

Springsteen, Bruce. (1975). *Born to run.* New York: Columbia Records.

Springsteen, Bruce. (1978). *Darkness on the edge of town.* New York: Columbia Records.

REVIEW QUESTIONS

1. Given Hemmens's examination of Springsteen's lyrics, do you feel you have a better understanding of Merton's ideas regarding strain? Does this differ from the understanding or feelings you had from Merton's original paper? If so, why?

2. Which portion of Springsteen's lyrics do you find most compelling or applicable in terms of Merton's ideas about strain or adaptations to strain? Which adaptation(s) to strain do you find are best represented in Springsteen's lyrics?

3. Can you think of lyrics from other musicians (or movies, books) that would better, or similarly, explain Merton's concept of strain or adaptations to strain?

In this selection, Robert Agnew explains how his extended model of general strain theory is an improvement over the traditional strain theory proposed by Merton. Specifically, general strain theory includes many elements that cause strain and frustration beyond the economic reasons that Merton emphasized. You will also see that Agnew's general strain theory places an emphasis on feelings of anger, as well as the primary causes of such feelings, especially the injustice that individuals tend to feel from not being treated fairly. You will see that the general strain theory framework is more elaborate, and hence more valid, than the traditional strain model by Merton, simply because it is far more versatile in terms of explaining what causes individuals to be strained or frustrated and thus more likely to commit criminal acts.

Building on the Foundation of General Strain Theory

Specifying the Types of Strain Most Likely to Lead to Crime and Delinquency

Robert Agnew

General strain theory (GST) argues that strains or stressors increase the likelihood of negative emotions like anger and frustration. These emotions create pressure for corrective action, and crime is one possible response (Agnew 1992). Crime may be a method for reducing strain (e.g., stealing the money you desire), seeking revenge, or alleviating negative emotions (e.g., through illicit drug use). GST builds on previous strain theories in several ways: most notably, by pointing to several new categories of strain, including the loss of positive stimuli (e.g., loss of a romantic partner, death of a friend), the presentation of negative stimuli (e.g., physical assaults and verbal insults), and new categories of goal blockage (e.g., the failure to achieve justice goals). Recent research demonstrates that many of the specific strains falling under these categories are related to crime and delinquency (see Agnew 2001a for a summary; Aseltine, Gore, and Gordon 2000; Mazerolle et al. 2000; Piquero and Sealock 2000). The specification of these new categories of strain in GST's greatest strength.

This strength, however, is also GST's biggest weakness. GST is so broad that researchers have little guidance as to the specific types of strain to examine in their research.

Hundreds of types of strain fall under the major categories of strain listed by GST, as reflected in recent inventories of stressful life events, chronic stressors, and daily life events or hassles (see Cohen, Kessler, and Gordon 1995; Herbert and Cohen 1996 for overviews). And even these inventories do not measure many of the strains described by GST. Furthermore, the broadness of GST makes it difficult to falsify. As Jensen (1995) stated, "If strain can be defined in so many different ways, then strain theory is virtually unfalsifiable. There is always a new measure that might salvage the theory" (p. 152).

It is therefore crucial that GST more precisely specify the types of strain most likely to lead to crime and delinquency. This article represents an attempt to do that. First, strain is defined. Although Agnew (1992) presented a general definition of strain, the term has nevertheless been used in different ways by researchers and it is important to clarify its meaning. Second, previous tests of GST are reviewed to determine what they say about the types of strain most likely to lead to crime. Third, the characteristics of those types of strain most likely to lead to crime are described. Briefly, such strains (1) are seen as unjust, (2) are seen as high in magnitude, (3) are associated with low social control, and

(4) create some pressure or incentive to engage in crime. Fourth, these characteristics are then used to predict the likelihood that several types of strain will result in crime. Fifth, suggestions for empirical research are provided.

What Is Strain?

Before discussing the types of strain most likely to lead to crime, it is first necessary to clarify what is meant by the term *strain.* Agnew (1992) stated that strain refers to "relationships in which others are not treating the individual as he or she would like to be treated" (p. 48). Even so, researchers use the term in different ways. Some refer to an objective event or condition (e.g., the infliction of physical abuse, the receipt of poor grades at school), some to the individual's evaluation of an event or condition (e.g., whether juveniles like the way their parents or teachers treat them), and some to the emotional reaction to an event or condition (e.g., whether respondents are angry at how others treat them). To help clarify the meaning of strain, the following definitions are proposed.

Objective strains refer to events or conditions that are disliked by most members of a given group. So, if we state that an individual is experiencing objective strain, we mean that he or she is experiencing an event or condition that is usually disliked by members of his or her group. Many events and conditions are disliked by most people, regardless of group membership (e.g., physical assault, lack of adequate food and shelter). The evaluation of other events and conditions varies with group characteristics, such as gender and age (e.g., Broidy and Agnew 1997; Elder, George, and Shanahan 1996). It is, of course, important for researchers to consider the possibility of such group differences when constructing measures of objective strain.

Empirically, it is possible to determine the objective strains for group members in several ways. Observational research is one method. Anderson (1999), for example, described many of the objective strains in a poor, inner-city, African American community. Surveying a representative sample of group members or people familiar with the group is another method, and both have been employed in the stress research (Turner and Wheaton 1995). In particular, respondents can be asked whether they (or group members) would dislike a range of events and conditions. It is important to present respondents with preestablished lists

of events/conditions and to ask them to list events/conditions not on the list. This helps to ensure that a complete list of objective strains is developed.[1]

Subjective strains refer to events or conditions that are disliked by the people who are experiencing (or have experienced) them. So, if we state that individuals are experiencing subjective strain, we mean that they are experiencing an event or condition that *they* dislike. One of the key findings to emerge from the stress research is that individuals often differ in their subjective evaluation of the same objective strains. For example, people differ in how they subjectively evaluate such objective strains as divorce and the death of a family member. The subjective evaluation of an objective strain is a function of a range of factors, including individual traits (e.g., irritability), personal and social resources (e.g., self-esteem, self-efficacy, social support), goals/values/identities, and a range of life circumstances (for overviews, see Dohrenwend 1998; Kaplan 1996; Lazarus 1999). Wheaton (1990), for example, found that the quality of a prior marriage strongly influenced how people evaluated their divorce, with people in bad marriages evaluating their divorce is positive terms. It is also important to note that an individual's evaluation of an objective strain frequently changes over time as the individual copes with the strain. So, although there is a relationship between objective and subjective strain, it is far from perfect.

Most of the research on strain theory employs measures of objective strain (although see Agnew and White 1992). Researchers ask individuals whether they have experienced a certain event or condition (e.g., Did you fail any classes? Do your parents yell at you?); no effort is made to measure the individual's subjective evaluation of this event/condition. This may cause researchers to underestimate the support for strain theory because objective strains sometimes create little subjective strain. This does not mean, however, that researchers should simply employ subjective measures of strain. It is important to examine objective strains as well because this allows us to better distinguish external events from the subjective evaluation of such events. We can then examine individual and group differences in both the exposure to external events/conditions likely to cause strain and the subjective evaluation of those events/conditions. Furthermore, we can explore the factors that influence individual and group differences in the subjective evaluation of the same external events and conditions. This is critical if we are to fully explain individual and group differences in crime. As an illustration, Bernard (1990) argued that poor, inner-city residents have higher rates of violence not only because they experience more objective strains but also because they are more sensitive to such strains (also see Thoits 1995 on individual and group differences in the "vulnerability" to stressors).

The emotional response to an event or condition is closely linked to subjective strain. Subjective strain deals with the individual's evaluation of an event or condition. There are many definitions of emotion, but most state that a central component of an emotion is an evaluation of or an affective response to some object or behavior or idea. Most theorists, however, go on to state that emotions involve more than an evaluation or affective response. For example, they also involve changes in physiological or bodily sensations (see Berkowitz 1993; Smith-Lovin 1995; Thoits 1989). Building on this argument, I would contend that subjective strain is distinct from the full emotional reaction to strain.

Two individuals may evaluate an event/condition in the same way; that is, they may both dislike it an equal amount. So, they have the same level of subjective strain. One may become angry in response to the strain, however, whereas the other may become depressed. And they may differ in the degree to which they experience certain emotions, so one may become quite angry, whereas the other may experience only mild anger. So the same subjective strain may result in rather different emotional reactions. Again, a range of individual and environmental factors influences the emotional reaction to subjective strain. The potential utility of distinguishing between subjective strain and the emotional reaction to strain is highlighted by Broidy and Agnew (1997). They argued that males and females often differ in their emotional reaction to subjective strains. Although both males and females may experience anger, the anger of females is more likely to be accompanied by feelings of guilt, depression, and anxiety. These additional emotions are said to reduce the likelihood of other-directed crime, thereby helping us explain gender differences in such crime.

 ## Research on the Types of Strain Most Likely to Lead to Crime and Delinquency

Agnew (1992) described those types of events and conditions most likely to be classified as objective strains and to result in subjective strain. Such events/conditions involve goal blockage, the loss of positive stimuli, and/or the presentation of negative stimuli. They are also high in magnitude (degree), recent, and of long duration. But as indicated earlier, hundreds of events/conditions meet these criteria, and so there are potentially hundreds of objective and subjective strains. Agnew did *not* discuss whether certain of these strains are more likely to result in crime than others. Rather, he treated these strains as more or less equivalent in terms of their impact on crime. He argued that whether they result in crime is largely a function of the characteristics of the individuals experiencing the strain. In particular, strain is most likely to lead to crime when individuals lack the skills and resources to cope with their strain in legitimate manner, are low in conventional social support, are low in social control, blame their strain on others, and are disposed to crime. This article builds on Agnew by arguing that the effect of strain on crime is a function not only of individual characteristics but also of the type of strain experienced by the individual. Certain types of strain—either objective or subjective strain—are more likely to result in crime than other types.

Previous research on GST provides some information about the types of strain most likely to lead to crime, although much of this research suffers from two problems that severely limit its utility. First, most tests of GST examine only a small portion of the strains described by Agnew (1992). These tests tend to make use of existing data sets, which were not collected for the purpose of testing GST. As a consequence, many key strain measures are missing—particularly measures of the types of goal blockage described by Agnew and measures of certain types of negative treatment, like peer abuse and experiences with racial discrimination and prejudice. So we have little idea whether these types of strain are related to delinquency. Second, most tests of GST examine the effect of a single, cumulative strain measure on delinquency. In some cases, a measure of stressful life events is employed. Hoffmann and associates, for example, tested GST using a 16- to 18-item measure that focuses on events like "death, illness, or accidents among family or friends; changes in school or residence; parental divorce or separation; and family financial problems" (Hoffmann and Cerbone 1999; Hoffmann and Miller 1998; Hoffmann and Su 1997; also see Aseltine et al. 2000). In other cases, the cumulative strain measure is a composite of several scales and/or items measuring a range of different types of strain, such as neighborhood problems, negative relations with adults, the failure to achieve educational and occupational goals, breaking up with a romantic partner or friend, and getting lower grades than you deserve (e.g., Mazerolle 1998; Mazerolle et al. 2000; Mazerolle and Piquero 1997). The use of such cumulative measures means that we lack information on the effect of the individual strain measures.

Researchers employ cumulative measures of strain because Agnew (1992) argued that it is not the effect of one specific strain or stressor that is important; rather, it is the cumulative effect of all the strains experienced by the individual. He recommended combining individual strain measures into a single scale so as to better estimate this cumulative effect (pp. 62–63). It is assumed that all or most of the individual strain measures in the cumulative scale make some contribution to crime. As will be argued below, there is good reason to question this assumption. Most cumulative measures encompass a wide range of strains, and it is likely that some contribute to crime and some do not. Given this fact, it is not surprising that most cumulative measures have only a moderate impact on crime. A consideration of different types of strain, however, might reveal that some have a strong impact on crime, whereas others have little or no impact.

Some tests of GST do examine the impact of different types of strain on crime among adolescents. Agnew and White (1992) examined the effect of eight strain measures on delinquency, including both general and specific measures. They found that negative life events, life hassles, negative relations with adults, and parental fighting are significantly associated with delinquency. Neighborhood problems, unpopularity with the opposite sex, occupational strain, and clothing strain are not associated with delinquency. Paternoster and Mazerolle (1994) examined the effect of five strain measures on delinquency. They found that neighborhood problems, negative life events, school/peer hassles, and negative relations with adults are significantly associated with subsequent delinquency, whereas a measure of educational and occupational expectations is not (see Mazerolle 1998 for information on gender differences in the effect of these strain measures). Aseltine et al. (2000) found that family and peer conflict (through anger) are related to selected types of delinquency. Agnew and Brezina (1997) found that poor relations with peers is related to delinquency, whereas unpopularity with peers is not. Piquero and Sealock (2000) found that physical and emotional abuse in the household (toward the juvenile and others) is related to

delinquency (also see Brezina 1999). Tests of classic strain theory typically find that the failure to achieve educational and occupational goals is *not* related to delinquency (see Agnew 1995a). The failure to achieve economic goals, however, may be related to delinquency (Burton and Dunaway 1994).

Many other studies have not set out to test GST but have examined types of strain that fall under the theory. Several studies found that adolescent crime is significantly related to criminal victimization; parental abuse and neglect; parental rejection; disciplinary techniques that are excessive, very strict, erratic, and/or punitive (e.g., nagging, yelling, threats, insults, and/or hitting); family conflict; parental divorce/separation; and negative experiences at school (low grades, poor relations with teachers, and the perception that school is boring and a waste of time). Summaries of these studies are provided in Agnew (1992, 1995b, 1997, 2001a, 2001b). Studies of adults suggest that crime is related to marital problems, work in the secondary labor market, unemployment in certain cases, and possibly the failure to achieve economic goals (Agnew et al. 1996; Baron and Hartnagel 1997; Cernkovich, Giordano, and Rudolph 2000; Colvin 2000; Crutchfield and Pitchford 1997; Sampson and Laub 1993; Uggen 2000). There has not been enough good research on other types of strain to draw any firm conclusions about their relationship to crime.

The above studies, then, suggested that certain types of strain are related to crime whereas others are not. At this point, it seems safe to conclude that crime is related to verbal and physical assaults, including assaults by parents, spouse/partners, teachers, and probably peers. Crime is also related to parental rejection, poor school performance, and work problems, including work in the secondary labor market. Crime is not related to the expected failure to achieve educational/occupational success or to unpopularity with peers. Beyond that, the relationship between various strains and crime is unclear.

These data pose a major problem for GST: Why is it that only some types of strain are related to crime? At present, GST offers little guidance in this area. GST, for example, does not allow us to explain why verbal and physical assaults are related to crime, but the failure to achieve educational/occupational goals and unpopularity with peers is not. All of these strains fall under the categories listed by Agnew (1992), and they are frequently high in magnitude (degree), recent, and of long duration.

Recent versions of GST do argue that certain types of strain are especially relevant to crime (Agnew and Brezina 1997; Broidy and Agnew 1997). Agnew (1997, 2001a, 2001b), for example, argued that although many types of goal blockage may lead to delinquency, the failure to achieve monetary, autonomy, and "masculinity" goals are of special importance. And he argued that although a range of negative or noxious stimuli may cause delinquency, physical and verbal assaults are of special importance. These suggestions, however, are not derived from theory. Rather, they represent ad hoc attempts to explain empirical findings or to incorporate other theoretical and empirical work into GST. Much theoretical and empirical work, for example, suggests that threats to one's status, particularly one's masculine status, contribute to crime in certain groups (Anderson 1999; Messerschmidt 1993). Likewise, some theoretical and empirical work suggests that the blockage of autonomy goals contributes to delinquency (Agnew 1984; Moffitt 1993; Tittle 1995).

And although empirical research is starting to point to those types of strain that are and are not related to delinquency, it is not wise to depend on such research to fully resolve this issue. There are hundreds of specific types of strain; it will take empirical researchers a long while to determine their relative importance (although observational research and open-ended, intensive interviews can be of some help here). Furthermore, we would still lack an explanation of why some types of strain have a greater effect on crime than other types. The lack of such an explanation might cause us to overlook certain important types of strain. It is therefore important for GST to better explain why some types of strain are more likely to lead to crime than other types.

Strain is most likely to lead to crime when it is seen as unjust, is seen as high in magnitude, is associated with low social control, and creates some pressure or incentive to engage in criminal coping. If these arguments are correct, types of strain that meet these conditions should be more strongly related to crime than types that do not (although the precise relationship between strain and crime is a function of the characteristics of *both* the strain and the people experiencing the strain). So at the most basic level, researchers should test the above arguments by classifying strains on the above characteristics and then examining the relative impact of these strains on crime. The classification of strains just presented can be used as a starting point for

such research. Ideally, researchers should compare the criminal behavior of people who have experienced the above strains. As an alternative, researchers can present people with vignettes describing these types of strain and then ask how likely they or others would be or respond to them with crime (see Mazerolle and Piquero 1997 for a model).

The Cumulative Effect of Strain

This strategy for testing strain theory differs from the approach now taken by most researchers, who examine the impact of cumulative measures of strain on crime—with these cumulative measures often containing types of strain that differ widely on the above characteristics. Although researchers should not ignore the argument that strains may have a cumulative effect on crime, it is most important at this point to determine which types of strain are most strongly related to crime. Once this is determined, researchers can then explore the cumulative impact of strain on crime. Cumulative scales can be created by combining those types of strain that have a significant impact on crime—perhaps weighting them by their regression coefficients. A similar strategy has been successfully employed in the stress literature (Herbert and Cohen 1996; Turner and Wheaton 1995; Wheaton et al. 1997; also see Agnew and White 1992). Or researchers can determine whether strains interact with one another in their impact on crime through the creation of interaction terms (see Wheaton et al. 1997; note the argument that moderate levels of prior stress sometimes *reduce* the negative effects of current stressors).

Distinguishing Strain from Social Control and Social Learning

Researchers testing GST all confront a major problem: Many of the "strain" measures they use—like low grades or harsh parental discipline—can also be taken as social control or social-learning measures. Researchers usually deal with this problem by assigning some measures to the strain camp, some to the social control camp, and some to the social-learning camp. They then try to justify these assignments, although their arguments are often less than convincing. Agnew (1995c) explained why this is so, noting that most variables have implications for strain, social control, *and* social-learning theories. Harsh discipline, for example, is often classified as a type of strain, but some claim that it leads to crime by reducing attachment to parents or implicitly teaching the child that violence is acceptable under certain conditions (see Brezina 1998). It is therefore difficult to classify an independent variable as a purely strain, social control, or social-learning variable. This article makes the same argument: Most types of strain have implications for social control and the social learning of crime. Furthermore, it is argued that those types of strain most likely to lead to crime are those that are associated with low social control and the social learning of crime.

This argument raises a major problem: If those types of strain most strongly related to crime are associated with low control and the social learning of crime, how do we know whether these strains affect crime for reasons related to strain, social control, or social-learning theories? Agnew's (1995c) solution to this problem was to examine the intervening processes described by these theories. Although these theories have many of the same independent variables in common, they differ in terms of their specification of intervening processes. Strain theory argues that these variables increase crime through their effect on negative emotions, control theory argues that they lower the perceived costs of crime, and social-learning theory argues that they influence the perceived desirability of crime. A few studies have attempted to examine such intervening processes, and they typically find that the processes associated with all three theories are operative (see Agnew 1985; Brezina 1998).[2] Unfortunately, most existing data sets do not allow for the proper examination of these intervening processes (see Schieman 2000 and Stone 1995 for discussions of certain of the problems involved in measuring the key negative emotion of anger).

There is a second strategy that may be employed to determine if a strain measure affects crime for reasons related to strain, social control, or social-learning theory. Certain strain measures may affect crime because they reduce social control and/or foster the social learning of crime. As indicated, harsh discipline is said to reduce attachment to parents and foster beliefs conducive to violence. In such cases, we can examine the effect of the strain measure on crime while controlling for the relevant social control and social-learning variables. For example, we can examine the effect of harsh discipline on crime while controlling for

parental attachment and beliefs conducive to violence. Or we can examine the effect of teacher conflicts while controlling for attachment to teachers, attachment to school, and grades. If the strain measure still affects crime after such controls, support for strain theory is increased. This strategy cannot be followed in all cases, however. Certain strain measures—like low grades—directly index the respondent's level of social control or social learning. Therefore, it is not possible to control for the relevant control or social-learning variables. Also, there is some risk in arguing that the *direct* effect of the strain measure on crime is best explained by strain theory. Researchers may have failed to control for or properly measure all relevant social control and social-learning variables. And it is possible that the strain measure affects crime for reasons other than those offered by strain, social control, and social-learning theories (e.g., genetic factors may influence both exposure to strain and levels of crime).

Finally, a third strategy sometimes allows us to determine whether strain variables affect crime for reasons distinct from those offered by social control theory. According to the logic of control theory, neutral relationships with other individuals and groups should have the same effect on crime as negative relationships. For example, a juvenile who does not care about her parents should be just as delinquent as a juvenile who dislikes or hates her parents. Both juveniles are equally free to engage in delinquency; that is, both have nothing to lose through delinquency. According to the logic of strain theory, however, the juvenile who hates her parents should be higher in delinquency than the juvenile who does not care about her parents. This is because the juvenile who hates her parents is under more strain. Her hatred likely stems from unpleasant relations with her parents, and it is stressful to live with people you hate. This prediction is easily tested with certain data sets, but researchers rarely compare juveniles who dislike/hate their parents with juveniles who neither like nor dislike their parents (see Nye 1958 for an exception). Similar analyses can be conducted in other areas. For example, researchers can compare the criminal behavior of individuals who hate their grades or jobs with those who do not care about their grades or jobs. If strain theory is correct, individuals who hate their grades or jobs should be higher in crime.

None of these strategies allows us to perfectly determine whether strain variables affect crime for reasons related to strain, social control, or social-learning theories, but taken together they can shed much light on this problem.

Measuring Strain

Many current measures of strain are quite simplistic; single-item measures of specific strains are often employed, with these measures providing little information about the magnitude, injustice, or other dimensions of the strain. A similar situation characterizes the stress literature, although stress researchers are starting to collect more detailed information on stressors to better estimate things like their magnitude. For example, some stress researchers have abandoned simple checklist measures and are employing intensive interviews with semistructured probes (see Herbert and Cohen 1996; Wethington et al. 1995; Wheaton 1996). Such techniques were developed because respondents often report trivial stressors when checklist measures are used—even when such checklists attempt to focus on serious stressors (Dohrenwend 2000; Herbert and Cohen 1996; Wethington et al. 1995). Also, many stress researchers now recognize that the circumstances associated with the stressors have an important effect on its impact. It is difficult to employ intensive interviews in the large-scale surveys often conducted by criminologists, but criminologists can do a much better job of measuring strain in such surveys. As an illustration, one need only compare the measures of economic strain typically employed by criminologists with those commonly used in the family research. Economic strain is not simply measured in terms of low income or a two- or three-item index of socioeconomic status. Rather, family researchers examine such things as (1) family per capita income; (2) unstable work history, which includes changing to a worse job, demotions, and being fired or laid off; (3) debt-to-asset ratio; and (4) increases or decreases in family income in the past year. Furthermore, researchers recognize that these types of economic strain do not affect all families in the same way. So, more direct measures of economic strain are sometimes employed as well. For example, parents are asked about the extent to which the family has enough money for clothing, food, medical care, and bills. They are also asked about the changes they have had to make to cope with economic hardship, like moving, taking an additional job, canceling medical insurance, and obtaining government assistance(e.g., Conger et al. 1992; Fox and Chancey 1998; Voydanoff 1990; also see Agnew et al. 1996; Cernkovich et al. 2000).

Conclusion

GST is usually tested by examining the effect of selected types of strain on crime. Researchers, however, have little guidance when it comes to selecting among the many hundreds of types of strain that might be examined. And they have trouble explaining why only some of the strains they do examine are related to crime. This article builds on GST by describing the characteristics of strainful events and conditions that influence their relationship to crime. As indicated, strains are most likely to lead to crime when they (1) are seen as unjust, (2) are seen as high in magnitude, (3) are associated with low social control, and (4) create some pressure or incentive to engage in criminal coping. Based on these characteristics, it is argued that certain types of strain will be unrelated or only weakly related to crime. Such strains include the failure to achieve educational and occupational success, the types of strain that have dominated the research on strain theory. Such strains also include many of the types of strain found in stressful life events scales, which are commonly used to test GST. And it is argued that other types of strain will be more strongly related to crime, including types that have received much attention in the criminology literature (e.g., parental rejection; erratic, harsh parental discipline; child abuse and neglect; negative school experiences) and types that have received little attention (e.g., the inability to achieve selected goals, peer abuse, experiences with prejudice and discrimination).

The arguments presented in this article should have a fundamental impact on future efforts to test GST because they identify those types of strain that should and should not be related to crime. And in doing so, these arguments make it easier to falsify GST. Furthermore, these arguments help explain the contradictory results of past research on strain theory; for example, they help explain why the failure to achieve educational and occupational success is usually not related to crime, whereas verbal and physical assaults usually have a relatively strong relationship to crime.

These arguments also have important policy implications. Agnew (1992) argued that two major policy recommendations flow from GST: reduce the exposure of individuals to strain and reduce the likelihood that individuals will cope with strain through crime (by targeting those individual characteristics conducive to criminal coping). This article suggests a third recommendation: alter the characteristics of strains in ways that reduce the likelihood they will result in crime. Despite our best efforts, many individuals will be exposed to strain. For example, parents, teachers, and criminal justice officials will continue to sanction individuals in ways that are disliked. We can, however, alter the ways in which these sanctions are administered so as to reduce the likelihood that they will (1) be seen as unjust, (2) be seen as high in magnitude, (3) reduce social control, and (4) create some pressure or incentive to engage in crime. In fact, this is one of the central thrusts behind the restorative justice and related movements (see Bazemore 1998; Briathwaite 1989; Sherman 1993, 2000; Tyler 1990). These movements point to ways in which criminal justice officials can increase the perceived justice of sanctions, reduce the perceived magnitude of sanctions, sanction in ways that increase rather than reduce social control, and sanction in ways that create little pressure or incentive for crime. Recommendations in these areas include treating offenders with respect; making them aware of the harm they have caused; giving them some voice in determining sanctions; tempering the use of severe, punitive sanctions; and reintegrating offenders with conventional society through a variety of strategies—like reintegration ceremonies and the creation of positive roles for offenders. Certain parent-training and school-based programs are also structured in ways that reduce the likelihood that strains like disciplinary efforts will be administered in ways that increase the likelihood of criminal coping (see Agnew 1995d, 2001b).

Notes

1. Most of the research in criminology simply assumes that certain events or conditions are disliked by most of the people being studied. This is probably a reasonable assumption in most cases (e.g., criminal victimization), although it is a more questionable assumption in other cases (e.g., changing schools). A potentially more serious problem with the criminology research is that researchers rarely employ a complete or comprehensive list of objective strains. Researchers usually examine only a few types of objective strain—often overlooking many of the most important types. For example, interviews with adolescents suggest that peer conflict and abuse are among the most important types of objective strain in this group, but such conflict/abuse is rarely considered by researchers (although see Agnew 1997; Agnew and Brezina 1997; Ambert 1994; Aseltine et al., 2000; Seiffge-Krenke 1995). Likewise, experiences with racial prejudice

and discrimination are seldom considered by researchers, despite evidence that such experiences are a major type of objective strain among African Americans and others (Ambert 1994; Anderson 1999). Recent research suggests that the failure to examine the full range of stressors can lead researchers to substantially underestimate the effect of stress or strain (Turner, Wheaton, and Lloyd 1995).

2. One should also take account of the possibility that anger may indirectly affect crime by reducing the perceived costs of crime and increasing the perceived desirability of crime, as indicated earlier in this article.

References

Agnew, Robert. 1984. "Autonomy and Delinquency." *Sociological Perspectives* 27: 219–36.

———. 1985. "A Revised Strain Theory of Delinquency." *Social Forces* 64: 151–67.

———. 1990. "The Origins of Delinquent Events: An Examination of Offender Accounts." *Journal of Research in Crime and Delinquency* 27: 267–94.

———. 1992. "Foundation for a General Strain Theory of Crime and Delinquency." *Criminology* 30: 47–87.

———. 1995a. "Strain and Subcultural Theories of Criminality." In *Criminology: A Contemporary Handbook*, edited by Joseph F. Sheley. Belmont, CA: Wadsworth.

———. 1995b. "The Contribution of Social-Psychological Strain Theory of the Explanation of Crime and Delinquency." In *The Legacy of Anomie Theory, Advances in Criminological Theory*, Vol. 6, edited by Freda Adler and William S. Laufer. New Brunswick, NJ: Transaction.

———. 1995c. "Testing the Leading Crime Theories: An Alternative Strategy Focusing on Motivational Processes." *Journal of Research in Crime and Delinquency* 32: 363–98.

———. 1995d. "Controlling Delinquency: Recommendations from General Strain Theory." In *Crime and Public Policy*, edited by Hugh D. Barlow. Boulder, CO: Westview.

———. 1997. "Stability and Change in Crime over the Life Course: A Strain Theory Explanation." In *Developmental Theories of Crime and Delinquency, Advances in Criminological Theory*, Vol. 7, edited by Terence P. Thornberry. New Brunswick, NJ: Transaction.

———. 2001a. "An Overview of General Strain Theory." In *Explaining Criminals and Crime*, edited by Raymond Paternoster and Ronet Bachman. Los Angeles: Roxbury.

———. 2001b. *Juvenile Delinquency: Causes and Control*. Los Angeles: Roxbury.

Agnew, Robert, and Timothy Brezina. 1997. "Relational Problems with Peers, Gender and Delinquency." *Youth and Society* 29: 84–111.

Agnew, Robert, Francis T. Cullen, Velmer S. Burton, Jr., T. David Evans, and R. Gregory Dunaway. 1996. "A New Test of Classic Strain Theory." *Justice Quarterly* 13: 681–704.

Agnew, Robert, and Helene Raskin White. 1992. "An Empirical Test of General Strain Theory." *Criminology* 30: 475–99.

Ambert, Ann-Marie. 1994. "A Qualitative Study of Peer Abuse and Its Effects: Theoretical and Empirical Implications." *Journal of Marriage and the Family* 56: 119–30.

Anderson, Elijah. 1999. *Code of the Street.* New York: Norton.

Aseltine, Robert H., Jr., Susan Gore, and Mary Ellen Colten. 1998. "The Co-occurrence of Depression and Substance Abuse in Late Adolescence." *Development and Psychopathology* 10: 549–70.

Aseltine, Robert H., Jr., Susan Gore, and Jennifer Gordon. 2000. "Life Stress, Anger and Anxiety, and Delinquency: An Empirical Test of General Strain Theory." *Journal of Health and Social Behavior* 41: 256–75.

Baron, Stephen W., and Timothy F. Hartnagel. 1997. "Attributions, Affect, and Crime: Street Youths' Reactions to Unemployment." *Criminology* 35: 409–34.

Bazemore, Gordon. 1998. "Restorative Justice and Earned Redemption." *American Behavioral Scientist* 41: 768–813.

Berkowitz, Leonard. 1993. *Aggression: Its Causes, Consequences, and Control.* New York: McGraw-Hill.

Bernard, Thomas J. 1990. "Angry Aggression among the 'Truly Disadvantaged.'" *Criminology* 28: 73–96.

Braithwaite, John. 1989. *Crime, Shame, and Reintegration.* Cambridge, UK: Cambridge University Press.

Brezina, Timothy. 1998. "Adolescent Maltreatment and Delinquency: The Question of Intervening Processes." *Journal of Research in Crime and Delinquency* 35: 71–99.

———. 1999. "Teenage Violence toward Parents as an Adaptation to Family Strain." *Youth and Society* 30: 416–44.

Broidy, Lisa, and Robert Agnew. 1997. "Gender and Crime: A General Strain Theory Perspective." *Journal of Research in Crime and Delinquency* 34: 275–306.

Brown, George W. 1998. "Loss and Depressive Disorders." In *Adversity, Stress, and Psychopathology,* edited by Bruce P. Dohrenwend. New York: Oxford University Press.

Burton, Velmer S., Jr., and R. Gregory Dunaway. 1994. "Strain, Relative Deprivation, and Middle-Class Delinquency." In *Varieties of Criminology,* edited by Greg Barak. Westport, CT: Praeger.

Cernkovich, Stephen A., Peggy C. Giordano, and Jennifer L. Rudolph. 2000. "Race, Crime, and the American Dream." *Journal of Research in Crime and Delinquency* 37: 131–70.

Cohen, Sheldon, Ronald C. Kessler, and Lynn Underwood Gordon. 1995. *Measuring Stress.* New York: Oxford University Press.

Colvin, Mark. 2000. *Crime and Coercion: An Integrated Theory of Chronic Criminality.* New York: St. Martin's.

Conger, Rand D., Katherine J. Conger, Glen H. Elder, Jr., Frederick O. Lorenz, Ronald L. Simons, and Lee B. Whitbeck. 1992. "A Family Process Model of Economic Hardship and Adjustment of Early Adolescent Boys." *Child Development* 63: 526–41.

Crutchfield, Robert D., and Susan R. Pitchford. 1997. "Work and Crime: The Effects of Labor Stratification." *Social Forces* 76: 93–118.

Dohrenwend, Bruce P. 1998. *Adversity, Stress, and Psychopathology.* New York: Oxford University Press.

———. 2000. "The Role of Adversity and Stress in Psychopathology: Some Evidence and Its Implications for Theory and Research." *Journal of Health and Social Behavior* 41: 1–19.

Elder, Glen H., Jr., Linda K. George, and Michael J. Shanahan. 1996. "Psychosocial Stress over the Life Course." In *Psychosocial Stress,* edited by Howard B. Kaplan. San Diego, CA: Academic Press.

Fox, Greer Linton, and Dudley Chancey. 1998. "Sources of Economic Distress." *Journal of Family Issues* 19: 725–49.

Herbert, Tracy B., and Sheldon Cohen. 1996. "Measurement Issues in Research on Psychosocial Stress." In *Psychosocial Stress,* edited by Howard B. Kaplan. San Diego, CA: Academic Press.

Hoffmann, John P., and Felice Gray Cerbone. 1999. "Stressful Life Events and Delinquency Escalation in Early Adolescence." *Criminology* 37: 343–74.

Hoffmann, John P., and Alan S. Miller. 1998. "A Latent Variable Analysis of Strain Theory." *Journal of Quantitative Criminology* 14: 83–110.

Hoffmann, John P., and S. Susan Su. 1997. "The Conditional Effects of Stress on Delinquency and Drug Use: A Strain Theory Assessment of Sex Differences." *Journal of Research in Crime and Delinquency* 34: 46–78.

Jensen, Gary F. 1995. "Salvaging Structure through Strain: A Theoretical and Empirical Critique." In *The Legacy of Anomie Theory, Advances in Criminological Theory,* Vol. 6, edited by Freda Adler and William S. Laufer. New Brunswick, NJ: Transaction.

Kaplan, Howard B. 1996. "Psychosocial Stress from the Perspective of Self Theory." In *Psychosocial Stress,* edited by Howard B. Kaplan. San Diego, CA: Academic Press.

Lazarus, Richard S. 1999. *Stress and Emotion: A New Synthesis.* New York: Springer.

Mazerolle, Paul. 1998. "Gender, General Strain, and Delinquency: An Empirical Examination." *Justice Quarterly* 15: 65–91.

Mazerolle, Paul, Velmer S. Burton, Jr., Francis T. Cullen, T. David Evans, and Gary L. Payne. 2000. "Strain, Anger, and Delinquency Adaptations: Specifying General Strain Theory." *Journal of Criminal Justice* 28: 89–101.

Mazerolle, Paul, and Alex Piquero. 1997. "Violent Responses to Strain: An Examination of Conditioning Influences." *Violence and Victims* 12: 323–43.

Messerschmidt, James W. 1993. *Masculinities and Crime.* Lanham, MD: Rowman and Littlefield.

Moffitt, Terrie E. 1993. "'Life-Course Persistent' and 'Adolescent-Limited' Antisocial Behavior: A Developmental Taxonomy." *Psychological Review* 100: 674–701.

Nye, Ivan. 1958. *Family Relationships and Delinquent Behavior.* New York: John Wiley.

Paternoster, Raymond, and Paul Mazerolle. 1994. "General Strain Theory and Delinquency: A Replication and Extension." *Journal of Research in Crime and Delinquency* 31: 235–63.

Piquero, Nicole Leeper, and Miriam D. Sealock. 2000. "Generalizing General Strain Theory: An Examination of an Offending Population." *Justice Quarterly* 17: 449–84.

Sampson, Robert J., and John H. Laub. 1993. *Crime in the Making.* Cambridge, MA: Harvard University Press.

Schieman, Scott. 2000. "Education and the Activation, Course, and Management of Anger." *Journal of Health and Social Behavior* 41: 20–39.

Seiffge-Krenke, Inge. 1995. *Stress, Coping, and Relationships in Adolescence.* Mahwah, NJ: Lawrence Erlbaum.

Sherman, Lawrence W. 1993. "Defiance, Deterrence, and Irrelevance: A Theory of Criminal Sanctions." *Journal of Research in Crime and Delinquency* 30: 445–73.

———. 2000. "The Defiant Imagination: Consilience and the Science of Sanctions." Presented at the University of Pennsylvania, Philadelphia.

Smith-Lovin, Lynn. 1995. "The Sociology of Affect and Emotion." In *Sociological Perspectives on Social Psychology,* edited by Karen S. Cook, Gary Alan Fine, and James S. House. Needham Heights, NY: Allyn and Bacon.

Stone, Arthur A. 1995. "Measurement of Affective Response." In *Measuring Stress,* edited by Sheldon Cohen, Ronald C. Kessler, and Lynn Underwood Gordon. New York: Oxford University Press.

Sykes, Gresham M., and David Matza. 1957. "Techniques of Neutralization: A Theory of Delinquency." *American Sociological Review* 22: 664–70.

Thoits, Peggy A. 1989. "The Sociology of Emotions." *Annual Review of Sociology* 15: 317–42.

———. 1995. "Stress, Coping, and Social Support Processes: Where Are We? What Next?" *Journal of Health and Social Behavior* (Extra Issue): 53–79.

Tittle, Charles R. 1995. *Control Balance: Toward a General Theory of Deviance.* Boulder, CO: Westview.

Turner, R. Jay, and Blair Wheaton. 1995. "Checklist Measurement of Stressful Life Events." In *Measuring Stress,* edited by Sheldon Cohen, Ronald C. Kessler, and Lynn Underwood Gordon. New York: Oxford University Press.

Turner, R. Jay, Blair Wheaton, and Donald A. Lloyd. 1995. "The Epidemiology of Social Stress." *American Sociological Review* 60: 104–25.

Tyler, Tom. 1990. *Why People Obey the Law.* New Haven, CT: Yale University Press.

Uggen, Christopher. 2000. "Work as a Turning Point in the Life Course of Criminals: A Duration Model of Age. Employment, and Recidivism." *American Sociological Review* 67: 529–46.

Voydanoff, Patricia. 1990. "Economic Distress and Family Relations: A Review of the Eighties." *Journal of Marriage and the Family* 52: 1099–115.

Wethington, Elaine, George W. Brown, and Ronald C. Kessler. 1995. "Interview Measurement of Stressful Life Events." In *Measuring Stress,* edited by Sheldon Cohen, Ronald C. Kessler, and Lynn Underwood Gordon. New York: Oxford University Press.

Wheaton, Blair. 1990. "Life Transitions, Role Histories, and Mental Health." *American Sociological Review* 55: 209–24.

———. 1996. "The Domains and Boundaries of Stress Concepts." In *Psychosocial Stress,* edited by Howard B. Kaplan. San Diego. CA: Academic Press.

Wheaton, Blair, Patricia Roszell, and Kimberlee Hall. 1997. "The Impact of Twenty Childhood and Adult Traumatic Stressors on the Risk of Psychiatric Disorder." In *Stress and Adversity over the Life Course: Trajectories and Turning Points,* edited by Ian H. Gottlib. New York: Cambridge University Press.

REVIEW QUESTIONS

1. What types of strain does Agnew propose in this article that go beyond those presented by Merton's strain theory? Explain these new forms/categories of strain.

2. Which types of strain or characteristics of strain does Agnew claim are most important in causing criminal activity? What other types of theories do these characteristics of strain involve?

3. What types of policy implications does Agnew claim arise from the findings of this study? Which of these do you believe is likely to be most effective and why?

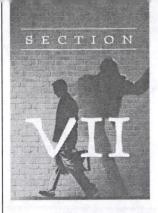

The Chicago School and Cultural and Subcultural Theories of Crime

This section will examine the origin and evolution of the Chicago or Ecological School theory, otherwise known as the ecological perspective or the theory of social disorganization. We will also discuss modern research on this theory, which assumes that the environments people live in determine their behavior. Finally, we will discuss the assumptions and dynamics of cultural and subcultural theory in society, highlighting differences in certain models emphasizing inner-city subcultures and other modern examples of subcultures (e.g., street gangs). We will finish by reviewing the policy implications that have been suggested by this perspective of crime.

The Chicago School evolved during the late 19th and early 20th centuries when the city of Chicago desperately needed answers for its exponentially growing problem of delinquency and crime. This became a primary focus in Chicago, where total chaos prevailed at the time.

A significant portion of the Chicago perspective focused on the transmission of cultural values to peers, and even across generations, as the older youths relayed their antisocial values and techniques to the younger children. Thus, the cultural and subcultural perspective is also a key area of this theoretical model. This cultural aspect of the Chicago model is also examined in this section, as are other subculture frameworks of offending behaviors.

The Ecological School and the Chicago School of Criminology

Despite the fact that its name specifies one city, the Chicago School of criminology represents one of the most valid and generalizable theories we will discuss in this book in the sense that many of its propositions can be readily applied to the growth and evolution of virtually all cities around the world. The Chicago School, which is often referred to as the Ecological School or the theory of social disorganization, also represents one of the earliest examples of balancing theorizing with scientific analysis and at the same time guiding important programs and policy implementations that still thrive today. Perhaps most important, the Chicago School of criminology was the epitome of using theoretical development and scientific testing to help improve conditions in society when it was most needed, which can be appreciated only by understanding the degree of chaos and crime that existed in Chicago in the late 1800s and early 1900s.

Cultural Context: Chicago in the 1800s and Early 1900s

Experts have determined that 19th-century Chicago was the fastest-growing city in U.S. history.[1] Census data show that the population went from about 5,000 in the early 1800s to more than 2 million by 1900; put another way, the population more than doubled every decade during the 19th century.[2] This massive rate of growth—much faster than that seen in other large U.S. cities such as Boston, Baltimore, New York, Philadelphia, and San Francisco—was due to Chicago's central geographic position. It was in many ways landlocked because, although it sits on Lake Michigan, there was no water route to the city from the Atlantic Ocean until the Erie Canal opened in 1825, which provided access to the Great Lakes region for shipping and migration of people. Three years later came the first U.S. passenger train, the Baltimore and Ohio railroad, whose route extended from the mid-Atlantic to central areas of the country. These two transportation advancements created a continual stream of migration to the Chicago area, which increased again when the transcontinental railroad was completed in 1869, linking both coasts with the U.S. Midwest.[3]

It is important to keep in mind that, in the early to mid 1800s, many large U.S. cities had virtually no formal social agencies to handle the problems of urbanization—no social workers, building inspectors, garbage collectors, or even police officers. Once police agencies were introduced, their duties often included finding lost children and collecting the garbage, primarily because there weren't other agencies to perform these tasks. Therefore, communities were largely responsible for solving their own problems, including crime and delinquency. By the late 1800s, however, Chicago was largely made up of citizens who did not speak a common language and did not share each other's cultural values. This phenomenon is consistent with Census Bureau data from that era, which show that 70% of Chicago residents were foreign born and another 20% were first-generation Americans. It was almost impossible for these citizens to organize themselves to solve community problems because, in most cases, they could not even understand each other.

This resulted in the type of chaos and normlessness that Durkheim predicted would occur when urbanization and industrialization occurred too rapidly; in fact, Chicago represented the archetype of a society in an anomic state, with almost a complete breakdown in control. One of the most notable manifestations of this breakdown in social control was that children were running wild on the streets in gangs, with adults making little attempt to intervene. So, delinquency was soaring, and it appeared that the gangs controlled the streets as much as any other group.

The leaders and people of Chicago needed theoretical guidance to develop solutions to their problems, particularly regarding the high rates of delinquency. This was a key factor in why the Department of Sociology at the

---

[1]For an excellent discussion of the early history of Chicago, see Thomas J. Bernard, *The Cycle of Juvenile Justice*, 2nd ed. (New York: Oxford University Press, 2010).

[2]See discussion in Thomas J. Bernard, Jeffrey B. Snipes, and Alexander L. Gerould, *Vold's Theoretical Criminology*, 6th ed. (Oxford: Oxford University Press, 2010), 117–22 (see chap. 1).

[3]These dates were taken from *The World Almanac, 2000*, Millennium Collector's Edition (Mahwah: Primedia Reference, 2000).

University of Chicago became so important and dominant in the early 1900s. Essentially, modern sociology developed in Chicago because this city needed it the most to solve its social problems. Thus, Chicago became a type of laboratory for sociological researchers, and they developed a number of theoretical models of crime and other social ills that are still shown to be empirically valid today.

Ecological Principles in City Growth and Concentric Circles

In the 1920s and 1930s, several new perspectives of human behavior and city growth were offered by sociologists at the University of Chicago. The first relevant model was proposed by Robert E. Park, who claimed that much of human behavior, especially the way cities grow, follows the basic principles of ecology that had been documented and applied to wildlife for many years at that point.[4] Ecology is essentially the study of the dynamics and processes through which plants and animals interact with the environment. In an application of Darwinian theory, Park proposed that the growth of cities follows a natural pattern and evolution.

Specifically, Park claimed that cities represent a type of complex organism with a sense of unity composed of the interrelations among its citizens and groups. Park applied the ecological principle of symbiosis to explain the dependency of various citizens and units on each other: Everyone is better off working together as a whole. Furthermore, Park claimed that all cities would contain identifiable clusters, which he called natural areas, that would take on a life or organic unity of their own. To clarify, many cities have neighborhoods that are made up of primarily one ethnic group or are distinguished by certain features. For example, New York City's Hell's Kitchen, Times Square, and Harlem represent areas of one city that have each taken on unique identities; however, each of them contributes to the whole makeup and identity of the city. The same can be seen in other cities, such as Baltimore, which in a two-mile area has the Inner Harbor, Little Italy, and Fell's Point, with each area complementing the other zones. From Miami to San Francisco to New Orleans, all cities across America, and throughout the world for that matter, contain these identifiable natural areas.

Applying several other ecological principles, Park also noted that some areas (or species) may invade and dominate adjacent areas (species). The dominated area or species can recede, migrate to another location, or die off. In wildlife, an example is the incredible proliferation of a plant called kudzu, which grows at an amazing pace and has large leaves. It grows on top of other plants, trees, fields, and even houses, seeking to cover everything in its path and steal all the sunlight needed by other plants. Introduced to the United States in the 1800s at a world exposition, this plant was originally used to stop erosion but got out of control, especially in the southeastern region of the United States. Now kudzu costs the government more than $350 million each year because of its destruction of crops and other flora. This is a good example of a species that invades, dominates, and causes the recession of other species in the area.

▲ Image 7.1   Virtually all large cities, like Chicago, New York, and Los Angeles, grew the same predictable way, and the formation of certain zones or types of areas follow ecological principles.

Source: © Ildar Sagdejev.

[4]Robert E. Park, "Human Ecology," *American Journal of Sociology* 42 (1936): 158–64; Robert E. Park, *Human Communities* (Glencoe: Free Press, 1952).

▲ Image 7.2 The American Buffalo was introduced to Catalina Island in California and destroyed much of the unique plant life there. This is an example of a foreign element creating chaos, such as crime does in residential areas.

Source: © Stefan Didam – Schmallenberg.

A similar example can be found in the introduction of bison on Santa Catalina Island off the Southern California coast in the 1930s. About three dozen buffalo were originally imported to the island for a movie shoot, and the producers decided not to spend the money to remove them after the project, so they have remained and multiplied. Had this occurred in other parts of the United States, it would not have caused a problem. However, the largest mammal native to the island before the bison was a 4-pound fox. So, the buffalo—now numbering in the hundreds, to the point where several hundred were recently shipped to their native Western habitat—have destroyed much of the environment, driving to extinction some plants and animals unique to Catalina Island. Like the kudzu, the bison came to dominate the environment; in this case, other species couldn't move off the island and died off.

Park claimed that a similar process occurs in human cities as some areas invade other zones or areas, and the previously dominant area must relocate or die off. This is easy to see in modern times with the growth of what is known as *urban sprawl*. Geographers and urban planners have long acknowledged the detriment to traditionally stable residential areas when businesses move in. Some of the most recent examples involve the battles of longtime homeowners against the introduction of malls, businesses, and other industrial centers in districts previously zoned residential. The media have documented such fights, especially with the proliferation of such establishments as Walmart and Kmart supercenters, which residents perceive, and perhaps rightfully so, as an invasion. Such an invasion can create chaos in a previously stable residential community due to increased traffic, transient populations, and perhaps most important, crime. Furthermore, some cities are granting power to such development through eminent domain, by which the local government can take land from homeowners to rezone and import businesses.

When Park developed his theory of ecology, he observed a trend in which businesses and factories were invading the traditionally residential areas of Chicago, which caused major chaos and breakdown in the stability of those areas. Readers, especially those who were raised in suburban or rural areas, can likely relate to this; going back to where they grew up, they can often see fast growth. Such development can devastate the informal controls (such as neighborhood networks or family ties) because it promotes invasion by a highly transient group of consumers and residents who do not have strong ties to the area.

This leads to a psychological indifference to the neighborhood in which no one cares about protecting the community any longer. Those who can afford to leave the area do, and those who can't afford to get out remain until they can save enough money to do so. When Park presented his theory of ecology in the 1920s, having factories that moved into the neighborhood often meant having a lot of smoke billowing out of chimneys. No one wanted to live in such a place, particularly at a time when the effects of pollution were not understood and smokestacks had no filters. Certain parts of Chicago and other U.S. cities were perpetually covered by the smog these factories created. In highly industrial areas, the constant and vast coverage of smoke and pollutants made it seem to be snowing or overcast most of the time. It is easy to see how such invasions can completely disrupt the previously dominant and stable residential areas of a community.

Park's ideas became even more valid and influential with the complementary perspective offered by Ernest W. Burgess,[5] who proposed a theory of city growth in which cities were seen as growing not simply on the edges but from the inside outward. It is easy to observe cities growing on the edges, as in the example of urban sprawl, but Burgess claimed that the source of growth was in the cities' centers. Growth of the inner city puts pressure on adjacent zones, which in turn begin to grow into the adjacent zones, following the ecological principle of *succession* identified by Park. This type of development is referred to as radial growth, meaning beginning on the inside and rippling outward.[6]

An example of this can be seen by watching a drop of water fall into the center of a bucket filled with water. The waves from the impact will form circles that ripple outward.

▲ Image 7.3   The Chicago/Ecological model proposed that as factories invaded and dominated residential areas, the residents who could afford to leave did and those left were the poor and deprived, which increased risk of crime.

Source: © Thinkstock Images / Stockbyte / Thinkstock.

This is exactly how Burgess claimed that cities grow. Although the growth of cities is most visible on the edges, largely due to development of business and homes where only trees or barren land existed before, the reason for growth there is the pressure forming at the very heart of the city. Another good analogy is the domino effect, because pressure from the center leads to growing pressure on the next zone, which leads to pressure on the adjacent zones, and so forth.

Burgess also specified the primary zones—five pseudodistinctive natural areas in a constant state of flux due to growth—that all cities appear to have. He depicted these zones as a set of concentric circles. The first, innermost circle was called Zone I, or the central business district. This area of a city contained the large business buildings, modern skyscrapers that are home to banks, chambers of commerce, courthouses, and other essential business, and political centers such as police headquarters and post offices.

Just outside the business district was the unnumbered factory zone. It was perhaps the most significant in terms of fostering crime because it invaded the previously stable residential areas in Zone II, which Burgess identified as the zone in transition. Zone II was appropriately named because it was truly in a state of transition from residential to industrial, primarily because this was the area of the city in which businesses and factories were invading residential areas. Zone II was the area

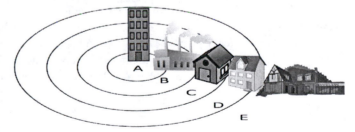

▲ Image 7.4   Virtually all large cities in the world historically developed and grew with the same basic design of concentric circles.

Source: http://commons.wikimedia.org/wiki/File:Burgess_model.svg

[5]Ernest W. Burgess, "The Growth of the City," in *The City*, ed. Robert Park, Ernest W. Burgess, and Roderick D. McKenzie (Chicago: University of Chicago Press, 1928).

[6]See George Vold, *Theoretical Criminology* (New York: Oxford University Press, 1958),118–21.

that was most significantly subjected to the ecological principles Park suggested: invasion, domination, recession, and succession. Subsequent criminological theorists focused on this zone.

According to Burgess's theory of concentric circles, Zone III was the workingmen's homes, relatively modest houses and apartment buildings; Zone IV consisted of higher-priced family dwellings and more expensive apartments; and Zone V was the suburban or commuter zone. These outer three zones Burgess identified were of less importance in terms of crime, primarily because, as a general rule, the farther a family could move out of the city, the better the neighborhood was in terms of social organization and the lower the rate of social ills (e.g., poverty, delinquency). The important point of this theory of concentric circles is that the growth of each inner zone puts pressure on the next zone to grow and push into the next adjacent zone.

It is easy for readers to see examples of concentric circles theory. Wherever you live in the United States, any major city provides real-life evidence of the validity of this perspective. For example, whether people drive on Interstate 95 through Baltimore or Interstate 5 through Los Angeles, they will see the same pattern of city structure. As they approach each of the cities, they see suburban wealth in the homes and buildings, often hidden by trees off the highway. Closer to the cities, they see homes and buildings deteriorating in terms of value. Because parts of the highway systems near Baltimore and Los Angeles are somewhat elevated, drivers entering Zone II can easily see the prevalence of factories and the highly deteriorated nature of the areas. Today, many 20th-century factories have been abandoned or have limited use; these factory zones consist of rusted-out or demolished buildings. Zone II is also often the location of subsidized or public housing. Only the people who can't afford to live anywhere else are forced to live in these neighborhoods. Finally, as drivers enter the inner city of skyscrapers, the conditions improve dramatically because the major businesses have invested their money there. Compared to Zone II, this innermost area is a utopia.

This theory applies around the world, and we challenge readers to find any major city throughout the world that did not develop this way. Nowadays, some attempts have been made to plan community development, and other cities have experienced the convergence of several patterns of concentric circles as central business districts (i.e., Zone Is) are developed in what was previously suburbia (i.e., Zone Vs). However, for the most part, the theoretical framework of concentric circles still has a great deal of support. In fact, even cities found in Eastern cultures have evolved this way. Therefore, Park's application appears to be correct: Cities grow in a natural way across time and place, abiding by the natural principles of ecology.

Shaw and McKay's Theory of Social Disorganization

Clifford Shaw and Henry McKay drew heavily on their colleagues at the University of Chicago in devising their theory of social disorganization, which became known as the Chicago School theory of criminology.[7] Shaw had been producing excellent case studies for years on the individual (i.e., micro) level before he took on theorizing on the macro (i.e., structural) level of crime rates.[8] However, once he began working with McKay, he devised perhaps the most enduring and valid model of why certain neighborhoods have more social problems, such as delinquency, than others.

In this model, Shaw and McKay proposed a framework that began with the assumption that certain neighborhoods in all cities have more crime than other parts of the city, most of them located in Burgess's Zone II, which is the zone in transition from residential to industrial due to the invasion of factories. According to Shaw and McKay, the neighborhoods that have the highest rates of crime typically have at least three common problems (see Figure 7.1): physical dilapidation, poverty, and heterogeneity (which is a fancy way of saying a high cultural mix).

[7]Clifford Shaw and Henry D. McKay, *Juvenile Delinquency and Urban Areas* (Chicago: University of Chicago Press, 1942); Clifford Shaw and Henry D. McKay, *Juvenile Delinquency and Urban Areas*, rev. ed. (Chicago: University of Chicago Press, 1969).

[8]Clifford Shaw, *Brothers in Crime* (Chicago: University of Chicago Press, 1938); Clifford Shaw, *The Jackroller* (Chicago: University of Chicago Press, 1930); Clifford Shaw, *The Natural History of a Delinquent Career* (Chicago: University of Chicago Press, 1931).

| Figure 7.1 | Model of Shaw and McKay's theory of social disorganization |

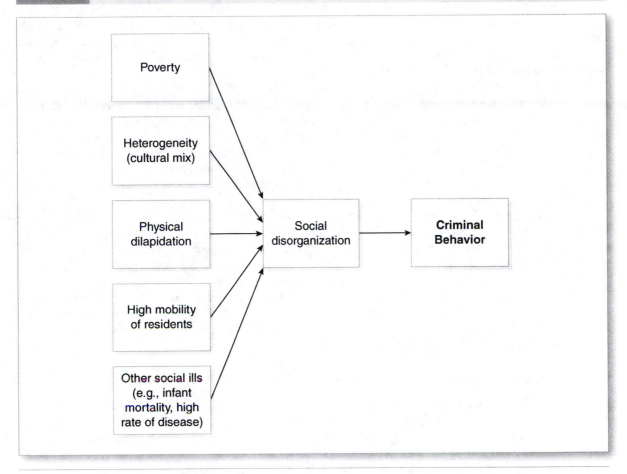

SOURCE: Tibbetts & Hemmens (2010).

There were other common characteristics that Shaw and McKay noted, such as a highly transient population, meaning that people constantly move in and out of the area, as well as unemployment among the residents of the neighborhood.

As noted in Figure 7.1, other social ills are included as antecedent factors in the theoretical model. The antecedent social ills tend to lead to a breakdown in social organization, which is why this model is referred to as the theory of social disorganization. Specifically, it is predicted that the antecedent factors of poverty, heterogeneity, and physical dilapidation lead to a state of social disorganization, which in turn leads to crime and delinquency. This means that in a neighborhood that fits the profile of having a high rate of poor, culturally mixed residents in a dilapidated area, people cannot come together to solve problems, such as delinquency among youth.

One of the most significant contributions of Shaw and McKay was that they demonstrated that the prevalence and frequency of various social ills—such as poverty, disease, and low birth weight—tend to overlap with higher delinquency rates. Regardless of what social problem is measured, higher rates are almost always clustered in the zone in transition. Shaw and McKay believed there is a breakdown of informal social controls in these areas and that children begin to learn offending norms from their interactions with peers on the street, through what the researchers call *play activities*.[9] Thus, the breakdown in the conditions of the neighborhood leads to social disorganization, which in turn leads to delinquency in children who learn criminal activities from older youths. Ultimately, the failure of the neighborhood residents to organize themselves allows the older youths to govern the behavior of the younger children. Basically, the older youths in the area provide a system of organization where the neighborhood adults cannot, so younger children follow them.

One of the best things about Shaw and McKay's theoretical model is that they supported their propositions with data from U.S. census and city records, showing that neighborhoods with high rates of poverty and physical dilapidation and high cultural mixes also had the highest rates of delinquency and crime. Furthermore, the high rates of delinquency and other social problems were consistent with Burgess's framework of concentric circles in that the highest rates were observed for the areas that were in Zone II, the zone in transition. There was one exception to the model: The Gold Coast area along the northern coast of Lake Michigan did not have the high rates of social problems, particularly delinquency, even though it was geographically in Zone II according to the otherwise consistent model of concentric circles and neighborhood zones.

Thus, the findings of Shaw and McKay were as predicted in the sense that high delinquency rates occurred in areas where factories were invading residential districts. Furthermore, Shaw and McKay's longitudinal data showed that it did not matter which ethnic groups lived in Zone II; all groups (with the exception of Asians) that lived in that zone had high delinquency rates during their residency. On the other hand, once most of an ethnic group had moved out of Zone II, the delinquency rate among its youths decreased significantly.

This finding rejects the notion of social Darwinism because it is clearly not the culture that influences crime and delinquency but rather the criminogenic nature of the environment. If ethnicity or race made a difference, the delinquency rates in Zone II would fluctuate based on who lived there, but the rates continued to be high from one group to the next. Rather, the zone determined the rates of delinquency.

Reaction and Research on Social Disorganization Theory

Over the last few decades, the Chicago School theoretical framework has received an enormous amount of attention from researchers.[10] Virtually all of the research has supported Shaw and McKay's version of social disorganization and the resulting high crime rates in neighborhoods that exhibit such deprived conditions. Modern research has supported the theoretical model proposed by Shaw and McKay, specifically in terms of the high crime rates in disorganized neighborhoods. Also, virtually every city that has an elevated highway (e.g., Richmond, Virginia; Baltimore, Maryland; Los Angeles, California) visually supports Shaw and McKay's model of crime in concentric circles. Drivers entering those cities can see the pattern of dilapidated structures in the zone of transition surrounding the

---

[9]Shaw, *Brothers in Crime*, 354–55.

[10]Wouter Steenbeek and John R. Hipp, "A Longitudinal Test of Social Disorganization Theory: Feedback Effects among Cohesion, Social Control, and Disorder," *Criminology* 49 (2011): 833–71; John Laub, "Urbanism, Race, and Crime," *Journal of Research in Crime and Delinquency* 20 (1983): 283–98; Robert Sampson, "Structural Sources of Variation In Race-Age-Specific Rate of Offending across Major U.S. Cities," *Criminology* 23 (1985): 647–73; J. L. Heitgard and Robert J. Bursik, "Extracommunity Dynamics and the Ecology of Delinquency," *American Journal of Sociology* 92 (1987): 775–87; Robert Bursik, "Social Disorganization and Theories of Crime and Delinquency: Problems and Prospects," *Criminology* 26 (1988): 519–51; Ralph Taylor and Jeanette Covington, "Neighborhood Changes in Ecology and Violence," *Criminology* 26 (1988): 553–89; Robert Bursik, "Ecological Stability and the Dynamics of Delinquency," in *Crime and Community*, ed. Albert J. Reiss and Morris H. Tonry (Chicago: University of Chicago Press, 1986), 35–66; Robert Sampson, "Transcending Tradition: New Directions in Community Research, Chicago Style—The American Society of Criminology 2001 Sutherland Address," *Criminology* 40 (2002): 213–30; Robert Sampson, J. D. Morenoff, and T. Gannon-Rowley, "Assessing 'Neighborhood Effects': Social Processes and New Directions in Research," *Annual Review of Sociology* 28 (2002): 443–78; P. O. Wikstrom and Rolf Loeber, "Do Disadvantaged Neighborhoods Cause Well-Adjusted Children to Become Adolescent Delinquents?" *Criminology* 38 (2000): 1109–42.

Figure 7.2   Zone map of male delinquents in Chicago, 1925–1933

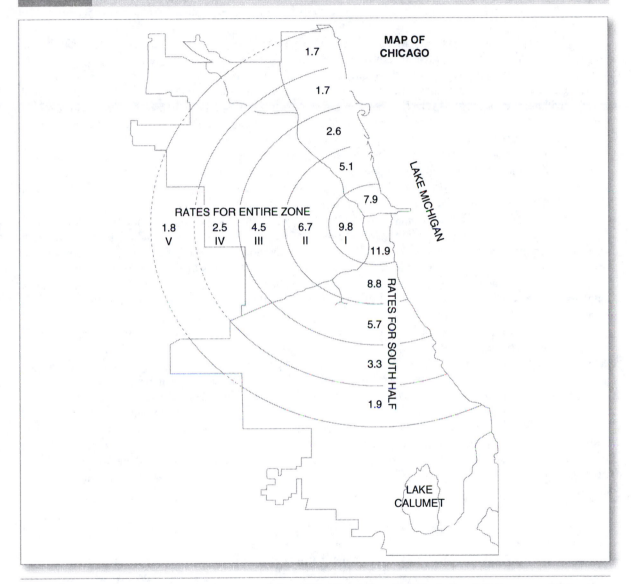

SOURCE: "Delinquency Rates and Community Characteristics," Shaw, Clifford R. and Henry D. McKay in Juvenile Delinquency and Urban Areas, 2nd edition, by C.R. Shaw and H.D. McKay. Copyright © 1969 University of Chicago Press. Reprinted by permission of The University of Chicago Press.

inner-city area. Before and after this layer of dilapidated structures, drivers encounter a layer of houses and residential areas that seem to increase in quality as the driver gets farther away from the inner-city area.

Some critics, however, have raised some valid concerns regarding the original model, arguing that Shaw and McKay's original research did not actually measure their primary construct: social disorganization. Although this criticism is accurate, recent research has shown that the model is valid even when valid measures of social disorganization are included.[11] Such measures of social disorganization include simply asking members of the neighborhood how many neighbors they know by name or how often they observe unsupervised peer groups in the area.

Additional criticisms of Shaw and McKay's formulation of social disorganization focus on the emphasis that the theory places on the macro, or aggregate, level of analysis. Although their theory does a good job of predicting which neighborhoods have higher crime rates, the model does not even attempt to explain why most youths in the worst areas do not become offenders. Furthermore, their model does not attempt to explain why some youths—although a very small number of them—in the best neighborhoods (i.e., in Zone V) choose to commit crime. However, the previously cited case studies completed and published by Clifford Shaw, such as *The Jackroller* and *Brothers in Crime*, attempted to address the individual (micro) level of offending.

Also, there was one notable exception to Shaw and McKay's proposition that all ethnic and racial groups have high rates of delinquency and crime while they live in Zone II. Evidence showed that when Japanese Americans made up a large portion of residents in this zone in transition, they had very low rates of delinquency. Thus, as in most theoretical models in social science, there was an exception to the rule.

Perhaps the biggest criticism of Shaw and McKay's theory, one that has yet to be adequately addressed, deals with the fact that they blatantly neglected to propose ways to ameliorate the most problematic source of criminality in Zone II neighborhoods. Although they clearly point to the invasion of factories and businesses into residential areas as a problem, they do not recommend how to slow such invasion. This is likely due to political and financial concerns: Owners of factories and businesses partially financed their research and later were the primary funders of implementation of their policies. Neglect is further represented in their failure to explain the exception of the Gold Coast in their results and conclusions.

Despite the criticisms and weaknesses of the Chicago School perspective of criminology, this theory resulted in one of the largest programs to date in attempting to reduce delinquency rates. Clifford Shaw was put in charge of establishing the Chicago Area Project (CAP), which created neighborhood centers in the most crime-ridden parts of Chicago. These centers offered activities for youths and tried to establish ties between parents and officials in the neighborhood. Although this program was never scientifically evaluated, it still exists, and many cities have implemented programs based on this model. For example, Boston implemented a very similar program, which was evaluated by Walter Miller.[12] This evaluation showed that, although the project was effective in establishing relationships and interactions between local gangs and community groups and in providing more educational and vocational opportunities, it seemed to fail in reducing delinquent and criminal behavior. Thus, the overall conclusion made by experts was that the Boston project and other similar programs, like the CAP, typically fail to prevent criminal behavior.[13]

Cultural and Subcultural Theories of Crime

Cultural and subcultural theories of crime assume that there are unique groups in society that socialize their children to believe that certain activities that violate conventional law are good and positive ways to behave. Although it is rather difficult to find large groups of people or classes who fit this definition, it may be that some subcultures or isolated groups of individuals buy into a different set of norms than the conventional, middle-class set of values.

---

[11]Robert Sampson and W. Byron Groves, "Community Structure and Crime: Testing Social Disorganization Theory," *American Journal of Sociology* 94 (1989): 774–802.

[12]Walter B. Miller, "The Impact of a 'Total-Community' Delinquency Control Project," *Social Problems* 10 (1962): 168–91.

[13]For a review, see Richard Lundman, *Prevention and Control of Juvenile Delinquency*, 2nd ed. (New York: Oxford University Press, 1993). See also Bernard et al., *Vold's Theoretical Criminology*, 125–26.

Early Theoretical Developments and Research in Cultural and Subcultural Theory

One of the key developments of cultural theory is the 1967 work of Ferracuti and Wolfgang, who examined the violent themes of a group of inner-city youths from Philadelphia.[14] Ferracuti and Wolfgang's primary conclusion was that violence is a culturally learned adaptation to deal with negative life circumstances and that learning such norms occurs in an environment that emphasizes violence over other options.[15] These researchers based their conclusion on an analysis of data that showed great differences in the rates of homicide across racial groups. However, Ferracuti and Wolfgang were clear that their theory was based on subcultural norms. Specifically, they proposed that no subculture can be totally different from or totally in conflict with the society of which it is a part.[16] This brings the distinction of culture and subculture to the forefront.

A culture represents a distinct set of norms and values among an identifiable group of people, values that are distinctly different from those of the mainstream culture. For example, communism is distinctly different from capitalism because it emphasizes equality over competition, and it values utopia (i.e., everyone gets to share all profits) over the idea that the best performer gets the most reward. So, it can be said that communists tend to have a different culture than capitalists. There is also a substantial difference between a culture and a subculture, which is typically only a pocket of individuals who may have a set of norms that deviate from conventional values. Therefore, what Ferracuti and Wolfgang developed is not so much a cultural theory as much as a subcultural theory.

This is also seen in the most prominent (sub)culture theory, which was presented by Walter Miller.[17] Miller's theoretical model proposed that the entire lower class had its own cultural value system. According to this model, virtually everyone in the lower class believes in and has been socialized to the values of six focal concerns: fate, autonomy, trouble, toughness, excitement, and smartness. Fate means luck, or whatever life has dealt you; it disregards responsibility and accountability for one's actions. Autonomy is the value of independence from authority. Trouble means staying out of legal problems, as well as getting into and out of personal difficulties (e.g., pregnancy). Toughness is maintaining your reputation on the street in many ways. Excitement is engagement in activities, some illegal, that help liven up an otherwise mundane existence of being lower class. Smartness emphasizes street smarts or the ability to con others. Miller thought that members of the lower class teach these six focal concerns as a culture or environment (or "milieu," as stated in the title of his work).

A more recent subculture model, proposed by Elijah Anderson, has received a lot of attention in the past few years.[18] This theory focuses on African Americans; because of the very deprived conditions in inner cities, Black Americans who live there feel a sense of hopelessness, isolation, and despair, Anderson asserts. He clearly notes that, although many African Americans believe in middle-class values, these values have no weight on the street, particularly among young urban males. According to Anderson, the "code of the street," which is the appropriate title of his book, is to maintain one's reputation and demand respect. For example, to be treated with disrespect ("dissed") is considered grounds for a physical attack. Masculinity and control of one's immediate environment are treasured characteristics; the immediate environment is perceived as the only thing people can control, given the harsh conditions (e.g., unemployment, poverty) in which they live.

Criticisms of Cultural Theories of Crime

Studies on cultural theories of crime, at least in the United States, find no large groups that blatantly deny the middle-class norms of society. Miller's model of lower class focal concerns is not consistent across the entire lower class.

[14]Bernard et al., *Vold's Theoretical Criminology*, 165–69; Frank Schmalleger, *Criminology Today*, 6th ed. (Upper Saddle River: Prentice Hall, 2011).

[15]Franco Ferracuti and Marvin Wolfgang, *The Subculture of Violence: Toward an Integrated Theory of Criminology* (London: Tavistock, 1967).

[16]As quoted in Schmalleger, *Criminology Today*, 230–31.

[17]Walter B. Miller, "Lower Class Culture as a Generating Milieu of Gang Delinquency," *Journal of Social Issues* 14 (1958): 5–19.

[18]Elijah Anderson, *Code of the Street* (New York: W. W. Norton, 2000).

Studies show that most adults in the lower class attempt to socialize their children to believe in conventional values, such as respect for authority, hard work, and delayed gratification, and not the focal concerns that Miller specified in his model.[19] Ferracuti and Wolfgang admitted that their research findings led them to conclude that their model had more of a subcultural perspective than one emphasizing a distinctly different culture. There may be small groups or gangs who have subcultural normative values, but that doesn't constitute a completely separate culture in society. Perhaps the best subculture theories are those presented by Cohen or Cloward and Ohlin (see Section VI) in their variations of strain theory that emphasize the formations of gangs among lower-class male youths. A recent example of a specific group that seems to embrace a different normative code is that of adult male bar fighters, which was presented by Heith Copes and his colleagues.[20] So apparently there are subcultural groups in U.S. society; however, they seem to make up a very small percentage of the population, which somewhat negates the cultural and subcultural perspective of criminality, which claims that crime-fostering subcultures make up a large, distinctive portion of the population. Still, this type of perspective may be important regarding the criminality of select subgroups of offenders, such as street gangs.

Policy Implications

Many of the policy implications suggested by the theoretical models proposed in this section are rather ironic. Regarding social disorganization, a paradox exists in the sense that the very neighborhoods most desperately in need of becoming organized to fight crime are the same inner-city ghetto areas where it is, by far, the most difficult to cultivate that organization (e.g., through neighborhood watch or block watch groups). Rather, the neighborhoods that have high levels of organization tend to be those that already have very low levels of crime because the residents naturally police their neighbors' well-being and property; they have a stake in the area's remaining crime free. Although there are some anecdotal examples of success of neighborhood watch programs in high-crime neighborhoods, most of the empirical evidence shows that this approach is "almost uniformly unsupportive" in its ability to reduce crime there.[21] Furthermore, many studies of these neighborhood watch programs find that the groups actually increase the fear of crime in some places, perhaps due to the heightened awareness of crime issues in these areas.[22]

Perhaps the most notable programs that resulted from the Chicago School or social disorganization model—the CAP and similar programs—have been dubbed failures in reducing crime rates among the participants. Still, there have been some advances in trying to get residents of high-crime areas to become organized in fighting crime. The more specific the goals regarding crime reduction (a specific goal might be careful monitoring of high-level offenders through more intensive supervised probation, or better lighting in dark places), the more effective the implementation.[23]

Regarding cultural and subcultural theories, some promising intervention and outreach programs have been suggested by such models. Many programs attempt to build prosocial attitudes among high-risk youths, often young children. For example, a recent evaluation showed that a program called Peace Builders, which focuses on children in early grades, was effective in producing gains in conflict resolution, development of prosocial values,

---

[19]Bernard et al., *Vold's Theoretical Criminology*.

[20] Heith Copes, Andy Hochstetler, and Craig Forsyth, "Peaceful Warriors: Codes for Violence among Adult Male Bar Fighters," *Criminology* 51 (2013): 761–94.

[21]John Worrall, *Crime Control in America: What Works?* 2nd ed. (Boston: Allyn & Bacon, 2008), 95.

[22]Ibid.

[23]Lundman, *Prevention and Control*; Sampson and Groves, "Community Structure"; Bernard et al., *Vold's Theoretical Criminology*.

and reductions in aggression; a follow-up showed that these attributes were maintained for a long period of time.[24] Another recent anti-aggression training program for boys in foster care showed positive effects in levels of empathy, self-efficacy, and attribution style among boys who had exhibited early-onset aggression.[25] Ultimately, there are effective programs out there that promote prosocial norms and culture. More effort should be given to promoting such programs to help negate the antisocial cultural norms of individuals, especially among high-risk youths.

Conclusion

In this section, we examined theoretical perspectives proposing that the lack of social organization in broken-down and dilapidated neighborhoods leads to the inability to contain delinquency and crime. Furthermore, we discussed how this model of crime was linked to processes derived from ecological principles. This type of approach has been tested numerous times, and virtually all studies show that the distribution of delinquents and crime activity is consistent with this model.

We then discussed the ability of cultural and subcultural theories to explain criminal activity. Empirical evidence shows that cultural values make a contribution to criminal behavior, but that the existence of an actual alternative culture in our society has not been found. However, some subcultural pockets, particularly inner-city youth gangs, certainly exist and provide some validity for this perspective of crime. Furthermore, the Chicago School perspective plays a role, because these subcultural groups tend to be found in zones of transition.

Finally, we examined policy implications suggested by these theoretical models. Regarding social disorganization, we noted that neighborhood crime-fighting groups are hardest to establish in high-crime neighborhoods and easiest to build in those neighborhoods with an already low rate of crime. Nevertheless, there have been some successes. We also looked at intervention and outreach programs based on cultural and subcultural perspectives.

Section Summary

- We examined how principles of ecology were applied to the study of how cities grow, as well as to the study of crime, by researchers at the University of Chicago, and how the resultant theories became known as the Chicago (or Ecological) School of criminology.
- We reviewed the various zones of the concentric circles theory, also a key contribution of the Chicago School of criminology, and explored which zones are most prone to crime.
- We examined why the findings from the Chicago School of criminology showed that social Darwinism was not accurate in attributing varying crime rates to ethnicity or race.
- We reviewed much of the empirical evidence regarding the theory of social disorganization and examined the strengths and weaknesses of this theoretical model.
- We discussed the cultural and subcultural model presented by Ferracuti and Wolfgang, as well as the cultural model of inner-city urban youths presented by Anderson.
- We discussed Miller's theory of lower-class culture, particularly its six focal concerns.
- We reviewed the strengths and weaknesses of cultural and subcultural theories of crime based on empirical evidence.

[24]Daniel J. Flannery, Mark I. Singer, and Kelly L. Wester, "Violence, Coping, and Mental Health in a Community Sample of Adolescence," *Violence and Victims* 18 (2003): 403–18. For a review of this research, see Stephen G. Tibbetts, "Perinatal and Developmental Determinants of Early Onset of Offending: A Biosocial Approach for Explaining the Two Peaks of Early Antisocial Behavior," in *The Development of Persistent Criminality*, ed. Joanne Savage (New York: Oxford University Press, 2009), 179–201.

[25]Karina Weichold, "Evaluation of an Anti-aggressiveness Training with Antisocial Youth," *Gruppendynamik* 35 (2004): 83–105. For a review, see Tibbetts, "Perinatal and Developmental."

KEY TERMS

Chicago School of criminology

cultural and subcultural theories

Ecological School

focal concerns

natural areas

social Darwinism

social disorganization

theory of concentric circles

zone in transition

DISCUSSION QUESTIONS

1. Identify and discuss an example of the ecological principles of invasion, domination, and succession among animals or plants that was not discussed in this section.

2. Can you see examples of the various zones that Shaw and McKay described in the town or city where you live (or the one nearest you)? Try obtaining a map or sketching a plot of this city or town, and then draw the various concentric circles where you think the zones are located.

3. What forms of organization and disorganization have you observed in your own neighborhood? Try to supply examples of both, if possible.

4. Can you provide modern-day examples of different cultures and subcultures in the United States? What regions or parts of the country would you say have cultures that are more conducive to crime?

5. Do you know people who believe most or all of Miller's focal concerns? What are their social classes? What are their other demographic features (age, gender, urban versus rural, etc.)?

6. Do you know individuals who seem to fit either Ferracuti and Wolfgang's cultural theory or Anderson's model of inner-city youths' street code? Why do you believe they actually fit such a model?

WEB RESOURCES

Chicago School of Criminology

http://criminology.fsu.edu/crimtheory/week6.htm

http://www.helium.com/items/865770-an-overview-of-the-chicago-school-theories-of-criminology

Subcultural Theories

http://www.umsl.edu/~keelr/200/subcult.html

READING 16

In this selection, Clifford Shaw and Henry McKay present a theoretical model of various characteristics of neighborhoods that contribute to higher crime and delinquency rates. Specifically, they examine physical, economic, and population factors that contribute to higher rates of delinquency in certain communities. Such observations of certain neighborhoods provide the basis for the theory of social disorganization (also known as the Chicago or Ecological School of criminology). While reading this selection, think about the places you have lived or visited that fit these characteristics; it is likely that such neighborhoods have high crime rates. Because this theory fits virtually all cities around the world, and because of their methodology, Shaw and McKay are generally considered two of the most prominent criminologists of the 20th century.

Delinquency Rates and Community Characteristics

Clifford R. Shaw and Henry D. McKay

The question has been asked many times: "What is it, in modern city life that produces delinquency?" Why do relatively large numbers of boys from the inner urban areas appear in court with such striking regularity, year after year, regardless of changing population structure or the ups and downs of the business cycle? [Elsewhere] a different series of male delinquents were presented which closely parallel one another in geographical distribution although widely separated in time, and the close resemblance of all these series to the distribution of truants and of adult criminals was shown. Moreover, many other community characteristics—median rentals, families on relief, infant mortality rates, and so on—reveal similar patterns of variation throughout the city. The next step would be to determine, if possible, the extent to which these two sets of data are related. How consistently do they vary together, if at all, and how high is the degree of association?

Where high zero-order correlations are found to exist uniformly between two variables, with a small probable error, it is possible and valid to consider either series as an approximate index, or indicator, of the other. This holds true for any two variables which are known to be associated or to vary concomitantly. The relationship, of course, may be either direct or inverse. In neither case, however, is there justification in assuming, on this basis alone, that the observed association is of a cause-and-effect nature; it may be, rather, that both variables are similarly affected by some third factor. Further analysis is needed. Controlled experimentation is often useful in establishing the degree to which a change in one variable "causes" or brings about a corresponding change in the other. In the social field, however, experimentation is difficult. Instead, it is often necessary to rely upon refined statistical techniques, such as partial correlation, which, for certain types of data, enable the investigator to measure the effects of one factor while holding others relatively constant. By the method of successive redistribution, also, the influence of one or more variables may be held constant. Thus, it is possible to study the relationship between rates of delinquents and economic status for a single nationality group throughout the city or for various nationality groups in the same area or class of areas. This process may be extended indefinitely, subject only to the limitations of the available data. In the analysis to be presented, both of the latter methods have been used in an attempt to determine how much weight should be given to various more or less influential factors.

Several practical considerations prevent the neat and precise statistical analysis which would be desirable. The characteristics studied represent only a sampling of the myriad forms in which community life and social relationships find expression. The rate of delinquents must itself be thought of as an imperfect enumeration of the delinquents and an index of the larger number of boys engaging in officially proscribed activities. Not only will there be chance fluctuations in the amount of alleged delinquency from year to year, but the policy of the local police officer in referring boys to the Juvenile Court, the focusing of the public eye upon conditions in an area, and numerous other matters may bring about a change in the index without any essential change in the underlying delinquency-producing influences in the community or in the behavior resulting therefrom. If the infant mortality rates or the rates of families on relief are looked upon as indexes of economic status or of the social organization of a community, it is obvious that they can be considered only very crude indicators at best. The perturbing influence of other variables must always be considered.

Certain exceptional conditions are known to limit the value of other variables chosen as indicators of local community differentiation. Median rental has been used widely because of its popularity as an index of economic status, although in Chicago such an index is far from satisfactory when applied to areas of colored population. The Negro is forced to pay considerably higher rents than the whites for comparable housing—thus his economic level is made to appear higher on the basis of rental than it actually is. Similarly, rates of increase or decrease of population are modified in Negro areas by restrictions on free movement placed upon the Negro population. Thus, in certain areas the population is increasing where it normally would be expected to decrease if there were no such barriers. Likewise, the percentage of families owning homes is not entirely satisfactory as an economic index in large urban centers, where many of the well-to-do rent expensive apartments. It is, however, an indication of the relative stability of population in an area.

Correlation of series of rates based on geographical areas is further complicated by the fact that magnitude of the coefficient is influenced by the size of the area selected.

This tendency has been noted by several writers, but no satisfactory solution of the problem has been offered. If it be borne in mind that a correlation of area data is an index of geographical association for a particular type of spatial division only, rather than a fixed measure of functional relationship, it will be apparent that a change in area size changes the meaning of the correlation. Thus, an r of .90 or above for two series of rates calculated by square-mile areas indicates a high degree of association between the magnitudes of the two rates in most of the square miles but does not tell us the exact degree of covariance for smaller or larger areas.

With these limitations clearly in mind, a number of correlation coefficients and tables of covariance are presented. The statistical data characterizing and differentiating local urban areas may be grouped under three headings: (1) physical status, (2) economic status, and (3) population composition. These will be considered, in turn, in relation to rates of delinquents.

Indexes of Physical Status in Relation to Rates of Delinquents

The location of major industrial and commercial developments, the distribution of buildings condemned for demolition or repair, and the percentage increase or decrease in population by square-mile areas were presented [elsewhere] as indications of the physical differentiation of areas within the city. Quantitative measures of the first two are not available, but inspection of the distribution maps shows clearly that the highest rates of delinquents are most frequently found in, or adjacent to, areas of heavy industry and commerce. These same neighborhoods have the largest number of condemned buildings. The only notable exception to this generalization, for Chicago, appears in some of the areas south of the central business district.

There is, of course, little reason to postulate a direct relationship between living in proximity to industrial developments and becoming delinquent. While railroads and industrial properties may offer a field for delinquent behavior, they can hardly be regarded as a cause of such activities. Industrial invasion and physical deterioration do, however, make an area less desirable for residential purposes. As a consequence, in time there is found a movement from this area of those people able to afford more attractive surroundings. Further, the decrease in the number of buildings available for residential purposes leads to a decrease in the population of the area.

Population Increase or Decrease. Increase or decrease of population and rates of delinquents, by square-mile areas, do not exhibit a linear relationship. A relatively slight difference in rate of decrease of population, or of rate of increase for areas where the increase is slight, is generally associated with a considerable change in rates of delinquents; while for large differences in rates of increase of population, where increase is great, there is little or no consistent difference in rates of delinquents. Thus, areas increasing more than 70 per cent show no corresponding drop in rates of delinquents, although the relationship is clear up to this point. . . .

[T]here is a similarity between the pattern of distribution of delinquency and that of population growth or decline. The data do not establish a causal relationship between the two variables, however. The fact that the population of an area is decreasing does not impel a boy to become delinquent. It may be said, however, that decreasing population is usually related to industrial invasion of an area and contributes to the development of a general situation conducive to delinquency.

 ## Population Composition in Relation to Rates of Delinquency

In Chicago, as in other northern industrial cities, as has been said, it is the most recent arrivals—persons of foreign birth and those who have migrated from other sections of this country—who find it necessary to make their homes in neighborhoods of low economic level. Thus the newer European immigrants are found concentrated in certain areas, while Negroes from the rural South and Mexicans occupy others of comparable status. Neither of these population categories, considered separately, however, is suitable for correlation with rates of delinquents, since some areas of high rates have a predominantly immigrant population and others are entirely or largely Negro. Both categories, however, refer to groups of low economic status making their adjustment to a complex urban environment. Foreign-born

and Negro heads of families will therefore be considered together in order to study this segregation of the newer arrivals, on a city-wide scale.

Percentage of Foreign-Born and Negro Heads of Families.[1] When the rates of delinquents in the 1927–33 series are correlated with the percentage of foreign-born and Negro heads of families as of 1930, by 140 square-mile areas, the coefficient is found to be .60 ± .03. Similarly, when the 1917–23 delinquency data are correlated with percentages of foreign-born and Negro heads of families for 1920, by the 113 areas into which the city was divided for that series, the coefficient is .58 ± .04. When rates of delinquents are calculated for the classes of areas . . . wide variations are found between the rates in the classes where the percentage of foreign-born and Negro heads of families is high and in those where it is low. . . . Since the number of foreign-born heads of families in the population decreased and the number of Negroes increased between 1920 and 1930, the total proportions of foreign-born and Negro heads of families in each class do not correspond. The variation with rates of delinquents, however, remains unchanged.

While it is apparent from these data that the foreign born and the Negroes are concentrated in the areas of high rates of delinquents, the meaning of this association is not easily determined. One might be led to assume that the relatively large number of boys brought into court is due to the presence of certain racial or national groups, were it not for the fact that the population composition of many of these neighborhoods has changed completely, without appreciable change in their rank as to rates of delinquents. Clearly, one must beware of attaching causal significance to race or nativity. For, in the present social and economic system, it is the Negroes and the foreign born, or at least the newest immigrants, who have least access to the necessities of life and who are therefore least prepared for the competitive struggle. It is they who are forced to live in the worst slum areas and who are least able to organize against the effects of such living.

In Chicago three kinds of data are available for the study of nativity, nationality, and race in relation to rates of delinquents. These data concern (1) the succession of nationality groups in the high-rate areas over a period of years; (2) changes in the national and racial backgrounds of children appearing in the Juvenile Court; and (3) rates of delinquents for particular racial, nativity, or nationality groups in different types of areas at any given moment.

In evaluating the significance of community characteristics found to be associated with high rates of delinquents, the relative weight of race, nativity, and nationality must be understood. . . .

It appears to be established, then, that each racial, nativity, and nationality group in Chicago displays widely varying rates of delinquents; that rates for immigrant groups in particular show a wide historical fluctuation; that diverse racial, nativity, and national groups possess relatively similar rates of delinquents in similar social areas; and that each of these groups displays the effect of disproportionate concentration in its respective areas at a given time. In the face of these facts it is difficult to sustain the contention that, by themselves, the factors of race, nativity, and nationality are vitally related to the problem of juvenile delinquency. It seems necessary to conclude, rather, that the significantly higher rates of delinquents found among the children of Negroes, the foreign born, and more recent immigrants are closely related to existing differences in their respective patterns of geographical distribution within the city. If these groups were found in the same proportion in all local areas, existing differences in the relative number of boys brought into court from the various groups might be expected to be greatly reduced or to disappear entirely.

It may be that the correlation between rates of delinquents and foreign-born and Negro heads of families is incidental to relationships between rates of delinquents and apparently more basic social and economic characteristics of local communities. Evidence that this is the case is seen in two partial correlation coefficients computed. Selecting the relief rate as a fair measure of economic level, the problem is to determine the relative weight of this and other factors. The partial correlation coefficient between rate of delinquents and percentage of families on relief, holding constant the percentage of foreign-born and Negro heads of families, in the 140 areas, is .76 ± .02. However, the coefficient for rates of delinquents and percentage of foreign-born and Negro heads of families, when percentage of families on relief is held constant, is only .26 ± .05. It is clear from these coefficients, therefore, that the percentage of families on relief is related to rates of delinquents in a more significant way than is the percentage of foreign-born and Negro heads of families.

It should be emphasized that the high degree of association between rates of delinquents and other community characteristics . . . does not mean that these characteristics must be regarded as causes of delinquency, or vice versa. Within certain types of areas differentiated in city growth,

these phenomena appear together with such regularity that their rates are highly correlated. Yet the nature of the relationship between types of conduct and given physical, economic, or demographic characteristics is not revealed by the magnitude either of zero-order or partial correlation coefficients, or of other measures of association.

A high degree of association may lead to the uncritical assumption that certain factors are causally related, whereas further analysis shows the existing association to be entirely adventitious. This is apparently the case with the data on nativity, nationality, and race. . . . That, on the whole, the proportion of foreign-born and Negro population is higher in areas with high rates of delinquents there can be little doubt; but the facts furnish ample basis for the further conclusion that the boys brought into court are not delinquent *because* their parents are foreign born or Negro but rather because of other aspects of the total situation in which they live. In the same way, the relationship between rates of delinquents and each associated variable should be explored, either by further analysis, by experimentation, or by the study of negative cases.

 ## Summary

It has been shown that, when rates of delinquents are calculated for classes of areas grouped according to rate of any one of a number of community characteristics studied, a distinct pattern appears—the two sets of rates in each case varying together. When values of these other community characteristics, in turn, are calculated for classes of areas grouped by rate of delinquents, the same consistent trends appear. . . . The data . . . indicate a high degree of association between rates of delinquents and other community characteristics when correlations are computed on the basis of values in square-mile areas or similar subdivisions, and a still closer general association by large zones or classes of areas. . . .

Note

1. The categories "foreign born" and "Negro" are not compatible, since the former group is made up primarily of adults, while the latter includes all members of the race. The classification "heads of families" has been used; therefore, foreign-born and Negro family heads are entirely comparable groupings. The census classification "other races" has been included—a relatively small group, comprising Mexicans, Japanese, Chinese, Filipinos, etc.

1. What do Shaw and McKay have to say about delinquency rates in neighborhoods located in or near heavy industrial areas? What types of physical indicators are present in such areas?

2. What do Shaw and McKay conclude regarding the crime rates of neighborhoods containing a population composition high in minorities or recent immigrants?

3. What do Shaw and McKay claim would happen to delinquency/crime rates if racial/ethnic groups, as well as recent immigrants, were equally distributed across all neighborhoods of a city (such as Chicago)?

READING 17

In this selection, Christopher Lowenkamp, Francis Cullen, and Travis Pratt present an empirical study that seeks to replicate the findings of a well-respected previous test of the Chicago School model of social disorganization theory (as originally presented by Clifford Shaw and Henry McKay). Specifically, this well-respected previous test of the theoretical model was performed by Robert Sampson and W. Byron Groves (1989) using data from the 1982 British Crime Survey. It generally supported the social disorganization theoretical framework, especially regarding the mediating effects of informal social controls in explaining the impact of structural factors (e.g., poverty) on neighborhood crime rates. In this study, Lowenkamp et al. find that a replication of this earlier study by Sampson and Groves (1989), which utilizes more recently collected data, also reveals a high level of empirical support for the social disorganization theoretical framework. The few differences between this and the earlier test (by Sampson and Groves) actually reveal more support for the Chicago School model. While reviewing this study, consider the places you have lived or visited that fit these characteristics.

Replicating Sampson and Groves's Test of Social Disorganization Theory

Revisiting a Criminological Classic

Christopher T. Lowenkamp, Francis T. Cullen, and Travis C. Pratt

Although Shaw and McKay's work linking social disorganization to community crime rates exerted considerable influence on criminological theory during the 1950s, by the mid-1980s, their perspective came to be considered by many as "little more than an interesting footnote in the history of community-related research" (Bursik 1986:36; see also, Pfohl 1985:158). Since that time, however, the social disorganization perspective has experienced a dramatic revitalization, reemerging from the dustbin of spent criminological paradigms to challenge for the status as a preeminent macro-level theory.

No single work did more to polish the tarnished image of social disorganization theory than Sampson and

Groves's essay, published in 1989, "Community Structure and Crime: Testing Social-Disorganization Theory." Their research ostensibly showed that consistent with the core predictions of the social disorganization perspective, the impact of structural factors on crime rates was mediated in important ways by direct measures of informal social controls (Taylor 2001). It is noteworthy that contemporary publications now cite Sampson and Groves's (1989) work as providing "a convincing test of Shaw and McKay's social disorganization thesis" (Bellair 1997:679) and as "one of the more important studies in criminological literature over the past decade" (Veysey and Messner 1999: 156). It is among the most cited criminological works and has become a staple in criminological textbooks published after 1989 (see, e.g., Akers 1999; Siegel 2000; Sykes and Cullen 1992; Tittle and Paternoster 2000).[1] In short, "Community Structure and Crime: Testing Social-Disorganization Theory" has emerged as a classic in the field of criminology.

As with other classic empirical works, however, the question arises as to whether Sampson and Groves's (1989) research offers virtually unshakable support for social disorganization theory or merely produced an idiosyncratic finding that was unique to a certain time and place. To gain insight on this issue, subsequent studies ideally would have replicated Sampson and Groves's work in different contexts and with refined measures of the study's core variables. But precise replications of their empirical test have been hampered by the failure of existing macro-level data sets to contain intervening, direct measures of informal social controls, including the full set of variables specified in the original study. A limited number of studies have moved beyond structural proxies to assess components of social disorganization or similar processes (Bellair 1997; Morenoff et al. 2001; Roundtree and Land 1996; Roundtree and Warner 1999; Sampson et al. 1997; Sampson, Morenoff, and Earls, 1999; Velez 2001; Warner and Roundtree 1997). Yet, again, none has attempted to provide a *systematic* test of Sampson and Groves's complete model. Accordingly, we have a classic study—cited repeatedly in the literature—that remains, in effect, nonreplicated.

In this context, we suggest an alternative strategy for replicating Sampson and Groves's (1989) apparent empirical confirmation of social disorganization theory. We propose to revisit the British Crime Survey (BCS) (Home Office Crime and Criminal Justice Unit 1994) a decade later

to investigate whether the findings reported in the original analysis will remain stable as social disorganization theory would predict. If the findings change in meaningful ways, it would suggest that the credence accorded Sampson and Groves's "classic" test is not warranted and that social disorganization theory cannot account for crime rates in a later time period, even though virtually the same data set and measures are being used. Phrased differently, it would call into question whether the social disorganization perspective is a "general theory" capable of accounting for ecological variations in crime rates across time and place.

If, however, their findings remain largely constant, it would suggest that the initial analysis by Sampson and Groves (1989) was not idiosyncratic but rather captured an ongoing empirical reality. Much as in other scientific fields, it would show that their conclusions could be reproduced under "laboratory conditions" (so to speak) that were similar to, but independent of, the original investigation. Admittedly, these findings would not necessarily mean that results from Britain would generalize, without specification, to the United States and other social contexts. Nonetheless, these results would bolster social disorganization theory's claim to be a perspective that warrants its place as a vital macro-level theory of crime and as deserving of further empirical investigation.

We begin by revisiting Sampson and Groves's (1989) classic test in more detail. This discussion serves as a prelude for a replication of their study using 1994 data from the BCS. This year of the BCS was chosen because it allows for the closest replication of Sampson and Groves's study. As we shall see, in important ways, their findings are largely replicated by our analysis, suggesting that social disorganization theory is potentially useful in accounting for variation in macro-level crime rates across communities.

Finally, we note the growing recognition within criminology—and social science generally—of the value of systematic replication (Gendreau in press). Breaking new theoretical and/or empirical ground is perhaps of prime importance, for such efforts potentially push the field to new horizons. Nevertheless, the emphasis on innovation over systematic replication has a cost: the inability to build cumulative knowledge and to be able to state with confidence what is, and is not, known. Even when theories have been subjected to tens of empirical tests, it is difficult to assess the perspectives' merits because of the failure of the research to build in an organized way on one another (e.g., measure all core constructs, include similar measures) (Kempf 1993). In this regard, the current study should be seen as an initial, but much needed, attempt to contribute to the cumulative knowledge base on Sampson and Groves's (1989) analysis of social disorganization theory.

Sampson and Groves's Test of Social Disorganization Theory

Measuring Social Disorganization: Intervening Variables

As Sampson and Groves (1989) noted, most ecological research inspired by Shaw and McKay (1972) examined the effects of structural antecedents (heterogeneity, socioeconomic status [SES], and mobility) on crime rates (see also Bursik 1986, 1988; Byrne and Sampson 1986). Although suggestive, these theoretical tests failed to provide direct measures of whether social disorganization prevailed within the ecological units under investigation (Veysey and Messner 1999). In essence, the lack of measures of the theorized mediators/intervening variables have created a "black box" phenomenon in which little is known about what exists between structural variables on the left side of a causal model and crimes rates on the other side of the model. Because there are no measures of the intervening variables, assumptions and inferences—plausible as they may be—must be invoked to explain the processes that might specify the relationships between the structural and dependent variables. Notably, this dearth of attention to measures of mediating processes plagues not only social disorganization theory, but also ecological theories in general (Byrne and Sampson 1986).

To test social disorganization theory with direct measures of intervening variables, Sampson and Groves (1989) used data from the 1982 BCS.[2] Their goal was to examine the mediating effects of intervening variables on the structural antecedents hypothesized to be causal influences on social disorganization and, subsequently, criminality within a community. Building on Shaw and McKay's (1972) original model of social disorganization, Sampson and Groves (1989) included three measures of community-level variables thought to cause social disorganization: low economic status, ethnic heterogeneity, residential mobility.

In extending Shaw and McKay's (1972) model, Sampson and Groves specified variables for two additional sources of social disorganization: urbanization and family disruption (a variable drawn from Sampson's [1987] earlier work).

The uniqueness of Sampson and Groves's (1989) work stems from the authors' construction of direct measures of social disorganization. These were treated as intervening variables in their main analyses. These measures include sparse local friendship networks, low organizational participation, and unsupervised teenage peer groups. These measures were largely developed based on works by Kasarda and Janowitz (1974), Krohn (1986) and on the relation of these works to Shaw and McKay's (1972) theoretical framework. Each measure was based on aggregated data from individual respondents in 238 communities.

Empirical Support for Social Disorganization Theory

To determine the impact of structural antecedents on social disorganization and on crime, Sampson and Groves (1989) developed and analyzed several weighted least squares (WLS) regression models. The results of their analyses indicated that each of the structural factors significantly predicted the degree to which respondents perceived unsupervised peer groups to be a problem in their community. The model predicting the level of local friendship networks indicated that only residential stability and urbanization had significant relationships with the dependent measure. Only one structural variable, SES, had a significant relationship with the level of organizational participation.

Turning to the results regarding the dependent variables, crime and delinquency, eight models were presented by Sampson and Groves (1989). Models predicting rates of mugging, stranger violence, total victimization, burglary, auto theft, and vandalism indicated, with few exceptions, that the intervening variables thought to measure social disorganization had significant relationships with the dependent variables and mediated some of the direct effects of the structural variables. Regarding rates of self-reported offending, unsupervised peer groups mediated much of the effects of the structural variables when predicting violent offending. Along with local friendship networks, unsupervised peer groups also mediated the effects of the structural variables when predicting self-reported property offenses.

Replicating Sampson and Groves's Test

Although Sampson and Groves's (1989) study has not been systematically replicated outside their article,[3] their original data have recently been reassessed by Veysey and Messner (1999) through the use of LISREL instead of WLS regression analysis. The findings from the reanalysis were largely consistent with those from Sampson and Groves (1989): (1) the social disorganization variables mediated, although not completely, the effect of structural characteristics on rates of community victimization, and (2) the variable of unsupervised peer groups had the largest impact on the outcome measures. We should also note, however, that Veysey and Messner's (1999) LISREL analysis revealed that the measures of structural antecedents had various direct effects on rates of crime (as measured by victimization data). This finding, they suggest, supports a position that is conceptually inconsistent with Sampson and Groves's (1989) version of social disorganization theory because the disorganization perspective would argue that the effects of structural factors should be completely mediated by measures of each community's level of disorganization.

Nevertheless, in their article, Sampson and Groves (1989) did not contend that the intervening variables in their model mediated fully the effects of the five structural factors. Their original path model showed direct effects of structural factors, although, admittedly, they highlighted the ability of their measures of neighborhood disorganization and informal social control to mediate the impact of these factors on levels of crime. Thus, Veysey and Messner's (1999) findings that the social disorganization variables did not completely mediate the relationships between the structural variables and rates of crime is perhaps best seen as an important clarification of, rather than a failure to replicate, Sampson and Groves's (1989) analysis. In any case, we also replicate Veysey and Messner's (1999) analysis and discuss its implications for social disorganization theory.

 ## Method

As with many surveys conducted repeated times, additions and deletions have been made to the content of information gathered in the BCS. After reviewing the codebooks for the BCSs conducted after 1982, we determined that the data from the 1994 survey contain those questions and information most similar to the data used by Sampson and Groves (1989). More recent BCSs no longer contain the same or, in some cases, similar questions employed by Sampson and Groves in the construction of their measures. In any event, the 1994 survey provided us with the data—collected a decade after the original study—to construct, in most instances, measures identical to those used by Sampson and Groves. In instances where identical measures could not be developed, very similar measures were constructed—each of which is noted below. The use of similar measures is significant because it means that differences in measurement cannot be employed to explain any divergent findings that might arise between the two studies.

Sample

The data for this study come from the 1994 BCS. The sampling method used is a multistage random probability design where 600 postal code sectors are selected by a systematic sampling method from a stratified list of postal code sectors. The probability for selection of any particular postal code sector was proportional to the total number of delivery points within that sector. Once 600 sectors were selected, 36 addresses were randomly selected from each sector yielding a total of 21,600 addresses. After removing all ineligible addresses and nonresponding households, the sample size was reduced to 14,617. This averages approximately 25 respondents per sector. The BCS collects data on the characteristics of adults and children that reside within the household as well as information pertaining to residential history, perceptions of crime, problems in the area, social habits, type of community, community involvement, social cohesion, criminal victimization, and experience with the police.

This sampling method differs from that used in 1982, where 60 addresses from 238 electoral wards were selected. After removing ineligible addresses and nonresponding households, the final sample size for 1982 was 10,905. Checks on the differences between these two sampling frames indicate no appreciable differences in crime rate trends due to the sampling frame (Lynn 1997).

Measures of Intervening Variables

The intervening variables in this model are very similar to those used by Sampson and Groves (1989). We have included measures of unsupervised teenage peer groups, local friendship networks, and organizational participation. Sampson and Groves measured *local friendship networks* based on responses to the question that asked the number of friends that lived in the local community. A mean was calculated for these responses and served as the measure of local friendship networks. Our local friendship indicator was derived from responses to the question, "Thinking of the people who live in this area, by this area, I mean a 10–15 minute walk from here, how many would you regard as friends or acquaintances?" We also calculated a mean response and used this as our measure.

As measured by Sampson and Groves (1989), *organizational participation* was the percentage of respondents that reported in meetings of clubs or committees the week before the interview. Our measure of organizational participation is the percentage of people that reported participating in a meeting of a club or committee the last time they were out in the evening.

The final intervening variable, *unsupervised peer groups*, was measured by Sampson and Groves (1989) as the percentage of respondents that reported groups of teenagers making a nuisance of themselves as a very common problem in their neighborhood. Our measure differed slightly in that the question relating to teenage groups asked respondents how big a problem teenage groups hanging around on the streets was in their neighborhood. We calculated the percentage of people that reported teenage groups to be a very big problem. Although this measure differs from the 1982 BCS, for the purpose at hand, it is most likely a preferable measure. As Sampson and Groves (1989) note, by removing the mention of "nuisance" behavior, the concern that respondents are confounding crime rates with "nuisance" behavior of teens is obviated.

Measures of Structural Variables

Consistent with Sampson and Groves (1989), we constructed measures of SES, residential stability, ethnic heterogeneity, family disruption, and urbanization. We followed identical processes in constructing these measures (e.g., formulas, summed z scores percentages, and means). Wherever possible, we used the same questions and responses.

SES is a composite of measure of z scores tapping education (the percentage of people with a higher degree or teaching certification), occupation (percentage in professional or managerial occupations using the BCS social class ratings), and income (percentage reporting incomes in the top two income brackets).

Residential stability, as measured by Sampson and Groves (1989), was the percentage of people that were brought up in the area within a 15-minute walk from home. Due to changes in the questions on the BCS main questionnaire, our measure of residential stability is the percentage of people that reported living in the area (within a 15-minute walk) for 10 or more years.

Ethnic *heterogeneity* is calculated using the same formula as Sampson and Groves (1989) $(1 - ?pi^2)$ where *pi* is the fraction of people in a particular group. Our measure of ethnic heterogeneity differed from Sampson and Groves's in that the 1994 BCS used seven rather than five categories of ethnicity.

Family disruption was the sum of *z* scores for the percentage of people surveyed that were either separated or divorced and the percentage of people that were separated, divorced, or single and had children in their household. This measure is identical to that used by Sampson and Groves (1989).

Urbanization, finally, was coded as either 0 or 1 according to the BCS data, where 1 represents an urban area. In 1982, the Planning and Research Applications Group's (PRAG) inner-city designations were used to determine which areas were inner-city areas. In 1984, the method for identifying inner-city areas was changed to where inner-city status is determined by the population density, percentage of owner occupied housing, and/or the social class of the areas based on standard occupational classification. This is the same procedure used in subsequent surveys.

Measure of Crime

Consistent with Sampson and Groves's (1989) final analysis (as well as the reanalysis of the 1982 BCS data by Veysey and Messner 1999), our measure of crime is the *total victimization rate*, which reflects the rate of personal and household victimization. This variable consists of the sum of crimes that can be classified as personal or household victimization and then standardizing it by the number of respondents in the area.

Results

The results of the replication of Sampson and Groves's (1989) analysis using the 1994 BCS data are presented here in two sections. First, we report the results of the social disorganization models using the 1994 BCS data to determine—on their own—whether they support the major propositions specified by social disorganization theory according to Sampson and Groves. Second, we present a series of statistical comparisons between the standardized parameter estimates from the 1982 wave of the BCS to determine whether any of the results from the present replication study are significantly different from those of the original study.

Social Disorganization Models from the 1994 BCS

As with Sampson and Groves's (1989) analysis, our replication using the 1994 BCS data proceeded in two stages. First, we examined the effect of the five structural characteristics on the three measures of social disorganization outlined by Sampson and Groves. Second, the effects of the social disorganization measures as "intervening" variables (i.e., as mediators of the effects of the structural characteristics) predicting neighborhood crime rates were assessed.

Structural Characteristics and Social Disorganization

Regarding the results of the WLS regression models testing the effects of the structural characteristics on the three dimensions of social disorganization using the 1994 BCS and consistent with the propositions set forth by Sampson and Groves, the first model indicates that SES, ethnic heterogeneity, and urbanization all exert a statistically significant inverse effect on local friendship networks. Family disruption was unrelated to local friendship networks, yet residential stability was positively and significantly related to this indicator of social disorganization.

The WLS model predicting unsupervised peer groups follows a similar pattern. Levels of ethnic heterogeneity, family disruption, and urbanization were all positively and significantly related to the existence of unsupervised peer groups. Unlike the previous model, however, residential stability was not a statistically significant predictor of this

dimension of social disorganization in this model. Nevertheless, also consistent with social disorganization theory, the effect of SES on unsupervised peer groups was inverse and statistically significant.

The WLS model predicting the social disorganization measure of organizational participation is not quite as robust as the previous two models. Even so, consistent with social disorganization theory, ethnic heterogeneity, residential stability, and family disruption were all significantly related to organizational participation in the theoretically expected direction. Inconsistent with the propositions made by Sampson and Groves (1989), however, SES and urbanization failed to significantly predict levels of organizational participation.

Social Disorganization and Total Victimization

Table 2 contains the results of the WLS model using the structural characteristics and the social disorganization measures to predict total criminal victimization. Two issues are important when examining this model: (1) whether the social disorganization measures significantly predict total

	Weighted Least Squares Regression Standardized Parameter Estimates of the Effects of Structural Variables and Measures of Social Disorganization on Total Victimization Rates ($N = 600$)
Table 2	

| | **Total Victimization Rate** | |
Independent Variable	**1982**	**1994**
Socioeconomic status	−.03	.06
Ethnic heterogeneity	.08	.06
Residential stability	.03	−.06
Family disruption	.20***	.17***
Urbanization	.21***	.03
Local friendship networks	−.12**	−.14***
Unsupervised peer groups	.34***	.40***
Organizational participation	−.11**	−.06
R-square	.42***	.28***

**P < .05. ***P < .01.

criminal victimization, and (2) whether the social disorganization measures mediate the effects of the structural characteristics on total victimization.

With regard to the first issue, all three of the social disorganization measures were significantly related to total criminal victimization in the theoretically expected direction. The effect is particularly strong for the relationship between unsupervised peer groups and total victimization. These results are generally supportive of the social disorganization model articulated by Sampson and Groves (1989). The issue of the mediating effects of the social disorganization variables, on the other hand, offers less support for the social disorganization paradigm. In particular, after controlling for the measures of social disorganization, the structural characteristics of residential stability and family disruption still maintained statistically significant relationships with total victimization. Alternatively, on controlling for the social disorganization measures, SES, ethnic heterogeneity, and urbanization failed to significantly predict total victimization.

Summary of 1994 BCS Replication

Our test of social disorganization theory using the 1994 BCS data is, on balance, supportive of the major propositions made by the theory in three respects. First, each of the five structural characteristics significantly predicted at least two of the three social disorganization measures specified by Sampson and Groves (1989). Second, each of the social disorganization measures was significantly related to rates of total criminal victimization. Finally, although the predicted relationships did not always occur, in the majority of cases, the social disorganization measures did mediate the effects of the structural characteristics on levels of total criminal victimization.

Social Disorganization and Total Victimization

As for the full model predicting total criminal victimization, only the effect of urbanization was significantly different from the 1982 to the 1994 BCS data. In Sampson and Groves's (1989) analysis, the direct effect of urbanization on total victimization was not fully mediated by the social disorganization variables. The magnitude of the urbanization coefficient in the 1994 analysis, however, is about

one-seventh of the size of the parameter estimate from the 1982 sample. This finding from the 1994 BCS data indicates greater support for social disorganization theory since the direct effect of this structural characteristic is even more dampened by the presence of the social disorganization variables.

As an added check on the direct and indirect effects of the structural characteristics on the total victimization rate, consistent with Veysey and Messner's (1999) analysis of the 1982 BCS data we reestimated the full model in LISREL. These results largely conform to the propositions set forth by Sampson and Groves (1989). To be sure, the overall model provides a relatively good fit to the data. It is noteworthy that much of the total effects of the structural characteristics on the total victimization rate are indirect through the social disorganization variables.

Summary on 1982 and 1994 BCS Comparisons

Our replication of the test of social disorganization theory conducted by Sampson and Groves (1989), using the 1994 BCS data, generally mirrors the results that were found using the 1982 BCS data. Like Sampson and Groves's study, our analysis reveals a relatively high level of empirical support for the social disorganization perspective. Furthermore, the magnitudes of the parameter estimates across the two samples are generally similar. Indeed, significant differences between the coefficients across the two data sets appeared in fewer than one-third of the comparisons. Notably, in each instance where the parameter estimates from the 1994 sample did differ significantly from the 1982 data source, the results generated from the more recent sample indicated a greater degree of support for social disorganization theory than was previously revealed. On balance, therefore, our analysis provides both empirical support for the social disorganization perspective and support for the conclusion that Sampson and Groves's results were not idiosyncratic to the 1982 BCS data.

 Notes

1. According to the Social Sciences Citation Index, Sampson and Groves's 1989 publication has been cited 232 times, including 96 times since 1999 and 32 times in the past 14 months. In a recent article, Wright, Malia, and Johnson (1999) reviewed

the most cited criminology and criminal justice works in 107 articles from the leading sociology journals. Sampson and Groves's publication ranked third, higher than a number of noteworthy works (e.g., Black 1976; Blau and Blau 1982; Cohen and Felson 1979; Gottfredson and Hirschi 1990; Kornhauser 1978; Merton 1968).

2. Sampson and Groves (1989) focused primarily on the 1982 BCS data. They supplemented their analysis with the 1984 BCS data, and the results were largely consistent with those from the 1982 sample. Thus, consistent with Sampson and Groves's original focus, in the present study, we compare our results to their analyses of the 1982 BCS data.

3. We should note that in their original article, Sampson and Groves (1989) attempted to confirm their 1982 analysis with a partial replication of data drawn from the 1984 BCS (e.g., there was no measure of organizational participation). Their results were consistent with the findings drawn from the 1982 analysis and lent added support to social disorganization theory. Our replication is patterned after the more complete 1982 study. In either case, however, our independent replication is conducted on BCS data collected a full decade after the surveys analyzed by Sampson and Groves.

 # References

Akers, Ronald L. 1999. *Criminological Theories: Introduction and Evaluation.* 2nd ed. Chicago: Fitzroy Dearborn.

Beckett, Katherine. 1997. *Making Crime Pay: Law and Order in Contemporary American Politics.* New York: Oxford University Press.

Bellair, Paul E. 1997. "Social interaction and Community Crime: Examining the Importance of Neighborhood Networks." *Criminology* 35: 677–703.

Bergen, Albert, and Max Herman. 1998. "Immigration, Race, and Riot: The 1992 Los Angeles Uprising." *American Sociological Review* 63: 39–54.

Black, Donald. 1976. *The Behavior of Law.* New York: Academic Press.

Blau, Judith R., and Peter M. Blau. 1982. "The Cost of Inequality: Metropolitan Structure and Violent Crime." *American Sociological Review* 47: 114–29.

Brame, Robert, Raymond Paternoster, Paul Mazerolle, and Alex Piquero. 1998. "Testing for the Equality of Maximum-Likelihood Regression Coefficients Between Two Independent Equations." *Journal of Quantitative Criminology* 14: 245–61.

Bursik, Robert J. 1986. "Delinquency Rates as Sources of Ecological Change." Pp. 63–74 in *The Social Ecology of Crime*, edited by James M. Byrne and Robert J. Sampson. New York: Springer-Verlag.

_____. 1988. "Social Disorganization and Theories of Crime and Delinquency: Problems and Prospects." *Criminology* 26: 519–51.

Bursik, Robert J., and Harold G. Grasmick. 1993. "Economic Deprivation and Neighborhood Crime Rates, 1960–1980." *Law and Society Review* 27: 263–83.

Byrne, James M., and Robert J. Sampson. 1986. "Key Issues in the Social Ecology of Crime." Pp. 1–22 in *The Social Ecology of Crime*, edited by James M. Byrne and Robert J. Sampson. New York: Springer-Verlag.

Clogg, Clifford C., Eva Petkova, and Adamantios Haritou. 1995. "Statistical Methods for Comparing Regression Coefficients Between Models." *American Journal of Sociology* 100: 1261–93.

Cohen, Ayala. 1983. "Comparing Regression Coefficients Across Subsamples: A Study of the Statistical Test." *Sociological Methods and Research* 12: 77–94.

Cohen, Lawrence E., and Marcus Felson. 1979. "Social Change and Crime Rate Trends: A Routine Activity Approach." *American Sociological Review* 44: 588–608.

Cole, Stephen. 1975. "The Growth of Scientific Knowledge: Theories of Deviance as a Case Study." Pp. 175–200 in *The Idea of Social Structure: Papers in Honor of Robert K. Merton* edited by Lewis A. Coser. New York: Harcourt Brace Jovanovich.

Cullen, Francis T. 1994. "Social Support as an Organizing Concept for Criminology: Presidential Address to the Academy of Criminal Justice Sciences." *Justice Quarterly* 11: 527–59.

DiIulio, John J. 1997. "Are Voters Fools? Crime, Public Opinion, and Democracy." *Corrections Management Quarterly* 1 (3): 1–5.

Dunford, Franklyn, David Huizinga, and Delbert S. Elliott 1990. "The Role of Arrest in Domestic Assault: The Omaha Experiment." *Criminology* 28: 183–206.

Gendreau, Paul. In press. "We Must Do a Better Job of Cumulating Knowledge." *Canadian Psychology.*

Gottfredson, Michael R., and Travis Hirschi. 1990. *A General Theory of Crime.* Stanford, CA: Stanford University Press.

Gould, Stephen Jay. 1996. *The Mismeasure of Man.* Rev. ed. New York: W. W. Norton.

Hagan, John. 1973. "Labeling and Deviance: A Case Study in the 'Sociology of the Interesting.'" *Social Problems* 20: 447–58.

Hall, Nancy S. 2000. "The Key Role of Replication in Science." *The Chronicle of Higher Education,* November 10, B14.

Hirschi, Travis, 1969. *Causes of Delinquency.* Berkeley: University of California Press.

Home Office Crime and Criminal Justice Unit Office of Population Census and Social Surveys Division. 1994. *British Crime Survey* (computer file). Colchester, Essex, UK: The Data Archive.

Kasarda, John D., and Morris Janowitz. 1974. "Community Attachment in Mass Society." *American Sociological Review* 39: 328–39.

Kempf, Kimberly L. 1993. "The Empirical Status of Hirschi's Control Theory." Pp. 143–85 in *New Directions in Criminological Theory: Advances in Criminological Theory*, Vol. 4, edited by Freda Adler and William S. Laufer. New Brunswick, NJ: Transaction.

Kornhauser, Ruth R. 1978. *Social Sources of Delinquency: An Appraisal of Analytic Models.* Chicago: University of Chicago Press.

Krivo, Lauren J., and Ruth D. Peterson. 1996. "Extremely Disadvantaged Neighborhoods and Urban Crime." *Social Forces* 75: 619–50.

Krohn, Marvin D. 1986. "The Web of Conformity: A Network Approach to the Explanation of Delinquent Behavior." *Social Problems* 33: 81–93.

Lilly, Robert J., Francis T. Cullen, and Richard A. Ball. 2002. *Criminological Theory: Context and Consequences.* 3rd ed. Thousand Oaks, CA: Sage.

Lynn, Peter. 1997. "Sampling Frame Effects on the British Crime Survey." *Journal of the Royal Statistical Society Series* 160 (2): 253–69.

Merton, Robert K. 1968. *Social Theory and Social Structure.* New York: Free Press.

Messner, Steven F., and Robert J. Sampson. 1991. "The Sex Ratio, Family Disruption, and Rates of Violent Crime: The Paradox of Demographic Structure." *Social Forces* 69: 693–713.

Miethe, Terance D., Michael Hughes, and David McDowall. 1991. "Social Change and Crime Rates: An Evaluation of Alternative Theoretical Approaches." *Social Forces* 70: 165–85.

Morenoff, Jeffrey D., and Robert J. Sampson. 1997. "Violent Crime and the Spatial Dynamics of Neighborhood Transition: Chicago, 1970-1990." *Social Forces* 76: 31–64.

Morenoff, Jeffrey D., Robert J. Sampson, and Stephen W. Raudenbush, 2001. "Neighborhood Inequality, Collective Efficacy, and the Spatial Dynamics of Urban Violence." *Criminology* 39: 517–59.

Pfohl, Stephen J. 1985. *Images of Deviance and Social Control: A Sociological History.* New York: McGraw-Hill.

Pratt, Travis C., and Francis T. Cullen. 2000. "The Empirical Status of Gottfredson and Hirschi's General Theory of Crime: A Meta-Analysis." *Criminology* 38: 931–64.

Roundtree, Pamela Wilcox, and Kenneth C. Land. 1996. "Burglary Victimization, Perceptions of Crime Risk, and Routine Activities: A Multilevel Analysis Across Seattle Neighborhoods and Census Tracts." *Journal of Research in Crime and Delinquency* 33: 147–80.

Roundtree, Pamela Wilcox, and Barbara D. Warner. 1999. "Social Ties and Crime: Is the Relationship Gendered?" *Criminology* 37: 789–812.

Sampson, Robert J. 1987. "Urban Black Violence: The Effect of Male Joblessness and Family Disruption." *American Journal of Sociology* 93: 348–82.

Sampson, Robert J., and W. Byron Groves. 1989. "Community Structure and Crime: Testing Social-Disorganization Theory." *American Journal of Sociology* 94: 774–802.

Sampson, Robert J., Jeffery D. Morenoff, and Felton Earls. 1999. "Beyond Social Capital: Spatial Dynamics of Collective Efficacy for Children." *American Sociological Review* 64: 633–60.

Sampson, Robert J., and Stephen W. Raudenbush. 1999. "Systematic Social Observation of Public Spaces: A New Look at Disorder in Urban Neighborhoods." *American Journal of Sociology* 105: 603–51.

Sampson, Robert J., Stephen W. Raudenbush, and Felton Earls. 1997. "Neighborhoods and Violent Crime: A Multilevel Study of Collective Efficacy." *Science* 277: 918–24.

Shaw, Clifford R., and Henry D. McKay. 1972. *Juvenile Delinquency and Urban Areas.* Chicago: University of Chicago Press.

Sherman, Lawrence W., and Richard A. Berk. 1984. "The Specific Deterrent Effects of Arrest for Domestic Assault." *American Sociological Review* 49: 261–72.

Sherman, Lawrence W., Janell D. Schmidt, Dennis P. Rogan, Patrick R. Gartin, Ellen G. Cohn, Dean J. Collins, and Anthony R. Bacich. 1991. "From Initial Deterrence to Long-Term Escalation: Short-Custody Arrest for Poverty Ghetto Domestic Violence." *Criminology* 29: 821–50.

Sherman, Lawrence W., Douglas A. Smith, Janell D. Schmidt, and Dennis P. Rogan. 1992. "Crime, Punishment, and Stake in Conformity: Legal and Informal Control of Domestic Violence." *American Sociological Review* 57: 680–90.

Siegel, Larry. 2000. *Criminology.* 7th ed. Belmont, CA: Wadsworth.

Skogan, Wesley G. 1992. *Disorder and Decline: Crime and the Spiral of Decay in American Neighborhoods.* Berkeley: University of California Press.

Sykes, Gresham M., and Francis T. Cullen. 1992. *Criminology.* 2nd ed. New York: Harcourt Brace Jovanovich.

Taylor, Ralph B. 2001. "The Ecology of Crime, Fear, and Delinquency: Social Disorganization Versus Social Efficacy. In *Explaining Criminals and Crime: Essays in Contemporary Criminological Theory,* edited by Raymond Paternoster and Ronet Bachman. Los Angeles: Roxbury.

Tittle, Charles R., and Raymond Paternoster. 2000. *Social Deviance and Crime: An Organizational and Theoretical Approach.* Los Angeles: Roxbury.

Velez, Maria B. 2001. "The Role of Public Social Control in Urban Neighborhoods: A Multi-Level Analysis of Victimization Risk." *Criminology* 39: 837–64.

Veysey, Bonita M., and Steven F. Messner. 1999. "Further Testing of Social Disorganization Theory: An Elaboration of Sampson and Groves's 'Community Structure and Crime.'" *Journal of Research in Crime and Delinquency* 36: 156–74.

Warner, Barbara D., and Glenn L. Pierce. 1993. "Reexamining Social Disorganization Theory Using Calls to the Police as a Measure of Crime." *Criminology* 31: 493–517.

Warner, Barbara D., and Pamela Wilcox Roundtree. 1997. "Local Ties in a Community and Crime Model: Questioning the Systemic Nature of Informal Social Control." *Social Problems* 44: 520–36.

Wilson, James Q., and George L. Kelling. 1982. "Broken Windows: The Police and Neighborhood Safety." *Atlantic Monthly,* March, 29–38.

Wright, Richard A., Michael Malia, and C. Wayne Johnson. 1999. "Invisible Influence: A Citation Analysis of Crime and Justice Articles Published in Leading Sociology Journal." *Journal of Crime and Justice* 22: 147–65.

REVIEW QUESTIONS

1. Identify and discuss the three types of variables used by Lowenkamp et al. (as well as Sampson and Groves) to measure the key intervening variables in the model of social disorganization. Which of these three do you feel is the best measure of community (i.e., informal) controls/organization, and why? Which of these do you feel is the least applicable, and why?

2. Identify and discuss the five types of structural variables of neighborhoods that Lowenkamp et al. (as well as Sampson and Groves) claim are mediated by the intervening variables (which you discussed in Review Question #1). Which of these structural variables do you think is most vital in predicting crime rates of neighborhoods, and why? Which structural variable do you think is least vital, and why?

3. If you were asked to make a conclusion as a social scientist regarding the current state of empirical evidence or support for Shaw and McKay's proposed model of social disorganization, what would you conclude? What key weaknesses do you see in the model or the way it has been tested?

4. To what extent do the findings presented by Lowenkamp et al. (or Samson and Groves) fit what you have observed in your own local community?

❖

READING 18

In this piece by Heith Copes, Andy Hochstetler, and Craig Forsyth, we see a type of subcultural normative code applied to the behavior of males who fight in bars. The authors elaborate on a particular code of behavior for honor and order as revealed by their sample of White, working-class males in the southeastern portion of the U.S. Interestingly, the authors find that some of the regulations of this normative code actually reduce violent behavior, or at least the degree to which it could escalate.

Peaceful Warriors: Codes for Violence among Adult Male Bar Fighters

Heith Copes, Andy Hochstetler, and Craig Forsyth

Understanding Codes of Conduct

The study of subcultures that endorse violence has a long history, and investigators have emphasized different influences on the content and development of codes for violence (Cohen 1955; Miller 1958; Wolfgang and Ferracuti 1967). Whereas theoretical explanations of violence that rely on value systems often have emphasized distinct aspects and origins, investigators have agreed that

SOURCE: Heith Copes, Andy Hochstetler, and Craig Forsyth, "Peaceful Warriors: Codes for Violence among Adult Male Bar Fighters," *Criminology* 51 (2013): 761–94.

codes for violence reflect that actors condone, justify, or legitimize violence as a means of grievance resolution or vengeance (Anderson 1999; Berg and Stewart 2013). In deciding to commit violence, actors often draw on portrayals of honor as well as on shared understandings of tolerance of provocation to determine the appropriate response to conflict. Accordingly, far from being senseless and random, aggression is patterned and expectable when considered in light of the subcultural values governing its use.

Wolfgang's (1958) research on the prevalence and incidence of violence paved the way for subcultural interpretations of violence by highlighting variation in the construction of meanings in confrontational situations between groups and subcultures and by nesting these meanings in general values and expectations:

> The significance of a jostle, a slightly derogatory remark, or the appearance of the weapon in the hands of an adversary are stimuli differentially perceived and interpreted. . . . Social expectations of response in particular types of social interaction result in differential "definitions of the situation." A male is usually expected to defend the name and honor of his mother, the virtue of womanhood . . . and to accept no derogation about . . . his masculinity. Quick resort to physical combat as a measure of daring, courage or defense of status appears to be a cultural expectation, especially for lower socio-economic class males of both races. (Wolfgang 1958:188–9)

Ethnographers with an interest in codes for violence often have emphasized urban decline, deindustrialization, and inner-city poverty as structural sources of cultural or cognitive landscapes that contribute to high rates of violence in some neighborhoods (Jacobs and Wright 2006; Sanders 1994; Vigil 1988), a finding that also has been borne out in the quantitative research (Piquero et al. 2012). The attitudes and beliefs thought to result from structural disadvantages also seem to influence violent behavior. Those in lower or working classes place greater emphasis on demonstrating courage and the willingness to escalate conflict than those from higher classes (Markowitz 2003). Additionally, those who commit violence endorse some forms of violent crime (Mills, Kroner, and Hemmati 2004), believe that the use of violence serves important purposes (Stewart, Simmons, and Conger 2002), perceive violence as

a demonstration of admirable character (Felson et al. 1994), emphasize courage and escalation in the face of conflict (Markowitz and Felson 1998), and endorse a code that calls for violence in the face of disrespect (Berg et al. 2012; Matsueda, Drakulich, and Kubrin 2006).

Methods

We base our findings on the narratives of 23 men who had been in multiple fights with nonfamily members as adults. These individuals lived in or near the city of Lafayette, Louisiana (population 120,623 as of 2010). Like most mid-sized cities in the southern United States, Lafayette has above average crime rates, especially violent crime. The number of assaults per 100,000 people in Lafayette was 579, whereas across the United States it was 254. The city's population is primarily White (63.5%) and Black (30.9%). The poverty rate is high (19.8% in 2010). The most central industry in the town is oil and gas extraction.

We located interviewees with the help of a lifelong resident who has a history of offenses related to drinking and fighting, and who is known for being a street fighter. He reported being in numerous bar fights (too many to list precisely), and several tavern owners have banned him entry for fighting. Although he has been arrested for disorderly conduct (including fighting), he denied taking part in other illegal activities and had no felony record. The recruiter relied on personal contacts and snowball sampling to locate the sample.

To be eligible, participants had to be White and male, and they had to have been in at least one nondomestic, physical fight within the past 3 months. The reason for restricting the racial composition of the sample was our hope to delve more deeply into how a particular group of persons (i.e., those inhabiting a social sphere of predominantly White, working-class taverns and neighborhoods) thought about fighting and their social world. We did so to act as a counterbalance to the numerous studies that focus on urban, minority youth (see also Jackson-Jacobs 2013). With such a purposive strategy, generalization to other populations is hazardous.

All the individuals we approached agreed to the interview, but one man never could arrange his schedule for a meeting time and was not interviewed. The age range of participants was 22 to 48; the average participant was 33 years of age. All participants feasibly can be classified as working class using their occupations and educational backgrounds at the time of the interview. Twenty were employed. The work these men performed included various labor jobs, such as plumbers' assistants, general contractors, and positions related to oil extraction. Two participants owned businesses (one a small restaurant and the other a screen-print shop). All graduated high school. Six participants graduated college or community college, but none worked in the white-collar workforce, in their major, or had advanced degrees. Eight participants were married. Whereas nearly all participants had been arrested for behaviors they defined as "little things, nothing serious," only one served time in prison. The majority identified with a Cajun ancestry, which is common in the area.

When asked how many fights they had been in as adults, all participants had a hard time providing accurate numbers and most provided ranges or estimates instead, which is common when repeat offenders report their crimes (Shover 1996). The estimated number of fights ranged from 5 to 50. The median range offered by participants was 12 to 15 fights. From their descriptions, participants had a high threshold for counting altercations as fights. They did not consider verbal arguments or quickly interrupted scuffles as fights.

We constructed an interview guide based on a consultation with the recruiter and prior literature on males who engaged in street fights (e.g., Oliver 2001). The recruiter also served as the interviewer. We trained him on proper interviewing techniques, such as probing and active listening. In addition, we listened to each of the first five interviews and offered feedback on how to improve or modify the interviews. Although he followed the same interview guide throughout, we read interviews as they progressed and encouraged him to pursue a few themes that he or we identified.

The interviewer conducted the interviews in private locations such as his home, the home of interviewees, or the homes of others they both knew. When recruiting participants, our contact explained that everything would be kept confidential and that there would be no financial compensation for participation. The interviews lasted between 30 and 45 minutes, and the interviewer recorded them with each participant's permission. We transcribed the interviews verbatim; however, on occasion we edited the text by dropping superfluous filler words and sounds, as well as using punctuation for clarity and readability. We also removed identifying remarks and assigned aliases to each.

To ensure interrater reliability in coding, each of us read the excerpts independently to identify relevant and common themes. We coded using strategies consistent with grounded theory, including open coding and axial coding (Charmaz 2006). We began our open coding by reading electronic versions of the transcripts and marking notes with editing functions in a word processor. We then compared coding and came to agreement on axial codes (theoretical and logical grouping of open codes). On the few cases where we differed on coding, we discussed the discrepancy and reached agreement. We then recoded transcripts using the axial codes we developed, which are reflected in the major themes discussed in the results.

Verifying Masculine Character

Defending and verifying character is a major motivator for violence among urban and rural residents in the United States and abroad (Anderson 1999; Brookman et al., 2011; Nisbett and Cohen 1996). Our participants were not exceptions, and many tied this belief directly to masculinity. When asked why it was important to fight when confronted, Kevin said:

> I think it's important to show who you are as a man, how you feel about yourself, and how you feel about your friends and loved ones. [To show] that you're there to protect them. People, even your friends, need to know that you're there for them, that you're there for yourself, that you have the strength to stand up for yourself and kinda prove you're a man.

David said the willingness to fight allows people to "keep their pride intact. Just sayin' that they're not chumps." Participants asserted that principled individuals know that their character is worth defending physically (Jackson-Jacobs 2013).

They believed that fights were an important part of maintaining self-image. This belief was evident when we asked what they would think of themselves if they did not fight when insulted. In response to this question, David said, "I hate to use the word, but the word pussy comes to mind. . . . That you punked out and you couldn't handle your own business." Similarly, Kevin answered:

> I'd feel guilty. I'd feel weak. I'd feel like I let myself down. I'd feel like I let anybody else that was involved down. I'd feel like the other person involved got the upper hand. I'd feel like I lost something. And most of all I wouldn't feel like a man.

Eric said that if he did not fight he would think:

> That I just wasn't a man, straight and simple. I feel like if I'm tested and I walk away, if I didn't fight that person or prove myself, you know, I'd just feel real down on myself and feel like I'm kind of a coward. They ain't nothin' more that I hate than feelin' like a coward. So, if I'm tested, I'm gonna do what I gotta do to not feel like a coward.

Fighting affirmed a sense of self as a capable and dependable man, but also it fended off powerful negative emotions and shame from refusal to meet the call when provoked.

Being perceived as men who are willing to defend principles was important for participants' sense of self. Using violence was more than saving face; it served internalized and private purposes. A desire to uphold their character led several participants to say that at times they were disappointed deeply in themselves for not fighting. Kevin explained:

> There's times when I kicked myself for days for not hurtin' somebody because I felt they disrespected me in front of people. And just to myself, I felt less of a man. I felt guilty for not doing anything. I felt like a chump. All around it affected me for a while.

Deterrence

There was a pragmatic reason for a firm and unyielding stance in the face of challenge or insult. Fighters believed that by violently responding to affronts they could prevent future insults and deter potential victimizers (Topalli, Wright, and Fornango 2002). Kelly said that, "Without

doing it [fighting], you'd just be a sitting duck. You'd be the one getting beaten up. Incidentally, laying the foundation to get beat up again, picked on, taken advantage of, or exploited later." Fred indicated that his latest fight was because, "I didn't want them to think that I was just some pussy. I wanted to show that I could take care of my business." In short, some violence was motivated by the desire to communicate that aggressors had selected the wrong person to confront.

Beaten rivals from the past also show that violence can be an effective specific deterrent. As Dana said:

> [If] you tell somebody not to keep hittin' on your wife, and they're not listenin' there's gotta be consequences. . . . I told him to back off, and he didn't so I knocked him out. After that he never fucked with her again. . . . [The police] wouldn't have solved anything. Really, I solved it. Maybe it wasn't the way everybody wants it to be handled, but it was handled. I got my point across and it never happened again.

Renee emphasized that his violence was a response to an insult, and for him the important thing was to show aggressors that they cannot insult with impunity:

> You give a man a warning, you ask him to respect it, and he doesn't want to listen to you, that's almost a sign of disrespect again. And if he already disrespected you once, he's gonna disrespect you again, and he's gonna always disrespect you. So you almost have to use physical violence, not to say teach him a lesson, but show him that you're not playin' around, and that you are willing to stand your ground and do it every time you see him.

> He tried talkin' his way out of it, but I didn't want to hear his talkin'. So, as soon as he was done talkin', I just hit him, and I hit him 'til I cut his eye, and I stopped. I told him, "Take your ass-beatin' like a man," and I walked back to the bar and he left.

By telling his opponent to follow the rule against retaliation for an honorable fight, he affirmed that the contest had ended, that the conflict was settled, and that no future violence should follow.

Conduct In Combat

Equal Combatants

One way to determine a "fair" fight was whether the combatants were matched equally, at least by appearances (see Garot 2010). As Kelly said, "A fair fight is when [they're] equally matched in physical stature, strength, age. Unfair would be age, physical stature, intoxication, outnumbered." Although any touching or attempt to intimidate by invading space during confrontation might set off a fight, participants claimed that they avoided throwing a first blow and would attempt to deescalate conflict when their opponent had lost the chance to win. Exceptions to the dictate to avoid the first blow were when they believed they were far outmatched and the fight was inevitable. They claimed that throwing the first blow in these situations might give a "puncher's chance" to escape unharmed. Still, several participants said that there is little purpose in fighting when there is no chance of winning, such as when a far superior fighter insults you. It is very bad form to bully far outside one's size and fighting ability; if personal pride allows, then there is little shame in letting it go when it happens. As Chris said, "If you're definitely gonna get your ass whipped, there's no point in fightin'. You might as well just walk away." It is possible to walk away from a fight and avoid humiliation when unquestionably outmatched (Garot 2010).

 ## Exceptions to Rules

Although participants articulated rules of combat, they also said that they sometimes abandoned these rules. Several indicated that for some transgressions—a sexual crime or other serious offense against those held close—the injured can cast rules aside. It may be acceptable to approach with stealth, gang up on, blindside, or pull a weapon first when the sole objective is vengeance and inflicting pain on dishonorable and egregious offenders who deserve it, but such events were rare among this group. Departures from the code also occurred for less intentional reasons; these events are much more common and received considerably more attention from participants. Here, we elaborate on the situations and circumstances where the participants did not follow the accepted rules of fighting.

Loyalty

Loyalty to friends or the unprotected can conflict with the imperative that fights be fair. Fighters often recognize that despite the need to let a fight proceed to culmination without interference, they should not let friends be injured severely or humiliated. Louis said that one must assist a friend in the fray "if they need it—if they're getting hurt or losing." David explained that he is sure to intervene in fights if a friend is outnumbered, but he said also that he would aid as a gesture of friendship and unwillingness to watch a compatriot suffer:

> Oh yeah, you jump in to help. Why? Because I guess it's your friend and it all depends, you know, how many friends they got with 'em. But yeah, I'd jump in for a friend of mine just 'cause it's your friend. You don't want to see them get hurt, get beat up.

Onlookers are attentive to how a battle unfolds and whether those with whom they side have the upper hand. If they judge that significant injury to their side is occurring or impending, or that the situation requires a demonstration of loyalty, then they may violate the abstract belief that people should fight their own battles. They cast such violations as reluctant, however. The following dialogue with Sal reflected his decision-making process for determining when to violate the ethic of fighting fair:

Interviewer:	Would you jump in even if it was a fair fight?
Sal:	Well, I guess it depends. I guess you'd have to be in the situation, see what it calls for.
Interviewer:	Let's say it's a fair fight and your friend's winning, would you jump in?
Sal:	No, I wouldn't jump in. I'd let him handle his business.
Interviewer:	But if he was getting beat up?
Sal:	I'd probably jump in, yeah.

Jason relied on loyalty to explain the use of a weapon in a fight where he normally would avoid it. He relayed a story of smashing a glass on an antagonist's head:

This big dude was harassing a guy I knew, who was pretty small. I told him, "don't worry that dude won't do nothing." Right after I said that, the big dude pushed my friend hard against the wall. I was like, "Fuck man, I just told him nothin' was going to happen to him." I had to do something. So I smashed my drink over the dude's head.

The participants were not blind to conflicting imperatives that shape how they should respond to a fight. Reportedly, it is a complicated decision determining when to intervene in an ongoing fight. The decision requires speedily considering the entirety of the situation; a significant part of the calculation is how much punishment one allows a friend who has lost momentum in a fight to take before intervening to assist. Onlookers should allow fights to proceed in most cases, but at some point, the beating of a friend must stop.

 ## Discussion

Our aims with this research were to explore the content and implementation of codes for fighting among a group of adult, working-class, White males and to determine how they talk about such codes in relation to constructing identities. In describing the content of their code for violence, participants said fighting was a means of constructing an identity as someone deserving respect, but only when conducted acceptably. They emphasized how defending honor, seeking quick conflict resolution, and establishing admirable qualities motivated them to fight. They were proud of their willingness and ability to oppose adversaries with violence when protecting honorable positions or defending character. They thought people should not seek out violence, but they should not back down from it either. They saw value in fighting to defend honor and to establish order. Defending themselves under the right circumstances enhanced self-respect and confidence that they were men of character and good repute. Failure to fight in appropriate circumstances led to self-doubt and regret.

They believed that fighting served functions beyond building a reputation, however. To them, fighting bolstered a confident demeanor, gave advantage in daily nonviolent interactions, and warded off future disrespectful interactions. They portrayed fighting as a reasonable means for dispute resolution because it ended verbal confrontation, brought conflicts to conclusion, and brought grudges out in the open. Completed fights settled disputes that if left untendered could fester and lead to nastier consequences, including shame associated with feeling cowed, gossip and other harmful talk, or sneaky vengeance. For these reasons and because fighting was an intimidating event, many believed it was the better strategy and found it psychologically easier to charge ahead and be done than to wait or act in hesitation.

Analyses of the codes that pertain to violence often contrast subcultural codes, which analysts cast as those that condone or allow violence, with those of the dominant culture, which they presume to proscribe violence. Our interviews imply that codes that are conducive to crime in some ways can be prohibitive in others. In some circumstances, a code for violence dissuades violent responses and limits the insults that lead to them. Therefore, a code may be useful to people who live within the law in general and think about the future; our participants defend it thus. Undoubtedly, few persons endorse codes for violence that condone ruthlessness, brutality, killing, and long-running cycles of escalating retaliation. Certainly, more individuals, like our participants, believe measured violence is appropriate when faced with certain insults and in a narrowly defined range of contexts. Restrictive codes for the use of violence may be enthusiastically perpetuated not only by the down-and-out but also by those rungs above on the class structure—say men who are solidly working class or pursuing college educations. Allowances for violence contained in these codes can contribute to violence, or help rationalize it, in situations clearly defined as appropriate and even in situations where misapplication occurs. Fighters often feel no regret when the former applies, as a code provides neat rationale, but in other cases, they may rest on good intentions, understandable mistakes, and circumstantial complexities. Flexibility in the implementation of codes and as a device for framing diverse violent events surely is one reason that codes for violence endure in so many contexts. For those avoiding callous or criminal reputations, the code may be durable and defensible not for its allowance but because of the restrictions it contains.

References

Agnew, Robert. 2006. "Storylines as a neglected cause of crime". *Journal of Research in Crime and Delinquency* 43:119–47.

Anderson, Elijah. 1999. *Code of the Street: Decency, Violence, and the Moral Life of the Inner City.* New York: Norton.

Athens, Lonnie. 1997. *Violent Criminal Acts and Actors Revisited.* Champaign: University of Illinois Press.

Berg, Mark T., and Eric Stewart. 2013. "Street Culture and Crime". In *Oxford Handbook of Criminological Theory*, eds. Francis T. Cullen and Pamela Wilcox. Oxford, UK.: Oxford University Press.

Berg, Mark T., Eric Stewart, Christopher Schreck, and Ronald L. Simons. 2012. The victim-offender overlap in context. Examining the role of neighborhood street culture. *Criminology* 50:359–90.

Brezina, Timothy, Robert Agnew, Francis T. Cullen, and John P. Wright. 2004. "The Code of the Street: A Quantitative Assessment of Elijah Anderson's Subculture of Violence Thesis". *Youth Violence and Juvenile Justice* 4:303–28.

Brookman, Fiona, Trevor Bennett, Andy Hochstetler, and Heith Copes. 2011. "The Role of the 'Code of the Street' in the Generation of Street Violence in the Uk". *European Journal of Criminology* 8:17–31.

Brookman, Fiona, Heith Copes, and Andy Hochstetler. 2011. "Street Codes, Accounts, and Rationales for Violent Crime". *Journal of Contemporary Ethnography* 40:397–424.

Charmaz, Kathy. 2006. *Constructing Grounded Theory.* Thousand Oaks, CA: Sage.

Cohen, Albert K. 1955. *Delinquent Boys: The Culture of the Gang.* Glencoe, IL: Free Press.

Copes, Heith, Fiona Brookman, and Anastasia Brown. 2013. "Accounting for Violations of the Convict Code". *Deviant Behavior.* In press. DOI: 10.1080/01639625.2013.781444.

DiMaggio, Paul. 1997. "Culture and Cognition". *Annual Review of Sociology* 23:263–87.

Faupel, Charles E. 1991. *Shooting Dope: Career Patterns of Hardcore Heroin Users.* Gainesville: University of Florida Press.

Felson, Richard B., Allen Liska, Scott J. South, and Thomas L. McNulty. 1994. "The Subculture of Violence: Individual vs. School Context Effects. *Social Forces* 73:155–73.

Ferguson, Ann A. 2001. *Bad Boys: Making of Black Masculinity.* Ann Arbor: University of Michigan Press.

Garot, Robert. 2010. *Who You Claim? Performing Gang Identity in School and on the Streets.* New York: New York University Press.

Guest, Greg, Arwen Bunce, and Laura Johnson. 2006. "How Many Interviews Are Enough? An Experiment with Data Saturation and Variability". *Field Methods* 24:59–82.

Harding, David. 2007. "Cultural Context, Sexual Behavior, and Romantic Relationships in Disadvantaged Neighborhoods". *American Sociological Review* 72:341–64.

Harding, David. 2010. *Living the Drama: Community, Conflict, and Culture among Inner-City Boys.* Cambridge, MA: Harvard University Press.

Hochstetler, Andy, Heith Copes, and Patrick Williams. 2010. "That's Not Who I Am: How Offenders Commit Violent Acts and Reject Authentically Violent Selves". *Justice Quarterly* 27:492–516.

Horowitz, Ruth. 1983. *Honor and the American Dream: Culture and Identity in a Chicano Community.* Newark, NJ: Rutgers University Press.

Jackson-Jacobs, Curtis. 2013. "Constructing Physical Fights: An Interactionist Analysis of Violence among Affluent, Suburban Youth". *Qualitative Sociology* 36:23–52.

Jacobs, Bruce A., and Richard Wright. 2006. *Street Justice: Retaliation in the Criminal Underworld.* New York: Cambridge University Press.

Jimerson, Jason B., and Matthew K. Oware. 2006. "Telling the Code: An Ethnomethodological Ethnography". *Journal of Contemporary Ethnography* 35:24–50.

Katz, Jack. 1988. *Seductions of Crime.* New York: Basic Books.

Klenowski, Paul, Heith Copes, and Christopher Mullins. 2011. "Gender, Identity and Accounts: How White Collar Offenders Do Gender When They Make Sense of Their Crimes". *Justice Quarterly* 28:46–69.

Kornhauser, Ruth. 1978. *The Social Sources of Delinquency: An Appraisal of Analytical Methods.* Chicago, IL: University of Chicago Press.

Lee, Matthew, and Edward S. Shihadeh. 2009. "The Spatial Concentration of Southern Whites and Argument-Based Lethal Violence". *Social Forces* 91:1671–94.

Loseke, Donileen R. 2007. "The Study of Identity as Cultural, Institutional, Organizational, and Personal Narratives: Theoretical and Empirical Integrations". *Sociological Quarterly* 48:661–88.

Markowitz, Fred E. 2003. "Socioeconomic Disadvantage and Violence: Recent Research on Culture and Neighborhood Control as Explanatory Mechanisms". *Aggression and Violent Behavior* 8:145–54.

Markowitz, Fred E., and Richard B. Felson. 1998. "Socio-demographic Differences in Attitudes and Violence". *Criminology* 36:117–38.

Maruna, Shadd, and Heith Copes. 2005. "What Have We Learned from Five Decades of Neutralization Research. In *Crime and Justice: A Review of Research*, Vol. 32, ed. Michael H. Tonry. Chicago, IL: University of Chicago Press.

Matsueda, Ross L., Kevin Drakulich, and Charis E. Kubrin. 2006. "Race and Neighborhood Codes of Violence". In *The Many Colors of Crime*, eds. Ruth D. Peterson, Lauren J. Krivo, and John Hagan. New York: New York University Press.

Miller, Walter. 1958. Lower class culture as a generating milieu of gang delinquency. *Journal of Social Issues* 1:5–20.

Mills, Jeremy F., Daryl G. Kroner, and Toni Hemmati. 2004. The measure of criminal attitudes and associates: The prediction of general and violent recidivism. *Criminal Justice and Behavior* 31:717–33.

Nisbett, Richard, and Dov Cohen. 1996. *Culture of Honor: The Psychology of Violence in the South.* Boulder, CO: Westview Press.

Oliver, William. 2001. *The Violent Social World of Black Men.* San Francisco, CA: Jossey-Bass.

Piquero, Alex, Jonathan Intravia, Eric Stewart, Nicole L. Piquero, Mark Gertz, and Jake Bratton. 2012. "Investigating the Determinants of the Street Code and its Relation to Offending Among Adults". *American Journal of Criminal Justice* 37:19–32.

Presser, Lois. 2010. "Collecting and Analyzing the stories of offenders". *Journal of Criminal Justice Education* 21:431–46.

Rosenfeld, Richard, Bruce Jacobs, and Richard Wright. 2003. "Snitching and the Code of the Street". *British Journal of Criminology* 43:291–309.

Sampson, Robert, and Lydia Bean. 2006. "Cultural Mechanisms and Killing Fields: A Revised Theory of Community-level Racial inequality". In *The Many Colors of Crime: Inequalities of Race, Ethnicity, and Crime in America*, eds. Ruth Peterson, Lauren Krivo, and John Hagan. New York: New York University Press.

Sampson, Robert, and William J. Wilson. 1995. "Toward a Theory of Race, Crime and Urban Inequality". In *Crime and Inequality*, eds. John Hagan and Ruth Peterson. Palo Alto, CA: Stanford University Press.

Sandberg, Sveinung. 2009a. "A Narrative Search for Respect". *Deviant Behavior* 30:487–510.

Sandberg, Sveinung. 2009b. "Gangster, Victim or Both? The Interdiscursive Construction of Sameness and Difference in Self-Presentations". *British Journal of Sociology* 60:523–42.

Sandberg, Sveinung. 2010. "What Can "Lies" Tell Us about Life? Notes towards a Framework of Narrative Criminology". *Journal of Criminal Justice Education* 21:447–65.

Sanders, William B. 1994. *Gangbangs and Drive-Bys: Grounded Culture and Juvenile Gang Violence*, New York: Aldine de Gruyter.

Scott, Marvin B., and Scott M. Lyman. 1968. "Accounts". *American Sociological Review* 33:46–62.

Shover, Neal. 1996. *Great Pretenders: Pursuits and Careers of Persistent Thieves*. Boulder, CO: Westview Press.

Spierenburg, Pieter. 1998. "Masculinity, Violence, and Honor". In *Men Violence: Gender, Honor, and Ritual in Modern Europe and America*, ed. Pieter Spierenburg. Athens: The Ohio State University Press.

Stewart, Eric A., and Ronald L. Simons. 2010. "Race, Code of the Street, and Violent Delinquency: A Multilevel Investigation of Neighborhood Street Culture and Individual Norms of Violence". *Criminology* 48:569–605.

Stewart, Eric A., Ronald L. Simons, and Rand Conger. 2002. "Assessing Neighborhood and Social Psychological Influences on Childhood Violence in an African-American Sample". *Criminology* 40:801–30.

Stokes, Randall, and John Hewitt. 1976. "Aligning Action". *American Sociological Review* 41:838–49.

Swidler, Ann. 1986. "Culture in Action: Symbols and Strategies". *American Sociological Review* 51:273–86.

Topalli, Volkan. 2005. "When Being Good Is Bad: An Expansion of Neutralization Theory". *Criminology* 43:797–836.

Topalli, Volkan, Richard Wright, and Robert Fornango. 2002. "Drug Dealers, Robbery, and Retaliation: Vulnerability, Deterrence and the Contagion of Violence. *British Journal of Criminology*" 42:337–351.

Vigil, James D. 1988. *Barrio Gangs: Street Life and Identity in Southern California*. Austin: University of Texas Press.

Wacquant, Loic. 2002. "Scrutinizing the Street: Poverty, Morality, and the Pitfalls of Urban Ethnography". *American Journal of Sociology* 107:1468–532.

Wieder, D. Lawrence. 1974. *Language and Social Reality: The Case of Telling the Convict Code*. The Hague, the Netherlands: Mouton.

Wilson, William J. 1996. *When Work Disappears: The World of the New Urban Poor*. New York: Knopf.

Wolfgang, Marvin E. 1958. *Patterns in Criminal Homicide*. Philadelphia: University of Pennsylvania Press.

Wolfgang, Marvin E., and Franco Ferracuti. 1967. *The Subculture of Violence: Towards an Integrated Theory in Criminology*. London, U.K.: Tavistock.

REVIEW QUESTIONS

1. What do the participants in this study reveal regarding the need to "verify" their masculinity?

2. What were some of the deterrents that prevented some of the subjects from committing further violence?

3. What was the overall conclusion of this study, in terms of subcultural codes for violence?

❖

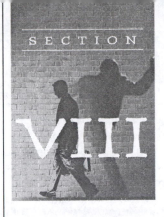
Social Process and Learning Theories of Crime

T his section will discuss Sutherland's development of differential association theory and how this evolved into Akers's work of differential reinforcement and other social learning theories, such as techniques of neutralization. Then, the modern state of research on these theories will be presented. We will also discuss the evolution of control theories of crime, with an emphasis on social bonding and the scientific evidence found regarding the key constructs in Hirschi's control theories, two of the most highly regarded perspectives according to criminological experts and their studies.[1]

Most of the social process theories assume that criminal behavior is learned behavior, which means that criminal activity is actually learned from others through social interaction, much like riding a bike or playing basketball. Namely, people learn criminal activity from significant others, such as family, peers, or coworkers. However, other social process theories, namely control theories, assume that offending is the result of natural tendencies and thus must be controlled by social processes. Social process theories examine how individuals interact with other individuals and groups and how the learning that takes place in these interactions leads to a propensity for criminal activity. This section will explore both of these theoretical frameworks and explain how social processes are vital to both perspectives in determining criminal behavior.

This section begins with social process theories known as learning theories. Such learning theories attempt to explain how and why individuals learn from significant others to engage in criminal rather than conventional behavior. Next, we discuss control theories, which emphasize personal or socialization factors that prevent individuals from engaging in selfish, antisocial behaviors.

---

[1]Anthony Walsh and Lee Ellis, "Political Ideology and American Criminologists' Explanations for Criminal Behavior," *The Criminologist* 24 (1999): 1, 14 (see chap. 1, n. 13).

Learning Theories

In this section, we review theories that emphasize how individuals learn criminal behavior through interacting with significant others, people with whom they typically associate. These learning theories assume that people are born with no tendency toward or away from committing crime. This concept is referred to as tabula rasa, or blank slate, meaning that all individuals are completely malleable and will believe what they are told by their significant others and act accordingly. Thus, such theories of learning tend to explain how criminal behavior is learned through cultural norms. One of the main concepts in learning theories is the influence of peers and significant others on an individual's behavior.

Here, three learning theories are discussed: (a) differential association theory, (b) differential identification theory, and (c) differential reinforcement theory; then we examine techniques of neutralization.

Differential Association Theory

Edwin Sutherland introduced his differential association theory in the late 1930s.[2] He proposed a theoretical framework that explained how criminal values could be culturally transmitted to individuals from their significant others. Sutherland proposed a theoretical model that included nine principles, but rather than list them all, we will summarize the main points of his theory.

Perhaps the most interesting principle is the first: Criminal behavior is learned. This was a radical departure from previous theories (e.g., Lombroso's "born criminal" theory, Goddard's feeblemindedness theory, Sheldon's body type theory). Sutherland was one of the first to state that criminal behavior is the result of normal social processes, resulting when individuals associate with the wrong type of people, often by no fault on their part. By associating with crime-oriented people, whether parents or peers, an individual will inevitably choose to engage in criminal behavior because that is what he or she has learned, Sutherland thought.

Perhaps the most important of Sutherland's principles, and certainly the most revealing one, was number six in his framework: "A person becomes delinquent because of an excess of definitions favorable to violation of law over definitions unfavorable to violation of law."[3] Sutherland noted that this principle represents the essence of differential association theory. It suggests that people can have associations that favor both criminal and noncriminal behavior patterns. If an individual is receiving more information and values that are pro-crime than anti-crime, the individual will inevitably engage in criminal activity. Also, Sutherland claimed that such learning can take place only in interactions with significant others and not via television, movies, radio, or other media.

It is important to understand the cultural context at the time Sutherland was developing his theory. In the early 20th century, most academics, and society for that matter, believed that there was something abnormal or different about criminals. Sheldon's body type theory was popular in the same period, as was the use of IQ to pick out people who were of lower intelligence and supposedly predisposed to crime (both of these theories were covered in Section IV). So, the common assumption when Sutherland created the principles of differential association theory was that there was essentially something wrong with individuals who commit crime.

In light of this common assumption, Sutherland's proposal—that criminality is learned just like any conventional activity—was extremely profound. This suggests that any normal person, when exposed to attitudes favorable to crime, will learn criminal activity, and that the processes and mechanisms of learning are the same for crime as for most legal, everyday behaviors, namely, social interaction with family and friends, and not reading books or watching movies. How many of us learned to play basketball or other sports by reading a book about

[2]Edwin H. Sutherland, *Principles of Criminology*, 3rd ed. (Philadelphia: Lippincott, 1939).

[3]Edwin H. Sutherland and Donald R. Cressey, *Principles of Criminology*, 5th ed. (Chicago: Lippincott, 1950), 78.

it? Virtually no one learns how to play sports this way. Rather, we learn the techniques (e.g., how to do a jump shot) and motivations for playing sports (e.g., it is fun or you might be able to earn a scholarship) through our friends, relatives, coaches, and other people close to us. According to Sutherland, crime is learned the same way; our close associates teach us both the techniques (e.g., how to steal a car) and the motivations (e.g., it is fun; you might be able to sell it or its parts). While most criminologists tend to take it for granted that criminal behavior is learned, the idea was rather unique and bold when Sutherland presented his theory of differential association.

It is important to keep in mind that differential association theory is just as positivistic as earlier biological and psychological theories. Sutherland clearly believed that, if people were receiving more information that breaking the law was good, then they would inevitably commit crimes. There is virtually no allowance for free will and rational decision making in this model of offending. Rather, people's choices to commit crime are determined through their social interactions with those close to them; they do not actually make the decisions to engage (or not engage) in criminal activities. So, differential association can be seen as a highly positive, deterministic theory, much like Lombroso's "born criminal" and Goddard's feeblemindedness theories (see Section IV), except that, instead of biological or psychological traits causing crime, it is social interaction and learning. Furthermore, Sutherland claimed that individual differences in biological and psychological functioning have little to do with criminality; however, this idea has been discounted by modern

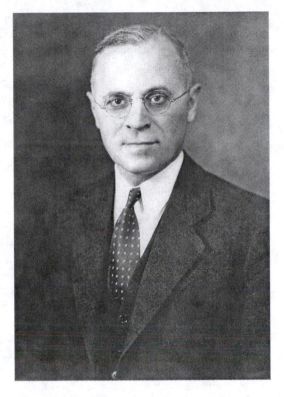

▲ Image 8.1   Edwin H. Sutherland (1883–1950), University of Chicago and Indiana University, author of differential association theory.

Source: The Estate of Donald Cressey.

research, which shows that such variations do in fact affect criminal behavior, largely because such biopsychological factors influence the learning processes of individuals, thereby directly impacting the basic principles of Sutherland's theory (see Sections IV and V).

Classical Conditioning: A Learning Theory with Limitations

Sutherland used the dominant psychological theory of learning in his era as the basis for his theory of differential association. This model was classical conditioning, which was primarily developed by Ivan Pavlov. Classical conditioning assumes that animals, as well as people, learn through associations between stimuli and responses.[4] Organisms, animals or people, are somewhat passive actors in this process, meaning that they simply receive and respond in natural ways to various forms of stimuli; over time, they learn to associate certain stimuli with certain responses.

For example, Pavlov showed that dogs, which are naturally afraid of loud noises such as bells, could be quickly conditioned not only to be less afraid of bells but to actually desire and salivate at their sound. A dog naturally

[4]For a discussion, see Thomas J. Bernard, Jeffrey B. Snipes, and Alexander L. Gerould, *Vold's Theoretical Criminology*, 6th ed. (Oxford: Oxford University Press, 2010), 156–57 (see chap. 2).

salivates when presented with meat, so when this presentation of an unconditioned stimulus (meat) is given, a dog will always salivate (unconditioned response) in anticipation of eating. Pavlov demonstrated through a series of experiments that, if a bell (conditioned stimulus) is always rung at the same time the dog is presented with meat, then the dog will learn to associate what was previously a negative stimulus with a positive stimulus (food). Thus, the dog will very quickly begin to salivate at the ringing of a bell, even when meat is not presented. When this occurs, it is called a conditioned response because it is not natural; however, it is a very powerful and effective means of learning, and it sometimes takes only a few occurrences of coupling the bell ringing with meat before the conditioned response takes place.

One modern use of this in humans is the administration of drugs that make people ill when they drink alcohol. Alcoholics are often prescribed drugs that make them very sick, often to the point of vomiting, if they ingest any alcohol. The idea is that they will learn to associate feelings of sickness with drinking and thus stop wanting to consume alcohol. One big problem with this strategy is that alcoholics often do not consistently take the drugs, so they quickly slip back into addiction. Still, if they were to maintain their regimen of drugs, it would likely work, because people do tend to learn through association.

This type of learning model was used in the critically acclaimed 1964 novel (and later motion picture) *A Clockwork Orange*. In this novel, the author, Anthony Burgess, tells the story of a juvenile murderer who is "rehabilitated" by doctors who force him to watch hour after hour of violent images while simultaneously giving him drugs that make him sick. In the novel, the protagonist is "cured" after only two weeks of this treatment, having learned to consistently associate violence with sickness. However, once he is let out, he lacks the ability to choose violence and other antisocial behavior, which is seen as losing his humanity. Therefore, the ethicists order a reversal treatment and make him back into his former self, a violent predator. Although a fictional piece, *A Clockwork Orange* is probably one of the best illustrations of the use of classical conditioning in relation to criminal offending and rehabilitation.

Another example of classical conditioning is the associations we make with certain smells and sounds. For example, all of us can relate good times to smells that were present during those occasions. If a loved one or someone we dated wore a certain perfume or cologne, smelling that scent at a later time can bring back memories. When our partner goes out of town, we can smell his or her pillow, and it will remind us of our partner because we associate his or her smell with his or her being. Or perhaps the smell of a turkey cooking in an oven always reminds us of Thanksgiving or another holiday. Regarding associations of sounds, we can all remember songs that remind us of happy and sad times in our lives. Often these songs will play on the radio, and they take us back to those occasions, whether good or bad. People with posttraumatic stress disorder (PTSD) also experience sound associations; war veterans, for example, may hit the deck when a car backfires. These are all clear examples of classical conditioning and associating stimuli with responses.

Since Sutherland's theory was published, many of the principles outlined in his model have come under scrutiny. Follow-up research has shown some flaws in, as well as misinterpretations of, his work.[5] Specifically, Sutherland theorized that crime occurs when associations favorable to violation of the law outweigh associations favorable to conforming to the law. However, measuring this type of ratio is nearly impossible for social scientists.[6]

Another topic of criticism involves Sutherland's claim that all criminals learn the behavior from others before they engage in such activity. However, many theorists have noted that an individual may engage in criminal activity without being taught such behavior, then seek out others with attitudes and behavior similar to their own.[7] So, do individuals learn to commit crime after they are taught by delinquent peers, or do they start associating with similar

---

[5]Edwin H. Sutherland and Donald R. Cressey, *Criminology*, 9th ed. (Philadelphia: Lippincott, 1974).

[6]Ross L. Matsueda and Karen Heimer, "Race, Family Structure, and Delinquency: A Test of Differential Association and Social Control Theories," *American Sociological Review* 47 (1987): 489–504; Charles R. Tittle, M. J. Burke, and E. F. Jackson, "Modeling Sutherland's Theory of Differential Association: Toward an Empirical Clarification," *Social Forces* 65 (1986): 405–32.

[7]Tittle et al., "Modeling Sutherland's Theory."

delinquents or criminals once they have initiated their offending career (i.e., "birds of a feather flock together")? This exact debate was examined by researchers, and the most recent studies point to the occurrence of both causal processes: Criminal associations cause more crime, and committing crime causes more criminal associations. Both are key in the causal process, so Sutherland was missing half of this equation.[8]

Another key criticism is that, if each individual is born with a blank slate and all criminal behavior is learned, then who committed crime in the first place? Who could expose the first criminal to the definitions favorable to violation of law? Furthermore, what factor(s) caused that individual to do the crime if it was not learned? Obviously, if it were due to any factor(s) other than learning—and it must have been because there was no one to teach it—then it obviously was not explained by learning theories. This criticism cannot be addressed, so it is somewhat ignored in the scientific literature.

Despite the criticisms and flaws, much research supports Sutherland's theory. For example, researchers have found that older criminals teach younger delinquents.[9] In addition, delinquents often associate with criminal peers prior to engaging in criminal activity.[10] Furthermore, research has shown that criminal friends, attitudes, and activity are highly associated.[11] Still, Sutherland's principles are quite vague and elusive in terms of measurement, which renders them difficult for social scientists to test.[12] Related to these issues, perhaps one of the biggest problems with Sutherland's formulation of differential association is that he used primarily one type of learning model—classical conditioning—to formulate most of his principles, and thus he neglected other important ways that we learn attitudes and behavior from others. Ultimately, Sutherland's principles are hard to test; more current versions of his framework have incorporated other learning models and thus are easier to test so that empirical validity can be demonstrated.

Glaser's Concept of Differential Identification

Another reaction to Sutherland's differential association dealt with the influence of movies and television, as well as other reference groups outside of one's significant others. As stated above, Sutherland claimed that learning of criminal definitions can take place only through social interactions with significant others as opposed to reading a book or watching movies. However, in 1956, Daniel Glaser proposed the idea of differential identification theory, which allows for learning to take place not only through people close to us but also through other reference groups, even distant ones, such as sports heroes or movie stars whom we have never actually met and with whom we have never corresponded.[13] Glaser claimed that it did not matter much whether an individual had a personal relationship with a reference group(s); in fact, he argued that a group could be imaginary, such as fictitious characters in a movie or book. The important thing, according to Glaser, was that an individual must identify with a person or character and thus behave in ways that fit the norm set of this reference group or person.

Glaser's proposition has been virtually ignored, with the exception of Dawes's study of delinquency in 1973, which found that identification with people other than parents was strong when youths perceived a greater degree of rejection from their parents.[14] Given the profound influence of movies, music, and television on today's youth

---

[8]Terence Thornberry, "Toward an Interactional Theory of Delinquency," *Criminology* 25 (1987): 863–87.

[9]Kenneth Tunnell, "Inside the Drug Trade: Trafficking from the Dealer's Perspective," *Qualitative Sociology* 16 (1993): 361–81.

[10]Douglas Smith, Christy Visher, and G. Roger Jarjoura, "Dimensions of Delinquency: Exploring the Correlates of Participation, Frequency, and Persistence of Delinquent Behavior," *Journal of Research in Crime and Delinquency* 28 (1991): 6–32.

[11]Matthew Ploeger, "Youth Employment and Delinquency: Reconsidering a Problematic Relationship," *Criminology* 35 (1997): 659–75.

[12]Reed Adams, "The Adequacy of Differential Association Theory," *Journal of Research in Crime and Delinquency* 1 (1974): 1–8; James F. Short, "Differential Association as a Hypothesis: Problems of Empirical Testing," *Social Problems* 8 (1960): 14–25.

[13]Daniel Glaser, "Criminality Theories and Behavioral Images," *American Journal of Sociology* 61 (1956): 433–44.

[14]Kenneth J. Dawes, "Family Relationships, Reference Others, Differential Identification and Their Joint Impact on Juvenile Delinquency," doctoral dissertation (Ann Arbor: University Mircrofilms, 1973).

culture, it is obvious that differential identification was an important addition to Sutherland's framework, and more research should examine the validity of Glaser's theory in contemporary society.

Although Glaser and others modified differential association, the most valid and respected variation is differential reinforcement theory.

Differential Reinforcement Theory

In 1965, C. R. Jeffery provided an extensive critique and reevaluation of Sutherland's differential association theory. He argued that the theory was incomplete without some attention to an updated social psychology of learning (e.g., operant conditioning and modeling theories of learning).[15] He wanted Sutherland to account for the fact that people can be conditioned into behaving certain ways, such as by being rewarded for conforming behavior. Then, in 1966, Robert Burgess and Ronald Akers criticized and responded to Jeffery's criticism by proposing a new theory that incorporated some of these learning models into Sutherland's basic framework.[16] The result was what is now known as differential reinforcement theory. Ultimately, Burgess and Akers argued that by integrating Sutherland's work with contributions from the field of social psychology, criminal behavior could be more clearly understood.

In some ways, differential reinforcement theory may appear to be no different than rational choice theory (see Section III). To an extent, this is true, because both models focus on reinforcements and punishments that occur after an individual offends. However, differential reinforcement theory can be distinguished from the rational choice perspective. The latter assumes that humans are born with the capacity for rational decision making, whereas the differential reinforcement perspective assumes people are born with a blank slate and, thus, must be socialized and taught how to behave through various forms of conditioning (e.g., operant and classical) as well as modeling.

Burgess and Akers developed seven propositions to summarize differential reinforcement theory, which largely represent efficient modifications of Sutherland's original nine principles of differential association.[17] The strong influence of social psychologists is illustrated in their first statement, as well as throughout the seven principles. Although differential reinforcement incorporates the elements of modeling and classical conditioning learning models in its framework, the first statement clearly states that the essential learning mechanism in social behavior is operant conditioning, so it is important to understand what operant conditioning is and how it is evident throughout life.

Operant Conditioning

The idea of operant conditioning was primarily developed by B. F. Skinner,[18] who ironically was working just across campus from Edwin Sutherland when he was developing differential association theory at Indiana University. As in modern times, academia was too intradisciplinary and intradepartmental. Had Sutherland been aware of Skinner's studies and theoretical development, he likely would have included it in his original framework. In his defense, operant conditioning was not well known or researched at the time; as a result, Sutherland incorporated the then-dominant learning model, classical conditioning. Burgess and Akers went on to incorporate operant conditioning into Sutherland's framework.

Operant conditioning concerns how behavior is influenced by reinforcements and punishments. Furthermore, operant conditioning assumes that an animal or human being is a proactive player in seeking out rewards and not

[15]C. Ray Jeffery, "Criminal Behavior and Learning Theory," *Journal of Criminal Law, Criminology, and Police Science* 56 (1965): 294–300.

[16]Robert Burgess and Ronald Akers, "A Differential Association-Reinforcement Theory of Criminal Behavior," *Social Problems* 14 (1966): 131.

[17]For a more recent version of these principles, see Ronald Akers, *Deviant Behavior: A Social Learning Approach*, 3rd ed. (Belmont: Wadsworth, 1985). See also Ronald L. Akers and Christine S. Sellers, *Criminological Theories: Introduction, Evaluation, and Application*, 6th ed. (Oxford: Oxford University Press, 2012).

[18]B. F. Skinner, *Science and Human Behavior* (New York: Macmillan, 1953).

just a passive entity that receives stimuli, as classical conditioning assumes. Behavior is strengthened or encouraged through reward (positive reinforcement) and avoidance of punishment (negative reinforcement). For example, if someone is given a car for graduation from college, that would be a positive reinforcement. On the other hand, if a teenager who has been grounded is allowed to start going out again because he or she has better grades, this would be a negative reinforcement, because he or she is now being rewarded via the avoidance of something negative. Like different types of reinforcement, punishment comes in two forms as well. Behavior is weakened, or discouraged, through adverse stimuli (positive punishment) or lack of reward (negative punishment). A good example of positive punishment would be a good, old-fashioned spanking, because it is certainly a negative stimulus; anything that directly presents negative sensations or feelings is a positive punishment. On the other hand, if parents take away car privileges from a teenager who broke curfew, that would be an example of negative punishment because the parents are removing a positive aspect or reward.

Some notable examples of operant conditioning include teaching a rat to successfully run a maze. When rats take the correct path and finish the maze quickly, they are either positively reinforced (e.g., rewarded with a piece of cheese) or negatively reinforced (e.g., not zapped with electricity as they were when they chose the wrong path). On the other hand, when rats take wrong turns or do not complete the maze in adequate time, they are either positively punished (e.g., zapped with electricity) or negatively punished (e.g., not given the cheese they expect to receive). The rats, like humans, tend to learn the correct behavior very fast using such consistent implementation of reinforcements and punishments.

In humans, such principles of operant conditioning can be found even at very early ages. In fact, many of us have implemented such techniques (or been subjected to them) without really knowing they were called operant conditioning. For example, during toilet training, children learn to use the bathroom to do their natural duty rather than doing it in their pants. To reinforce the act of going to the bathroom on a toilet, we encourage the correct behavior by presenting positive rewards, which can be as simple as applauding the child or giving him or her a piece of candy for a successful job. While parents (we hope) rarely proactively use spanking in toilet training, there is an inherent positive punishment involved when children go in their pants; namely, they have to be in their dirty diaper for a while, not to mention the embarrassment that most children feel when they do this. Furthermore, negative punishments are present in such situations because the child does not get the applause or candy, so the rewards have been removed.

Of course, this does not apply only to early behavior. An extensive amount of research has shown that humans learn attitudes and behavior best through a mix of reinforcements and punishments throughout life. In terms of criminal offending, studies have clearly shown that the rehabilitative programs that appear to work most effectively in reducing recidivism in offenders are those that provide opportunities for reward as well as threats of punishment. Empirical research has combined the findings from hundreds of such studies of rehab programs, showing that the programs that are most successful in changing the attitudes and behavior of previous offenders are those that offer at least four reward opportunities for every one possible punishment.[19] So, whether it is training children to go potty correctly or altering criminals' thinking and behavior, operant conditioning is a well-established form of learning that makes differential reinforcement theory a more valid and specified model of offending than differential association.

Whether deviant or conforming behavior occurs and continues "depends on the past and present rewards or punishment for the behavior, and the rewards and punishment attached to alternative behavior."[20] In contrast to Sutherland's differential association model, which looks only at what happens before an act (i.e., classical conditioning), not at what happens after the act is completed (i.e., operant conditioning), Burgess and Akers's model looks at both. Criminal behavior is likely to occur, Burgess and Akers theorized, when its rewards outweigh the punishments.

[19]Patricia Van Voorhis and Emily Salisbury, *Correctional Counseling and Rehabilitation*, 8th ed. (Cincinnati: Anderson, 2013).

[20]Ronald L. Akers, *Deviant Behavior: A Social Learning Approach*, 2nd ed. (Belmont: Wadsworth, 1977), 57.

Bandura's Theory of Modeling and Imitation

Another learning model that Burgess and Akers emphasized in their formulation of differential reinforcement theory was the element of modeling and imitation. Although Sutherland's original formulation of differential association theory was somewhat inspired by Gabriel Tarde's concept of imitation,[21] the nine principles did not adequately emphasize the importance of modeling in the process of learning behavior. Sutherland's failure was likely due to the fact that Albert Bandura's primary work in this area had not occurred when Sutherland was formulating differential association theory.[22]

Through a series of experiments and theoretical development, Bandura demonstrated that a significant amount of learning takes place without any form of conditioning. Specifically, he claimed that individuals can learn even if they are not rewarded or punished for behavior (i.e., operant conditioning) and even if they have not been exposed to associations between stimuli and responses (i.e., classical conditioning). Rather, Bandura proposed that people learn much of their attitudes and behavior from simply observing the behavior of others, namely through mimicking what others do. This is often referred to as *monkey see, monkey do*, but it is not just monkeys that do this. Like most animal species, humans are biologically hardwired to observe and learn the behavior of others, especially elders, to see what behavior is essential for survival and success.

Bandura showed that simply observing the behavior of others, especially adults, can have profound learning effects on the behavior of children. Specifically, he performed experiments in which a randomized experimental group of children watched a video of adults acting aggressively toward Bo-Bo dolls (which are blow-up plastic dolls); the control group of children did not watch such a video. Both groups of children were then sent into a room containing Bo-Bo dolls, and the experimental group, who had seen the adult behavior, mimicked their elders by acting far more aggressively toward the dolls than the children in the control group. The experimental group had no previous associations of more aggressive behavior toward the dolls and no good feelings or motivations, let alone rewards, for such behavior. Rather, the children became more aggressive themselves simply because they were imitating what they had seen older people do.

Bandura's findings have important implications for the modeling behavior of adults (and peers) and for the influence of television, movies, video games, and other factors. Furthermore, the influences demonstrated by Bandura supported a phenomenon commonplace in everyday life. Mimicking is the source of fashion trends—wearing low-slung pants or baseball hats turned a certain way. Styles tend to ebb and flow based on how some respected person (often a celebrity) wears clothing. This can be seen very early in life; parents must be careful what they say and do because their children, as young as two years old, imitate what their parents do. This continues throughout life, especially in the teenage years as young persons imitate the cool trends and styles as well as behaviors. Of course, sometimes this behavior is illegal, but individuals are often simply mimicking the way their friends or others are behaving with little regard for potential rewards or punishments. Ultimately, Bandura's theory of modeling and imitation adds a great deal of explanation to a model of learning, and differential reinforcement theory includes such influences, whereas Sutherland's model of differential association does not, largely because the psychological perspective had not yet been developed.

Burgess and Akers's theory of differential reinforcement has also been the target of criticism by theorists and researchers. Perhaps the most important criticism of differential reinforcement theory is that it appears *tautological*, meaning that the variables and measures used to test its validity are true by definition. To clarify, studies testing this theory have been divided into four groups based on variables or factors: associations, reinforcements, definitions, and modeling.

---

[21]Gabriel Tarde, *Penal Philosophy*, trans. Rapelje Howell (Boston: Little, Brown, 1912).

[22]See Albert Bandura, *Principles of Behavior Modification* (New York: Holt, Rinehart & Winston, 1969); Albert Bandura, *Aggression: A Social Learning Analysis* (Englewood Cliffs: Prentice Hall, 1973); Albert Bandura, *Social Learning Theory* (Englewood Cliffs: Prentice Hall, 1977).

Some critics have noted that, if individuals who report that they associate with those who offend are rewarded for offending, believe offending is good, and have seen many of their significant others offend, they will inevitably be more likely to offend. In other words, if your friends and family are doing it, there is little doubt that you will be doing it.[23] For example, critics would argue that a person who primarily hangs out with car thieves, knows he will be rewarded for stealing cars, believes stealing cars is good and not immoral, and has observed many respected others stealing cars, will inevitably commit auto theft himself. However, it has been well argued that such criticisms of tautology are not valid because none of these factors necessarily makes offending by the respondent true by definition.[24]

Differential reinforcement theory has also faced the same criticism that was addressed to Sutherland's theory, namely, that delinquent associations may take place after criminal activity rather than before. However, Burgess and Akers's model clearly has this area of criticism covered in the sense that differential reinforcement includes what comes after the activity, not just what happens before it. Specifically, it addresses the rewards or punishments that follow criminal activity, whether those rewards come from friends, parents, or other members or institutions of society.

It is arguable that differential reinforcement theory may have the most empirical validity of any contemporary (nonintegrated) model of criminal offending, especially considering that studies have examined a variety of behaviors, ranging from drug use to property crimes to violence. The theoretical model has also been tested in samples across the United States as well as in other cultures, such as South Korea, with the evidence being quite supportive of the framework. Furthermore, a variety of age groups have been examined, ranging from teenagers to middle-aged adults to the elderly, with all studies providing support for the model.[25]

Specifically, researchers found that the major variables of the theory had a significant effect in explaining marijuana and alcohol use among adolescents.[26] The researchers concluded that the "study demonstrates that central learning concepts are amenable to meaningful questionnaire measurement and that social learning theory can be adequately tested with survey data."[27] Other studies have also supported the theory when attempting to understand delinquency, cigarette smoking, and drug use.[28] Therefore, the inclusion of three psychological learning models, namely, classical conditioning, operant conditioning, and modeling and imitation, appears to have made differential reinforcement one of the most valid theories of human behavior, especially in regard to crime.

---

[23]Mark Warr, "Parents, Peers, and Delinquency," *Social Forces* 72 (1993): 247–64; Mark Warr and Mark Stafford, "The Influence of Delinquent Peers: What They Think or What They Do?" *Criminology* 29 (1991): 851–66.

[24]Akers and Sellers, *Criminological Theories*, 98–101.

[25]See studies including Ronald Akers and Gang Lee, "A Longitudinal Test of Social Learning Theory: Adolescent Smoking," *Journal of Drug Issues* 26 (1996): 317–43; Ronald Akers and Gang Lee, "Age, Social Learning, and Social Bonding in Adolescent Substance Abuse," *Deviant Behavior* 19 (1999): 1–25; Ronald Akers and Anthony J. La Greca, "Alcohol Use among the Elderly: Social Learning, Community Context, and Life Events," in *Society, Culture, and Drinking Patterns Re-examined*, ed. David J. Pittman and Helene Raskin White (New Brunswick: Rutgers Center of Alcohol Studies, 1991), 242–62; Sunghyun Hwang, "Substance Use in a Sample of South Korean Adolescents: A Test of Alternative Theories," doctoral dissertation (Ann Arbor: University Microfilms, 2000); and Sunghyun Hwang and Ronald Akers, "Adolescent Substance Use in South Korea: A Cross-Cultural Test of Three Theories," in *Social Learning Theory and the Explanation of Crime: A Guide for the New Century*, ed. Ronald Akers and Gary F. Jensen (New Brunswick: Transaction, 2003).

[26]Ronald Akers, Marvin D. Krohn, Lonn Lanza-Kaduce, and Marcia Radosevich, "Social Learning and Deviant Behavior: A Specific Test of a General Theory," *American Sociological Review* 44 (1979): 638.

[27]Akers et al., "Social Learning and Deviant Behavior," 651.

[28]Richard Lawrence, "School Performance, Peers and Delinquency: Implications for Juvenile Justice," *Juvenile and Family Court Journal* 42 (1991): 59–69; Marvin Krohn, William Skinner, James Massey, and Ronald Akers, "Social Learning Theory and Adolescent Cigarette Smoking: A Longitudinal Study," *Social Problems* 32 (1985): 455–71; L. Thomas Winfree, Christine Sellers, and Dennis Clason, "Social Learning and Adolescent Deviance Abstention: Toward Understanding the Reasons for Initiating, Quitting, and Avoiding Drugs," *Journal of Quantitative Criminology* 9 (1993): 101–23; Ronald Akers and Gang Lee, "A Longitudinal Test of Social Learning Theory: Adolescent Smoking," *Journal of Drug Issues* 26 (1996): 317–43.

Neutralization Theory

Neutralization theory is associated with Gresham Sykes and David Matza's techniques of neutralization[29] and Matza's drift theory.[30] Like Sutherland, both Sykes and Matza thought that social learning influences delinquent behavior, but they also asserted that most criminals hold conventional beliefs and values. Specifically, Sykes and Matza argued that most criminals are still partially committed to the dominant social order. According to Sykes and Matza, youths are not immersed in a subculture that is committed to either extreme: complete conformity or complete nonconformity. Rather, these individuals vacillate, or drift, between these two extremes and are in a state of *transience*.[31]

While remaining partially committed to the conventional social order, youths can drift into criminal activity, Sykes and Matza claimed, and avoid feelings of guilt for these actions by justifying or rationalizing their behavior. This typically occurs in the teenage years, when social controls (parents, family, etc.) are at their weakest point and peer pressures and associations are at their highest level. Why is this called neutralization theory? The answer is that people justify and rationalize behavior through neutralizing it or making it appear not so serious. They make up situational excuses for behavior that they know is wrong to alleviate the guilt they feel for doing such immoral acts. In many ways, this resembles Freud's defense mechanisms, which allow us to forgive ourselves for the bad things we do even when we know they are wrong. The specific techniques of neutralization outlined by Sykes and Matza in 1957 are much like excuses for inappropriate behavior.

Techniques of Neutralization

Sykes and Matza identified methods or techniques of neutralization[32] that people use to justify their criminal behavior. These techniques allow people to neutralize or rationalize their criminal and delinquent acts by making themselves look as though they are conforming to the rules of conventional society. If individuals can create such rationalizations, then they are free to engage in criminal activities without serious damage to their consciences or self-images. According to Sykes and Matza, there are five common techniques of neutralization:

1. *Denial of responsibility:* Individuals may claim they were influenced by forces outside themselves and that they are not responsible or accountable for their behavior. For example, many youths blame their peers for their own behavior.

2. *Denial of injury:* This is the rationalization that no one was actually hurt by the offender's behavior. For instance, if someone steals from a store, he or she may rationalize this by saying that the store has insurance, so there is no direct victim.

3. *Denial of the victim:* Offenders see themselves as avengers and the victims as the wrongdoers. For example, some offenders believe that a person who disrespects or "disses" them deserves what he or she gets, even if it means serious injury.

4. *Condemnation of the condemners:* Offenders claim that the condemners (usually the authorities who catch them) are hypocrites. For instance, one may claim that police speed on the highway all the time, so everyone else is entitled to drive higher than the speed limit.

---

[29]Gresham M. Sykes and David Matza, "Techniques of Neutralization: A Theory of Delinquency," *American Sociological Review* 22 (1957): 664–70.

[30]David Matza, *Delinquency and Drift* (New York: Wiley, 1964).

[31]Ibid., 28.

[32]Sykes and Matza, "Techniques of Neutralization."

5. *Appeal to higher loyalties:* Offenders often overlook the norms of conventional society in favor of the rules of a belief they have or of a group to which they belong. For example, people who kill doctors who perform abortions tend to see their crimes as above the law because they are serving a higher power.

Although Sykes and Matza specifically labeled only five techniques of neutralization, it should be clear that there may be endless excuses people make up to rationalize behaviors they know are wrong. Techniques of neutralization have been applied to white-collar crime, for example. Several studies have examined the tendency to use such excuses to alleviate guilt for engaging in illegal corporate crime; they point out new types of excuses white-collar criminals use to justify their acts, techniques that were not discussed in Sykes and Matza's original formulation.[33]

Studies that have attempted to empirically test neutralization theory are, at best, inconsistent. For example, Agnew argued that there are essentially two general criticisms of studies that support neutralization theory.[34] First, theorists and researchers have noted that some neutralization techniques are much more difficult to measure than commitment to unconventional attitudes or norms.[35] The second major criticism is the concern that criminals may not use techniques of neutralization prior to committing a criminal offense but rather only after committing a crime. As estimated by previous studies, temporal ordering can be problematic in terms of causal implications when neutralization follows a criminal act.[36] This temporal ordering problem results from research conducted at a single point in time. Some would argue that the temporal ordering problem is not a major criticism because individuals may be predisposed to make up such rationalizations for their behavior regardless of whether they do it before or after the act of offending. Such a propensity may be related to low self-control theory, which we will examine later in this section.

Summary of Learning Theories

Learning theories tend to emphasize the social processes of how and why individuals learn criminal behavior. These theories also focus on the impact of significant others involved in the socialization process, such as family, friends, and teachers. Ultimately, empirical research has shown that learning theories are key in our understanding of criminal behavior, particularly in terms of whether criminal behavior is rewarded or punished. In summary, if individuals are taught and rewarded for performing criminal acts by the people they interact with on a day-to-day basis, they will in all likelihood engage in illegal activity.

 ## Control Theories

The learning theories discussed in the previous section assume that individuals are born with a conforming disposition. By contrast, control theories assume that all people would naturally commit crimes if it weren't for restraints on their innate selfish tendencies. Social control perspectives of criminal behavior thus assume that there is some

---

[33]For a review and a study on this topic, see Nicole Piquero, Stephen Tibbetts, and Michael Blankenship, "Examining the Role of Differential Association and Techniques of Neutralization in Explaining Corporate Crime," *Deviant Behavior* 26 (2005): 159–88. See also Lynne Vieraitis, Nicole Leeper Piquero, Alex R. Piquero, Stephen G. Tibbetts, and Michael B. Blankenship, "Do Women and Men Differ in Their Neutralizations of Corporate Crime?" *Criminal Justice Review* 37 (2012): 478–93.

[34]Robert Agnew, "The Techniques of Neutralization and Violence," *Criminology* 32 (1994): 563–64.

[35]W. William Minor, "The Neutralization of Criminal Offense," *Criminology* 18 (1980): 116; W. William Minor, "Neutralization as a Hardening Process: Considerations in the Modeling of Change," *Social Forces* 62 (1984): 995–1019. See also Roy L. Austin, "Commitment, Neutralization, and Delinquency," in *Juvenile Delinquency: Little Brother Grows Up*, ed. Theodore N. Ferdinand (Beverly Hills: Sage, 1977); and Quint C. Thurman, "Deviance and the Neutralization of Moral Commitment: An Empirical Analysis," *Deviant Behavior* 5 (1984): 291–304.

[36]Travis Hirschi, *Causes of Delinquency* (Berkeley: University of California Press, 1969), 207. See also Mark Pogrebin, Eric Poole, and Amos Martinez, "Accounts of Professional Misdeeds: The Sexual Exploitation of Clients by Psychotherapists," *Deviant Behavior* 13 (1992): 229–52; and John Hamlin, "The Misplaced Concept of Rational Choice in Neutralization Theory," *Criminology* 26 (1988): 425–38.

type of basic human nature and that all human beings exhibit antisocial tendencies. Such theories are concerned with why individuals don't commit crime or deviant behaviors. Control theorists ask questions like this: What is it about society and human interaction that causes people not to act on their impulses?

The assumption that people have innate antisocial tendencies is a controversial one because it is nearly impossible to test. Nevertheless, some recent evidence supports the idea that human beings are inherently selfish and antisocial by nature. Specifically, researchers have found that most individuals are oriented toward selfish and aggressive behaviors at an early age, with such behaviors peaking at the end of the second year (see Figure 8.1).[37]

An example of antisocial dispositions appearing early in life was reported by Tremblay and LeMarquand, who found that most young children's (particularly boys') aggressive behaviors peaked at age 27 months. These behaviors included hitting, biting, and kicking others.[38] Their research is not isolated; virtually all developmental experts acknowledge that toddlers exhibit a tendency to show aggressive behavior toward others. This line of research would seem to support the notion that people are predisposed toward antisocial, even criminal, behavior.

| Figure 8.1 | Frequencies of hitting, biting, and kicking at ages 2 to 12 years |

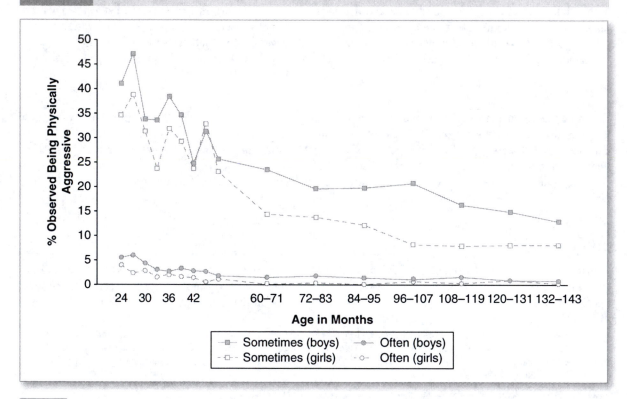

[37]Michael Lewis, Steven Alessandri, and Margaret Sullivan, "Expectancy, Loss of Control, and Anger in Young Infants," *Developmental Psychology* 25 (1990): 745–51; Albert Restoin, Dayana Rodriguez, V. Ulmann, and Hubert Montagner, "New Data on the Development of Communication Behavior in the Young Child with His Peers," *Recherches de Psychologie Sociale* 5 (1985): 31–56; Richard Tremblay, Christa Japel, Daniel Perusse, Pierre McDuff, Michel Boivin, Mark Zoccolillo, and Jacques Montplaisir, "The Search for the Age of 'Onset' of Physical Aggression: Rousseau and Bandura Revisited," *Criminal Behaviour and Mental Health* 9 (1999): 8–23.

[38]Richard Tremblay and David LeMarquand, "Individual Risk and Protective Factors," in *Child Delinquents: Development, Intervention, and Service Needs*, ed. Rolf Loeber and David Farrington (London: Sage, 2001): 137–64.

Control theorists do not necessarily assume that people are predisposed toward crime in a way that remains constant throughout life. On the contrary, research shows that most individuals begin to desist from such behaviors starting at around age two. This trend continues until approximately age five, with only the most aggressive individuals (i.e., chronic offenders) continuing such behavior at higher ages.

It is important to note that, at the same time selfish and aggressive behaviors decline, self-consciousness is formed. In addition, social emotions—such as shame, guilt, empathy, and pride—begin to appear.[39] This observation is critical because it is what separates control theories from the Classical School of criminology and the predispositional theories that we already discussed. According to control theories, without appropriate socialization, people act on their preprogrammed tendency toward crime and deviance.

In short, control theories claim that all individuals have natural tendencies to commit selfish, antisocial, and even criminal behavior. So, what is it that curbs this natural propensity? Many experts believe the best explanation is that individuals are socialized and controlled by social attachments and investments in conventional society. This assumption regarding the vital importance of early socialization is probably the primary reason why control theories are currently the most popular and accepted theories among criminologists.[40] We will now discuss several early examples of these control theories.

Early Control Theories of Human Behavior

Thomas Hobbes

Control theories are found in a variety of disciplines, including biology, psychology, and sociology. Perhaps the earliest significant use of social control in explaining deviant behavior is found in a perspective offered by the 17th-century Enlightenment philosopher Thomas Hobbes (see Section II). Hobbes claimed that the natural state of humanity is one of selfishness and self-centeredness to the point of constant chaos, characterized by a state of warfare between individuals. He stated that all individuals are inherently disposed to take advantage of others in order to improve their own personal well-being.[41]

However, Hobbes also claimed that the constant fear created by such selfishness results in humans rationally coming together to create binding contracts that will keep individuals from violating others' rights. Even with such controlling arrangements, however, Hobbes was clear that the selfish tendencies people exhibit can never be extinguished. In fact, they explain why punishments are necessary to maintain an established social contract among people.

Durkheim's Idea of Awakened Reflection and Collective Conscience

Consistent with Hobbes's view of individuals as naturally selfish, Durkheim later proposed a theory of social control in the late 1800s that suggested that humans have no internal mechanism to let them know when they are fulfilled.[42] To this end, Durkheim coined the terms *automatic spontaneity* and *awakened reflection*. Automatic spontaneity can be understood with reference to animals' eating habits. Specifically, animals stop eating when they are full, and they are content until they are hungry again; they don't start hunting right after they have filled their stomachs with food. In contrast, awakened reflection concerns the fact that humans do not have such an internal, regulatory mechanism. That is because people often acquire resources beyond what is immediately required. Durkheim went so far as to say

---

[39]For reviews of supporting studies, see June Price Tangney and K. W. Fischer, *Self-Conscious Emotions: The Psychology of Shame, Guilt, Embarrassment, and Pride* (New York: Guilford Press, 1995); and Michael Lewis, *Shame: The Exposed Self* (New York: Macmillan, 1992).

[40]Walsh and Ellis, "Political Ideology."

[41]Thomas Hobbes, *Leviathan* (Cambridge: Cambridge University Press, 1651/1904).

[42]Émile Durkheim, *The Division of Labor in Society* (New York: Free Press, 1893/1965); Émile Durkheim, *Suicide* (New York: Free Press, 1897/1951) (see chap. 6, n. 18).

that "our capacity for feeling is in itself an insatiable and bottomless abyss."[43] This is one of the reasons that Durkheim believed crime and deviance are quite normal, even essential, in any society.

Durkheim's awakened reflection has become commonly known as greed. People tend to favor better conditions and additional fulfillment because they apparently have no biological or psychological mechanism to limit such tendencies. As Durkheim noted, the selfish desires of humankind "are unlimited so far as they depend on the individual alone. . . . The more one has, the more one wants."[44] Thus, society must step in and provide the regulative force that keeps humans from acting too selfishly.

One of the primary elements of this regulative force is the *collective conscience*, which is the extent of similarities or likenesses that people share. For example, almost everyone can agree that homicide is a serious and harmful act that should be avoided in any civilized society. The notion of collective conscience can be seen as an early form of the idea of social bonding, which has become one of the dominant theories in criminology.[45]

According to Durkheim, the collective conscience serves many functions in society. One such function is the establishment of rules that keep individuals from following their natural tendencies toward selfish behavior. Durkheim also believed that crime allows people to unite together in opposition against deviants. In other words, crime and deviance allow conforming individuals to be bonded together in opposition against a common enemy, as can be seen in everyday life when groups come together to face opposition. This enemy consists of the deviants who have not internalized the code of the collective conscience.

Many of Durkheim's ideas hold true today. Just recall a traumatic incident you may have experienced with other strangers (e.g., being stuck in an elevator during a power outage, weathering a serious storm, or being involved in a traffic accident). Incidents such as these bring people together and permit a degree of bonding that would not take place in everyday life. Crime, Durkheim argued, serves a similar function.

How is all of this relevant today? Most control theorists claim that individuals commit crime and deviant acts not because they are lacking in any way but because certain controls have been weakened in their development. This assumption is consistent with Durkheim's theory, which we discussed previously (see Section VI).

Freud's Concepts of the Id, Superego, and Ego

Although psychoanalytic theory would seem to have few similarities with sociological positivistic theory, in this case, it is extremely complementary. One of Freud's most essential propositions is that all individuals are born with a tendency toward inherent drives and selfishness due to the id domain of the psyche (see Figure 8.2).[46] According to Freud, all people are born with equal amounts of id drives (e.g., libido, food) and motivations toward selfishness and greed. Freud said this inherent selfish tendency must be countered by controls produced from the development of the superego, which is the subconscious domain of the psyche that contains our conscience. According to Freud, the superego is formed through the interactions between a young infant or child and his or her significant others. As you can see, the control perspective has a long history in many philosophical and scientific disciplines.

These two drives of the subconscious domains of the id and superego are regulated, Freud thought, by the only conscious domain of the psyche: the ego. This ego mediates the battles between our innate drives (id) and our socialized constraints (superego); it represents our personality. There have been a number of applications of Freud's theoretical model to criminality, such as the concept of a deficient superego (due to a lack of early attachments) or

---

[43]Durkheim, *Suicide*, 246–47. Also, much of this discussion is adapted from Raymond Paternoster and Ronet Bachman, *Explaining Criminals and Crime* (Los Angeles: Roxbury, 2001) (see chap. 5, n. 10).

[44]Durkheim, *Suicide*, 254.

[45]A good discussion of Durkheim's concepts, particularly that of the collective conscience, can be found in Bernard et al., *Vold's Theoretical Criminology*, 124–39 (see chap. 2).

[46]Sigmund Freud, "The Ego and the Id," in *The Complete Psychological Works of Sigmund Freud*, Vol. 19, ed. James Strachey (London: Hogarth Press, 1923/1959).

| **Figure 8.2** | Freud's model of the three domains of the psyche |

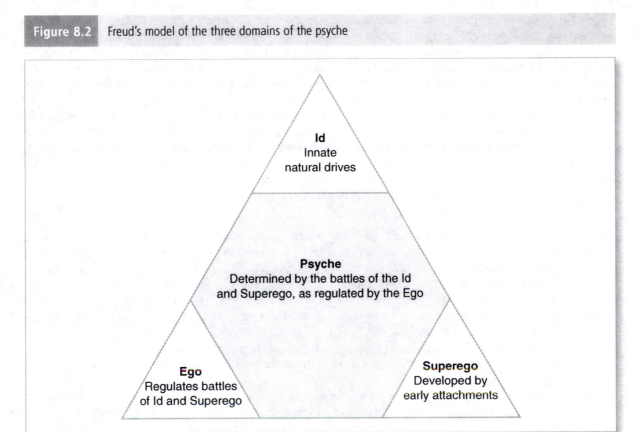

a weak ego (which fails to properly regulate the battle between the id and superego). The main point is that Freud was an early control theorist and that his theoretical model was highly influential among psychologists in the early 1900s as they tried to determine why certain individuals committed criminal offenses.[47]

Early Control Theories of Crime

Throughout the 1950s and 1960s, criminologists borrowed and built on some of the ideas just discussed. Until that time, most research in the criminological literature was dominated by the learning theories discussed earlier in this section, or social structure theories such as the Chicago School or Merton's strain theory (see Sections VI and VII). While early control theories may not be particularly popular in this day and age, they were vitally important in the sense that they laid the groundwork for future theoretical development.

Reiss's Control Theory

One of the first control theories of crime was proposed by Albert Reiss in 1951. Reiss claimed that delinquency was a consequence of weak ego or superego controls among juvenile probationers.[48] Reiss found no explicit motivation for delinquent activity. Rather, he thought it would occur in the absence of controls or restraints against such behavior.

[47]Ibid.

[48]Albert Reiss, "Delinquency as the Failure of Personal and Social Controls," *American Sociological Review* 16 (1951): 196–207.

Like Freud, Reiss believed that the family was the primary source through which deviant predispositions were discouraged. Furthermore, Reiss claimed that a sound family environment would provide for an individual's needs and the essential emotional bonds that are so important in socializing individuals. Another important factor in Reiss's model was close supervision, not only by the family but also by the community. He said that individuals must be closely monitored for delinquent behavior and adequately disciplined when they break the rules.

Personal factors, such as the ability to restrain one's impulses and delay gratification, were also important in Reiss's framework. These concepts are very similar to later, more modern concepts of control theory, which have been consistently supported by empirical research.[49] For this reason, Reiss was ahead of his time when he first proposed his control theory. Although the direct tests of Reiss's theory have provided only partial support for it, his influence is apparent in many contemporary criminological theories.[50]

Toby's Concept of Stake in Conformity

Soon after Reiss's theory was presented, a similar theory was developed. In 1957, Jackson Toby proposed a theory of delinquency and gangs.[51] He claimed that individuals were more inclined to act on their natural inclinations when the controls on them were weak. Like most other control theorists, Toby claimed that such inclinations toward deviance were distributed equally across all individuals. Furthermore, he emphasized the concept of a stake in conformity that supposedly prevents most people from committing crime. The stake in conformity Toby was referring to is the extent to which individuals have investments in conventional society. In other words, how much is a person willing to risk when he or she violates the law?

Studies have shown that stake in conformity is one of the most influential factors in individuals' decisions to offend. People who have nothing to lose are much more likely to take risks and violate others' rights than those who have relatively more invested in social institutions.[52]

One distinguishing feature of Toby's theory is his emphasis on peer influences in terms of both motivating and inhibiting antisocial behavior depending on whether most peers have low or high stakes in conformity. Toby's stake in conformity has been used effectively in subsequent control theories of crime.

Nye's Control Theory

A year after Toby introduced the stake in conformity, F. Ivan Nye proposed a relatively comprehensive control theory that placed a strong focus on the family.[53] Following the assumptions of early control theorists, Nye claimed that there was no significant positive force that caused delinquency because such antisocial tendencies are universal and would be found in virtually everyone if not for certain controls usually found in the home.

Nye's theory consisted of three primary components of control. The first component was internal control, which is formed through social interaction. This socialization, he claimed, assists in the development of a conscience. Nye further claimed that if individuals are not given adequate resources and care, they will follow their natural tendencies toward doing what is necessary to protect their interests.

---

[49]For a comprehensive review of studies of low self-control, see Travis Pratt and Frank Cullen, "The Empirical Status of Gottfredson and Hirschi's General Theory of Crime: A Meta-analysis," *Criminology* 38 (2000): 931–64.

[50]See Bernard et al., *Vold's Theoretical Criminology*, 202–3.

[51]Jackson Toby, "Social Disorganization and Stake in Conformity: Complementary Factors in the Predatory Behavior of Hoodlums," *Journal of Criminal Law, Criminology, and Police Science* 48 (1957): 12–17.

[52]Hirschi, *Causes of Delinquency*; Robert Sampson and John Laub, *Crime in the Making: Pathways and Turning Points in Life* (Cambridge: Harvard University Press, 1993).

[53]F. Ivan Nye, *Family Relationships and Delinquent Behavior* (New York: Wiley, 1958).

Nye's second component of control was direct control, which consists of a wide range of constraints on individual propensities to commit deviant acts. Direct control includes numerous types of sanctions, such as jail and ridicule, and the restriction of one's chances to commit criminal activity. Nye's third component of control was indirect control, which occurs when individuals are strongly attached to their early caregivers. For most children, it is through an intense and strong relationship with their parents or guardians that they establish an attachment to conventional society. However, Nye suggested that when the needs of an individual are not met by their caregivers, inappropriate behavior can result.

As shown in Figure 8.3, Nye predicted a U-shaped curve of parental controls in predicting delinquency. Specifically, he argued that either no controls (i.e., complete freedom) or too much control (i.e., no freedom at all) would predict the most chronic delinquency. He believed that a healthy balance of freedom and parental control was the best strategy for inhibiting criminal activity. Some recent research supports Nye's prediction.[54] Contemporary control theories, such as Tittle's control-balance theory, draw heavily on Nye's idea of having a healthy balance of controls and freedom.[55]

Reckless's Containment Theory

Another control theory, known as containment theory, has been proposed by Walter Reckless.[56] This theory emphasizes both inner containment and outer containment, which can be viewed as internal and external controls. Reckless broke from traditional assumptions of social control theories by identifying predictive factors that push or pull individuals toward antisocial behavior. However, the focus of his theory remained on the controlling elements, which can be seen in the emphasis placed on containment in the theory's name.

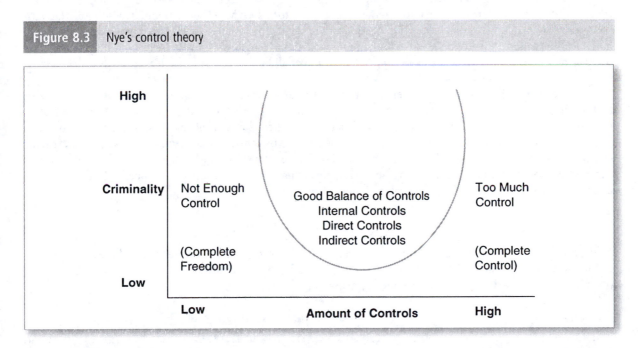

Figure 8.3 Nye's control theory

---

[54]Ruth Seydlitz, "Complexity in the Relationships among Direct and Indirect Parental Controls and Delinquency," *Youth and Society* 24 (1993): 243–75.

[55]Charles Tittle, *Control Balance: Toward a General Theory of Deviance* (Boulder: Westview, 1995).

[56]Walter Reckless, *The Crime Problem*, 4th ed. (New York: Appleton-Century-Crofts, 1967).

Reckless claimed that individuals can be pushed into delinquency by their social environment, such as by a lack of opportunities for education or employment. Furthermore, he pointed out that some individual factors, such as brain disorders or risk-taking personalities, could push some people to commit criminal behavior. Reckless also noted that some individuals could be pulled into criminal activity by hanging out with delinquent peers, watching too much violence on television, and so on. All told, Reckless went beyond the typical control theory assumption of inborn tendencies. In addition to these natural dispositions toward deviant behavior, containment theory proposes that extra pushes and pulls can motivate people to commit crime.

Reckless further claimed that the pushes and pulls toward criminal behavior could be enough to force individuals into criminal activity unless they are sufficiently contained or controlled. Reckless claimed that such containment should be both internal and external. By *internal containment*, he meant building a person's sense of self, which helps the person resist the temptations of criminal activity. According to Reckless, other forms of internal containment include the ability to internalize societal norms. With respect to *external containment*, Reckless claimed that social organizations, such as school, church, and other institutions, are essential in building bonds that inhibit individuals from being pushed or pulled into criminal activity.

Reckless offered a visual image of containment theory, which we present in Figure 8.4. The outer circle (Circle 1) in the figure represents the social realm of pressures and pulls (e.g., peer pressure), whereas the innermost circle (Circle 4) symbolizes a person's individual-level pushes to commit crime, such as predispositions or personality traits that are linked to crime. In between these two circles are the two layers of controls, external containment (Circle 2) and internal containment (Circle 3). The structure of Figure 8.4 and the examples included in each circle are those specifically noted by Reckless.[57]

While some studies have shown general support for containment theory, others offer more support for some components, such as internalization of rules, than for other factors, such as self-perception, in accounting for variations in delinquency.[58] External factors may be more important than internal ones. Furthermore, some studies have noted weaker support for Reckless's theory among minorities and females, who may be more influenced by their peers or other influences. Thus, the model appears to be most valid for White males, at least according to empirical studies.[59]

One of the problems with containment theory is that it does not go far enough toward specifying the factors that are important in predicting criminality, especially regarding specific groups of individuals. For example, an infinite number of concepts could potentially be categorized either as a push or pull toward criminality or as an inner or outer containment of criminality. Thus, the theory could be considered too broad or vague and not specific enough to be of practical value. To Reckless's credit, however, containment theory has increased the exposure of control theories of criminal behavior. And although support for containment theory has been mixed, there is no doubt that it has influenced other, more recent control theories.[60]

Modern Social Control Theories

As the previous sections attest, control theory has been around in various forms for some time. Modern social control theories build on these earlier versions and add levels of depth and sophistication. Two modern social control theories are Matza's drift theory and Hirschi's social bonding theory.

---

[57]Ibid., 479.

[58]Richard Lawrence, "School Performance, Containment Theory, and Delinquent Behavior," *Youth and Society* 7 (1985): 69–95; Richard A. Dodder and Janet R. Long, "Containment Theory Reevaluated: An Empirical Explication," *Criminal Justice Review* 5 (1980): 74–84.

[59]William E. Thompson and Richard A. Dodder, "Containment Theory and Juvenile Delinquency: A Reevaluation through Factor Analysis," *Adolescence* 21 (1986): 365–76.

[60]Ronald L. Akers, *Criminological Theories: Introduction, Evaluation, and Application*, 3rd ed. (Los Angeles: Roxbury, 2000), 103–4.

Figure 8.4	Reckless's containment theory

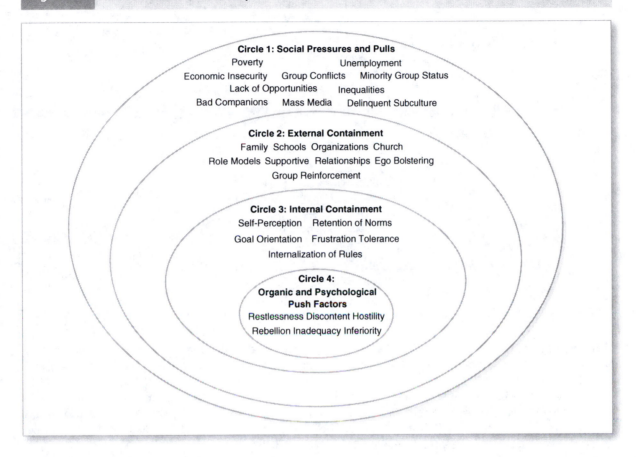

Circle 1: Social Pressures and Pulls
Poverty   Unemployment
Economic Insecurity   Group Conflicts   Minority Group Status
Lack of Opportunities   Inequalities
Bad Companions   Mass Media   Delinquent Subculture

Circle 2: External Containment
Family Schools Organizations Church
Role Models Supportive Relationships Ego Bolstering
Group Reinforcement

Circle 3: Internal Containment
Self-Perception   Retention of Norms
Goal Orientation   Frustration Tolerance
Internalization of Rules

Circle 4:
Organic and Psychological
Push Factors
Restlessness Discontent Hostility
Rebellion Inadequacy Inferiority

Matza's Drift Theory

The theory of drift, or drift theory, presented by David Matza in 1964, claims that individuals offend at certain times in their lives when social controls—such as parental supervision, employment, and family ties—are weakened.[61] In developing his theory, Matza criticized earlier theories and their tendency to predict too much crime. For example, the Chicago School would incorrectly predict that all individuals in bad neighborhoods will commit crime. Likewise, strain theory predicts that all poor individuals will commit crime. Obviously, this is not true. Thus, Matza claimed that there is a degree of determinism (i.e., Positive School) in human behavior but also a significant amount of free will (i.e., Classical School). He called this perspective soft determinism, which is the gray area between free will and determinism. This is illustrated in Figure 8.5.

Returning to the basics of Matza's theory, he claimed that individuals offend at the time in life when social controls are most weakened. As is well known, social controls are most weakened for most individuals during the teenage years. At this time, parents and other caretakers stop having a constant supervisory role, and at the same time, teenagers generally do not have too many responsibilities—such as careers or children—that would inhibit

---

[61]Matza, *Delinquency and Drift.*

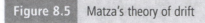

Figure 8.5 Matza's theory of drift

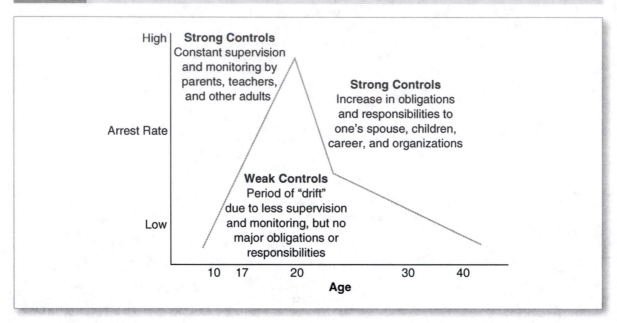

them from experimenting with deviance. This is very consistent with the well-known age–crime relationship; most individuals who are arrested experience this in their teenage years.[62] Once sufficient ties are developed, people tend to mature out of criminal lifestyles.

Matza further claimed that when supervision is absent and ties are minimal, the majority of individuals are the most free to do what they want. Where, then, does the term *drift* come from? During the times when people have few ties and obligations, they will drift in and out of delinquency, Matza proposed. He pointed out that previous theories were unsuccessful in explaining this age–crime relationship:

> Most theories of delinquency take no account of maturational reform; those that do often do so at the expense of violating their own assumptions regarding the constrained delinquent.[63]

Matza insisted that drifting is not the same as a commitment to a life of crime. Instead, it is experimenting with questionable behavior and then rationalizing it. The way youths rationalize behavior that they know to be wrong is through learning the techniques of neutralization discussed earlier.

Drift theory goes on to say that individuals do not reject the conventional normative structure. On the contrary, much offending is based on neutralizing or adhering to subterranean values, which young people have been socialized to use as a means of circumventing conventional values. This is basically the same as asserting one's independence, which tends to occur with a vengeance during the teenage years.

[62]*OJJDP Statistical Briefing Book.* Unpublished arrest data for 1980–1997 from the Federal Bureau of Investigation for 1998, 1999, and 2000 from *Crime in the United States* reports (Washington, DC: Government Printing Office, 1999, 2000, and 2001, respectively).

[63]"Age-arrest rate curve" is loosely based on data provided by Federal Bureau of Investigation, *Crime in the United States* report (Washington, DC: Government Printing Office, 1997).

Subterranean values are quite prevalent and underlie many aspects of our culture, which is why Matza's drift theory is also classified as a learning theory. For example, while it is conventional to believe that violence is wrong, boxing matches and sports that commonly lead to injury are some of the most popular spectator activities. Such phenomena create an atmosphere that readily allows neutralization or rationalization of criminal activity.

We will see other forms of subterranean values when we discuss risk-taking and low self-control later in this section. In many contexts, such as business, risk-taking and aggressiveness are seen as desirable characteristics, so many individuals are influenced by such subterranean values. This, according to Matza, adds to individuals' likelihood of drifting into crime and delinquency.

Matza's theory of drift seems sensible on its face, but empirical research examining the theory has shown mixed results.[64] One of the primary criticisms of Matza's theory, which even he acknowledged, is that it does not explain the most chronic offenders, the people who are responsible for the vast majority of serious, violent crimes. Chronic offenders often offend long before and well past their teenage years, which clearly limits the predictive value of Matza's theory.

Despite its shortcomings, Matza's drift theory appears to explain why many people offend exclusively during their teenage and young adult years but then grow out of it. Also, the theory is highly consistent with several of the ideas presented by control theorists, including the assumption that (a) selfish tendencies are universal, (b) these tendencies are inhibited by socialization and social controls, and (c) the selfish tendencies appear at times when controls are weakest. The theory goes beyond previous control theories by adding the concepts of soft determinism, neutralization, and subterranean values, as well as the idea that, in many contexts, selfish and aggressive behaviors are not wrong but actually desirable.

Hirschi's Social Bonding Theory

Perhaps the most influential social control theory was presented by Travis Hirschi in 1969.[65] Hirschi's model of social bonding theory takes an assumption from Durkheim that "we are all animals, and thus naturally capable of committing criminal acts."[66] However, as Hirschi acknowledged, most humans can be adequately socialized to become tightly bonded to conventional entities, such as families, schools, and communities. Hirschi said that the more strongly a person is bonded to conventional society, the less prone to engaging in crime he or she will be. More specifically, the stronger the social bond, the lower the likelihood that an individual will commit criminal offenses.

As shown in Figure 8.6, Hirschi's social bond is made up of four elements: (a) attachment, (b) commitment, (c) involvement, and (d) moral belief. The stronger or more developed the person in each of the four elements, the lower the likelihood that he or she will commit crime. Let us now consider each element in detail.

The most important factor in the social bond is *attachment*, which consist of affectionate bonds between an individual and his or her significant others. Attachment is vitally important for the internalization of conventional values. Hirschi said, "The essence of internalization of norms, conscience, or superego thus lies in the attachment of the individual to others."[67] Hirschi made it clear, as did Freud, that strong, early attachments are the most important factor in developing a social bond. The other constructs in the social bond—commitment, involvement, and belief—are contingent on adequate attachment to others, he argued. That is, without healthy attachments, especially early in life, the probability of acting inappropriately increases.

---

[64] See Bernard et al., *Vold's Theoretical Criminology*, 205–7.

[65] Hirschi, *Causes of Delinquency* (see chap. 6, n. 30).

[66] Ibid., 31, in which Hirschi cites Durkheim.

[67] Ibid., 18.

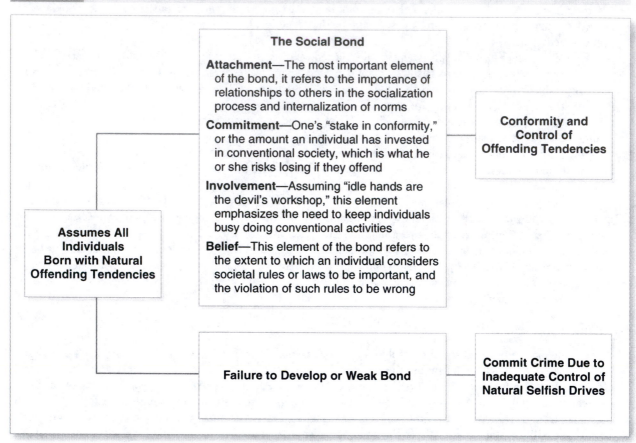

Figure 8.6   Hirschi's social bonding theory

Commitment, the second element of Hirschi's social bond, is the investment a person has in conventional society. This has been explained as one's stake in conformity, or what is at risk of being lost if one gets caught committing crime. If people feel they have much to lose by committing crime, they will probably not do it. In contrast, if someone has nothing to lose, what is to prevent that person from doing something he or she may be punished for? The answer is, of course, not much. And this, some theorists claim, is why it is difficult to control so-called chronic offenders. Trying to instill a commitment to conventional society in such individuals is extremely difficult.

Another element of the social bond is *involvement*, which is the time spent in conventional activities. The assumption is that time spent in constructive activities will reduce time devoted to illegal behaviors. This element of the bond goes back to the old adage that "idle hands are the devil's workshop."[68] Hirschi claimed that participating in conventional activities can inhibit delinquent and criminal activity.

The last element of the social bond is *beliefs*, which have generally been interpreted as moral beliefs concerning the laws and rules of society. This is one of the most examined and consistently supported aspects of the social bond. Basically, individuals who feel that a course of action is against their moral beliefs are much less likely to pursue it

[68]Ibid., 22.

than individuals who don't see a breach of morality in such behavior. For example, we all probably know some people who see drunk driving as a very serious offense because of the injury and death it can cause. However, we also probably know individuals who don't see a problem with such behavior. The same can be said about speeding in a car, shoplifting from a store, or using marijuana; people differ in their beliefs about most forms of criminal activity.

Hirschi's theory has been tested by numerous researchers and has, for the most part, been supported.[69] However, one criticism is that the components of the social bond may predict criminality only if they are defined in a certain way. For example, with respect to the involvement element of the bond, studies have shown that not all conventional activities are equal when it comes to preventing delinquency. Only academic or religious activities seem to have consistent effects in inhibiting delinquency. In contrast, many studies show that teenagers who date or play sports actually have an increased risk of committing crime.[70]

Another major criticism of Hirschi's theory is that the effect of attachment on crime depends on to whom one is attached. Studies have clearly and consistently shown that attachment to delinquent peers is a strong predictor of criminal activity.

Finally, some evidence indicates that social bonding theory may better explain why individuals start offending than why they continue or escalate in their offending. One reason for this is that Hirschi's theory does not elaborate on what occurs after an individual commits criminal activity. This is likely the primary reason why some of the more complex, integrated theories of crime often attribute the initiation of delinquency to a breakdown in the social bond. However, other theories (such as differential reinforcement) are typically seen as better predictors of what happens after the initial stages of the criminal career.[71]

Despite the criticism it has received, Hirschi's social bonding theory is still one of the most accepted theories of criminal behavior.[72] It is a relatively convincing explanation for criminality because of the consistent support that it has found among samples of people taken from all over the world.[73]

Integrated Social Control Theories

Although we will review integrated theories in detail in Section XI, it is worthwhile to briefly discuss the two integrated models that most incorporate the control perspective into their frameworks. These two integrated models are control-balance theory and power-control theory. Both have received considerable attention in the criminological literature. Other integrated theories that incorporate control theory to a lesser extent include Braithwaite's shaming theory and Sampson and Laub's life-course theory. These will be covered in more detail in Sections XI and XII.

Tittle's Control-Balance Theory

Presented by Charles Tittle in 1995, control-balance theory proposes that (a) the amount of control to which one is subjected and (b) the amount of control one can exercise determine the probability that deviance will occur. The balance between these two types of control, he argued, can even predict the type of behavior that is likely to be committed.[74]

---

[69]For a review, see Akers, *Criminological Theories*, 105–10.

[70]Ibid.

[71]Delbert Elliott, David Huizinga, and Suzanne Ageton, *Explaining Delinquency and Drug Use* (Beverly Hill: Sage, 1985).

[72]Walsh and Ellis, "Political Ideology."

[73]Dennis Wong, "Pathways to Delinquency in Hong Kong and Guangzhou, South China," *International Journal of Adolescence and Youth* 10 (2001): 91–115; Alexander Vazsonyi and Martin Killias, "Immigration and Crime among Youth in Switzerland," *Criminal Justice and Behavior* 28 (2001): 329–66; Manuel Eisner, "Crime, Problem Drinking, and Drug Use: Patterns of Problem Behavior in Cross-National Perspective," *Annals of the American Academy of Political and Social Science* 580 (2002): 201–25.

[74]Charles Tittle, *Control Balance: Toward a General Theory of Deviance* (Boulder: Westview, 1995).

Tittle argued that a person is least likely to offend when he or she has a balance of controlling and being controlled. Furthermore, the likelihood of offending increases when these become unbalanced. If individuals are more controlled (Tittle calls this *control deficit*), then the theory predicts that they will commit predatory or defiant acts. In contrast, if an individual possesses an excessive level of control (Tittle calls this *control surplus*), then he or she will be more likely to commit acts of exploitation or decadence. Note that excessive control is not the same as excessive self-control. Tittle argues that people who are controlling, that is, who have excessive control over others, will be predisposed toward inappropriate activities.

Initial empirical tests of control-balance theory have reported mixed results, with both surpluses and deficits predicting the same types of deviance.[75] In addition, researchers have uncovered differing effects of the control-balance ratio on two types of deviance that are contingent on gender. This finding is consistent with the gender-specific support found for Reckless's containment theory, described earlier in this section.[76]

Hagan's Power-Control Theory

Power-control theory is an integrated theory that was proposed by John Hagan and his colleagues.[77] The primary focus of this theory is on the level of control and patriarchal attitudes, as well as structure in the household, which are influenced by parental positions in the workforce. Power-control theory assumes that, in households where the mothers and fathers have relatively similar levels of power at work (i.e., balanced households), mothers will be less likely to exert control on their daughters. These balanced households will be less likely to experience gender differences in the criminal offending of the children. However, households in which mothers and fathers have dissimilar levels of power in the workplace (i.e., unbalanced households) are more likely to suppress criminal activity in daughters. In addition, assertiveness and risky activity among the males in the house will be encouraged. This assertiveness and risky activity may be a precursor to crime.

Most empirical tests of power-control have provided moderate support for the theory, while more recent studies have further specified the validity of the theory in different contexts.[78] For example, one recent study reported that the influence of mothers, not fathers, on sons had the greatest impact on reducing the delinquency of young males.[79] Another researcher found that differences in perceived threats of embarrassment and formal sanctions varied between more patriarchal and less patriarchal households.[80] Finally, studies have also started measuring the effect of patriarchal attitudes on crime and delinquency.[81] Power-control theory is a good example of a social control

---

[75]Alex Piquero and Matthew Hickman, "An Empirical Test of Tittle's Control Balance Theory," *Criminology* 37 (1999): 319–42; Matthew Hickman and Alex Piquero, "Exploring the Relationships between Gender, Control Balance, and Deviance," *Deviant Behavior* 22 (2001): 323–51.

[76]Hickman et al., "Exploring the Relationships," 323–51.

[77]John Hagan, *Structural Criminology* (Newark: Rutgers University Press, 1989); John Hagan, A. Gillis, and J. Simpson, "The Class Structure of Gender and Delinquency: Toward a Power-Control Theory of Common Delinquent Behavior," *American Journal of Sociology* 90 (1985): 1151–78; John Hagan, A. Gillis, and J. Simpson, "Clarifying and Extending Power-Control Theory," *American Journal of Sociology* 95 (1990): 1024–37; John Hagan, J. Simpson, and A. Gillis, "Class in the Household: A Power-Control Theory of Gender and Delinquency," *American Journal of Sociology* 92 (1987): 788–816.

[78]Hagen et al., "Class in the Household," 788–816; B. McCarthy and John Hagan, "Gender, Delinquency, and the Great Depression: A Test of Power-Control Theory," *Canadian Review of Sociology and Anthropology* 24 (1987): 153–77; Merry Morash and Meda Chesney-Lind, "A Reformulation and Partial Test of the Power-Control Theory of Delinquency," *Justice Quarterly* 8 (1991): 347–77; Simon Singer and Murray Levine, "Power-Control Theory, Gender, and Delinquency: A Partial Replication with Additional Evidence on the Effects of Peers," *Criminology* 26 (1988): 627–47.

[79]B. McCarthy, John Hagan, and T. Woodward, "In the Company of Women: Structure and Agency in a Revised Power-Control Theory of Gender and Delinquency," *Criminology* 37 (1999): 761–88.

[80]Brenda Sims Blackwell, "Perceived Sanction Threats, Gender, and Crime: A Test and Elaboration of Power-Control Theory," *Criminology* 38 (2000): 439–88.

[81]Blackwell, "Perceived Sanction Threats," 439–88; Kristin Bates and Chris Bader, "Family Structure, Power-Control Theory, and Deviance: Extending Power-Control Theory to Include Alternate Family Forms," *Western Criminology Review* 4 (2003).

theory in that it is consistent with the idea that individuals must be socialized and that the gender differences in such socialization make a difference in how people will act throughout life.

A General Theory of Crime: Low Self-Control

In 1990, Travis Hirschi, along with his colleague Michael Gottfredson, proposed a general theory of low self-control, which is often referred to as *the general theory of crime*.[82] This theory has led to a significant amount of debate and research in the field since its appearance—more than any other contemporary theory of crime. Like previous control theories of crime, this theory assumes that individuals are born predisposed toward selfish, self-centered activities and that only effective child rearing and socialization can create self-control. Without such adequate socialization (i.e., social controls) and reduction of criminal opportunities, individuals will follow their natural tendencies to become selfish predators. Furthermore, the general theory of crime assumes that self-control must be established by age 10. If it has not formed by that time, then, according to the theory, individuals will forever exhibit low self-control.

Although Gottfredson and Hirschi still attribute the formation of controls to the socialization processes, the distinguishing characteristic of this theory is its emphasis on the individual's ability to control himself or herself. That is, the general theory of crime assumes that people can take a degree of control over their own decisions and, within certain limitations, control themselves.

The general theory of crime is accepted as one of the most valid theories of crime.[83] This is probably because it identifies only one primary factor that causes criminality—low self-control. But, low self-control theory may actually implicate a series of personality traits and behavior, including risk-taking, impulsiveness, self-centeredness, short-term orientation, and quick temper. For example, recent research has supported the idea that inadequate child-rearing practices tend to result in lower levels of self-control among children and that these low levels produce various risky behaviors, including criminal activity.[84] Such propensities toward low self-control can manifest in varying forms across an individual's life. For example, teenagers with low self-control will likely hit or steal from peers, and as they grow older, they will be more likely to gamble or cheat on taxes.

Psychological Aspects of Low Self-Control

Criminologists have recently claimed that low self-control may be due to the emotional disposition of individuals. For example, one study showed that the effects of low self-control on intentions to commit drunk driving and shoplifting were tied to individuals' perceptions of pleasure and shame. More specifically, the findings of this study showed that individuals who had low self-control had significantly lower levels of anticipated shame but significantly higher levels of perceived pleasure in committing both drunk driving and shoplifting.[85] These results suggest that individuals who lack self-control will be oriented toward gaining pleasure and taking advantage of resources and toward avoiding negative emotional feelings (e.g., shame) that are primarily induced through socialization.

---

[82]Michael Gottfredson and Travis Hirschi, *A General Theory of Crime* (Palo Alto: Stanford University Press, 1990).

[83]For an excellent review of studies regarding low self-control theory, see Travis Pratt and Frank Cullen, "The Empirical Status of Gottfredson and Hirschi's General Theory of Crime: A Meta-analysis," *Criminology* 38 (2000): 931–64. For critiques of this theory, see Ronald Akers, "Self-Control as a General Theory of Crime," *Journal of Quantitative Criminology* 7 (1991): 201–11. For a study that demonstrates the high popularity of the theory, see Walsh and Ellis, "Political Ideology."

[84]Carter Hay, "Parenting, Self-Control, and Delinquency: A Test of Self-Control Theory," *Criminology* 39 (2001): 707–36; Karen Hayslett-McCall and Thomas Bernard, "Attachment, Masculinity, and Self-Control: A Theory of Male Crime Rates," *Theoretical Criminology* 6 (2002): 5–33.

[85]Alex Piquero and Stephen Tibbetts, "Specifying the Direct and Indirect Effects of Low Self-Control and Situational Factors in Offenders' Decision Making: Toward a More Complete Model of Rational Offending," *Justice Quarterly* 13 (1996): 481–510.

Physiological Aspects of Low Self-Control

Low self-control can also be tied to physiological factors. Interestingly, research has shown that chronic offenders show greater arousal toward danger and risk-taking than toward the possibility of punishment.[86] This arousal has been measured by monitoring brain activity in response to certain stimuli. The research suggests that individuals are encouraged to commit risky behavior due to physiological mechanisms that reward their risk-taking activities by releasing pleasure chemicals in their brains.[87]

In a similar vein, recent studies show that chronic gamblers tend to get a physiological high (such as a sudden, intense release of brain chemicals similar to that following a small dose of cocaine) from the activity of betting, particularly when they are gambling with their own money and risking a personal loss.[88] Undoubtedly, a minority of individuals thrive off of risk-taking behaviors significantly more than others. This suggests that physiological as well as psychological differences may explain why certain individuals favor risky behaviors.

Researchers have also found that criminal offenders generally perceive a significantly lower level of internal sanctions (e.g., shame, guilt, embarrassment) than do nonoffenders.[89] So, in summary, a select group of individuals appear to derive physiological and psychological pleasure from engaging in risky behaviors while simultaneously being less likely to be inhibited by internal emotional sanctions. Such a combination, Gottfredson and Hirschi claimed, is very dangerous and helps explain why impulsive individuals often end up in prison.

Finally, the psychological and physiological aspects of low self-control may help explain the gender differences observed between males and females. Specifically, studies show that females are significantly more likely than males to experience internal emotional sanctioning for offenses they have committed.[90] In other words, there appears to be something innately different about males and females that helps explain the differing levels of self-control each possesses.

Summary of Control Theories

Control perspectives are among the oldest and most respected explanations of criminal activity. The fundamental assumption that humans have an inborn, selfish disposition that must be controlled through socialization distinguishes control theories from other theories of crime. The control perspective's longevity as one of the most popular criminological theories demonstrates its legitimacy as an explanation of behavior. This is likely due to the dedication and efforts of criminologists who are constantly developing new and improved versions of control theory, many of which we have discussed here.

 Policy Implications

Numerous policy implications can be taken from the various types of social learning and control theories presented here. We will concentrate on those that are likely to be most effective and pragmatic in helping to reduce criminal behavior.

A number of policy implications can be drawn from the various learning models. Perhaps their most important suggestion is to supply many opportunities for positive reinforcements, or rewards, for good behavior. Such

---

[86]Adrian Raine, *The Psychopathology of Crime* (San Diego: Academic Press, 1993).

[87]Anthony Walsh, *Biosocial Criminology: Introduction and Integration* (Cincinnati: Anderson, 2002).

[88]Christopher D. Fiorillo, Phillippe N. Tobler, and Wolfram Schultz, "Discrete Coding of Reward Probability and Uncertainty by Dopamine Neurons," *Science* 299 (2003): 1898–1902.

[89]Harold Grasmick and Robert Bursik, "Conscience, Significant Others, and Rational Choice: Extending the Deterrence Model," *Law and Society Review* 24 (1990): 837–61; Stephen Tibbetts, "Shame and Rational Choice in Offending Decisions," *Criminal Justice and Behavior* 24 (1997): 234–55.

[90]Stephen Tibbetts and Denise Herz, "Gender Differences in Factors of Social Control and Rational Choice," *Deviant Behavior* 17 (1996): 183–208.

reinforcements have been found to be far more effective than punishments, especially among criminal offenders.[91] Furthermore, studies show that the most effective rehabilitation programs for offenders should be based on a cognitive behavioral approach, which teaches individuals to think before they act.[92] Furthermore, evaluation studies have shown that simply grouping offenders together for counseling or peer-therapy sessions is not an effective strategy; rather, it appears that such programs often show no effect, or actually increase offending among participants, perhaps because they tend to learn more antisocial attitudes from such sessions.[93] Ultimately, offender programs that emphasize positive reinforcements and are based on a cognitive behavioral approach show the greatest success.

Regarding the policy implications of control theories, we will focus on the early social bonding that must take place and the need for more parental supervision to help an individual develop or learn self-control and create healthy, strong bonds to conventional society. Most control theories assume that individuals are predisposed to criminal behavior, so the primary focus of programs should be to reduce this propensity toward such behavior. According to most control perspectives, the most important factor in preventing or controlling this predisposition involves early parenting and building attachments or ties to prosocial aspects of the individual's environment.

Thus, perhaps the most important policy recommendation is to increase the ties between early caregivers or parents and their children. A variety of programs try to increase the relationship and bonding that takes place between infants and young children and their parents, as well as to monitor the supervision that takes place in this dynamic. Such programs have consistently been shown to be effective in preventing and reducing criminality in high-risk children, especially when such programs involve home visitations by health care providers (e.g., nurses) and social care experts (e.g., social workers).[94] By visiting the homes of high-risk children, workers can provide more direct, personal attention in aiding and counseling parents about how best to nurture, monitor, and discipline their young children.[95] These types of programs may lead to more control over behavior while building stronger bonds to society and developing self-control among these high-risk individuals.

 ## Conclusion

In this section, we have discussed a wide range of theories that may appear to be quite different. However, all of the criminological theories here share an emphasis on social processes as the primary reason why individuals commit crime. This is true of the learning theories, which propose that people are taught to commit crime, as well as the control theories, which claim that people offend naturally and must be taught not to commit crime. Despite their seemingly opposite assumptions of human behavior, the fact is that learning and control theories both identify socialization, or the lack thereof, as the key cause of criminal behavior.

We also examined some of the key policy recommendations that have been suggested by both of these theoretical perspectives. Specifically, we noted that programs that simply group offenders together only seem to reinforce their tendency to offend, whereas programs that take a cognitive behavioral approach and use many reward opportunities appear to have some effect in reducing recidivism. Also, we concluded that programs that involve home visitations by experts (e.g., nurses, counselors) tend to aid in developing more effective parenting and building social bonds among young individuals, which helps them to build strong attachments to society and develop self-control.

[91]Van Voorhis and Salisbury, *Correctional Counseling.*

[92]Ibid.

[93]Ibid. See also reviews of such programs in Richard J. Lundman, *Prevention and Control of Juvenile Delinquency* (New York: Oxford University Press, 1993); and Akers and Sellers, *Criminological Theories*, 101–8.

[94]Joycen Carmouche and Joretta Jones, "Her Children, Their Future," *Federal Prisons Journal* 1 (1989): 23, 26–27.

[95]For a review, see Stephen G. Tibbetts, "Perinatal and Developmental Determinants of Early Onset of Offending: A Two-Peak Model Approach," in *The Development of Persistent Criminality*, ed. Johanna Savage (New York: Oxford University Press, 2009), 179–201.

Section Summary

- First, we discussed what distinguishes learning theories of crime from other perspectives.
- Then we reviewed Glaser's differential identification theory, which emphasizes the learning that takes place via reference groups or role models.
- We then discussed Sutherland's differential association theory and how this framework was improved by Akers's differential reinforcement theory.
- We examined in depth the psychological learning model of classical conditioning, as well as its limitations.
- We then explored two other learning models that formed the basis of differential reinforcement theory, namely, operant conditioning and learning according to modeling or imitation.
- We reviewed the theory of neutralization, including the five original techniques of neutralization presented by Sykes and Matza.
- We also reviewed several early forms of social control theory, such as Hobbes's, Freud's, and Durkheim's.
- Then we examined the early social control theories of crime, presented by Reiss, Toby, and Nye, along with Reckless's containment theory.
- We then examined more modern social control theories, such as Matza's drift theory and Hirschi's social bonding theory.
- Integrated social control theories were briefly examined, including Tittle's control-balance theory and Hagan's power-control theory.
- Finally, we reviewed low self-control theory from both a psychological and a physiological perspective.

KEY TERMS

classical conditioning	id	power-control theory
containment theory	learning theories	social bonding theory
control-balance theory	modeling and imitation	soft determinism
control theories	negative punishment	stake in conformity
differential association theory	negative reinforcement	subterranean values
differential identification theory	neutralization theory	superego
differential reinforcement theory	operant conditioning	tabula rasa
drift theory	positive punishment	theory of low self-control
ego	positive reinforcement	

DISCUSSION QUESTIONS

1. What distinguishes learning theories from other criminological theories?

2. What distinguishes differential association from differential reinforcement theory?

3. What did differential identification add to learning theories?

4. Which technique of neutralization do you use or relate to the most? Why?

5. Which technique of neutralization do you find least valid? Why?

6. Which element of Hirschi's social bond do you find you have highest levels of?

7. Which element of Hirschi's social bond do you find you have lowest levels of?

8. Can you identify someone you know who fits the profile of a person with low self-control?

9. Which aspects of the low self-control personality do you think you fit?

10. Do you think Matza's theory of drift relates to when you or your friends have committed crime in life? Studies show that most people commit crimes when they are in their teens or 20s, or at least know people who do (e.g., drinking under age 21, speeding).

WEB RESOURCES

Differential Association Theory

http://www.criminology.fsu.edu/crimtheory/sutherland.html

Differential Reinforcement Theory

http://www.criminology.fsu.edu/crimtheory/akers.htm

Social and Self-Control Theory

http://www.criminology.fsu.edu/crimtheory/hirschi.htm

Techniques of Neutralization

http://www.criminology.fsu.edu/crimtheory/matza.htm

READING 19

This selection may be one of the most important entries in the book, primarily because it is written by Edwin H. Sutherland, who is generally regarded as the most important criminologist of the 20th century. One of the key reasons that Sutherland is held in such high regard is because of his proposed theoretical model of criminal behavior, which is known as differential association theory. This theory contains nine propositions, which are the focus of this selection. Readers should keep in mind that when these nine propositions were presented in the early to mid-1900s, the primary emphasis of criminological theory and research was on how offenders are physically (e.g., body type theories) or psychologically (e.g., IQ) different from nonoffenders. Although the social learning of criminal behavior is often assumed by modern criminologists, at that time Sutherland's emphasis was seen as a major break from widely accepted theoretical frameworks.

Specifically, Sutherland claims that offenders are no different, physically or psychologically, from nonoffenders. Rather, he concludes that individuals engage in offending because they are exposed to significant others (e.g., family, friends) who teach them the norms and techniques beneficial for committing crime. It is also important to keep in mind that Sutherland's theory is just as deterministic as previous theories (e.g., Lombroso's theory, Goddard's feeblemindedness theory, Sheldon's body type theory) in the sense that Sutherland claims that people do not have free choice or free will in determining their actions; rather, it all comes down to whom they associate with the most, and their attitudes regarding the violation of law.

It is also important to note that Sutherland bases his theory on classical conditioning, which was the dominant psychological model of learning when Sutherland developed differential association theory. Classical conditioning is based on Pavlov's concept of learning through association between stimuli and responses. Good examples can be easily found in everyday life, such as when people hear a certain song on the radio or smell a certain scent that reminds them of a particular event from their past. Although there is no doubt that classical conditioning, or learning via association, is a valid way that individuals learn, we will see later in this section that Sutherland's reliance on only this one model of learning somewhat limited his theory because it does not take other learning models into account.

A Sociological Theory of Criminal Behavior

Edwin H. Sutherland

 ## Explanation of Criminal Behavior

The following statement refers to the process by which a particular person comes to engage in criminal behavior.

1. *Criminal behavior is learned.* Negatively, this means that criminal[ity] is not inherited, as such;

also, the person who is not already trained in crime does not invent criminal behavior, just as a person does not make mechanical inventions unless he has had training in mechanics.

2. *Criminal behavior is learned in interaction with other persons in a process of communication.* This communication is verbal in many respects but includes also "the communication of gestures."

SOURCE: Edwin H. Sutherland and Donald Cressey, *Principles of Criminology*, 5th ed., ed. E. H. Sutherland and D. Cressey (Chicago: Lippincott, 1955), 77–80. Copyright © 1955 by J.B. Lippincott Company. Reprinted by permission of the Estate of Donald Cressey, via The Copyright Clearance Center.

3. *The principal part of the learning of criminal behavior occurs within intimate personal groups.* Negatively, this means that the impersonal agencies of communication, such as movies and newspapers, play a relatively unimportant part in the genesis of criminal behavior.

4. When criminal behavior is learned, the learning includes (a) techniques of committing the crime, which are sometimes very complicated, sometimes very simple; (b) the specific direction of motives, drives, rationalizations, and attitudes.

5. *The specific direction of motives and drives is learned from definitions of the legal codes as favorable or unfavorable.* In some societies an individual is surrounded by persons who invariably define the legal codes as rules to be observed, while in others he is surrounded by persons whose definitions are favorable to the violation of the legal codes. In our American society these definitions are almost always mixed, with the consequences that we have culture conflict in relation to the legal codes.

6. A person becomes delinquent because of an excess of definitions favorable to violation of law over definitions unfavorable to violation of law. This is the principle of differential association. It refers to both criminal and anti-criminal associations and has to do with counteracting forces. When persons become criminal, they do so because of contacts with criminal patterns and also because of isolation from anti-criminal patterns. Any person inevitably assimilates the surrounding culture unless other patterns are in conflict; a Southerner does not pronounce "r" because other Southerners do not pronounce "r." Negatively, this proposition of differential association means that associations which are neutral so far as crime is concerned have little or no effect on the genesis of criminal behavior. Much of the experience of a person is neutral in this sense, e.g., learning to brush one's teeth. This behavior has no negative or positive effect on criminal behavior except as it may be related to associations which are concerned with the legal codes.

This neutral behavior is important especially as an occupier of the time of a child so that he is not in contact with criminal behavior during the time he is so engaged in the neutral behavior.

7. *Differential associations may vary in frequency, duration, priority, and intensity.* This means that associations with criminal behavior and also associations with anti-criminal behavior vary in those respects. "Frequency" and "duration" as modalities of associations are obvious and need no explanation. "Priority" is assumed to be important in the sense that lawful behavior developed in early childhood may persist throughout life, and also that delinquent behavior developed in early childhood may persist throughout life. This tendency, however, has not been adequately demonstrated, and priority seems to be important principally through its selective influence. "Intensity" is not precisely defined but it has to do with such things as the prestige of the source of a criminal or anti-criminal pattern and with emotional reactions related to the associations. In a precise description of the criminal behavior of a person these modalities would be stated in quantitative form and a mathematical ratio be reached. A formula in this sense has not been developed, and the development of such a formula would be extremely difficult.

8. The process of learning criminal behavior by association with criminal and anti-criminal patterns involves all of the mechanisms that are involved in any other learning. Negatively, this means that the learning of criminal behavior is not restricted to the process of imitation. A person who is seduced, for instance, learns criminal behavior by association, but this process would not ordinarily be described as imitation.

9. While criminal behavior is an expression of general needs and values, it is not explained by those general needs and values since non-criminal behavior is an expression of the same needs and values. Thieves generally steal in order to secure money, but likewise honest laborers work in order to secure money. The attempts by many scholars to explain criminal behavior by general

drives and values, such as, the happiness principle, striving for social status, the money motive, or frustration, have been and must continue to be futile since they explain lawful behavior as completely as they explain criminal behavior. They are similar to respiration, which is necessary for any behavior but which does not differentiate criminal from non-criminal behavior.

It is not necessary, at this level of explanation, to explain why a person has the associations which he has; this certainly involves a complex of many things. In an area where the delinquency rate is high a boy who is sociable, gregarious, active, and athletic is very likely to come in contact with the other boys in the neighborhood, learn delinquent behavior from them, and become a gangster; in the same neighborhood the psychopathic boy who is isolated, introvert, and inert may remain at home, not become acquainted with the other boys in the neighborhood, and not become delinquent. In another situation, the sociable, athletic, aggressive boy may become a member of a scout troop and not become involved in delinquent behavior. The person's associations are determined in a general context of social organization. A child is ordinarily reared in a family; the place of residence of the family is determined largely by family income; and the delinquency rate is, in many respects, related to the rental value of the houses. Many other factors enter into this social organization, including many of the small personal group relationships.

The preceding explanation of criminal behavior is stated from the point of view of the person who engages in criminal behavior. As indicated earlier, it is possible, also, to state sociological theories of criminal behavior from the point of view of the community, nation, or other group. The problem, when thus stated, is generally concerned with crime rates and involves a comparison of the crime rates of various groups or the crime rates of a particular group at different times. The explanation of a crime rate must be consistent with the explanation of the criminal behavior of the person, since the crime rate is a summary statement of the number of persons in the group who commit crimes and the frequency with which they commit crimes. One of the best explanations of crime rates from this point of view is that a high crime rate is due to social disorganization. The term "social disorganization" is not entirely satisfactory and it seems preferable to substitute for it the term "differential social organization." The postulate on which this theory is based, regardless of the name, is that crime is rooted in the social organization and is an expression of that social organization. A group may be organized for criminal behavior or organized against criminal behavior. Most communities are organized both for criminal and anti-criminal behavior and in that sense the crime rate is an expression of the differential group organization. Differential group organization as an explanation of variations in crime rates is consistent with the differential association theory of the processes by which persons become criminals. . . .

REVIEW QUESTIONS

1. Using Sutherland's first three propositions, how does he claim criminal behavior is learned? What does he have to say about the effect of movies and media on the learning of criminal behavior?

2. What two types of learning does Sutherland claim takes place in his fourth proposition? Provide an example of each of these two types.

3. Sutherland's sixth proposition is often considered the best summary of his theory. Explain what this proposition means as if you were trying to tell a person who knows nothing about criminology. Also, do you agree with it? Why or why not?

4. What four types of associations are identified by Sutherland in his seventh proposition? Explain each, and provide your opinion on which of the four types is most important in determining criminal activity.

❖

In this selection, Ron Akers presents a theoretical model known as differential reinforcement theory. Although some, including Akers himself, often refer to this theory as social learning theory, this label is a bit confusing because there are many social learning theories. We prefer differential reinforcement theory as the name of this framework because, when you say this, criminologists know exactly which theoretical model you are referring to, and also because the term *reinforcement* specifies the key concept that distinguishes this model from all other social learning theories.

Differential reinforcement theory builds on the framework provided by Sutherland's differential association theory but adds two important models of social learning that were not included in Sutherland's theory. Specifically, Sutherland based his differential association model on only one type of social learning: classical conditioning. While including classical conditioning in its framework, Akers's theory of differential reinforcement adds two additional learning models: operant conditioning and modeling and imitation. Operant conditioning is based on B. F. Skinner's work in psychology, which emphasizes whether punishments or reinforcements (i.e., rewards) occur after a given activity. The other learning model is modeling and imitation, which is largely based on Bandura's psychological model of learning through observation, such as what happens when children watch what adults do and then imitating their behavior—in other words, "monkey see, monkey do." Differential reinforcement theory is an improvement over Sutherland's differential association theory because it takes all three learning processes—classical conditioning, operant conditioning, and modeling and imitation—into account in the theoretical model. While reading this selection, readers are encouraged to consider how the primary concepts and propositions of the theory occur in their lives, not necessarily in terms of criminal behavior, but in the learning of any behavior. Another important aspect of Sutherland's theory that Akers's differential reinforcement theory adopts is that the processes involved in the learning of criminal behavior are the same as the processes for learning all types of conventional behavior.

A Social Learning Theory of Crime

Ronald L. Akers

Concise Statement of the Theory

The basic assumption in social learning theory is that the same learning process, operating in a context of social structure, interaction, and situation, produces both conforming and deviant behavior. The difference lies in the direction of the process in which these mechanisms operate. In both, it is seldom an either-or, all-or-nothing process; what is involved, rather, is the balance of influences on behavior. That balance usually exhibits some stability over time, but it can become unstable and change with time or circumstances. Conforming and deviant behavior is learned by all of the mechanisms in this process, but the theory proposes that the principal mechanisms are in that part of the process in which differential reinforcement (instrumental learning through rewards and punishers) and imitation (observational learning) produce both overt behavior and cognitive definitions that function as discriminative (cue) stimuli for the behavior. Always implied, and

SOURCE: R. L. Akers, *A Social Learning Theory of Crime* (Piscataway, NJ: Transaction, 2009), 50–59. Copyright © 2009 Transaction Publishers. Reprinted with permission of Transaction Publishers.

sometimes made explicit when these concepts are called upon to account for deviant/conforming behavior, is the understanding that the behavioral processes in operant and classical conditioning are in operation (see below). However, social learning theory focuses on four major concepts—differential association, differential reinforcement, imitation, and definitions. The central proposition of the social learning theory of criminal and deviant behavior can be stated as a long sentence proposing that criminal and deviant behavior is more likely when, on balance, the combined effects of these four main sets of variables instigate and strengthen nonconforming over conforming acts:

> The probability that persons will engage in criminal and deviant behavior is increased and the probability of their conforming to the norm is decreased when they differentially associate with others who commit criminal behavior and espouse definitions favorable to it, are relatively more exposed in-person or symbolically to salient criminal/deviant models, define it as desirable or justified in a situation discriminative for the behavior, and have received in the past and anticipate in the current or future situation relatively greater reward than punishment for the behavior.

> The probability of conforming behavior is increased and the probability of deviant behavior is decreased when the balance of these variables moves in the reverse direction.

Each of the four main components of this statement can be presented as a separate testable hypothesis. The individual is more likely to commit violations when:

1. He or she differentially associates with other[s] who commit, model, and support violations of social and legal norms.

2. The violative behavior is differentially reinforced over behavior in conformity to the norm.

3. He or she is more exposed to and observes more deviant than conforming models.

4. His or her own learned definitions are favorable toward committing the deviant acts.

General Principles of Social Learning Theory

Since it is a general explanation of crime and deviance of all kinds, social learning is not simply a theory about how novel criminal behavior is learned or a theory only of the positive causes of that behavior. It embraces variables that operate to both motivate and control delinquent and criminal behavior, to both promote and undermine conformity. It answers the questions of why people do and do not violate norms. The probability of criminal or conforming behavior occurring is a function of the variables operating in the underlying social learning process. The main concepts/variables and their respective empirical indicators have been identified and measured, but they can be viewed as indicators of a general latent construct, for which additional indicators can be devised (Akers & La Greca, 1991; Akers & Lee, 1996).

Social learning accounts for the individual becoming prone to deviant or criminal behavior and for stability or change in that propensity. Therefore, the theory is capable of accounting for the development of stable individual differences, as well as changes in the individual's behavioral patterns or tendencies to commit deviant and criminal acts, over time and in different situations. . . . The social learning process operates in each individual's learning history and in the immediate situation in which the opportunity for a crime occurs.

Deviant and criminal behavior is learned and modified (acquired, performed, repeated, maintained, and changed) through all of the same cognitive and behavioral mechanisms as conforming behavior. They differ in the direction, content, and outcome of the behavior learned. Therefore, it is inaccurate to state, for instance, that peer influence does not explain adolescent deviant behavior since conforming behavior is also peer influenced in adolescence. The theory expects peer influences to be implicated in both; it is the content and direction of the influence that is the key.

The primary learning mechanisms are differential reinforcement (instrumental conditioning), in which behavior is a function of the frequency, amount, and probability of experienced and perceived contingent rewards and punishments, and imitation, in which the behavior of others and its consequences are observed and modeled. The process of stimulus discrimination/generalization is another important mechanism; here, overt and covert stimuli, verbal and cognitive, act as cues or signals for behavior to occur. As I point out below, there are other behavioral mechanisms in the learning process, but these are not as important and are usually left implied rather than explicated in the theory.

The content of the learning achieved by these mechanisms includes the simple and complex behavioral sequences and the definitions (beliefs, attitudes, justifications, orientations) that in turn become discriminative for engaging in deviant and criminal behavior. The probability that conforming or norm-violative behavior is learned and performed, and the frequency with which it is committed, are a function of the past, present, and anticipated differential reinforcement for the behavior and the deviant or nondeviant direction of the learned definitions and other discriminative stimuli present in a given situation.

These learning mechanisms operate in a process of differential association—direct and indirect, verbal and nonverbal communication, interaction, and identification with others. The relative frequency, intensity, duration, and priority of associations affect the relative amount, frequency, and probability of reinforcement of conforming or deviant behavior and exposure of individuals to deviant or conforming norms and behavioral models. To the extent that the individual can control with whom she or he associates, the frequency, intensity, and duration of those associations are themselves affected by how rewarding or aversive they are. The principal learning is through differential association with those persons and groups (primary, secondary, reference, and symbolic) that comprise or control the individual's major sources of reinforcement, most salient behavioral models, and most effective definitions and other discriminative stimuli for committing and repeating behavior. The reinforcement and discriminative stimuli are mainly social (such as socially valued rewards and punishers contingent on the behavior), but they are also nonsocial (such as unconditioned physiological reactions to environmental stimuli and physical effects of ingested substances and the physical environment).

Sequence and Reciprocal Effects in the Social Learning Process

Behavioral feedback effects are built into the concept of differential reinforcement—actual or perceived changes in the environment produced by the behavior feed back on that behavior to affect its repetition or extinction, and both prior and anticipated rewards and punishments influence present behavior. Reciprocal effects between the individual's behavior and definitions or differential association are also reflected in the social learning process. This process is one in which the probability of both the initiation and the repetition of a deviant or criminal act (or the initiation and repetition of conforming acts) is a function of the learning history of the individual and the set of reinforcement contingencies and discriminative stimuli in a given situation. The typical process of initiation, continuation, progression, and desistance is hypothesized to be as follows:

1. The balance of past and current associations, definitions, and imitation of deviant models, and the anticipated balance of reinforcement in particular situations, produces or inhibits the initial delinquent or deviant acts.

2. The effects of these variables continue in the repetition of acts, although imitation becomes less important than it was in the first commission of the act.

3. After initiation, the actual social and nonsocial reinforcers and punishers affect the probability that the acts will be or will not be repeated and at what level of frequency.

4. Not only the overt behavior, but also the definitions favorable or unfavorable to it, are affected by the positive and negative consequences of the initial acts. To the extent that they are more rewarded than alternative behavior, the favorable definitions will be strengthened and the unfavorable definitions will be weakened, and it becomes more likely that the deviant behavior will be repeated under similar circumstances.

5. Progression into more frequent or sustained patterns, rather than cessation or reduction, of criminal and deviant behavior is promoted to the extent that reinforcement, exposure to deviant models, and norm-violating definitions are not offset by negative formal and informal sanctions and norm abiding definitions.

The theory does not hypothesize that definitions favorable to law violation always precede and are unaffected by the commission of criminal acts. Although the probability of a criminal act increases in the presence of favorable definitions, acts in violation of the law do occur (through imitation and reinforcement) in the absence of any thought given to whether the acts are right or wrong. Furthermore, the individual may apply neutralizing definitions retroactively to excuse or justify an act without having contemplated them beforehand. To the extent that such excuses become associated with successfully mitigating others' negative sanctions or one's self-punishment, however, they become cues for the repetition of deviant acts. Such definitions, therefore, precede committing the same acts again or committing similar acts in the future.

Differential association with conforming and nonconforming others typically precedes the individual's committing crimes and delinquent acts. This sequence of events is sometimes disputed in the literature because it is mistakenly believed to apply only to differential peer association in general or to participation in delinquent gangs in particular without reference to family and other group associations. It is true that the theory recognizes peer associations as very important in adolescent deviance and that differential association is most often measured in research by peer associations. But the theory also hypothesizes that the family is a very important primary group in the differential association process, and it plainly stipulates that other primary and secondary groups besides peers are involved (see Sutherland, 1947, pp. 164–65). Accordingly, it is a mistake to interpret differential association as referring only to peer associations. The theoretical stipulation that differential association is causally prior to the commission of delinquent and criminal acts is not confined to the balance of peer associations; rather, it is the balance (as determined by the modalities) of family, peer, and other associations. According to the priority principle, association, reinforcement, modeling, and exposure to conforming and deviant definitions occurring within the family during childhood, and such antisocial conduct as aggressiveness, lying, and cheating learned in early childhood, occur prior to and have both direct and selective effects on later delinquent and criminal behavior and associations. . . .

The socializing behavior of parents, guardians, or caretakers is certainly reciprocally influenced by the deviant and unacceptable behavior of the child. However, it can never be true that the onset of delinquency precedes and initiates interaction in a particular family (except in the unlikely case of the late-stage adoption of a child who is already delinquent or who is drawn to and chosen by deviant parents). Thus, interaction in the family or family surrogate always precedes delinquency.

But this is not true for adolescent peer associations. One may choose to associate with peers based on similarity in deviant behavior that already exists. Some major portion of this behavioral similarity results from previous association with other delinquent peers or from anticipatory socialization undertaken to make one's behavior match more closely that of the deviant associates to whom one is attracted. For some adolescents, gravitation toward delinquent peers occurs after and as a result of the individual's involvement in delinquent behavior. However, peer associations are most often formed initially around interests, friendships, and such circumstances as neighborhood proximity, family similarities, values, beliefs, age, school attended, grade in school, and mutually attractive behavioral patterns that have little to do directly with co-involvement or similarity in specifically law-violating or serious deviant behavior. Many of these factors in peer association are not under the adolescents' control, and some are simply happenstance. The theory does not, contrary to the Gluecks' distorted characterization, propose that "accidental differential association of non-delinquents with delinquents is the basic cause of crime" (Glueck & Glueck, 1950, p. 164). Interaction and socialization in the family precedes and affects choices of both conforming and deviant peer associations.

Those peer associations will affect the nature of models, definitions, and rewards/ punishers to which the person is exposed. After the associations have been established, their reinforcing or punishing consequences as well as direct and vicarious consequences of the deviant behavior will affect both the continuation of old and the seeking of new associations (those over which one has any choice). One may choose further interaction with others based on whether they too are involved in deviant or criminal behavior; in such cases, the outcomes of that interaction are more rewarding than aversive and it is anticipated that the associates will more likely approve or be permissive toward one's own deviant behavior. Further interaction with delinquent peers, over which the individual has no choice, may also result from being apprehended and confined by the juvenile or criminal-justice system.

These reciprocal effects would predict that one's own deviant or conforming behavioral patterns can have effects on choice of friends; these are weaker in the earlier years, but should become stronger as one moves through adolescence and gains more control over friendship choices. The typical sequence outlined above would predict that deviant associations precede the onset of delinquent behavior more frequently than the sequence of events in which the delinquent associations begin only after the peers involved have already separately and individually established similar patterns of delinquent behavior. Further, these behavioral tendencies that develop prior to peer association will themselves be the result of previous associations, models, and reinforcement, primarily in the family. Regardless of the sequence in which onset occurs, and whatever the level of the individual's delinquent involvement, its frequency and seriousness will increase after the deviant associations have begun and decrease as the associations are reduced. That is, whatever the temporal ordering, differential association with deviant peers will have a causal effect on one's own delinquent behavior (just as his actions will have an effect on his peers).

Therefore, both "selection," or "flocking" (tendency for persons to choose interaction with others with behavioral similarities), and "socialization," or "feathering" (tendency for persons who interact to have mutual influence on one another's behavior), are part of the same overall social learning process and are explained by the same variables. A peer "socialization" process and a peer "selection" process in deviant behavior are not mutually exclusive, but are simply the social learning process operating at different times. Arguments that social learning posits only the latter, that any evidence of selective mechanisms in deviant interaction run counter to social learning theory (Strictland, 1982; Stafford & Ekland-Olson, 1982), or that social learning theory recognizes only a recursive, one-way causal effect of peers on delinquent behavior (Thornberry et al., 1994; Catalano et al., 1996) are wrong.

Behavioral and Cognitive Mechanisms in Social Learning

The first statement in Sutherland's theory was a simple declarative sentence maintaining that criminal behavior is learned, and the eighth statement declared that this involved all the mechanisms involved in any learning. What little Sutherland added in his (1947, p. 7) commentary downplayed imitation as a possible learning mechanism in

criminal behavior. He mentioned "seduction" of a person into criminal behavior as something that is not covered by the concept of imitation. He defined neither imitation nor seduction and offered no further discussion of mechanisms of learning in any of his papers or publications. Recall that filling this major lacuna in Sutherland's theory was the principal goal of the 1966b Burgess-Akers reformulation. To this end we combined Sutherland's first and eighth statements into one: "Criminal behavior is learned according to the principles of operant conditioning." The phrase "principles of operant conditioning" was meant as a shorthand reference to all of the behavioral mechanisms of learning in operant theory that had been empirically validated.

Burgess and I delineated, as much as space allowed, what these specific learning mechanisms were: (1) operant conditioning, differential reinforcement of voluntary behavior through positive and negative reinforcement and punishment; (2) respondent (involuntary reflexes), or "classical," conditioning; (3) unconditioned (primary) and conditioned (secondary) reinforcers and punishers; (4) shaping and response differentiation; (5) stimulus discrimination and generalization, the environmental and internal stimuli that provide cues or signals indicating differences and similarities across situations that help elicit, but do not directly reinforce, behavior; (6) types of reinforcement schedules, the rate and ratio in which rewards and punishers follow behavior; (7) stimulus-response constellations; and (8) stimulus satiation and deprivation. We also reported research showing the applicability of these mechanisms of learning to both conforming and deviant behavior.

Burgess and I used the term "operant conditioning" to emphasize that differential reinforcement (the balance of reward and punishment contingent upon behavioral responses) is the basic mechanism around which the others revolve and by which learning most relevant to conformity or violation of social and legal norms is produced. This was reflected in other statements in the theory in which the only learning mechanisms listed were differential reinforcement and stimulus discrimination.

We also subsumed imitation, or modeling, under these principles and argued that imitation "may be analyzed quite parsimoniously with the principles of modern behavior theory," namely, that it is simply a sub-class of behavioral shaping through operant conditioning (Burgess and Akers, 1966b, p. 138). For this reason we made no specific mention of imitation in any of the seven statements. Later, I became persuaded that the operant principle of gradual shaping of responses through "successive approximations" only incompletely and awkwardly incorporated the processes of observational learning and vicarious reinforcement that Bandura and Walters (1963) had identified. Therefore, without dismissing successive approximation as a way in which some imitative behavior could be shaped, I came to accept Bandura's conceptualization of imitation. That is, imitation is a separate learning mechanism characterized by modeling one's own actions on the observed behavior of others and on the consequences of that behavior (vicarious reinforcement) prior to performing the behavior and experiencing its consequences directly. Whether the observed acts will be performed and repeated depends less on the continuing presence of models and more on the actual or anticipated rewarding or aversive consequences of the behavior. I became satisfied that the principle of "observational learning" could account for the acquisition, and to some extent the performance, of behavior by a process that did not depend on operant conditioning or "instrumental learning." Therefore, in later discussions of the theory, while continuing to posit differential reinforcement as the core behavior-shaping mechanism, I included imitation as another primary mechanism in acquiring behavior. Where appropriate, discriminative stimuli were also specifically invoked as affecting behavior, while I made only general reference to other learning mechanisms.

Note that the term "operant conditioning" in the opening sentence of the Burgess-Akers revision reflected our great reliance on the orthodox behaviorism that assumed the empirical irrelevance of cognitive variables. Social behaviorism, on the other hand, recognizes "cognitive" as well as "behavioral" mechanisms (see Bandura, 1969; 1977a; 1977b; 1986; 1989; Grusec, 1992; Staats, 1975). My social learning theory of criminal behavior retains a strong element of the symbolic interactionism found in Sutherland's theory (Akers, 1985, pp. 39–70). As a result, it is closer to cognitive learning theories, such as Albert Bandura's, than to the radical operant behaviorism of B. F. Skinner with which Burgess and I began. It is for this reason, and the reliance on such concepts as imitation, anticipated reinforcement, and self-reinforcement, that I have described social learning theory as "soft behaviorism" (Akers, 1985, p. 65).

The unmodified term "learning" implies to many that the theory only explains the acquisition of novel behavior

by the individual, in contrast to behavior that is committed at a given time and place or the maintenance of behavior over time (Cornish and Clarke, 1986). It has also been interpreted to mean only "positive" learning of novel behavior, with no relevance for inhibition of behavior or of learning failures (Gottfredson and Hirschi, 1990). As I have made clear above, neither of these interpretations is accurate. The phrase that Burgess and I used, "effective and available reinforcers and the existing reinforcement contingencies," and the discussion of reinforcement occurring under given situations (Burgess & Akers, 1966b, pp. 141, 134) make it obvious that we were not proposing a theory only of past reinforcement in the acquisition of a behavioral repertoire with no regard for the reward/cost balance obtaining at a given time and place. There is nothing in the learning principles that restrict[s] them to prior socialization or past history of learning. Social learning encompasses both the acquisition and the performance of the behavior, both facilitation and inhibition of behavior, and both learning successes and learning failures. The learning mechanisms account not only for the initiation of behavior but also for repetition, maintenance and desistance of behavior. They rely not only on prior behavioral processes but also on those operating at a given time in a given situation. . . .

Definitions and Discriminative Stimuli

[In] *The Concept of Definitions,* Sutherland asserted that learning criminal behavior includes "techniques of committing the crime which are sometimes very complicated, sometimes very simple" and the "specific direction of motives, drives, rationalizations and attitudes" (1947, p. 6). I have retained both definitions and techniques in social learning theory, with clarified and modified conceptual meanings and with hypothesized relationships to criminal behavior. The qualification that "techniques" may be simple or complex shows plainly that Sutherland did not mean to include only crime-specific skills learned in order to break the law successfully. Techniques also clearly include ordinary, everyday abilities. This same notion is retained in social learning theory.

By definition, a person must be capable of performing the necessary sequence of actions before he or she can carry out either criminal or conforming behavior—inability to perform the behavior precludes committing the crime. Since many of the behavioral techniques for both conforming and criminal acts are the same, not only the simple but even some of the complex skills involved in carrying out crime are not novel to most or many of us. The required component parts of the complete skill are acquired in essentially conforming or neutral contexts to which we have been exposed—driving a car, shooting a gun, fighting with fists, signing checks, using a computer, and so on. In most white-collar crime, the same skills needed to carry out a job legitimately are put to illegitimate use. Other skills are specific to given deviant acts—safe cracking, counterfeiting, pocket picking, jimmying doors and picking locks, bringing off a con game, and so on. Without tutelage in these crime-specific techniques, most people would not be able to perform them, or at least would be initially very inept.

Sutherland took the concept of "definitions" in his theory from W. I. Thomas's "definition of the situation" (Thomas and Thomas, 1928) and generalized it to orienting attitudes toward different behavior. It is true that "Sutherland did not identify what constitutes a definition 'favorable to' or 'unfavorable to' the violation of law" (Cressey, 1960, p. 53). Nevertheless . . . there is little doubt that "rationalizations" and "attitudes" are subsumed under the general concept of definitions—normative attitudes or evaluative meanings attached to given behavior. Exposure to others' shared definitions is a key (but not the only) part of the process by which the individual acquires or internalizes his or her own definitions. They are orientations, rationalizations, definitions of the situation, and other attitudes that label the commission of an act as right or wrong, good or bad, desirable or undesirable, justified or unjustified.

In social learning theory, these definitions are both general and specific. General beliefs include religious, moral, and other conventional values and norms that are favorable to conforming behavior and unfavorable to committing any of a range of deviant or criminal acts. Specific definitions orient the person to particular acts or series of acts. Thus, there are people who believe that it is morally wrong to steal and that laws against theft should be obeyed, but at the same time see little wrong with smoking marijuana and rationalize that it is all right to violate laws against drug possession. The greater the extent to which one holds attitudes that disapprove of certain acts, the less

likely one is to engage in them. Conventional beliefs are negative toward criminal behavior. The more strongly one has learned and personally believes in the ideals of honesty, integrity, civility, kindness, and other general standards of morality that condemn lying, cheating, stealing, and harming others, the less likely he or she is to commit acts that violate social and legal norms. Conversely, the more one's own attitudes approve of, or fail to condemn, a behavior, the greater the chances are that he or she will engage in it. For obvious reasons, the theory would predict that definitions in the form of general beliefs will have less effect than specific definitions on the commission of specific criminal acts.

Definitions that favor criminal or deviant behavior are basically positive or neutralizing. Positive definitions are beliefs or attitudes that make the behavior morally desirable or wholly permissible. They are most likely to be learned through positive reinforcement in a deviant group or subculture that carries values conflicting with those of conventional society. Some of these positive verbalizations may be part of a full-blown ideology of politically dissident, criminal, or deviant groups. Although such ideologies and groups can be identified, the theory does not rest only on this type of definition favorable to deviance; indeed, it proposes that such positive definitions occur less frequently than neutralizing ones.

Neutralizing definitions favor violating the law or other norms not because they take the acts to be positively desirable but because they justify or excuse them. Even those who commit deviant acts are aware that others condemn the behavior and may themselves define the behavior as bad. The neutralizing definitions view the act as something that is probably undesirable but, given the situation, is nonetheless justified, excusable, necessary, all right, or not really bad after all. The process of acquiring neutralizing definitions is more likely to involve negative reinforcement; that is, they are verbalizations that accompany escape or avoidance of negative consequences like disapproval by one's self or by society.

While these definitions may become part of a deviant or criminal subculture, acquiring them does not require participation in such subcultures. They are learned from carriers of conventional culture, including many of those in social control and treatment agencies. The notions of techniques of neutralization and subterranean values (Sykes and Matza, 1957; Matza and Sykes, 1961; Matza, 1964) come from the observation that for nearly every social norm there is a norm of evasion. That is, there are recognized exceptions or ways of getting around the moral imperatives in the norms and the reproach expected for violating them. Thus, the general prohibition "Thou shalt not kill" is accompanied by such implicit or explicit exceptions as "unless in time of war," "unless the victim is the enemy," "unless in self-defense," "unless in the line of duty," "unless to protect others"! The moral injunctions against physical violence are suspended if the victim can be defined as the initial aggressor or is guilty of some transgression and therefore deserves to be attacked.

The concept of neutralizing definitions in social learning theory incorporates not only notions of verbalizations and rationalizations (Cressey, 1953) and techniques of neutralization (Sykes & Matza, 1957) but also conceptually similar if not equivalent notions of "accounts" (Lyman & Scott, 1970), "disclaimers" (Hewitt & Stokes, 1975), and "moral disengagement" (Bandura, 1976, 1990). Neutralizing attitudes include such beliefs as "Everybody has a racket"; "I can't help myself, I was born this way"; "It's not my fault"; "I am not responsible"; "I was drunk and didn't know what I was doing"; "I just blew my top"; "They can afford it"; "He deserved it." Some neutralizations (e.g., nonresponsibility) can be generalized to a wide range of disapproved and criminal behavior. These and other excuses and justifications for committing deviant acts and victimizing others are definitions favorable to criminal and deviant behavior.

Exposure to these rationalizations and excuses may be through after-the-fact justifications for one's own or others' norm violations that help to deflect or lessen punishment that would be expected to follow. The individual then learns the excuses either directly or through imitation and uses them to lessen self-reproach and social disapproval. Therefore, the definitions are themselves behavior that can be imitated and reinforced and then in turn serve as discriminative stimuli accompanying reinforcement of overt behavior. Deviant and criminal acts do occur without being accompanied by positive or neutralizing definitions, but the acts are more likely to occur and recur in situations the same as or similar to those in which the definitions have already been learned and applied. The extent to which one adheres to or rejects the definitions favorable to crime is itself affected by the rewarding or punishing consequences that follow the act.

 # References

Akers, R. L. (1985). *Deviant behavior: A social learning approach.* Belmont, CA: Wadsworth.

Akers, R. L., & La Greca, A. J. (1991). Alcohol use among the elderly: Social learning, community context, and life events. In D. J. Pittman & H. R. White (Eds.), *Society, culture, and drinking patterns re-examined* (pp. 242–262). New Brunswick, NJ: Rutgers Center of Alcohol Studies.

Akers, R. L., & Lee, G. (1996). A longitudinal test of social learning theory: Adolescent smoking. *Journal of Drug Issues, 26,* 317–343.

Bandura, A. (1969). *Principles of behavior modification.* New York: Holt, Rinehart & Winston.

Bandura, A. (1976). *Analysis of delinquency and aggression.* New York: Lawrence Erlbaum.

Bandura, A. (1977a). Self-efficacy: Toward a unifying theory of behavioral change. *Psychological Review, 84,* 191–215.

Bandura, A. (1977b). *Social learning theory.* Englewood Cliffs, NJ: Prentice Hall.

Bandura, A. (1986). Social foundations of thought and action: A social cognitive theory. Englewood Cliffs, NJ: Prentice Hall.

Bandura, A. (1989). Human agency and social cognitive theory. *American Psychologist, 44,* 1175–1184.

Bandura, A. (1990). Selective activation and disengagement of moral control. *Journal of Social Issues, 46,* 27–46.

Bandura, A., & Walters, R. H. (1963). *Social learning and personality development.* New York: Holt, Rinehart & Winston.

Burgess, R. L., & Akers, R. L. (1966b). A different association-reinforcement theory of criminal behavior. *Social Problems, 14,* 128–147.

Catalano, R. F., Kosterman, R., Hawkins, J. D., Newcomb, M. D., & Abbott, R. D. (1996). Modeling the etiology of adolescent substance use: A test of the social development model. *Journal of Drug Issues, 26,* 429–455.

Cornish, D. B., & Clarke, R. V. (1986). *The reasoning criminal: Rational choice perspectives on offending.* New York: Springer-Verlag.

Cressey, D. R. (1953). *Other people's money.* Glencoe, IL: Free Press.

Cressey, D. (1960). Epidemiology and individual conduct. *Pacific Sociological Review, 3,* 47–58.

Glueck, S., & Glueck, E. (1950). *Unraveling juvenile delinquency.* Cambridge, MA: Harvard University Press.

Gottfredson, M., & Hirschi, T. (1990). *A general theory of crime.* Stanford, CA: Stanford University Press.

Grusec, J. E. (1992). Social learning theory and developmental psychology: The legacies of Robert Sears and A. Bandura. *Developmental Psychology, 28,* 776–786.

Hewitt, J. P., & Stokes, R. (1975). Disclaimers. *American Sociological Review, 40,* 1–11.

Lyman, S. M., & Scott, M. B. (1970). *A sociology of the absurd.* New York: Appleton-Century-Crofts.

Matza, D. (1964). *Delinquency and drift.* New York: Wiley.

Matza, D., & Sykes, G. M. (1961). Juvenile delinquency and subterranean values. *American Sociological Review, 26*, 712–719.

Staats, A. (1975). *Social behaviorism.* Homewood, IL: Dorsey.

Stafford, M. C., & Ekland-Olson, S. (1982). On social learning and deviant behavior: A reappraisal of the findings. *American Sociological Review, 47*, 167–169.

Strictland, D. E. (1982). Social learning and deviant behavior: A specific test of a general theory: A comment and critique. *American Sociological Review, 47*, 162–167.

Sutherland, E. H. (1947). *Criminology.* Philadelphia: J. B. Lippincott.

Sykes, G. M., & Matza, D. (1957). Techniques of neutralization: A theory of delinquency. *American Sociological Review, 22*, 664–670.

Thomas, W. I., & Thomas, D. S. (1928). *The child in America: Behavior problems and programs.* New York: Knopf.

Thornberry, T. P., Lizotte, A. J., Krohn, M. D., Farnworth, M., & Jang, S. J. (1994). Delinquent peers, beliefs, and delinquent behavior: A longitudinal test of interactional theory. *Criminology, 32*, 47–83.

REVIEW QUESTIONS

1. What are the four main components of the theory of differential reinforcement according to Akers? Which of these propositions is primarily based on Sutherland's differential association theory? Which of these components is based on operant conditioning? Which of these are based on imitation/modeling? Explain your reasons in each case.

2. Akers seems to emphasize the importance of behavioral feedback and reciprocal effects. Explain what these concepts mean and why they are important.

3. What does Akers mean when he talks about the concept of definitions? Provide a thorough explanation and some examples.

Reading 21

In this selection, Lynne Vieraitis, Nicole and Alex Piquero, Stephen Tibbetts, and Michael Blankenship examine gender differences in the effects of techniques of neutralization in decisions to engage in unethical decision making in a corporate setting. One very interesting aspect of this study is that their sample is made up of students in a master of business administration (MBA) program, and a significant portion of this group were in an executive MBA program, meaning that they had many years of corporate experience. The students were asked how they would deal with the knowledge that a drug their company sold was found to be harmful to those who take it. Readers will likely find the results quite surprising and insightful.

Do Women and Men Differ in Their Neutralizations of Corporate Crime?

Lynne M. Vieraitis,[1] Nicole Leeper Piquero,
Alex R. Piquero, Stephen G. Tibbetts,[2] and Michael Blankenship[3]

SOURCE: Lynne M. Vieraitis, Nicole Leeper Piquero, Alex R. Piquero, Stephen G. Tibbetts, & Michael Blankenship. "Do Women and Men Differ in Their Neutralizations of Corporate Crime?" *Criminal Justice Review* 37 (2012): 478–93.

[1]University of Texas at Dallas, Richardson, TX, USA

[2]Department of Criminal Justice, California State University, San Bernardino, CA, USA

[3]Department of Criminal Justice and Criminology, Boise State University, Boise, ID, USA

Since its publication in 1957, Sykes and Matza's "Techniques of Neutralization: A Theory of Delinquency" has been one of the most influential and most frequently cited articles in the criminological literature—accounting for over 2,800 citations in Google Scholar as of September 2012. Their work was groundbreaking for its divergence from the then current assumption by criminological theorists that most delinquents were "committed" to delinquent values. It also marked a departure from the dominant thinking in psychology that individual behavior was undertaken in response to a series of positive and negative stimuli. In contrast, Sykes and Matza argued that most delinquents were not committed to delinquent values and did not conceive of themselves as delinquents or criminals. To maintain this "noncriminal" self-image, offenders justified their behaviors by employing one or more of the five techniques of neutralization as delineated by Sykes and Matza (1957), including denial of responsibility ("It's not my fault"), denial of injury ("No one got hurt"), denial of victim ("The victim had it coming"), appeal to higher loyalties ("I didn't do it for myself, I did it for my children"), and condemnation of the condemners ("The police are corrupt"). Subsequent studies on neutralization theory have produced additional excuses and justifications, including metaphor of the ledger ("I've done a lot of good things in my life"; Klockars, 1974), the claim of normality ("Everyone else is doing it"; Benson, 1985; Coleman, 2006), the defense of necessity ("I didn't have a choice"; Benson, 1985; Coleman, 2006; Minor, 1981), justification by comparison ("I'm not as bad as others"; Cromwell & Thurman, 2003), and the claim of entitlement ("I deserve this, they owed me"; Coleman, 2006).

Yet despite the number and scope of crimes and criminals examined by researchers, the gender differences among offenders' use of neutralizations are rarely examined and the differences between men and women remain an underexplored area of criminological research (for exceptions, see Copes & Vieraitis, 2012; Daly, 1989; Klenowski et al., 2011; Zietz, 1981).

 ## Background

Current Focus

This article builds on prior research in the application of techniques of neutralization to white-collar/corporate crime by examining the degree to which men and women use specific techniques to account for their corporate offending. To the extent that techniques of neutralization operate as a general theoretical process, then we should find that men and women do or do not use the techniques in the same manner. Such a view does not negate the possibility of differences in the average values of techniques themselves. On the other hand, some gender-specific theoretical models and more gendered theories of crime would suggest that the theoretical processes underlying the gender–corporate crime relationship will evince differences not only in degree but also differences in kind. That is, the techniques men and women rely on to rationalize the same offending behavior should be used in different ways, such that some should matter for one group but not the other.

 ## Data and Method

Data were obtained from a questionnaire administered to a convenience sample of 133 students enrolled in either a traditional MBA program (80%) or the executive MBA program (20%) at a single university.[1] The use of a sample of MBA students for this particular study is justified for at least three reasons. First, MBA students include a cadre of persons with knowledge about the business world and thus find themselves in situations where the opportunity for corporate misbehavior may occur. Second, although on the younger side of a typical business age structure, MBA students are to become future managers and corporate executives over the next few decades of their professional careers and understanding their decision-making styles provides a unique window into the sorts of things that may influence their decision making. Finally, on a practical level, there are very few secondary sources available that

---

[1]The academic content of the executive MBA program does not significantly differ from that of the traditional MBA program but is designed to accommodate full-time working professionals and business executives. As such, those enrolling in the executive MBA program tend to have much more business or "real-world" experience than their counterparts in the traditional MBA program.

permit analyses of corporate malfeasance and none that contain the array of theoretical variables elaborated in neutralization theory with respect to corporate crime decision making.

The survey included a range of questions about attitudes toward business practices and also asked respondents to indicate their purported intentions to engage in a specific behavior after reading a scenario about a hypothetical drug (see Appendix A). All 133 students were presented with the purpose of the study, were asked to participate, and all of them gave voluntary consent and completed the full survey. On average, the sample was over 30 years of age ($M = 30.70$, $SD = 7.37$, range: 22–55), mostly White (77%), and predominately male (67%).[2]

Dependent Variable

The use of scenarios (or vignettes) has been common in previous white-collar/corporate crime research (Paternoster & Simpson, 1996; N. L. Piquero, 2012; N. L. Piquero et al., 2005; N. L. Piquero, Exum, & Simpson, 2005; Simpson, Paternoster, & Piquero, 1998; Simpson & Piquero, 2002). This methodology presents a scenario to respondents depicting a hypothetical situation in which a character engages in a particular behavior or act. Following each scenario, respondents are typically asked (on a Likert-type scale) whether they would do what the character in the scenario did. The current study presented respondents with a scenario regarding the inhibition or promotion of a hypothetical drug, Panalba, which was banned by the Food and Drug Administration (see Appendix A). Serving as the main outcome variable, respondents were asked to report the extent to which they would promote or inhibit the distribution of Panalba, which is known to harm persons.

This measure was coded on a scale ranging from 1 to 6 as follows: (1) *recall Panalba immediately and destroy all existing inventories, (2) stop production of Panalba immediately but allow existing inventories to be sold, (3) stop all advertising and promotion of Panalba, but continue distribution to those physicians who request it, (4) continue efforts to effectively market Panalba until its sale is actually banned, (5) continue efforts to market Panalba while taking legal, political, and other actions to prevent its banning,* and (6) *continue efforts to market Panalba in other countries after the FDA bans the drug in the U.S.* The average score was 2.57 ($SD = 1.70$), which suggests that the average respondent chose to either stop production but allow existing inventories to be sold or to stop all advertising and promotion but continue distribution to physicians who request it.[3]

Techniques of Neutralization

Our measures of the techniques of neutralization are informed by the early research on neutralization, where studies used scenarios to assess the degree to which people accepted neutralizing statements under the assumption that delinquents would be more accepting of neutralizing statements than nondelinquents. Maruna and Copes's (2005) review of these studies provides strong validity for the techniques measures, and we use these as the starting point for our measures that are reoriented to the business domain. Specifically, we operationalize Sykes and Matza's five techniques of neutralization with modifications to reflect the context of the workplace environment and workplace decision making (see Hollinger, 1991; N. L. Piquero, Tibbetts, & Blankenship, 2005). All 5 items had response options that ranged from 1 (*strongly disagree*) to 3 (*neutral*) to 5 (*strongly agree*). Higher scores on all 5 items, which did

---

[2]As with any sampling frame, the use of university students, even in MBA programs, is limited. Still, given the lack of available data on business decision making within a criminological context (Simpson & Piquero, 2002), the application of techniques of neutralization across gender in the current study provides a baseline to which future studies can be modeled after and results compared against.

[3]We recognize that there may be some concerns over the use of the vignette methodology and the solicitation of purported offending intentions. For example, the method has been criticized because it places individuals in a hypothetical situation that may not be realistic or that such persons may not (now or ever) find themselves in. And while such methods have been routinely used in criminology generally (Nagin & Paternoster, 1993; A. Piquero & Tibbetts, 1996) and the study of white-collar/corporate crime in particular (Simpson et al., 1998; Simpson & Piquero, 2002; N. L. Piquero, 2012; N. L. Piquero, Tibbetts, & Blankenship, 2005), there is the issue about whether purported intentions equate perfectly with actual behavior. Importantly, the survey used in our study was modeled closely after those that have been successfully administered and judged valid and realistic by survey respondents (including our own, who rated the scenario as very believable) and furthermore there are a sizable number of studies showing a strong concordance between projected and actual behavior (Pogarsky, 2004).

not lead to concerns over multicollinearity as judged by variance inflation factors (VIFs) and the fact that the highest correlation among the five techniques items was $r = .435$, indicate stronger levels of neutralization and should be positively associated with increased intentions to promote and sell Panalba.

Denial of injury (government exaggerates dangers to consumers). Respondents were asked, "The government exaggerates the danger to consumers from most products." According to N. L. Piquero et al. (2005, p. 170), by agreeing with this statement, respondents are able "to deny the injury of the act by claiming that the government is overly cautious in assessing the danger to the public. This belief also relates to denial of responsibility in the sense that it implies that there is minimal danger in the use of marketed products, so the companies that produce such items should not be held responsible if injuries do happen to occur from usage."

Condemnation of the condemners (regulations impede). Respondents were asked: "Government regulations impede business." Here, the blame of the act is deflected to the government and the strict regulations it places on business.

Appeal to higher loyalty (profit most important). Respondents were asked: "Profit is emphasized above everything else at my place of work." By placing the blame onto the organization or company for which the respondent works for, he or she is able to deflect feelings of guilt associated with the behavior and its outcomes.

Denial of victim (Caveat emptor motto). Respondents were asked: "'Caveat emptor' (let the buyer beware) is the motto of my employer." By deflecting the blame of the act onto the victim the respondent can claim that the victim should have known better.

Denial of responsibility (anything to make a profit). Respondents were asked: "Where I work, it is all right to do anything to make a profit unless it is against the law." Here, the individual places the responsibility of the act onto the organization (by its rules and culture of how it does its business) in which he or she is employed and thus can deny his or her own individual responsibility for the behavior and its outcomes.

Table 1 presents descriptive statistics for study variables.

Table 1	Descriptive Statistics
Variable	**M (SD)**
Denial of injury	2.82 (1.09)
Condemnation of condemners	2.55 (1.00)
Appeal to higher loyalty	2.90 (1.24)
Denial of victim	2.30 (1.07)
Denial of responsibility	2.42 (1.11)
Gender (1 = M, 2 = F)	1.33 (0.47)
Age	30.70 (7.37)
Race (1 = W, 2 = NW)	1.77 (0.42)
Program (1 = MBA, 2 = Exc)	1.21 (0.41)
Intentions to offend	2.57 (1.67)

Analytic Plan

To examine the extent to which techniques of neutralization relate to the marketing and sale of the unsafe drug Panalba across gender, we begin by examining the extent to which there are any gender differences with respect to (a) intentions to offend and (b) techniques of neutralization. To presuppose our findings, we do indeed observe some average differences for these two constructs. These preliminary results support the need to examine split-gender models where we examine the extent to which the techniques of neutralization relate to offending intentions in similar or unique ways for males and females using ordinary least squares (OLS) regression models.[4] A series of coefficient comparison tests will also be conducted to examine the equality of regression coefficients across gender (see Paternoster, Brame, Mazerolle, & Piquero, 1998).

 Results

Bivariate Analysis

Initial results show that men and women significantly differ on the overall intentions outcome variable, with men ($M = 2.82$) reporting a significantly higher average value

---

[4]Although the distribution of the outcome variable did not evince any extreme skew, we also estimated supplemental Ordered Logistic Regression models, the results of which were substantively the same as those reported in the main text with OLS.

compared to women (M = 2.04; t = 2.78, p < .05). Figure 1 provides a graphical portrayal of this relationship. Here, it can be seen that while there are a higher percentage of women at the two lower decision options (recalling Panalba, stopping production of Panalba), at the other end of the continuum there is a higher percentage of men who would impede the ban of Panalba or who would continue to market Panalba outside the United States.

Having established a bivariate relationship between gender and offending intentions, we next examine how men and women responded to the five techniques of neutralization items. As seen in Table 2, there are significant differences on two of the items and no differences on the other three items. With respect to the two items that differ across gender, (a) men are more likely than women to agree that the government exaggerates the danger to consumers from most products (denial of injury) and (b) women are more likely to agree that government regulations impede business (condemnation of the condemners).

Full-Sample Analysis

Next, we estimated a full-sample OLS regression model predicting offending intentions with the five techniques of neutralization measures, gender, and three control variables (age, race, MBA program status). Three of the techniques variables are significantly associated with higher intentions to offend: denial of injury (government exaggerates), condemnation of the condemners (regulations impede), and appeal to higher loyalty (profit is most important), and the model explains almost 20% of the variation in offending intentions.[5] Higher agreement with each of these techniques was associated with continued interest in marketing and selling Panalba. Confirming the bivariate results, we found that women were less likely to market and sell Panalba and instead more likely to recall it or stop its production. Of the control variables, only program status was significant, indicating that executive MBA enrollees were less likely to report affirmative intentions to offend.[6] In short, these findings show that techniques of

neutralization relate to corporate misbehavior in some similar ways when compared to how neutralizations have been found to relate to other deviant acts. Yet, we also find some differences in that not all techniques that have been found to relate to deviance in other studies relate similarly to corporate deviance, supporting Sykes and Matza's suggestion that certain techniques are better adapted to particular deviant acts than others (p. 670). Further, the results indicate that certain techniques of neutralization appear better adapted to corporate misbehavior than other techniques, but whether this pattern of findings replicates across gender is unknown and becomes the focus of the next set of analyses.

Gender-Specific Models Predicting Offending Intentions

Next, we estimate split-gender models to ascertain the relationship between the techniques of neutralization and

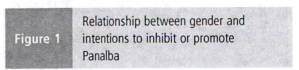

Figure 1 Relationship between gender and intentions to inhibit or promote Panalba

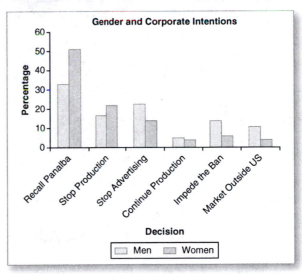

---

[5]There were no problems with multicollinearity in this (nor subsequent) model estimations.

[6]Caution should be exercised with respect to the MBA program status effect as there were only 31 enrollees in the executive MBA program. We nevertheless felt the need to control for program status because there may be a "different kind" of student in the executive compared to traditional program.

Table 2	Mean Differences for Techniques of Neutralization by Gender	
Technique of Neutralization	**Men** M (SD)	**Women** M (SD)
Denial of injury	3.02 (1.12)	2.41 (0.89)*
Condemnation of condemners	2.36 (0.97)	2.96 (0.96)*
Appeal to higher loyalty	2.93 (1.24)	2.86 (1.25)
Denial of victim	2.28 (1.03)	2.31 (1.14)
Denial of responsibility	2.50 (1.11)	2.24 (1.10)

NOTE: *p < .05.

offending intentions for men and women[7] (see Table 3). Among men, two of the five techniques were significantly associated with offending intentions: denial of injury (government exaggerates) and appeal to higher loyalties (profit most important). Once again, agreeing with these techniques was associated with continued efforts to impede the ban of Panalba or market the sale of Panalba

Table 3	Split-Gender OLS Regressions Predicting Intentions to Inhibit or Promote Panalba	
	Men B (SE)	**Women** B (SE)
Denial of injury	0.40 (0.17)*	0.62 (0.27)*
Condemnation of condemners	0.22 (0.21)	0.15 (0.24)
Appeal to higher loyalty	0.41 (0.16)*	−0.24 (0.21)
Denial of victim	−0.03 (0.21)	−0.14 (0.19)
Denial of responsibility	−0.08 (0.19)	0.53 (0.24)*
Age	0.04 (0.03)	−0.01 (0.04)
Race (1 = W, 2 = NW)	−0.54 (0.52)	0.33 (0.43)
Program (1 = MBA, 2 = Exec)	−0.70 (0.54)	−1.48 (0.63)*
Constant	0.82 (1.73)	1.49 (2.30)
R^2	.16	.39

NOTE: *< .05, unstandardized coefficient reported.

outside the United States. Among women, two of the five techniques of neutralization were significantly associated with offending intentions. Specifically, women who agreed that the government exaggerates the danger from most products (denial of injury) to consumers were more likely to report affirmative offending intentions. On the other hand, and opposite of the corresponding male coefficient, women who believed that their place of business eschewed the belief that it was acceptable to do anything to make a profit unless it was against the law (denial of responsibility) were more likely to report higher offending intentions. None of the other three techniques of neutralization were significantly related to offending intentions among women. One control variable, MBA program status, had a negative and significant effect on offending intentions among women, with women in the executive MBA program reporting lower offending intentions. However, there were only eight women in the executive MBA program and this effect should be interpreted with caution.[8] In short, we find that some techniques operate in the same way across gender (denial of injury), others are gender-specific (i.e., higher loyalties for males but denial of responsibility for females), and others that are unimportant for either males or females. Thus, some neutralizations appear gender-neutral while others may be gender-specific.

Discussion

Sykes and Matza's neutralization theory has been applied to a wide variety of offenders. Although a sound empirical knowledge base has accumulated (Maruna & Copes, 2005), the examination of the role of gender has received limited attention. The present study assessed the extent to which techniques of neutralization related to corporate offending decisions varied across gender. In doing so, it sought to contribute to underdeveloped and underexplored research areas in criminology more generally, by focusing on potential gender differences in corporate offending (see N. L. Piquero & Moffitt, 2012). Using a sample of MBA students, four key findings emerged from our analysis.

[7]Since the sample size for female respondents is small, caution should be exercised when interpreting these results.

[8]A series of coefficient comparison tests indicated that only one coefficient (denial of responsibility technique: anything to make a profit) approached being significantly different across gender (z = 1.47). Although not statistically significant at conventional levels, this is a potentially interesting difference as the effect was negative and insignificant for males but positive and significant for females.

First, bivariate comparisons showed that men were more likely than women to indicate their intention to commit corporate crime by agreeing to continue to market or sell the banned drug Panalba. Second, men and women differed from one another on two of the five techniques of neutralization: Men were most likely to rely on denial of injury to justify their intention to offend, while women reported greater agreement with condemnation of condemners. Third, regression analyses of the full sample indicated that women were less likely to continue to market and sell Panalba and more likely to recall the drug or stop its production and that three techniques of neutralization (appeal to higher loyalties, condemnation of condemners, and denial of injury) were associated with greater corporate offending intentions. Finally, split-gender analysis indicated that one of the techniques, denial of injury, was significantly associated with greater intentions to offend for both men and women, while appeal to higher loyalties was a significant predictor among men and denial of responsibility was a significant predictor among women. A series of coefficient comparison tests of the relationship between the five techniques of neutralization measures and corporate offending intentions across gender failed to indicate any significant difference between men and women.

In short, our analyses showed gender differences in intentions to offend and minor mean-level differences between men and women for only a few of the techniques of neutralization. Our finding that women were less likely than men to report intentions to engage in corporate crime (by marketing and continuing to sell Panalba) is consistent with what little is known about white-collar offending differences between men and women. Data from convicted white-collar offenders repeatedly suggest that men are more commonly involved in the more complex white-collar crimes (i.e., antitrust and securities fraud), while women are involved in the less complex offenses such as bank embezzlement (Weisburd, Waring, & Chayet, 2001; Weisburd et al., 1991). In fact, Daly (1989) found that the female share of corporate crime was quite low, approximately 1%, and thus, noted that almost all of women's white-collar crimes were petty offenses.

Authors' Note

Michael Blankenship passed away on April 21, 2011. He was responsible for the data collection used in this study and we are indebted to his contribution and friendship.

Declaration of Conflicting Interests

The authors declared no potential conflicts of interest with respect to the research, authorship, and/or publication of this article.

Funding

The authors received no financial support for the research, authorship, and/or publication of this article.

 ## References

Benson, M. L. (1985). Denying the guilty mind: Accounting for involvement in white-collar crime. *Criminology, 23,* 583–608.

Borkowski, S. C., & Ugras, Y. J. (1998). Business students and ethics: A meta-analysis. *Journal of Business Ethics, 17,* 117–127.

Brookman, F., Mullins, C., Bennett, T., & Wright, R. (2007). Gender, motivation and the accomplishment of street robbery in the United Kingdom. *British Journal of Criminology, 47,* 861–884.

Brooks-Gordon, B., & Gelsthorpe, L. (2003). What men say when apprehended for kerb crawling: A model of prostitutes clients' talk. *Psychology, Crime and Law, 9,* 145–171.

Byers, B. D., & Crider, B. W. (2002). Hate crimes against the Amish: A qualitative analysis of bias motivation using routine activities theory. *Deviant Behavior, 23,* 115–148.

Cohen, A. K. (1955). *Delinquent boys: The culture of the gang.* New York, NY: Free Press.

Coleman, J. W. (2006). *The criminal elite: Understanding white-collar crime* (6th ed.). New York, NY: Worth.

Copes, H. (2003). Societal attachments, offending frequency, and techniques of neutralization. *Deviant Behavior, 24,* 101–127.

Copes, H. & Vieraitis, L. M. (2009). Bounded rationality of identity thieves: Using offender-based research to inform policy. *Criminology & Public Policy, 8,* 101–126.

Copes, H., & Vieraitis, L. M. (2012). *Identity thieves: Motives and methods.* Boston, MA: Northeastern University Press.

Copes, H., Vieraitis, L. M., & Jochum, J. (2007). Bridging the gap between research and practice: How neutralization theory can inform Reid interrogations of identity thieves. *Journal of Criminal Justice Education, 18,* 444–459.

Copes, H., & Williams, P. (2007). Techniques of affirmation: Deviant behavior, moral commitment, and resistant subcultural identity. *Deviant Behavior, 28,* 247–272.

Cressey, D. R. (1953). *Other people's money: A study in the social psychology of embezzlement.* Glencoe, IL: Free Press.

Cromwell, P., & Thurman, Q. (2003). The devil made me do it: Use of neutralizations by shoplifters. *Deviant Behavior, 24,* 535–550.

Dabney, D. A. (1995). Neutralization and deviance in the workplace: Theft of supplies and medicines by hospital nurses. *Deviant Behavior, 16,* 313–331.

Daly, K. (1989). Gender and varieties of white collar crime. *Criminology, 27,* 769–794.

DeYoung, M. (1988). The indignant page: Techniques of neutralization in the publications of pedophile organizations. *Child Abuse and Neglect, 12,* 583–591.

Durkin, K. F., & Bryant, C. (1999). Propagandizing pederasty: A thematic analysis of the on-line exculpatory accounts of unrepentant pedophiles. *Deviant Behavior, 20,* 103–127.

Edelhertz, H. (1970). *The nature, impact and prosecution of white-collar crime.* Washington, DC: U.S. Department of Justice.

Eliason, S. L., & Dodder, R. (1999). Techniques of neutralization used by deer poachers in the Western United States. *Deviant Behavior, 20,* 233–252.

Evans, R. D., & Porche, D. A. (2005). The nature and frequency of medicare/medicaid fraud and neutralization techniques among speech, occupational, and physical therapists. *Deviant Behavior, 26,* 253–270.

Ferraro, K. J., & Johnson, J. M. (1983). How women experience battering: The process of victimization. *Social Problems, 30,* 325–339.

Goode, S., & Cruise, S. (2006). What motivates software crackers? *Journal of Business Ethics, 65,* 173–201.

Greenberg, J. (1990). Employee theft as a reaction to underpayment inequity: The hidden cost of pay cuts. *Journal of Applied Psychology, 75,* 561–568.

Higginson, J. G. (1999). Defining, excusing, and justifying deviance: Teen mothers' accounts of statutory rape. *Symbolic Interaction, 22,* 25–44.

Hollinger, R. C. (1991). Neutralizing in the workplace: An empirical analysis of property theft and production deviance. *Deviant Behavior, 12,* 169–202.

Holt, T. J., & Copes, H. (2010). Transferring subcultural knowledge online: Practices and beliefs of persistent digital pirates. *Deviant Behavior, 31,* 625–654.

Holtfreter, K. (2005). Is occupational fraud "typical" white-collar crime? A comparison of individual and organizational characteristics. *Journal of Criminal Justice, 33,* 353–365.

Ingram, J. R., & Hinduja, S. (2008). Neutralizing music piracy: An empirical examination. *Deviant Behavior, 29,* 334–366.

Jesilow, P., Pontell, H. N., & Geis, G. (1993). *Prescription for profit: How doctors defraud Medicaid.* Berkeley: University of California Press.

Klenowski, P. M., Copes, H., & Mullins, C. W. (2011). Gender, identity, and accounts: How white collar offenders do gender when making sense of their crimes. *Justice Quarterly, 28,* 46–69.

Klockars, C. B. 1974. *The professional fence.* New York, NY: Free Press.

Levi, K. 1981. Becoming a hit man: Neutralization in a very deviant career. *Urban Life, 10,* 47–63.

Maruna, S., & Copes, H. (2005). What have we learned from five decades of neutralization research? *Crime and Justice: A Review of Research, 32,* 221–320.

Miller, J. (1998). Up it up: Gender and the accomplishment of street robbery. *Criminology, 36,* 37–66.

Minor, W. W. (1981). Techniques of neutralization: A reconceptualization and empirical examination. *Journal of Research in Crime and Delinquency, 18,* 295–318.

Mullins, C., & Cherbonneau, M. (2011). Establishing connections: Gender, motor vehicle theft, and disposal networks. *Justice Quarterly, 28,* 278–302.

Mullins, C., Wright, R., & Jacobs, B. A. (2004). Gender, streetlife, and criminal retaliation. *Criminology, 42,* 911–940.

Nagin, D. S., & Paternoster, R. (1993). Enduring individual differences and rational choice theories of crime. *Law & Society Review, 27,* 467–469.

Paternoster, R., Brame, R., Mazerolle, P., & Piquero, A. (1998). Using the correct statistical test for the equality of regression coefficients. *Criminology, 36,* 859–866.

Paternoster, R., & Simpson, S. (1996). Sanction threats and appeals to morality: Testing a rational choice model of corporate crime. *Law and Society Review, 30,* 549–583.

Peretti-Watel, P. (2003). Neutralization theory and the denial of risk: Some evidence from cannabis use among French adolescents. *British Journal of Sociology, 54,* 21–42.

Piquero, A., & Tibbetts, S. G. (1996). Specifying the direct and indirect effects of low self-control and situational factors in offender decision making: Toward a more complete model of rational offending. *Justice Quarterly, 13,* 601–631.

Piquero, A. R., Farrington, D. P., & Blumstein, A. (2003). The criminal career paradigm. In M. Tonry (Ed.), *Crime and justice: A review of research (Vol 30).* Chicago, IL: University of Chicago Press.

Piquero, N. L. (2012). The only thing we have to fear is fear itself: Investigating the relationship between fear of falling and white-collar crime. *Crime and Delinquency, 58,* 362–379.

Piquero, N. L., & Moffitt, T. E. (2012). Can childhood factors explain workplace deviance? *Justice Quarterly,* doi: 10.1080/07418825. 2012.661446

Piquero, N. L., Exum, M. L., & Simpson, S. S. (2005). Integrating the desire for control and rational choice in a corporate crime context. *Justice Quarterly, 22,* 252–280.

Piquero, N. L., Tibbetts, S. G., & Blankenship, M. B. (2005). Examining the role of differential association and techniques of neutralization in explaining corporate crime. *Deviant Behavior, 26,* 159–188.

Pogarsky, G. (2004). Projected offending and contemporaneous rule violation: Implications for heterotypic continuity. *Criminology, 42,* 111–135.

Pogrebin, M. R., Poole, E. D., & Martinez, A. (1992). Accounts of professional misdeeds: The sexual exploitation of clients by psychotherapists. *Deviant Behavior, 13,* 229–252.

Pogrebin, M. R., Stretesky, P. B., Unnithan, N. P., & Venor, G. (2006). Retrospective accounts of violent events by gun offenders. *Deviant Behavior, 27,* 479–501.

Presser, L. (2003). Remorse and neutralization among violent male offenders. *Justice Quarterly, 20,* 801–825.

Priest, T. B., & McGrath, J. H., III. (1970). Techniques of neutralization: Young adult marijuana smokers. *Criminology, 8,* 185–194.

Ray, M. C., & Simons, R. L. (1987). Convicted murderers' accounts of their crimes: A study of homicide in small communities. *Symbolic Interaction, 10,* 57–70.

Scully, D., & Marolla, J. (1984). Convicted rapists' vocabulary of motive: Excuses and justifications. *Social Problems, 31*, 530–544.

Shapiro, S. P. (1990). Collaring the crime, not the criminal: Reconsidering the concept of white-collar crime. *American Sociological Review, 55*, 346–365.

Shover, N., Coffey, G., & Sanders, C. R. (2004). Dialing for dollars: Opportunities, justifications, and telemarketing fraud. *Qualitative Sociology, 27*, 59–75.

Simpson, S. S., Paternoster, R., & Piquero, N. L. (1998). Exploring the micro-macro link in corporate crime research. In P. A. Bamberger & W. J. Sonnenstuhl (Eds.), *Research in the sociology of organizations* (Vol. 15, pp. 35–68). Stamford, CT: JAI Press.

Simpson, S. S., & Piquero, N. L. (2002). Low self-control, organizational theory, and corporate crime. *Law & Society Review, 36*, 509–547.

Sutherland, E. H. (1983). *White collar crime: The uncut version.* New Haven, CT: Yale University Press.

Sutherland, E. H. (1940). White-collar criminality. *American Sociological Review, 5*, 1–12.

Sykes, G. M., & Matza, D. (1957). Techniques of neutralization: A theory of delinquency. *American Sociological Review, 22*, 664–670.

Thurman, Q. C., St. John, C. & Riggs, L. (1984). Neutralizations and tax evasion: How effective would a moral appeal be in improving compliance to tax laws? *Law and Policy, 6*, 309–328.

Vaughan, D. (1996). *The challenger launch decision: Risky technology, culture and deviance at NASA.* Chicago, IL: University of Chicago Press.

Weisburd, D., Waring, E., & Chayet, E. (2001). *White-collar crime and criminal careers.* New York, NY: Cambridge University Press.

Weisburd, D., Wheeler, S., Waring, E., & Bode, N. (1991). *Crimes of the middle classes.* New Haven, CT: Yale University Press.

Zietz, D. (1981). *Women who embezzle or defraud: A study of convicted felons.* New York, NY: Praeger Publishers.

REVIEW QUESTIONS

1. What are some of the additional neutralization techniques that have been added over the years to Sykes and Matza's original five that they presented back in 1957?

2. Which gender showed significantly higher intentions to engage in unethical corporate practices?

3. According to the reported results of the split-gender regression models, did the estimated model do a better job of explaining unethical decision making by women or men?

READING 22

In this selection, David May estimates the influence of fear on carrying firearms to school among approximately 8,000 public high school students. He bases this test on two theories, the first being a variation of Sutherland's differential association theory, which we have examined in previous selections in this section. The second is Travis Hirschi's social bonding theory, which we have not examined in previous selections, so we will now briefly review it here, and a more elaborate explanation can be found in the section introduction.

Hirschi's social bonding theory, a well-known control theory, is actually quite straightforward. First, like all other control theories, Hirschi's theory assumes that individuals are born selfish, greedy, and so on; thus, it assumes that criminal offending is a natural state of human beings, which is consistent with Sigmund Freud's concept of being born with an "id" that constantly seeks pleasure even if it means violating others. So instead of explaining why people offend, the challenge is to explain why human beings actually conform or do not violate the law. Hirschi's social bonding theory claims that what inhibits individuals from engaging in offending behavior is the strength of one's "social bond" to conventional society. According to Hirschi, this social bond is made up of four components, which we will now briefly review.

Specifically, the social bond consists of four elements or components: (a) attachments to others, (b) commitment to conventional society, (c) involvement in conventional activities, and (d) moral beliefs that violation of law is wrong.

The stronger or higher the levels on each of these components of the social bond, the lower the likelihood that individuals will conform to rules of society and the lower the likelihood that they will follow their natural tendencies to commit crimes against others.

While reading this selection, readers are encouraged to put themselves in the shoes of public high school students and imagine the fear they may have of being victimized, as well as whether such fear could justify carrying a firearm to school. In addition, consider the validity of the two theoretical models that were used by the author to explain this phenomenon and whether you feel these two models were good choices. Would you have chosen other theoretical frameworks if you had performed this study?

Scared Kids, Unattached Kids, or Peer Pressure

Why Do Students Carry Firearms to School?

David C. May

Firearm homicides are the second leading cause of death for youngsters 15 to 19 years old and are the leading cause of death for Black males aged 10 to 34 years (Fingerhut, 1993). Between 1980 and 1990, there was a 79% rise in the number of juveniles committing murder with guns (Senate Hearings, 1993) and in 1990, 82% of all murder victims aged 15 to 19 years and 76% of victims aged 20 to 24 years were killed by firearms (Roth, 1994).

The problem of violent crime among adolescents is particularly acute in places where youth spend much of their time. Arguably, there is no single place where youth consistently congregate more than at school. Although deaths at school as a result of violence are rare events (76 violent student deaths in the 1992–1994 academic years), the general perception is that school-associated violence is on the increase (Kachur et al., 1996). Although Kachur et al. indicate that this does not appear to be the case, school violence, and particularly gun violence at school, is a problem that is not easily ignored. Some have argued that approximately 100,000 students take guns to school every day (Senate Hearings, 1993; Wilson & Zirkel, 1994). Estimates of the percentage of students who take guns to school vary widely, however; the percentage has been determined to be anywhere from .5% (Chandler, Chapman, Rand, & Taylor, 1998) to approximately 9% who carry a gun to school at least "now and then" (Sheley & Wright, 1993, p. 5). Furthermore, a majority of students say it would be little or no trouble to get a gun if they wanted one (Sheley & Wright, 1993). It is obvious that firearms in our schools are a problem.

Although numerous studies have examined prevalence of firearms possession among school-aged adolescents (Callahan & Rivara, 1992; Center to Prevent Handgun Violence, 1993; Chandler et al. 1998; Hechinger, 1992; Roth, 1994; Wilson & Zirkel, 1994), the study of causes of firearm possession at school has all but been neglected. Of those researchers who have attempted to examine determinants of adolescent firearm possession, many argue that protection is an often cited reason for weapon possession and provide various explanations for this finding (Asmussen, 1992; Bergstein, Hemenway, Kennedy, Quaday, & Ander, 1996; Blumstein, 1995; Hemenway, Prothrow-Stith, Bergstein, Ander, & Kennedy, 1996; Sheley, 1994; Sheley & Wright, 1993); in fact, Sheley and Wright (1995) determined that 89% of the gun carriers in their sample of youth in correctional facilities and inner-city youth felt that self-protection was a *very important* reason for owning a handgun. Only one study (Sheley & Brewer, 1995), however, examines the association between fear and firearm possession at school (see below for detailed discussion).

There have been many studies that have attempted to determine characteristics of adult firearms owners as well as research that seeks to determine individuals' motivation for owning guns. One explanation that has surfaced to account for why adults own firearms is the "fear and loathing hypothesis" (Wright, Rossi, & Daly, 1983, p. 49). The fear and loathing hypothesis suggests that people buy guns in response to their fear of crime and other incivilities present in our society. According to the fear and loathing hypothesis, individuals, fearful of elements of the larger society (e.g., crime and violence), go through a mental process in which they begin to deplore crime, criminals, and the like and purchase firearms for protection. Recently, many researchers have diminished the loathing aspect of the hypothesis and have examined what would more accurately be called the fear of criminal victimization hypothesis.

Several studies have attempted to test this hypothesis, with mixed results (Arthur, 1992; Lizotte, Bordua, & White, 1981; Smith & Uchida, 1988; Wright & Marston, 1975). These studies, however, are limited in that they use only adult populations; excluding the study conducted by Sheley and Brewer (1995), the fear of criminal victimization hypothesis has never been tested using a sample of adolescents.

Sheley and Brewer (1995), in an examination of suburban high school students in Louisiana, were the first to specifically test the fear of criminal victimization hypothesis among adolescents by investigating the effect of fear on adolescent gun possession at school. They determined that fear had a nonsignificant association with carrying firearms to school, particularly for males. Their study was limited, however, by the fact that they used a single-item indicator of fear of criminal victimization, a method often criticized in the fear of crime literature (see Ferraro, 1995, for a review).

Although there may be no reason to treat gun ownership among adults as a deviant behavior, gun possession among juveniles should be treated as such. Despite the fact that legislation allows adults to carry firearms in many areas, it is illegal in all areas for juveniles to carry firearms to school. This act is not only a violation of the law, it also undermines the authority of schoolteachers and other officials. For these reasons, this act must be considered delinquent.

Furthermore, it is expected that the correlates of delinquency should be the same as the correlates of juvenile gun ownership. Although many of the aforementioned evaluations offer various explanations as to why youths possess firearms, often arguing that the possession is due to structural or personality factors, none attempt to test the effects of fear of criminal victimization on adolescent firearm possession, while controlling for competing explanations of delinquent behavior. These studies, although accepting that carrying a weapon for protection may be due to fear of criminal victimization, fail to examine the specific relationship between fear of criminal victimization and firearm possession. This study attempts to fill that void.

The study makes two major contributions to the literature concerning adolescent firearm possession. First, I test the effect of the fear of criminal victimization hypothesis on juvenile firearms possession at school using a cumulative index to represent fear of criminal victimization, an effort heretofore unexplored. Second, this analysis enhances the relevant scholarship by controlling for variables in Hirschi's (1969) social control theory and a derivative of Sutherland's (1939/1947) differential association theory, a much-needed improvement in this area (see Benda & Whiteside, 1995, for a discussion).

Following social control theory, youth whose bond to society is weakest will be more likely to carry guns to school; advocates of differential association would argue that delinquent tendencies of a juvenile's associates would induce the adolescent to carry firearms to school. On the other hand, following the fear of criminal victimization hypothesis, those youth who are most fearful would be most likely to carry guns to school. Thus, this study seeks to determine if fear of criminal victimization is associated with juvenile gun possession at school, controlling for two acknowledged explanations of delinquency.

 ## Fear of Criminal Victimization Hypothesis

The fear of criminal victimization hypothesis argues that firearm ownership and possession among some people has been motivated by fear of criminal victimization

(Newton & Zimring, 1969). Consequently, according to the fear of criminal victimization hypothesis, a group of gun owners purchase guns for protection from crime and criminals; consequently, those who are most fearful of criminal victimization will be those most likely to own a firearm.

According to the fear of crime literature, females, the elderly, those with lower income and education, urban residents, and African Americans are more fearful than their counterparts (Baumer, 1985; Belyea & Zingraff, 1988; Box, Hale, & Andrews, 1988; Braungart, Braungart, & Hoyer, 1980; Clemente & Kleiman, 1976, 1977; Garofalo, 1979; Kennedy & Krahn, 1984; Kennedy & Silverman, 1984; Larson, 1982; Lawton & Yaffee, 1980; Parker, 1988; Sharp & Dodder, 1985). It follows that these groups would also be the most likely to purchase and carry guns.

As alluded to earlier, tests of this hypothesis have produced inconclusive results. Some authors find that those who are most fearful are most likely to own guns for protection (Lizotte et al., 1981; Smith & Uchida, 1988); other researchers have found little evidence that fear of crime influences carrying a gun for protection (Adams, 1996; Arthur, 1992; Bankston & Thompson, 1989; Bankston, Thompson, Jenkins, & Forsyth, 1990; Williams & McGrath, 1976; Wright et al., 1983).

Although a tremendous volume of research has been produced in the area of fear of criminal victimization and its effect on adult gun ownership and use, two glaring inadequacies remain. The fear of criminal victimization hypothesis has not been tested on adolescents; by the same token, it has not been tested either against, or along with, any other theory of juvenile delinquency or as an explanation for delinquent behavior. The purpose of this study is to fill this void within the literature. This study will attempt to determine the impact of the fear of criminal victimization on juvenile firearms possession. This relationship then will be tested against the relationship between the control that social instructions (such as family and school) have and the influence that peers have on adolescents' firearm possession, to determine the association that these factors have on adolescent gun possession.

The fear of criminal victimization hypothesis, social control theory, and differential association all offer explanations for juvenile firearm possession; the substance of each theory's explanation, however, varies greatly. According to the fear of criminal victimization hypothesis, adolescents who are more fearful would be more likely to carry

guns; advocates of control theory would argue that adolescents with weaker bonds to society would be more likely to carry guns; and finally, proponents of differential association theory would argue that youth whose peers were most approving of engagement in delinquency would be most likely to carry guns. Thus, if, after controlling for two known explanations of deviance, the relationship between fear of criminal victimization and adolescent firearm possession still persists, support for the fear of criminal victimization hypothesis will increase.

 Method

Sample

Data for this study were obtained from a study of Mississippi high school students conducted in the spring of 1992. As the South has the highest rate of gun ownership by region (Kleck, 1997), and Mississippi was the site of the first of several highly publicized schoolyard shootings in the academic year of 1997–1998, gun-carrying behavior of Mississippi adolescents is of particular interest in this field of inquiry.

Dependent Variable

The dependent variable is juvenile firearm possession at school and was operationalized through the questions, "How many times have you carried a gun to school?" Responses were collapsed into two categories, with those who answered *never* coded (0) and those who responded *one or more* times coded as (1). Only 637 students (8.1%) indicated that they had carried a firearm to school one or more times.

Independent Variables

The independent variables include an index representing fear of criminal victimization, an index representing the strength of the adolescent's bond to society (social control), and a similar index representing deviant attitudes of the adolescent's peers (differential association). Due to their significant associations with delinquent behavior found in the literature, race, gender, residence, number of parental figures in the household, socioeconomic status, and gang membership are used as control variables. Finally, as neighborhood incivility has been determined to be a strong predictor of fear of crime among adults (Bursik & Grasmik,

1993; Will & McGrath, 1995), an index of perceived neighborhood incivility is included as a control variable as well.

Perceived Neighborhood Incivility Index

The exogenous variable, perceived neighborhood incivility, was obtained by constructing an index using responses to statements concerning how the respondent viewed his or her neighborhood, such as "There are drug dealers in my neighborhood." The construct demonstrated an internal reliability of .753, indicating that the index is a reliable measure of perceived neighborhood incivility.

Fear of Criminal Victimization Index

The fear of criminal victimization hypothesis states that those who are more fearful will be more likely to carry guns (Wright et al., 1983). This hypothesis does not postulate that excessive fear leads to crime commission. In contrast, its premise is that the fearful will carry firearms to protect themselves from crime.

Fear of crime among the adolescents was measured through construction of a fear of criminal victimization index composed of nine items. The Cronbach's alpha for the scale was .896. It is hypothesized that those respondents scoring higher on the fear scale will be more likely to have carried a gun to school.

Social Control Index

The research reviewed earlier suggests that those adolescents with stronger bonds between themselves and family and school institutions will be less likely to commit delinquent acts (Hirschi, 1969; Jensen, 1972; Reiss, 1951; Wiatrowski, Griswold, & Roberts, 1981). The adolescent's involvement with social institutions was measured by creating a social control index. The index consists of 11 questions or statements. The Cronbach's alpha for the scale was .734. It is hypothesized that those adolescents scoring at the lower end of the scale will be more likely to carry a firearm to school than those on the higher end of the scale.

Differential Association Index

As noted from the research reviewed earlier, those adolescents whose peers have the greatest amount of definitions favorable to violation of the law and engage in the most deviant acts are more likely to engage in delinquent acts (see Williams & McShane, 1999, for a review). Following differential association theory, an index was created to represent the deviant definitions and activities of one's peers.

Cronbach's alpha, used to measure the reliability of the index, was 614. It is hypothesized that those adolescents scoring at the higher end of the scale will be more likely to carry a firearm to school than those on the lower end of the scale.

Demographic Characteristics

It is feasible to suggest that as adolescents age and become familiar with their school surroundings and peers, they will be more able and thus more likely to obtain a firearm if they desire. Thus, it is hypothesized that older youth will be more likely to bring firearms to school than their younger counterparts.

Race will also be used as a control variable. As the overwhelming majority of Mississippi residents fall into one of two racial categories (White and African American), responses to the race question were dichotomized into two categories: White and Black. Several researchers have determined that Whites are less delinquent than Blacks (Cernkovich & Giordano, 1987; Rosen, 1985) and Whites are less fearful than non-Whites; subsequently, Blacks will be more likely to carry guns to school.

Regardless of the theory employed when predicting delinquency, males are more likely than females to be delinquent (Cernkovich & Giordano, 1987, 1992; Hirschi & Gottfredson, 1994). However, the fear of criminal victimization hypothesis would predict that females, the more fearful group, would be more likely to carry firearms. Sheley and Wright (1995) further determined that protective gun possession was more common among females than males in their sample. The question used to assess firearm possession in this study, however, does not allow the researcher to gauge reasons for possession. Thus, even though females may be more likely to possess firearms for protection, it is hypothesized that males will be much more likely to carry guns to school than will their female counterparts, a finding confirmed in numerous studies (e.g. Arria, Wood, & Anthony, 1995; Sheley & Wright, 1995).

Several researchers have identified an inverse relationship between socioeconomic status and delinquency (Reiss, 1951; Rosen, 1985; Wiatrowski et al., 1981). People with lower incomes also are more fearful. Thus, those youth from households with lower household income will be more likely to carry firearms to school.

Although some have argued that family structure does not affect delinquency, particularly violent delinquency (Salts, Lindholm, Goddard, & Duncan, 1995), many have indicated that juveniles from disrupted households (those with one parent) will be more likely than those from intact households (two or more adults in the household) to commit delinquent acts (Gove & Crutchfield, 1982; Hirschi & Gottfredson, 1994; Matsueda & Heimer, 1987; Reiss, 1951). Such findings support Hirschi's control theory. According to Hirschi (1969), two parents will have more control over the juvenile and his or her whereabouts than will one, especially if one of the two parents is not employed. It is reasonable to assume that the relationship will be the same for firearm possession at school as well. Following control theory, it is expected that those juveniles from disrupted family settings will be more likely to carry a gun to school than will their counterparts from households with two parents.

Finally, gang members have been demonstrated to engage in disproportionate amounts of delinquency, including carrying guns (Block & Block, 1993; Blumstein, 1995; Dukes, Martinez, & Stein, 1997; Knox, 1991; Spergel, 1990). Thus, it is hypothesized that gang members will be more likely to carry guns as well.

 Results

Characteristics of the sample are presented in Table 1. Table 1 classifies the sample into gun carriers and nongun carriers. There were several statistically significant differences between the two groups. First, the mean score was significantly higher for the gun carriers than for the nongun carriers on the fear scale (17.101 vs. 14.271, p < .001) and the perceived incivility scale (7.139 vs. 5.842, p < .001). Gun carriers also scored significantly lower on the social control index (27.250) than did the nongun carriers (30.568, p < .001) and significantly higher on the differential association index (6.932 vs. 5.394, p < .001).

The percentage distributions in Table 1 also reveal important differences between gun and nongun carriers. As expected, the percentage of gun carriers who were male (83.7%) is much larger than the percentage of nongun carriers who were male (41.5%), as was the percentage of gun

carriers who were gang members (61.5% vs. 4.6%). The percentage of gun carriers who were Black (55.4%) was also larger than the percentage of nongun carriers who were Black (46.2%). A lower proportion of the gun carriers came from two-parent households (50.7%) than did nongun carriers (58.0%). Furthermore, a larger percentage of youth from the 17 to 18 years and 19 to 20 years age groups (61.1% and 11.8%, respectively) were found among the gun carriers than among the nongun carriers (54.6% and 5.2%, respectively). Finally, there was little difference between gun carriers and nongun carriers across household income or place of residence.

The results presented in Table 1 indicate that significant associations exist between adolescent firearm possession and the independent variables included in this study. To determine the effect of the factors reflected in the perceived incivility index, the fear index, the social control index, and the differential association index on adolescent firearm possession, controlling for the demographic variables, logistic regression will be used.

The results obtained from regressing adolescent firearm possession on the demographic variables not shown indicate that, as expected, gender, race, age, parental structure, income, and gang membership had statistically significant associations with adolescent firearm possession. The regression coefficients indicate that males were six times as likely as females to possess a firearm at school, whereas Blacks were 1.4 times as likely as Whites to carry a firearm to school. Older adolescents were also more likely to carry guns to school than were their younger counterparts. The association between parental structure and adolescent firearm possession was also significant, as those youth from households with other than two adults were significantly more likely than their counterparts from two-parent homes to carry a firearm to school. Those students from families with higher incomes were more likely than students from families with lower incomes to carry guns to school. Finally, gang members were nine times as likely to carry firearms to school as adolescents who were not in gangs. Place of residence had no statistically significant effect on adolescent firearm possession at school.

The second model regressed adolescent firearm possession on the variables included in the first model with the addition of the perceived neighborhood incivility index and the fear of criminal victimization index. Males were again six times as likely as females to indicate that they had carried a firearm to school. Interestingly, however,

Table 1 Characteristics of Gun Carriers and Nongun Carriers

	Gun Carriers		Nongun Carriers	
Variable	M	SD	M	SD
Social control scale	27.250***	4.915	30.568	4.599
Differential association scale	6.932***	1.946	5.394	1.598
Fear scale	17.101***	6.215	14.271	4.812
Perceived incivility	7.139***	2.302	5.842	2.048
	n	%	n	%
Gender				
Male	533	83.7	3,011	41.5
Female	104	16.3	4,238	58.5
Total n	637		7,249	
Race				
White	284	44.6	3,901	53.8
Black	353	55.4	3,348	46.2
Total n	637		7,249	
Age (years)				
13–14	6	0.9	50	0.7
15–16	166	26.1	2,866	39.6
17–18	389	61.1	3,954	54.6
19–20	75	11.8	376	5.2
Total n	636		7,246	
Parental arrangement				
2 or more parents (intact) household	323	50.7	4,205	58.0
Single-parent (disrupted) household	313	49.1	3,036	41.9
Total n	636		7,241	
Family income				
Less than $10,000	8	13.8	922	12.7
$10,000–$19,999	101	15.9	1,368	18.9
$20,000–$29,999	140	22.0	1,546	21.3
$30,000–$39,999	120	18.8	1,503	20.7
More than $40,000	159	25.0	1,652	22.8
Total n	608		6,991	
Gang membership				
Yes	286	61.5	315	4.6
No	179	38.5	6,523	95.4
Total n	465		6,838	
Place of residence				
Rural farm	72	11.3	579	8.0
Rural nonfarm	101	15.9	1,580	21.8
Outside suburbs	90	14.1	1,020	14.1
In suburbs	169	26.5	1,831	25.3
Near center of city	202	31.7	2,212	30.5
Total *n*	634		7,222	

***$p < .001$

with the addition of perceived neighborhood incivility and the fear of crime index, the effect of race became nonsignificant. Youth from two-parent homes were again significantly less likely than youth from other than two-parent homes to carry a firearm to school, whereas older youth continued to be significantly more likely than younger youth to carry a firearm to school. Gang members remained significantly more likely to carry a firearm to school than youth who were not in gangs. The association between household income and adolescent firearm possession remained statistically significant, with those youth from households with greater income again significantly more likely to carry a gun to school than their counterparts from households with lower incomes. The perceived incivility index and the fear of criminal victimization index had statistically significant effects on adolescent firearm possession at school, indicating that those youth who perceived their neighborhood to be most disorderly and those youth who were most fearful of criminal victimization were significantly more likely to carry a gun to school than their counterparts, who perceived their neighborhood to be less disorderly and who were less fearful, respectively. Thus, following the fear of criminal victimization hypothesis, those youth who are most fearful and who perceive their neighborhoods as most disorderly are most likely to carry a gun to school.

The third model in Table 2 presents the results of regressing adolescent firearm possession on the variables included in the second model with the addition of the social control index and the differential association index. Males, Blacks, older respondents, youth from other than two-parent homes, gang members, and respondents with higher levels of household income continued to be significantly more likely than their counterparts to carry a firearm to school, whereas those adolescents who perceived their neighborhoods as disorderly and those adolescents who were most fearful were again significantly more likely than their counterparts to indicate that they had carried a firearm to school. Moreover, those who scored lower on the social control index and those who scored higher on the differential association index respectively were significantly more likely to indicate that they had carried a firearm to school. Thus, as expected, those youth with weaker bonds to society and those youth with more deviant friends were more likely to carry a firearm to school.

 ## Discussion

The results of this study generally support the findings of previous studies dealing with social control, differential association, and delinquent acts. Those children who scored lower on the social control scale, exhibiting lower parental and familial attachment, were significantly more likely to possess firearms at school, as were those youth who scored higher on the index measuring differential association. Both of these findings are consistent with the literature reviewed earlier.

The findings concerning family structure also conform with those from other studies; namely, those children from single-parent homes were significantly more likely to carry guns to school. The evaluation also is consistent with previous studies in demonstrating that males, Blacks, and gang members were more likely to commit the delinquent act in question. As expected, age was positively associated with gun carrying; the older youth were more likely to carry guns to school than were their younger counterparts.

Household income also had a statistically significant positive association with carrying firearms to school; those youth who were from families with higher household income were more likely to carry firearms to school. As this finding is contrary to the literature concerning social control, differential association, and the fear of criminal victimization hypothesis, this finding deserves some explanation. There are two divergent explanations for this finding. It could be that those youth from homes with higher household income had greater financial resources to purchase firearms, thus allowing them to carry a gun to school, whereas other youth might choose some less expensive weapon. This study is limited in that it is unable to examine that relationship.

A second, and perhaps more likely, explanation is that the relationship between household income and adolescent firearm possession may be due to the methodology of the study. Adolescents were asked to estimate their household income; it is quite probable that many of the youth did not have this knowledge and may have exaggerated their household income. Finally, the size of the sample also leads one to question the substantive value of this finding. In a sample this large, associations may achieve statistical significance ($p < .05$) but not substantive significance. Whatever the explanation, this finding should be viewed with extreme caution.

Place of residence had no statistically significant association with adolescent firearm possession. This contradicted the hypothesis concerning the relationship between these variables. One explanation for this might be that the adolescents are unaware of the actual size of their residence; furthermore, inasmuch as the sample consists of adolescents from Mississippi, a primarily rural state, even those who classified themselves as living at the center of the city probably live in areas that could not be characterized as traditional, urban residents.

The most interesting finding from this study concerns the relationship between perceived neighborhood incivility, fear of criminal victimization, and adolescent firearm possession. Adolescents who perceived their neighborhoods as most disorderly and who were most fearful were significantly more likely to carry a gun to school. These findings support the fear of criminal victimization hypothesis: at least in part, students carry guns to school because of the fear of classmates and the perceived criminogenic conditions of their neighborhoods that they experience. It is evident that fear of criminal victimization in juveniles creates similar reactions to fear of criminal victimization in adults.

On further review, the association might not be as peculiar as it sounds. With the prevalence of guns in our society, guns are readily available for juveniles. As mentioned earlier, a majority of students know where to get a gun if they desire. Those students who are most fearful might take action to get a gun and take that gun to school for protection. Another plausible explanation might be that those juveniles who are most delinquent are also most fearful of other delinquents with whom they may interact. If this is the case, their fear might be a result instead of a cause of delinquency. It could be that the delinquents develop their fear after they have committed delinquent acts.

It also could be that adolescents' fear might be explained by the lifestyles approach, which states that those individuals who put themselves in situations in which crimes will occur are more likely to commit crimes and to be victimized by them (Cohen & Felson, 1979; Hindelang, Gottfredson, & Garofalo, 1978). These adolescents could very well develop the fear because they see so many delinquent acts being committed by their peers (as this study shows, those adolescents whose peers were most delinquent, as well as those youth who were gang members,

were also more likely to carry firearms) and thus become fearful that one day their delinquent friends, or adversaries of their friends, might harm them. It is beyond the nature of this study to test this temporal relationship. However, further research in this area would be beneficial. A longitudinal study might be used to determine which occurs first: the fear or the firearm-related delinquency.

 Implications

The purpose of this study was to examine the association between the fear of criminal victimization hypothesis and adolescent firearm possession, while controlling for more traditional explanations of delinquency—namely, differential association and social control theory. Analysis of the results indicate that the fear of criminal victimization hypothesis, social control theory, and differential association are all statistically significant indicators of adolescent firearm possession.

The implications of this study are twofold. First, social control theory, differential association theory, and the fear of criminal victimization hypothesis have a significant association with firearms possession. Second, the fear of criminal victimization hypothesis seems to apply to gun ownership and possession at least as well among juveniles as among adults.

As the findings from this study indicate, at least part of the reason that youth carry firearms to school is because of a fear of criminal victimization at school and a perception that their neighborhoods are dens of criminal activity. The findings from this study explicate a phenomenon known to social science researchers for quite some time but only recently identified and prioritized by policy makers. To reduce the number of firearms in school, the circumstances that cause youth to bring firearms to school must be reduced. Although taking steps to alleviate the problem of fear on the school grounds is important, it is equally important that these steps be taken in the neighborhoods where these youth live as well. It is imperative that we find measures to reduce the fear of crime of students at school, as well as their fear of crime in their neighborhoods.

There are a number of steps that could be implemented in this regard that are already in place with adult populations. First, as Kenney and Watson (1998) suggest, adolescents should be empowered to make use of school and police resources to reduce fear and disorder problems at school and at home. By implementing problem-solving methods widely used by police and Neighborhood Watch programs throughout the country, adolescents can be empowered to identify sources of fear of crime in their environment and identify and implement steps aimed at alleviating those conditions.

Second, it is well demonstrated that much of the public perception of crime in the United States is strongly influenced by the media. Thus, it is imperative that more accurate information about the problem of guns and violence in schools be presented. Universities throughout the country regularly publish reports identifying the crime that goes on at their campus. It is quite possible that if junior high and high schools throughout the country were to implement a similar reporting system, the perception that crime, particularly crime with guns, is rampant at schools could be alleviated and thus reduced.

Finally, an important step in this effort to curb violence and fear of violence among adolescents might be to ensure that adolescents do not carry firearms to school. Although various measures have been implemented in an attempt to curb this activity (e.g., metal detectors, banning book bags, increased use of locker searches), each needs to be evaluated to determine its effectiveness in combating crime at school. Those measures that are most effective subsequently can be implemented in schools throughout the country. When these measures are institutionalized, the first step will be taken in reducing firearm possession at school and concomitantly reducing school violence.

⧖ References

Adams, K. (1996). Guns and gun control. In T. J. Flanagan & D. R. Longtime (Eds.), *Americans view crime and justice: A national public opinion survey* (pp. 109–123). Thousand Oaks, CA: Sage.

Arria, A. M., Wood, N. P., & Anthony, J. (1995). Prevalence of carrying a weapon and related behaviors in urban schoolchildren, 1989 to 1993. *Archives of Pediatric and Adolescent Medicine, 149,* 1345–1350.

Arthur, J. A. (1992). Criminal victimization, fear of crime, and handgun ownership among Blacks: Evidence from national survey data. *American Journal of Criminal Justice, 16*(2), 121–141.

Asmussen, K. J. (1992). Weapon possession in public high schools. *School Safety, 28,* 28–30.

Bankston, W., & Thompson, C. (1989). Carrying firearms for protection: A causal model. *Sociological Inquiry, 59*(1), 75–87.

Bankston, W., Thompson, C., Jenkins, Q., & Forsyth, C. (1990). The influence of fear of crime, gender, and Southern culture on carrying firearms for protection. *Sociological Quarterly, 31*(2), 287–305.

Baumer, T. (1985). Testing a general model of fear of crime: Data from a national sample. *Journal of Research in Crime and Delinquency, 22*(3), 239–255.

Belyea, M. J., & Zingraff, M. T. (1988). Fear of crime and residential location. *Rural Sociology, 53*(4), 473–486.

Benda, B. B., & Whiteside, L. (1995). Testing an integrated model of delinquency using LISREL. *Journal of Social Service Research, 21*(2), 1–32.

Bergstein, J. M., Hemenway, D., Kennedy, B., Quaday, S., & Ander, R. (1996). Guns in young hands: A survey of urban teenagers' attitudes and behaviors related to handgun violence. *Journal of Trauma, Injury, Infection, and Critical Care, 41*(5), 794–798.

Block, C. R., & Block, R. (1993). *Street gang crime in Chicago.* Washington, DC: National Institute of Justice.

Blumstein, A. (1995). *Violence by young people: Why the deadly nexus?* Washington, DC: National Institute of Justice.

Box, S., Hale, C., & Andrews, G. (1988). Explaining fear of crime. *British Journal of Criminology, 28*(3), 340–356.

Braungart, M., Braungart, R., & Hoyer, W. (1980). Age, sex, and social factors in fear of crime. *Sociological Focus, 13*(1), 55–66.

Bursik, R. J., Jr., & Grasmick, H. G. (1993) *Neighborhoods and crime: The dimensions of effective community control.* Lexington, MA: Lexington Books.

Callahan, C. M., & Rivara, F. P. (1992). Urban high school youth and handguns: A school-based survey. *Journal of the American Medical Association, 267*(22), 3038–3042.

Center to Prevent Handgun Violence. (1993). *Kids carrying guns.* Washington, DC: Government Printing Office.

Cernkovich, S. A., & Giordano, P. C. (1987). Family relationships and delinquency. *Criminology, 25*(2), 295–321.

Cernkovich, S. A., & Giordano, P. C. (1992). School bonding, race, and delinquency. *Criminology, 30*(2), 261–289.

Chandler, K. A., Chapman, C. D., Rand, M. R., & Taylor, B. M. (1998). *Students' reports of school crime: 1989 and 1995.* Washington, DC: Department of Education and Justice.

Clemente, F., & Kleiman, M. (1976). Fear of crime among the aged. *The Gerontologist, 16*(3), 207–210.

Clemente, F., & Kleiman, M. (1977, December). Fear of crime in the United States: A multivariate analysis. *Social Forces, 56,* 519–531.

Cohen, L. E., & Felson, M. (1979). Social change and crime rate trends: A routine activities approach. *American Sociological Review, 44,* 588–608.

Dukes, R. L., Martinez, R. O., & Stein, J. A. (1997). Precursors and consequences of membership in youth gangs. *Youth and Society, 29*(2), 139–165.

Ferraro, K. F. (1995). *Fear of crime: Interpreting victimization risk.* Albany: State University of New York Press.

Fingerhut, L. (1993, March 23). Firearm mortality among children, youth, and young adults 1–34 years of age, trends and current status: United States, 1985–90: Advance Data. Hyattsville, MD: National Center for Health Statistics.

Garofalo, J. (1979). Victimization and the fear of crime. *Journal of Research on Crime and Delinquency, 16,* 80–97.

Gove, W. R., & Crutchfield, R. D. (1982). The family and juvenile delinquency. *Sociological Quarterly, 23*(3), 301–319.

Hechinger, F. M. (1992). *Fateful choice: Healthy youth for the 21st century.* New York: Hill and Wang.

Hemenway, D., Prothrow-Stith, D., Bergstein, J. M., Ander, R., & Kennedy, B. P. (1996). Gun carrying among adolescents. *Law and Contemporary Problems, 59*(1), 39–53.

Hindelang, M., Gottfredson, M., & Garofalo, J. (1978). *Victims of personal crime: An empirical foundation for a theory of personal victimization.* Cambridge, MA: Ballinger.

Hirschi, T. (1969). *Causes of delinquency.* Berkeley: University of California Press.

Hirschi, T, & Gottfredson, M. (1994). *The generality of deviance.* New Brunswick, NJ: Transaction Publishers.

Jensen, G. F. (1972). Parents, peers, and delinquent action: A test of the differential association perspective. *American Journal of Sociology, 78*(3), 562–575.

Kachur, S. P., Stennies, G. M., Powell, K. E., Modzeleski, W., Stephens, R., Murphy, R., Kresnow, M., Sleet, D., & Lowry, R. (1996). School-associated violent deaths in the United States, 1992 to 1994. *Journal of the American Medical Association, 275*(22), 1729–1733.

Kennedy, L. W., & Krahn, H. (1984). Rural-urban origin and fear of crime: The case for rural baggage. *Rural Sociology, 49*(2), 247–260.

Kennedy, L. W., & Silverman, R. A. (1984). Significant others and fear of crime among the elderly. *International Journal of Aging and Human Development, 20*(4), 241–256.

Kenney, D. J., & Watson, T. S. (1998). *Crime in the schools: Reducing fear and disorder with student problem solving.* Washington, DC: Police Executive Research Forum.

Kleck, G. (1997). *Targeting guns: Firearms and their control.* Hawthorne, NY: Aldine.

Knox, G. W. (1991). *An introduction to gangs.* Berrien Springs, MI: Vande Vere.

Larson, C. J. (1982). City size, fear, and victimization. *Free Inquiry in Creative Sociology, 10*(1), 13–22.

Lawton, M. P., & Yaffee, S. (1980). Victimization and fear of crime in elderly housing tenants. *Journal of Gerontology, 35,* 768–79.

Lizotte, A. J., Bordua, D. J., & White, C. S. (1981). Firearms ownership for sport and protection: Two not so divergent models. *American Sociological Review, 46,* 499–503.

Matsueda, R. L., & Heimer, K. (1987). Race, family structure, and delinquency: A test of differential association and social control theories. *American Sociological Review, 52*(6) 826–840.

Newton, G. D., & Zimring, F. E. (1969). Firearms and violence in American life: A staff report to the national commission on the causes and prevention of violence. Washington, DC: Government Printing Office.

Parker, K. D. (1988). Black-White differences in perceptions of fear of crime. *Journal of Social Psychology, 128*(4), 487–494.

Reiss, A. J. Jr. (1951). Delinquency as the failure of personal and social controls. *American Sociological Review, 16*(2), 196–206.

Rosen, L. (1985). Family and delinquency: Structure or function? *Criminology, 23*(3), 553–573.

Roth, J. A. (1994). *Firearms and violence.* Washington, DC: National Institute of Justice.

Salts, C. J., Lindholm, B. W., Goddard, H. W., & Duncan, S. (1995). Predictive variables of violent behavior in adolescent males. *Youth and society, 26*(3), 377–399.

Senate Hearings. (1993). *Children and gun violence.* Washington, DC: Government Printing Office.

Sharp, P. M., & Dodder, R. A., (1985). Victimization and the fear of crime: Some consequences by age and sex. *International Journal of Contemporary Sociology, 22*(1, 2), 149–161.

Sheley, J. F. (1994). Drug activity and firearms possession and use by juveniles. *The Journal of Drug Issue, 24*(3), 363–382.

Sheley, J. F., & Brewer, V. E. (1995). Possession and carrying of firearms among suburban youth. *Public Health Reports, 110,* 18–26.

Sheley, J. F., & Wright, J. D. (1993). *Gun acquisition and possession in selected juvenile samples.* Washington, DC: National Institute of Justice.

Sheley, J. F., & Wright, J. D. (1995). *In the line of fire: Youth, guns, and violence in urban America.* Hawthorne, NY: Aldine.

Smith, D. A., & Uchida, C. D. (1988). The social organization of self-help: A study of defensive weapon ownership. *American Sociological Review, 53,* 94–102.

Spergel, I. A. (1990). Youth gangs: Continuity and change. In M. Tonry & N. Morris (Eds.), *Crime and justice: A review of research* (Vol. 12, pp. 171–275). Chicago: University of Chicago Press.

Sutherland, E. H. (1947). *Principles of Criminology* (4th ed.). Philadelphia: J. B. Lippincott. (Original work published 1939)

Wiatrowski, M. D., Griswold, D. B., & Roberts, M. K. (1981). Social control theory and delinquency. *American Sociological Review, 46,* 525–541.

Will, J. A., & McGrath, J. H. (1995). Crime, neighborhood perceptions, and the underclass: The relationship between fear of crime and class position. *Journal of Criminal Justice, 23*(2), 163–176.

Williams, F. P., III, & McShane, M. D. (1999). *Criminological theory* (3d ed.). Englewood Cliffs, NJ: Prentice Hall.

Williams, J. S., McGrath, J. H., III. (1976). Why people own guns. *Journal of Communication, 26,* 22–30.

Wilson, J. M., & Zirkel, P. A. (1994). When guns come to school. *American School Board Journal, 181,* 32–34.

Wright, J. D., & Marston, L. (1975). The ownership of the means of destruction: Weapons in the United States. *Social Problems, 23,* 92–107

Wright, J. D., Rossi, P., & Daly, K. (1983). *Under the gun: Weapons, crime, and violence in America.* Hawthorne, NY: Aldine.

REVIEW QUESTIONS

1. What does the author have to say about the impact of firearms in causing injury or death among juveniles and the existing research regarding this phenomenon? Do these statistics and findings convince you that this is a major problem in U.S. society? State your reasons.

2. How important do you feel the fear of victimization is among public high school students? How important do you feel it is for other individuals in U.S. society? Do you feel it justifies carrying weapons, even if it is illegal to do so?

3. How does fear of crime affect your daily life? For example, do you lock your doors and windows at home when you leave, or do you lock your car doors, or do you avoid going to certain places at certain times? If not, why don't you take any of these precautions against crime?

4. According to the findings of the study, to what extent do the two theories (Sutherland's and Hirschi's) appear to have importance in explaining why high school students carry firearms to school? What does the author propose as policy implications? Do you agree with these recommendations? Explain your reasoning.

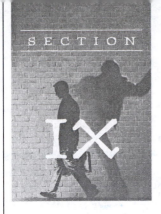

Social Reaction, Critical, and Feminist Models of Crime

T his section will discuss the evolution of social reaction and labeling theory, reviewing contributions made by early theorists as well as modern developments in this area. We will then discuss social conflict and reaction models of criminal behavior, emphasizing the foundational assumptions and principles of Marx as well as the more criminological applications of Marxist and conflict theory by Bonger, Turk, Vold, and others. We'll also review modern applications of various forms of feminist theory.

During the 1960s and early 1970s, social reaction and labeling theories, as well as various critical, conflict, and feminist theories, became popular. At the time, society was looking for theories that placed the blame for criminal offending on government authorities—either the police or societal institutions like economic or class structures. Here we explore these various theories with a special emphasis on how they radically altered the way that crime and law were viewed, as well as how these perspectives highly represented the overall climate in the United States at that time. Specifically, many groups of people—particularly the lower class, minorities, and women—were fighting for their rights during this period, and this manifested itself in criminological theory and research.

Labeling and Social Reaction Theory

Social reaction theory, otherwise referred to as labeling theory, is primarily concerned with how individuals' personal identities are highly influenced by the way that society or authorities tend to categorize them as offenders. With such categorization or labeling, an offender becomes a self-fulfilling prophecy, from this perspective, and results in individuals confirming their status as criminals or delinquents by increasing the frequency or seriousness of their illegal activity. Furthermore, this perspective assumes that there is a tendency to put negative labels on lower-class individuals or minorities as offenders significantly more often than on middle- or upper-class White people.[1]

This perspective assumes that people who are labeled offenders have virtually no choice but to conform to the role that they have been "assigned" by society. Thus, social reaction theory claims that recidivism can be reduced by limiting stigmatization by authorities (e.g., law enforcement) and society. This is referred to as the *hands-off policy*, and it became very popular in the 1960s and early 1970s.[2] Policies that became popular during this period were diversion, decriminalization, and deinstitutionalization (known as the *Ds*). (See Section XII for a discussion of these policies.) All of these attempted to get youthful or first-time offenders out of the formal justice system as soon as possible to avoid stigmatizing or labeling them as offenders. Today, these very policies have led critics to dismiss labeling theory by claiming that it promotes lenient and ineffective sentencing.[3]

Labeling theory was based on seminal work by George Mead and Charles Cooley, which emphasized the importance of the extreme ways that individuals react to and are influenced by the social reaction to their roles and behavior. George Herbert Mead, who was a member of the Chicago School (see Section VII), said that a person's sense of self is constantly constructed and reconstructed through the various social interactions a person has on a daily basis.[4] Every person is constantly aware of how she or he is judged by others through social interactions.

Readers can probably relate to this in the sense that they have experienced how differently they are treated in stores or restaurants if they are dressed nicely as opposed to being less well dressed; as you have observed, there is a significant difference in the way one is treated. Also, when growing up, you probably heard your parents or guardians warn that you should not hang out with Johnny or Sally because they were "bad" kids. Or perhaps you were a Johnny or Sally at some point. Either way, you can see how certain individuals can be labeled by authorities or society and then ostracized by mainstream groups. This can lead to isolation and typically results in a person having only other "bad" kids or adults to hang out with. This results in a type of feedback system, in which the person begins associating with others who will only increase their propensity for illegal activity.[5]

Many strain theorists claim that certain demographic factors, such as social class or the neighborhood where a certain offense took place, may make it more likely that the offender will be caught and labeled by authorities. This claim is quite likely to be true, especially given recent policing strategies that target areas or neighborhoods that have high rates of crime. This is the side of social reaction and labeling theory that deals with the disproportionate rate at which members of the lower class and minorities are labeled as offenders.

Some of the earliest labeling theorists laid the groundwork for this perspective long before it became popular in the 1960s. For example, in the 1930s, Frank Tannenbaum noted the dramatization of evil that occurred when youth were arrested and charged with their first offense.[6] Later, other theorists such as Edwin Lemert contributed a highly important causal sequence to how labeling affects criminality among those who are labeled. Lemert said that individuals, typically youths, commit primary deviance, which is not serious (i.e., it is nonviolent) and not frequent, but they happen to be caught by police and are subsequently labeled.[7] The stigma of the label makes them think of

---

[1]Thomas J. Bernard, Jeffrey B. Snipes, and Alexander L. Gerould, *Vold's Theoretical Criminology*, 6th ed. (Oxford: Oxford University Press, 2010) (see chap. 2).

[2]Edwin Schur, *Radical Nonintervention: Rethinking the Delinquency Problem* (Englewood Cliffs: Prentice Hall, 1973).

[3]Ronald L. Akers and Christine S. Sellers, *Criminological Theories: Introduction, Evaluation, and Application*, 6th ed. (Oxford: Oxford University Press, 2012) (see chap. 8).

[4]George H. Mead, *Mind, Self, and Society* (Chicago: University of Chicago, 1934).

[5]Howard S. Becker, *Outsiders: Studies in the Sociology of Deviance* (New York: Free Press, 1963).

[6]Frank Tannenbaum, *Crime and the Community* (Boston: Ginn, 1938).

[7]Edwin Lemert, *Human Deviance, Social Problems, and Social Control*, 2nd ed. (Englewood Cliffs: Prentice Hall, 1972).

themselves as offenders and forces them to associate only with other offenders. This results in what Lemert referred to as secondary deviance, in which offending is more serious (often violent) and far more frequent. Thus, the causal model that Lemert describes is illustrated as

Primary Deviance → Caught and Labeled → Secondary Deviance

According to Lemert's model, if the label or stigma is not placed on a young or first-time offender, then the more serious and more frequent offending of secondary deviance will not take place. Therefore, Lemert's model is highly consistent with the labeling approach's hands-off policies, such as diversion, decriminalization, and deinstitutionalization. If you ignore such behavior, Lemert reasons, it will tend to go away. However, since the mid-1970s, the get-tough approach has become highly dominant, so such policies are not emphasized by society or policy makers today.

Research on labeling theory suffered a significant blow in the 1970s and 1980s when empirical findings consistently showed that formal arrests and sanctions did not tend to have results that supported traditional labeling theory.[8] In fact, most people who are arrested once are never arrested again, which tends to support deterrence theory and does not support labeling theory. In addition, some experts have concluded that "the preponderance of research finds no or very weak evidence of [formal] labeling effects. . . . The soundest conclusion is that official sanctions by themselves have neither strong deterrent nor a substantial labeling effect."[9] Furthermore, some theorists have questioned the basic assumptions of labeling theory, pointing out that the label does not cause the initial (or primary) offending and that labeling theorists largely ignore the issue of what is causing individuals to engage in illegal activity in the first place. Also, labeling theorists do not recognize the fact that offenders who are caught tend to be the ones who are committing more crimes than those who are not caught; in fact, there tends to be a strong relationship between being caught and committing multiple offenses.[10]

However, more contemporary research and theorizing have emphasized more informal forms of labeling, such as labeling by the community, parents, or friends. Studies have shown more support for the influence of this informal labeling on individuals' behavior.[11] After all, it only makes sense that informal labeling by people with whom you interact on a daily basis (i.e., parents, friends, neighbors, employers, etc.) will have more impact in terms of how you feel about yourself than labeling by police or other authorities, which tends to be temporary or situational.

KARL MARX

▲ Image 9.1   Karl Marx.

Source: © Photos.com / Photos.com / Thinkstock

[8]Marvin Wolfgang, Robert Figlio, and Thorsten Sellin, *Delinquency in a Birth Cohort* (Chicago: University of Chicago Press, 1972).

[9]Akers and Sellers, *Criminological Theories*, 142.

[10]Charles Wellford, "Labeling Theory and Criminology," *Social Problems* 22 (1975): 313–32.

[11]Lening Zhang, "Informal Reactions and Delinquency," *Criminal Justice and Behavior* 24 (1997): 129–50.

Marxist Theories of Crime

Based on the writings of Karl Marx, Marxist theories of crime focus on the fact that people from the lower classes (i.e., the poor) are arrested and charged with crimes at a disproportionate rate. Like conflict criminology, Marxist theories emphasize the effects of a capitalistic society on how justice is administered, describing how society is divided by money and power.[12] Marx said the law is the tool by which the bourgeoisie (the ruling class in a country without a ruling aristocracy, e.g., industrialists and financiers in Western industrialized countries) controls the lower classes (the proletariat and the lowest group, the *lumpenproletariat*) and keeps them in a disadvantaged position. In other words, the law is used as a mechanism by which the middle or upper class maintains its dominance over the lower classes. More specifically, Marx claimed that law is used as a tool to protect the economic interests and holdings of the bourgeoisie, as well as to prevent the lower classes from gaining access to financial resources.[13] Thus, Marxist theories propose that economic power can be translated into legal or political power and substantially accounts for the general disempowerment of the majority.

Willem Bonger

One early key theorist who applied Marxist theory to crime was Willem Bonger, who emphasized the relationship between economy and crime but did not believe simply being poor would cause criminal activity. Rather, he thought crime came about because capitalism caused a difference in the way individuals felt about society and their place in it. In the early 1900s, Bonger said that the contemporary economic structure, particularly capitalism, was the cause of crime in the sense that it promoted a system based on selfishness and greed.[14] Such selfishness manifests itself in competition among individuals, which is obvious in interactions and dealings carried out for the purpose of obtaining goods and resources. This competition and selfishness lead to more isolation, individualism, and egoistic tendencies, which promote a strong focus on self-interests at the expense of communitarianism and societal well-being. Bonger believed that this strong focus on the individual leads to criminal behavior.[15] He also stressed the association between social conditions (largely the result of economic systems) and criminal offending; because of cultural differences, crime can be a normal, adaptive response to social and economic problems, he argued. The poor often develop a strong feeling of injustice, which also contributes to their entering into illegal activity.[16]

Richard Quinney

Although Bonger's theory did not become popular in the early 1900s, when his book was originally published, his ideas received a lot of attention when a neo-Marxist period began in the early 1970s. This renewed interest in Marxist theory was coupled with harsh criticisms leveled at the existing theoretical frameworks, which is why these neo-Marxist theories are often referred to as critical theories. This time, Marxist theories of crime became quite popular, largely because the social climate desired such perspectives. Whereas notable European theorists in this vein include Ian Taylor, Paul Walton, and Jock Young,[17] one of the key figures in this neo-Marxist perspective in the United States was Richard Quinney.[18]

---

[12]Karl Marx, *Selected Works of Karl Marx and Frederick Engels* (Moscow: Foreign Languages Publishing House, 1962).

[13]Bernard et al., *Vold's Theoretical Criminology.*

[14]Willem Bonger, *Criminality and Economic Conditions* (Bloomington: Indiana University Press, 1905/1969).

[15]Bernard et al., *Vold's Theoretical Criminology*; Akers and Sellers, *Criminological Theories.*

[16]Bonger, *Criminality and Economic Conditions.*

[17]Ian Taylor, Paul Walton, and Jock Young, *The New Criminology: For a Social Theory of Deviance* (New York: Harper & Row, 1973).

[18]Richard Quinney, *Critique of Legal Order: Crime Control in Capitalist Society* (Boston: Little, Brown, 1974).

Like Bonger, Quinney claimed that crime was caused by the capitalistic economic structure and the emphasis on materials that this system produced. One way that Quinney's theory goes beyond Bonger is that Quinney further proposed that even the crimes committed by the upper classes are caused by capitalism. To clarify, Quinney claimed that such acts are crimes of "domination and repression" committed by the elite to keep the lower classes down or to protect their property, wealth, and power.[19] A good example is white-collar crimes, which almost always involve raising profits or income, whether for individual or company advantage; such crimes often result in losses to the relatively lower-income clients or customers.

Evidence regarding Marxist Theories of Crime

Many critics noted that these seminal Marxist theories of crime were too simplistic, as well as somewhat naive in the sense that they seemed to claim that the capitalistic economic system was the only reason for crime and that socialism or communism was the only sure way to reduce crime in the United States.[20] Now, even most Marxist theorists reject this proposition. Thus, more modern frameworks have been presented that place more emphasis on factors that stem from capitalism. For example, Colvin and Pauly presented a theoretical model that claims that delinquency and crime are the result of problematic parenting, which results from the degrading and manipulative treatment that parents of lower-class children get in the workplace.[21] However, the empirical tests of this more modern Marxist theory have demonstrated rather weak effects regarding the importance of capitalism (or parenting practices resulting from employment positions or social class).[22] Thus, there does not seem to be much empirical support for Marxist or neo-Marxist theories of crime, which is perhaps why this theoretical framework is not one of the primary models currently accepted by most criminologists.[23]

Conflict Theories of Crime

Conflict theories of crime assume that all societies are in a process of constant change and that this dynamic process inevitably creates conflicts among various groups.[24] Much of the conflict is due to the competition to have each group's interests promoted, protected, and often put into law. If all groups were equally powerful and had the same amount of resources, such battles would involve much negotiation and compromise; however, groups tend to differ significantly in the amount of power or resources that they have. Thus, laws can be created and enforced such that powerful groups can exert dominance over the weaker groups. So, like Marxist theories, law is seen as a tool by which some groups gain and maintain dominance over less powerful groups. Furthermore, this state of inequality and resulting oppression creates a sense of injustice and unfairness among members of the less powerful groups, and such feelings are a primary cause of crime.[25]

There are several types of conflict theory, and fittingly for this framework (as well as inherently supportive of the model), theorists of varying types often give scathing reviews of the other types of conflict theory. Marxist

---

[19]Quinney, *Critique of Legal Order*. See also Akers and Sellers, *Criminological Theories*, 224–26, for a discussion.

[20]For a discussion, see Akers and Sellers, *Criminological Theories*, 226–31.

[21]Mark Colvin and John Pauly, "A Critique of Criminology: Toward an Integrated Structural Marxist Theory of Delinquency Production," *American Journal of Sociology* 89 (1983): 513–51.

[22]See Sally Simpson and Lori Elis, "Is Gender Subordinate to Class? An Empirical Assessment of Colvin and Pauly's Structural Marxist Theory of Delinquency," *Journal of Criminal Law and Criminology* 85 (1994): 453–80. See further discussion in Akers and Sellers, *Criminological Theories*.

[23]Lee Ellis and Anthony Walsh, "Criminologists' Opinions about the Causes and Theories of Crime and Delinquency," *The Criminologist* 24 (1999): 1–4.

[24]William Chambliss and Robert Seidman, *Law, Order, and Power* (Reading: Addison-Wesley, 1971).

[25]Bernard et al., *Vold's Theoretical Criminology*.

theories are one example. Critics have noted that many communistic countries (e.g., Cuba, Russia) have high rates of crime, whereas some countries that have capitalistic economic structures have very low crime rates, such as Sweden.

Another type of conflict theory is referred to as *pluralistic*; it argues that, instead of one or a few groups holding power over all the other groups, a multitude of groups must compete on a relatively fair playing field.[26] However, this latter type of conflict theory is not one of the more popular versions among critical theorists because it is sometimes seen as rather naive and idealistic.[27] Some of the key theorists in the pluralistic (conflict) perspective are Thorsten Sellin, George Vold, and Austin Turk.

Thorsten Sellin

Thorsten Sellin applied Marxist and conflict perspectives, as well as numerous other types of models, to studying the state of cultural diversity in industrial societies. Sellin claimed that separate cultures will diverge from a unitary, mainstream set of norms and values held by the dominant group in society.[28] Thus, these minority groups that break off from the mainstream will establish their own norms. Furthermore, when laws are enacted, they will reflect only the values and interests of the dominant group, which causes what Sellin referred to as *border culture conflict.* This conflict of values, which manifests itself when different cultures interact, can cause a backlash by the weaker groups, which tend to react defiantly or defensively. According to Sellin, the more unequal the balance of power, the worse the conflict tends to be.[29]

George Vold

Another key conflict theorist was George Vold, who presented his model in his widely used textbook, *Theoretical Criminology.*[30] Vold claimed that people are naturally social and inevitably form groups out of shared needs, values, and interests. Because various groups compete with each other for power and to promote their values and interests, each group competes for control of political processes, including the power to create and enforce laws that can suppress the other groups. Some critics have argued that Vold put too much emphasis on the battle for creation of laws as opposed to the power to enforce laws.[31]

Austin Turk

Like the other conflict theorists, Austin Turk assumed that the competition for power among various groups in society is the primary cause of crime.[32] Turk emphasized the idea that a certain level of conflict among groups can be very beneficial because it reminds citizens to consider whether the status quo or conventional standards can be improved. This type of idea is very similar to Durkheim's proposition that a certain level of crime is healthy for society because it defines moral boundaries and sometimes leads to progress (see Section VI). Another aspect of Turk's theorizing, which separates him from other conflict theorists, is that he saw conflict among the various components of the criminal justice system. For example, the police often are at odds with the courts and district attorney's office. Such tension or conflict among formal agencies that should be on the same side of the playing field leads to even more frustration and inefficiency when it comes to fighting crime and ensuring that justice is served.

---

[26]Akers and Sellers, *Criminological Theories.*

[27]Quinney, *Critique of Legal Order.*

[28]Thorsten Sellin, *Culture Conflict and Crime* (New York: Social Science Research Council, 1938).

[29]Ibid.

[30]George Vold, *Theoretical Criminology* (New York: Oxford University Press, 1958).

[31]Akers and Sellers, *Criminological Theories.*

[32]Austin Turk, *Criminality and Legal Order* (Chicago: Rand McNally, 1969).

Evidence regarding Conflict Theories of Crime

Empirical tests of conflict theories are rare, likely because of the nature of the framework, which lends itself to a global view of societal structure and a perhaps infinite number of interest groups who are constantly in play for power.[33]

However, one notable study found evidence of a relationship between U.S. states that had large numbers of interest groups and violent crime but not property crime.[34] The authors concluded that these findings demonstrated the need for more discussion about how competitiveness in the United States affects criminal behavior, but no other studies have examined the influence of political interest groups on criminal behavior. It is rather difficult to test conflict theory in other ways. Perhaps conflict theory researchers should build an agenda of more rigorous ways to test the propositions of their theoretical perspective; as it stands, it remains quite vague. The few studies there are do not seem rigorous enough to persuade other criminologists or readers toward accepting the validity of this model.[35]

Despite the lack of empirical research supporting the conflict (and Marxist or critical) theories of crime, there is little doubt that such perspectives have contributed much to the theorizing and empirical studies of criminologists regarding this framework. In fact, the American Society of Criminology (ASC)—which is probably the largest and best-known professional society in the discipline—has a special division made up of experts devoted to this area of study. Thus, it is likely that theorizing and empirical research will be greatly enhanced in the near future. Furthermore, it is clear that criminologists have acknowledged the need to explore the various issues presented by the conflict and Marxist perspectives in research in criminal justice and offending.

Feminist Theories of Crime

About the same time that Marxist theories of crime were becoming popular in the early 1970s, the feminist perspective began to receive attention; this was a key period in the women's rights movement. The Feminist School of criminology began largely as a reaction to the lack of rational theorizing about why females commit crime and why they tend to be treated far differently by the criminal justice system.[36] Prior to the 1970s, theories of why girls and women engage in illegal activities were primarily based on false stereotypes.

Much of the attention of theorists in this area can be broken into two categories: the *gender ratio* issue and the *generalizability* issue. The gender ratio issue refers to theorizing and research that examines why females so often commit less serious, less violent offenses than males. Some experts feel that this does not matter; however, if we understood why females commit far less violence, then perhaps we could apply such knowledge to reducing male offending.[37] The generalizability argument is consistent with the ideas some have about the gender ratio issue; specifically, many of the same critics argue that theorists should simply take the findings found for male offending and generalize them to females. However, given the numerous differences found between males and females in what predicts their offending patterns, simply generalizing across gender is not a wise thing to do.[38]

---

[33]See discussion by Akers and Sellers, *Criminological Theories*, 210–12.

[34]Gregory G. Brunk and Laura A. Wilson, "Interest Groups and Criminal Behavior," *Journal of Research in Crime and Delinquency* 28 (1991): 157–73.

[35]Ellis and Walsh, "Criminologists' Opinions."

[36]Meda Chesney-Lind and Lisa Pasko, *The Female Offender: Girls, Women, and Crime* (Thousand Oaks: Sage, 2004).

[37]For a discussion, see Stephen Tibbetts and Denise Herz, "Gender Differences in Factors of Social Control and Rational Choice," *Deviant Behavior* 17 (1996): 183–208.

[38]Tibbetts and Herz, "Gender Differences."

▲ Image 9.2   Female gang members.

SOURCE: © Jupiterimages / liquidlibrary / Thinkstock

Another important issue in feminist research on crime is that women today have more freedom and rights than those in past generations. Seminal theories of female crime in the 1970s predicted that this would result in far higher offending rates for women.[39] However, this has not been seen in serious, violent crimes. Rather, increases have been observed in property and public order crimes, typically committed by girls or women who have not benefited from such freedom and rights—for example, those who do not have much education or who lack strong employment records.

Also, there are numerous forms of feminism and, thus, many types of feminist theories of crime, as pointed out by Daly and Chesney-Lind.[40] One of the earliest was liberal feminism, which assumed that differences between males and females in offending were due to the lack of opportunities for females in education and employment and that, as more females were given such opportunities, they would come to resemble males in terms of offending.

Another major feminist perspective of crime is critical feminism or radical feminism, which emphasizes the idea that many societies (such as the United States) are based on a structure of patriarchy, in which males dominate virtually every aspect of society, including politics, family structure, and the economy. It is hard to contest the primary assumption of this theory. Despite the fact that more women than ever hold professional, white-collar jobs, men still get paid a significant amount more than women for the same positions, on average. Furthermore, the U.S. Senate and House of Representatives—and other high political offices, such as president, vice president, cabinet posts, U.S. Supreme Court justices—are still held primarily (or exclusively) by men. So the United States, like most other countries in the world, appears to be based in patriarchy.

The extent to which this model explains female criminality, however, remains to be seen. Regarding serious crimes, it is not clear why this perspective would expect higher or lower rates of female criminal behavior. Regarding some delinquent offenses, it may partially explain the greater tendency to arrest females. For example, virtually every self-report study ever conducted shows that males run away far more than females; however, FBI data show that female juveniles are arrested for running away far more often than males. Critical feminism may provide the best explanation for this difference. Females are more protected—that is, reported and arrested for running away—because they are considered to be more like property in our patriarchal society. This is just one explanation, but it appears to be somewhat valid.

Similar to critical or radical feminism is Marxist feminism, which emphasizes men's ownership and control of the means of economic production, thus focusing solely on the economic structure. Marxist feminists point out that men control economic success in our country, as well as in virtually every country in the world, and that this flows from capitalism. One of the primary assumptions of capitalism is *survival of the fittest* or *the best person for the job*, which would seem to favor women. Studies have found that women in the United States do far better, despite our capitalistic system, than those in most other countries. Furthermore, women in countries based on Marxism have a less favorable lifestyle and are no better off economically than those in the United States. Whether or not one believes in a Marxist economic structure, it does not readily explain female criminality.

[39]Freda Adler, *Sisters in Crime: The Rise of the New Female Criminal* (New York: McGraw-Hill, 1975).

[40]Kathleen Daly and Meda Chesney-Lind, "Feminism and Criminology," *Justice Quarterly* 5 (1988): 536–58.

Another feminist perspective is that of socialist feminism, which moved away from focusing on economic structure (e.g., Marxism) as the primary detriment for females and instead emphasized control of reproductive systems. This model believes that women should take control of their own bodies and their reproductive functions in order to control their criminality. It is not entirely clear how females' taking charge of their reproductive destinies can increase or reduce their crime rates. Although no one can deny that data show that females who reproduce frequently, especially in inner-city, poor environments, tend to offend more often than other females, it appears that other factors mediate these effects. Women who want good futures tend to take more precautions against becoming pregnant; on the other hand, the very females who most need to take precautions against getting pregnant are the least likely to do so, despite the availability of numerous forms of contraception. This is one of the many paradoxes in our field. It is unclear how much socialist feminism has contributed to an understanding of female criminality.

An additional perspective of feminist criminology is that of postmodern feminism, which holds that an understanding of women as a group, even by other women, is impossible because every person's experience is unique. If this is true, we should give up discussing female criminal theory and theories of criminality in general—along with all studies of medicine, astronomy, psychology, and so on—because every person interprets each observation subjectively. According to postmodern feminists, there is no point in measuring anything. Thus, this model is based on anti-science and has contributed nothing to the study of female criminality.

In all these variations of feminist perspectives, little emphasis is placed on parental differences in how children are disciplined and raised. Studies have clearly shown that parents, often without realizing it, tend to globally reward young boys for completing a task (e.g., "You are such a good boy"), whereas they tend to tell a young girl that she did a good job. On the other hand, when young boys do not successfully complete a task, most parents tend to excuse the failure (e.g., "It was a hard thing to do; don't worry"), whereas for young girls, the parents will often globally evaluate them for the task (e.g., "Why couldn't you do it?"). Although numerous psychological studies have found this tendency, it has yet to make it into the mainstream criminological theories of crime.

Evidence regarding Feminist Theories of Crime

As discussed above, there is no doubt that female offenders were highly neglected by traditional models of criminological theory, and given that they make up at least 50% of the population of the world, it is important that they be covered and explained by such theories. Furthermore, we also discussed the fact that if we knew why females everywhere commit far less violence than men, it would likely go a long way toward devising policies to reduce the extremely higher rates of violence among males. However, in other ways, the feminist theories of crime have not been supported.

For instance, as noted above, the seminal feminist crime theories specifically proposed that, as women became liberated, their rates of crime would become consistent with the rates of male offending.[41] Not only did this fail to occur, but the evidence actually supports the opposite trend; specifically, the females who were given the most opportunities (e.g., education, employment, status) were the *least* likely to offend, whereas the women who were not liberated or given such opportunities were the *most* likely to engage in criminal behavior.[42]

On the other hand, one major strength of feminist theories of crime is that they have led to a number of studies showing that the factors causing crime in males are different than those for females. For example, females appear to be far more influenced by internal, emotional factors; they are more inhibited by moral emotions, such as shame, guilt, and embarrassment.[43] Ultimately, there is no doubt that feminist theories of crime have contributed much to the discourse and empirical research regarding why females (as well as males) commit crime. In fact, some highly

---

[41]Adler, *Sisters in Crime.*

[42]For a discussion, see Akers and Sellers, *Criminological Theories.* See also discussion in Bernard et al., *Vold's Theoretical Criminology.*

[43]For a review, see Tibbetts and Herz, "Gender Differences."

respected criminology and criminal justice journals have been created to deal with that very subject. So, in that sense, the field has recognized and accepted the need to examine feminist theorizing and research on offending and the justice system and explore the various issues involved.

Policy Implications

A variety of policy implications have come from the theoretical perspectives reviewed in this section. Regarding social reaction and labeling theory, several policies have evolved, known as the *Ds*: diversion, decriminalization, and deinstitutionalization. Diversion, which is now commonly used, involves trying to get cases out of the formal justice system as soon as possible. Courts try to get many juvenile cases and, in recent times, drug possession cases diverted to a less formal, more administrative process (e.g., drug courts, youth accountability boards or teams). Such diversion programs appear to have saved many billions of dollars, since the offenders would otherwise have been incarcerated, while providing a way for first-time or relatively nonserious offenders not to experience the stigmatizing effects of being incarcerated. Although empirical evaluations of such diversion programs are mixed and suffer from methodological problems (i.e., the individuals who volunteer or qualify for such programs are likely the better cases among the sample population), some studies have shown their potential promise.[44]

There have also been numerous examples of decriminalization, which refers to reducing the criminality of certain illegal activities. A good example is the legal approach to marijuana possession in California. Unlike other jurisdictions, California does not incarcerate individuals for possessing less than an ounce of marijuana; rather, they receive a citation, similar to a parking ticket. There are many other forms of decriminalization (which is distinguished from legalization, which makes an act completely legal and not subject to legal sanction). The purpose of decriminalization is to deemphasize less dangerous crimes and decrease the resources devoted to offenders who pose less danger to society. In terms of social reaction and labeling theory, decriminalization also reduces the stigmatization of individuals who are relatively minor offenders but would likely become more serious offenders if they were incarcerated with more chronic offenders.

Another policy implication of this section is deinstitutionalization. In the early 1970s, federal laws were passed that ordered all youth status offenders to be removed from incarceration facilities. This has not been accomplished; some are still being placed in such facilities. However, the number and rate of status offenders being placed in incarceration facilities has declined, avoiding any further stigmatization and integration into further criminality. Overall, this deinstitutionalization has kept relatively minor, often first-time offenders from experiencing the ordeals of incarceration.

Additional policy implications that can be inferred from this section involve providing more economic and employment opportunities to those who do not typically have access to such options. From a historical perspective, such as the New Deal, which was meant to deal with the effects of the Great Depression of the 1930s, providing more employment opportunities can greatly enhance the well-being of the population, and in that period, there was a very significant decrease in crime and homicide rates (see Section I). Today, perhaps nothing could be more important in our nation than creating jobs; the ability to do this will largely determine future crime rates.

Finally, there are numerous policy implications regarding feminist theory and feminist perspectives of crime. It is of primary importance to include such perspectives in future research and theoretical developments. Furthermore, it is important to realize that females offend far less than males; if criminologists could figure out why, this could be a landmark finding in efforts to reduce crime. Ultimately, this section reveals that the more attention and resources given to disenfranchised groups (e.g., youth, minorities, women), the lower the likelihood that they will offend, and the better we will understand the reasons why they offend.

[44]For a review, see John Worrall, *Crime Control in America: What Works?* 2nd ed. (Boston: Allyn & Bacon, 2008): 228–29.

Conclusion

This section examined the theories that place responsibility for individuals' criminal behavior on societal factors. Specifically, this section discussed theories of social reaction or labeling, critical perspectives, and feminist theories of criminal behavior. All of these theories have a common theme: They emphasize the use of legal or criminal justice systems to target or label certain groups of people (the poor, women, etc.) as criminals while protecting the interests of those who have power (i.e., White males). Given the evidence discussed here, you will have enough evidence to make objective conclusions about whether this perspective is valid, as well as which aspects of these theories are more supported by empirical research and which are more in question.

 Section Summary

- First, we explored the basic assumptions of social reaction and labeling theory.
- We then reviewed the primary theoretical concepts and propositions of labeling theory, especially the importance of distinguishing primary deviance from secondary deviance.
- We discussed the current state of labeling theory, which emphasizes informal sources of social reaction, not just the formal sources as in traditional models.
- Then we examined Marxist theories of crime, as well as numerous subsequent versions of this theory, such as those developed by Bonger and Quinney.
- We also examined conflict theories, including theories by Sellin, Vold, and Turk.
- Finally, we examined the basic assumptions of feminist perspectives of crime, as well as some of the more notable implications that can be derived from these perspectives.

KEY TERMS

bourgeoisie	dramatization of evil	primary deviance
conflict theories	labeling theory	proletariat
critical feminism	liberal feminism	radical feminism
decriminalization	Marxist feminism	secondary deviance
deinstitutionalization	pluralistic (conflict) perspective	socialist feminism
diversion	postmodern feminism	

DISCUSSION QUESTIONS

1. What are the major assumptions of labeling and social reaction theory, and how do they differ significantly from other traditional theories of crime?

2. According to Lemert, what is the difference between primary deviance and secondary deviance?

3. How can you relate personally to being labeled, even if not for offending?

4. How do Marx's ideas relate to the study of crime? Provide some examples.

5. Which conflict theory do you buy into the most? The least? Why?

6.   What are the key assumptions and features of the various feminist perspectives?

7.   Which type of feminist theory do you believe is the most helpful for explaining crime?

WEB RESOURCES

Conflict Theories

http://www.criminology.fsu.edu/crimtheory/conflict.htm

Feminist Theories of Crime

http://www.youtube.com/watch?v=wIdzD8kpYwk

Labeling Theory

http://www.criminology.fsu.edu/crimtheory/week_10.htm

Marxist Theory

http://law.jrank.org/pages/819/Crime-Causation-Sociological-Theories-Critical-theories.html
www.sociology.org.uk/pcdevmx.doc

In this selection, Lening Zhang provides a brief review of the history of labeling theory, discussing its prominence in the 1960s and the declaration in 1985 that labeling theory was "dead," largely because the tests of the theory up to that time had been based solely on formal labeling, such as that given by law enforcement, courts, or corrections, which showed little or no effect for the labeling perspective. Then Zhang reviews the various studies and perspectives that revitalized labeling theory in the 1990s, largely by introducing the informal labeling process by significant others (peers, parents, employers, etc.), in other words, the labeling that takes place during interactions with people or agencies who are not part of the formal justice system (i.e., police, courts, and corrections).

Zhang then presents a test of this informal labeling process. Specifically, Zhang uses a national sample of youths, called the National Youth Survey (NYS), to test his predictions that delinquency produces informal labeling; that such informal labeling by parents produces social isolation; and that this social isolation increases the likelihood of recidivism or subsequent delinquency.

While reading this selection, readers are encouraged to think about when they were a teenager and their parents may have told them to stay away or not hang out with certain youths in their neighborhood or school. Readers are also encouraged to consider what types of effects this had on such people, who were likely socially isolated and in many cases had only other "bad" kids to hang out with, which likely increased their delinquent activity. Perhaps you have siblings or cousins who experienced such informal labeling, or maybe you actually experienced this type of labeling personally.

Informal Reactions and Delinquency

Lening Zhang

In formulating a symbolic interaction theory of delinquency, Matsueda (1992) recently developed a model of reflected appraisals and behavior based on Felson's (1985, 1989) and Kinch's (1963) work. A reflected appraisal is how one perceives the way others see one. Matsueda's model predicts that actual delinquent acts affect both actual and reflected appraisals by significant others. In turn, both actual and reflected appraisals influence subsequent delinquent behavior. Also, actual appraisals by significant others have an effect on reflected appraisals of others, and prior delinquent behavior directly affects subsequent delinquency.[1] Drawing on labeling theory,

Matsueda also argued that these predictions derived from the model implied the role of informal labeling in accounting for subsequent delinquency. Youths who have engaged in delinquent behavior should be more likely to be labeled delinquent by significant others. Significant others' labeling increases the probability of further delinquency. Although his study shed light on the relationship between informal labeling processes and subsequent life and behavioral adjustments, Matsueda did not fully address the issue because the focus of his study was not on this issue. Using Matsueda's basic framework, the present research specified a comprehensive theoretical model of the informal labeling

Source: Lening Zhang, "Informal Reactions and Delinquency." *Criminal Justice and Behavior* 24, no. 1 (1997): 129–50. Copyright © 1997 Sage Publications, Inc. Used by permission of Sage Publications, Inc.

process and tested this model with data from the National Youth Survey (NYS; Elliott & Ageton 1980), a longitudinal study of delinquency and drug use.

The labeling perspective on deviance has undergone an uneven development. During the 1960s, labeling, or reaction, theory emerged as a new and dominant perspective in criminology. In the mid-1970s, the perspective was subjected to serious critiques (Gibbs, 1966, 1972; Gove, 1980; Hagan, 1974; Tittle, 1975, 1980a; Wellford, 1975) and by 1985 was pronounced "dead" (Paternoster & Iovanni, 1989, p. 359). After its unpopular position in the study of crime for several years, the perspective has been revitalized since the late 1980s and the early 1990s (Berk, Campell, Klap, & Western, 1992; Farrell, 1989; Gove & Hughes, 1989; Hagan & Palloni, 1990; Heimer & Matsueda, 1994; Link, 1982, 1987; Link & Cullen, 1983; Link, Cullen, Frank, & Wozniak, 1987; Link, Cullen, Struening, Shrout, & Dohren-wend, 1989; Matsueda, 1992; Palamara, Cullen, & Gersten, 1986; Pate & Hamilton, 1992; Paternoster & Iovanni, 1989; Sampson, 1986; Sherman & Smith, 1992; Tittle, 1988; Tittle & Curran, 1988; Triplett & Jarjoura, 1994).

This revitalization reflects new theoretical and research interests in labeling theory, which indicate the potential power and capacity of the theory for explaining deviance and crime. However, the new developments do not represent a simple return to the traditional version of labeling theory. They entail new attempts to elaborate, to specify, and to expand the theory in a new context of studies in criminology. As Paternoster and Iovanni (1989) pointed out, the above-mentioned efforts suggested some of the components that might constitute a *neolabeling theory.*

Consistent with these new research interests in the labeling perspective, the present study addressed an important but relatively neglected issue—the informal labeling process and delinquency.

Despite this relative neglect, a few scattered early studies (Alvarez, 1968; Black, 1970; Black & Reiss, 1970; DeLamater, 1968; Orcutt, 1973; Swigert & Farrell, 1978; Tittle, 1975) involved attempts to explore the issues of informal reactions. A notable example was Orcutt's (1973) research, in which he differentiated between formal and informal reactions on the basis of the labeling perspective and noted the underemphasis on informal reactions. He argued that studies of the labeling perspective must pay greater attention to informal reactions.

According to Swigert and Farrell (1978), the evaluations and views of social audiences, such as parents and close friends, might have significant effects on the self-evaluations of labeled deviants. Hence informal groups may be crucial for self-identity and behavioral adjustment of labeled individuals. A similar argument was offered by Tittle (1975). He suggested that cultural patterns in different communities might serve as important variables that could interact with official formal reactions and affect the outcome of formal reactions. However, Tittle observed, these effects of cultural patterns had not yet been addressed theoretically and empirically.

In addition, several early studies dealt with family reactions to drinking problems and mental disorders (Jackson, 1954, 1962; Sampson, Messinger, & Towne, 1962; Yarrow, Schartz, Murphy, & Deasy, 1955). These studies indicated how family reactions change in response to drinking and mental problems from "inclusive" to "exclusive" reactions (Orcutt, 1973). Although these early studies appealed for attention to informal reactions to deviance, studies of labeling phenomena have focused primarily on formal official reactions.

Recently, in the resurgence of labeling theory, some scholars (Braithwaite, 1989; Heimer & Matsueda, 1994; Matsueda, 1992; Pate & Hamilton, 1992; Paternoster & Iovanni, 1989; Tittle, 1988; Triplett & Jarjoura, 1994) again have called attention to informal reactions to deviance. An interesting formulation of this issue was Braithwaite's (1989) specification of informal reactions associated with "reintegrative shaming." He argued that

if the labeling perspective is to be the stimulus to testable propositions with any hope of consistent empirical support, then a strategy is required for predicting the circumstances where labeling will be counterproductive and where it will actually reduce crime. (p. 20)

To meet this challenge, he identified two types of shaming: reintegrative and disintegrative (stigmatization) shaming. Reintegrative shaming refers to expressions of community disapproval with gestures of reacceptance into the community of law-abiding citizens. Such informal labeling reduces crime. In contrast, disintegrative shaming divides the community by creating a class of outcasts. It is conceived of as criminogenic labeling.

In discussing the secondary deviance hypothesis of labeling theory, Paternoster and Iovanni (1989) similarly called for more attention to informal rather than official reactions, whereas Triplett and Jarjoura (1994) formulated an integrated model of the labeling perspective and social learning theory. In their model, (a) parents' labeling of their child and (b) the youth's interpretation that parents are labeling him or her as delinquent are treated as key variables that may predict parental attachment, school attachment, and subsequent delinquency. Their findings indicate that both objective and subjective labels are factors in accounting for a child's relationship with major socialization sources, such as school and friends and subsequent delinquency. Thus they concluded that the labeling perspective could contribute more to criminological theory and research than it did in the past.

In the deterrence literature, informal sanctions have been demonstrated to have much stronger effects on deviance than do formal sanctions, and they significantly mediate the relationship between formal sanctions and deviance. As Tittle (1980b) observed,

> Social control as a general process seems to be rooted almost completely in informal sanctioning. Perceptions of formal sanction probabilities or severities do not appear to have much of an effect, and those effects that are evident turn out to be dependent upon perceptions of informal sanctions. (p. 241)

For a review of the deterrence literature, see Braithwaite (1989) and Williams and Hawkins (1986). Recently, on the basis of the Dade County spouse assault experiment, Pate and Hamilton (1992) examined the interaction effects between formal and informal deterrents on domestic violence. They found that formal arrest had no independent effect on the occurrence of a subsequent domestic assault. Its effect was contingent on employment status, with formal arrest more likely to exhibit a significant deterrent effect for employed suspects than for unemployed suspects. These observations in the deterrence literature also may be valuable and useful in exploring the role of informal reactions in the labeling process.

All of these studies suggest that informal reactions play an important role in explaining deviant behavior. Following this general line of studies, the present study attempted to further clarify some conceptual issues by specifying informal reactions as a dependent variable, an independent variable, and an intervening variable in the labeling process.

Treating informal reactions as a dependent variable is concerned with explaining why some people come to be labeled deviant by significant others, such as parents, friends, and neighbors or the public (for a general discussion of societal reaction as a dependent variable, see Gove, 1980; Orcutt, 1973). The explanation involves three analytic dimensions: (a) Informal labeling is caused by formal labeling such as police arrest and court hearings; (b) actual deviant behavior leads to informal reactions; and (c) status characteristics of individuals, including those of both labelee and labeler (e.g., race, sex, social status) are relevant to informal reactions.

Viewing informal reaction as an independent variable focuses on the consequences that follow if a person is labeled deviant by significant others or the public. Four possible consequences can be specified. First, informal reactions may lead to formal (official) reactions. For instance, neighbors' complaints of someone's behavior may lead to formal actions by official agencies (Black, 1970; Black & Reiss, 1970). Second, informal reactions may push the labeled person to commit further deviance. Third, informal reactions may have negative consequences in other areas of the labeled person's life, such as interpersonal relationships. Finally, as deterrence theory predicts, informal reactions may be important factors in deterring further deviance.

In considering informal reactions as an intervening variable, the major concerns are with the mediating role of informal reactions in explaining the effects of formal reactions and actual deviant behavior on further deviance and other areas of a person's life. The role can be specified in two possibly opposite directions underlying efforts at social control. If informal labeling following and accompanying formal labeling or actual deviant behavior comes with reintegrative shaming, it may play an important and positive role in rehabilitating a rule breaker. This is a positive direction expected by a society. For example, Braithwaite (1989) emphasized the contributions of the informal mechanisms to low crime rate in Japanese society. In contrast, informal reactions may reinforce the stigma imposed by official agencies and thereby become a significant factor leading to further deviance.

These conceptual specifications suggest a framework for examining the relationship of informal labeling processes to delinquency. On the basis of available data from the NYS, the author developed a specific model focused on this relationship (see Figure 1). The model uses Matsueda's (1992) symbolic interactionist framework and extends his study to reflect the conceptual specifications proposed in the present study. The key extension is that the present study introduces an important variable—social isolation—into the model. First, in the model, social isolation from significant others is treated as a dependent variable caused by informal labeling. As previously specified, informal reactions may have negative consequences for other areas of the labeled person's life, one of which is negative change in interpersonal relations. Recently, an important dimension of the trend to revitalize labeling theory has involved efforts to focus on the effect of formal reactions on other areas of a person's life rather than just on subsequent deviance. Specifically, in the research areas of labeling theory and mental illness, Link and his colleagues (Link, 1982, 1987; Link et al., 1987, 1989) noted the previous overemphasis on the effect of formal labeling on subsequent mental disorders in comparison with the neglect of specifying the direct effect of formal labeling on problems of life adjustment, such as marriage and job problems, experienced by ex-mental patients. Their studies provided evidence for the relationship between formal labeling and life

adjustment. Similarly, it is reasonable to speculate that informal labeling not only increases the possibility of further delinquency involvement but also has negative consequences for other areas of the labeled person's life, such as interpersonal relationships.

Second, social isolation is also treated as an intervening variable between informal reactions and subsequent delinquency. The theoretical hypothesis is that informal reactions result in social isolation from significant others, and, in turn, such isolation increases the probability of further delinquency. It is possible that a negative label, through a series of reinforcing conditions, such as rejection by significant others, increases the probability of further deviance. Link (1982) pointed out that if this were demonstrated by further research, the eventual results of such a program of research offered the genuine possibility of developing a theory that assigned a partial role to labeling in the etiology of deviance. Similarly, Liska (1987) proposed a clear diagram regarding the association of labeling with further deviance. His diagram assumed that the effect of societal reaction on further deviance was through its effect on self-concept, interpersonal networks, and structured opportunities. Therefore, the present model posits that social isolation has a mediating role for the effect of informal labeling on subsequent delinquency involvement, even though this mediating role may be only partial.

Figure 1   A causal model for informal reactions and delinquency

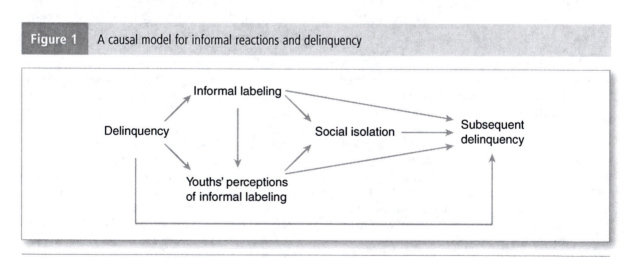

NOTE: Controls for gender, race, age, parent education, and family income are included in all regressions but are not shown in the diagram.

In summary, the predictions from this model are as follows:

1. Delinquent acts are a significant predictor of informal labeling.

2. Both delinquent acts and informal labeling positively affect youths' perceptions of informal labeling.

3. Both informal labeling and youths' perceptions of informal labeling lead to two possible consequences: social isolation from significant others experienced by the labeled youths and subsequent delinquency.

4. Social isolation, in turn, increases the likelihood of subsequent delinquency.

Finally, as previous studies (see Gibbons & Krohn, 1991, for a review) have indicated, stable delinquent patterns exist. Therefore, a path included in the model predicts that prior delinquency is a significant predictor of subsequent delinquency.

An additional dimension of efforts to revitalize labeling theory involves attempts to specify a variety of contingencies that potentially influence the effect of official labeling on subsequent deviance (Berk et al., 1992; Palamara et al., 1986; Ray & Downs, 1986; Sherman & Smith, 1992). Studies have demonstrated that official reactions do affect the likelihood of subsequent deviance but that the effects are contingent on specific circumstances, such as gender, marital status, and employment status. The effect of official punishment on subsequent deviance is not uniform across different individual characteristics and different social contexts. In this vein, the present study, hypothesizing that women are more vulnerable to informal reactions than are men, assessed gender differences with the model. In addition, the present study also speculated that youth's perceptions of different kinds of informal labeling by different significant others (e.g. parents, friends, and teachers) may have differential associations with preceding variables such as delinquent behavior and subsequent variables such as social isolation. Therefore, the present study assessed the model with respect to youths' perceptions of different kind of informal labeling.

 ## Method

Sample

The data used for the present study came from the NYS, conducted by Elliott and his colleagues (Elliott & Ageton, 1980, Elliot, Huizinga, & Ageton, 1985; Elliot, Huizinga, & Menard, 1989). The original sample size of 1,725 youths was obtained from a national probability sample of households by employing a multistage cluster sample frame. The age range of these youths at the first wave was 11 to 17 years.

The data from the first two waves of the NYS were used for the present study. The first wave survey was conducted in early 1977 and the second in early 1978.

Measurement

The NYS used personal interview to collect self-reports of delinquent acts; parents' labeling of their child; the child's perceptions of parents', friends', and teachers' labeling; and the child's perceptions of social isolation from family, from friends, and at school. The variables included in the model presented above were measured as follows:

Informal labeling. Because only data concerning parents' attitudes toward their child were available in the NYS, the informal labeling was reflected in parents' labeling. The parents' labeling consisted of a set of four measures, including "bad kid," "gets into trouble," "breaks rules," and "does things against the law." These measures reflected the extent to which parents labeled their child as deviant, with a 5-point scale ranging from 1 (*strongly disagree*) to 5 (*strongly agree*).

Child's perceptions of informal labeling. Youth respondents were asked to indicate the extent to which their parents, their friends, and their teachers labeled them as deviant. The items and scoring for youth responses were the same as those for parents' labeling.

Social isolation. Youth respondents reported their perceptions of interpersonal relationships with their families, their friends, and at school. Each type of relationship was assesed by five items. A 5-point scale ranging from 1 (*strongly disagree*) to 5 (*strongly agree*) was used for each item.

The scoring for these items was rearranged by the present investigator so that high scores represented high isolation. For isolation related to family, the items were as follows: "outsider with family," "feel lonely with family," "family not interested in problems," "family listens to problems," and "feel close to family." For isolation from friends, the five items were the following: "don't fit with friends," "friends don't take interest," "feel lonely with friends," "feel close to friends," and "friends listen to problems." Similarly, five items reflected isolation at school: 'Teachers don't call on me," "nobody at school cares," "don't belong at school," "feel lonely at school," and "teachers don't ask me to work on projects."

Delinquent acts. The NYS included a delinquency inventory to represent the entire range of delinquent acts. Each of the self-reported delinquent acts was coded in two parts: (a) absolute frequency and (b) categorical responses, ranging from 1 (*never*) to 9 (*two to three times per day*). Following Elliott et al. (1985) and Matsueda (1992), the present study used a 24-item scale of general delinquency with the categorical responses because the categorical responses have less skewed distributions. The delinquency items included auto theft, $5 theft, $5 to $50 theft, buying stolen goods, runaway, concealed weapon, aggravated assault, prostitution, sexual intercourse, gang fights, sold marijuana, hit parents, hit teachers, hit students, disorderly conduct, sold drugs, joyriding, sexual assault, strongarmed students, strong-armed teachers, strong-armed others, breaking and entering, panhandled.

The present study created several additive indexes to represent these variables in the model (i.e., indexes for parents' labeling; youths' perceptions of parents', friends', and teachers' labeling; social isolation from family, from friends, and at school; and delinquency) by using the above items. The standardized reliability coefficient for each index ranged from .65 to .75.

In addition to these key variables in the model, the present study included the following control variables that may be related to the informal labeling process: race; age; family income, measured by a 10-point scale ranging from 1 (*$6,000 or less*) to 10 (*$38,001 or more*); and parental education, measured by a 7-point scale ranging from 1 (*some grade school*) to 7 (*graduate degree*).

Based on time and logical order, self-reported delinquency in the first wave of the NYS consisted of delinquent acts prior to parents' labeling and youths' perceptions of informal labeling. In the first wave, the adolescent respondents reported their delinquency during the previous year. Also, in the first wave, parents were interviewed to report their current attitudes toward their child, and youths reported their current perceptions of parents', friends', and teacher's labeling and their perceptions of isolation from family, from friends, and at school. Thus parents' labeling, youths' perceptions of informal labeling, and social isolation were measured in the first wave. In addition, race, age, family income, and parental education were measured in the first wave. The measure of subsequent self-reported delinquency occurred in the second wave.

Ordinary least squares regression (OLS) was employed to assess the model. In addition, the present study examined the interactions between gender and each of the primary independent variables to assess the possible role of gender differences in the informal labeling process.

Results

The present study begins its analysis with the effect of delinquency on parents' labeling (see Table 1). Delinquency significantly and positively affected parents' labeling of their child (β = 23). Also, there were significant associations between race, age, and parental education and parents' labeling, which indicated that younger and non-White youths and youths whose parents' education was lower were more likely to be labeled as deviant by their parents. These results supported the predictions of labeling theory that individual and social disadvantages are related to the labeling process.

Table 1	Regression for Effects of Delinquency on Parents' Labeling, with Control Variables Included

Independent Variable	β	t
Delinquency	.23	9.54*
Gender	.04	1.72
Race	−.13	−4.96*
Age	−.07	−2.93*
Parent education	−.13	−4.83*
Family income	−.03	−1.21

NOTE: Beta (β) = Standardized regression coefficient. $R^2 = .12$.

*$p < .05$.

Table 2 presents the effects of delinquency and parents' labeling on youths' perceptions of parents,' friends,' and teachers' labeling. Three equations are included in Table 2 for the three dependent variables—perceived parents,' friends,' and teachers' labeling. Both parents' labeling and delinquency had significant effects on youths' perceptions of parents' labeling (β =.29 and .25, respectively), friends' labeling, (β =.22 and .35, respectively), and teachers' labeling (β =.23 and .36, respectively).

In addition to the direct effect of delinquency on youths' perceptions of significant others' labeling, delinquency had indirect effects on these youths' perceptions through parents' labeling. However, these indirect effects were fairly small. On the basis of the direction of these indirect effects, they increased the amount of total positive effects of delinquency on youths' perceptions of informal labeling.

Furthermore, both gender and parent education were significantly associated with youths' perceptions of parents,' friends,' and teachers' labeling, whereas family income exhibited significant effects on youths' perceptions of parents' and friends' labeling. Men and youths whose parental education was lower were more likely to perceive labeling by parents, friends, and teachers. Youths who came from families with lower income were more likely to perceive labeling by parents and friends.

Table 3 presents the results of regressions of social isolation on parents' labeling and youths' perceptions of significant others' labeling. Similar to Table 2, Table 3 includes three equations for the three dependent variables—isolation from family, from friends, and at school. First, youths' perceptions of parents' labeling were a significant predictor of isolation from family (β = .31), from friends (β = .20), and at school (β = .24). The greater the youths' perceptions of parents' labeling, the greater were their perceptions of isolation from all three kinds of significant others. Second, youths' perceptions of friends' labeling had a positive effect only on isolation from friends (β = .18), and youths' perceptions of teachers' labeling had a positive effect only on isolation at school (β = .13). Third, parents' labeling significantly affected isolation from family (β = .05). Furthermore, on the basis of the causal order, parents' labeling had indirect effects on isolation from significant others through youths' perceptions of significant others' labeling. All of these findings were consistent with propositions of labeling theory. Informal labeling appears to lead to negative changes in interpersonal relationships, as assessed by degree of isolation.

Finally, the results in Table 3 also show that delinquency was negatively related to youths' perceptions of friends' isolation (β =−11). This may imply that delinquency is an important factor leading to closer group association. In addition, non-White youths were more likely to perceive isolation from family, from friends, and at school. Older and female youths were more likely to perceive isolation from family, whereas younger and male youths were more likely to perceive isolation from friends. Family income was significantly and negatively related to isolation from friends.

| Table 2 | Regression for Effects of Delinquency and Parents' Labeling on Youths' Perceptions of Informal Labeling by Parents, Friends, and Teachers, with Control Variables Included |

| | Youths' Perceptions of Informal Labeling | | | | | |
| | Parents | | Friends | | Teachers | |
Independent Variable	β	t	β	t	β	t
Parents' labeling	.29	12.00*	.22	9.28*	.23	10.04*
Delinquency	.25	10.57*	.35	15.19*	.36	15.41*
Gender	.05	2.19*	.11	4.68*	.09	4.05*
Race	.02	0.02	−.01	−0.71	−.01	−0.31
Age	−.04	−1.86	.03	1.53	−.01	−0.62
Parent education	−.06	−2.54*	−.08	−3.17*	−.08	−3.32*
Family income	−.05	−1.97*	.06	2.37*	.03	1.18

NOTE: Beta (β) = Standardized regression coefficient. R^2 = .22 for parents, .25 for friends, and .26 for teachers.

*$p < .05$.

Table 3	Regression for Effects of Delinquency; Parents' Labeling; Youths' Perceptions of Informal Labeling by Parents, Friends, and Teachers on Youths' Perceptions of Social Isolation from Family, Friends, and at School, with Control Variables Included

| | Youths' Perceptions of Informal Labeling | | | | | |
| | Family | | Friends | | School | |
Independent Variable	β	t	β	t	β	t
Parents' labeling	.05	2.10*	−.01	−0.33	.01	0.43
Delinquency	.04	1.38	−.11	−3.81*	.01	0.25
Youths' perceptions of parents' labeling	.31	9.43*	.20	5.84*	.24	7.05*
Youths' perceptions of friends' labeling	.05	1.30	.18	4.32*	.03	0.77
Youths' perceptions of teachers' labeling	.06	1.60	−.06	−1.34	.13	3.10*
Gender	−.12	−4.97*	.07	2.81*	−.03	−1.41
Race	−.07	−2.77*	−.12	−4.51*	−.05	−2.04*
Age	.13	5.69*	−.07	−2.84*	−.04	−1.86
Parent education	−.04	−0.02	.02	0.89	−.04	−1.42
Family income	−.02	−0.56	−.06	−2.24*	−04	−1.31

NOTE: Beta (β) = Standardized regression coefficient. R^2 = .22 for isolation from family, .13 for isolation from friends, and .16 for isolation at school.

*$p < .05$.

The results of a full regression equation predicting subsequent delinquency are reported in Table 4. Consistent with labeling theory, parents' labeling and youths' perceptions of teachers' labeling yielded significantly positive coefficients (β = .08 and .08, respectively). They predicted an increased possibility of subsequent delinquency. Also, parents' labeling had an indirect effect on subsequent delinquency via perceived teachers' labeling. Inconsistent with labeling theory, social isolation from family, from friends, and at school evidenced no significant positive effects on subsequent delinquency. Thus social isolation had no mediating role for the relationship between informal labeling and subsequent delinquency.[2]

The results in Table 4 also revealed that, as predicted, prior delinquency was significantly and positively related to subsequent delinquency (β = .50). Furthermore, consistent with labeling theory, part of the total effect of prior delinquency on subsequent delinquency was positively mediated by parents' labeling and youths' perceptions of teachers' labeling. Finally, the significant coefficients for gender (β = .09) and age (β = .09) indicated that older and male youths were more likely to be involved in delinquency.

Table 4	Regression for Effects Hypothesized Predictors on Subsequent Delinquency

Independent Variable	β	t
Parents' labeling	.08	3.66*
Prior delinquency	.50	21.17*
Youths' perceptions of parents' labeling	−.01	−0.26
Youths' perceptions of friends' labeling	.03	0.93
Youths' perceptions of teachers' labeling	.08	2.41*
Family isolation	−.02	−0.94
Friends' isolation	−.01	−0.06
School isolation	−.02	−0.81
Gender	.09	4.18*
Race	.01	0.52
Age	.09	4.04*
Parent education	−.01	−0.11
Family income	−.03	−1.10

NOTE: Beta (β) = Standardized regression coefficient. R^2 = .39.

*$p < .05$.

The present study also examined possible interactions between gender and the primary variables. The results revealed three kinds of significant interaction effects. First, there was a significant interaction of delinquency and gender on parents' labeling ($\beta = -.56$), which indicated that delinquency exerted a greater effect on parents' labeling for women than for men. This was consistent with the hypothesis that women are more likely to suffer informal labeling. Second, parents' labeling and gender had an interaction effect on subsequent delinquency ($\beta = .20$), which indicated that parents' labeling was more likely to increase the probability of delinquency involvement for men than for women. This was at odds with the hypothesis proposed in the present study. Third, there was a significant interaction effect between prior delinquency and gender on subsequent delinquency ($\beta = .57$). Consistent with previous research, prior delinquency exhibited a greater effect on further delinquency for men than for women. That is, a stable delinquent pattern was more likely to exist among men than women.

Discussion

There were several noteworthy findings in the present study. First, delinquent behavior significantly increased the probability of parents' labeling of their child, with the probability greater for women than men. Also, as Matsueda (1992) reported, some demographic variables exhibited significant effects on parents' labeling of their children as deviant. Non-White, younger youths and youths whose parents had lower education were more likely to be labeled as deviant by their parents. These findings were consistent with the propositions of labeling theory, which predict that individual and social disadvantages are related to the labeling process.

Second, delinquent behavior and parents' labeling exerted significant effects on youths' perceptions of labeling by significant others, including parents, friends, and teachers. This implies that delinquent behavior and informal labeling may damage youths' previous conventional self-identity through their self-perceptions of their own delinquent acts and significant others' labeling, thereby increasing the probability of their self-degradation

and self-labeling. This finding was also consistent with the labeling perspective.

Third, youths' perceptions of parents' labeling were significantly and positively related to their perceptions of isolation from family, from friends, and at school. Parents' labeling was more likely to increase the probability of family isolation, and youths' perceptions of friends' and teachers' labeling exerted, respectively, positive and significant effects on isolation from friends and at school. Thus labeling by significant others and perceptions of the labeling were more likely to lead to feelings of social rejection. Although youths' perceptions of parents' labeling were a source of feelings of isolation from all three kinds of significant others (i.e., family, friends, and school); specificity of effects also existed, in that (a) parents' labeling led to feelings of isolation from family, (b) youths' perceptions of friends' labeling led to feelings of isolation from friends, and (c) youths' perceptions of teachers' labeling led to feelings of isolation from school. These findings were consistent with the hypothesis that informal labeling has direct and negative consequences for other areas of a person's life.

Fourth, prior delinquency significantly affected subsequent delinquency, with the effect greater for male youths than female youths. This was consistent with previous findings of stable delinquent patterns among youths and among male youths in particular. Furthermore, parents' labeling and youths' perceptions of teachers' labeling were significantly and positively related to subsequent delinquency. Also, a gender difference was uncovered, indicating that parents' labeling was more likely to be a negative factor leading to subsequent delinquency for male youths than for female youths. Again, these results were in agreement with the prediction of labeling theory that deviant labels increase the likelihood of further delinquency involvement, and they reaffirmed the importance of recent efforts to specify the variety of contingencies that may influence the effect of a deviant label on further deviant behavior.

Fifth, youths' perceptions of social isolation from significant others had no direct and significant effect on subsequent delinquency and thus had no mediating role for the effect of informal labeling on subsequent delinquency. This was at odds with the hypothesis derived from labeling theory.

Finally, some indirect effects were found in the present study. For instance, part of the total effect of delinquency on social isolation from significant others was mediated by parents' labeling and youths' perceptions of parents', friends', and teachers' labeling. These findings were consistent with recent studies of labeling theory, which have adopted a "softer" rather than a "harder" stance by specifying a variety of intervening variables that may, in part, account for the association of labeling with delinquency. As Paternoster and Iovanni (1989) pointed out, this softer stance, compared with a deterministic one, can represent more plausibly the classic implication of labeling theory.

In addition to these major results related to the predictions derived from the model, an unanticipated but important finding was the negative relationship between delinquency and youths' perceptions of isolation from their friends. This finding may have two implications. First, delinquency may be a medium or vehicle that ties youths together, even though their relationships are not close and intimate. Second, according to self-derogation theory (Kaplan, 1975, 1980), adolescents are motivated to commit delinquency in order to enhance their self-esteem, and, thus, appreciative companionship is necessary to satisfy the motivation. Therefore, delinquency and peer companionship may be positively correlated.

The informal labeling process appears to play an important role in explaining youths' life and behavioral adjustments. Elaborations and specifications of this informal labeling process should be valuable in the development of "neolabeling" theory. Second, in some important aspects, such as parents' labeling, the informal labeling process is not uniform across gender. This reaffirms the trend of revitalizing labeling theory by specifying a variety of contingencies. Such specifications of contingencies should be an important requirement for any attempts to develop a neolabeling theory. Third, social isolation from significant others appears to have no significant effect on further delinquency. This challenges the proposition derived from labeling theory that social rejection caused by deviant labels necessarily results in further deviance. It may be that any such relationship, if it exists, depends on the nature and type of social rejection and deviant behavior. Future research is needed to address these important issues. Such research would contribute to the further development of neolabeling theory.

 ## Notes

1. More recent work by Heimer and Matsueda (1994) has extended Matsueda's study by adding some variables of social control, such as attachment to family and friends. This social control model, based on Matsueda's (1992) model of reflected appraisals, has been tested by Heimer and Matsueda.

2. Tests for multicollinearity among youths' perceptions of parents', friends', and teachers' labeling and among youths' perceptions of isolation from family, from friends, and at school indicated no multicollinearity problems in each equation.

 ## References

Alvarez, R. (1968). Informal reactions to deviance in simulated work organizations: A laboratory experiment. *American Sociological Review, 33,* 895–912.

Berk, R. A., Campell, A., Klap. R., & Western, B. (1992). The deterrent effect of arrest: A Bayesian analysis of four field experiments. *American Sociological Review, 57,* 689–708.

Black, D. J. (1970). Production of crime rates. *American Sociological Review, 35,* 733–748.

Black, D. J., & Reiss. A. J. (1970). Police control of juveniles. *American Sociological Review, 35,* 63–47.

Braithwaite, J. (1989). *Crime, shame, and reintegration.* Cambridge, England: Cambridge University Press.

DeLamater, J. (1968). On the nature of deviance. *Social Forces, 46,* 445–455.

Elliott, D. S., & Ageton, S. S. (1980). Reconciling race and class differences in self-reported and official estimates of delinquency. *American Sociological Review, 40,* 95–110.

Elliott, D. S., Huizinga, D., & Ageton, S. S. (1985). *Explaining delinquency and drug use.* Beverly Hills. CA: Sage.

Elliott, D. S., Huizinga. D., & Menard, S. (1989). Multiple problem youth: Delinquency, substance use, and mental health problems. New York: Springer-Verlag.

Farrell, R. A. (1989). Cognitive consistency in deviance causation: A psychological elaboration of an integrated system model. In S. F. Messner, M. D. Krohn, & A. E. Liska (Eds.), *Theoretical integration in the study of deviance and crime: Problems and prospects* (pp. 77–92). Albany: State University of New York Press.

Felson, R. B. (1985). Reflected appraisal and the development of self. *Social Psychology Quarterly, 48,* 71–77.

Felson, R. B. (1989). Parents and reflected appraisal process: A longitudinal analysis. *Journal of Personality and Social Psychology, 56,* 965–971.

Gibbons, D. C., & Krohn, M. D. (1991). *Delinquent behavior* (5th ed.). Eaglewood Cliffs, NJ: Prentice Hall.

Gibbs, J. P. (1966). Conception of deviant behavior: The old and the new. *Pacific Sociological Review, 9*, 9–14.

Gibbs, J. P. (1972). Issues in defining deviant behavior. In R. A. Scott & J. D. Douglas (Eds.), *Theoretical perspectives on deviance* (pp. 39–68). New York: Basic Books.

Gove, W. R. (1980). The labeling perspective: An overview. In W. R. Gove (Ed.), *The labeling of deviance: Evaluating a perspective* (2nd ed., pp. 9–33). Beverly Hills, CA: Sage.

Gove, W. R., & Hughes, M. (1989). A theory of mental illness: An attempted integration of biological, psychological, and social variables. In S. F. Messner, M. D. Krohn, & A. E. Liska (Eds.), *Theoretical integration in the study of deviance and crime: Problems and prospects* (pp. 61–76). Albany: State University of New York Press.

Hagan, J. (1974). Extra-legal attitudes and criminal sanctioning: An assessment and a sociological view. *Law and Society Review, 8*, 357–383.

Hagan, J., & Palloni, A. (1990). The social reproduction of a criminal class in working-class London. *American Journal of Sociology, 96*, 265–299.

Heimer, K., & Matsueda, R. L. (1994). Role-taking, role commitment, and delinquency: A theory of differential social control. *American Sociological Review, 59*, 356–390.

Jackson, J. K. (1954). The adjustment of the family to the crisis of alcoholism. *Quarterly Journal of Studies on Alcohol, 15*, 564–586.

Jackson, J. K. (1962). Alcoholism and the family. In D. J. Pittman & C. R. Snyder (Eds.), *Society, culture, and drinking patterns* (pp. 472–479). New York: Wiley.

Kaplan, H. B. (1975). Increase in self-rejection as an antecedent of deviant responses. *Journal of Youth and Adolescence, 4*, 438–458.

Kaplan, H. B. (1980). *Deviant behavior in defense of self.* New York: Academic Press.

Kinch, J. W. (1963). A formalized theory of the self-concept. *American Journal of Sociology, 68*, 481–486.

Link, B. (1982). Mental patient status, and income: An examination of the effects of a psychiatric label. *American Sociological Review, 47*, 456–478.

Link, B. (1987). Understanding labeling effects in the area of mental disorders: An assessment of the effects of expectations of rejection. *American Sociological Review, 52*, 1004–1081.

Link, B., & Cullen, F. T. (1983). Reconsidering the social rejection of external patients: Levels of attitudinal response. *American Journal of Community Psychology, 11*, 261–273.

Link, B., Cullen, F. T., Frank, J., & Wozniak, J. F. (1987). The social rejection of former mental patients: Understanding why labels matter. *American Journal of Sociology, 92*, 1461–1500.

Link, B., Cullen, F. T., Struening, E., Shrout, P. E., & Dohrenwend, B. P. (1989). A modified labeling theory approach to mental disorders: An empirical assessment. *American Sociological Review, 54*, 400–423.

Liska, A. E. (1987). *Perspectives on deviance.* Englewood Cliffs, NJ: Prentice Hall.

Matsueda, R. L. (1992). Reflected appraisals, parental labeling, and delinquency: Specifying a symbolic interactionist theory. *American Journal of Sociology, 97*, 1577–1611.

Orcutt, J. D. (1973). Social reaction and the response to deviation in small groups. *Social Forces, 52*, 259–267.

Palamara, F., Cullen, F. T., & Gersten, J. C. (1986). The effect of police and mental health intervention on juvenile delinquency: Specifying contingencies in the impact of formal reaction. *Journal of Health and Social Behavior, 27*, 90–105.

Pate, A. M., & Hamilton, E. E. (1992). Formal and informal deterrents to domestic violence: The Dade County spouse assault experiment. *American Sociological Review, 57*, 691–697.

Paternoster, R., & Iovanni, L. (1989). The labeling perspective and delinquency: An elaboration of the theory and an assessment of the evidence. *Justice Quarterly, 6*, 395–394.

Ray, M. C., & Downs, W. R. (1986). An empirical test of labeling theory using longitudinal data. *Journal of Research in Crime and Delinquency, 23*, 169–194.

Sampson, H., Messinger, S. L., & Towne, R. D. (1962). Family processes and becoming a mental patient. *American Journal of Sociology, 68*, 88–96.

Sampson, R. J. (1986). Effects of socioeconomic context on social reaction to juvenile delinquency. *American Sociological Review, 51*, 876–885.

Sherman, L. W., & Smith, D. A. (1992). Crime, punishment, and stake in community: Legal and informal control of domestic violence. *American Sociological Review, 57*, 680–690.

Swigert, L. V., & Farrell, R. A. (1978). Referent others and deviance causation; A neglected dimension in labeling research. In M. D. Krohn & R. L. Akers (Eds.), *Crime, law, and sanctions; theoretical perspectives* (pp. 59–72). Beverly Hills, CA: Sage.

Tittle, C. R. (1975). Deterrence or labeling? *Social Forces, 53*, 399–410.

Tittle, C. R. (1980a). Labeling and crime: An empirical evaluation. In W. R. Gove (Ed.), *The labeling of deviance: Evaluating a perspective* (2nd ed., pp. 241–263). Beverly Hills, CA: Sage.

Tittle, C. R. (1980b). *Sanctions and social deviance: The question of deterrence.* New York: Praeger.

Tittle, C. R. (1988). Two empirical regularities (maybe) in search of an explanation: Commentary on the age/crime debate. *Criminology, 26*, 75–86.

Tittle, C. R., & Curran, D. A. (1988). Contingencies for dispositional disparities in juvenile justice. *Social Forces, 67*, 23–58.

Triplett, R. A., &. Jarjoura, G. R. (1994). Theoretical and empirical specification of a model of informal labeling. *Journal of Quantitative Criminology, 10*, 241–276.

Wellford, G. F. (1975). Labeling theory and criminology: An assessment. *Social Problems, 22*, 332–345.

Williams, K. R., & Hawkins, R. (1986). Perceptual research on general deterrence: A critical review. *Law and Society Review, 20*, 545–547.

Yarrow, M. R., Schartz, C. G., Murphy, H. S., & Deasy, L. C. (1955). The psychological meaning of mental illness in the family. *Journal of Social Issues, 11*, 12–24.

REVIEW QUESTIONS

1. How does Zhang measure informal labeling, the child's perceptions of informal labeling, and social isolation? Do you agree that such measures are valid? How would you improve such measures?

2. What did findings from this study show regarding parents' labeling? Which types of the youths' perceptions of labeling had the greatest effect on their subsequent delinquency? Explain these findings.

3. Given the findings of this study, do you believe that informal labeling has an important impact on recidivism or reoffending by youths who have been labeled "bad" kids? What types of policies would you advise based on these findings?

❖

READING 24

In this reading, Stanley Eitzen applies principles and concepts of conflict theory to deviance in the area of sports. After briefly reviewing traditional conflict perspectives, such as those of Marx and Weber, he generally applies various conflict theory ideas to social organizations in general, with an emphasis on the power of certain groups over others. Eitzen then narrows his scope specifically to sports, and demonstrates how the conflict perspective can readily be applied to this beloved realm of social life.

Conflict Theory and Deviance in Sport

D. Stanley Eitzen

The purpose of this essay is to elaborate the conflict paradigm with emphasis on its insights for understanding deviance in sport using the American case for illustrative purpose. To accomplish this the discussion is organized to: (1) enumerate the assumptions of the conflict perspective; (2) define deviance and establish its parameters as dictated by the conflict model; and (3) examine the structural roots of deviance in sport.*

 ## The Assumptions of Conflict Theory

The conflict perspective has a long tradition in sociology with such early giants as Marx and Weber and later theorists such as Mills, Dahrendorf, Habermas, Collins, Chambliss, Domhoff, Zeitlin, and Useem. These theorists and others have provided a unique and important paradigm for

SOURCE: D. Stanley Eitzen, "Conflict Theory and Deviance in Sport," *International Review for Sociology of Sport* 23 (1988): 193–203.

*Portions of this paper are adapted from Eitzen (1981a; 1981b; 1984a; 1984b; 1988)

understanding social structure, the social sources of social problems, and social change.

A problem in applying this perspective to social phenomena is that the vision and emphasis of conflict theorists vary considerably. Conflict theorists may be Marxists, neo-Marxists, or nonMarxists. Critical theorists from the Frankfurt school are included as are some phenomenologists. The analytical focus of conflict theorists may be on power structures, the role of institutions in legitimizing the status quo, how individuals are dominated through the shaping of their consciousnesses and world views, the connection between the personal troubles of individuals and the structure of society, or the efforts by the advantaged to retain power and the disadvantaged to increase theirs.

The conflict perspective, while not a unified theory, does have a unique way of interpreting social life that unites its somewhat diverse adherents. In this section I will present the general principles common to conflict theorists (taken in part from Bowles and Gintis 1976; Chambliss 1976; Collins 1975; Hansen 1976; Johnson 1981; Lenski 1966; Parenti 1978; Reasons and Perdue 1981; Turner 1974).

A major premise of the conflict perspective is that conflict is endemic in social organizations resulting from social structure itself. The things that people desire such as property, prestige, and power are not distributed equally in social organizations, resulting in a fundamental cleavage between the advantaged and the disadvantaged (Dahrendorf 1959; Marks and Engels 1951).

Related to the above is the assumption of conflict theorists that group interests are the basic elements of social life. Those persons in a similar social condition will organize to maximize their effectiveness in the struggles to preserve or promote vital group interests.

Next, there is the assumption that the powerful use their power to keep themselves in power. They are effective in controlling the powerless in three fundamental ways. Foremost, they claim a monopoly on the legitimate power including the use of force. Any threat to this power is considered illegitimate and the dissenters coerced to conform or face punishment. Next, directly or indirectly, the powerful control the decision-making apparatus. At the societal level, for example, they claim that the state and the law are instruments of the powerful (Wolfe 1978). Finally, the powerful control the production and distribution of information thus achieving ideological conformity among members (Bagdikian 1983). In Marx's memorable words, "The ideas of the ruling class are in every epoch the ruling ideas . . ." (1947:39). At the societal level, this ideological hegemony is accomplished by controlling the media, schools, churches, and other institutions (Ingham 1976:246–247). Through the socialization process individuals are taught the cultural norms, values, and ideologies and thus to accept the status quo as normal and right, thereby preserving the interests of the dominant (Parenti, 1978; Bowles and Gintis, 1976). This last process is a most effective social control mechanism, even resulting in individuals defining conditions against their interests as appropriate—a condition that Marx called false consciousness (Marx, in Johnson, 1981:130–131).

Another assumption common to conflict theorists is that the inequities in wealth, power, and prestige plus the coercion and exploitation by the powerful aimed at the disadvantaged inevitably lead to conflicts between them. There is a dynamic tension between the haves and have nots with discrimination and power plays. A wide variety of street politics develop to change power and class relations. This tension and the resulting struggles shape the relations within the social organization and the direction and magnitude of social change within it (Chambliss and Ryther 1975:55–56).

A prominent assumption of the conflict perspective is that the understanding of society or any of its institutions requires the analysis of the political economy. Power and wealth are inextricably intertwined and they dominate the rest of society. Social relations are the consequence of society's economic organization. Therefore, the analyst must consider the type of economy, the ways that members are organized for production and consumption, the distribution of material goods, the way decisions are made, and the distribution of power (Hoch 1972:1–15). In short, although conflict theorists may be interested in a number of social institutions, they show a distinct preference in their description, analysis, and explanation for the two "master" institutions of the economy and the polity (Forcese and Richer 1975:92–101).

Another assumption of the conflict perspective has to do with the consequences of social structure for individuals. Conflict theorists believe that the conditions of social organization, domination, and exploitation are not impersonal forces but have alienating, repressive, and frustrating effects on individuals. The important concept here is alienation, which refers to estrangement resulting from the lack of control over the conditions of one's own life (see Horton 1966; Marx 1962). The individual may be alienated from work, the products of labor, from others, and from oneself. Relations of powerlessness and estrangement prevail in social organizations characterized by impersonal bureaucracy, undemocratic decision-making, class inequality, and where system needs supersede individual needs.

The final assumption of the conflict perspective is that human beings are the architects of social organization and history. Individuals as members of groups define their form and content. The extent to which the powerless are able to accomplish radical change depends on their understanding of the bias of the system and their ability to mobilize others in the same condition (Anderson and Gibson 1978:7). Poor theory produces bad politics, however, pre-theoretical resistance and rebellion entail such destruction, responses as crime, capitalist religion, petty tyranny in the home, or psychological anguish. Social conditions, then, are subject to the collective actions of human actors, which may have good or bad consequences (Flacks and Turkel 1978:193–194).

 ## Toward a Definition of Deviance in Sport

Typically, sociologists define deviance as behavior that violates the norms. The rules are taken as morally correct, and the focus is on what kinds of people deviate. Conflict theorists interpret deviance quite differently. They assume that the rules are instruments of the ruling class to maintain and perpetuate the existing social order and therefore its advantage (Quinney 1974; 1977). Society's rules are believed to be *not* based on a consensus of the members but rather express the interests of those powerful who make the rules (McCaghy 1985:88). Conflict theorists argue that the traditional view of taking the rules of the social order as the foundation of what is and what is not deviance, results in an analysis that supports the social order (Braithwaite and Wilson 1978:4). To do so ignores the pernicious consequences of power, privilege, domination, and oppression.

Conflict theorists, then, do not focus on rule breakers but rather on rule makers. They do not focus on troublemakers but rather on the troubles caused by the macro

structural forces of the larger society (Miller 1976). Thus, conflict theory directs our attention to the covert, institutional, and normal activities in society that do physical and psychic harm (Liazos 1972; Thio 1973). The conflict theorist, then, focuses, for example, on the law, the quality of life, the economy, and institutional racism and sexism. We ask: How does the economy, the educational system, or the organization of sport really work? Who benefits from these arrangements and who does not (Eitzen 1984b: 11)?

Implicit in this discussion is the assumption by conflict theorists that there are objective conditions, regardless of the rules, that do harm and are therefore deviant (see Eitzen 1984a, 1988). I believe that conflict theorists would tend to agree that the following principles should be applied to assess right or wrong behavior by organizations and individuals in the sports context.

1. *Athletes must always be considered ends and not means.* In other words, the outcome for the participants in sport is infinitely more important than the outcome of the contest, the money generated, or other extraneous consideration. In practice this means that athletes must be treated by coaches and administrators with dignity and respect; they must not be exploited; and they must not be demeaned and dehumanized. This means, further, that athletes must respect their opponents and not condone or engage in tactics of intimidation or willful injury. As philosopher Paul Weiss has argued: "Sports should begin and be carried out with a concern for the rights of others" (1969:180).

Obviously this principle is violated and deviance occurs when:

- Athletes are physically and mentally abused by coaches as Gary Shaw has documented in his description of the football program at the University of Texas (1972), and as described of the basketball program under Coach Bob Knight at Indiana University (1986).

- Coaches encourage disrespect for opponents as the legendary Vince Lombardi did when he counseled "To play this games [football] you must have that fire in you, and nothing stokes that fire like hate" (quoted in Kramer, 1981:x).

- Athletes are expected by their superiors to use excessive violence to intimidate opponents and to injure them.

- Injured athletes are administered pain killing drugs so that they can return to action sooner than is prudent for their long term health.

- Administrators and owners insist on using artificial turf regardless of the evidence that it increases the probability of injuries to athletes (Johnson, 1985).

- Especially strong teams schedule the especially weak to enhance their records and the weak do so to make money, although often at the expense of their player's health.

- College athletes are exploited through low pay, excessive demand on their time and energies, ignoring their educational goals, treating them as interchangeable parts, and by a system of rules and enforcements that punishes athletes more than those who coax them to break the rules (Purdy, Eitzen, and Hufnagel 1982; Sack and Thiel 1985; and Underwood 1984).

2. *The competition must be fair.* The administration of leagues and the supervision of contests must be governed by rules applied impartially to all parties. There must be not taint of bias.

An implication of this fairness principle has to do with the nature of sport itself. Sport, by definition, is a competition involving physical prowess. Thus, athletic contests, true to the ideals of sport, must be decided only by differences in physical skills, motivation, strategy, and luck. This rules out those activities that give an athlete or team an unfair advantage such as cheating (Luschen 1976) or the use of drugs to enhance performance artificially. Obvious, too, is that efforts to fix the outcome of athletic contests by gamblers and corrupt athletes violates the spirit of sport.

The temptation to cheat by individuals and sports organizations is great because the psychic and material rewards for winning are so great. For the athletes winning brings adulation, fame, records, and, depending on the sport, the possibility of great material gains. For coaches winning translates into celebrity status, contracts with shoe manufacturers, gifts from generous fans, television contracts, and ever higher salaries. For team owners winning increases gate receipts, brings invitations to lucrative tournaments and bowl games, and raises television revenues.

In short, sport is not a pristine activity in a Utopia but rather one that occurs in a society where only the fittest survive. The doctrine of "winning is the only thing" means that the end justifies the means. As one football coach stated:

> Until three years ago we obeyed every rule and where did it get us? We finished last in the conference. Since that time there isn't a rule we haven't broken. And where are we now? This year we're playing in the Orange Bowl (quoted in Shea 1978:145).

One might argue that when unethical practices such as cheating are widespread, then they do not constitute deviance. If "everyone is doing it" how can it be deviance? Most big-time college sports programs break the rules in recruiting. Most offensive linemen illegally hold their opponents. Every major league baseball team probably has at least one pitcher who illegally applies a foreign substance to the baseball for an unfair advantage. And, most world class weight lifters use illegal anabolic steroids to increase bulk, strength, and muscle definition. Does a majority flaunting a rule negate it? Does the rationale that "everyone is doing it" justify it? Conflict theorists would argue that if a widespread practice in sport provides an unfair advantage in athletic contests, then it is deviant no matter how many are doing it. Rules intended to provide equity for all participants and teams are unconditional and thus constitute imperatives (Shea 1978:149).

3. *Participation, leadership, resources, and rewards must be based on achievement rather than ascribed characteristics.* This means that sports activities must be characterized by equal access and equal opportunity. Thus ability coupled with motivation shall decide who participates rather than race, creed, gender, or social position. Sport, however, has a long and sordid history in violating this principle. The structures of class, gender, and racial privilege have always dominated sport with the rules guiding amateur sport and in the societal wide practices that denied equal opportunity in sport to women and people of color.

The battle for equality in sport continues. Unequal opportunity structures still deny access to the poor. Blacks remain virtually absent from some sports. Where blacks do participate and even dominate on the field in a sport, they are vastly underrepresented in leadership roles as players, coaches, and administrators (Eitzen and Sage 1986). The patriarchal power structures in sport remain in power, resisting for the most part efforts to achieve gender equality whether it be equal resources, equal and nonsexist media coverage, or whatever.

 ## The Structural Roots of Deviance in Sport

How are we to understand the cheating, the exploitation, and the other forms of deviance so commonplace in sport? Obviously, there are some bad people who, when given an option, gravitate toward these behaviors, but this explanation is shallow and does not get at the source. The conflict approach to rule-breaking and other deviant acts locates them not in original sin, in the genes, or in the psyches of evil persons, but in the structural conditions of society and in the organization found therein.

Deviance in American sport does not occur in a vacuum. Deviance is rooted in the political economy of society. The insights of the conflict theorists within the Marxist tradition are especially instructive in aiding our understanding of deviance in sport. They argue that society in monopoly capitalism is dominated by two structural conditions—massification and commodification—both of which help to explain why individuals *qua* individuals and as decision-makers in organizations make deviant choices in all areas of social life including sport.

When sport becomes an activity of *dis*-play, it destroys what is valuable in sport altogether. Sport becomes transformed into a spectacle, played for and shaped into a form which will be "consumed" by spectators searching for titillating entertainment (Sewart 1981:49).

Violence attracts spectators even more and is therefore encouraged. Sport, because of its attractiveness to so many in mass society, is a particularly effective vehicle for advertising. Many athletes, male and female, are objectified as sex objects to sell products. As Brohm has put it: "They [athletes] are very often advertising 'sandwich-board' men" (1978:176). Today's top-level athletes, whether so-called amateur or professional, are workers who sell their labor power—their ability to draw crowds—to employers. Thus, players are purchased, bought, and sold for profit. So, too, are franchises

leaving fans feeling abused and used. As a final example, athletes are treated like machines, as instruments, for producing victories and income. This is seen in the total mobilization of the athletes to produce maximum performance.

Every sport now involves a fantastic *manipulation of human robots* by doctors, psychologists, bio-chemists and trainers. The "manufacturing of champions" is no longer a craft but an industry, calling on specialized laboratories, research institutes, training camps and experimental sport centers. Most top-level athletes are reduced to the status of more or less voluntary guinea pigs. "Hopefuls" are spotted young, the less talented are methodically weeded out and those that remain are then systematically oriented according to their potential . . . The specialists in this sporting Gulag stop at no human sacrifice in their drive to push back the limits of human capacity and transcend biological barriers (Brohm 1978:18–19).

In short, sport and its participants are like any other commodity—"something to be marketed, packaged, and sold . . . The consequence of the process of commodification is that the multifarious forms of human activity lose their unique and distinct qualities to the principles of the market" (Sewart 1981:47–48).

Under the social conditions resulting from the massification and commodification of sport, coaches, athletes, and spectators are increasingly objects to be manipulated and exploited. Winning is the all consuming goal, and participants will be judged exclusively in terms of instrumental rationality. The unsuccessful will be replaced, just as the defective parts in a machine. Under these circumstances opponents *are* enemies. So, too, are teammates since they compete among themselves for starting positions. Under these conditions the humans actors view themselves as objects and others as objects to be used.

In viewing himself as an object, the worker increasingly relates to other people as objects; he is alienated from the species whereby instead of celebrating his existence through meaningful interaction, he is isolated, asocial and ultimately, like the market within which he exists, amoral (Sugden 1981:59).

Under these conditions, then, the actors are alienated individuals who are exploited and see others as means to their ends. Thus, the common *modus operandi* of "whatever it takes to win."

Organizational deviance. We have seen that conflict theory points to the structural sources of deviance. In

American society the rewards for winning are so great that coaches, athletes, and others often use and abuse others for personal gain. But deviance is not just the behavior of unethical individuals. Organizations, too, may be deviant (Santomier et al. 1980; Santomier and Cautilli 1985). Some deviant acts are perpetrated by individuals concerned with achieving organizational goals. The owners of professional baseball, for example, once conspired to keep the sport racially segregated. Throughout their histories professional leagues have worked to retain their power over athletes through the reserve clause, Rozelle Rule, the player draft, and other unfair mechanisms. Some universities have repeatedly been found guilty of "buying" athletes regardless of the personel. When Clemson University was found guilty of multiple violations, its President, William Atchely, wanted to clean up the program. The Board of Regents fired him for advocating such a plan.

The controlling body of intercollegiate sport, the National Collegiate Athletic Association (NCAA) is, in many respects, a deviant organization. The NCAA has monopolistic control over big-time college athletic programs. Most significantly, this monopoly is used to the one-sided detriment of the worker-athletes and to the benefit of the member schools. Four examples forcefully make this point: (1) scholarship athletes make a four-year commitment to a school, yet the schools only make a commitment to the athletes on a year-to-year basis; (2) athletes must wait a year to play if they change schools even if the coach they signed to play for has left the institution; (3) athletes are paid only for room, board, tuition, and books yet they may be in a sport generating many millions of dollars to the school; and (4) by insisting that an athletic scholarship is not paid, the NCAA has helped keep injured athletes from receiving workers' compensation (Porto, 1985).

The NCAA is also deviant, I would argue, when it resists government regulations that would move toward gender equality in school sports. The NCAA maintains that big-time athletic programs are revenue-producing businesses and that sacrificing these revenues for gender equality is bad business. The NCAA argues that the schools are businesses but the athletes generating the income are not workers but amateurs engaged in an educational experience. Somehow this twisted logic is permitted by its member institutions to justify the continued second class status of womens' sports (Sack 1981).

To conclude, this essay has demonstrated how sport is a microcosm of society and how the origins of deviance in sport are structural. The conflict perspective, however, does not stop with these insights. This theoretical stance demands that we *not* accept "the way things are" (Birrell 1984). Rather, we must work to improve the human condition, and this requires not reform but the transformation of society and its institutions—in this case the institution of sport.

 ## References

Anderson, Charles H. and Jeffry R. Gibson, 1978. *Toward a New Sociology*, 3rd ed. Homewood, IL: Dorsey.

Bagdikian, Ben. 1983. *The Media Monopoly.* Boston: Beacon Press.

Birrell, Susan, 1984. "Separation as an Issue in Women's Sport," *Arena Review* 8, (July):21–29.

Bowles, Samuel and Herbert Gintis. 1976. *Schooling in Capitalist America.* New York: Basic Books.

Braithwaite, John and Paul R. Wilson, 1978: "Pervs, Pimps, and Powerbrokers. " Pp. 1–12 in *Two Faces of Deviance*, edited by Paul R. Wilson and John Braithwaite. Queensland, Australia: University of Queensland Press.

Brohm, Jean-Marie, 1978: *Sport: A Prison of Measured Time.* London: Ink Links.

Chambliss, William J., 1976: "Functional and Conflict Theories of Crime: The Heritage of Emile Durkheim and Karl Marx." Pp. 1–28 in *Whose Law? What Order? A Conflict Approach to Criminology,* edited by William J. Chambliss and Milton Mankoff. New York: John Wiley & Sons.

Chambliss, William J. 1984. "Crime and Conflict Theory," *Criminal Law in Action.* 2nd ed. New York: John Wiley & Sons, pp. 1–9.

Chambliss, William J. and Thomas E. Ryther. 1975. *Sociology.* New York: McGraw-Hill.

Collins, Randall. 1975. *Conflict Sociology.* New York: Academic Press.

Dahrendorf, Ralf. 1958. "Out of Utopia: Toward a Reorientation of Sociological Analysis," *American Journal of Sociology* 64:115–127.

Dahrendorf, Ralf. 1959. *Class and Class Conflict in Industrial Society.* Stanford, Calif.: Stanford University Press.

Eitzen, D. Stanley. 1981a. "Athletics and Higher Education: A Conflict Perspective," paper presented at the annual meeting of the North American Society for the Sociology of Sport, Fort Worth, Texas (November, 12–15).

Eitzen, D. Stanley. 1981b. "Sport and Deviance." In *Handbook of Social Science of Sport*, edited by Gunther R. F. Luschen and George H. Sage. Champaign, IL: Stipes.

Eitzen, D. Stanley. 1984a Teaching Social Problems: Implications of the Objectivist-Subjectivist Debate," *Society for the Study of Social Problems Newsletter* 16 (Fall): 10–12.

Eitzen, D. Stanley. 1984b. "Conflict Theory and the Sociology of Sport," *Arena Review* 8 (November):45–54.

Eitzen, D. Stanley. 1988. "Ethical Problems in Sport," *Journal of Sport and Social Issues* 12:17–30.

Eitzen, D. Stanley and George H. Sage. 1986. *Sociology of North American Sport*, 3rd ed. Dubuque, IA: Wm. C. Brown.

Feinstein, John. 1986. *A Season on the Brink*. New York: Macmillan.

Forcese, Dennis and Stephen Richer. 1975. *Issues in Canadian Society*. Scarborough, Ontario: Prentice Hall.

Flacks, Richard and Gerald Turkel. 1978. "Radical Sociology: The Emergence of Neo-Marxian Perspectives in U.S. Sociology." *Annual Review of Sociology* 4:193–238.

Hansen, Donald A., 1976: *An Invitation to Critical Sociology*. New York: Free Press.

Hargreaves, John, 1982: "Theorizing Sport," *Culture and Ideology*, edited by John Hargreaves. London: Routledge & Kegan Paul.

Hoch, Paul. 1972. *Rip Off the Big Game*. Garden City, New York: Doubleday.

Horton, John. 1966. "Order and Conflict Theories of Social Problems in Competing Ideologies," *American Journal of Sociology* 71 (May): 701–713.

Hughes, Robert and Jay J. Coakley. 1984. "Mass Society and the Commercialization of Sport," *Sociology of Sport Journal* 1 (1): 57–63.

Ingham, Alan G. 1976. "Sport and the 'New Left': Some Reflections Upon Opposition without Praxis Pp. 238–248 in" *Social Problems in Athletics*, edited by Daniel M. Landers. Urbana: University of Illinois Press.

Johnson, Doyle Paul. 1981. *Sociological Theory*. New York: John Wiley & Sons.

Johnson, William Oscar. 1985. "The Tyranny of Phony Grass," *Sports Illustrated* 63 (August 12):34–44.

Kramer, Jerry , ed. 1981. *Lombardi: Winning Is the Only Thing*. New York: Pocket Books.

Lenski, Gerhard E. 1966. *Power and Privilege: A Theory of Social Stratification*. New York: McGraw-Hill.

Liazos, Alexander. 1972. "The Poverty of Sociology of Deviance: Nuts, Sluts, and 'Preverts," *Social Problems* 20 (Summer): 103–120.

Luschen, Gunther R. F. 1976. "Cheating in Sport," *Social Problems in Athletics*, edited by Daniel M. LANDERS. Urbana: University of Illinois Press, pp. 67–77.

Marx, Karl. 1947. *The German Ideology*. New York: International Publishers. (originally published in 1846)

Marx, Karl. 1963. "Economic and Philosphical Manuscripts," in *Karl Marx Early Writings*, edited by T. B. Bottomore New York: McGraw-Hill.

Marx, Karl and Friedrich Engels. 1951. *The Communist Manifesto*, volume 1. Moscow: Foreign Languages Publishing House. (originally published in 1848)

Mccaghy, Charles H. 1985. *Deviant Behavior: Crime, Conflict, and Interest Groups*, 2nd ed. New York: Macmillan.

Miller, S. M. 1976. "The Political Economy of Social Problems: From the Sixties to the Seventies," *Social Problems* 24 (October): 131–141.

Parenti, Michael. 1978. *Power and the Powerless*. New York: St. Martin's Press.

Porto, Brian L. 1985. "Athletic Scholarships as Contracts of Employment: The Rensing Decisions and the Future of College Sports," *Journal of Sport and Social Issues* 9 (Winter/Spring):20–37.

Purdy, Dean A., D. Stanley Eitzen, and Rick Hufnagel, 1982: "Are Athletes Also Students?" *Social Problems* 29 (April):439–47.

Quinney, Richard. 1974. *Critique of Legal Order*. Boston: Little, Brown.

Quinney, Richard. 1977. *Class, State and Crime*. New York: David McKay.

Reasons, Charles E. and William D. Perdue. 1981. *The Ideology of Social Problems*. Sherman Oaks, CA: Alfred.

Sack, Allen L. 1981. "College Sports Much Choose: Amateur or Pro?" *The New York Times* (May 3):2S.

Sack, Allen L. and Robert Thiel. 1985. "College Basketball and Role Conflict: A National Survey," *Sociology of Sport Journal* 2 (September): 195–209.

Santomier, James P. and Peter Cautelli. 1985. "Controlling Deviance in Intercollegiate Athletics." Pp. 397–403 in *Sport and Higher Education*, edited by Donald Chu, Jeffrey O. Segrave, and Beverly J. Becker (eds.). Champaign, IL: Human Kinetics.

Santomier, James P., William G. Howard Wendy L. Pilz, and Thomas J. Romance, 1980: "White Sock Crime: Organizational Deviance in Intercollegiate Athletics," *Journal of Sport and Social Issues* 4 (Fall/Winter): 26–32.

Sewart, John J. 1981. "The Rationalization of Modern Sport: The Case of Professional Football, "*Arena Review* 5 (September) :45–53.

Shaw, Gary. 1972. *Meat on the Hoof: The Hidden World of Texas Football*. New York: St. Martin's Press.

Shea, E. J. 1978. *Ethical Decisions in Physical Education and Sport*. Springfield, IL: Charles C Thomas.

Sugden, J. P. 1981. "The Sociological Perspective: The Political Economy of Violence in American Sport," *Arena Review* 5 (February):57–62.

Thio, Alex. 1973. "Class Bias in the Sociology of Deviance," *The American Sociologist* 8 (February): 1–12.

Turner, Jonathan H. 1974. *The Structure of Sociological Theory*. Homewood, IL: Dorsey.

Underwood, John. 1984. *Spoiled Sport*. Boston: Little, Brown.

Weiss, Paul. 1969. *Sport: A Philosophic Inquiry*. Carbondale: Southern Illinois University Press.

Whitson, David J. n.d. "Research Methodology in Sport Sociology". *CAHPER Sociology of Sport Monograph Series*. Ottawa, Canada: CAHPER.

Wolfe, Alan. 1978. *The Seamy Side of Democracy: Repression in America*. New York.

Young, T. R. 1972. *New Sources of Self*. London: Pergamon Press.

Young, T. R. 1984. "The Sociology of Sport: A Critical Overview," *Arena Review* 8 (November) 1–14.

Young, T. R. and Garth Massey. 1980. "The Dramaturgical Society: A Macro-Analytic Approach to Dramaturgical Analysis," *Qualitative Sociology* 1(2):78–98.

1. What does the author mean when he says, "Athletes must always be considered ends and not means"? Try to provide an example, even if hypothetical.

2. Give your reaction to the author's point that "the competition must be fair," especially in light of the cited interview with the football player who says that breaking rules got him to the Orange Bowl.

3. Toward the end of the piece, what does the author conclude about the NCAA? How does this fit with the theme of the paper/topic?

READING 25

In this selection, Amanda Burgess-Proctor presents a theoretical piece that examines the interplay among the various concepts that are so vital in conflict perspectives of criminality, namely, race/ethnicity, socioeconomic status, and gender. She reveals the established and potential interactions between these various concepts, particularly their importance in terms of why people commit crime, as well as the handling of such persons by the justice system. Although the author places a high emphasis on feminism, this selection includes important discussions about demographic characteristics that are key in virtually all conflict perspectives of crime and formal handling by the system.

While reading the first portion of Burgess-Proctor's article, pay attention to the idea that there does not exist a single, unitary perspective of feminist criminology. Rather, there are various perspectives of crime that exist under the heading of feminist theories in the discipline. The categories included in Burgess-Proctor's review are liberal feminism, radical feminism, Marxist feminism, socialist feminism, and postmodern feminism. Although this list is not exhaustive, these categories are currently the most common forms of feminist criminology and are largely based on what is most vital to their respective frameworks. For example, while Marxist feminists claim that women's economic oppression in capitalistic societies is the primary issue, liberal feminists claim that the differential way that males and females are socialized toward gender-specific roles in society is the primary problem facing women. This is just one example of the way feminist criminology is far more complex than most people, including many criminologists, realize.

While reading this selection, readers are also encouraged to consider the importance of each of these demographic characteristics—race/ethnicity, social class, and gender—in terms of their impact on crime and how such cases are treated in the criminal justice system. More than half of the readers of this selection may themselves be underrepresented minorities, women, or members of the working class, and the other readers likely know offenders who fit into these groups. Thus, all readers are encouraged to examine whether they can relate to this perspective, either for themselves or others they know well. Ultimately, Burgess-Proctor presents an important framework in her presentation of multi-class and multi-racial feminism, and the issues she proposes regarding the interactions among these concepts represent the current state of understanding and recommendations for future research regarding race, class, and gender.

Intersections of Race, Class, Gender, and Crime

Future Directions for Feminist Criminology

Amanda Burgess-Proctor

Feminist criminology has survived the growing pains of its development during the 1970s to emerge as a mature theoretical orientation. Thanks to the pioneering generation of feminist criminologists who insisted that women's deviance was worthy of academic inquiry, as well as to the contemporary generation of feminist criminologists who have contributed immensely to our understanding of women as victims, offenders, and practitioners of the criminal justice system, feminist criminology now is routinely recognized by the broader discipline as a legitimate theoretical perspective (or more accurately, set of perspectives). More than 30 years after the first scholarship of its kind was produced, feminist studies of crime are more commonplace than ever before.

Two recent milestone events remind us of just how powerful an influence feminists have had in criminology during the past three decades. First, 2004 marked the 20th anniversary of the Division on Women and Crime, the unit of the American Society of Criminology whose members are dedicated to feminist criminology and to the study of issues related to women, gender, and crime. Second, the creation of this journal, the official publication of the Division on Women and Crime, serves as a testament to the demand that exists for feminist criminological scholarship. Together, these two important achievements provide the perfect opportunity to reflect on what lies ahead for feminist criminology. Now is the time to ask ourselves, in what direction is contemporary feminism heading, and how will developments in the broader feminist movement influence the future of feminist criminology in particular? How will the work of feminist criminologists be defined in the 21st century, and what opportunities exist for the advancement of feminist criminology in the coming years?

Throughout this article, I argue that the future of feminist criminology lies in our willingness to embrace a theoretical framework that recognizes multiple, intersecting inequalities. Contemporary feminist criminologists bear the responsibility of advancing an inclusive feminism, one that simultaneously attends to issues of race, class, gender, sexuality, age, nationality, religion, physical ability, and other locations of inequality as they relate to crime and deviance. Put simply, to advance an understanding of gender, crime, and justice that achieves universal relevance and is free from the shortcomings of past ways of thinking, feminist criminologists must examine linkages between inequality and crime using an intersectional theoretical framework that is informed by multiracial feminism.

To present a persuasive argument for using an intersectional approach in feminist studies of crime, I have divided this article into four sections. First, I start by tracing the development of feminist criminology from its inception in the early 1970s. This section begins with a brief discussion of various feminist perspectives and then outlines the development of feminist criminology within the context of the broader feminist movement. Second, I describe the evolution of feminist approaches to gender that occurred during second-wave feminism of the 1970s and 1980s. Specifically, this section considers the transition from "sameness" and "difference" models, which are informed by liberal feminism, to a "dominance" model informed by radical feminism. Third, I discuss the emergence during contemporary third-wave feminism of an alternative approach to gender: an intersectional model informed by multiracial feminism. Fourth, I underscore the importance of this intersectional model for feminist criminology by highlighting its theoretical, methodological, and praxis-related relevance, and I suggest future directions for feminist criminology with respect to intersections of race, class, gender, and crime.

The Emergence of Feminist Criminology

The first wave of feminism began in the United States with the birth of the abolitionist and women's suffrage movements in the mid- to late 1800s. Criminology itself was still developing at this time, as scholars such as Lombroso and Durkheim (in Europe) and Kellor (in the United States) began theorizing about crime and deviance (Beirne & Messerschmidt, 2000). Some 100 years later, the women's liberation and civil rights movements of the 1960s and 1970s marked the genesis of second-wave feminism. It is during this era that feminism made its appearance in criminology.

Theoretically speaking, feminist criminology developed because (primarily liberal) feminist scholars objected to the exclusion of gender from criminological analyses, an omission that seemed particularly glaring given that gender is such a strong predictor of offending (Blumstein, Cohen, Roth, & Visher, 1986; Steffensmeier & Allan, 1996), arrest (Stolzenberg & D'Alessio, 2004) and sentencing outcomes (Daly, 1994; Daly & Tonry, 1997). Feminist scholars were dissatisfied with the failure of mainstream criminology to recognize issues of gender inequality at all, as well as with the failure of critical and radical criminology to consider the relationship between inequality and crime outside of the narrow context of economic disparities, under which were subsumed issues of race and gender (see Beirne & Messerschmidt, 2000). In particular, feminist criminologists protested the exclusion of women's experiences in emerging "general" theories of crime, which were being developed by mainstream criminologists using almost exclusively male samples to predict patterns of male delinquency (Barak, 1998; Belknap, 2001; Chesney-Lind & Pasko, 2004; Daly & Chesney-Lind, 1988; Flavin, 2004; Miller, 2004; Milovanovic & Schwartz, 1996; Morash, 1999). These early feminist criminologists demanded that analyses of crime include consideration of gender in ways that had not occurred before.

It is important to note here that feminist criminology was born during a crucial juncture of the feminist movement. Shortly after the beginning of the second wave in the 1970s, feminists of minority-group status found that their experiences were underrepresented in mainstream feminism and subsequently levied sharp criticism toward their majority-group counterparts whose voices were purported to speak on behalf of all women. Feminists of color, lesbian feminists, Third World feminists, and feminists from other marginalized groups condemned the hegemony of White, middle-class, heterosexual experience that characterized mainstream second-wave feminism at that time. As I discuss more fully in the following section, it is against this backdrop that feminist criminology emerged, and claims of essentialism and reductionism soon plagued the broader feminist movement as well as feminist criminology in particular.

Finally, second-wave feminism gave way to third-wave feminism during the 1980s and 1990s. A defining feature of third-wave feminism is its focus on multiplicities or the belief that there exist multiple genders, races, and sexualities. With this idea in mind and echoing earlier criticisms, many third-wave feminists expressed dissatisfaction with the insufficient treatment of race, class, sexuality, and other locations of inequality in mainstream feminist scholarship. As a result, it is during contemporary third-wave feminism that intersectionality first appeared (Price & Sokoloff, 2004).[1] Intersectionality recognizes that systems of power such as race, class, and gender do not act alone to shape our experiences but rather, are multiplicative, inextricably linked, and simultaneously experienced. Feminist criminologists writing at this time also recognized the need for intersectionality (Daly, 1993; Daly & Stephens, 1995). For example, Daly and Stephens (1995) observed that an intersectional approach to studying crime explores

> how class, gender, and race (and age and sexuality) construct the normal and deviant . . . how these inequalities put some societal members at risk to be rendered deviant or to engage in law-breaking, and . . . how law and state institutions both challenge and reproduce these inequalities. (p. 193)

This timeline of events allows for a more thorough understanding of the development of feminist thought during second-wave and early third-wave feminism. In the following section, I describe in detail how feminist approaches to studying gender have evolved in the past 30 years, largely in response to the events outlined above.

The Evolution of Feminist Approaches to Gender: Sameness, Difference, and Dominance

Shortly after the inception of second-wave feminism, one question divided feminists more sharply than perhaps any other: Are women essentially similar to men such that the sexes should be treated equally (i.e., the sameness approach) or do women have distinctive characteristics that require special treatment to overcome their gender-based discrimination (i.e., the difference approach)? This question loomed large among feminists, with proponents of each side lamenting the threat posed by the opposing viewpoint to the advancement of women's rights. For example, opponents of the difference approach argued that difference often is nothing more than a euphemism for discrimination, as well as that championing women's differences ultimately leads to their exclusion from certain roles, particularly within the workplace (MacKinnon, 1991; Nagel & Johnson, 2004; Williams, 1991). Conversely, opponents of the sameness approach believed in a gender dichotomy and claimed that women suffer from an equal-treatment model because, under the guise of gender neutrality, women's status ultimately is measured against a dominant male norm (Daly & Chesney-Lind, 1988; MacKinnon, 1991; Nagel & Johnson, 2004).

The sameness/difference debate that surfaced in the broader feminist movement also appeared in feminist criminology. For example, advocates of the sameness approach supported gender-neutral, "equal treatment under the law" measures, such as symmetrical correctional programming meant to guarantee male and female inmates access to the same vocational and educational resources (Barak et al., 2001). Furthermore, supporters of this equal-treatment model worried about the hidden dangers of the difference approach, wherein women's difference from men translates into their need for greater legal protection, as in the case of statutory rape laws:

> Statutory rape is, in criminal law terms, a clear instance of a victimless crime, since all parties are, by definition, voluntary participants. In what sense, then, can [Supreme Court Justice] Rehnquist assert [in a 1981 decision upholding California's statutory rape law] that the woman is victim and the man offender? One begins to get an inkling when, later, the Justice explains that the statutory rape law is "protective" legislation. . . . The notion that men are frequently the sexual aggressors and that the law ought to be able to take that reality into account in very concrete ways is hardly one that feminists could reject out of hand . . . it is therefore an area . . . in which we need to pay special attention to our impulses lest we inadvertently support and give credence to the very social constructs and behaviors we so earnestly mean to oppose. (Williams, 1991, pp. 20–21)

However, critics of the sameness approach argued that this model actually harms women because the law is not gender neutral but in fact assumes a male standard (MacKinnon, 1991; Williams, 1991). Given this male standard, women's legal claims have the potential to be regarded as requiring special or preferential treatment (Daly & Chesney-Lind, 1988). For example, considering parenthood as a mitigating factor in sentencing decisions, although applied "equally" to all defendants, disproportionately benefits female defendants with children (or "familied" women) and unintentionally punishes childless women (Barak et al., 2001; Daly, 1989; Daly & Tonry, 1997). Furthermore, critics recognized that the desire to standardize sentencing practices in the name of "equal justice" may carry unintended consequence for women:

> A major problem is that [equal-treatment] sentencing reforms are designed to reduce race- and class-based disparities in sentencing men. Their application to female offenders may yield equality with a vengeance: a higher rate of incarceration and for longer periods of time than in the past. Like reforms in divorce . . . and in child custody . . . devised with liberal feminist definitions of equality, sentencing reform also may prove unjust and may work ultimately against women. (Daly & Chesney-Lind, 1988, p. 525)

Despite the stark contrast in the orientation of the sameness and difference models, both approaches share a commonality: They are rooted in simplistic notions of women's and men's equality that are characteristic of liberal feminism. Recall that liberal feminism emphasizes political, social, legal, and economic equality between the sexes. Therefore, theoretical paradigms such as the sameness and difference models that fail to place gender relations in the context of patriarchy fit squarely within the perspective of liberal feminism. Furthermore, as many feminists have observed, the sameness and difference models also share the same fundamental flaw: They essentially ignore issues of power and privilege (Barak et al., 2001; MacKinnon, 1991; Sokoloff, Price, & Flavin, 2004). Put differently, both approaches fail to acknowledge disparities in power between the sexes; consequently, sameness and/or difference cannot be considered meaningfully without regard for women's subordinate status in a patriarchal society. As MacKinnon (1991) noted, although "men's differences from women are equal to women's differences from men . . . the sexes are not socially equal" (p. 85).

In an effort to improve upon previous models that were informed by liberal feminism and that offered elementary comparisons of men and women without regard for the effects of patriarchy, radical feminists writing at the beginning of the third wave argued for the adoption of a dominance approach to studying gender. The dominance approach is informed by radical feminism because it recognizes how patriarchy shapes gender relations and considers gender difference within the context of power and oppression (Barak et al., 2001; MacKinnon, 1991). "For women to affirm difference, when difference means dominance, as it does with gender, means to affirm the qualities and characteristics of powerlessness" (MacKinnon, 1991, p. 86). Moreover, supporters argued that the dominance approach was the only truly feminist paradigm. According to radical feminists, the sameness and difference approaches are masculinist insomuch as they use a male referent, whereas the dominance approach, "in that it sees the inequalities of the social world from the standpoint of the subordination of women to men, is feminist" (MacKinnon, 1991, p. 86).

Feminist criminologists also recognized the value of using the dominance approach. For example, Barak et al. (2001) maintain that the utility of the dominance model for feminist criminologists rests in its attention to power: "For example, proponents of the dominance approach have been instrumental in pressuring the legal system to abandon its 'hands-off' attitude toward domestic violence and to define wife battering and marital rape as crimes" (p. 154).

Furthermore, the dominance approach has value for feminist criminologists because its emphasis on power and privilege dovetails with related issues of inequality in the criminal justice system.

However, despite its appeal, the dominance approach was criticized by many early third-wave feminists—primarily women of color, lesbian women, and women from other marginalized groups—for essentializing women (Andersen & Collins, 2004; Baca Zinn, Hondagneu-Sotello, & Messner, 2000; Barak et al., 2001; Belknap, 2001; Daly & Chesney-Lind, 1988). "Essentialism occurs when a voice—typically a white, heterosexual, and socioeconomically privileged voice—claims to speak for everyone" (Sokoloff et al., 2004, p. 12). By asserting that women universally suffer the effects of patriarchy, the dominance approach rests on the dubious assumption that all women, by virtue of their shared gender, have a common "experience" in the first place. In short, the dominance approach is reductionist because it assumes that all women are oppressed by all men in exactly the same ways or that there is one unified experience of dominance experienced by women. Soon after these criticisms first emerged in the broader feminist movement, feminist criminologists began contemplating their own acts of essentialism. In the words of Daly and Chesney-Lind (1988), "One of the many challenges for feminism in general and feminist criminology in particular is the paradox of acknowledging diversity among women while claiming women's unity in experiences of oppression and sexism" (p.502).

 ## Beyond Dominance: Multiracial Feminism and Intersections of Race, Class, and Gender

As discussed in the previous section, the promise of the dominance approach was not shared by women who felt marginalized by "the hegemony of feminisms constructed primarily around the lives of white-middle class women" (Baca Zinn & Thornton Dill, 1996, p. 321).[2] Moreover, the dominance approach, for all of its positive attributes, is unidimensional in the sense that it merely examines women's experiences vis-à-vis men's experiences. In contrast, contemporary feminists now face a more multidimensional question: How do we move away from the "false universalism embedded in the concept 'woman'" toward an examination of gender in the context of other locations of inequality (Baca Zinn & Thornton Dill, 1996, p. 322)?

This question is not easily answered, and previous attempts by feminist scholars to acknowledge systems of power other than gender resulted in a rather benign emphasis on "diversity." As Baca Zinn and Thornton Dill (1996) comment,

> Despite the much heralded diversity trend within feminist studies, difference is often reduced to mere pluralism; a "live and let live" approach where principles or relativism generate a long list of diversities which begin with gender, class, and race and continue through a range of social structural as well as personal characteristics. . . . The major limitation of these approaches is the failure to attend to the power relations that accompany difference. Moreover, these approaches ignore the inequalities that cause some characteristics to be seen as "normal" while others are seen as "different" and thus, deviant. (p. 323)

For example, as "outsiders within" the feminist movement, women of color protested the complicity of "unitary theories of gender" in mainstream feminism (Baca Zinn & Thornton Dill, 1996, p. 321; see also Collins, 2000). Building on the criticisms wielded by feminists of color, a new paradigm has emerged in contemporary third-wave feminism that advances feminist thought beyond issues of sameness, difference, or dominance.[3] The "intersectional" model, informed by multiracial feminism, has succeeded in examining gender through the lens of difference while at the same time acknowledging the instrumental role of power in shaping gender relations. That is, guided by the perspective of multiracial feminism, the intersectional approach successfully attends to issues of power and dominance while achieving a universal relevance that has eluded previous approaches to studying gender.

It is sometimes difficult to disentangle concepts embedded in multiracial feminism from concepts embedded in intersections of race, class, and gender. In an attempt to elucidate these ideas, I have divided the following section in half. The first half describes key conceptual features of multiracial feminism. The second half discusses the advantages of adopting an intersectional (or "race-class-gender")

approach to studying gender that is informed by multiracial feminism. Together, both halves of the following section are intended to highlight the importance of intersectionality for feminist criminology.

Multiracial Feminism

Multiracial feminism was pioneered by women of color who recognized the need to construct approaches to studying gender that attended to issues of power and difference in ways that previous models had not (Baca Zinn & Thornton Dill, 1996). Although this perspective is known by a variety of names, including intersectionality theory and multicultural feminism, the term multiracial feminism is preferred because it emphasizes "race as a power system that interacts with other structured inequalities to shape genders" (Baca Zinn & Thornton Dill, 1996, p. 324). Still, the main focus is on interlocking and multiple inequalities (Baca Zinn & Thornton Dill, 1996; Thompson, 2002).

Multiracial feminism has several key conceptual features that distinguish it from other feminist perspectives and that make it ideal for promoting theoretical advancement for feminist criminology. First, multiracial feminism proposes that gender relations do not occur in a vacuum but, instead, that men and women also are characterized by their race, class, sexuality, age, physical ability, and other locations of inequality (Baca Zinn & Thornton Dill, 1996). Put differently, this perspective emphasizes that a power hierarchy—what Collins (2000) calls the "matrix of domination"—exists in which people are socially situated according to their differences from one another. Feminists who operate within this perspective interpret gender as being socially constructed through interlocking systems of race, class, gender, and other sources of inequality (Baca Zinn & Thornton Dill, 1996). In turn,

> this structural pattern affects individual consciousness, group interaction, and group access to institutional power and privileges . . . within this framework, [the focus is] less on the similarities and differences among race, class, and gender than on patterns of connection that join them. (Andersen & Collins, 2004, p. 7)

In a related manner, multiracial feminism proposes that these intersections occur simultaneously and, therefore, create a distinct social location for each individual (Baca Zinn & Thornton Dill, 1996). In other words, the various axes of the matrix of domination intersect to create a particular status within the broader social structure, which constitutes one's social location (Andersen & Collins, 2004). "A key element to class-race-gender is that social relations are viewed in multiple and interactive terms—not as additive" (Daly, 1993, p. 56). Thus, the main point here is that these elements work multiplicatively to shape one's social location. Although at a given time race, class, or gender might feel more relevant, "they are overlapping and cumulative in their effect on people's experience" (Andersen & Collins, 2004, p. 7).

Second, multiracial feminism calls attention to the ways in which intersecting systems of power act on all social-structural levels:

> Class, race, gender, and sexuality are components of *both* social structure and social interaction. Women and men are differently embedded in locations created by these cross-cutting hierarchies. As a result, women and men throughout the social order experience different forms of privilege and subordination. (Baca Zinn & Thornton Dill, 1996, p. 327, italics added)[4]

One important concept of multiracial feminism that underscores this point is "both/and" (e.g., see Collins, 2000). That is, all people simultaneously experience both oppression and privilege; no individual or group can be entirely privileged or entirely oppressed. In other words,

> the theoretical starting point [of this perspective] is that there are multiple and cross-cutting relations of class, race-ethnicity, gender, sexuality and age. This produces a matrix of domination taking a "both/and" form . . . not a simple additive model of structural subordinate relations. (Daly & Stephens, 1995, pp. 206–207)

Third, multiracial feminism is centered on the concept of relationality; that is, it assumes that groups of people are socially situated in relation to other groups of people based on their differences. "This means that women's differences are connected in systematic ways" (Baca Zinn & Thornton Dill, 1996, p. 327, emphasis in original). More important,

relationality should not be thought of as a unilateral concept. To illustrate, multiracial feminism assumes that the experiences of women are structurally linked, such that some women benefit from the oppression of other women who occupy a lower social position, even when (or perhaps especially when) the former are not cognizant of the benefits that their privileged status provides. In this way, multiracial feminism retains an emphasis on power and privilege but avoids essentializing women's experiences. As Baca Zinn and Thornton Dill (1996) observe, "Multiracial feminism highlights the relational nature of dominance and subordination. Power is the cornerstone of women's differences" (p. 327).

Last, other key conceptual features of multiracial feminism include a focus on the interaction of social structure and women's agency, a reliance on a variety of methodological approaches, and an emphasis on understandings grounded in the lived experiences of dynamic groups of women (Baca Zinn & Thornton Dill, 1996). Together, these features distinguish multiracial feminism from other feminist perspectives. Although some feminist perspectives share certain of these conceptual features (e.g., postmodern feminism's emphasis on the social construction of reality; socialist, Black, and critical race feminism's attention to interacting systems of power), taken in total these characteristics make multiracial feminism truly unique among feminist perspectives.

The Intersectional Approach to Gender: Using a Race-Class-Gender Framework

Feminists who operate from the perspective of multiracial feminism advocate for an intersectional approach to studying gender. The intersectional approach recognizes that race, class, gender, sexuality, and other locations of inequality are dynamic, historically grounded, socially constructed power relationships that simultaneously operate at both the micro-structural and macro-structural levels (Andersen & Collins, 2004; Weber, 2001; Weber & Parra-Medina, 2003).

In many ways, the development of this intersectional approach to studying gender may be viewed as a natural progression of feminist thought. Recall that the sameness and difference approaches, which are informed by liberal feminism, were criticized by radical feminists who favored the dominance approach because it attends to issues of power and privilege. Likewise, feminists dissatisfied with the primacy of gender in the dominance approach have advocated for the adoption of the intersectional approach, which is informed by multiracial feminism and which does not prioritize gender over other systems of power. Thus, applying a race-class-gender framework to the study of gender may be regarded as the next step in the evolution of feminist thought.

An example from the sentencing literature helps to clarify this point. According to Daly and Tonry (1997), criminologists and legal scholars have adopted three modes of conceptualizing race and gender in criminal law and criminal justice practice: (a) law and practices as racist/sexist, (b) law and practices as White/male, and (c) law and practices as racialized/gendered. The first mode (racist/sexist) parallels the sameness approach because "differential treatment is seen as synonymous with discrimination" and because liberal feminists would "be most comfortable" with this mode (p. 236). The second mode (White/male) is equivalent to the dominance approach because it is concerned with challenging the use of a White, male referent. As Daly and Tonry note,

> Virtually all empirical work on race and gender disparities (and our assessment of it) is framed within a racist/sexist perspective in that the research centers on whether sanctions are applied differently across varied racial-ethnic, gender groups. However, a new generation of feminists and critical race scholars has raised questions about the limits this conceptualization imposes on theory, research and policy . . . [and] are more likely to embrace the latter two modes. (p. 235)

The third mode (racialized/gendered) corresponds to the intersectional approach because it "assumes that race and gender relations structure criminal law and justice system practices" in important ways (p. 237). Thus, the third (intersectional) mode of conceptualizing race and gender has evolved in response to the inadequacies of previous paradigms.

For these reasons, the intersectional approach that is informed by multiracial feminism offers feminists the broadest, richest, and most complete theoretical framework for studying gender. Because all social relations are racialized, including those that appear not to be, multiracial feminism achieves a universal relevance that remains elusive to other feminist perspectives. In Daly and Stephens's (1995) words,

> Although many claim that black women are at the intersection of class, race, and gender, that statement is misleading. Black women are marked at the intersection as being on the subordinate side of these three relations, but all social groups (including middle-class white men) are at the intersection. (p. 205)

A race-class-gender framework is applicable to the lives of all people, regardless of their social location:

> At the same time that structures of race, class, and gender create disadvantages for women of color, they provide unacknowledged benefits for those who are at the top of these hierarchies—Whites, members of upper classes, and males. Therefore, multiracial feminism applies not only to racial ethnic women but also to women and men of all races, classes, and genders. (Baca Zinn & Thornton Dill, 1996, p. 327)

It is clear, then, that multiracial feminism and the intersectional framework through which it operates hold great promise for contemporary feminist scholarship.

 ## Multiracial Feminism and Criminology: Intersections of Race, Class, Gender, and Crime

For several reasons, multiracial feminism and the intersectional approach can make important contributions to feminist criminology. Although still an emerging body of scholarship, some feminists (as well as some nonfeminists) have already begun urging the adoption of an intersectional approach to studying crime (e.g., Barak et al., 2001; Belknap, 2001; Britton, 2004; Daly, 1993, 1997; Daly & Chesney-Lind, 1988; Daly & Stephens, 1995; Flavin, 2004; Lynch, 1996; Milovanovic & Schwartz, 1996; Price & Sokoloff, 2004; Sokoloff & Dupont, 2005; Zatz, 2000). However, despite this support for a race-class-gender framework, to date few feminist criminologists have embraced the intersectional approach. Below I outline several reasons why contemporary third-wave feminist criminologists should adopt an intersectional framework.

The Theoretical Relevance of Intersections

Criminologists have begun to recognize the importance of developing integrated criminological theories. As Barak (1998) argues, criminology stands to benefit from the integration of criminological perspectives. Although a thorough discussion of integrating criminologies is beyond the scope of this article, Barak's overall point helps justify the use of the intersectional approach and multiracial feminism. For example, Barak observes that race, class, and gender have been "autonomously" applied to the study of crime, whereas in the past decade feminist criminologists have begun to focus on the interaction between two or more of these variables as they relate to crime (p. 251). According to Barak, an integrated theoretical perspective "incorporates an appreciation of differences in the patterns of crime attributed to socialization, opportunities, and bias in the context that everyone's life is framed by inequalities of race, class, and gender" (p. 251).

In a similar manner, multiracial feminism emphasizes that intersecting system of race, class, and gender act as "structuring forces" affecting how people act, the opportunities that are available to them, and the way in which their behavior is socially defined (Lynch, 1996, p. 4). For criminologists, this includes examining how the legal system responds to individual offenders based on their social locations (Barak et al., 2001). For example, Steffensmeier, Ulmer, and Kramer (1998) studied the interaction of race, gender, and age in sentencing decisions and discovered that outcomes are most punitive for defendants whose social locations place them at the margins of race, age, and gender systems—in other words, young Black men. The findings of Steffensmeier et al. "demonstrate the importance of considering the joint effects of race, gender, and age on sentencing, and of using interactive rather than additive models" (p. 763). In a similar manner, Spohn and Holleran (2000) discovered that punishment penalties also are paid by defendants in other marginalized social locations: young, unemployed Black and Hispanic men.

Therefore, concepts and propositions found in multiracial feminism may be integrated with concepts and propositions found in existing criminological theories to achieve the type of integrated perspective that Barak (1998) described. To illustrate, the preceding examples from the sentencing literature represent conceptual theoretical integration. That is, the concept of social location from multiracial feminism and the concept (or "focal concern") of offender blameworthiness from sentencing theory overlap in a meaningful, theoretical way to explain how defendants' demographic characteristics influence judicial decision making (Steffensmeier et al., 1998).

Moreover, initial attempts at theorizing about inequality and crime using an intersectional framework have already occurred. For example, Sampson and Wilson (1995) developed their theory of race, crime, and urban inequality by examining intersecting race and class inequalities. Taking this approach one step further, Lynch (1996) has attempted to develop a theory of race, class, gender inequality, and crime in four ways by (a) "linking race, class, and critical criminology to life course or life history research"; (b) "connecting race, class, and gender to the types of choices that are structured into people's lives"; (c) "demonstrating life course and structured choice effects by reviewing data on income, wealth, and power disparities that arise from race, gender and class inequality"; and (d) "examining how race, class, and gender intersect to affect the production of crime" (p. 3).

Finally, several feminist criminologists have used intersectionality to theorize about the relationship between inequality and crime. For example, Richie (1996) shows how intersecting systems of race, class, and gender can lead battered Black women to commit criminal offenses. In her analysis, Richie uses the concept of gender entrapment to explain how "some women are forced or coerced into crime by their culturally expected gender roles, the violence in their intimate relationships, and their social position in the broader society" (p. 133). In a similar manner, Maher (1997) explores intersections of race, class, and gender in the lives of women who participate in the street-level drug economy. In her study, Maher describes how explanations of women's involvement with the drug economy have shifted from "primarily class-based explanations towards acknowledgement of a more complex set of cross-cutting influences—race/ethnicity, sex/gender, age, immigrant status, and other social relations" (p. 169). Most recently, Sokoloff and Dupont

(2005) argue for the use of an intersectional framework in developing theories of domestic violence (see also Sokoloff & Pratt, 2005). Sokoloff and Dupont (2005) observe that intersectional approaches to domestic violence

> question the monolithic nature of woman batter-ing, call for a greater emphasis on the structural causes of woman battering, caution against dis-empowering representations of marginalized bat-tered women, and explore the complex role of culture in understanding woman abuse and our responses to it. (p. 40)

As these examples illustrate, an intersectional theoret-ical framework that is informed by multiracial feminism can be instrumental to the advancement of criminological theory.

Conclusion

For the reasons outlined in this article, feminist criminolo-gists wishing to advance inclusive analyses of race, class, gender, and crime would do well to adopt an intersectional framework that is informed by multiracial feminism. In one of the few existing criminological texts advocating the use of the intersectional approach, Barak et al. (2001) noted several promising developments for intersectionality in criminology. Of these, perhaps most relevant to feminist criminology is "scholarship that shifts the emphasis [of criminology] on identifying systems of privilege that sup-port existing systems of oppression but are rarely acknowl-edged by those who reap the benefits" (p. 234).

Indeed, feminist criminologists have long been critical of scholarship that remains blind to issues of power and privilege. For contemporary third-wave feminist criminol-ogists, the time has come to build on the foundation that has been laid for us by our predecessors and to advance a feminist criminology that embraces all sources of oppres-sion without prioritizing gender. After all, as multiracial feminism reveals, power, privilege, and oppression are multiplicative and intersecting according to race, class, gender, sexuality, nationality, age, and other defining social characteristics. As we take stock of our field and look ahead to the future, the words of Daly and Chesney-Lind (1988) are instructive:

Turning to the future, we wonder what will happen as increasing numbers of white women, as well as men and women of color, enter the discipline and try to find their place in it. One cannot expect that the first generation of new scholars will be confi-dent or surefooted after centuries of exclusion from the academy. One might expect, however, that we will ask different questions or pursue prob-lems which our discipline has ignored. (p. 506)

In the coming years, successful examination of the ways in which women (and men) in the criminal justice system experience oppression by virtue of their race, class, and gender characteristics must be grounded in an intersectional framework that is informed by multiracial feminism:

> Research and theorizing must continue to reject the essentialism inherent in treating women as a unitary category . . . . We already know much about the ways in which race, class, and sexual inequality interweave with women's experiences as victims, offenders, and workers. The challenge for feminist criminology in the years to come lies in formulating theory and carrying out empirical studies that prioritize all of these dimensions, rather than relegating one or more of them to the background for the sake of methodological convenience. (Britton, 2004, p. 71)

In time, such advances will no doubt constitute the very core of feminist criminology in the 21st century.

Notes

1. According to Thompson (2002), intersectionality actu-ally emerged during the 1970s. That is, at the beginning of the second wave of the feminist movement, women of color (as well as White antiracist women and others who felt marginalized by mainstream feminism) began calling for scholarship that simulta-neously attended to issues of race, class, gender, and sexuality. However, the concept of intersecting inequalities first appeared in criminology during the 1980s, corresponding to feminism's third wave. Therefore, for the purposes of this article, intersectionality is presented as a product of third-wave feminism.

2. In fact, the mainstream second-wave feminist movement was labeled "hegemonic feminism" by some women of color and White antiracist women for its exclusive use of a White, middle-class, heterosexual female standard (Thompson, 2002).

3. Again, see Thompson (2002) for a discussion of the timing of the emergence of multiracial feminism.

4. However, Sokoloff and Dupont (2005) have argued that social structure is "rarely" the focus of analyses rooted in multiracial feminism.

⊠ References

Andersen, M., & Collins. P. H. (2004). *Race, class, and gender* (5th ed.). Belmont, CA: Wadsworth.

Baca Zinn, M., Hondagneu-Sotello, P., & Messner, M. A. (Eds.). (2000). *Gender through the prism of difference* (2nd ed.). Boston: Allyn & Bacon.

Baca Zinn, M., & Thornton Dill, B. (1996). Theorizing difference from multiracial feminism. *Feminist Studies, 22,* 321–331.

Barak, G. (1998). *Integrating criminologies.* Boston: Allyn & Bacon.

Barak, G., Flavin, J., & Leighton, P. S. (2001). *Class, race, gender, and crime: Social realities of justice in America.* Los Angeles: Roxbury.

Beirne, P., & Messerschmidt, J. (2000). *Criminology* (3rd ed.). Boulder, CO: Westview.

Belknap, J. (2001). *The invisible woman: Gender, crime, and justice* (2nd ed.). Belmont, CA: Wadsworth.

Blumstein, A., Cohen, J., Roth, J. A., & Visher, C. (1986). Introduction: Studying criminal careers. In A. Blumstein, J. Cohen. J. A. Roth. & C. Visher (Eds.), *Criminal careers and "career criminals"* (pp. 12–30). Washington, DC: National Academy Press.

Britton, D. M. (2004). Feminism in criminology: Engendering the outlaw. In P. J. Schram & B. Koons-Witt (Eds.), *Gendered (in) justice: Theory and practice in feminist criminology* (pp. 49–67). Long Grove. IL: Waveland Press.

Bui, H. (2004). In the adopted land: Abused immigrant women and the criminal justice system. Westport, CT: Praeger.

Chesney-Lind, M., & Pasko, L. (Eds.). (2004). *Girls, women, and crime.* Thousand Oaks, CA: Sage.

Collins, P. H. (2000). Black feminist thought: Knowledge, consciousness, and the politics of empowerment (2nd ed.). New York: Routledge.

Crenshaw, K. (1991). Demarginalizing the intersection of race and sex: A Black feminist critique of antidiscrimination doctrine, feminist theory, and antiracist politics. In K. Bartlett & R. Kennedy (Eds.), *Feminist legal theory* (pp. 57–80). Boulder, CO: Westview.

Daly, K. (1989). Rethinking judicial paternalism: Gender, work-family relations, and sentencing. *Gender & Society, 3,* 9–36.

Daly, K. (1993). Class-race-gender: Sloganeering in search of meaning. *Social Justice, 20,* 56–71.

Daly, K. (1994). Gender and punishment disparity. In M. Myers & G. Bridges (Eds.), *Inequality, crime, and social control* (pp. 117–133). Boulder, CO: Westview.

Daly, K. (1997). Different ways of conceptualizing sex/gender in feminist theory and their implications for criminology. *Theoretical Criminology, 1,* 25–51.

Daly, K., & Chesney-Lind, M. (1988). Feminism and criminology. *Justice Quarterly, 5,* 497–538.

Daly, K., & Maher. L. (1998). Crossroads and intersections: Building from feminist critique. In K. Daly & L. Maher (Eds.), *Criminology at the crossroads: Feminist readings in crime and justice* (pp. 1–17). New York: Oxford University Press.

Daly, K., & Stephens, D. J. (1995). The "dark figure" of criminology: Towards a Black and multi-ethnic feminist agenda for theory and research. In N. Hahn Rafter & F. Heidensohn (Eds.), *International feminist perspectives in criminology: Engendering a discipline* (pp. 189–215). Philadelphia: Open University Press.

Daly, K., & Tonry, M. (1997). Gender, race, and sentencing. In M. Tonry (Ed.), *Crime and justice: An annual review of research* (Vol. 22, pp. 201–252). Chicago: University of Chicago.

Flavin. J. (2004). Feminism for the mainstream criminologist: An invitation. In P. J. Schram & B. Koons-Witt (Eds.), *Gendered (in) justice: Theory and practice in feminist criminology* (pp. 68–92). Long Grove, IL: Waveland Press.

Gaarder, E., & Belknap, J. (2002). Tenuous borders: Girls transferred to adult court. *Criminology, 40,* 481–518.

Hajjar, L. (2004). Religion, state power, and domestic violence in Muslim societies: A framework for comparative analyses. *Law & Social Inquiry, 29,* 1–38.

Lorber, J. (Ed.). (2001). *Gender inequality: Feminist theories and politics* (2nd ed.). Los Angeles: Roxbury.

Lynch, M. J. (1996). Class, race, gender, and criminology: Structured choices and the life course. In D. Milovanovic & M. D. Schwartz (Eds.), *Race, gender, and class in criminology: The intersections* (pp. 3–28). New York: Garland.

MacKinnon, C. A. (1991). Difference and dominance: On sex discrimination. In K. T. Bartlett & R. Kennedy (Eds.), *Feminist legal theory* (pp. 81–94). Boulder, CO: Westview.

Maher, L. (1997). Sexed work: Gender, race, and resistance in a Brooklyn drug market. Oxford, UK: Oxford University Press.

Miller, J. (2004). Feminist theories of women's crime: Robbery as a case study. In B. R. Price & N. Sokoloff (Eds.), *The criminal justice system and women* (3rd ed., pp. 51–67). New York: McGraw-Hill.

Milovanovic, D., & Schwartz, M. D. (Eds.). (1996). *Race, gender, and class in criminology: The intersections.* New York: Garland.

Moe, A. (2004). Blurring the boundaries: Women's criminality in the context of abuse. *Women's Studies Quantity, 32,* 116–138.

Morash, M. (1999). A consideration of gender in relation to social learning and social structure: A general theory of crime and deviance. *Theoretical Criminology, 3,* 451–462.

Nagel, I., & Johnson, B. (2004). The role of gender in a structured sentencing system: Equal treatment, policy choices, and the sentencing of female offenders. In P. J. Schram & B. Koons-Witt (Eds.), *Gendered (in)justice: Theory and practice in feminist criminology* (pp. 198–235). Long Grove, IL: Waveland Press.

Price, B. R., & Sokoloff, N. (2004). *The criminal justice system and women* (3rd ed.). New York: McGraw-Hill.

Renzetti, C. (1992). Violent betrayal: Partner abuse in lesbian relationships. Newbury Park, CA: Sage.

Richie, B. (1996). Compelled to crime: The gender entrapment of Black battered women. New York: Routledge.

Sampson, R., & Wilson, W. J. (1995). Toward a theory of race, crime, and urban inequality. In J. Hagan & R. D. Peterson (Eds.), *Crime and inequality* (pp. 37–54). Stanford, CA: Stanford University Press.

Sokoloff, N., & Dupont, I. (2005). Domestic violence at the intersections of race, class, and gender. *Violence Against Women, 11,* 38–64.

Sokoloff, N., & Pratt, C. (2005). *Domestic violence at the margins: Readings on race, class, gender, and culture.* New Brunswick, NJ: Rutgers University Press.

Sokoloff, N., Price, B. R., & Flavin, J. (2004). The criminal law and women. In B. R. Price & N. Sokoloff (Eds.), *The criminal justice system and women* (3rd ed., pp. 11–29). New York: McGraw-Hill.

Spohn, C., & Holleran, D. (2000). The imprisonment penalty paid by young, unemployed Black and Hispanic male offenders. *Criminology, 38,* 281–306.

Steffensmeier, D., & Allan, E. (1996). Gender and crime: Toward a gendered theory of female offending. *Annual Review of Sociology, 22,* 459–487.

Steffensmeier, D., Ulmer, J., & Kramer, J. (1998). The interaction of race, gender, and age in criminal sentencing: The punishment cost of being young, Black, and male. *Criminology, 36,* 763–793.

Stolzenberg, L., & D'Alessio, S. (2004). Sex differences in the likelihood of arrest. *Journal of Criminal Justice, 32,* 443–454.

Thompson, B. (2002). Multiracial feminism: Recasting the chronology of second wave feminism. *Feminist Studies, 28,* 337–360.

Weber, L. (2001). Understanding race, class, gender, and sexuality: A conceptual framework. Boston: McGraw-Hill.

Weber, L., & Parra-Medina, D. (2003). Intersectionality and women's health: Charting a path to eliminating health disparities. In M. Texler Segal, V. Demos, & J. Jacobs Kronenfeld (Eds.), *Gender perspectives on health and medicine: Key themes* (pp. 181–229). Oxford, UK: Elsevier.

Williams, W. (1991). The equality crisis: Some reflections on culture, courts, and feminism. In K. T. Bartlett & R. Kennedy (Eds.), *Feminist legal theory* (pp. 15–34). Boulder, CO: Westview.

Zatz, M. (2000). Convergence of race, ethnicity, and class on court decision-making: Looking toward the 21st century. In J. Horney (Ed.), *Policies, process, & decisions of the criminal justice system: Criminal justice 2000* (Vol. 3, pp. 503–552). Washington, DC: U.S. Department of Justice.

REVIEW QUESTIONS

1. Burgess-Proctor asserts that all three factors—race/ethnicity, social class, and gender—are equally important when it comes to engaging in criminal behavior or processing by the criminal justice system. From your own experience, do you agree? If so, why? If not, which characteristic of these do you think is most important, and why?

2. Studies have consistently shown that most victims of homicide by rate are lower-class, Black males, and that the offenders by rate are lower-class, Black males. How do you think these findings relate to Burgess-Proctor's discussion? Is it consistent or not?

3. How do you think an upper-class White male would be treated by the criminal justice system as compared to a lower-class Black female? What advice would you offer to the latter defendant?

4. Which of the five feminist criminological perspectives do you most agree with? Which of these five types do you least agree with? Do your selections vary depending on whether you are contemplating the reasons why females commit crime or considering how females are handled by the criminal justice system? If so, how?

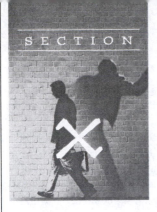
Life-Course Perspectives of Criminality

T his section will discuss the development of the life-course perspective in the late 1970s and its influence on modern research on criminal trajectories. We will explain the various concepts in the life-course perspective, such as onset, desistence, and frequency, as well as the arguments against this perspective. Finally, we will review the current state of research regarding this perspective.

This section will present one of the most current and progressive approaches to explaining why individuals engage in criminal activity, namely, developmental theories of criminal behavior. Developmental theories are explanatory models of criminal behavior that follow individuals throughout their life courses of offending, thus explaining the development of offending over time. Such developmental theories represent a break with traditional theoretical frameworks, which typically focused on the effects of constructs and variables on behavior at a given point in time. Virtually no theories attempted to explain the various stages (e.g., onset, desistence) of individuals' criminal careers, and certainly no models differentiated the varying factors that are important at each stage. Developmental theories have been prominent in modern times, and we believe that readers will agree that developmental theories have added a great deal to our understanding of and thinking about why people commit criminal behavior.

Developmental Theories

Developmental theories, which are also to some extent integrated, are distinguished by their emphasis on the evolution of individuals' criminality over time. Developmental theories tend to look at the individual as the unit of analysis, and such models focus on the onset, frequency, intensity, duration, desistence, and other aspects of the individual's criminal career. The onset of offending is when the offender first begins offending, and desistence is when an individual stops committing crime. Frequency refers to how often the individual offends, whereas intensity is the degree of seriousness of the offenses he or she commits. Finally, duration is the length of an individual's criminal career.[1]

Experts have long debated and examined these various aspects of the development of criminal behavior. For example, virtually all studies show an escalation from minor status offending (e.g., truancy, underage drinking, smoking tobacco) to petty crimes (e.g., shoplifting, smoking marijuana) to far more serious criminal activity, such as robbery and aggravated assault, and then murder and rape. This development of criminality is shown across every study that has ever been performed and demonstrates that, with very few exceptions, people begin with relatively minor offending and progress toward more serious, violent offenses.

Although this trend is undisputed, other issues are not yet resolved. For example, studies have not yet determined when police contact or an arrest becomes *early onset*. Most empirical studies draw the line at age 14, so that any arrest or contact prior to this time is considered early onset.[2] However, other experts would disagree and say that this line should be drawn earlier (say, 12 years old) or even later (such as 16 years old). Still, however it is defined, early onset is one of the most important predictors of any of the measures we have in determining who is most at risk for developing serious, violent offending behavior.

Perhaps the most discussed and researched aspect of developmental theory is *offender frequency*, which has been referred to as *lambda*. Estimates of lambda, or average frequency of offending by criminals over a year's time, vary greatly.[3] Some estimates of lambda are in the high single digits, and some are in the triple digits. Given this large range, it does not do much good to estimate what the frequency of most offenders is. Rather, the frequency depends on many, many variables, such as what type of offenses the individual commits. Perhaps if we were studying only drug users or rapists, it would make sense to determine lambda, but given the general nature of most examinations of crime, such estimates are not useful. Even within the same crime type, the frequency of offending varies so widely across individuals that we question its use in understanding criminal careers.

Before we discuss the dominant models of developmental theory, it is important to discuss the opposing viewpoint, which is that of complete stability in offending. Such counterpoint views assume that the developmental approach is a waste of time because the same individuals who show antisocial behavior at early ages (before age 10) are those who will exhibit the most criminality in their teenage years, 20s, 30s, 40s, and so on. This framework is most notably represented by the theoretical perspective proposed by Gottfredson and Hirschi in their model of low self-control.

Antidevelopmental Theory: Low Self-Control Theory

In 1990, Travis Hirschi, along with his colleague Michael Gottfredson, proposed a general theory of low self-control as the primary cause of all crime and deviance (see prior discussion in Section VIII); this is often referred to as *the*

---

[1]Matt DeLisi and Kevin M. Beaver, eds., *Criminological Theory: A Life-Course Approach*, 2nd ed. (Burlington, MA: Jones & Bartlett, 2014). See also Alex R. Piquero, David P. Farrington, and Alfred Blumstein, "Criminal Career Paradigm: Background, Recent Developments, and the Way Forward," *International Annals of Criminology* 41 (2003): 243–69; and Robert Brame, Michael Turner, Raymond Paternoster, and Shawn Bushway, "Cumulative Prevalence of Arrest from Ages 8 to 23 in a National Sample," *Pediatrics* 129 (2012): 21–27.

[2]For more discussion, see Stephen G. Tibbetts, "Perinatal and Developmental Determinants of Early Onset of Offending: A Biosocial Approach for Explaining the Two Peaks of Early Antisocial Behavior," pp. 179–201 in Joanne Savage, ed., *The Development of Persistent Criminality* (New York: Oxford University Press, 2009); Matt DeLisi, "Zeroing in on Early Arrest Onset: Results from a Population of Extreme Career Criminals," *Journal of Criminal Justice* 34 (2006): 17–26; Stephen Tibbetts and Alex Piquero, "The Influence of Gender, Low Birth Weight, and Disadvantaged Environment in Predicting Early Onset of Offending: A Test of Moffitt's Interactional Hypothesis," *Criminology* 37 (1999): 843–78; and Chris L. Gibson and Stephen Tibbetts, "A Biosocial Interaction in Predicting Early Onset of Offending," *Psychological Reports* 86 (2000): 509–18.

[3]For a review, see Samuel Walker, *Sense and Nonsense about Crime and Drugs: A Policy Guide*, 7th ed. (Belmont: Cengage, 2011). See also Piquero et al., "Criminal Career Paradigm."

Figure 10.1 Gottfredson and Hirschi's theory of low self-control

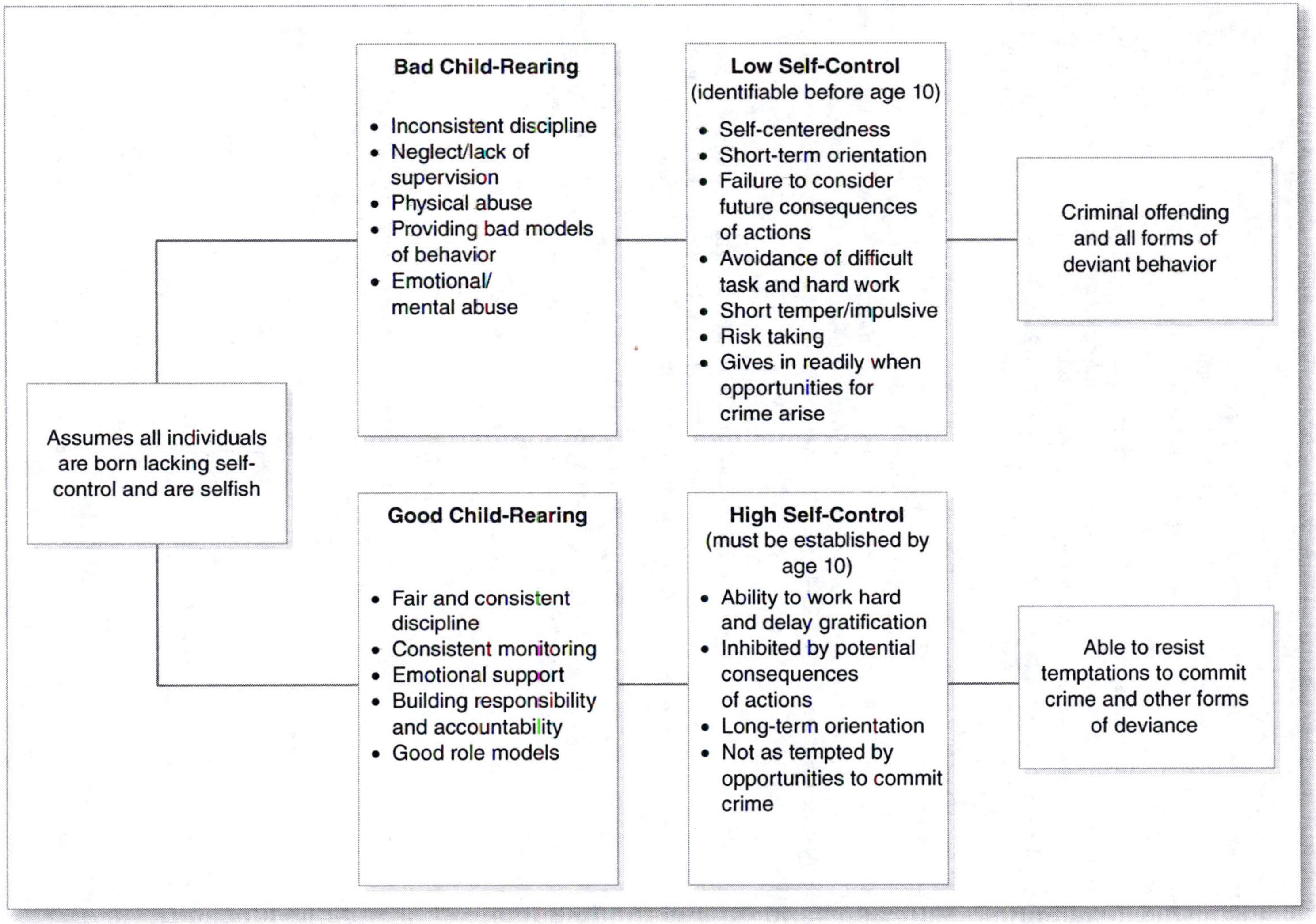

Bad Child-Rearing

- Inconsistent discipline
- Neglect/lack of supervision
- Physical abuse
- Providing bad models of behavior
- Emotional/mental abuse

Low Self-Control (identifiable before age 10)

- Self-centeredness
- Short-term orientation
- Failure to consider future consequences of actions
- Avoidance of difficult task and hard work
- Short temper/impulsive
- Risk taking
- Gives in readily when opportunities for crime arise

Criminal offending and all forms of deviant behavior

Assumes all individuals are born lacking self-control and are selfish

Good Child-Rearing

- Fair and consistent discipline
- Consistent monitoring
- Emotional support
- Building responsibility and accountability
- Good role models

High Self-Control (must be established by age 10)

- Ability to work hard and delay gratification
- Inhibited by potential consequences of actions
- Long-term orientation
- Not as tempted by opportunities to commit crime

Able to resist temptations to commit crime and other forms of deviance *general theory of crime.*[4] This theory has led to a significant amount of debate and research in the field since its appearance, more than any other contemporary theory of crime.

Like other control theories of crime, this theory (see Figure 10.1) assumes that individuals are born predisposed toward selfish, self-centered activities, and that only effective child rearing and socialization can create self-control. Without such adequate socialization (i.e., social controls) and reduction of criminal opportunities, individuals will follow their natural tendencies to become selfish predators. The general theory of crime assumes that self-control must be established by age 10. If it has not formed by that time, then according to the theory, individuals will forever exhibit low self-control. The assumption that self-control must be formed by age 10 is the feature of this theory that opposes the developmental perspective. The authors assert that once low self-control is set by age 10, there is no way to develop it afterward. In contrast, developmental theory assumes that people can indeed change over time.

Like others, Gottfredson and Hirschi attribute the formation of controls to socialization processes in the first years of life; the distinguishing characteristic of this theory is its emphasis on the individual's ability to control himself or herself. That is, the general theory of crime assumes that people can take a degree of control over their own decisions and, within certain limitations, control themselves. The general theory of crime is accepted as one of the most valid theories of crime.[5] This is probably due to the parsimony, or simplicity, of the theory, as it identifies only one primary cause of criminality—low self-control. However, low self-control may actually consist of a series of personality traits, including risk-taking, impulsiveness, self-centeredness, short-term orientation, and quick temper. Recent research has supported the idea that inadequate child-rearing practices tend to result in lower levels of self-control among children and that these low levels produce various risky behaviors, including criminal activity.[6] It is important to note that this theory has a developmental component in the sense that it proposes that self-control develops during early years from parenting practices; thus, even this most notable antidevelopment theory actually includes a strong developmental aspect.

In contrast to Gottfredson and Hirschi's model, one of the most dominant and researched frameworks of the last 20 years, another sound theoretical model shows that individuals can change their life trajectories in terms of crime. Research shows that events or realizations can occur that lead people to alter their frequency or incidence of offending, sometimes to zero. To account for such extreme transitions, we must turn to the dominant life-course model of offending, which is Sampson and Laub's developmental model.

Sampson and Laub's Developmental Model

Perhaps the best-known and best-researched developmental theoretical model to date is that of Robert Sampson and John Laub.[7] Sampson and Laub have proposed a developmental framework that is largely based on a reanalysis of

[4]Michael Gottfredson and Travis Hirschi, *A General Theory of Crime* (Palo Alto: Stanford University Press, 1990).

[5]For reviews of studies regarding low self-control theory, see John P. Wright, Stephen G. Tibbetts, and Leah Daigle, *Criminals in the Making: Criminality across the Life Course*, 2nd ed. (Thousand Oaks: Sage, 2015) (see chap. 1); George E. Higgins and Margaret Mahoney, "Self-Control Theory and Antisocial Behavior," in *Criminological Theory: A Life-Course Approach*, 2nd ed., ed. Matt DeLisi and Kevin M. Beaver (Burlington, MA: Jones & Bartlett, 2014), 249–60; and Travis Pratt and Frank Cullen, "The Empirical Status of Gottfredson and Hirschi's General Theory of Crime: A Meta-analysis," *Criminology* 38 (2000): 931–64. For critiques of this theory, see Ronald Akers, "Self-Control as a General Theory of Crime," *Journal of Quantitative Criminology* 7 (1991): 201–11. For a study that demonstrates the high popularity of the theory, see Anthony Walsh and Lee Ellis, "Political Ideology and American Criminologists' Explanations for Criminal Behavior," *The Criminologist* 24 (1999): 1, 14 (see chap. 1, n. 13).

[6]Carter Hay, "Parenting, Self-Control, and Delinquency: A Test of Self-Control Theory," *Criminology* 39 (2001): 707–36; K. Hayslett-McCall and T. Bernard, "Attachment, Masculinity, and Self-Control: A Theory of Male Crime Rates," *Theoretical Criminology* 6 (2002): 5–33.

[7]Robert Sampson and John Laub, "Crime and Deviance over the Life Course: The Salience of Adult Social Bonds," *American Sociological Review* 55 (1990): 609–27; Robert Sampson and John Laub, "Turning Points in the Life Course: Why Change Matters to the Study of Crime," *Criminology* 31 (1993): 301–26; Robert Sampson and John Laub, *Crime in the Making: Pathways and Turning Points through Life* (Cambridge: Harvard University Press, 1993).

original data collected by Sheldon and Eleanor Glueck in the 1940s. As a prototypical developmental model, this theoretical perspective focuses primarily on individual stability and change.

Most significantly, Sampson and Laub emphasized the importance of certain events and life changes, which can alter an individual's decisions to commit (or not commit) criminal activity. Although based on a social control framework, this model contains elements of other theoretical perspectives. First, Sampson and Laub's model assumes, like other developmental perspectives, that early antisocial tendencies among individuals, regardless of social variables, are often linked to later adult criminal offending. Furthermore, some social structure factors (e.g., family structure, poverty) also tend to lead to problems in social and educational development, which then leads to crime. Another key factor in this development of criminality is the influence of delinquent peers or siblings, which further increases an individual's likelihood for delinquency.

However, Sampson and Laub also strongly emphasize the importance of transitions, or events that are important in altering life trajectories, such as marriage, employment, or military service, drastically changing a person's criminal career. Sampson and Laub show sound evidence that many individuals who

▲ Image 10.1　Robert Sampson (1956-) and John Laub (1954-)

Source: Robert Sampson and John Laub.

were once on a path toward a consistent form of behavior—in this case, serious, violent crime—suddenly (or gradually) halted due to such a transition or series of transitions. In some ways, this model is a more specified form of David Matza's theory of drift, which we discussed in Section VIII, in which individuals tend to grow out of crime and deviance due to the social controls imposed by marriage, employment, and so on. Still, Sampson and Laub's framework contributed much to the knowledge of criminal offending by providing a more specified and grounded framework that identified the ability of individuals to change their criminal trajectories via life-altering transitions. In fact, recent research has consistently shown that marriage and full-time employment significantly reduce the recidivism of California parolees, and other recent studies have shown similar results from employment in later years.[8]

Moffitt's Developmental Taxonomy

Another primary developmental model that has had a profound effect on the current state of criminological thought and theorizing is Terrie Moffitt's developmental theory (taxonomy), proposed in 1993.[9] Moffitt's framework distinguishes two types of offenders: adolescence-limited offenders and life-course-persistent offenders.

---

[8]Alex Piquero, Robert Brame, Paul Mazzerole, and Rudy Haapanen, "Crime in Emerging Adulthood," *Criminology* 40 (2002): 137–70; Chris Uggen, "Work as a Turning Point in the Life Course of Criminals: A Duration Model of Age, Employment, and Recidivism," *American Sociological Review* 65 (2000): 529–46.

[9]Terrie Moffitt, "Adolescence Limited and Life Course Persistent Antisocial Behavioral: A Developmental Taxonomy," *Psychological Review* 100 (1993): 674–701. For a review, see Savage, *Development of Persistent Criminality*.

▲ Image 10.2   Life-course theories attempt to uncover points of desistence, critical events that may change a person's life path from deviant behavior back to law-abiding status. Getting married and being employed are considered some of the most significant events. Once one is married or gains steady employment, free time to hang out with one's friends tends to disappear.

Source: © Jupiterimages / Photos.com / Thinkstock.

Adolescence-limited offenders make up most of the general public and include all persons who committed offenses when they are teenagers or young adults. Their offending is largely caused by association with peers and a desire to engage in activities exhibited by the adults that they are trying to be. Such activities are a type of rite of passage and quite normal among all people who have normal social interactions with their peers in their teenage or young adult years. It should be noted that a very small percentage of the population (about 1% to 3%) are nonoffenders who quite frankly do not have normal relations with their peers and therefore do not offend at all, even in adolescence.

On the other hand, there exists another small group of offenders, referred to in this model as *life-course-persistent offenders*. This small group, estimated to be 4% to 8% of offenders—albeit the most violent and chronic—commit the vast majority of the serious, violent offenses in any society, such as murder, rape, and armed robbery. In contrast to the adolescence-limited offenders, the disposition of life-course-persistent offenders toward offending is caused by an entirely different model: an interaction between neurological problems and the disadvantaged or criminological environments in which they are raised.

For example, if an individual has only neurological problems or only a poor, disadvantaged environment, then that individual will be unlikely to develop a life-course-persistent trajectory toward crime. However, if a person has both neurological problems and a disadvantaged environment, then that individual will have a very high likelihood of becoming a chronic, serious, violent offender. This proposition, which has been supported by empirical studies,[10] suggests that it is important to pay attention to what happens early in life. Because illegal behaviors are normal among teenagers or young adults, more insight can be gained by looking at the years prior to age 12 to determine who is most likely to become a chronic, violent offender. Life-course-persistent offenders begin offending very early in life and continue to commit crime far into adulthood, even to middle age, whereas adolescence-limited offenders tend to engage in criminal activity only during their teenage and young adult years. Moffitt's model suggests that more than one

---

[10]See Tibbetts and Piquero, "Influence of Gender." For a recent review of such studies, see Wright et al., *Criminals in the Making* (see chap. 1). See also Savage, *Development of Persistent Criminality*.

type of development explains criminality. Furthermore, this framework shows that different types of offenders commit crime due to entirely different causes and factors.

Policy Implications

There are many, perhaps an infinite number of, policy implications that can be derived from developmental theories of criminality. Thus, we will focus on the most important, which concerns the prenatal and perinatal stages of life, because the most significant and effective interventions can occur during this time. If policy makers hope to reduce early risk factors for criminality, they must insist on universal health care for pregnant women as well as their newborn infants through the first few years of life. The United States is one of the few developed nations that do not guarantee this type of maternal and infant medical care and supervision. Doing so would go a long way toward avoiding the costly (in many ways) damages of criminal behavior among youths at risk.[11]

▲ Image 10.3   Terrie Moffitt (1955-)

Source: Terrie Moffitt.

Furthermore, there should be legally mandated interventions for pregnant women who are addicted to drugs or alcohol. Although this is a highly controversial topic, it appears to be a no-brainer that women who suffer from such addictions may become highly toxic to the child(ren) they carry and should receive closer supervision and more health care. There may be no policy implementation that would have as much influence on reducing future criminality in children as making sure their mothers do not take toxic substances while they are pregnant.[12]

Other policy implications include assigning special caseworkers to high-risk infants, such as those with low birth weight or low Apgar scores. Another advised intervention would be to have a centralized medical system that provides a flag for high-risk infants who have numerous birth or delivery complications, so that the doctors who are seeing them for the first time are aware of their vulnerabilities.[13] Finally, universal preschool should be funded and provided to all young children; studies have shown that this leads to better performance once they enter school, both academically and socially.[14]

Ultimately, as the many developmental theories have shown, there are many concepts and stages of life that can have a profound effect on the criminological trajectories that lives can take. However, virtually all of these models propose that the earlier stages of life are likely the most important in determining whether an individual will engage in criminal activity throughout life or not. Therefore, policy makers should focus their efforts on providing care and interventions in this time period.

[11]Wright et al., *Criminals in the Making*, 260–62.

[12]Ibid., 184–86, 258.

[13]Ibid., 259–62.

[14]Ibid.

Conclusion

This section presented a brief discussion of the importance of developmental or life-course theories of criminal behavior. This perspective, having become popular in the 1970s, is relatively new compared to other traditional theories explored in this text. Ultimately, this is one of the most cutting-edge areas of theoretical development, and life-course theories are likely to be the most important frameworks in the future of the field of criminological theory.

Then we examined the policy implications of this developmental approach, emphasizing the need to provide universal care for pregnant mothers as well as their newborn children. Other policy implications include legally mandated interventions for mothers who are addicted to toxic substances (e.g., alcohol, drugs) and assignment of caseworkers to high-risk infants and children, such as those with a history of complications at birth. Such interventions would go a long way toward saving society the many problems (e.g., financial difficulties, victimization) that will persist without such interventions. Ultimately, a focus on the earliest stages of intervention will provide "the biggest bang for the buck."

 ## Section Summary

* Developmental or life-course theory focuses on the individual, following people throughout life to examine their offending careers. In-depth consideration of changes during the life course are of highest concern, especially regarding general conclusions that can be made about the factors that tend to increase or decrease the risk that individuals will continue offending.
* Life-course perspectives emphasize onset of offending, frequency of offending, duration of offending, seriousness of offending, desistence of offending, and other factors that play key roles in when individuals offend and why they do so—or don't do so—at certain times of their lives.
* There are many critics of the developmental or life-course perspective, particularly those who buy into the low self-control model, which is antidevelopmental in the sense that it assumes that propensities for crime do not change over time but rather remain unchanged across life.
* One of the developmental models that has received the most attention is that of Sampson and Laub, which emphasizes transitions in life (e.g., marriage, military service, employment) that alter trajectories either toward or away from crime.
* Moffitt's developmental theory of chronic offenders (whom she labeled *life-course-persistent offenders*) versus more normal offenders (whom she labeled *adolescence-limited offenders*) is the developmental model that has received the most attention over the last decade, and much of this research is supportive of the interactive effects of biology and environment that combine to create chronic, habitual offenders.

KEY TERMS

adolescence-limited offenders	life-course-persistent-offenders	trajectory
developmental theories	Moffitt's developmental theory (taxonomy)	transitions

DISCUSSION QUESTIONS

1. What characteristic distinguishes developmental theories from traditional theoretical frameworks?

2. What aspects of a criminal career do experts consider important in such a model? Describe all of the aspects they look at in a person's criminal career.

3. Discuss the primary criticisms of the developmental perspective, particularly that presented by Gottfredson and Hirschi. Which theoretical paradigm do you consider most valid? Why?

4. What transitions or trajectories have you seen in your life or your friends' lives that support Sampson and Laub's developmental model? What events encouraged offending or inhibited it?

5. Given Moffitt's dichotomy of life-course-persistent offenders and adolescence-limited offenders, which of these should be given more attention by research? Why do you feel this way?

WEB RESOURCES

Developmental Theories of Crime

http://cooley.libarts.wsu.edu/garina/Soc3612/Documents/Lecture_20.ppt

Sampson and Laub's Model

http://harvardmagazine.com/2004/03/twigs-bent-trees-go-stra.html

Terrie Moffitt's Theory

http://www.wpic.pitt.edu/research/famhist/PDF_Articles/APA/BF16.pdf

READING 26

In this selection, Alex Piquero, David Farrington, and Alfred Blumstein provide a comprehensive review of the concepts, issues, and propositions presented by the criminal career framework, on which developmental theories are based. The developmental paradigm is, by definition, based on following the criminal activity of individuals over time and exploring the reasons why they offend when they do, as well as why these individuals don't offend at certain times. The authors explore the history of the criminal career perspective, as well as the key concepts of participation, offending frequency, duration, and co-offending patterns. Piquero et al. also explore the policy implications that can be gathered, given the current state of research on these various dimensions.

Then the authors explore the issues related to chronic offenders, who are the small percentage of society (approximately 5% to 8% of the population) who commit the vast majority of violent and serious offenses. Piquero et al. also provide policy recommendations, especially regarding incarceration policies. Finally, the authors review the extant research on career length and desistence (or the ceasing of offending in an individual's life), as well as prescribing issues that future research should examine.

While reading this selection, readers should consider the various concepts, such as frequency and duration, in regard to their own offending careers, or the offending careers of people they know well. Furthermore, readers should examine the incarceration policies suggested by Piquero et al. and consider whether they agree or disagree with their suggestions.

Criminal Career Paradigm

Background, Recent Developments, and the Way Forward

Alex R. Piquero, David P. Farrington, and Alfred Blumstein

Researchers have long been interested in the patterning of criminal activity throughout the course of criminal careers. Early on, Quetelet (1831) recognized that the age was closely related to the propensity for crime. Using data on crimes committed against persons and property in France from 1826 to 1829, Quetelet found that crimes peaked in the late teens through the mid twenties. Since Quetelet's findings, a number of researchers have pursued the relationship between age and crime, across cultures and historical periods, and for a number of different crime types (Hirschi and Gottfredson 1983). Research on the relationship between age and crime has been one of the most studied issues within criminology (Farrington 1986; Steffensmeier et al. 1989; Tittle and Grasmick 1993).

The relationship between age and crime raises the question of the degree to which the aggregate pattern displayed in the age/crime curve is similar to—or different from—the pattern of individual careers and whether conclusions about individuals can be validly drawn from aggregate data. For example, how far does the observed peak of the aggregate age/crime curve reflect changes within individuals as opposed to changes in the composition of offenders? In other words, is the peak in the age/crime curve a function of active offenders committing more crime, or is it a function of more individuals actively offending during those peak years?

Within individuals, to what extent is the slowing past the peak age a function of deceleration in continued criminal activity or stopping by some of the individuals? Across individuals, how much of the age/crime curve can be attributed to the arrival/initiation and departure/termination of different individuals? How about the role of co-offending? How much of the continuation of offending by lone/solo offenders is attributable to identifying theirs as the key criminal careers of long duration, with their co-offenders serving merely as transients with shorter careers? How much of the age/crime curve for any particular crime type is a consequence of individuals persisting in offending, but switching from less serious crime types early in the career to more serious crime types as they get older? What about the relationship between past and future offending? Is it due to some causal factors or changes in causal factors (state dependence), unobserved individual differences (persistent heterogeneity), or some combination?

These questions are central to theory, as well as policy, especially those policies that are geared toward incapacitive effects of criminal sanctions, as well as to changes in the criminal career (e.g., rehabilitation or criminalization patterns as a result of actions by the criminal justice system). For example, if crime commission and arrest rates differ significantly among offenders and over the career, the effect of sentence length on overall crime will depend on who is incarcerated, and for how long (Petersilia 1980:325). Addressing these and related issues requires knowledge about individual criminal careers, their initiation, their termination and the dynamic changes between these end points (Blumstein et al. 1986).

In 1983, a Panel on Research on Criminal Careers was convened by the National Academy of Science at the request of the U. S. National Institute of Justice and was charged with evaluating the feasibility of predicting the future course of criminal careers, assessing the effects of prediction instruments in reducing crime through incapacitation, and reviewing the contribution of research on criminal careers to the development of fundamental knowledge about crime and criminals. This report outlined a novel approach of asking questions regarding the longitudinal patterning of criminal activity over the life course, i.e., the criminal career paradigm (Blumstein et al. 1986).

Since publication of the report, numerous theoretical, empirical, and policy issues have surfaced regarding the longitudinal patterning of criminal careers. One concerned the relevance (or lack thereof) of criminal career research for criminology generally, and public policy in particular. Gottfredson and Hirschi (1990) levied a series of critiques against the criminal career approach in which they claimed that attempts to identify career criminals and other types of offenders were doomed to failure. Perhaps the most important issue they raised concerns causality. Although the criminal career paradigm necessitates a longitudinal focus in order to study both the between- and within-individual patterning of criminal activity, Gottfredson and Hirschi questioned whether longitudinal research designs could actually resolve questions of causal order. They also argued that, since correlations with offending were relatively stable over the life-course, cross-sectional designs were suitable for studying the causes of crime.

This paper summarizes background and recent developments regarding the criminal career paradigm. Section I provides a brief review of the criminal career paradigm, as well as an overview of the empirical findings generated by criminal careers research, with a concentration on the dimensions of criminal careers. Section II presents a discussion of selected policy implications including the identification of career criminals and policies associated with sentence duration. Section III offers an agenda for future theoretical, empirical, and methodological research. The full conclusion of our report may be found in the essay "The Criminal Career Paradigm," published in *Crime and Justice: A Review of Research, Volume 30* (Piquero, Farrington, and Blumstein 2003).

I. The Criminal Career Paradigm

At its most basic level, a criminal career is the "characterization of the longitudinal sequence of crimes committed by an individual offender" (Blumstein et al. 1986:12). This definition helps to focus researchers' attention on entry into a career when or before the first crime is committed and dropout from the career when or after the last crime is committed. The criminal career paradigm recognizes that individuals start their criminal activity at some age, engage in crime at some individual crime rate, commit a mixture of crimes, and eventually stop. Hence, the criminal career approach emphasizes the need to investigate issues related to why and when people start offending (onset), why and how they continue offending (persistence), why and if offending becomes more frequent or serious (escalation) or specialized, and why and when people stop offending (desistance). The study of criminal careers does not imply that offenders necessarily derive their livelihood exclusively or even predominantly from crime; instead, the concept is intended only as a means of structuring the longitudinal sequence of criminal events associated with an individual in a systematic way (Blumstein et al. 1982:5). In sum, the criminal career approach focuses on both between- and within-individual changes in criminal activity over time.

A. Dimensions of a Criminal Career

1. Participation

The criminal career approach partitions the aggregate crime rate into two primary components: "participation," the distinction between those who commit crime and those who do not; and "frequency," the rate of offending among active offenders, commonly denoted by the Greek letter λ (Blumstein et al. 1986:12). Participation is measured by the fraction of a population ever committing at least one crime before some age or currently active during some particular observation period. In any period, active offenders include both new offenders whose first offense occurs during the observation period, and persisting offenders who began criminal activity in an earlier period and continue to be active during the observation period. Importantly, the longer the average duration of offending, the greater the contribution of persisters to measured participation in successive observation periods.

Estimates of ever-participation in criminal activity vary across reporting method (they tend to be much higher with self-report than with official records which are a filtered subset of self-reports), the crimes in which participation is being measured (there is more participation in less serious criminal activity), the level of threshold of involvement (police contact, arrest, conviction), and the characteristics and representativeness of the sample (high school students, college students, general population, offender-based, etc.). In general, ever-participation estimates are fairly common across data sets and consistent with most criminological findings.

There is a relatively high rate of participation among males in criminal activity (Elliott et al. 1987:502). Blumstein et al. (1986) reported that about 15 percent of urban males are arrested for an index offense by age eighteen, and about 25 to 45 percent of urban males are arrested for a non-traffic offense by age eighteen. Visher and Roth's (1986) overview of several longitudinal studies employing police and court records indicates a lifetime prevalence estimate of 40 to 50 percent, with slightly higher rates for blacks and much lower rates among females. Stattin et al.'s (1989) longitudinal study of Swedish males and females revealed that by age 30, 37.7% of Swedish males and 9% of Swedish females were registered for a criminal offense. The cumulative prevalence of self-reported offenses is even more striking. For example, in the Cambridge study, Farrington (2003) found that 96 percent of the males had reported committing at least one of ten specified offenses (including burglary, theft, assault, vandalism, and drug abuse) up to age thirty-two. Kelley et al. (1997) used self-reported data on serious violence from three longitudinal studies funded by the Office of Juvenile Justice and Delinquency Prevention, the Causes and Correlates studies, and found that 39 percent of Denver males, 41 percent of Pittsburgh males, 40 percent of Rochester males, 16 percent of Denver females, and 32 percent of Rochester females reported committing at least one serious violent act by age sixteen.

Regardless of whether official or self-report records are used to study prevalence, three main conclusions emerge. First, male participation rates are typically higher than those for females, and especially so for the more serious offenses. Second, black participation rates are typically higher than those for whites, especially when participation is examined via official records as opposed to self-reports (Hindelang et al. 1981). In self-reports, blacks have also been found to report continuing their violent offending at higher rates than whites (Elliott 1994). Third, there is a strong relationship between age and participation. In particular, the probability of initiating a criminal career at a given age is highest between thirteen and eighteen, on the lower end for self-report estimates and on the higher end for arrest and conviction records, with little to no gender difference (Moffitt et al. 2001). Also, evidence on the probability of committing an offense at a given age is mixed, with some research indicating a consistent increase through the mid-teens to a peak at age nineteen and then subsequent decline, while other research indicates a decline in self-reported participation through the teens (Elliott et al. 1983; Lauritsen 1998; Thornberry 1989). Studying demographic differences in prevalence remains controversial. For example, Hindelang et al. (1981) argued that there is a race difference in the validity of self-reported delinquency measures, which leads to a serious underestimation of black males' prevalence rates.

2. Key Dimensions of Active Criminal Careers

The criminal career paradigm encompasses several dimensions of active criminal careers including offending frequency, duration, crime type mix and seriousness, and co-offending patterns.

a. Offending Frequency. The offending rate for individual offenders, λ, reflects the frequency of offending by individuals who are actively engaged in crime (Blumstein et al. 1986:55). Much criminal career research has been concerned with estimating the individual offending frequency of active offenders during their criminal careers (Blumstein and Cohen 1979; Cohen 1986; Loeber and Snyder 1990).

Blumstein et al. (1986) summarized variation in λ for active offenders by gender, age, and race. Regarding gender, they found little variation in frequency across males and females (i.e., the ratios are generally 2:1 or less) for most crimes (Blumstein at al. 1986:67–68). Thus, if active in a crime type, females commit crimes at rates similar to those of males (for an exception see Wikström 1985). Regarding age, Blumstein et al. reported little change with age in offense-specific frequency rates for active offenders, but when all offense types are combined, there tended to be an increase during the juvenile years and a decrease during the adult years. In the Rand Inmate surveys, there appeared to be some evidence of general stability of λ over age (Chaiken and Chaiken 1982). The number of active crime types declined with age in the Rand survey, but crime-specific frequencies tended to be stable (Peterson and Braiker 1980). Finally, although research based on official records tends to indicate that there is not a strong relationship between offending frequency and demographic characteristics, some recent self-report data on serious violence tends to indicate otherwise (Elliott 1994).

Spelman (1994) summarized current knowledge on offending frequencies. First, there are different values for the average offense frequencies across studies because researchers provide different definitions and operationalizations of the offense rate. Second, most of the variation in offense rates can be attributed to differences in the populations sampled and especially where in the criminal justice system they are sampled. Third, the average offender commits around eight crimes per year, while offenders who are incarcerated at some point in their lives commit thirty to fifty crimes per year, and the average member of an incoming prison cohort commits between sixty and 100 crimes per year. Fourth, criminals do not commit crimes all the time; in other words, there is evidence that many offenders spend long periods of time in which they commit no crimes. Fifth, the distribution of offending frequencies is highly skewed, with a few offenders committing crimes at much higher than average rates.

b. Duration, *the Interval between Initiation and Termination*. One aspect of the criminal career paradigm that has received a great deal of research attention is initiation, or the onset of antisocial and criminal activity (Farrington et al. 1990). Several studies have reported higher recidivism rates among offenders with records of early criminal activity as juveniles (Blumstein et al. 1986). Although many researchers argue that individuals who begin offending early will desist later, and thus have lengthy careers (Hamparian et al. 1978; Krohn et al. 2001), there has been much less research on the duration of criminal careers, or an individual's criminal career (Piquero, Brame, and Lynam 2003). It is more tenable, however, to measure a rate of desistance for an identified group of offenders (Bushway et al. 2001). Research on desistance, or the termination of a criminal career, has received even less attention because of difficulties in measurement and operationalization (Laub and Sampson 2001).

The two most common approaches for studying career termination have been through providing estimates of termination probabilities after each arrest, and estimating the time between the first and last crimes committed. Regarding termination probabilities, Blumstein et al. (1986) calculated persistence probabilities for six different data sets and found that after each subsequent event (i.e., police contact, arrest, conviction, etc.), the persistence probability increases, reaching a plateau of .7 to .9 by the fourth event across all data sets. Farrington, Lambert, and West (1998) used conviction data to calculate recidivism probabilities for Cambridge study males through age thirty-two and found that after the third offense, the recidivism probability ranged from .79 to .91 through the tenth offense.

A number of studies have attempted to derive estimates of career duration, typically measured as career length in years. Three major studies conducted in the 1970s estimated career lengths to be between five and fifteen years (Greenberg 1975; Greene 1977; Shinnar and Shinnar 1975). In 1982, Blumstein, Cohen, and Hsieh conducted the most detailed study of criminal career duration and used data on arrests rather than on arrestees to estimate career lengths, and concluded that criminal careers are relatively short, averaging about five years for offenders who are active in index offenses as young adults. Residual careers, or the length of time still remaining in careers, increase to an expected ten years for index offenders still active in their thirties. Persistent offenders who begin their adult careers at age eighteen or earlier and who are still active in their thirties are most likely to be persistent offenders and are likely to continue to commit crimes for about another ten years (Visher 2000).

Spelman (1994) studied career lengths with data from the three-state Rand Inmate Survey, and developed estimates of total career lengths of about six or seven years (Spelman 1994). Spelman showed that young and inexperienced offenders, those in the first five years of their career, were more likely than older offenders to drop out each year, but after five years the rate of dropout leveled off, rising only after the twentieth year as an active offender. Farrington (2003) examined the duration of criminal careers in the Cambridge study using conviction data to age forty and found that the average duration of criminal careers was 7.1 years. Excluding one-time offenders, whose duration was zero, the average duration of criminal careers was 10.4 years. Piquero, et al. (2003) studied the length of criminal careers using data from a sample of serious offenders paroled from California Youth Authority institutions in the 1970s and found that the average career length was 17.27 years, with little difference between white (16.7 years) and non-white parolees (17.7 years).

c. Crime Type Mix and Seriousness. The mix of different offense types among active offenders is another important criminal career dimension. The study of crime-type mix involves studying seriousness (the tendency to commit serious crimes throughout one's criminal career), escalations

(the tendency to move toward more serious crimes as one's career progresses), specialization (the tendency to repeat the same offense type on successive crimes), and crime-type switching (the tendency to switch types of crimes and/or crime categories on successive crimes).

Diverse methodological techniques have been employed to investigate specialization, or the tendency to repeat the same offense type on successive crimes. Using official records, some research provides evidence in favor of some small degree of specialization (Bursik 1980; Rojek and Erickson 1982; Smith and Smith 1984), but most find that generality is the norm throughout offending careers (Farrington et al. 1988; Wolfgang et al. 1972; Nevares et al. 1990; Tracy et al. 1990). At the same time, important differences in specialization are observed between adults and juveniles such that specialization appears to be stronger in magnitude for adult rather than for juvenile offenders (Le Blanc and Fréchette 1989; Piquero et al. 1999). On the other hand, self-report data from the Rand studies suggest that, although there is some evidence of property specialization (Spelman 1994), incarcerated offenders tend to report much more generality than speciality (Petersilia et al. 1978; Peterson and Braiker 1980; Chaiken and Chaiken 1982).

Some scholars have investigated specialization in violence. Using official records, Farrington (1989) and Piquero (2000) reported little evidence of specialization in violence in the Cambridge study or the Philadelphia perinatal cohort, and that the commission of a violent offense in a criminal career is a function of offending frequency: frequent offenders are more likely to accumulate a violent offense in their career. Similar results have been obtained by Capaldi and Patterson (1996) with self-report data from the Oregon Youth Study.

Directly related to the specialization issue is the switching that occurs across clusters of crime types. Clusters represent natural groupings of offense types (violence, property, other), and research indicates that adult offenders display a stronger tendency to switch among offense types within a cluster and a weaker tendency to switch to offense types outside a cluster, but the strong partitioning is not as sharp among juveniles (Blumstein et al. 1986; Cohen 1986). Adult offenders and incarcerated juveniles are more likely to commit offenses within a cluster than to switch to offenses outside a cluster (Rojek and Erickson 1982; Blumstein et al. 1988). Drug offenders, however, do not tend to switch to either violent or property offenses.

d. Co-offending Patterns. Another important criminal career feature is whether a person commits on offense alone or with others (Reiss 1986). Little empirical work has been completed on co-offending, and even less information exists regarding the group criminal behavior of youths in transition to adult status or of adult offenders at different ages. In the Cambridge Study, Reiss and Farrington (1991) report that the incidence of co-offending is greatest for burglary and robbery, and that juvenile offenders primarily commit their crimes with others, whereas adult offenders primarily commit their crimes alone. Although the decline in co-offending may, at first glance, be attributed to co-offenders dropping out, it seems to occur because males change from co-offending in their teenage years to lone offending in their twenties. In the Swedish Borlänge study, Sarnecki (1990) found that 45 percent of all youths suspected of offense at some stage during the six-year study period could be linked together in a single large network that accounted for most offenses. Recently, Sarnecki (2001) used data from all individuals aged twenty or less who were suspected of one or more offenses in Stockholm during 1991–1995 to study the extent and role of co-offending and uncovered that 60 percent of the individuals had a co-offender at some point. Interestingly, he also found that males tended to co-offend primarily with other males, but among females, the proportion of girls choosing other females was lower than the proportion of boys choosing other males as co-offenders. Conway and McCord (2002) conducted the first co-offending study designed to track patterns of violent criminal behavior over an eighteen-year period (1976–1994) among a random sample of 400 urban offenders and their accomplices in Philadelphia. Using crime data collected from court records and "rap sheets," they found that nonviolent offenders who committed their first co-offense with a violent accomplice were at increased risk for subsequent serious violent crime, independent of the effects of age and gender.

B. Policy Issues

The criminal career paradigm suggests three general orientations for crime control strategies: prevention, career modification, and incapacitation. Knowledge concerning the patterning of criminal careers is intimately related to these policy issues. Prevention strategies, including general deterrence, are intended to reduce the number of nonoffenders who become offenders. Career modification strategies, including individual deterrence and rehabilitation, are focused on persons already known to be criminals and seek to reduce the frequency or seriousness of their crimes. In addition, these strategies encourage the termination of ongoing criminal careers through mechanisms such as job training and drug treatment. Incapacitative strategies focus on the crimes reduced as a result of removing offenders from society during their criminal careers. Two types of incapacitation are general, or collective, and selective, which focuses on the highest frequency offenders. These three crime control strategies are intimately related to specific laws, including habitual offender statutes, truth-in-sentencing laws, three-strikes laws, and mandatory minimum sentences laws.

1. Crime Control Strategies

Of all crime control strategies, the criminal career paradigm has focused extensive attention on incapacitation. General or collective incapacitation strategies aim to reduce criminal activity as a consequence of increasing the total level of incarceration while selective incapacitation policies focus primarily on offenders who represent the greatest risk of future offending. The former approach is consistent with the equal treatment concerns of a just-deserts sentencing policy while the latter focuses as much on the offenders as the offense. Importantly, the degree to which selective incapacitation policies are effective depends on the ability to distinguish high- and low-risk offenders, and to identify them early enough before they are about to terminate criminal activity. Three related issues arise: the ability to classify individual offenders in terms of their projected criminal activity; the quality of the classification rules; and the legitimacy of basing punishment of an individual on the possibility of future crimes rather than only on the crimes already committed (and the consequent level of disparity that is considered acceptable).

Regarding collective incapacitation, Blumstein et al. (1986) suggest that achieving a 10 percent reduction in crime may require more than doubling the existing inmate population. However, under selective incapacitation policies, long prison terms would be reserved primarily for offenders identified as most likely to continue committing serious crimes at high rates. Blumstein et al. conclude that selective incapacitation policies could achieve 5 to 10 percent reductions in robbery with 10 to 20 percent increases in the population of robbers in prison, while much larger increases in prison populations are required for collective incapacitation policies.

2. Relationship to Laws

Both collective and selective incapacitation policies are directly influenced by laws and policies that govern criminal justice decisions regarding the punishment of offenders. For example, habitual offender statutes give special options to prosecutors for dealing with repeat offenders. Truth-in-sentencing laws are intended to increase incapacitation by requiring offenders, particularly violent offenders, to serve a substantial portion of their prison sentence, and parole eligibility and good-time credits are restricted or eliminated. Three-strikes laws provide that any person convicted of three, typically violent, felony offenses, must serve a lengthy prison term, usually a minimum term of twenty-five-years-to-life. Mandatory-minimum sentence laws require a specified sentence and prohibit offenders convicted of certain crimes from being placed on probation, while other statutes prohibit certain offenders from being considered for parole. Mandatory-minimum sentence laws can also serve as sentencing enhancement measures, requiring that offenders spend additional time in prison if they commit particular crimes in a particular manner (e.g., committing a felony with a gun). The net effect of these laws is to increase prison populations by incarcerating certain kinds of offenders or increasing the sentence length of those offenders convicted for certain types of crimes.

C. "Chronic" Offenders

Criminologists have long recognized that a small group of individuals is responsible for a majority of criminal activity. Wolfgang et al. (1972) focused attention on the chronic offender by applying that label to the small group of 627 delinquents in the 1945 Philadelphia birth cohort who committed five or more offenses by age seventeen (hereafter five-plus). This group constituted just 6 percent of the full cohort of 9,945 males and 18 percent of the delinquent subset of 3,475, but was responsible for 5,305 offenses, or 52 percent of all delinquency in the cohort through age

seventeen. The chronic offenders were responsible for an even larger percentage of the more serious, violent offenses. The finding that a small subset of sample members are responsible for a majority of criminal activity is supported by data from other longitudinal data sets, including the second 1958 Philadelphia birth cohort (Tracy et al., 1990), the Puerto Rico Birth Cohort Study (Nevares et al., 1990), the Dunedin New Zealand Multidisciplinary Health Study (Moffitt et al. 2001), the Philadelphia (Piquero 2000) and Providence (Piquero and Buka 2002) perinatal projects, the Racine, WI, birth cohorts (Shannon 1982), the Cambridge study (Farrington 2003), and also by cohort studies in Sweden (Wikström 1985), Finland (Pulkkinen 1988), and Denmark (Guttridge et al. 1983). The finding is also replicated across gender and race (Moffitt et al. 2001; Piquero and Buka 2002), and emerges from both official and self-report data. Research also indicates that chronic offenders exhibit an early onset, a longer career duration, and involvement in serious offenses—including person/violent-oriented offenses—than other offenders (Loeber and Farrington 1998).

The five-plus cutoff advanced by Wolfgang et al. (1972) has been employed in several studies; however, since theoretical and empirical definitions of chronicity have yet to be established, questions have been raised about the extent to which similar definitions of chronicity should be used across gender (Farrington and Loeber 1998; Piquero 2000), as well as the relatively arbitrary designation of five-plus offenses as characteristic of chronicity (Blumstein et al. 1985). Blumstein et al. (1985) raised other concerns with the use of five-plus as the chronicity cut point. They argued that the chronic offender calculation, which was based on the full cohort, overestimates the chronic offender effect because many cohort members will never be arrested. Instead, they urge that the ever-arrested subjects should be the base used to calculate the chronic offender effect. With the base, the 627 chronics with five-plus arrests represented 18 percent of those arrested, as opposed to 6 percent of the cohort. Blumstein and colleagues also argued that the proportion of chronic offenders observed by Wolfgang et al. (1972) could have resulted from a homogenous population of persisters. Blumstein et al. (1985) tested the hypothesis that all persisters (those with more than three arrests) could be viewed as having the same rearrest probability. Such an assumption could not be rejected. Although those with five-plus arrests accounted for the majority of arrests among the persisters, such a result could have occurred even if all subjects with three or more arrests had identical recidivism probabilities. Thus, the chronic offenders who were identified retrospectively as those with five or more arrests could not have been distinguished prospectively from nonchronics with three or four arrests.

II. Policy Implications

Research on criminal careers has direct import for decision-making in the criminal justice system. In this section, we address four implications of criminal career research: the role of criminal career research in policy and individual decision-making, individual prediction of offending frequencies (λ), sentence duration, and research on career length and desistance and its relation to intelligent sentencing policy.

A. Role of Criminal Career Research in Policy and Individual Decision-Making

A principal example of the importance of criminal career research for criminal justice policy is criminal career length. Three-strikes and selective incapacitation philosophies assume that high-rate offenders will continue to offend at high rates and for long periods of time if they are not incarcerated. From an incapacitative perspective, incarceration is only effective in averting crimes when it is applied during an active criminal career. Thus, incarceration after the career ends or when a career is abating, is wasted for incapacitation purposes (Blumstein et al. 1982:70). By identifying career lengths, especially residual career lengths, policymakers can better target incarceration on offenders whose expected remaining careers are longest. Incarceration policies should be based on career duration distribution information. The more hardcore committed offenders with the longest remaining careers are identifiable only after an offender has remained active for several years (Blumstein et al. 1982). Earlier and later in criminal careers, sanctions will be applied to many offenders who are likely to drop out shortly anyway (Blumstein et al. 1982:71). The benefits derived from incapacitation will vary depending on an individual's crime rate and the length of his or her remaining criminal career. Continuing to incarcerate an offender after his/her career ends limits the usefulness of incarceration.

B. Individual Prediction of λ

Rand's second inmate survey highlighted the extreme skewness of the distribution of λ for a sample of serious criminals (Chaiken and Chaiken 1982; Visher 1986). Naturally, the identification of a small number of inmates who reported committing several hundred crimes per year led to the search for a method to identify these offenders in advance. If high-rate offenders cannot be identified prospectively, then crime control efforts will be hampered (Visher 1987). In this section, we highlight two related issues: the difficulty in identifying high-λ individuals, and the alleviation of the concern over prediction by "stochastic selectivity."

1. Difficulty in Identifying High-λ Individuals

Although high-λ individuals emerge in the aggregate, it has been difficult to identify specific individuals. Greenwood and Turner (1987) used data consisting of follow-up criminal history information on the California inmates who were included in the original Rand survey and who had been out of prison for two years to examine the extent to which Greenwood's seven-item prediction scale succeeded in predicting recidivism. The scale was not very effective in predicting post-release criminal activity when the recidivism measure was arrest. The majority of released inmates, regardless of whether they were predicted to be low- or high-rate offenders, were rearrested within two years. Greenwood and Turner also created a measure of the offender's annual arrest rate (i.e., the number of arrests per year of street time) for the follow-up sample and defined high-rate offenders as those inmates who had an actual arrest rate greater than 0.78. They found that the seven-item scale was less accurate in predicting annual arrest rates than it was in predicting re-incarceration.

There are also concerns related to the false positive prediction problem in identifying high-λ individuals. For example, Visher (1986:204-5) reanalyzed the Rand second inmate survey and found that not only were the estimates of λ for robbery and burglary sensitive to choices in computation (i.e., handling missing data, street time, etc.), but also that some inmates reported annual rates of 1,000 or more robberies or burglaries, thus strongly affecting the distribution of λ, and especially its mean. Finally, Visher's analysis of the Greenwood scale for identifying high-rate offenders indicated that 55 percent of the classified high-rate group

(27 percent of the total sample) were false positives who did not commit crimes at high rates. In fact, the prediction scale worked better in identifying low-rate offenders. Recently, Auerhahn (1999) replicated Greenwood and Abrahams's (1982) selective incapacitation study with a representative sample of California state prison inmates, and found that the scale's overall predictive accuracy was 60 percent, indicating a great deal of error in identifying serious, high-rate offenders.

2. Concern and Need for Prediction Alleviated by "Stochastic Selectivity"

Many analyses of the crime control potential of increasing incarceration rely on a single estimate of mean λ derived from prison inmates and applying it indiscriminately to all related populations of offenders (Canela-Cacho et al. 1997). This assumes that all offenders engage in the same amount (λ) of criminal behavior—regardless of whether they are in prison or jail, or free in the community—and that the probability of their detection and incarceration is equal. However, measures of λ derived from arrestee/convictee populations display a strong selection bias because individuals who have gone through the criminal justice process are unlikely to be representative of the total offender population. This selection bias could be because samples of arrestees have a higher propensity for arrest or different offending frequencies. A highly heterogeneous distribution of offending frequency in the total population of offenders combines with relatively low imprisonment levels to lead to substantial selectivity of high-λ offenders among resident inmates and a correspondingly low mean value of λ among those offenders who remain free (Canela-Cacho et al. 1997). "Stochastic selectivity," then, draws into prison new inmates disproportionately from the high end of the λ distribution of free offenders. Further, the higher the incarceration probability following a crime, the deeper into the offender pool incarceration will reach, and the lower will be the incapacitation effect associated with the incoming cohorts (Canela-Cacho et al. 1997).

Using data from the second Rand inmate survey, Canela-Cacho et al. (1997) studied the issue of stochastic selectivity and found that the proportion of low-λ burglars and robbers among free offenders was much larger than among resident inmates, while at the high end of the offending frequency distribution there was a larger proportion of high-λ burglars and robbers among resident inmates

than among free offenders. Thus, selectivity occurred naturally as high-λ offenders experienced greater opportunities for incarceration through the greater number of crimes they committed (Canela-Cacho el al. 1997:142), thereby obviating the need for efforts to explicitly identify individual high-λ offenders.

C. Sentence Duration

Information about crime rates and career lengths is particularly useful for incapacitation and incarceration decisions and policies, and such knowledge can also provide useful information regarding the intelligent use of incapacitation and may even provide powerful arguments against lengthy incapacitation policies. Principal among these is the decision regarding sentence length. Many current sentencing policies are based on the assumption that high-rate offenders will continue committing crimes at high rates and for lengthy periods, and thus prescribe lengthy incarceration stints. The extent to which this policy is effective, however, is contingent on the duration of a criminal career.

Much debate regarding sentence length has centered on three-strikes policies. These policies severely limit judges' discretion because they prescribe a mandatory prison sentence of (typically) twenty-five-years-to-life. The incapacitation effectiveness of three-strikes laws, however, depends on the duration of criminal careers. To the extent that sentencing decisions incarcerate individuals with short residual career lengths, a three-strikes law will waste incarceration resources (Stolzenberg and D'Alessio 1997:466).

Stolzenberg and D'Alessio (1997) used aggregate data drawn from the ten largest cities in California to examine the impact of California's three-strikes law on serious crime rates and found that the three-strikes law did not decrease serious crime or petty theft rates below the level expected on the basis of preexisting trends. Zimring et al. (1999) obtained a sample of felony arrests (and relevant criminal records) in Los Angeles, San Francisco, and San Diego, both before and after the California law went into effect to study the three-strikes issue. Two key findings emerged from their study. First, the mean age at arrest for two strikes and above was 34.6 years. This is particularly important because: "[O]n average the two or more strikes defendant has an almost 40 percent longer criminal adult career behind him (estimated at 16.6 years) than does the no-strikes felony defendant. All other things being equal, this means that the twenty-five-years-to-life mandatory prison sentence will prevent fewer crimes among the third-strike group than it would in the general population of felons because the group eligible for it is somewhat older" (Zimring et al. 1999:34). Second, when comparing crime trends in the three cities before and after the law, Zimring et al. found that there was no decline in the crimes committed by those targeted by the new law. In particular, the lower crime rates in 1994 and 1995 (just immediately after the three-strikes law went into effect) were evenly spread among targeted and non-targeted populations, suggesting that the decline in crime observed after the law went into effect was not due to the law.

D. Research on Career Length and Desistance

Sentencing practices involving lengthy sentence durations assume that affected offenders will continue to commit crime at a high rate and for a long period. To the extent that this is the case, incapacitation policies will avert crimes and thwart continued careers. However, to the extent that offenders retire before the expiration of a lengthy sentence, shorter career durations will reduce the effects of lengthy sentences. Using data from Florida, Schmertmann et al. (1998) concluded that the aging of prison populations under three-strikes policies in that state will undermine their long-run effectiveness. In particular, they noted that the policies will cause increases in prison populations due to the addition of large numbers of older inmates who are unlikely to commit future offenses.

The key to the sentence duration issue, and why estimates of criminal career duration are so important, rests on the characteristics of the person years—not the people—that are removed from free society as a result of such policies (Schmertmann et al. 1998:458). Such policies will be effective only to the extent that they incarcerate offenders during the early stages of their criminal careers when they are committing crimes at a high-rate.

Unfortunately, research on career duration and desistance is in its infancy. Knowledge on this subject will be important for furthering criminal justice policy and the cost-effective use of criminal justice resources.

 ## III. Directions for Future Criminal Career Research

Evidence on criminal career issues cuts to the heart of theory and policy. On the theoretical side, knowledge on the correlates of criminal career dimensions is relevant to the necessity for general versus typological models. If research indicates that the correlates of one offending dimension are similar to another offending dimension, then more general and non-dimension-specific theories are warranted. If the correlates of one offending dimension are different from another offending dimension, then the causal process(es) underlying these two particular dimensions are probably different and different explanations and theories are required.

Better knowledge on various criminal career dimensions would aid policy initiatives designed to prevent initial involvement, curtail current offending, and accelerate the desistance process. If research suggests that poor parental socialization is related to early initiation, then prevention efforts should include parent-training efforts. Similarly, if drug use is associated with continued involvement in delinquent and criminal behavior, then intervention efforts should include drug treatment. Finally, if some set of correlates is associated with desistance, then policy efforts may wish to provide for specific prevention and intervention efforts.

Knowledge on career length and residual career length could best inform criminal justice policies because it deals directly with sentencing and incapacitation policies that are now driven more by ideology than by empirical knowledge. For example, if residual criminal career lengths average around five years, criminal justice policies advocating multi-decade sentences waste scarce resources. Similarly, if offenders are incarcerated in late adulthood when their residual career lengths have diminished, incarceration space will be wasted, and health care costs will increase, thereby further straining scarce resources.

Empirical study of criminal careers requires data collection for large samples of individuals beginning early in life and continuing for a lengthy period into adulthood. Such data are needed if questions surrounding initiation, continuation, and desistance are to be adequately addressed, and this is especially the case among serious offenders for which little longitudinal data exists (Laub and Sampson

2001; Piquero et al. 2002). The use of such longitudinal data, of course, brings with it several potential problems that need to be considered including methodological issues such as street time (Piquero et al. 2001), mortality (Eggleston, Laub, and Sampson 2003) and sample attrition (Brame and Piquero 2003), as well as statistical issues that deal with various modeling strategies and assumptions (Bushway et al. 1999; Nagin 1999; Raudenbush 2001). Nevertheless, continued data collection and research are important to identify and study unaddressed and unresolved criminal career issues, and to update thirty-year-old estimates.

Information derived from criminal career research is important to advance fundamental knowledge about offending and to assist criminal justice decision-makers in dealing with offenders. Much more important criminal career research lies on the horizon nationally and internationally, and we look forward to seeing this research emerge.

 ## References

Auerhahn, Kathleen. 1999. "Selective Incapacitation and the Problem of Prediction." *Criminology* 37: 703–34.

Blumstein, Alfred, and Jacqueline Cohen. 1979. "Estimation of Individual Crime Rates from Arrest Records." *Journal of Criminal Law and Criminology* 70: 561–85.

Blumstein, Alfred, Jacqueline Cohen, Somnath Das, and Soumyo D. Moitra. 1988. "Specialization and Seriousness during Adult Criminal Careers." *Journal of Quantitative Criminology* 4: 303–45.

Blumstein, Alfred, Jacqueline Cohen, and Paul Hsieh. 1982. *The Duration of Adult Criminal Careers*. Final report submitted to National Institute of Justice, August 1982. Pittsburgh, PA: School of Urban and Public Affairs, Carnegie-Mellon University.

Blumstein, Alfred, Jacqueline Cohen, Jeffrey A. Roth, and Christy A. Visher, eds. 1986. *Criminal Careers and "Career Criminal."* 2 vols. Panel on Research on Criminal Careers, Committee on Research on Law Enforcement and the Administration of Justice. Commission on Behavioral and Social Sciences and Education, National Research Council. Washington, DC: National Academy Press.

Blumstein, Alfred, David P. Farrington, and Soumyo Moitra. 1985. "Delinquency Careers: Innocents, Desisters, and Persisters." In *Crime and Justice: An Annual Review of Research*, Vol. 6, ed. Michael Tonry and Norval Morris. Chicago: University of Chicago Press.

Brame. Robert, and Alex R. Piquero. 2003. "The Role of Sample Attrition in Studying the Longitudinal Relationship between Age and Crime." *Journal of Quantitative Criminology*.

Bursik, Robert J., Jr. 1980. "The Dynamics of Specialization in Juvenile Offenses." *Social Forces* 58: 851–64.

Bushway, Shawn, Robert Brame, and Raymond Paternoster. 1999. "Assessing Stability and Change in Criminal Offending: A Comparison of Random Effects, Semiparametric, and Fixed Effects Modeling Strategies." *Journal of Quantitative Criminology* 15: 23–64.

Bushway, Shawn D., Alex R. Piquero, Lisa M. Broidy, Elizabeth Cauffman, and Paul Mazerolle. 2001. "An Empirical Framework for Studying Desistance as a Process." *Criminology* 39: 491–515.

Canela-Cacho, José E., Alfred Blumstein, and Jacqueline Cohen. 1997. "Relationship between the Offending Frequency (λ) of Imprisoned and Free Offenders." *Criminology* 35: 133–76.

Capaldi, Deborah N., and Gerald R. Patterson. 1996. "Can Violent Offenders Be Distinguished from Frequent Offenders: Prediction from Childhood to Adolescence." *Journal of Research in Crime and Delinquency* 33: 206–31.

Chaiken, Jan M., and Marcia R. Chaiken. 1982. *Varieties of Criminal Behavior*. Rand Report R-2814-NIJ. Santa Monica, CA: Rand Corporation.

Cohen, Jacqueline. 1986. "Research on Criminal Careers: Individual Frequency Rates and Offense Seriousness." In *Criminal Careers and "Career Criminals,"* Vol. 1, ed. Alfred Blumstein, Jacqueline Cohen, Jeffrey A. Roth, and Christy A. Visher. Washington, DC: National Academy Press.

Conway, Kevin P., and Joan McCord. 2002. "A Longitudinal Examination of the Relation between Co-offending with Violent Accomplices and Violent Crime." *Aggressive Behavior* 28: 97–108.

Eggleston, Eliane, John H. Laub, and Robert J. Sampson. 2003. "Examining Long-term Trajectories of Criminal Offending: The Glueck Delinquents from Age 7 to 80." *Journal of Quantitative Criminology*, forthcoming.

Elliott, Delbert S. 1994. "1993 Presidential Address—Serious Violent Offenders: Onset, Developmental Course, and Termination." *Criminology* 32: 1–22.

Elliott, Delbert S., Suzanne S. Ageton, David Huizinga, Barbara Knowles, and R. Canter. 1983. *The Prevalence and Incidence of Delinquent Behavior: 1976–1980*. National Youth Survey, Report No. 26. Boulder, CO: Behavioral Research Institute.

Elliott, Delbert S., David Huizinga, and Barbara Morse. 1987. "Self-Reported Violent Offending: A Descriptive Analysis of Juvenile Violent Offenders and Their Offending Careers." *Journal of Interpersonal Violence* 1: 472–514.

Farrington, David P. 1986. "Age and Crime." In *Crime and Justice: An Annual Review of Research*, Vol. 7, ed. Michael Tonry and Norval Morris. Chicago: University of Chicago Press.

———. 1989. "Self-Reported and Official Offending from Adolescence to Adulthood." In *Cross-National Research in Self-Reported Crime and Delinquency*, ed. Malcolm W. Klein. Dordrecht: Kluwrer.

———. 2003. "Key Results from the First Forty Years of the Cambridge Study in Delinquent Development." In *Taking Stock of Delinquency: An Overview of Findings from Contemporary Longitudinal Studies*, ed. Terence P. Thornberry and Marvin D. Krohn. New York: Kluwer/Plenum.

Farrington, David P., Sandra Lambert, and Donald J. West. 1998. "Criminal Careers of Two Generations of Family Members in the Cambridge Study in Delinquent Development." *Studies on Crime and Crime Prevention* 7: 85–106.

Farrington, David P., and Rolf Loeber. 1998. "Major Aims of This Book." In *Serious & Violent Juvenile Offenders: Risk Factors and Successful Interventions*, ed. Rolf Loeber and David P. Farrington. Thousand Oaks, CA: Sage.

Farrington, David P., Rolf Loeber, Delbert S. Elliott, J. David Hawkins, Denise Kandel, Malcolm Klein, Joan McCord, David Rowe, and Richard Tremblay. 1990. "Advancing Knowledge about the Onset of Delinquency and Crime." In *Advances in Clinical and Child Psychology*, ed. Bernard Lahey and A. Kazdin. New York: Plenum.

Farrington, David P., Howard N. Snyder, and Terrence A. Finnegan. 1988. "Specialization in Juvenile Court Careers." *Criminology* 26: 461–87.

Gottfredson, Michael R., and Travis Hirschi. 1990. *A General Theory of Crime*. Stanford, CA: Stanford University Press.

Greenberg, David F. 1975. "The Incapacitative Effect of Imprisonment: Some Estimates." *Law and Society Review* 9: 541–80.

Greene, M. A. 1977. The Incapacitive Effect of Imprisonment on Policies of Crime. Unpublished PhD thesis, School of Urban and Public Affairs, Carnegie-Mellon University, Pittsburgh, PA (University Microfilms, Ann Arbor, MI).

Greenwood, Peter W., and Allan Abrahams. 1982. *Selective Incapacitation*. Rand Report R-2815-NIJ. Santa Monica, CA: Rand.

Greenwood, Peter W., and Susan Turner. 1987. *Selective Incapacitation Revisited: Why the High-Rate Offenders Are Hard to Predict*. Rand Report R-3397-NIJ. Santa Monica, CA: Rand.

Guttridge, P., W. F. Gabrielli, Jr., Sarnoff A. Mednick, and Kathertne T. Van Dusen. 1983. "Criminal Violence in a Birth Cohort." In *Prospective Studies of Crime and Delinquency,*, ed. Katherine T. Van Dusen and Sarnoff A. Mednick. Boston: Kluwer-Nijhoff.

Hamparian, D. M., R. Schuster, S. Dinitz, and J. Conrad. 1978. *The Violent Few: A Study of Dangerous Juvenile Offenders*. Lexington, MA: Lexington Books.

Hindelang, Michael, Travis Hirschi, and Joseph Weis. 1981. *Measuring Delinquency*. Beverly Hills, CA: Sage.

Hirschi, Travis, and Michael G. Gottfredson. 1983. "Age and the Explanation of Crime." *American Journal of Sociology* 89: 552–84.

Kelley, Barbara Tatem, David Huizinga, Terence P. Thornberry, and Rolf Loeber. 1997. *Epidemiology of Serious Violence*. Office of Juvenile Justice Bulletin. Washington, DC: U.S. Department of Justice, Office of Juvenile Justice and Delinquency Prevention.

Krohn, Marvin D., Terence P. Thornberry, Craig Rivera, and Marc Le Blanc. 2001. "Later Delinquency Careers." In *Child Delinquents: Development, Intervention, and Service Needs*, ed. Rolf Loeber and David P. Farrington. Thousand Oaks, CA: Sage.

Laub, John H., and Robert J. Sampson. 2001. "Understanding Desistance from Crime." In *Crime and Justice: A Review of Research*, Vol. 28, ed. Michael Tonry. Chicago: University of Chicago Press.

Lauritsen, Janet. 1998. "The Age-Crime Debate: Assessing the Limits of Longitudinal Self-Report Data." *Social Forces* 77: 127–55.

Le Blanc, Marc, and Marcel Fréchette. 1989. *Male Criminal Activity from Childhood through Youth: Multilevel and Developmental Perspectives*. New York: Springer-Verlag.

Loeber, Rolf, and David P. Farrington, eds. 1998. *Serious & Violent Juvenile Offenders: Risk Factors and Successful Interventions*. Thousand Oaks, CA: Sage.

Loeber, Rolf, and Howard N. Snyder. 1990. "Rate of Offending in Juvenile Careers: Findings of Constancy and Change in Lambda." *Criminology* 28: 97–110.

Moffitt, Terrie E., Avshalom Caspi, Michael Rutter, and Phil A. Silva. 2001. *Sex Differences in Antisocial Behaviour: Conduct Disorder, Delinquency, and Violence in the Dunedin Longitudinal Study*. Cambridge, UK: Cambridge University Press.

Nagin, Daniel S. 1999. "Analyzing Developmental Trajectories: A Semi-Parametric, Group-Based Approach." *Psychological Methods* 4: 139–77.

Nevares, Dora, Marvin E. Wolfgang, and Paul E. Tracy. 1990. *Delinquency in Puerto Rico: The 1970 Birth Cohort Study*. New York: Greenwood Press.

Petersilia, Joan. 1980. "Criminal Career Research: A Review of Recent Evidence." In *Crime and Justice: An Annual Review of Research*, Vol. 2, ed. Norval Morris and Michael Tonry. Chicago: University of Chicago Press.

Petersilia, Joan, Peter W. Greenwood, and Marvin Lavin. 1978. *Criminal Careers of Habitual Felons*. Washington, DC: National Institute of Law Enforcement and Criminal Justice, Law Enforcement Assistance Administration, U.S. Government Printing Office.

Peterson, Mark A., and Harriet B. Braiker. 1980. *Doing Crime: A Survey of California Prison Inmates*. Report R-2200-DOJ. Santa Monica, CA: Rand.

Piquero, Alex R. 2000. "Assessing the Relationships between Gender, Chronicity, Seriousness, and Offense Skewness in Criminal Offending." *Journal of Criminal Justice* 28:103–16.

Piquero, Alex R., Alfred Blumstein, Robert Brame, Rudy Haapanen, Edward P. Mulvey, and Daniel S. Nagin. 2001. "Assessing the Impact of Exposure Time and Incapacitation on Longitudinal Trajectories of Criminal Offending." *Journal of Adolescent Research* 16:54–74.

Piquero, Alex R., Robert Brame, and Donald Lynam. 2003. "Do the Factors Associated with Life-Course-Persistent Offending Relate to Career Length?" *Crime and Delinquency,* forthcoming.

Piquero, Alex R., David P. Farrington, and Alfred Blumstein. 2003. "The Criminal Career Paradigm." In *Crime and Justice: A Review of Research*, Vol. 30, ed. Michael Tonry. Chicago: University of Chicago Press.

Piquero, Alex R., Robert Brame, Paul Mazerolle, and Rudy Haapanen. 2002. "Crime in Emerging Adulthood." *Criminology* 40: 137–70.

Piquero, Alex R., and Stephen L. Buka. 2002. "Linking Juvenile and Adult Patterns of Criminal Activity in the Providence Cohort of the National Collaborative Perinatal Project." *Journal of Criminal Justice* 30: 1–14.

Piquero, Alex R., Raymond Paternoster, Paul Mazerolle, Robert Brame, and Charles W. Dean. 1999. "Onset Age and Offense Specialization." *Journal of Research in Crime and Delinquency* 36: 275–99.

Pulkkinen, L. 1988. "Delinquent Development: Theoretical and Empirical Considerations." In *Studies of Psychosocial Risk: The Power of Longitudinal Data*, ed. Michael Rutter. Cambridge, UK: Cambridge University Press.

Quetelet, Adolphe. 1831. *Research on the Propensity for Crime at Different Ages.* 1984 edition translated by Sawyer F. Sylvester. Cincinnati, OH: Anderson Publishing Company.

Raudenbush, Stephen W. 2001. "Toward a Coherent Framework for Comparing Trajectories of Individual Change." In *New Methods for the Analysis of Change*, ed. Linda M. Collins and Aline G. Sayers. Washington, DC: American Psychological Association.

Reiss, Albert J., Jr. 1986. "Co-Offender Influences on Criminal Careers." In *Criminal Careers and "Career Criminals,"* ed. Alfred Blumstein, Jacqueline Cohen, Jeffrey A. Roth, and Christy A. Visher. Washington, DC: National Academy Press.

Reiss, Albert J., Jr., and David P. Farrington. 1991. "Advancing Knowledge about Co-Offending: Results from a Prospective Longitudinal Survey of London Males." *Journal of Criminal Law and Criminology* 82: 360–95.

Rojek, D. G., and M. L. Erickson. 1982. "Delinquent Careers: A Test of the Career Escalation Model." *Criminology* 20: 5–28.

Sarnecki, Jerzy. 1990. "Delinquent Networks in Sweden." *Journal of Quantitative Criminology* 6: 31–51.

———. 2001. *Delinquent Networks. Youth Co-Offending in Stockholm.* Cambridge, UK: Cambridge University Press.

Schmertmann, Carl P., Adansi A. Amankwaa, and Robert D. Long. 1998. "Three Strikes and You're Out: Demographic Analysis of Mandatory Prison Sentencing." *Demography* 35: 445–63.

Shannon, Lyle. 1982. *Assessing the Relationship of Adult Criminal Careers to Juvenile Careers.* Washington, DC: U.S. Department of Justice, Office of Juvenile Justice and Delinquency Prevention.

Shinnar, Shlomo, and Reuel Shinnar. 1975. "The Effects of the Criminal Justice System on the Control of Crime: A Quantitative Approach." *Law and Society Review* 9: 581–611.

Smith, D. Randall, and William R. Smith. 1984. "Patterns of Delinquent Careers: An Assessment of Three Perspectives." *Social Science Research* 13: 129–58.

Spelman, William. 1994. *Criminal Incapacitation.* New York: Plenum.

Stattin, Håkan, David Magnusson, and Howard Reichel. 1989. "Criminal Activity at Different Ages: A Study Based on a Swedish Longitudinal Research Population." *British Journal of Criminology* 29: 368–85.

Steffensmeier, Darrell J., Emilie Andersen Allan, Miles D. Harer, and Cathy Streifel. 1989. "Age and the Distribution of Crime." *American Journal of Sociology* 94: 803–31.

Stolzenberg, Lisa, and Stewart J. D'Alessio. 1997. "'Three Strikes and You're Out': The Impact of California's New Mandatory Sentencing Law on Serious Crime Rates." *Crime and Delinquency* 43: 457–69.

Thornberry. Terence P. 1989. "Panel Effects and the Use of Self-Reported Measures of Delinquency in Longitudinal Studies." In *Cross-National Research in Self-Reported Crime and Delinquency,* ed. Malcolm W. Klein. Dordrecht: Kluwer Academic.

Tittle, Charles R., and Harold G. Grasmick. 1993. "Criminal Behavior and Age: A Test of Three Provocative Hypotheses." *Journal of Criminal Law and Criminology* 88: 309–42.

Tracy, Paul E., Marvin E. Wolfgang, and Robert M. Figlio. 1990. *Delinquency Careers in Two Birth Cohorts.* New York: Plenum.

Visher, Christy A. 1986. "The Rand Inmate Survey: A Re-Analysis." In *Criminal Careers and "Career Criminals,"* Vol. 2, ed. Alfred Blumstein, Jacqueline Cohen, Jeffrey A. Roth, and Christy A. Visher. Washington, DC: National Academy Press.

———. 1987. "Incapacitation and Crime Control: Does a 'Lock 'em Up' Strategy Reduce Crime?" *Justice Quarterly* 4: 513–43.

———. 2000. "Career Criminals and Crime Control." In *Criminology: A Contemporary Handbook,* ed. Joseph F. Sheley. 3rd ed. Belmont, CA: Wadsworth.

Visher, Christy A., and Jeffrey A Roth. 1986. "Participation in Criminal Careers." In *Criminal Careers and "Career Criminals,"* Vol. 1, ed. Alfred Blumstein, Jacqueline Cohen, Jeffrey A. Roth, and Christy A. Visher. Washington, DC: National Academy Press.

Wikström, Per-Olof H. 1985. *Everyday Violence in Contemporary Sweden: Situational and Ecological Aspects.* Stockholm: National Council for Crime Prevention, Sweden, Research Division.

Wolfgang, Marvin E., Robert M. Figlio, and Thorsten Sellin. 1972. *Delinquency in a Birth Cohort.* Chicago: University of Chicago Press.

Zimring, Franklin E., Sam Kamin, and Gordon Hawkins. 1999. *Crime and Punishment in California: The Impact of Three Strikes and You're Out.* Berkeley, CA: Institute of Governmental Studies Press, University of California.

REVIEW QUESTIONS

1. Explain in your own words some of the concepts that Piquero et al. point out as key concepts of the career criminal paradigm, such as offending frequency and duration. Which of the concepts do you feel are most important in determining which individuals pose the greatest danger to society?

2. Which policy implications suggested by Piquero et al. do you feel make the most sense? Which make the least sense to you, and why?

3. Do you know any individuals in your life whom you would classify as chronic offenders? (If not, consider stories in the media.) What do you think caused them to become such habitual offenders? What do you think are the primary causes for their chronic offending, and what types of policies would you implement to prevent others from becoming such persistent offenders?

READING 27

In this selection by Michael Turner, Jennifer Hartman, and Donna Bishop, the authors test a biosocial interaction in predicting life-course-persistent offending using the National Longitudinal Survey of Youth. Further, the authors examine the predictive ability of this biosocial interaction across different racial and neighborhood contexts. Importantly, the results show that the effects are quite varied depending on the types of groups in these different contexts. This study further advances our understanding of the interplay between biosocial dispositions and developmental environments.

The Effects of Prenatal Problems, Family Functioning, and Neighborhood Disadvantage in Predicting Life-Course-Persistent Offending

Michael G. Turner, Jennifer L. Hartman, and Donna M. Bishop

For at least three decades, there have been a number of attempts at theoretical integration (see, e.g., Messner, Krohn, & Liska, 1989). Although most of these integrations have involved attempts to marry various micro-level social theories (e.g., Cullen, 1994; Elliott, Ageton, & Canter, 1979; Thornberry, 1987), integrations that cross the traditional theoretical and disciplinary boundaries have also been proposed. Some of the most promising are the biosocial theories that focus on neuropsychological problems that place individuals at risk for maladaptive responses to adverse social environments (e.g., Eysenck, 1977; Mednick, 1977; Moffitt, 1993). In this framework, neuropsychological problems may contribute to delinquent and criminal behavior, depending on the nature of the social environment. In other words, it is the interaction of physiological features and social conditions that enhances the risk of delinquent behavior. Research has thus far produced some fairly compelling evidence of interactions between neuropsychological factors and family environments in the

Source: Michael G. Turner, Jennifer L. Hartman, and Donna M. Bishop, "The Effects of Prenatal Problems, Family Functioning, and Neighborhood Disadvantage in Predicting Life-Course-Persistent Offending," *Criminal Justice and Behavior* 34 (2007): 1241–61.

co-production of juvenile delinquency and adult crime (Brennan, Mednick, & Raine, 1997; Gibson & Tibbetts, 2000; Raine, Brennan, & Mednick, 1994; for a review of this literature, see Raine, 2002). The most robust effect involves the interaction of neuropsychological deficits (frequently stemming from oxygen deprivation in utero or at birth) and disadvantaged family environments (e.g., those characterized by low socioeconomic status [SES], parental criminality, harsh or erratic discipline) to increase the risk of aggressive, and especially violent, behavior. This research helps to explain why only some of the individuals exposed to aversive home environments, and only some of the individuals with neuropsychological impairments, engage in delinquency and crime.

Concomitant with this trend toward integration of biological and social theories at the individual level, a movement has also developed to integrate the micro and macro levels of analysis (R. J. Sampson, 1997; Wikstrom & Loeber, 2000). An integration of micro and macro theories recognizes the possibility that the relationships among individual traits, family characteristics, and offending may be conditioned by the community context in which individuals and families are embedded. It is increasingly recognized that multilevel multidisciplinary models that integrate biological-, family-, and community-level influences have the potential to provide a much more complete accounting of crime. For example, Tonry, Ohlin, and Farrington (1991) have observed that "most individual-level research is inadequate because it neglects variation in community characteristics, while community-level research fails to take account of individual differences" (p. 42). Despite this recognition, there has been limited theorizing and research on how the additive and joint effects of these influences work to produce crime.

This article contributes to the integration of individual-biological, individual-social, and macro-level theories by exploring (a) whether the confluence of certain individual-level physiological and family characteristics increases the explanatory power of these variables to explain delinquent behavior and, if so, (b) whether the effects of Person x Family interactions are exacerbated or tempered by conditions within the larger community environment. These goals are accomplished by testing Moffitts (1993) biosocial theory of life-course-persistent offending both within and across different neighborhood contexts.

 ## Moffitt's Biosocial Theory

One of the most promising of the integrated biosocial approaches is that put forth by Terrie Moffitt (1993, 1994), who distinguishes between adolescent-limited and life-course-persistent offenders in explaining the aggregate age—crime curve. According to Moffitt, the vast majority of delinquents are normal adolescents who participate in offending for a relatively short period. Frustrated by the mismatch between their adult biological development and societal expectations that they refrain from adult behaviors, they commit illegal acts symbolic of claims to adult status (e.g., curfew violations, auto theft, underage drinking, retail theft, drug use), from which they desist once they gain access to adult roles. Moffitt refers to this group as the "adolescence-limiteds."

A much smaller group of offenders, referred to as the "life-course-persistents," begins to manifest conduct problems in very early childhood and continues to engage in antisocial behavior well into adulthood. Moffitt attributes life-course-persistent offending to the interface between neuropsychological deficits and disadvantaged social environments. More specifically, Moffitt suggests that neuropsychological impairments, which are most commonly generated in utero or in the early postnatal period, disrupt normal development of verbal and executive functions of the brain. These disruptions have negative effects on learning, reasoning, memory, problem solving, temperament, and impulse control, each of which increases the propensity toward antisocial, and especially aggressive and violent, behavior. This propensity may be ameliorated or exacerbated by the home environment.

Moffitt argues that a child with even mild neuropsychological dysfunction living in an adverse environment for childrearing is at risk for developing a constellation of negative traits—poor self-control, ill temper, low cognitive ability, and hyperactivity. These traits are likely to strain social relationships and provoke hostility and rejection from both adults and conventional peers. An invidious pattern of negative interaction between these youths and those around them prevents them from acquiring and practicing prosocial behaviors (see also Patterson, 1976, 1995; Patterson, Dishion, & Bank, 1984), eventuating in the gradual elaboration of a style of hostile attributions and responses that pervades all domains of behavior. By the time these youths reach adolescence, frequently they have sabotaged the formation of prosocial skills and relationships and initiated a pattern of serious and violent offending that persists into adult life.

To date, several tests of Moffitt's theory have provided support for the notion that the interaction of child neuropsychological vulnerabilities and adverse family environments predicts precocious, persistent, and violent behavior (e.g., Moffitt, 1990; Moffitt, Lynam, & Silva, 1994; Piquero & Tibbetts, 1999; Tibbetts & Piquero, 1999). Moffitt (1993, 1997) has also suggested, however, that the vulnerability of children with neuropsychological risks to criminogenic environments may also extend beyond the home. More specifically, she argues that both neuropsychological risks and risk factors in the immediate family are likely to be exacerbated by poverty and by life in disorganized, economically disadvantaged neighborhoods.[1] Nevertheless, few studies of the relationship between individual or family characteristics and offending have explored the possibility that neighborhood environments may exacerbate or ameliorate these risks.

To be sure, research on the effects of neighborhood context on individual-level outcomes is in its infancy. There is some evidence that neighborhood features are at least modestly related to a variety of youth behavioral outcomes, including cognitive development (Brooks-Gunn, Duncan, Klebanov, & Sealand, 1993; Chase-Lansdale & Gordon, 1996), school performance (Garner & Raudenbush, 1991; Halpern-Felsher et al., 1997), and peer-reported aggression (Kupersmidt, Griesler, DeRosier, Patterson, & Davis, 1995). In addition, researchers have reported significant but weak correlations between neighborhood context and delinquency at the individual level of analysis (Elliott et al., 1996; Gottfredson, McNeill, & Gottfredson, 1991; Loeber & Wikstrom, 1993).

Although these studies are important, they do not address the question of whether the relationship between offending, individual vulnerabilities, and family disadvantage is affected by neighborhood conditions. If Moffitt is correct, the effect of neuropsychological risk on offending will be contingent on both family and neighborhood characteristics.

 ## The Effects of Neighborhood on Individuals and Families

There are many reasons to expect that the likelihood of offending for neuropsychological vulnerable youths from adverse home environments may be different for those living in wealthy and well-organized neighborhoods than for those living in poor and socially disorganized ones (Wikstrom & Loeber, 2000). A number of mechanisms have been proposed through which neighborhoods might affect individual-level outcomes (Jencks & Mayer, 1990; Leventhal & Brooks-Gunn, 2000, 2003; R. J. Sampson, 1997). For example, R. J. Sampson (1997) proposed a social capital/collective efficacy model that is unique in linking neighborhood context, family characteristics, and individual-level outcomes. He suggests that social capital—defined as the extent to which adults are involved in stable social networks with the parents and relatives of their children's friends—is a critical feature of neighborhoods that affects parental socialization. These networks transmit norms regarding parenting and supervision and also share parental responsibility for the informal social control (monitoring and discipline) of children. Thus, family management practices—level of parental supervision, parental warmth, parental rejection, parent–child attachment—are mediated by the social organization of the community. Parenting styles and levels of child supervision are not only a function solely of the characteristics and interactional patterns of parents and children but also are influenced by the larger community context in which families are embedded. Sampson hypothesizes that because high levels of poverty, family disruption, and residential instability tend to weaken social networks, the collective socialization of children in disadvantaged neighborhoods suffers.

 ## Current Focus

First, this study used a national sample of relatively high-risk adolescents. This sample is particularly noteworthy given that most previous research has relied on smaller samples

---

[1]In neighborhoods characterized by concentrated poverty, unemployment, and family disruption, pregnant women are less likely to receive adequate prenatal care, both mother and child are more likely to be malnourished, and there is greater risk of exposure to environmental toxins and infectious disease. Consequently, Moffitt contends that children born in these environments are at greater risk for neuropsychological deficits.

that are less representative. In addition, a higher risk sample should yield a greater number of life-course-persistent offenders, supporting statistical analyses that might not be possible otherwise. Second, in categorizing offenders as either life-course-persistents or adolescence-limiteds, this study made use of a self-report measurement protocol. In doing so, two of Moffitt's (1994) criteria for identifying life-course-persistent offending were used: (a) involvement in violent offending and (b) involvement in offending over multiple measurement points. Third, following the advice of previous researchers who examined neighborhood contextual effects (Furstenburg, 1993), this study used perceptual measures of neighborhood disadvantage. Such measures are particularly advantageous in understanding youths' views of, and responses to, criminogenic influences within their neighborhoods. Finally, this study examined the preceding hypotheses across categories of race. This effort is important in this regard given that no previous research has tested Moffitt's theory of life-course-persistent offending within and across different neighborhood contexts using perceptual measures of neighborhood disadvantage in a national sample of relatively high-risk youths.

Method

Data for this research were drawn from the National Longitudinal Survey of Youth, Child–Mother data (hereafter referred to as the NLSY). The NLSY is a prospective, longitudinal data-collection effort supported by the U.S. Department of Labor and administered by the National Opinion Research Center. First administered in 1979 to 12,686 individuals aged 14 to 21, the main purpose of the original NLSY was to assess youths as they completed high school and entered the workforce. A separate biennial data collection effort began in 1986 that included detailed assessments of each child born to the girls and women in the original NLSY data cohort (referred to as the NLSY Child–Mother data). As of January 1, 1998, a total of seven waves had been administered to individuals who range in age from birth to 27 years (Center for Human Resource Research, 2000).

Participants

To investigate the hypotheses, this study restricted the analyses to a subsample of 513 individuals who had reached the age of 15 by 1994 and who provided valid interviews during the years 1994, 1996, and 1998. These restrictions were placed on the sample for two reasons: First, individuals who reached the age of 15 by December 31, 1994—termed the "young adults"—were the only individuals in the main sample who received a self-administered questionnaire that contained detailed delinquency and crime measures, including violent behavior. It should also be noted that these items were not available in the survey prior to the 1994 wave. Second, although the rate of sample attrition in this study (never exceeding 6.7% in any one wave) is consistent with similar longitudinal research designs investigating adolescent problem behavior (see Jessor, Van Den Bos, Vanderryn, Costa, & Turbin, 1995; Smith, Lizotte, Thornberry, & Krohn, 1995), the restriction to respondents who completed all three interviews circumvented missing data problems (see Jessor et al., 1995).

We examined the effects of the attrition of the 467 participants who were interviewed in 1994 but not in one or more of the two subsequent waves. In particular, comparisons were made on the main variables of interest across the final sample and the attrition subsample. No significant differences emerged between the two samples, suggesting that those excluded experienced similar levels of prenatal problems, family disadvantage, and neighborhood disadvantage. In addition, we examined the differences across the two samples on the standard demographic measures of age, race, and sex. Although no race differences emerged, the attrition subsample possessed significantly more males and older individuals. Despite these differences, the intercorrelations among the measures were similar for the final sample and the attrition subsample. Therefore, although there are modest differences between the sample used in this research and the attrition subsample, relationships among the variables used in the subsequent analyses most likely would not have been significantly different had the attrition not occurred.

Dependent Variable

Moffitt argues that life-course-persistent offending can be manifested in a number of ways. The measure of life-course-persistent offending used in this study combines two of Moffitt's parameters of antisocial behavior, self-reported involvement in violent offending and chronicity in offending (see Moffitt, 1994). To measure violent offending, at each of the three waves, individuals were asked whether, in the preceding year, they had "hit or seriously threatened to hit someone," "attacked someone with the idea of seriously hurting or killing them," and "hurt someone badly enough to need bandages or a doctor." The responses for each year were summed and collapsed so that involvement in the incident equaled 1 and no involvement equaled 0. The chronicity dimension of the life-course-persistent offending measure was operationalized using individuals' involvement in any offending (i.e., violent or nonviolent) in at least two of the three waves (see the appendix for the list of these items). In sum, an individual is categorized as a life-course-persistent offender (1) if he or she self-reported a violent offense in at least one wave *and* self-reported some offending in at least two waves of data collection. Those not meeting this threshold but reporting at least some nonviolent delinquency were categorized as adolescence-limited offenders (0).

Independent Variables

Prenatal Problem Index. Research has shown that disruption to the neuropsychological development of the fetus can result from maternal involvement in risky behaviors during pregnancy (Kandel, Brennan, & Mednick, 1989; P. D. Sampson et al., 1997; Wakschlag & Hans, 2002). Among these, cigarette smoking and alcohol use are two of the most important. An abundance of research has documented that mothers who smoke during pregnancy place their children at an increased risk of crime in general (e.g., Brennan, Grekin, Mortensen, & Mednick, 2002; Rasanen et al., 1999) and life-course-persistent offending in particular (Brennan, Grekin, & Mednick, 1999; Gibson, Piquero, & Tibbetts, 2000; Piquero, Gibson, Tibbetts, Turner, & Katz, 2002). Moreover, the relationship between maternal smoking and childhood behavior survives statistical controls for a wide range of social factors, including SES, maternal age, maternal IQ, home environment, maternal rejection, parenting style, and parental criminality (for a review and discussion, see Wakschlag, Pickett, Cook, Benowitz, & Leventhal, 2002).

Although the links are less strong and consistent, research suggests that maternal alcohol use during pregnancy is also associated with a host of negative outcomes, including lower IQ scores, learning problems, cognitive deficits, and behavioral problems (e.g., attention deficit hyperactivity disorder, conduct disorder, oppositional-defiant behaviors, and delinquency; see

Hill, Lowers, Locke-Wellman, & Shen, 2000; Streissguth, Barr, Brookstein, Sampson, & Olson, 1999; West, Chen, & Pantazis, 1994).

Because the data lack direct measures of neuropsychological deficits, consistent with prior research (see Piquero & Tibbetts, 1999; Tibbetts & Piquero, 1999), measures of prenatal problems were used as a proxy for neuropsychological deficits. To measure prenatal problems, a summative index was constructed based on items measuring maternal smoking and drinking behaviors during pregnancy. Consistent with previous research examining prenatal risks (Raine, Brennan, & Mednick. 1997), this measure combines a dichotomous measure of maternal cigarette smoking with a dichotomous measure of maternal alcohol use during pregnancy to create the Prenatal Problems Index. Those reporting any involvement in these behaviors during pregnancy received a score of 1 and those not reporting involvement received a score of 0. Therefore, the Prenatal Problems Index will range from 0 to 2, with higher values being indicative of greater prenatal risk.

Family Disadvantage Index. Individuals evidencing neuropsychological deficits are often born into families that are incapable of providing environments conducive to the healthy growth and development of their children. As Moffitt (1997) indicated, "Vulnerable infants are disproportionately found in environments that will not be ameliorative because many sources of neural maldevelopment co-occur with family disadvantage or parental deviance" (p. 126). Consistent with prior research, this study measures family disadvantage using the sum of four dichotomized items collected early in the youth's life (Kolvin, Miller, Fleeting, & Kolvin, 1988; Rutter, 1978; Stanton, McGee, & Silva, 1989). These items include (a) age of the mother at childbirth (1 = *younger than 18 years,* 0 = *18 years and older*), (b) maternal educational attainment at childbirth (1 = *less than high school graduate,* 0 = *at least high school graduate*), (c) maternal poverty status at childbirth (1 = *in poverty,* 0 = *not in poverty*), and (d) maternal marital status at childbirth (1 = *not married,* 0 = *married*). Higher scores on the family disadvantage measure are indicative of more disadvantaged familial environments.

Neighborhood Disadvantage. Measuring neighborhood disadvantage is a particularly daunting task considering the absence of a clear consensus in the literature regarding the relative benefits of objective measures (e.g., census data) and perceptual measures (e.g., reports from respondents regarding their immediate neighborhood surroundings). Each measurement strategy has advantages. Objective measures provide insight into the structural characteristics of a neighborhood (e.g., population density, ethnic heterogeneity, SES). Alternatively, perceptual measures provide insight into social ties that members with neighborhoods have with one another. Furthermore, to the extent that behavior is affected by individual perceptions of neighborhood conditions, rather than the objective conditions themselves, perceptual measures are preferable. Because Moffitt's theory is particularly concerned with the extent to which neighborhood socialization experiences exacerbate disadvantaged familial environments, this study measures neighborhood disadvantage in terms of respondents' perceptions. This falls comfortably in line with Furstenberg's (1995) research, which suggests that familial perceptions of the neighborhood context influenced youths' behavioral outcomes.

Similar to prior research (see Pratt, Turner, & Piquero, 2004; Turner, Piquero, & Pratt, 2005) that measured neighborhood disadvantage, this study uses maternal reports of seven items collected during Wave 4 (1992), when offspring were at a mean age of 13. Mothers responded to seven items assessing a variety of neighborhood problems. For example, they were asked to respond using a three-category response set to items such as "people in your neighborhood don't have enough respect for rules or laws," "too many parents in your neighborhood don't supervise their children," "there is not enough police protection in your neighborhood," and "people keep to themselves and don't care what goes on in the neighborhood." Responses were categorized as follows: 1 = *big problem*, 2 = *somewhat of a problem*, and 3 = *not a problem*. Items were recoded so that higher scores reflected a greater degree of neighborhood disadvantage. Analyses of the overall scale indicated that it was highly reliable (alpha = .88), and factor analyses indicate that it formed a unitary factor (KMO = .82).

In many of the subsequent analyses, this study examined the biosocial interaction (between prenatal problems and family disadvantage) across different neighborhood contexts. That is this study investigated the hypothesis that the biosocial interaction is intensified in bad neighborhoods while having weaker, if not insignificant, effects in better neighborhoods. To capture unique neighborhoods,

and consistent with past risk-related research (see Farrington & Loeber, 1999), this study dichotomized responses on the Neighborhood Disadvantage scale, categorizing those falling in the top quartile of the neighborhood measure as bad neighborhoods (1) and those falling below this threshold as good neighborhoods (0).[2]

Biosocial interaction. At the core of Moffitt's theory is the importance of a biosocial interaction between neuropsychological risks and disadvantaged familial environments. This study computed this interaction term by mean-centering the raw scores of the component factors and multiplying these factors. This method produces an interaction term that is not collinear with each of its component factors (Aiken & West, 1991; Jaccard, Turrisi, & Wan, 1990). Higher scores on the interaction term correspond with a higher degree of risk.

Control Variables

This study controlled for the age, sex, and race of the individual. Specifically, age was a continuous measure, capturing respondents' age in 1998. Sex was coded as females = 0 and males = 1. Race was also coded dichotomously: White = 0 and non-White = 1. Table 1 contains descriptive statistics for the full sample and race-specific samples (White/non-White). Presenting the data in such a format allows one to compare the distribution of each of the variables across categories of race and to illustrate the bivariate relationships in preparation for the race-specific analyses presented below.

Results

Table 1 presents the means and standard deviations of each of the variables for the nonoffenders as well as for each category of offender. Offender groups differed significantly on sex, prenatal problems (and each of its components), and maternal marital status. That is, compared to the adolescence-limited group, the life-course-persistent group is comprised of a significantly greater proportion of males ($F = 9.818$; $p < .05$), who had higher levels of prenatal problems ($F = 8.012$; $p < .05$) and who were more likely to be born to a nonmarried mother ($F = 4.030$; $p < .05$). It is also

---

[2]We assessed the sensitivity of this measure by creating different cutoff points (i.e., mean splits, median splits, etc.). The results did not substantively change the importance of the main exogenous variables of interest.

| Table 1 | Variables and Descriptive Statistics of Sample |

| | Nonoffenders (n = 20) | | Adolescent-Limited (n = 263) | | | | Life-Course-Persistent (n = 130) | | | | |
| | | | White | | Non-White | | White | | Non-White | | |
Variable	M	SD	M	SD	M	SD	M	SD	M	SD	F
Age (1998)	19.20	0.86	19.00	0.81	19.11	0.83	18.92	0.82	19.21	0.80	2.769
Sex (1 = male)	0.40	0.49	0.48	0.50	0.41	0.49	0.62	0.49	0.68	0.51	9.818[*]
Prenatal Problem Index	0.52	0.68	0.78	0.80	0.85	0.78	0.80	0.73	0.89	0.75	8.012[*]
Maternal alcohol use	0.23	0.42	0.39	0.47	0.38	0.51	0.40	0.50	0.42	0.49	6.044[*]
Maternal smoking	0.27	0.45	0.39	0.50	0.47	0.49	0.40	0.51	0.47	0.48	4.632[*]
Family Disadvantage	1.54	1.15	1.67	1.16	1.72	1.15	1.77	1.16	1.83	1.19	1.496
Maternal age at childbirth	0.43	0.50	0.45	0.49	0.47	0.51	0.46	0.50	0.50	0.49	0.283
Maternal education	0.37	0.48	0.36	0.47	0.36	0.48	0.34	0.47	0.36	0.48	0.121
Maternal poverty status	0.38	0.49	0.40	0.49	0.42	0.49	0.46	0.50	0.47	0.50	0.948
Maternal marital status	0.34	0.48	0.45	0.50	0.47	0.51	0.50	0.50	0.52	0.49	4.030[*]
Neighborhood Disadvantage	11.42	3.91	11.65	3.90	11.73	3.94	12.03	3.81	12.11	3.83	0.895
Bad neighborhood (1 = bad)	0.22	0.41	0.09	0.45	0.39	0.48	0.12	0.47	0.46	0.44	2.034
Biosocial interaction	0.03	0.89	−0.11	0.91	−0.15	0.90	0.00	0.85	0.02	0.91	1.765

NOTE: F values represent differences across the three groupings (i.e., nonoffenders, adolescent-limiteds, and life-course-persistents).

[*]$p < .05$.

noteworthy that, although not significant, differences in the predicted direction existed on each of the remaining independent variables of interest.

As can be seen in Table 1, the life-course-persistent offending group is considerably larger than has typically been reported in prior research. Specifically, life-course-persistent offenders in the present sample represent approximately one third of the offending population; Moffitt (1993) has proffered that this group should constitute 5% to 8% of the offending population. Two explanations are offered to account for this finding. First, the NLSY is comprised of a relatively high-risk sample. The survey oversamples African Americans, Hispanics, and economically disadvantaged Whites—populations that Moffitt has pointed out should evidence the highest proportions of life-course-persistent offenders (Moffitt, 1997). Second, and perhaps more important, the measurement protocol identifying life-course-persistent offenders was based on self-reported offending. Self-reports typically uncover a great deal more delinquency than that reported in official data. Although self-reports of offending have been used in previous research testing Moffitt's theory (see Moffitt &

Caspi, 2001; Piquero et al., 2002), they have generally been used in conjunction with official data. That is, no previous research has operationalized life-course-persistent offending relying solely on self-reported offending. It is likely that the use of self-reports, along with a high-risk sample, produced a higher proportion of life-course-persistent offenders than would be expected in the general population using official data.

As a first step in testing the biosocial hypothesis, the estimates of two separate models are presented in Table 2. Model 1 is a base model that examines the influence of the control variables, the Prenatal Problem Index, and the Family Disadvantage Index on life-course-persistent offending. This model indicates that only sex is a significant predictor of life-course-persistent offending ($B = 0.85$; $p < .01$). That is, males have a higher likelihood of engaging in a course of persistent and violent offending.

Model 2 in Table 2 adds the Prenatal Problem x Familial Disadvantage interaction term into the base equation. Similar to Model 1, this model suggests that, although the effect of the interaction term is in the predicted direction, only sex remains a significant predictor

Table 2	Logistic Regression Coefficients Predicting Self-Reported Violence: Models Examining Main and Interaction Effects ($n = 393$)					
	Model 1			**Model 2**		
Variable	**B**	**SE**	**Exp (b)**	**B**	**SE**	**Exp (b)**
Age	−0.08	0.14	0.928	−0.08	0.14	0.928
Sex	0.85**	0.22	2.350	0.86**	0.22	2.353
Non-White	−0.05	0.26	0.955	−0.08	0.25	0.925
Prenatal Problem (PP) Index	0.06	0.15	1.062	0.02	0.14	1.018
Family Disadvantage (FD)	0.12	0.10	1.129	0.10	0.10	1.107
PP x FD Interaction	−		−	0.18	0.12	1.190
Constant	0.02	2.61		0.31	2.63	
Nagelkerke R^2	0.06			0.06		

*$p < .05$. **$p < .01$.

of life-course-persistent offending ($B = 0.86$; $p < .01$). Thus, the biosocial interaction does not emerge as a significant predictor of life-course-persistent offending in the full offending sample.

The Biosocial Hypothesis Within and Across Different Neighborhood Contexts

The biosocial hypothesis was then tested within and across different neighborhood contexts. Table 3 presents the findings of the identical equations in Model 2 of Table 2 across different neighborhood contexts. Specifically, two separate equations were estimated to examine the effects of the biosocial interaction separately for those who scored in the top quartile of the Neighborhood Disadvantage scale (i.e., those in the worst neighborhoods) and those below this threshold. If the neighborhood context conditions antisocial behavior, and in light of the findings presented in Table 2, it should be expected that a significant biosocial interaction would emerge in the worst neighborhoods and insignificant effects in the less disadvantaged neighborhoods.

The first set of columns is identical to Model 2 in Table 2 and is only used for comparison purposes. Turning to the neighborhood-specific models, and as predicted, the findings suggest that the biosocial interaction significantly predicts life-course-persistent offending for those residing in the worst neighborhoods ($B = 0.54$; $p < .05$) while having

a nonsignificant effect among those living in the less disadvantaged neighborhoods. Once again, being male ($B = 1.12$; $p < .01$) emerged as the only significant predictor of life-course-persistent offending for those residing in the lower three quartiles of the neighborhood disadvantage measures. In short, the effects of the biosocial interaction were exacerbated in the most disadvantaged neighborhoods but were insignificant in less disadvantaged neighborhoods.[3]

The Biosocial Hypothesis Across Different Neighborhood Contexts and Racial Backgrounds

Next, the equations examined above were estimated across groups defined by race and neighborhood context. That is, the biosocial hypothesis was estimated among Whites and non-Whites who resided in the more and less disadvantaged neighborhoods. If Moffitt's theory is correct, the biosocial interaction should significantly predict life-course-persistent offending for Whites and non-Whites in the most disadvantaged neighborhoods, with non-Whites potentially experiencing the strongest effects. The results displayed in Table 4 provide estimates for each of the four groupings.

Focusing first on the good neighborhoods, the results in Table 4 suggest that being male corresponded with a higher propensity to manifest life-course-persistent offending for Whites and non-Whites ($B = 1.78$; $p < .05$ for

---

[3]A coefficient comparison test revealed that these differences were significant at the .10 level ($z = 1.78$).

| Table 3 | Logistic Regression Coefficients Predicting Self-Reported Violence: Full Model and Neighborhood-Specific Models |

| | Full Model (n = 393) | | | | Neighborhood-Specific Models | | | | | | | |
| | | | | | Top 25% (n = 116) | | | | Lower 75% (n = 277) | | | |
Variables	B	SE	Wald	Exp(b)	B	SE	Wald	Exp(b)	B	SE	Wald	Exp(b)
Age	0.05	0.13	0.12	1.047	−0.02	0.25	0.01	0.977	−0.12	0.17	0.46	0.891
Sex	0.70	0.21	10.97*	2.005	0.41	0.40	1.02	1.500	1.12	0.28	15.58**	3.070
Non-White	0.15	0.24	0.39	1.163	−0.40	0.68	0.36	0.668	−0.19	0.29	0.40	0.831
Prenatal Problem (PP) Index	0.08	0.14	0.31	1.081	0.21	0.25	0.71	1.238	−0.06	0.17	0.15	0.938
Family Disadvantage (FD)	0.14	0.09	2.07	1.147	0.04	0.19	0.05	1.041	0.16	0.13	1.50	1.168
PP × FD interaction	0.16	0.12	1.94	1.178	0.54	0.25	4.83*	1.717	0.02	0.15	0.02	1.020
Constant	−1.60	2.47	0.41		0.11	4.81	0.00		0.86	3.24	0.07	
Nagelkerke R^2	.06				.09				.09			

$^*p < .05.$ $^{**}p < .01.$

| Table 4 | Logistic Regression Coefficients Predicting Self-Reported Violence: Race/Neighborhood-Specific Models |

| | Whites | | | | | | Non-Whites | | | | | |
| | Good Neighborhood | | | Bad Neighborhood | | | Good Neighborhood | | | Bad Neighborhood | | |
Variable	B	SE	Exp(b)	B	SE	Exp(b)	B	SE	Exp(b)	B	SE	Exp(b)
Age	−0.31	0.29	0.73	2.39	1.75	10.91	0.05	0.22	1.05	−0.16	0.26	0.85
Sex	1.78	0.51*	5.92	0.34	1.93	1.41	0.85	0.36*	2.34	0.47	0.43	1.59
Prenatal Problem (PP) Index	−0.46	0.32	0.63	0.24	0.90	1.27	0.27	0.21	1.31	0.25	0.27	1.29
Family Disadvantage (FD)	0.34	0.25	1.41	0.66	0.73	1.93	−0.06	0.17	0.94	−0.04	0.20	0.96
PP × FD interaction	0.13	0.30	1.14	1.53	1.28	4.60	−0.36	0.23	0.70	−0.61	0.27*	1.84
Constant	4.36	5.55		−46.22	33.59		−2.23	4.28		2.29	4.98	
Nagelkerke R^2	.25			.45			.07			0.11		

$^*p < .05$

Whites; $B = 0.85$; $p < .05$ for non-Whites). Notably, the biosocial interaction was insignificant for both racial categories with good neighborhoods. Turning to the models estimated for those residing in the most disadvantaged neighborhoods, the results indicate that the biosocial interaction significantly predicted life-course-persistent offending only for non-Whites ($B = 0.61$; $p < .05$), though having insignificant effects for Whites. That is, non-Whites living in the most disadvantaged neighborhoods who were at risk because of prenatal problems and familial disadvantage

were significantly more likely to be life-course-persistent offenders. The null results of the biosocial interaction for Whites living in disadvantaged neighborhoods, however, should be tempered because of low sample size. More specifically, only 9.6% ($n = 12$) of the Whites resided in the most disadvantaged neighborhoods, compared to 38.8% ($n = 104$) of non-Whites. This latter finding is consistent with much prior research showing that non-Whites are greatly overrepresented in the most disadvantaged neighborhoods (R. J. Sampson & Wilson, 1995; Wilson, 1987).

Discussion

During the past decade, Moffitt's biosocial hypothesis predicting life-course-persistent offending has received a fair amount of empirical scrutiny. Past research has rather consistently found that individuals suffering from early neuropsychological dysfunction and who are raised in disadvantaged familial environments have a higher propensity to manifest life-course-persistent offending (Moffitt Lynam, & Silva, 1994; Raine et al., 1994, 1997). Although informative, the vast majority of this research has failed to examine the effects of this interaction within and across different neighborhood contexts (but see Moffitt, 1997; Piquero et al., 2005). Investigation of this hypothesis is important given that emerging research is beginning to suggest that individual differences are enhanced or exacerbated within disadvantaged environments (e.g., Lynam et al., 2000). Toward this end, this study made use of a national sample of adolescents to investigate Moffitt's biosocial hypothesis within and across different types of neighborhoods. In addition, guided by the extant literature on race and neighborhood disadvantage (see Massey, 1995; R. J. Sampson & Wilson, 1995; Wilson, 1987, 1991, 1996), this study also explored how Moffitt's biosocial hypothesis fared among Whites and non-Whites in different neighborhood contexts.

The study produced three important findings. First, the biosocial interaction failed to predict life-course-persistent offending within the full sample. Although generally inconsistent with previous research, this finding may be a function of two important considerations: (a) the measurement of life-course-persistent offending and (b) the fact that interaction effects are difficult to uncover with research designs that are not truly experimental in nature. As discussed previously, little research has relied solely on self-reports to operationalize life-course-persistent offending. Rather, efforts have tended to rely on official reports of formal contact with the criminal justice system (i.e., age of first arrest and/or conviction). It is therefore possible that the measurement strategy—based on self-reports—yielded a group of life-course-persistent offenders that included individuals who might not have been categorized as life-course-persistents if official measures of delinquency were used. In fact, prior research has suggested that predicting life-course-persistent offending is at least somewhat dependent on the measurement strategy used (see Brennan et al.,

1999; Piquero et al, 2002). Future research should attempt to replicate this study's use of self-reports to operationalize life-course-persistent offending before definitive conclusions can be drawn.

Second, the biosocial interaction was found to predict life-course-persistent offending for individuals living in the most disadvantaged neighborhoods. In other words, the neighborhood context conditioned the effects of the biosocial interaction. This finding is important because it is consistent with a growing body of research suggesting that individual risks, particularly those occurring early in the life course, are exacerbated in disadvantaged neighborhoods (Lynam et al., 2000). In addition, this study's findings are consistent with previous efforts examining similar hypotheses that relied solely on objective versus perceptual measures of neighborhood disadvantage (Piquero et al., 2005). As such, it appears that regardless of how it is measured (via objective or perceptual measures), the neighborhood context in which a youth is raised is an important determinant of behavioral outcomes (Klebanov et al., 1997).

Third, when the data were analyzed by race and neighborhood context, this study found that the biosocial interaction was a significant predictor of life-course-persistent offending for certain groups of individuals living within the most disadvantaged neighborhoods. Specifically, the biosocial interaction was only significant in predicting life-course-persistent offending for non-Whites living in disadvantaged neighborhoods; each of the remaining categorizations produced null results. Although this finding is somewhat consistent with Moffitt's (1993) predictions that the biosocial interaction would be stronger for non-Whites in disadvantaged neighborhoods, it is somewhat inconsistent given that the interaction should also emerge as being significant for the White population residing within disadvantaged neighborhoods.

References

Aiken, L. S., & West, S. G. (1991). *Multiple regression: Testing and interpreting interactions.* London: Sage.

Brame, R., & Piquero. A. R. (2003). The role of sample attrition in studying the longitudinal relationship between age and crime. *Journal of Quantitative Criminology, 19,* 107–128.

Brennan, P. A., Grekin, E. R., & Mednick, S. A. (1999). Maternal smoking during pregnancy and adult male criminal outcomes. *Archives of General Psychiatry, 56,* 215–219.

Brennan, P., Grekin, E. R., Mortensen, E. L., & Mednick, S. A. (2002). Relationship of maternal smoking during pregnancy with criminal arrest and hospitalization for substance abuse in male and female adult offspring. *American Journal of Psychiatry, 159,* 48–54.

Brennan, P., Mednick, S. A., & Raine, A. (1997). Biosocial interactions and violence: A focus on perinatal factors. In A. Raine, P. Brennan, D. Farrington, & S. A. Mednick (Eds.), *Biosocial bases of violence* (pp. 163–174). New York: Plenum.

Brooks-Gunn, J., Duncan, G. J., Klebanov, P. K., & Sealand, N. (1993). Do neighborhoods influence child and adolescent development? *American Journal of Sociology, 99,* 353–395.

Bursik, R. J., Jr. (1986). Ecological stability and the dynamics of delinquency. In A. J. Reiss, Jr. & M. Tonry (Eds.), *Communities and crime* (pp. 35–66). Chicago: University of Chicago Press.

Center for Human Resource Research, The Ohio State University. (2000). *National longitudinal surveys handbook.* Columbus, OH: Author.

Cernkovich, S. A., & Giordano, P. A. (1985). Chronic offenders: The missing cases in self-report delinquency research. *Journal of Criminal Law and Criminology, 76,* 705–732.

Chase-Lansdale, P. L., & Gordon, R. A. (1996). Economic hardship and the development of five- and six-year-olds: Neighborhood and regional perspectives. *Child Development, 67,* 3338–3367.

Coullon, C. J. (1996). Effects of neighborhoods on families and children: Implications for services. In A. J. Kahn & S. B. Kamerman (Eds.), *Children and their families in big cities: Strategies for service reform* (pp. 87–120). New York: Columbia University School of Social Work.

Cullen, F. T. (1994). Social support as an organizing concept for criminology: Presidential address to the Academy of Criminal Justice Sciences. *Justice Quarterly, 11,* 527–560.

Earls, F., McGuire, J., & Shay, S. (1994). Evaluating a community intervention to reduce the risk of child abuse: Methodological strategies in conducting neighborhood surveys. *Child Abuse and Neglect, 18,* 473–485.

Elliott, D. S., Ageton, S. S., & Canter, R. J. (1979). An integrated perspective on delinquent behavior. *Journal of Research in Crime and Delinquency, 16,* 3–27.

Elliott, D. S., Wilson, W. J., Huizinga, D., Sampson, R. J., Elliott, A. J., & Rankin, B. (1996). The effects of neighborhood disadvantage on adolescent development. *Journal of Research in Crime and Delinquency, 33,* 389–426.

Eysenck, H. (1977). *Crime and personality* (Rev. ed.). London: Routledge Kegan Paul.

Farrington, D. P., & Loeber, R. (1999). Some benefits of dichotomization in psychiatric and criminological research. *Criminal Behavior and Mental Health, 10,* 100–122.

Furstenberg, F. F. (1993). How families manage risk and opportunity in dangerous neighborhoods. In W. J. Wilson (Ed.). *Sociology and the public agenda* (pp. 231–258). Newbury Park, CA: Sage.

Furstenberg, F. F. (1995). Social capital and successful development among at-high-risk youth. *Journal of Marriage and the Family, 57,* 580–592.

Garner, C. L., & Raudenbush, S. W. (1991). Neighborhood effects on educational attainment: A multilevel analysis. *Sociology of Education, 64,* 251–262.

Gibson, C. L., Piquero, A. R., & Tibbetts, S. G. (2000). Assessing the relationship between maternal cigarette smoking during pregnancy and age at first police contact. *Justice Quarterly, 17,* 519–542.

Gibson, C. L., & Tibbetts, S. G. (2000). A biosocial interaction in predicting early onset of offending. *Psychological Reports, 56,* 509–518.

Goddard, H. H. (1914). *Feeblemindedness: Its causes and consequences.* New York: Macmillan.

Gottfredson, D. C., McNeill, R. G., & Gottfredson, G. D. (1991). Social area influences on delinquency: A multilevel analysis. *Journal of Research in Crime and Delinquency, 28,* 197–226.

Halpern, R. (1990). Poverty and early childhood parenting: Toward a framework for intervention. *American Journal of Orthopsychiatry, 60,* 6–18.

Halpern-Felsher, B. L., Connell, J. P., Spencer, M. B., Aber, J. L., Duncan, G. J., Clifford, E., et al. (1997). Neighborhood and family factors predicting educational risk and attainment in African American and White children and adolescents. In J. Brooks-Gunn, G. J. Duncan, & J. L. Aber (Eds.), *Neighborhood poverty: Context and consequences for children* (Vol. I. pp. 146–173). New York: Russell Sage.

Hanson, T. L., McLanahan, S., & Thomson, E. (1997). Economic resources, parental practices, and children's well-being. In G. J. Duncan & J. Brooks-Gunn (Eds.), *Consequences of growing up poor* (pp. 190–238). New York: Russell Sage.

Hill, S. Y., Lowers, L., Locke-Wellman. J., & Shen, S. (2000). Maternal smoking and drinking during pregnancy and the risk for child and adolescent psychiatric disorders. *Journal of Studies on Alcohol. 61,* 661–668.

Jaccard, J., Turrisi, R., & Wan, C. K. (1990). *Interaction effects in multiple regression.* Newbury Park, CA: Sage.

Jarrett, R. L. (1997). Bringing families back in: Neighborhood effects on child development. In J. Brooks-Gunn, G. J. Duncan, & J. L., Aber (Eds.). *Neighborhood poverty: Policy implications in studying neighborhoods* (Vol. 2, pp. 48–64). New York: Russell Sage.

Jencks, C. & Mayer, S. E. (1990). The social consequences of growing up in a poor neighborhood. In L. E. Lynn, Jr. & M. G. H. McGeary (Eds.), *Inner-city poverty in the United States* (pp. 48–64). Washington, DC: National Academy Press.

Jessor, R., Van Den Bos, J., Vanderryn, J., Costa, F. M., & Turbin, M. S. (1995). Protective factors in adolescent problem behavior: Moderator effects and developmental change. *Developmental Psychology, 31,* 923–933.

Kandel, E., Brennan. P., & Mednick, S. A. (1989). Minor physical anomalies and parental modeling of aggression predict violent offending. *Journal of Consulting and Clinical Psychology, 78,* 1–5.

Klebanov, P. K., Brooks-Gunn. J., Chase-Lansdale. P. L., & Gordon, R. A. (1997). Are neighborhood effects on young children mediated by features of home environment? In J. Brooks-Gunn, G. J. Duncan, & J. L. Aber (Eds.), *Neighborhood poverty: Context and consequences for children* (Vol. 1, pp. 119–145). New York: Russell Sage.

Kolvin, I., Miller, F., Fleeting. M., & Kolvin. P. (1988). Social and parenting factors affecting criminal-offense rates. *British Journal of Psychiatry, 152*, 80–90.

Kupersmidt, J. B., Griesler, P. C., DeRosier, M. E., Patterson. C. .J., & Davis, P. W. (1995). Childhood aggression and peer relations in the context of family and neighborhood factors. *Child Development, 66*, 360–375.

Leventhal, T., & Brooks-Gunn, J. (2000). The neighborhoods they live in: The effects of neighborhood residence on child and adolescent outcomes. *Psychological Bulletin, 126*, 309–337.

Leventhal, T., & Brooks-Gunn, J. (2003). Children and youth in neighborhood contexts. *Current Directions in Psychological Science, 12*, 27–31.

Loeber, R., & Stouthamer-Loeber, M. (1986). Family factors as correlates and predictors of juvenile conduct problems and delinquency. In M. Tonry & N. Morris (Eds.). *Crime and justice: An annual review of research* (Vol. 7). Chicago: University of Chicago Press.

Loeber, R., & Wikstrom, P. (1993). Individual pathways to crime in different types of neighborhoods. In D. P. Farrington, R. J. Sampson, & P. Wikstrom (Eds.), *Integrating individual and ecological aspects of crime* (pp. 169–204). Stockholm, Sweden: National Council for Crime Prevention.

Lombroso, C. (1876). *L'uomo delinquente* [The criminal man]. Milan, Italy: Hoepli.

Lynam, D. R., Caspi, A., Moffitt. T. E., Wikstrom, P., Loeber, R., & Novak, S. (2000). The interaction between impulsivity and neighborhood context on offending: The effects of impulsivity are stronger in poorer neighborhoods. *Journal of Abnormal Psychology, 109*, 563–574.

Massey, D. S. (1995). Getting away with murder: Segregation and violent crime in urban America. *University of Pennsylvania Law Review, 143*, 1203–1232.

Massey, D. S., & Denton. N. A. (1993). *American apartheid: Segregation and the making of the underclass*. Cambridge. MA: Harvard University Press.

McLoyd, V. C. (1990). The impact of economic hardship on Black families and children: Psychological distress, parenting, and socioemotional development. *Child Development, 61*, 311–346.

Mednick, S. A. (1977). A bio-social theory of the learning of law-abiding behavior. In S. Mednick & K. O. Christiansen (Eds.). *Biosocial bases of criminal behavior* (pp. 153–178). New York: Gardner.

Messner, S. F., Krohn, M. D., & Liska, A. E. (1989). *Theoretical integration in the study of deviance and crime: Problems and prospects*. Albany: State University of New York Press.

Moffitt, T. E. (1990). The neuropsychology of delinquency: A critical review of theory and research. In N. Morris & M. Tonry (Eds.), *Crime and justice* (pp. 99–169). Chicago: University of Chicago Press.

Moffitt, T. E. (1993). "Life-course-persistent" and "adolescent-limited" antisocial behavior: A developmental taxonomy. *Psychological Review, 100*, 674–701.

Moffitt, T. E. (1994). Natural histories of delinquency. In E. Weitekamp & H. Kerner (Eds.), *Cross-national longitudinal research on human development and criminal behavior* (pp. 3–61). Dordrecht, the Netherlands: Kluwer.

Moffitt, T. E. (1997). Neuropsychology, antisocial behavior, and neighborhood context. In J. McCord (Ed.), *Violence and childhood in the inner city* (pp. 116–170). New York: Cambridge University Press.

Moffitt, T. E., & Caspi, A. (2001). Childhood predictors differentiate life-course-persistent and adolescence-limited antisocial pathways among males and females. *Development and Psychopathology, 13*, 355–375.

Moffitt, T. E., Lynam, D. R., & Silva, P. A. (1994). Neuropsychological tests predicting persistent male delinquency. *Criminology, 32*, 277–300.

Park, R. E. (1926). The urban community as a special pattern and moral order. In E. W. Burgess (Ed.), *The urban community* (pp. 3–18), Chicago: University of Chicago Press.

Park, R. E., Burgess, E. W., & McKenzie, R. (1925). *The city*. Chicago: University of Chicago Press.

Patterson, G. R. (1976). The aggressive child: Victim and architect of a coercive system. In E. J. March, L. C. Hand, & L. A. Hamerlynck (Eds.), *Behavior modification and families, volume 1: Theory and research* (pp. 267–316). New York: Brunner/Mazel.

Patterson, G. R. (1995). Coercion as a basis for early age of onset for arrest. In J. McCord (Ed.), *Coercion and punishment in long-term perspective* (pp. 81–105). New York: Cambridge University Press.

Patterson, G. R., Dishion, T. J., & Bank, L. (1984). Family interaction: A process model of deviancy training. *Aggressive Behavior, 10*, 253–267.

Peeples, R. & Loeber, R. (1994). Do individual factors and neighborhood context explain ethnic differences in juvenile delinquency? *Journal of Quantitative Criminology, 10*, 141–157.

Piquero, A. R., Gibson, C., Tibbetts, S., Turner, M. G., & Katz, S. H. (2002). Maternal prenatal cigarette smoking and life-course-persistent offending. *International Journal of Offender Therapy and Comparative Criminology, 46*, 231–248.

Piquero, A. R., Moffitt, T. E., & Lawton, B. (2005). Race differences in life-course-persistent offending. In D. Hawkins & K. Kempf-Leonard (Eds.), *Our children, their children: Race, development and juvenile justice* (pp. 202–244). Chicago: University of Chicago Press.

Piquero, A. R., & Tibbetts, S. G. (1999). The impact of pre/perinatal disturbances and disadvantaged familial environment in predicting criminal offending. *Studies on Crime and Crime Prevention, 8*, 52–70.

Pratt, T., Turner, M. G., & Piquero, A. R. (2004). Parental socialization and community context: A longitudinal analysis of the structural sources of low self-control. *Journal of Research in Crime and Delinquency, 41*, 219–243.

Raine, A. (2002). Biosocial studies of antisocial and violent behavior in children and adults: A review. *Journal of Abnormal Child Psychology, 30*, 311–327.

Raine, A., Brennan, P., & Mednick. S. A. (1994). Birth complications combined with early maternal rejection at age 1 year predispose to violent crime at age 18 years. *Archives of General Psychiatry, 51*, 984–988.

Raine, A., Brennan, P., & Mednick. S. A. (1997). Interaction between birth complications and early maternal rejection in predisposing individuals to adult violence: Specificity to serious, early-onset violence. *American Journal of Psychiatry, 154*, 1265–1271.

Rankin, B. H., & Quane, J. M. (2002). Social contexts and urban adolescent outcomes: The interrelated effects of neighborhoods, families, and peers on African-American youth. *Social Problems, 49*, 79–91.

Rasanen, P., Hakko, H., Isohanni, M., Hodgins, S., Jarvelin, M., & Tihonen, J. (1999). Maternal smoking during pregnancy and risk of criminal behavior among adult male offspring in the northern Finland 1966 birth cohort. *American Journal of Psychiatry, 156*, 857–862.

Rutter, M. (1978). Family, area and school influences in the genesis of conduct disorders. In L. A. Hersov, M. Berger, & D. Shaffer (Eds.). *Aggression and antisocial behavior in childhood and adolescence* (pp. 95–114). Oxford, UK: Pergamon.

Sampson, P. D., Kerr, B., Olson, H. C., Streissguth, A. P., Hunt, E., Barr, H. M., et. al. (1997). The effects of prenatal alcohol exposure on adolescent cognitive processing: A speed-accuracy trade-off. *Intelligence, 24*, 329–353.

Sampson, R. J. (1997). The embeddedness of child and adolescent development: A community-level perspective on urban violence. In J. McCord (Ed.). *Violence and childhood in the inner city* (pp. 31–77). New York: Cambridge University Press.

Sampson, R. J., & Groves, W. B. (1989). Community structure and crime: Testing social disorganization theory. *American Journal of Sociology, 94*, 774–802.

Sampson, R. J., & Lauritsen, J. L. (1997). Racial and ethnic disparities in crime and criminal justice in the United States. In M. Tonry (Ed.). *Ethnicity, crime, and immigration: Comparative and cross-national perspectives* (pp. 311–374). Chicago: University of Chicago Press.

Sampson, R. J., & Wilson. W. J. (1995). Toward a theory of race, crime, and urban inequality. In J. Hagan & R. Peterson (Eds.). *Crime and inequality* (pp. 37–56). Palo Alto, CA: Stanford University Press.

Shaw, C. R., & McKay, H. D. (1942). *Juvenile delinquency and urban areas.* Chicago: University of Chicago Press.

Smith, C., Lizotte, A. J., Thornberry, T. P., & Krohn, M. D. (1995). Resilient youth: Identifying factors that prevent high-risk youth from engaging in delinquency and drug use. In Z. S. Belau & J. Hagan (Eds.), *Current perspectives on aging and the life cycle* (pp. 217–247). Greenwich, CT: JAI.

Stanton, W. R., McGee, R., & Silva, P. A. (1989). A longitudinal study of the interactive effects of perinatal complications and early family adversity on cognitive ability. *Australian Pediatric Journal, 25*, 130–133.

Streissguth, A. P., Barr, H. M., Brookstein, F. L., Sampson, P. D., & Olson, H. C. (1999). The long term neurocognitive consequences of prenatal alcohol exposure: A 14-year study. *Psychological Science, 10*, 186–190.

Thornberry, T. P. (1987). Toward an integrated theory of delinquency. *Criminology, 35*, 863–891.

Tibbetts, S. G., & Piquero, A. R. (1999). The influence of gender, low birth weight, and disadvantaged environment in predicting early onset of offending: A test of Moffitt's interactional hypothesis. *Criminology, 37*, 843–877.

Tonry, M., Ohlin. L., & Farrington, D. P. (1991). *Human development and criminal behavior.* New York: Springer-Verlag.

Turner, M. G., Piquero. A. R., & Pratt, T. (2005). The school context as a source of self-control. *Journal of Criminal Justice, 33*, 327–339.

Wakschlag, L. S., & Hans, S. L. (2002). Maternal smoking during pregnancy and conduct problems in high-risk youth: A developmental framework. *Development and Psychopathology, 14*, 351–369.

Wakschlag, L. S., Pickett, K. E., Cook, E., Jr., Benowitz, N. L., & Leventhal, B. L. (2002). Maternal smoking during pregnancy and severe antisocial behavior in offspring: A review. *American Journal of Public Health, 92*, 966–974.

West, J. R., Chen, W. A., & Pantazis, N. J. (1994). Fetal alcohol syndrome: The vulnerability of the developing brain and possible mechanisms of damage. *Metabolic Brain Disease, 9*, 291–322.

Wikstrom, P. H., & Loeber, R. (2000). Do disadvantaged neighborhoods cause well-adjusted children to become adolescent delinquents? A study of male juvenile serious offending, individual risk and protective factors, and neighborhood context. *Criminology, 38*, 1109–1142.

Wilson, W. J. (1987). *The truly disadvantaged: The inner city, the underclass, and public policy.* Chicago: Chicago University Press.

Wilson, W. J. (1991). Studying inner-city dislocations: The challenge of public agenda research. *American Sociological Review, 56*, 1–14.

Wilson, W. J. (1996). *When work disappears.* New York: Knopf.

AUTHORS' NOTE: *Correspondence concerning this article may be sent to Michael G. Turner, PhD. Department of Criminal Justice, University of North Carolina at Charlotte. 5070 Colvard, Charlotte, NC 28223-0001; e-mail: mgturner@email.uncc.edu.*

REVIEW QUESTIONS

1. Which theoretical biosocial model do the authors base their study on? Briefly explain the primary concepts and propositions of this model, as well as the theorist who developed this theoretical framework.

2. Regarding the Prenatal Problem Index the authors used for their primary independent variable, explain the key constructs that went into this measure, as well as the justification for including them in this scale.

3. The authors conclude that when the data were analyzed by race and neighborhood, the biosocial interaction was significant in predicting life-course-persistent offending for only a certain group. What was this group, and is it consistent with previous studies?

READING 28

In this reading by Edward Mulvey, the author reviews a number of studies that have focused on reducing offending among youth offenders. Although the author notes that most young offenders show a decrease in serious offending as they grow older, regardless of any intervention, he also points out a number of strategies that seem to show effectiveness in helping in this process. Further, he also notes some intervention strategies that tend to hinder such reductions in recidivism. Readers should focus in on exactly which policies seem to work best, and which don't seem to be effective.

Highlights from Pathways to Desistance:
A Longitudinal Study of Serious Adolescent Offenders

Edward P. Mulvey

The Pathways to Desistance Study is a large collaborative, multidisciplinary project that is following 1,354 serious juvenile offenders ages 14–18 (184 females and 1,170 males) for 7 years after their conviction (for more detailed information, see "Study Design").[1] This study has collected the most comprehensive data set currently available about serious adolescent offenders and their lives in late adolescence and early adulthood. It looks at the factors that lead youth who have committed serious offenses to continue or desist from offending, including individual maturation, life changes, and involvement with the criminal justice system.

[1]OJJDP is sponsoring the Pathways to Desistance study in partnership with the National Institute of Justice, the Centers for Disease Control and Prevention, the John D. and Catherine T. MacArthur Foundation, the William T. Grant Foundation, the Robert Wood Johnson Foundation, the William Penn Foundation, the National Institute on Drug Abuse (Grant Number R01DA019697), the Pennsylvania Commission on Crime and Delinquency, and the Arizona State Governor's Justice Commission. Investigators for this study are Edward P. Mulvey, Ph.D. (University of Pittsburgh), Robert Brame, Ph.D. (University of North Carolina—Charlotte), Elizabeth Cauffman, Ph.D. (University of California—Irvine), Laurie Chassin, Ph.D. (Arizona State University), Sonia Cota-Robles, Ph.D. (Temple University), Jeffrey Fagan, Ph.D. (Columbia University), George Knight, Ph.D. (Arizona State University), Sandra Losoya, Ph.D. (Arizona State University), Alex Piquero, Ph.D. (Florida State University), Carol A. Schubert, M.P.H. (University of Pittsburgh), and Laurence Steinberg, Ph.D. (Temple University). The rationale for the study may be found in Mulvey et al., 2004, and the details of operations can be found in Schubert et al., 2004.

Source: Edward P. Mulvey. "Highlights from Pathways to Desistance: A Longitudinal Study of Serious Adolescent Offenders" (U.S. Department of Justice, OJJDP Juvenile Justice Fact Sheet, 2010), 1-4.

Study Findings

The primary findings of the study to date deal with the decrease in self-reported offending over time by most serious adolescent offenders, the relative inefficacy of longer juvenile incarcerations in decreasing recidivism, the effectiveness of community-based supervision as a component of aftercare for incarcerated youth, and the effectiveness of substance abuse treatment in reducing both substance use and offending by serious adolescent offenders.

Most youth who commit felonies greatly reduce their offending over time, regardless of the intervention. Approximately 91.5 percent of youth in the study reported decreased or limited illegal activity during the first 3 years following their court involvement. In particular, two groups of male offenders—those with high, stable offending rates, and those with high, but declining offending rates—had very different outcomes despite similar treatment by the juvenile justice system (see Figure 1). For both groups, approximately 40 percent of offenders were in jail or prison across the 3-year followup period (see "Study Design"); each group also had similar percentages under detention or in a contracted residential placement (about 20 percent of each group was in each of these forms of supervision). Overall, approximately 50 percent of the youth in each group were under some form of supervision during the followup period, and about 20 percent were receiving community-based services.

Therefore, institutional placement and the type of setting appeared to have little effect on which high-end offenders persisted in offending and which reduced their offending (Mulvey, Steinberg, et al., 2010).

Longer stays in juvenile institutions do not reduce recidivism, and some youth who had the lowest offending levels reported committing more crimes after being incarcerated. The researchers looked at two groups of cases that were adjudicated in juvenile court at both the Philadelphia and metropolitan Phoenix sites. Of 921 offenders who remained in the juvenile system, 502 received probation and 419 were placed in institutions. The researchers then matched the two groups based on 66 variables that would

affect the probability that an individual offender would be placed in an institution to rule out those variables as potential causes of different outcomes between the placement and probation groups. After 64 of those 66 variables were ruled out, the two groups showed no significant differences in their rate either of rearrest or of self-reported offending. Also, when the researchers matched groups of offenders with similar backgrounds, they found that, for lengths of stay between 3 and 13 months, youth who stayed in institutions longer showed little or no decrease in their rates of rearrest compared with those with shorter stays (Loughran et al., 2009). Moreover, in another set of analyses, the study found that the group of offenders with the lowest levels of self-reported offending actually raised their levels of offending by a small but statistically significant amount following stays in institutions (Mulvey, Steinberg, et al., 2010).

Community-based supervision as a component of aftercare is effective for youth who have committed serious offenses, and offenders who receive community-based services following incarceration are more likely to attend school, go to work, and reduce offending. Because the project collects monthly data about institutional placement, probation, and involvement in community-based services, investigators were able to examine the effects of aftercare services for 6 months after a court-ordered placement (the period when such services are presumably provided with greater intensity in most locales). Increasing the duration of community supervision reduced reported reoffending. In addition, although returning offenders generally received supervision only, rather than treatment, the research showed that in the 6 months after release, youth who were involved in community-based services were more likely to avoid further involvement with the juvenile justice system (Chung, Schubert, and Mulvey, 2007).

Substance abuse treatment reduces both substance use and criminal offending, at least in the short term. Research has consistently shown that substance use among adolescents is linked to serious juvenile offending. The adolescent offenders profiled in the Pathways to Desistance

---

[2]During their baseline interviews, 57 percent of the respondents reported that they had smoked marijuana in the previous 6 months, 40 percent had drunk alcohol during that time, and 27 percent had used cocaine, hallucinogens, or other drugs. Approximately 48 percent of the study participants had used multiple substances during the 6 months before the baseline interviews and, in each followup interview, about 28 to 30 percent reported using multiple substances in the previous 6 months. In addition, at the time of the baseline interview, 37 percent of male study participants and 35 percent of female participants were diagnosed with a substance use disorder in the previous year, three to four times the rate in the general youth population (Mulvey, Schubert, and Chassin, 2010).

study reported very high levels of substance use and substance use problems.[2] Substance use was linked to other illegal activities engaged in by the study participants. It is a strong, prevalent predictor of offending. The presence of a drug or alcohol disorder and the level of substance use were both shown to be strongly and independently related to the level of self-reported offending and the number of arrests. This relationship held even when drug-related offenses and behaviors were removed from the offending measures, and characteristics including socioeconomic status, gender, and ethnicity were controlled statistically (Mulvey, Schubert, and Chassin, 2010). The good news, however, is that treatment appears to reduce both substance use and offending, at least in the short term. Youth whose treatment lasted for at least 90 days and included significant family involvement showed significant reductions in alcohol use, marijuana use, and offending over the following 6 months (Chassin et al., 2009).

Study Design

The study involved extensive interviews with young offenders at enrollment, followup interviews every 6 months for the first 3 years and annually thereafter, interviews following release from residential facilities, collateral interviews with family members and friends, data collection about significant life events recorded at the monthly level, and reviews of official records data. Enrollment took place between November 2000 and March 2003, and the research team concluded data collection in 2010.

The study followed young offenders in two metropolitan areas: Maricopa County (metropolitan Phoenix), AZ, and Philadelphia County, PA. Youth enrollees in the study were 14 to 17 years old and found guilty of at least one serious (almost exclusively felony-level) violent crime, property offense, or drug offense as the result of their current petition to court. The study limited the proportion of male drug offenders to 15 percent at each site to ensure a heterogeneous sample of serious offenders. Because investigators also wanted to ensure a large enough sample of female offenders—a group neglected in previous research—they did not apply this limit to female drug offenders. In addition, youth whose cases

were considered for trial in the adult criminal justice system were still enrolled.

Conclusions

The most important conclusion of the study is that even adolescents who have committed serious offenses are not necessarily on track for adult criminal careers. Only a small proportion of the offenders studied continued to offend at a high level throughout the followup period. The great majority reported low levels of offending after court involvement, and a significant portion of those with the highest levels of offending reduced their reoffending dramatically. Two factors that appear to distinguish high-end desisters from persisters are lower levels of substance use and greater stability in their daily routines, as measured by stability in living arrangements and work and school attendance.

The second conclusion is that incarceration may not be the most appropriate or effective option, even for many of the most serious adolescent offenders. Longer stays in juvenile facilities did not reduce reoffending; institutional placement even raised offending levels in those with the lowest level of offending. Youth who received community-based supervision and aftercare services were more likely to attend school, go to work, and avoid further offending during the 6 months after release, and longer supervision periods increased these benefits.

Finally, substance use is a major factor in continued criminal activity by serious adolescent offenders. Substance abuse treatment for young offenders reduces both substance use and non-drug-related offending in the short term, if the treatment period is long enough and if families take part in the treatment with the offender. Most young offenders who are diagnosed with substance abuse disorders, however, do receive treatment in institutions or community-based settings. Given that community-based supervision may reduce reoffending and promote pro-social attitudes and behaviors, and that continued substance abuse treatment may be needed to prevent longer term relapses, integrating substance abuse treatment into community-based services may realize greater benefits in reducing serious adolescent offending while providing more efficient and effective delivery of services.

References

Chassin, L., Knight, G., Vargas-Chanes, D., Losoya, S., and Naranjo, D. (2009). Substance use treatment outcomes in a sample of male serious juvenile offenders. *Journal of Substance Abuse Treatment* 36:183–194.

Chung, L., Schubert, C. A., and Mulvey, E. P. (2007). An empirical portrait of community reentry among serious juvenile offenders in two metropolitan cities. *Criminal Justice and Behavior* 34(11): 1402–1426.

Loughran, T., Mulvey, E. P., Schubert, C. A., Fagan, J., Losoya, S. H., and Piquero, A. R. (2009). Estimating a dose-response relationship between length of stay and future recidivism in serious juvenile offenders. *Criminology* 47(3):699–740.

Mulvey, E. P., Schubert, C. A., and Chassin, L. (2010). *Substance Use and Offending in Serious Adolescent Offenders.* Washington, DC:

U.S. Department of Justice, Office of Justice Programs, Office of Juvenile Justice and Delinquency Prevention.

Mulvey, E. P., Steinberg, L., Fagan, J., Cauffman, E., Piquero, A., Chassin, L., Knight, G., Brame, R., Schubert, C., Hecker, T., and Losoya, S. 2004. Theory and research on desistance from antisocial activity in serious juvenile offenders. *Youth Violence and Juvenile Justice* 2(3):213–236.

Mulvey, E. P., Steinberg, L., Piquero, A. R., Besana, M., Fagan, J., Schubert, C. A., and Cauffman, E. (2010). Longitudinal offending trajectories among serious adolescent offenders. *Development & Psychopathology* 22:453–475.

Schubert, C., Mulvey, E., Cauffman, E., Steinberg, L., Losoya, S., Hecker, T., Chassin, L., and Knight, G. (2004). Operational lessons from the Pathways to Desistance Study. *Youth Violence and Juvenile Justice* 2(3):237–255.

REVIEW QUESTIONS

1. What does the author conclude regarding the effectiveness of longer stays in juvenile institutions in reducing recidivism for youth offenders?

2. What does the author conclude regarding the effectiveness of substance abuse treatment in reducing offending and substance use for young offenders?

3. What does the author conclude regarding the effectiveness of community-based supervision for youth offenders?

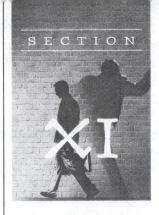

Integrated Theoretical Models and New Perspectives of Crime

T his section will introduce integrated theories, those in which two or more traditional theories are merged into one cohesive model. We will then discuss the pros and cons of integrating theories and explain the various ways theories can be integrated. A review of integrated theories will demonstrate the many ways different theories have been merged to form more empirically valid explanations for criminal behavior.

This section examines relatively recent changes in criminological development, with virtually all of these advances having taken place in the last few decades. Specifically, we discuss the types of models that modern explanatory formulations seem to have adopted, namely integrated theories. Of course, other unique theoretical frameworks have been presented in the last 30 years, but most of the dominant models presented during this time fall into the category of integrated theories.

Integrated theories attempt to put together two or more traditionally separate models of offending to form one unified explanatory theory. Given the empirical validity of most of the theories discussed in previous sections, as well as the failure of these previously examined theories to explain all variation in offending behavior, it makes sense that theorists would try to combine the best of several theories while disregarding or deemphasizing the concepts and propositions that don't seem to be as scientifically valid. Furthermore, some forms of theoretical integration deal with only concepts or propositions, while others vary by level of analysis (micro vs. macro, or both). Although such integrated formulations sound attractive and appear to be surefire ways to develop sounder explanatory models of behavior, they have a number of weaknesses and criticisms. Here, we explore these issues, as well as the best-known and most accepted integrated theories that are currently being examined and tested in the criminological literature.

Integrated Theories

About 30 years ago at a conference at the State University of New York at Albany, leading scholars in criminological theory development and research came together to discuss the most important issues in the growing area of theoretical integration.[1] Some integrated theories go well beyond formulating relationships between two or more traditionally separate explanatory models; they actually fuse the theories into one, all-encompassing framework. The following sections will examine why integrated theories became popular over the last several decades while discussing different types of integrated theories, the strengths and weaknesses of theoretical integration, and several of the better-known and better-respected integrated theories.

The Need for Integrated Theories in Criminology

The emphasis on theoretical integration is a relatively recent development that has evolved due to the need to improve the empirical validity of traditional theories, which suffer from lack of input from various disciplines.[2] This was the result of the history of criminological theory, which we discussed in prior sections of this book. Specifically, most 19th-century theories of criminal behavior are best described as based on single-factor (e.g., IQ) or limited-factor (e.g., stigmata) reductionism. Later, in the early 1900s, a second stage of theoretical development involved the examination of various social, biological, and psychological factors, which became known as the multiple-factor approach and is most commonly linked with the work of Sheldon and Eleanor Glueck.

Finally, in the latter half of the 20th century, a third stage of theoretical development and research in criminology became dominant, which represented a backlash against the multiple-factor approach. This stage has been called *systemic reductionism*, which refers to pervasive attempts to explain criminal behavior in terms of a particular system of knowledge.[3] For example, a biologist who examines only individuals' genotypes will likely not be able to explain much criminal behavior because he is missing a lot of information about the environment in which the people live, such as their levels of poverty or unemployment. For the last 60 years, the criminological discipline in the United States has been dominated by sociologists, which is largely due to the efforts and influence of Edwin Sutherland (see Section VIII). Thus, as one expert has observed:

> It is not surprising to find that most current explanations of criminal behavior are sociologically based and are attempts to explain variations in the rates of criminal behavior as opposed to individual instances of that behavior. . . . [E]ven when the effort is to explain individual behavior, the attempt is to use exposure to or belief in cultural or social factors to explain individual instances or patterns of criminal behavior. . . . We find ourselves at the stage of development in criminology where a variety of sociological systemic reductionistic explanations dominate, all of which have proven to be relatively inadequate (to the standard of total explanation, prediction, or control) in explaining the individual occurrence or the distribution of crime through time or space.[4]

---

[1]For a compilation of the papers presented at this conference, see Steven F. Messner, Marvin D. Krohn, and Allen E. Liska, eds., *Theoretical Integration in the Study of Deviance and Crime: Problems and Prospects* (Albany: State University of New York Press, 1989).

[2]This discussion is largely drawn from Charles F. Wellford, "Towards an Integrated Theory of Criminal Behavior," in Messner et al., *Theoretical Integration*, 119–27.

[3]Ibid., 120.

[4]Ibid., 120–21.

Other criminologists have also noted this sociological dominance, with some going as far to claim that:

Sutherland and the sociologists were intent on turning the study of crime into an exclusively sociological enterprise and . . . they overreacted to the efforts of potential intruders to capture some of what they regarded as their intellectual turf.[5]

This dominance of sociology over the discipline is manifested in many obvious ways. For example, virtually all professors of criminology have doctorates of philosophy (PhDs) in sociology or criminal justice, and virtually no professors have a degree in biology, neuropsychology, or other fields that obviously have important influence on human behavior. Furthermore, virtually no undergraduate (or even graduate) programs in criminal justice and criminology currently require students to take a course that covers principles in biology, psychology, anthropology, or economics; rather, virtually all the training is sociology based. In fact, most criminal justice programs in the United States do not even offer a course in biopsychological approaches to understanding criminal behavior, despite the obvious need for and relevance of such perspectives.

Many modern criminologists now acknowledge the limitations of this state of systemic reductionism, which limits theories to only one system of knowledge, in this case sociology.[6] What resulted is a period of relative stagnation in theoretical development, with experts regarding the 1970s as "one of the least creative periods in criminological history."[7] In addition, the mainstream theories that were introduced for most of the 1900s (such as differential association, strain, social bonding, and labeling, which we reviewed in previous sections) received limited empirical support, which should not be too much of a surprise given that they were based on principles of only one discipline, namely, sociology. Thus, it has been proposed that integrated theories evolved as a response to such limitations and the need to revitalize progress in the area of criminological theory building.[8] After reviewing some of the many integrated theories that have been proposed in the last two decades, we think readers will agree that combining explanatory models has indeed helped stimulate much growth in the area of criminological theory development. But, before examining these theories, it is important to discuss the varying forms they take.

Different Forms of Integrated Theories

There are several different types of integrated theories, which are typically categorized by the way that their creators propose that the theories should be fused together. The three most common forms of propositional theoretical integration, meaning synthesis of theories based on their postulates, are known as end-to-end, side-by-side, and up-and-down integration.[9] We will first explore each of these types before discussing a few more variations of combining theoretical concepts and propositions.

[5]This quote is taken from Stephen E. Brown, Finn-Aage Esbensen, and Gilbert Geis, *Criminology: Explaining Crime and Its Context*, 8th ed. (Cincinnati: Anderson, 2013), 251 (see chap. 6), regarding claims made by Robert Sampson and John Laub, "Crime and Deviance over the Life Course: The Salience of Adult Social Bonds," *American Sociological Review* 55 (1990): 609–27. See also discussion in Richard A. Wright, "Edwin H. Sutherland," *Encyclopedia of Criminology*, Vol. 1, ed. Richard A. Wright and J. Mitchell Miller (New York: Routledge, 2005).

[6]Wellford, "Towards an Integrated Theory"; Sampson and Laub, "Crime and Deviance."

[7]Wellford, "Towards an Integrated Theory," 120, citing Frank P. Williams III, "The Demise of Criminological Imagination: A Critique of Recent Criminology," *Justice Quarterly* 1 (1984): 91–106.

[8]Wellford, "Towards an Integrated Theory."

[9]This typology is largely based on Travis Hirschi, "Separate and Unequal Is Better," *Journal of Research in Crime and Delinquency* 16 (1979): 34–37.

End-to-End Integration

The first type, end-to-end theoretical integration, typically is used when theorists expect that one theory will come before or after another in terms of temporal ordering of causal factors. This type of integration is more developmental in the sense that it tends to propose a certain ordering of the component theories that are being merged. For example, an integrated theory may claim that most paths toward delinquency and crime have their early roots in the breakdown of social attachments and controls (i.e., social bonding theory), but later, the influence of negative peers (i.e., differential association) becomes more emphasized. Thus, such a model would look like this:

Weak Social Bond → Negative Peer Associations → Crime

Such an integrated model is referred to as an *end-to-end* (or *sequential*) integration, which is appropriately named because it conveys the linkage of the theories based on the temporal ordering of two or more theories in their causal timing.[10] Specifically, the breakdown of social bonds comes first, followed by the negative peer relations. Another way of saying this is that the breakdown of social bonds is expected to have a more remote or indirect influence on crime, which is mediated by differential peer influences; on the other hand, according to this model, peer influences are expected to have a more immediate or direct effect on crime, with no mediating influences of other variables. This model is hypothetical and presented to illustrate the end-to-end form of integration, but we will see that some established frameworks have incorporated similar propositions regarding social bonding and differential association and reinforcement theories.

Many of the traditionally separate theories that we have examined in previous sections tend to differ in their focus on either remote or immediate causal factors.[11] For instance, one of the assumptions of differential association theory is that psychological learning of crime is based on day-to-day (or even moment-to-moment) learning, so the emphasis is on more immediate causes of crime, namely, interactions with peers and significant others. On the other hand, other theories tend to focus more on remote causes of crime, such as social disorganization and strain theory, which place the emphasis on social structure factors (e.g., relative deprivation or industrialization) that most experts would agree are typically not directly implicated in situational decisions to engage in an actual criminal act but are extremely important nonetheless.

This situation seems conducive to the use of end-to-end integration, and often, the theories seem to complement each other quite well, as in our hypothetical example in which social control theory proposes the remote cause (i.e., weakened bonds) and differential association theory contributes the more direct, proximate cause (i.e., negative peer influence). On the other hand, two or more theories that focus only on more immediate causes of crime would be harder to combine because they both claim they are working at the same time, each in a sense competing against the other for being the primary direct cause of criminal activity; thus, they would be unlikely to fuse together as nicely and would not complement one another. Also, some theorists have argued that end-to-end integration is simply a form of theoretical elaboration, which we will discuss later. Another major limitation of end-to-end integration is the issue of whether the basic assumptions of the included theories are consistent with one another. We will investigate this in the following section, which discusses criticism of integration. But first, we must examine the other forms of theoretical integration.

Side-by-Side Integration

Another type of integrated theory is called side-by-side (or horizontal) integration. In the most common form of side-by-side integration, cases are classified by a certain criterion (e.g., impulsive vs. planned), and two or

---

[10]Allen E. Liska, Marvin D. Krohn, and Steven F. Messner, "Strategies and Requisites for Theoretical Integration in the Study of Crime and Deviance," in Messner et al., *Theoretical Integration*, 1–19.

[11]Much of our discussion of these forms of integration is taken from ibid.

more theories are considered parallel explanations depending on what type of case is being considered. So, when the assumptions or target offenses of two or more theories are different, a side-by-side integration is often the most natural way to integrate them. For example, low self-control theory may be used to explain impulsive criminal activity, whereas rational choice theory may be used to explain criminal behavior that involves planning, such as white-collar crime. Traditionally, many theorists would likely argue that low self-control and rational choice theory are quite different, almost inherently opposing perspectives of crime. However, contemporary studies and theorizing have shown that the two models complement and fill gaps in the other.[12] Specifically, the rational choice and deterrence framework has always had a rather hard time explaining and predicting why individuals often do very stupid things for which there is little payoff and a high likelihood of getting in serious trouble, so the low self-control perspective helps fill in this gap by explaining that some individuals are far more impulsive and are more concerned about the immediate payoff (albeit often small) than they are about any long-term consequences.

An illustration of side-by-side integration of these two theories might thus look something like this:

For most typical individuals

High Self-Control → Consideration of Potential Negative
Consequences → Deterred from Committing Crime

For more impulsive individuals or activities

Low Self-Control → Desire for Immediate Payoff → Failure to
Consider Consequences → Decision to Commit Criminal Act

This side-by-side integration shows how two different theories can each be accurate, depending on what type of individual or criminal activity is being considered. As some scholars have concluded, rational choice theory is likely not a good explanation for homicides between intimates (which tend to be spontaneous acts), but it may be very applicable to corporate crime.[13]

Up-and-Down Integration

Another way of combining two or more theories is referred to as up-and-down (or deductive) integration. It is generally considered the classic form of theoretical integration because it has been done relatively often in the history of criminological theory development, even before it was considered integration. It often involves increasing

---

[12]Daniel Nagin and Raymond Paternoster, "Enduring Individual Differences and Rational Choice Theories of Crime," *Law and Society Review* 27 (1993): 467–96; Alex Piquero and Stephen Tibbetts, "Specifying the Direct and Indirect Effects of Low Self-Control and Situational Factors in Offenders' Decision Making: Toward a More Complete Model of Rational Offending," *Justice Quarterly* 13 (1996): 481–510; Stephen Tibbetts and Denise Herz, "Gender Differences in Factors of Social Control and Rational Choice," *Deviant Behavior* 17 (1996): 183–208 (chap. 8, n. 90); Stephen Tibbetts and David Myers, "Low Self-Control, Rational Choice, and Student Test Cheating," *American Journal of Criminal Justice* 23 (1999): 179–200; Bradley Wright, Avshalom Caspi, and Terrie Moffitt, "Does the Perceived Risk of Punishment Deter Criminally Prone Individuals? Rational Choice, Self-Control, and Crime," *Journal of Research in Crime and Delinquency* 41 (2004): 180–213. For a review, see Stephen Tibbetts, "Individual Propensities and Rational Decision-Making: Recent Findings and Promising Approaches," in *Rational Choice and Criminal Behavior: Recent Research and Future Challenges*, ed. Alex Piquero and Stephen Tibbetts (New York: Routledge, 2002), 3–24.

[13]Liska et al., "Strategies and Requisites." For a review, see Brown et al., *Criminology: Explaining Crime*. For a recent study of rational choice applied to corporate crime, see Nicole Leeper Piquero, M. Lyn Exum, and Sally S. Simpson, "Integrating the Desire-for-Control and Rational Choice in a Corporate Crime Context," *Justice Quarterly* 22 (2005): 252–81.

the level of abstraction of a single theory so that postulates seem to follow from a conceptually broader theory. Up-and-down integration can take two prevalent forms: theoretical reduction and theoretical synthesis.

Theoretical reduction is typically done when it becomes evident "that theory A contains more abstract or general assumptions than theory B and, therefore, that key parts of theory B can be accommodated within the structure of theory A."[14] We have discussed this form of integration previously in this book without actually calling it by name. For example, in Section VIII, we discussed how differential reinforcement theory subsumed Sutherland's differential association theory. By equating concepts contained in both theories, the authors of differential reinforcement argued somewhat effectively that the learning that takes place through interactions with primary groups is one type of conditioning.[15] As you will recall, the main point is that the concepts and propositions of differential reinforcement theory are more general than, but entirely consistent with, those of differential association theory, such that the latter is typically a specific form of the former model. In other words, differential reinforcement is a much more broad, general theory, which accounts for not only differential association (i.e., classical conditioning) but also many other theoretical concepts and propositions (operant conditioning, modeling, or imitation).

This same type of theoretical reduction was also discussed in Section VI when we noted that general strain theory subsumed Merton's traditional strain theory. Specifically, traditional strain theory focused on only one type of strain: failure to achieve positively valued goals. While general strain theory also places an emphasis on failure to achieve positively valued goals, it is more general and broader because it also focuses on two other forms of strain: loss of positively valued stimuli and exposure to noxious stimuli. Therefore, it seems to make sense that general strain theory would subsume traditional strain theory, because the concepts and principles of traditional strain appear to simply represent a specific type of general strain and can be fully accounted for by the more general version of the theory.[16]

Despite the obvious efficiency in theoretical reduction, many theorists have criticized such subsuming of theories by another. Specifically, many experts in the social sciences view such deduction as a form of theoretical imperialism, because the theory being deduced essentially loses its unique identity.[17] Therefore, the very phrase *theoretical reduction* generally has a negative connotation among scholars. In fact, one of the most accepted reductions in 20th-century criminological literature, the differential association–differential reinforcement synthesis we referred to above, has been condemned as a "revisionist takeover . . . a travesty of Sutherland's position."[18] So, even the most widely known and cited forms of theoretical reduction have been harshly criticized, which gives readers some idea of how much social scientists can frown upon the subsuming of one theory by another.

The other form of up-and-down integration is referred to as *theoretical synthesis*, which is "done by abstracting more general assumptions from theories A and B, allowing parts of both theories to be incorporated in a new theory C."[19] This form of up-and-down integration is more uncommon in social science than theoretical reduction, perhaps because it is more difficult to achieve successfully, since by definition it requires the formulation of a new theory with new concepts or hypotheses that are not already found in the original component models. Furthermore, if the constituent theories are competing explanations, then it is quite likely that new terminology will have to be created

---

[14]Liska et al., "Strategies and Requisites," 10.

[15]Liska et al., "Strategies and Requisites," 13; Robert L. Burgess and Ronald Akers, "Differential Association-Reinforcement Theory of Criminal Behavior," *Social Problems* 14 (1966): 128–46; Ronald Akers, *Deviant Behavior: A Social Learning Approach*, 3rd ed. (Belmont: Wadsworth, 1985) (see chap. 8).

[16]Robert Agnew, "Foundation for a General Strain Theory of Crime and Delinquency," *Criminology* 30 (1992): 47–87; Robert Agnew and Helen R. White, "An Empirical Test of General Strain Theory," *Criminology* 30 (1992): 475–99.

[17]Liska et al., "Strategies and Requisites."

[18]This quote is from Ian Taylor, Paul Walton, and Jock Young, *The New Criminology* (New York: Harper & Row, 1973), 131–32. See discussion in Liska et al., "Strategies and Requisites," 13.

[19]Liska et al., "Strategies and Requisites," 10.

or incorporated to resolve these differences.[20] However, if theoretical synthesis can be done correctly, it is perhaps the type of integration that provides the most advancement of theory development because, in addition to bringing together previously independent models, it also results in a new theory with predictions and propositions that go beyond the original frameworks.

One of the best-known and most accepted (despite its critics) examples of theoretical synthesis is Elliott's integrated model, which we review in detail later in this section.[21] For our purposes here, it is important only to understand why Elliott's model is considered theoretical synthesis. This is because Elliott's model integrates the concepts and propositions of various theories (e.g., social control and differential association) and contributes additional propositions that did not exist in the component theories.

Levels of Analysis of Integrated Theories

Beyond the variation in types of propositional theoretical integration discussed above, such synthesis of explanatory models also differs in terms of the level of analysis that is being considered. Specifically, the integrated models can include component theories of micro-micro, macro-macro, or even micro-macro (called *cross-level*) combinations. For example, Elliott's integrated theory is a micro-micro level theory, which means that all of the component theories that make up the synthesized model refer to the individual as the unit of analysis. Although these models can provide sound understanding for why certain individuals behave in certain ways, they typically do not account for differences in criminality across groups (gender, socioeconomic groups, etc.).

On the other hand, some integrated models include theories from only macro levels. A good example of this type of integration is seen in Bursik's synthesis of conflict theory and the social disorganization framework.[22] Both of these component theories focus only on the macro (group) level of analysis, thus neglecting the individual level; for example, they would fail to explain why some individuals do or do not commit crime even in the same structural environment.

The most complicated integrated theories, at least in terms of levels of analysis, are those that include both micro and macro models. Such models are likely the most difficult to synthesize successfully because this involves bringing together rather unnatural relationships between individual-based propositions and group-level postulates. However, when done effectively, such a model can be rather profound in terms of explanation of crime. After all, one of the primary objectives of a good theory is to explain behavior across as many circumstances as possible. Thus, a theory that can effectively explain why crime occurs in certain individuals as well as certain groups would be better than a theory that explains crime across only individuals or only groups.

An example of such a theory is Braithwaite's reintegrative shaming theory, which begins with an individual (or micro) level theory of social control and bonding—which he refers to as interdependency—and then relates levels of this concept to a group or community (or macro) level theory of bonding—which he refers to as communitarianism.[23] This theory will be discussed in far more detail later, but it is important here to acknowledge the advantages of explaining both the micro (individual) and macro (group) level of analysis in explanations of criminal behavior, such as in the theory of reintegrative shaming.

---

[20]David Wagner and Joseph Berger, "Do Sociological Theories Grow?" *American Journal of Sociology* 90 (1985): 697–728.

[21]Delbert Elliott, Suzanne S. Ageton, and Rachelle J. Canter, "An Integrated Theoretical Perspective on Delinquent Behavior," *Journal of Research in Crime and Delinquency* 16 (1979): 3–27. See also discussion in Delbert Elliott, "The Assumption That Theories Can Be Combined with Increased Explanatory Power: Theoretical Integrations," in *Theoretical Methods in Criminology*, ed. Robert F. Meier (Beverly Hills: Sage, 1985), 123–49. Discussion of Elliott's model as an example of theoretical synthesis can be found in Charles R. Tittle, "Prospects for Synthetic Theory: A Consideration of Macrolevel Criminological Activity," in Messner et al., *Theoretical Integration*, 161–78.

[22]Robert J. Bursik, "Political Decision Making and Ecological Models of Delinquency, Conflict and Consensus," in Messner et al., *Theoretical Integration*, 105–18.

[23]John Braithwaite, *Crime, Shame and Reintegration* (Cambridge: Cambridge University, 1989).

Ultimately, the levels of analysis of any component theories are important considerations in the creation of integrated models of crime. It is particularly important to ensure that the merging of certain theories from within or across particular levels makes rational sense and, most important, advances our knowledge and understanding of the causes of crime.

Additional Considerations regarding Types of Integration

Beyond the basic forms of propositional integration models and levels of analysis, there are two additional types of integration—conceptual integration and theoretical elaboration—that are quite common, perhaps even more common than the traditional forms discussed above. Conceptual integration involves the synthesis of models in which "the theorist equates concepts in different theories, arguing that while the words and terms are different, the theoretical meanings and operations of measurement are similar."[24] Essentially, the goal in such a formulation is to take the primary constructs of two or more theories and merge them into a more general framework that aids understanding in explaining behavior by unifying terms that represent fundamentally similar phenomena or issues. Such formulations are considered less intrusive on the component theories than the propositional integrations we discussed previously.

One of the first and most cited examples of conceptual integration was provided by Pearson and Weiner in 1985.[25] As shown in Table 11.1, Pearson and Weiner attempted to map the various concepts of numerous criminological theories. This was done by creating categories that numerous concepts from various theories would appear to fit into through their inclusion in explanatory models of criminal behavior and across levels of explanation. Although based on a social learning and differential reinforcement perspective, Pearson and Weiner's model attempts to include concepts of virtually all existing theories of crime and delinquency. A particular strength is that this model includes feedback or behavioral consequence elements, as well as classifying each model by unit of measurement and analysis.

For example, as illustrated in Table 11.1, the conceptual model shows that differential association theory has concepts that apply to all internal aspects and one of the two concepts under consequences or feedback at the micro level but none of the aspects under the external micro level or any of the four macro-level concepts. On the other hand, Marxist-critical theory is shown to apply to three of the internal micro and one of the consequences or feedback level concepts and to most of the macro-level concepts as well. Although only some of the theories that we have discussed in this book are included, largely because Pearson and Weiner's conceptual integration was done in the mid-1980s, this model includes most of the dominant theoretical frameworks that were prevalent in the criminological literature at the time of their formulation. Thus, this conceptual model remains as a sort of prototype for future attempts to conceptually integrate established theories explaining criminal conduct.

One notable strength of Pearson and Weiner's conceptual integration is the inclusion of most mainstream theories—differential association, labeling, social control, deterrence, economic, routine activities, neutralization, strain, normative (culture) conflict, generalized strain, and Marxist-critical group conflict—in existence at the time in which they created their integrated framework. Another strength of their integrated framework is the fact that they account for concepts at different levels of analysis, namely the micro (individual) and macro (group) levels, as shown in Table 11.1. So, the framework clearly does a good job at creating links between the most prominent theories in terms of the concepts they propose as the primary causes of crime.

However, Pearson and Weiner's conceptually integrated framework does have several notable weaknesses. One of the most prominent criticisms of the conceptual model is that it is based on a single theory, specifically social

[24]Liska et al., "Strategies and Requisites," 15; definition adapted from Frank S. Pearson and Neil Alan Weiner, "Toward an Integration of Criminological Theories," *Journal of Criminal Law and Criminology* 76 (1985): 116–50.

[25] Frank S. Pearson and Neil Alan Weiner, "Toward an Integration." See review in Thomas J. Bernard and Jeffrey B. Snipes, "Theoretical Integration in Criminology," in *Crime and Justice Review*, Vol. 20, ed. Michael Tonry (Chicago: University of Chicago Press, 1996), 301–48.

Table 11.1 Mapping of the Selected Criminological Theories into the Integrative Structure

INTEGRATIVE CONSTRUCTS

Selected Criminological Theories	MICRO LEVEL — Antecedent — INTERNAL				EXTERNAL		CONSEQUENCES OR FEEDBACK		MACRO LEVEL — SOCIAL STRUCTURAL PRODUCTION AND DISTRIBUTION OF:			
	Utility Demand (Deprivation)	Behavioral Skill	Rules of Expedience	Rules of Morality	Signs of Favorable Opportunities (Descriminative Stimuli)	Behavioral Resources	Utility Reception	Information Acquisition	Utilities	Opportunities	Rules of Expedience and Morality	Belief about Sanctioning Practices
Differential association	✓	✓	✓	✓			✓					
Negative labeling	✓	✓	✓	✓			✓					
Social control:												
1. Attachment	✓		✓		✓		✓					
2. Commitment	✓		✓		✓			✓				
3. Involvement			✓		✓			✓				
4. Belief				✓	✓			✓				
Deterrence	✓		✓	✓	✓		✓	✓				✓
Economic	✓	✓	✓	✓	✓		✓		✓	✓	✓	
Routine activities	✓		✓		✓	✓			✓	✓		
Neutralization	✓	✓	✓		✓			✓	✓	✓	✓	
Relative deprivation	✓	✓	✓		✓		✓		✓	✓		
Strain	✓	✓	✓	✓			✓	✓	✓	✓	✓	
Normative (culture) conflict				✓						✓	✓	
Generalized strain and normative (culture) conflict	✓	✓	✓		✓	✓	✓	✓	✓	✓	✓	
Marxist-critical/group conflict	✓		✓	✓			✓		✓	✓	✓	

Source: From Frank S. Pearson and Neil Alan Weiner, "Toward an Integration of Criminological Theories," *Journal of Criminal Law and Criminology* 76 (1985): 116–50 (table p.130).

© 2004-2008: *The Journal of Criminal Law and Criminology*—Northwestern University School of Law.

learning theory (tied to Akers's differential reinforcement and social learning theory, discussed in Section VIII), and the authors never really provide a strong argument for why they chose this particular base framework for their model. Another major weakness of this conceptual framework is that it completely neglects many biological and biosocial factors—hormones, neurotransmitters, toxins—that have been consistently shown to have profound effects on human behavior. Still, despite the criticisms of this integrated framework, respected theorists have noted that Pearson and Weiner's "integration of these concepts into a consistent, coherent framework is impressive," but the model has never received much attention in the criminological literature.[26]

However, despite the obvious tendency to simplify formulations through conceptual integration, many critics have claimed that such attempts are simply a means toward propositional integration. Thus, despite its categorization as conceptual, this type of integration is not necessarily seen as such, and it may be seen by many as a form of deductive integration. However, many experts have noted that conceptual integration is actually not a form of side-by-side integration, nor is it end-to-end integration. Rather, it is what it says it is: conceptual integration. It is nothing more and nothing less.[27] Therefore, it appears that conceptual integration is a distinct derivative form of integration and that it can and should occur independently if it helps to advance understanding of why people commit crime. As the most knowledgeable experts recently concluded, "establishing some conceptual equivalence is necessary for deductive integration."[28]

An additional variation of integration is theoretical elaboration, which is a strategy that takes an existing theory that is arguably underdeveloped and then further develops it by adding concepts and propositions from other theories. Many critics of traditional theoretical integration have argued that theoretical elaboration is a more attractive strategy because existing theories of offending are not developed enough to fully integrate them.[29] An example of theoretical integration can be seen in the expansion of rational choice theory, which had traditionally focused on ratios of perceived costs and benefits, to include deontological constructs, such as moral beliefs. Specifically, studies have consistently shown that ethical constraints condition the influence of expected consequences on criminal behavior ranging from violence to academic dishonesty to white-collar crime.[30] Although they are not without critics, most rational choice scholars appear to agree that such elaboration advanced the theoretical framework and made it a more accurate explanation of human behavior. In sum, theoretical integration, like conceptual integration, is an option for merging and improving theoretical models without completely synthesizing two or more entire paradigms.

Criticisms and Weaknesses of Integrated Theories

A number of criticisms have been leveled at theoretical integration. Perhaps one of the most obvious and prevalent, not to mention extremely valid, criticisms is the argument that caution should be taken in attempting to integrate

[26]Ronald L. Akers and Christine S. Sellers, *Criminological Theories: Introduction, Evaluation, and Application*, 6th ed. (Oxford: Oxford University Press, 2012), 288 (see chap. 8).

[27]Liska et al., "Strategies and Requisites," 15.

[28]Ibid., 16.

[29]Liska et al., "Strategies and Requisites," 16; Travis Hirschi, "Exploring Alternatives to Integrated Theory," in Messner et al., *Theoretical Integration*, 37–50; Terence P. Thornberry, "Reflections on the Advantages and Disadvantages of Theoretical Integration," in Messner et al., *Theoretical Integration*, 51–60; Robert F. Meier, "Deviance and Differentiation," in Messner et al., *Theoretical Integration*, 199–212.

[30]Amitai Etzioni, *The Moral Dimension: Toward a New Economics* (New York: Free Press, 1988); Ronet Bachman, Raymond Paternoster, and Sally Ward, "The Rationality of Sexual Offending: Testing a Deterrence/Rational Choice Conception of Sexual Assault," *Law and Society Review* 26 (1992): 401–19; Raymond Paternoster and Sally Simpson, "Sanction Threats and Appeals to Morality: Testing a Rational Choice Model of Corporate Crime," *Law and Society Review* 30 (1996): 378–99; Stephen G. Tibbetts, "College Student Perceptions of Utility and Intentions of Test Cheating," doctoral dissertation, University of Maryland—College Park (Ann Arbor: UMI, 1997). For a review and discussion, see Sally Simpson, Nicole Leeper Piquero, and Raymond Paternoster, "Rationality and Corporate Offending Decisions," in Piquero and Tibbetts, *Rational Choice*, 25–40.

theories that have apparent contradictions or inconsistencies in their postulates.[31] As we have seen, different theories are based on varying, often opposite, perspectives of human nature. While most versions of strain theory (e.g., Merton's theory) assume that human beings are born with a natural tendency toward being good, most variations of control theory (e.g., Hirschi's social bonding and self-control theories) assume that humans are innately selfish and hedonistic. At the same time, most versions of learning theory (e.g., Sutherland's theory of differential association and Akers's differential reinforcement theory) assume that humans are born with a blank slate; in other words, people are born with neither good nor bad tendencies but rather learn their morality moment to moment from social interaction.

Obviously, attempts to integrate these theories face the hurdles of dealing with such obvious contradictions, and many formulations that do merge some of these perspectives simply do not deal with this issue. The failure to acknowledge, let alone explain, such inconsistencies is likely to result in regression of theoretical development instead of leading to progress in understanding, which is the primary goal of integrating theories in the first place.

Other experts have argued that any attempts to integrate theories must unite three different levels of analysis, including individual (micro), group (macro), and micro-situational, which merges the micro level with the spontaneous context.[32] While we agree that this would be the ideal for theory formulation, we know of no theory that does so. Therefore, this proposition is more of an ideal that has not yet been attempted. Thus, we are inclined to go with the best that has been offered by expert theorists. Still, in the future, it is hoped that such an integrated model will be offered that addresses all of these aspects in an explanatory model.

Another argument against theoretical integration is the stance that explanatory perspectives of crime are meant to stand alone. This is the position taken by Travis Hirschi, who has been one of the most cited and respected scholars in criminology over the last 40 years.[33] As others have noted, Hirschi confirmed his position on this debate unequivocally when he stated that "separate and unequal is better" than integrating traditionally independent theoretical models.[34]

This type of perspective is also called *oppositional tradition* or *theoretical competition*, because the separate theories are essentially pitted against one another in a form of battle or opposition. Although scientists are trained to always be skeptical of their own beliefs and open to other possibilities, especially the desire to refine theoretical models that are shown to be invalid, it is surprising that such a position exists. Despite the rather unscientific nature of this stance, such a position of oppositional tradition has many supporters. Specifically, one of the most respected and cited criminologists, Travis Hirschi, claimed:

> The first purpose of oppositional theory construction is to make the world safe for a theory contrary to currently accepted views. Unless this task is accomplished, there will be little hope for the survival of the theory and less hope for its development. Therefore, oppositional theorists should not make life easy for those interested in preserving the status quo. They should instead remain at all times blind to the weaknesses of their own position and stubborn in its defense. Finally, they should never smile.[35]

Unfortunately, this position against theoretical integration is presented in a very unscientific tone. After all, scientists should always be critical of their own views and theories. By stating that theorists should be "blind" to

---

[31]Much of this discussion is taken from Brown et al., *Criminology: Explaining Crime*; and Messner et al., *Theoretical Integration*.

[32]James Short, "The Level of Explanation Problem in Criminology," in *Theoretical Methods in Criminology*, ed. Robert Meier (Beverly Hills: Sage, 1985), 42–71. See also James Short, "On the Etiology of Delinquent Behavior," *Journal of Research in Crime and Delinquency* 16 (1979): 28–33.

[33]Bernard and Snipes, "Theoretical Integration"; Hirschi, "Exploring Alternatives."

[34]Hirschi, "Separate but Unequal."

[35]Hirschi, "Exploring Alternatives," 45.

opposing viewpoints and "stubborn" in their own perspective's defense, Hirschi advocates a position that is absolutely against science. Still, this statement, albeit flawed, demonstrates the extreme position against theoretical integration that is favorable toward having each independent theory standing opposed to others. It is our position that this stand does not have much defense, which is shown by Hirschi's lack of rational argument. Furthermore, it is generally acceptable to smile when presenting any theoretical or empirical conclusions, even when they involve opposition to or acceptance of integrated theoretical models of criminal behavior.

Perhaps one of the most important criticisms against Hirschi's and others' criticisms of integrated models is that most traditional models alone only explain a limited amount of variation in criminal activity. Elliott and colleagues have claimed the following:

> Stated simply, the level of explained variance attributable to separate theories is embarrassingly low, and, if sociological explanations for crime and delinquency are to have any significant impact upon future planning and policy, they must be able to demonstrate greater predictive power.[36]

While some put this estimate at 10% to 20% of the variance in illegal activities, this is simply an average across different theories and various forms of deviant behavior.[37] However, this range is an overestimate based on many studies investigating the accuracy of separate theories, which tend to show weak support (explaining well under 10% of the variation in offending), particularly social bonding and strain models.[38]

On the other hand, this estimated range of explained variance underestimates the empirical validity of some theoretical frameworks that consistently show high levels of explained variation in certain criminal behaviors. For example, a large number of studies investigating Akers's differential reinforcement and social learning theory (discussed in Section VIII), which examine not only a wide range of samples (in terms of age, nationality, and other demographic characteristics) but also a large range of deviant activities (e.g., cigarette smoking, drug usage, violent sexual crimes), consistently account for more than 20% of variation in such behaviors.[39] Specifically, most of these studies estimate that Akers's social learning model explains up to 68% or more of the variation in certain deviant behaviors, with the lowest estimate being around 30%.

Obviously, not all independent theories of crime lack empirical validity, so this does not support critics' claims that traditionally separate theories of crime do not do a good job of explaining criminal behavior. However, it is also true that many of the theories that do the best job in empirical tests for validity are those that are somewhat integrated

---

[36]Delbert Elliott, David Huizinga, and Suzanne Ageton, *Explaining Delinquency and Drug Use* (Beverly Hills: Sage, 1985), 125, as quoted in Bernard and Snipes, "Theoretical Integration," 306.

[37]This estimate can be found in Bernard and Snipes, "Theoretical Integration," 306, but is based on the estimates of others, as discussed in this work.

[38]See review in Akers and Sellers, *Criminological Theories.*

[39]Ronald Akers, Marvin Krohn, Lonn Lanza-Kaduce, and Maria Radosevich, "Social Learning and Deviant Behavior: A Specific Test of a General Theory," *American Sociological Review* 44 (1979): 635–55; Marvin Krohn and Lonn Lanza-Kaduce, "Community Context and Theories of Deviant Behavior: An Examination of Social Learning and Social Bonding Theories," *Sociological Quarterly* 25 (1984): 353–71; Lonn Lanza-Kaduce, Ronald Akers, Marvin Krohn, and Marcia Radosevich, "Cessation of Alcohol and Drug Use among Adolescents: A Social Learning Model," *Deviant Behavior* 5 (1984): 79–96; Ronald Akers and John Cochran, "Adolescent Marijuana Use: A Test of Three Theories of Deviant Behavior," *Deviant Behavior* 6 (1985): 323–46; Ronald Akers and Gang Lee, "Age, Social Learning, and Social Bonding in Adolescent Substance Use," *Deviant Behavior* 19 (1999): 1–25; Marvin Krohn, William Skinner, James Massey, and Ronald Akers, "Social Learning Theory and Adolescent Cigarette Smoking: A Longitudinal Study," *Social Problems* 32 (1985): 455–73; Ronald Akers and Gang Lee, "A Longitudinal Test of Social Learning Theory: Adolescent Smoking," *Journal of Drug Issues* 26 (1996): 317–43; Ronald Akers, Anthony La Greca, John Cochran, and Christine Sellers, "Social Learning Theory and Alcohol Behavior among the Elderly," *Sociological Quarterly* 30 (1989): 625–38; Scot Boeringer, Constance Shehan, and Ronald Akers, "Social Contexts and Social Learning in Sexual Coercion and Aggression: Assessing the Contribution of Fraternity Membership," *Family Relations* 40 (1991): 558–64; Sunghyun Hwang and Ronald Akers, "Adolescent Substance Use in South Korea: A Cross-Cultural Test of Three Theories," in *Social Learning Theory and the Explanation of Crime: A Guide for the New Century,* ed. Ronald Akers and Gary Jensen (New Brunswick: Transaction, 2003), 39–64.

in the sense that they often have been formed by merging traditional theories with other constructs and propositions, much like Akers's differential reinforcement theory, which added more modern psychological concepts and principles (e.g., operant conditioning and modeling) to Sutherland's traditional theory of differential association (see Section VIII). So, in a sense, an argument can be made that theoretical integration (or at least theoretical elaboration) had already occurred, which made this theory far more empirically valid than the earlier model.

Another example of the high level of empirical validity of existing models of offending can be found in some models of rational choice, which have been revised through theoretical elaboration and have explained more than 60% of the explained variation in deviant behavior.[40] However, much of the explanatory power of such frameworks relies on incorporating the constructs and principles of other theoretical models, which is what science is based on; specifically, they revise and improve theory based on what is evident from empirical testing. After all, even some of the harshest critics of theoretical integration admit that traditional theories do not own variables or constructs.[41] For example, Hirschi claimed:

> Integrationists somehow conclude that variables appear . . . with opposition theory labels attached to them. This allows them to list variables by the theory that owns them. Social disorganization theory . . . might own economic status, cultural heterogeneity, and mobility. . . . Each of the many variables is measured and . . . the theories are ranked in terms of the success of their variables in explaining variation in delinquency . . . such that integration is in effect *required* by the evidence and surprisingly easily accomplished.[42]

This is the way that science and theoretical development and revision are supposed to work, so in our opinion, this is exactly as it should be. All scientists and theoreticians should constantly be seeking to improve their explanatory models and be open to ways to do so, as opposed to being staunch supporters of one position and blind to existing evidence.

Despite the criticisms against theoretical integration, a strong argument has been made that theoretical competition and oppositional tradition are generally pointless.[43] A big reason for this belief among proponents of theoretical integration is that various theories tend to explain different types of crime and varying portions of the causal processes for behavior. For example, some theories focus more on property crimes while others focus on violent crimes, and some theories emphasize the antecedent or root causes of crime (e.g., genetics, poverty) while others emphasize more immediate causes (e.g., current social context at the scene). Given that there are multiple factors that contribute to crime and that different factors are more important for different types of crime, it only makes sense that a synthesis of traditionally separate theories must come together to explain the wide range of criminal activity that occurs in the real world.

Ultimately, there are both pros and cons of integrating theories. It is our belief that theoretical integration is generally a good thing, as long as there is caution and attention given to merging models that have opposing assumptions, such as those regarding the natural state of human beings (e.g., good vs. bad vs. blank slate). But only after considerable empirical research will the true validity of integrated models be tested, and many have already been put to the test. We will now examine a handful of integrated theories that have been proposed over the last couple of decades as well as the studies that have examined their empirical validity. Not surprisingly, some integrated and elaborated theories appear to be more valid than others, with most adding considerably to our understanding of

---

[40]For example, see Tibbetts, "College Student Perceptions," which showed that an elaborated rational choice model explained more than 60% of variation in test cheating among college students.

[41]See discussion in Bernard and Snipes, "Theoretical Integration," 306–7.

[42]Hirschi, "Exploring Alternatives," 41, as cited (revised) in Bernard and Snipes, "Theoretical Integration," 307.

[43]Bernard and Snipes, "Theoretical Integration," 306, based on the rationale provided by Elliott et al., *Explaining Delinquency.*

human behavior and contributing to explaining the reasons why certain individuals or groups commit criminal behavior more than others.

Examples of Integrated Criminological Theory

We have already discussed the advantages and disadvantages of theoretical integration, as well as the ways in which traditionally separate explanatory models are combined to form new, synthesized frameworks. We will now review a number of the most prominent examples of theoretical integration that have been proposed in the last 35 years, which is largely the time period when most attempts at integration have been presented. We hope that readers will critique each theory based on the criteria that we have already discussed, particularly noting the empirical validity of each model based on scientific observation and the logical consistency of its propositions.

Elliott's Integrated Model

Perhaps the first and certainly the most prominent integrated model is that proposed by Delbert Elliott and his colleagues in 1979, which has become known as Elliott's integrated model.[44] In fact, this model "opened the current round of debate on integration," because it was essentially the first major perspective proposed that clearly attempted to merge various traditionally separate theories of crime.[45] Elliott's integrated framework attempts to merge strain, social disorganization, control, and social learning and differential association-reinforcement perspectives for the purpose of explaining delinquency, particularly in terms of drug use but also for other forms of deviant behavior (see Figure 11.1).

As can be seen in Figure 11.1, the concepts and propositions of strain and social disorganization, as well as inadequate socialization, are considered antecedent (or root) causes of delinquency. In other words, failing to achieve one's goals (i.e., strain theory) and coming from a disadvantaged neighborhood (i.e., social disorganization) are key factors predisposing people to criminal behavior. Furthermore, the fact that many low-income households tend to lack adequate socialization, such as when a single parent has to work two or three jobs to make ends meet, is also a major root cause of delinquency.

Because this model clearly shows some constructs that lead to criminality as coming first (e.g., strain, social disorganization) and others as coming later (e.g., weak bonding and then affiliations with delinquents), this is a good example of end-to-end theoretical integration. In other words, this is an end-to-end form of integration because some models or concepts, such as strain, occur first, which then lead chronologically to other models and concepts, such as weak conventional bonding or strong delinquent bonding, which then lead to crime.

The notable ways in which this perspective becomes a true integrated model is seen in the mediating or intervening variables. Although some antecedent variables (such as strain) can lead directly to delinquent activity, most of the criminal activity is theoretically predicted through a process that would include a breakdown of conventional bonding (i.e., social control and bonding theory), which occurs in many individuals who experience strain or social disorganization in their neighborhoods along with inadequate socialization. Furthermore, individuals who have such a breakdown in conventional bonding tend to be more highly influenced by the associations that they make in the streets among their peers (i.e., differential association-reinforcement and social learning theory). According to Elliott's integrated theory, this factor—strong delinquent bonding—most directly results in delinquent behavior among most juvenile offenders.

One of the notable features of this theoretical model is that it allows for various types of individuals to become criminal. In other words, unlike traditionally separate frameworks that assume that offenders expect not to achieve

---

[44]Delbert Elliott, S. Ageton, and R. Cantor, "An Integrated Theoretical Perspective on Delinquent Behavior," *Journal of Research in Crime and Delinquency* 16 (1979): 3–27. For further elaboration and refinement of this theory, see Elliott et al., *Explaining Delinquency*.

[45]Bernard and Snipes, "Theoretical Integration," 310.

Figure 11.1	Elliott et al.'s integrated theoretical model

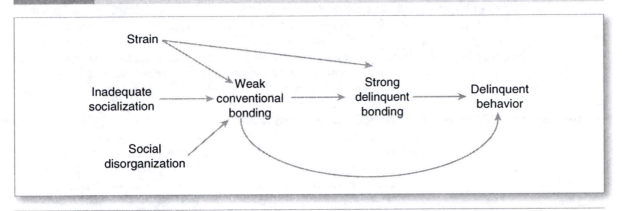

SOURCE: Elliott, Huizinga, & Ageton, 1985.

their goals (e.g., strain theory) or come from bad neighborhoods (e.g., Chicago or social disorganization theory), Elliott's integrated theory allows for a variety of possibilities when it comes to causal paths that explain how crime and delinquency develop in certain people and groups. This is what makes integrated models so much more powerful; namely, they bring several valid explanations together and allow for various possibilities to occur, all of which explain some criminality. Whereas traditional theories largely provide for only one causal process, Elliott and his colleagues showed right from the first major integrated theory that different types of trajectories, or paths to crime, are possible.

One of the major criticisms of merging such theories, particularly strain (which assumes individuals are born relatively good) and control or social bonding (which clearly assumes that people are born relatively bad [i.e., selfish, greedy, aggressive, etc.]), is that they tend to have extremely different, even opposite, assumptions of human behavior. As a recent review of theoretical integration noted, Elliott and his colleagues attempted to circumvent this obvious contrast in basic assumptions by claiming that the model allows for variation in individual motivations for why people engage in delinquency and crime.[46] For example, they claimed that failure to achieve one's goals (i.e., strain theory) is not always the motivation for crime; rather, crime can result from inadequate socialization or from coming from a disadvantaged neighborhood.

Furthermore, Elliott's integrated model allows for different forms of control or social bonding, with not all of the delinquents being required to have weak social bonds with conventional society. For instance, as can be seen in Figure 11.1, a person who has experienced strain (or failure to achieve her or his goals) can move directly to the social learning and differential association-reinforcement variables of strong delinquent bonding, so that the weak conventional bonding construct is not a required causal process in this theoretical model. So, while some critics claim that Elliott and his colleagues have combined theories that simply cannot be synthesized due to contrasting assumptions, we believe that this integrated theory did, in fact, find a logical and consistent way of showing how both models can be merged in a way that makes a lot of sense in the real world. On the other hand, the model does indeed claim that strain directly causes weak conventional bonding, and the theoretical framework implies that the probability of delinquency is highest when an individual experiences both strain and weak conventional bonding, so to some extent, the critics make an important point regarding the logical consistency of the full model, which Elliott and his colleagues have not adequately addressed.[47]

[46]Ibid.

[47]Ibid.

Despite the presence of elements of four traditionally separate theories (strain, social disorganization, social control or bonding, and social learning or differential association-reinforcement), Elliott and his colleagues identify this integrated theory with social control, as opposed to any of the other perspectives, which they argue is a more general theory and can explain crime and delinquency across different levels of explanation. They also note that the social control perspective is more sociological in the sense that it places more importance on the role of institutional structures in controlling criminal behavior.[48] Perhaps another reason why they identified their model with social control or bonding theory was because both intervening constructs represent types of bonds formed or not formed with others: weak conventional bonding and strong delinquent bonding. However, it is important to keep in mind that these constructs actually represent two traditionally separate theories, namely, social bonding theory and differential association-reinforcement or social learning, respectively.

The authors of this textbook believe that when an integrated theory (which claims to be such an integrated model) chooses a primary or dominant theory as its basis, this does not help in selling it to the scientific community, let alone others. A similar problem was seen in Pearson and Weiner's conceptual integration in their identifying a single traditionally separate theory—social learning or differential association-reinforcement—as the foundation or basis for their framework. Obviously, the first reaction by many theorists, even those that are not inherently against theoretical integration, would be somewhat cautious or even resistant. After all, why would a theory that claims to be integrated outright claim a single explanatory framework as its basis?

Rather, such models may be seen more as examples of theoretical elaboration, which tends to start with the assumptions and concepts of one theory and draw from other models to improve the base model. Still, despite the criticisms against identifying a single model as a basis for developing an integrated framework for explaining criminality, it is apparent that latitude has been granted. It is important to note that Elliott's model is considered the first true attempt at theoretical integration and is still widely respected as the prototype and example of what an integrated model could and should be.

Much of the empirical evidence supporting Elliott's integrated model has been provided by Elliott and his colleagues themselves through their testing of the theory. Specifically, much of the testing they have done has been via the National Youth Survey (NYS), a national survey collected and synthesized by criminologists at the University of Colorado, Boulder, which is where Elliott and most of the colleagues with whom he works are professors. This longitudinal measure of delinquency has been administered and analyzed for several decades, and it represents perhaps the most systematic collection of information from youths regarding key developmental variables and delinquency rates that has ever existed.

Most of the evidence from the NYS shows general strong support for Elliott's model.[49] However, some evidence has shown few direct effects of the strain and social control concepts, which is surprising given that the basis of the model was the social control and bonding elements of the theory.[50] In fact, the original hypothesis in the model—that strain and social control or bonding theories would have a direct effect on delinquency—was not observed.[51] Rather, only bonding to delinquent peers had a significant and strong effect on future criminality, which supports social learning and differential association-reinforcement theory. This strongly supports the social learning variables in the model and diminishes the claim made by Elliott and his colleagues about the fundamental theoretical perspective of social control and bonding.

Furthermore, a critical review of Elliott's framework, as presented in his 1985 book (with Huizinga and Ageton), notes that a major problem is that its "most puzzling feature . . . is the inclusion of social disorganization in

---

[48]Ibid., 311–12.

[49]See review in Akers and Sellers, *Criminological Theories*, 273–76.

[50]Elliott et al., *Explaining Delinquency*.

[51]Akers and Sellers, *Criminological Theories*, 275.

it as a causal factor, in the absence of any attempt to measure or test the importance of this factor. Presumably, the authors wished to claim that their theory was 'more sociological than psychological.'"[52]

This point is particularly important, given that virtually none of the tests of Elliott's integrated model have included social disorganization factors in their studies, even after this critical review was published more than 25 years ago. So, Elliott and his colleagues should either drop this portion from consideration in the model or provide an adequate test of it in relation to the rest of the framework. Although we would opt for the latter, one of these two alternatives must be chosen.

However, from the presentation that Elliott gave as his presidential address to the American Society of Criminology in 1993, it appears that the former alternative was chosen. Specifically, in his model of the onset of serious violent offending, all of the antecedent variables could be explained by the other traditionally separate theoretical models in his framework. He included two bonding constructs (family and school), parental sanctions, stressful life events (i.e., strain), and early exposure to crime and victimization. Perhaps the last factor could be construed as related to social disorganization theory, but it is probably regarded more as a social learning and differential association-reinforcement variable, as is suggested from the original model.

In addition, this critique noted that the existing evidence shows that most delinquent activity is committed among groups of juveniles, and thus, youths who tend to commit illegal acts naturally associate with delinquents. Yet, the affiliation with delinquent peers is not considered the basic foundation of the theory—as tests of this model demonstrated—but rather an intervening variable in the model. The author of this critique claims that Elliott's model does not emphasize this point strongly enough and thereby does not provide convincing evidence that delinquent peers cause or facilitate offending.[53]

In light of these findings, even Elliott and his colleagues acknowledged that their integrated model best fit the data as a social learning and differential association-reinforcement framework of delinquency.[54] However, they chose to retain social control and bonding theory as the primary foundation of their integrated model, stating that "it is not clear that a social learning model would have predicted a conditional relationship between conventional bonding . . . and deviant bonding."[55] Elliott and colleagues went on to say that they did not attribute most of the explained variation in the model to social learning and differential reinforcement as being the most important construct because they claimed that such variables did not play a strong enough part in the indirect effects that were seen in the estimated models.

This is actually a logical position, given the fact that their integrated framework would, in fact, predict that social learning and differential association-reinforcement variables were the primary direct effects on delinquency, and social control, strain, and social disorganization variables were considered primarily indirect all along, according to their model. However, some critics, especially the proponents of social learning and differential reinforcement theory, have claimed that

> Even with the addition of the interactive effects of conventional bonding, the final model reported by Elliott et al. is more of a variation on social learning theory (with bonding modifications) than it is a variation on social bonding theory (with learning modifications).[56]

---

[52]David Farrington, book review of Elliott et al., *Explaining Delinquency*, in *British Journal of Addiction* 81 (1986): 433; embedded quote taken from p. 67 in Elliott et al.'s book.

[53]Farrington, book review, 433.

[54]Ibid.

[55]Ibid., based on quote from Elliott et al., *Explaining Delinquency*, 137.

[56]Akers and Sellers, *Criminological Theories*, 275.

After all, the measures of delinquent peer bonds used by Elliott and his colleagues are essentially measures that have been used by theorists and researchers of social learning theory over the last few decades regarding differential associations, reinforcements, and modeling.[57]

Additional analyses using the NYS have tended to agree with the critics regarding the importance of social learning and differential reinforcement variables in predicting crime and delinquency. Specifically, one relatively recent reanalysis of NYS data showed that social learning variables appeared to predict more variation in deviance than did the other models or constructs in the model.[58] The assumption that strong attachments to others, regardless of who they are, reduces offending, has been shown by empirical research to be false (see Section VIII). This is true, and all future integrated models must address this issue if they include social control or bonding propositions or constructs in their models.

Despite these criticisms and empirical observations, it appears that Elliott's integrated model has contributed to our understanding of the development of delinquent behavior. In the least, it inspired other theoretical frameworks, some of which we review here. However, it should also be obvious that there are some valid criticisms of this model, such as the claim that it is based on social control and bonding theory while depending heavily on the strong delinquent bonding that takes place in most cases of criminality, clearly implicating social learning and differential reinforcement theory. Again, we want to stress that a true integrated model should not place any emphasis on a particular theory; otherwise, the critics will have a sound argument when findings show that one theory is more influential than another.

Thornberry's Interactional Theory

After Elliott's integrated model, presented in 1979, the next major integrated framework was that of Terrence Thornberry in 1987.[59] This model incorporated empirical evidence drawn since Elliott's presentation to create a unique and insightful model of criminality, which addressed an extremely important aspect that had never been addressed previously in criminological theory. Specifically, Thornberry's interactional theory was the first to emphasize reciprocal, or feedback, effects in the causal modeling of the theoretical framework.

As a basis for his model, Thornberry combined social control and social learning models. According to Thornberry, both of these theories try to explain criminality in a straightforward, causal process and are largely targeted toward a certain age population.[60] Thornberry uniquely claims that the processes of both social control and social learning theory affect each other in a type of feedback process.

Thornberry's integrated model incorporates five primary theoretical constructs, which are synthesized in a comprehensive framework to explain criminal behavior. These five concepts include the following: commitment to school; attachment to parents; belief in conventional values (these first three are taken from social control and bonding theory); adoption of delinquent values; and association with delinquent peers (these last two are drawn from social learning and differential association-reinforcement theory). These five constructs, which most criminologists would agree are important in the development of criminality, are obviously important in a rational model of crime, so at first it does not appear that Thornberry has added much to our understanding of criminal behavior. Furthermore, Thornberry's

---

[57]Ibid., 276.

[58]Robert Agnew, "Why Do They Do It? An Examination of the Intervening Mechanisms between 'Social Control' Variables and Delinquency," *Journal of Research in Crime and Delinquency* 30 (1993): 245–66.

[59]Terrence Thornberry, "Toward an Interactional Theory of Delinquency," *Criminology* 25 (1987): 863–87. See also Thornberry, "Reflections"; Terrence Thornberry, Alan Lizotte, Marvin Krohn, Margaret Farnworth, and Sung Jang, "Testing Interactional Theory: An Examination of Reciprocal Causal Relationships among Family, School and Delinquency," *Journal of Criminal Law and Criminology* 82 (1991): 3–35; Terrance Thornberry, Alan Lizotte, Marvin Krohn, Margaret Farnworth, and Sung Joon Jang, "Delinquent Peers, Beliefs, and Delinquent Behavior: A Longitudinal Test of Interactional Theory," *Criminology* 32 (1994): 47–83.

[60]Much of this discussion is taken from Bernard and Snipes, "Theoretical Integration," 314–16; and also Akers and Sellers, *Criminological Theories*, 278.

model clearly points out that different variables will have greater effects at certain times; for example, he claims that association with delinquent peers will have more effect in the midteenage years than at other ages.

What Thornberry adds beyond other theories is the idea of reciprocity or feedback loops, which no previous theory had mentioned, much less emphasized. In fact, much of the previous criminological literature had spent much time debating whether individuals become delinquent and then start hanging out with similar peers or whether individuals start hanging out with delinquent peers and then begin engaging in criminal activity. This has been the traditional chicken-or-egg question in criminology for most of the 20th century; namely, which came first, delinquency or bad friends? It has often been referred to as the *self-selection* versus *social learning* debate; in other words, do certain individuals decide to hang out with delinquents based on their own previous behavior, or do they learn criminality from delinquents with whom they start associating? One of the major contributions of Thornberry's interactional model is that he directly answered this question.

Specifically, Thornberry noted that most, if not all, contributors to delinquency (and criminal behavior itself) are related reciprocally. Thus, Thornberry postulated that engaging in crime leads to hanging out with other delinquents and that hanging out with delinquents leads to committing crimes. It is quite common for individuals to commit crime and then start hanging out with other peers who are doing the same, and it is also quite common for people to start hanging out with delinquent peers and then start committing offenses. Furthermore, it is perhaps the most likely scenario for a person who is offending to be dealing with both the influences of past experiences and peer effects as well.

As mentioned previously, Thornberry considers the social control and bonding constructs, such as attachment to parents and commitment to school, the most essential predictors of delinquency. Like previous theoretical models of social bonding and control, Thornberry's model puts the level of attachment and commitment to conventional society ahead of the degree of moral beliefs that individuals have regarding criminal offending. However, lack of such moral beliefs leads to delinquent behavior, which in turn negatively affects the level of commitment or attachments an individual may have built in her or his development. As Thornberry claimed:

> While the weakening of the bond to conventional society may be an initial cause of delinquency, delinquency eventually becomes its own indirect cause precisely because of its ability to weaken further the person's bonds to family, school, and conventional beliefs.[61]

Thus, the implications of this model are that variables relating to social control or bonding and other sources cause delinquency, which then becomes, in itself, a predictor and cause for the breakdown of other important causes of delinquency and crime.

For example, consider a person we shall call Johnny, who has an absent father, and a mother who uses inconsistent discipline and sometimes harsh physical abuse of her son. He sees his mother's state of constant neglect and abuse as proof that belief in conventional values is wrong, and he becomes indifferent toward governmental laws; after all, his main goal is to survive and be successful. Because of his mother's psychological and physical neglect, Johnny pays no attention to school and rather turns to his older peers for guidance and support. These peers guide him toward behavior that gives him both financial reward (selling what they steal) and status in their group (respect from performing well in illegal acts). At some point, Johnny gets caught, and this makes the peers who taught him how to engage in crime very proud, while alienating him from the previous bonds he had with his school, from which he is either suspended, and with his mother, who further distances herself from him. This creates a reciprocal effect or feedback loop to the previous factors, which were lack of attachment to his mother and lack of commitment to school. The lowered level of social bonding and control with conventional institutions and factors (mother, school) and increased influence by delinquent peers then leads Johnny to commit more frequent and more serious crimes.

---

[61]Thornberry, "Toward an Interactional Theory," 876, as quoted by Bernard and Snipes, "Theoretical Integration," 315.

Such a model, although complex and hard to measure, is logically consistent, and the postulates are sound. However, the value of any theory has to be determined by the empirical evidence that is found regarding its validity. Much of the scientific evidence regarding Thornberry's empirical model has been contributed by Thornberry and his colleagues.

Although the full model has yet to be tested, the researchers "have found general support for the reciprocal relationships between both control concepts and learning concepts with delinquent behavior."[62] One test of Thornberry's model used the longitudinal Rochester Youth Development Study to test its postulates.[63] This study found that the estimates of previous unidirectional models (nonreciprocal models) did not adequately explain the variation in the data. Rather, the results supported the interactional model, with delinquent associations leading to increases in delinquency, delinquency leading to reinforcing peer networks, and both directional processes working through the social environment. In fact, this longitudinal study demonstrated that, once the participants had acquired delinquent beliefs from their peers, the effects of these beliefs had further effects on their future behavior and associations, which is exactly what Thornberry's theory predicts.[64]

Perhaps the most recent test of Thornberry's interactional model examined the age-varying effects of the theory.[65] This study incorporated hierarchical linear modeling in investigating a sample of the NYS. The results showed that, while the effects of delinquent peers were relatively close to predictions, peaking in the midteenage years, the predictions regarding the effects of family on delinquency were not found to be significant in the periods that were expected, although family was important during adolescence.

Unlike other authors of integrated theories, Thornberry specifically notes that he prefers to see his approach as theoretical elaboration and not full theoretical integration. While we commend Thornberry for addressing this concern, virtually all criminologists still consider his framework a fully integrated model. And, in many ways, Thornberry's interactional model is far more integrated than others discussed here because it gives equal weight to the traditionally separate theoretical frameworks that are combined into his model in the sense that both are considered antecedent and reciprocal in their effects on criminal behavior.

Braithwaite's Theory of Reintegrative Shaming

A unique integrated model that proposed the synthesis of several traditionally separate theories was presented in 1989 in a book titled *Crime, Shame, and Reintegration*.[66] The theory of reintegrative shaming merges constructs and principles from several theories, primarily social control or bonding theory and labeling theory, with elements of strain theory, subculture and gang theory, and differential association theory. All of these theories are synthesized in a clear and coherent framework that is presented in both descriptive and graphic form. We will spend extra time discussing Braithwaite's theory because it addresses not only U.S. culture but also cultural and justice tendencies in Japanese culture.

Braithwaite's idea for the theory was obviously inspired by the cultural differences he observed in Eastern (particularly Japanese) culture, in terms of both socialization practices and the justice system, as compared to the Western world. (Note that Braithwaite is from Australia, which uses the same Western practices as England and the United States.) Specifically, he emphasizes the Japanese focus on the aggregate, such as the family, school, or business, to which the individual belongs. In contrast, in many Western cultures, epitomized by U.S. culture, the emphasis is clearly placed on the individual.

---

[62]Bernard and Snipes, "Theoretical Integration," 316.

[63]Thornberry et al., "Delinquent Peers."

[64]Ibid.

[65]Sung Joon Jang, "Age-Varying Effects of Family, School, and Peers on Delinquency: A Multilevel Modeling Test of Interactional Theory," *Criminology* 37 (1999): 643–85.

[66]John Braithwaite, *Crime, Shame, and Reintegration* (New York: Cambridge University Press, 1989).

This contrast has often been referred to as the *we* culture versus the *me* culture (Eastern versus Western emphases, respectively). Although this is seen in virtually all aspects of culture and policy practices, it is quite evident in people's names. In most Eastern cultures, people are known by their family name, which is placed first in the ordering. This shows the importance that is placed on the group to which they belong. In contrast, Western societies list individual names first, implying a focus on the individual herself or himself. These naming practices are a manifestation of a virtually all-encompassing cultural difference regarding group dynamics and social expectations across societies, especially in their justice systems. For example, it is quite common in Japan to receive a sentence of apologizing in public, even for the most serious violent crimes.[67] In his book, Braithwaite points out that, after World War II, Japan was the only highly industrialized society that showed a dramatic decrease in its crime rate.

Criminological theory would predict an increasing crime rate in Japan, given the extremely high density of urban areas due to rapid industrialization, especially on such a small amount of land, Japan being a large island. As Braithwaite describes it, the Japanese suffered from anomie after the war in the sense of a general breakdown of cultural norms, but the nation was able to deal with this anomic state despite the odds. Japan definitively decided not to follow the Western model of justice after the war; rather, it rejected the Western system of stigmatizing convicted felons. Instead, the Japanese implemented a system in which offenders are reintroduced (hence *reintegration*) via a formal ceremony in which citizens accept the offenders back into conventional society. In contrast, in the United States, we typically give our ex-cons about $200 on average and make them promise always to identify themselves as felons on legal documents.

Japan is also extremely lenient in sentencing offenders to prison. In contrast, by rate of incarceration, the United States is the most punitive developed nation. In Japan, Braithwaite notes:

> Prosecution only proceeds in major cases . . . where the normal process of apology, compensation, and forgiveness by the victim breaks down. Fewer than 10 percent of those offenders who are convicted receive prison sentences, and for two-thirds of these, prison sentences are suspended. Whereas 45 percent of those convicted of a crime serve a jail sentence in the U.S., in Japan the percentage is under two.[68]

Public apology is the most common punishment among the Japanese, which strongly reflects the nature of honor in Japanese society, as well as pointing out the fundamental differences between how we deal with offenders. Braithwaite claims that this cultural and political difference has a huge impact on why crime rates in both nations have experienced such different trends.

Most developing Western nations, including the United States, experienced a rising crime rate in the 1950s, 1960s, and 1970s. Braithwaite argues that this was likely due to culture and the differential treatment of its offenders:

> It might be argued that this [the downward trend in crime rates after World War II in Japan] was a result of the re-establishment of cultural traditions of shaming wrongdoers, including the effective coupling of shame and punishment. . . . [O]ne contention . . . is that the uncoupling of shame and punishment manifested in a wide variety of ways in many Western countries is an important factor in explaining the rising crime rates in those countries."[69]

Furthermore, in contrast to American society, the Japanese are typically less confrontational with authority. For example, some scholars have noted that the Japanese accept the authority of law, and police officers are considered

---

[67]Ibid., 62.

[68]Ibid., citing findings from J. Haley, "Sheathing the Sword of Justice in Japan: An Essay on Law without Sanctions," *Journal of Japanese Studies* 8 (1982): 265–81.

[69]Braithwaite, *Crime Shame*, 61; brackets are authors' paraphrasing.

similar to "elder brothers" who rely "on positive rather than negative reinforcement" when it comes to crime control.[70] This difference in the way officers and other authority figures are considered is likely due to the way that the Japanese view society in terms of neighborhood, community, school, and work—the informal institutions of control that we have mentioned earlier in this book as having more effect on the crime rate than formal institutions (i.e., police, courts, prisons).

Beyond discussing the cultural differences, Braithwaite's integrated theory addresses some of the most notable scientific observations regarding which types of individuals and groups are likely to commit crime. Specifically, Braithwaite states that most crime is committed by young, poor, single males who live in urban communities that have high levels of residential mobility; they are likely to be unattached to or to do poorly in school, have low educational or occupational aspirations, are not strongly attached to their parents, associate with delinquent peers, and do not have moral beliefs against violating law.[71]

It is obvious from this list that Braithwaite incorporated some of the major theories and corresponding variables into his theoretical perspective. The emphasis on poor people who do not have high educational or occupational aspirations obviously supports strain theory, whereas the inclusion of urban individuals who live in communities with high residential mobility reflects the Chicago School or social disorganization theory. At the same time, Braithwaite clearly highlights the predisposition of people who have limited moral beliefs and weak attachments, which conjures up images of social bonding and control theory; individuals having delinquent peers obviously supports differential association and reinforcement theory. Thus, a handful of theories are important in the construction of Braithwaite's integrated theory.

Braithwaite notes that much of the effectiveness of the Japanese system of crime control depends on two constructs: interdependency and communitarianism. Interdependency is the level of bonding of an individual to conventional society, such as the degree to which she or he is involved with or attached to conventional groups in society, which would include employment, family, church, and organizations. According to Braithwaite, interdependency is the building block of the other major theoretical construct in his integrated model: communitarianism. Communitarianism is the macro (group) level of interdependency, meaning that it is the cumulative degree of the bonds that individuals have with conventional groups and institutions (e.g., family, employment, organizations, church, etc.) in a given society. Obviously, these theoretical constructs are mostly based on the theory of social bonding and control in the sense that they are based on attachments, commitment, and involvement in conventional society.

Braithwaite's model has a causal ordering that starts with largely demographic variables, such as age, gender, marital status, employment, and aspirations, on the individual level and urbanization and residential mobility on the macro (group) level. All of these factors are predicted to influence the level of interdependency and communitarianism in the model, which as we previously discussed, is largely based on social control and bonding theory. Depending on which type of culture is considered, or what forms of shaming are used in a given jurisdiction, the various types of shaming that are administered are key in this integrated model.

According to Braithwaite, societies that emphasize reintegrative shaming, such as Japan, will reduce the rates of crime in their societies. When an offender in Japan completes her or his sentence or punishment for committing a crime, the government will often sponsor a formal ceremony in which the offender is reintroduced or reintegrated back into conventional society. According to Braithwaite, we in the United States do not reintegrate offenders into our society after shaming them but rather stigmatize them, which leads them to associate only with people from criminal subcultures (e.g., drug users, gang members). Braithwaite claims that this leads to the formation of criminal groups and the grasping of illegitimate opportunities offered in the local community. Ultimately, this means

---

[70]David H. Bayley, *Forces of Order: Police Behavior in Japan and the United States* (Berkeley: University of California Press, 1976).

[71]Braithwaite, *Crime, Shame*, 44–53.

that people who are not reintegrated into conventional society will inevitably be stigmatized and labeled as offenders, preventing them from becoming productive members of the community, even if their intentions are to do such.

Most empirical studies of Braithwaite's theory show mixed results, with most being in favor of this theory, especially regarding its implementation for policy. Some tests have shown that reintegrative ideology regarding violations of law can have a positive impact on future compliance with the law; others have found that high levels of shaming in parental practices do not increase offending.[72] Studies in other countries, such as China and Iceland, show partial support for Braithwaite's theory.[73] While some studies have found encouraging results,[74] other recent studies have also found weak or no support for the theory.[75]

The most recent reports regarding the effects of shame show that outcomes largely depend on how shame is measured, which Braithwaite's theory largely ignores. There are, for example, episodic or situational shame states as well as long-term shame traits or propensities. Recent reviews of the literature and studies of how different types of shame are measured show that certain forms of shame are positively correlated with offending, whereas other forms of shame tend to inhibit criminal behavior.[76] If individuals persistently feel shame, they are more likely to commit criminal activity, but if persons who are not predisposed to feel shame perceive that they would feel shame for doing a given illegal activity, then they would be strongly inhibited from engaging in such activity.[77] This is consistent with findings from another recent study that demonstrated that the effect of reintegrative shaming had an interactive effect on delinquency.[78]

Furthermore, Braithwaite's theory does not take into account other important self-conscious emotions, such as guilt, pride, embarrassment, and empathy, that are important when individuals are deciding whether to commit criminal behavior. Although some theorists claim that shame is the key social emotion, studies show that they are clearly wrong. Rather, many emotions, such as guilt and embarrassment, are based on social interaction and self-consciousness; in many ways, they are just as inhibitory or rehabilitating as shame.[79] The literature examining rational choice theory is also an indication of the effects of emotions other than shame in influencing decisions on offending.[80]

[72]Toni Makkai and John Braithwaite, "Reintegrative Shaming and Compliance with Regulatory Standards," *Criminology* 32 (1994): 361–86; Carter Hay, "An Exploratory Test of Braithwaite's Reintegrative Shaming Theory," *Journal of Research in Crime and Delinquency* 38 (2001): 132–53.

[73]Lu Hong, Zhang Lening, and Terance Miethe, "Interdependency, Communitarianism, and Reintegrative Shaming in China," *Social Science Journal* 39 (2002): 189–202; Eric Baumer, Richard Wright, Kristrun Kristinsdottir, and Helgi Gunnlaugsson, "Crime, Shame, and Recidivism: The Case of Iceland," *British Journal of Criminology* 42 (2002): 40–60.

[74]Nathan Harris, Lode Walgrave, and John Braithwaite, "Emotional Dynamics in Restorative Conferences," *Theoretical Criminology* 8 (2004): 191–210; Eliza Ahmed and Valerie Braithwaite, "'What, Me Ashamed'? Shame Management and School Bullying," *Journal of Research in Crime and Delinquency* 41 (2004): 269–94.

[75]Bas Van Stokkom, "Moral Emotions in Restorative Justice Conferences: Managing Shame, Designing Empathy," *Theoretical Criminology* 6 (2002): 339–61; Charles Tittle, Jason Bratton, and Marc Gertz, "A Test of a Microlevel Application of Shaming Theory," *Social Problems* 50 (2003): 592–617; Lening Zhang and Sheldon Zhang, "Reintegrative Shaming and Predatory Delinquency," *Journal of Research in Crime and Delinquency* 41 (2004): 433–53.

[76]Stephen Tibbetts, "Shame and Rational Choice in Offending Decisions," *Criminal Justice and Behavior* 24 (1996): 234–55.

[77]Stephen Tibbetts, "Self-Conscious Emotions and Criminal Offending," *Psychological Reports* 93 (2003): 201–31; Stephen G. Tibbetts, "Traits and States of Self-Conscious Emotions in Criminal Decision Making," in *Affect and Cognition in Criminal Decision Making*, ed. Jean-Louis Van Gelder, Henk Elffers, Danielle Reynald, and Daniel Nagin (London: Routledge, 2014), 221–38.

[78]Hay, "An Exploratory Test."

[79]For an excellent review, see June Price Tangney and Kurt Fischer, *Self-Conscious Emotions: The Psychology of Shame, Guilt, Embarrassment, and Pride* (New York: Guilford Press, 1995).

[80]See Harold Grasmick, Brenda Sims Blackwell, and Robert Bursik, "Changes over Time in Gender Differences in Perceived Risk of Sanctions," *Law and Society Review* 27 (1993): 679–705; Harold Grasmick, Robert Bursik, and Bruce Arneklev, "Reduction in Drunk Driving as a Response to Increased Threats of Shame, Embarrassment, and Legal Sanctions," *Criminology* 31 (1993): 41–67; and Tibbetts, "College Student Perceptions."

Still, Braithwaite's reintegrative theory provides an important step ahead in theoretical development, particularly in terms of combining explanatory models to address crime rates, as well as correctional policies and philosophies, across various cultures. Specifically, Braithwaite's theory makes a strong argument that Eastern (particularly Japanese) policies of reintegration and apology for convicted offenders are beneficial for that culture. Would this system work in Western culture, especially the United States? The answer is definitely unknown, but it is unlikely that such a model would work well in the United States. After all, most of the chronic, serious offenders in the United States would not be highly deterred by having to apologize to the public, and many might consider such an apology or reintegration ceremony an honor, or a way to show that they really hadn't been punished. This may not be true, but we would not know this until such policies were implemented fully in our system. However, programs along these lines have been implemented in our country, and some of these programs will be reviewed later in this book.

Tittle's Control-Balance Theory

One of the more recently proposed models of theoretical integration is Charles Tittle's control-balance theory. Presented by Tittle in 1995, control-balance integrated theory proposes that (a) the amount of control to which one is subjected and (b) the amount of control that one can exercise determine the probability of deviance occurring. In other words, the balance between these two types of control, he argued, can predict the type of behavior that is likely to be committed.[81]

In this integrated theoretical framework, Tittle claimed that a person is least likely to offend when she or he has a balance of controlling and being controlled. On the other hand, the likelihood of offending will increase when these become unbalanced. If individuals are more controlled by external forces, which Tittle calls *control deficit*, then the theory predicts that they will commit predatory or defiant criminal behavior. In contrast, if an individual possesses an excessive level of control by external forces, which Tittle refers to as *control surplus*, then that individual will be more likely to commit acts of exploitation or decadence. It is important to realize that this excessive control is not the same as excessive self-control, which would be covered by other theories examined in this section. Rather, Tittle argues that people who are controlling, that is, who have excessive control over others, will be predisposed toward inappropriate activities.

Early empirical tests of control-balance theory have reported mixed results, with both surpluses and deficits predicting the same types of deviance.[82] Furthermore, researchers have uncovered differing effects of the control-balance ratio on two types of deviance that are contingent on gender. This finding is consistent with the gender-specific support found for Reckless's containment theory and with the gender differences found in other theoretical models.[83] Despite the mixed findings for Tittle's control-balance theory of crime, this model of criminal offending still gets a lot of attention, and most of the empirical evidence has been in favor of this theory.

Hagan's Power-Control Theory

The final integrated theory that we will cover in this section deals with the influence of familial control and how this relates to criminality across gender. Power-control theory is another integrated theory that was proposed by John

---

[81]Charles Tittle, *Control Balance: Toward a General Theory of Deviance* (Boulder: Westview, 1995) (see chap. 8, n. 55).

[82]Alex Piquero and Matthew Hickman, "An Empirical Test of Tittle's Control Balance Theory," *Criminology* 37 (1999): 319–42 (see chap. 8, n. 75); Matthew Hickman and Alex Piquero, "Exploring the Relationships between Gender, Control Balance, and Deviance," *Deviant Behavior* 22 (2001): 323–51 (see chap. 8, n. 75).

[83]Hickman and Piquero, "Exploring the Relationships." For contrast and comparison, see Grasmick et al., "Changes over Time"; Grasmick et al., "Reduction in Drunk Driving"; and Tibbetts, "College Student Perceptions."

Hagan and his colleagues.[84] The primary focus of this theory is on the level of patriarchal attitudes and structure in the household, which are influenced by parental positions in the workforce.

Power-control theory assumes that, in households where the mother and father have relatively similar levels of power at work (i.e., balanced households), mothers will be less likely to exert control on their daughters. These balanced households will be less likely to experience gender differences in the criminal offending of the children. However, households in which mothers and fathers have dissimilar levels of power in the workplace (i.e., unbalanced households) are more likely to suppress criminal activity in daughters. In such families, it is assumed that daughters will be taught to be less risk-taking than the males in the family. In addition, assertiveness and risky activity among the males in the house will be encouraged. This assertiveness and risky activity may be precursors to crime, which is highly consistent with the empirical evidence regarding trends in crime related to gender. Thus, Hagan's integrated theory seems to have a considerable amount of face validity.

Most empirical tests of power-control theory have provided moderate support, while more recent studies have further specified the validity of the theory in different contexts.[85] For example, one recent study reported that the influence of mothers, not fathers, on sons had the greatest impact on reducing the delinquency of young males.[86] Another researcher has found that differences in perceived threats of embarrassment and formal sanctions vary between more patriarchal and less patriarchal households.[87] Finally, studies have also started measuring the effect of patriarchal attitudes on crime and delinquency.[88] However, most of the empirical studies that have shown support for the theory have been done by Hagan or his colleagues. Still, power-control theory is a good example of a social control theory in that it is consistent with the idea that individuals must be socialized and that the gender differences in such socialization make a difference in how people will act throughout life.

 Policy Implications

Many policy implications can be drawn from the various integrated theoretical models that we have discussed in this section. We will focus on the concepts that were most prominent, which are parenting and peer influences. Regarding the former, numerous empirical studies have examined programs for improving the ability of parents and expecting parents to be effective.[89] Such programs typically involve training high school students—or individuals or couples who are already parents—on how to be better parents. Additional programs include

[84]John Hagan, *Structural Criminology* (Newark: Rutgers University Press, 1989) (see chap. 8, n. 77); John Hagan, A. Gillis, and J. Simpson, "The Class Structure of Gender and Delinquency: Toward a Power-Control Theory of Common Delinquent Behavior," *American Journal of Sociology* 90 (1985): 1151–78 (see chap. 8, n. 77); John Hagan, A. Gillis, and J. Simpson, "Clarifying and Extending Power-Control Theory," *American Journal of Sociology* 95 (1990): 1024–37 (see chap. 8, n. 77); John Hagan, J. Simpson, and A. Gillis, "Class in the Household: A Power-Control Theory of Gender and Delinquency," *American Journal of Sociology* 92 (1987): 788–816 (see chap. 8, n. 77).

[85]John Hagan et al., "Class in the Household"; B. McCarthy and John Hagan, "Gender, Delinquency, and the Great Depression: A Test of Power-Control Theory," *Canadian Review of Sociology and Anthropology* 24 (1987): 153–77 (see chap. 8, n. 78); Merry Morash and Meda Chesney-Lind, "A Reformulation and Partial Test of the Power-Control Theory of Delinquency," *Justice Quarterly* 8 (1991): 347–77 (see chap. 8, n. 78); Simon Singer and Murray Levine, "Power-Control Theory, Gender, and Delinquency: A Partial Replication with Additional Evidence on the Effects of Peers," *Criminology* 26 (1988): 627–47 (see chap. 8, n. 78).

[86]B. McCarthy, John Hagan, and T. Woodward, "In the Company of Women: Structure and Agency in a Revised Power-Control Theory of Gender and Delinquency," *Criminology* 37 (1999): 761–88 (see chap. 8, n. 79).

[87]Brenda Sims Blackwell, "Perceived Sanction Threats, Gender, and Crime: A Test and Elaboration of Power-Control Theory," *Criminology* 38 (2000): 439–88 (see chap. 8, n. 80).

[88]Blackwell, "Perceived Sanction Threats"; Kristin Bates and Chris Bader, "Family Structure, Power-Control Theory, and Deviance: Extending Power-Control Theory to Include Alternate Family Forms," *Western Criminology Review* 4 (2003): 170–90 (see chap. 8, n. 81).

[89]See review in Brown et al., *Criminology: Explaining Crime*, 425.

Head Start and other preschool programs that attempt to prepare high-risk youth for starting school; these have been found to be effective in reducing disciplinary problems.[90]

Regarding peer influences, numerous programs and evaluations have examined the effects of reducing negative peer influences regarding crime.[91] Programs that emphasize prosocial peer groups are often successful, whereas others show little or no success.[92] The conclusion from most of these studies is that the most successful programs of this type are those that focus on learning life skills and prosocial skills and use a curriculum based on a cognitive behavioral approach.[93] This strategy includes reinforcing positive behavior, clarifying rules of behavior in social settings, teaching life and thinking skills, and, perhaps most important, thinking about the consequences of a given behavior before acting (hence, the cognitive behavioral approach). Studies consistently show that programs using a cognitive behavioral approach (i.e., think before you act) are far more successful than programs that emphasize interactions among peers or use psychoanalysis or other forms of therapy.[94]

Many other policy implications can be derived from integrated theories explaining criminal behavior, but parenting practices and peer influences are the primary constructs in most integrated models. Thus, these are the two areas that should be targeted for policy interventions, but this must be done correctly. For a start, policy makers could review the findings from empirical studies and evaluations and see that the earlier parenting programs start, particularly for high-risk children, the more effective they can be. Regarding the peer influence programs, a combination of cognitive behavioral therapy and training in life skills appears to be more effective than other approaches.

Conclusion

In this section, we have reviewed which factors determine the types of integrated theories and which criteria make an integrated theory a good explanation of human behavior. We have also examined examples of integrated theories that have been proposed in the criminological literature in the last 30 years. All of the examples represent the most researched and discussed integrated theories, and they demonstrate both the advantages and disadvantages of theoretical integration or elaboration. We hope that readers will be able to determine for themselves which of these integrated theories are the best in explaining criminal activity.

In this section, we have examined the various ways in which theoretical integration can be done, including forms of conceptual integration and theoretical elaboration. Furthermore, the criticisms of the different variations of integration and elaboration have been discussed. In addition, numerous examples of theoretical integration have been presented, along with the empirical studies that have been performed to examine their validity.

Finally, we discussed the policy implications that can be recommended from such integrated theories. Specifically, we concluded that early parenting and peer influences are the two most important influences across these theoretical models. Furthermore, we concluded that when it comes to parenting programs, the earlier, the better. We also concluded that a cognitive behavioral approach that includes the teaching of life skills is most effective for peer influence programs.

Section Summary

♦ Theoretical integration is one of the more contemporary developments in criminological theorizing. This approach brings with it many criticisms, yet arguably many advantages.

[90]Ibid.

[91]For a review, see Akers and Sellers, *Criminological Theories*, 102–8.

[92]Ibid.

[93]Ibid., 108.

[94]Ibid.

- Types of theoretical integration include end-to-end, side-by-side, and up-and-down.
- Conceptual integration appears to be a useful, albeit rarely explored, form of theoretical integration.
- Theoretical elaboration is another form of integration, which involves using one theory as the base or primary model and then incorporating concepts and propositions from other theories to make the primary model stronger.
- A number of seminal integrated theories have been examined using empirical evidence and appear to have enhanced our understanding of criminal behavior.
- Some of the theoretical models that have been proposed (such as Elliott et al.'s model) have been supported by empirical research.
- Theoretical integration models have many critics, who claim that the assumptions, concepts, and propositions of the mixed theories are counterintuitive.

KEY TERMS

Braithwaite's reintegrative shaming theory

communitarianism

conceptual integration

Elliott's integrated model

end-to-end theoretical integration

integrated theories

interdependency

side-by-side (or horizontal) integration

theoretical elaboration

Thornberry's interactional model

up-and-down (or deductive) integration

DISCUSSION QUESTIONS

1. What is the definition of theoretical integration, and why can such theories be beneficial?

2. Describe what end-to-end theoretical integration is, and provide an example of such integration.

3. Describe what side-by-side theoretical integration is, and provide an example of such integration.

4. Describe what up-and-down theoretical integration is, and provide an example of such integration.

5. Discuss the difference between theoretical elaboration, theoretical integration, and conceptual integration.

6. What are the major strengths and weaknesses of theoretical integration?

7. In your opinion, what is the best of the integrated models? Why do you believe this is the best integrated model?

8. What do you believe is the weakest integrated model? Why?

WEB RESOURCES

Integrated Theories of Crime

http://en.wikipedia.org/wiki/integrative_criminology

John Braithwaite/Reintegrative Theory

https://www.anu.edu.au/fellows/jbraithwaite/_documents/Chapters/Shame_Restorative_2005.pdf

Various Integrated Theories of Crime

http://law.jrank.org/pages/821/Crime-Causation-Sociological-Theories-Integrated-theories.html

READING 29

In this selection, Delbert Elliott, Suzanne Ageton, and Rachelle Canter provide one of the earliest, and still one of the best-known and best-respected, examples of theoretical integration. We shall see that Elliott and his colleagues merge various concepts and propositions from at least three traditional theoretical perspectives, namely, strain theory, social control theory, and various social learning theories.

One of the beneficial aspects of Elliott and his colleagues' integrated theory is that it attempts to merge various versions of each of these perspectives into a cohesive, unitary explanation of delinquency and criminal behavior. For example, the authors go beyond the original strain theory proposed by Merton in 1938 and also take into consideration the subsequent versions of strain theory that appeared in later decades (such as Cloward and Ohlin's theory of differential opportunities, as well as Cohen's ideas regarding the formation of gang subcultures). Also, when explaining how control theories were integrated into Elliott and his colleagues' model, the authors do not simply rely on Hirschi's version of social bonding but also consider some of the other versions of control theory (such as control theories by Reiss, Nye, and Reckless as well as Matza's theory of drift). Finally, the authors don't simply merge Sutherland's theory of differential association but also take into account the more modern versions of social learning theory, such as Akers's model of differential reinforcement and Bandura's model of imitation and modeling. Although even more modern versions of each of these theoretical perspectives have been introduced (e.g., general strain theory) since Elliott and his colleagues proposed this model in 1979, it is obvious from this selection that the authors did their best to integrate these three major perspectives using the most recent scientific evidence they had in the late 1970s.

While reading this selection, readers are encouraged to consider the validity of the model by considering themselves or others they grew up with and examining whether the development of the various stages proposed by Elliott and his colleagues seems to fit with the delinquents or criminals they have known. Furthermore, if you were to create such an integrated model, would you emphasize any concepts or propositions from these three theoretical perspectives (or those from other theories) that the authors do not seem to focus on or merge into their "comprehensive" explanation of why individuals become delinquents? Finally, consider whether it is rational to merge theoretical perspectives that have opposing basic assumptions, such as merging strain theory, which claims that individuals are born good, with perspectives such as control theory, which claims that people are born bad and must be taught or controlled to be good.

An Integrated Theoretical
Perspective on Delinquent Behavior

Delbert S. Elliott, Suzanne S. Ageton, and Rachelle J. Canter

SOURCE: Delbert Elliott, Suzanne S. Ageton, and Rachelle J. Canter, "An Integrated Theoretical Perspective on Delinquent Behavior," *Journal of Research in Crime and Delinquency* 16 (1979): 3–27. Copyright © 1979 Sage Publications, Inc. Used by permission of Sage Publications, Inc.

Previous Theories: Strain and Control

Anomie/Strain Perspective

. . . Strain theory has become the most influential and widely used contemporary formulation in the sociology of delinquent behavior. A specific application of strain theory to delinquency has been proposed by Cloward and Ohlin (1960) and, more recently, by Elliott and Voss (1974). Cloward and Ohlin's work is of particular interest to us because their formulation, like that proposed here, represents an attempt to integrate and extend current theoretical positions. Although their theory has been viewed primarily as an extension of the earlier work of Durkheim and Merton, it is equally an extension of the differential association perspective and the prior work of Sutherland (1947). Indeed, much of its significance lies in the fact that it successfully integrated these two traditional perspectives on the etiology of delinquent behavior. Cloward and Ohlin maintain that limited opportunity for achieving conventional goals is the motivational stimulus for delinquent behavior. The specific form and pattern of delinquent behavior are acquired through normal learning processes within delinquent groups. Experiences of limited or blocked opportunities (a result of structural limitations on success) thus lead to alienation (perceived anomie) and an active seeking out of alternative groups and settings in which particular patterns of delinquent behavior are acquired and reinforced (social learning).

Merton, Cloward, and Ohlin have conceptualized the condition leading to anomie in terms of differential opportunities for achieving socially valued goals. Differential access to opportunity creates strain; this is postulated to occur primarily among disadvantaged, low-SES [socioeconomic status] youths, resulting in the concentration of delinquent subcultures in low-SES neighborhoods. It is important to note, however, that Cloward and Ohlin have changed the level of explanation from the macrosociological level which characterized Durkheim's work to an individual level. It is the *perception* of limited access to conventional goals that motivates the *individual* to explore deviant means. This change in level of explanation was essential for the integration of strain and learning perspectives.

Elliott and Voss's more recent work (1974) has attempted to deal with the class-bound assumptions inherent in strain theory. Their formulation extends Cloward and Ohlin's classic statement in the following three ways: (1) The focus on limited opportunities was extended to a wider range of conventional goals. (2) The goal-means disjunction was modified to be logically independent of social class. (3) The role of social learning in the development of delinquent behavior was further emphasized. Elliott and Voss have proposed a sequential, or developmental, model of delinquency: (1) Limited opportunities or failure to achieve conventional goals serves to (2) attenuate one's initial commitment to the normative order and (3) results in a particular form of alienation (normlessness), which serves as a "permitter" for delinquency, and (4) exposure to delinquent groups, which provides learning and rewards for delinquent behavior for those whose bonds have undergone the attenuation process.

From this perspective, aspiration-opportunity disjunctions provide motivation for delinquent behavior. As compared with Merton and Cloward and Ohlin, Elliott and Voss view *both* goals and opportunities as variables. They postulate that middle-class youths are just as likely to aspire beyond their means as are low-SES youths. While the absolute levels of aspirations and opportunities may vary by class, the discrepancies between personal goals and opportunities for realizing these goals need not vary systematically by class. Given Durkheim's (1897/1951, p. 254) view that poverty restrains aspirations, Elliott and Voss have postulated that aspiration-opportunity disjunctions would be at least as great, if not greater, among middle-class youths. In any case, the motivational stimulus for delinquent behavior in the form of aspiration-opportunity discrepancies or goal failure is viewed as logically independent of social class.

Normlessness, the expectation that one must employ illegitimate means to achieve socially valued goals (Seeman, 1959), is postulated to result from perceived aspiration-opportunity disjunctions. When a person cannot reach his or her goals by conventional means, deviant or illegitimate means become rational and functional alternatives. When the source of failure or blockage is perceived as external—resulting from institutional practices and policies—the individual has some justification for withdrawing his or her moral commitment to these conventional norms. In this manner, a sense of injustice mitigates ties to conventional norms and generates normlessness.

Once at this point in the developmental sequence, the relative presence or absence of specific delinquent learning and performance structures accounts for the likelihood of one's behavior. The time-ordering of the exposure to delinquency variable is not explicit. It may predate failure or it may be the result of seeking a social context in which one can achieve some success. While the exposure may result in the acquisition of delinquent behavior patterns, actual delinquent behavior (performance) will not result until one's attachment to the social order is neutralized through real or anticipated failure, and the delinquent behavior has been reinforced. The results of research relative to this set of propositions have been generally encouraging. . . .

While considerable empirical support for an integrated strain-learning approach to delinquency has been amassed, most of the variance in delinquency remains unexplained. If the power of this theoretical formulation is to be improved, some basic modification is required. One avenue is suggested by the weak predictive power of the aspiration-opportunity discrepancy variables. . . . [In some studies], limited academic success at school and failure in one's relationship with parents were predictive, but only weakly. To some extent, the low strength of these predictors might be anticipated, since they are the initial variables in the causal sequence and are tied to delinquency only through a set of other conditional variables. On the other hand, the strong emphasis placed on these specific variables in strain theories seems questionable, given the available data. It might be argued that the difficulty lies in the operationalization or measurement of the relevant goal-opportunity disjunctions. However, we are inclined to reject this position because previous findings as to this postulated relationship have been generally weak and inconclusive (Brennan, 1974; Elliot, 1962; Hirschi, 1969; Jessor et al., 1968; Liska, 1971; Short, 1964; Short, Rivera, & Tennyson: Spergel, 1967). Furthermore, there is substantial evidence in the above-mentioned studies that many adolescents engaging in significant amounts of delinquent behavior experience no discrepancies between aspirations and perceived opportunities. The lack of consistent support for this relationship suggests that failure or anticipated failure constitutes only one possible path to an involvement in delinquency.

The Control Perspective

The different assumptions of strain and control theories are significant. Strain formulations assume a positively socialized individual who violates conventional norms only when his or her attachment and commitment are attenuated. Norm violation occurs only after the individual perceives that opportunities for socially valued goals are blocked. Strain theory focuses on this attenuation process. Control theories, on the other hand, treat the socialization process and commitment to conventional norms and values as problematic. Persons differ with respect to their commitment to and integration into the conventional social order. . . .

From a control perspective, delinquency is viewed as a consequence of (1) lack of internalized normative controls, (2) breakdown in previously established controls, and/or (3) conflict or inconsistency in rules or social controls. Strain formulations of delinquency appear to be focusing on those variables and processes which account for the second condition identified by Reiss (1951): attenuation or breakdown in previously established controls. On the other hand, most control theorists direct their attention to the first and third conditions, exploring such variables as inadequate socialization (failure to internalize conventional norms) and integration into conventional groups or institutions which provide strong external or social controls on behavior. From our perspective, these need not be viewed as contradictory explanations. On the contrary, they may be viewed as alternative processes, depending on the outcome of one's early socialization experience.

For example, Hirschi (1969) has argued that high aspirations involve a commitment to conventional lines of action that functions as a positive control or bond to the social order. Strain theories, on the other hand, view high aspirations (in the face of limited opportunities) as a source of attenuation of attachment to the conventional order. Recognizing this difference, Hirschi suggested that the examination of this relationship would constitute a crucial test of the two theories. Empirically, the evidence is inconsistent and far from conclusive. One possible interpretation is that both hypotheses are correct and are part of different etiological sequences leading to delinquent behavior.

Empirical studies using the control perspective have focused almost exclusively on the static relation of weak internal and external controls to delinquency without considering the longer developmental processes. These processes may involve an initially strong commitment to and integration into society which becomes attenuated over time, with the attenuation eventually resulting in delinquency. The source of this difficulty may lie in the infrequent use of longitudinal designs. Without a repeated-measure design, youths with strong bonds which subsequently become attenuated may be indistinguishable from those who never developed strong bonds.

An Integrated Strain-Control Perspective

Our proposed integrated theoretical paradigm begins with the assumption that different youths have different early socialization experiences, which result in variable degrees of commitment to and integration into conventional social groups. The effect of failure to achieve conventional goals on subsequent delinquency is related to the strength of one's initial bonds. Limited opportunities to achieve conventional goals constitute a source of strain and thus a motivational stimulus for delinquency only if one is committed to these goals. In contrast, limited opportunities to achieve such goals should have little or no impact on those with weak ties and commitments to the conventional social order.

Limited opportunities to achieve conventional goals are not the only experiences which weaken or break initially strong ties to the social order. Labeling theorists have argued that the experience of being apprehended and publicly labeled delinquent initiates social processes which limit one's access to conventional social roles and statuses, isolating one from participation in these activities and relationships and forcing one to assume a delinquent role (Ageton & Elliott; Becker, 1963; Goldman, 1963; Kitsuse, 1962; Rubington & Weinberg, 1968; Schur, 1971). It has also been argued that the effects of social disorganization or crisis in the home (divorce, parental strife and discord, death of a parent) and/or community (high rates of mobility, economic depression, unemployment) attenuate or break one's ties to society (Andry, 1962; Glueck & Glueck, 1970; Monahan, 1957; Rosen, 1970; Savitz, 1970; Shaw, 1931; Thomas & Znaniecki, 1927; Toby, 1957).

In sum, we postulate that limited opportunities, failure to achieve valued goals, negative labeling experiences, and social disorganization at home and in the community are all experiences which may attenuate one's ties to the conventional social order and may thus be causal factors in the developmental sequence leading to delinquent behavior for those whose early socialization experiences produced strong bonds to society. For those whose attachments to the conventional social order are already weak, such factors may further weaken ties to society but are not necessary factors in the etiological sequence leading to delinquency.

Our basic conceptual framework comes from control theory, with a slightly different emphasis placed on participation in and commitment to delinquent groups. Further, it identifies a set of attenuating/bonding experiences which weaken or strengthen ties to the conventional social order over time. Our focus is on experiences and social contexts which are relevant to adolescents. A diagram of our proposed theoretical scheme is shown in Figure 1. The rows in Figure 1 indicate the direction and sequence of the hypothesized relationships. While the time order designated in Figure 1 is unidirectional, the actual relationships between initial socialization, bonding/attenuation processes, normative orientations of groups, and behavior are often reciprocal and reinforcing. We have also presented the variables in dichotomized form to simplify the model and the discussion of its major elements.

Bonds

Control theorists disagree about sources of control, but they all accept the central proposition that delinquent behavior is a direct result of weak ties to the conventional normative order. In operationalizing control theory, major emphasis has been placed on the bond(s) which tie a person to society. Hirschi (1969) conceptualized four elements of this bond. First, attachment implies a moral link to other people and encompasses such concepts as conscience, superego, and internalization of norms. Commitment, the second factor, is the rational element in the bond. Hirschi views commitment to conformity as an investment in conventional lines of action, such as an educational or occupational career. Other theorists have tied the concept of commitment to such notions as "stake in conformity" (Goode, 1960) and "side bets" (Becker, 1960). Involvement is the time and energy dimension of the bond for Hirschi. Given the limits of time and energy, involvement in conventional activities acts as a social constraint on delinquent behavior. The final bond, *belief*, refers to one's acceptance of the moral validity of social rules and norms. According to Hirschi, this psychological element of the bond is effective as long as a person accepts the validity of the rules. If one denies or depreciates the validity of the rules, one source of control is neutralized.

Figure 1	Integrated Strain-Control Paradigm

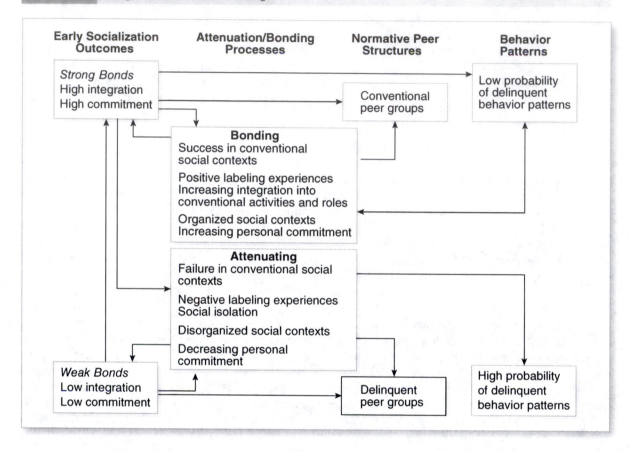

Other control theorists, such as Reiss (1951), Nye (1958), and Reckless (1967) use a more general classification of bonds as internal (personal) and external (social) controls. Hirschi's dimensions are not easily placed into these two general categories, although Hirschi identifies attachment as an internal and involvement as an external element of the bond (1969, p. 19). We believe that distinguishing internal controls, whose locus is within the person (beliefs, commitment, attitudes, perceptions), from external controls, whose locus is in the surrounding social and physical milieu, poses fewer difficulties and produces greater conceptual clarity than is found in Hirschi's four concepts.

The external, or social, bond we have defined as *integration*. By this, we refer to involvement in and attachment to conventional groups and institutions, such as the family,

school, peer networks, and so on. Those persons who occupy and are actively involved in conventional social roles are, by this definition, highly integrated. Group controls exist in the form of sanctioning networks (the formal and informal rules and regulations by which the behavior of social role occupants or group members is regulated). This conceptualization of integration is akin to Hirschi's concepts of involvement and commitment.

The internal, or personal, bond is defined as *commitment*. Commitment involves personal attachment to conventional roles, groups, and institutions. At another level, it reflects the extent to which one feels morally bound by the social norms and rules and the degree to which one internalizes or adopts those norms as directives for action. Our notion of commitment is akin to Hirschi's concepts of attachment and belief. Integration and commitment together constitute the bonds which tie an individual to the prevailing social order. High levels of integration and commitment imply strong bonds and general insulation from delinquent behavior. Conversely, low social integration and commitment presuppose weak bonds and a susceptibility to delinquent behavior. All gradations of integration and commitment are possible.

Building Social Control: The Bonding/Attenuation Processes

The inclusion of the bonding/attenuation process in the model suggests that, throughout adolescence, youths are involved in experiences and processes which attenuate or reinforce their childhood bonds to the conventional social order. Adolescence is a critical life period, both psychologically and socially. As youths make the transition from childhood to adulthood, the level of involvement in the immediate family declines and they move into new and more complex social settings at school and in the community. For one who developed strong childhood bonds, such factors as (1) success experiences at school and in the larger community, (2) positive labeling in these new settings, and (3) a continuous, stable, harmonious home life constitute positive reinforcements of initially strong bonds and continuing insulation from delinquency. For some, the transition is not as smooth, and failure, negative labeling, isolation, and rejection occur in these new social settings; these, in turn, may create difficulties in the youth's relationship with his family. The net effect of these new experiences may be a weakening of one's integration into . . . these social groups and institutions and an increasing likelihood of involvement in delinquent behavior. Finally, for those who never developed strong bonds during childhood, bonding/attenuation experiences will either strengthen the weak bonds, thus reducing the likelihood of delinquency, or further attenuate them, thus maintaining or increasing the probability of delinquent behavior.

We do not propose that this specific set of variables exhausts the possible experiences or conditions which might attenuate or reinforce one's bonds to society during adolescence. Rather, we have purposely selected those conditions and experiences which prior theory and research have suggested as critical variables to illustrate the major dimensions of the paradigm.

Delinquent Learning and Performance Structures

A major criticism of control theory has been that weak bonds and the implied absence of restraints cannot alone account for the specific form or content of the behavior which results. They may account for a state of "drift," as described by Matza (1964), but they do not explain why some youths in this state turn to delinquency, drug use, and various unconventional subcultures, while others maintain an essentially conforming pattern of behavior; nor can they account for emerging patterns of delinquency which may be unique to particular ages or birth cohorts. We therefore postulate that access to and involvement in delinquent learning and performance structures is a necessary (but not sufficient) variable in the etiology of delinquent behavior. Following Sutherland (1947), we maintain that delinquent behavior, like conforming behavior, presupposes a pattern of social relationships through which motives, rationalizations, techniques, and rewards can be learned and maintained (Akers, 1977; Bandura, 1969, 1973; Burgess & Akers, 1966a, 1966b; Mischel, 1968). Delinquent behavior is thus viewed as behavior which has social meaning and must be supported and rewarded by social groups if it is to persist.

By the time children enter adolescence, virtually all have been sufficiently exposed to criminal forms of behavior to have "learned" or acquired some potential for such acts. The more critical issue for any theory of delinquency is why and how this universal potential is transformed into delinquent acts for some youths and not others. For most learning theorists, a distinction is made between learning and performance and the latter is directly tied to reinforcements (Bandura, 1969; Bandura & Walters, 1963; Mischel, 1968; Rotter, 1954). . . .

According to the present social learning formulation, learning or acquisition of novel responses is regulated by sensory and cognitive processes; learning may be facilitated by reinforcement but does not depend on it (e.g., Bandura & Walters, 1963; Hebb, 1966). Direct and vicarious reinforcements are, however, important determinants of response selection in performance.

The delinquent peer group thus provides a positive social setting that is essential for the performance and maintenance of delinquent patterns of behavior over time. Those committed to conventional goals, although they may have been exposed to and learned some delinquent behaviors, should not establish patterns of such behavior unless (1) their ties to the conventional social order are neutralized through some attenuating experiences and (2) they are participating in a social context in which delinquent behavior is rewarded. In social learning terms, they may have acquired or learned delinquent behavior patterns, but the actual performance and maintenance of such behavior are contingent on attenuation of their commitment to conventional norms and their participation in a social context supportive of delinquent acts. Alternatively, for those with weak ties and commitments to the conventional social order, there is no reason for a delay between acquisition and performance of delinquent acts.

In the causal sequence described by strain theory, the individual holds conventional goals but is unable to attain them by conventional means. If attachment to the goals is strong enough, it may support delinquent behavior without participation in delinquent groups, for attaining these goals may provide sufficient reinforcement to maintain the behavior. Therefore, our model shows one direct route to delinquent behavior from attenuating experiences, without mediating group support for delinquency. We view this as the atypical case, however, and postulate that it is difficult to sustain this causal sequence for extended periods of time.

Involvement in a delinquent group is a necessary condition for sustained patterns of delinquency among persons who do not subscribe to conventional goals (the weakly socialized person described by control theory). Individual patterns of delinquency (without group support) are more viable for those committed to conventional goals because there are generally shared expectations and social supports for achievement of those goals. For youths with weak bonds, involvement in a delinquent peer group serves this support function. Cohen (1966) has observed that delinquency often involves a desire for recognition and social acceptance, and, therefore, requires group visibility and support. Maintenance of delinquent behavior patterns should require some exposure to and participation in groups supporting delinquent activities. Though not a necessary condition for delinquent behavior among those with initially strong bonds, contact with delinquent groups should, nevertheless, increase the likelihood of sustained delinquent behavior.

Delineation of the delinquent peer group as a necessary condition for maintenance of delinquent behavior patterns represents an extension of previous statements of control theory. . . . It is one thing to be a social isolate with weak bonds to conventional peer groups and another to be highly committed to and integrated into a delinquent peer group. Both persons may be characterized as having weak bonds to the social order, with few conventional restraints on their behavior; but those committed to and participating in delinquent peer groups have some incentive and social support for specifically delinquent forms of behavior. We agree with Hirschi's (1969) and Hepburn's (1976) argument that those with a large stake in conformity (strong bonds) are relatively immune to delinquent peer group influence. However, we postulate that, in addition to weak bonding and an absence of restraints, some positive motivation is necessary for sustained involvement in delinquent behavior. In the absence of positive motivation, we would not predict significant involvement in delinquency across time even for those with weak bonds, for there is no apparent mechanism for maintaining such behavior (Brennan, Huizinga, & Elliott, 1978). It may be that some exploratory, "primary" forms of delinquency (Lemert, 1951) may occur without group support, or that this constitutes a pathological path to delinquency, but the maintenance of delinquent behavior patterns usually requires some exposure to and participation in groups supporting delinquent activity.

In sum, we postulate that bonding to conventional groups and institutions insulates one from involvement in delinquent patterns of behavior and that bonding to deviant groups or subcultures facilitates and sustains delinquent behavior. When examining the influence of social bonds, it is critical that the normative orientation of particular groups be taken into account. This focus on the normative orientations of groups is the central theme in subcultural theories of delinquency (Cloward & Ohlin, 1960; Cohen, 1955; Miller, 1958) and constitutes an important qualification to a simple interpretation of the relationship between social bonds and delinquency. This position has an empirical as well as a theoretical base. . . .

Delinquent Behavior

Delinquent behavior is viewed as a special subclass of deviant behavior. While deviance includes all violations of all prevailing norms, delinquent behavior includes only violations of statutory proscriptive norms, or, as they are usually called, laws. Thus, delinquent behavior takes on special meaning because (1) there is generally broad community consensus for these norms, (2) virtually all persons are aware that these specific proscriptions are enforced by official sanctions, and (3) the risk of detection and punishment influences the performance of delinquent acts.

We are not concerned here with the isolated delinquent act. Our focus is on sustained patterns of delinquent behavior, whether the person involved is socially or self-defined as a delinquent or nondelinquent person. Although our definition of delinquency subsumes one characteristic of a delinquent role (sustained patterns of delinquent behavior), it is our view that continuing involvement in delinquency may not necessarily involve the enactment of a delinquent role (Becker, 1963). There is empirical evidence that many embezzlers, auto thieves, check forgers, shoplifters, and persons involved in violent assaults against persons (including rape) do not view themselves as criminal or delinquent (Cameron, 1964; Gauthier, 1959; Gebhard et al., 1965; Lemert, 1951, 1953; Robin, 1974). Furthermore, many adolescents involved in sustained patterns of delinquent behavior are never apprehended and publicly labeled as delinquent persons, and have neither a public nor a self-definition as a delinquent or criminal person (Cameron, 1964; Hirschi, 1969; Jensen, 1972; Kelly, 1977; Reiss, 1961; Sykes & Matza, 1957). Thus, our conceptualization of delinquency focuses on sustained patterns of illegal behavior and is logically independent of the concept of delinquent role.

Etiological Paths to Delinquency

There are two dominant etiological paths to delinquency in the paradigm shown in Figure 1. The first involves an integration of traditional control theory and social-learning theory. Weak integration into and commitment to the social order, absence of conventional restraints on behavior, and high vulnerability to the influence of delinquent peer groups during adolescence characterize the socialization experiences related to the first path. Depending on the presence and accessibility of conventional and delinquent peer groups, some weakly bonded youths turn to delinquency while others maintain an essentially conforming pattern of behavior or a legal, but

unconventional, lifestyle. The crucial element in this path is the delinquent peer group. Weakly bonded youths may not hold conventional aspirations (as for academic success), but they do share in more general aspirations for friendship and acceptance, as well as status and material rewards, which may be offered through participation in a group. Given an absence of conventional restraints and access to delinquent groups, the reasons for involvement are not unlike those for involvement in more conventional peer groups during adolescence.

The second path represents an integration of traditional strain and social-learning perspectives. Youths who follow this path develop strong bonds to the conventional social order through their socialization experiences. The crucial element in this sequence is the attenuation, or weakening, of these bonds. Attenuating experiences during adolescence involve personal failure to achieve conventional goals and/or threats to the stability and cohesion of one's conventional social groups. Once one's bonds are effectively weakened, like those who never developed strong bonds, one is free to explore alternative means for goal achievement and to participate in delinquent or unconventional groups.

In most instances, this path also involves participation in peer groups which tolerate or encourage delinquent forms of behavior. It is our view that truly individual adaptations to this situation are unlikely to survive long enough to generate detectable patterns of delinquent behavior. However, two possible subtypes deserve mention. The diagram of this integrated paradigm shows a direct causal path from initially strong bonds and subsequent attenuation experiences to delinquent behavior patterns. Under some circumstances, participation in groups providing reinforcements for delinquent acts is unnecessary. Attenuating experiences are sufficient to motivate repeated acts of delinquency, which are attempts to regain conventional rewards through unconventional means. This pattern involves the classic strain model, in which the person retains a strong commitment to conventional goals and values and uses illegal means as a temporary expedient. The attenuation process is only partial, and these youths retain some commitment to and integration into conventional groups. We anticipate such patterns to be of relatively short duration and to involve highly instrumental forms of delinquent behavior. Patterns of theft may characterize this etiological path.

A second subtype corresponds to that described generally by Simon and Gagnon (1976) in their article on the anomie of affluence. This path involves those whose commitments to conventional goals are attenuated by a decreasing gratification derived from goal achievement. Unlike the previously described subtype, which involved failure to achieve conventional success goals because of limited means or abilities, this type has ability and a ready access to legitimate means and is successful by conventional standards. The failure to derive personal gratification from "success" results in an attenuation of the commitment to these success goals and sets in motion a search for alternative goals whose attainment will provide a greater measure of personal gratification. This path to delinquency clearly requires participation in social groups in which delinquent behavior patterns can be learned and reinforced. This pattern of delinquency is characterized by a search for new experiences, which frequently involves illegal forms of behavior, such as illicit drug use and sex-related offenses.

At a more tentative level, we postulate that the two major paths (1) typically involve different forms of personal alienation and (2) result in different self-images and social labels. Conceptually, alienation plays a slightly different role within strain and control perspectives. From a control perspective, alienation, in the form of powerlessness, societal estrangement, and social isolation, directly reflects a weak personal commitment to conventional groups and norms. For strain theory, however, alienation represents a crucial intervening variable linking failure to delinquency. It is evidence of the attenuation of one's commitment bond or, in Hirschi's (1969) terms, the neutralization of "moral obstacles" to delinquency. In the form of alienation described by Cloward and Ohlin (1960), the neutralization is achieved through a blaming process in which failure is attributed to others or to general societal injustice. These same elements are present in Sykes and Matza's (1957) techniques of neutralization. Cartwright et al. (1966) and Cartwright (1971) identify four types of alienation which provide this direct encouragement, justification, or permission for delinquency: normlessness, futility, lack of trust, and perceived indifference. If we assume some relationship between the two causal paths and social class, there is some indirect empirical support for the hypothesis that the form of alienation is tied to the strength of one's initial commitment bond. . . .

We also hypothesize that those with initially strong bonds are less likely to view themselves as delinquent, even when they are involved in sustained patterns of delinquent behavior. Such persons are more likely to come from advantaged backgrounds and to have prosocial self-images. Consequently, they are likely to view their delinquent acts as temporary expedients, retaining at least a partial commitment to conventional goals. The probability of apprehension and public labeling by the police and courts is also much lower for such youths. In contrast, those who never developed strong bonds to the social order are more vulnerable to labeling processes and thus more likely to be viewed as delinquents by themselves and by others (Jensen, 1972). This may account, in part, for the persistent view among law enforcement officials and the general public that most delinquents are poor and/or nonwhite, in spite of the compelling evidence that the incidence of delinquent behavior is unrelated to these variables.

▧ Summary and Discussion

. . . . We believe the synthesis of traditional strain, social control, and social-learning perspectives into a single paradigm has several advantages over a conceptualization which treats each theory as separate and independent. First, the provision for multiple etiological paths to delinquency in a single paradigm presents a more comprehensive view. The integration of strain and control perspectives assumes that these two paths are independent and additive and that their integration will account for more variance in sustained patterns of delinquent behavior than either can explain independently. Independent tests of these traditional perspectives in the past have often failed to include the variables necessary to test alternative explanations, and even when such variables were available, the alternative explanations were assumed to be competitive and were thus evaluated with respect to the relative strengths of the two competing hypotheses (Eve, 1977: Hirschi, 1969). Such an approach misses the possibility that both hypotheses are correct and are accounting for different portions of the variance in delinquency. We have also suggested that different patterns of delinquency may be tied to alternative etiological paths; for example, we postulated that one of the strain paths (limited means/goal failure) should produce forms of delinquency which are considered very instrumental by conventional values. The alternative strain path (attenuated commitment to conventional goals) should result in less instrumental forms of delinquency, since it characteristically involves a search for new experiences (e.g., drug use) rather than attempts to achieve conventional goals.

Second, we believe that our integrated paradigm is consistent with previous empirical findings and offers some insight into contradictory findings. Previous research using the social control perspective has established a relationship between the strength of one's bonds and social class, with low-SES and minority youths characterized by weaker bonds (Gold, 1963; Hirschi, 1969; McKinley, 1964; Nye, 1958). In contrast, the attenuated commitment strain path has been associated with affluence, and the limited means-strain path seems most relevant to working-class youths. The combined effect seems consistent with the observed class distribution of self-reported delinquent behavior. Our assumption that weakly bonded youths run the greatest risk of official processing (because of greater surveillance in their neighborhoods, more traditional forms of delinquent behavior, and limited resources with which to avoid processing in the justice system) would account for the observed class distribution of official measures of delinquency. . . .

References

Ageton, S., & Elliott, D. S. (1974). The effects of legal processing on delinquent orientations. *Social Problems, 22,* 87–100.

Akers, R. (1977). *Deviant behavior: A social learning perspective.* Belmont, CA: Wadsworth.

Andry, R. G. (1962). Parental affection and delinquency. In M. E. Wolfgang, L. Savitz, & N. Johnston (Eds.), *The sociology of crime and delinquency* (pp. 342–352). New York: Wiley.

Bandura, A. (1969). *Principles of behavior modification.* New York: Holt, Rinehart & Winston.

Bandura, A. (1973). *Aggression: A social learning analysis.* Englewood Cliffs, NJ: Prentice Hall.

Bandura, A., & Walters, R. H. (1963). *Social learning and personality development.* New York: Holt, Rinehart & Winston.

Becker, H. S. (1960). Notes on the concept of commitment. *American Journal of Sociology, 66,* 32–40.

Becker, H. S. (1963). *Outsiders.* New York: Free Press.

Brennan, T. (1974). *Evaluation and validation regarding the National Strategy for Youth Development: A review of findings* (Report submitted to the Office of Youth Development). Boulder, CO: Behavioral Research and Evaluation Corporation.

Brennan, T., Huizinga, D., & Elliott, D. S. (1978). *The social psychology of runaways.* Lexington, MA: D. C. Heath.

Burgess, R. L., & Akers, R. L. (1966a). Are operant principles tautological? *Psychological Record, 16,* 305–312.

Burgess, R. L., & Akers, R. L. (1966b). A different association-reinforcement theory of criminal behavior. *Social Problems, 14,* 128–147.

Cameron, M. O. (1964). *The booster and the snitch.* New York: Free Press.

Cartwright, D. S. (1971). *Summary of conceptual issues in the National Strategy for Delinquency Prevention* (Document No. 34 in Center for Action Research). Boulder, CO: University of Colorado, Bureau of Sociological Research.

Cartwright, D. S., Reuterman, N. A., & Vandiver, R. I. (1966). *Multiple-factor approach to delinquency.* Boulder: Department of Psychology, University of Colorado.

Cloward, R. A., & Ohlin, L. E. (1960). *Delinquency and opportunity—A theory of delinquent gangs.* New York: Free Press.

Cohen, A. K. (1955). *Delinquent boys: The culture of the gang.* Glencoe, IL: Free Press.

Cohen, A. (1966). *Deviance and control.* Englewood Cliffs, NJ: Prentice Hall.

Durkheim, E. (1951). *Suicide: A study of sociology.* Glencoe, IL: Free Press. (Original work published 1897)

Elliott, D. S. (1962). Delinquency and perceived opportunity. *Sociological Inquiry, 32,* 216–227.

Elliott, D. S., & Voss, H. (1974). *Delinquency and dropout.* Lexington, MA: D. C. Heath.

Eve, R. (1977). *The efficacy of strain, culture conflict and social control theories for explaining rebelliousness among high school students.* Unpublished manuscript, University of Texas at Arlington.

Gauthier, M. (1959). The psychology of the compulsive forger. *Canadian Journal of Corrections, 1,* 62–69.

Gebhard, P. H., et al. (1965). *Sex offenders.* New York: Harper & Row.

Gibbons, D. C. (1977). *Society, crime and criminal careers* (3rd ed.). Englewood Cliffs, NJ: Prentice Hall.

Glueck, S., & Glueck, E. (1950). *Unraveling juvenile delinquency.* Cambridge, MA: Harvard University Press.

Gold, M. (1963). *Status forces in delinquent boys.* Ann Arbor: University of Michigan, Institute for Social Research.

Goldman, N. (1963). *The differential selection of juvenile offenders for court appearance.* Washington, DC: National Council on Crime and Delinquency.

Goode, W. J. (1960). Norm commitment and conformity to role status obligation. *American Journal of Sociology, 64,* 246–258.

Hebb, D. O. (1966). *Psychology.* Philadelphia: Saunders.

Hepburn, J. R. (1976). Testing alternative models of delinquency causation. *Journal of Criminal Law and Criminology, 67,* 450–460.

Hirschi, T. (1969). *Causes of delinquency.* Berkeley: University of California Press.

Jensen, G. F. (1972). Delinquency and adolescent self-conceptions: A study of the personal relevance of infraction. *Social Problems, 20*, 84–103.

Jessor, R., et al. (1968). *Society, personality and deviant behavior: A study of a tri-ethnic community.* New York: Holt, Rinehart & Winston.

Kelly, D. H. (1977). The effects of legal processing upon a delinquent's public identity: An analytical and empirical critique. *Education, 97*, 280–289.

Kitsuse, J. I. (1962). Societal reaction to deviant behavior: Problems of theory and method. *Social Problems, 9*(Winter), 247–256.

Lemert, E. M. (1951). *Social pathology.* New York: McGraw-Hill.

Lemert, E. M. (1953). An isolation and closure theory of naive check forgery. *Journal of Criminal Law, Criminology and Police Science, 44*, 296–307.

Liska, A. E. (1971). Aspirations, expectations and delinquency: Stress and additive models. *Sociological Quarterly, 12*, 99–107.

Matza, D. (1964). *Delinquency and drift.* New York: Wiley.

McKinley, D. G. (1964). *Social class and family life.* New York: Free Press.

Miller, W. B. (1958). Lower class culture as a generating milieu of gang delinquency. *Journal of Social Issues, 14*(3), 5–19.

Mischel, W. (1968). *Personality and assessment.* New York: Wiley.

Monahan, T. P. (1957). Family status and the delinquent child: A reappraisal and some new findings. *Social Forces, 35*, 250–258.

Nye, F. I. (1958). *Family relationships and delinquent behavior.* New York: Wiley.

Reckless, Walter. (1967). *The Crime Problem* (4th ed.). New York: Appleton-Century-Crofts.

Reiss, A. J., Jr. (1951). Delinquency as the failure of personal and social controls. *American Sociological Review, 16*, 196–207.

Reiss, A. J., Jr. (1961). The social integration of queers and peers. *Social Problems, 9*, 102–120.

Robin, G. (1974). The American customer: Shopper or shoplifter? *Police, 8*, 6–14.

Rosen, L. (1970). The broken home and male delinquency. In M. E. Wolfgang, L. Savitz, & N. Johnston (Eds.), *The sociology of crime and delinquency* (2nd ed., pp. 484–495). New York: Wiley.

Rotter, J. B. (1954). *Social learning and clinical psychology.* Englewood Cliffs, NJ: Prentice Hall.

Rubington, E. R., & Weinberg, M. S. (Eds.). (1968). *Deviance: The interactionist perspective.* New York: Macmillan.

Savitz, L. (1970). Delinquency and migration. In M. E. Wolfgang, L. Savitz, & N. Johnston (Eds.), *The sociology of crime and delinquency* (2nd ed., pp. 473–480). New York: Wiley.

Schur, E. M. (1971). *Labeling deviant behavior.* New York: Harper & Row.

Seeman, M. (1959). On the meaning of alienation. *American Sociological Review, 24*, 783–791.

Shaw, G. (1931). *Delinquency areas.* Chicago: University of Chicago Press.

Short, J. F., Jr. (1964). Gang delinquency and anomie. In M. B. Clinard (Ed.), *Anomie and deviant behavior* (pp. 98–127). New York: Free Press.

Short, J. F., Jr., Rivera, R., & Tennyson, R. A. (1965). Perceived opportunities, gang membership and delinquency. *American Sociological Review, 30*, 56–67.

Simon, W., & Gagnon, J. H. (1976). The anomie of affluence: A post Mertonian conception. *American Journal of Sociology, 82*, 356–378.

Spergel, I. (1967). Deviant patterns and opportunities of pre-adolescent Negro boys in three Chicago neighborhoods. In M. W. Klein (Ed.), *Juvenile gangs in context: Theory, research and action* (pp. 38–54). Englewood Cliffs, NJ: Prentice Hall.

Sutherland, E. H. (1947). *Criminology.* Philadelphia: J. B. Lippincott.

Sykes, G. M., & Matza, D. (1957). Techniques of neutralization: A theory of delinquency. *American Sociological Review, 22*, 664–670.

Thomas, W. I., & Znaniecki, F. (1927). *The Polish peasant in Europe and America.* New York: Knopf.

Toby, J. (1957). The differential impact of family disorganization. *American Sociological Review, 22*, 505–512.

REVIEW QUESTIONS

1. In the integrated model proposed by Elliott and his colleagues, which theoretical perspective is considered to be antecedent, or most important in the early stages, for developing delinquent or criminal tendencies? Do you agree with this portion of the model?

2. Do you think it is rational to merge theoretical perspectives that have opposing basic assumptions, such as merging strain theory, which claims that individuals are born good, with perspectives such as control theory, which claims that people are born bad and must be taught or controlled to be good? Or to merge them with learning theories, such as differential association/reinforcement, that assume individuals are born neither good nor bad, but rather as a "blank slate"? If you agree with such integration, explain your reasoning. If not, why?

3. Ultimately, what do you think of Elliott and his colleagues' model? Do you think it was a good early attempt at an integrated theory, or do you think it was rather weak given the information they had at that time (1979)?

❖

READING 30

In this selection, Carter Hay examines the empirical validity of a more modern and well-respected integrated theoretical model, namely, John Braithwaite's theory of reintegrative shaming. We examined Braithwaite's integrated model in the introduction to this section, and Hay provides one of the first empirical tests of the theory's propositions regarding individuals. The author does this with an American sample, which consists of 197 adolescents from one region in the United States.

While reading this selection, readers should consider the extent to which the primary concepts or variables in the model are represented, such as the way youths are shamed negatively or in a more positive, reintegrative form. Also, readers should consider whether the effects of reintegrative shaming reduce delinquency among youth.

An Exploratory Test of Braithwaite's Reintegrative Shaming Theory

Carter Hay

Reintegrative Shaming Theory

John Braithwaite first put forth reintegrative shaming theory (RST) in the book *Crime, Shame and Reintegration* (Braithwaite 1989). The theory's essential argument is that the precise ways in which societies, communities, and families sanction deviance affect the extent to which their members engage in predatory criminal behavior. The key explanatory variable in the theory is shaming, which Braithwaite defines as any social process that expresses disapproval of a sanctioned act such that there is the intent or effect of invoking moral regret in the person being shamed (p. 100). Braithwaite is explicit about how shaming contrasts with a more classical view of sanctioning: "Shaming, unlike purely deterrent punishment, sets out to *moralize* [emphasis added] with the offender to communicate reasons for the evil of her actions" (p. 100).

Shaming is not, however, a uniform type of sanctioning—it can be done in different ways and in different contexts. Braithwaite (1989) distinguishes between two types of shaming. First, shaming is reintegrative when it reinforces an offender's membership in the community of law-abiding citizens. This prevents the shamed individual from adopting a deviant master status and is accomplished when shaming (1) maintains bonds of love or respect between the person being shamed and the person doing the shaming, (2) is directed at the evil of the act rather than the evil of the person, (3) is delivered in a context of general social approval, and (4) is terminated with gestures or ceremonies of forgiveness (pp. 100–1).

Reintegrative shaming is contrasted with stigmatization, which is disintegrative shaming in which little or no effort is made to forgive offenders or affirm the basic goodness of their character and thus reinforce their membership in the community of law-abiding citizens. Stigmatization can be seen essentially as shaming in the absence of reintegration—it is the converse of each of the four aspects of reintegration mentioned earlier. The primary importance of stigmatization is that it treats offenders as outcasts and provokes a rebellious and criminal reaction from them: "Shaming that is stigmatizing ... makes criminal subcultures

SOURCE: Hay, Carter. "An Exploratory Test of Braithwaite's Reintegrative Shaming Theory," *Journal of Research in Crime and Delinquency*, 38(2):132–153.

more attractive because these are in some sense subcultures which reject the rejectors" (Braithwaite 1989:102).

RST's basic prediction therefore is quite simple: There should be a negative relationship between the use of reintegrative shaming and the extent of criminal behavior. This prediction is applicable to both micro- and macro-level units of analysis. That is, just as individuals who are exposed to reintegrative shaming should commit fewer crimes, communities or societies with high levels of reintegrative shaming should have low aggregate rates of crime.

The focus of this study is the micro-level portion of the theory, and three further points about the theory should be emphasized. First, Braithwaite (1989) specifies the antecedent of reintegrative shaming: Whether individuals are exposed to reintegrative shaming to begin with should be a function of their involvement in interdependent relationships. Braithwaite describes interdependency in the following way:

> Interdependency is a condition of individuals. It means the extent to which individuals participate in networks wherein they are dependent on others to achieve valued ends and others are dependent on them. . . . Interdependency is approximately equivalent to the social bonding, attachment and commitment of control theory. (pp. 99–100)

Braithwaite (1989) argues that several individual characteristics generally found to reduce crime—age (being younger than 15 and older than 25), being married, being female, and having a job—do so because they increase involvement in interdependent relationships and therefore increase the chances that rule-violating behavior will be met with reintegrative shaming rather than stigmatization.

Second, key to the theory is the interaction between reintegration and shaming: The combination of reintegration and shaming should have an effect on offending that exceeds the sum of each variable's independent effects. In fact, strictly speaking, neither variable should have an independent effect on offending (Braithwaite 1989:99; Makkai and Braithwaite 1994:371–72). Instead, the effects of shaming should be conditional on the level of reintegration. When reintegration is high, shaming should be negatively related to offending. When reintegration is low, shaming has a stigmatizing effect and should be positively related to offending.

A third point to emphasize about RST is that it limits its scope to the explanation of predatory offenses against persons and property. The reason for this restricted focus is that reintegrative shaming is thought to be relevant only for offenses in which there is consensus regarding their moral wrongfulness. When such consensus is lacking, shaming should not be influential.

 ## The Current Study

This study reports an exploratory test of the micro-level predictions of RST. As has been noted elsewhere (Braithwaite 1989:120–21; Hay 1998:424), there are substantial barriers to testing the macro-level portions of RST. Using survey research to measure reintegrative shaming across a sample of communities or societies would be prohibitively expensive. Moreover, researchers have yet to identify proxies for community- or societal-wide levels of reintegrative shaming.

This study instead will examine the more testable micro-level arguments of RST. Specifically, adolescents are taken as the units of analysis, and the focus is on the relationship between their perceptions of their parents' sanctioning methods and their reports of predatory delinquency. This strategy would seem acceptable to Braithwaite (1989), who noted that "the best place to see reintegrative shaming at work is in loving families" (p. 56). The analysis will address three principal research questions: (1) What variables predict the extent to which parents respond to adolescent rule-violating behavior with reintegration and shaming? (2) Do reintegration and shaming statistically interact to affect predatory delinquency, or are their effects additive? (3) Are any observed effects of reintegration and shaming on delinquency merely a result of spuriousness?

Data and Method

Sample. The data used to examine the research questions mentioned above come from anonymous, self-administered questionnaires completed by a sample of 197 adolescents taken from a single urban area in a southwestern state of the United States. Respondents were located through their attendance in a single high school located in the central part of the urban area. This school was chosen because of its diversity in race/ethnicity and socioeconomic status. All students enrolled in physical education classes during the fall of 1998 were invited to participate in the study.[1] Roughly 60 percent of students completed and returned the necessary consent forms and took part in the study.

Table 1	Characteristics of the Sample (N = 197)	
Variable	**Category**	**Percentage of Sample**
Age	14	25.8
	15	30.8
	16	24.7
	17	13.2
	Other	5.5
Sex	Male	47.8
	Female	52.2
Race	White	40.9
	Hispanic	32.0
	African American	19.9
	Other	7.2
Family structure	Mother and father	44.8
	Two-parent other	16.0
	Single parent	39.2
Mother's education	High school diploma or less	44.8
Father's education	High school diploma or less	43.2

Table 1 shows the demographic characteristics of the sample. Most respondents are between the ages of 14 and 17, and the sex ratio of the sample is roughly 1 to 1. The sample is diverse in terms of race/ethnicity, with Whites, Hispanics, and Africans Americans all highly represented. Family disruption is common, with only 45 percent of respondents living in a household with their biological mother and father. Also, close to 45 percent of respondents' parents have a high school diploma or less.

Measurement of key variables. As more quantitative tests of RST emerge, knowledge of how reintegration and shaming should be measured will emerge as well. For now, however, this study makes essentially the same qualifying statement that has appeared in two prior quantitative analyses of RST (Makkai and Braithwaite 1994:368; Zhang 1995:251): Measuring reintegration and shaming is no easy task, and the measures used in this study should be improved on as more research is conducted.

Consistent with Braithwaite's (1989:100) discussion of shaming, the key measurement concern was to identify sanctions that involved "moralizing." Three survey items were selected and scaled. With these items, respondents were asked to indicate how much importance their mother and father place on three goals when reacting to a violation of any rule considered important by the parent: convincing the adolescent that what he or she did was immoral or unfair, making him or her feel guilty or ashamed for what was done, and having him or her "make up" for the actions by apologizing or helping to erase any harm that was done."[2]

Parents' use of reintegration was measured with a scale comprising four items that correspond to the four aspects of reintegration discussed earlier. The first two items asked respondents to indicate how much they agreed or disagreed that their parents see them as good people even when upset with them and treat them with respect when they are disciplining them. For the last two items, respondents assessed how likely it is that in response to their rule violations, parents would tell them that they are "bad kids" and eventually express their forgiveness to the adolescents.

All of the shaming and reintegration items asked respondents to assess their mother and father separately. Preliminary analyses indicated that mothers and fathers did not differ in terms of their use of shaming and reintegration or the effects of those variables on predatory offending. Scores for mothers and fathers were therefore combined to create an overall score for parents. Responses to the shaming and reintegration scales were coded so that high scorers perceive high levels of the two variables.

Delinquency was measured with two different variables. The first is a nine-item scale of early childhood antisocial behavior that will be used to protect against spuriousness and examine whether childhood behavioral problems predict parents' use of reintegrative shaming. For these items, respondents were asked to indicate the earliest age at which they committed nine offenses: breaking into a building or house, stealing things worth $50 or less, stealing things worth more than $50, purposely damaging or destroying property, taking a car for a drive without the owner's permission, getting in a fight with someone with the idea of seriously hurting him or her, carrying a hidden weapon such as a knife or gun, drinking alcohol, and using marijuana or some other drug. For each item, responses were coded 1 if the respondent reported committing the act by age 11 or earlier and 0 if he or she had not. The nine items were summed to produce a measure of childhood antisocial behavior, with possible scores ranging from 0 to 9 and a mean of 1.24.

The second delinquency variable is a measure of adolescents' projected involvement in the first seven offenses listed above. Importantly, each of the seven acts is an illegal violent or property offense and therefore fits within RST's emphasis on predatory offenses. These survey items asked respondents the following question: "If you found yourself in a situation where you had the chance to do the following things [each of the seven offenses], how likely is it that you would do each one?" Respondents chose an answer from a scale of 0 to 10, where 0 means there is no chance that they would commit the act, 5 means there is a "50–50 chance," and 10 means that they definitely would commit the act. The seven items were averaged to create a projected predatory delinquency scale, with scores ranging from 0 to 10 and a mean of 2.55. The Cronbach's alpha for the scale is .90.

This measure of projected delinquency—rather than self-reported past delinquency—was used as a dependent variable to avoid the causal order problems that often arise in cross-sectional delinquency research. Cross-sectional studies that use self-reported past offending as the dependent variable suffer inherent causal order problems if independent variables are measured with items about respondents' current attitudes and perceptions—any assertion of appropriate causal order is questionable if current attitudes and perceptions are used to explain past behavior. Thus, the clear strength of a projected offending variable is that it allows for clear conceptualization of causal ordering with cross-sectional data (Tittle 1977:586).

Measures of projected offending have been used effectively by a number of other researchers (e.g., Bachman, Paternoster, and Ward 1992; Grasmick, Bursik, and Arneklev 1993; Grasmick and Bursik 1990; Jensen and Stitt 1982; Tittle 1980). A few things attest to their validity. First, variables that are known to predict self-reported offending in longitudinal designs have also been found to predict projected offending (Jensen and Stitt 1982; Tittle 1980). Second, using a two-wave panel design, Green (1989) found that projections of future deviance were highly correlated with actual subsequent deviance (r =.80). The current evidence therefore suggests that measures of projected

offending are useful for avoiding the causal order problems associated with cross-sectional data.

Analysis

The Prediction of Reintegration and Shaming

The first issue to consider involves the antecedents of parental reintegration and shaming—that is, what variables predict that adolescents' parents will respond to their rule-violating behavior with reintegration and shaming? Braithwaite (1989) argues that involvement in interdependent relationships should be the most important factor; moreover, many demographic variables known to predict offending may do so because they increase involvement in interdependent relationships.

To consider that possibility, three regression equations were estimated for both dependent variable, reintegration and shaming. Equation (1) includes five exogenous variables: four demographic variables (age, sex, family structure, and race/ethnicity) and a measure of childhood antisocial behavior.[3] Although Braithwaite (1989) makes no reference to how childhood behavior problems affect parental reintegration and shaming during adolescence, much research suggests that parent-child interactions are highly reciprocal (e.g., Cohen and Brook 1995; Kandel and Wu 1995; Sampson and Laub 1993).

Equations (2) and (3) consider the role of parent-child interdependency. Equation (2) adds individual measures of three parent-child interdependency variables—adolescent attachment to parents, adolescent perceptions of parents' feelings of attachment for them, and adolescent reports of instrumental and intimate communication with parents.[4] If Braithwaite's (1989) predictions are correct, the parent-child interdependency variables should have significant effects on reintegration and shaming, and their inclusion in the model should substantially weaken any effects of the exogenous variables that are observed in equation (1). Equation (3) examines the same issue, but rather than considering interdependency as three separate variables, a combined measure is used. This combined measure is simply an average of its three component parts.

Table 2 shows the results of the analysis and reveals moderate support for RST's predictions. Looking first at the results of equation (1) for reintegration, only race/ethnicity

Table 2	Standardized Coefficients and Fit for Ordinary Least Squares Regressions of Reintegration and Shaming on Exogenous Variables and Parent-Child Interdependency		
Independent Variable	**1**	**2**	**3**
Reintegration			
Age	−.04	−.03	−.04
Sex	.02	−.04	−.03
Race/ethnicity	−.13*	−.09*	−.08
Family structure	−.11	−.08	−.09
Childhood antisocial behavior	−.23*	−.05	−.04
Attachment to parents	—	.40*	—
Perceived parental attachment to child	—	.30*	—
Parent-child communication	—	.12	—
Parent-child interdependency	—	—	.72*
R^2	.09	.57	.56
Shaming			
Age	−.01	.00	−.01
Sex	−.05	−.07	−.06
Race/ethnicity	−.05	−.02	−.04
Family structure	−.11	−.10	−.10
Childhood antisocial behavior	−.06	−.01	−.01
Attachment to parents	—	−.01	—
Perceived parental attachment to child	−.17	—	—
Parent-child communication	—	.08	—
Parent-child interdependency	—	—	.20*
R^2	.02	.07	.06

NOTE: Age was measured as a continuous variable in years. Sex, race/ethnicity, and family structure were measured with dummy variables: Sex was coded 1 for males and 0 for females, race/ethnicity was coded 1 for non-Whites and 0 for Whites, and family structure was coded 1 for non-intact and 0 for intact homes.

*$p < .05$.

and childhood antisocial behavior significantly affect parents' use of reintegration. Consistent with Braithwaite's (1989) predictions, both effects are reduced (childhood antisocial behavior is rendered insignificant) when the interdependency variables are introduced into equation (2). The effects of both attachment to parents and perceived parental attachment to the child are statistically and substantively significant. The effect of parent-child communication is less impressive but is nevertheless in the predicted direction and higher than those observed for the exogenous variables. Equation (3) shows a similar pattern, revealing that the combined interdependency variable has a substantial effect (β =.72) on reintegration.

Perhaps most notable about these results is the substantial increase in explained variance that occurs when the interdependency variables are included in the model. In

equation (1), the explained variance for reintegration is less than 10 percent, but in equations (2) and (3), explained variance is nearly 60 percent.

The results for shaming are generally less supportive of RST's predictions. The results for equation (1) reveal that none of the exogenous variables have an effect on shaming, and they combine to explain just 2 percent of the variation in parental shaming. When the three interdependency variables are included in equation (2), explained variance improves to 7 percent, although none of the three have a statistically significant effect on shaming. This is due in part to the shared variance between the three measures of interdependency—equation (3) reveals that when they are combined into a single measure, the effect of interdependency on shaming (β = .20) is significant. Nevertheless, the explained variance (6 percent) in equation (3) remains low. By and large, the effect of parent-child interdependency on parental shaming is relatively modest but apparent nonetheless.

Testing for a Reintegration-Shaming Interaction

The next issue to consider involves the way in which reintegration and shaming affect predatory delinquency. RST predicts that the two interact, but it may be that their effects are additive rather than interactive—that is, the combination of reintegration and shaming may not produce an effect that exceeds the sum of each variable's independent effects on delinquency (Hay 1998:430–31).

The typical strategy for detecting an interaction between two variables is to enter a multiplicative term into an ordinary least squares (OLS) equation that includes parameters for the two main effects. This is not the preferred strategy, however, for assessing the interaction in question here. Jointly considering reintegration and shaming yields four parental sanctioning combinations, including sanctioning that is (1) high in both reintegration and shaming, (2) high in reintegration but low in shaming, (3) low in reintegration but high in shaming, and (4) low in both reintegration and shaming. Using a multiplicative term to express this interaction would obscure how each combination is distinct from the others.

To capture these distinctions, respondents' reintegration and shaming scores were collapsed into two categories—high or low—on the basis of whether they were above or below the median. This created the four combinations listed above: high reintegration/high shaming, high reintegration/low shaming, low reintegration/high shaming, and low reintegration/low shaming. Dummy variables were then constructed to represent the four categories.

Equation (1) of Table 3 regresses projected predatory offending on three of the dummy variables (low reintegration/low shaming is the reference category) as well as control variables for sex, age, family structure, race/ethnicity, and childhood antisocial behavior. This model does not directly bear on the issue of interaction but rather reveals how projected offending is distributed across the four categories of reintegration and shaming. The relatively large, negative coefficient for each dummy variable indicates that each category is associated with lower projected offending than the low-reintegration/low-shaming category omitted from the model. Consistent with RST,

| Table 3 | Standardized Coefficients and Fit for Ordinary Least Squares Regression of Predatory Crime on Reintegration and Shaming Dummy Variables and Main Effects |

Independent Variable	1	2
High reintegration/high shaming	−.27*	.07
High reintegration/low shaming	−.25*	−.02
Low reintegration/high shaming	−.24*	−.08
Reintegration	—	−.29*
Shaming	—	−.16**
R^2	.33	.36

NOTE: Low reintegration/low shaming is the omitted category. Both equations include controls for age, sex, race/ethnicity, and childhood antisocial behavior.

*$p < .05$. **$p < .08$.

this strongly suggests the delinquency-generating effects of being exposed to neither reintegration nor shaming.

In contrast to the RST's predictions, however, the negative effect of the high-reintegration/high-shaming category—the reintegrative shaming category—is not statistically different from the effects of the other two categories included in the model. In fact, that the low-reintegration/high-shaming category—what Braithwaite (1989) refers to as stigmatization—has a negative rather than positive coefficient is itself contradictory to RST. Braithwaite clearly predicts that stigmatization should produce a higher rate of projected offending than any other category.

Although informative, equation (1) does not address the issue of interaction because main effects for reintegration and shaming were not included in the model and thus not partialled out from the effects of the dummy variables. Equation (2) includes the two main effects. The results for equation (2) suggest that reintegration and shaming affect offending additively rather than interactively. The main effects of reintegration ($\beta = .29$) and shaming ($\beta = .16$) on predatory delinquency are significant (at $p = .08$ for shaming) and of at least moderate strength. Of principal importance is that none of the three dummy variables has an effect on delinquency that is significantly different from the omitted category.[5]

Two things should be noted about this finding of no interaction. First, it runs counter to the findings of Makkai and Braithwaite (1994), who observed that reintegration and shaming from health inspectors interact to affect nursing homes' compliance with regulatory standards. Second, although a finding of no interaction runs counter to RST, it does not suggest that reintegration and shaming are without importance. Quite the opposite, both variables are significantly and negatively related to projected offending, even after controlling for one another; dummy variables representing the different categories of reintegration and shaming; and theoretically relevant control variables, including childhood antisocial behavior. A tentative conclusion that can therefore be made is that reintegration and shaming appear to affect delinquency additively in these data. Each variable—but especially reintegration—exerts an independent effect on delinquency, but the combination of the two produces no effect marginal to those independent effects.

Testing for Spuriousness

Before concluding that reintegration and shaming are significant causes of offending, the possibility of spuriousness must be ruled out. The apparent effect of reintegration and shaming on delinquency may simply reflect that all three result from the same prior cause. The analyses shown in Table 3 partially protected against this by including controls for basic demographic variables and childhood antisocial behavior. Perhaps the most important source of spuriousness, however, may be parent-child interdependency—that is, reintegration and shaming may appear to be causes of delinquency only because all three are by-products of parent-child interdependency.

To consider that possibility, two OLS equations were estimated, and the results are shown in Table 4. Equation (1) regresses projected predatory delinquency on reintegration, shaming, and controls for age, sex, family structure, race/ethnicity, and childhood antisocial behavior. Consistent with the earlier findings, moderately large effects of reintegration and shaming are revealed. Both effects are statistically significant, but the standardized effect of reintegration ($\beta = .24$) is greatest. Equation (2) of Table tests for spuriousness by adding the composite parent-child interdependency variable that combines the three separate interdependency variables used earlier. If the

Table 4	Standardized Coefficient and Fit for Ordinary Least Squares Regressions of Predatory Crime on Reintegration, Shaming, and Parent-Child Interdependency	
Independent Variable	1	2
Reintegration	−.24*	.05
Shaming	−.17*	−.12*
Parent-child interdependency	—	−.41*
R^2	.35	.42

NOTE: Both equations include controls for age, sex, race/ethnicity, family structure, and childhood antisocial behavior.

*$p < .05$.

effects of reintegration and shaming are causal effects, they should persist even when controlling for interdependency, given RST's clear prediction that interdependency is a cause of reintegration and shaming rather than a mediator of their effects on offending (Braithwaite 1989:99).

The results for equation (2) suggest that reintegration's effect is spurious but that the effect of shaming is not. When parent-child interdependency is included in the equation, the effect of reintegration is entirely eliminated (the beta goes from .24 to .05), whereas the negative effect of shaming is reduced less dramatically (the beta goes from .17 to .12) and remains statistically significant. Including the interdependency variable resulted in only a moderate increase (from .35 to .42) in R^2, pointing to the overlap between reintegration and interdependency.[6]

Admittedly, the failure of reintegration to retain its significance when interdependency was controlled may result from inadequate measurement of reintegration. Recall that reintegration was measured with just 4 items, whereas interdependency was measured with 12. Moreover, the newness of RST and the lack of prior quantitative tests precluded the use of empirically validated measures of either reintegration or shaming. Most of the interdependency items, on the other hand, have been used effectively in delinquency research over the past several decades. Given the obvious conceptual overlap between parental reintegration and parent-child interdependency, this analysis may have favored the better measured variable.

The enduring effect of shaming, however, is worth emphasizing. Despite the same measurement limitations faced with reintegration, equation (2) of Table 4 reveals that shaming significantly reduces predatory delinquency even after controlling for reintegration, parent-child interdependency, childhood antisocial behavior, and important demographic variables such as age, sex, race/ethnicity, and family structure. Shaming is arguably the most novel aspect of RST, and this analysis suggests its potential importance to the explanation of predatory delinquency.

Discussion and Conclusion

The past two decades have seen an explosion in theories of crime and delinquency causation, but these theories have received limited empirical attention. This article sought to address that void by testing the micro-level portion of reintegrative shaming theory as it applies to the sanctioning methods used by parents with adolescents. Because this is one of the first explicit tests of RST, firm conclusions about the theory's validity and defects are not warranted. Nevertheless, three key findings are worth reflecting on: (1) the strong relationship between parent-child interdependency and reintegration, (2) the apparent spuriousness of the reintegration-delinquency relationship, and (3) the durable independent effect of shaming on delinquency.

First, consistent with RST's predictions, this study revealed a strong relationship between the level of parent-child interdependency and parents' use of reintegration. Interdependency also had a significant effect on shaming, but its effect on reintegration was notably stronger—interdependency and reintegration share about 50 percent of their variation. If nothing else, this strong effect clearly supports the idea that parents who have a close relationship with their children are likely to sanction in such away that reinforces that close relationship.

But this strong statistical relationship between parent-child interdependency and reintegration contributes to a second key finding: An initial effect of reintegration on delinquency disappeared when parent-child interdependency was held constant. This was interpreted as evidence that the initial effect of reintegration was spurious—reintegration was related to delinquency only because each was the result of interdependency. This interpretation is consistent with RST's specification of causal order: Interdependency affects the level of reintegration, which in turn affects delinquency. Because reintegration is supposed to be the variable most proximate to delinquency, its effect should have remained.

An alternative possibility with these two variables is that their actual causal order is opposite what RST predicts—it may be that reintegrative sanctioning of children leads to high parent-child interdependency rather than vice versa. If that were the case, the findings presented here would be just as expected. Future research might be usefully directed toward sorting out the causal order of these variables, paying special attention to the possibility that parental reintegration and parent-child interdependency are reciprocally related to one another in the same way that many other delinquency-causing variables are (Thornberry et al. 1994).

A third key finding of this study involves the durable, independent effect of shaming on delinquency. Shaming—arguably the most novel aspect of RST (see Hay 1998:423)—was significantly and negatively related to projected delinquency even when controlling for age, sex, family structure, race/ethnicity, childhood antisocial behavior, and parent-child interdependency. Moreover the negative effect of shaming was not dependent on the level of reintegration—the effect was strong when reintegration was at both high and low levels (see equation [1] of Table 4). Although this clearly suggests the potential importance of shaming, strictly speaking, it is not entirely supportive of RST, which argues that shaming should be negatively related to delinquency only when reintegration is high.

One possibility to consider in future research is that contrary to RST, moral-based sanctions such as shaming may rarely be stigmatizing, even when used in the absence of high reintegration or interdependency. Research in developmental psychology has consistently shown that moral- and reason-based sanctions are generally effective at controlling adolescents, especially relative to sanctions based on coercion and intimidation (see, e.g., Bandura and Walters 1959; Baumrind 1991; Patterson, Reid, and Dishion 1992; Sears, Maccoby, and Levin 1957). In short, RST's emphasis on the harmful effects of stigmatization may be appropriate, but shaming as defined by RST may not be a source of such stigmatization, even in the absence of reintegration. Future research may consider that stigmatization is likely to result not from moral-based sanctions such as shaming but rather, from such things as physical punishment, harsh verbal attacks, and similar forms of intensely antagonistic sanctioning.

In concluding, it can be noted that like most empirical tests of theory, the findings in this study are neither uniformly supportive nor unsupportive. The findings here do suggest, however, that RST and its central concept of shaming are worthy of greater empirical attention than they have received thus far. Future empirical tests may involve micro-level tests of the theory such as the one reported here or, conversely, macro-level analyses of community or societal rates of crime. Or better yet, future tests should consider the micro/macro linkages that can be derived from RST. At any rate, increased attention to RST and other recent theories will be necessary if those theories are to contribute to rather than complicate our understanding of the causes of crime.

 Notes

1. Physical education is a required course for all students except those on athletic teams. Rather than taking normal physical education classes, athletes enroll in a class specific to their sport. Most students at this school fulfill the physical education requirement during their first two years of high school.

2. There is some question as to whether RST is a theory of crime causation or recidivism (Hay 1998:432). From a measurement standpoint, this is an important question. If RST is a theory of crime causation, then measurement should focus on reintegration and shaming in response to *any* rule-violating behavior, including noncriminal acts. On the other hand, if RST is solely a theory of recidivism, reintegration and shaming should be relevant only in response to criminal acts.

Braithwaite (1989) is not clear on the issue, so different interpretations are possible. The position taken here is that RST is a theory of both causation and recidivism. Whether it is treated as one or the other in a given study will depend largely on which sanctioning institution is the focus. For example, if the micro-level theory is tested by examining the extent of reintegrative shaming found in juvenile court dispositions, this would obviously be examining RST as a theory of recidivism because individuals would not be exposed to the sanctioning had they not already committed a crime. However, when parental sanctioning is the focus, it makes more sense to examine RST as a theory of crime causation because the vast majority (perhaps all) of parental sanctions will be directed at noncriminal rule violations. Moreover, parental sanctioning begins at an age prior to when crime is possible. So the question here becomes, "How does parental reintegrative shaming in response to *all* rule-violations, including noncriminal violations, prevent involvement in serious criminal violations?"

3. Admittedly, RST makes no prediction that age differences within this range (roughly 14–17) will explain offending or exposure to reintegration and shaming. Rather, it predicts that age differences should exist between those inside this range and those outside of it. Thus, including this demographic variable does not explicitly test RST's predictions about the effects of age on reintegration and shaming.

4. The interdependency variables were measured in a way consistent with Braithwaite's (1989) argument that interdependency approximates Hirschi's (1969) notion of the social bond. Because parental sanctioning is the focus of this study, interdependency between the parent and child in particular was emphasized. The following scales were used, with adolescents indicating how much they agree or disagree with each statement. Each item was answered separately for mothers and fathers, and the scores were combined to create an overall score for parents. All items were coded so that high values correspond to high interdependency.

Adolescent attachment to parents:

I'm closer to my mother/father than a lot of kids are to theirs.

Having a good relationship with her/him is important to me.

I would like to be the kind of person she/he is.

Adolescent perceptions of parents' feelings of attachment:

She/he is interested in what I do.

She/he encourages me to discuss my problems with her/him.

I think she/he shows more interest in my brothers and sisters than in me.

Other mothers/fathers seem to show more interest in their children than mine does in me.

She/he tries to understand my problems and worries.

Parent-child communication:

I often share my thoughts and feelings with my mother/father.

I enjoy letting her/him in on my "big" moments.

I often talk to her/him about problems that I am facing.

I often talk to her/him about my plans for the future.

5. Multicollinearity is a concern with regression equations that include interaction terms and the variables used to construct them. In this case, examination of variance inflation factors (VIFs) indicated no cause for concern. VIFs for the three interaction dummy variables were 3.35, 3.23, and 4.49—well below the point at which multicollinearity typically is seen as problematic (see Myers 1990:369; Stevens 1992:77). An additional equation was estimated without the control variables. This lowered the VIFs for the dummy variables slightly to 3.17, 3.10, and 4.23. This equation once again indicated that the interaction dummy variables were not significantly related to crime, but the two main effects were.

6. The F test ($F = 19.9$, $df = 1,166$) for this difference is, however, significant at $p < .01$. Other analyses indicate that the R^2 for the model in equation (2) of Table 4 is also marginally higher than that found for an equation that only includes interdependency ($R^2 = 40$), but this difference ($F = 2.00$, $df = 2.168$) is not significant.

References

Agnew, Robert. 1992. "Foundation for a General Strain Theory of Crime and Delinquency." *Criminology* 30: 47–87.

Bachman, Ronet, Raymond Paternoster, and Sally Ward. 1992. "The Rationality of Sexual Offending: Testing a Deterrence/Rational Choice Conception of Sexual Assault." *Law and Society Review* 26: 343–72.

Bandura, Albert, and Richard H. Walters, 1959. *Adolescent Aggression.* New York: Ronald Press.

Baumrind, Diana. 1991. "The Influence of Parenting Style on Adolescent Competence and Substance Use." *Journal of Early Adolescence* 11: 56–95.

Bernard, Thomas J. 1989. "A Theoretical Approach to Integration." Pp.137–59 in *Theoretical Integration in the Study of Crime and Deviance: Problems and Prospects,* ed. Steven F. Messner, Marvin D. Krohn, and Allen E. Liska. Albany: State University of New York Press.

Bernard, Thomas J., and Jeffrey B. Snipes. 1996. "Theoretical Integration in Criminology." Pp. 301–48 in *Crime and Justice: A Review of Research,* ed. Michael Tonry. Chicago: University of Chicago Press.

Braithwaite, John. 1989. *Crime, Shame and Reintegration.* New York: Cambridge University Press.

———. 1999. "Restorative Justice: Assessing Optimistic and Pessimistic Accounts." *Crime and Justice: A Review of Research* 25: 1–127.

Cohen, Lawrence E., and Richard Machalek. 1988. "A General Theory of Expropriative Crime." *American Journal of Sociology* 94: 465–501.

Cohen, Patricia and Judith Brook. 1995. "The Reciprocal Influence of Punishment and Child Behavior Disorder." In *Coercion and Punishment in Long-Term Perspectives,* ed. Joan McCord. New York: Cambridge University Press.

Colvin, Mark, and John Pauly. 1983. "A Critique of Criminology: Toward an Integrated Structural-Marxist Theory of Delinquency Production." *American Journal of Sociology* 89: 513–51.

Cornish, Derek B., and Ronald V. Clarke, eds. 1986. *The Reasoning Criminal: Rational Choice Perspectives on Offending.* New York: Springer-Verlag.

Cullen, Francis T. 1994. "Social Support as an Organizing Concept for Criminology: Presidential Address to the Academy of Criminal Justice Sciences." *Justice Quarterly* 11: 527–59.

Currie, Elliott. 1997. "Market, Crime, and Community: Toward a Mid-Range Theory of Post-Industrial Violence." *Theoretical Criminology* 2: 147–72.

Elliott, Delbert. 1985. "The Assumption That Theories Can Be Combined with Increased Explanatory Power." Pp.123–49 in *Theoretical Methods in Criminology,* ed. Robert F. Meier. Beverly Hills, CA: Sage.

Gottfredson, Michael R., and Travis Hirschi. 1990. *A General Theory of Crime.* Stanford, CA. Stanford University Press.

Grasmick, Harold G., and Robert J. Bursik, Jr. 1990. "Conscience, Significant Others, and Rational Choice: Extending the Deterrence Model." *Law and Society Review* 24: 837–61.

Grasmick, Harold G., Robert J. Bursik, Jr., and Bruce J. Arneklev. 1993. "Reduction in Drunk Driving as a Response to Increased Threats of Shame, Embarrassment, and Legal Sanctions." *Criminology* 31: 41–67.

Green, Donald E. 1989. "Measures of Illegal Behavior in Individual Level Deterrence Research." *Journal of Research in Crime and Delinquency* 26: 253–75.

Hagan, John. 1988. *Structural Criminology.* New Brunswick. NJ: Rutgers University Press.

Hay, Carter. 1998. "Parental Sanctions and Delinquent Behavior: Toward Clarification of Braithwaite's Theory of Reintegrative Shaming." *Theoretical Criminology* 2: 419–43.

Heimer, Karen, and Stacy De Coster. 1999. "The Gendering of Violent Delinquency." *Criminology* 37: 277–317.

Hirschi, Travis. 1969. *Causes of Delinquency.* Berkeley: University of California Press.

Jeffery, C. R. 1989. *Criminology.* Englewood Cliffs. NJ: Prentice Hall.

Jensen, Gary, and B. Grant Stitt. 1982. "Words and Misdeeds: Hypothetical Choices versus Past Behavior as Measures of Deviance." Pp. 33–54 in *Deterrence Reconsidered,* ed. John Hagan. Beverly Hills, CA: Sage.

Kandel, Denise, and Ping Wu. 1995. "Disentangling Mother-Child Effects." In *Coercion and Punishment in Long-Term Perspectives,* ed. Joan McCord. Cambridge, UK: Cambridge University Press.

Katz, Jack. 1988. *The Seductions of Crime.* New York: Basic Books.

Liska, Allen E., Marvin D. Krohn, and Steven F. Messner. 1989. "Strategies and Requisites for Theoretical Integration in the

Study of Crime and Deviance." Pp. 1–19 in *Theoretical Integration in the Study of Deviance and Crime: Problem and Prospects,* ed. Steven F. Messner, Marvin D. Krohn, and Allen E. Liska. Albany: State University of New York Press.

Makkai, Toni, and John Braithwaite. 1994. "Reintegrative Shaming and Compliance with Regulatory Standards." *Criminology* 32: 361–83.

Matsueda, Ross L. 1992. "Reflected Appraisals, Parental Labeling, and Delinquency: Specifying a Symbolic Interactionist Theory." *American Journal of Sociology* 97: 1577–1611.

Mawson, A. R. 1987. *Transient Criminality* New York: Praeger.

Messerschmidt, James M. 1993. *Masculinities and Crime: Critique and Reconceptualization of Theory.* Lanham, MD: Rowman & Littlefield.

Messner, Steven F., and Richard Rosenfeld. 1994. *Crime and the American Dream.* Belmont. CA: Wadsworth.

Moffitt, Terrie E. 1993. "Adolescence-Limited and Life-Course-Persistent Antisocial Behavior: A Developmental Taxonomy." *Psychological Review* 100: 674–701.

Myers, R. 1990. *Classical and Modern Regression with Applications.* 2nd ed. Boston: Duxbury.

Patterson, Gerald R., John B. Reid, and Thomas J. Dishion. 1992. *Antisocial Boys.* Eugene, OR: Castalia.

Pearson, Frank, and Neil Alan Weiner. 1985. "Toward an Integration of Criminological Theories." *Journal of Criminal Law and Criminology* 76: 116–50.

Sampson, Robert, and John Laub. 1993. *Crime in the Making: Pathways and Turning Points through Life.* Cambridge, MA: Harvard University Press.

Schwendinger, H., and J. S. Schwendinger. 1985. *Adolescent Subcultures and Delinquency.* New York: Praeger.

Sears, R., E. Maccoby, and H. Levin. 1957. *Patterns of Child Rearing.* Evanston. IL: Row, Peterson.

Sherman, Lawrence W. 1993. "Defiance, Deterrence, and Irrelevance: A Theory of the Criminal Sanction." *Journal of Research in Crime and Delinquency* 30: 445–73.

Stevens, James. 1992. *Applied Multivariate Statistics for the Social Sciences.* 2nd ed. Hillsdale, NJ: Lawrence Erlbaum.

Tittle, Charles. 1977. "Sanction Fear and the Maintenance of Social Order." *Social Forces* 55: 579–96.

———. 1980. *Sanctions and Social Deviance: The Question of Deterrence.* New York: Praeger.

———. 1995. *Control Balance: Toward a General Theory of Deviance.* Boulder, CO: Westview.

Thornberry, Terence P. 1987. "Toward an Interactional Theory of Delinquency." *Criminology* 25: 863–91.

Thornberry, Terence P., Alan J. Lizotte, Marvin D. Krohn, Margaret Farnsworth, and Sung Joon Jang. 1994. "Delinquent Peers, Beliefs, and Delinquent Behavior: A Longitudinal Test of Interactional Theory." *Criminology* 32: 47–84.

Tyler, Tom R. 1990. *Why People Obey the Law.* New Haven. CT: Yale University Press.

Vila, Bryan J. 1994. "A General Paradigm for Understanding Criminal Behavior: Extending Evolutionary Ecological Theory." *Criminology* 32: 311–60.

Walters, G. 1992. *Foundations of Criminal Science.* New York: Praeger.

Wilson, James Q., and Richard J. Herrnstein. 1985. *Crime and Human Nature.* New York: Simon & Schuster.

Wood, Peter B., Walter R. Gove, James A. Wilson, and John K. Cochran. 1997. "Nonsocial Reinforcement and Habitual Criminal Conduct: An Extension of Learning Theory." *Criminology* 35: 335–66.

Zhang, Sheldon X. 1995. "Measuring Shaming in an Ethnic Context." *British Journal of Criminology* 35: 248–62.

REVIEW QUESTIONS

1. According to Hay, what types of factors seem to be important in determining whether parents use reintegrative disciplinary strategies as opposed to more stigmatizing techniques? If you were (or are) a parent, do these strategies make sense to you in the disciplining of your own child(ren)?

2. From the results of this study, do the effects of reintegration and shaming tend to interact to predict offending? If so, how? If not, give your reasons why they do not seem to interact.

3. What other factors may account for the findings of this study, specifically reintegration and shaming? Did Hay find evidence that other such factors seemed to account for such findings?

4. Do you think Braithwaite's model of reintegrative shaming could work in the United States as a whole? Explain your reasoning for your answer.

❖

READING 31

In this selection, Terence Thornberry presents an integrated model that primarily merges two theoretical perspectives, specifically control theory and differential reinforcement/social learning theory. However, the primary distinction between previous integrated frameworks and Thornberry's model is that Thornberry takes into account the reciprocal, or feedback, effects that certain variables may have on the increase of delinquent/criminal behavior.

For example, Thornberry claims that weak bonds to parents (a control concept) may lead to association with delinquent peers (a differential association/social learning concept), which is likely to lead to parents having even weaker bonds with the individual/youth. So it is proposed that a youth's getting in trouble is likely to lead to more alienation or weaker bonds with the youth's parents, which is quite likely in reality. Such an effect is a good example of a reciprocal effect or feedback effect, and this is just one of the many reciprocal effects that are proposed in this model. Thornberry's integrated model of offending is full of such reciprocal (or feedback) effects, and this is what distinguishes his model from previous integrated frameworks, or any of the traditional theoretical models that attempted to explain offending.

While reading this selection, readers should consider their own experience or those of others they know who were caught once (and maybe arrested) for a relatively minor charge. The social "fallout" from this initial arrest may have resulted in more adverse reactions from parents (or others), and that may have made the other factors, such as delinquent peers, more prominent. Readers may notice that this type of reciprocal or feedback loop resembles labeling theory, in which a person commits an initial (often minor) offense and is labeled as an offender, leading to worse and more frequent offending. Although Thornberry does not specifically invoke labeling theory in his theory, there is an obvious comparison to be made between the reciprocal effects he discusses and the effects of stigmatization that labeling theorists include in their explanatory models. Still, Thornberry's integrated model was one of the first integrated frameworks that actually incorporated such reciprocal or feedback effects into the theory of why individuals engage in offending behavior.

Toward an Interactional Theory of Delinquency

Terence P. Thornberry

 Origins and Assumptions

The basic premise of the model proposed here is that human behavior occurs in social interaction and can therefore best be explained by models that focus on interactive processes. Rather than viewing adolescents as propelled along a unidirectional pathway to one or another outcome—that is, delinquency or conformity—it argues that adolescents interact with other people and institutions and that behavioral outcomes are formed by that interactive process. For example, the delinquent behavior of an adolescent is formed in part by how he and his parents *interact*

SOURCE: "Toward an Interactional Theory of Delinquency," Thornberry, Terence P. in *Criminology*, 25, pp. 863–891. Copyright © 1987 American Society of Criminology. Reprinted with permission.

over time, not simply by the child's perceived, and presumably invariant, *level* of attachment to parents. Moreover, since it is an interactive system, the behaviors of others—for example, parents and school officials—are influenced both by each other and by the adolescent, including his or her delinquent behavior. If this view is correct, then interactional effects have to be modeled explicitly if we are to understand the social and psychological processes involved with initiation into delinquency, the maintenance of such behavior, and its eventual reduction.

Interactional theory develops from the same intellectual tradition as the theories mentioned above, especially the Durkheimian tradition of social control. It asserts that the fundamental cause of delinquency lies in the weakening of social constraints over the conduct of the individual. Unlike classical control theory, however, it does not assume that the attenuation of controls leads directly to delinquency. The weakening of controls simply allows for a much wider array of behavior, including continued conventional action, failure as indicated by school dropout and sporadic employment histories, alcoholism, mental illness, delinquent and criminal careers, or some combination of these outcomes. For the freedom resulting from weakened bonds to be channeled into delinquency, especially serious prolonged delinquency, requires an interactive setting in which delinquency is learned, performed, and reinforced. This view is similar to Cullen's structuring perspective which draws attention to the [indeterminacy] of deviant behavior. "It can thus be argued that there is an *indeterminate* and not a determinate or etiologically specific relationship between motivational variables on the one hand and any particular form of deviant behavior on the other hand" (Cullen, 1984, p. 5).

Although heavily influenced by control and learning theories, and to a lesser extent by strain and culture conflict theories, this is not an effort at theoretical integration as that term is usually used (Elliott, 1985). Rather, this paper is guided by what we have elsewhere called theoretical elaboration (Thornberry, 1987a). In this instance, a basic control theory is extended, or elaborated upon, using available theoretical perspectives and empirical findings to provide a more accurate model of the causes of delinquency. In the process of elaboration, there is no requirement to resolve disputes among other theories—for example, their different assumptions about the origins

of deviance (Thornberry, 1987a, pp. 15–18); all that is required is that the propositions of the model developed here be consistent with one another and with the assumptions about deviance stated above.

 ## Organization

The presentation of the interactional model begins by identifying the central concepts to be included in the model. Next, the underlying theoretical structure of the proposed model is examined and the rationale for moving from unidirectional to reciprocal causal models is developed. The reciprocal model is then extended to include a developmental perspective, examining the theoretical saliency of different variables at different developmental stages. Finally, the influence of the person's position in the social structure is explored. Although in some senses the last issue is logically prior to the others, since it is concerned with sources of initial variation in the causal variables, it is discussed last so that the reciprocal relationships among the concepts—the heart of an interactional perspective—can be more fully developed.

 ## Theoretical Concepts

Given these basic premises, an interactional model must respond to two overriding issues. First, how are traditional social constraints over behavior weakened and, second, once weakened, how is the resulting freedom channeled into delinquent patterns? To address these issues, the present paper presents an initial version of an interactional model, focusing on the interrelationships among six concepts: attachment to parents, commitment to school, belief in conventional values, associations with delinquent peers, adopting delinquent values, and engaging in delinquent behavior. These concepts form the core of the theoretical model since they are central to social psychological theories of delinquency and since they have been shown in numerous studies to be strongly related to subsequent delinquent behavior (see Elliott et al., 1985, Chs. 1–3, for an excellent review of this literature).

The first three derive from Hirschi's version of control theory (1969) and represent the primary mechanisms by which adolescents are bonded to conventional middle-class society. When those elements of the bond are weakened, behavioral freedom increases considerably. For that freedom to lead to delinquent behavior, however, interactive settings that reinforce delinquency are required. In the model, those settings are represented by two concepts: associations with delinquent peers and the formation of delinquent values which derive primarily from social learning theory. For the purpose of explicating the overall theoretical perspective, each of these concepts is defined quite broadly. Attachment to parents includes the affective relationship between parent and child, communication patterns, parenting skills such as monitoring and discipline, parent-child conflict, and the like. Commitment to school refers to the stake in conformity the adolescent has developed and includes such factors as success in school, perceived importance of education, attachment to teachers, and involvement in school activities. Belief in conventional values represents the granting of legitimacy to such middle-class values as education, personal industry, financial success, deferral of gratification, and the like.

Three delinquency variables are included in the model. Association with delinquent peers includes the level of attachment to peers, the delinquent behavior and values of peers, and their reinforcing reactions to the adolescent's own delinquent or conforming behavior. It is a continuous measure that can vary from groups that are heavily delinquent to those that are almost entirely nondelinquent. Delinquent values refer to the granting of legitimacy to

delinquent activities as acceptable modes of behavior as well as a general willingness to violate the law to achieve other ends. Delinquent behavior, the primary outcome variable, refers to acts that place the youth at risk for adjudication; it ranges from status offenses to serious violent activities. Since the present model is an interactional one, interested not only in explaining delinquency but in explaining the effects of delinquency on other variables, particular attention is paid to prolonged involvement in serious delinquency. . . .

 ## Model Specification

A causal model allowing for reciprocal relationships among the six concepts of interest—attachment to parents, commitment to school, belief in conventional values, association with delinquent peers, delinquent values, and delinquent behavior—is presented in Figure 1. This model refers to the period of early adolescence, from about ages 11 to 13, when delinquent careers are beginning, but prior to the period at which delinquency reaches its apex in terms of seriousness and frequency. In the following sections the model is extended to later ages.

The specification of causal effects begins by examining the three concepts that form the heart of social learning theories of delinquency—delinquent peers, delinquent values, and delinquent behavior. For now we focus on the

Figure 1   A reciprocal model of delinquent involvement at early adolescence

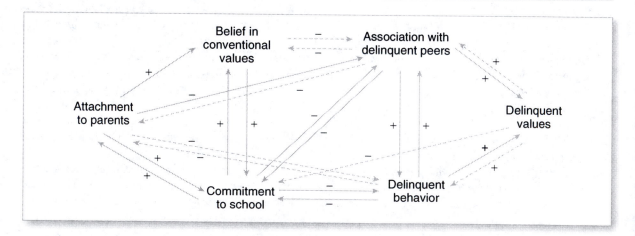

reciprocal nature of the relationships, ignoring until later variations in the strength of the relationships. Traditional social learning theory specifies a causal order among these variables in which delinquent associations affect delinquent values and, in turn, both produce delinquent behavior (Akers, Krohn, Lanza-Kaduce, & Radosevich, 1979; Matsueda, 1982). Yet, for each of the dyadic relationships involving these variables, other theoretical perspectives and much empirical evidence suggest the appropriateness of reversing this causal order. For example, social learning theory proposes that associating with delinquents, or more precisely, people who hold and reinforce delinquent values, increases the chances of delinquent behavior (Akers, 1977). Yet, as far back as the work of the Gluecks (1950) this specification has been challenged. Arguing that "birds of a feather flock together," the Gluecks propose that youths who are delinquent seek out and associate with others who share those tendencies. From this perspective, rather than being a cause of delinquency, associations are the result of delinquents seeking out and associating with like-minded peers.

An attempt to resolve the somewhat tedious argument over the temporal priority of associations and behavior is less productive theoretically than capitalizing on the interactive nature of human behavior and treating the relationship as it probably is: a reciprocal one. People often take on the behavioral repertoire of their associates but, at the same time, they often seek out associates who share their behavioral interests. Individuals clearly behave this way in conventional settings, and there is no reason to assume that deviant activities, such as delinquency, are substantially different in this regard.

Similar arguments can be made for the other two relationships among the delinquency variables. Most recent theories of delinquency, following the lead of social learning theory, posit that delinquent associations lead to the formation of delinquent values. Subcultural theories, however, especially those that derive from a cultural deviance perspective (Miller, 1958) suggest that values precede the formation of peer groups. Indeed, it is the socialization of adolescents into the "lower-class culture" and its particular value system that leads them to associate with delinquent peers in the first place. This specification can also be derived from a social control perspective as demonstrated in Weis and Sederstrom's social development model (1981) and Burkett and Warren's social selection model (1987).

Finally, the link between delinquent values and delinquent behavior restates, in many ways, the basic social psychological question of the relationship between attitudes and behavior. Do attitudes form behavior patterns or does behavior lead to attitude formation? Social psychological research, especially in cognitive psychology and balance models (for example, Festinger, 1957; Brehm and Cohen, 1962), points to the reciprocal nature of this relationship. It suggests that people indeed behave in a manner consistent with their attitudes, but also that behavior is one of the most persuasive forces in the formation and maintenance of attitudes.

Such a view of the relationship between delinquent values and behavior is consistent with Hindelang's findings: this general pattern of results indicates that one can "predict" a respondent's self approval [of illegal behaviors] from knowledge of that respondent's involvement/non-involvement [in delinquency] with fewer errors than vice-versa (1974, p. 382). It is also consistent with recent deterrence research which demonstrates that the "experiential effect," in which behavior affects attitudes, is much stronger than the deterrent effect, in which attitudes affect behavior (Paternoster, Saltzman, Waldo, & Chiricos, 1982; Paternoster, Saltzman, Chiricos, & Waldo, 1983).

Although each of these relationships appears to be reciprocal, the predicted strengths of the associations are not of equal strength during the early adolescent period (see Figure 1). Beliefs that delinquent conduct is acceptable [and] positively valued may be emerging, but such beliefs are not fully articulated for 11- to 13-year-olds. Because of their emerging quality, they are viewed as more effect than cause, produced by delinquent behavior and associations with delinquent peers. As these values emerge, however, they have feedback effects, albeit relatively weak ones at these ages, on behavior and associations. That is, as the values become more fully articulated and delinquency becomes positively valued, it increases the likelihood of such behavior and further reinforces associations with like-minded peers.

Summary. When attention is focused on the interrelationships among associations with delinquent peers, delinquent values, and delinquent behavior, it appears that they are, in fact, reciprocally related. The world of human behavior is far more complex than a simple recursive one in which a temporal order can be imposed on interactional variables of this nature. Interactional theory sees these three concepts as embedded in a causal loop, each reinforcing the others over time. Regardless of where the individual enters the loop the following obtains: delinquency increases associations with delinquent peers and delinquent values; delinquent values increase delinquent behavior and associations with delinquent peers; and associations with delinquent peers increases delinquent behavior and delinquent values. The question now concerns the identification of factors that lead some youth, but not others, into this spiral of increasing delinquency.

▨ Social Control Effects

As indicated at the outset of this reading, the promise of interactional theory is that the fundamental cause of delinquency is the attenuation of social controls over the person's conduct. Whenever bonds to the conventional world are substantially weakened, the individual is freed from moral constraints and is at risk for a wide array of deviant activities, including delinquency. The primary mechanisms that bind adolescents to the conventional world are attachment to parents, commitment to school, and belief in conventional values, and their role in the model can now be examined.

During the early adolescent years, the family is the most salient arena for social interaction and involvement and, because of this, attachment to parents has a stronger influence on other aspects of the youth's life at this stage than it does at later stages of development. With this in mind, attachment to parents is predicted to affect four other variables. Since youths who are attached to their parents are sensitive to their wishes (Hirschi, 1969, pp. 16–19), and, since parents are almost universally supportive of the conventional world, these children are likely to be strongly committed to school and to espouse conventional values. In addition, youths who are attached to their parents, again because of their sensitivity to parental wishes, are unlikely to associate with delinquent peers or to engage in delinquent behavior.

In brief, parental influence is seen as central to controlling the behavior of youths at these relatively early ages. Parents who have a strong affective bond with their children, who communicate with them, who exercise appropriate parenting skills, and so forth, are likely to lead their children towards conventional actions and beliefs and away from delinquent friends and actions.

On the other hand, attachment to parents is not seen as an immutable trait, impervious to the effects of other variables. Indeed, associating with delinquent peers, not being committed to school, and engaging in delinquent behavior are so contradictory to parental expectations that they tend to diminish the level of attachment between parent and child. Adolescents who fail at school, who associate with delinquent peers, and who engage in delinquent conduct are, as a consequence, likely to jeopardize their affective bond with their parents, precisely because these behaviors suggest that the "person does not care about the wishes and expectations of other people" (Hirschi, 1969, p. 18), in this instance, his or her parents.

Turning next to belief in conventional values, this concept is involved in two different causal loops. First, it strongly affects commitment to school and in turn is affected by commitment to school. In essence, this loop posits a behavioral and attitudinal consistency in the conventional realm. Second, a weaker loop is posited between belief in conventional values and associations with delinquent peers. Youths who do not grant legitimacy to conventional values are more apt to associate with delinquent friends who share those views, and those friendships are likely to attenuate further their beliefs in conventional values. This reciprocal specification is supported by Burkett and Warren's findings concerning religious beliefs and peer associations (1987). Finally, youths who believe in conventional values are seen as somewhat less likely to engage in delinquent behavior.

Although belief in conventional values plays some role in the genesis of delinquency, its impact is not particularly strong. For example, it is not affected by delinquent behavior, nor is it related to delinquent values. This is primarily because belief in conventional values appears to be quite invariant; regardless of class of origin or delinquency status, for example, most people strongly assert conventional values (Short & Strodtbeck, 1965, Ch. 3). Nevertheless, these beliefs do exert some influence in the model, especially with respect to reinforcing commitment to school.

Finally, the impact of commitment to school is considered. This variable is involved in reciprocal loops with both of the other bonding variables. Youngsters who are attached to their parents are likely to be committed to and succeed in school, and that success is likely to reinforce the close ties to their parents. Similarly, youths who believe in conventional values are likely to be committed to school, the primary arena in which they can act in accordance with those values, and, in turn, success in that arena is likely to reinforce the beliefs.

In addition to its relationships with the other control variables, commitment to school also has direct effects on two of the delinquency variables. Students who are committed to succeeding in school are unlikely to associate with delinquents or to engage in substantial amounts of serious, repetitive delinquent behavior. These youths have built up a stake in conformity and should be unwilling to jeopardize that investment by either engaging in delinquent behavior or by associating with those who do. Low commitment to school is not seen as leading directly to the formation of delinquent values, however. Its primary effect on delinquent values is indirect, via associations with delinquent peers and delinquent behavior (Conger, 1980, p. 137). While school failure may lead to a reduced commitment to conventional values, it does not follow that it directly increases the acceptance of values that support delinquency.

Commitment to school, on the other hand, is affected by each of the delinquency variables in the model. Youths who accept values that are consistent with delinquent behavior, who associate with other delinquents, and who engage in delinquent behavior are simply unlikely candidates to maintain an active commitment to school and the conventional world that school symbolizes.

Summary. Attachment to parents, commitment to school, and belief in conventional values reduce delinquency by cementing the person to conventional institutions and people. When these elements of the bond to conventional society are strong, delinquency is unlikely, but when they are weak the individual is placed at much greater risk for delinquency. When viewed from an interactional perspective, two additional qualities of these concepts become increasingly evident.

First, attachment to parents, commitment to school, and belief in conventional values are not static attributes of the person, invariant over time. These concepts interact with one another during the developmental process. For some youths the levels of attachment, commitment, and belief increase as these elements reinforce one another,

while for other youths the interlocking nature of these relationships suggests a greater and greater attenuation of the bond will develop over time.

Second, the bonding variables appear to be reciprocally linked to delinquency, exerting a causal impact on associations with delinquent peers and delinquent behavior; they also are causally affected by these variables. As the youth engages in more and more delinquent conduct and increasingly associates with delinquent peers, the level of his bond to the conventional world is further weakened. Thus, while the weakening of the bond to conventional society may be an initial cause of delinquency, delinquency eventually becomes its own indirect cause precisely because of its ability to weaken further the person's bonds to family, school, and conventional beliefs. The implications of this amplifying causal structure [are] examined below. First, however, the available support for reciprocal models is reviewed and the basic model is extended to later developmental stages. . . .

Developmental Extensions

The previous section developed a strategy for addressing one of the three major limitations of delinquency theories mentioned in the introduction, namely, their unidirectional causal structure. A second limitation is the non-developmental posture of most theories which tend to provide a cross sectional picture of the factors associated with delinquency at one age, but which do not provide a rationale for understanding how delinquent behavior develops over time. The present section offers a developmental extension of the basic model.

Middle Adolescence

First, a model for middle adolescence, when the youths are approximately 15 or 16 years of age is presented (Figure 2). This period represents the highest rates of involvement in delinquency and is the reference period, either implicitly or explicitly, for most theories of delinquent involvement. Since the models for the early and middle adolescent periods have essentially the same structure and causal relationships (Figures 1 and 2), discussion focuses on the differences between them and does not repeat the rationale for individual causal effects.

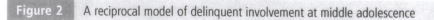

Figure 2 A reciprocal model of delinquent involvement at middle adolescence

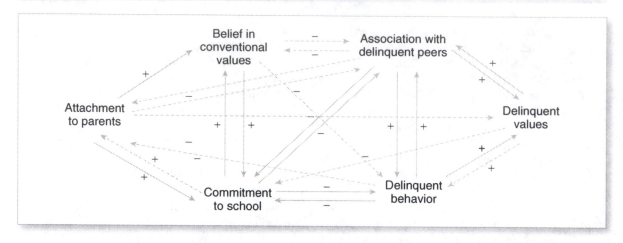

Perhaps the most important difference concerns attachment to parents which is involved in relatively few strong relationships. By this point in the life cycle, the most salient variables involved in the production of delinquency are likely to be external to the home, associated with the youth's activities in school and peer networks. This specification is consistent with empirical results for subjects in this age range (Johnson, 1979, p. 105; and Schoenberg, 1975, quoted in Johnson. Indeed, Johnson concludes that "an adolescent's public life has as much or more to do with his or her deviance or conformity than do 'under-the-roof' experiences" (1979, p. 116).

This is not to say that attachment to parents is irrelevant; such attachments are involved in enhancing commitment to school and belief in conventional values, and in preventing associations with delinquent peers. It is just that the overall strength of parental effects [is] weaker than at earlier ages when the salience of the family as a locus of interaction and control was greater. The second major change concerns the increased importance of delinquent values as a causal factor. It is still embedded in the causal loop with the other two delinquency variables, but now it is as much cause as effect. Recall that at the younger ages delinquent values were seen as emerging, produced by associations with delinquent peers and delinquent behavior. Given their emergent nature, they were not seen as primary causes of other variables. At mid-adolescence, however, when delinquency is at its apex, these values are more fully articulated and have stronger effects on other variables. First, delinquent

values are seen as major reinforcers of both delinquent associations and delinquent behavior. In general, espousing values supportive of delinquency tends to increase the potency of this causal loop. Second, since delinquent values are antithetical to the conventional settings of school and family, youths who espouse them are less likely to be committed to school and attached to parents. Consistent with the reduced saliency of family at these ages, the feedback effect to school is seen as stronger than the feedback effect to parents.

By and large, the other concepts in the model play the same role at these ages as they do at the earlier ones. Thus, the major change from early to middle adolescence concerns the changing saliency of some of the theoretical concepts. The family declines in relative importance while the adolescent's own world of school and peers takes on increasing significance. While these changes occur, the overall structure of the theory remains constant. These interactive variables are still seen as mutually reinforcing over time.

Later Adolescence

Finally, the causes of delinquency during the transition from adolescence to adulthood, about ages 18 to 20, can be examined (Figure 3). At these ages one should more properly speak of crime than delinquency, but for consistency we will continue to use the term delinquency in the causal diagrams and employ the terms delinquency and crime interchangeably in the text.

Figure 3   A reciprocal model of delinquent involvement at later adolescence

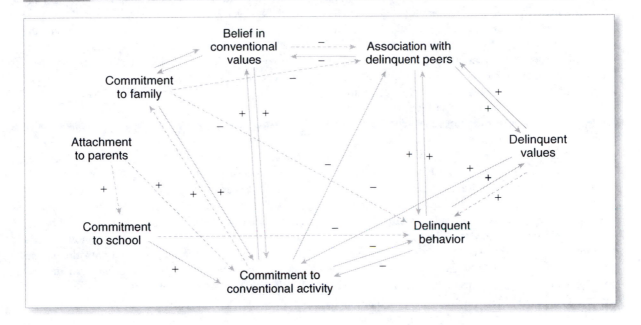

Two new variables are added to the model to reflect the changing life circumstances at this stage of development. The more important of these is commitment to conventional activities which includes employment, attending college, and military service. Along with the transition to the world of work, there is a parallel transition from the family of origin to one's own family. Although this transition does not peak until the early 20s, for many people its influence is beginning at this stage. Included in this concept are marriage, plans for marriage, and plans for childrearing. These new variables largely replace attachment to parents and commitment to school in the theoretical scheme; they represent the major sources of bonds to conventional society for young adults. Both attachment to parents and commitment to school remain in the model but take on the cast of exogenous variables. Attachment to parents has only a minor effect on commitment to school, and commitment to school is proposed to affect only commitment to conventional activities and, more weakly, delinquent behavior.

The other three variables considered in the previous models—association with delinquent peers, delinquent values, and delinquent behavior—are still hypothesized to be embedded in an amplifying causal loop. As indicated above, this loop is most likely to occur among adolescents who, at earlier ages, were freed from the controlling influence of parents and school. Moreover, via the feedback paths delinquent peers, delinquent values, and delinquent behavior further alienate the youth from parents and diminish commitment to school. Once this spiral begins, the probability of sustained delinquency increases.

This situation, if it continued uninterrupted, would yield higher and higher rates of crime as the subjects matured. Such an outcome is inconsistent with the desistance that has been observed during this age period (Wolfgang, Thornberry, and Figlio, 1987). Rates of delinquency and crime begin to subside by the late teenage years, a phenomenon often attributed to "maturational reform." Such an explanation, however, is tautological since it claims that crime stops when adolescents get older, because they get older. It is also uninformative since the concept of maturational reform is theoretically undefined. A developmental approach, however, offers an explanation for desistance. As the developmental process unfolds, life circumstances change, developmental milestones are met (or, for some, missed), new social roles are created, and new networks of attachments and commitments emerge. The effects of these changes enter the processual model to explain new and often dramatically different behavioral patterns. In the present model, these changes are represented by commitment to conventional activity and commitment to family.

Commitment to conventional activity is influenced by a number of variables, including earlier attachment to parents, commitment to school, and belief in conventional values. And once the transition to the world of work is made, tremendous opportunities are afforded for new and different effects in the delinquency model. Becoming committed to conventional activities, work, college, military service, and so on—reduces the likelihood of delinquent behavior and associations with delinquent peers because it builds up a stake in conformity that is antithetical to delinquency. Moreover, since the delinquency variables are still embedded in a causal loop, the effect of commitment to conventional activities tends to resonate throughout the system. But, because of the increased saliency of a new variable, commitment to conventional activities, the reinforcing loop is now set in motion to *reduce* rather than increase delinquent and criminal involvement. The variable of commitment to family has similar, albeit weaker, effects since the transition to the family is only beginning at these ages. Nevertheless, commitment to family is proposed to reduce both delinquent associations and delinquent values and to increase commitment to conventional activity. In general, as the individual takes on the responsibilities of family, the bond to conventional society increases, placing additional constraints on behavior and precluding further delinquency.

These changes do not occur in all cases, however, nor should they be expected to since many delinquents continue on to careers in adult crime. In the Philadelphia cohort of 1945, 51% of the juvenile delinquents were also adult offenders, and the more serious and prolonged the delinquent careers were, the greater the odds of an adult career (Wolfgang et al., 1987, Ch. 4). The continuation of criminal careers can also be explained by the nature of the reciprocal effects included in this model. In general, extensive involvement in delinquency at earlier ages feeds back upon and weakens attachment to parents and commitment to school (see Figures 1 and 2). These variables, as well as involvement in delinquency itself, weaken later commitment to family and to conventional activities (Figure 3). Thus, these new variables, commitment to conventional

activities and to family, are affected by the person's situation at earlier stages and do not "automatically" alter the probability of continued criminal involvement. If the initial bonds are extremely weak, the chances of new bonding variables being established to break the cycle towards criminal careers are low and it is likely that criminal behavior will continue. . . .

 ## Structural Effects

Structural variables, including race, class, sex, and community of residence, refer to the person's location in the structure of social roles and statuses. The manner in which they are incorporated in the interactional model is illustrated here by examining only one of them, social class of origin. Although social class is often measured continuously, a categorical approach is more consistent with the present model and with most theories of delinquency that incorporate class as a major explanatory variable—for example, strain and social disorganization theories. For our purposes, the most important categories are the lower class, the working lower class, and the middle class.

The lower class is composed of those who are chronically or sporadically unemployed, receive welfare, and subsist at or below the poverty level. They are similar to Johnson's "underclass" (1979). The working lower class is composed of those with more stable work patterns, training for semiskilled jobs, and incomes that allow for some economic stability. For these families, however, the hold on even a marginal level of occupational and economic security is always tenuous. Finally, the middle class refers to all families above these lower levels. Middle-class families have achieved some degree of economic success and stability and can reasonably expect to remain at that level or improve their standing over time.

The manner in which the social class of origin affects the interactional variables and the behavioral trajectories can be demonstrated by comparing the life expectancies of children from lower- and middle-class families. As compared to children from a middle-class background, children from a lower class background are more apt to have (1) disrupted family processes and environments (Conger, McCarty, Wang, Lahey, & Kroop, 1984; Wahler, 1980); (2) poorer preparation for school (Cloward and Ohlin, 1960); (3) belief structures influenced by the traditions of the American lower class (Miller, 1958); and (4) greater exposure to neighborhoods with high rates of crime (Shaw & McKay, 1942; Braithwaite, 1981). The direction of all these effects is such that we would expect children from lower-class families to be initially less bonded to conventional society and more exposed to delinquent values, friends, and behaviors.

As one moves towards the working lower class, both the likelihood and the potency of the factors just listed decrease. As a result, the initial values of the interactional variables improve but, because of the tenuous nature of economic and social stability for these families, both the bonding variables and the delinquency variables are still apt to lead to considerable amounts of delinquent conduct. Finally, youths from middle-class families, given their greater stability and economic security, are likely to start with a stronger family structure, greater stakes in conformity, and higher chances of success, and all of these factors are likely to reduce the likelihood of initial delinquent involvement.

In brief, the initial values of the interactional variables are systematically related to the social class of origin. Moreover, since these variables are reciprocally related, it follows logically that social class is systematically related to the behavioral trajectories described above. Youngsters from the lowest classes have the highest probability of moving forward on a trajectory of increasing delinquency. Starting from a position of low bonding to conventional institutions and a high delinquency environment, the reciprocal nature of the interrelationships leads inexorably towards extremely high rates of delinquent and criminal involvement. Such a view is consistent with prevalence data which show that by age 18, 50%, and by age 30, 70% of low SES minority males have an official police record (Wolfgang et al., 1987).

On the other hand, the expected trajectory of middle-class youths suggests that they will move toward an essentially conforming life-style, in which their stakes in conformity increase and more and more preclude serious and prolonged involvement in delinquency. Finally, because the initial values of the interactional variables are mixed and indecisive for children from lower working-class homes, their behavioral trajectories are much more volatile and the outcome much less certain.

Summary. Interactional theory asserts that both the initial values of the process variables and their development over time are systematically related to the social class of origin. Moreover, parallel arguments can be made for other structural variables, especially those associated with class, such as race, ethnicity, and the social disorganization of the neighborhood. Like class of origin, these variables are systematically related to variables such as commitment to school and involvement in delinquent behavior, and therefore, as a group, these structural variables set the stage on which the reciprocal effects develop across the life cycle. . . .

 # References

Akers, R. (1977). *Deviant behavior: A social learning perspective.* Belmont, CA: Wadsworth.

Akers, R. L., Krohn, M. D., Lanza-Kaduce, L., & Radosevich, M. (1979). Social learning theory and deviant behavior. *American Sociological Review, 44,* 635–655.

Braithwaite, J. (1981). The myth of social class and criminality reconsidered. *American Sociological Review, 46,* 36–58.

Brehm, J. W., & Cohen, A. R. (1962). *Explorations in cognitive dissonance.* New York: Wiley.

Burkett, S. R., & Warren, B. O. (1987). Religiosity, peer influence, and adolescent marijuana use: A panel study of underlying causal structures. *Criminology, 25,* 109–131.

Cloward, R. A., & Ohlin, L. E. (1960). *Delinquency and opportunity—A theory of delinquent gangs.* New York: Free Press.

Conger, R. D. (1980). Juvenile delinquency: Behavior restraint or behavior facilitation? In T. Hirschi & M. Gottfredson (Eds.), *Understanding crime.* Beverly Hills, CA: Sage.

Conger, R. D., McCarty, J. A., Wang, R. K., Lahey, B. B., & Kroop, J. P. (1984). Perception of child, child-rearing values, and emotional distress as mediating links between environmental stressors and observed maternal behavior. *Child Development, 55,* 2234–2247.

Cullen, F. T. (1984). *Rethinking crime and deviance theory: The emergence of a structuring tradition.* Totowa, NJ: Rowman and Allanheld.

Elliott, D. S. (1985). The assumption that theories can be combined with increased explanatory power: Theoretical integrations. In R. F. Meier (Ed.), *Theoretical methods in criminology.* Beverly Hills, CA: Sage.

Elliott, D. S., Huizinga, D., & Ageton, S. S. (1985). *Explaining delinquency and drug use.* Beverly Hills, CA: Sage.

Festinger, L. (1957). *A theory of cognitive dissonance.* Stanford, CA: Stanford University Press.

Glueck, S., & Glueck, E. (1950). *Unraveling juvenile delinquency.* Cambridge, MA: Harvard University Press.

Hindelang, M. J. (1974). Moral evaluations of illegal behaviors. *Social Problems, 21,* 370–384.

Hirschi, T. (1969). *Causes of delinquency.* Berkeley: University of California Press.

Johnson, R. E. (1979). *Juvenile delinquency and its origins.* Cambridge, UK: Cambridge University Press.

Matsueda, R. (1982). Testing social control theory and differential association. *American Sociological Review, 47,* 489–504.

Miller, W. B. (1958). Lower class culture as a generating milieu of gang delinquency. *Journal of Social Issues, 14*(3), 5–19.

Paternoster, R., Saltzman, L. E., Chiricos, T. G., & Waldo, G. P. (1983). Perceived risk and social control: Do sanctions really deter? *Law and Society Review, 17,* 457–479.

Paternoster, R., Saltzman, L. E., Waldo, G. P., & Chiricos, T. G. (1982). Perceived risk and deterrence: Methodological artifacts in perceptual deterrence research. *Journal of Criminal Law and Criminology, 73,* 1238–1258.

Shaw, C., & McKay, H. D. (1942). *Juvenile delinquency and urban areas.* Chicago: University of Chicago Press.

Short, J. F., Jr., & Strodtbeck, F. L. (1965). *Group process and gang delinquency.* Chicago: University of Chicago Press.

Thornberry, T. P. (1987a). *Reflections on the advantages and disadvantages of theoretical integration.* Paper presented at the Albany Conference on Theoretical Integration in the Study of Crime and Deviance.

Thornberry, T. P. (1987b). Towards an interactional theory of delinquency. *Criminology, 25,* 863–891.

Wahler, R. (1980). The insular mother: Her problems in parent-child treatment. *Journal of Applied Behavior Analysis, 13,* 207–219.

Weis, J. G., & Sederstrom, J. (1981). *The prevention of serious delinquency: What to do?* Washington, DC: U.S. Department of Justice.

Wolfgang, M. E., Thornberry, T. P., & Figlio, R. M. (1987). *From boy to man—From delinquency to crime: Followup to the Philadelphia Birth Cohort of 1945.* Chicago: University of Chicago Press.

REVIEW QUESTIONS

1. Explain what is meant by reciprocal (or feedback) effects. Use a noncrime example to explain such effects.

2. Can you think of concepts or theoretical models other than labeling that Thornberry could or should have incorporated into his integrated model of crime? Explain your rationale for including such concepts or models.

3. Using your own life, or others you know, give an example of someone who follows the causal model proposed by Thornberry. If you can't come up with one, explore the media for someone who does.

❖

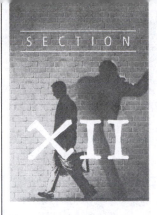

Applying Criminological Theory to Policy

This section will discuss how criminological theories that we have discussed throughout the book have been used to make current criminal justice policies more effective in preventing and reducing crime. Given that we have examined many of the policy implications derived from theoretical models at the end of each section throughout this book, here we will provide only a brief review regarding each category of theories. Thus, this section is meant to summarize the way policy has been altered by criminological research in U.S. history, as well as to suggest future policy changes based on the current state of research in criminology and criminal justice.

Criminological theories have been used to inform development of policy ever since the father of deterrence, Cesare Beccaria, developed the first rational theory of crime in the mid-18th century. We will focus on the policies that have received the most attention by researchers and policy makers. Readers should realize that this section is not meant to be a conclusive review of all policies that can be based on a particular type of theory; on the contrary, this is only a short list of the numerous policies that can be derived from a given theoretical framework.

 Policy Applications Derived from the Classical School: Deterrence Theory

Although most modern criminologists and theoreticians in the field do not consider deterrence theory to be one of the more robust models for understanding or reducing illegal activity,[1] there is no doubt that policy making in

---

[1] Lee Ellis and Anthony Walsh, "Criminologists' Opinions about the Causes and Theories of Crime and Delinquency," *The Criminologist* 24 (1999): 1–4 (see chap. 1, n.6).

our criminal justice system is dominated by the ideas of the Classical School, especially deterrence theory.[2] This is seen in most policies used throughout the system by its three major components: law enforcement, courts, and corrections.

Law Enforcement

Perhaps the most important assumption in applying deterrence theory to policy making in the criminal justice system is that individuals are rational. Unfortunately, much research suggests that people often engage in behaviors that they know are irrational and that individuals' cognitive differences can limit rational decision making.[3] Criminologists often refer to this limitation as *bounded rationality*.[4] Therefore, it is not surprising that many attempts by police and other criminal justice authorities to deter potential offenders do not seem to have much effect in preventing crime.

Of course, the simple existence of a policing authority tends to deter people to some extent. When policing breaks down in given jurisdictions, riots and looting often follow, and it can become a free-for-all among a large mob, which typically contains otherwise law-abiding people. This is one of the reasons why it is typically illegal for police unions to conduct a strike that would leave no police officers available for responding to calls.

Looking at deterrence another way, studies show that the vast majority of drivers speed on highways. For example, one recent study by researchers at Purdue University revealed that 21% of motorists think it's perfectly safe to exceed the speed limit by 5 miles per hour, another 43% saw no risk in going 10 miles per hour over the limit, and another 36% saw no risk in driving 20 miles per hour over the speed limit.[5] This finding is consistent with other studies on drivers' attitudes regarding speeding.

However, when police cruisers are seen, most people will slow down and be more careful, which is in a sense a form of deterrence. For example, most individuals' heart rates will go up a few notches when they see a police cruiser or highway patrol car, even if they are not doing anything wrong. This is a good example of how deterrence can result from simply seeing a police presence. It is likely we can all relate to this, especially if we are speeding or engaging in other illegal behavior (e.g., talking on the cell phone while driving).

On the other hand, research is less clear about whether increasing the number of police in a given area, often referred to as *saturated patrol*, can significantly reduce crime. Some early studies, especially one key experiment involving increased random patrol in certain beats in Kansas City, found no deterrent effect from saturated patrol.[6] However, a recent review of the extant literature, hereafter referred to as the Maryland Report (because all key authors of the report were professors at University of Maryland), concluded that extra police who focus on specific locations (i.e., hot spots), as opposed to larger beat areas, can prevent crime.[7] This strategy of cracking down on specific locations applies to deterrence theory and also incorporates another type of theory that assumes a rational individual: routine activities theory. This theory assumes that motivated offenders will be less likely to commit an

[2]Thomas J. Bernard, Jeffrey B. Snipes, and Alexander L. Gerould, *Vold's Theoretical Criminology*, 6th ed. (Oxford: Oxford University Press, 2010) (see chap. 1).

[3]For a review of the extant research on this topic, see Alex Piquero and Stephen Tibbetts, *Rational Choice and Criminal Behavior* (New York: Routledge, 2002) (see chap. 3).

[4]For more recent discussion on the complexity of developing policies based on deterrence and rational choice models, see Travis Pratt, "Rational Choice Theory, Crime Control Policy, and Criminological Relevance," *Criminology and Public Policy* 7 (2008): 43–52.

[5]For an example, see a news report regarding a study by researchers at Purdue University in which the vast majority of drivers believed going over the speed limit was acceptable and safe: http://www.themotorreport.com.au/12358/study-shows-motorists-ambivalent-to-speed-limits/

[6]George Kelling, *The Kansas City Preventive Patrol Experiment* (Washington, DC: Police Foundation, 1974).

[7]Lawrence Sherman, Denise Gottfredson, Doris MacKenzie, John Eck, Peter Reuter, and Shawn Bushway, *Preventing Crime: What Works, What Doesn't, What's Promising: A Report to the United States Congress* (Washington, DC: U.S. Department of Justice, 1997) (see chap. 2).

offense if there is a presence of guardianship, so adding police to a specific location reduces the likelihood that they will have the opportunity to commit criminal activity at that hot spot.

This same Maryland Report also noted that proactive arrests for drunk driving have consistently been found to reduce such behavior.[8] The effectiveness of reducing drunk driving this way probably has to do with deterring individuals from continuing such activity; that effect is not surprising given the fact that drunk driving often is committed by middle- and upper-class people who have a lot to lose if they don't alter their behavior. The Maryland Report also concludes that the same type of phenomenon is seen with arresting employed (but not unemployed) individuals for domestic violence; to clarify, the employed people have more to lose, so they tend to be deterred from recidivating for domestic violence.[9]

The Maryland Report also offers conclusions about which policing strategies do not seem to prevent or deter crime: more rapid response time to 911 calls, arrests of juveniles for minor crimes, arrest crackdowns at drug markets, and community policing programs with no clear focus on crime risk factors.[10] Finally, it is interesting to note that the Maryland Report acknowledges that the government invests far more federal funds in policing—$2 billion per year—than in any other crime prevention institution, despite the fact that there are still many questions about how effective this funding strategy is, given the wide variation in how each police agency uses this funding and the departments' lack of understanding about what types of programs may be effective versus those that aren't.[11] Thus, it would be very beneficial if policy makers and policing authorities examined the findings of recent empirical research to direct their resources to policies that actually work in reducing crime.

Courts, Diversion Programs, and Corrections

Numerous policies implemented by courts and diversion strategies are based, at least to a large extent, on deterrence. One of the most notorious of the diversion programs is *scared straight*, which became popular in the 1970s.[12] These programs involved having prisoners talk to youths about the realities of their lives, which was supposed to scare them into refraining from recidivating and make them decide to go straight. Unfortunately, virtually all of these programs were found to be ineffective, and some evaluations showed that young participants had significantly higher rates of recidivism.[13] Perhaps the intense experience of being scared by actual inmates had the effect of stigmatizing the youths who went through these programs. Regardless of the reasons, empirical research has consistently found that scared straight programs do not deter or prevent future offending, and the Maryland Report concluded this after reviewing the evaluation literature.

In quite a different strategy, some judges have moved toward using shaming strategies to deter offenders from recidivating.[14] For example, many cities have begun posting the names (and sometimes pictures) of men who are arrested for soliciting prostitutes. Also, some judges have started forcing individuals convicted of drunk driving to place glow-in-the-dark bumper stickers on their cars, as a condition of their probations, that state "BEWARE: Convicted Drunk Driver"; or having shoplifters walk in front of stores with signs that say, "I am a thief. I stole from Walmart!" These are just some of the examples of a growing trend that attempts to deter individuals by threatening

---

[8]Ibid.

[9]Ibid.

[10]Ibid.

[11]Ibid.

[12]For a review of these programs and evaluations of them, see Richard Lundman, *Prevention and Control of Juvenile Delinquency*, 3rd ed. (Oxford: Oxford University Press, 2001).

[13]Lundman, *Prevention and Control*.

[14]For a variety of examples of judges using such shaming sanctions, see story at http://www.msnbc.msn.com/id/19957110/

them with shaming practices if they choose to engage in illegal behavior. Such sentences apply elements of rational choice theory, particularly its ideas about the strong deterrent influence of informal factors, such as community, family, employment, and church. Unfortunately, there have been virtually no empirical evaluations of the effectiveness of such shaming penalties.

Another strategy courts have used for deterring individuals is to develop special sentencing enhancements for habitual offenders, such as California's *three strikes you're out*. Using the common term from baseball, the three-strikes-you're-out policy refers to sentencing schemes that mandate life imprisonment for three-time felons, although each state differs in how this formula works. Washington state was the first to implement a three-strikes law, and today most states have some version of it.[15] As a specific deterrent, such a strategy clearly works because a third-time felon will be in prison for life; however, the three-strikes law was also intended to be a general deterrent and to prevent offenders from recidivating.

Empirical evaluations of the deterrent effect of this law provide no clear result. One study of California's three-strikes law suggests that it has reduced crime,[16] whereas several other studies have shown negligible effects. In some cases, three-strikes laws may have actually increased violence,[17] perhaps due to the desperation and nothing-left-to-lose mentality of offenders who know they face a life sentence if apprehended.[18] Also, the vast majority of offenders prosecuted under the three-strikes penalty are nonviolent (i.e., drug offenders, property offenders, etc.). This is true in California, one of the states that most frequently uses this type of sentencing policy. For example, a man who had no violent crime on his record stole some DVDs from a store and was given a life sentence, which was upheld by the U.S. Supreme Court because of two prior offenses. In some cases, these types of sentencing policies have actually forced the release of violent offenders to make room for habitual nonviolent drug and property offenders. This issue was mentioned as a serious problem in the Maryland Report.

Thus far, successful deterrent policies in the courts and corrections components of the criminal justice system seem rare. According to the Maryland Report, one of the only court-mandated policies that seems promising in deterring offending behavior is orders of protection for battered women.[19] Still, far more brainstorming and evaluations of deterrence-based policies are needed.

 Policy Applications Derived from Biosocial Theories

Although a multitude of policy strategies are related to the biosocial perspective (see Section V), there has been a reluctance to claim that these policies derive from such a theoretical framework due to the stigma of any reference to biology in curbing crime. However, the Maryland Report suggests the importance of identifying and quickly treating any head and bodily trauma early in development among infants and toddlers, concluding that some of the most consistently supported early-intervention programs for such physiological problems are those that involve

---

[15]David Shichor and Dale K. Sechrest, eds., *Three Strikes and You're Out: Vengeance as Social Policy* (Thousand Oaks: Sage, 1996).

[16]Joanna Shepherd, "Fear of the First Strike: The Full Deterrent Effect of California's Two- and Three-Strikes Legislation," *Journal of Legal Studies* 31 (2002): 159–201.

[17]Steven N. Durlauf and Daniel S. Nagin, "Imprisonment and Crime: Can Both be Reduced?," *Criminology and Public Policy* 10 (2011): 13–54; Lisa Stolzenberg and Stewart J. D'Alessio, "Three-Strikes-You're-Out: The Impact of California's New Mandatory Sentencing Law on Serious Crime Rates," *Crime and Delinquency* 43 (1997): 457–469; Mike Males and Dan Macallair, "Striking Out: The Failure of California's Three-Strikes and You're Out Law," *Stanford Law and Policy Review* 11 (1999): 65–72.

[18]Tomislav Kovandzic, John J. Sloan III, and Lynne M. Vieraitis, "Unintended Consequences of Politically Popular Sentencing Policy: The Homicide-Promoting Effects of 'Three Strikes' in U.S. Cities (1980–1999)," *Criminology and Public Policy* 1 (2002): 399–424.

[19]Sherman et al., *Preventing Crime*.

weekly infant home visitation.[20] Experts have recently suggested many more strategies, such as mandatory health insurance for pregnant mothers and their children, which is likely one of the most efficient ways to reduce crime in the long run.[21] Furthermore, all youths should be screened for levels of toxins (e.g., lead), as well as abnormal levels of neurotransmitters (e.g., serotonin) and hormones (e.g., testosterone).[22] Furthermore, greater efforts should be made to ensure that any type of abuse or other form of head trauma gets special attention.

Ultimately, despite the neglect that biosocial models of crime receive in terms of both recognition and policy implications, there is no doubt that this area is crucial if we hope to advance our understanding and create more efficient policies regarding criminal behavior. It is time that all criminologists recognize the degree to which human behavior results from physiological disorders. We all have brains, each about 3 pounds in weight, that determine the choices we make. Criminologists must acknowledge the influence of biological or physiological factors that influence this vital organ, or the discipline will be behind the curve in terms of understanding why people commit (or do not commit) criminal offenses.

▲ Image 12.1   Scared straight programs were designed to expose delinquents to heart-to-heart talks with inmates with the aim of literally scaring them into becoming straight or nondelinquent.

Source: © AP Photo/Wisconsin State Journal, Craig Schreiner.

Policy Applications Derived from Social Structure Theories

Since the introduction of Shaw and McKay's theory of social disorganization (see Section VII), there have been numerous attempts to prevent crime in lower-class, urban areas, where crime is concentrated. One of the most straightforward strategies involves forming a neighborhood watch in high-risk neighborhoods.[23] After reviewing the extant evaluations of such neighborhood watch programs, the Maryland Report concluded that they do not seem to work in reducing crime in neighborhoods. Perhaps this is because the cohesive communities that form such watches already have low crime rates; the neighborhoods that have the highest crime rates tend to be those that are the least cohesive. Furthermore, the report explicitly concludes that community mobilization against crime in high-crime, inner-city, poor areas does not work, probably for the same reasons. Specifically, the most crime-ridden areas tend to have a high turnover of poor residents, who have virtually no investment in the neighborhood; they plan on moving out of the area as soon as they can.

Also related to Shaw and McKay's theory of social disorganization, the Maryland Report concluded that some promising strategies (although there was not enough information to make strong conclusions) included gang

---

[20]Ibid.

[21]John P. Wright, Stephen G. Tibbetts, and Leah Daigle, *Criminals in the Making: Criminality across the Life Course*, 2nd ed. (Thousand Oaks: Sage, 2015) (see chap. 5).

[22]Ibid.

[23]Sherman et al., *Preventing Crime.*

violence prevention programs that focus on reducing gang cohesion, as well as volunteer mentoring programs, such as the Big Brothers Big Sisters program, which appears to be especially good for reducing substance abuse among youths.[24] Thus, it appears that focusing on high-risk youths may be one way of effectively targeting resources and strategies for reducing crime, as opposed to trying to address the crime issues of an entire neighborhood or area of a city. This is consistent with meta-analyses of evaluation studies, which show that the most effective programs are those that focus on the individuals that have the highest risk for offending or recidivism.[25] It is also consistent with studies showing that diversion and rehabilitation programs that target the offenders who are most at risk tend to have more effect than those targeting medium- or low-risk offenders, probably due to the fact that the lower-risk offenders likely won't offend again anyway.[26]

In regard to Merton's strain theory (see Section VI), there have been significant attempts to address the more global issues of deprivation that result from poverty in U.S. society. Perhaps the best example is the War on Poverty, a federal program introduced by President Lyndon B. Johnson during the 1960s. Although an enormous amount of money and other resources were spent in trying to aid the poor in order to reduce crime rates in America, crime rates soared during this period. Many experts noted that the federal investment was not efficiently handed out, but the rise in crime during this period still casts doubt on the effectiveness of such a strategy.

Rather, the Maryland Report concludes that vocational training for adult male offenders has consistently lowered offending rates, as have intensive residential training programs for at-risk youth (such as Job Corps).[27] This conclusion appears consistent with our previous finding that a focus on certain high-risk individuals is more effective than programs addressing an entire group, such as all types of offenders. Perhaps this is because not all offenders have the target characteristic, but such programs tend to be effective for those who do. For example, some offenders are thrust into drug programs even though they have never used drugs or alcohol. Also, some offenders are coerced into engaging in vocational programs when they already have skills in a certain trade. Thus, it makes sense to focus resources (e.g., vocational programs, drug programs.) on the people who are most at risk for the given risk factor.

Policy Applications Derived from Social Process Theories

Ever since the introduction of Sutherland's differential association theory in the 1930s (see Section VIII), numerous programs to reduce crime and delinquency have been based on the assumption that youths must be provided with prosocial interactions with their parents and peers. Many of these programs have shown poor results, probably due to the fact that mixing offenders with other offenders only leads to more offending, ironically due to associations with other offenders. However, many of these programs have shown success or at least promise.

According to the Maryland Report, evidence consistently supports programs that involve long-term, frequent home visitation combined with preschool, as well as family therapy by clinical staff for at-risk youth.[28] Furthermore, the Maryland Report stresses the success of school programs that aim to clarify and communicate norms for various behaviors by establishing school rules and consistently enforcing them through positive reinforcement and schoolwide campaigns.[29] Other effective school programs focus on various competency skills, such as developing

---

[24]Ibid.

[25]Patricia Van Voorhis and Emily Salisbury, *Correctional Counseling and Rehabilitation*, 8th ed. (Cincinnati: Anderson, 2013).

[26]Ibid.

[27]Sherman et al., *Preventing Crime.*

[28]Ibid.

[29]Ibid.

self-control, stress management, responsible decision making, problem solving, and communication skills.[30] On the other hand, the Maryland Report noted some school programs that do not reduce delinquent behavior, such as those that counsel students in a peer-group context (see reasoning above), as well as substance use programs that simply rely on information dissemination or fear arousal (such as the traditional DARE program).[31] Ultimately, programs that teach youths to develop cognitive or thinking skills are beneficial, as opposed to those that simply focus on providing information about drugs or criminal offending. The bottom line for successful programs appears to be that they must instruct youths to deal with everyday influences in a healthy way (according to a cognitive behavioral model), as opposed to just giving them information about crime and drugs.

Policy Applications Derived from Social Reaction and Conflict Theories

Most of the policy implications that were derived from labeling and other forms of social reaction theories (see Section IX) are often referred to as *the Ds* because they include diversion, decriminalization, and deinstitutionalization, which all became very popular in the late 1960s and early 1970s, when the popularity of labeling theory peaked. Consistent with labeling theory, all three emphasize the hands-off doctrine, which seeks to reduce the stigmatization that may occur from being processed or incarcerated by the formal justice system. Diversion includes a variety of programs, such as drug courts or community service programs, which attempt to remove an offender from the traditional prosecutorial and trial process as soon as possible, often with the promise of the charge being expunged or removed from his or her permanent record. Despite empirical research showing mixed results, some of these diversion programs, such as drug courts, have shown promise.[32]

Decriminalization is the lessening of punishments, which is typically recommended for nonviolent crimes to reduce the stigma and penalty related to an offense. This can be distinguished from legalization, which makes an act completely legal; rather, when a certain behavior is decriminalized, it remains illegal, but the penalties are significantly reduced. For example, the possession of small amounts of marijuana is decriminalized in some states (e.g., California): Instead of being arrested and possibly jailed, a person found holding only a small amount is given a ticket, similar to a speeding ticket, which requires payment of a fine. Similarly, deinstitutionalization refers to the avoidance of incarcerating minor, nonviolent offenders, especially if they are juveniles committing status offenses (running away, truancy, etc.). Some have argued that this policy will lead to higher rates of recidivism, but this has not become a problem according to statistics from police and FBI reports.

The bulk of policies that have been derived from conflict theories have emphasized attempting to make laws, enforcement, and processing through the justice system more equitable in terms of social class. For example, the federal sentencing guidelines were recently reviewed for drug possession because it became clear that they were unfair in how they punished drug possession offenders. Specifically, according to the 1980s guidelines, possession of an ounce of crack cocaine earned a defendant a sentence 100 times longer than an offender who possessed an ounce of powder cocaine. Not surprisingly, crack cocaine is typically used and sold by lower-class minorities, whereas cocaine powder is typically used and sold by upper- or middle-class Whites. The disparity in this form of sentencing, which clearly penalizes a certain group of people more than another, has recently become a target for reform by the Obama administration, so there are current efforts to address this issue. This is just one example of how laws and processing are significantly disproportionate in the sense that certain groups (typically lower-class minorities) are arrested, punished, and locked up far more than well-to-do offenders. Studies showing higher

---

[30]Ibid.

[31]Ibid.

[32]Ibid.

conviction rates and longer sentences for offenders who must rely on public defenders to represent them consistently support the high degree of disparities in the criminal justice system, which policies derived from conflict theory attempt to address.

Recently, these hands-off policies have been less attractive to authorities and politicians who want to be seen as hard on criminal offenders so they will be elected or retained in office. Still, due to recent economic crises in many state and local communities, it is likely that many jurisdictions will reconsider these approaches and find alternative strategies for dealing with nonviolent offenders.

 ## Policy Applications Derived from Integrated and Developmental Theories

Few policy strategies have been derived from integrated or developmental theories, probably because most policy makers are either unaware of such theoretical frameworks or because the theories are so complicated that it is difficult for practitioners to apply them. However, one exception to this rule is Braithwaite's theory of shaming and reintegration (see Section XI). Braithwaite has gone to great lengths to apply his theory in Australia, and some evaluations of this approach have shown promise, even if not in the United States. Interventions stress the restorative concepts of his theory, particularly the idea of reintegrating offenders back into society as opposed to stigmatizing them.[33] This strategy emphasizes holding offenders accountable, yet it tries to bring them back into conventional society as quickly and efficiently as possible. In contrast, the U.S. system typically gives prisoners a nominal sum of money (in most jurisdictions, about $200), and they must report themselves as convicted felons for the rest of their lives on all job applications. Would Braithwaite's model work here in the United States? We don't know, but it seems that there could be a better way to incorporate offenders back into society in such a way that they are not automatically set up to fail.

Another area of policy implications from developmental theory is that involving early childhood. Recent research has shown that the earlier that resources are provided—for maternal care during pregnancy, as well as infant care, especially for high-risk infants—the lower the likelihood that such infants will be disposed toward engaging in criminal offending.[34] Thus, far more resources and funding should be given to early development of youths, especially in regard to high-risk pregnant mothers.

 ## Conclusion

This section briefly examined some of the policy implications that can be derived from the theories discussed throughout this text. Other policy strategies have been tried, but we have focused on those that have received the most attention. It is up to each reader to consider what other types of programs can or should be derived from the various theories explored in this book.

 ## Section Summary

◆   Ever since the beginning of rational criminological theorizing in the 18th century, policy implications have always been derived from the popular theories of a given time period.

---

[33]John Braithwaite, "Restorative Justice: Assessing Optimistic and Pessimistic Accounts," in *Crime and Justice: A Review of Research*, Vol. 25, ed. Michael Tonry (Chicago: University of Chicago Press, 1999), 1–27.

[34]Wright et al., *Criminals in the Making*.

◆ Policies derived from Classical School or deterrence theory have seen mixed results, largely because of the limited rationality of people due to psychological and physiological propensities. However, some of these policy implications appear to have had some success, such as proactive policing and the targeting of high-crime locations, known as hot spots. On the other hand, many of the court-implemented policies based on deterrence principles, such as three strikes you're out, have not shown much promise as they are currently administered.

◆ Policies derived from biosocial theories emphasize the need for more medical care, especially during the prenatal and perinatal stages of life. The earlier that biological and social risk factors can be addressed, the better.

◆ Many policies can be derived from social structure theories, but these have not always been found successful, for example, the War on Poverty in the 1960s and various forms of neighborhood watch programs in the last few decades. However, some programs do appear to work, such as those that provide vocational training so people can pull themselves out of poverty.

◆ Social process theories also have numerous policy applications, many of them successful, such as visitations by professionals to make sure the family environment is not problematic, as well as programs that teach individuals (typically youths) cognitive behavioral skills for handling peer pressure and other social situations.

◆ Social reaction theories have inspired policies such as diversion and decriminalization. Conflict theories have inspired policies such as revising sentencing guidelines to make them more equitable according to the seriousness of a given act.

◆ Developmental and integrative theories have not inspired too many policies yet, due to the complexity of such models. However, it is quite likely that, in the near future, such theoretical frameworks will be able to inform policy makers.

DISCUSSION QUESTIONS

1. What types of policies have been derived from the Classical School or deterrence theory? Which have been found to be successful, and which have not?

2. What types of policies have been derived from biosocial theories?

3. What types of policies have been derived from social structure theories?

4. What types of policies have been derived from social process theories?

5. What types of policies have been derived from social reaction and conflict theories?

6. What types of policies have been derived from integrated and developmental theories?

7. What pattern can be seen from the successful programs across all the theories discussed in this book? What patterns do you see in the failure of programs across all theories in this book?

WEB RESOURCES

Policy Implications Derived from Criminological Theories

http://www.cjpf.org/crime/crime.html

http://www.crimepolicy.org/

University of Maryland Report of What Works and What Doesn't

http://www.ncjrs.gov/works/

READING 32

In this selection, James Q. Wilson gives a contemporary review of the various policies that are recommended by the most recent research that exists in the scientific criminological literature. However, keep in mind while reading this selection that Wilson does have some bias toward certain types of theories and assumptions, as does every researcher (whether or not he or she will admit to it).

Wilson provides a variety of explanations for the recent reduction in crime, such as his claim that when crimes decreased in the mid-1990s, one "of the reasons may have been a drop in crack dealing." Wilson explains that another reason for the large decrease is that "crime is also reduced when a nation increases its use of prisons." These two factors are the primary criteria that Wilson acknowledges as important as determinants in why crime/ delinquency reduced so much in the last decade.

While reading this selection, readers should consider whether they agree with Wilson's policy recommendations. Furthermore, they should consider the fact that the data are on Wilson's side; specifically, as incarceration rates have soared over the last 40 years, the rate of serious street crimes (e.g., homicide) has fallen drastically. Still, other crimes have increased substantially, and it is up to readers to decide what types of policy recommendations make the most sense with crimes in the future.

Crime and Public Policy

James Q. Wilson

There are two great questions about crime: Why do people differ in the rate at which they break the law, and why do crime rates in a society rise and fall? You might think that the answer to each question would be the same, but they are not. As Terrie Moffitt and her colleagues explain in chapter 3 of this volume, some people are biologically more likely to commit crimes than are others. But when our nation's crime rate rose sharply, as it did in the 1960s and 1970s, it was not because there was a sudden increase in our biological predisposition to crime. Other factors must have played a role. We also know that young men are much more likely to commit crimes than are young women, but most societies have the same proportion of men and women, even though their crime rates differ sharply.

The chapters in this book provide fascinating answers to both questions: we know much more than we used to about why people differ in how many crimes they commit, and we have learned a lot (though not yet enough) about what factors make the crime rate go up or down. In this chapter I will draw on these findings to provide my overview of what this knowledge means for public policy, but in doing so I am not providing an agreed-upon summary of what has been learned. The authors of the other chapters have not reviewed what I have written here; some may agree, some may not. If you are a student, do not read this chapter to find a condensed version of the whole book; instead, read the book.

SOURCE: "Crime and Public Policy," by James Q. Wilson, in *Crime and Public Policy*, edited by James Q. Wilson and Joan Petersilia. Copyright © 2011 by Oxford University Press. Reprinted with permission.

Crime Rates

Everyone knows that the United States has a high level of homicide, though one much reduced from what it was 20 years ago. But some people forget, as James Lynch and William Pridemore point out in chapter 2, that this country has a level of less-serious crime, including most property crimes, that is about the same as what we find in other democratic countries.

Explaining why we have so many murders and (relatively) so few burglaries is not an easy task. We have probably kept the burglary rate lower than what one finds in some European nations because we are more likely to imprison burglars. Lynch and Pridemore point out that this country is more likely to convict a person for burglary and robbery than are England, Scotland, and Switzerland and more likely to send convicted persons to prison than are Australia, England, Scotland, and Sweden, and to keep people in prison for longer periods than are England, the Netherlands, Scotland, Sweden, and Switzerland.

These differences suggest, but do not prove, that America's criminal justice system has helped keep the rates of burglary and robbery lower than what one finds in many comparable nations. To prove this argument, of course, would require us to take into account all of the many differences among the countries, an analysis that is very difficult to do. One personal anecdote may explain why I take this possibility seriously. When I visited England in the 1980s, that country sent a higher fraction of its robbers to prison than did California, and the English robbery rate was lower than California's. When I returned to England 20 years later, the situation had reversed itself: now the English sent a much smaller fraction of robbers to prison than did California, and its robbery rate had become higher than here. One is entitled to suppose that imprisonment affects national differences in crime rates (Wilson 1976, 1997).

But if that is so, it does not explain why this country has so high a homicide rate. We convict and imprison murderers at about the same rate as do European nations, but our homicide rate is more than five times higher than England's. The only answer we can give is that America is a more murderous country than is England or any other European nation. We have been that way for a long time. The late Eric Monkkonen has shown that the homicide rate in New York City has been 10 to 15 times higher than it has been in London for at least 200 years (Monkkonen 2001).

That level of violence occurred long before televised violence, widespread drug use, and the advent of semiautomatic weapons.

Why is that so? Imagine that you are asked this question on an exam. Your answer could plausibly list all of the distinctive features of American history. We are a nation of immigrants; we never had a powerful aristocracy that could keep ordinary people in their place; our government has always been weaker and more decentralized than most governments abroad; we had to settle an open frontier inhabited by sometimes hostile Native Americans; we settled it before there was a government to manage it; we practiced racial slavery that used force to suppress black Americans and when they became free, especially during the Jim Crow period, we did not have the police enforce criminal laws if the offense took place among blacks. Prohibition created violent gangs that outlasted the dry years. The South has long had a culture of honor that placed a high value on maintaining status by means of dueling. And so on.

Some may suppose that the prevalence of guns in this country may explain our high homicide rate. No doubt it explains some of it; as Philip Cook and his colleagues point out in chapter 10, we do not have drive-by knifings, but we do have drive-by shootings. But guns cannot explain the whole difference. As Franklin Zimring and Gordon Hawkins have pointed out, in 1984 the rate at which we kill people *without* using guns (with knives, clubs, fists, and poison) is three times higher than the rate at which British kill each other without using guns (Zimring and Hawkins 1997). With the recent decline in homicide rates that connection may or may not still be true, but it remains the case that Americans are more violent with or without guns.

The Recent Decline in Crime

Crime rates rose from the early 1960s until the early 1980s, then leveled off a bit, then increased sharply in the late 1980s and early 1990s, and then dropped again right into 2009. Part of this decline is the result, as Greenwood and Turner show, of a decline in the proportion of juveniles in the population. When there are fewer young people, there is less crime. But that is not the whole story; the late Marvin Wolfgang and his colleagues have shown us that young people in the 1970s were not only a bigger share of the population, they had also become, as individuals, more likely to commit serious crimes (Tracy, Wolfgang, and Figlio 1990).

Several authors suggest that the spike in violent crime in the late 1980s was the result of the emergence of street-level crack dealing, an enterprise that involved young people who, in order to protect themselves and harass other dealers, acquired guns. But as the crack trade either diminished or came under tighter control in the mid-1990s, the need for violence declined (Blumstein, Rivara, and Rosenfeld 2000).

In addition, we made heavier use of prison. The number of people in prison rose from about 320,000 in 1980 to 1.1 million in 1995. This country is often criticized for putting a lot of people in prison, but as Apel and Nagin point but in chapter 14, there are several important studies that show that increasing the risk of going to prison for a crime reduces the rate at which that crime is committed. Deterrence works, though the studies disagree about how large this deterrent effect is.

One reason for this uncertainty is that the effect of prison on crime rates changes with the amount of imprisonment. Piehl and Useem make this point in chapter 18. If a state imprisons very few people, adding more prisoners drives the crime rate down by a large amount. But if the state already imprisons a lot of offenders, adding more prisoners has only a modest effect on the crime rate.

If punishment reduces crime, why doesn't every nation punish more? There are several reasons. One is cost: it takes a lot of money to build and manage a prison. But an even more important reason is politics. In this country, the criminal justice system is under popular control: district attorneys and many judges are elected. When people worry about crime, prosecutors and judges worry also. But in most industrialized nations, prosecutors and judges are appointed by the national government, and these officials are sensitive, not to what the public wants, but to what their national superiors prefer. These superiors are upper-middle-class people who can afford to protect themselves against crime and who may be more concerned with other issues.

But there is much we still need to know. Gangs cause a lot of crime; in some cities, such as Los Angeles, they may cause most of the murders. It would be nice to know how gang activity changes and in response to what political or community activities. Maxson in chapter 6 shows that, in many cities, gangs have become less common in recent

years, though in some large ones, such as Chicago and Los Angeles, they remain powerful and increase sharply the number of crime that their young members commit.

There are accounts by journalists suggesting that, in some large cities, gangs have reduced the conflict among them and may even have begun to cooperate in selling drugs and other criminal activities. If true, this suggests that we may have less violence but more illegal business transactions, a trade-off that, though worrisome, may make people safer from drive-by shootings.

People have also invested more heavily in self-defense. They have moved to the suburbs, hired security guards to watch over their big-city apartments, equipped their cars with alarms and special locks, and stayed away from dangerous neighborhoods. We do not know how big a difference this change has made, but we do know that much street crime is committed by people who live near their targets. Crime not only requires criminals, it also requires opportunities. When there are fewer opportunities, there is less crime because most offenders do not travel far to find new targets.

But when middle-class people move out of a crime-ridden neighborhood in order to be safer, they leave behind people who cannot or will not move out and who therefore become less safe. As Robert Sampson points out in chapter 8, crime is more common in unstable neighborhoods where it is hard to maintain an adequate sense of mutual trust and a shared willingness to act to reduce crime. What Sampson calls the "collective efficacy" of a neighborhood is reduced when people with a commitment to sustaining it move away.

Our culture changes also, with people at some times being somewhat tolerant of crime or at least resigned to its being commonplace and at other times being intolerant of it and determined to do something about it. Public policies aimed at solving other problems may also reduce crime rates. The spread of shelters for abused women has not only helped them but may well have reduced the rate at which women are killed by abusive males. There is evidence that in the 1960s and 1970s that crime rose not only in America but everywhere in Europe despite rising levels of economic progress, because people, especially young ones, felt that they had been freed from traditional restraints on their behavior (Wilson 1983). Today society seems less tolerant of "doing your own thing"; perhaps that has helped reduce crime rates.

Police tactics have also changed. Sherman points out in chapter 20 that some departments have become skillful at reducing crime rates by improving how they manage police patrols, respond to calls for help, and manage the ways in which officers spend their time. When the police focus on known offenders and the "hot spots" where crime is likely to occur, they can have a larger impact than when they merely drive around on patrol or wait for 911 calls. In several cities the police are directed, through management techniques like CompStat that was pioneered in New York City by William Bratton, to focus not on maximizing arrests but on reducing crime. This police management technique makes detailed analyses of crime rates in particular neighborhoods and holds the precinct or district commanders accountable for reducing those rates, sometimes by arrests but sometimes by relocating patrols or changing the physical environment.

Finally, changes in public health affect crime rates. Lead can cause reductions in intelligence and increases in crime. When government policies led to a reduction in the amount of leaded gasoline and paint, data suggest that this may have helped reduce crime levels (Reyes 2007).

 ## Can More Be Done to Reduce Crime?

When the crime rate in America began rising sharply in the early 1960s, scholars did not know much about how it might be controlled. Many denied that deterrence works; to them, crime was entirely the result of human factors (attitudes, peer connections, family difficulties, school problems, and the like) that made would-be offenders immune to the risk of punishment. It was customary then to say that crime could only be reduced by changing its "root causes."

No doubt reducing the causes of crime would help, but 40 years ago we did not have a very good idea of what those causes were. Many people thought that unemployment caused crime, but in the 1960s that was a curious view since the American economy was booming and unemployment rates were quite low.

The connection between crime and the economy is much more complicated than popular discussions recognize. As Bushway shows in chapter 7, the link between unemployment and crime is dependent on time. When people first become unemployed, they stay at home, draw on savings, or work on homely tasks. Crime rates stay low. But if unemployment persists it may well drive up crime rates. And more is at stake than unemployment. One is the share of people who participate in the labor market. When this is high, people feel connected to work even when they are unemployed. But when people have never joined the labor market or have left it because they have a prison record or are engaged in drug dealing, they become detached from the goal of finding legitimate work.

Moreover, it may be the condition of the economy as a whole (the gross domestic product, or GDP) rather than the unemployment rate that affects human behavior. A decline in GDP may push burglary rates up, but an *increase* in GDP may drive auto theft rates up. Economists continue to puzzle over these connections. One possibility is that imprisonment has affected so many offenders that they find the legal labor market either unappealing or inaccessible.

Others thought that family problems were the cause, but no one knew much about how the government could affect family life. Still others blamed gangs and bad companions and urged gang workers to reduce these bad influences. That was a good idea except that then—and to a considerable extent, still today—we do not know very much about reducing gang influences.

But the rising crime rate produced at least one good result: a sharp increase in intelligent research on crime. Today we know vastly more than we once did about individual differences in the tendency to break the law and about the effect (or in some cases, the non-effect) of policies aimed at reducing crime rates. The most important thing to do is to move toward evidence-based criminal justice policies. This book contains a summary of much of that evidence.

 ## Deterrence

We know that punishment deters crime, but we also know that it is probably the swiftness and certainty of being imprisoned more than the severity of the penalty that has the largest effect. This raises the question of whether we keep some people in prison too long. Typical offenders commit most of their crimes when they are in their early twenties, and very few after they reach their forties. Perhaps we could cut prison costs and open up more prison space by shortening sentences.

But we can only do that if we think that the chief purpose of punishment is deterrence. If punishment also has a moral role by conveying society's view about the wrongness of some behavior, then there are important limits to how short sentences can be. You go to prison if you are convicted of murdering your spouse, but how long you stay there does not depend on whether, after your release, you will murder your next spouse; indeed, convicted wife murderers are not likely to marry again. You are kept in prison for a long time because society thinks murder is a terrible crime, not because we simply want to discourage more murders. Prison terms for some offenses can be safely reduced; for example, it may make little sense to keep an auto thief in prison for a long time since theft, though a serious crime, is not one that arouses powerful (and desirable) retributive instincts.

And it may make even less sense to keep a drug dealer in prison very long because when one dealer leaves, a rival takes his place on the street. Punishing people who deal in certain drugs is a good idea because we want to make it clear that using these substances is a big mistake, but long sentences for drug dealing are not likely to reduce that dealing.

A better way to shorten prison terms and thus create more space for new offenders is to rethink the practice, common in many states, of sending people who violate the terms of their parole back to prison. Some parolees do things that merit reimprisonment, but others commit only technical violations that could be handled more easily by toughening up community controls.

The creation of global positioning satellites makes it possible today to require people on probation or parole to wear a GPS monitor around their ankles, accompanied by a device that warns the police if they try to remove it. The GPS monitor can tell probation and parole officers exactly where their charges are and can be fitted with devices that set off an alarm if they go to forbidden places (for example, a school or a dangerous bar).

Another strategy is to give an incentive to persons to avoid crime. Project HOPE, described by Boyum, Caulkins, and Kleiman in chapter 13, is a major advancement in how to keep people on probation, most of whom have committed felonies, from committing more. It shows how overworked probation officers can be mobilized to write up short, simple violation notices and get judges quickly to warn and then punish with short jail terms people who fail

to obey the terms of probation. The result of swift deterrence was a sharp drop in crime rates, even though no "root causes" were eliminated.

Preventing Crime

Preventing people from becoming criminal is an ideal strategy: it spares us the later and high costs of more police, more judges, and more prison time. The problem is to discover and test programs that in fact prevent crime and to be sure that a program that works on a few people in one place when it is run by gifted researchers will work across the country for thousands of people when it is run by ordinary employees.

Happily, we have learned a lot about what works. There are several sources of such knowledge. One is the Center for the Study and Prevention of Violence at the University of Colorado, which has produced short, readable accounts of prevention programs that meet at least two tests. The first is that they have been evaluated by randomly assigning people to either the program or to the status quo. Random assignment is important because it eliminates the possibility that a program only appears to work owing to the fact that those in the program are predisposed to benefit and those not in it are inclined to resist change. Random assignment means that both participants and the control group are equal. The second requirement is to test the program in more than one place. This is important because it reduces the chance that some exceptional feature of one locale, or the people in that locale, explain the gains.

The University of Colorado survey lists about a dozen programs that have survived these two tests. Some of them seem obvious: for example, a program that teaches children to avoid drug use (Project STAR), another that makes foster homes work better (Treatment Foster Care), and yet another that helps improve family life (Functional Family Therapy). But some successes may strike you as puzzling. One is the Nurse Home Visitation Program, which sends trained nurses into the homes of poor young girls who have just become pregnant. The nurses explain how to care for newborn babies by feeding, clothing, and handling their health care needs. Why should any of this affect later criminality? But it does: in one study, done in Elmira, New York, the female children of these mothers 19 years later were one-fifth as likely to be arrested or convicted of a crime as those in the control group (Eckenrode, 2010). But there was no improvement for the male children. For the girls, early care made a difference.

There no doubt are other good programs, but because they have not been rigorously evaluated we do not know that they work. One may be the High/Scope Perry Preschool Project in Ypsilanti, Michigan. About one hundred three- or four-year-old children were randomly divided between being in and out of a new preschool project. They were followed for over 20 years, and those in the program were less likely than those not in it to have been arrested, to be unemployed, or to receive welfare (Schweinhart, Barnes, and Weikart 2005). But for reasons that I do not know, the program was only done in one city and so it did not meet the Colorado test.

As David Farrington shows in chapter 5, we have learned some things about reducing the extent to which bad families can cause crime among their children. These programs are not easily managed, as many involve dealing with family members in special clinics or as part of a program that involves children, their schoolteachers, and their parents.

Unfortunately, programs that work are not nearly as well-known as those that do not. Millions of people have heard of DARE (Drug Abuse Resistance Education), a program that sends police officers into fifth-grade classes to teach students to avoid drugs. The several studies that have been done show that it has not reduced later drug use. (It may still be a helpful program if it makes the police and young people get along better, but that was not what it was intended to achieve.) Everybody knows about DARE; hardly anybody knows about nurse home visitations.

Guns and Crime

For many people, America's high homicide rate would go down sharply if we just got guns off the street. But public opinion polls and a recent Supreme Court decision make it clear that this will not happen. The Court held that the Second Amendment gives to individual citizens the right to own a gun, but it allows the states to impose reasonable restrictions on the kinds of guns and how they may be purchased (*District of Columbia v. Heller* 2008). However, if guns did disappear, we would still have a higher murder rate than does England because we kill people at a higher rate without using guns than does England.

Government restrictions may limit gun purchases to people who are not criminals but they may not ban (as has been tried in a few places) every citizen from owning any gun. And such bans would probably not make much difference; after they were enacted, violent crime rates in many of those places continued to rise. The reason is simple: there are hundred of millions of guns in private possession. A criminal can easily steal one or, in places where their sale is legal, get a person without a criminal record to buy one and pass it on to him.

But surely we can reduce the number of guns carried by people who are ready to use them for criminal purposes. Yes, but this tactic requires certain restrictions on civil rights and a great need for a better technology.

The civil rights problem is that the police must be able to justify a search of another person. That is easily done if the person is arrested or the police have a search warrant. But it is not so easily done if the police spot a suspicious person on the street and try to search him. It can be done under certain circumstances. The Supreme Court has ruled that the police may stop and frisk someone if an officer observes unusual conduct that leads him or her reasonably to conclude that the person may be armed or dangerous (*Terry v. Ohio* 1968). A "stop and frisk" means patting down a person's clothing and, if a gun is felt, seizing it. These street stops have become very important in some big cities, with thousands of guns being taken off the streets.

The police can also search for guns when they make traffic stops; Lawrence Sherman has reported that when this was done in a part of Kansas City, many guns were seized and in that neighborhood the crime rate fell.

The police in some cities have asked parents to allow their homes to be searched for guns that might be owned by their children on the understanding that, if a gun is found, no one will be arrested. And in every state, probation and parole officers have the authority to take guns from anyone under their supervision.

It is possible that technology might be devised that would allow the police to detect from a distance whether a person was carrying a concealed weapon on the street. Of course, some people carrying a concealed weapon may have a permit that allows this. But others who lack such permits could have their gun seized. This technology has been produced. It uses millimeter-band radar. But the device is too cumbersome for the police to carry. More research is needed to create a more useful apparatus.

Guns play a role in self-defense. Studies have been done to estimate how frequently a gun protects a person threatened with assault or robbery. The results vary; no one is sure what the correct number is, but it is much larger than zero. One study argues that places where people find it easy to get a permit to carry a concealed weapon have, other things being equal, a lower risk of being murdered (Lott 2000). Other studies have challenged this finding (Donohue and Ayres 2003; Black and Nagin 1998). A committee appointed by the National Academy of Sciences examined the issue and, with one dissent, agreed with the critics. I was the dissenter (Wellford, Pepper, and Petrie 2004).

 ## Reducing Crime Among Ex-Convicts

About two-thirds of the people released from prison commit new crimes. This high recidivism rate is a major source of our crime rate. If we could reduce this rate, it would make a big difference in how many new crimes are committed.

But this is a very hard task. Unlike crime prevention programs for children, treatment programs for adults must cope with people who, in most cases, are leading completely dysfunctional lives. Most are on drugs, many belong to gangs, few have much education or job skills, some are psychopaths who find it very hard to learn any rules, and a lot leave prison to go back to neighborhoods where circumstances had already pushed them into crime.

Joan Petersilia in chapter 17 writes about the importance of this group. Judging from how many are involved (there were 828,000 adults on parole in 2008), it may be impossible to deal effectively with many of them. That means, I imagine, dealing with those that are either amenable to change or who constitute the greatest risk.

I have written "dealing" with them, but frankly we do not yet know how best to deal with them. One possibility is to keep them under close supervision using a GPS anklet that cannot be removed without sending out a signal. We might then be able to keep close track of them and be able to intervene if they go to places (a dangerous barroom, a place where drugs are sold, a public school) that we wish them to avoid.

But today we know more than we used to. Forty years ago a committee from the National Academy of Science wrote that there was very little evidence that any program to rehabilitate criminals worked. But today, as Francis Cullen and Cheryl Jonson point out in chapter 11, we can say with some confidence that there are such programs that make a difference. By looking at all such efforts taken together (the process is called meta-analysis) we learn that they will, on average, reduce the recidivism rate by about 10 percent. A gain, but a small one, and we are not certain it is worth the cost.

But the same meta-analysis tells us that certain kinds of programs will reduce recidivism by much more, perhaps by 20 to 30 percent. These successful programs focus on what specialists call cognitive-behavioral or social learning approaches. In plain language, they involve helping criminals learn how to handle the environment they face. They do this in two ways. First, they alter what the offenders think about crime (for example, by learning that it is they, and not some outside force, that is to blame for what they do). A striking finding about criminals is they often think that "outside forces" explain their behavior. Second, offenders are taught how to manage themselves as they confront the environment (by, for example, controlling their anger and their impulsive urges).

We have also learned what does not work, such as boot camps and "scared straight" programs. And there is much about which we are uncertain, such as the effect on crime of many educational and job training programs. If there is any one area of criminal justice on which new research is most needed, handling ex-cons is it.

 ## Justice and Crime

Policies to deal with crime must not only be effective and worth the cost, they must be just. In chapter 9, Randall Kennedy describes the long and still incomplete struggle this country has had in trying to ensure that crime control policies are not racially biased.

But even when we try to be fair, we are still likely to think up policies to deal with crime on the basis of our ideological predispositions. If you are a liberal, you will tend to blame crime on poverty, too many guns, and unemployment and argue for more civil rights and more jobs—whatever the facts may be. If you are a conservative, you will be inclined to blame crime on personal irresponsibility and lenient courts that have hurt the police and argue in favor of capital punishment and longer prison terms—whatever the facts may be. Picking your way through this ideological swamp is difficult, and no one, including the authors in this book, is entirely successful at doing it.

Crime control in this country is essentially a local matter, but there is one thing that local authorities find it hard to do, and that is to find out what works. A local police chief may be eager to learn what patrol strategy is best, but he faces two problems: he or she needs to find enough money to test different strategies (but money is scare at the local level), and he or she has to be willing to risk political embarrassment if a strategy fails. To help with these problems, it is important that the federal government give money to carefully test new ideas.

In the past, federal authorities, notably the National Institute of Justice, have done this, but only on occasion. Politically, it is much easier to send money to law enforcement agencies without asking them to find out what works. That episodic approach is a mistake. The nation needs a continuous and systematic commitment to the development of evidence-based law enforcement.

 ## References

Black, D. A., and D. S. Nagin. 1998. "Do Right-to-Carry Laws Deter Violent Crime?" *Journal of Legal Studies* 27: 221.

Blumstein, A., F. P. Rivara, and R. Rosenfeld. 2000. "The Rise and Decline of Homicide—and Why." *Annual Review of Public Health* 21: 505–541.

Bureau of Justice Statistics, *Key Facts at A Glance,* Available at http://bjs.ojp.usdoj.gov/content/glance/tables/corr2tab. cfm.

District of Columbia v. Heller. 2008. 554 U.S. 128 S. Ct. 2783, 171 L. Ed 2d 637.

Donohue, J., and I. Ayres. 2003. "Shooting Down the "More Guns, Less Crime' Hypothesis." *Stanford Law Review* 51: 4.

Eckenrode et al., 2010. "Long-Term Effects of Prenatal and Infancy Nurse Home Visitation on the Life Course of Youths: 19-Year Follow-Up of a Randomized Trial." *Archives of Pediatric Adolescent Medicine* 164: 9–15.

Lott, J. R. 2000. *More Guns, Less Crime: Understanding Crime and Gun Control Laws,* 2d ed. Chicago: University of Chicago Press.

Monkkonen, E. 2001. *Murder in New York City.* Berkeley: University of California Press.

Reyes, J. W. 2007. "Environmental Policy as Social Policy? The Impact of Childhood Lead Exposure on Crime," National Bureau of Economic Research, Working Paper 13097, 2007. Available at http://www.nber.org/papers/w13097.

Schweinhart, L. J., H. V. Barnes, and D. P. Weikart. 2005. *Significant Benefits: The High/Scope Perry Preschool Program Through Age 40.* Ypsilanti: High/Scope Press. Available at http://www.highscope.org/content.asp?contentid=219.

Terry v. Ohio. 1968. 392 U.S. 1.

Tracy, P. E., M. E. Wolfgang, and R. M. Figlio. 1990. *Delinquency Careers in Two Birth Cohorts.* New York: Plenum.

Wellford, C. F., J. V. Pepper, and C. V. Petrie, eds. 2004. *Firearms and Violence: A Critical Review.* Washington, DC: National Academy Press.

Wilson, J. Q. 1976. "Crime and Punishment in England." *The Public Interest* 43 (Spring): 3–25.

Wilson, J. Q. 1983. "Crime and American Culture." *The Public Interest* 70 (Winter): 22–48.

Wilson, J. Q. 1997. "Criminal Justice in England and America." *The Public Interest* 126 (Winter): 3–14.

Zimring, F. E., and G. Hawkins. 1997. *Crime Is Not the Problem: Lethal Violence in America.* New York: Oxford University Press.

READING 33

In this selection by Craig Schwalbe, the author claims that efforts to strengthen probation programs are quite often hindered by a lack of a sound theoretical framework for probation practice. The study closely examined the insights of 31 probation officers via interviews about their probation work. The author uses these insights to develop a framework to guide future program practices and policies as well as research development.

Toward an Integrated Theory of Probation

Craig S. Schwalbe

Despite the advanced age of juvenile probation, a unified, coherent practice theory of probation has yet to emerge in the literature. As probation is the focal point of a majority of juvenile court interventions, the lack of scholarship in this area is startling. Across the United States, approximately 60% of all youth referred to the juvenile court will have some form of probation supervision as their final disposition (Snyder & Sickmund, 2006). Probation officers carry out the will of the court and, by extension, the policies of the legislative bodies that formulate juvenile justice policy (Howell, 2003; Maloney, Romig, & Armstrong, 1988). Because the field lacks a coherent practice theory, probation programs vacillate over time between the enforcement/control function of the court and its rehabilitative mission in response to shifting public opinion about crime rates and its concern for disadvantaged youth. More important, initiatives to strengthen probation programs often lack a strong theoretical footing and fail to produce their promised results.

This article uses a grounded theory approach, the study developed the *participation process model of probation*. The participation process model advances criminal justice scholarship by describing mechanisms of change hypothesized to promote the achievement of policy-informed objectives and goals. Thus, this framework reconciles historical debates about the control versus rehabilitation function of probation and illustrates how strategies and tactics representative of these perspectives work in tandem to achieve the desired aims of effective probation supervision.

 ## Current State of Probation Theory

Care and Control in Probation

Implied or explicit in much probation scholarship is the tension arc that exists between care and control, with *care* usually referencing therapeutic programming aimed at treatment and *control* usually referencing deterrence and punishment approaches. This tension arc is often cast in either–or terms and has spawned a modest number of

surveys aimed at describing where individual officers position themselves and what factors predict officer beliefs about their rehabilitation versus control responsibilities. In recent studies, surveys indicate that many officers hold mixed attitudes that blend care and control, that juvenile probation officers are more likely to hold attitudes favorable to rehabilitation compared to adult probation officers, and that education level and length of service, among other things, predict the strength of officers' attitudes toward punishment (Leiber, Schwarze, Mack, & Farnworth, 2002; Lopez & Russell, 2008; Moak & Wallace, 2000; Polcin & Greenfield, 2003). Although useful for predicting officer propensities toward various types of probation strategies (Schwalbe & Maschi, 2009), this research is insufficient on its own to develop a coherent theory of probation because it does not inform testable hypotheses about the relative influence of care and control strategies on probation outcomes.

The theoretical work of Klockars (1972) and Skeem and Manchak (2008) represents an advance toward a normative practice theory for probation. Klockars established a typology of probation based on an in-depth ethnographic study of a large, urban probation department. The typology addressed the problem of how probation officers integrated their rehabilitative mission, which requires trust and self-disclosure on the part of probationers, with their control mission, which threatens punishment to probationers when rule-violating or illegal behavior is brought to light. Three officer types emerged in this research: law enforcers, therapeutic agents, and synthetic officers. It is not surprising that the law enforcers and therapeutic agents emphasized one or the other competing missions of probation (control and rehabilitation, respectively) whereas the synthetic officer sought integration. Synthetic officers resolved the inherent contradiction between care and control by establishing a fictional negotiating triad where officer authority was attributed to an external force, such as a supervisor or judge. Klockars found that success on probation required rule compliance that was ostensibly monitored by the external authority. However, the force of the external authority could be deferred in the face of rule violations when probationers established rapport with their officers. The model paradox rests in the hidden

SOURCE: Craig S. Schwalbe, "Toward an Integrated Theory of Probation," *Criminal Justice and Behavior* 39 (2012): 185–201.

authority of the officer—the negotiating triad is fictional in the sense that all information needed by the external authority flows through the officer, making the whole process dependent on officer discretion.

Skeem and Manchak (2008) conducted a literature review to evaluate the relative effectiveness of the three probation types identified by Klockars (1972). Overall, the weight of evidence reviewed by Skeem and Manchak favored the synthetic approach. Studies of individual officer orientation showed that probationers supervised by officers who were "firm but fair" and officers who were "balanced" had lower rates of violations and reconvictions compared to officers who emphasized either the control orientation of the law enforcer or the exclusive treatment orientation of the therapeutic agent (Andrews & Kiessling, 1980; Paparozzi & Gendreau, 2005). Evidence from probation program evaluations reinforced these findings. For example, when intensive supervision programs emphasized monitoring and surveillance to the exclusion of treatment and rehabilitation, failure rates were disappointingly high and programs had no effect on recidivism (Petersilia & Turner, 1993). On the other hand, Intensive Supervision Programs (ISP) that blended treatment with the threat of sanctions through monitoring increased service utilization and reduced recidivism (Aos, Miller, & Drake, 2006; Paparozzi & Gendreau, 2005).

Risk/Need/Responsivity (RNR)

Paralleling the care/control debate, the RNR paradigm is derived from empirical research conducted over the past 20 years about factors associated with recidivism reduction in the juvenile and adult justice systems (Andrews, Bonta, & Hoge, 1990). This body of literature suggests that the effect of justice system rehabilitation efforts are conditioned on the risk and need characteristics of individual offenders matched with the intervention characteristics provided through justice system involvement. Andrews et al. (1990) isolated these conditions in their now classic work introducing the RNR model. They argued that rehabilitative interventions are most effective when they target probationers who are at high risk of recidivism (the *risk principle*), when they target specific malleable risk factors known to predict offending (the *need principle*), and when they are implemented in accordance with the learning styles of individual offenders (the *responsivity principle*).

A growing body of research supports the RNR paradigm. Andrews and Bonta (2010) reviewed this literature and the meta-analyses that have contributed to it. The preponderance of evidence suggests that although the overall effect of offering social services to offenders is small ($r = .12$), the effect increases markedly in programs that maintain fidelity to the RNR model ($r = .26$). Several empirical studies have isolated the specific effects of RNR-informed probation strategies on offender outcomes. For instance, Bonta, Rugge, Scott, Bourgon, and Yessine (2008) showed in their study of 62 probation officers who supervised juveniles, adults, or both in Manitoba that amount of time in officer–client meetings devoted to a discussion of client needs rather than probation conditions was positively associated with reductions in recidivism. Vieira, Skilling, and Peterson-Badali (2009) found that the degree of concordance between case plans and assessed need reduced the hazard of recidivism by 18 times in their sample of 122 youth. Findings such as these, in conjunction with extensive meta-analyses about the effectiveness of psychosocial interventions for offender populations (Landenberger & Lipsey, 2005), provide compelling evidence that rehabilitation efforts led by probation officers can increase public safety and reduce recidivism, rebutting Martinson (1974), whose essay launched the "get tough" era of juvenile and criminal justice in which the prevailing sentiment was that "nothing works" to prevent recidivism.

Toward an Integrated, Coherent Theory

Together, Klockars's (1972) probation typology and the RNR paradigm (Andrews & Bonta, 2010; Andrews et al., 1990) are suggestive that a synthetic approach blending care and control with an intervention focus on criminogenic need are necessary to reduce recidivism and to promote public safety among probationers. Missing are the hypothesized mechanisms that join the synthetic officer type with the RNR framework. The grounded theory presented in this article proposes just such a mechanism. The original intent of this study was to outline a grounded theory of probation based on officer-reported descriptions of their practice strategies; theoretical integration was not the planned outcome. Yet the perspectives of officers, who in this case supervise juvenile offenders, points to the establishment of a more unified, coherent, practice theory for probation.

Method

Participants

Participants were juvenile probation officers recruited from a pool of respondents who completed an online survey about probation strategies in 2008 (Schwalbe & Maschi, 2009, 2011). Of 308 survey respondents, 206 indicated their willingness to participate in a follow-up study. The list of officers willing to be recontacted was sorted randomly using a random number generator. Officers were contacted in blocks of 10 via e-mail with a second contact attempted for nonresponders. Those who expressed willingness to participate were scheduled for telephone interviews. A target sample of 30 officers was sought to ensure saturation in the main study aims (Onwuegbuzie & Leech, 2007; Sandelowski, 1995). In total, 110 officers were contacted, 14 e-mail messages were returned as undeliverable, and 31 officers who expressed their willingness to participate were interviewed.

The median participant in this study was female (*n* = 21), had 10 years of experience in juvenile probation (*M* = 9.5, *SD* = 6.2, range = 1.5–25 years), and was educated at the bachelor's level (bachelor's = 22, master's = 6, other = 2) with a major in criminal justice *(N* = 11; sociology = 4, social work = 3, psychology = 4, other = 10). Officers in the current study were representative of the original survey sample in gender and education level. However, participants in the current study had about twice the level of experience compared to respondents in the original survey sample (Schwalbe & Maschi, 2009). Officers most often described their caseloads as general (*n* = 13) or specialized (*n* = 14) with a small number describing their caseloads as adult–juvenile mixed (*n* = 1) or intake (*n* = 2). Specialized caseloads included high-risk, serious offenders (*n* = 5), intensive probation (*n* = 2), mental health/substance abuse (*n* = 2), sex offenders (*n* = 3), and gender specialization (*n* = 2). One supervisor who no longer carried a caseload was also interviewed.

Procedures

Interviews were conducted by telephone by the study author following a semistructured format. The interviews were designed to elicit officers' individual theories of probation. That is, they were asked to describe and elaborate how the use of specific probation strategies and tactics achieved their long-range goals and to identify the mechanisms of change that mediate these hypothesized relations. After verbal informed consent, officers were asked to (a) describe the overall objectives of probation, (b) describe their general approach to probation, (c) identify a youth on their caseload who is considered "high risk" and known to have mental health problems, (d) describe the youth case-plan goals, (e) describe an intervention or probation strategy that officers would judge to have led to progress on their case-plan goals, and (f) describe their experience, education, and training. Throughout the interviews, participants were prompted to provide behavioral descriptions where possible (e.g., "If I was to watch you clarifying your role as a probation officer, what would I see you do?") and to describe specific linkages between probation strategies and outcomes (e.g., "When you ask open-ended questions about a youth's long-term goals, what should change for the youth?"). In addition, they were prompted to describe conditions under which probation strategies employed were more or less successful (e.g., "Are there times when monitoring strategies do not cause youths to 'think twice'? Please elaborate."). Because detailed data were collected about specific youth on participants' caseloads, geographic data about the officers (i.e., county or state of employment) were not collected to preserve officer and youth confidentiality.

Analysis

Interviews were digitally recorded and transcribed to facilitate analysis using Atlas-ti software (Atlas.ti, 2010). A grounded theory approach using open coding and constant comparison was employed throughout the study (Charmaz, 2006; Denzin & Lincoln, 2005; Padgett, 2008). During interviews, follow-up questions to respondents were used to elaborate hypotheses generated in earlier interviews, and memos were developed to track investigator interpretations, questions, and hypotheses. A code matrix of literal codes was derived for the first 10 transcripts when high levels of repetition among codes between transcripts indicated that saturation in the main study aims had been achieved. The literal codes were classified into conceptual clusters. The literal codes and conceptual clusters were then verified by double coding three transcripts with a colleague experienced in qualitative methods. After revising the code matrix, all transcripts were recoded with new codes added as they emerged in subsequent interview transcripts. A theory of probation practice was derived for each officer based on quotations from the coded transcripts. As a final step, each transcript was reread in totality to confirm that the theories of probation derived in the coding procedure reflected perceptions of probation practice as described by the participants.

Results

A conceptual model of probation practices, summarized in Figure 1, was derived from across all interviews. According to this model, three types of probation strategies (casework, communication, leverage) are employed by officers to achieve three long-term objectives (risk/need reduction, public safety, accountability). Additionally, four proximal change mechanisms both mediate and

moderate the relation between probation tactics and long-term objectives (youth participation, officer–youth relationship, parental support, youth motivational processes). As elaborated in more detail below, notable features of this theoretical model are (a) the central role of youth participation as a moderator of risk/need reduction and accountability; (b) the mediating role of motivational processes, officer–youth relationship quality, and parental support; and (c) the general rather than specific effects of the probation tactics on the proximal change mechanisms. As a synthesis of 31 individual theories of probation, it should be noted that no officers endorsed all theoretical paths as illustrative of their typical probation practices. However, the theoretical framework presented here encompasses the diversity of perspectives reflected in the probation officers' interpretations of their own practice strategies.

Objectives of Probation

Public safety, that is, prevention of recidivism, is the penultimate objective of most probation interventions. To achieve public safety, officers endorsed two long-term objectives: risk/need reduction and offender accountability.

Figure 1   Participation process model of probation

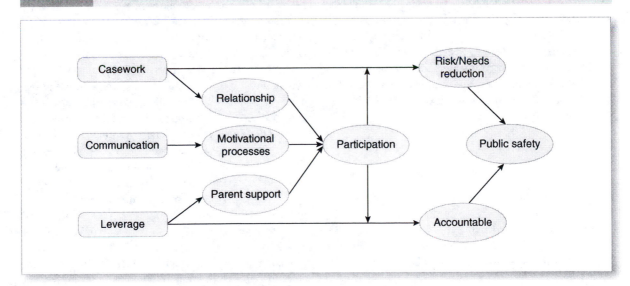

Youth risks and needs were understood to be psychosocial conditions or circumstances that are hypothesized to predict recidivism, often including such factors as substance abuse, school problems, and family dysfunction. Risk/need reduction was primarily achieved through case management activities including assessment, case planning, and referrals to community programs and services. Successful risk/need reduction was thought to reduce youth propensity to offend through mechanisms such as the development of skills (e.g., "We also need to assess and develop skills to help the client manage their own lives") and an increase in prosocial community involvements (e.g., "It just goes back to, the more positive things that they have to take up their time, the less time they have to be running around with [delinquent peers], drinking or using").

Youth accountability was defined as "paying back" the community for harm caused by delinquency as well as accepting consequences for delinquency. In terms of probation, this meant following through on community service orders, paying restitution, writing victim apology letters, participating in victim-offender mediation, and complying with conditions of probation, which commonly included curfew restrictions and school attendance, among others. Youth accountability and public safety were linked when youth were able to consider the consequences of their behaviors (e.g., "So [adolescent female client] can talk her way out of a lot of things. And just having her realize that this wasn't something that she was going to be able to talk her way out of, I think was a good life lesson for her"). When youth accepted consequences for their behavior and paid back victims of their offenses, their subsequent decisions about delinquency and rule-violating behaviors would tend toward more prosocial goals, thereby increasing public safety.

Strategies for Meeting Probation Objectives

Table 1 presents a matrix of conceptual clusters for three types of probation strategies commonly endorsed by participants. Overall, probation strategies were coded 859 times. Communication strategies were most common (coded 414 times, average = 13.3), followed by casework strategies (coded 346 times, average = 9.9), and leverage strategies (coded 302 times, average = 8.4). Officers described 8.4 discrete strategies on average, including 3.4 types of communication strategies, 2.9 types of casework strategies, and 2.1 types of leverage strategies. Overlap across strategies was the norm, with all officers describing their specific communication strategies, 30 of 31 officers describing the use of casework strategies, and 28 of 31 officers describing the use of leverage strategies.

Communication strategies are a range of interpersonal tactics deployed by officers in their meetings with youth and their families. Of the seven categories reported, dialogue/asking questions was the most frequently coded (coded 119 times, average = 3.5). Types of questions included those that elicit information or feelings, as well as Socratic questions that were employed to lead youth and parents to new learning. Other communication strategies frequently coded included clarifying (e.g., informing youth about probation officer roles and expectations of probation), praise/encouragement (e.g., cheerleader for tasks yet to be done and affirmation for tasks already completed), persuasion (e.g., making an argument for change including pointing out consequences and benefits), and confrontation (e.g., pointing out misbehavior and making demands for changes).

Casework strategies were coded whenever officers reported elements of the casework process, including assessing problems, establishing case goals, planning interventions, and implementing interventions (excluding sanctions and other leverage interventions, described below). The most common casework strategy coded was linking/referral (coded 143 times, average = 4.1). Linking/referral codes were applied whenever officers described referring youth to formal service providers or to informal service community resources, or made reference to the use of specific evidence-based interventions. Other casework strategies included case planning (e.g., establishing goals and intervention plans, either collaboratively or via court order) and assessment (e.g., referral for psychological testing, structured risk/needs assessment, unstructured interview). Fifteen officers reported the use of incentives that involved tokens (e.g., bus passes or food treats), privileges (e.g., relaxed curfew), or early discharge.

Leverage strategies are aversive sanctions, either applied or threatened, that are imposed by the courts and probation officers as a consequence for rule-violating behavior. Across all strategy types, monitoring was the most frequently coded strategy (coded 153 times,

Table 1	Conceptual Clusters of Communication Strategies, Casework Strategies, and Leverage Strategies					
Tactic	**Example**	**Frequency**	**M**	**(SD)**	**Mdn**	**Range**
Communication		414	13.3	(8.1)	13	2–42
Dialogue/asking questions	Elicit information Socratic questioning	119	3.5	(4.2)	2	0–19
Clarify roles	Expectations of probation Approach of probation officer	74	2.4	(2.0)	2	0–8
Praise/encouragement	Affirm youth capabilities Validate youth accomplishments	73	2.4	(3.1)	1	0–10
Persuasion	Appeal to reason Appeal to success of role models	57	1.8	(2.4)	1	0–9
Confrontation	Demand backed by threat Point out misbehavior	51	1.6	(1.8)	1	0–8
Problem solving	Define problems Suggest solutions	20	0.6	(1.0)	0	0–4
Listen	Empathy	21	0.7	(1.1)	0	0–4
Casework		346	9.9	(5.2)	10	0–26
Referral/linking/EBP	Formal programs Informal community resources	143	4.1	(3.7)	3	0–17
Assessment	Structured assessments Subjective assessment	65	1.8	(1.7)	1	0–6
Case planning	Collaborative approach Court-mandated goals	87	2.6	(2.7)	2	0–10
Incentives	Early discharge Relax probation conditions	35	0.9	(1.3)	0	0–5
Other	Advocacy Provide concrete assistance	16	0.5	(1.3)	0	0–6
Leverage		302	8.4	(6.5)	8	0–29
Monitoring	Frequency of check-in visits Team meetings	153	4.3	(4.5)	3	0–16
Sanctions	Restrict freedom of movement inconvenience	103	2.8	(2.6)	2	0–8
Placement	Detention center Commitment to state	46	1.2	(1.7)	0	0–6

average = 4.3). Monitoring codes were applied whenever officers described following up on youth to validate youth- or parent-reported compliance or to ensure that youth were following rules. Specific types of monitoring endorsed by officers included check-in visits with youth, drug testing, the use of electronic monitoring technologies, and close collaboration with service providers to ensure that youth knew that treatment team members were "on the same page." Sanctions included restrictions to youth freedom such as house arrest and penalties such as fines and community service. Out-of-home placements were a special class of sanction that included short-term stays in detention centers and longer term placements in youth development centers.

Proximal Change Mechanisms

All officers hypothesized one or more of a set of proximal change mechanisms that linked probation strategies shown in Table 1 with the long-range objectives as illustrated in Figure 1. As shown in Figure 1, youth participation in probation-directed interventions and activities is the principle moderator of probation success and is the short-term objective of a majority of probation tactics and strategies.

Participation is central to the model, as many officers noted that holding youth accountable for delinquent behaviors meant ensuring compliance with court-ordered probation conditions (e.g., "I'm not your friend [to the client]. And I have to do what the court is ordering me to do, and that includes your curfews that the court placed on you"). Moreover, the many officers who endorsed the case management–risk/need reduction pathway assumed that success was only possible if youth were full participants in programs and services (e.g., "And so, as a probation officer that's our goal, to refer them to the appropriate programs. And if they're not complying with that, or if other issues are coming about that they're not willing to address then those are, you know, ultimately we have to get that information back to the court"). Thus, pathways to youth participation are of central importance to the theory of probation.

Three change mechanisms—officer–youth relationship quality, parental support, and youth motivational processes—mediate the effects of probation tactics and strategies on youth participation. These proximal change mechanisms are the immediate effect of specific probation tactics and strategies and have a direct bearing on youth cooperativeness and participation in probation programming.

Officer–youth relationship strength. The nature of the officer–youth relationship was described as pivotal to probation success. For example, a female officer with 17 years of probation experience in a rural county shared this story about how the officer–youth relationship was a motivating factor for a 12-year-old who was diagnosed with a serious mental illness:

> I remember one day, he was sitting in the middle of the road, and he wouldn't let the school bus go by. . . . And, I said, "Get out of the road." And, he got up out of the road and went in the house. And, I asked him later, I said, "why do you do those things? And, why when I call you on the phone, and say 'Get out of the road,' why do you do that? Why do you treat people that way?" And, he said, "Because they don't treat me the way you treat me."

Most officers endorsed a diverse array of probation tactics to build strong, trusting, respectful relationships with juvenile offenders. In the case introduced above, the officer described her persistent efforts to advocate for the child to obtain needed mental health services. Other officers described establishing "partnerships" with youth to work toward mutually agreed goals, and they frequently endorsed specific communication skills involving dialogue about youth's feelings, aspirations, interests, problems, and strengths. Sanctions and consequences, when paired with role clarity and a respectful rather than punitive communication style, were an important avenue toward strong working relationships. By clarifying roles and expectations and providing consistent application of sanctions when warranted, officers believed that youth were more likely to accept sanctions such as detention placements and house arrest. This led to an increase in trust and respect that allowed the officer–youth relationship to withstand the life disruptions that occur when youth liberty is restricted and indeed led youth to cooperate with consequences rather than to fight against them.

Parental support. Alongside strong, trusting officer–youth relationships, officers prized parental support of probation as a critical ingredient for youth participation. In the words of one officer, parental support of probation case plans

> . . . makes a major difference in the success of the, of the juvenile on probation . . . if they're not supportive of what the juvenile is trying to do, you see a real breakdown. Uh, generally, we end up with a lot of violations. Uh, we end up doing tech boards, and going back to court. These are the kids I see that run. You know, exhibit a lot of those behaviors. Pick up new charges.

This officer was contrasting problems associated with poor parental support with a case involving a single parent who was highly supportive of probation for her 14-year-old son. She expressed her support through her direct involvement with his mental health providers by arranging appointments, participating in counseling sessions, and supervising his medications. She acknowledged academic and social problems he had in school and accepted the support of the probation officer to remedy these problems. In a way, she and the probation officer became partners in the care of her son, increasing the effectiveness of informal and formal social controls on his behavior. When parents withhold their support of probation, officers' chief concern was that uncooperative parents undermine youth participation in probation by sending negative verbal messages (e.g., "Eh, you know, it's all this [stuff], you don't really have to follow through with it"), withholding information about serious youth misbehavior, and refusing to help youth fulfill their obligations.

Youth motivational processes. Officers described at least three distinct themes related to increasing motivation among probationers. They include thinking twice, future orientation, and self-esteem/confidence. These motivational processes were reported to mediate youth participation and for some officers were hypothesized to have a direct effect on risk/need reduction.

Of the three, *thinking twice* was most frequently coded. "Thinking twice" was coded whenever officers sought to instill in youth a state of constant awareness of probation-related consequences as an avenue to alter youth decision making. This was usually done through the use of monitoring interventions or more intensive supervision to create a deterrent effect on rule violating behaviors but was also influenced through the use of incentives such as relaxed curfews and early release. In essence, youth would be motivated to participate in probation based on a risk–reward calculation. Of note was a broader purpose to interventions aimed at helping youth to "think twice." Many officers shared the hypothesis that helping youth to more consciously consider the consequences and rewards of behavior in the short term helps deepen their capacity for judgment and improves their social problem-solving skills in the long term. This hypothesis led them to frequently employ communication strategies in addition to leverage strategies, sanctions, and incentives. One officer with 6 years of experience in probation intake discussed her approach when youth systematically broke rules at home and at school. She believed that immature decision-making processes, whereby youth fail to consider the potential consequences of their behavior, contributed to their rule-violating behavior. Thus, an objective of hers shared by many officers was simply that youth more readily identify the potential positive and negative consequences when they are confronted with choices. This officer used interviewing strategies such as Socratic questions and problem solving in addition to leverage interventions and sanctions to

> [get] them to slow down, to think about the actions that they did, and the choices that they have, and try to get them to realize that, you know, if you continue to make the right choices, in the long run . . . you will be rewarded.

As a mediating motivational process, *future orientation* was closely related to thinking twice and judgment, and indeed was endorsed by participants nearly as often. Both involve mature decision making and a calculation of rewards and consequences. But whereas thinking twice focused on immediate consequences facing youth, future orientation focused on long-term aspirations and decisions about what kind of life youth desired. A prototypical example is the experience of a 17-year-old female who was assaultive to members of her family and who was noncompliant with probation conditions. The experience of several out-of-home placements led her to "gain perspective about what, what kind of freedom you can lose." Frequently, officers paired communication strategies with sanctions and other leverage strategies to teach life lessons about freedom as in the previous example or to encourage youth to have "epiphanies" about their need for help with substance abuse or other psychosocial problems. Officers also employed casework strategies to foster community engagement and to help youth see alternatives and to learn basic life lessons. For example,

> one of our kids, um, was really interested in, in wrestling . . . so he served as, kind of like a coach-manager for a year, and kind of learned the ins and outs and all the techniques and stuff. And then the next year he tried out and, and actually made the team because, you know, he had bought into the whole notion of, you know, "if I work hard I get a reward."

Such insights increase youth's motivation to cooperate with probation supervision by connecting their present probation imperatives with their long-term aspirations. Repeatedly, officers noted that youth participation was strongest when probation interventions were aligned with their priorities and goals. To promote future orientation, officers used probation tactics strategically to help youth develop an awareness of what their priorities and goals really were.

Finally, officers elaborated on *self-esteem* as the third motivational mediating mechanism. Self-esteem was coded when officers made reference to how interventions improved youth's sense of self-worth and confidence. Thus, self-esteem in this model is a composite of global self-worth and more specific efficacy beliefs. Praising accomplishments was a typical tactic of officers who emphasized the development of youth self-esteem. For example, a 10-year veteran of juvenile probation assigned to an intensive drug court program described her approach with youth who were noted in interdisciplinary team meetings as "doing a fantastic job" in a treatment program. In her view, the tactic—praise—had an indirect effect on participation through an increase in esteem, or "sense of pride" in the current example. The officer noted that "some of these kids have been told by their parents, for years, 'You can't do anything good,' or whatever. Everybody sees them as a bad kid "cause they've been smokin' weed, or doin' whatever." But the sense of "pride that you see in their faces" derived from the success they experience reinforces continued participation in treatment.

 ## Discussion

The original purpose of this research was to develop a grounded theory of probation from the perspective of officers who currently provide supervision to delinquent juveniles. In the end, the theory synthesized from the perspective of the interview participants yielded an integrative theoretical framework for probation practice. The participation process model generated in this research integrates Klockars's (1972) theory of the synthetic officer, emphasizing as it does a balanced approach inclusive of care and accountability strategies, with the RNR model, which emphasizes an evidence-based approach to reducing recidivism and increasing public safety through the reduction of criminogenic needs (Andrews & Bonta, 2010; Andrews et al., 1990). In so doing, this research generated a cohesive, comprehensive framework that makes possible future research to establish the construct validity of the causal linkages hypothesized in the theory, provides a framework for ongoing theoretical development, and suggests a rationale for the design and testing of specific probation strategies to strengthen probation outcomes.

The participation process model integrates assumptions from existing theories from criminology and social psychology. For example, theories of procedural justice are embedded within the hypothesis that strong officer–youth relationships lead to greater youth participation (Leiber, Nalla, & Farnworth, 1998; Skeem, Louden, Polaschek, & Camp, 2007; Tyler, 2006; Wells, 2007). Repeatedly throughout

the interviews, officers reported the importance of transparency and being forthright about the likely consequences of behavior so as to increase youth's trust and perceptions of fairness. Theories of social control inform hypotheses that parental support and parental involvement in probation increase youth participation in the probation (Hepburn & Griffin, 2004; Skeem, Louden, Manchak, Vidal, & Haddad, 2009). As probation can be conceptualized as an event occurring within probationers' social networks, strategic involvement of network actors such as family members should increase informal social controls on youth behaviors toward greater probationer participation and cooperation (Hawe, Shiell, & Riley, 2009). Likewise, the roles of deterrence theory and social learning theory inform hypotheses about how probation officers can influence motivational processes. Perceptions of sanction certainty and severity are embedded within the theme of thinking twice (Maxwell & Gray, 2000), and the role of long-term goals and efficacy beliefs as keystone motivators of behavior are embedded within the themes of future orientation and esteem/efficacy (Bandura, 1977, 1997). The integration of these complementary theoretical assumptions (i.e., social control, procedural justice, deterrence, social learning) provides a comprehensive explanation for how probation practices such as casework strategies, leverage tactics, and communication strategies may influence youth participation in probation interventions.

The importance of participation and compliance to the success of probation stands as a paramount assumption of the model. Findings from this study make clear that probation officers perceived youth participation in the probation process to be a prerequisite of risk reduction and accountability. In general, youth participation was a taken-for-granted assumption and was not the subject of critical appraisal. Rather, their overall sentiment was that noncompliance with probation was an indicator of probation failure; alternative strategies that did not require direct participation of the probationer were not reported. Had officers adopted perspectives from the field of environmental criminology (Cullen, Eck, & Lowenkamp, 2002), for example, their probation tactics and strategies would have focused on ensuring the presence of capable "guardians" and on managing aspects of the youth's daily routines rather than placing a preeminent focus on youth participation and cooperation. As theoretical advances in probation continue, more attention to the assumption of youth participation and cooperation is needed in light of potential competing explanations.

The integration of these theoretical perspectives within a coherent model suggests a set of innovations that may strengthen probation outcomes. To be sure, work is ongoing to strengthen the casework activities of probation officers toward more effective risk reduction including the implementation of fourth-generation risk and needs assessment instruments and the implementation of evidence-based interventions and youth development principles to address specific psychosocial needs (Bonta, 1996; Ferguson, 2002). Alongside these initiatives, the participation process model suggests that systematic strategies that affect the mediating mechanisms of participation (i.e., relationship, motivational processes, parental support) may be needed. The adaptation of motivational interviewing and cognitive behavioral techniques for probation holds promise in this regard (Hartzler & Espinosa, 2011; Landenberger & Lipsey, 2005; Walters, Vader, Nguyen, Harris, & Eells, 2010). Both strategies emphasize collaboration, which may strengthen the officer–client relationship as well as influence youth decision making. However, as these strategies are developed, constant attention needs to be given to how they can be integrated into the synthetic approach that strategically embraces both the enforcement and rehabilitative functions of the probation officer.

 # References

Andrews, D. A., & Bonta, J. (2010). Rehabilitating criminal justice policy and practice. *Psychology, Public Policy, and Law, 16*, 39–55.

Andrews, D. A., Bonta, J., & Hoge, R. D. (1990). Classification for effective rehabilitation: Rediscovering psychology. *Criminal Justice and Behavior, 17*, 19–52.

Andrews, D. A., & Kiessling, J. (1980). Program structure and effective correctional practice: A summary of CaVIC research. In R. Ross & P. Gendreau (Eds.), *Effective correctional treatment* (pp. 441–463). Toronto, Canada: Butterworths.

Aos, S., Miller. M., & Drake, E. (2006). *Evidence-based adult corrections programs: What works and what does not.* Olympia: Washington State Institute for Public Policy.

Atlas.ti (Version 6.1.11) [Computer software]. (2010). ATLAS.ti Scientific Software Development GmbH, Berlin, Germany.

Bandura, A. (1977). *Social learning theory.* Upper Saddle River, NJ: Prentice Hall.

Bandura, A. (1997). *Self-efficacy: The exercise of control.* New York, NY: Freeman.

Bazemore, G., & Schiff, M. (2005). *Juvenile justice reform and restorative justice: Building theory and policy from practice.* Portland, OR: Willan.

Bender, V., King, M, & Torbet, P. (2006). Advancing accountability: Moving toward victim restoration. *Juvenile & Family Court Journal, 57*, 53–67.

Bonta, J. (1996). Risk-needs: Assessment and treatment. In A. T. Harland (Ed.), *Choosing correctional options that work: Defining the demand and evaluating the supply* (pp. 18–32). Thousand Oaks, CA: Sage.

Bonta, J., Rugge, T., Scott, T., Bourgon, G., & Yessine, A. (2008). Exploring the black box of community supervision. *Journal of Offender Rehabilitation, 47*, 248–270.

Bradshaw, W., & Roseborough, D. (2005). An empirical review of family group conferencing in juvenile offenses. *Juvenile & Family Court Journal, 56*, 21–28.

Charmaz, K. (2006). *Constructing grounded theory: A practical guide through qualitative analysis.* Thousand Oaks, CA: Sage.

Cullen, F. T., Eck, J., & Lowenkamp, C. (2002). Environmental corrections: A new framework for effective probation and parole supervision. *Federal Probation, 66*, 28–37.

Denzin, N. K., & Lincoln, Y. S. (Eds.). (2005). *Handbook of qualitative research* (3rd ed.). Thousand Oaks, CA: Sage.

Dodge, K. A., & Pettit, G. S. (2003). A biopsychosocial model of the development of conduct problems in adolescence. *Developmental Psychology, 39*, 349–371.

Dodge, K. A., & Price, J. M. (1994). On the relation between social information processing and socially competent behavior in early school-aged children. *Child Development, 65*, 1385–1397.

Eisenberg, N., Spinard, T. L., & Eggum, N. D. (2010). Emotion-related self-regulation and its relation to children's maladjustment. *Annual Review of Clinical Psychology, 6*, 495–525.

Ferguson, J. L. (2002). Putting the "what works" research into practice: An organizational perspective. *Criminal Justice and Behavior, 29*, 472–492.

Ghetti, S., & Redlich, A. D. (2001). Reactions to youth crime: Perceptions of accountability and competency. *Behavioral Science and Law, 19*, 33–52.

Griffin. P., & Torbet, P. (2002). *Desktop guide to good juvenile probation practice.* Pittsburgh, PA: National Center for Juvenile Justice.

Hartzler, B., & Espinosa, E. M. (2011). Moving criminal justice organizations toward adoption of evidence-based practice via advanced workshop training in motivational interviewing: A research note. *Criminal Justice Policy Review, 22*, 235–253.

Hawe, P., Shiell, A., & Riley, T. (2009). Theorising interventions as events in systems. *American Journal of Community Psychology, 43*, 267–276.

Hepburn, J. R., & Griffin, M. L. (2004). The effect of social bonds on successful adjustment to probation: An event history analysis. *Criminal Justice Review, 29*, 46–75.

Howell, J. C. (2003). *Preventing and reducing juvenile delinquency: A comprehensive, framework.* Thousand Oaks, CA: Sage.

Klockars, C. B. (1972). A theory of probation supervision. *Journal of Criminal Law, Criminology, and Police Science, 63*, 550–557.

Kurlychek, M., Torbet, P., & Bozynski, M. (1999). *Focus on accountability: Best practices for juvenile court probation.* Washington, DC: U.S. Department of Justice, Office of Justice Programs, Office of Juvenile Justice and Delinquency Prevention.

Landenberger, N. A., & Lipsey, M. W. (2005). The positive effects of cognitive-behavioral programs for offenders: A meta-analysis of factors associated with effective treatment. *Journal of Experimental Criminology, 1*, 451–476.

Lane, J., Turner, S., Fain, T., & Sehgal, A. (2007). Implementing "corrections of place" ideas: The perspective of clients and staff. *Criminal Justice and Behavior, 34*, 76–95.

Leiber, M. J., Nalla, M. K., & Farnworth, M. (1998). Explaining juveniles' attitudes toward the police. *Justice Quarterly, 15*, 151–174.

Leiber, M. J., Schwarze, K., Mack, K. Y., & Farnworth, M. (2002). The effects of occupation and education on punitive orientations among juvenile justice personnel. *Journal of Criminal Justice, 30*, 303–316.

Lipsey, M. W., & Cullen, F. T. (2007). The effectiveness of correctional rehabilitation: A review of systematic reviews. *Annual Review of Law and Social Science, 3*, 297–320.

Lopez, V., & Russell, M. (2008). Examining the predictors of juvenile probation officers' rehabilitation orientation. *Journal of Criminal Justice, 36*, 381–388.

MacKenzie, D. L., Browning, K., Skroban, S. B., & Smith, D. A. (1999). The impact of probation on the criminal activities of offenders. *Journal of Research in Crime and Delinquency, 36*, 423–453.

MacKenzie, D. L., & De Li, S. (2002). The impact of formal and informal social controls on the criminal activities of probationers. *Journal of Research in Crime and Delinquency, 39*, 243–276.

Maloney, D., Romig, D., & Armstrong, T. (1988). The balanced approach to juvenile probation. *Juvenile & Family Court Journal, 39*, 1–4.

Martinson, R. (1974). What works? Questions and answers about prison reform. *The Public Interest, 35*, 22–54.

Maxwell, S. R., & Gray, M. K. (2000). Deterrence: Testing the effects of perceived sanction certainty on probation violations. *Sociological Inquiry, 70*, 117–136.

Moak, S. C., & Wallace, L. H. (2000). Attitudes of Louisiana practitioners toward rehabilitation of juvenile offenders. *American Journal of Criminal Justice, 24*, 271–285.

Mullins, T. G., & Toner, C. (2008). *Implementing the family support approach for community supervision.* Lexington, KY: Family Justice and the American Probation and Parole Association.

Onwuegbuzie, A. J., & Leech, N. L. (2007). A call for qualitative power analysis. *Quality & Quantity, 41*, 105–121.

Padgett, D. K. (2008). *Qualitative methods in social work research* (2nd ed.). Thousand Oaks, CA: Sage.

Paparozzi, M. A., & Demichele, M. (2008). Probation and parole: Overworked, misunderstood, and under-appreciated: But why? *Howard Journal, 47*, 275–296.

Paparozzi, M. A., & Gendreau, P. (2005). An intensive supervision program that worked: Service delivery, professional orientation, and organizational supportiveness. *Prison Journal, 85*, 445–466.

Petersilia, J., & Turner, S. (1993). Intensive probation and parole. *Crime and Justice, 17*, 281–335.

Pogarsky, G. (2007). Deterrence and individual differences among convicted offenders. *Journal of Quantitative Criminology, 23*, 59–74.

Polcin, D. L., & Greenfield, T. K. (2003). Factors associated with probation officers' use of criminal justice coercion to mandate alcohol treatment. *American Journal of Drug and Alcohol Abuse, 29*, 647–670.

Pratt, T. C, Cullen, F T., Blevins, K. R., Daigle, L. E., & Madensen, T. D. (2006). The empirical status of deterrence theory: A meta-analysis. In F. T. Cullen, J. P. Wright, & K. R. Blevins (Eds.), *Taking stock: The status of criminological theory* (pp. 367–395). New Brunswick, NJ: Transaction.

Ruback, R. B., & Bergstrom, M. H. (2006). Economic sanctions in criminal justice: Purposes, effects, and implications. *Criminal Justice and Behavior, 33*, 242–273.

Sandelowski, M. (1995). Sample size in qualitative research. *Research in Nursing & Health, 18*, 179–183.

Schwalbe, C. S., & Maschi, T. M. (2009). Investigating probation strategies with juvenile offenders: The influence of officers' attitudes and youth characteristics. *Law and Human Behavior, 33*, 357–367.

Schwalbe, C. S., & Maschi, T (2011). Confronting delinquency: Probation officers' use of coercion and client centered tactics to foster youth compliance. *Crime and Delinquency, 57*, 801–822.

Skeem, J. L., Louden, J. E., Manchak, S., Vidal. S., & Haddad, E. (2009). Social networks and social control of probationers with co-occuring mental health and substance abuse problems. *Law and Human Behavior, 33*, 122–135.

Skeem, J. L., Louden, J. E., Polaschek, D., & Camp, J. (2007). Assessing relationship quality in mandated community treatment: Blending care with control. *Psychological Assessment, 19*, 397–410.

Skeem, J. L., & Manchak, S. (2008). Back to the future: From Klockars' model of effective supervision to evidence-based practice in probation. *Journal of Offender Rehabilitation, 47*, 220–247.

Snyder, H. N., & Sickmund, M. (2006). *Juvenile Offenders and Victims: 2006 National Report.* Washington, DC: U.S. Department of Justice. Office of Justice Programs, Office of Juvenile Justice and Delinquency Prevention.

Taxman, F. S. (2002). Supervision—Exploring the dimensions of effectiveness. *Federal Probation, 66*, 14–27.

Tyler, T. R. (2006). Restorative justice and procedural justice: Dealing with rule breaking. *Journal of Social Issues, 62*, 307–326.

Vieira, T. A., Skilling, T. A., & Peterson-Badali, M. (2009). Matching court-ordered services with treatment needs: Predicting treatment success with young offenders. *Criminal Justice and Behavior, 36*, 385–401.

Walsh, A. (2001). *Correctional assessment, casework, and counseling* (3rd ed.). Alexandria, VA: American Correctional Association.

Walters, S. T., Vader, A. M., Nguyen, N., Harris, T. R., & Eells, J. (2010). Motivational interviewing as a supervision strategy in probation: A randomized effectiveness trial. *Journal of Offender Rehabilitation, 49,* 309–323.

Ward, D. A., Stafford, M. C, & Gray, L. N. (2006). Rational choice, deterrence, and theoretical integration. *Journal of Applied Social Psychology, 36,* 571–585.

Wells, W. (2007). Type of contact and evaluations of police officers: The effects of procedural justice across three types of police-citizen contacts. *Journal of Criminal Justice, 35,* 612–621.

Yeh, S. S. (2010). Cost-benefit analysis of reducing crime through electronic monitoring of parolees and probationers. *Journal of Criminal Justice, 38,* 1090–1096.

REVIEW QUESTIONS

1. The author bases much of his discussion on the RNR paradigm. What does this acronym stand for? Briefly explain what it means.

2. What three types of probation practices does the author focus on in his study? How do they differ?

3. What does the author conclude is the best approach for strengthening probation outcomes? What specific policies does the author promote for enhancing the effectiveness of probation of juvenile offenders?

Glossary

Actus reus: In legal terms, whether the offender actually engaged in a given criminal act. This concept can be contrasted with *mens rea*, which is a concept regarding whether the offender had the intent to commit a given act. This concept is important, especially in situations in which juveniles or mentally disabled individuals engage in offending.

Adaptations to strain: As proposed by Merton, the five ways that individuals deal with feelings of strain; see Conformity, Innovation, Rebellion, Retreatism, and Ritualism.

Adolescence-limited offenders: A type of offender labeled in Moffitt's developmental theory; such offenders commit crimes only during adolescence and desist from offending once they reach their twenties or adulthood.

Adoption studies: Studies that examine the criminality of adoptees as compared to the criminality of their biological and adoptive parents; such studies consistently show that biological parents have more influence on children's criminal behavior than the adoptive parents who raised them.

Age of Enlightenment: A period of the late 17th to 18th century in which philosophers and scholars began to emphasize the rights of individuals in society. This movement emphasized the rights of individuals to have a voice in their government and to exercise free choice; it also included the idea of the social contract and other important assumptions that influenced our current government and criminal justice system.

Anomie: A concept originally proposed by Durkheim, which meant "normlessness" or the chaos that takes place when a society (e.g., economic structure) changes very rapidly. This concept was later used by Merton in his strain theory of crime, where he redefined it as a disjunction between the emphasis placed on conventional goals and the conventional means used to achieve such goals.

Atavistic/Atavism: The belief that certain characteristics/behaviors of a person are a throwback to an earlier stage of evolutionary development.

Autonomic nervous system/ANS: The portion of the nervous system that consists of our anxiety levels, such as the "fight or flight" response, as well as our involuntary motor activities (e.g., heart rate). Studies consistently show that lower levels of ANS functioning are linked to criminality.

Bourgeoisie: A class/status that Karl Marx assigned to the dominant, oppressing owners of production, who are considered the elite class due to ownership of companies, factories, and so on. Marx proposed that this group created and implemented laws that helped retain the dominance of this class over the proletariat or working class.

Braithwaite's reintegrative shaming theory: This integrated theoretical model merges constructs and principles from several theories, primarily social control/bonding theory and labeling theory, with elements of strain theory, subculture/gang theory, and differential association theory.

Brutalization effect: The predicted tendency of homicides to increase after an execution, particularly after high-profile executions.

Central nervous system/CNS: The portion of the nervous system that largely consists of the brain and spinal column and is responsible for our voluntary motor activities. Studies consistently show that low functioning of the CNS (e.g., slower brain wave patterns) is linked to criminal behavior.

Cerebrotonic: The type of temperament or personality associated with an ectomorphic (thin) body type; these people tend to be introverted and shy.

Certainty of punishment: Certainty of punishment is one of the key elements of deterrence; the assumption is that when people commit a crime, they will perceive a high likelihood of being caught and punished.

Chicago School of criminology: A theoretical framework of criminal behavior that is often referred to as the Ecological School or the theory of social disorganization; it emphasizes the environmental impact of living in a high-crime neighborhood and asserts that this increases criminal activity. This model applies ecological principles of invasion, domination, and succession in explaining how cities grow and the implications this has on crime rates. Also, this model emphasizes the level of organization (or lack thereof) in explaining crime rates in a given neighborhood.

Classical conditioning: A learning model that assumes that animals, as well as people, learn through associations between stimuli and responses; this model was primarily promoted by Pavlov.

Classical School: The Classical School of criminological theory is a perspective that is considered the first rational model of crime, one that was based on logic rather than supernatural/demonic factors; it assumes that crime occurs after a rational individual mentally weighs the potential good and bad consequences of crime and then makes a decision about whether or not to engage in a given behavior; this model is directly tied to the formation of deterrence theory and assumes that people have free will to control their behavior.

Clearance rate: The percentage of crimes reported to police that result in an arrest, or an identification of a suspect who cannot be apprehended (due to death of suspect, or fleeing, etc.) In other words, the authorities essentially have a very good idea of who committed the crime, so it is considered "solved." The clearance rate can be seen as rough estimate of the rate at which crimes are solved.

Collective conscience: According to Durkheim, the extent of similarities or likeness that people in a society share. The theory assumes that the stronger the collective conscience, the less crime in that community.

College boy: A type of lower-class male youth identified by Cohen who has experienced the same strains and status frustration as his peers but responds to his disadvantaged situation by dedicating himself to overcoming the odds and competing in the middle-class schools despite the unlikely chances for success.

Communitarianism: A concept in Braithwaite's theory of reintegration, which is a macro-level measure of the degree to which the individuals are connected or interdependent on mainstream society (via organizations or groups).

Conceptual integration: A type of theoretical integration in which a theoretical perspective consumes or uses concepts from many other theoretical models.

Concordance rates: Rates at which twin pairs either share a trait (e.g., criminality) or the lack of the trait; for example, either both twins are criminal or neither is criminal; discordant would be if one of the pair is criminal, and the other is not.

Conflict gangs: A type of gang identified by Cloward and Ohlin that tends to develop in neighborhoods with weak stability and little or no organization; gangs are typically relatively disorganized and lack the skills and knowledge to make a profit through criminal activity. Thus, their primary illegal activity is violence, which is used to gain prominence and respect among themselves and the neighborhood.

Conflict theories: Theories of criminal behavior which assume that most people disagree on what the law should be and/or that law is used as a tool by those in power to keep down other groups.

Conformity: In strain theory, an adaptation to strain in which an individual buys into the conventional means of success and also buys into the conventional goals.

Consensual perspective: Theories that assume virtually everyone is in agreement on the laws and therefore assume no conflict in attitudes regarding the laws/rules of society.

Containment theory: A control theory proposed by Reckless in the 1960s, which presented a model that emphasized internal and social pressures to commit crime, which range from personality predispositions to peer influences, as well as internal and external constraints, ranging from personal self-control to parental control, that determine whether an individual will engage in criminal activity. This theory is often criticized as being too vague or general, but it advanced criminological theory by providing a framework in which many internal and external factors were emphasized.

Control-balance theory: An integrated theory originally presented by Tittle, which assumes that the amount of control to which one is subjected, as compared to the amount of control that one can exercise, determines the probability of deviant behavior and the types of deviance that are committed by that individual. In other words, the balance or imbalance between these two types of control can predict the amount and type of behavior likely to be committed.

Control theories: A group of theories of criminal behavior that emphasize the assumption that humans are born selfish and have tendencies to be aggressive and offend and that individuals must be controlled, typically by socialization and discipline, or from internalized self-control that has been developed in their upbringing.

Corner boy: A type of lower-class male youth identified by Cohen who has experienced the same strains and status frustration as others but responds to his disadvantaged situation by accepting his place in society as someone who will somewhat passively make the best of life at the bottom of the social order. As the label describes, they often "hang out" on corners.

Correlation or covariation: A criterion of causality that requires a change in a predictor variable (X) to be consistently associated with some change (either positive or negative) in the explanatory variable (Y). An example would be unemployment (X) being related to criminal activity (Y).

Craniometry: The field of study that emphasized the belief that the size of the brain or skull reflected superiority or inferiority, with larger brains/skulls being considered superior.

Criminal gangs: A type of gang identified by Cloward and Ohlin that forms in lower-class neighborhoods with an organized structure of adult criminal behavior. Such neighborhoods are so organized and stable that their criminal networks are often known and accepted by the conventional citizens. In these neighborhoods, the adult gangsters mentor neighborhood youth and take them under their wing. Such gangs tend to be highly organized and stable.

Criminology: The scientific study of crime and the reasons why people engage (or don't engage) in criminal behavior, as well as the study of why certain trends occur or groups of people seem to engage in criminal behavior more than others.

Critical/radical feminism: A perspective of feminist theory that emphasizes the idea that many societies (such as the United States) are based on a structure of patriarchy, in which males dominate virtually every aspect of society, such as law, politics, family structure, and the economy.

Cross-sectional studies: A form of research design modeling in which a collection of data is taken at one point in time (often in survey format).

Cultural/subcultural theories: A perspective of criminal offending which assumes that many offenders believe in a normative system that is distinctly different than, and often at odds with, the norms accepted by conventional society.

Cytogenetic studies: Studies of crime that focus on the genetic makeup of individuals, with a specific focus on abnormalities in their chromosomal makeup. An example is XYY instead of the normal XX (females) and normal XY (males).

Dark figure: The vast majority of major crime incidents that never get reported to police due to the failure of victims to file a police report; covers most criminal offending, with the exception of homicide and motor vehicle theft, which are almost always reported to police.

Decriminalization: A policy related to labeling theory, which proposes less harsh punishments for some minor offenses, such as the possession of small amounts of marijuana; for example, in California, an offender gets a ticket/fine for this offense rather than being officially charged and prosecuted.

Deinstitutionalization: A policy related to labeling theory; proposes that juveniles or those accused of relatively minor offenses should not be locked up in jail or prison.

Delinquent boy: A type of lower-class male youth identified by Cohen who responds to strains and status frustration by joining with similar others in a group to commit a crime.

Determinism: The assumption that human behavior is caused by factors outside of free will and rational decision-making (e.g., biology, peer influence, poverty, bad parenting); it is the distinctive, primary assumption of positivism (as opposed to the Classical School of criminological theory, which assumes free will/free choice).

Deterrence theory: The theory of crime associated with the Classical School, which proposes that individuals will make rational decisions regarding their behavior. This theory focuses on three concepts: the individual's perception of (1) certainty of punishment, (2) severity of punishment, and (3) the swiftness of punishment.

Developmental theories: Perspectives of criminal behavior, which are also to some extent integrated but are distinguished by their emphasis on the evolution of individuals' criminality over time. Specifically, developmental theories tend to look at the individual as the unit of analysis, and such models focus on the various aspects of the onset, frequency, intensity, duration, desistence, and other aspects of the individuals' criminal career.

Deviance: Behaviors that are not normal; includes many illegal acts, as well as activities that are not necessarily criminal but are unusual and often violate social norms, such as burping loudly at a formal dinner or wearing inappropriate clothing.

Differential association theory: A theory of criminal behavior that emphasizes the association with significant others (peers, parents, etc.) in learning criminal behavior. This theory was originally presented by Sutherland.

Differential identification theory: A theory of criminal behavior that is very similar to differential association theory; the major difference is that differential identification theory takes into account associations with persons/images that are presented in the media (e.g., movies, TV, sports, etc.). This model was originally proposed by Glaser.

Differential reinforcement theory: A theory of criminal behavior that emphasizes various types of social learning, specifically classical conditioning, operant conditioning, and imitation/modeling. This theory was originally presented by Burgess and Akers and is one of the most supported theories according to empirical studies.

Diversion: A set of policies related to labeling theory that attempt to get an offender out of the formal justice system as quickly as possible; an offender might perform a service or enter a rehabilitation program instead of serving time in jail or prison. Often, if an offender successfully completes the contract, the official charge/conviction for the crime is expunged or eliminated from the official record.

Dizygotic twins: Also referred to as fraternal/nonidentical twins, these are twin pairs that come from two separate eggs (zygotes) and thus share only 50% of the genetic makeup that can vary.

Dopamine: A neurotransmitter that is largely responsible for "good feelings" in the brain; it is increased by many illicit drugs (e.g., cocaine).

Dramatization of evil: A concept proposed by Tannenbaum in relation to labeling theory, which states that often when relatively minor laws are broken, the community tends to overreact and make a rather large deal out of it ("dramatizing" it). A good example is when a very young offender sprays graffiti on a street sign, and the neighborhood ostracizes that youth.

Drift theory: A theory of criminal behavior in which the lack of social controls in the teenage years allows for individuals to experiment in various criminal offending, often due to peer influence, without the individuals buying into a criminal lifestyle; this theory was introduced by David Matza.

Ecological School/perspective: See Chicago School of criminology.

Ectoderm: A medical term for the outer layer of tissue in our bodies (e.g., skin, nervous system).

Ectomorphic: The type of body shape associated with an emphasis on the outer layer of tissue (ectoderm) during development; these people are disposed to be thin.

Ego: The only conscious domain of the psyche; according to Freud; it functions to mediate the battle between id and superego.

Elliott's integrated model: Perhaps the first major integrated perspective proposed that clearly attempted to merge various traditionally separate theories of crime. Elliott's integrated framework attempts to merge strain, social disorganization, control, and social learning/differential association-reinforcement perspectives for the purpose of explaining delinquency, particularly in terms of drug use, as well as other forms of deviant behavior.

Empirical validity: Refers to the extent to which a theoretical model is supported by scientific research. In criminology, empirical research has consistently supported a number of theories and consistently refuted others.

Endoderm: A medical term for the inner layer of tissue in our bodies (e.g., digestive organs).

Endomorphic: The type of body shape associated with an emphasis on the inner layer of tissue (endoderm) during development; these people are disposed to be obese.

End-to-end theoretical integration: A type of theoretical integration that conveys the linkage of the theories based on the temporal ordering of two or more theories in their causal timing. This means that one theory (or concepts from one theory) precedes another theory (or concepts from another theory) in terms of causal ordering or timing.

Equivalency hypothesis: A "mirror image" tendency, which is the observed phenomenon that virtually all studies have shown; the characteristics, such as young, male, urban, poor, or minority, tend to have the highest rates of criminal offending *and* the highest rates of victimization. This hypothesis has one important exception, namely lower class offenders tend to have higher rates of theft against middle- to upper-class households/individuals).

Eugenics: The study of and policies related to the improvement of the human race via discriminatory control over reproduction.

Experiential effect: The extent to which individuals' previous experience has an effect on their perceptions of how certain or severe criminal punishment will be when they are deciding whether or not to offend again.

Family studies: Studies that examine the clustering of criminality in a given family.

Feeblemindedness: A technical, scientific term in the early 1900s meaning those who had significantly below average levels of intelligence.

Focal concerns: The primary concept of Walter Miller's theory, which asserts that all members of the lower class focus on a number of concepts they deem important: fate, autonomy, trouble, toughness, excitement, and smartness.

Formal controls: Factors that involve the official aspects of criminal justice, such as police, courts, and corrections (e.g., prisons, parole, probation).

Frontal lobes: A region of the brain that is, as its name suggests, located in the frontal portion of the brain; most of the "executive functions" of the brain, such as problem solving, take place here, so it is perhaps the most vital portion of the brain and what makes us human.

General deterrence: Punishments given to an individual are meant to prevent or deter other potential offenders from engaging in such criminal activity in the future.

General strain theory: Although derived from traditional strain theory, this theoretical framework assumes that people of all social classes and economic positions deal with frustrations in routine daily life, to which virtually everyone can relate; includes more sources of strain than traditional strain theory.

Hot spots: Specific locations, such as businesses, residences, or parks, that experience a high concentration of crime incidents; a key concept in routine activities theory.

Hypotheses: Specific predictions that are based on a scientific theoretical framework and tested via observation.

Id: A subconscious domain of the psyche, according to Freud, with which we are all born; it is responsible for our innate desires and drives (such as libido [sex drive]); it battles the moral conscience of the superego.

Imitation and modeling: A learning model that emphasizes that humans (and other animals) learn behavior simply by observing others; this model was most notably proposed by Bandura. See Modeling/Imitation.

Index Offenses: Also known as Part I offenses, according to the FBI Uniform Crime Report, these are eight common offenses: murder, forcible rape, aggravated assault, robbery, burglary, motor vehicle theft, larceny, and arson. All reports of these crimes, even when they do not result in an arrest, are recorded to estimate crime in the nation and various states/regions.

Informal controls: Factors like family, church, or friends that do not involve official aspects of criminal justice, such as police, courts, and corrections (e.g., prisons).

Innovation: In strain theory, an adaptation to strain in which an individual buys into the conventional goals of success but does not buy into the conventional means for getting to the goals.

Integrated theories: Theories that combine two or more traditional theories into one combined model.

Interdependency: A concept in Braithwaite's theory of reintegration, which is a micro-level measure of the degree to which the individuals are connected or interdependent on mainstream society (via organizations or groups).

Interracial: When an occurrence (such as a crime event) involves people of different race/ethnicity, such as a White person committing crime against a Black person.

Intraracial: When an occurrence (such as a crime event) involves people of the same race/ethnicity, such as a White person committing crime against another White person.

Labeling theory: A theoretical perspective that assumes that criminal behavior increases because certain individuals are caught and labeled as offenders; their offending increases because they have been stigmatized as "offenders." Most versions of this perspective also assume that certain people (e.g., lower class or minorities) are more likely to be caught and punished. Another assumption of most versions is that if such labeling did not occur, the behavior would stop; this assumption led to numerous policy implications, such as diversion, decriminalization, and deinstitutionalization.

Learning theories: Theoretical models that assume criminal behavior of individuals is due to a process of learning from others the motivations and techniques for engaging in such behavior. Virtually all of the variations of the learning perspective propose that the processes involved in a person learning how and why to commit crimes are the same as those involved in learning to engage in conventional activities (e.g., riding a bike, playing basketball).

Legalistic approach: A way of defining behaviors as crime; includes only acts that are specifically against the legal codes of a given jurisdiction. The problem with such a definition is that what is a crime in one jurisdiction is not necessarily a crime in other jurisdictions.

Liberal feminism: One of the areas of feminist theories of crime that emphasizes the assumption that differences between males and females in offending were due to the lack of female opportunities in education, employment, etc., as compared to males.

Life-course-persistent offenders: A type of offender, as labeled by Moffitt's developmental theory; such people start offending early and persist in offending through adulthood.

Logical consistency: Refers to the extent to which concepts and propositions of a theoretical model makes sense, in terms of both face value and regarding the extent to which the model is consistent with what is readily known about crime rates/trends.

Macro level of analysis: Theories that focus on group or aggregated scores and measures as the unit of analysis, as opposed to individual rates.

Mala in se: Acts that are considered inherently evil and that virtually all societies consider to be serious crimes; an example is murder.

Mala prohibita: The many acts that are considered crimes primarily because they have been declared bad by the legal codes in that jurisdiction; in other places and times, they are not illegal; examples are gambling, prostitution, and drug usage.

Marxist feminism: A perspective of crime that emphasizes men's ownership and control of the means of economic production; similar to critical/radical feminism but distinguished by its reliance on the sole concept of economic structure, in accordance with Marx's theory.

Mechanical societies: In Durkheim's theory, these societies were rather primitive with a simple distribution of labor (e.g., hunters and gatherers) and thus a high level of agreement regarding social norms and rules because nearly everyone is engaged in the same roles.

Mens rea: In legal terms, this means "guilty mind" or intent. This concept involves whether or not offenders actually knew what they were doing and meant to do it.

Mesoderm: A medical term for the middle layer of tissue in our bodies (e.g., muscles, tendons, bone structure).

Mesomorphic: The type of body shape associated with an emphasis on the middle layer of tissue (mesoderm) during development; these people are disposed to be athletic or muscular.

Micro level of analysis: Theories that focus on individual scores and measures as the unit of analysis, as opposed to group or aggregate rates.

Minor physical anomalies (MPAs): Physical features, such as asymmetrical or low-seated ears, which are believed to indicate developmental problems, typically problems in the prenatal stage in the womb.

Modeling/Imitation: A major factor in differential reinforcement theory, which proposes that much social learning takes place via imitation or modeling of behavior; for example, when adults/parents say "bad" words, their children begin using those words.

Moffitt's developmental theory/taxonomy: A theoretical perspective proposed by Moffitt, in which criminal behavior is believed to be caused by two different causal paths: (1) adolescence-limited offenders commit their crimes during teenage years due to peer pressure (2) life-course persistent offenders commit antisocial behavior throughout life, starting very early and continuing on throughout their lives, because of the interaction between their neuropsychological deficits and criminogenic environments in their upbringing.

Monozygotic twins: Also referred to as identical twins, these are twin pairs that come from a single egg (zygote) and thus share 100% of their genetic makeup.

National Crime Victimization Survey (NCVS): One of the primary measures of crime in the United States; collected by the Department of Justice and the Census Bureau, based on interviews with victims of crime. This measure started in the early 1970s.

Natural areas: The Chicago School's idea that all cities naturally contain identifiable clusters, such as a Chinatown or Little Italy, and neighborhoods that have low or high crime rates.

Negative punishment: A concept in social learning in which people are given a punishment by removing something that they enjoy/like (e.g., taking away driving privileges for a teenager).

Negative reinforcement: A concept in social learning in which people are given a reward by removing something that they dislike (e.g., not being on curfew or not having to do their "chores").

Neoclassical School: Neoclassical School of criminological theory is virtually identical to the Classical School (both assume free will, rationality, social contract, deterrence, etc.), except that it assumes that aggravating and mitigating circumstances should be taken into account for purposes of sentencing/punishing an offender.

Neurotransmitters: Nervous system chemicals in the brain and body that help transmit electric signals from one neuron to another, thus allowing healthy communication in the brain and to the body.

Neutralization theory: A theory of criminal behavior that emphasizes the excuses or neutralization techniques that are used by offenders to alleviate the guilt (or to excuse) their behavior, when they know that their behavior is immoral; this theory was originally presented by Gresham Sykes and David Matza. In their theory, they presented five key "techniques," ways that offenders alleviate their guilt or excuse their behavior, which they know is wrong; since they presented this idea in the 1960s, other techniques have been added, especially regarding white-collar crime.

Non-index offenses: Also known as Part II offenses, more than two dozen crimes that are considered relatively less serious than Index crimes and must result in an arrest to be recorded by the FBI; therefore, the data on such results are far less reliable because the vast majority of reports of these crimes do not result in an arrest and are not in the annual FBI report.

Operant conditioning: The learning model that takes place in organisms (such as humans), based on association between an action and feedback that occurs after it has taken place; for example,

a rat running a maze can be trained to run the maze faster based on rewards (reinforcement), such as cheese, as well as punishments, such as electric shocks; introduced and promoted by B. F. Skinner.

Organic societies: In the Durkheimian model, those societies that have a high division of labor and thus a low level of agreement about societal norms, largely because everyone has such different roles in society, leading to very different attitudes about the rules and norms of behavior.

Paradigm: A unique perspective of a phenomenon; has an essential set of assumptions that significantly oppose those of other existing paradigms or explanations of the same phenomenon.

Parsimony: Essentially means "simple"; a characteristic of a good theory, meaning that it explains a certain phenomenon, in our case criminal behavior, with the fewest possible propositions/concepts.

Phenotype: An observed manifestation of the interaction of genotypical traits with the environment, such as height (which depends largely on genetic disposition and diet, as exhibited by Asians or Mexicans who are raised in the United States and thus grow taller).

Phrenology: The science of determining human dispositions based on distinctions (e.g., bumps) in the skull, which was believed to conform to the shape of the brain.

Physiognomy: The study of facial and other bodily aspects to identify developmental problems, such as criminality.

Pluralistic (conflict) perspective: A theoretical assumption that instead of one dominant and other inferior groups in society, there are a variety of groups that lobby and compete to influence changes in law; most linked to Vold's theoretical model.

Policy implications: The extent to which a theory can be used to inform authorities about how to address a given phenomenon; in this case, ways to help law enforcement, court, and prison officials reduce crime/recidivism.

Positive punishment: A concept in social learning in which an individual is given a punishment by doing something they dislike (e.g., spanking, time-out, grounding, etc.).

Positive reinforcement: A concept in social learning in which an individual is given a reward by providing something they like (e.g., money, extending curfew, etc.).

Positive School: The Positive School of criminological theory is a perspective that assumes individuals have no free will to control their behavior. Rather, the theories of the Positive School assume that criminal behavior is "determined" by factors outside of free choices made by the individual, such as peers, bad parenting, poverty, or biology.

Postmodern feminism: A perspective that says women as a group cannot be understood, even by other women, because every person's experience is unique; therefore, there is no need to measure or research such experiences. This perspective has been criticized as being "anti-science" and thus, irrelevant; from this perspective, there is no need to investigate any cases because the findings cannot be generalized beyond the specific individual.

Power-control theory: An integrated theory of crime that assumes that in households where the mother and father have relatively similar levels of power at work (i.e., balanced households), mothers will be less likely to exert control on their daughters. These balanced households will be less likely to experience gender differences in the criminal offending of the children. However, households in which mothers and fathers have dissimilar levels of power in the workplace (i.e., unbalanced households) are more likely to suppress criminal activity in daughters, but more criminal activity is likely in the boys of the household.

Primary deviance: A concept in labeling theory originally presented by Lemert; the type of minor, infrequent offending that people commit before they are caught and labeled as offenders. Most normal individuals commit this type of offending due to peer pressure and normal social behavior in their teenage years.

Proletariat: In Marx's conflict theory, the proletariat is the oppressed group of workers who are exploited by the bourgeoisie, an elite class that owns the means of production; according to Marx, the proletariat will never truly profit from their efforts because the upper class owns and controls the means of production.

Radical (or critical) feminism: see Critical/radical feminism.

Rational choice theory: A modern, Classical School-based framework for explaining crime that includes the traditional formal deterrence aspects, such as police, courts, and corrections and adds other informal factors that studies show consistently and strongly influence behavior, specifically informal deterrence factors (such as friends, family, community, etc.) and also the benefits of offending, whether they be monetary, peer status, or physiological (the "rush" of engaging in deviance).

Reaction formation: A Freudian defense mechanism applied to Cohen's theory of youth offending, which involves adopting attitudes or committing behaviors that are opposite of what is expected, for example, by engaging in malicious behavior as a form of defiance; youth buy into this antinormative belief system so that they will feel less guilt for not living up to the standards they are failing to achieve and so they can achieve status among their delinquent peers.

Rebellion: In strain theory, an adaptation to strain in which an individual buys into the idea of conventional means and goals of success but does not buy into the current conventional means or goals.

Reintegrative Shaming theory: See Braithwaite's Reintegrative shaming theory.

Relative deprivation: The perception that results when relatively poor people live in close proximity to relatively wealthy people. This concept is distinct from poverty in the sense that a poor area could mean that nearly everyone is poor, but relative deprivation inherently suggests that there is a notable amount of wealth and poor in a given area.

Retreatism: In strain theory, an adaptation to strain in which an individual does not buy into the conventional goals of success and also does not buy into the conventional means.

Retreatist gangs: A type of gang identified by Cloward and Ohlin that tends to attract individuals who have failed to succeed in both the conventional world and the criminal or conflict gangs of their neighborhoods. Members of retreatist gangs are no good at making a profit from crime, nor are they good at using violence to achieve status, so the primary form of offending in retreatist gangs is usually drug usage.

Ritualism: In strain theory, an adaptation to strain in which an individual buys into the conventional means of success (e.g., work, school, etc.) but does not buy into the conventional goals.

Routine activities theory: An explanation of crime that assumes that most crimes are committed during the normal daily activities of people's lives; it assumes that crime/victimization is highest in places where three factors come together in time and place: motivated offenders, suitable/attractive targets, and absence of guardian; this perspective assumes a rational offender who picks targets due to opportunity.

Scenario (vignette) research: Studies that involve providing participants with specific hypothetical scenarios and then asking them what they would do in that situation; typically, they are also asked about their perceptions of punishment and other factors related to that particular situation.

Scientific Method: The method used in all scientific fields to determine the most objective results and conclusions regarding empirical observations. This method involves testing hypotheses via observation/data collection and then making conclusions based on the findings.

Scope: Refers to the range of criminal behavior that a theory attempts to explain, which in our case can be seen as the amount of criminal activity a theory can account for, such as only violent crime or only property crime, or only drug usage; if a theory has a very large scope, it would attempt to explain all types of offending.

Secondary deviance: A concept in labeling theory originally presented by Lemert; the type of more serious, frequent offending that people commit after they get caught and are labeled offenders. Individuals commit this type of offending because they have internalized their status as offenders and often have resorted to hanging out with other offenders.

Selective placement: A criticism of adoption studies, arguing that adoptees tend to be placed in households that resemble that of their biological parents; thus, adoptees from rich biological parents are placed in rich adoptive households.

Self-report data: One of the primary ways that crime data are collected, typically by asking offenders about their own offending; the most useful for examining key causal factors in explaining crime (e.g., personality, attitudes, etc.).

Serotonin: A neurotransmitter that is key in information processing; low levels are linked to depression and other mental illnesses; the neurotransmitter most consistently linked to criminal behavior in its deficiency.

Severity of punishment: One of the key elements of deterrence; the assumption is that a given punishment must be serious enough to outweigh any potential benefits gained from a crime (but not too severe, so that it causes people to commit far more severe offenses to avoid apprehension); in other words, this theoretical concept advises graded penalties that increase as the offender recidivates/reoffends.

Side-by-side (or "horizontal") integration: A type of theoretical integration in which cases are classified by a certain criteria (e.g., impulsive versus planned) and two or more theories are considered parallel explanations based on what type of case is being considered. Thus, there are two different paths in which a case is predicted to go, typically based on an initial variable (such as low or high self-control).

Social bonding theory: A control theory proposed by Hirschi in 1969 which assumes that individuals are predisposed to commit crime and that the conventional bond that is formed with the individual prevents or reduces their offending. This bond is made up of four constructs: attachments, commitment, involvement, and moral beliefs regarding committing crime.

Social contract: An Enlightenment ideal/assumption that stipulates there is an unspecified arrangement among citizens of a society in which they promise the state/government not to commit offenses against other citizens (to follow the rules of a society), and in turn they gain protection from being violated by other citizens; violators will be punished.

Social Darwinism: The belief that only the beneficial (or "fittest") societal institutions or groups of people survive or thrive in society.

Social disorganization. *See* Chicago School of criminology.

Social dynamics: A concept proposed by Comte that describes aspects of social life that alter how societies are structured and that pattern the development of societal institutions.

Socialist feminism: Feminist theories that moved away from economic structure (e.g., Marxism) as the primary detriment for females and placed a focus on control of reproductive systems. This model believes that women should take control of their own bodies and their reproductive functions via contraceptives.

Social sciences: A category of scientific disciplines or fields of study that focus on various aspects of human behavior, such as criminology, psychology, economics, sociology, or anthropology; typically use the scientific method for gaining knowledge.

Social statics: A concept proposed by Comte to describe aspects of society that relate to stability and social order, which allow societies to continue and endure.

Soft Determinism: The assumption that both determinism (the fundamental assumption of the Positive School of criminology) and free will/free choice (the fundamental assumption of the Classical School) play a role in offenders' decisions to engage in criminal behavior. This perspective can be seen as a type of compromise or "middle-road" concept.

Somotonic: The type of temperament or personality associated with a mesomorphic (muscular) body type; these people tend to be risk-taking and aggressive.

Somatotyping: The area of study, primarily linked to William Sheldon, that links body type to risk for delinquent/criminal behavior. Also, as a methodology, it is a way of ranking body types based on three categories: endomorphy, mesomorphy, and ectomorphy (see other entries).

Specific deterrence: Punishments given to an individual are meant to prevent or deter that particular individual from committing crime in the future.

Spuriousness: When other factors (often referred to as Z factors) are actually causing two variables (X and Y) to occur at the same time; it may appear as if X causes Y, when in fact they are both being caused by other Z factor(s). To account for spuriousness, which is required for determining causality, researchers must ensure that no other factors are causing the observed correlation between X and Y. An example is when ice cream sales (X) are related to crime rates (Y); the Z variable is warm weather, which increases the opportunity for crime because more people and offenders are interacting.

Stake in conformity: A significant portion of Toby's control theory, which applies to virtually all control theories, which refers to the extent to which individuals have investments in conventional society. It is believed, and supported by empirical studies, that the higher the stake in conformity an individual has, the less likely he or she will engage in criminal offending.

Stigmata: The physical manifestations of atavism (biological inferiority), according to Lombroso; he claimed that if a person had more than 5, he/she was a born criminal, meaning that a person or feature of an individual is a throwback to an earlier stage of evolutionary development and inevitably would be a chronic offender. An example is very large ears, or very small ears.

Strain theory: A category of theories of criminal behavior in which the emphasis is placed on a sense of frustration (e.g., economy) in crime causation; hence, the name "strain" theories.

Structural-functional theory: The theoretical framework proposing that society is similar to a living organism, in that all portions of society function together to form a functioning system. Specifically, like a human body, which depends on numerous interrelated organs to survive, a society depends on a variety of vital parts (i.e., societal institutions such as education, economy, family) that work together as a well-functioning system.

Subterranean values: Those norms that individuals have been socialized to accept (e.g., violence) in certain contexts in a given society; an example would be the popularity of boxing or Ultimate Fighting Championship events in American society, even though violence is generally viewed negatively. Another example is the romanticized nature and popularity of crime movies, such as *The Godfather* and *Pulp Fiction*.

Superego: A subconscious domain of the psyche, according to Freud; it is not part of our nature but must be developed through early social attachments; it is responsible for our morality and conscience; it battles the subconscious drives of the id.

Swiftness of punishment: Swiftness of punishment is one of the key elements of deterrence; the assumption is that the faster punishment occurs after a crime is committed, the more an individual will be deterred in the future.

Symbolic interaction: The theoretical perspective proposed by Mead and related to the labeling perspective; proposes that many social interactions involve symbolism, which occurs when individuals interpret each other's words or gestures and then act based on the meaning of those interactions.

Tabula rasa: The assumption that when people are born, they have a "blank slate" regarding morality and that every portion of their ethical/moral beliefs is determined by the interactions that occur in the way they are raised and socialized. This is a key assumption of virtually all learning theories.

Techniques of neutralization: See Neutralization theory.

Telescoping: The human tendency in which events are perceived to occur much more recently in the past than they actually did, causing estimates of crime events to be overreported; in the NCVS measure asking respondents to estimate their victimization over the last six months, respondents often report victimization that happened before the six month cut-off date.

Temporal lobes: The region of the brain located above our ears, which is responsible for a variety of functions; located right above many primary limbic structures, which govern our emotional and memory functions.

Temporal ordering: The criterion for determining causality; requires that the predictor variable (X) precedes the explanatory variable (Y) in time.

Testability: Refers to the extent that a theoretical model can be empirically or scientifically tested through observation and empirical research.

Theoretical elaboration: A form of theoretical integration that uses a traditional theory as the framework for the theoretical model but also adds concepts/propositions from other theories.

Theoretical reduction: *See* Up-and-down integration.

Theory: A set of concepts linked together by a series of propositions in an organized way to explain a phenomenon.

Theory of Concentric theories: A model proposed by Chicago School theorists; assumes that all cities grow in a natural way that universally has the same five zones (or circles/areas). For example, all cities have a central Zone I, which contains basic government buildings, as well as a Zone II, which was once residential but is being "invaded" by factories. The outer three zones involve various forms of residential areas.

Theory of low self-control: A theory that proposes that individuals either develop self-control by the time they are about age 10 or do not. Those who do not develop self-control will manifest criminal/deviant behaviors throughout life. This perspective was originally proposed by Gottfredson and Hirschi.

Thornberry's interactional model: This integrated model of crime was the first major perspective to emphasize reciprocal, or feedback effects, in the causal modeling of the theoretical framework.

Trajectory: A path that someone takes in life, often due to the transitions (see Transitions).

Transitions: Events that are important in altering trajectories toward or against crime, such as marriage, employment, or military service.

Twins-separated-at-birth studies: Studies that examine the similarities between identical twins who are separated in infancy; research indicates that such twins are often extremely similar even though they grew up in completely different environments.

Twin studies: Studies that examine the relative concordance rates for monozygotic versus dizygotic twins, with virtually every study showing that identical twins (monozygotic) tend to be far more concordant for criminality than fraternal (dizygotic) twins.

Uniform Crime Report (UCR): An annual report published by the FBI in the Department of Justice, which is meant to estimate most of the major street crimes in the United States. It is based on police reports/arrests throughout the nation, and started in the 1930s.

Up-and-down integration: A type of theoretical integration that is generally considered the classic form of theoretical integration because it has been done relatively often in the history of criminological theory development. This often involves increasing the level of abstraction of a single theory so that postulates seem to follow from a conceptually broader theory, such as differential reinforcement theory assuming virtually all of the concepts and assumptions of differential association theory.

Utilitarianism: A philosophical concept that is often applied to social policies of the Classical School of criminology, which relates to the "greatest good for the greatest number."

Viscerotonic: The type of temperament or personality associated with an endomorphic (obese) body type; these people tend to be jolly, lazy, and happy-go-lucky.

Zone in transition: In the Chicago School/social disorganization theory, this zone (labeled Zone II) was once residential but is becoming more industrial because it is being invaded by the factories; this area of a city tends to have the highest crime rates due to the chaotic effect that the invasion of factories has on the area.

Index

Note: Page numbers in italic type indicate figures, images, or tables.

Actus reus, 45, 55

Adaptations to strain, 224–226, 245

Adler, Freda, 7

Adolescence-limited offenders, 403–404

Adoption studies, 176–177

Adult male bar fighters, 288–293

Age

    crime rates by, 21, 227

    developmental theories and, 399–406, 408–418

Age of Enlightenment, 30–31, 39, 42–44

Ageton, Suzanne S., "An Integrated Theoretical Perspective on Delinquent Behavior," 466–475

Aggression, neuroimaging of, 198–205

Agnew, Robert, 232–233, 235, 307

    "Building on the Foundation of General Strain Theory," 250–257

Akers, Ronald, 302–305, 450

    "Social Learning Theory of Crime," 329–336

American Dream, 223–224, 228, 229–232

American Revolution, 216, 219, 221, 225

American Society of Criminology (ASC), 363, 388

"An Exploratory Test of Braithwaite's Reintegrative Shaming Theory" (Hay), 477–487

Analytic criminology, 30–37

Anderson, Elijah, 271

Androgens, 191–197

Anomie, 215, 221–224, 235, 238–243, 244, 467

Anthropometry, 151–154

Asians, intelligence scores of, 144

Atavism, 136–138, 156

Attachment, 317

Attention deficit hyperactivity disorder (ADHD), 185

Australia, 504

Automatic spontaneity, 309

Autonomic nervous system, 183–185

Awakened reflection, 309–310

Baby boom, 18–19

Baltzell, E. Digby, 31

Bandura, Albert, 304, 329

Beccaria, Cesare, 44–54, *45*

    death penalty, 47–49

    deterrence theory, 49–52

    influence of, 52–54

    influences on, 44

    "On Crimes and Punishments," 61–64

    origins of criminology, 32–33

    punishment, 45, 47, 49–51, 61–65

    reforms proposed by, 44–47

Benedict XVI, Pope, 40–41

Bentham, Jeremy, 32–34, 54, *54*

Binet, Alfred, 140–141

Biosocial perspectives, 173–188. *See also* Positive School

    adoption studies, 176–177

    brain injuries, 182–183

    cytogenetic studies, 178–179

    explanations of criminal behavior, 186–187

    explanatory model of, 191–197

    family studies, 174

    hormones and neurotransmitters, 179–182

    nature vs. nurture, 174–177, 186–187

    nervous system activity, 183–185

    neuroimaging of aggressive and violent behavior, 198–205

    policy implications, 187–188, 202–205, 502–504

    twins separated at birth, 177

    twin studies, 174–176

Bishop, Donna M., "The Effects of Prenatal Problems, Family Functioning, and Neighborhood Disadvantage in Predicting Life-Course-Persistent Offending," 421–430

BJS. *See* U.S. Bureau of Justice Statistics

Blacks

    crime rates among, 23–24

    intelligence scores, 144

    subcultural theory of, 271

Blankenship, Michael, "Do Women and Men Differ in Their Neutralizations of Corporate Crime?," 337–343

Blumstein, Alfred, "Criminal Career Paradigm," 408–418

Body type theory, 144–147

Bonger, Willem, 360

Boot camps, 35

Border culture conflict, 362

Born criminals, 136–138, 151–160

Bounded rationality, 57, 500

Bourgeoisie, 360

Braga, Anthony A., "The Effects of Focused Deterrence Strategies on Crime," 87–92

Brain

   emotion regulation, 199–202

   neuroimaging of, 198–205

Brain injuries, 182–183

Brain waves, 196

Braithwaite's reintegrative shaming theory, 445, 458–462, 477–487, 506

Brewer, Victoria, "Capital Punishment and Deterrence," 66–71

Broken windows theory, 8, 83, 118

Brutalization effect, 48

Buck v. Bell (1927), 143

Buddha, 220

Buerger, Michael E., "Hot Spots of Predatory Crime," 109–115

Bufkin, Jana L., "Neuroimaging Studies of Aggressive and Violent Behavior," 198–205

"Building on the Foundation of General Strain Theory" (Agnew), 250–257

Burgess, Anthony, *A Clockwork Orange*, 300

Burgess, Ernest W., 265–266

Burgess, Robert, 302–305

Burgess-Proctor, Amanda, "Intersections of Race, Class, Gender, and Crime," 388–396

Bursik, Robert J., 445

Bush, George W., 46, 146

Cabot, Richard Clark, 34

Caning, 42

Canter, Rachelle J., "An Integrated Theoretical Perspective on Delinquent Behavior," 466–476

Capitalism, 360–361, 364

Capital punishment. *See* Death penalty

"Capital Punishment and Deterrence" (Sorensen, Wrinkle, Brewer, and Marquart), 66–72

Catherine the Great, 52

Causality, 8–10

Center for the Study and Prevention of Violence, University of Colorado, 512

Central nervous system, 183–185

Cerebrotonic, 146

Certainty of punishment, 50, 63

Chicago Area Project, 270

Chicago School of criminology, 261–270. *See also* Cultural and subcultural theory; Social disorganization theory

   Chicago in 1800s and early 1900s, 262–263

   city growth and ecology, 263–266

   concentric circles theory, 265–266

   critiques of, 268–270

   ecological theory of city growth, 263–264

   social disorganization theory, 266–270, 279–285

Children, victimization of, 14–15

Chivalry model, 22

Chronic offenders. *See also* Born criminals

   age as predictor, 21

   biosocial interaction and, 162–168, 421–430

   Moffitt's developmental theory, 403

   nervous system activity, 183–185

   physical characteristics, 146–147

   physiological factors, 322

   policy implications, 414–415

Cities, growth and ecology of, 263–266

Clarke, Ron, 78

Class. *See* Social class

Classical conditioning, 299–300

Classical School, 44–54

   characteristics of, 4–5, 39–40

   decline of, 55–56, 74

   influence of, 40

   modern applications, 73–84

   origins of, 32

   policy implications, 56–57, 83–84, 501–504

   Positive School vs., 138–139

   preclassical perspectives, 40–42

Clearance rate, 13, 50

Clinton, Hillary Rodham, 146

Cloward, Richard A., 229–232, 235, 466

Cohen, Albert, 228–229, 235, 466

Cohen, Lawrence, 80

Collective conscience, 219, 310

Collectivity theories, 109–110

College boy, 228

Colvin, Mark, 361

Commitment, 318

Communitarianism, 445, 460

Competitive/victimizing behavior, 191–197

Comte, Auguste, 216–217

Concentric circles. *See* Theory of concentric circles

Conceptual integration, 446, *447*

Concordance rates, 175

Conflict gangs, 230–231

Conflict theories, 5–6, 361–363, 380–385, 505–506
"Conflict Theory and Deviance in Sport" (Eitzen), 380–385
Conformity, 219, 224, 312
Consensual perspective, 5
Containment theory, 313–314, *315*
"Contribution of Family Adversity and Verbal IQ to Criminal Behavior, The" (Gibson, Piquero, and Tibbetts), 161–168
Control-balance theory, 319–320, 462
Control deficit, 462
Control surplus, 462
Control theories, 6, 307–322
    in integrated models, 468–474, 488–498
    integrated, 319–321, 452–458
    low self-control, 321–322, 400–402
    modern, 314–319
    of crime, early, 311–314
    of human behavior, early, 309–311
    policy implications, 322–323
Cooley, Charles, 358
Copes, Heith, "Peaceful Warriors," 288–293
Corner boy, 228–229
Cornish, Derek, 78
Corporal punishment, 42
Corporate crime. *See* White-collar crime
Correlation, 9
Cortisol, 196
Courts, 501–502
Covariation. *See* Correlation
Craniometry, 134
Crime. *See also* Measures of crime
    definitions, 3–4, 11
    distribution of, 16–19
    preventing, 512–513
"Crime and Public Policy" (Wilson), 508–515
Crime rates, 509–511. *See also* Measures of crime
    age as factor in, 21, 227
    gender as factor in, 22
    geographical differences, 20
    historical, 16–19
    population density as factor in, 22–23
    race/ethnicity as factors in, 23–24
    social class as factor in, 23
    social functions of, 219–220
    time as influence on, 20–21
    UCR vs. NCVS, 14
Criminal career, 408–418
"Criminal Career Paradigm" (Piquero, Farrington, and Blumstein), 408–418
Criminal gangs, 230

"Criminal Man, The" (Lombroso), 151–160
Criminological theories. *See also* Theory
    classification of, 4–6
    influence of, 31
Criminology
    defined, 2
    history of, 30–37
    Lombroso as father of, 138–139
    origins of, 32–34
    perspectives on, 2
    scientific perspective on, 2, 3
Critical feminism, 364
Critical theories, 5–6, 360
Cross-sectional studies, 75
Cuban, Mark, 223
Cullen, Francis T., "Replicating Sampson and Groves's Test of Social Disorganization Theory," 279–285
Cultural and subcultural theory, 261, 270–273, 288–293. *See also* Chicago School of criminology
Cytogenetic studies, 178–179

DARE program, 505, 513
Dark figure, 12, 14
Darwin, Charles, *56,* 74, 148
    The Origin of Species, 55, 136
Davis, Gray, 143
Death penalty
    Beccaria on, 47–49
    deterrent effect, 56, 67–71
Decriminalization, 358–359, 366, 505
Deinstitutionalization, 358–359, 366, 507
Delinquency
    community characteristics, 275–278
    defined, 472
    drift theory, 315–317
    etiological paths to, 473–474
    firearms in schools, 346–354
    integrated theory of, 466–476
    interactional theory of, 488–498
    labeling theory and, 369–378
    learning theories and, 298–307, 326–328
    strain theory and, 228–229
"Delinquency Rates and Community Characteristics" (Shaw and McKay), 275–278
Delinquent boy, 228
Determinism, 138–139. *See also* Soft determinism
Deterrence theory, 39, 51–512
    Beccaria and, 49–52
    characteristics of effective punishment, 49–51
    death penalty, 56, 67–71
    effectiveness of, 74–78, 87–92

formal vs. informal, 78–80
policy making based on, 56–57, 501–502
revival of, 74–78
specific vs. general, 51–52
Developmental theories, 399–406
    antidevelopment theory, 400, *401*, 402
    criminal career, 408–418
    Moffitt's developmental taxonomy, 162–168, 403–405, 422–430
    Pathways to Desistance, 434–436
    policy implications, 405, 413–417, 504
    Sampson and Laub's developmental model, 402–403
Deviance, 4
Differential association theory, 6, 298–302, 326–328, 348–354, 452–456, 504
Differential identification theory, 301–302
Differential opportunity theory, 229–232
Differential reinforcement theory, 8, 302–305, 329–336, 452–456, 488–494
Distribution of crime, 16–19
Diversion, 358–359, 366, 501, 505
Dizygotic twins, 175
Dopamine, 181
"Do Women and Men Differ in Their Neutralizations of Corporate Crime?" (Vieraitis, Piquero, Piquero, Tibbetts, and Blankenship), 337–343
Dramatization of evil, 358
Drift theory, 315–317, *316*
Drug courts, 35
Drunk driving, 75
Dugdale, Richard, 174
Durkheim, Émile, 23, 218–222, *220*, 235, 244, 309–310

Ecological School. *See* Chicago School of criminology
Ectoderm, 145
Ectomorph, 145, *145*
"Effects of Focused Deterrence Strategies on Crime, The" (Braga and Weisburd), 87–92
"Effects of Prenatal Problems, Family Functioning, and Neighborhood Disadvantage in Predicting Life-Course-Persistent Offending, The" (Turner, Hartman, and Bishop), 421–430
Ego, 310
Eisenhower, Dwight D., 34
Eitzen, D. Stanley, "Conflict Theory and Deviance in Sport," 380–385
Elliott, Delbert, 450, 452
    "Integrated Theoretical Perspective on Delinquent Behavior, An," 466–476
Elliott's integrated model, 445, 452–456, *453*, 466–476
Ellis, Lee, "A Theory Explaining Biological Correlates of Criminality," 191–197

Ellis Island, 141, *142*
Embezzlement, 22
Emotions
    criminals', 156–160
    regulation of, 199–202
Empirical validity, 8
Endoderm, 145
Endomorph, *145*, 145
End-to-end integration, 442, 452
Enlightenment. *See* Age of Enlightenment
Epilepsy, 195
Equivalency hypothesis, 23
Ethnicity. *See* Race/ethnicity
Eugenics, 133–135, 141, 143
Evolutionary neuroandrogenic theory, 191–197
Executive cognitive functioning, 194
Exorcisms, 40–41
The Exorcist (film), 40
Experiential effect, 75
Experimental criminology, 30–37

Family adversity, 162–168, 421–430
Family studies, 174
Farnworth, M., 227
Farrington, David P., "Criminal Career Paradigm," 408–418
Fascism, 138, 139, 148
Faulkner, William, 244
Federal Bureau of Investigation (FBI), 10, 11
Feeblemindedness, 141–143
Felson, Marcus, *80*, 80
Feminist criminology, 22, 363–366, 388–396
    dominance approach, 391
    history of, 389
    impact of, 365
    intersectional approach, 391–396
    policy implications, 366
    sameness vs. difference approaches, 363, 390–391
    types of, 364–365
Ferracuti, Franco, 271–272
Ferri, Enrico, 139
Fielding, Henry, 32–33
Firearms, in school, 346–354
Focal concerns, 271–272
Focused deterrence, 88–92
Formal controls, 22
Formal deterrence, 78–80
Forsyth, Craig, "Peaceful Warriors," 288–293
France, 54–55
Free will, 4–5, 39, 44, 138–139, 221
French Revolution, 216, 219, 221

Freud, Sigmund, 8, 228, 306, 310–311
Frontal lobes, 182–183
Frustration. *See* Strain theory
Full-moon theory, 41

Gacy, John Wayne, *182*
Galileo Galilei, 220
Galvanic Skin Response, 195–196
Gandhi, Mohandas, 220
Gang formation, 228–232
Gang types, 230–231
Garrofalo, Raphael, 139
Gartin, Patrick R., "Hot Spots of Predatory Crime," 109–115
Gauss, K. F., 134
Gender. *See also* Women
    crime rates by, 22
    evolutionary explanations of crime, 191–197
    hormonal differences, 179–180
    neutralizations of corporate crime, 337–343
    power-control theory, 320
General deterrence, 51–52
General strain theory, 232–235, 250–257
General theory of crime, 321–322, 400, *401*, 402
Generation X, 19
Geographic distribution of crime, 20, 109–115, 118–128
Gibson, Chris L., "The Contribution of Family Adversity and Verbal IQ to Criminal Behavior," 161–168
Glaser, Daniel, 301–302
Glueck, Eleanor, 403, 440
Glueck, Sheldon, 403, 440
Goddard, H. H., *141,* 141–143, 174
Gonzales, Alberto, 46
Gottfredson, Michael, 6, 95, 235, 321–322, 400–402
Great Depression, 17–18, 222, 235
Groves, W. Byron, 279–285
Guerry, André-Michel, 217
Guns
    crime and, 511–512
    school and, 346–354

Hagan, John, 320, 462–463
Hands-off policy, 358–359
Hartman, Jennifer L., "The Effects of Prenatal Problems, Family Functioning, and Neighborhood Disadvantage in Predicting Life-Course-Persistent Offending," 421–430
Hawthorne, Nathaniel, 244
    The Scarlet Letter, 23
"An Exploratory Test of Braithwaite's Reintegrative Shaming Theory," 477–487
Heart rate, 195

Hedonistic calculus, 54
Hemmens, Craig, "There's a Darkness on the Edge of Town," 244–249
Herrnstein, Richard, 144
"Highlights from Pathways to Desistance" (Mulvey), 434–436
High/Scope Perry Preschool Project, 511
Hindelang, Michael, 143
Hirschi, Travis, 7, 95, 143, 235, 317–319, 321–322, 345–346, 400–402, 449–451, 466
Hobbes, Thomas, 42–44, 76, 309
Hochstetler, Andy, "Peaceful Warriors," 288–293
Holmes, Oliver Wendell, Jr., 143
Homeless people, victimization of, 14–15
Homicide rates, *18,* 509
Hormones, 179–181
Hot spots, 20, 81, 109–115, 500, 511. *See also* Geographic distribution of crime
"Hot Spots of Predatory Crime" (Sherman, Gartin, and Buerger), 109–115
Human nature, 6
Hutcheson, Frances, 32
Hypoglycemia, 195
Hypotheses, 2, 27

Id, 310
Imitation. *See* Modeling and imitation
"Impact of Neighborhoods, Schools, and Malls on the Spatial Distribution of Property Damage, The" (LaGrange), 118–128
Incarceration rate, 19, 35, 509, 510
Index offenses, 11–13
Industrial Revolution, 216, 219, 221
Informal controls, 22–23, *24*
Informal deterrence, 78–80
"Informal Reactions and Delinquency" (Zhang), 369–378
Innovation, 225
"Integrated Theoretical Perspective on Delinquent Behavior, An" (Elliott, Ageton, and Canter), 466–476
Integrated theories, 439–464
    Braithwaite's reintegrative shaming theory, 458–462, 477–487
    characteristics of, 5
    conceptual integration of, *447*
    control-balance theory, 462
    critiques of, 448–452
    Elliott's integrated model, 452–456, 466–476
    examples of, 452–463
    levels of analysis, 445–446
    need for, 440–441
    policy implications, 463–464, 504
    power-control theory, 462–463
    probation and, 515–525
    social control, 319–321, 452–458

Thornberry's interactional model, 456–458, 488–498
types of, 441–445, 446, 448
validity of, 8
Interaction hypothesis, 162–168, 421–430
Interdependency, 445, 460
Interracial crime, 23
Intersectional approach to gender, 391–396
"Intersections of Race, Class, Gender, and Crime"
 (Burgess-Proctor), 388–396
Intraracial crime, 23
Involvement, 318
IQ testing, 140–144, 148
Islamic justice, 42

Japan, 459–460
Jeffery, C. R., 302
Jesus, 220
Jews, intelligence scores of, 144
Job Corps, 18, 504
Johnson, Lyndon B., 14, 19, 504
Jury trials, 47
Justice, 507, 516–517
Juvenile Delinquency Prevention and Control Act (1961), 231

Kaczynski, Ted (Unabomber), 225
Kant, Immanuel, 31
Katz, Jack, 78
Kennedy, Robert, 231
King, Martin Luther, 220
King, Rodney, 43

Labeling theory, 357–359, 366, 369–378, 507–509
LaGrange, Teresa C., "The Impact of Neighborhoods, Schools,
 and Malls on the Spatial Distribution of Property
 Damage," 118–128
Larceny, 22
Laub, John H., 235, 402–403, *403*
Law enforcement, 502–503. *See also* Police
Learning theories, 297–307
 differential association, 298–302, 326–328
 differential identification, 301–302
 differential reinforcement, 302–305, 329–336
 integrated models and, 452–458
 neutralization theory, 306–307, 337–343
 policy implications, 322–323
Lee, David Sang-Yoon, 218
Legalistic approach to crime, 3
Leiber, M. J., 227
LeMarquand, David, 308
Lemert, Edwin, 358–359
Lenin, Vladimir, 47

Liberal feminism, 364
"Life-Course Analysis of the Criminogenic Effects of Maternal
 Cigarette Smoking during Pregnancy" (McGloin, Pratt,
 and Piquero), 206–211
Life-course-persistent offenders, 162–168, 403–404, 421–430.
 See also Chronic offenders
Life-course perspectives. *See* Developmental theories
Lifestyle theory. *See* Routine activities theory
Lipton, D., 34–35
Literature reviews, 27
Logical consistency, 7
Lombroso, Cesare, 7, 9, 10, 136–140, *137*, 148
 "Criminal Man, The," 151–160
 father of criminology, 138–139
 list of stigmata, 137–138
 policy implications, 139–140
 theory of crime, 136–137
Lowenkamp, Christopher T., "Replicating Sampson and Groves's
 Test of Social Disorganization Theory," 279–285
Low self-control. *See also* Theory of low self-control
Luttrell, Vickie R., "Neuroimaging Studies of Aggressive and
 Violent Behavior," 198–205

Macro level of analysis, 5, 445
Mala in se, 3–4
Mala prohibita, 3–4
Mandela, Nelson, 220
Marquart, James, "Capital Punishment and Deterrence," 67–71
Martinson, R., 34–35
Marx, Karl, 225, 359, 360
Marxist feminism, 364
Marxist theories, 360–361
Maryland Report, 500–505
Massachusetts Bay Colony, 22
Maternal smoking during pregnancy, 194–195, 206–211
Matza, David, 306–307, 315–317, 338, 466
May, David C., "Scared Kids, Unattached Kids, or Peer
 Pressure," 346–354
McCord, Joan, 36
McGloin, Jean Marie, "A Life-Course Analysis of the
 Criminogenic Effects of Maternal Cigarette Smoking
 during Pregnancy," 206–211
McKay, Henry, 266–270, 279–280, 503
 "Delinquency Rates and Community Characteristics," 275–278
Mead, George Herbert, 358
Measures of crime, 10–16. *See also* Crime rates
 distribution of crime, 16–19
 National Crime Victimization Survey, 10, 14–15
 reporting/nonreporting of crime, 11–12, 14–15
 self-report data, 10–11, 15–16
 Uniform Crime Report, 10–13

Mechanical societies, 219

Me culture, 459

Mednick, Sarnoff, 176

Mens rea, 45, 55

Merton, Robert K., 222–227, *224,* 235, 244–249, 467, 504
  "Social Structure and Anomie," 238–243

Mesoderm, 145

Mesomorph, *145,* 145, 194

Methodology, of research, 27

Micro level of analysis, 5, 445

Miller, Arthur, 244

Miller, Walter, 271–272

Minor physical anomalies (MPAs), 140, 147

Mobilization for Youth, 231

Modeling and imitation, 304

Moffitt, Terrie, 405

Moffitt's developmental theory (taxonomy), 162–168, 403–405, 422–430

Mohammed, 220

Monoamine oxidase, 196

Monozygotic twins, 175

Montesquieu, Baron de, 44

Moral beliefs, 98, 318–319

Morality
  insensitivity in, 157
  sentencing as reflection of, 512

Moral reasoning, brain activity associated with, 193–194

Multiracial feminism, 392–396

Mulvey, Edward P., "Highlights from Pathways to Desistance," 434–436

Murray, Charles, 144

National Crime Victimization Survey (NCVS), 10, 14–15

National Institute of Justice, 35

National Longitudinal Survey of Youth, 424

National Youth Survey, 369–370, 454

Native Americans, 23

Natural areas, 263

Natural selection, 55, 74, 136

Nature vs. nurture, 174–177, 186–187

Nazism, 138, 139

NCVS. *See* National Crime Victimization Survey

Negative punishment, 303

Negative reinforcement, 303

Neighborhood watch programs, 503

Neoclassical School, 54–57
  decline of, 55–56, 74
  policy implications, 56–57

Neo-Marxist theories, 360–361

"Neuroimaging Studies of Aggressive and Violent Behavior" (Bufkin and Luttrell), 198–205

Neuropsychological risk, 162–168, 421–430

Neurotransmitters, *181,* 181–182

Neutralization theory, 306–307, 337–343

New Deal, 18, 366

Nonindex offenses, 11, 13

Nurse Home Visitation Program, 512

Nye, F. Ivan, 312–313, 466

Offender frequency, 400, 411, 415–416

Ohlin, Lloyd E., 229–232, 235, 467

Olds, David, 35

"On Crimes and Punishments" (Beccaria), 61–64

Operant conditioning, 302–303

Opportunities for crime, 9, 17, 21, 22, 41, 80–82, 217

Oppositional tradition, 449, 451

Organic societies, 219

Panopticon, 33–34, 54

Paradigms, 4

Park, Robert E., 263–265

Parsimony, 6–7

Pathways to Desistance Study, 434–436

Patriarchy, 22, 364, 391

Pauly, John, 361

Pavlov, Ivan, 299–300

Pearson, Frank S., 446–448

Phrenology, 134–135, *135*

Physiognomy, 135–136, 151–154

Piquero, Alex R.
  "Contribution of Family Adversity and Verbal IQ to Criminal Behavior, The," 161–168
  "Criminal Career Paradigm," 408–418
  "Do Women and Men Differ in Their Neutralizations of Corporate Crime?," 337–343
  "Life-Course Analysis of the Criminogenic Effects of Maternal Cigarette Smoking during Pregnancy," 206–211
  "Specifying the Direct and Indirect Effects of Low Self-Control and Situational Factors in Offenders' Decision Making," 95–105

Piquero, Nicole Leeper, "Do Women and Men Differ in Their Neutralizations of Corporate Crime?," 337–343

Place. *See* Geographic distribution of crime; Hot spots

Pleasure, of criminal behavior, 78, 80, 96–97

Pluralistic (conflict) perspective, 362

Police
  crime definition and recording by, 13
  crime-reduction strategies, 56–57
  deterrent effect of, 500–502
  origins of, 16–17, 33
  public attitudes toward, 12

Policy making. *See* Public policy
Population density, 22–23
Positive punishment, 303
Positive reinforcement, 303
Positive School, 133–149. *See also* Biosocial perspectives
    characteristics of, 5, 138–139
    Classical School vs., 138–139
    Comte as precursor of, 217
    IQ testing, 140–144
    learning theories, 299
    Lombroso and, 136–140
    origins of, 133–136
    policy implications, 139–140, 147–148
    stigmata indicating born criminals, 137–140
Postmodern feminism, 365
Poverty
    crime associated with, 23–24
    relative deprivation, 218
Powell, Colin, 223
Power-control theory, 320–321, 462–463
Pratt, Travis C.
    "Life-Course Analysis of the Criminogenic Effects of Maternal Cigarette Smoking during Pregnancy," 206–211
    "Replicating Sampson and Groves's Test of Social Disorganization Theory," 279–285
Preclassical perspectives on crime, 40–42
Prefrontal regions, 193, 199–202
President's Commission on Law Enforcement and Administration of Justice, 14
Primary deviance, 358
Prison design, 33–34, 54
Probation, 515–525
Prohibition, *16*, 17
Proletariat, 360
Public policy, 8, 24, 497–504
    Beccaria's influence on, 52–53
    biosocial factors and, 187–188, 202–205, 499–506
    Classical and Neoclassical influences on, 56–57, 83–84, 502–504
    conflict theories and, 505–505
    control theories and, 322–323
    developmental theories and, 405, 413–417, 508
    feminist theories and, 366
    integrated theories and, 463–464, 506
    labeling theory and, 366, 507–508
    learning theories and, 322–323
    Positivist influences on, 139–140, 147–148
    review of, 508–515
    social process theories and, 322–323, 506–508
    social structure theories and, 236, 505–506
    strain theory and, 231–232, 236, 256–257

Pulse rate, 195
Punishment
    Beccaria on, 45, 47, 49–51, 61–64
    certainty of, 50, 63
    characteristics of effective, 49–51
    corporal, 42
    in preclassical period, 41–42
    intent as influence on, 45
    nervous system response to, 185
    operant conditioning, 302–303
    right to administer, 62
    severity of, 50–51, 63–64
    swiftness of, 49–50, 62–63

Quetelet, Adolphe, *217*, 217–218
Quinney, Richard, 360–361

Race/ethnicity
    crime influenced by, 23–24
    delinquency rates, 277–278
    inferiority and criminality, 133–136
    intelligence scores, 144
Radical feminism, 364
Rational choice theory, 78–80, 95–105, 302
Rational decision making, 5, 39–40, 44
Reaction formation, 228
Rebellion, 225
Recidivism, 512
Reckless, Walter, 313–314, 466
Reinforcement theory, 6. *See also* Differential reinforcement theory
Reintegrative shaming. *See* Braithwaite's reintegrative shaming theory
Reiss, Albert, 311–312, 466
Relative deprivation, 218
Reliability, of research, 27
Religious perspectives on crime, 2, 40–42
"Replicating Sampson and Groves's Test of Social Disorganization Theory" (Lowenkamp, Cullen, and Pratt), 279–285
Research articles, how to read, 27–29
Retreatism, 225
Retreatist gangs, 231
Rights, Enlightenment concept of, 43, 44, 46, 52, 53
Ritualism, 224–225
Rochester Youth Development Study, 458
Roman Catholic Church, 40–41, 52
Roosevelt, Franklin D., 18
Ross, H. L., 75
Routine activities theory, 20, 80–82, 110–115, 118–128
Runaways, 22
Russia, 47, 52

Sampling design, 14

Sampson, Robert J., 235, 279–285, 402–403, *403*

Saturated patrol, 500

"Scared Kids, Unattached Kids, or Peer Pressure" (May), 346–354

Scared-straight approach, 57

Scared-straight programs, 501, 503

Scenario (vignette) research, 77–78

Schools, as crime sites, 12, 21, 35, 120–121, 124–128, 346–354

Schwalbe, Craig S., "Toward an Integrated Theory of Probation," 515–525

Schwarzenegger, Arnold, 223

Scientific method, 2, 216

Scope, 7

Search and seizure practices, 511

Secondary deviance, 359

Securities and Exchange Commission, 75

Selective placement, 176

Self-control theory, 6. *See also* Low self-control

Self-report data (SRD), 10–11, 15–16

Self-selection, 457

Sellin, Thorsten, 362

Serotonin, 181–182, 196

Severity of punishment, 50–51, 63–64

Shame, 78–79, 97–105

Shaming strategies, 23, *24*, 84, 503–505. *See also* Braithwaite's reintegrative shaming theory

Shaw, Clifford, 266–270, 279–280, 503
 "Delinquency Rates and Community Characteristics," 275–278

Sheldon, William, 144–147

Sherman, Lawrence W.
 "Hot Spots of Predatory Crime," 109–115
 "Use and Usefulness of Criminology, 1751–2005, The," 28–37

Shopping malls, as crime sites, 120, 124–128

Side-by-side integration, 442–443

Situational factors, 95–105

Skin conductivity, 195–196

Skinner, B. F., 302, 329

Smith, Adam, 32

Smoking. *See* Maternal smoking during pregnancy

Social bonding theory, 317–319, *318*, 345–346, 348–354

Social class, 23
 equal justice regardless of, 507
 gang formation, 228–229
 strain theory, 228–229, 238–243
 subcultural theory of, 271–272

Social contract, 43

Social control, 254–256. *See also* Control theories

Social Darwinism, 268

Social disorganization theory, 262, 266–270, 279–285, 452–456, 503. *See also* Chicago School of criminology

Social dynamics, 216

Socialist feminism, 365

Social learning, 254–256, 457, 471–473. *See also* Learning theories

"Social Learning Theory of Crime" (Akers), 329–336

Social process theories, 297–323
 control theories, 307–322
 learning theories, 297–307
 policy implications, 322–323, 506–508

Social reaction theories. *See* Labeling theory; Marxist theories

Social sciences, 2, 31

Social statics, 216

"Social Structure and Anomie" (Merton), 238–243

Social structure theories, 215–222. *See also* Strain theory
 Comte, 216–217
 Durkheim, 218–222
 Guerry, 217
 policy implications, 236, 503–504
 Quetelet, 217–218

"Sociological Theory of Criminal Behavior" (Sutherland), 326–328

Sociology
 Comte as founder of, 216–217
 dominance of, in criminology, 440–441

Soft determinism, 315

Somatotyping, 144–147

Somotonic, 146

Sorensen, Jon, "Capital Punishment and Deterrence," 67–71

Spatial distribution of crime, 109–115, 118–128

Specific deterrence, 51–52

"Specifying the Direct and Indirect Effects of Low Self-Control and Situational Factors in Offenders' Decision Making" (Piquero and Tibbetts), 95–105

Spiral of decay, 118, 121

Sport, deviance in, 380–385

Springsteen, Bruce, 244–249

Spuriousness, 9–10

SRD. *See* Self-report data

Stake in conformity, 312

Status frustration, 228

Sterilizations, 143

Stewart, James K., 35

Stigmata, 151–160

Stimulus hunger, 185

Stoker, Bram, *Dracula*, 138

Stoning, 42

Strain
 cumulative effect of, 254
 defining, 251–252
 measuring, 256

social control and social learning vs., 254–256
types of, leading to crime and delinquency, 252–254
Strain theory, 6, 215, 222–235
  critiques of, 226–227, 229, 231, 233–235
  differential opportunities, 229–232
  general strain theory, 232–235, 250–257
  in integrated models, 452–456, 467–474
  low-class status, 228–229
  Merton, 222–227, 238–249, 504
  policy implications, 231–232, 236, 256–257
  Springsteen's lyrics and, 244–249
  summary of, 235
Structural functionalism, 219
Subterranean values, 316–317
Suicide, 221
Superego, 310
Sutherland, Edwin, 230, 298–302, 299, 304, 440–441, 504
"Sociological Theory of Criminal Behavior," 326–328
Swank, Hillary, 223
Swiftness of punishment, 49–50, 62–63
Sykes, Gresham, 306–307, 338

Tabula rasa, 6, 298
Tannenbaum, Frank, 358
Tarantino, Quentin, 223
Tarde, Gabriel, 304
Tattoos, 7, 9–10, 137, 154–156
Taylor, Ian, 360
Telescoping, 15
Temporal lobes, 182–183
Temporal ordering, 9
Tennessee Valley Authority, 18
Testability, 8
Testosterone, 179–180, 193–194
Texas, death penalty in, 68–71
Theoretical competition, 449, 451
Theoretical elaboration, 448, 454
Theoretical reduction, 444
Theoretical synthesis, 444–445
Theory, 2–3, 6–8. See also Criminological theories
"Theory Explaining Biological Correlates of Criminality" (Ellis), 191–197
Theory of concentric circles, 265, 265–266
Theory of low self-control, 6–7, 95–105, 321–322, 400, 401, 402
"There's a Darkness on the Edge of Town" (Hemmens), 244–249
Thornberry, Terrence, 456
  "Toward an Interactional Theory of Delinquency," 488–498
Thornberry's interactional model, 456–458, 488–497
Three-strikes sentencing laws, 50–51, 83, 504

Tibbetts, Stephen G.
  "Contribution of Family Adversity and Verbal IQ to Criminal Behavior, The," 161–168
  "Do Women and Men Differ in Their Neutralizations of Corporate Crime?," 337–343
  "Specifying the Direct and Indirect Effects of Low Self-Control and Situational Factors in Offenders' Decision Making," 95–105
Time of day and year, 20–21
Tittle, Charles, 319–320, 462
Toby, Jackson, 312
Torture, 46
"Toward an Integrated Theory of Probation" (Schwalbe), 515–525
"Toward an Interactional Theory of Delinquency" (Thornberry), 488–497
Trajectory, 404
Transitions, 402, 403
Tremblay, Richard, 308
Turk, Austin, 362
Turner, Michael G., "The Effects of Prenatal Problems, Family Functioning, and Neighborhood Disadvantage in Predicting Life-Course-Persistent Offending," 421–430
Twins-separated-at-birth studies, 177
Twin studies, 174–176

Uniform Crime Report (UCR), 10–13
United States. See also American Dream; American Revolution
  IQ testing and public policy, 141–143
  Neoclassical School, 54–55
  reintegration of offenders in, 459–462, 506
  violence in, 507
Up-and-down integration, 443–445
U.S. Bill of Rights, 31, 53
U.S. Bureau of Justice Statistics (BJS), 10, 14
U.S. Bureau of the Census, 10, 14
U.S. Constitution, 53
U.S. Declaration of Independence, 44
U.S. Justice Department, 10
U.S. Supreme Court, 511
"Use and Usefulness of Criminology, The, 1751–2005" (Sherman), 28–37
Utilitarianism, 44

Validity. See Empirical validity
Verbal IQ, 143–144, 162–168
Victimization
  equivalency hypothesis, 23
  fear of, 347–354
  groups susceptible to, 14–15
  nonreporting of crime, 11–12, 14–15

Vieratis, Lynne M., "Do Women and Men Differ in Their Neutralizations of Corporate Crime?," 337–343
Violence
  codes for, 288–293
  in United States, 507
  neuroimaging of, 198–205
Viscerotonic, 146
Vold, George, 362

Walton, Paul, 360
War on Drugs, 17
War on Poverty, 504
We culture, 459
Weiner, Neil Alan, 446–448
Weisburd, David L., "The Effects of Focused Deterrence Strategies on Crime," 87–92
White-collar crime
  experiential effect and, 75

gender differences in neutralizations of, 337–343
  neo-Marxist theory of, 361
Wilks, J., 34–35
Wilson, James Q., "Crime and Public Policy," 508–514
Witchcraft, 23
Wolfgang, Marvin, 271–272
Women. *See also* Gender
  anthropometry of, 153–154
  feminist criminology, 363–366, 388–396
World War II, 18
Wrinkle, Robert, "Capital Punishment and Deterrence," 67–71

XYY factor, 178–179

Young, Jock, 360

Zhang, Lening, "Informal Reactions and Delinquency," 369–378
Zone in transition, 265

About the Authors

Stephen G. Tibbetts has been pursuing an understanding of criminal offending for the past two decades. He has attempted to discover the extent to which individuals' inherent dispositions and attitudinal traits contribute to their offending decisions, especially in relation to other factors, such as demographic, developmental, and situational factors. Dr. Tibbetts' research has included work on the differences between men and women in their decisions to commit deviant behavior, as well as their perceptions of risk and consequences of getting caught. His additional research interests include the effects of perinatal disorders as an influence in future criminality, the etiology of white-collar crime, gang intervention, and citizens' attitudes regarding various forms of pornography. Dr. Tibbetts has published nine books and more than 50 scholarly papers examining various issues in criminology. He recently received the annual Outstanding Professor Award at California State University, San Bernardino, in 2011. Dr. Tibbetts taught at East Tennessee State University for four years prior to coming to CSUSB. He served as a Court Appointed Special Advocate in Washington County, Tennessee, for several years, in which he directed the disposition of numerous juvenile court cases. He continued this work as a child advocate in San Bernardino County from 2000 to 2006.

Craig Hemmens is Department Chair and Professor in the Department of Criminal Justice and Criminology at Washington State University. In addition to being the editor for the SAGE Text/Reader Series in Criminology/Criminal Justice, he has published several books, including *Law, Justice and Society* (Oxford University Press, ©2012), *Legal Guide for Police* (Anderson, ©2011) and *An Introduction to Criminal Evidence* (Oxford University Press, ©2009). He holds a JD from North Carolina Central University School of Law and a PhD in Criminal Justice from Sam Houston State University. He served as the President of the Association of Criminal Justice Sciences (ACJS) from 2012 to 2013.

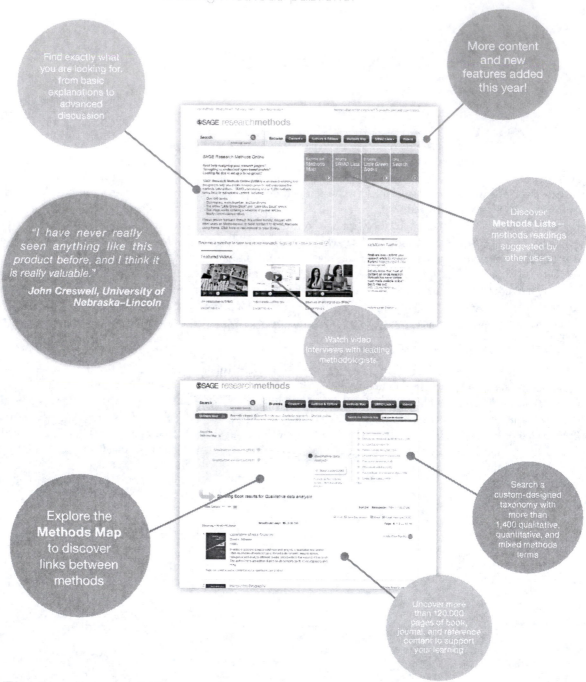

⑤SAGE research**methods**

The essential online tool for researchers from the world's leading methods publisher

Find exactly what you are looking for, from basic explanations to advanced discussion

More content and new features added this year!

"I have never really seen anything like this product before, and I think it is really valuable."

John Creswell, University of Nebraska–Lincoln

Discover **Methods Lists** — methods readings suggested by other users

Watch video interviews with leading methodologists

Explore the **Methods Map** to discover links between methods

Search a custom-designed taxonomy with more than 1,400 qualitative, quantitative, and mixed methods terms

Uncover more than 120,000 pages of book, journal, and reference content to support your learning

Find out more at
www.sageresearchmethods.com

CPSIA information can be obtained
at www.ICGtesting.com
Printed in the USA
FSOW02n0745291217
42473FS

TEACHING THE
SOCIAL SCIENCES AND
HISTORY IN
SECONDARY SCHOOLS

A Methods Book